GIRL TWIRL
COMICS

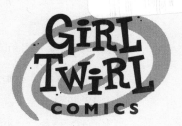

Special thanks to:

Zan and all the guys at Prism Comics
www.PrismComics.org

Brian Miller
Hi-Fi colour design
www.hifidesign.com

Terry and Robyn Moore

Stephan Pastis

Jean Schulz

Karen Johnson

Joe and Dottie

Guy and Stacy

Jane's World, Collection 1
ISBN 978-0-9766707-8-0

Jane's World
P.O. Box 88
Sebastopol, CA 95473

JanesWorld@mac.com

www.JaneComics.com

Webmaster:
Michael Shermis
3WD World Wide Web Design
www.3WD.com

Printed in Canada

jane's world

STORY AND ART BY
PAIGE BRADDOCK

jane's world

BY PAIGE BRADDOCK

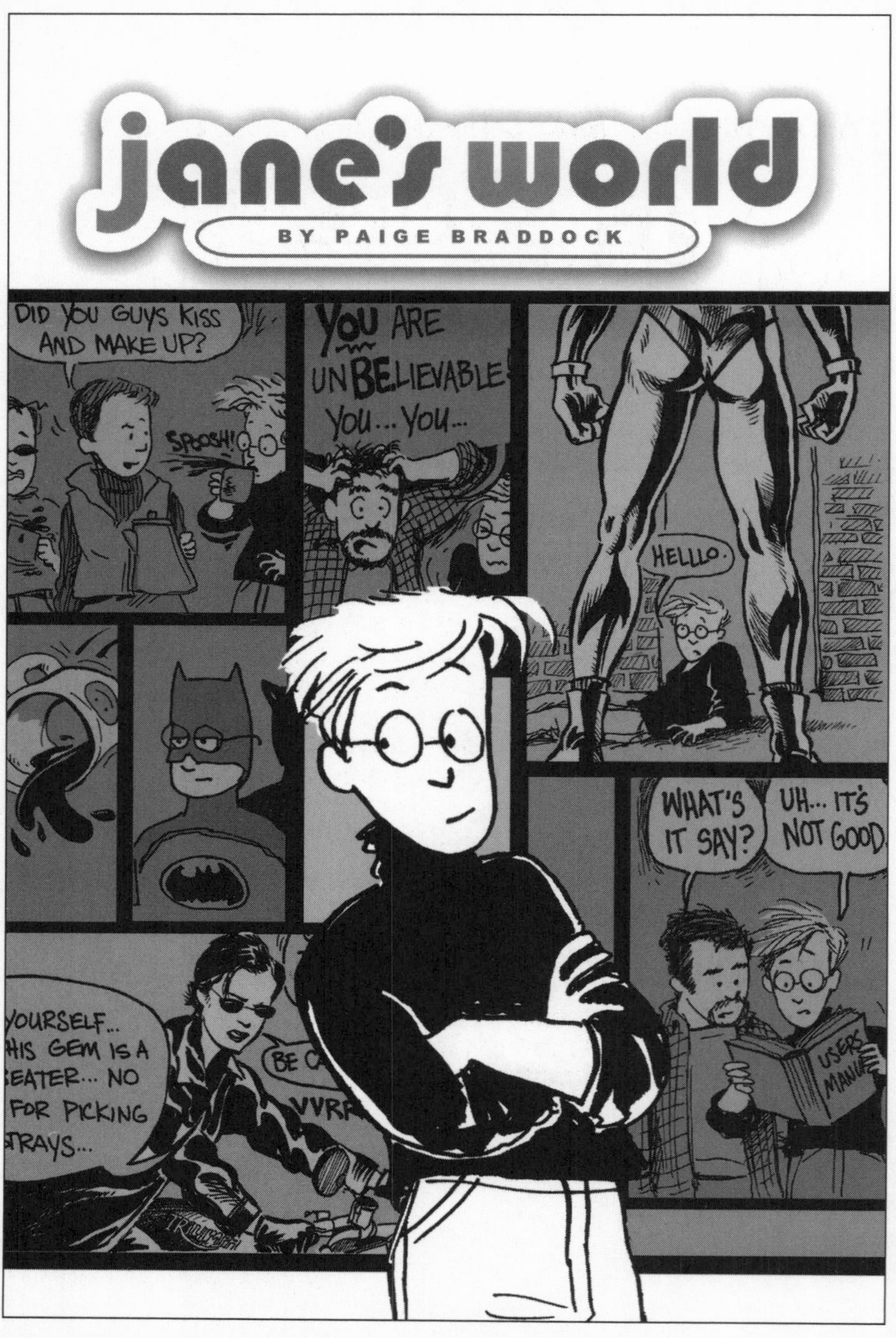
DID YOU GUYS KISS AND MAKE UP?
SPOOSH!
YOU ARE UNBELIEVABLE! YOU... YOU...
HELLLO.
WHAT'S IT SAY?
UH... IT'S NOT GOOD.

WHO'S WHO AND WHAT'S THE STORY IN JANE'S WORLD:

JANE
CENTER OF
JANE'S KNOWN
UNIVERSE

SARAH
JANE'S
GIRLFRIEND

BECCA
JANE'S
PERFECT
LAWYER
SISTER

CHELLE
CENTER OF
CHELLE'S
KNOWN
UNIVERSE

ETHAN
JANE'S
ROOMMATE
AND CHRONIC
NET SURFER

SEE, JANE HAD THIS GREAT JOB AT THE NEWSPAPER... WELL, IT **WAS** A GREAT JOB... BUT THEN YOU KNOW HOW IT GOES WITH EVERY JOB... IT STARTS TO BE NOT SO GREAT. OR MAYBE IT WAS NEVER GREAT, BUT JANE WAS JUST TOO GREEN TO KNOW THE DIFFERENCE...

SORRY, I'M GETTING A LITTLE AHEAD HERE... WHAT I WANTED TO TELL YOU HAS NOTHING TO DO WITH A CAREER PATH - GOOD OR OTHERWISE. THIS ALL STARTED WHEN JANE'S TRAINER, CINDY, HAD A BIT OF A CRUSH ON JANE'S ROOMMATE, ETHAN. ACTUALLY, MAYBE IT STARTED JUST BEFORE THAT... THE REASON JANE WAS AT THE GYM IN THE FIRST PLACE WAS TO TRY TO BECOME A JOCK TO WIN SARAH, HER EX, BACK... CHICKS DIG JOCKS, RIGHT?

BUT BEFORE SARAH NOTICED ANY SIGNIFICANT JANE-THE-JOCK BEHAVIOR, THE WHOLE THING WITH CINDY AND ETHAN CAME UP.

JANE THOUGHT SHE HAD THE PERFECT PLAN TO HELP ETHAN EASE OUT OF A POTENTIALLY BRUISING SITUATION... OF COURSE, AS IS TYPICAL WITH MOST "JANE" SCHEMES, THINGS GOT A BIT OFF TRACK AND THERE WAS THIS UNFORTUNATE INCIDENT WITH A FALLING SIGN. THEN THERE WAS JANE'S SHORT TRIP TO A PARALLEL UNIVERSE INHABITED ONLY BY FEMALE SUPER HEROES, BUT I'M SURE NO ONE IS INTERESTED IN THAT.

WHAT YOU REALLY WANT TO KNOW IS HOW JANE MET CHELLE...

Chapter 1

CLOWN PRINCESS

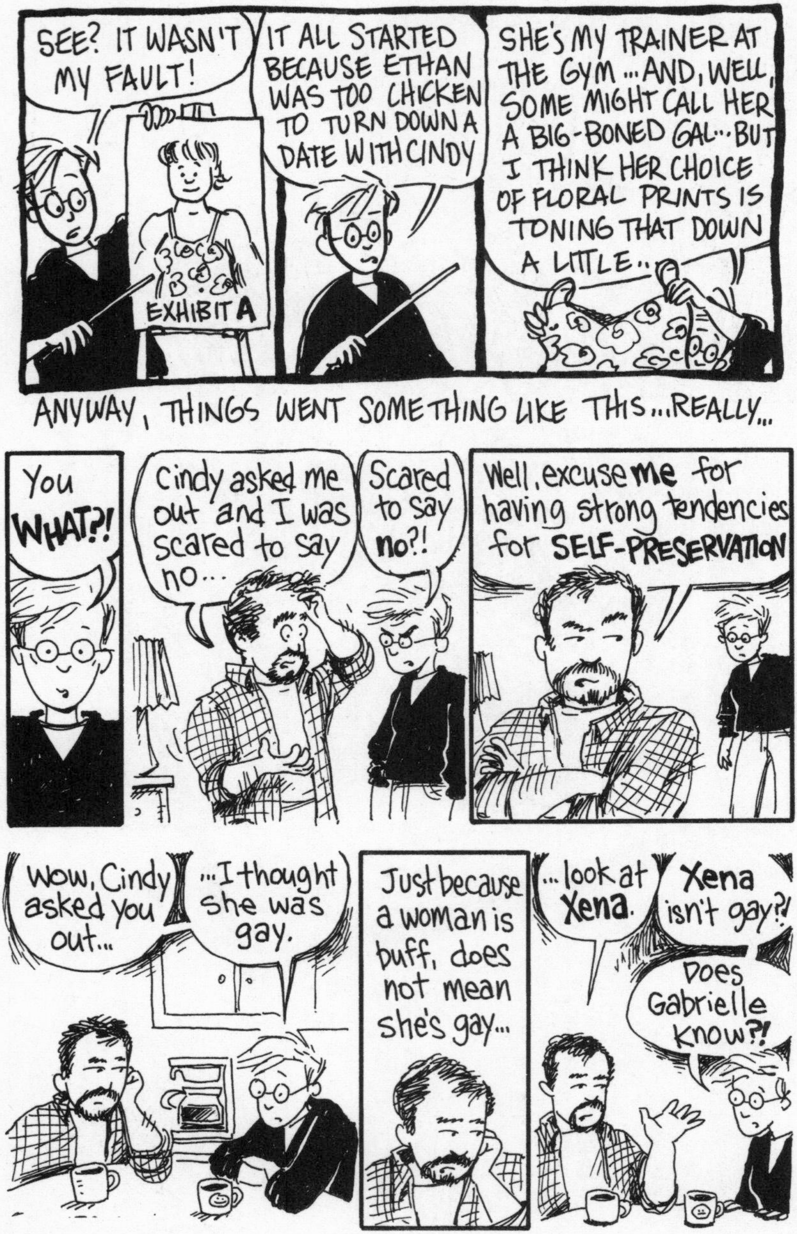

SEE? IT WASN'T MY FAULT!
EXHIBIT A
IT ALL STARTED BECAUSE ETHAN WAS TOO CHICKEN TO TURN DOWN A DATE WITH CINDY
SHE'S MY TRAINER AT THE GYM ... AND, WELL, SOME MIGHT CALL HER A BIG-BONED GAL... BUT I THINK HER CHOICE OF FLORAL PRINTS IS TONING THAT DOWN A LITTLE...
ANYWAY, THINGS WENT SOMETHING LIKE THIS...REALLY...
You WHAT?!
Cindy asked me out and I was scared to say no...
Scared to say no?!
Well, excuse me for having strong tendencies for SELF-PRESERVATION
Wow, Cindy asked you out...
...I thought she was gay.
Just because a woman is buff, does not mean she's gay...
...look at Xena.
Xena isn't gay?!
Does Gabrielle know?!

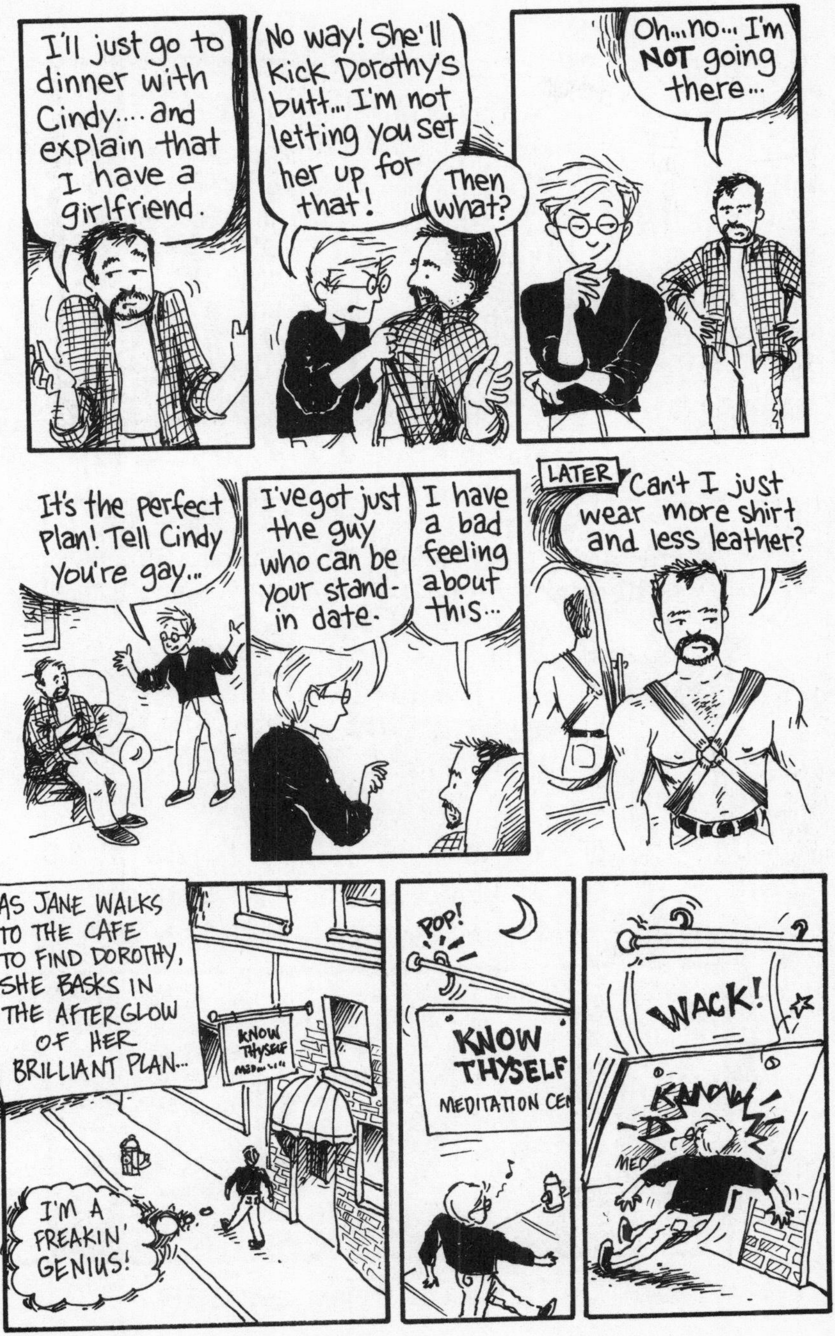
I'll just go to dinner with Cindy.... and explain that I have a girlfriend.
No way! She'll kick Dorothy's butt... I'm not letting you set her up for that!
Then what?
Oh...no... I'm **NOT** going there...
It's the perfect plan! Tell Cindy you're gay...
I've got just the guy who can be your stand-in date.
I have a bad feeling about this...
LATER
Can't I just wear more shirt and less leather?
AS JANE WALKS TO THE CAFE TO FIND DOROTHY, SHE BASKS IN THE AFTERGLOW OF HER BRILLIANT PLAN...
KNOW THYSELF
I'M A FREAKIN' GENIUS!
POP!
KNOW THYSELF
MEDITATION CEN
WACK!
KANOW!
MED

OH SURE, SO THERE WAS THAT UNFORTUNATE FALLING SIGN INCIDENT... I MEAN, THAT WASN'T MY FAULT EITHER... I WAS JUST MINDING MY OWN BUSINESS... AND **BOOM!** I WAKE UP IN THIS PARALLEL UNIVERSE POPULATED SOLEY BY FEMALE SUPER HEROS... YEAH, EVEN TRINITY WAS THERE... COMPLETE WITH **TRIUMPH**...

MEANWHILE, IN A REALITY NOT SO FAR AWAY!

HELLO...

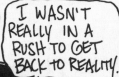

YOU GET THE PICTURE...

I WASN'T REALLY IN A RUSH TO GET BACK TO REALITY.

UNFORTUNATELY, THE **POWERS THAT BE** HAD OTHER NOTIONS AND I HAD TO BID FAREWELL TO THE LAND OF **WONDERBRAS**... AND CAN YOU BELIEVE IT?... I CAME BACK TO REALITY WITH NOT ONE PERK!

YOU'D THINK A HEAD INJURY WOULD AT LEAST SCORE SOME SYMPATHY... AND MAYBE EVEN AN EXTRA DESSERT!

I'M REALLY OKAY, BUT IF YOU INSIST ON BRINGING ME A CUP-CAKE FOR BREAKFAST THAT'D BE GREAT...

CUPCAKE?! HERE, YOU'RE HAVING YOGURT AND FRUIT.

CUPCAKE!...PULEEZE... BUT..BUT... I THOUGHT A HEAD INJURY WAS ALL ABOUT JELLO, ICE CREAM AND CUPCAKES?

...BUT, WAIT!... IT GETS EVEN BETTER...

MY BOSS COULD CARE LESS... SEE, I'M A COG IN THIS CORPORATE MEDIA MACHINE, ONCE FONDLY REFERRED TO BY MY GRANDPA AS A "DAILY **NEWS**-PAPER"... YEAH... MAYBE IN HIS DAY... NOW, IT'S "SEXY" NEWS THAT SELLS... SCANDAL IS WHAT EVERYONE WANTS. UNFORTUNATELY FOR ME, I'M NOT ON THE "SEXY" BEAT...

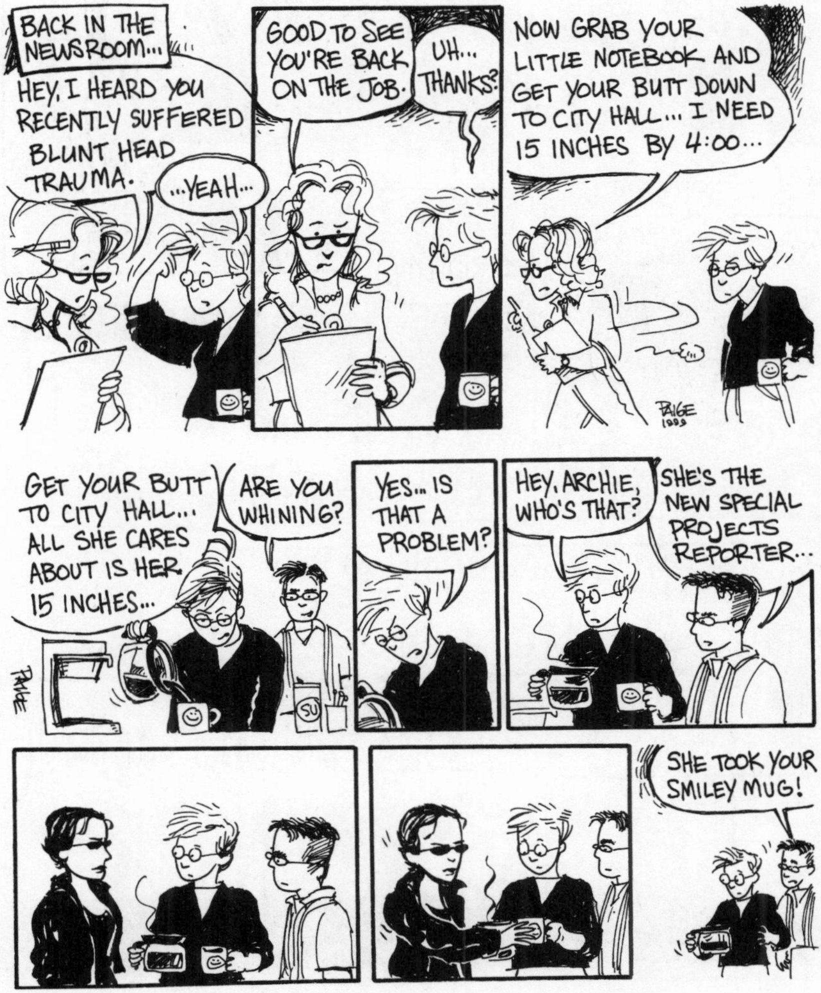
BACK IN THE NEWSROOM...
HEY, I HEARD YOU RECENTLY SUFFERED BLUNT HEAD TRAUMA.
...YEAH...
GOOD TO SEE YOU'RE BACK ON THE JOB.
UH... THANKS?
NOW GRAB YOUR LITTLE NOTEBOOK AND GET YOUR BUTT DOWN TO CITY HALL... I NEED 15 INCHES BY 4:00...
GET YOUR BUTT TO CITY HALL... ALL SHE CARES ABOUT IS HER 15 INCHES...
ARE YOU WHINING?
YES... IS THAT A PROBLEM?
HEY, ARCHIE, WHO'S THAT?
SHE'S THE NEW SPECIAL PROJECTS REPORTER...
SHE TOOK YOUR SMILEY MUG!

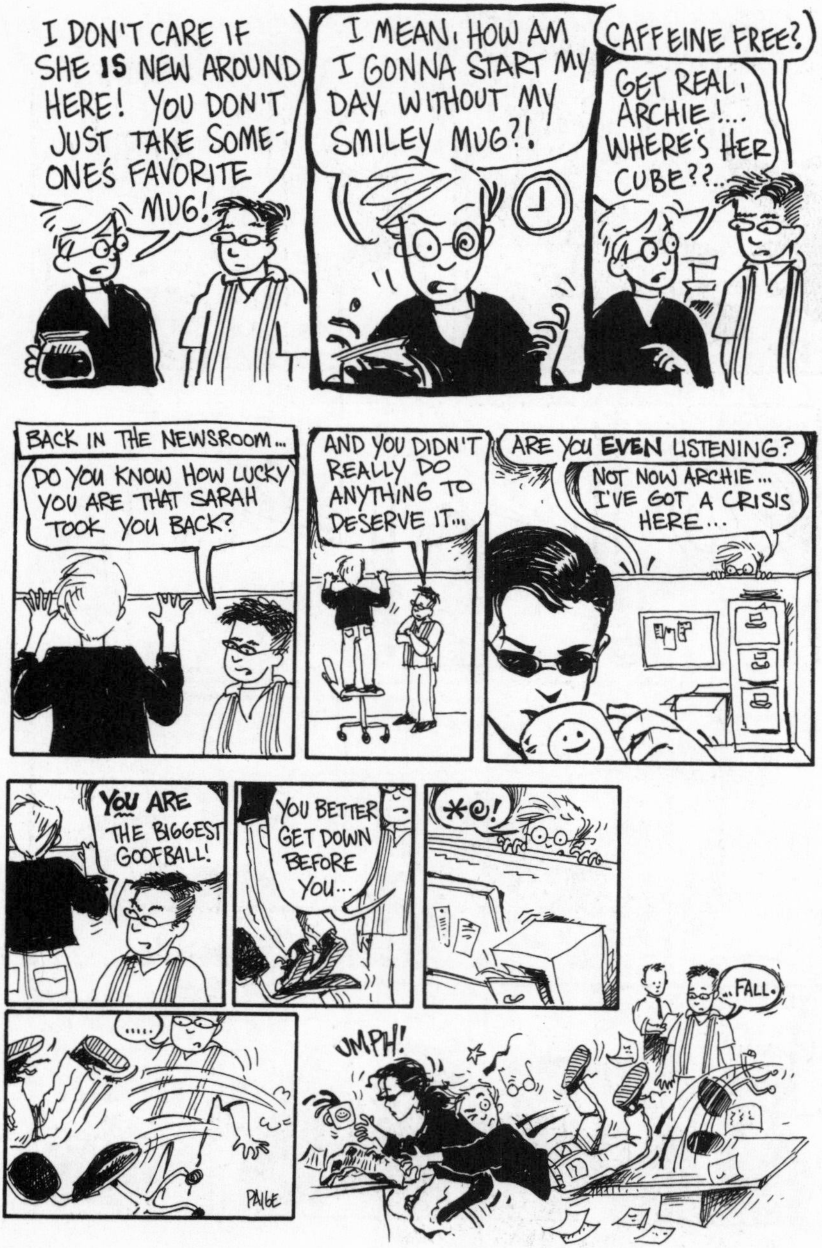

I DON'T CARE IF SHE **IS** NEW AROUND HERE! YOU DON'T JUST TAKE SOME-ONE'S FAVORITE MUG!
I MEAN, HOW AM I GONNA START MY DAY WITHOUT MY SMILEY MUG?!
CAFFEINE FREE?
GET REAL, ARCHIE!... WHERE'S HER CUBE??...
BACK IN THE NEWSROOM...
DO YOU KNOW HOW LUCKY YOU ARE THAT SARAH TOOK YOU BACK?
AND YOU DIDN'T REALLY DO ANYTHING TO DESERVE IT...
ARE YOU **EVEN** LISTENING?
NOT NOW ARCHIE... I'VE GOT A CRISIS HERE...
YOU ARE THE BIGGEST GOOFBALL!
YOU BETTER GET DOWN BEFORE YOU...
*@!
.....
..FALL.
UMPH!
PAIGE

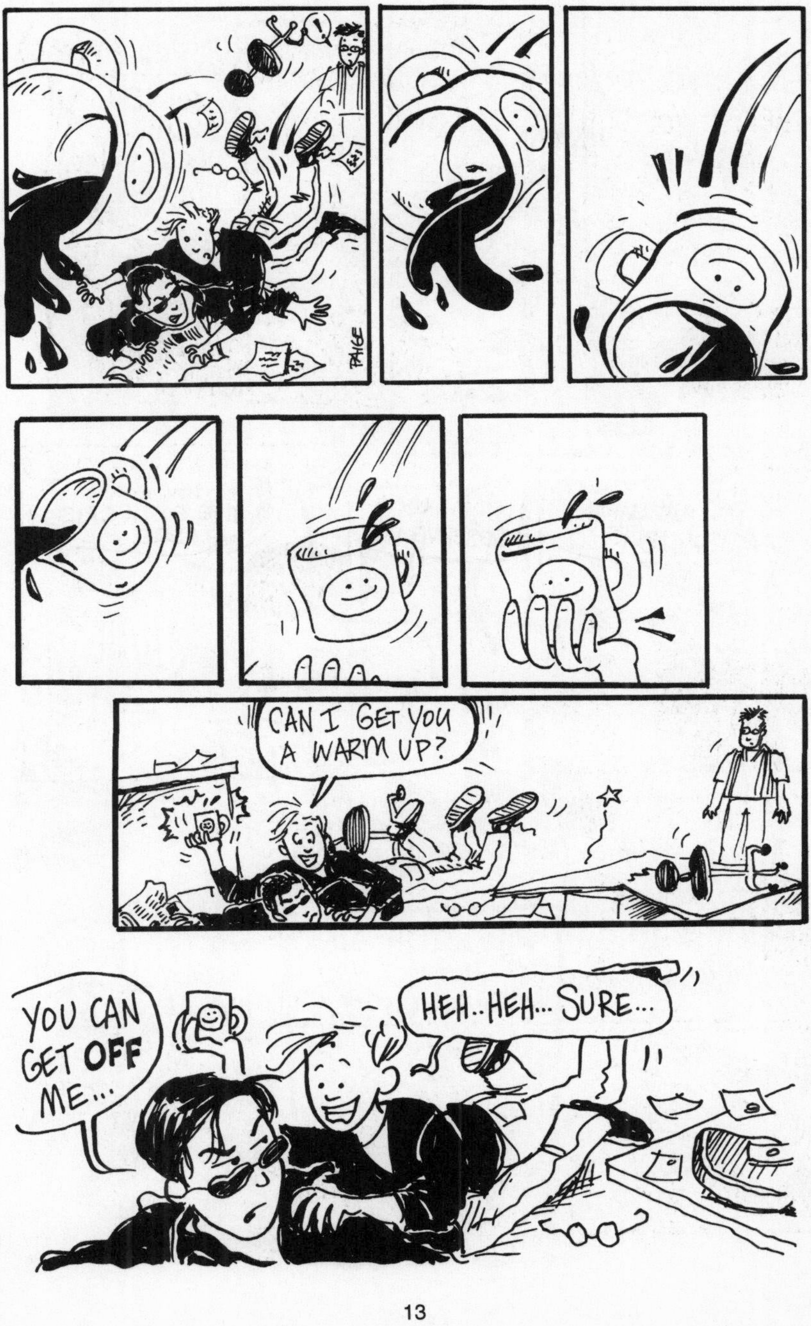
PAIGE
CAN I GET YOU A WARM UP?
YOU CAN GET OFF ME...
HEH.. HEH... SURE...

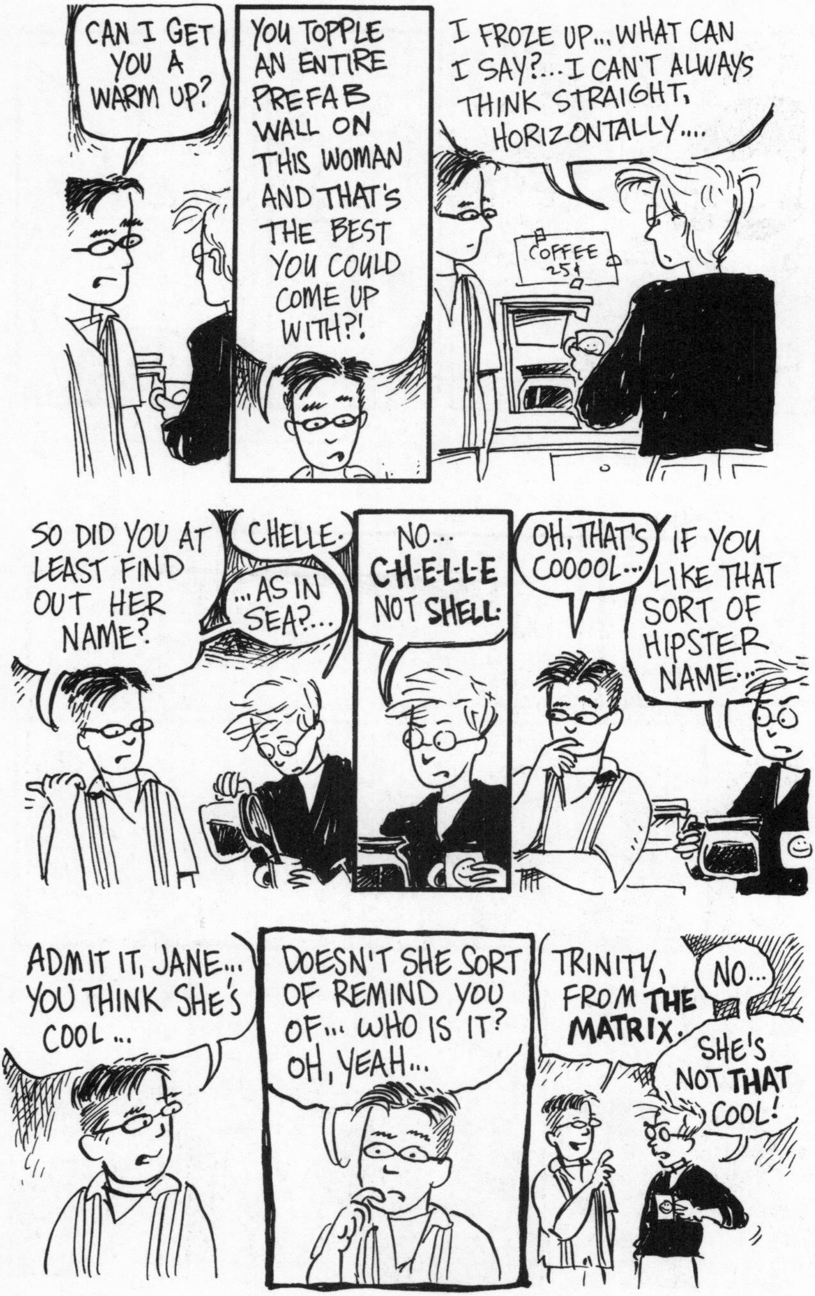
CAN I GET YOU A WARM UP?
YOU TOPPLE AN ENTIRE PREFAB WALL ON THIS WOMAN AND THAT'S THE BEST YOU COULD COME UP WITH?!
I FROZE UP... WHAT CAN I SAY?... I CAN'T ALWAYS THINK STRAIGHT, HORIZONTALLY....
COFFEE 25¢
SO DID YOU AT LEAST FIND OUT HER NAME?
CHELLE.
...AS IN SEA?...
NO... C-H-E-L-L-E NOT SHELL.
OH, THAT'S COOOOL...
IF YOU LIKE THAT SORT OF HIPSTER NAME...
ADMIT IT, JANE... YOU THINK SHE'S COOL...
DOESN'T SHE SORT OF REMIND YOU OF... WHO IS IT? OH, YEAH...
TRINITY, FROM THE MATRIX.
NO...
SHE'S NOT THAT COOL!

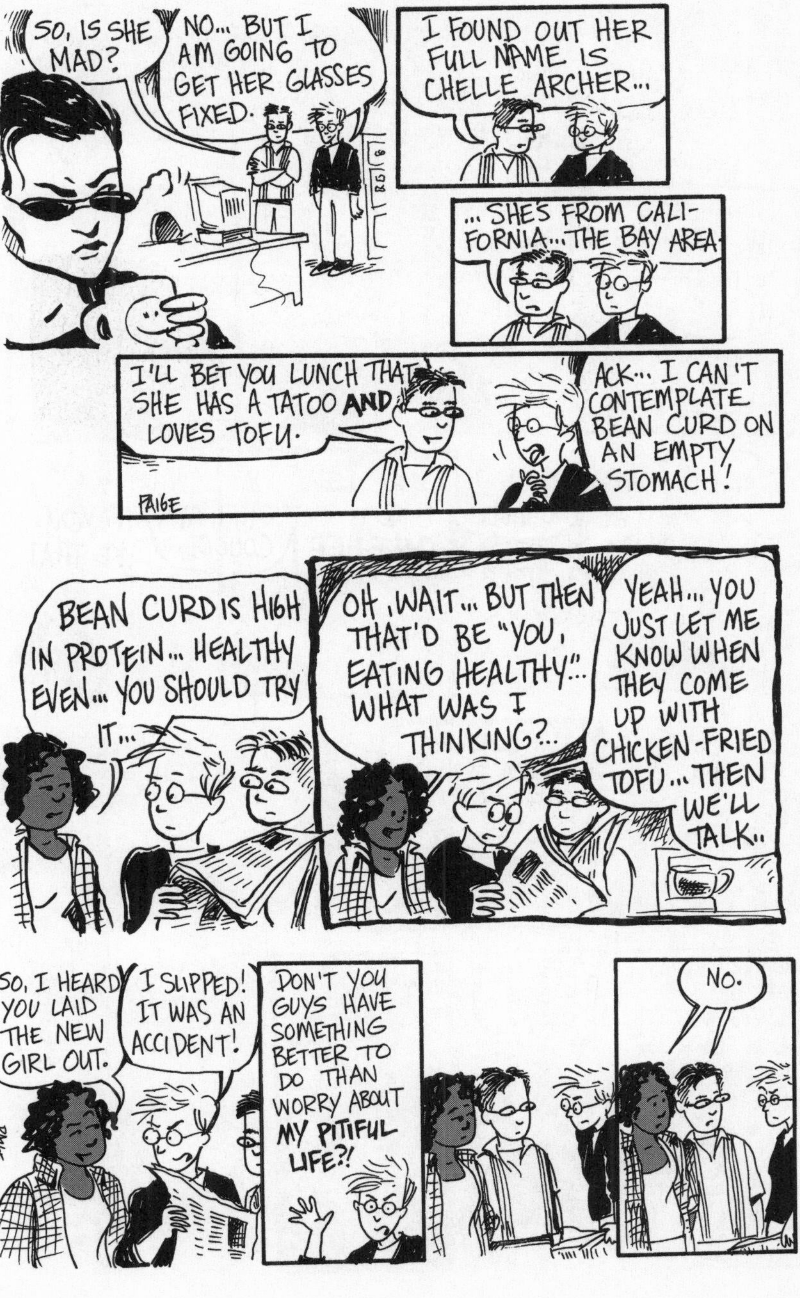
SO, IS SHE MAD?
NO... BUT I AM GOING TO GET HER GLASSES FIXED.
I FOUND OUT HER FULL NAME IS CHELLE ARCHER...
... SHE'S FROM CALI-FORNIA... THE BAY AREA.
I'LL BET YOU LUNCH THAT SHE HAS A TATOO **AND** LOVES TOFU.
ACK... I CAN'T CONTEMPLATE BEAN CURD ON AN EMPTY STOMACH!
PAIGE
BEAN CURD IS HIGH IN PROTEIN... HEALTHY EVEN... YOU SHOULD TRY IT...
OH, WAIT... BUT THEN THAT'D BE "YOU, EATING HEALTHY"... WHAT WAS I THINKING?...
YEAH... YOU JUST LET ME KNOW WHEN THEY COME UP WITH CHICKEN-FRIED TOFU... THEN WE'LL TALK..
SO, I HEARD YOU LAID THE NEW GIRL OUT.
I SLIPPED! IT WAS AN ACCIDENT!
DON'T YOU GUYS HAVE SOMETHING BETTER TO DO THAN WORRY ABOUT **MY PITIFUL LIFE?!**
NO.
PAIGE

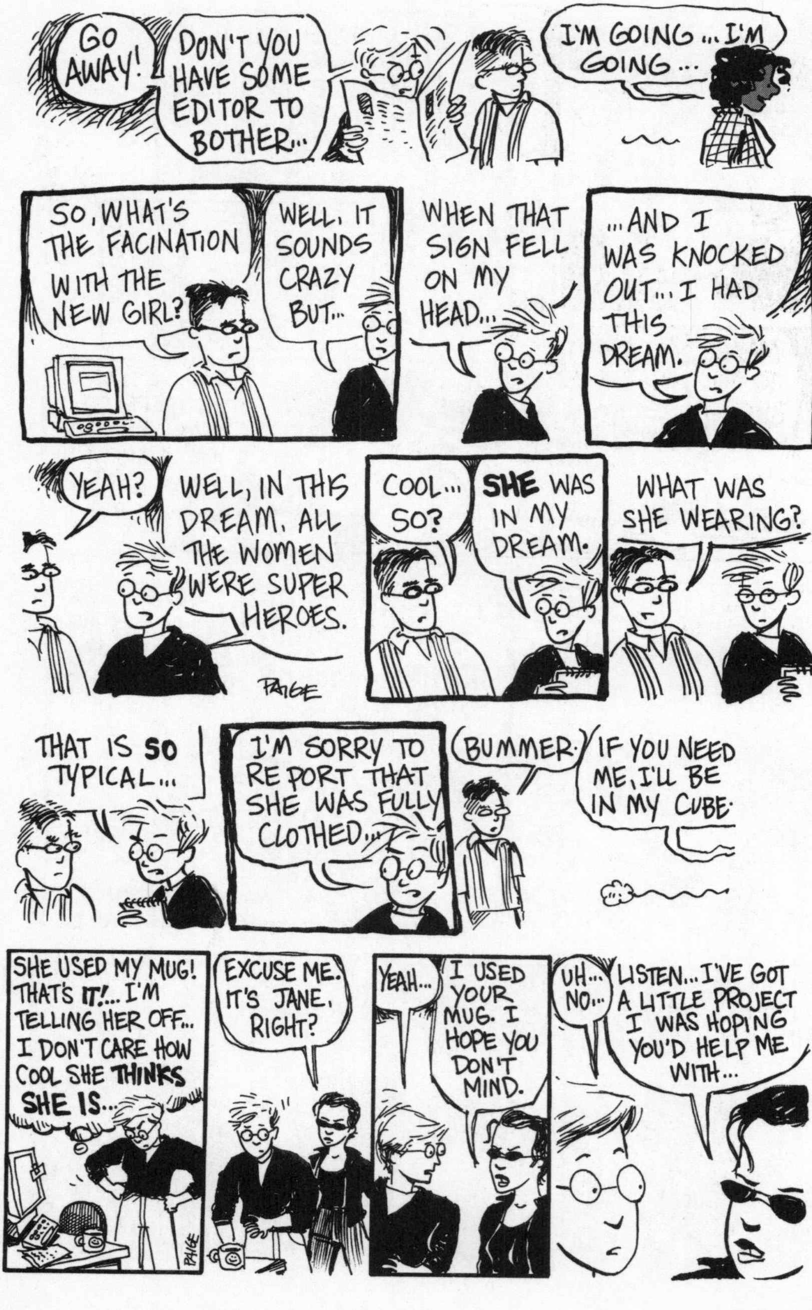
GO AWAY!
DON'T YOU HAVE SOME EDITOR TO BOTHER...
I'M GOING... I'M GOING...
SO, WHAT'S THE FACINATION WITH THE NEW GIRL?
WELL, IT SOUNDS CRAZY BUT...
WHEN THAT SIGN FELL ON MY HEAD...
...AND I WAS KNOCKED OUT... I HAD THIS DREAM.
YEAH?
WELL, IN THIS DREAM, ALL THE WOMEN WERE SUPER HEROES.
PAIGE
COOL... SO?
SHE WAS IN MY DREAM.
WHAT WAS SHE WEARING?
THAT IS SO TYPICAL...
I'M SORRY TO REPORT THAT SHE WAS FULLY CLOTHED...
BUMMER.
IF YOU NEED ME, I'LL BE IN MY CUBE.
SHE USED MY MUG! THAT'S IT!... I'M TELLING HER OFF... I DON'T CARE HOW COOL SHE THINKS SHE IS...
PAIGE
EXCUSE ME. IT'S JANE, RIGHT?
YEAH...
I USED YOUR MUG. I HOPE YOU DON'T MIND.
UH... NO...
LISTEN... I'VE GOT A LITTLE PROJECT I WAS HOPING YOU'D HELP ME WITH...

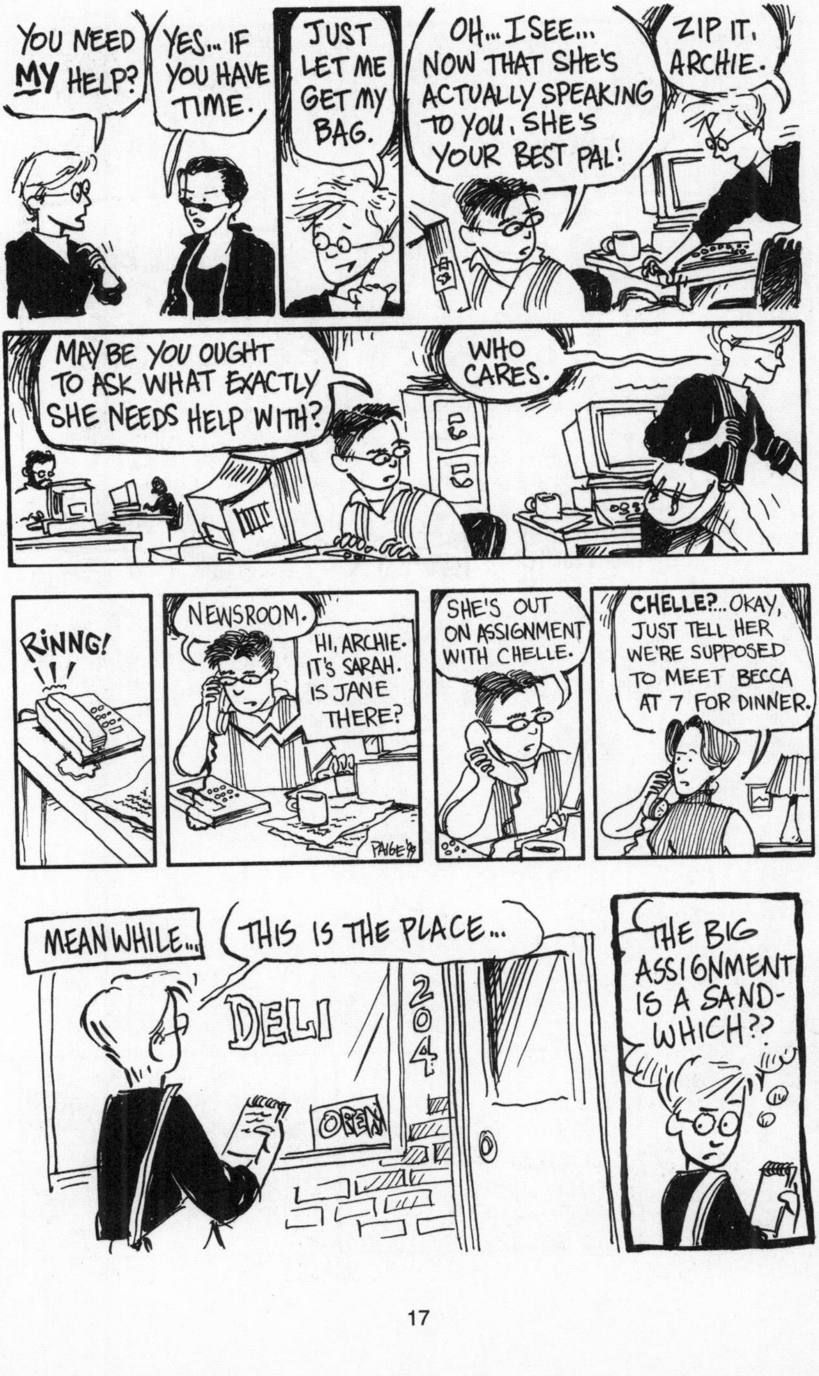

YOU NEED MY HELP?
YES... IF YOU HAVE TIME.
JUST LET ME GET MY BAG.
OH... I SEE... NOW THAT SHE'S ACTUALLY SPEAKING TO YOU, SHE'S YOUR BEST PAL!
ZIP IT, ARCHIE.
MAYBE YOU OUGHT TO ASK WHAT EXACTLY SHE NEEDS HELP WITH?
WHO CARES.
RiNNG!
NEWSROOM.
HI, ARCHIE. IT'S SARAH. IS JANE THERE?
SHE'S OUT ON ASSIGNMENT WITH CHELLE.
CHELLE?... OKAY, JUST TELL HER WE'RE SUPPOSED TO MEET BECCA AT 7 FOR DINNER.
PAIGE '98
MEANWHILE...
THIS IS THE PLACE...
DELI
204
OPEN
THE BIG ASSIGNMENT IS A SAND-WHICH??

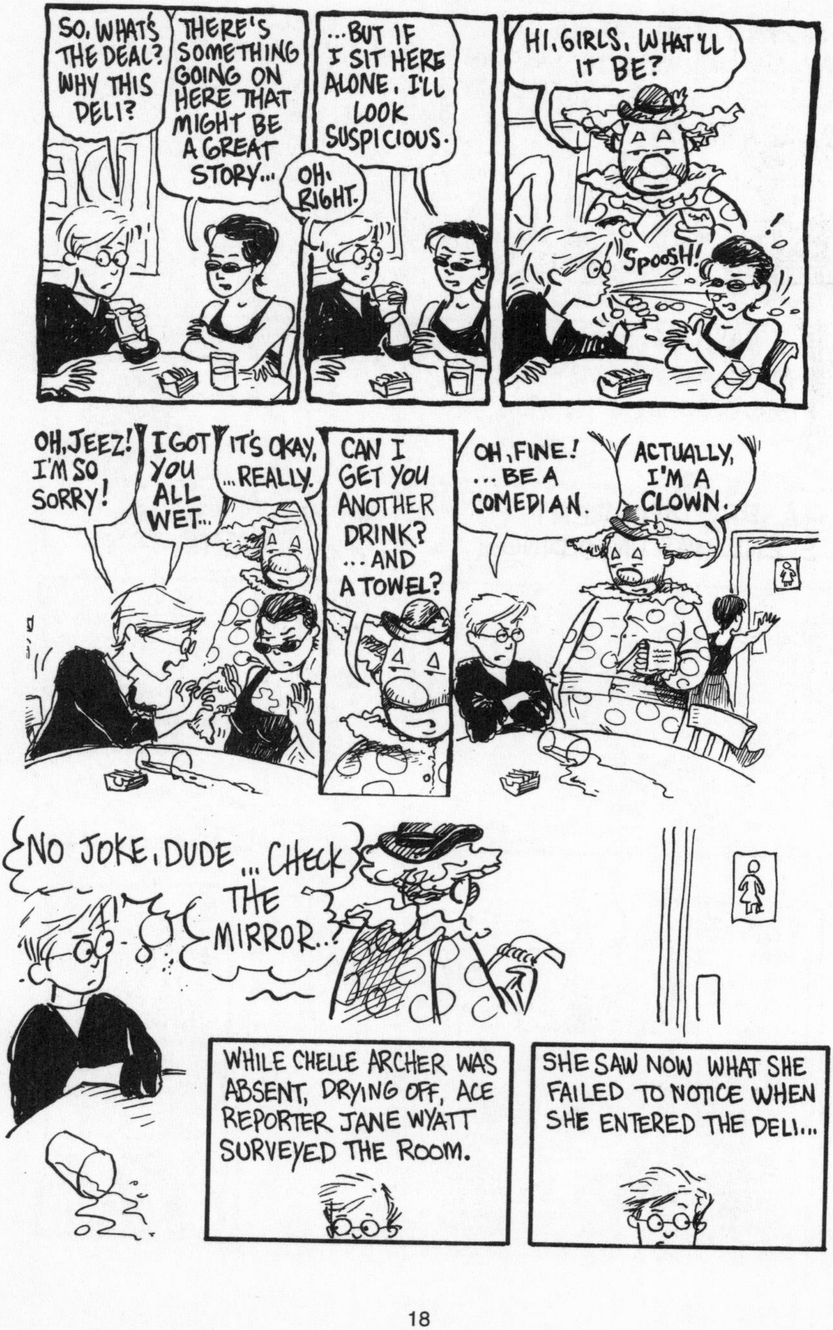
SO, WHAT'S THE DEAL? WHY THIS DELI?
THERE'S SOMETHING GOING ON HERE THAT MIGHT BE A GREAT STORY...
...BUT IF I SIT HERE ALONE, I'LL LOOK SUSPICIOUS.
OH, RIGHT.
HI, GIRLS. WHAT'LL IT BE?
!
SPOOSH!
OH, JEEZ! I'M SO SORRY!
I GOT YOU ALL WET...
IT'S OKAY, ...REALLY.
CAN I GET YOU ANOTHER DRINK? ...AND A TOWEL?
OH, FINE! ...BE A COMEDIAN.
ACTUALLY, I'M A CLOWN.
NO JOKE, DUDE... CHECK THE MIRROR...
WHILE CHELLE ARCHER WAS ABSENT, DRYING OFF, ACE REPORTER JANE WYATT SURVEYED THE ROOM.
SHE SAW NOW WHAT SHE FAILED TO NOTICE WHEN SHE ENTERED THE DELI...

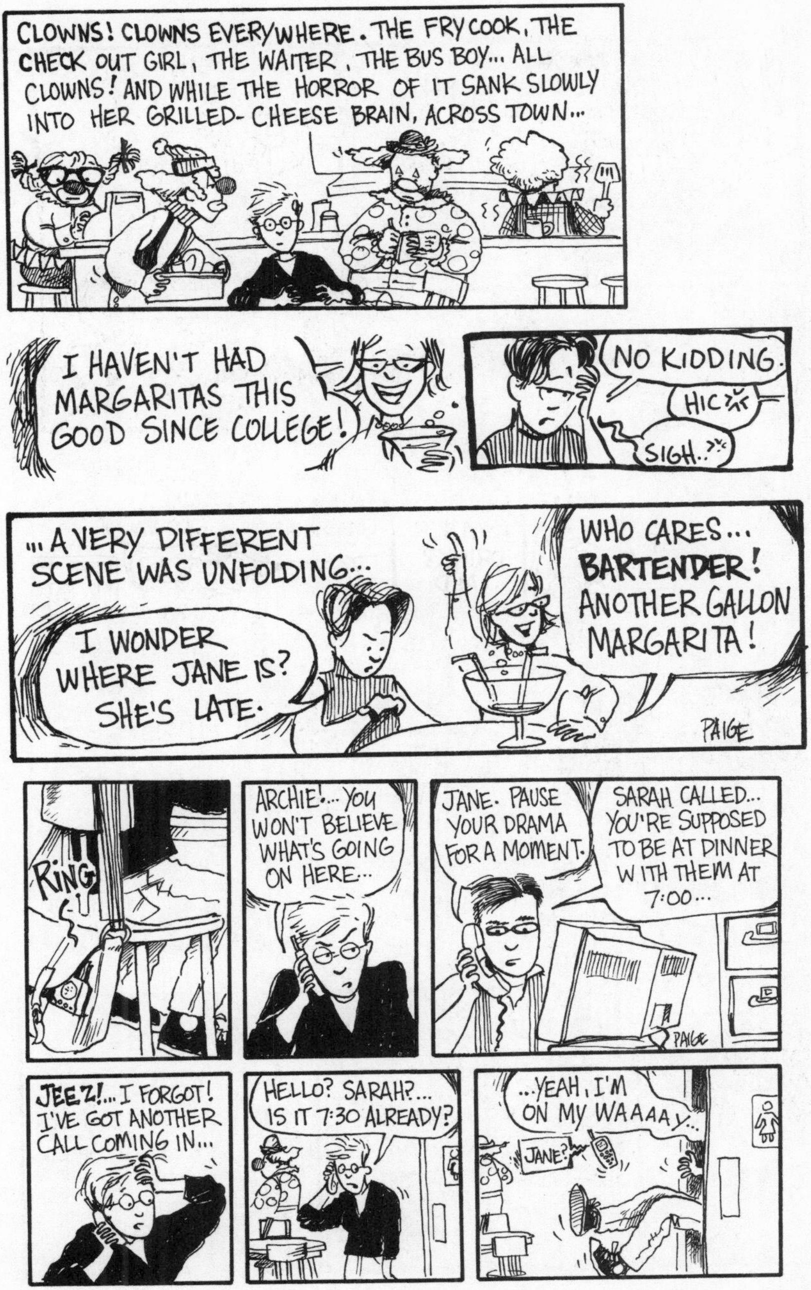
CLOWNS! CLOWNS EVERYWHERE. THE FRY COOK, THE CHECK OUT GIRL, THE WAITER, THE BUS BOY... ALL CLOWNS! AND WHILE THE HORROR OF IT SANK SLOWLY INTO HER GRILLED-CHEESE BRAIN, ACROSS TOWN...
I HAVEN'T HAD MARGARITAS THIS GOOD SINCE COLLEGE!
NO KIDDING.
HIC
SIGH..
...A VERY DIFFERENT SCENE WAS UNFOLDING...
I WONDER WHERE JANE IS? SHE'S LATE.
WHO CARES... BARTENDER! ANOTHER GALLON MARGARITA!
PAIGE
RING
ARCHIE!... YOU WON'T BELIEVE WHAT'S GOING ON HERE...
JANE. PAUSE YOUR DRAMA FOR A MOMENT.
SARAH CALLED... YOU'RE SUPPOSED TO BE AT DINNER WITH THEM AT 7:00...
PAIGE
JEEZ!... I FORGOT! I'VE GOT ANOTHER CALL COMING IN...
HELLO? SARAH?... IS IT 7:30 ALREADY?
...YEAH, I'M ON MY WAAAAY...
JANE?

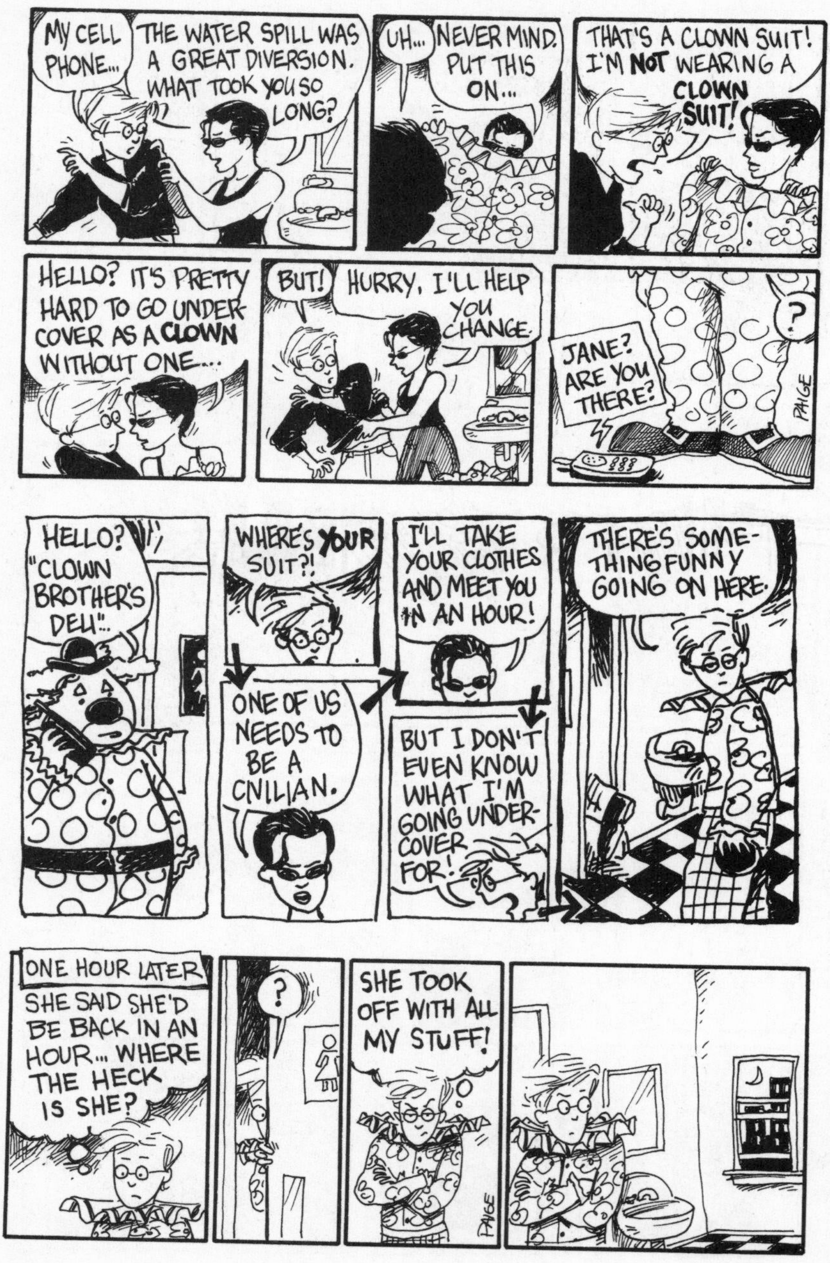
MY CELL PHONE...
THE WATER SPILL WAS A GREAT DIVERSION. WHAT TOOK YOU SO LONG?
UH...
NEVER MIND. PUT THIS ON...
THAT'S A CLOWN SUIT! I'M NOT WEARING A CLOWN SUIT!
HELLO? IT'S PRETTY HARD TO GO UNDER-COVER AS A CLOWN WITHOUT ONE...
BUT!
HURRY, I'LL HELP YOU CHANGE.
JANE? ARE YOU THERE?
?
PAIGE
HELLO? "CLOWN BROTHER'S DELI"...
WHERE'S YOUR SUIT?!
ONE OF US NEEDS TO BE A CIVILIAN.
I'LL TAKE YOUR CLOTHES AND MEET YOU IN AN HOUR!
BUT I DON'T EVEN KNOW WHAT I'M GOING UNDER-COVER FOR!
THERE'S SOME-THING FUNNY GOING ON HERE.
ONE HOUR LATER
SHE SAID SHE'D BE BACK IN AN HOUR... WHERE THE HECK IS SHE?
?
SHE TOOK OFF WITH ALL MY STUFF!
PAIGE

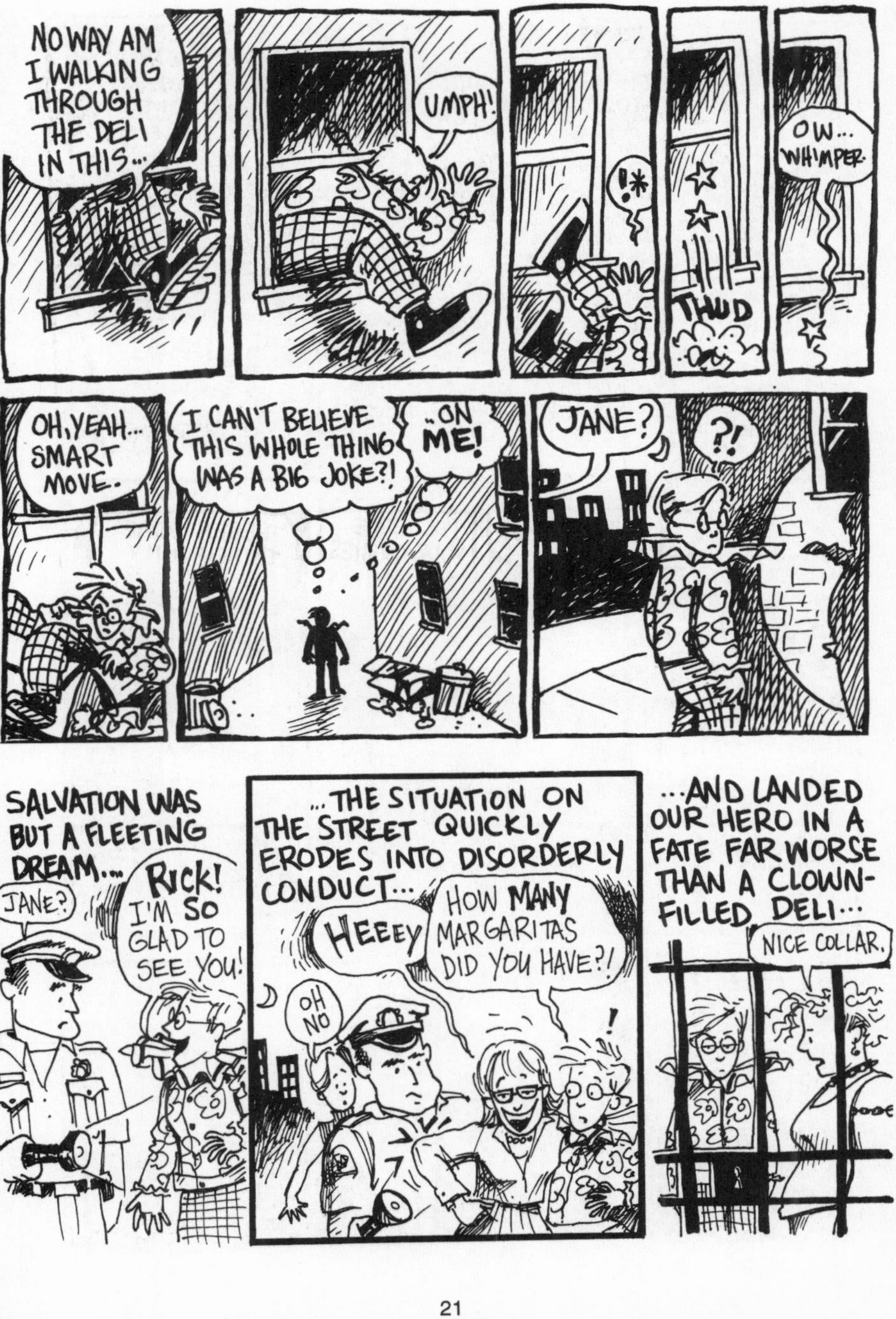
NO WAY AM I WALKING THROUGH THE DELI IN THIS...
UMPH!
!*
THUD
OW... WHIMPER
OH, YEAH... SMART MOVE.
I CAN'T BELIEVE THIS WHOLE THING WAS A BIG JOKE?!
..ON ME!
JANE?
?!
SALVATION WAS BUT A FLEETING DREAM....
JANE?
RICK! I'M SO GLAD TO SEE YOU!
...THE SITUATION ON THE STREET QUICKLY ERODES INTO DISORDERLY CONDUCT...
HEEEY
HOW MANY MARGARITAS DID YOU HAVE?!
OH NO
!
...AND LANDED OUR HERO IN A FATE FAR WORSE THAN A CLOWN-FILLED DELI...
NICE COLLAR.

THANKS ALOT!
DID YOU HAVE TO MAKE SUCH A DRUNKEN SCENE?... IN PUBLIC?!
HUH, WHAT? (HIC)
NEVER MIND.
WE WOULDN'T EVEN HAVE BEEN THERE IF THAT CLOWN HADN'T ANSWERED YOUR CELL PHONE.
UMPH!
SPEAKING OF CLOWNS... WHAT ARE YOU WEARING?
Z
WANNA TRADE COLLARS?
I WANT MY PHONE CALL!!
OKAY... MAKE YOUR PHONE CALL AND MOVE ALONG.
FINALLY!
OH NO...
BUSY SIGNAL
NO! HE'S SURFING!
NEXT!
Nooooo...
MEANWHILE, AT JANE'S HOUSE...
COOL... I JUST BOUGHT A KARMANN GHIA ON EBAY...
I WONDER WHY JANE ISN'T HOME YET...
IT'S GREAT TO HAVE THE PHONE LINE ALL TO MY-SELF... I'LL JUST SURF A LITTLE MORE...
I'M GONNA KILL ETHAN..
MIND IF I SIT DOWN?..

A FEW HOURS LATER...

SEE. I LEFT MY FIRST HUSBAND BECAUSE... WELL IT WAS VERY COMPLICATED...
I CALLED KATE. SHE'LL BE HERE IN A HALF HOUR...
...OH... MY HEAD.
PAIGE
HE WAS BAD. BUT SO GOOD... IF YOU KNOW WHAT I MEAN.
OKAY, LADIES... YOU'RE FREE TO GO... LET'S TRY AND STAY OUT OF TROUBLE FROM NOW ON...
CLICK
NICE OUTFIT, FUNNY GIRL...
BECCA!
SHHH... DON'T YELL...
HUNG OVER?
NICE COLLAR.
IF YOU WEREN'T MY SISTER I'D BELT YOU...
PAIGE
YOU AND WHAT CLOWN ARMY?

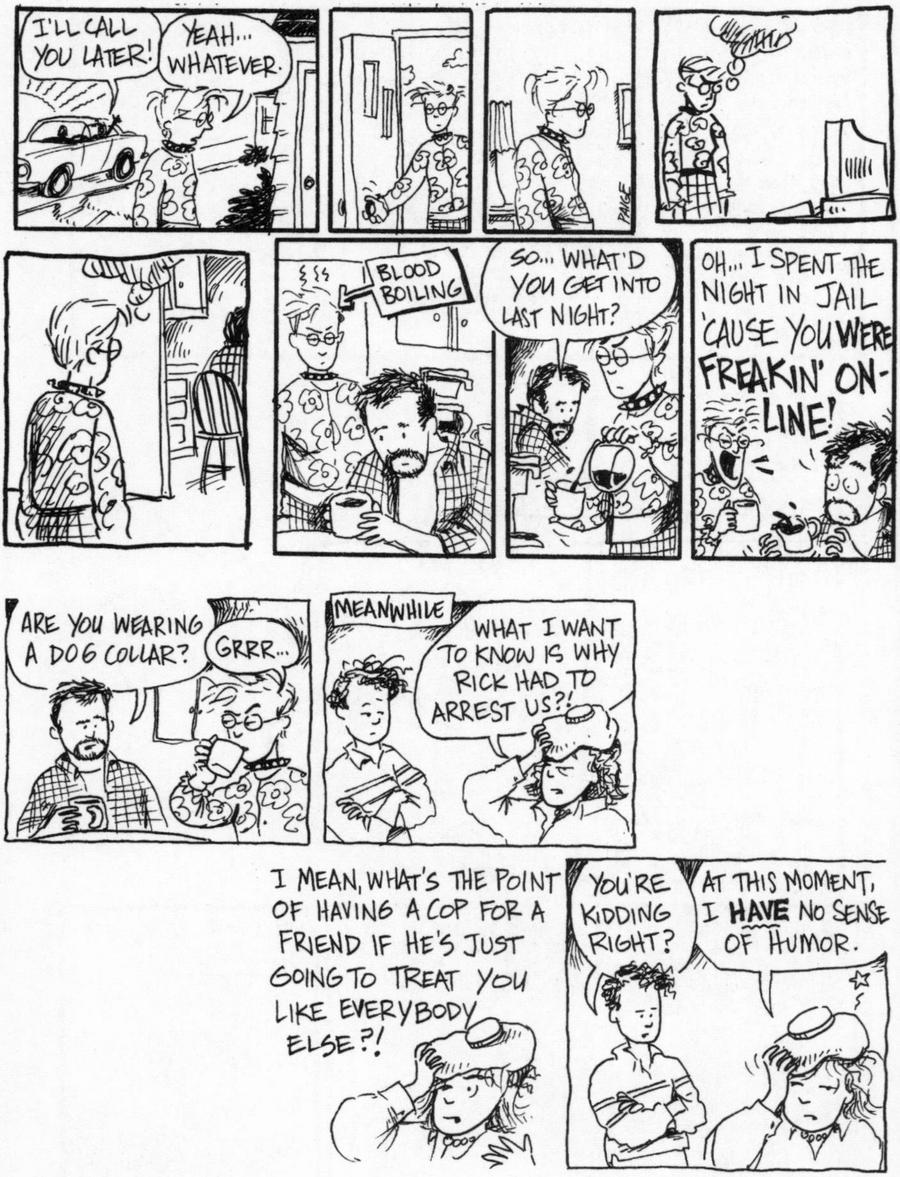
I'LL CALL YOU LATER!
YEAH... WHATEVER.
PAIGE
BLOOD BOILING
SO... WHAT'D YOU GET INTO LAST NIGHT?
OH... I SPENT THE NIGHT IN JAIL 'CAUSE YOU WERE FREAKIN' ON-LINE!
ARE YOU WEARING A DOG COLLAR?
GRRR...
MEANWHILE
WHAT I WANT TO KNOW IS WHY RICK HAD TO ARREST US?!
I MEAN, WHAT'S THE POINT OF HAVING A COP FOR A FRIEND IF HE'S JUST GOING TO TREAT YOU LIKE EVERYBODY ELSE?!
YOU'RE KIDDING RIGHT?
AT THIS MOMENT, I HAVE NO SENSE OF HUMOR.

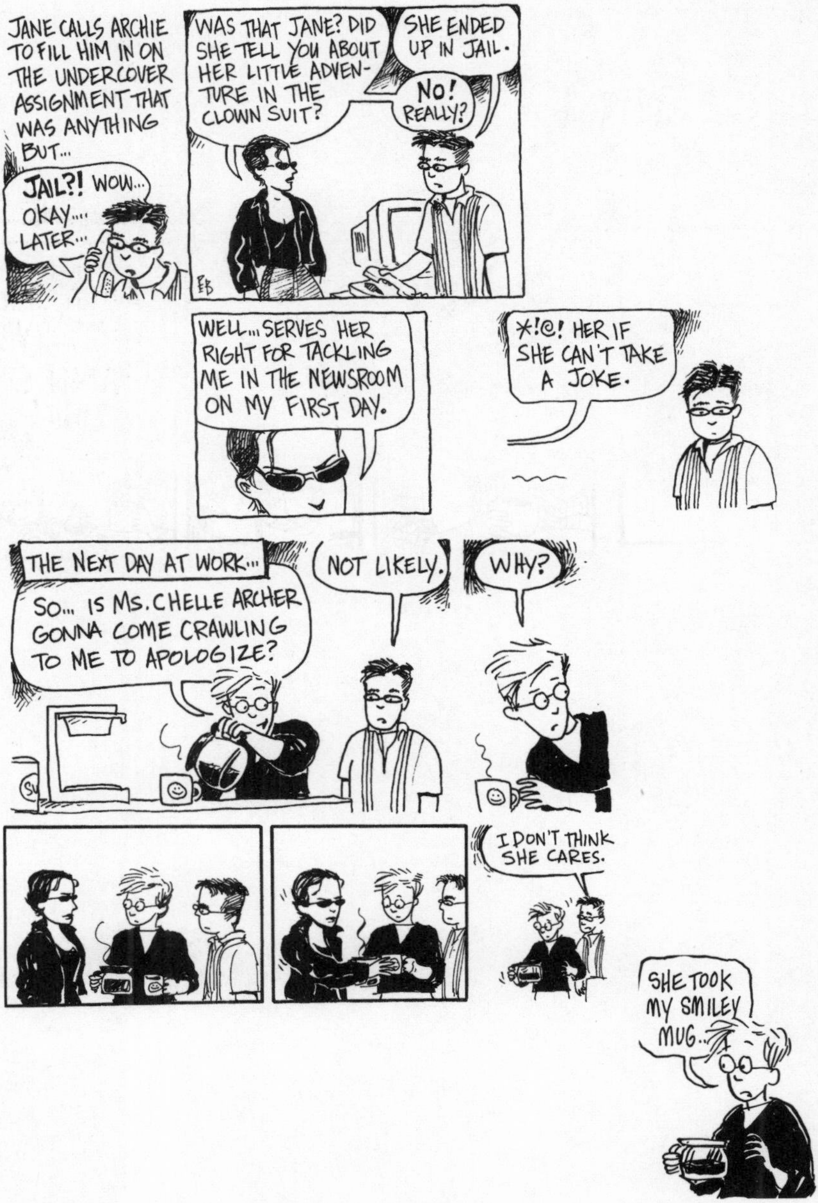
JANE CALLS ARCHIE TO FILL HIM IN ON THE UNDERCOVER ASSIGNMENT THAT WAS ANYTHING BUT...
JAIL?! WOW... OKAY.... LATER...
WAS THAT JANE? DID SHE TELL YOU ABOUT HER LITTLE ADVENTURE IN THE CLOWN SUIT?
SHE ENDED UP IN JAIL.
NO! REALLY?
WELL... SERVES HER RIGHT FOR TACKLING ME IN THE NEWSROOM ON MY FIRST DAY.
*!@! HER IF SHE CAN'T TAKE A JOKE.
THE NEXT DAY AT WORK...
SO... IS MS. CHELLE ARCHER GONNA COME CRAWLING TO ME TO APOLOGIZE?
NOT LIKELY.
WHY?
I DON'T THINK SHE CARES.
SHE TOOK MY SMILEY MUG...

Chapter 2

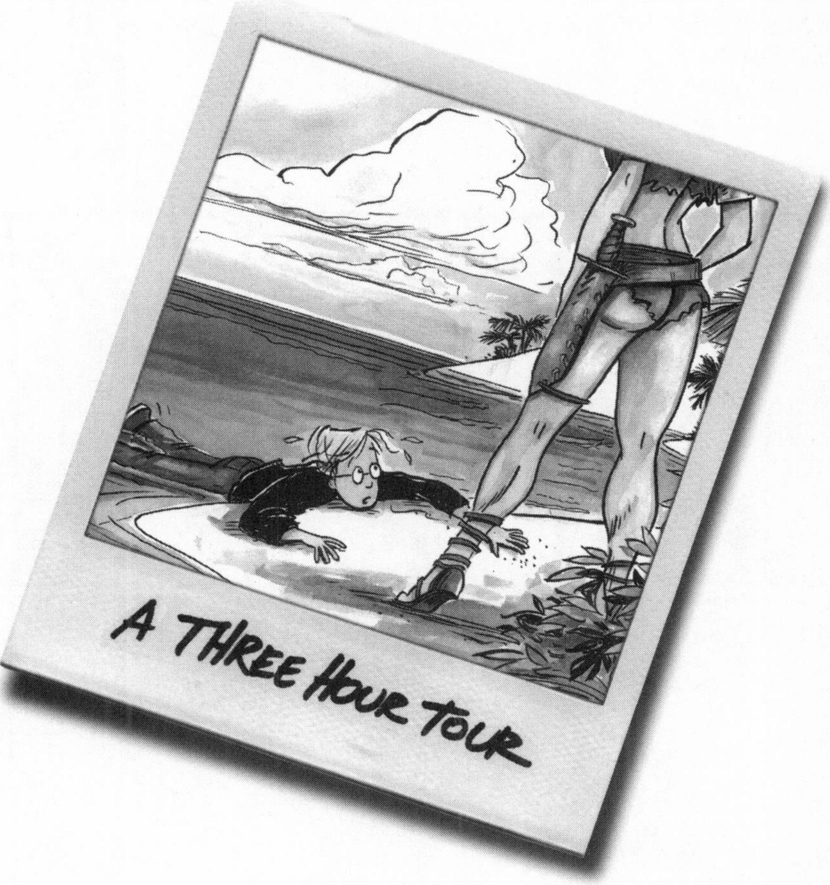
A THREE HOUR TOUR

DAYS HAVE PASSED SINCE JANE'S EMBARRASSING ARREST IN THE CLOWN SUIT. JANE HAS RECOVERED A BIT OF HER COMPOSURE ABOUT THE WHOLE EXPERIENCE, BUT SHE STILL ISN'T ALL THAT SURE SHE CAN TRUST CHELLE'S MOTIVES. MAYBE THAT IS JUST JANE, BEING SELF-ABSORBED... ASSUMING THAT WHATEVER CHELLE'S MOTIVES MIGHT BE, THEY MUST REVOLVE AROUND HER.

WE NOW REJOIN OUR STORY, ALREADY IN PROGRESS....

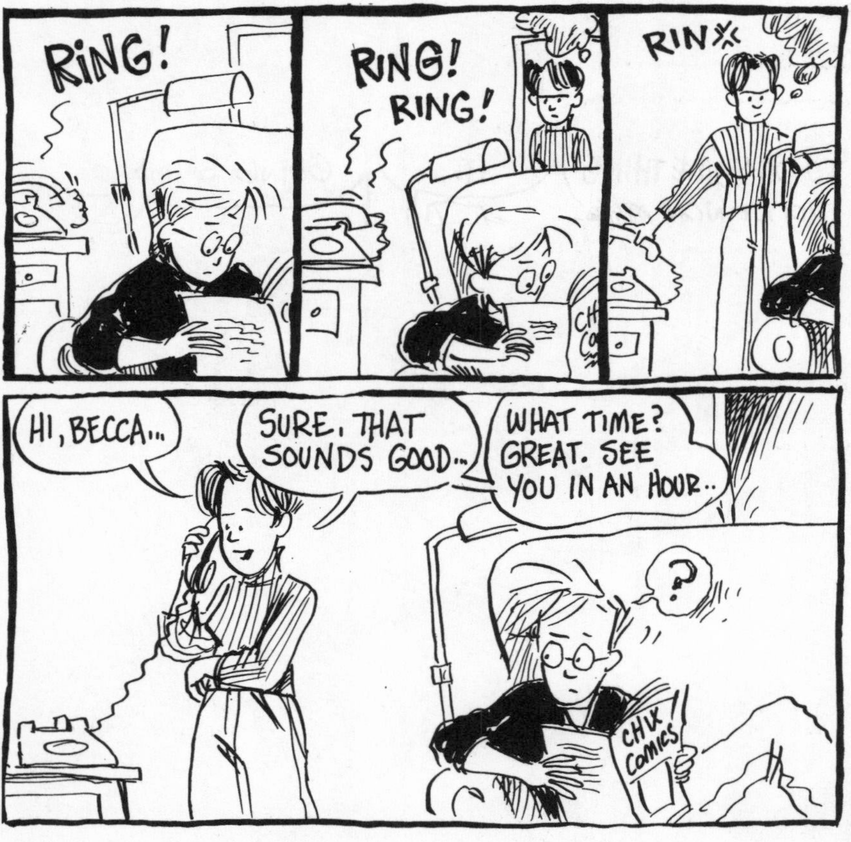

RING!
RING!
RING!
RIN
HI, BECCA...
SURE, THAT SOUNDS GOOD...
WHAT TIME? GREAT. SEE YOU IN AN HOUR..
?
CHIX COMICS

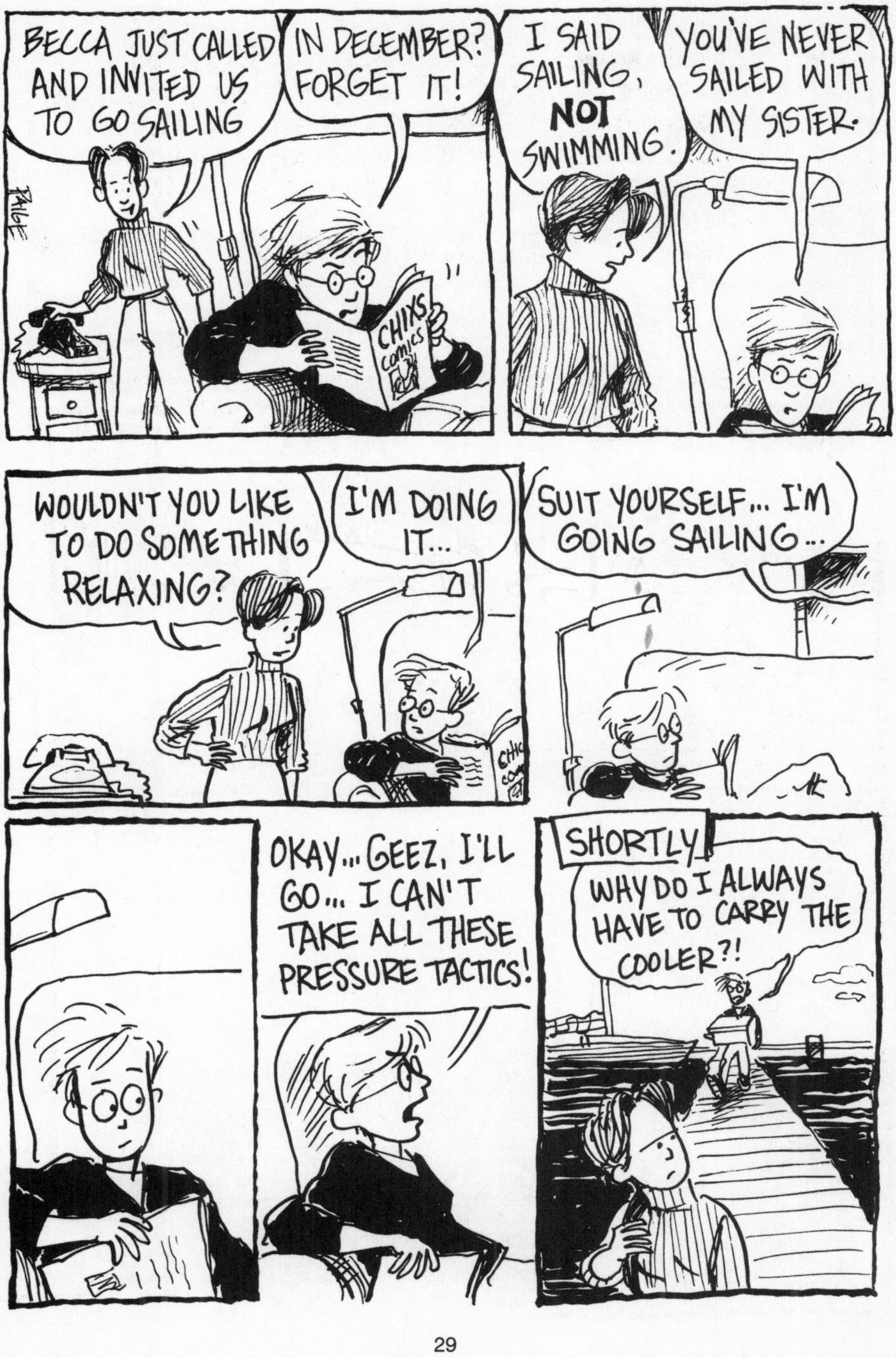
BECCA JUST CALLED AND INVITED US TO GO SAILING
IN DECEMBER? FORGET IT!
I SAID SAILING, NOT SWIMMING.
YOU'VE NEVER SAILED WITH MY SISTER.
WOULDN'T YOU LIKE TO DO SOMETHING RELAXING?
I'M DOING IT...
SUIT YOURSELF... I'M GOING SAILING...
OKAY... GEEZ, I'LL GO... I CAN'T TAKE ALL THESE PRESSURE TACTICS!
SHORTLY
WHY DO I ALWAYS HAVE TO CARRY THE COOLER?!

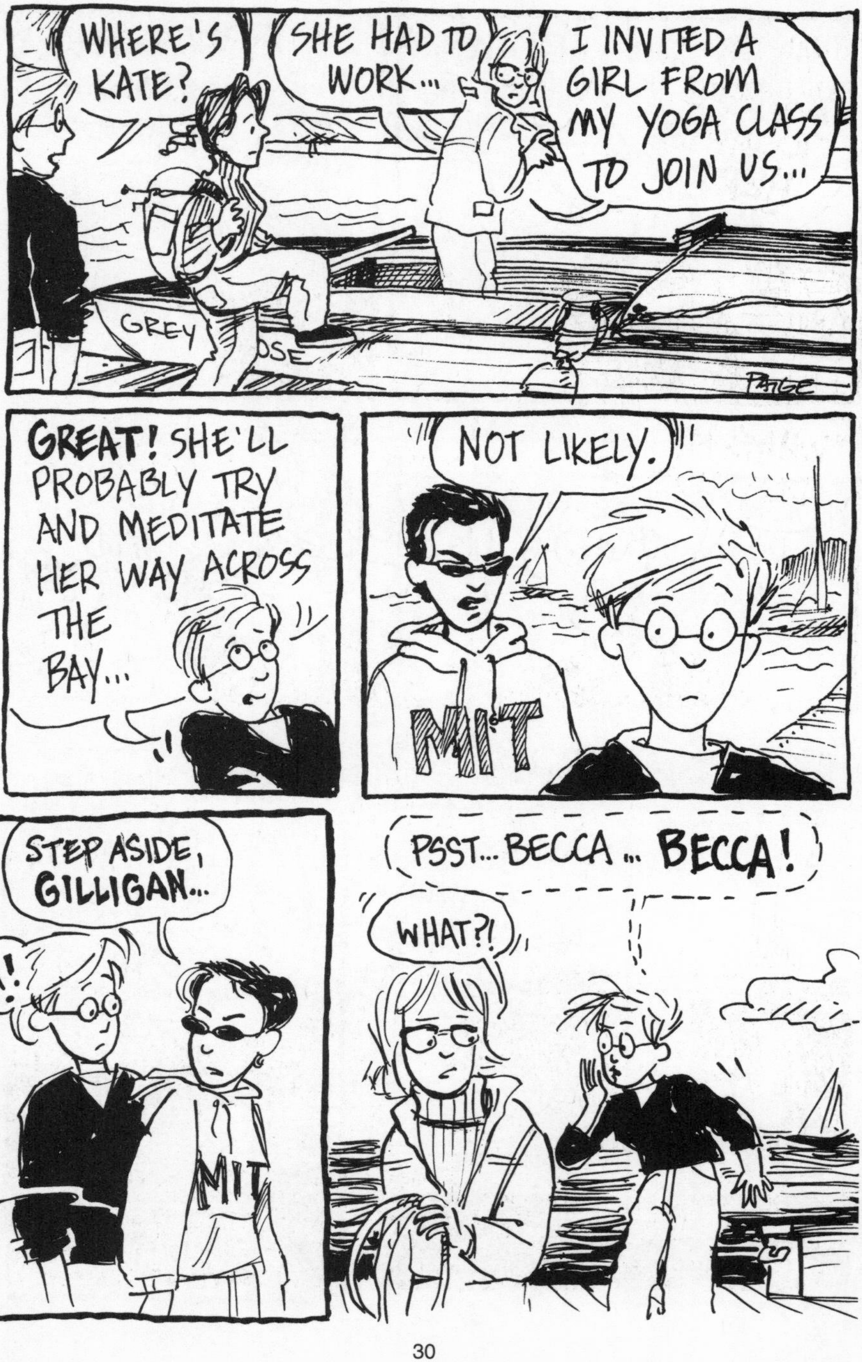
WHERE'S KATE?
SHE HAD TO WORK...
I INVITED A GIRL FROM MY YOGA CLASS TO JOIN US...
GREY
OSE
PAIGE
GREAT! SHE'LL PROBABLY TRY AND MEDITATE HER WAY ACROSS THE BAY...
NOT LIKELY.
MIT
STEP ASIDE, GILLIGAN...
!!
MIT
PSST... BECCA ... BECCA!
WHAT?!

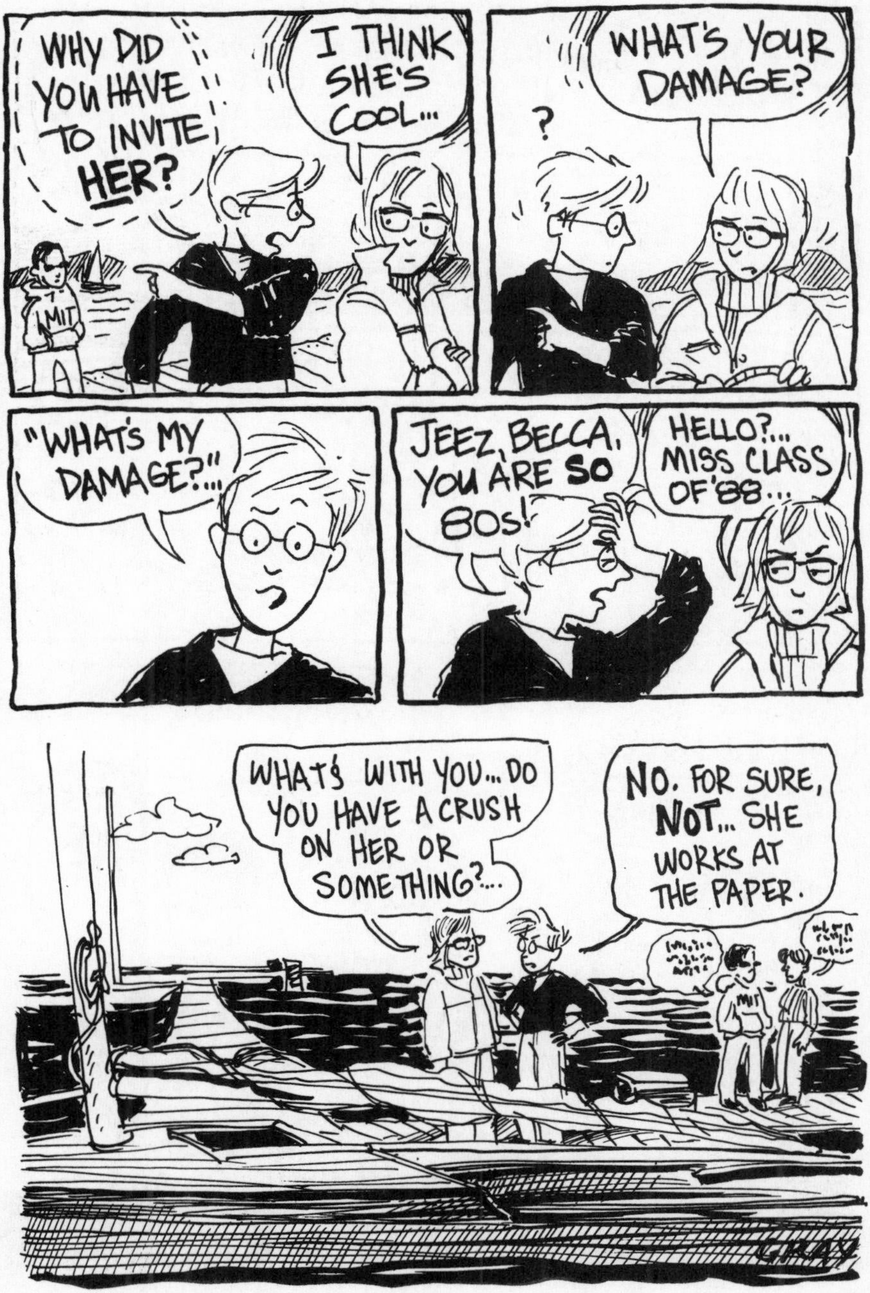
WHY DID YOU HAVE TO INVITE HER?
I THINK SHE'S COOL...
MIT
?
WHAT'S YOUR DAMAGE?
"WHAT'S MY DAMAGE?"...
JEEZ, BECCA, YOU ARE SO 80s!
HELLO?... MISS CLASS OF '88...
WHAT'S WITH YOU... DO YOU HAVE A CRUSH ON HER OR SOMETHING?...
NO. FOR SURE, NOT... SHE WORKS AT THE PAPER.
MIT
GRAY

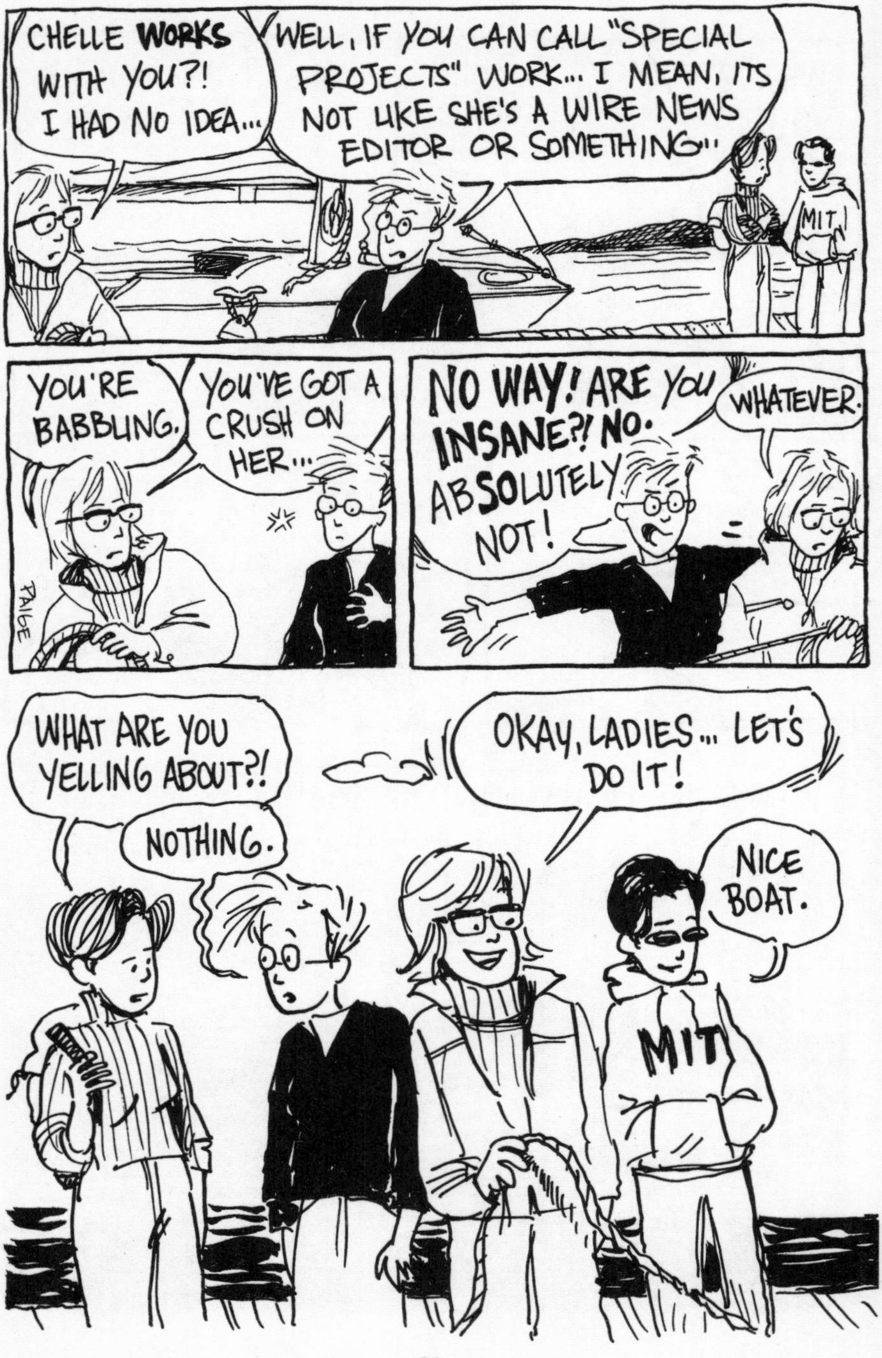
CHELLE **WORKS** WITH YOU?! I HAD NO IDEA...
WELL, IF YOU CAN CALL "SPECIAL PROJECTS" WORK... I MEAN, ITS NOT LIKE SHE'S A WIRE NEWS EDITOR OR SOMETHING...
MIT
YOU'RE BABBLING.
YOU'VE GOT A CRUSH ON HER...
PAIGE
NO WAY! ARE YOU **INSANE?! NO.** AB**SO**LUTELY NOT!
WHATEVER.
WHAT ARE YOU YELLING ABOUT?!
NOTHING.
OKAY, LADIES... LET'S DO IT!
NICE BOAT.
MIT

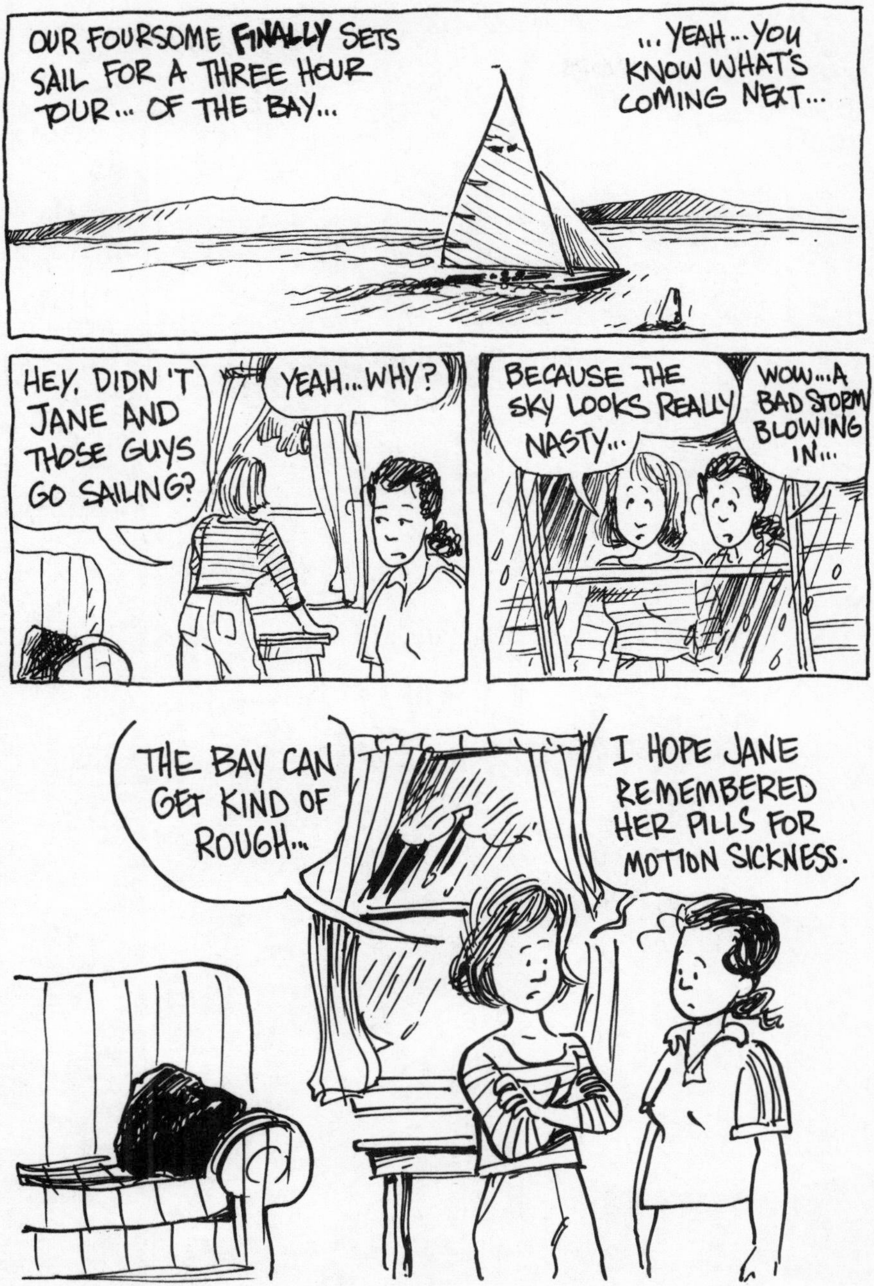
OUR FOURSOME FINALLY SETS SAIL FOR A THREE HOUR TOUR... OF THE BAY...
...YEAH...YOU KNOW WHAT'S COMING NEXT...
HEY, DIDN'T JANE AND THOSE GUYS GO SAILING?
YEAH...WHY?
BECAUSE THE SKY LOOKS REALLY NASTY...
WOW...A BAD STORM BLOWING IN...
THE BAY CAN GET KIND OF ROUGH...
I HOPE JANE REMEMBERED HER PILLS FOR MOTION SICKNESS.

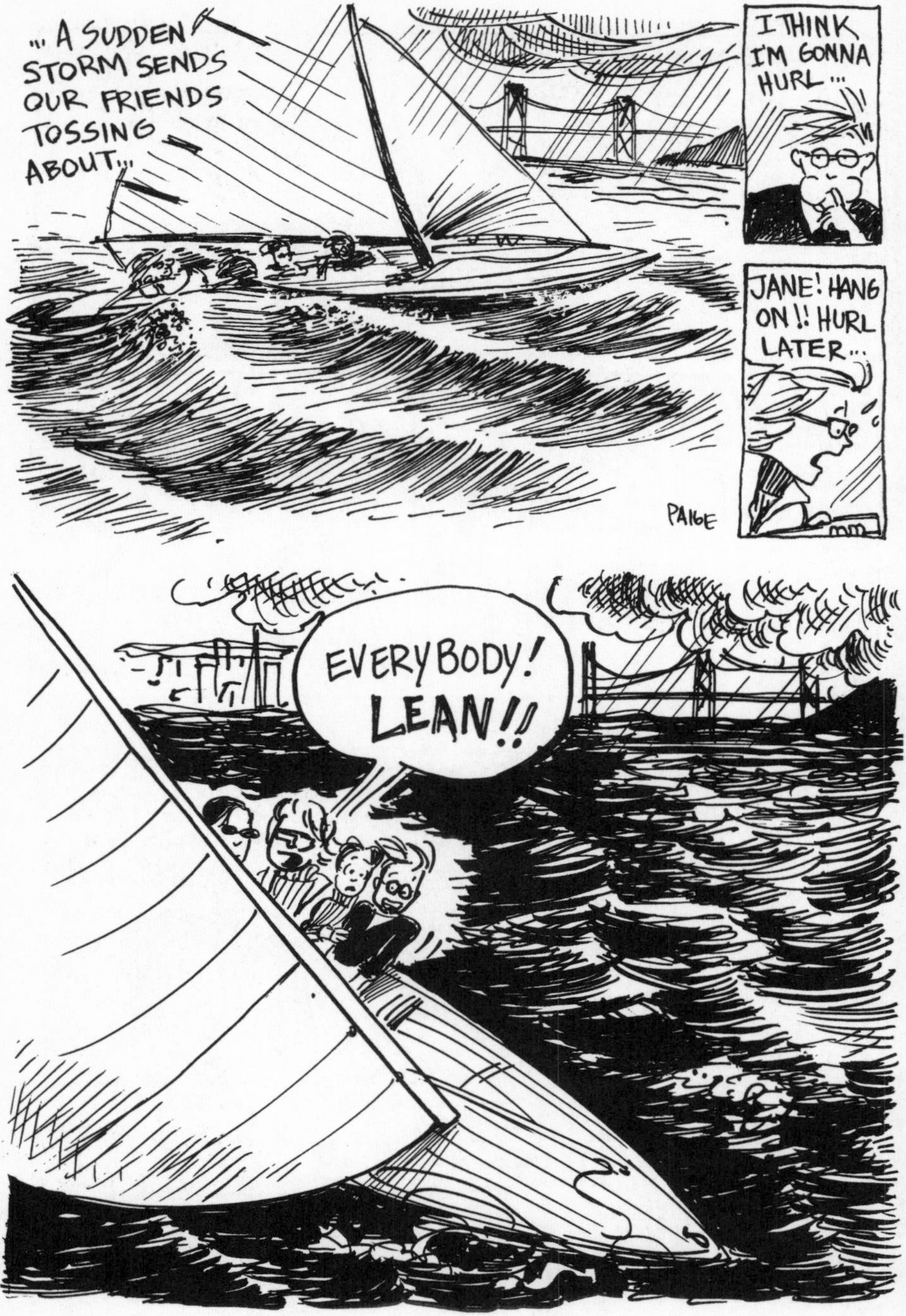
... A SUDDEN STORM SENDS OUR FRIENDS TOSSING ABOUT...
I THINK I'M GONNA HURL...
JANE! HANG ON!! HURL LATER...
PAIGE
EVERYBODY! LEAN!!

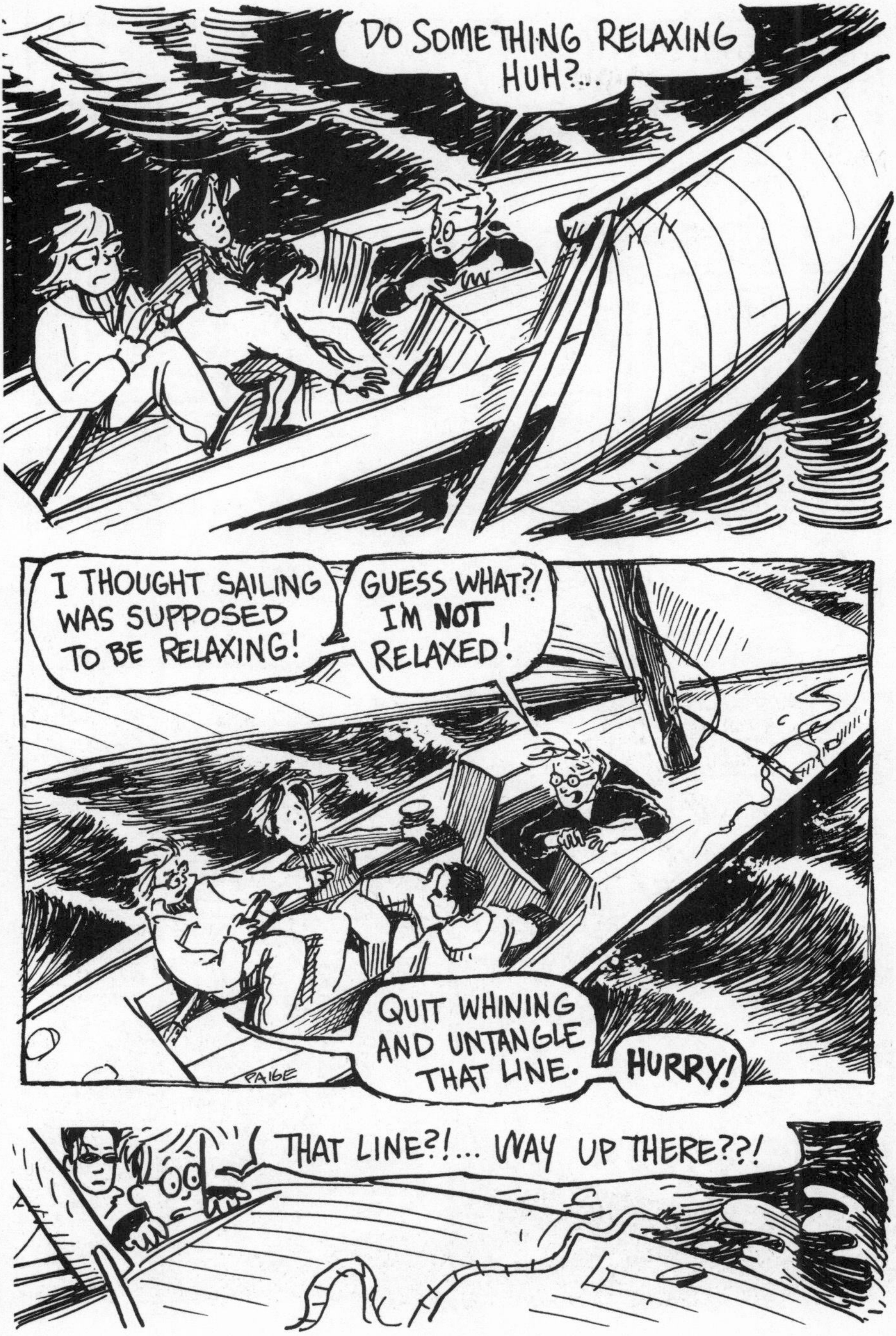
DO SOMETHING RELAXING HUH?...
I THOUGHT SAILING WAS SUPPOSED TO BE RELAXING!
GUESS WHAT?! I'M **NOT** RELAXED!
QUIT WHINING AND UNTANGLE THAT LINE.
HURRY!
PAIGE
THAT LINE?!... WAY UP THERE??!

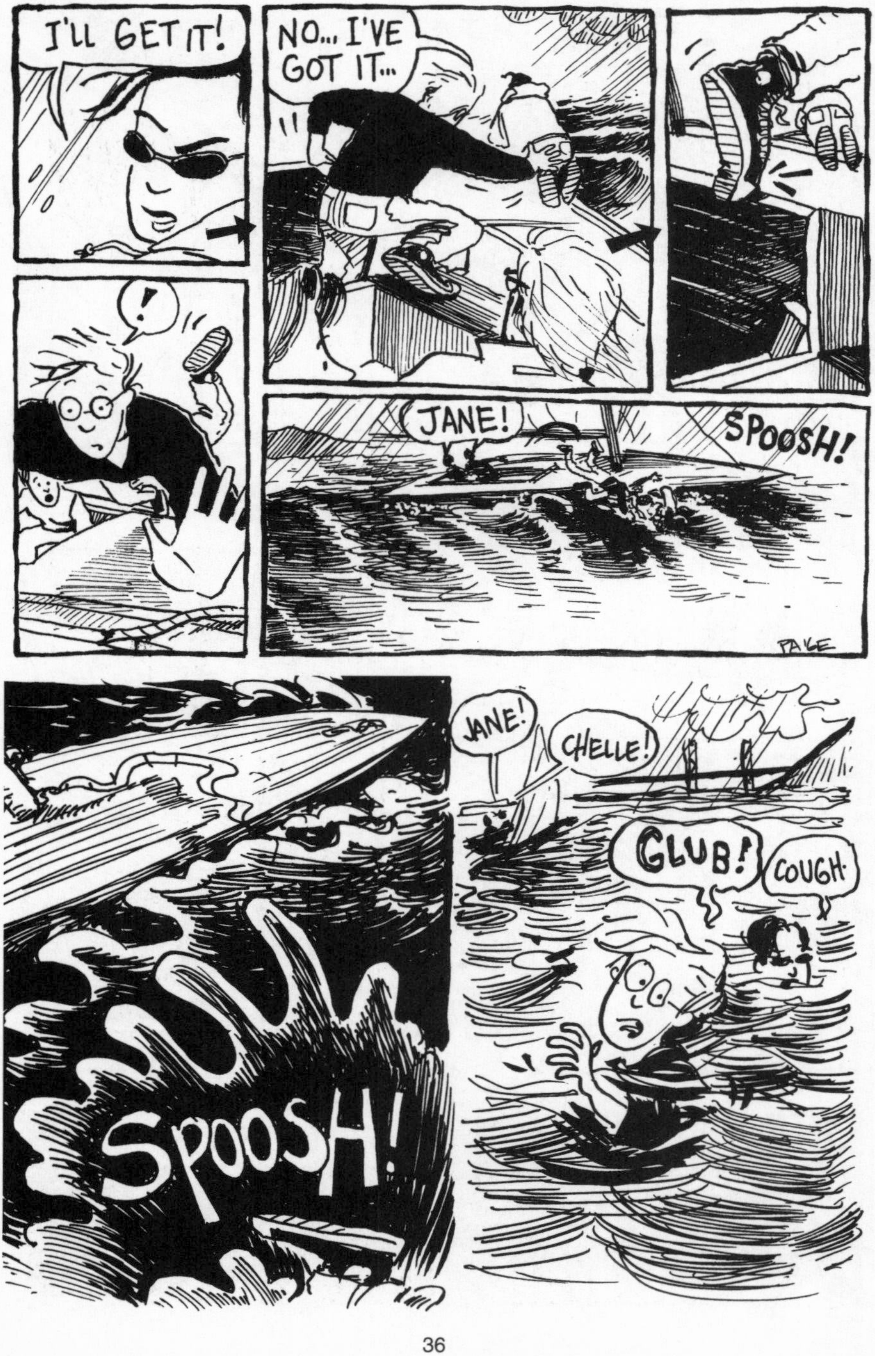
I'LL GET IT!
NO... I'VE GOT IT...
!
JANE!
SPOOSH!
PAIGE
SPOOSH!
JANE!
CHELLE!
GLUB!
COUGH·

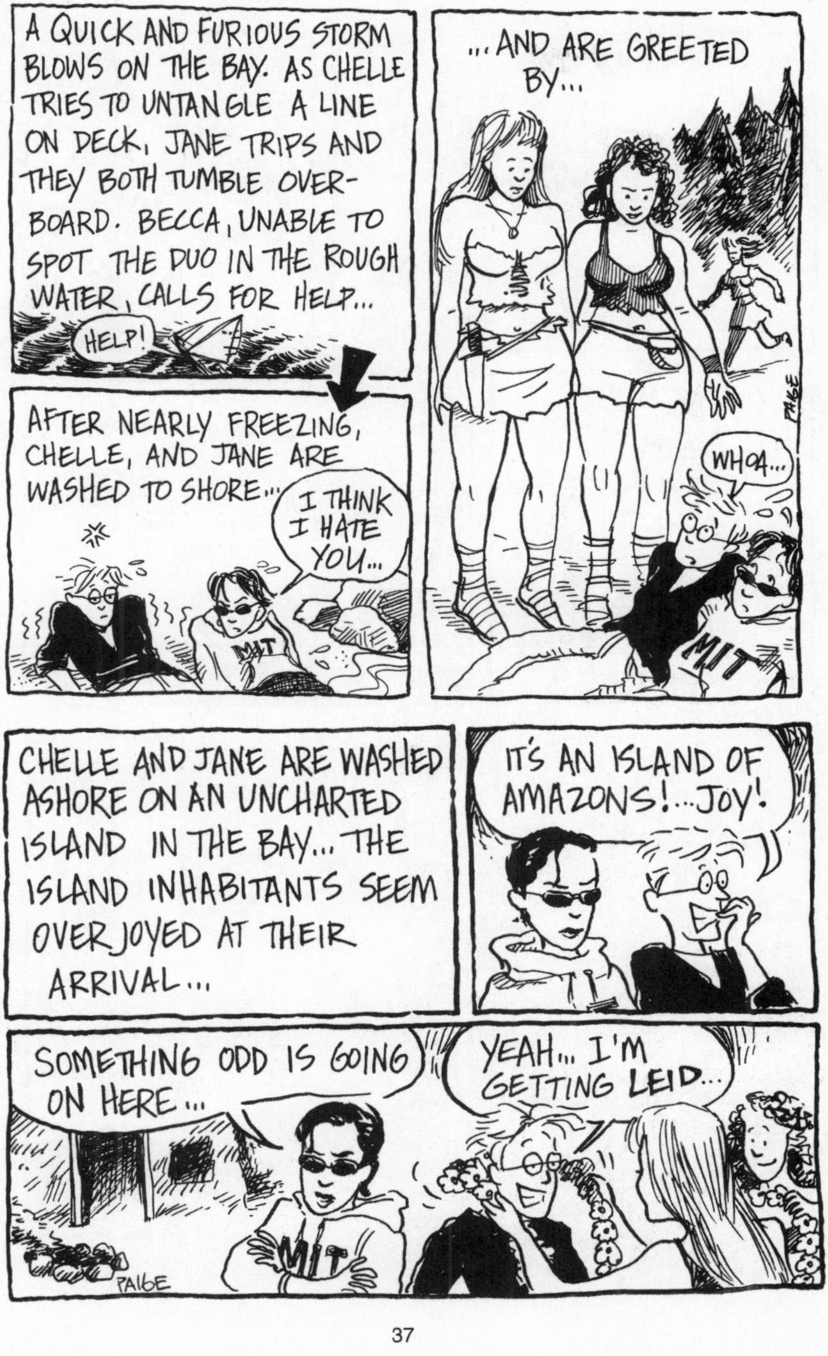
A QUICK AND FURIOUS STORM BLOWS ON THE BAY. AS CHELLE TRIES TO UNTANGLE A LINE ON DECK, JANE TRIPS AND THEY BOTH TUMBLE OVER-BOARD. BECCA, UNABLE TO SPOT THE DUO IN THE ROUGH WATER, CALLS FOR HELP...
HELP!
AFTER NEARLY FREEZING, CHELLE, AND JANE ARE WASHED TO SHORE...
I THINK I HATE YOU...
MIT
...AND ARE GREETED BY...
PAIGE
WHOA...
MIT
CHELLE AND JANE ARE WASHED ASHORE ON AN UNCHARTED ISLAND IN THE BAY... THE ISLAND INHABITANTS SEEM OVERJOYED AT THEIR ARRIVAL...
IT'S AN ISLAND OF AMAZONS!...JOY!
SOMETHING ODD IS GOING ON HERE...
YEAH... I'M GETTING **LEID**...
MIT
PAIGE

WELL, DON'T YOU FIND IT STRANGE THAT THEY SEEM SO HAPPY TO SEE TWO WOMEN WASH UP ON THE BEACH?

MAYBE THEY'RE HARD UP FOR DATES...

LOOK AROUND...

PAIGE

I SEE YOUR POINT.

AND IF THEY DID WANT DATES, SAN FRANCISCO IS RIGHT OVER...

..WHERE IS IT?!

MAYBE IT'S TOO FOGGY...

MAYBE WE'RE NO WHERE **NEAR** SAN FRANCISCO!

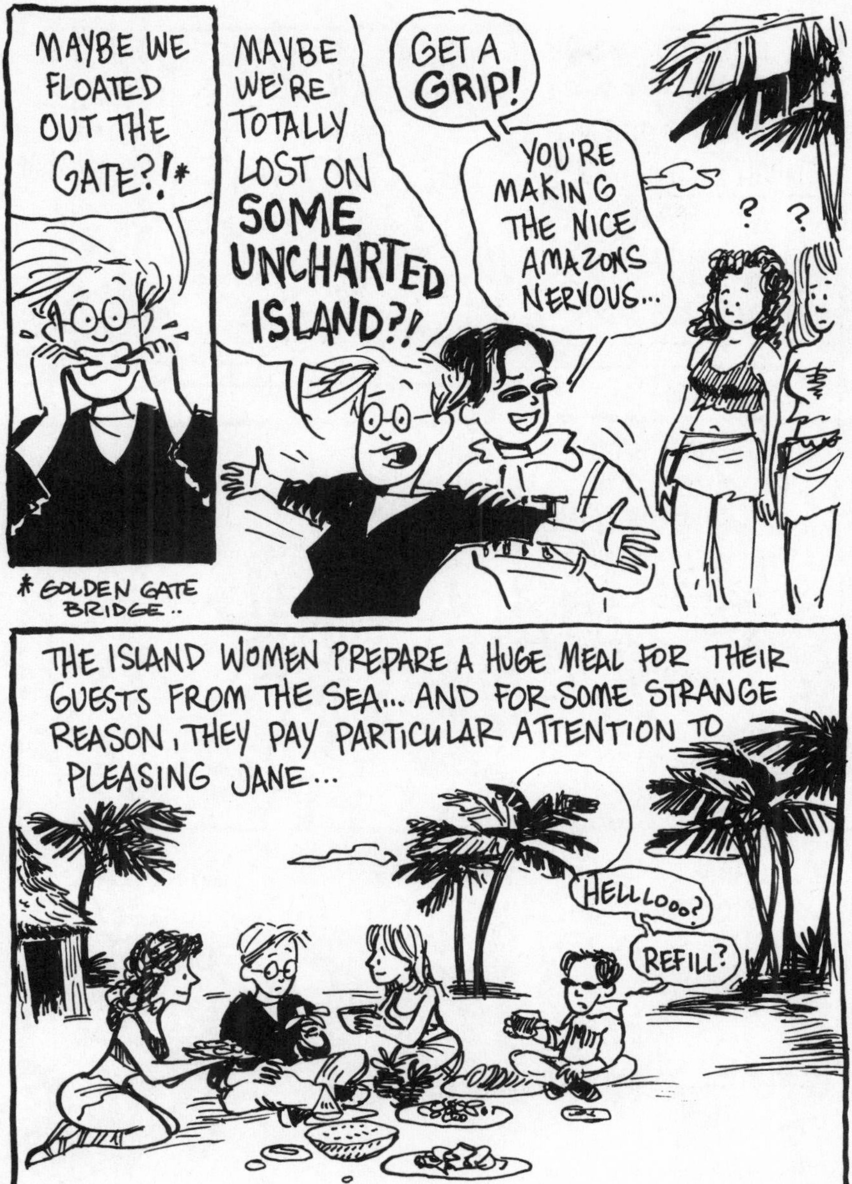
MAYBE WE FLOATED OUT THE GATE?!*
MAYBE WE'RE TOTALLY LOST ON SOME UNCHARTED ISLAND?!
GET A GRIP!
YOU'RE MAKING THE NICE AMAZONS NERVOUS...
? ?
* GOLDEN GATE BRIDGE..
THE ISLAND WOMEN PREPARE A HUGE MEAL FOR THEIR GUESTS FROM THE SEA... AND FOR SOME STRANGE REASON, THEY PAY PARTICULAR ATTENTION TO PLEASING JANE...
HELLLOOO?
REFILL?

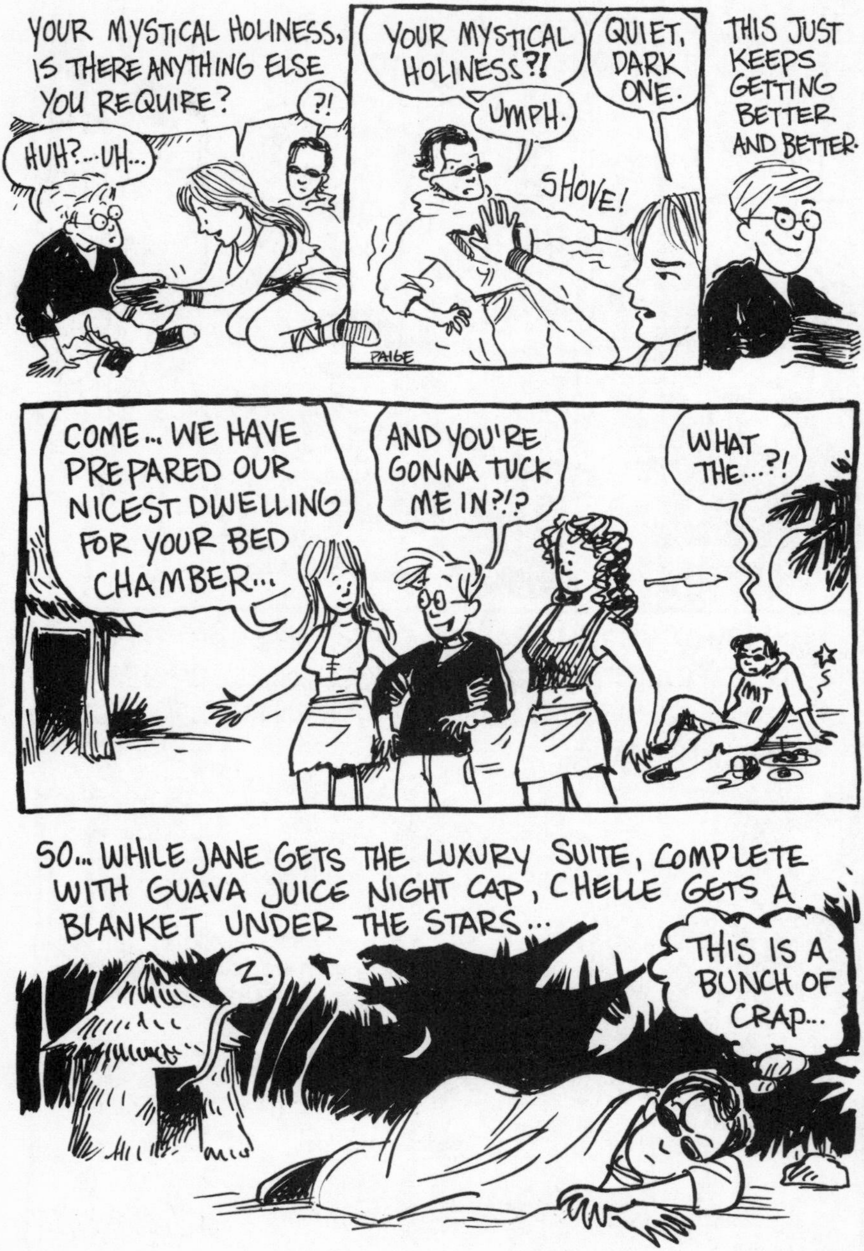
YOUR MYSTICAL HOLINESS, IS THERE ANYTHING ELSE YOU REQUIRE?
HUH?...UH...
?!
YOUR MYSTICAL HOLINESS?!
UMPH.
QUIET, DARK ONE.
SHOVE!
PAIGE
THIS JUST KEEPS GETTING BETTER AND BETTER.
COME... WE HAVE PREPARED OUR NICEST DWELLING FOR YOUR BED CHAMBER...
AND YOU'RE GONNA TUCK ME IN?!?
WHAT THE...?!
SO... WHILE JANE GETS THE LUXURY SUITE, COMPLETE WITH GUAVA JUICE NIGHT CAP, CHELLE GETS A BLANKET UNDER THE STARS...
Z.
THIS IS A BUNCH OF CRAP...

LATER THAT NIGHT...

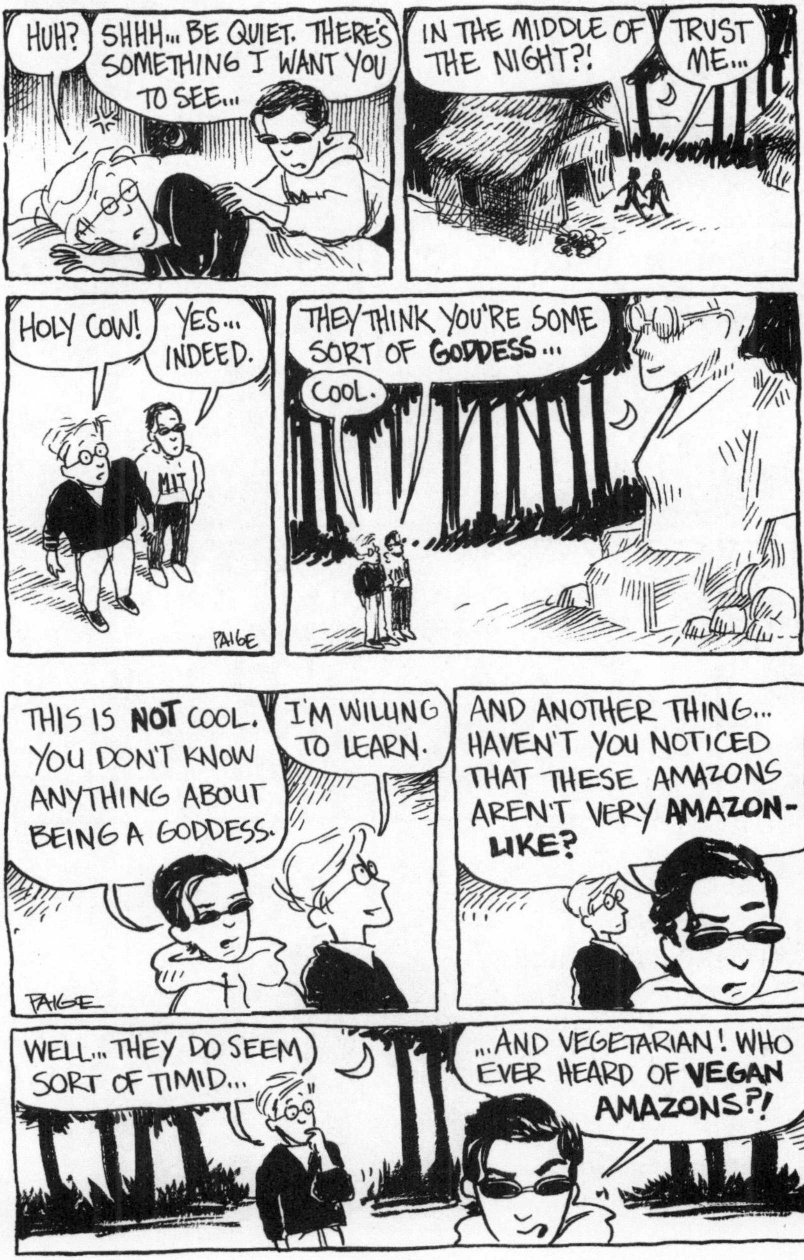
HUH?
SHHH... BE QUIET. THERE'S SOMETHING I WANT YOU TO SEE...
IN THE MIDDLE OF THE NIGHT?!
TRUST ME...
HOLY COW!
YES... INDEED.
MIT
PAIGE
THEY THINK YOU'RE SOME SORT OF GODDESS...
COOL.
THIS IS NOT COOL. YOU DON'T KNOW ANYTHING ABOUT BEING A GODDESS.
I'M WILLING TO LEARN.
PAIGE
AND ANOTHER THING... HAVEN'T YOU NOTICED THAT THESE AMAZONS AREN'T VERY AMAZON-LIKE?
WELL... THEY DO SEEM SORT OF TIMID...
...AND VEGETARIAN! WHO EVER HEARD OF VEGAN AMAZONS?!

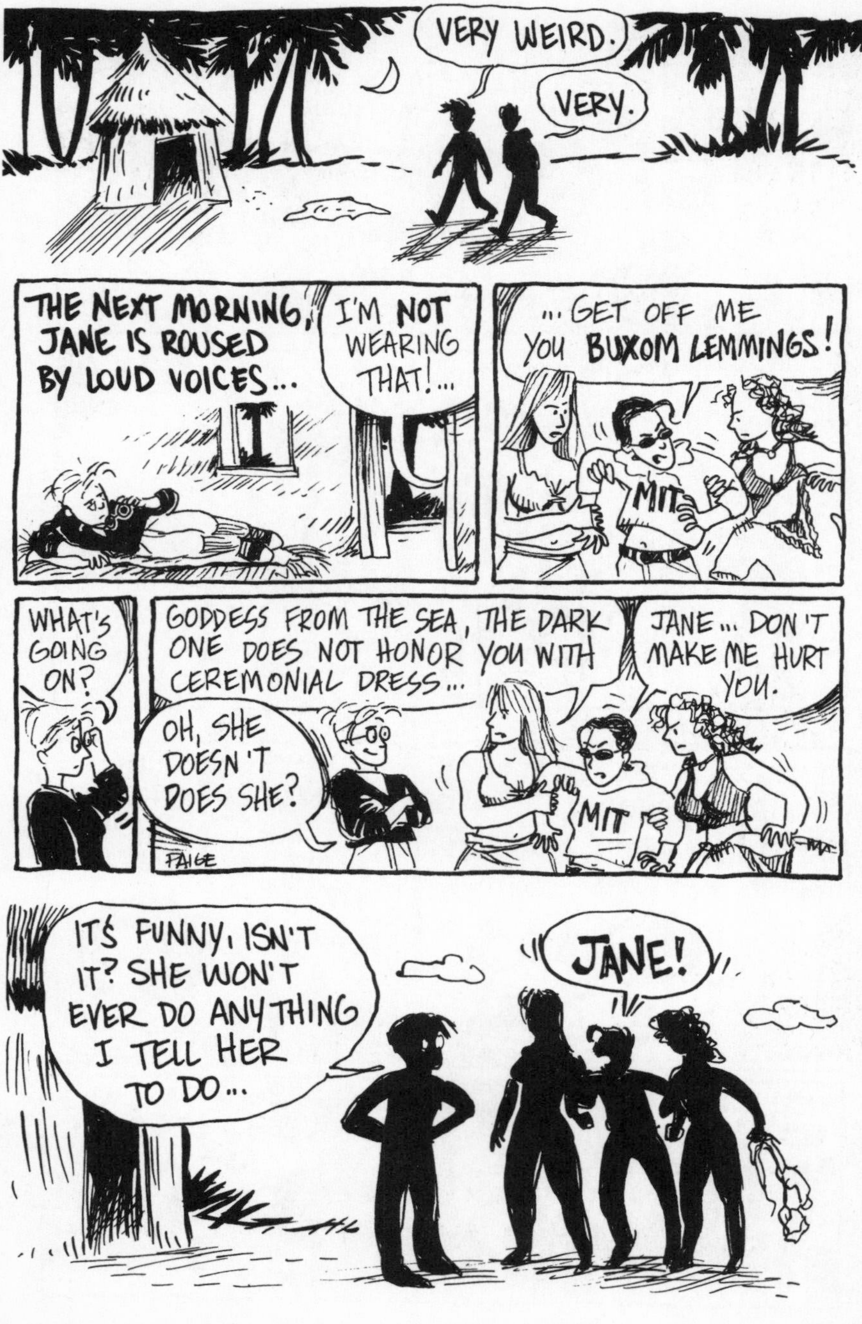
VERY WEIRD.
VERY.
THE NEXT MORNING, JANE IS ROUSED BY LOUD VOICES...
I'M NOT WEARING THAT!...
... GET OFF ME YOU BUXOM LEMMINGS!
MIT
WHAT'S GOING ON?
GODDESS FROM THE SEA, THE DARK ONE DOES NOT HONOR YOU WITH CEREMONIAL DRESS...
JANE... DON'T MAKE ME HURT YOU.
OH, SHE DOESN'T DOES SHE?
MIT
FAIGE
IT'S FUNNY, ISN'T IT? SHE WON'T EVER DO ANYTHING I TELL HER TO DO...
JANE!

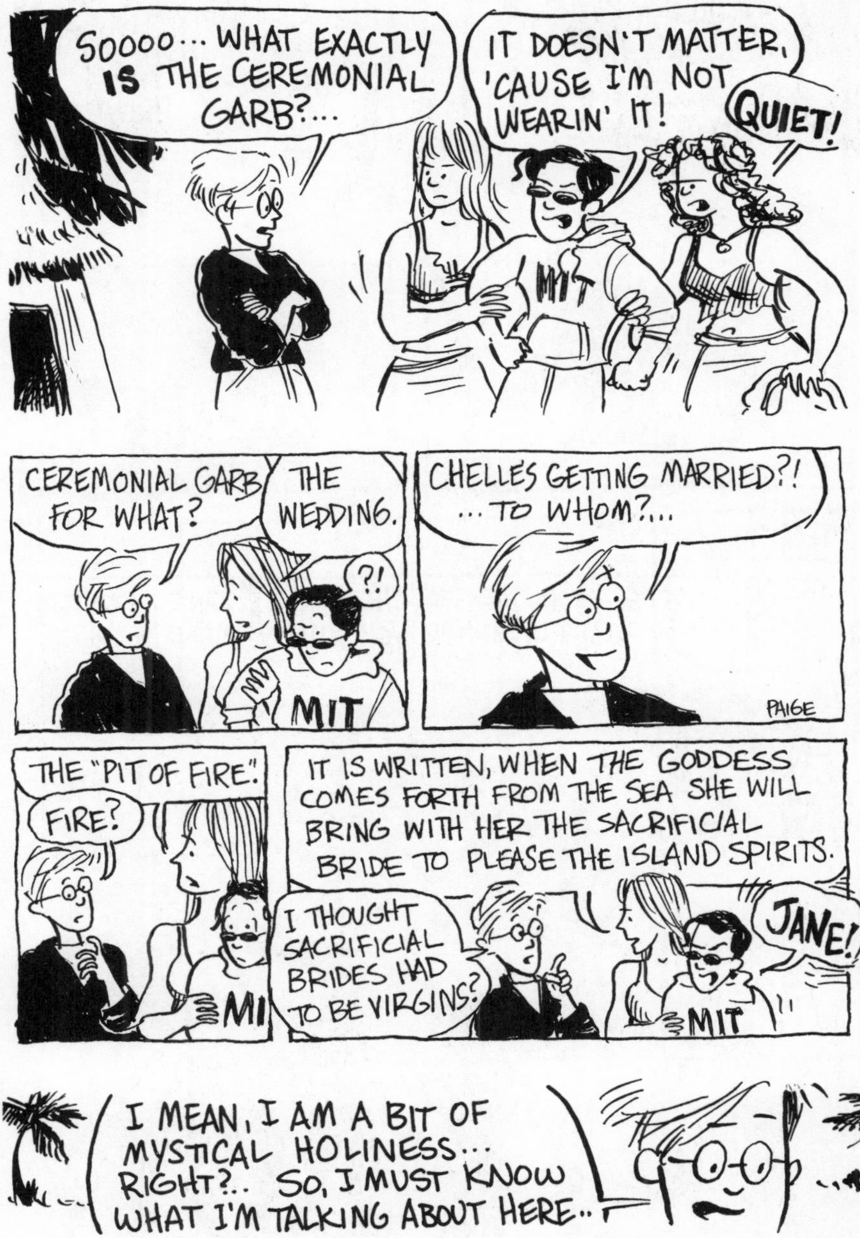
SOOOO... WHAT EXACTLY IS THE CEREMONIAL GARB?...
IT DOESN'T MATTER, 'CAUSE I'M NOT WEARIN' IT!
QUIET!
CEREMONIAL GARB FOR WHAT?
THE WEDDING.
?!
CHELLE'S GETTING MARRIED?! ... TO WHOM?...
PAIGE
THE "PIT OF FIRE."
FIRE?
MI
IT IS WRITTEN, WHEN THE GODDESS COMES FORTH FROM THE SEA SHE WILL BRING WITH HER THE SACRIFICIAL BRIDE TO PLEASE THE ISLAND SPIRITS.
I THOUGHT SACRIFICIAL BRIDES HAD TO BE VIRGINS?
JANE!
MIT
I MEAN, I AM A BIT OF MYSTICAL HOLINESS... RIGHT?.. SO, I MUST KNOW WHAT I'M TALKING ABOUT HERE..

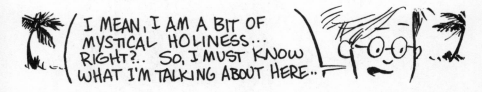

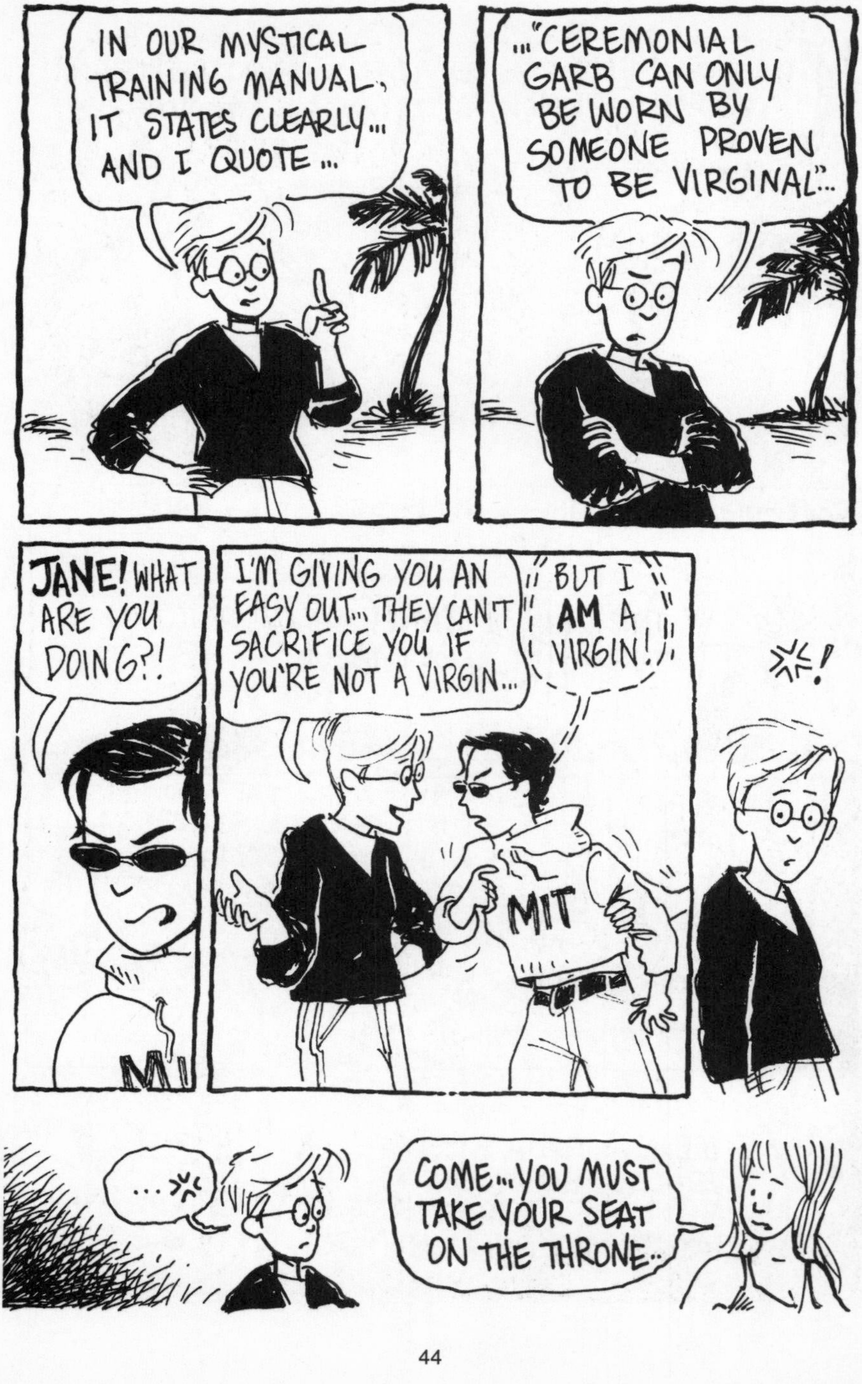
IN OUR MYSTICAL TRAINING MANUAL, IT STATES CLEARLY... AND I QUOTE ...
..."CEREMONIAL GARB CAN ONLY BE WORN BY SOMEONE PROVEN TO BE VIRGINAL"...
JANE! WHAT ARE YOU DOING?!
I'M GIVING YOU AN EASY OUT... THEY CAN'T SACRIFICE YOU IF YOU'RE NOT A VIRGIN...
BUT I AM A VIRGIN!
MIT
...
COME... YOU MUST TAKE YOUR SEAT ON THE THRONE..

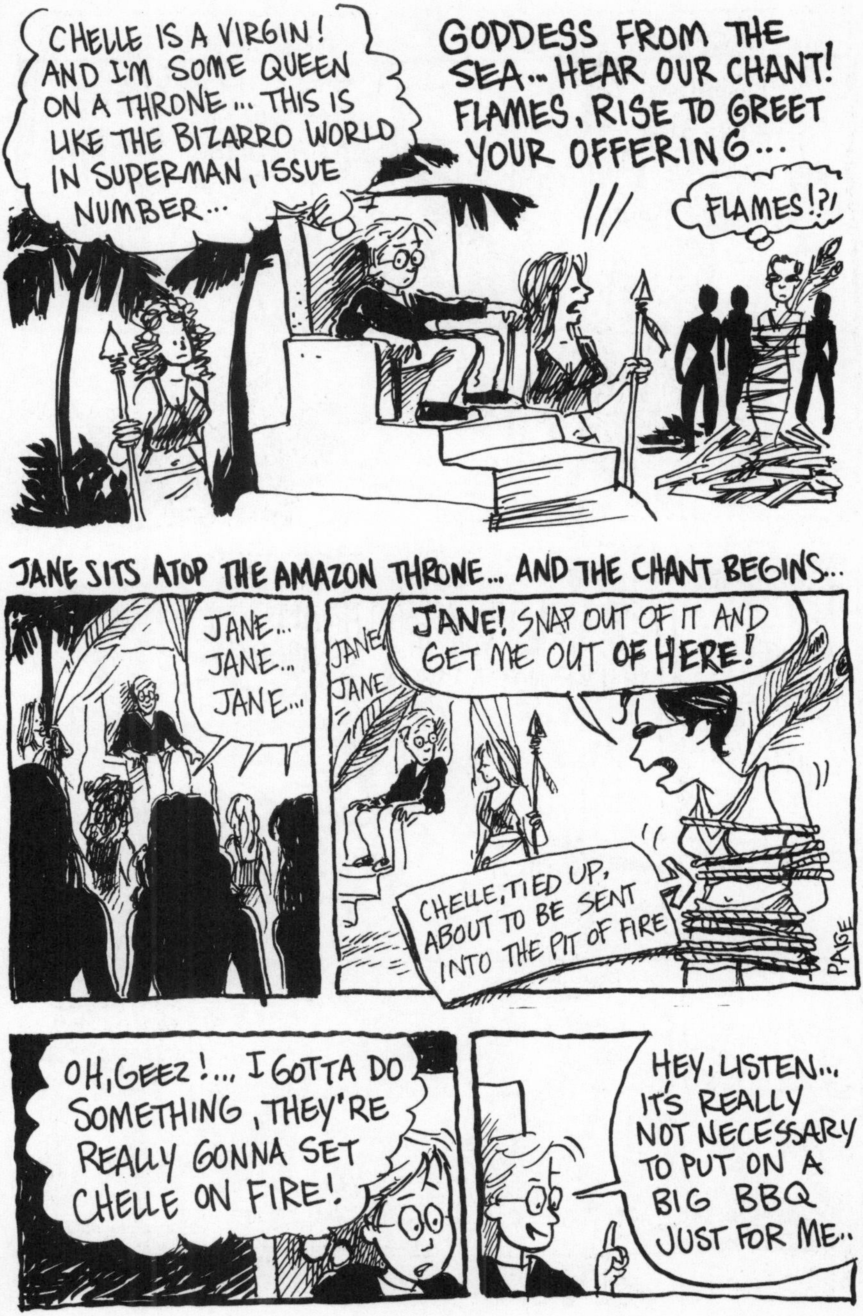
CHELLE IS A VIRGIN! AND I'M SOME QUEEN ON A THRONE... THIS IS LIKE THE BIZARRO WORLD IN SUPERMAN, ISSUE NUMBER...
GODDESS FROM THE SEA... HEAR OUR CHANT! FLAMES, RISE TO GREET YOUR OFFERING...
FLAMES!?!
JANE SITS ATOP THE AMAZON THRONE... AND THE CHANT BEGINS...
JANE... JANE... JANE...
JANE JANE
JANE! SNAP OUT OF IT AND GET ME OUT OF HERE!
CHELLE, TIED UP, ABOUT TO BE SENT INTO THE PIT OF FIRE
PAIGE
OH, GEEZ!... I GOTTA DO SOMETHING, THEY'RE REALLY GONNA SET CHELLE ON FIRE!
HEY, LISTEN... IT'S REALLY NOT NECESSARY TO PUT ON A BIG BBQ JUST FOR ME..

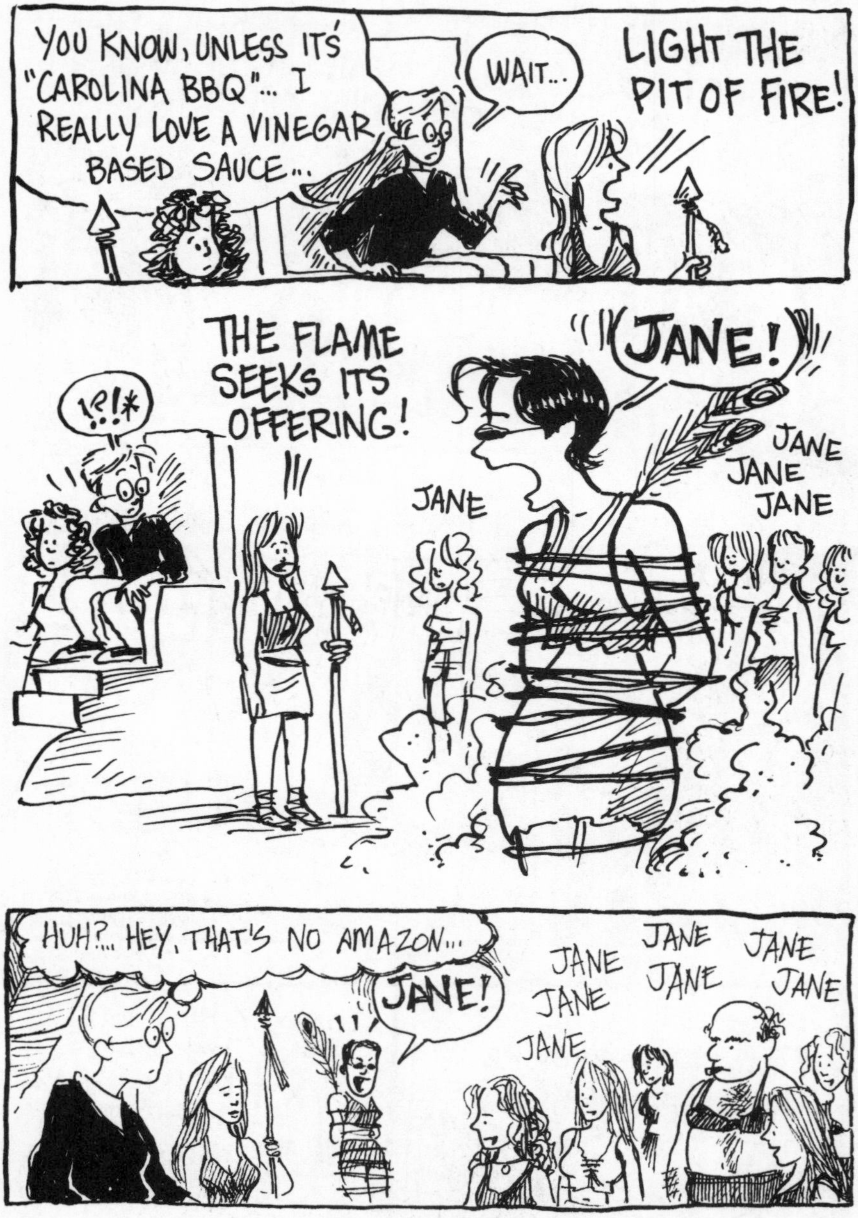

YOU KNOW, UNLESS IT'S "CAROLINA BBQ"... I REALLY LOVE A VINEGAR BASED SAUCE...
WAIT...
LIGHT THE PIT OF FIRE!
!?!*
THE FLAME SEEKS ITS OFFERING!
JANE!
JANE
JANE
JANE
JANE
HUH?... HEY, THAT'S NO AMAZON...
JANE!
JANE
JANE
JANE
JANE
JANE
JANE
JANE

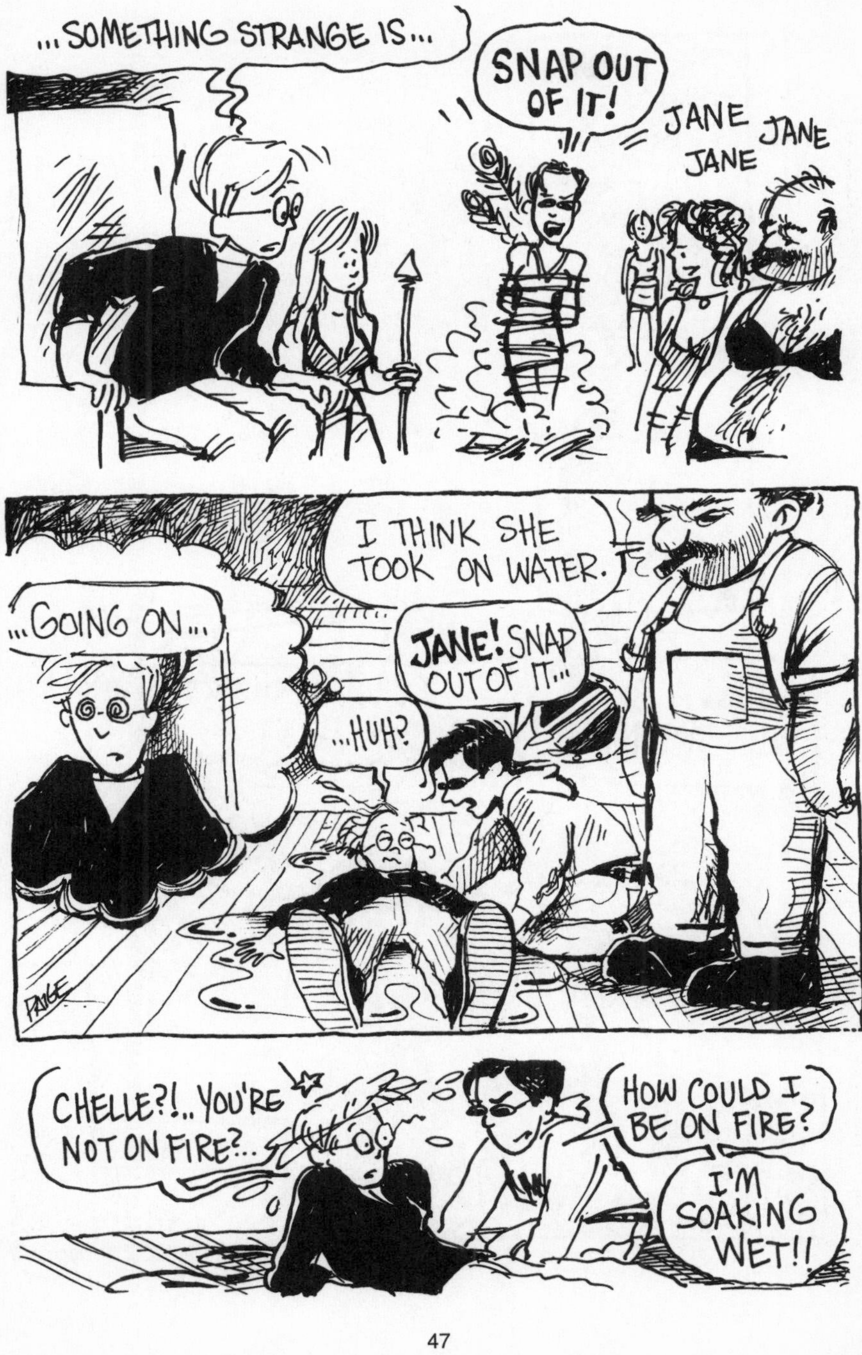
...SOMETHING STRANGE IS...
SNAP OUT OF IT!
JANE JANE JANE
I THINK SHE TOOK ON WATER.
...GOING ON...
JANE! SNAP OUT OF IT...
...HUH?
PAIGE
CHELLE?!.. YOU'RE NOT ON FIRE?...
HOW COULD I BE ON FIRE?
I'M SOAKING WET!!

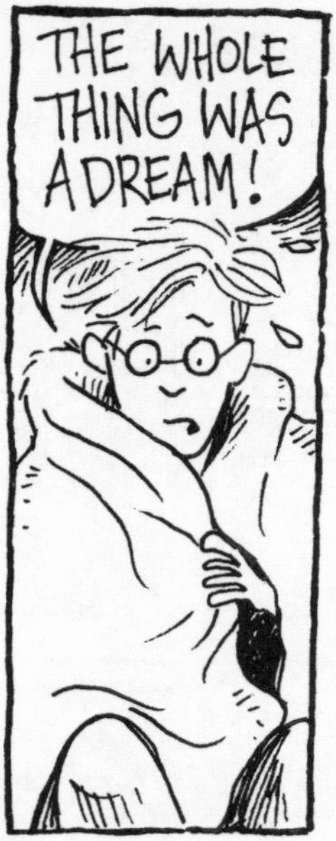
THE WHOLE THING WAS A DREAM!

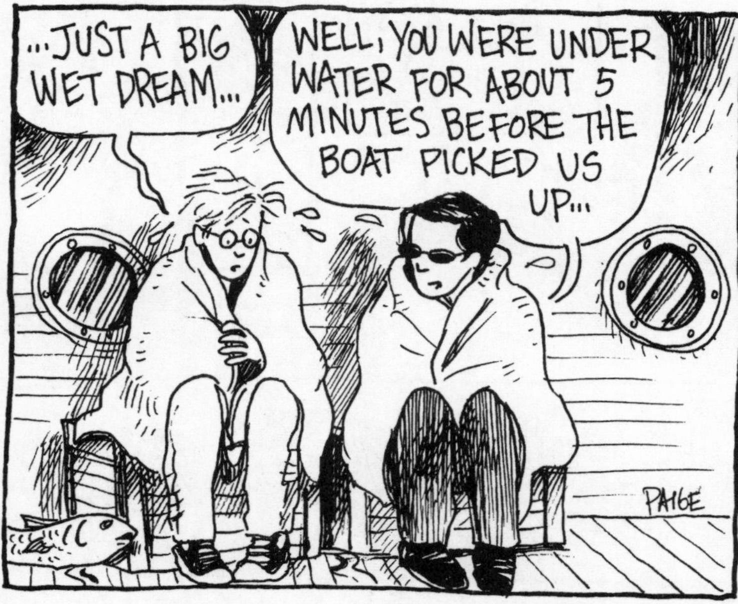
...JUST A BIG WET DREAM...
WELL, YOU WERE UNDER WATER FOR ABOUT 5 MINUTES BEFORE THE BOAT PICKED US UP...
PAIGE

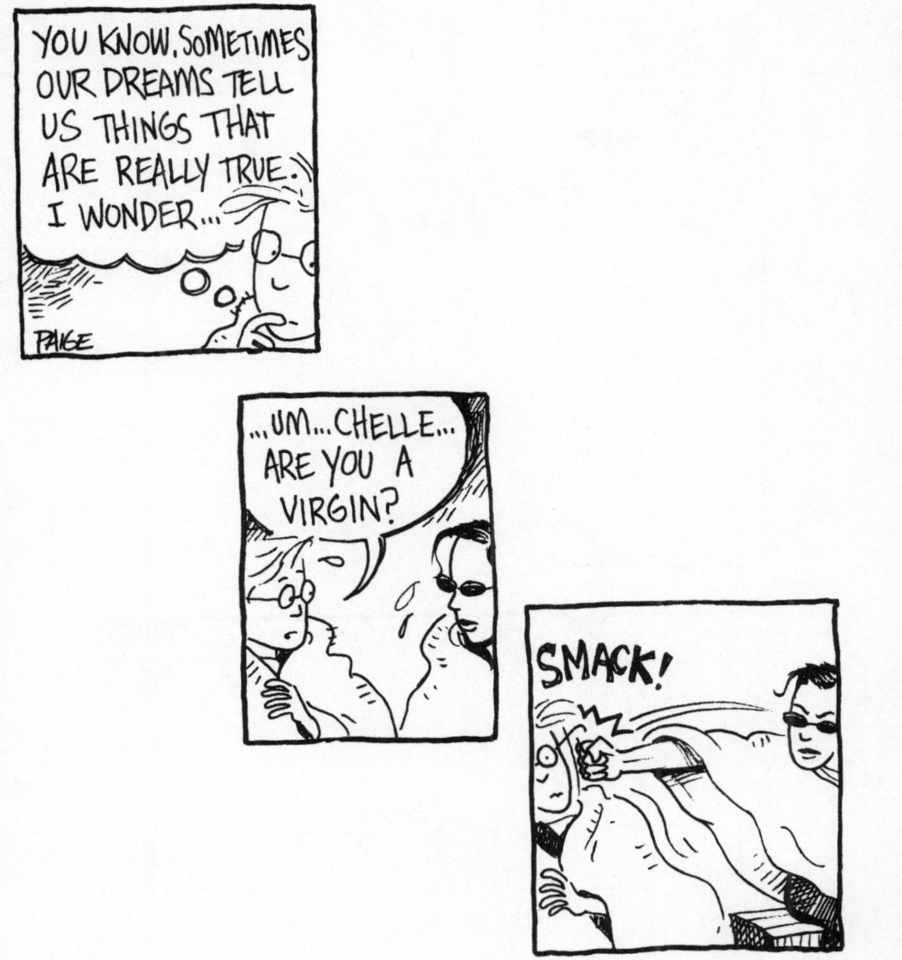
YOU KNOW, SOMETIMES OUR DREAMS TELL US THINGS THAT ARE REALLY TRUE. I WONDER...
PAIGE
...UM...CHELLE... ARE YOU A VIRGIN?
SMACK!
OW.

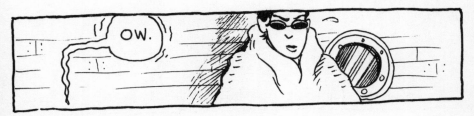

Chapter 3

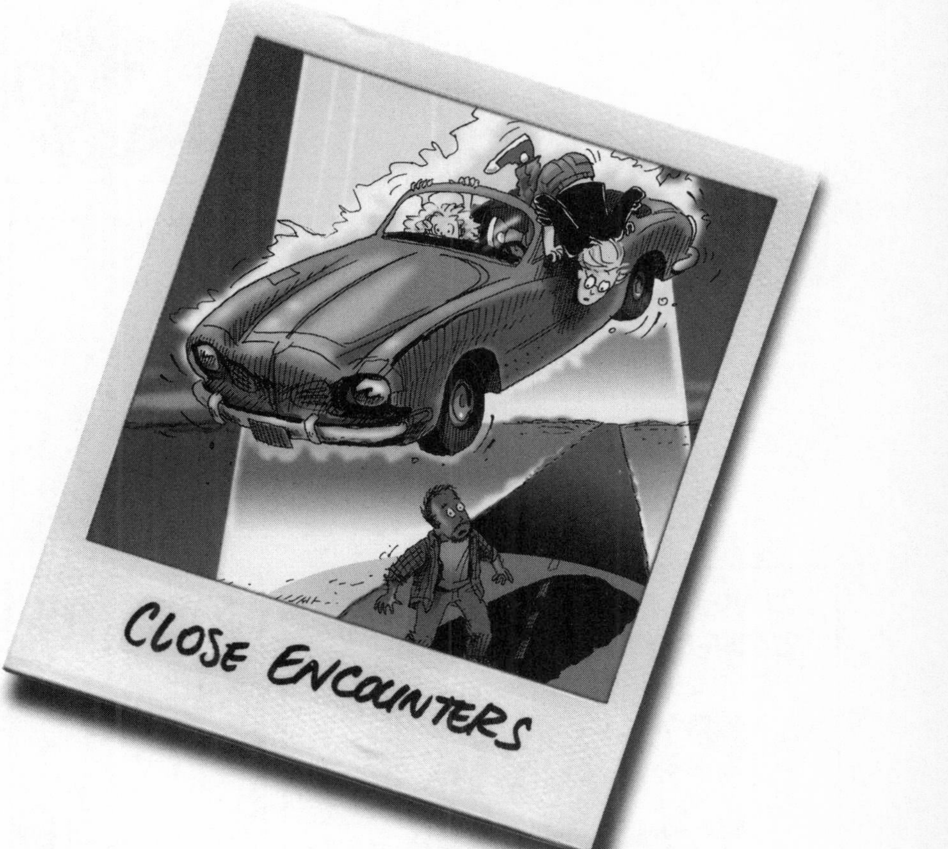
CLOSE ENCOUNTERS

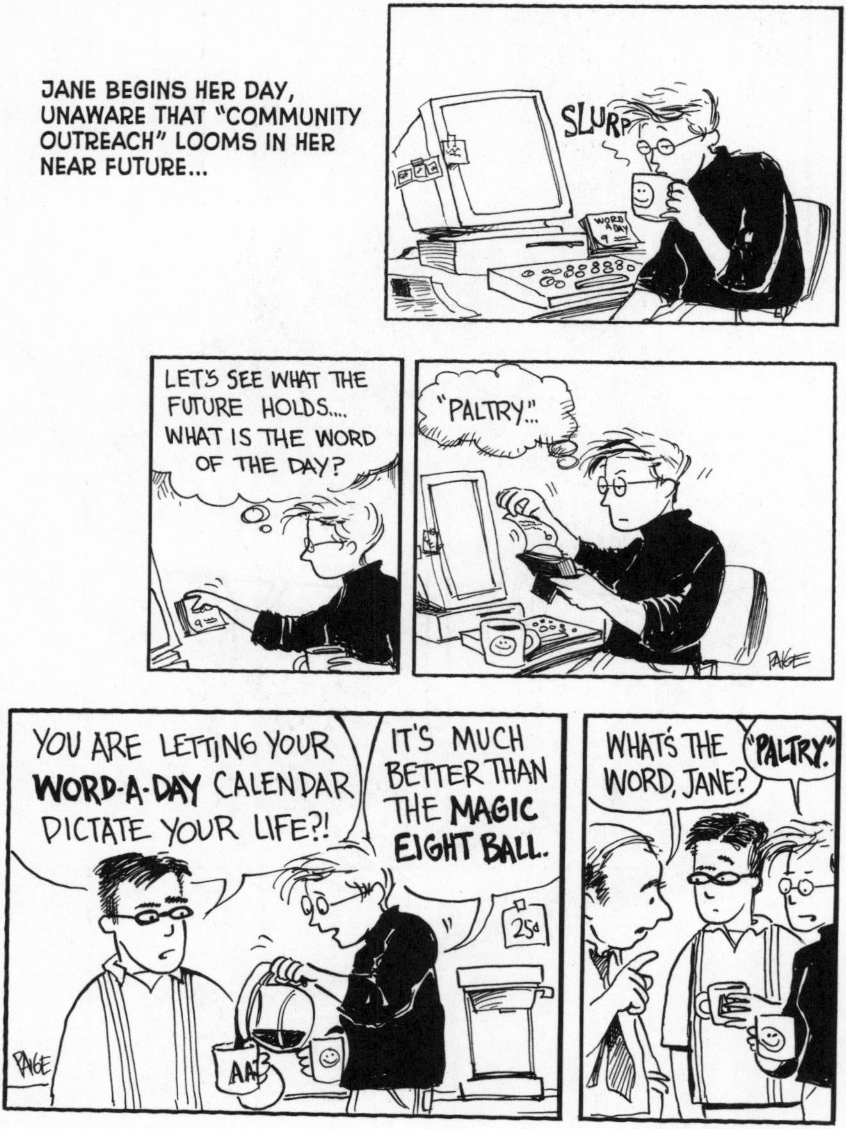
JANE BEGINS HER DAY, UNAWARE THAT "COMMUNITY OUTREACH" LOOMS IN HER NEAR FUTURE...
SLURP
WORD A DAY
LET'S SEE WHAT THE FUTURE HOLDS.... WHAT IS THE WORD OF THE DAY?
"PALTRY."
PAGE
YOU ARE LETTING YOUR WORD-A-DAY CALENDAR DICTATE YOUR LIFE?!
IT'S MUCH BETTER THAN THE MAGIC EIGHT BALL.
25¢
AA
PAGE
WHAT'S THE WORD, JANE?
"PALTRY."

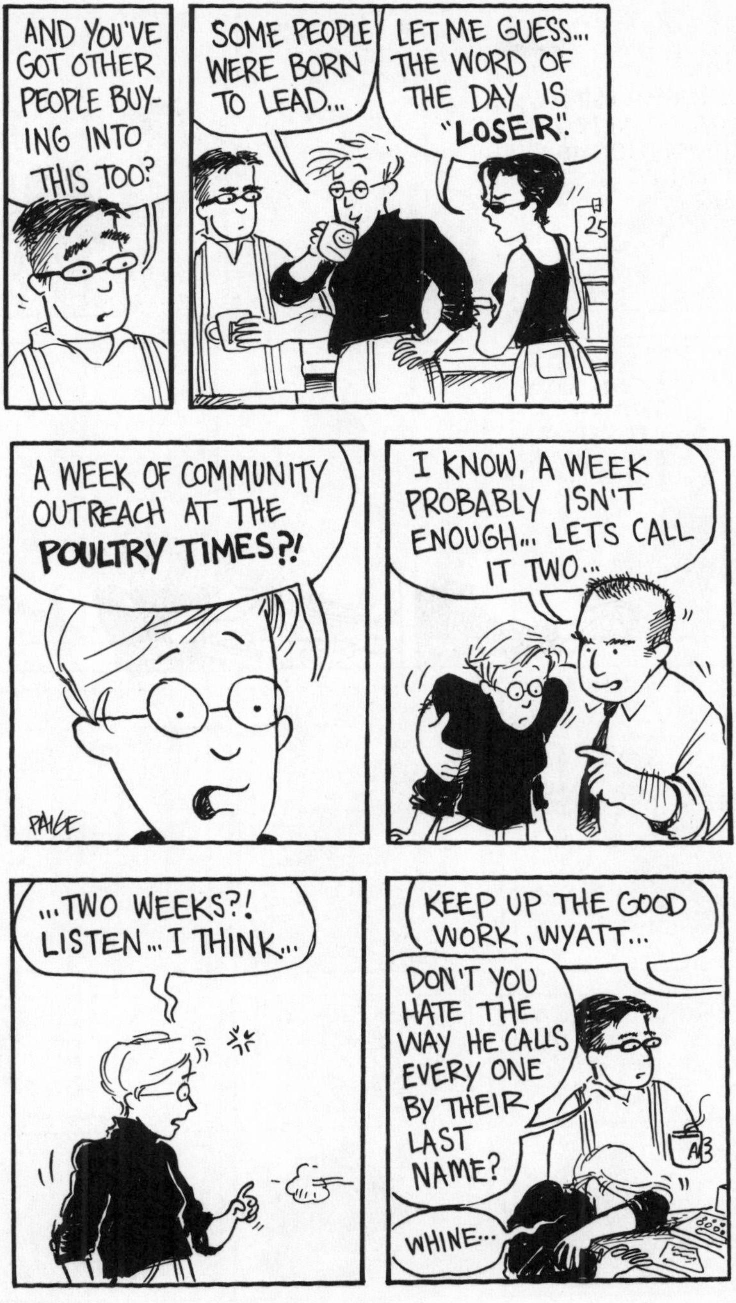
AND YOU'VE GOT OTHER PEOPLE BUY-ING INTO THIS TOO?
SOME PEOPLE WERE BORN TO LEAD...
LET ME GUESS... THE WORD OF THE DAY IS "LOSER".
25
A WEEK OF COMMUNITY OUTREACH AT THE POULTRY TIMES?!
PAIGE
I KNOW, A WEEK PROBABLY ISN'T ENOUGH... LETS CALL IT TWO...
...TWO WEEKS?! LISTEN... I THINK...
KEEP UP THE GOOD WORK, WYATT...
DON'T YOU HATE THE WAY HE CALLS EVERY ONE BY THEIR LAST NAME?
WHINE...

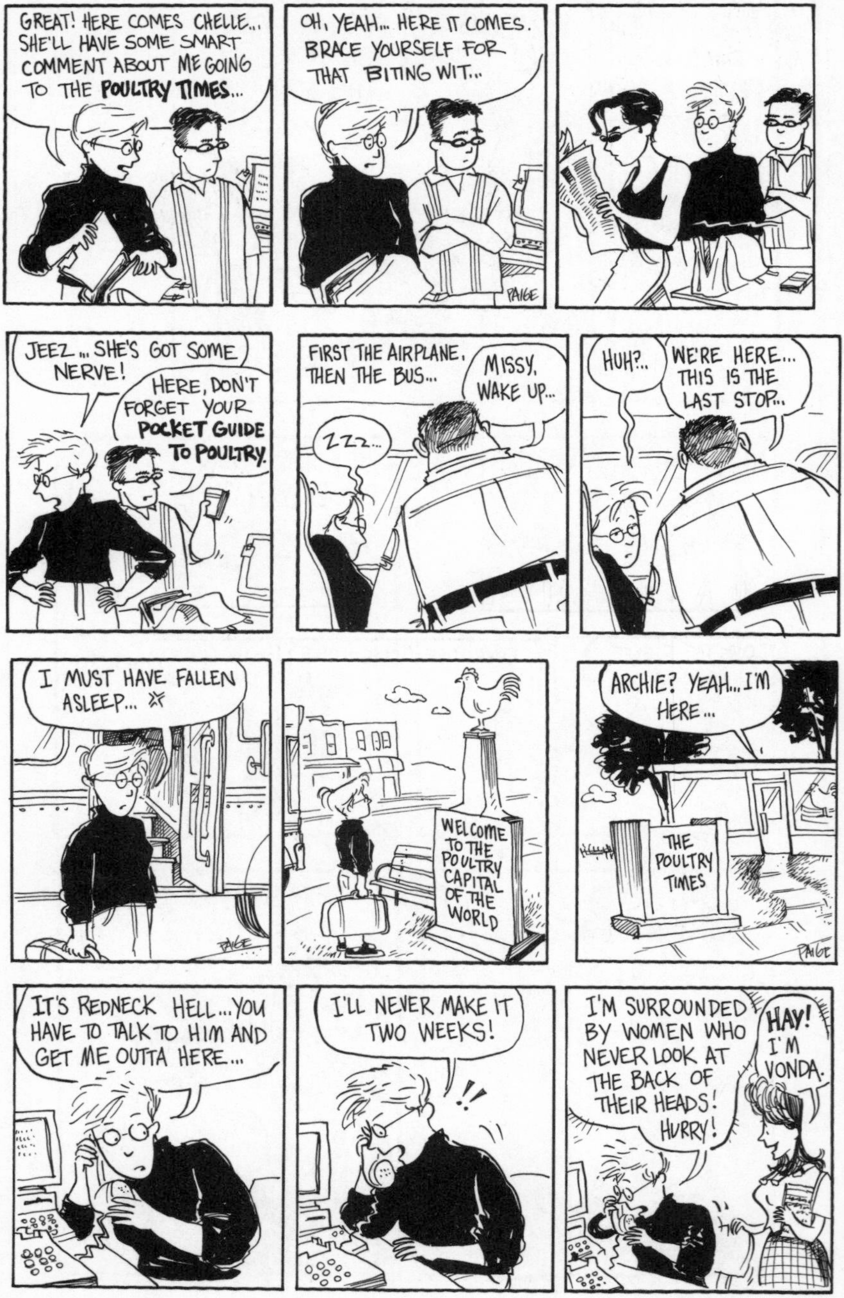
GREAT! HERE COMES CHELLE... SHE'LL HAVE SOME SMART COMMENT ABOUT ME GOING TO THE POULTRY TIMES...
OH, YEAH... HERE IT COMES. BRACE YOURSELF FOR THAT BITING WIT...
PAIGE
JEEZ... SHE'S GOT SOME NERVE!
HERE, DON'T FORGET YOUR POCKET GUIDE TO POULTRY.
FIRST THE AIRPLANE, THEN THE BUS...
MISSY, WAKE UP...
ZZZ...
HUH?..
WE'RE HERE... THIS IS THE LAST STOP...
I MUST HAVE FALLEN ASLEEP...
PAIGE
WELCOME TO THE POULTRY CAPITAL OF THE WORLD
ARCHIE? YEAH... I'M HERE...
THE POULTRY TIMES
PAIGE
IT'S REDNECK HELL... YOU HAVE TO TALK TO HIM AND GET ME OUTTA HERE...
I'LL NEVER MAKE IT TWO WEEKS!
I'M SURROUNDED BY WOMEN WHO NEVER LOOK AT THE BACK OF THEIR HEADS! HURRY!
HAY! I'M VONDA.

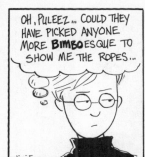

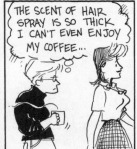

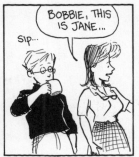

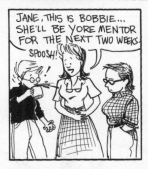

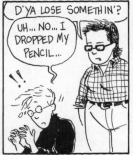

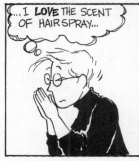

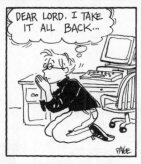

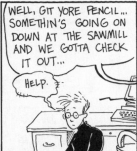

OH, PULEEZ... COULD THEY HAVE PICKED ANYONE MORE BIMBOESQUE TO SHOW ME THE ROPES...
THE SCENT OF HAIR SPRAY IS SO THICK I CAN'T EVEN ENJOY MY COFFEE...
SIP...
BOBBIE, THIS IS JANE...
JANE, THIS IS BOBBIE... SHE'LL BE YORE MENTOR FOR THE NEXT TWO WEEKS.
SPOOSH!
DEAR LORD. I TAKE IT ALL BACK...
PAIGE
...I LOVE THE SCENT OF HAIRSPRAY...
D'YA LOSE SOMETHIN'?
UH... NO... I DROPPED MY PENCIL...
WELL, GIT YORE PENCIL... SOMETHIN'S GOING ON DOWN AT THE SAWMILL AND WE GOTTA CHECK IT OUT...
HELP.
A FEW MOMENTS LATER, IN THE PARKING LOT AT THE POULTRY TIMES...
WHERE'D SHE GO? I THOUGHT SHE GOT IN HER TRUCK...
HEY, BOBBIE!... I'M READY TO GO WHENEVER YOU ARE...
PAIGE

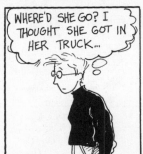

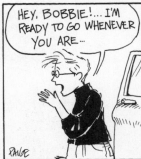

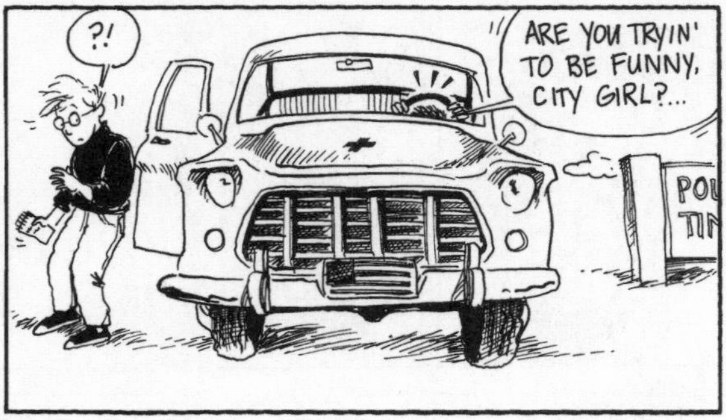
?!
ARE YOU TRYIN' TO BE FUNNY, CITY GIRL?...

JANE SOON DISCOVERS THAT BOBBIE'S VIEW OF THE ROAD IS SOMEWHAT VERTICALLY CHALLENGED...

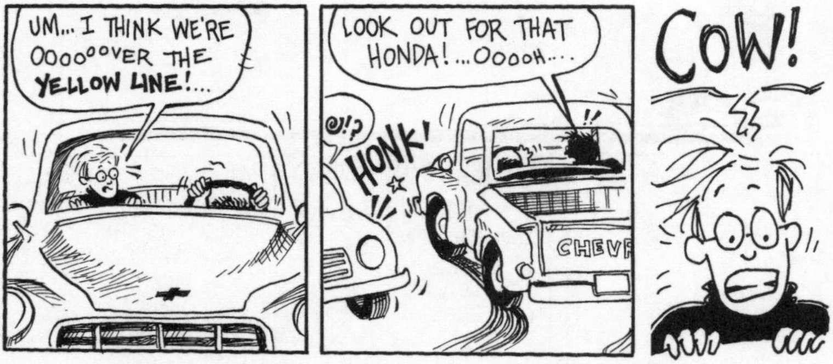
UM... I THINK WE'RE OOOOOOVER THE YELLOW LINE!...
LOOK OUT FOR THAT HONDA! ...OOOOH....
@!?
HONK!
!!
COW!

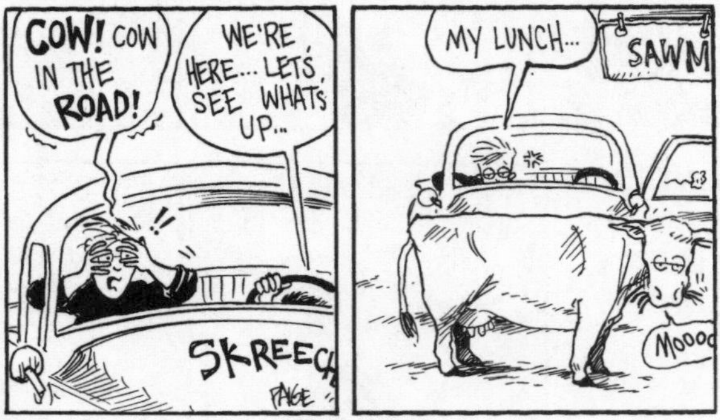
COW! COW IN THE ROAD!
WE'RE HERE... LETS SEE WHATS UP...
SKREECH
PAGE
MY LUNCH...

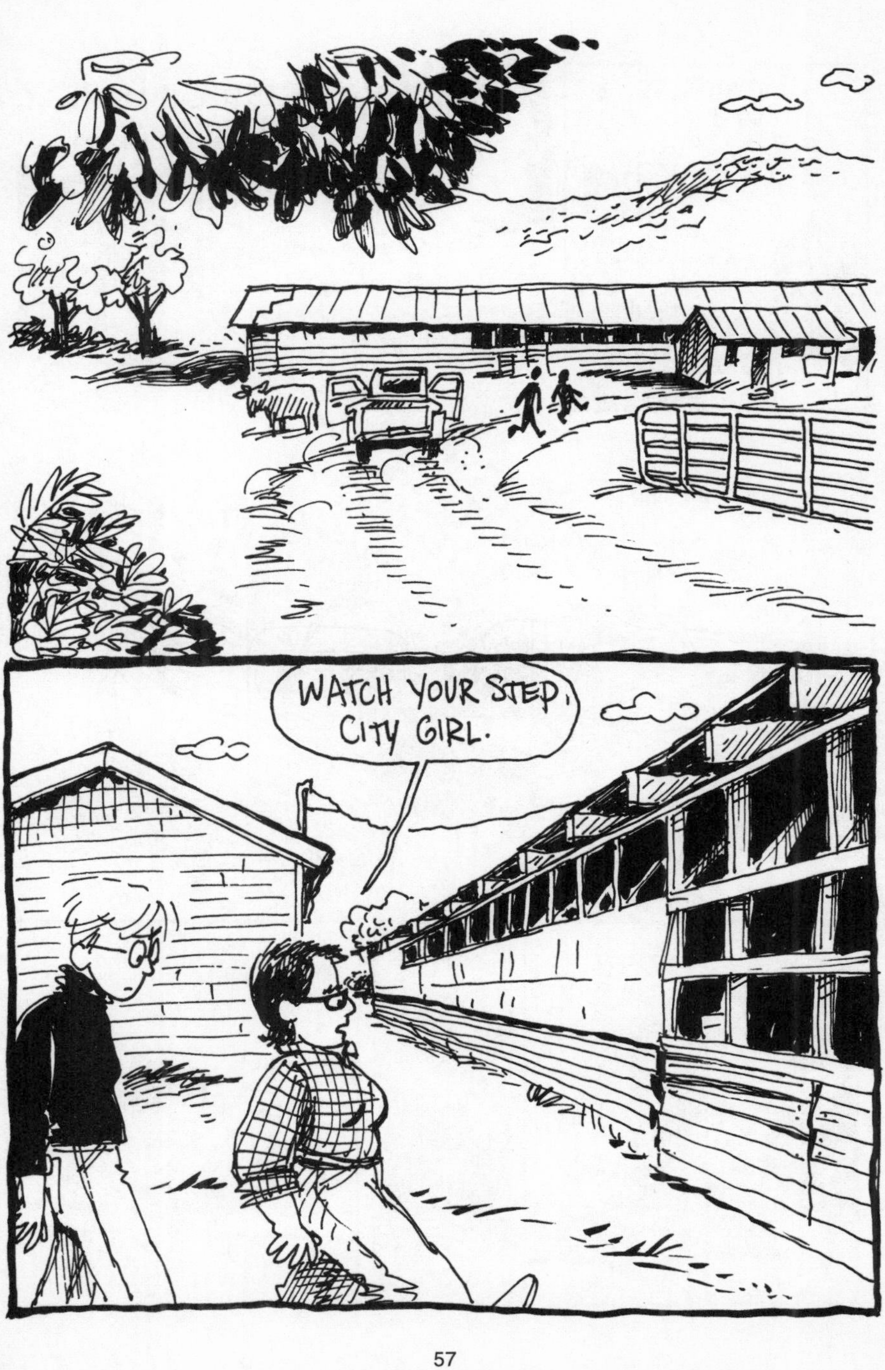
WATCH YOUR STEP, CITY GIRL.

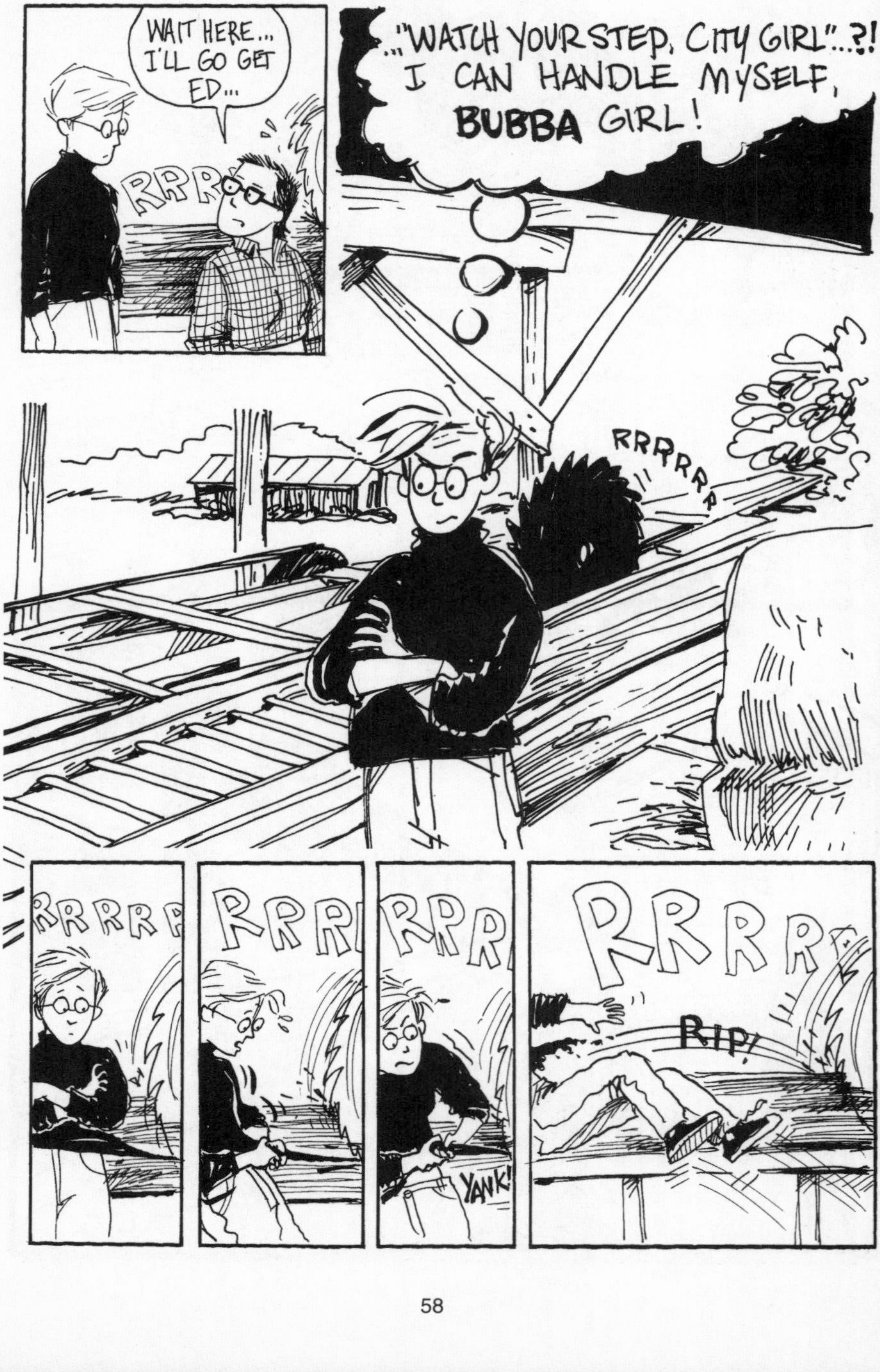
WAIT HERE... I'LL GO GET ED...
RRR
..."WATCH YOUR STEP, CITY GIRL"...?! I CAN HANDLE MYSELF, BUBBA GIRL!
RRRRRRR
RRRRR
RRR
RRR
YANK!
RRRR
RIP!

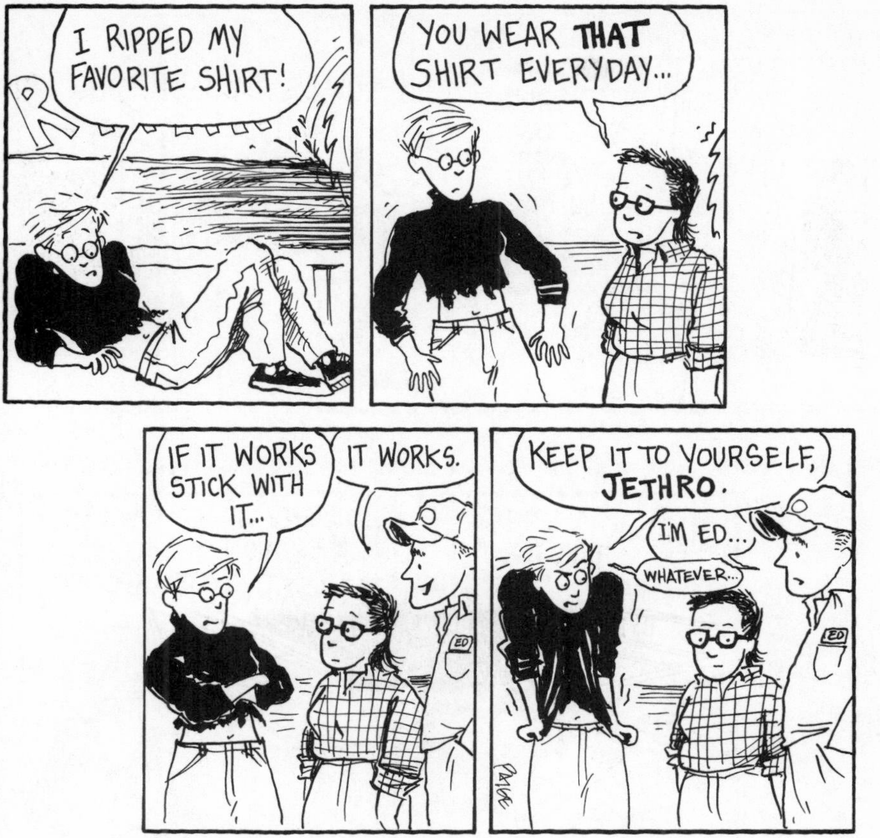
I RIPPED MY FAVORITE SHIRT!
YOU WEAR **THAT** SHIRT EVERYDAY...
IF IT WORKS STICK WITH IT...
IT WORKS.
KEEP IT TO YOURSELF, **JETHRO**.
I'M ED...
WHATEVER...

LATER...

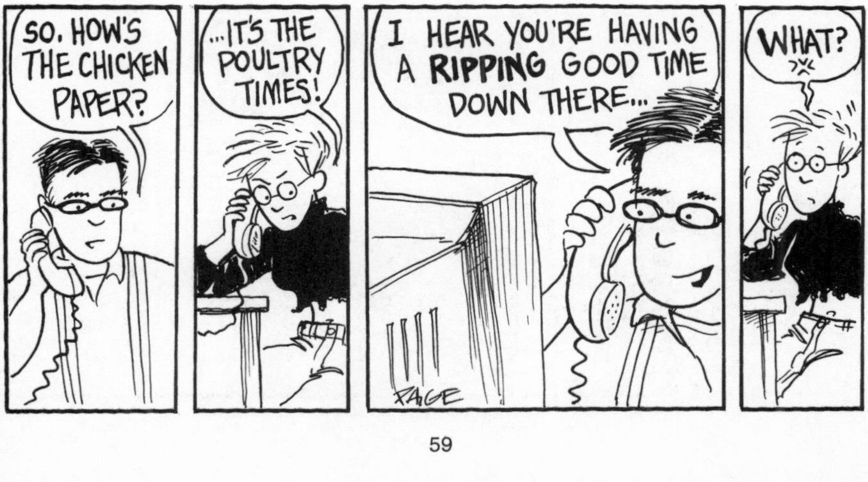
SO. HOW'S THE CHICKEN PAPER?
...IT'S THE POULTRY TIMES!
I HEAR YOU'RE HAVING A **RIPPING** GOOD TIME DOWN THERE...
WHAT?
PAGE

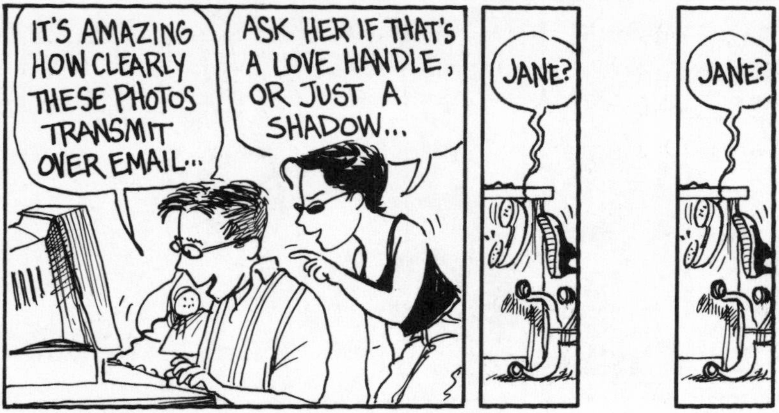
IT'S AMAZING HOW CLEARLY THESE PHOTOS TRANSMIT OVER EMAIL...
ASK HER IF THAT'S A LOVE HANDLE, OR JUST A SHADOW...
JANE?
JANE?

LATER THAT NIGHT, JANE TAKES A PRIVATE MOMENT FOR SELF-REFLECTION...

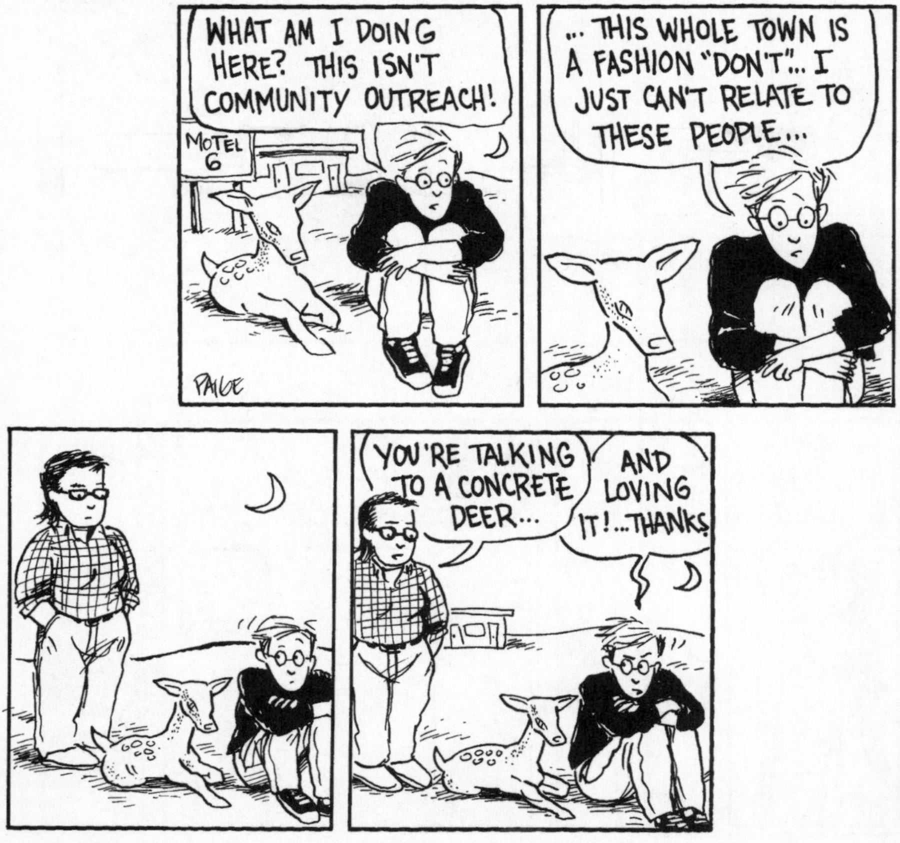
WHAT AM I DOING HERE? THIS ISN'T COMMUNITY OUTREACH!
MOTEL 6
PAIGE
... THIS WHOLE TOWN IS A FASHION "DON'T"... I JUST CAN'T RELATE TO THESE PEOPLE...
YOU'RE TALKING TO A CONCRETE DEER...
AND LOVING IT!...THANKS

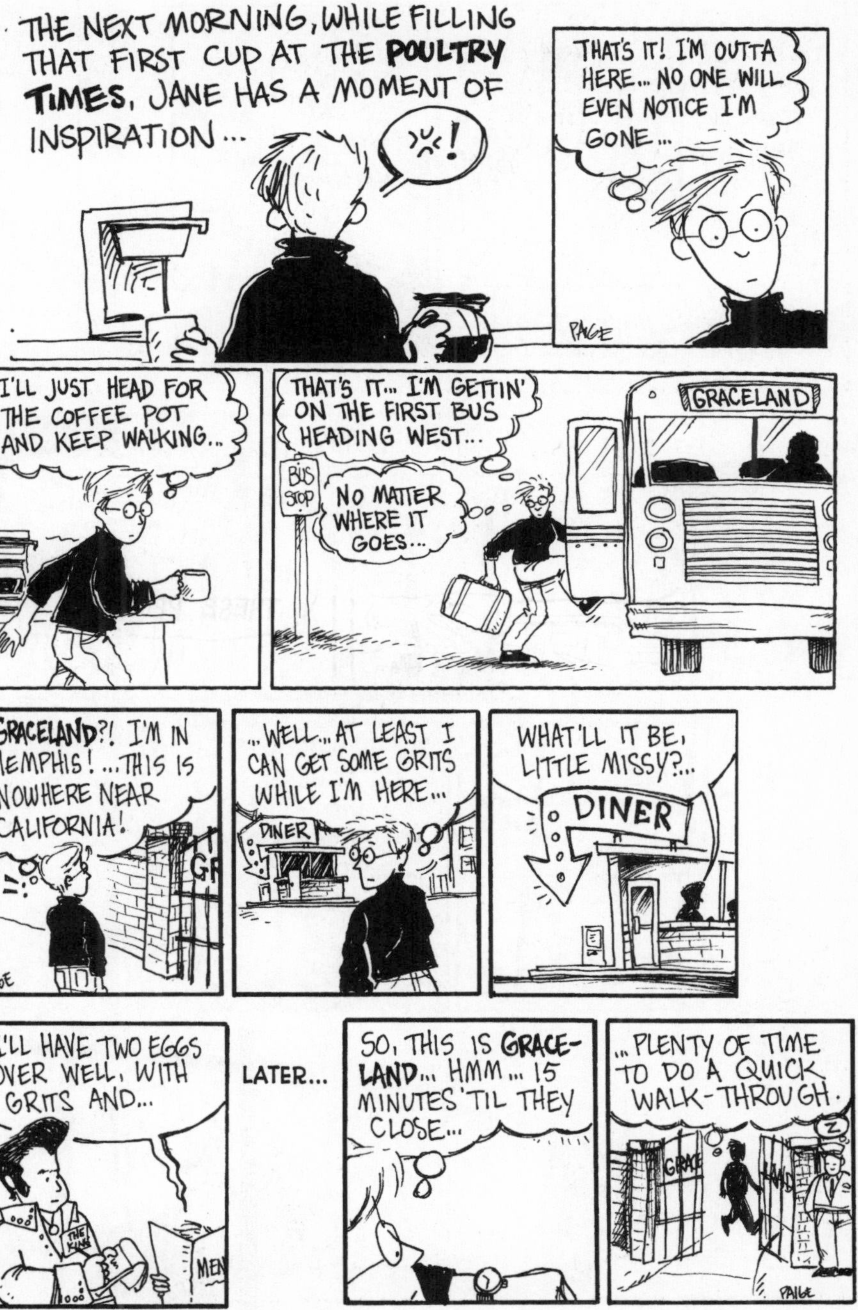

THE NEXT MORNING, WHILE FILLING THAT FIRST CUP AT THE **POULTRY TIMES**, JANE HAS A MOMENT OF INSPIRATION...
!
THAT'S IT! I'M OUTTA HERE... NO ONE WILL EVEN NOTICE I'M GONE...
PAIGE
I'LL JUST HEAD FOR THE COFFEE POT AND KEEP WALKING...
THAT'S IT... I'M GETTIN' ON THE FIRST BUS HEADING WEST...
BUS STOP
NO MATTER WHERE IT GOES...
GRACELAND
GRACELAND?! I'M IN MEMPHIS! ...THIS IS NOWHERE NEAR CALIFORNIA!
PAIGE
...WELL... AT LEAST I CAN GET SOME GRITS WHILE I'M HERE...
DINER
WHAT'LL IT BE, LITTLE MISSY?...
DINER
I'LL HAVE TWO EGGS OVER WELL, WITH GRITS AND...
THE KING
LATER...
SO, THIS IS **GRACELAND**... HMM... 15 MINUTES 'TIL THEY CLOSE...
...PLENTY OF TIME TO DO A QUICK WALK-THROUGH.
GRACE
LAND
Z
PAIGE

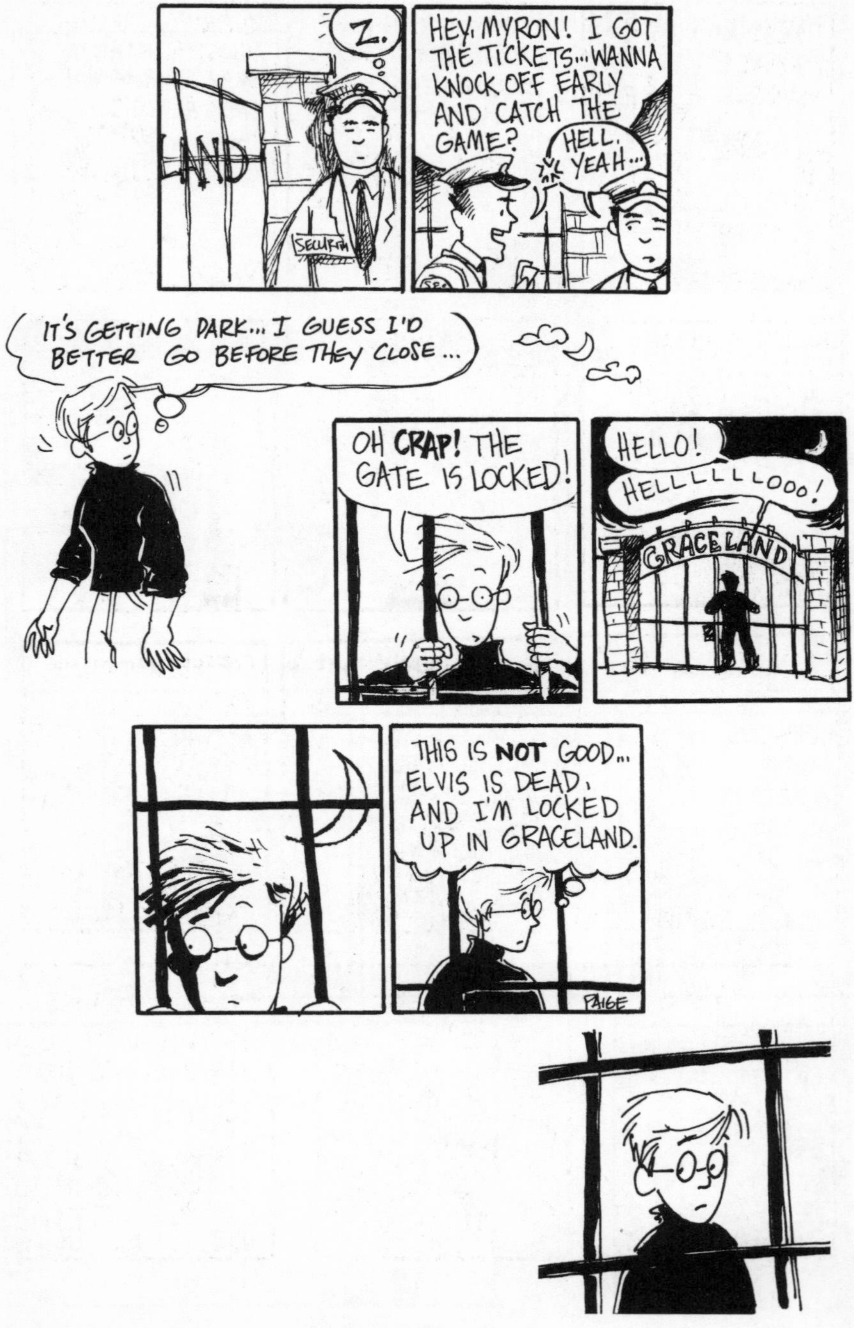
Z.
SECURITY
HEY, MYRON! I GOT THE TICKETS...WANNA KNOCK OFF EARLY AND CATCH THE GAME?
HELL, YEAH...
IT'S GETTING DARK... I GUESS I'D BETTER GO BEFORE THEY CLOSE...
OH CRAP! THE GATE IS LOCKED!
HELLO!
HELLLLLLLOOO!
GRACELAND
THIS IS NOT GOOD... ELVIS IS DEAD, AND I'M LOCKED UP IN GRACELAND.
PAIGE

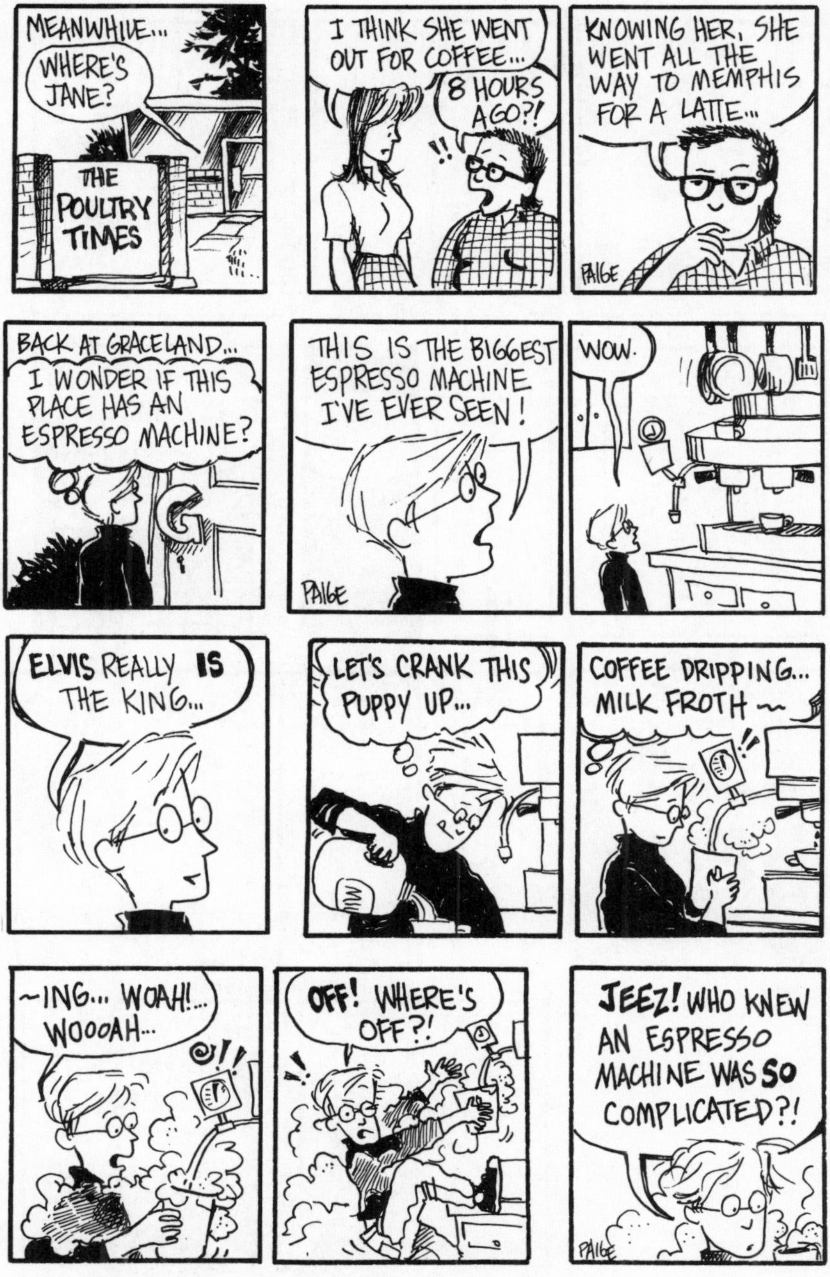
MEANWHILE...
WHERE'S JANE?
THE POULTRY TIMES
I THINK SHE WENT OUT FOR COFFEE...
8 HOURS AGO?!
!!
KNOWING HER, SHE WENT ALL THE WAY TO MEMPHIS FOR A LATTE...
PAIGE
BACK AT GRACELAND...
I WONDER IF THIS PLACE HAS AN ESPRESSO MACHINE?
THIS IS THE BIGGEST ESPRESSO MACHINE I'VE EVER SEEN!
PAIGE
WOW.
ELVIS REALLY IS THE KING...
LET'S CRANK THIS PUPPY UP...
COFFEE DRIPPING... MILK FROTH ~
~ING... WOAH!... WOOOAH...
OFF! WHERE'S OFF?!
JEEZ! WHO KNEW AN ESPRESSO MACHINE WAS SO COMPLICATED?!
PAIGE

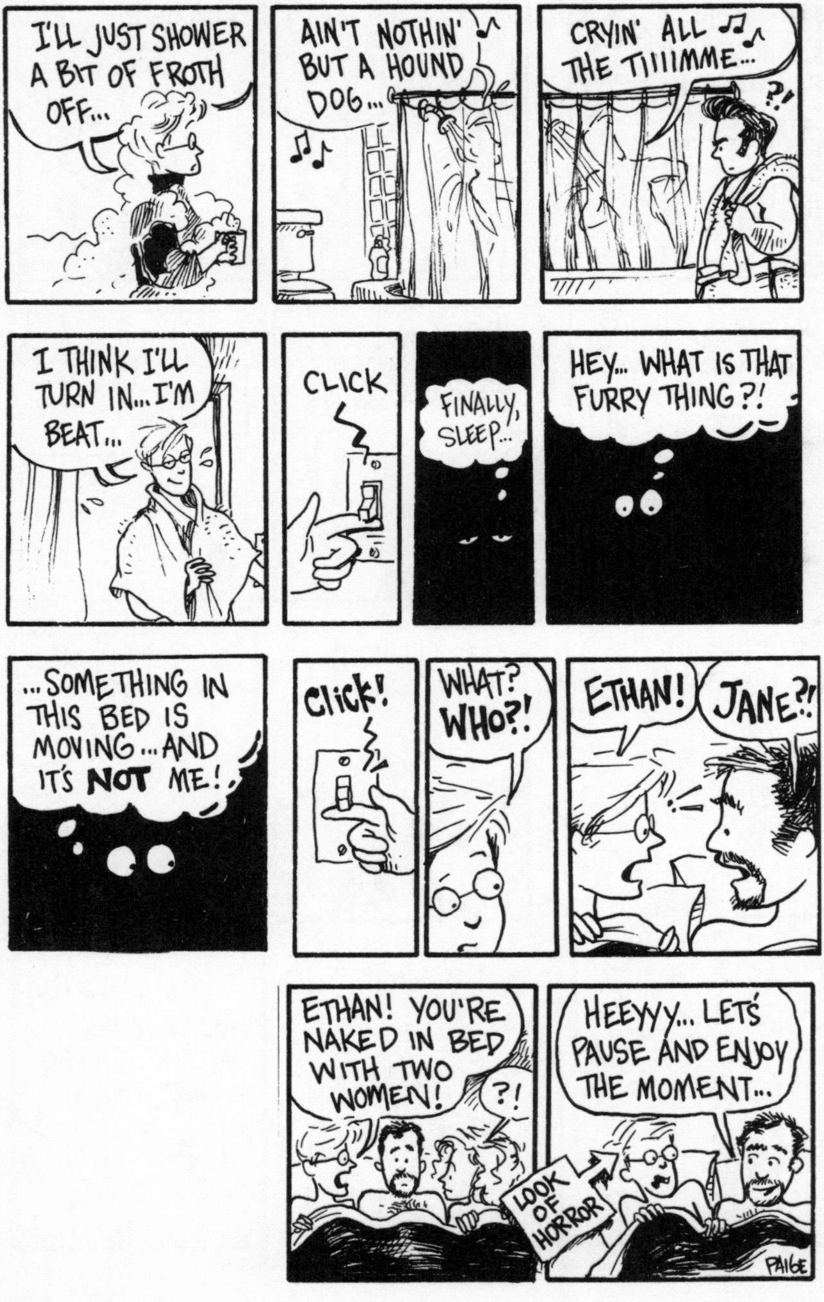

I'LL JUST SHOWER A BIT OF FROTH OFF...
AIN'T NOTHIN' BUT A HOUND DOG...
CRYIN' ALL THE TIIIIMME...
?!
I THINK I'LL TURN IN... I'M BEAT...
CLICK
FINALLY, SLEEP...
HEY... WHAT IS THAT FURRY THING?!
...SOMETHING IN THIS BED IS MOVING... AND IT'S **NOT** ME!
CLICK!
WHAT? **WHO?!**
ETHAN!
JANE?!
ETHAN! YOU'RE NAKED IN BED WITH TWO WOMEN!
?!
LOOK OF HORROR
HEEYYY... LET'S PAUSE AND ENJOY THE MOMENT...
PAIGE

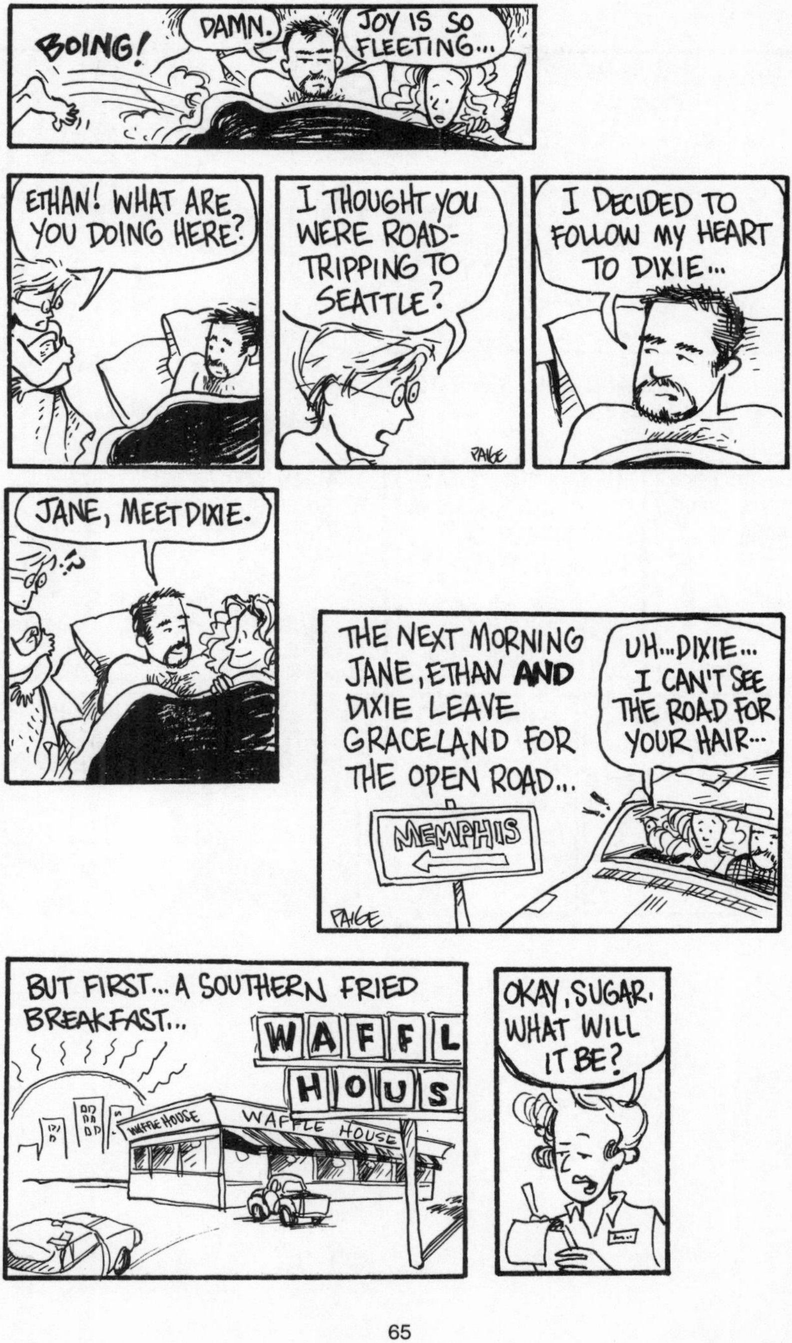
BOING!
DAMN.
JOY IS SO FLEETING...
ETHAN! WHAT ARE YOU DOING HERE?
I THOUGHT YOU WERE ROAD-TRIPPING TO SEATTLE?
PAIGE
I DECIDED TO FOLLOW MY HEART TO DIXIE...
JANE, MEET DIXIE.
THE NEXT MORNING JANE, ETHAN **AND** DIXIE LEAVE GRACELAND FOR THE OPEN ROAD...
UH...DIXIE... I CAN'T SEE THE ROAD FOR YOUR HAIR...
MEMPHIS
PAIGE
BUT FIRST... A SOUTHERN FRIED BREAKFAST...
WAFFL HOUS
WAFFLE HOUSE
WAFFLE HOUSE
OKAY, SUGAR. WHAT WILL IT BE?

WHAT DO YOU HAVE THAT'S FRESH?
LOU!
THERE'S A GIRL OUT HERE WHO WANTS TO MEET YOU!
?!
LOOK OF HORROR
ME
PAIGE

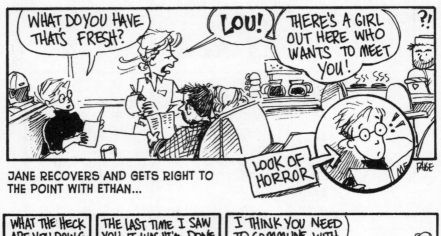

JANE RECOVERS AND GETS RIGHT TO THE POINT WITH ETHAN...

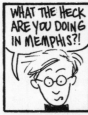

WHAT THE HECK ARE YOU DOING IN MEMPHIS?!
THE LAST TIME I SAW YOU IT WAS "I'M DONE WITH WOMEN, I'M HEADING TO CANADA"...
I THINK YOU NEED TO COMMUNE WITH A ROAD ATLAS...
...YOU ARE NO WHERE NEAR CANADA...
I HAD A LITTLE CLASH WITH AN EX IN SEATTLE SO I CHANGED COURSE.
BESIDES, I NEEDED A LITTLE EGO STROKING AND DIXIE NEEDED A RIDE...
OOH, STOP! TOO MUCH INFORMATION.
PAIGE

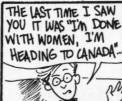

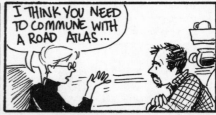

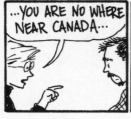

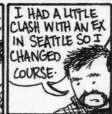

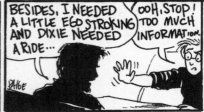

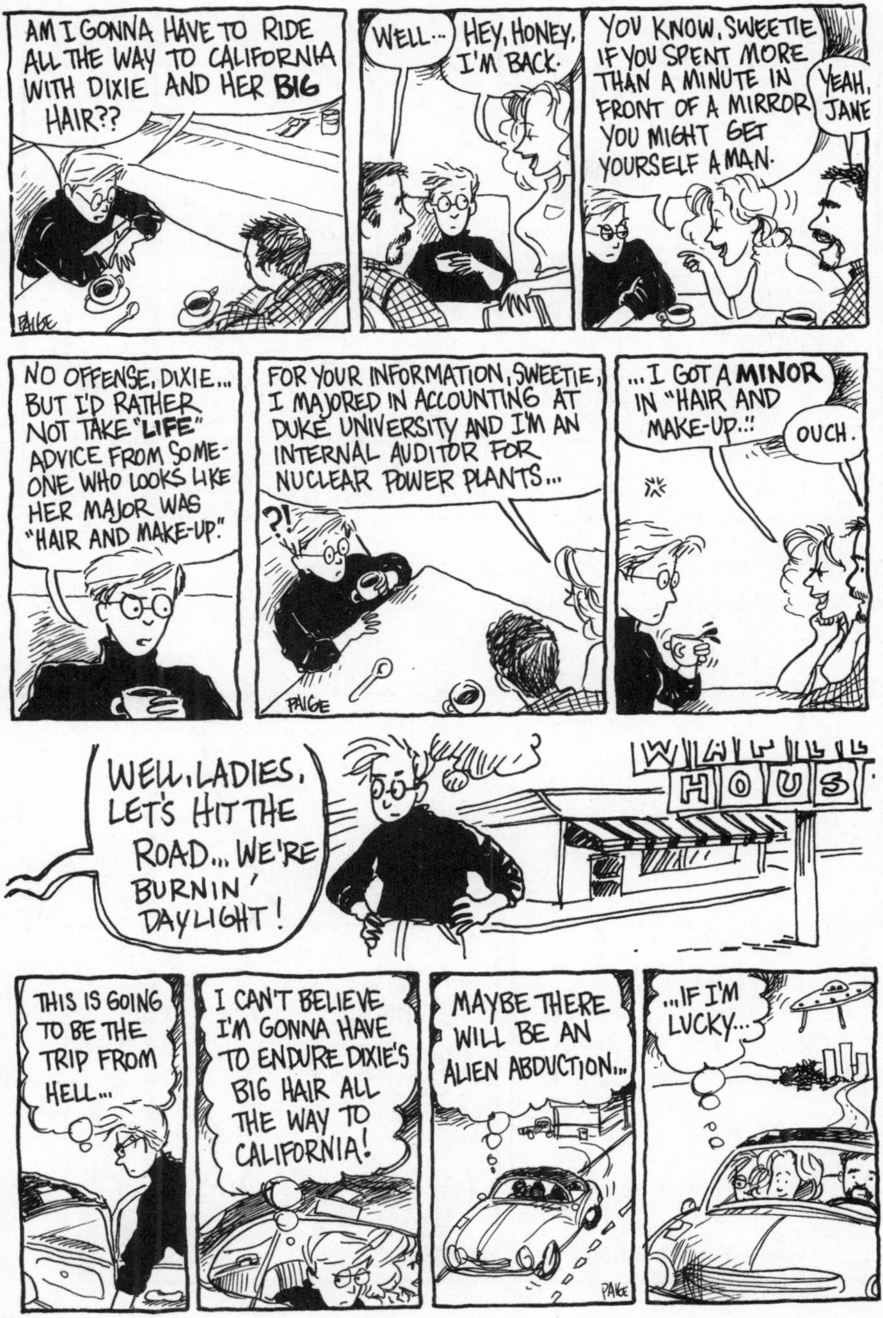
AM I GONNA HAVE TO RIDE ALL THE WAY TO CALIFORNIA WITH DIXIE AND HER **BIG** HAIR??
PAIGE
WELL...
HEY, HONEY, I'M BACK.
YOU KNOW, SWEETIE IF YOU SPENT MORE THAN A MINUTE IN FRONT OF A MIRROR YOU MIGHT GET YOURSELF A MAN.
YEAH, JANE
NO OFFENSE, DIXIE... BUT I'D RATHER NOT TAKE "**LIFE**" ADVICE FROM SOME-ONE WHO LOOKS LIKE HER MAJOR WAS "HAIR AND MAKE-UP."
FOR YOUR INFORMATION, SWEETIE, I MAJORED IN ACCOUNTING AT DUKE UNIVERSITY AND I'M AN INTERNAL AUDITOR FOR NUCLEAR POWER PLANTS...
?!
PAIGE
...I GOT A **MINOR** IN "HAIR AND MAKE-UP."!
OUCH.
WELL, LADIES, LET'S HIT THE ROAD... WE'RE BURNIN' DAYLIGHT!
HOUS
THIS IS GOING TO BE THE TRIP FROM HELL...
I CAN'T BELIEVE I'M GONNA HAVE TO ENDURE DIXIE'S BIG HAIR ALL THE WAY TO CALIFORNIA!
MAYBE THERE WILL BE AN ALIEN ABDUCTION...
PAIGE
...IF I'M LUCKY...

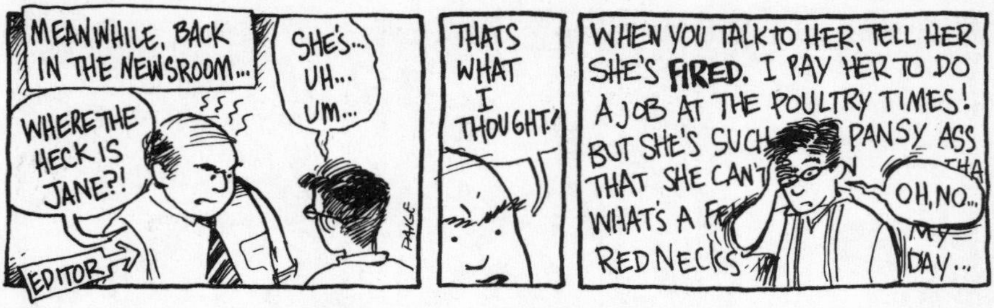
MEANWHILE, BACK IN THE NEWSROOM...
WHERE THE HECK IS JANE?!
EDITOR
SHE'S... UH... UM...
PAIGE
THATS WHAT I THOUGHT!
WHEN YOU TALK TO HER, TELL HER SHE'S FIRED. I PAY HER TO DO A JOB AT THE POULTRY TIMES! BUT SHE'S SUCH PANSY ASS THAT SHE CAN'T WHAT'S A REDNECKS
OH, NO... DAY...

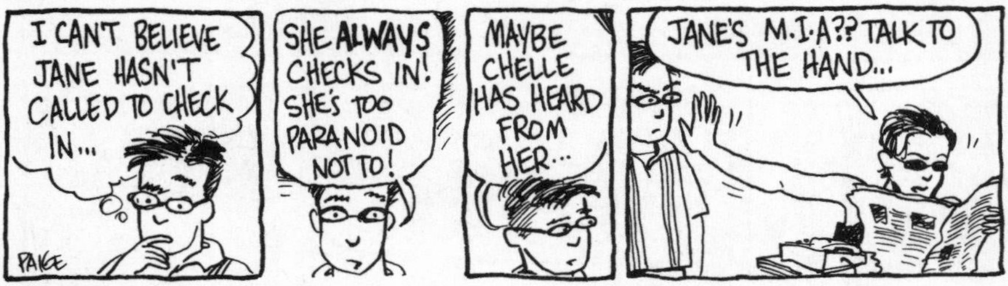
I CAN'T BELIEVE JANE HASN'T CALLED TO CHECK IN...
PAIGE
SHE ALWAYS CHECKS IN! SHE'S TOO PARANOID NOT TO!
MAYBE CHELLE HAS HEARD FROM HER...
JANE'S M.I.A?? TALK TO THE HAND...

MEANWHILE, ON THE OPEN ROAD, OUR TRIO DRIVES INTO THE DESCENDING OKLAHOMA DUSK...

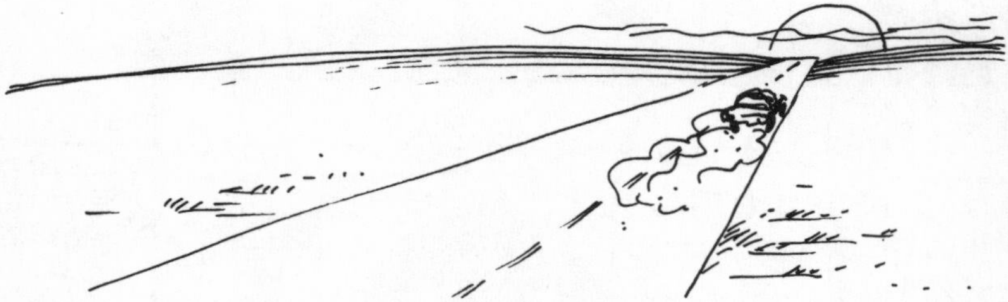

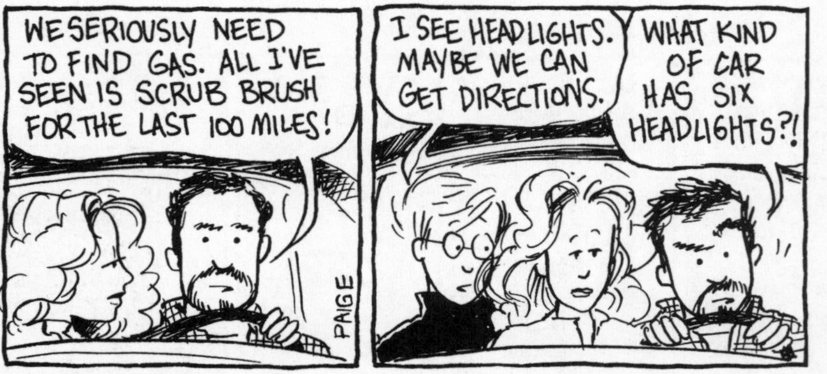
WE SERIOUSLY NEED TO FIND GAS. ALL I'VE SEEN IS SCRUB BRUSH FOR THE LAST 100 MILES!
PAIGE
I SEE HEADLIGHTS. MAYBE WE CAN GET DIRECTIONS.
WHAT KIND OF CAR HAS SIX HEADLIGHTS?!

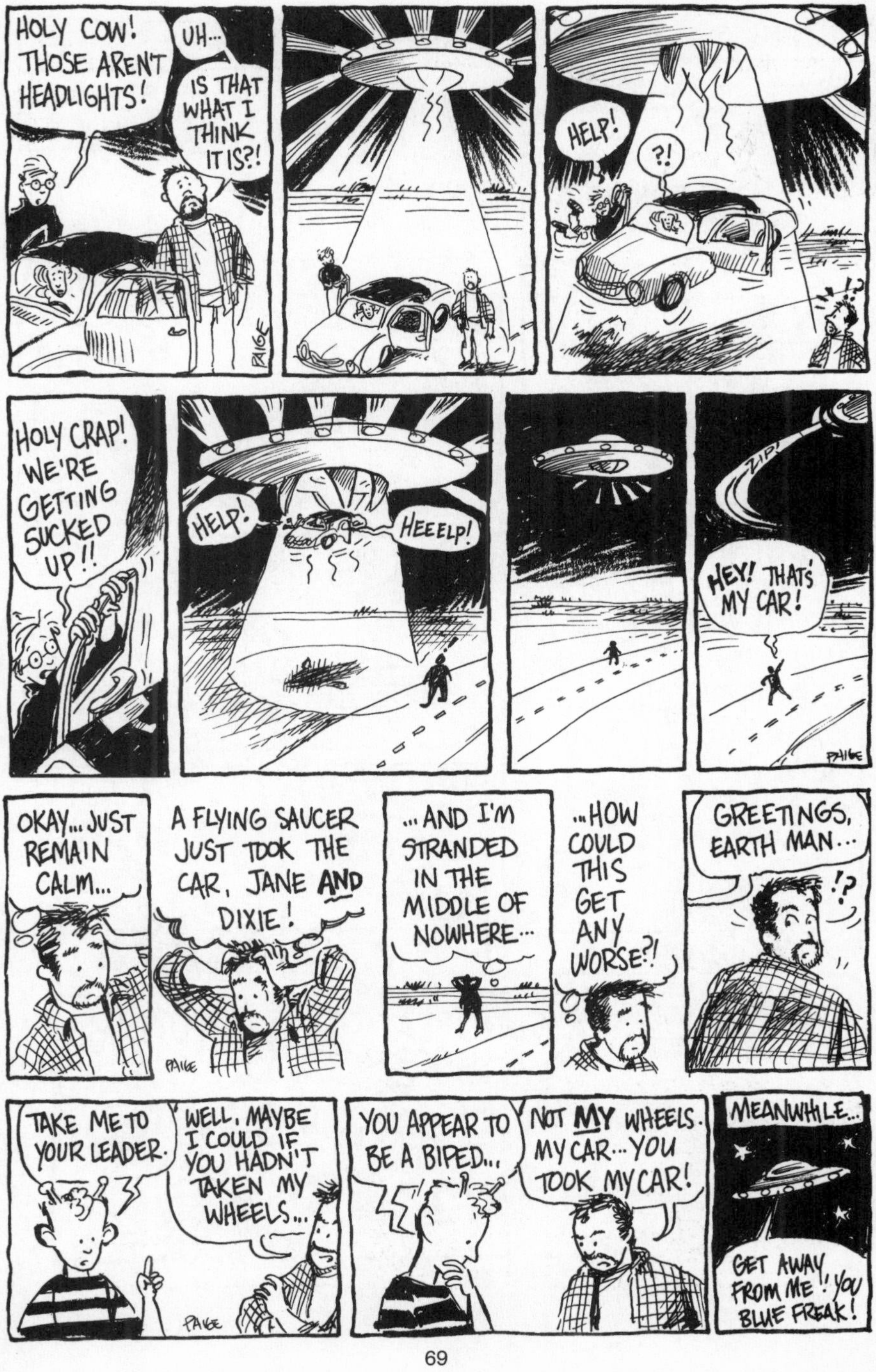
HOLY COW! THOSE AREN'T HEADLIGHTS!
UH...
IS THAT WHAT I THINK IT IS?!
PAIGE
HELP!
?!
!?
HOLY CRAP! WE'RE GETTING SUCKED UP!!
HELP!
HEEELP!
ZIP!
HEY! THAT'S MY CAR!
PAIGE
OKAY... JUST REMAIN CALM...
A FLYING SAUCER JUST TOOK THE CAR, JANE AND DIXIE!
PAIGE
...AND I'M STRANDED IN THE MIDDLE OF NOWHERE...
...HOW COULD THIS GET ANY WORSE?!
GREETINGS, EARTH MAN...
!?
TAKE ME TO YOUR LEADER.
WELL, MAYBE I COULD IF YOU HADN'T TAKEN MY WHEELS...
PAIGE
YOU APPEAR TO BE A BIPED...
NOT MY WHEELS. MY CAR... YOU TOOK MY CAR!
MEANWHILE...
GET AWAY FROM ME! YOU BLUE FREAK!

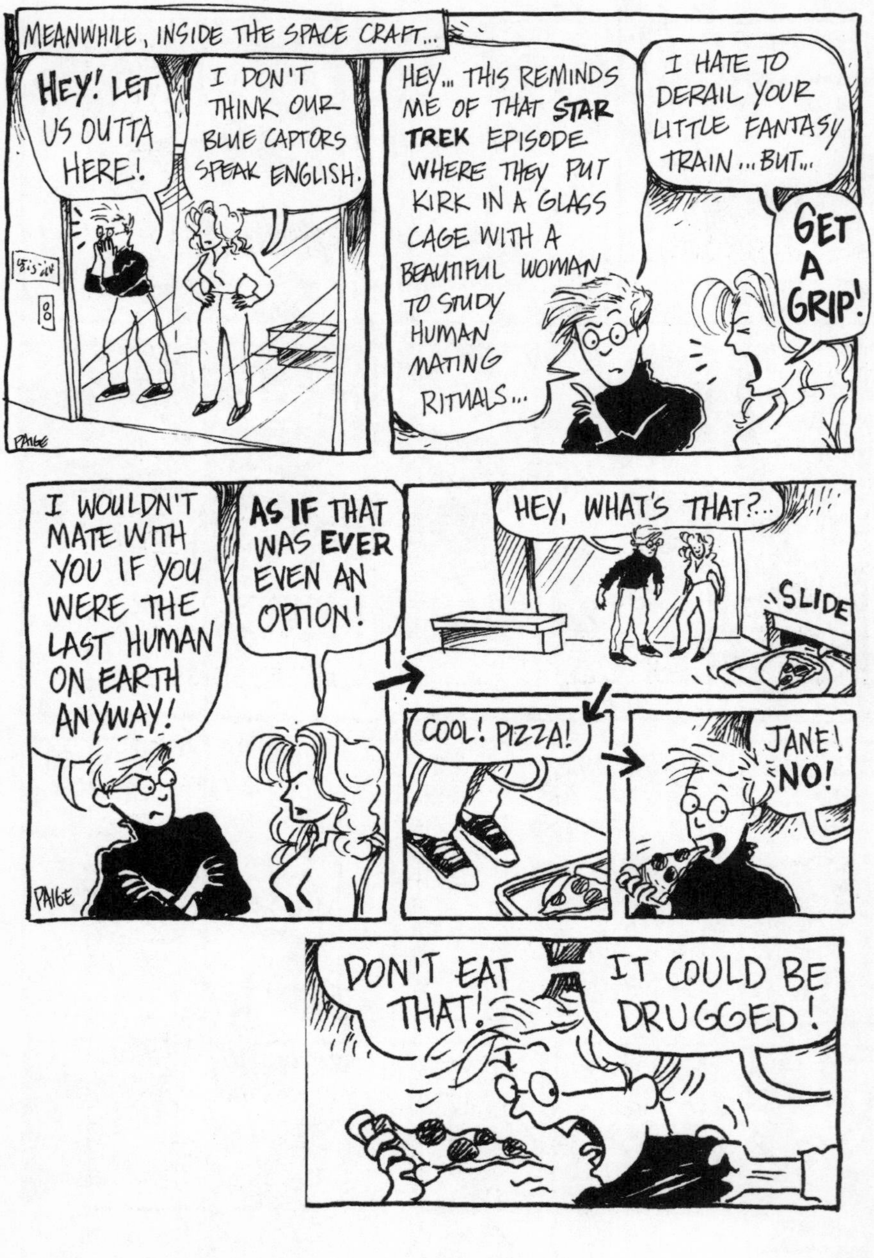
MEANWHILE, INSIDE THE SPACE CRAFT...
HEY! LET US OUTTA HERE!
I DON'T THINK OUR BLUE CAPTORS SPEAK ENGLISH.
HEY... THIS REMINDS ME OF THAT STAR TREK EPISODE WHERE THEY PUT KIRK IN A GLASS CAGE WITH A BEAUTIFUL WOMAN TO STUDY HUMAN MATING RITUALS...
I HATE TO DERAIL YOUR LITTLE FANTASY TRAIN... BUT...
GET A GRIP!
PAIGE
I WOULDN'T MATE WITH YOU IF YOU WERE THE LAST HUMAN ON EARTH ANYWAY!
AS IF THAT WAS EVER EVEN AN OPTION!
HEY, WHAT'S THAT?...
SLIDE
COOL! PIZZA!
JANE! NO!
PAIGE
DON'T EAT THAT!
IT COULD BE DRUGGED!

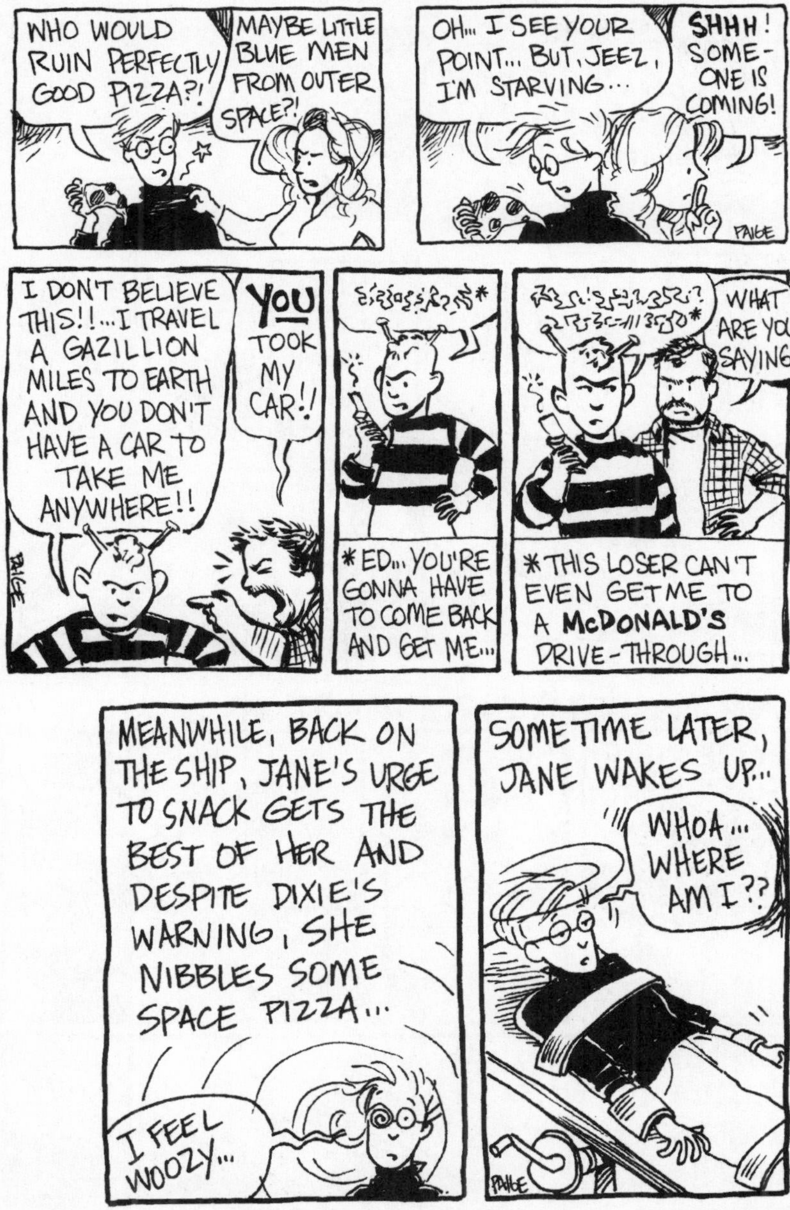
WHO WOULD RUIN PERFECTLY GOOD PIZZA?!
MAYBE LITTLE BLUE MEN FROM OUTER SPACE?!
OH... I SEE YOUR POINT... BUT, JEEZ, I'M STARVING...
SHHH! SOME-ONE IS COMING!
PAIGE
I DON'T BELIEVE THIS!!...I TRAVEL A GAZILLION MILES TO EARTH AND YOU DON'T HAVE A CAR TO TAKE ME ANYWHERE!!
YOU TOOK MY CAR!!
PAIGE
*ED... YOU'RE GONNA HAVE TO COME BACK AND GET ME...
WHAT ARE YOU SAYING?
*THIS LOSER CAN'T EVEN GET ME TO A McDONALD'S DRIVE-THROUGH...
MEANWHILE, BACK ON THE SHIP, JANE'S URGE TO SNACK GETS THE BEST OF HER AND DESPITE DIXIE'S WARNING, SHE NIBBLES SOME SPACE PIZZA...
I FEEL WOOZY...
SOMETIME LATER, JANE WAKES UP...
WHOA... WHERE AM I??
PAIGE

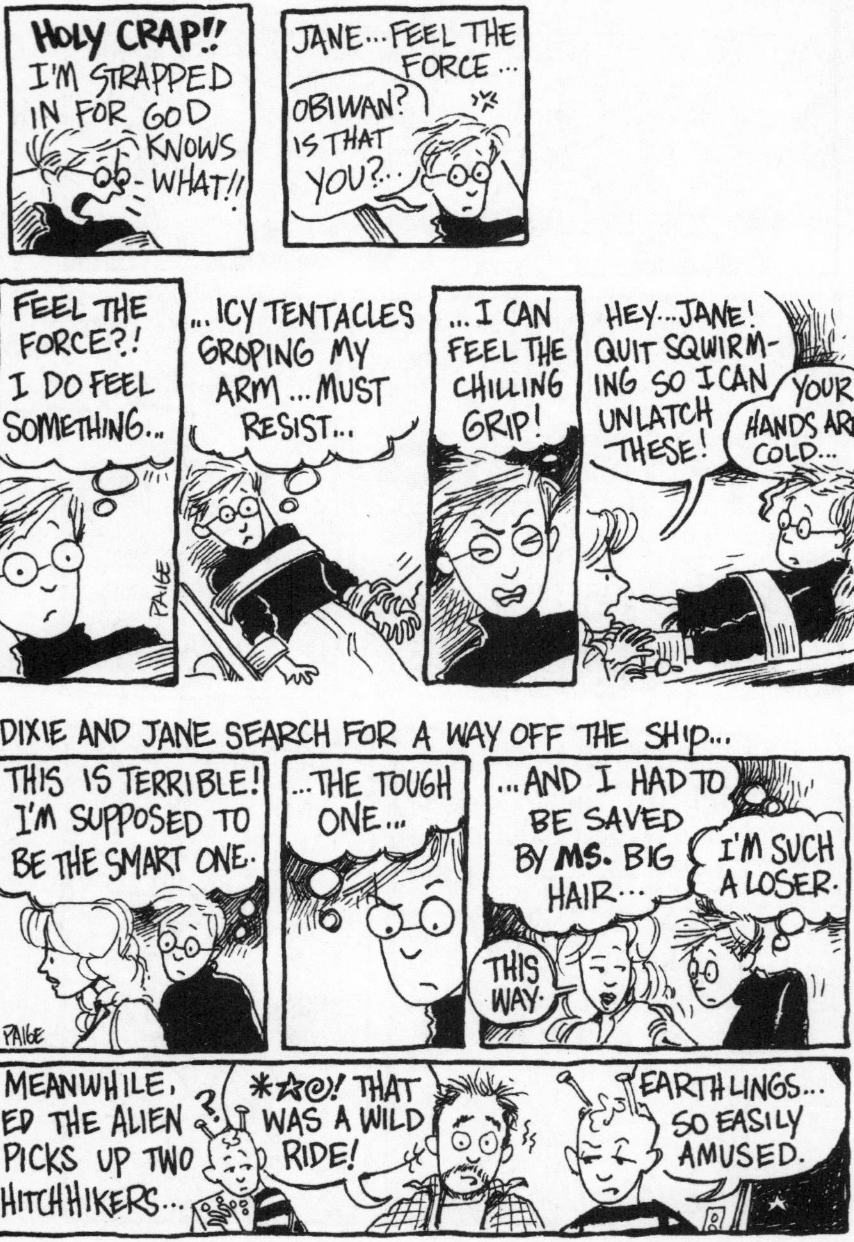
HOLY CRAP!! I'M STRAPPED IN FOR GOD KNOWS WHAT!!
JANE... FEEL THE FORCE...
OBIWAN? IS THAT YOU?...
FEEL THE FORCE?! I DO FEEL SOMETHING...
PAIGE
...ICY TENTACLES GROPING MY ARM ... MUST RESIST...
...I CAN FEEL THE CHILLING GRIP!
HEY...JANE! QUIT SQWIRMING SO I CAN UNLATCH THESE!
YOUR HANDS ARE COLD...
DIXIE AND JANE SEARCH FOR A WAY OFF THE SHIP...
THIS IS TERRIBLE! I'M SUPPOSED TO BE THE SMART ONE.
PAIGE
...THE TOUGH ONE...
...AND I HAD TO BE SAVED BY MS. BIG HAIR...
I'M SUCH A LOSER.
THIS WAY.
MEANWHILE, ED THE ALIEN PICKS UP TWO HITCHHIKERS...
?
*☆@! THAT WAS A WILD RIDE!
EARTHLINGS... SO EASILY AMUSED.

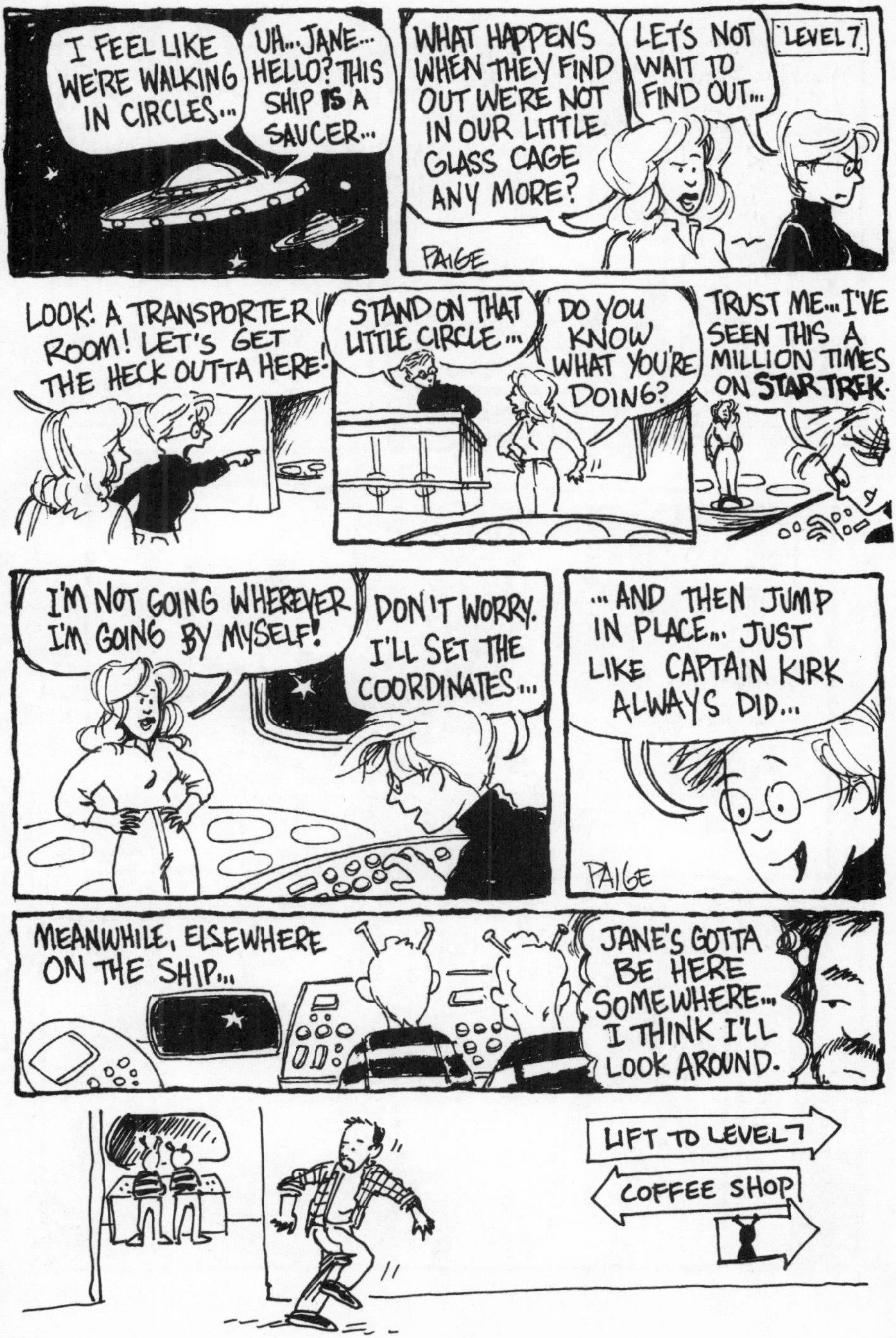
I FEEL LIKE WE'RE WALKING IN CIRCLES...
UH... JANE... HELLO? THIS SHIP IS A SAUCER...
WHAT HAPPENS WHEN THEY FIND OUT WE'RE NOT IN OUR LITTLE GLASS CAGE ANY MORE?
LET'S NOT WAIT TO FIND OUT...
LEVEL 7
PAIGE
LOOK! A TRANSPORTER ROOM! LET'S GET THE HECK OUTTA HERE!
STAND ON THAT LITTLE CIRCLE...
DO YOU KNOW WHAT YOU'RE DOING?
TRUST ME... I'VE SEEN THIS A MILLION TIMES ON STAR TREK.
I'M NOT GOING WHEREVER I'M GOING BY MYSELF!
DON'T WORRY. I'LL SET THE COORDINATES...
...AND THEN JUMP IN PLACE... JUST LIKE CAPTAIN KIRK ALWAYS DID...
PAIGE
MEANWHILE, ELSEWHERE ON THE SHIP...
JANE'S GOTTA BE HERE SOMEWHERE... I THINK I'LL LOOK AROUND.
LIFT TO LEVEL 7
COFFEE SHOP

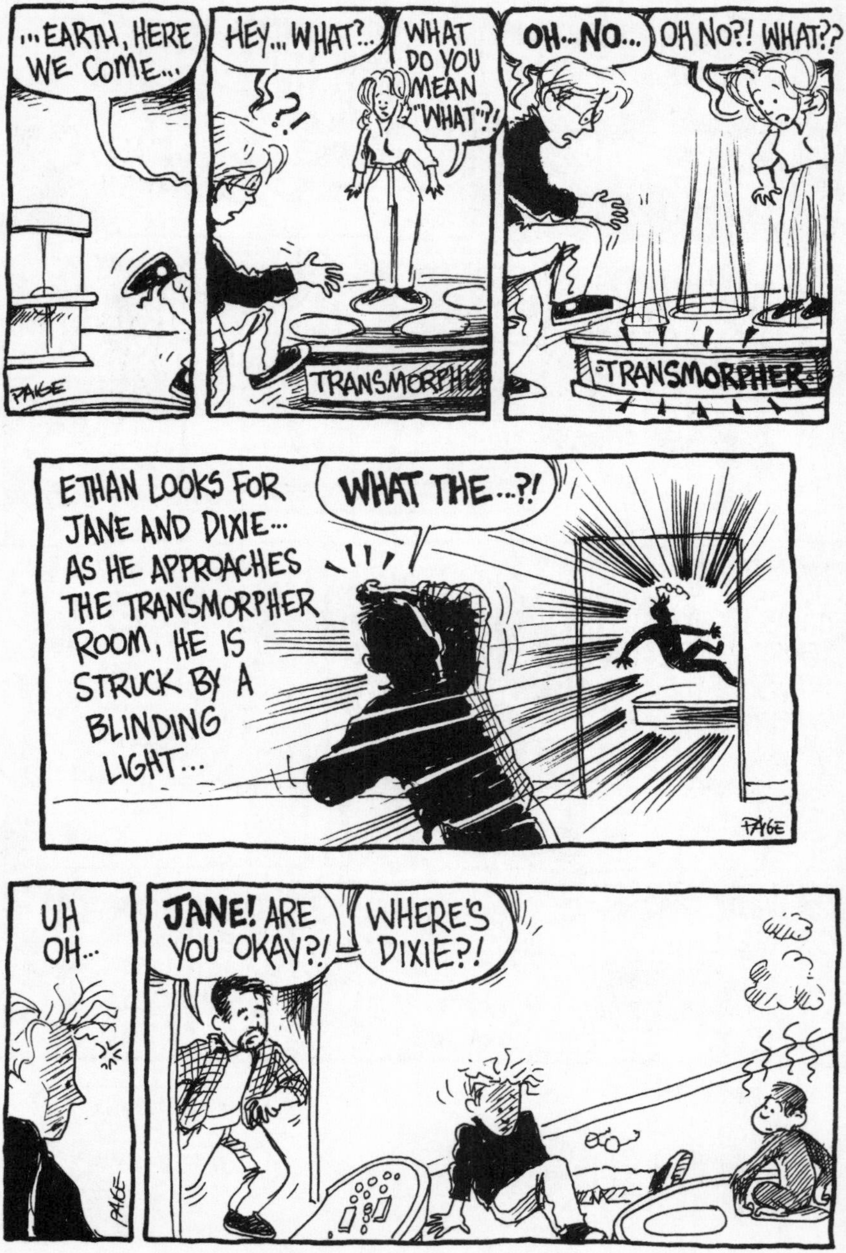

...EARTH, HERE WE COME...
PAIGE
HEY... WHAT?...
?!
WHAT DO YOU MEAN "WHAT"?!
TRANSMORPH
OH.. NO...
OH NO?! WHAT??
TRANSMORPHER
ETHAN LOOKS FOR JANE AND DIXIE... AS HE APPROACHES THE TRANSMORPHER ROOM, HE IS STRUCK BY A BLINDING LIGHT...
WHAT THE...?!
PAIGE
UH OH...
PAIGE
JANE! ARE YOU OKAY?!
WHERE'S DIXIE?!

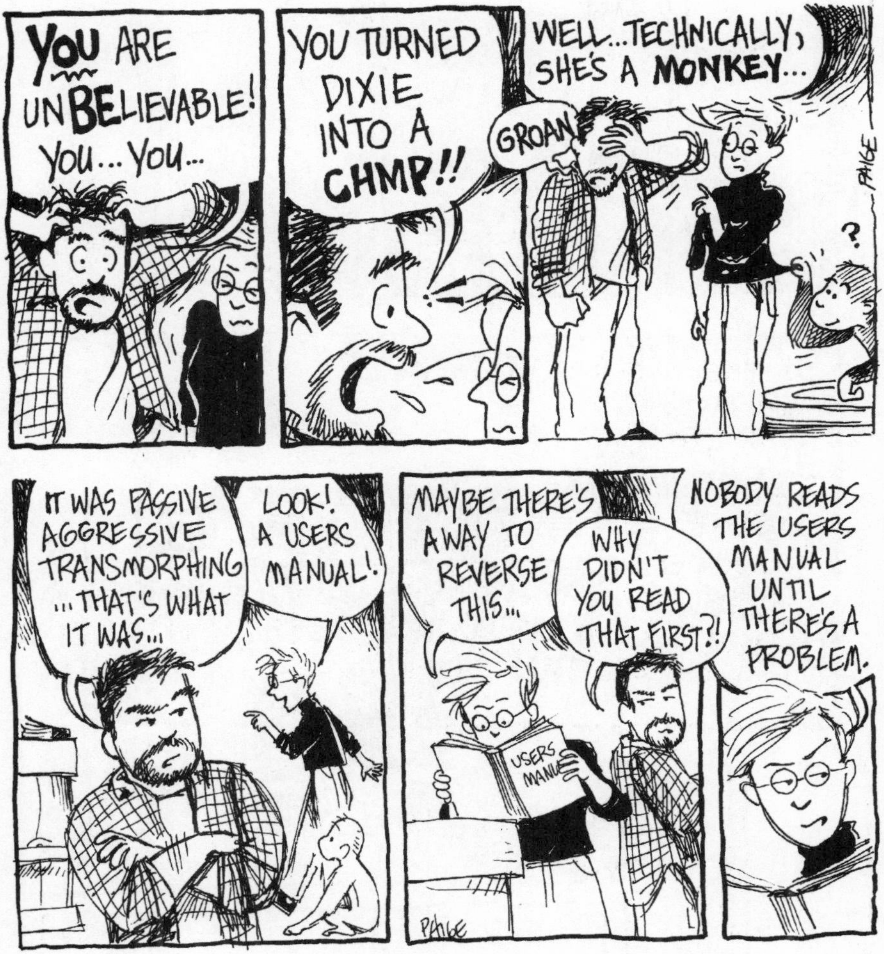
YOU ARE UNBELIEVABLE! YOU... YOU...
YOU TURNED DIXIE INTO A CHMP!!
WELL...TECHNICALLY, SHE'S A MONKEY...
GROAN
?
PAIGE
IT WAS PASSIVE AGGRESSIVE TRANSMORPHING ...THAT'S WHAT IT WAS...
LOOK! A USERS MANUAL!
MAYBE THERE'S A WAY TO REVERSE THIS...
WHY DIDN'T YOU READ THAT FIRST?!
USERS MANU
NOBODY READS THE USERS MANUAL UNTIL THERE'S A PROBLEM.
PAIGE

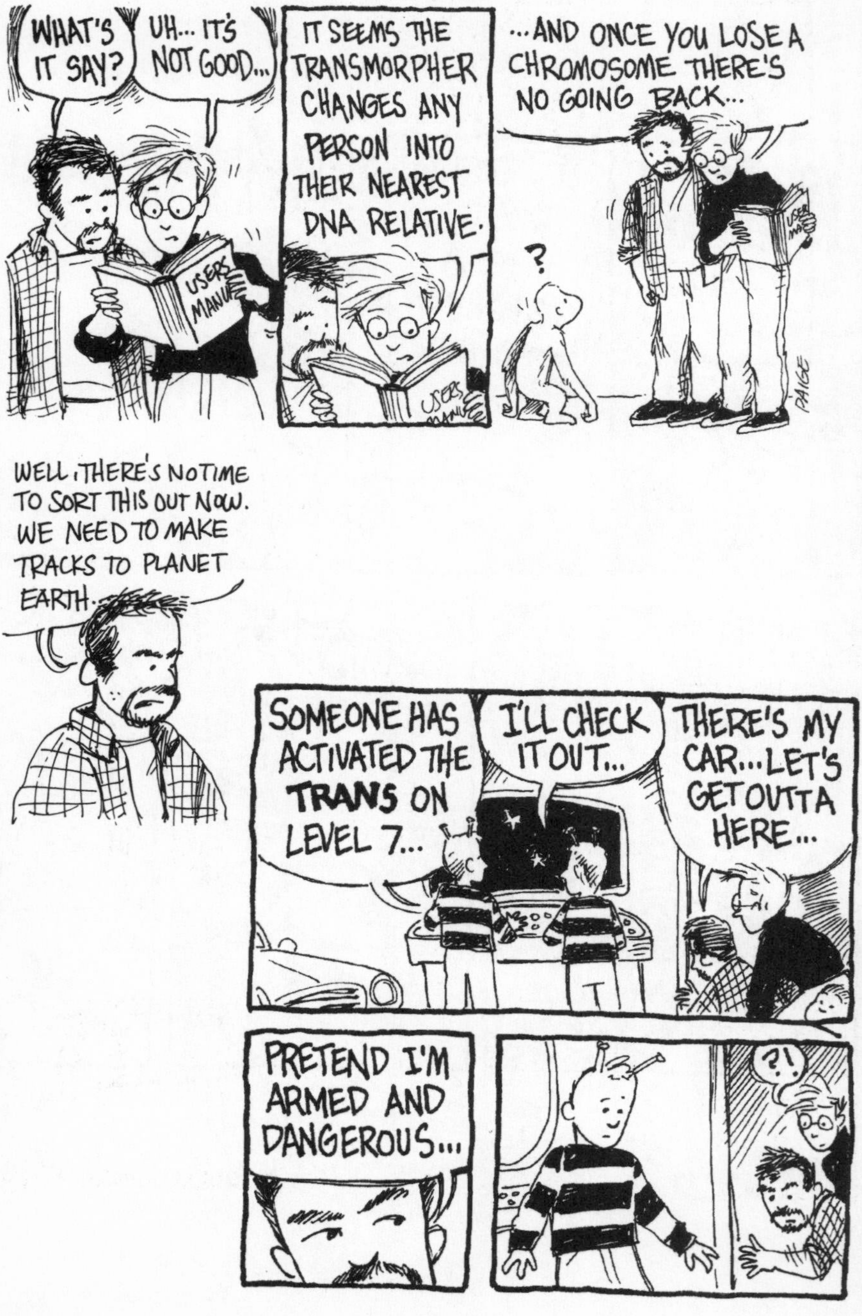
WHAT'S IT SAY?
UH... IT'S NOT GOOD...
IT SEEMS THE TRANSMORPHER CHANGES ANY PERSON INTO THEIR NEAREST DNA RELATIVE.
USERS MANU
...AND ONCE YOU LOSE A CHROMOSOME THERE'S NO GOING BACK...
?
PAIGE
WELL, THERE'S NO TIME TO SORT THIS OUT NOW. WE NEED TO MAKE TRACKS TO PLANET EARTH...
SOMEONE HAS ACTIVATED THE TRANS ON LEVEL 7...
I'LL CHECK IT OUT...
THERE'S MY CAR...LET'S GET OUTTA HERE...
PRETEND I'M ARMED AND DANGEROUS...
?!

HEY! SMURFBOY! ZAP US OUT OF HERE, OR YOUR PAL GETS IT...
PAIGE

ED! THIS EARTH MAN HAS VIOLENT URGES! DO WHAT HE SAYS!!
YEAH!

MEANHHILE, BACK HOME, ARCHIE IS WORRIED...
HI, SARAH.. HAVE YOU HEARD FROM JANE YET?
NO...AND I'M MAD... BUT I'M SURE SHE HAS SOME TALL TALE ABOUT WHERE SHE'S BEEN...
PAIGE
MOMENTS LATER...
WHERE ARE WE?
...AND WHO'S THE MONKEY?

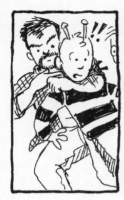

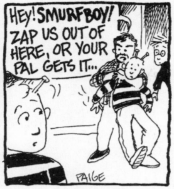

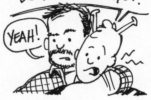

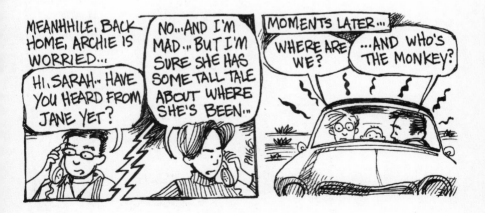

Chapter 4

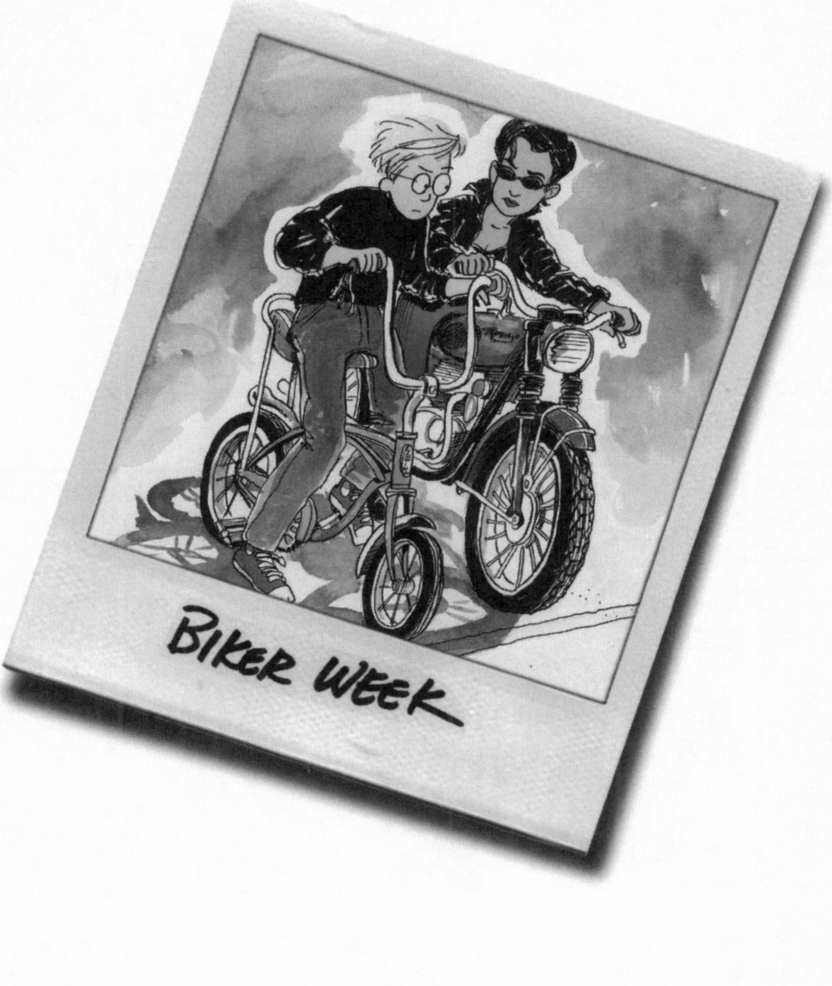
BIKER WEEK

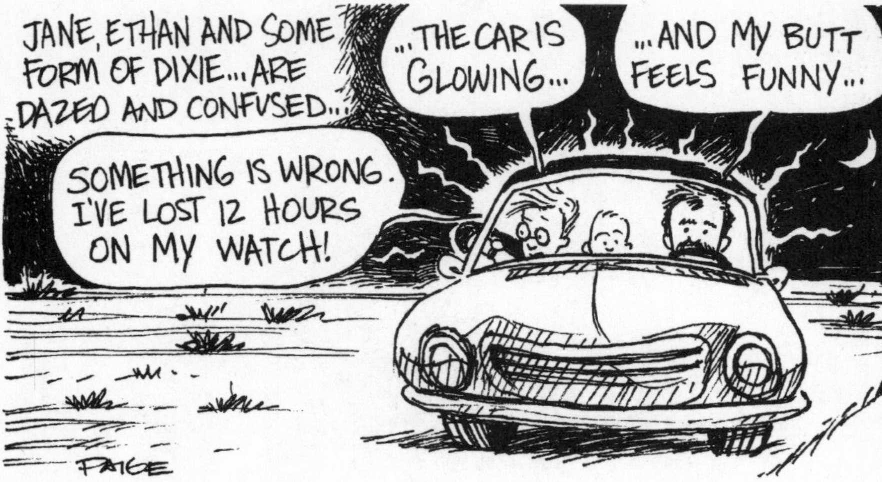
JANE, ETHAN AND SOME FORM OF DIXIE... ARE DAZED AND CONFUSED...
...THE CAR IS GLOWING...
...AND MY BUTT FEELS FUNNY...
SOMETHING IS WRONG. I'VE LOST 12 HOURS ON MY WATCH!
PAIGE

AFTER SOME DELIBERATION, ETHAN AND JANE DECIDE THE BEST WAY TO SOLVE A PROBLEM IS TO FEED IT...

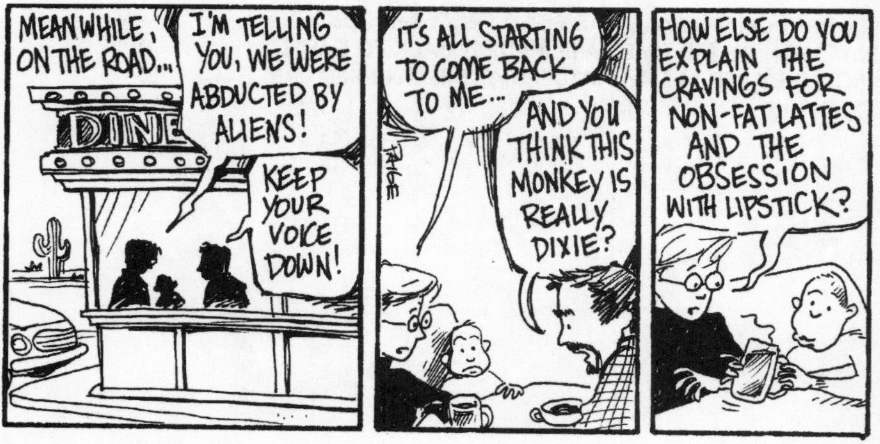
MEANWHILE, ON THE ROAD...
I'M TELLING YOU, WE WERE ABDUCTED BY ALIENS!
KEEP YOUR VOICE DOWN!
IT'S ALL STARTING TO COME BACK TO ME...
AND YOU THINK THIS MONKEY IS REALLY DIXIE?
PAIGE
HOW ELSE DO YOU EXPLAIN THE CRAVINGS FOR NON-FAT LATTES AND THE OBSESSION WITH LIPSTICK?

LIPSTICK NOTWITHSTANDING, ETHAN STILL ISN'T SURE, BUT THINKS IT'S BEST TO TAKE THE MONKEY WITH THEM... AND BEFORE HITTING THE HIGHWAY AGAIN, JANE DECIDES TO CHECK IN WITH ARCHIE AT THE NEWSPAPER...

JANE CALLS FROM THE ROAD, ONLY TO FIND OUT THAT SHE'S BEEN...
FIRED!!.. THAT JERK FIRED ME! IT'S NOT MY FAULT WE GOT ABDUCTED BY ALIENS!
YOU'RE RIGHT. IT COULD HAPPEN TO ANYONE.
HOW CAN THIS DAY GET ANY WORSE?..
HEY, SISSY BOY... IS THAT YOUR FOREIGN CAR OVER THERE?
!

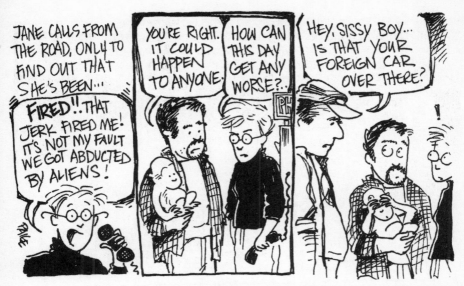

... UNFORTUNATELY, OUR FRIENDS SUFFER ONE SETBACK AFTER ANOTHER. BEING ABDUCTED BY SPACE ALIENS WAS AN EXCITING SIDE TRIP FOR JANE, BUT IT WAS HELL FOR HER CAREER. WHILE CIRCLING THE PLANET WITH A WOMAN SOON TO BECOME A CHIMP, JANE WAS FIRED FROM HER JOB AT THE NEWSPAPER. NOT ONLY THAT, BY THE TIME JANE MADE IT BACK TO CALIFORNIA, SARAH WAS SO ANNOYED BY HER M.I.A. STATUS THAT SHE PLUNKED JANE'S BELONGINGS INTO A BOX AND LEFT THEM ON THE FRONT LAWN. GRANTED, THE BOX ONLY CONTAINED A FEW INDIGO GIRLS CD'S AND A PAIR OF VALENTINE BOXER SHORTS... OH, AND A SLIGHTLY WILTED NEW YEAR'S EVE PARTY HAT... BUT STILL, THAT'S GOTTA HURT. IT DIDN'T HURT NEARLY AS MUCH AS WHAT HAPPENED NEXT! WITH PROXIMITY AND A VINTAGE TRIUMPH IN HER POSSESSION, CHELLE SEIZES THIS OPENING TO MAKE A MOVE ON SARAH! HOW CAN JANE COMPETE WITH ALL THAT COOLNESS?!

SARAH! WOW, CHECK THE NEW LOOK!
DO YOU LIKE THE NEW HAIRCUT?
YEAH... AND I DON'T THINK I'M THE ONLY ONE...
PAIGE

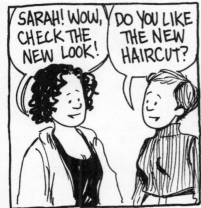

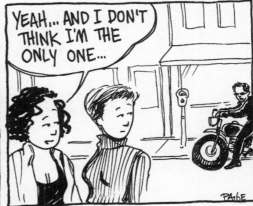

BEING GENERALLY UNINFORMED AND VICTIM OF A CAREFREE, TYPE "B" PERSONALITY, JANE DECIDES TO LET THINGS COOL OFF WITH SARAH A BIT. SHE MISTAKENLY ASSUMES THAT ONCE SARAH HAS CALMED DOWN ALL WILL RETURN TO NORMAL. UNFORTUNATELY, INERTIA IS NOT NECESSARILY THE PATH TO ROMANCE...

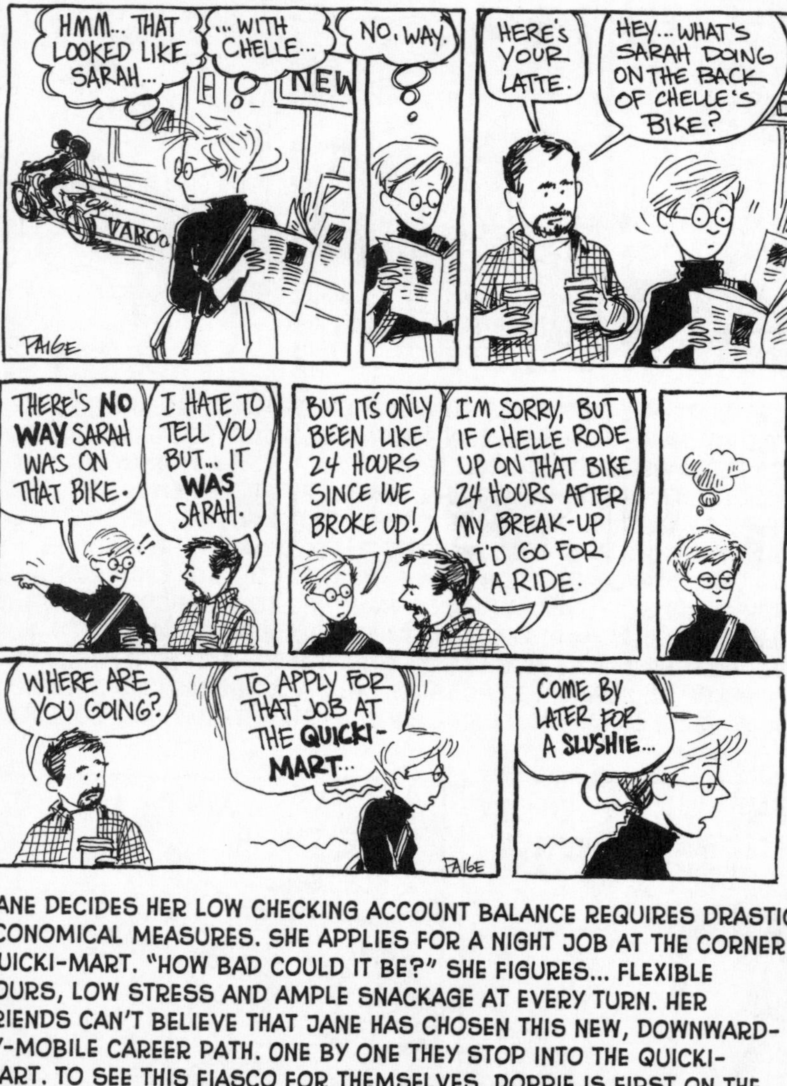
HMM... THAT LOOKED LIKE SARAH...
...WITH CHELLE...
VAROO
PAIGE
NO, WAY.
HERE'S YOUR LATTE.
HEY... WHAT'S SARAH DOING ON THE BACK OF CHELLE'S BIKE?
THERE'S NO WAY SARAH WAS ON THAT BIKE.
I HATE TO TELL YOU BUT... IT WAS SARAH.
BUT IT'S ONLY BEEN LIKE 24 HOURS SINCE WE BROKE UP!
I'M SORRY, BUT IF CHELLE RODE UP ON THAT BIKE 24 HOURS AFTER MY BREAK-UP I'D GO FOR A RIDE.
WHERE ARE YOU GOING?
TO APPLY FOR THAT JOB AT THE QUICKI-MART...
PAIGE
COME BY LATER FOR A SLUSHIE...

JANE DECIDES HER LOW CHECKING ACCOUNT BALANCE REQUIRES DRASTIC ECONOMICAL MEASURES. SHE APPLIES FOR A NIGHT JOB AT THE CORNER QUICKI-MART. "HOW BAD COULD IT BE?" SHE FIGURES... FLEXIBLE HOURS, LOW STRESS AND AMPLE SNACKAGE AT EVERY TURN. HER FRIENDS CAN'T BELIEVE THAT JANE HAS CHOSEN THIS NEW, DOWNWARDLY-MOBILE CAREER PATH. ONE BY ONE THEY STOP INTO THE QUICKI-MART. TO SEE THIS FIASCO FOR THEMSELVES. DORRIE IS FIRST ON THE SCENE. SHE TRIES TO OFFER SOME SORT OF MORAL SUPPORT FOR HER PAL JANE.

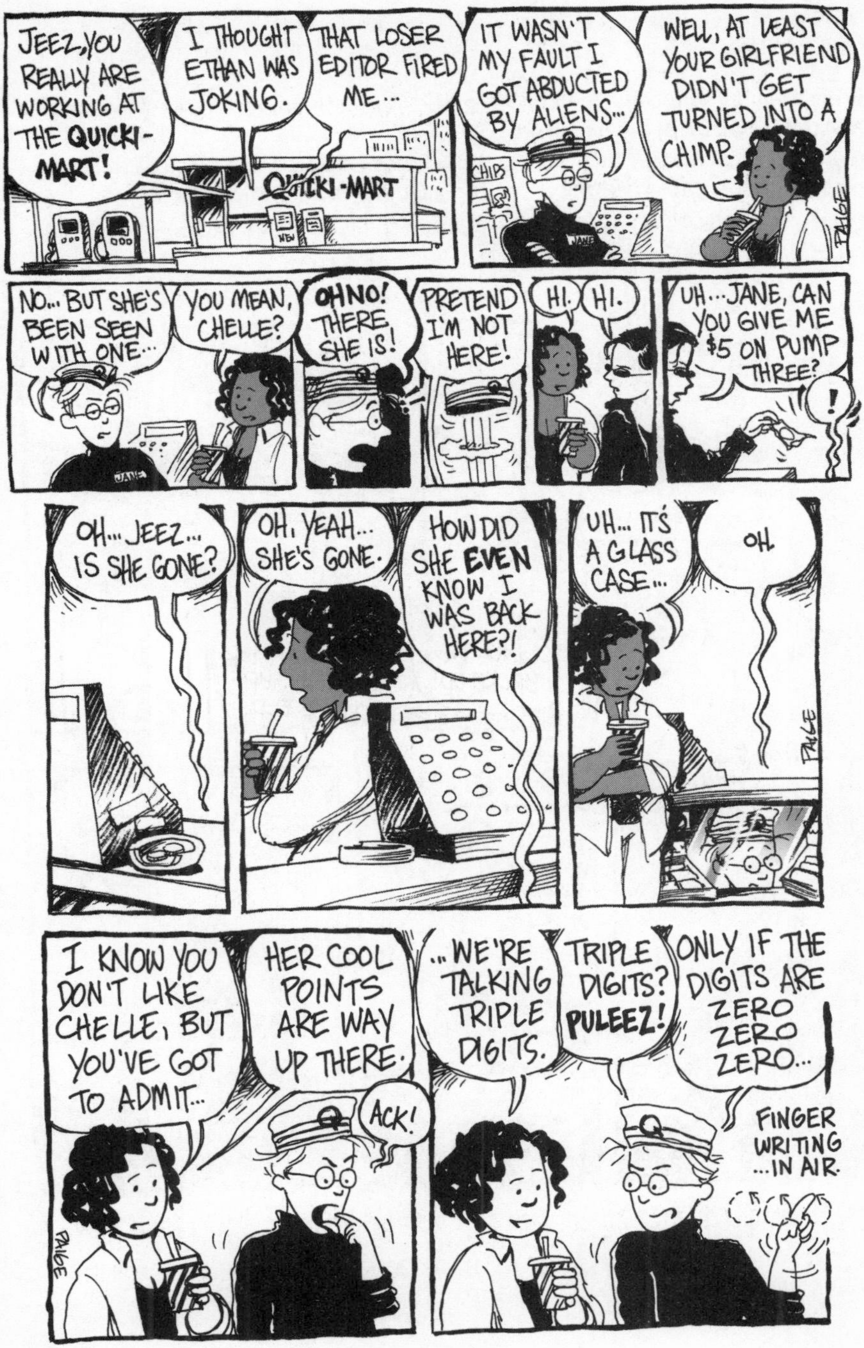

JEEZ, YOU REALLY ARE WORKING AT THE **QUICKI-MART**!
I THOUGHT ETHAN WAS JOKING.
THAT LOSER EDITOR FIRED ME...
QUICKI-MART
IT WASN'T MY FAULT I GOT ABDUCTED BY ALIENS...
WELL, AT LEAST YOUR GIRLFRIEND DIDN'T GET TURNED INTO A CHIMP.
NO... BUT SHE'S BEEN SEEN WITH ONE...
YOU MEAN, CHELLE?
OH NO! THERE SHE IS!
PRETEND I'M NOT HERE!
HI.
HI.
UH... JANE, CAN YOU GIVE ME $5 ON PUMP THREE?
!
OH... JEEZ... IS SHE GONE?
OH, YEAH... SHE'S GONE.
HOW DID SHE **EVEN** KNOW I WAS BACK HERE?!
UH... IT'S A GLASS CASE...
OH.
I KNOW YOU DON'T LIKE CHELLE, BUT YOU'VE GOT TO ADMIT...
HER COOL POINTS ARE WAY UP THERE.
ACK!
... WE'RE TALKING TRIPLE DIGITS.
TRIPLE DIGITS? **PULEEZ!**
ONLY IF THE DIGITS ARE ZERO ZERO ZERO...
FINGER WRITING ...IN AIR.

JANE WASN'T THE ONLY ONE HAVING AN ISSUE WITH DOWNWARD MOBILITY. MIA AND DOROTHY HAD HIT A ROUGH SPOT WHILE JANE AND ETHAN WERE AWAY. IT HAD SOMETHING TO DO WITH AN EX-HOOTER'S GIRL, TURNED MASSAGE THERAPIST, NAMED INGA... BUT IT'S PROBABLY NOT WORTH GOING INTO HERE. IT WAS PRIDE WEEK, SO THERE WERE BIGGER THINGS A FOOT...

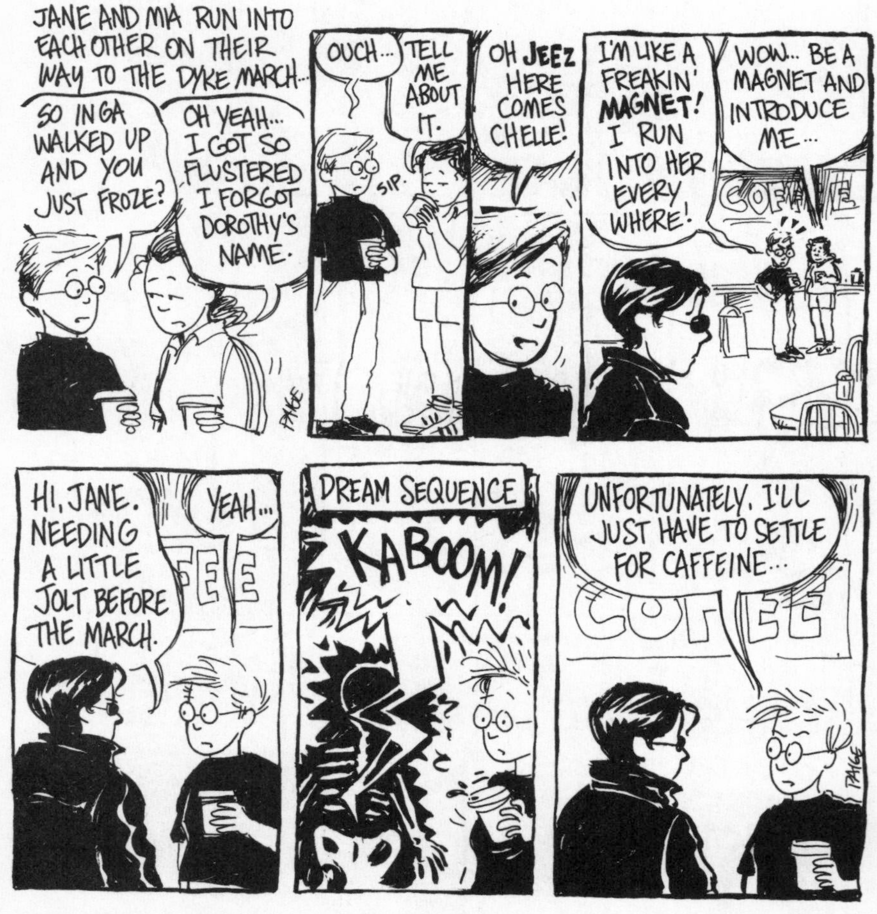

JANE AND MIA RUN INTO EACH OTHER ON THEIR WAY TO THE DYKE MARCH...
SO INGA WALKED UP AND YOU JUST FROZE?
OH YEAH... I GOT SO FLUSTERED I FORGOT DOROTHY'S NAME.
PAIGE
OUCH...
TELL ME ABOUT IT.
SIP.
OH JEEZ HERE COMES CHELLE!
I'M LIKE A FREAKIN' MAGNET! I RUN INTO HER EVERY WHERE!
WOW... BE A MAGNET AND INTRODUCE ME...
COFFEE
HI, JANE. NEEDING A LITTLE JOLT BEFORE THE MARCH.
YEAH...
DREAM SEQUENCE
KABOOM!
UNFORTUNATELY. I'LL JUST HAVE TO SETTLE FOR CAFFEINE...
COFFEE
PAIGE

A FEW MOMENTS LATER, JANE AND MIA RUN INTO ETHAN... COFFEE IN TOW...

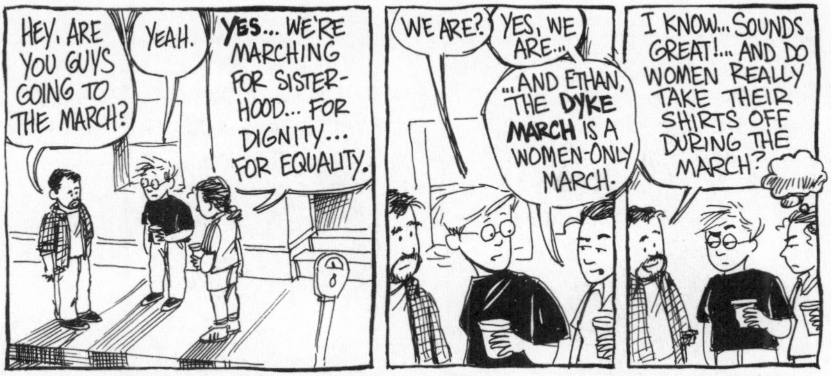
HEY, ARE YOU GUYS GOING TO THE MARCH?
YEAH.
YES... WE'RE MARCHING FOR SISTER-HOOD... FOR DIGNITY... FOR EQUALITY.
WE ARE?
YES, WE ARE...
...AND ETHAN, THE DYKE MARCH IS A WOMEN-ONLY MARCH.
I KNOW... SOUNDS GREAT!... AND DO WOMEN REALLY TAKE THEIR SHIRTS OFF DURING THE MARCH?

THEN IT HAPPENED... JANE GOT A GLIMPSE OF HER WORST NIGHTMARE... HER EX AND HER NEMESIS, COZIED UP TOGETHER ON A VINTAGE MOTORCYCLE FOR THE PARADE. JANE WAS IN SHOCK!... UNTIL ETHAN SWOOPED IN WITH A LITTLE DOSE OF "REALITY." AT SOME POINT, JANE WILL REALIZE THAT A FRIEND WHO ISN'T AFRAID TO BE BRUTALLY HONEST IS A RARE GIFT... BUT IT WON'T BE TODAY...

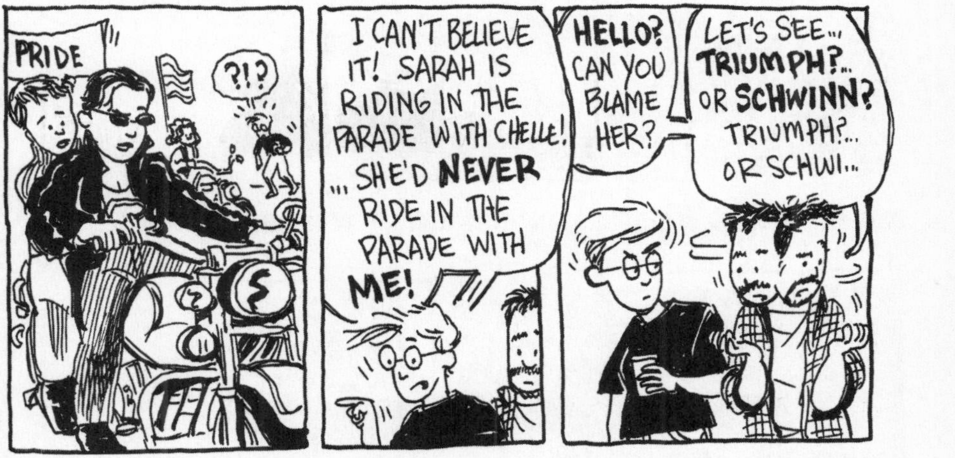
PRIDE
?!?
I CAN'T BELIEVE IT! SARAH IS RIDING IN THE PARADE WITH CHELLE! ...SHE'D NEVER RIDE IN THE PARADE WITH ME!
HELLO? CAN YOU BLAME HER?
LET'S SEE... TRIUMPH?... OR SCHWINN? TRIUMPH?... OR SCHWI...

A WEEK OR SO PASSED... AND JANE CAME UP WITH A BRILLIANT PLAN TO GET SARAH BACK. IT ALL STARTED WITH A FAILED LUNCH DATE...

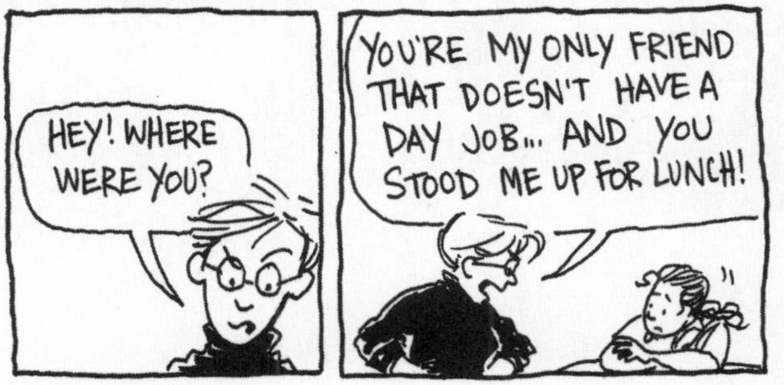
HEY! WHERE WERE YOU?
YOU'RE MY ONLY FRIEND THAT DOESN'T HAVE A DAY JOB... AND YOU STOOD ME UP FOR LUNCH!

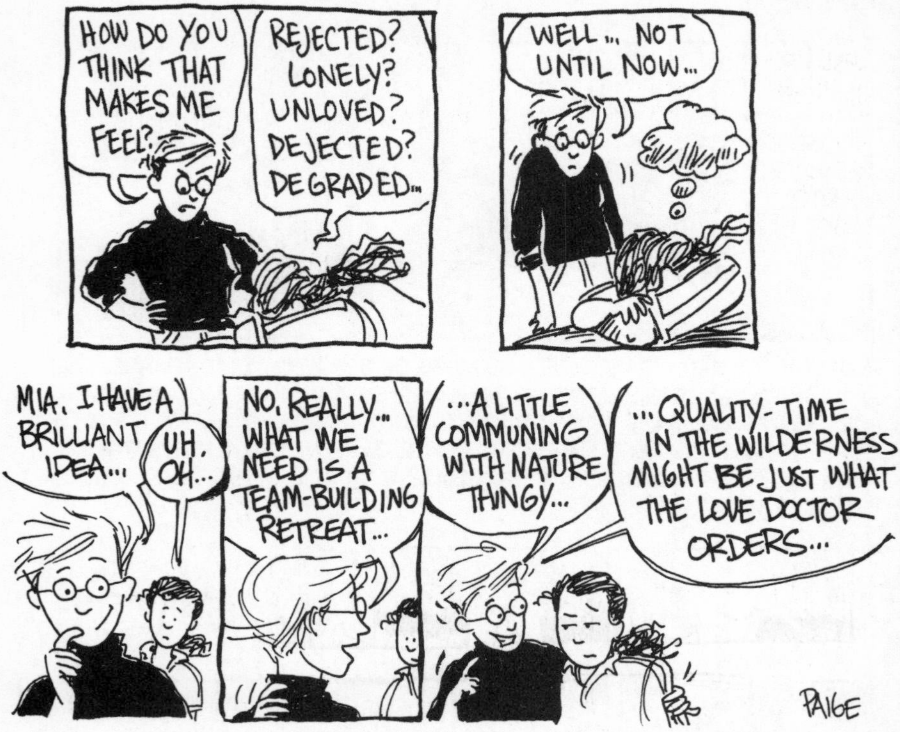

HOW DO YOU THINK THAT MAKES ME FEEL?
REJECTED? LONELY? UNLOVED? DEJECTED? DEGRADED...
WELL... NOT UNTIL NOW...
MIA, I HAVE A BRILLIANT IDEA...
UH, OH...
NO, REALLY... WHAT WE NEED IS A TEAM-BUILDING RETREAT...
...A LITTLE COMMUNING WITH NATURE THINGY...
...QUALITY-TIME IN THE WILDERNESS MIGHT BE JUST WHAT THE LOVE DOCTOR ORDERS...
PAIGE

JANE SHARES HER "MASTER PLAN" WITH ETHAN... HE IS UNDERWHELMED...

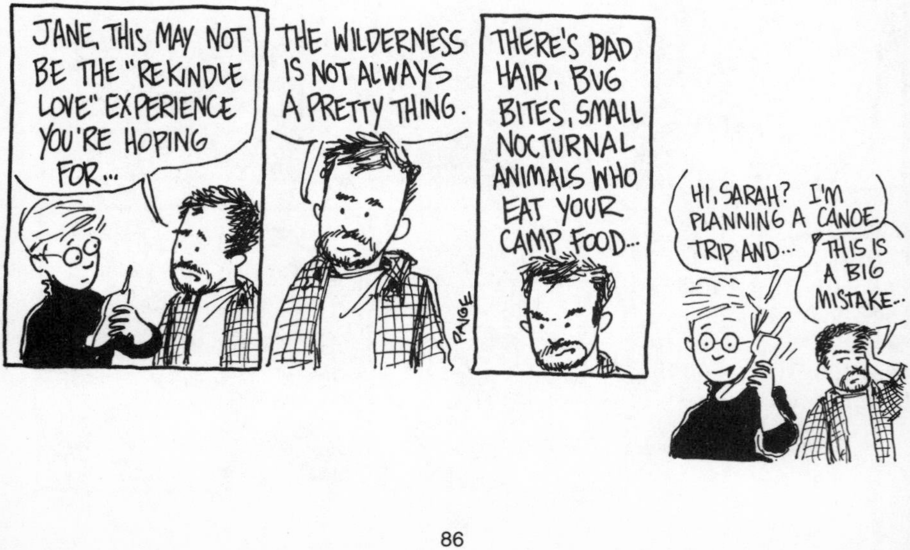

JANE, THIS MAY NOT BE THE "REKINDLE LOVE" EXPERIENCE YOU'RE HOPING FOR...
THE WILDERNESS IS NOT ALWAYS A PRETTY THING.
PAIGE
THERE'S BAD HAIR, BUG BITES, SMALL NOCTURNAL ANIMALS WHO EAT YOUR CAMP FOOD...
HI, SARAH? I'M PLANNING A CANOE TRIP AND...
THIS IS A BIG MISTAKE...

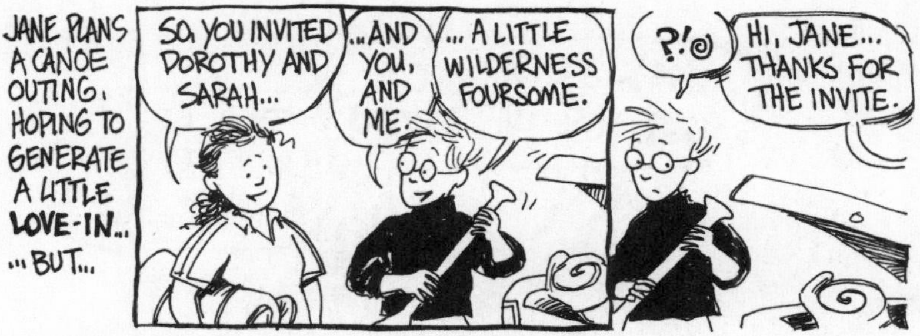
JANE PLANS A CANOE OUTING, HOPING TO GENERATE A LITTLE LOVE-IN... ...BUT...
SO, YOU INVITED DOROTHY AND SARAH...
...AND YOU, AND ME
... A LITTLE WILDERNESS FOURSOME.
?!
HI, JANE... THANKS FOR THE INVITE.

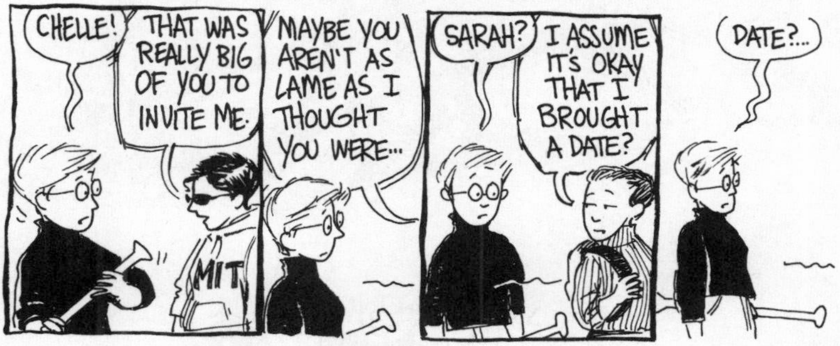
CHELLE!
THAT WAS REALLY BIG OF YOU TO INVITE ME.
MAYBE YOU AREN'T AS LAME AS I THOUGHT YOU WERE...
MIT
SARAH?
I ASSUME IT'S OKAY THAT I BROUGHT A DATE?
DATE?...

LATER...

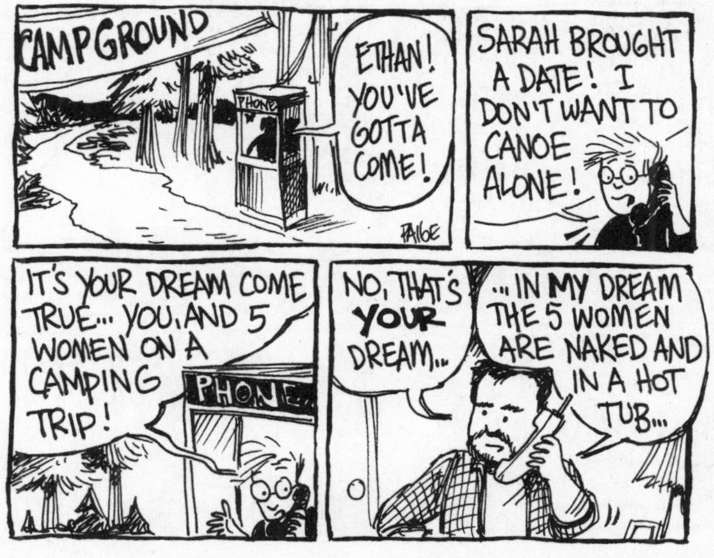
CAMPGROUND
PHONE
ETHAN! YOU'VE GOTTA COME!
PAIGE
SARAH BROUGHT A DATE! I DON'T WANT TO CANOE ALONE!
IT'S YOUR DREAM COME TRUE... YOU, AND 5 WOMEN ON A CAMPING TRIP!
PHONE
NO, THAT'S YOUR DREAM...
...IN MY DREAM THE 5 WOMEN ARE NAKED AND IN A HOT TUB...

... DESPITE HIS UNREQUITED DREAM, ETHAN SHOWS UP TO HELP JANE OUT...

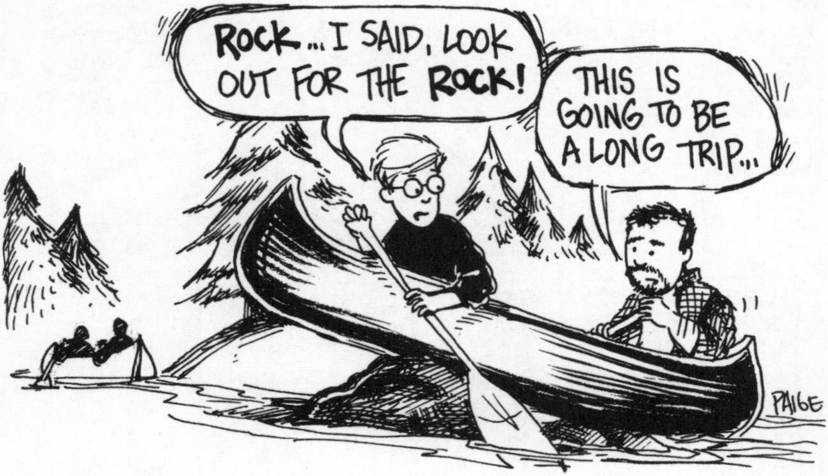
ROCK... I SAID, LOOK OUT FOR THE ROCK!
THIS IS GOING TO BE A LONG TRIP...
PAIGE

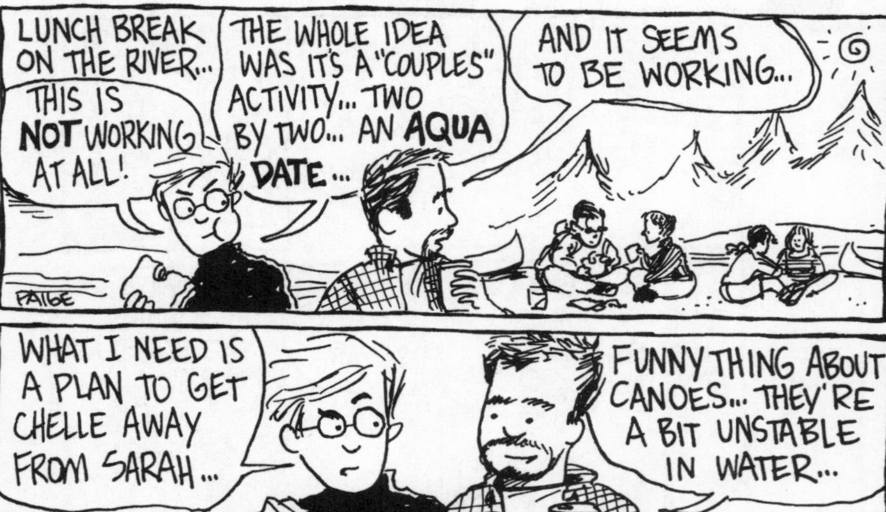
LUNCH BREAK ON THE RIVER...
THIS IS NOT WORKING AT ALL!
THE WHOLE IDEA WAS IT'S A "COUPLES" ACTIVITY... TWO BY TWO... AN AQUA DATE...
AND IT SEEMS TO BE WORKING...
PAIGE
WHAT I NEED IS A PLAN TO GET CHELLE AWAY FROM SARAH...
FUNNY THING ABOUT CANOES... THEY'RE A BIT UNSTABLE IN WATER...

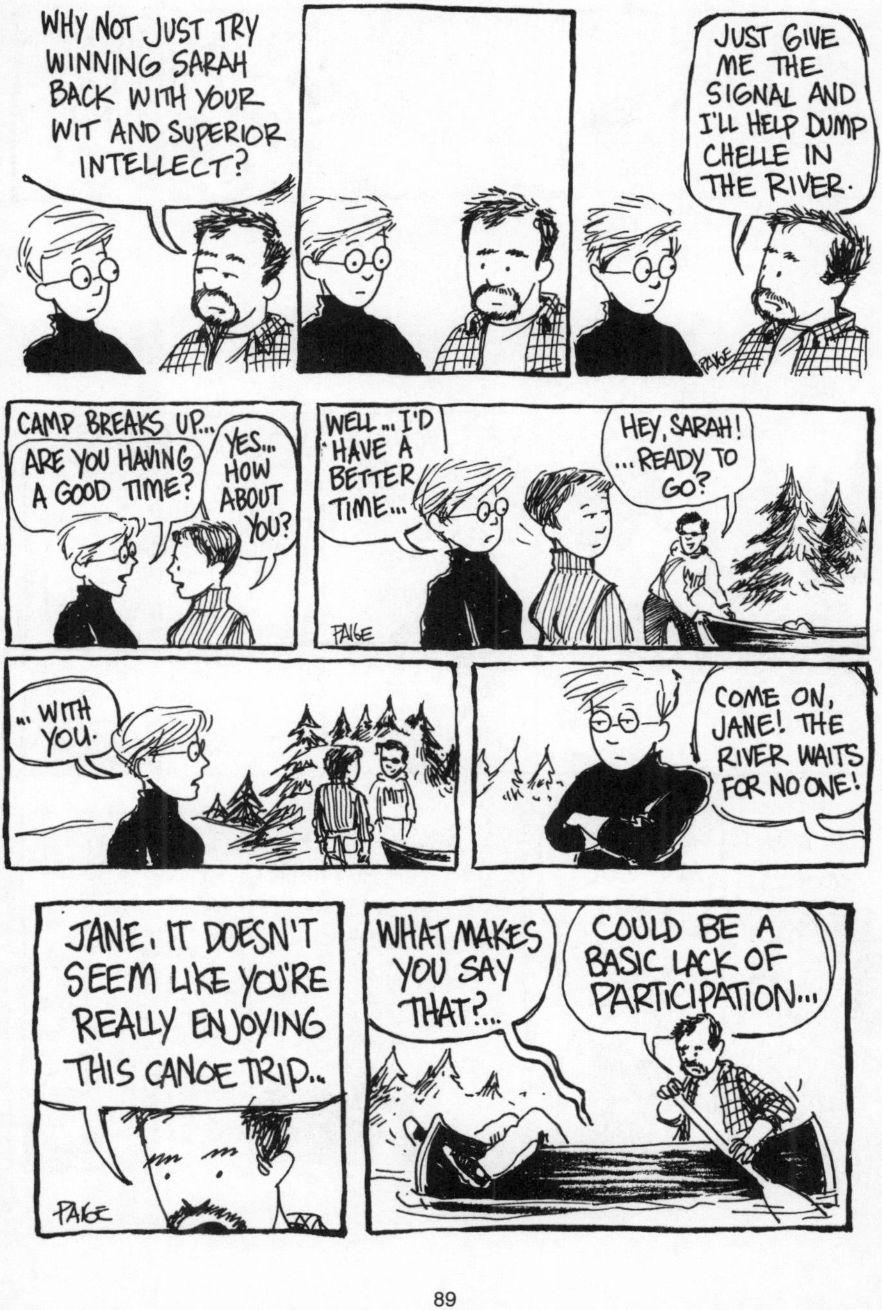

WHY NOT JUST TRY WINNING SARAH BACK WITH YOUR WIT AND SUPERIOR INTELLECT?
JUST GIVE ME THE SIGNAL AND I'LL HELP DUMP CHELLE IN THE RIVER.
PAIGE
CAMP BREAKS UP...
ARE YOU HAVING A GOOD TIME?
YES... HOW ABOUT YOU?
WELL... I'D HAVE A BETTER TIME...
HEY, SARAH! ...READY TO GO?
MIT
PAIGE
... WITH YOU.
MIT
COME ON, JANE! THE RIVER WAITS FOR NO ONE!
JANE, IT DOESN'T SEEM LIKE YOU'RE REALLY ENJOYING THIS CANOE TRIP...
PAIGE
WHAT MAKES YOU SAY THAT?...
COULD BE A BASIC LACK OF PARTICIPATION...

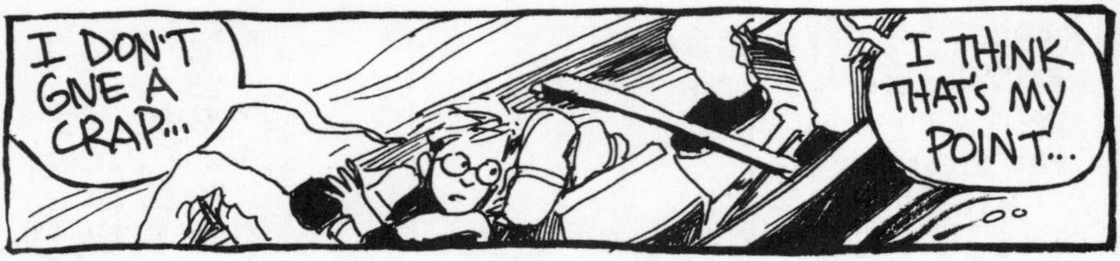
I DON'T GIVE A CRAP...
I THINK THAT'S MY POINT...

LATER THAT NIGHT IN CAMP...

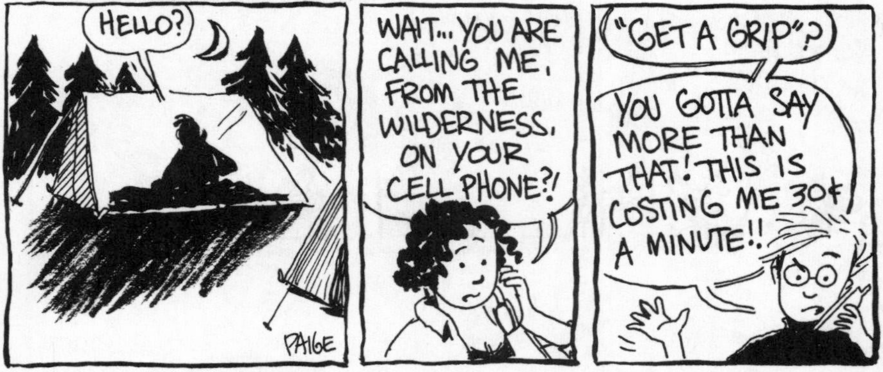
HELLO?
PAIGE
WAIT... YOU ARE CALLING ME, FROM THE WILDERNESS, ON YOUR CELL PHONE?!
"GET A GRIP"?
YOU GOTTA SAY MORE THAN THAT! THIS IS COSTING ME 30¢ A MINUTE!!

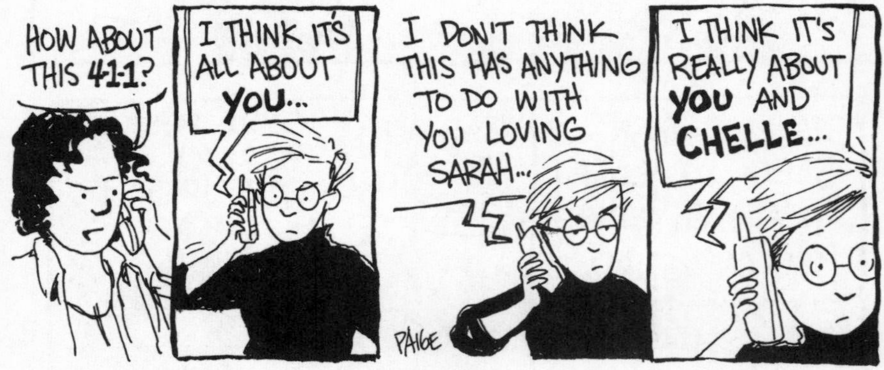
HOW ABOUT THIS 4-1-1?
I THINK IT'S ALL ABOUT **YOU**...
I DON'T THINK THIS HAS ANYTHING TO DO WITH YOU LOVING SARAH...
PAIGE
I THINK IT'S REALLY ABOUT **YOU** AND **CHELLE**...

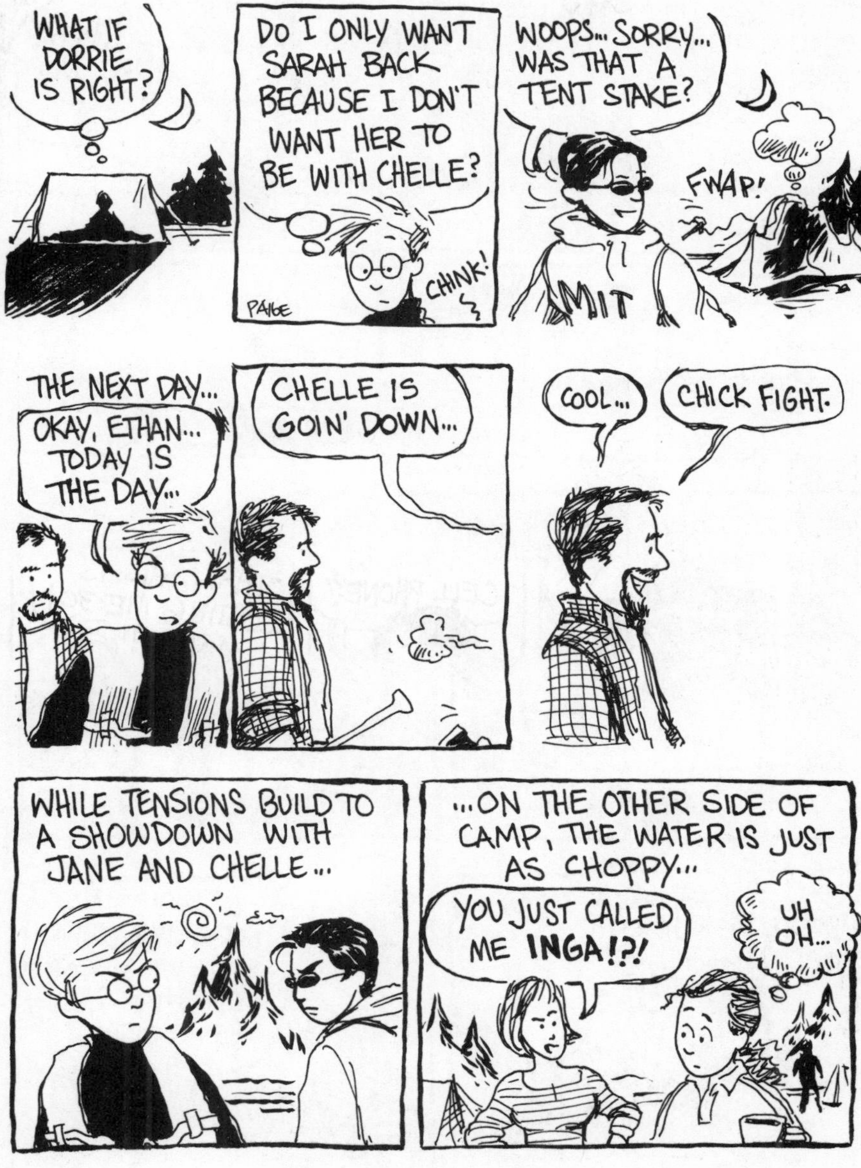
WHAT IF DORRIE IS RIGHT?
DO I ONLY WANT SARAH BACK BECAUSE I DON'T WANT HER TO BE WITH CHELLE?
CHINK!
PAIGE
WOOPS... SORRY... WAS THAT A TENT STAKE?
FWAP!
MIT
THE NEXT DAY...
OKAY, ETHAN... TODAY IS THE DAY...
CHELLE IS GOIN' DOWN...
COOL...
CHICK FIGHT.
WHILE TENSIONS BUILD TO A SHOWDOWN WITH JANE AND CHELLE...
...ON THE OTHER SIDE OF CAMP, THE WATER IS JUST AS CHOPPY...
YOU JUST CALLED ME INGA!?!
UH OH...

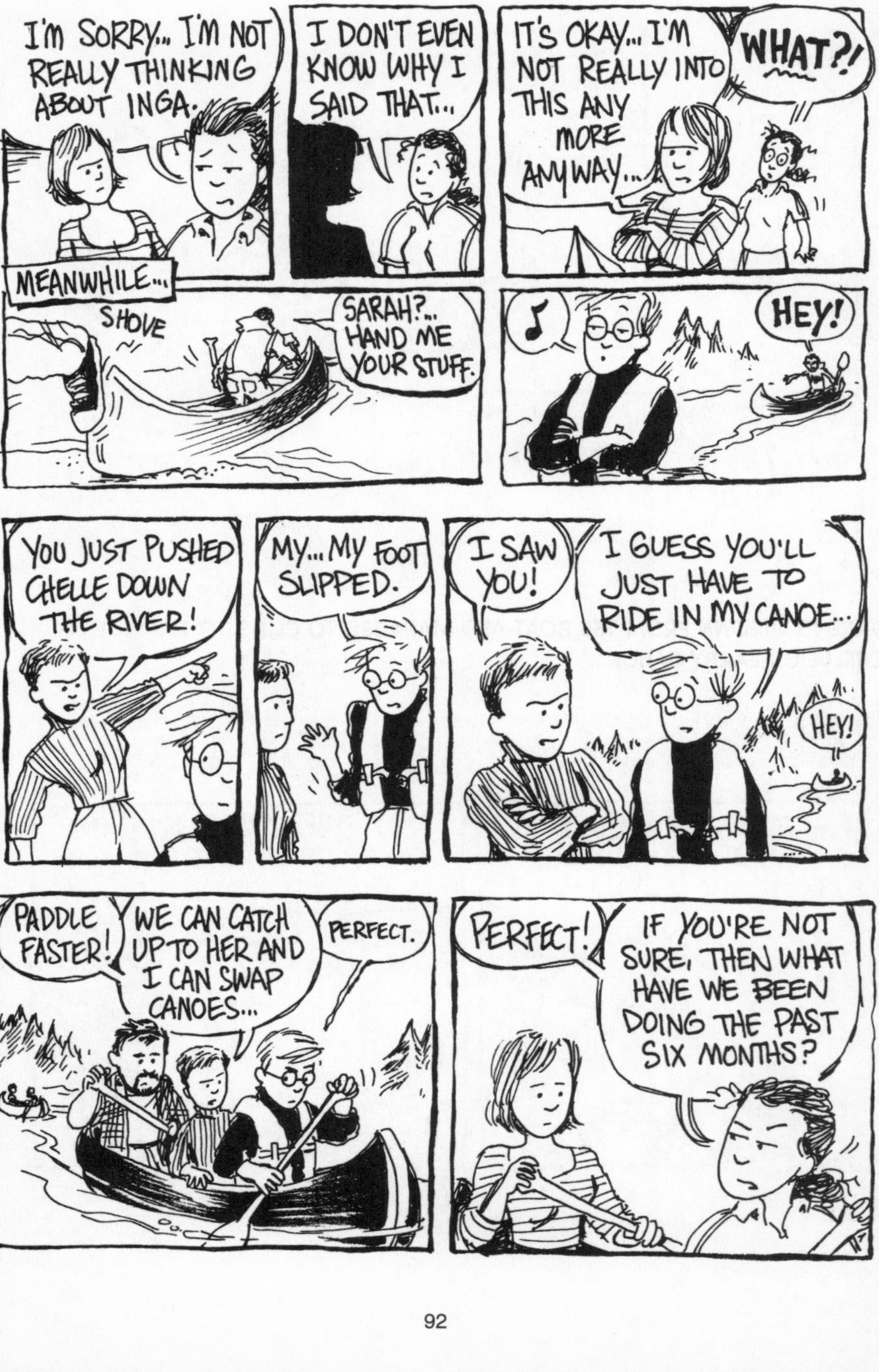
I'M SORRY... I'M NOT REALLY THINKING ABOUT INGA.
I DON'T EVEN KNOW WHY I SAID THAT...
IT'S OKAY... I'M NOT REALLY INTO THIS ANY MORE ANYWAY...
WHAT?!
MEANWHILE...
SHOVE
SARAH?... HAND ME YOUR STUFF.
HEY!
YOU JUST PUSHED CHELLE DOWN THE RIVER!
MY... MY FOOT SLIPPED.
I SAW YOU!
I GUESS YOU'LL JUST HAVE TO RIDE IN MY CANOE...
HEY!
PADDLE FASTER!
WE CAN CATCH UP TO HER AND I CAN SWAP CANOES...
PERFECT.
PERFECT!
IF YOU'RE NOT SURE, THEN WHAT HAVE WE BEEN DOING THE PAST SIX MONTHS?

AS THE RIVER NARROWS, JANE PULLS THE CANOE CLOSE TO CHELLE, WHILE MIA AND DOROTHY TRAIL A BIT, ARGUING SEMANTICS...

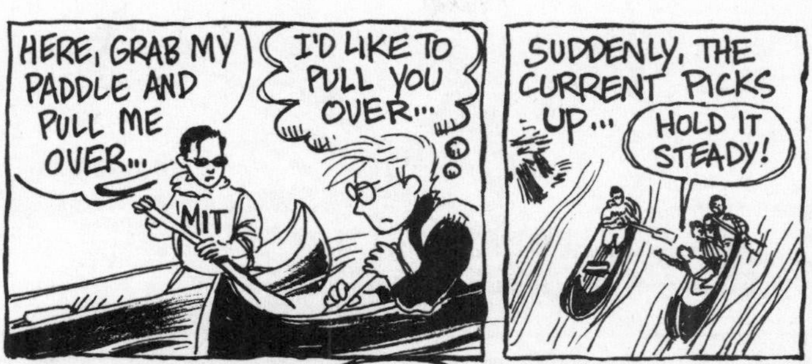
HERE, GRAB MY PADDLE AND PULL ME OVER...
I'D LIKE TO PULL YOU OVER...
MIT
SUDDENLY, THE CURRENT PICKS UP...
HOLD IT STEADY!

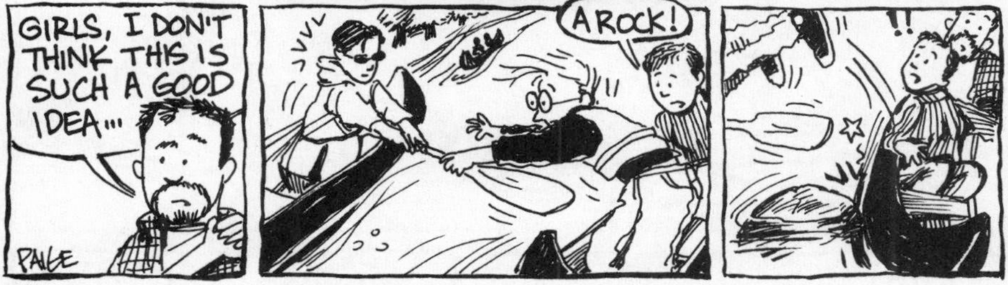
GIRLS, I DON'T THINK THIS IS SUCH A GOOD IDEA...
PAIGE
A ROCK!
!!

JANE IS THROWN FROM THE BOAT AND MANAGES TO CLING TO THE SIDE OF CHELLE'S NEARBY CANOE...

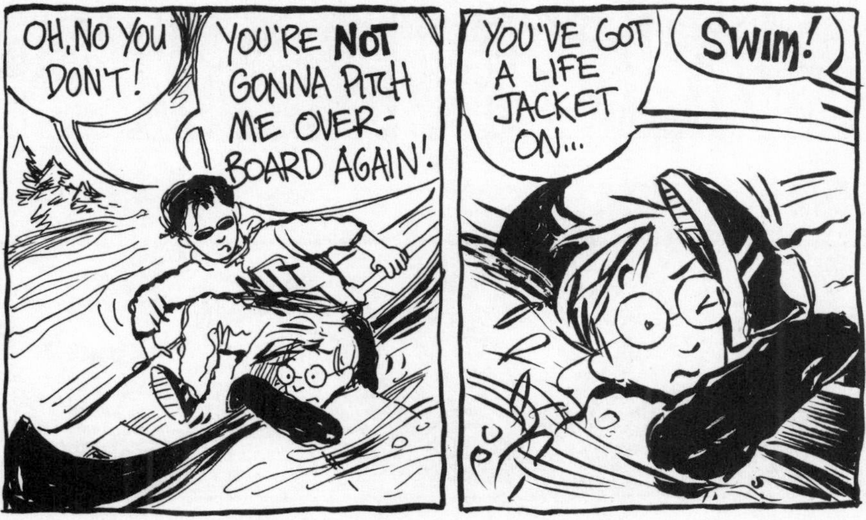
OH, NO YOU DON'T!
YOU'RE **NOT** GONNA PITCH ME OVER-BOARD AGAIN!
MIT
YOU'VE GOT A LIFE JACKET ON...
SWIM!

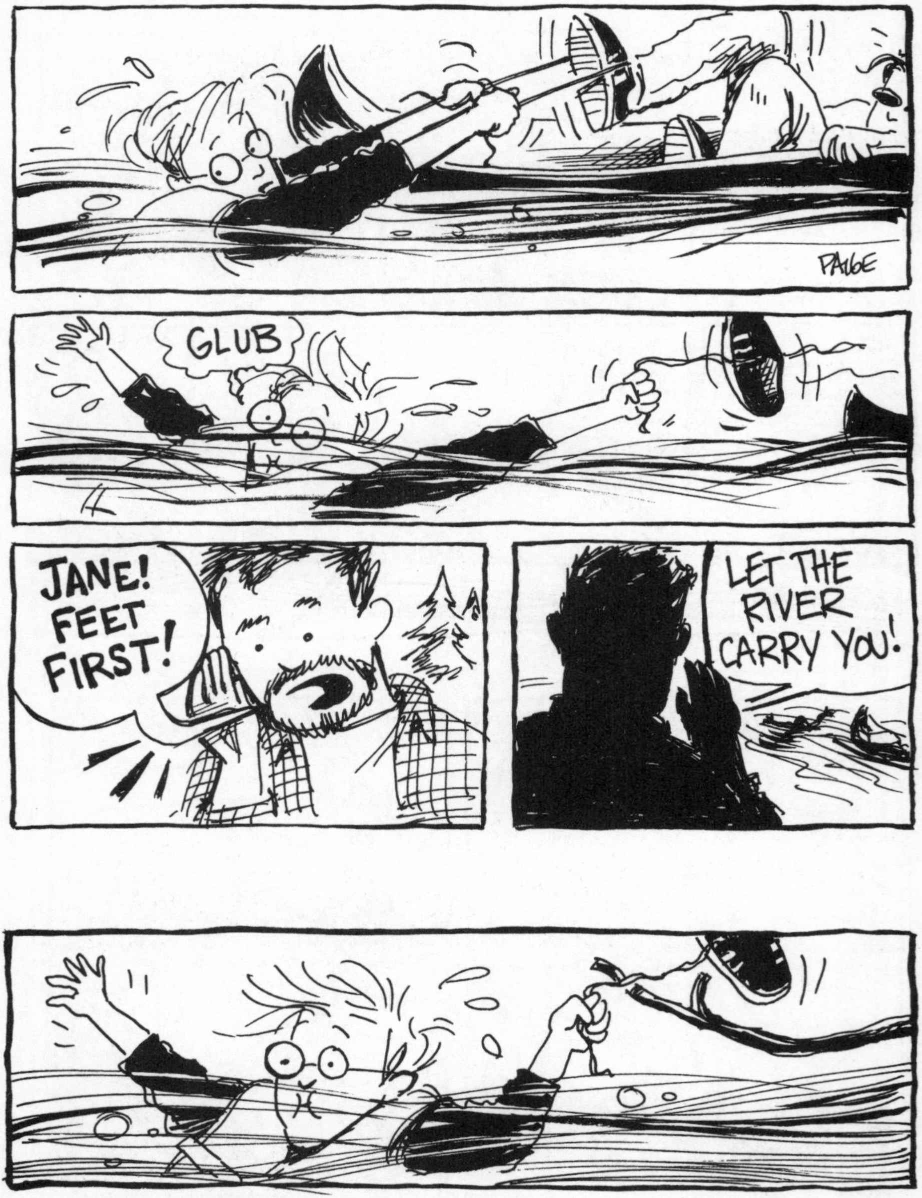
PAIGE
GLUB
JANE! FEET FIRST!
LET THE RIVER CARRY YOU!

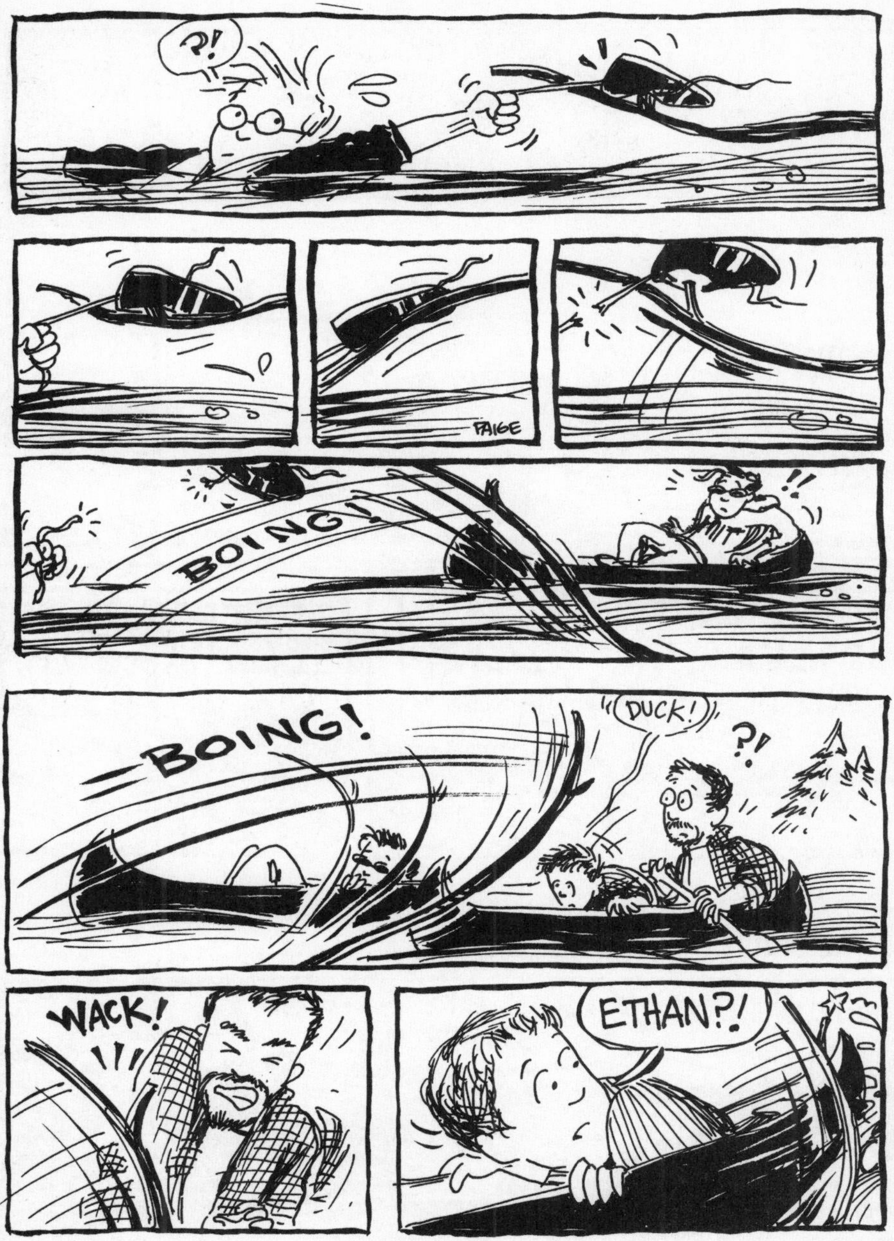
?!
PAIGE
BOING!
BOING!
DUCK!
?!
WACK!
ETHAN?!

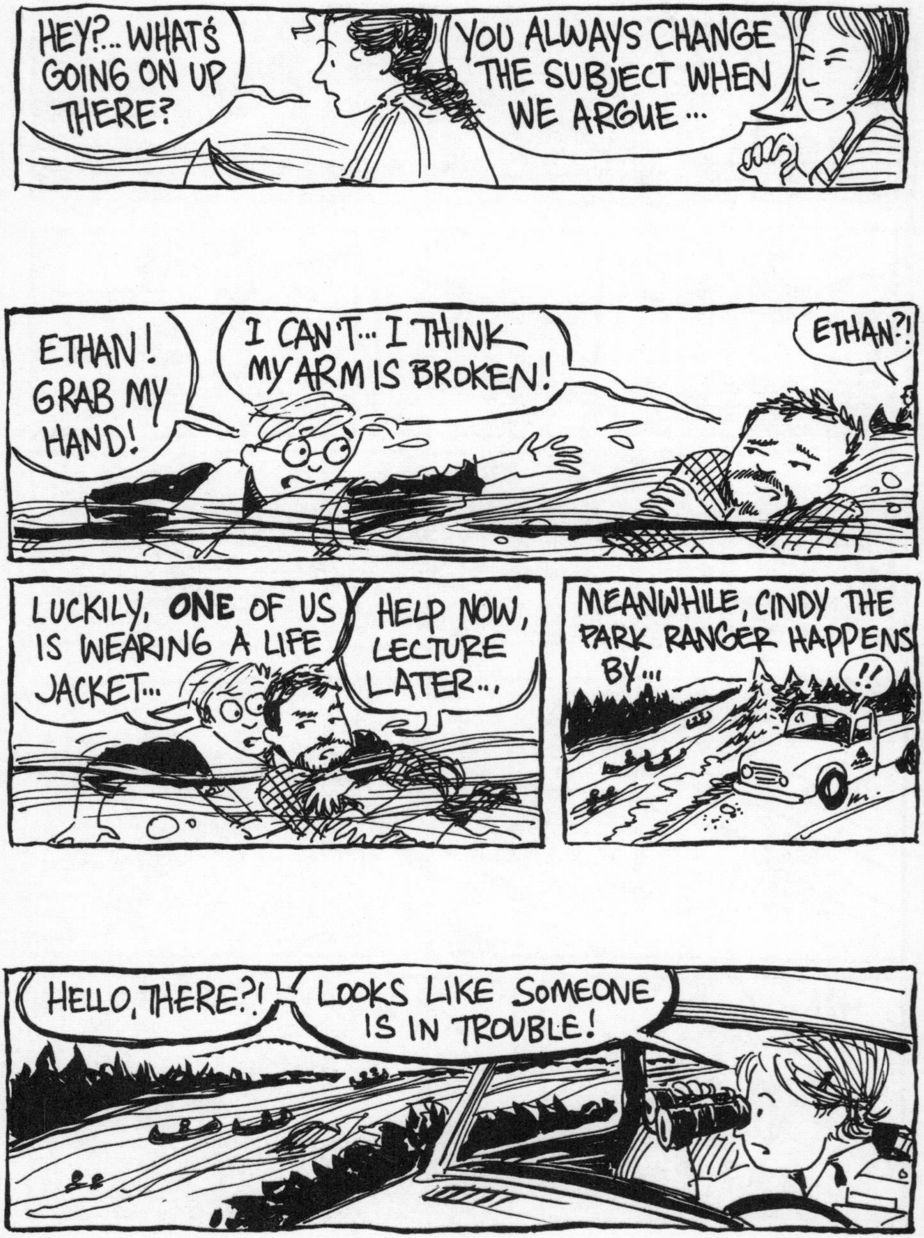
HEY?... WHAT'S GOING ON UP THERE?
YOU ALWAYS CHANGE THE SUBJECT WHEN WE ARGUE...
ETHAN! GRAB MY HAND!
I CAN'T... I THINK MY ARM IS BROKEN!
ETHAN?!
LUCKILY, ONE OF US IS WEARING A LIFE JACKET...
HELP NOW, LECTURE LATER...
MEANWHILE, CINDY THE PARK RANGER HAPPENS BY...
!!
HELLO, THERE?!
LOOKS LIKE SOMEONE IS IN TROUBLE!

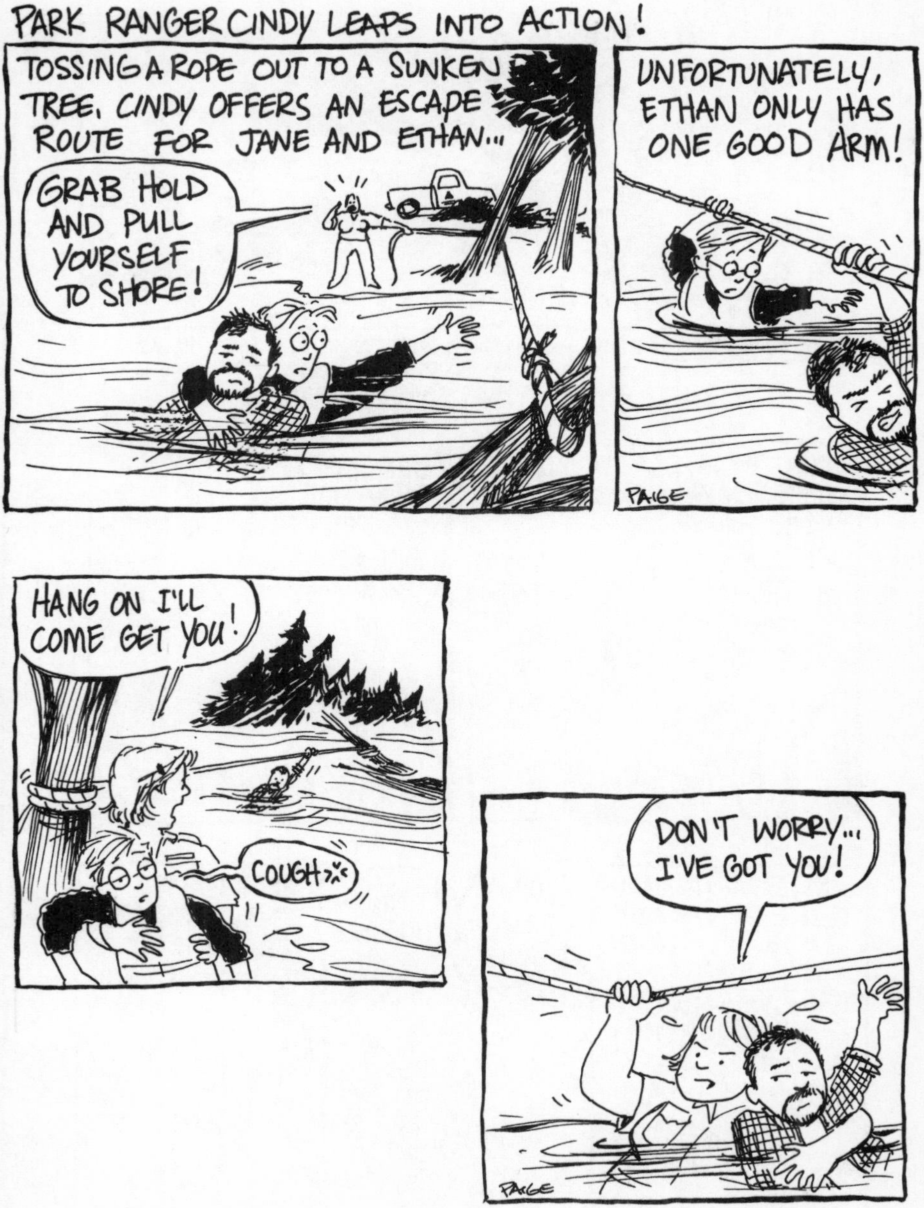
PARK RANGER CINDY LEAPS INTO ACTION!
TOSSING A ROPE OUT TO A SUNKEN TREE, CINDY OFFERS AN ESCAPE ROUTE FOR JANE AND ETHAN...
GRAB HOLD AND PULL YOURSELF TO SHORE!
UNFORTUNATELY, ETHAN ONLY HAS ONE GOOD ARM!
PAIGE
HANG ON I'LL COME GET YOU!
COUGH
DON'T WORRY... I'VE GOT YOU!
PAIGE

THE REST OF THE GROUP PADDLES TO SHORE AND JOINS THE TRIO...

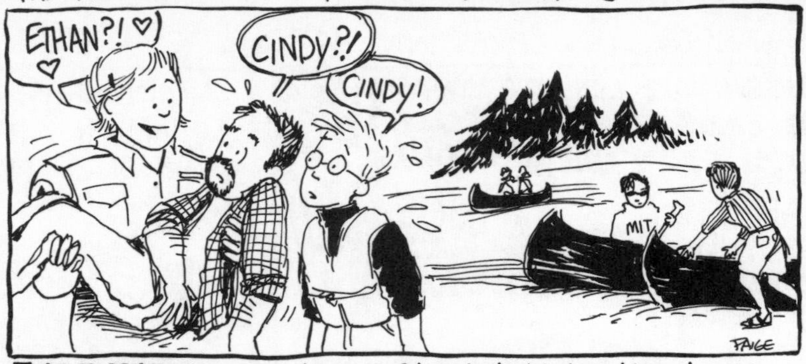
ETHAN?!
CINDY?!
CINDY!
MIT
PAIGE

JANE FLASHBACK: CINDY HAD A CRUSH ON ETHAN A YEAR AGO... HE WAS TOO SCARED TO GO OUT WITH HER BECAUSE SHE WAS MORE BUFF THAN HE WAS!

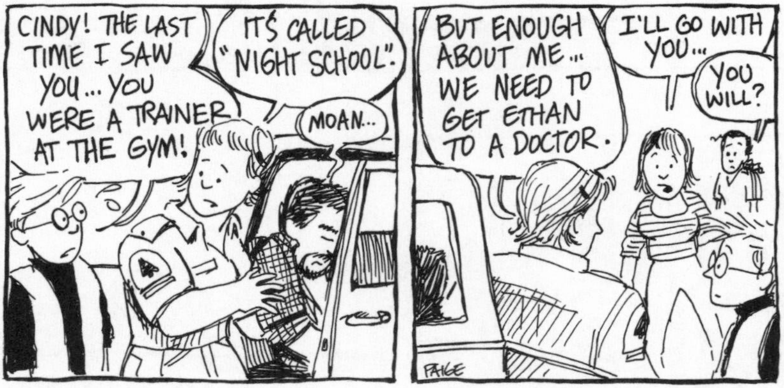
CINDY! THE LAST TIME I SAW YOU... YOU WERE A TRAINER AT THE GYM!
IT'S CALLED "NIGHT SCHOOL".
MOAN...
BUT ENOUGH ABOUT ME... WE NEED TO GET ETHAN TO A DOCTOR.
I'LL GO WITH YOU...
YOU WILL?
PAIGE

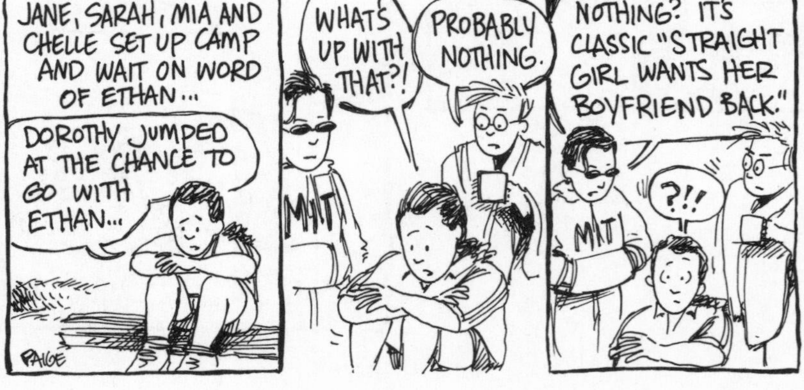
JANE, SARAH, MIA AND CHELLE SET UP CAMP AND WAIT ON WORD OF ETHAN...
DOROTHY JUMPED AT THE CHANCE TO GO WITH ETHAN...
PAIGE
WHAT'S UP WITH THAT?!
PROBABLY NOTHING.
MIT
NOTHING? IT'S CLASSIC "STRAIGHT GIRL WANTS HER BOYFRIEND BACK."
?!!
MIT

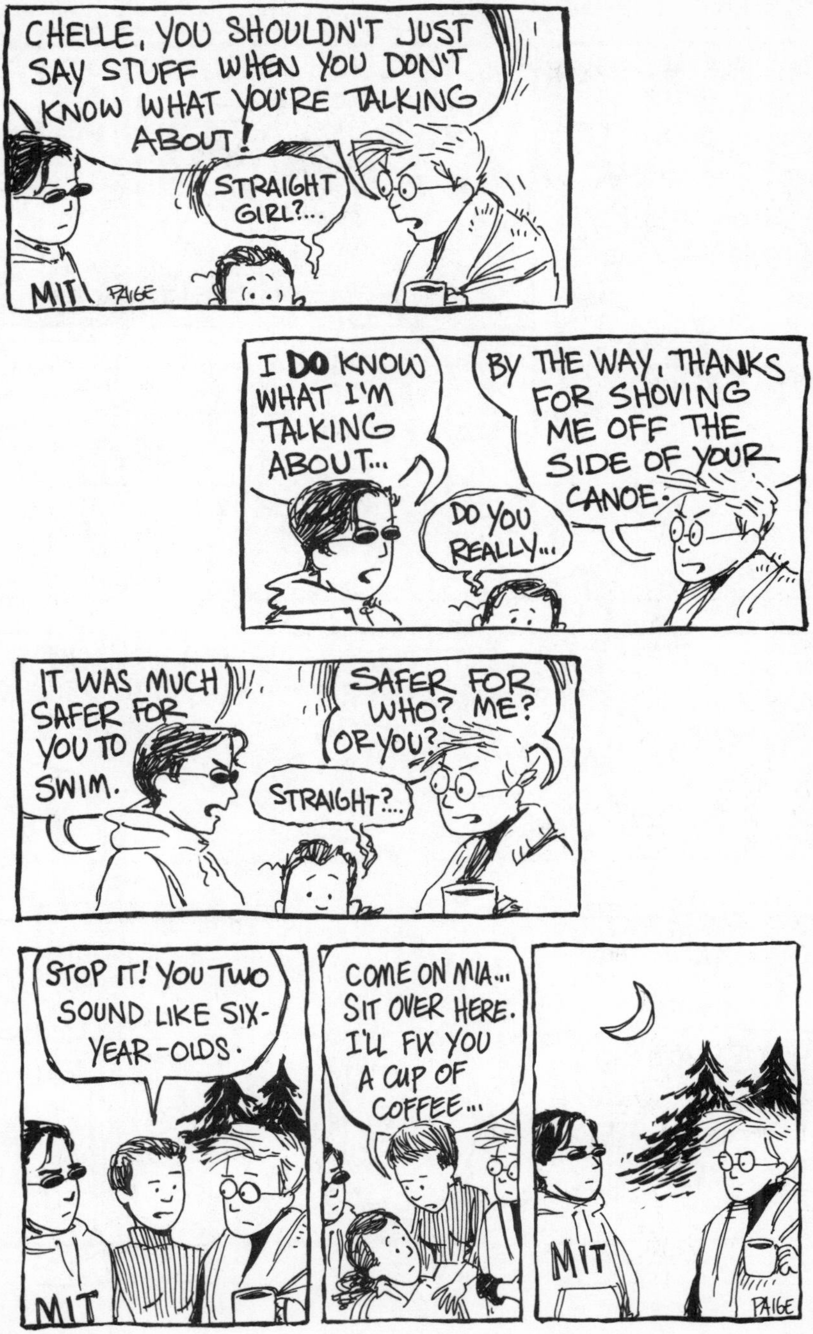
CHELLE, YOU SHOULDN'T JUST SAY STUFF WHEN YOU DON'T KNOW WHAT YOU'RE TALKING ABOUT!
STRAIGHT GIRL?...
MIT
PAIGE
I **DO** KNOW WHAT I'M TALKING ABOUT...
BY THE WAY, THANKS FOR SHOVING ME OFF THE SIDE OF YOUR CANOE.
DO YOU REALLY...
IT WAS MUCH SAFER FOR YOU TO SWIM.
SAFER FOR WHO? ME? OR YOU?
STRAIGHT?...
STOP IT! YOU TWO SOUND LIKE SIX-YEAR-OLDS.
MIT
COME ON MIA... SIT OVER HERE. I'LL FIX YOU A CUP OF COFFEE...
MIT
PAIGE

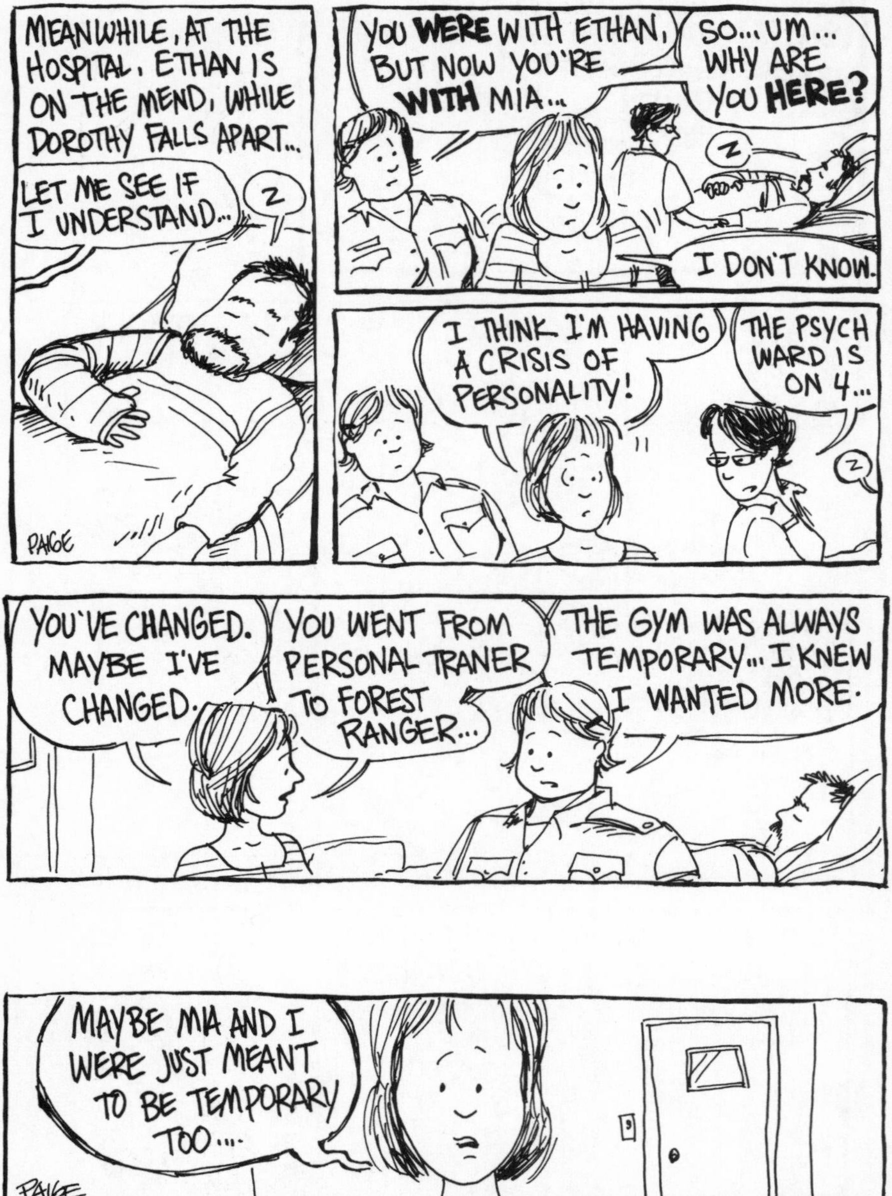
MEANWHILE, AT THE HOSPITAL, ETHAN IS ON THE MEND, WHILE DOROTHY FALLS APART...
LET ME SEE IF I UNDERSTAND...
Z
PAIGE
YOU **WERE** WITH ETHAN, BUT NOW YOU'RE **WITH** MIA...
SO... UM... WHY ARE YOU **HERE?**
Z
I DON'T KNOW.
I THINK I'M HAVING A CRISIS OF PERSONALITY!
THE PSYCH WARD IS ON 4...
Z
YOU'VE CHANGED. MAYBE I'VE CHANGED.
YOU WENT FROM PERSONAL TRANER TO FOREST RANGER...
THE GYM WAS ALWAYS TEMPORARY... I KNEW I WANTED MORE.
MAYBE MIA AND I WERE JUST MEANT TO BE TEMPORARY TOO....
PAIGE

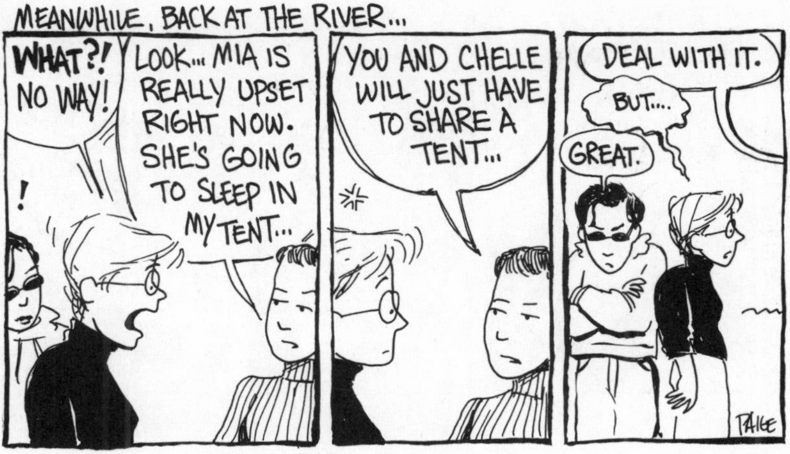
MEANWHILE, BACK AT THE RIVER...
WHAT?! NO WAY!
LOOK... MIA IS REALLY UPSET RIGHT NOW. SHE'S GOING TO SLEEP IN MY TENT...
YOU AND CHELLE WILL JUST HAVE TO SHARE A TENT...
DEAL WITH IT.
BUT....
GREAT.
PAIGE

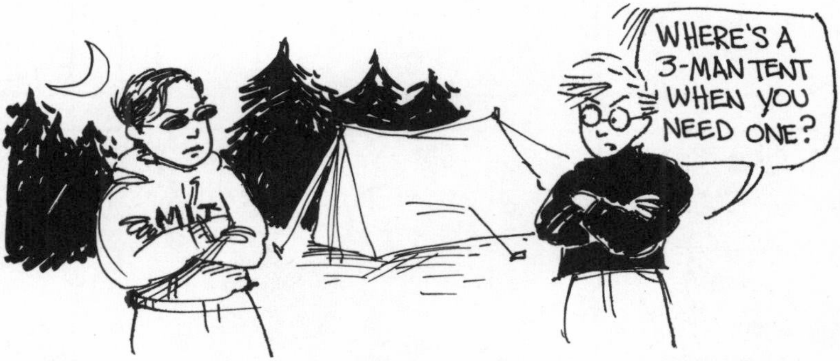
WHERE'S A 3-MAN TENT WHEN YOU NEED ONE?

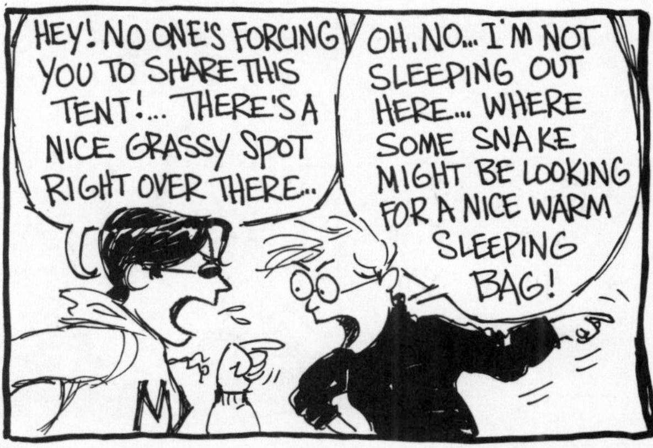
HEY! NO ONE'S FORCING YOU TO SHARE THIS TENT!... THERE'S A NICE GRASSY SPOT RIGHT OVER THERE...
OH, NO... I'M NOT SLEEPING OUT HERE... WHERE SOME SNAKE MIGHT BE LOOKING FOR A NICE WARM SLEEPING BAG!

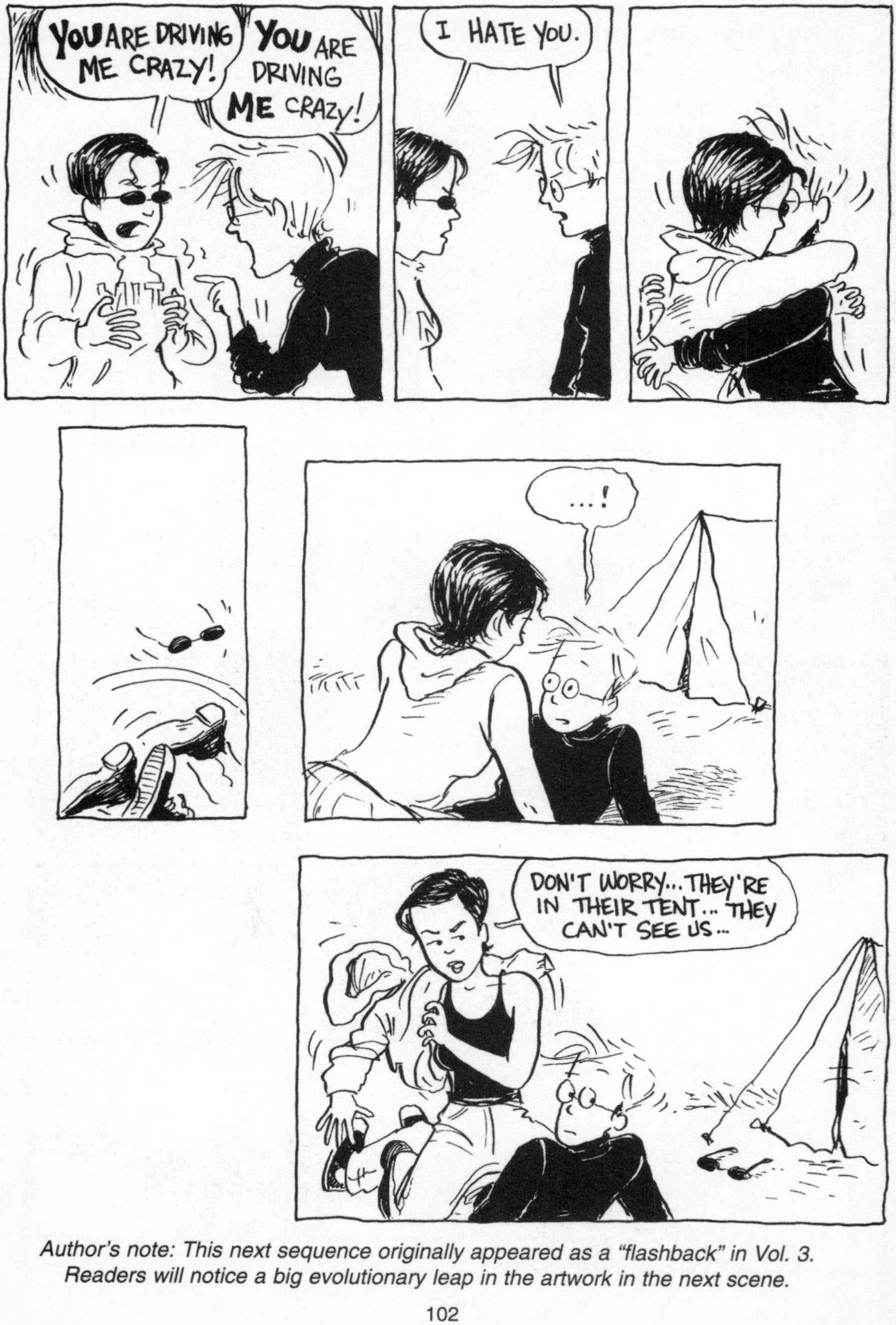
YOU ARE DRIVING ME CRAZY!
YOU ARE DRIVING ME CRAZY!
I HATE YOU.
...!
DON'T WORRY... THEY'RE IN THEIR TENT... THEY CAN'T SEE US...

Author's note: This next sequence originally appeared as a "flashback" in Vol. 3. Readers will notice a big evolutionary leap in the artwork in the next scene.

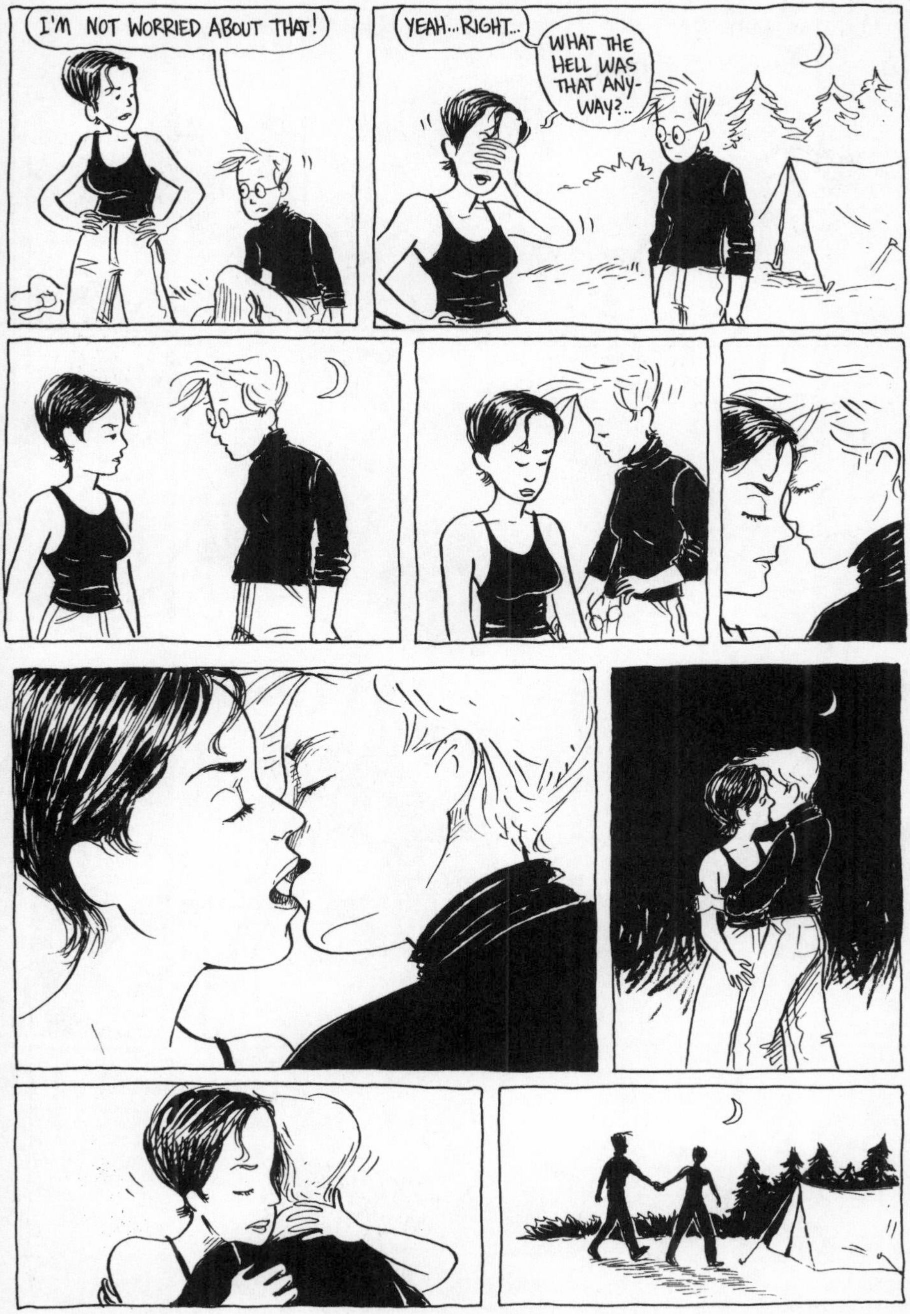
I'M NOT WORRIED ABOUT THAT!
YEAH...RIGHT...
WHAT THE HELL WAS THAT ANY-WAY?...

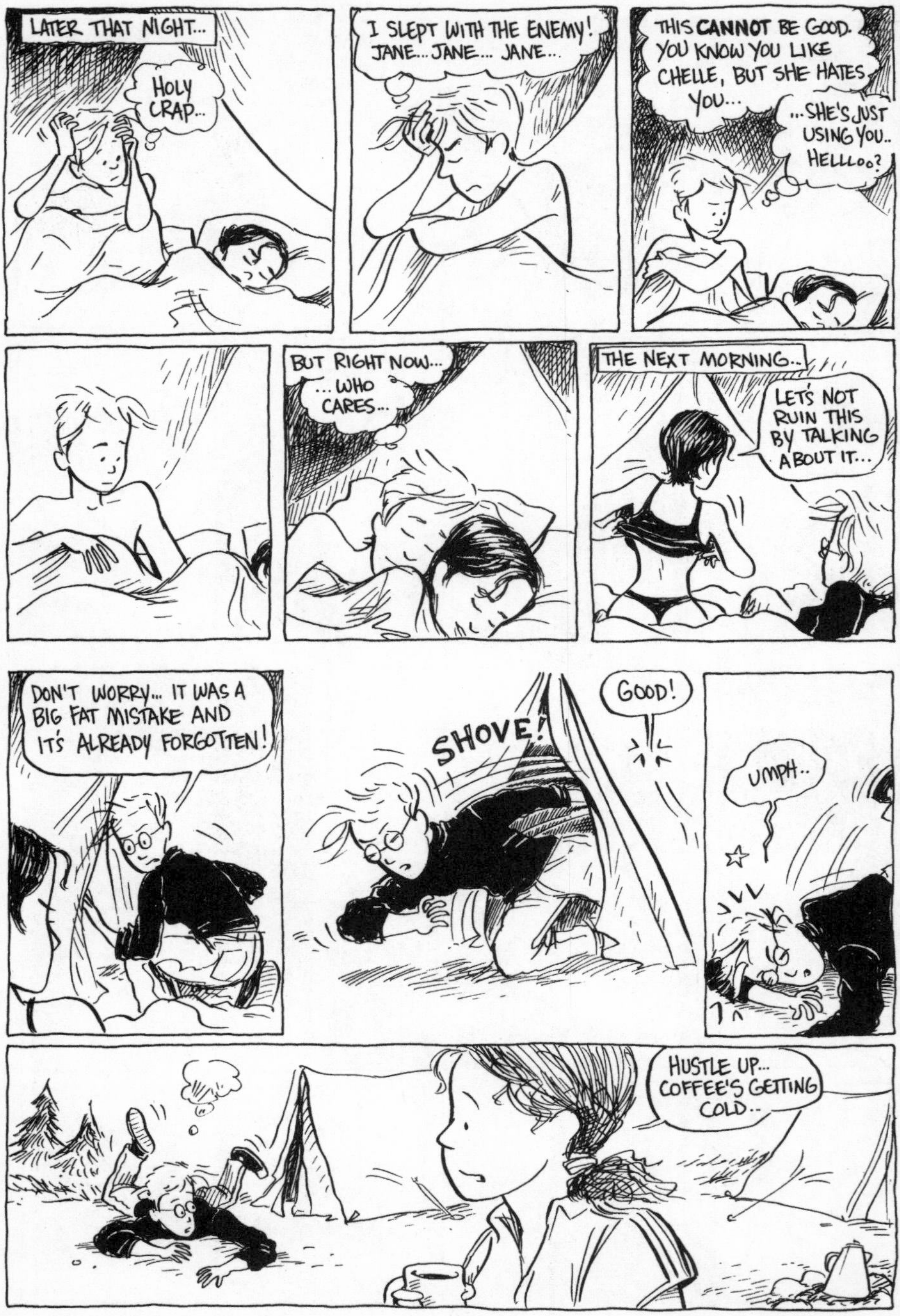
LATER THAT NIGHT...
HOLY CRAP...
I SLEPT WITH THE ENEMY! JANE... JANE... JANE...
THIS CANNOT BE GOOD. YOU KNOW YOU LIKE CHELLE, BUT SHE HATES YOU...
...SHE'S JUST USING YOU.. HELLLoo?
BUT RIGHT NOW...
...WHO CARES...
THE NEXT MORNING..
LET'S NOT RUIN THIS BY TALKING ABOUT IT...
DON'T WORRY... IT WAS A BIG FAT MISTAKE AND IT'S ALREADY FORGOTTEN!
SHOVE!
GOOD!
UMPH..
HUSTLE UP... COFFEE'S GETTING COLD..

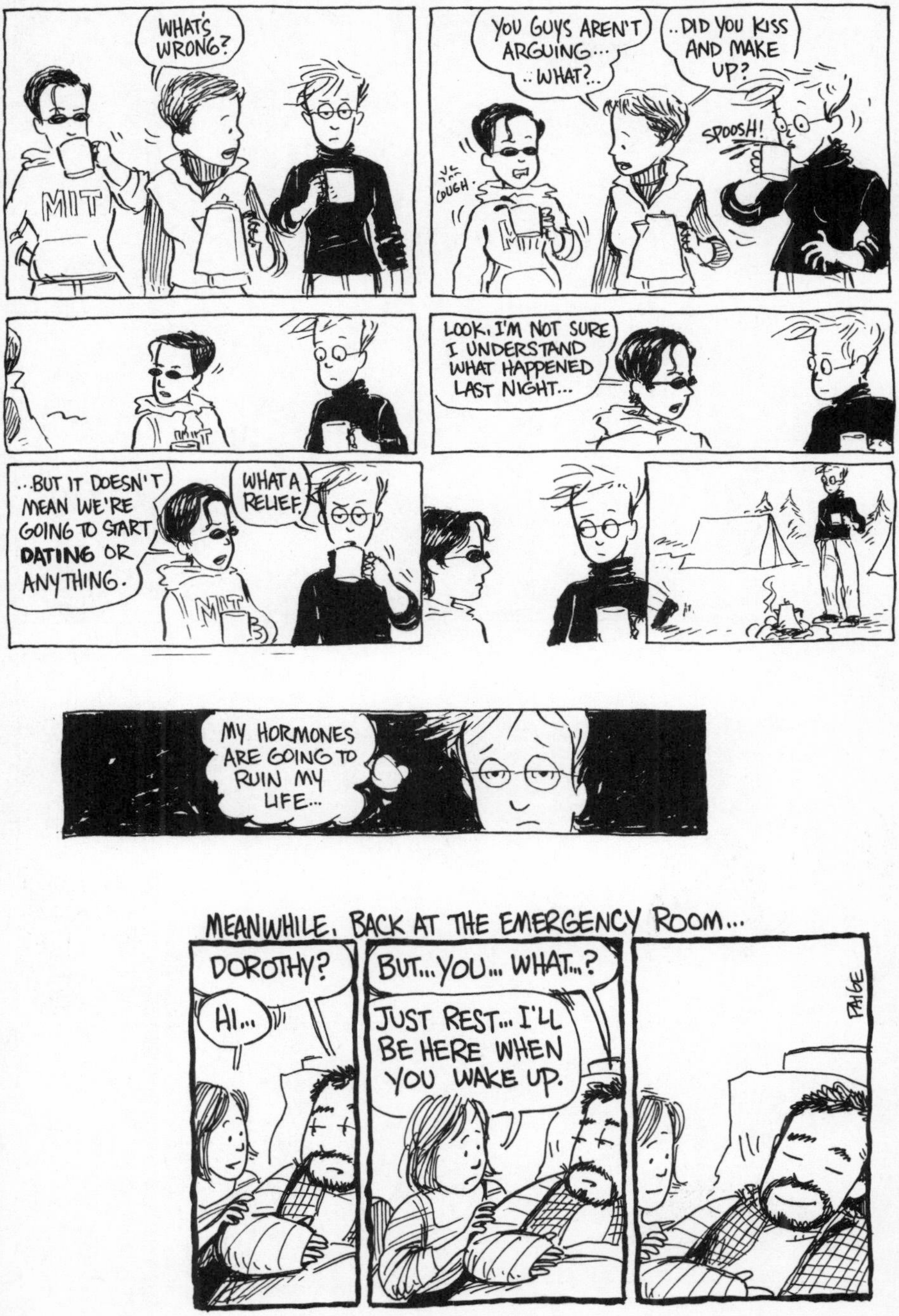
WHAT'S WRONG?
YOU GUYS AREN'T ARGUING... ..WHAT?..
..DID YOU KISS AND MAKE UP?
SPOOSH!
COUGH.
LOOK, I'M NOT SURE I UNDERSTAND WHAT HAPPENED LAST NIGHT...
...BUT IT DOESN'T MEAN WE'RE GOING TO START **DATING** OR ANYTHING.
WHAT A RELIEF.
MY HORMONES ARE GOING TO RUIN MY LIFE...
MEANWHILE, BACK AT THE EMERGENCY ROOM...
DOROTHY?
HI...
BUT... YOU... WHAT...?
JUST REST... I'LL BE HERE WHEN YOU WAKE UP.
PAIGE

Chapter 5

BAT GEEK

PARK RANGER, CINDY, PICKS UP THE SOMEWHAT SULLEN FOURSOME ON THE RIVER BANK AND TAKES THEM BACK TO CITY LIFE... FINALLY... IT'S A LONG RIDE... FIVE WOMEN ON A BENCH SEAT PROVIDES A LITTLE TOO MUCH TOGETHERNESS FOR THE RIDE HOME. AFTER CINDY DROPS JANE OFF, JANE DECIDES TO CHECK IN WITH DORRIE ABOUT THE CHIMP... OR SHOULD WE SAY, THE CHIMP THAT ONCE WAS, DIXIE...

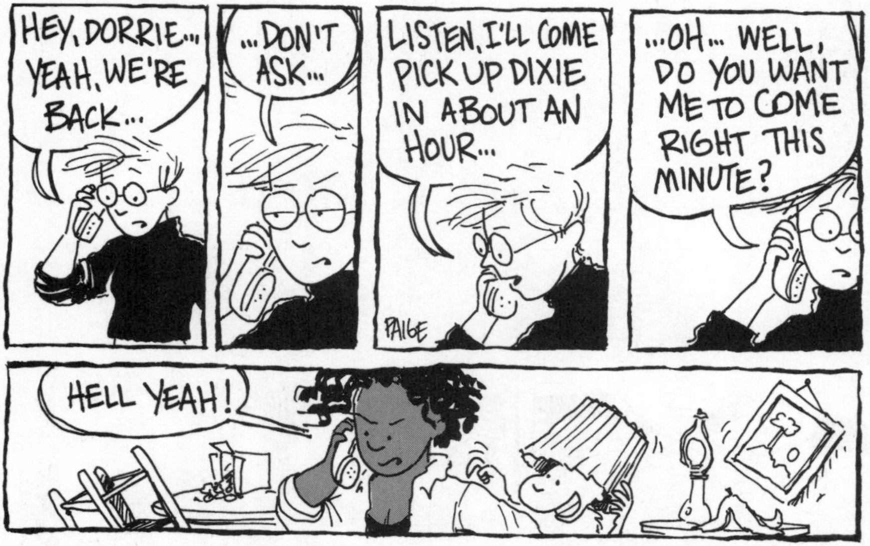
HEY, DORRIE... YEAH, WE'RE BACK...
...DON'T ASK...
LISTEN, I'LL COME PICK UP DIXIE IN ABOUT AN HOUR...
PAIGE
...OH... WELL, DO YOU WANT ME TO COME RIGHT THIS MINUTE?
HELL YEAH!

SINCE ETHAN IS HAVING TO COPE WITH AN ARM IN A CAST, JANE OFFERS TO PICK UP HIS EX-GIRLFRIEND, TURNED CHIMP. DORRIE WAS UNLUCKY ENOUGH TO GET TO PET SIT... MAYBE THAT'S NOT THE BEST WAY TO PUT IT... BUT YOU KNOW WHAT WE MEAN... MOMENTS LATER, JANE ARRIVES TO RESCUE DORRIE...

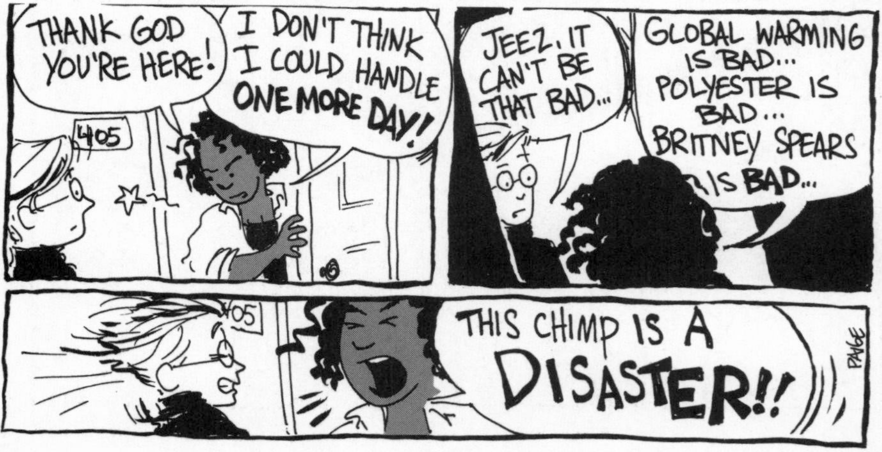
THANK GOD YOU'RE HERE!
I DON'T THINK I COULD HANDLE ONE MORE DAY!
405
JEEZ, IT CAN'T BE THAT BAD...
GLOBAL WARMING IS BAD... POLYESTER IS BAD... BRITNEY SPEARS IS BAD...
405
THIS CHIMP IS A DISASTER!!
PAIGE

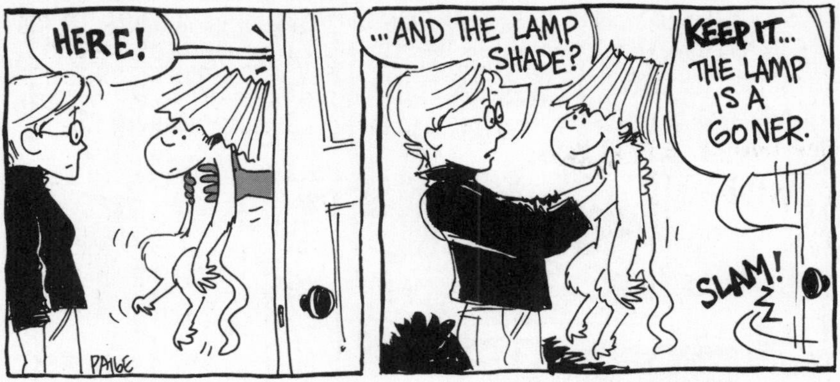
HERE!
...AND THE LAMP SHADE?
KEEP IT... THE LAMP IS A GONER.
SLAM!
PAIGE

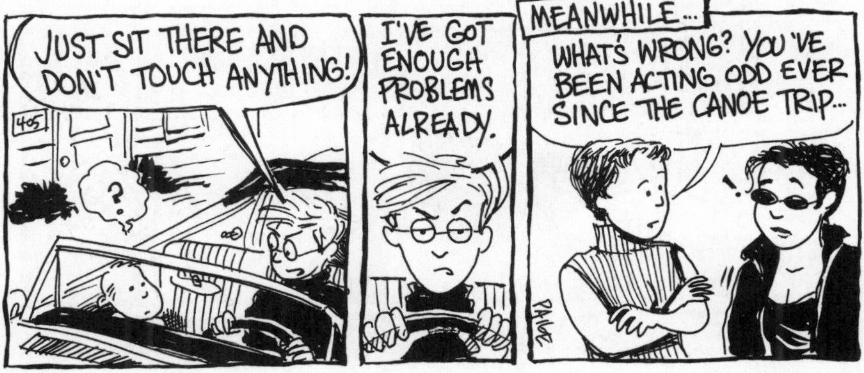
JUST SIT THERE AND DON'T TOUCH ANYTHING!
405
?
I'VE GOT ENOUGH PROBLEMS ALREADY.
MEANWHILE...
WHAT'S WRONG? YOU'VE BEEN ACTING ODD EVER SINCE THE CANOE TRIP...
!
PAIGE

LATER, BACK AT JANE'S...

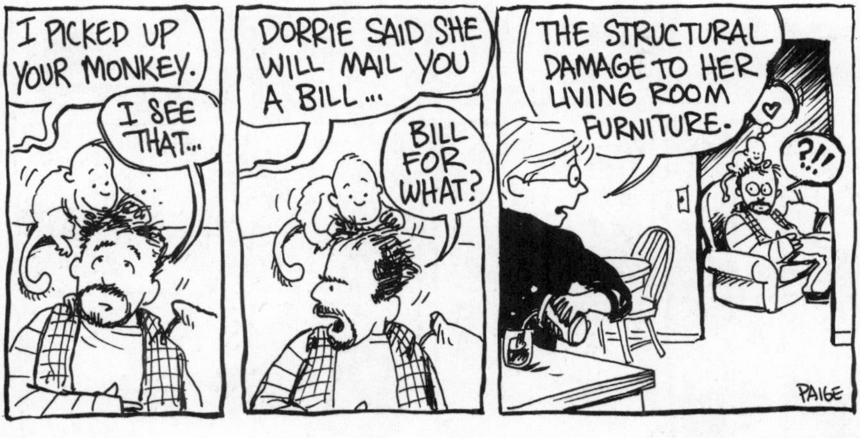
I PICKED UP YOUR MONKEY.
I SEE THAT...
DORRIE SAID SHE WILL MAIL YOU A BILL...
BILL FOR WHAT?
THE STRUCTURAL DAMAGE TO HER LIVING ROOM FURNITURE.
?!!
PAIGE

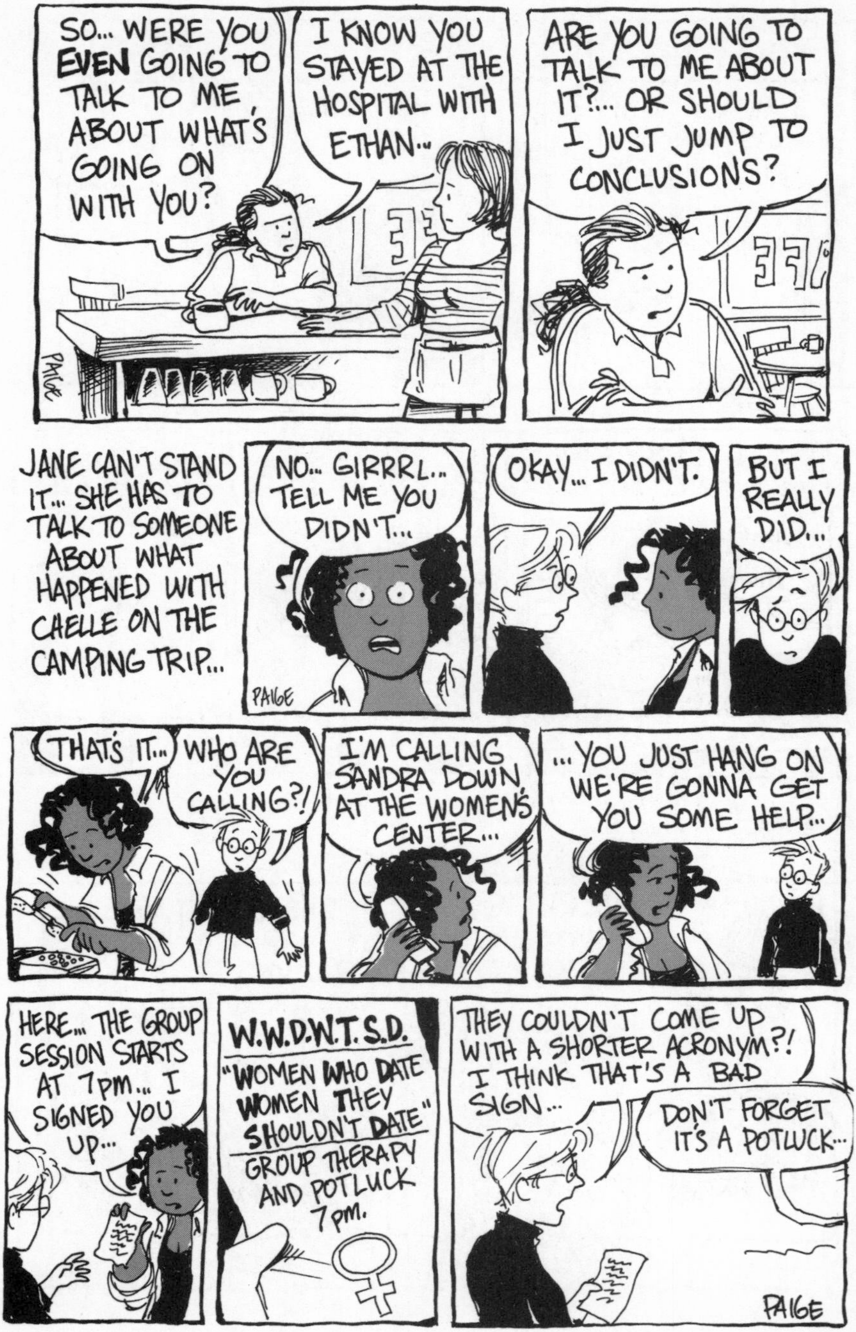

SO... WERE YOU EVEN GOING TO TALK TO ME, ABOUT WHAT'S GOING ON WITH YOU?
I KNOW YOU STAYED AT THE HOSPITAL WITH ETHAN...
ARE YOU GOING TO TALK TO ME ABOUT IT?... OR SHOULD I JUST JUMP TO CONCLUSIONS?
PAIGE
JANE CAN'T STAND IT... SHE HAS TO TALK TO SOMEONE ABOUT WHAT HAPPENED WITH CAELLE ON THE CAMPING TRIP...
NO... GIRRRL... TELL ME YOU DIDN'T...
PAIGE
OKAY... I DIDN'T.
BUT I REALLY DID...
THAT'S IT...
WHO ARE YOU CALLING?!
I'M CALLING SANDRA DOWN, AT THE WOMEN'S CENTER...
...YOU JUST HANG ON WE'RE GONNA GET YOU SOME HELP...
HERE... THE GROUP SESSION STARTS AT 7pm... I SIGNED YOU UP...
W.W.D.W.T.S.D.
"WOMEN WHO DATE WOMEN THEY SHOULDN'T DATE"
GROUP THERAPY AND POTLUCK 7pm.
THEY COULDN'T COME UP WITH A SHORTER ACRONYM?! I THINK THAT'S A BAD SIGN...
DON'T FORGET IT'S A POTLUCK...
PAIGE

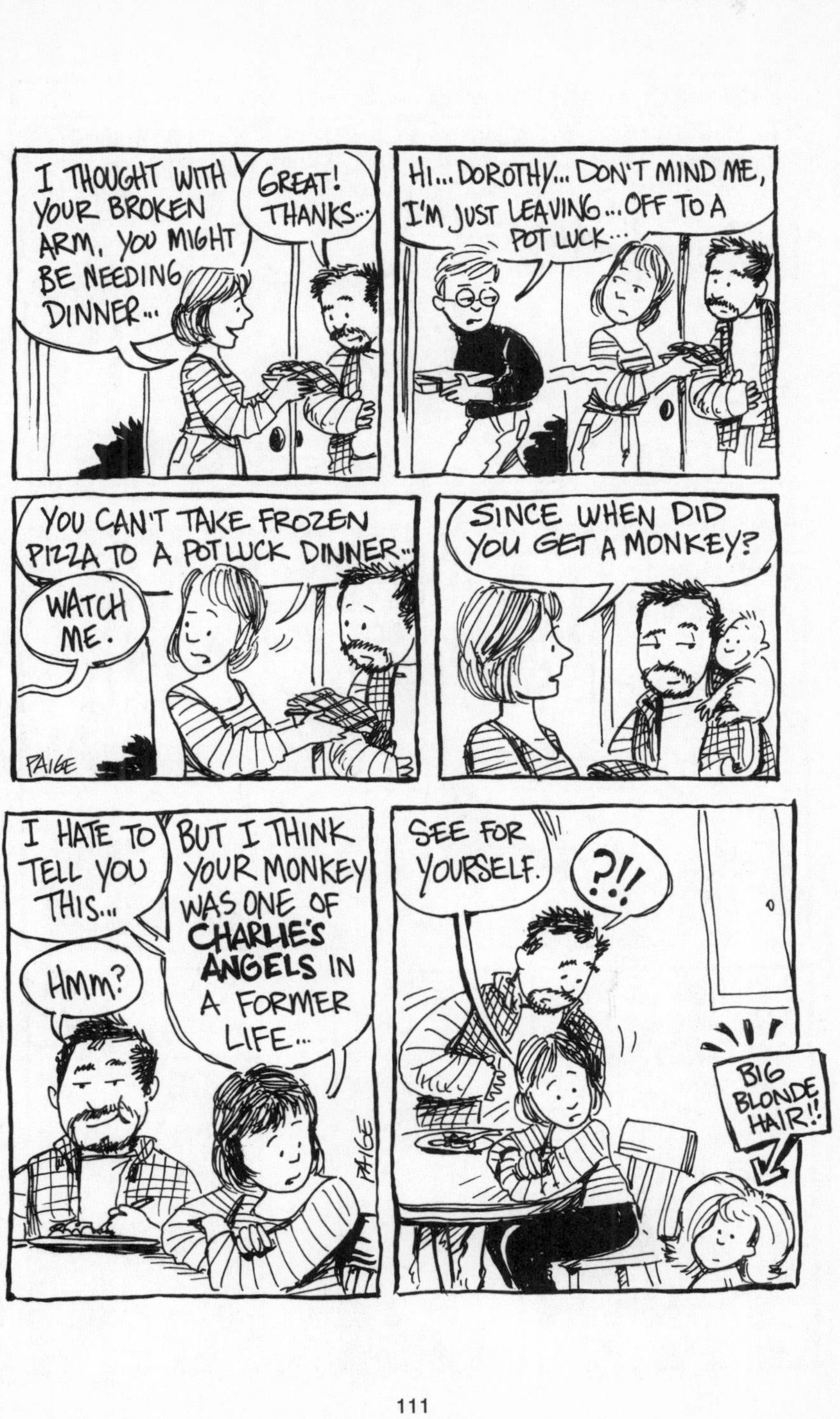
I THOUGHT WITH YOUR BROKEN ARM, YOU MIGHT BE NEEDING DINNER...
GREAT! THANKS...
HI... DOROTHY... DON'T MIND ME, I'M JUST LEAVING... OFF TO A POT LUCK...
YOU CAN'T TAKE FROZEN PIZZA TO A POT LUCK DINNER...
WATCH ME.
PAIGE
SINCE WHEN DID YOU GET A MONKEY?
I HATE TO TELL YOU THIS...
BUT I THINK YOUR MONKEY WAS ONE OF CHARLIE'S ANGELS IN A FORMER LIFE...
HMM?
PAIGE
SEE FOR YOURSELF.
?!!
BIG BLONDE HAIR!!

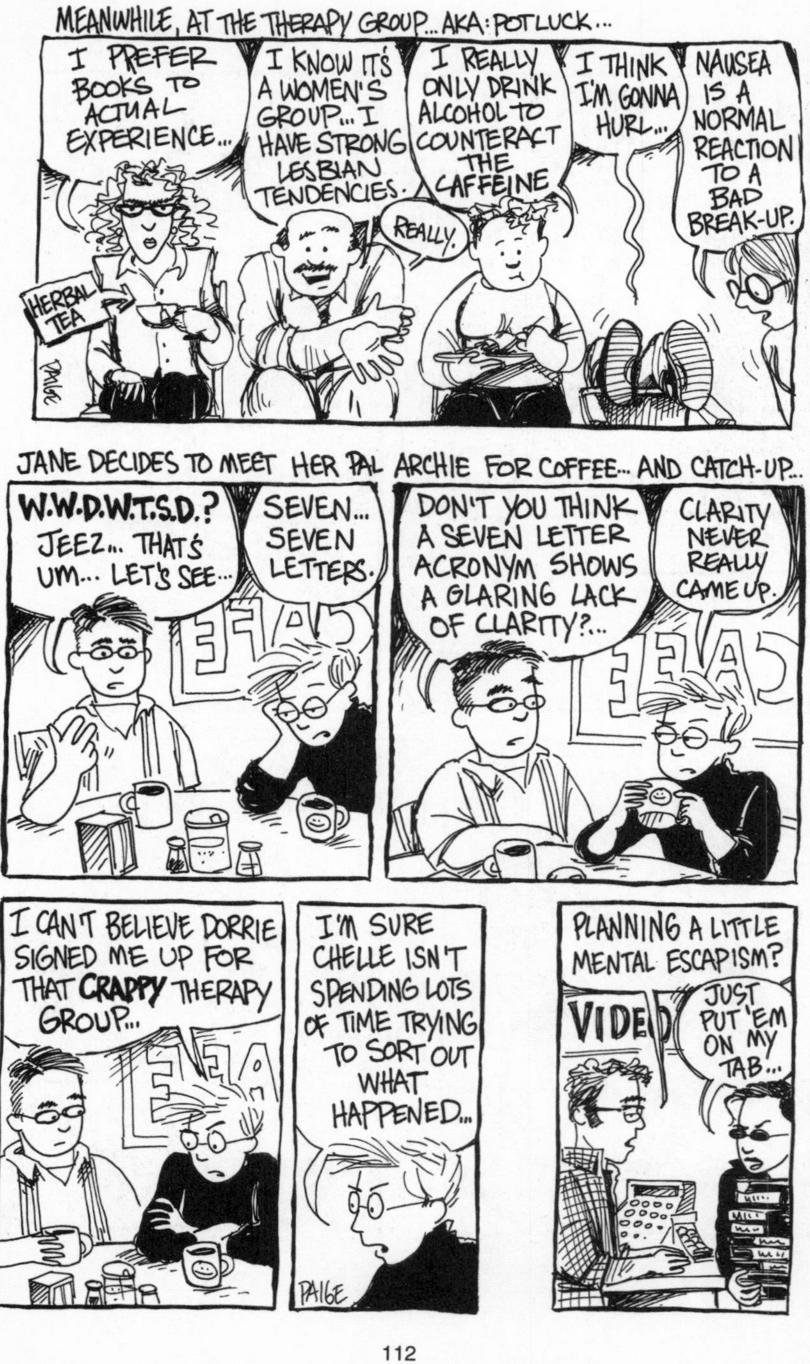
MEANWHILE, AT THE THERAPY GROUP... AKA: POTLUCK...
I PREFER BOOKS TO ACTUAL EXPERIENCE...
HERBAL TEA
I KNOW IT'S A WOMEN'S GROUP... I HAVE STRONG LESBIAN TENDENCIES.
REALLY.
I REALLY ONLY DRINK ALCOHOL TO COUNTERACT THE CAFFEINE
I THINK I'M GONNA HURL...
NAUSEA IS A NORMAL REACTION TO A BAD BREAK-UP.
PAIGE
JANE DECIDES TO MEET HER PAL ARCHIE FOR COFFEE... AND CATCH-UP...
W.W.D.W.T.S.D.? JEEZ... THAT'S UM... LET'S SEE...
SEVEN... SEVEN LETTERS.
CAFE
DON'T YOU THINK A SEVEN LETTER ACRONYM SHOWS A GLARING LACK OF CLARITY?...
CLARITY NEVER REALLY CAME UP.
I CAN'T BELIEVE DORRIE SIGNED ME UP FOR THAT CRAPPY THERAPY GROUP...
I'M SURE CHELLE ISN'T SPENDING LOTS OF TIME TRYING TO SORT OUT WHAT HAPPENED...
PAIGE
PLANNING A LITTLE MENTAL ESCAPISM?
VIDEO
JUST PUT 'EM ON MY TAB...

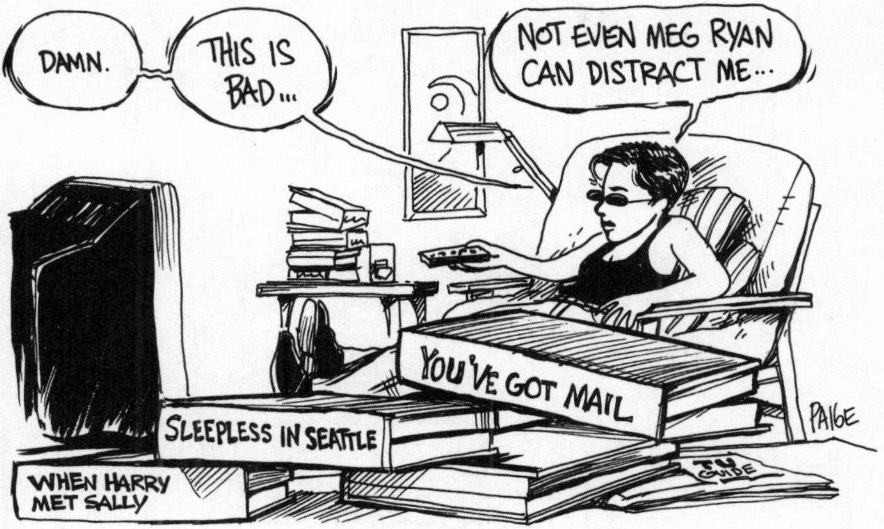
DAMN.
THIS IS BAD...
NOT EVEN MEG RYAN CAN DISTRACT ME...
YOU'VE GOT MAIL
SLEEPLESS IN SEATTLE
WHEN HARRY MET SALLY
TV GUIDE
PAIGE

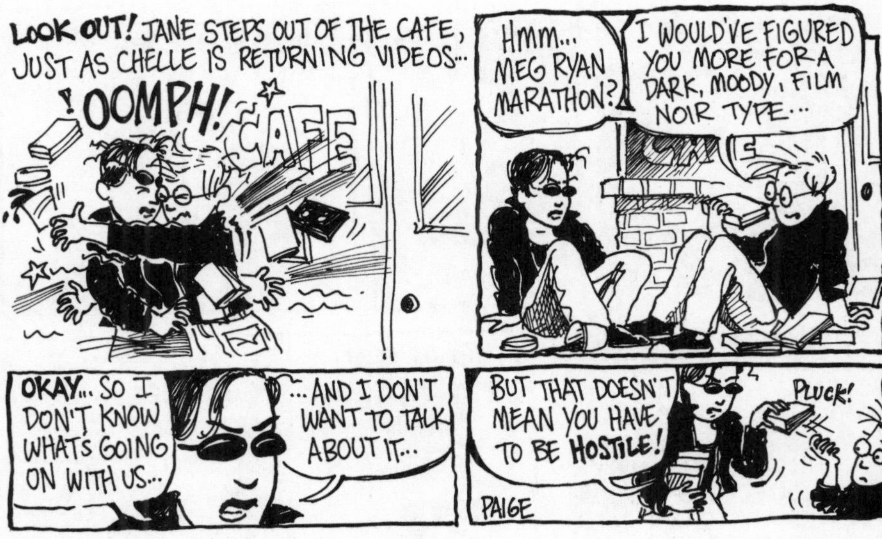
LOOK OUT! JANE STEPS OUT OF THE CAFE, JUST AS CHELLE IS RETURNING VIDEOS...
!OOMPH!
CAFE
Hmm... MEG RYAN MARATHON?
I WOULD'VE FIGURED YOU MORE FOR A DARK, MOODY, FILM NOIR TYPE...
OKAY... SO I DON'T KNOW WHATS GOING ON WITH US...
...AND I DON'T WANT TO TALK ABOUT IT...
BUT THAT DOESN'T MEAN YOU HAVE TO BE HOSTILE!
PLUCK!
PAIGE

WHAT HAPPENED?!

I DON'T EVEN KNOW...

IT WAS LIKE... LIKE, CHELLE WAS ALMOST BEING **SENSITIVE**...?!

PAIGE

UH...OH...

IT'S MONDAY... AND JANE AND DORRIE MEET AT THE CAFE...

I CAN'T BELIEVE YOU SIGNED ME UP FOR THAT **LOSER** THERAPY GROUP!

I DIDN'T THINK YOU'D ACTUALLY GO.

IT WAS SORT OF A JOKE...

A **JOKE**?!

OH CRAP... DON'T LOOK...

PAIGE

WHAT? IT'S EVELYN... FROM THE THERAPY GROUP... SHE'S WALKING THIS WAY...

HI... IT'S **JANE** ISN'T IT?

HI.

TRUE TO FORM, JANE CAN'T SEEM TO ESCAPE UNCOMFORTABLE SOCIAL MEETINGS. SHE'S FORCED TO SMALL TALK WITH EVELYN FOR AT LEAST THREE MINUTES... JUST LONG ENOUGH FOR A SPARK TO GENERATE FOR DORRIE... CAN YOU SAY "SPEED DATING?"

EVELYN IS AN INTERESTING WOMAN...

OH...YEAH...ABOUT AS INTERESTING AS A TOOTH ACHE!

SIP

114

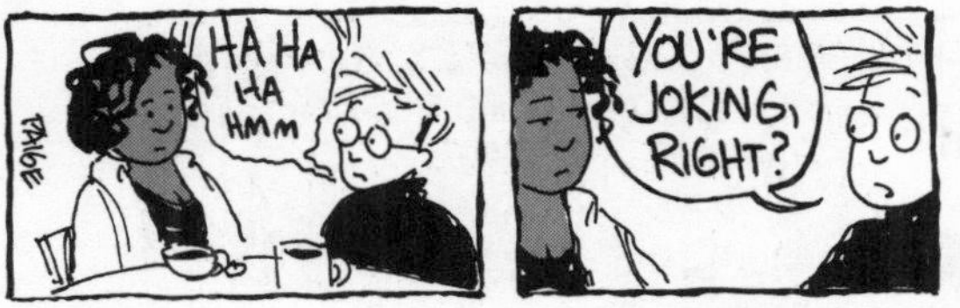
HA HA HA HMM
YOU'RE JOKING, RIGHT?

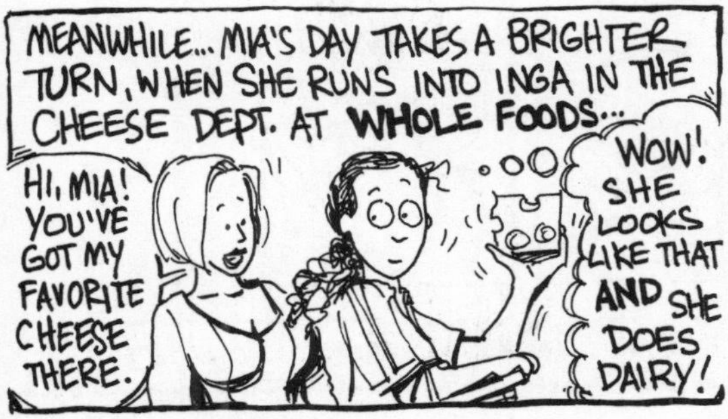
MEANWHILE... MIA'S DAY TAKES A BRIGHTER TURN, WHEN SHE RUNS INTO INGA IN THE CHEESE DEPT. AT WHOLE FOODS...
HI, MIA! YOU'VE GOT MY FAVORITE CHEESE THERE.
WOW! SHE LOOKS LIKE THAT AND SHE DOES DAIRY!

REMEMBER INGA? SHE'S WHO GOT MIA INTO SO MUCH TROUBLE WITH DOROTHY ON THE CANOE TRIP. HOW DID ALL THAT START ANYWAY? WHO IS INGA? HOW ABOUT A LITTLE FLASHBACK?... IT ALL STARTED BECAUSE DOROTHY TALKED MIA INTO A MUD BATH AT A SPA... ONLY MIA WASN'T INTO THE WHOLE GROUP NUDITY FACTOR...

FLASHBACK... ROLL TAPE!

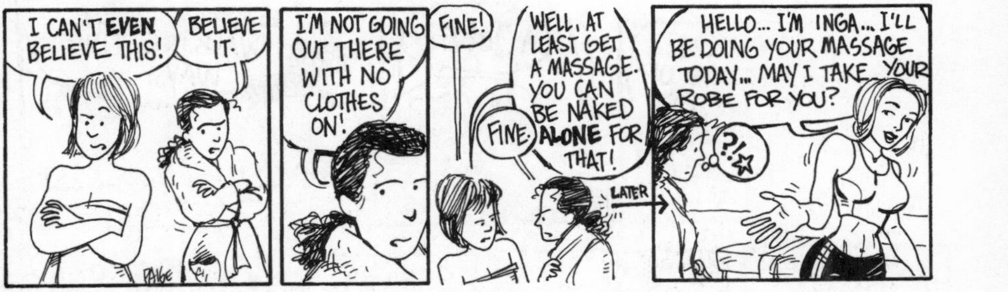
I CAN'T EVEN BELIEVE THIS!
BELIEVE IT.
I'M NOT GOING OUT THERE WITH NO CLOTHES ON!
FINE!
WELL, AT LEAST GET A MASSAGE. YOU CAN BE NAKED ALONE FOR THAT!
FINE.
LATER
HELLO... I'M INGA... I'LL BE DOING YOUR MASSAGE TODAY... MAY I TAKE YOUR ROBE FOR YOU?

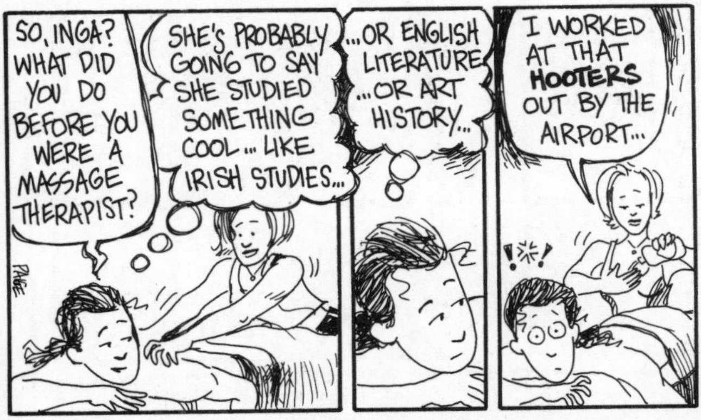
SO, INGA? WHAT DID YOU DO BEFORE YOU WERE A MASSAGE THERAPIST?
SHE'S PROBABLY GOING TO SAY SHE STUDIED SOMETHING COOL... LIKE IRISH STUDIES...
...OR ENGLISH LITERATURE ...OR ART HISTORY...
I WORKED AT THAT HOOTERS OUT BY THE AIRPORT...

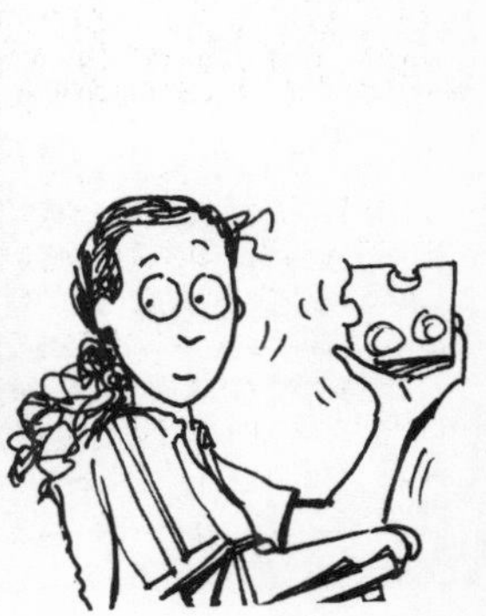

WE NOW REJOIN OUR STORY, WHERE MIA'S ROMANTIC IMAGINATION HAS CAUGHT UP WITH HER AT THE CHEESE COUNTER...

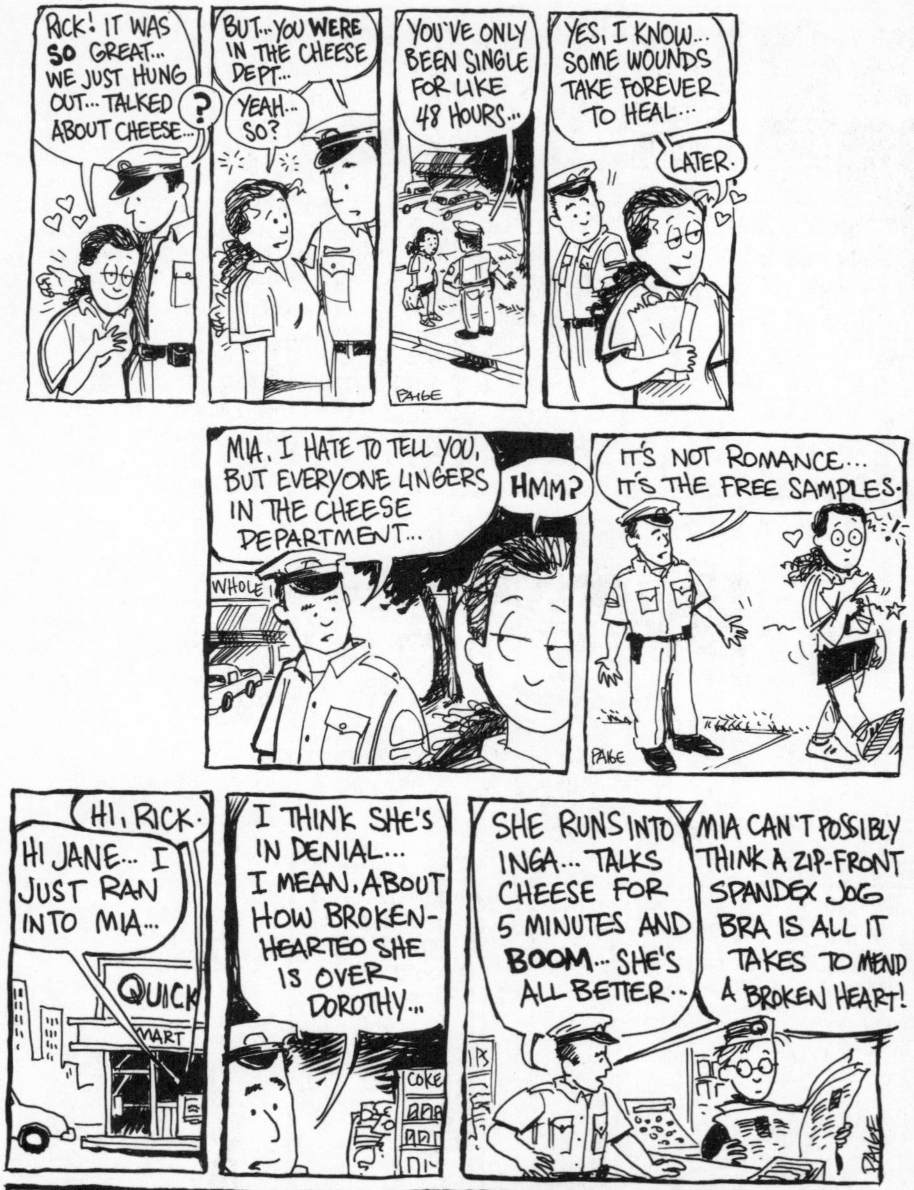

RICK! IT WAS SO GREAT... WE JUST HUNG OUT... TALKED ABOUT CHEESE...
?
BUT... YOU WERE IN THE CHEESE DEPT...
YEAH... SO?
YOU'VE ONLY BEEN SINGLE FOR LIKE 48 HOURS...
PAIGE
YES, I KNOW... SOME WOUNDS TAKE FOREVER TO HEAL...
LATER.
MIA, I HATE TO TELL YOU, BUT EVERYONE LINGERS IN THE CHEESE DEPARTMENT...
HMM?
WHOLE
IT'S NOT ROMANCE... IT'S THE FREE SAMPLES.
PAIGE
HI, RICK.
HI JANE... I JUST RAN INTO MIA...
QUICK
MART
I THINK SHE'S IN DENIAL... I MEAN, ABOUT HOW BROKEN-HEARTED SHE IS OVER DOROTHY...
COKE
SHE RUNS INTO INGA... TALKS CHEESE FOR 5 MINUTES AND BOOM... SHE'S ALL BETTER...
MIA CAN'T POSSIBLY THINK A ZIP-FRONT SPANDEX JOG BRA IS ALL IT TAKES TO MEND A BROKEN HEART!
CHIPS
UH... I HATE TO BE THE SHALLOW ONE HERE BUT...

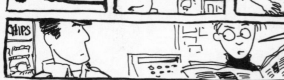

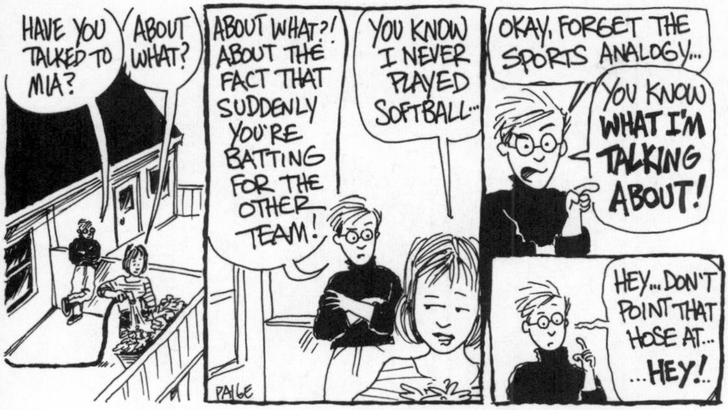
HAVE YOU TALKED TO MIA?
ABOUT WHAT?
ABOUT WHAT?! ABOUT THE FACT THAT SUDDENLY YOU'RE BATTING FOR THE OTHER TEAM!
YOU KNOW I NEVER PLAYED SOFTBALL...
OKAY, FORGET THE SPORTS ANALOGY...
YOU KNOW **WHAT I'M TALKING ABOUT!**
HEY... DON'T POINT THAT HOSE AT... ...**HEY!**..
PAIGE

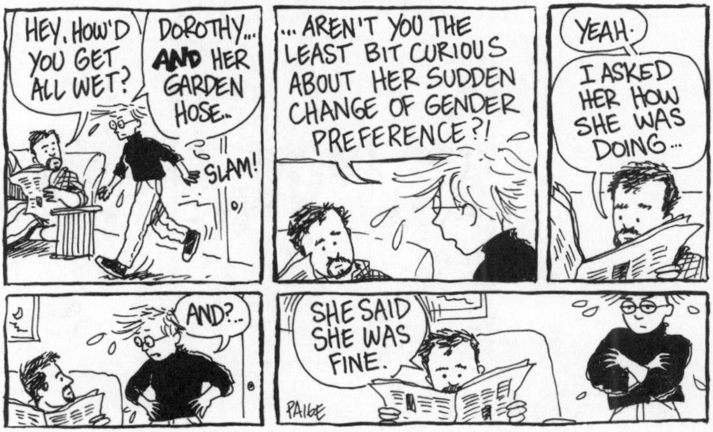
HEY, HOW'D YOU GET ALL WET?
DOROTHY... **AND** HER GARDEN HOSE..
SLAM!
... AREN'T YOU THE LEAST BIT CURIOUS ABOUT HER SUDDEN CHANGE OF GENDER PREFERENCE?!
YEAH.
I ASKED HER HOW SHE WAS DOING...
AND?..
SHE SAID SHE WAS FINE.
PAIGE

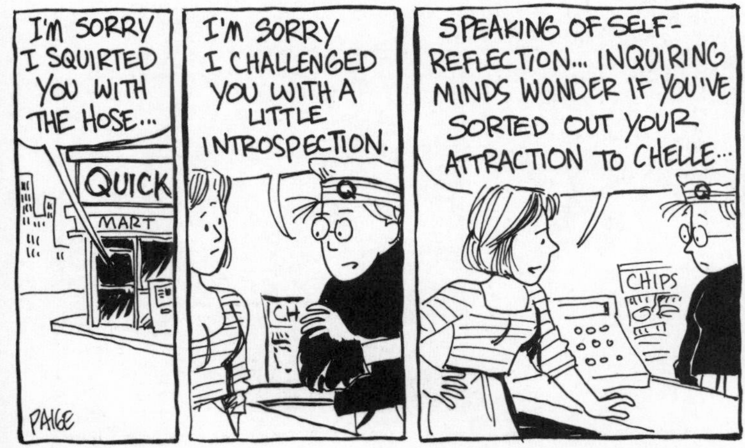
I'M SORRY I SQUIRTED YOU WITH THE HOSE...
QUICK MART
PAIGE
I'M SORRY I CHALLENGED YOU WITH A LITTLE INTROSPECTION.
SPEAKING OF SELF-REFLECTION... INQUIRING MINDS WONDER IF YOU'VE SORTED OUT YOUR ATTRACTION TO CHELLE...
CHIPS

LUCKILY, JANE WAS AT THE END OF HER SHIFT... SO SHE DIDN'T HAVE TO SELF-REFLECT IN PUBLIC... SHE COULD SAVE IT FOR THE DRIVE HOME...

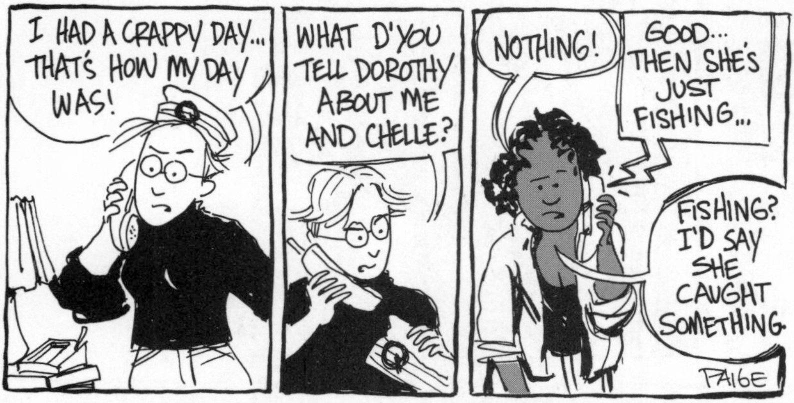
I HAD A CRAPPY DAY... THAT'S HOW MY DAY WAS!
WHAT D'YOU TELL DOROTHY ABOUT ME AND CHELLE?
NOTHING!
GOOD... THEN SHE'S JUST FISHING...
FISHING? I'D SAY SHE CAUGHT SOMETHING.
PAIGE

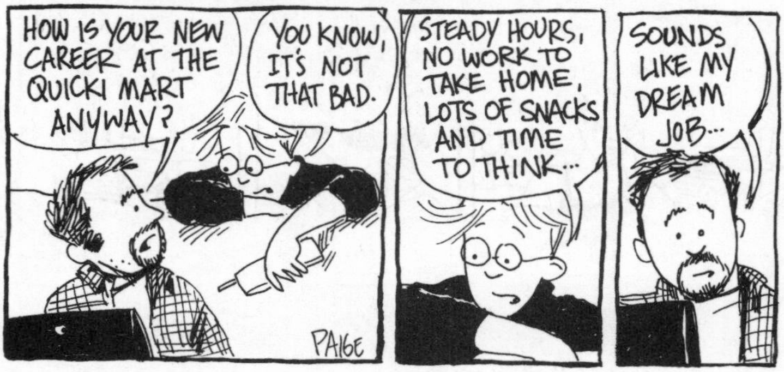
HOW IS YOUR NEW CAREER AT THE QUICKI MART ANYWAY?
YOU KNOW, IT'S NOT THAT BAD.
PAIGE
STEADY HOURS, NO WORK TO TAKE HOME, LOTS OF SNACKS AND TIME TO THINK...
SOUNDS LIKE MY DREAM JOB...

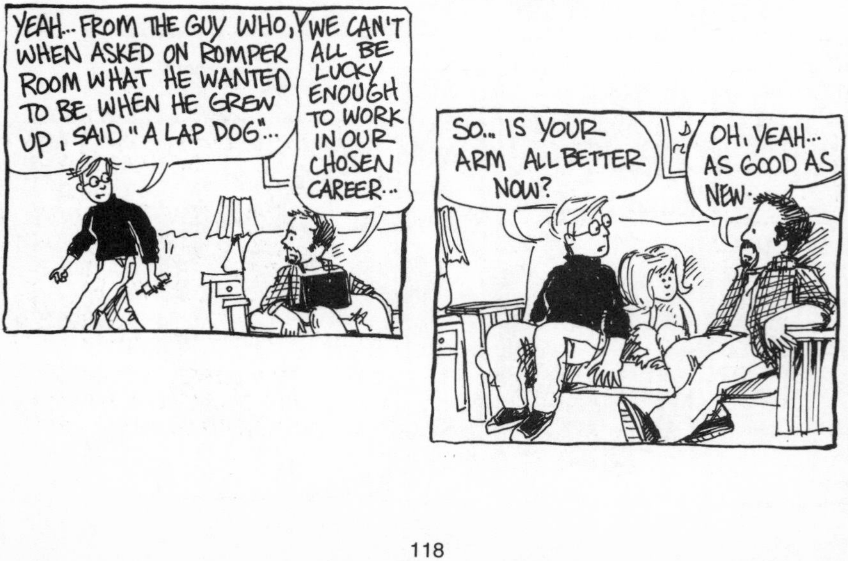
YEAH... FROM THE GUY WHO, WHEN ASKED ON ROMPER ROOM WHAT HE WANTED TO BE WHEN HE GREW UP, SAID "A LAP DOG"...
WE CAN'T ALL BE LUCKY ENOUGH TO WORK IN OUR CHOSEN CAREER...
SO... IS YOUR ARM ALL BETTER NOW?
OH, YEAH... AS GOOD AS NEW.

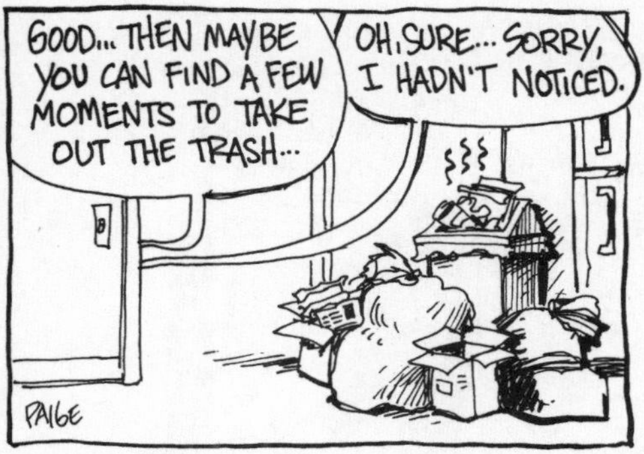
GOOD... THEN MAYBE YOU CAN FIND A FEW MOMENTS TO TAKE OUT THE TRASH...
OH, SURE... SORRY, I HADN'T NOTICED.
PAIGE

BACK IN THE NEWSROOM, CHELLE CONTEMPLATES HER NEXT STEPS...

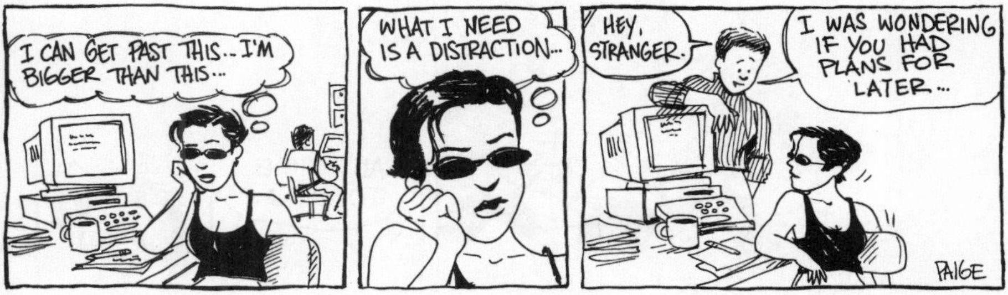
I CAN GET PAST THIS... I'M BIGGER THAN THIS...
WHAT I NEED IS A DISTRACTION...
HEY, STRANGER.
I WAS WONDERING IF YOU HAD PLANS FOR LATER...
PAIGE

THE NEXT NIGHT, AT THE CAFE, JANE IS HAVING HER USUAL LATTE WITH DORRIE, WHEN EVELYN WALKS IN.

"SINCE WHEN DID THIS BECOME HER HANG OUT?!" SAID JANE, ANNOYED... "SCOOT DOWN IN YOUR CHAIR... MAYBE SHE WON'T SEE US."

"IF YOU WERE REALLY MY FRIEND, YOU'D GET HER NUMBER FOR ME," DORRIE TAUNTED, TRYING TO GUILT JANE INTO ACTION.

"NO..." JANE QUIPPED, "IF I WAS REALLY YOUR FRIEND, I WOULD-N'T."

"TRUST ME ON THIS," ADDED JANE, "SHE'S ONE OF THOSE FEMINIST THEORIST TYPES... SHE'LL JUST RAIL ON NEO-FEMINISM AND SIP ORGANIC HERBAL TEA..."

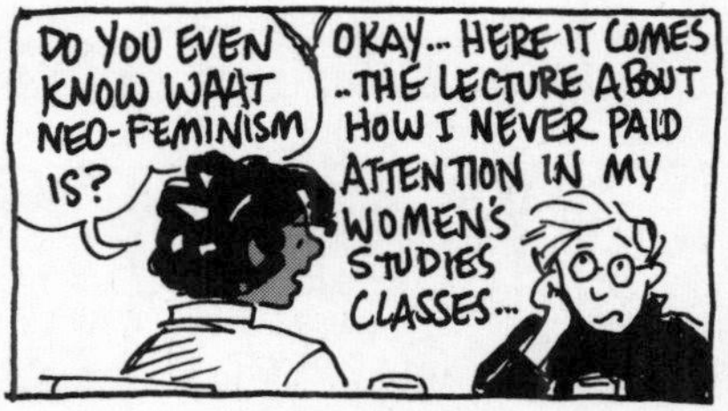
DO YOU EVEN KNOW WHAT NEO-FEMINISM IS?
OKAY... HERE IT COMES ...THE LECTURE ABOUT HOW I NEVER PAID ATTENTION IN MY WOMEN'S STUDIES CLASSES...

JANE LOSES THE ARGUMENT AND SLINKS OFF TO DO DORRIE'S BIDDING...

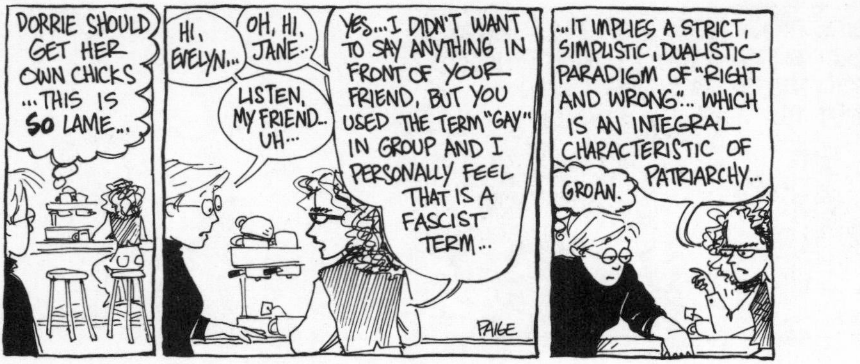
DORRIE SHOULD GET HER OWN CHICKS ...THIS IS SO LAME...
HI, EVELYN...
OH, HI, JANE...
LISTEN, MY FRIEND.. UH...
YES...I DIDN'T WANT TO SAY ANYTHING IN FRONT OF YOUR FRIEND, BUT YOU USED THE TERM "GAY" IN GROUP AND I PERSONALLY FEEL THAT IS A FASCIST TERM...
PAIGE
...IT IMPLIES A STRICT, SIMPLISTIC, DUALISTIC PARADIGM OF "RIGHT AND WRONG"... WHICH IS AN INTEGRAL CHARACTERISTIC OF PATRIARCHY...
GROAN.

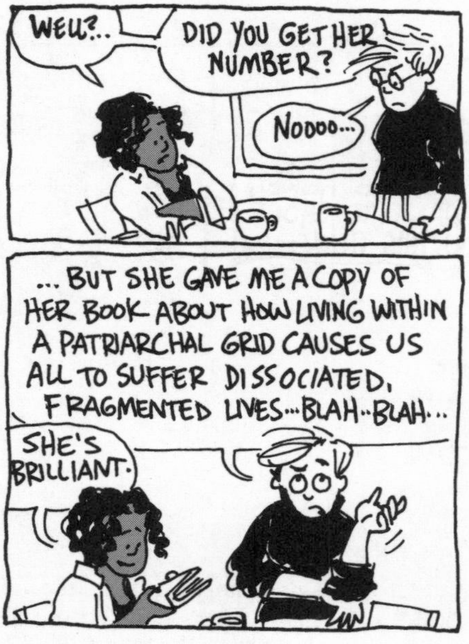
WELL?...
DID YOU GET HER NUMBER?
NOOOO...
... BUT SHE GAVE ME A COPY OF HER BOOK ABOUT HOW LIVING WITHIN A PATRIARCHAL GRID CAUSES US ALL TO SUFFER DISSOCIATED, FRAGMENTED LIVES...BLAH..BLAH...
SHE'S BRILLIANT.

DORRIE DISCOVERED LATER THAT EVELYN HAD WRITTEN HER NAME INSIDE THE BOOK.... WITH A LITTLE SLEUTHING, DORRIE WAS ABLE TO GET EVELYN'S NUMBER HERSELF. A FEW DAYS LATER, JANE BUMPED INTO DORRIE AND GOT THE UPDATE...

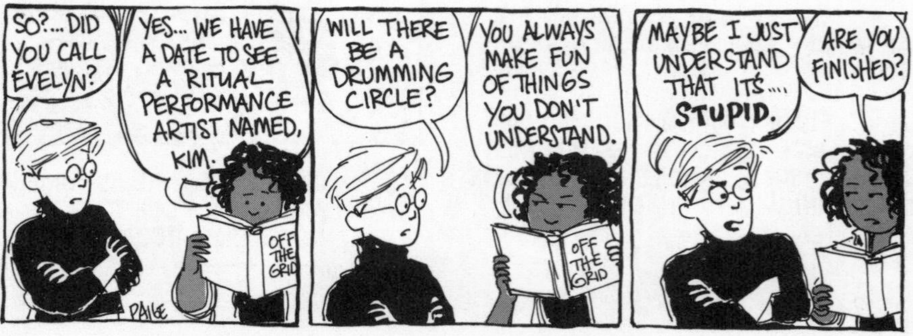
SO?... DID YOU CALL EVELYN?
YES... WE HAVE A DATE TO SEE A RITUAL PERFORMANCE ARTIST NAMED, KIM.
OFF THE GRID
PAIGE
WILL THERE BE A DRUMMING CIRCLE?
YOU ALWAYS MAKE FUN OF THINGS YOU DON'T UNDERSTAND.
OFF THE GRID
MAYBE I JUST UNDERSTAND THAT IT'S.... STUPID.
ARE YOU FINISHED?

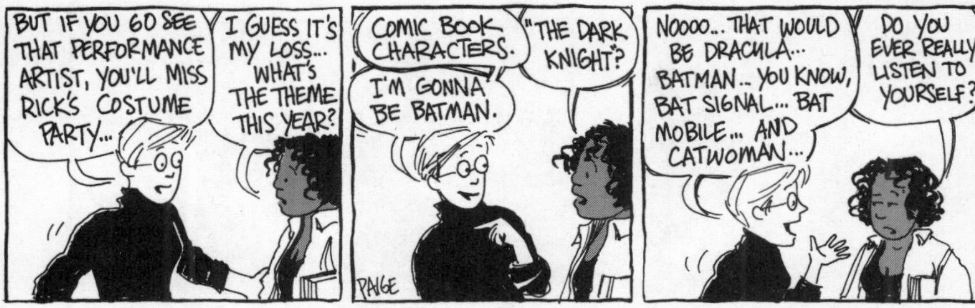

BUT IF YOU GO SEE THAT PERFORMANCE ARTIST, YOU'LL MISS RICK'S COSTUME PARTY...
I GUESS IT'S MY LOSS... WHAT'S THE THEME THIS YEAR?
COMIC BOOK CHARACTERS.
I'M GONNA BE BATMAN.
"THE DARK KNIGHT"?
NOOOO... THAT WOULD BE DRACULA... BATMAN... YOU KNOW, BAT SIGNAL... BAT MOBILE... AND CATWOMAN...
DO YOU EVER REALLY LISTEN TO YOURSELF?
PAIGE

NEEDLESS TO SAY, DORRIE DECIDES TO SKIP RICK'S ANNUAL COSTUME PARTY EXTRAVAGANZA... AND ETHAN MISTAKENLY AGREES TO LET JANE PICK THEIR COSTUMES FOR THE EVENT...

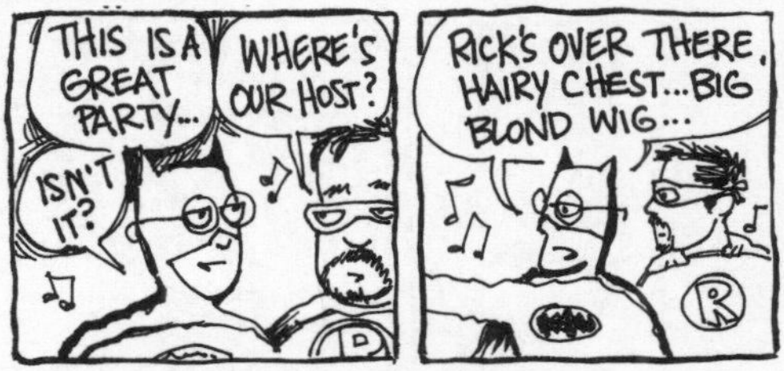

THIS IS A GREAT PARTY...
ISN'T IT?
WHERE'S OUR HOST?
RICK'S OVER THERE. HAIRY CHEST... BIG BLOND WIG...

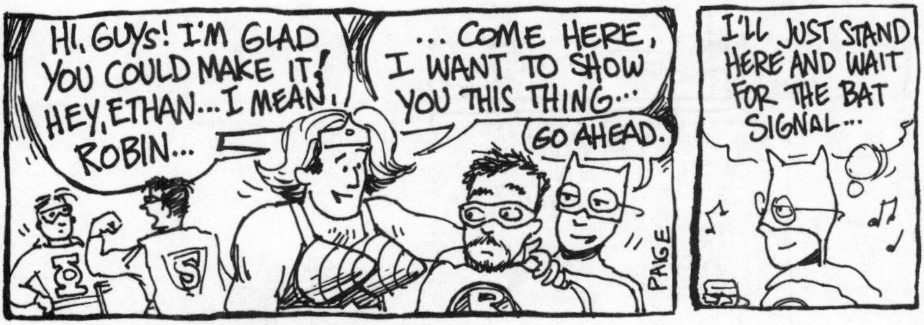

HI, GUYS! I'M GLAD YOU COULD MAKE IT! HEY, ETHAN... I MEAN, ROBIN...
... COME HERE, I WANT TO SHOW YOU THIS THING...
GO AHEAD.
PAIGE
I'LL JUST STAND HERE AND WAIT FOR THE BAT SIGNAL...

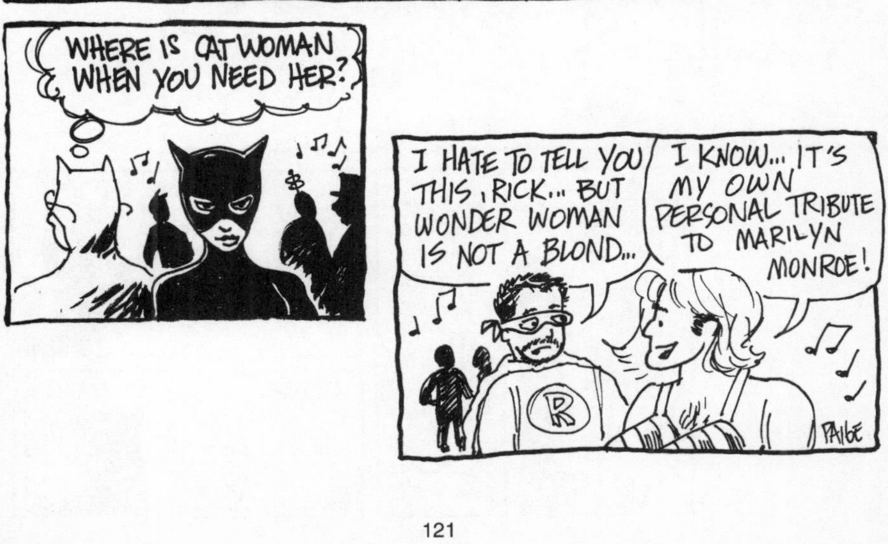

WHERE IS CATWOMAN WHEN YOU NEED HER?
I HATE TO TELL YOU THIS, RICK... BUT WONDER WOMAN IS NOT A BLOND...
I KNOW... IT'S MY OWN PERSONAL TRIBUTE TO MARILYN MONROE!
PAIGE

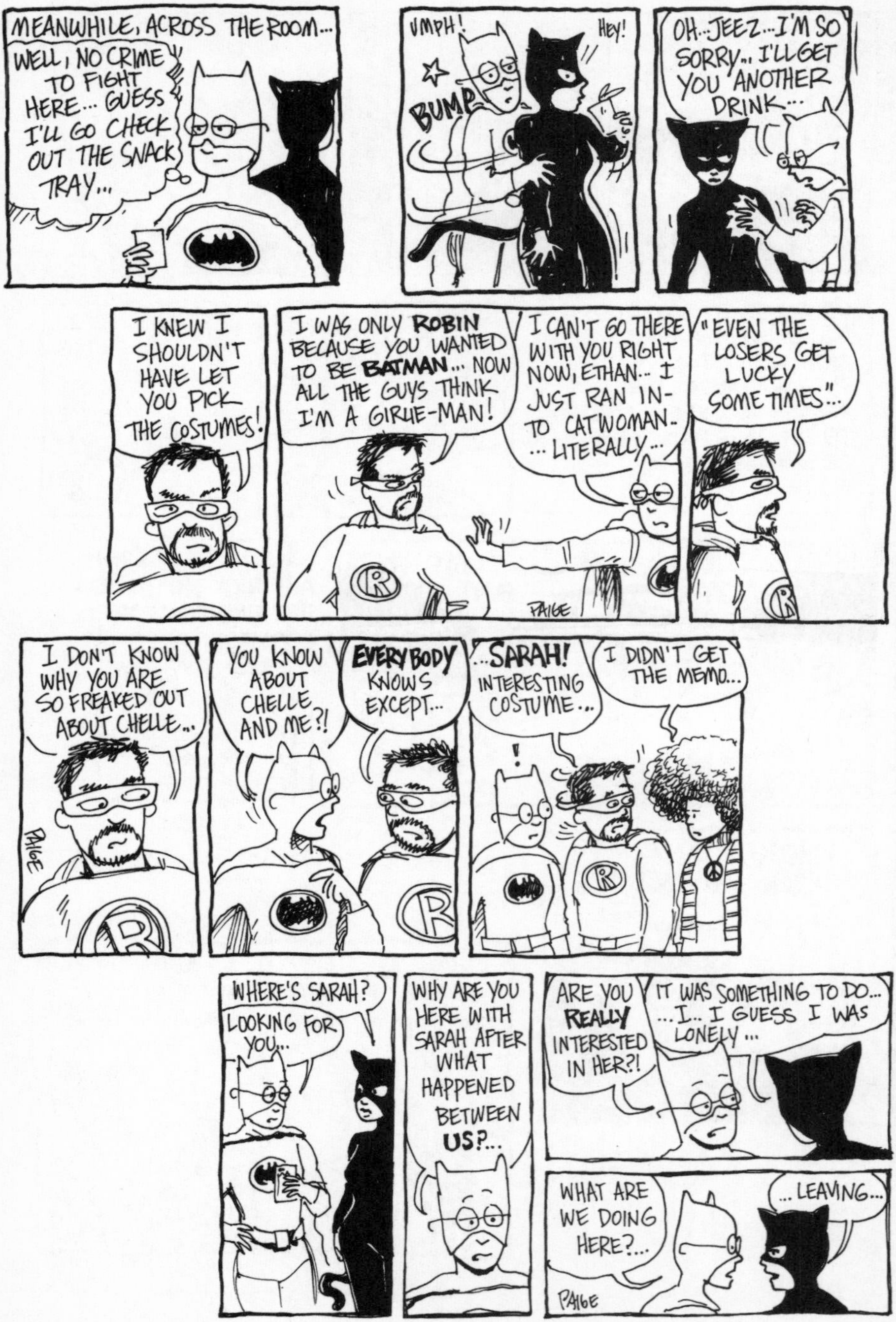
MEANWHILE, ACROSS THE ROOM...
WELL, NO CRIME TO FIGHT HERE... GUESS I'LL GO CHECK OUT THE SNACK TRAY...
UMPH!
HEY!
BUMP
OH...JEEZ...I'M SO SORRY... I'LL GET YOU ANOTHER DRINK...
I KNEW I SHOULDN'T HAVE LET YOU PICK THE COSTUMES!
I WAS ONLY ROBIN BECAUSE YOU WANTED TO BE BATMAN... NOW ALL THE GUYS THINK I'M A GIRLIE-MAN!
I CAN'T GO THERE WITH YOU RIGHT NOW, ETHAN... I JUST RAN IN-TO CATWOMAN... ... LITERALLY...
PAIGE
"EVEN THE LOSERS GET LUCKY SOME-TIMES"...
I DON'T KNOW WHY YOU ARE SO FREAKED OUT ABOUT CHELLE...
PAIGE
YOU KNOW ABOUT CHELLE AND ME?!
EVERYBODY KNOWS EXCEPT...
...SARAH! INTERESTING COSTUME...
I DIDN'T GET THE MEMO...
WHERE'S SARAH?
LOOKING FOR YOU...
WHY ARE YOU HERE WITH SARAH AFTER WHAT HAPPENED BETWEEN US?...
ARE YOU REALLY INTERESTED IN HER?!
IT WAS SOMETHING TO DO... ...I... I GUESS I WAS LONELY...
WHAT ARE WE DOING HERE?...
...LEAVING...
PAIGE

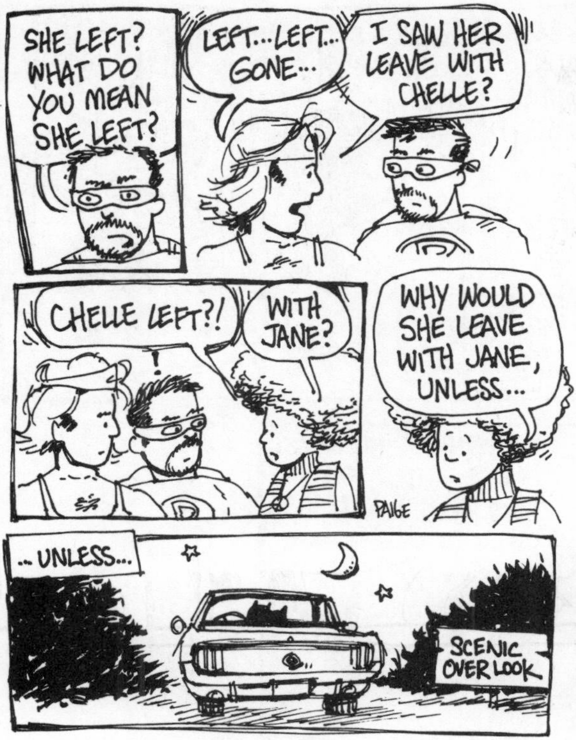
SHE LEFT? WHAT DO YOU MEAN SHE LEFT?
LEFT...LEFT... GONE...
I SAW HER LEAVE WITH CHELLE?
CHELLE LEFT?!
!
WITH JANE?
WHY WOULD SHE LEAVE WITH JANE, UNLESS...
PAIGE
... UNLESS...
SCENIC OVERLOOK

POOR SARAH... ETHAN AND RICK TRY TO HELP HER FIND COMFORT IN "COMFORT FOOD" AT AN ALL NIGHT DINER AFTER THE PARTY...

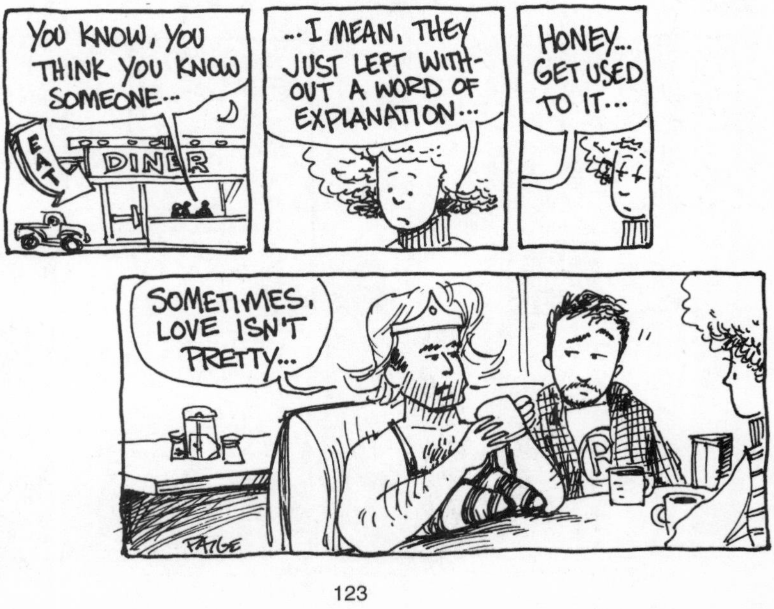
YOU KNOW, YOU THINK YOU KNOW SOMEONE...
EAT
DINER
... I MEAN, THEY JUST LEFT WITHOUT A WORD OF EXPLANATION...
HONEY... GET USED TO IT...
SOMETIMES, LOVE ISN'T PRETTY...
PAIGE

THE NEXT DAY AT WORK, THE HOURS SEEM TO DRAG, BUT...

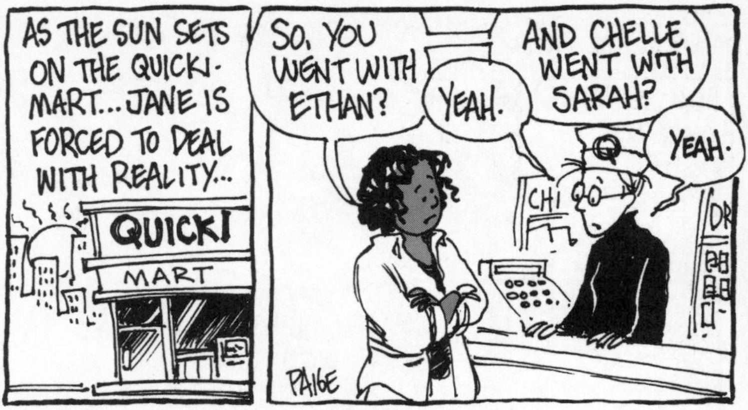
AS THE SUN SETS ON THE QUICKI-MART... JANE IS FORCED TO DEAL WITH REALITY...
QUICKI
MART
SO, YOU WENT WITH ETHAN?
YEAH.
AND CHELLE WENT WITH SARAH?
YEAH.
CHI
PAIGE

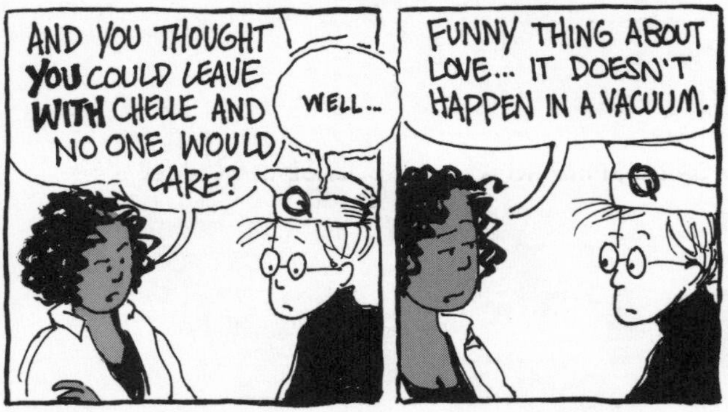
AND YOU THOUGHT **YOU** COULD LEAVE **WITH** CHELLE AND NO ONE WOULD CARE?
WELL...
FUNNY THING ABOUT LOVE... IT DOESN'T HAPPEN IN A VACUUM.

JANE LEAVES WORK AND A BIT OF INTROSPECTION FINALLY SETS IN...

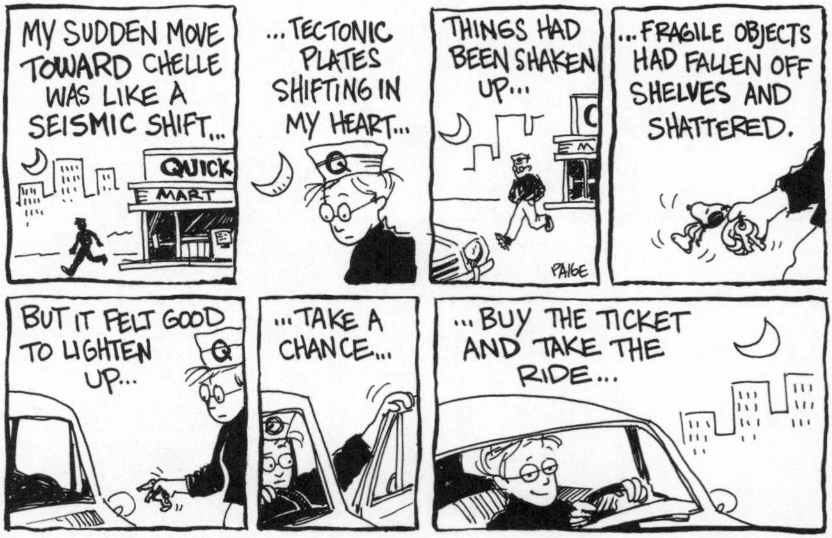
MY SUDDEN MOVE TOWARD CHELLE WAS LIKE A SEISMIC SHIFT...
QUICK
MART
...TECTONIC PLATES SHIFTING IN MY HEART...
THINGS HAD BEEN SHAKEN UP...
PAIGE
...FRAGILE OBJECTS HAD FALLEN OFF SHELVES AND SHATTERED.
BUT IT FELT GOOD TO LIGHTEN UP...
...TAKE A CHANCE...
...BUY THE TICKET AND TAKE THE RIDE...

... BUT BEFORE SHE PULLS AWAY IN HER CAR, SHE NOTICES A FOLDED SCRAP OF NOTEBOOK PAPER...

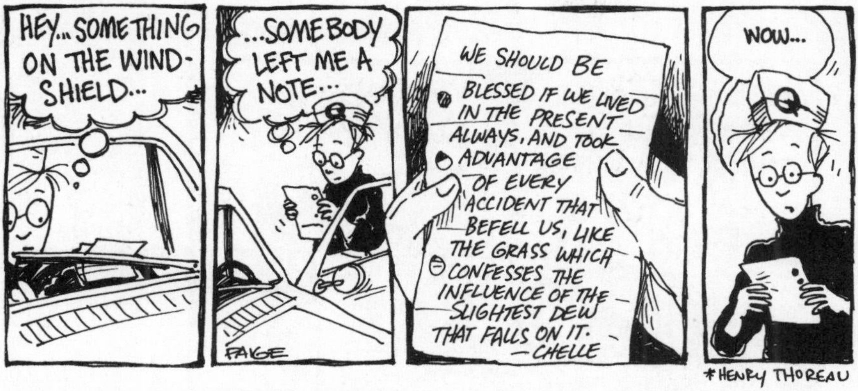
HEY... SOMETHING ON THE WIND-SHIELD...
...SOMEBODY LEFT ME A NOTE...
PAIGE
WE SHOULD BE BLESSED IF WE LIVED IN THE PRESENT ALWAYS, AND TOOK ADVANTAGE OF EVERY ACCIDENT THAT BEFELL US, LIKE THE GRASS WHICH CONFESSES THE INFLUENCE OF THE SLIGHTEST DEW THAT FALLS ON IT. —CHELLE
WOW...
*HENRY THOREAU

JANE SITS AT THE WHEEL OF HER CAR... SUCH A SURPRISING NOTE MADE HER FEEL A BIT LIGHT -HEADED... AND ALL THE SENSATIONS OF THAT UNEXPECTED NIGHT TOGETHER ON THE RIVER CAME RUSHING BACK... MEANWHILE, AT THE CAFE, MIA BUMPS INTO SARAH, FINDING A LITTLE SOLACE IN MARCEL PROUST... WHO ELSE?!

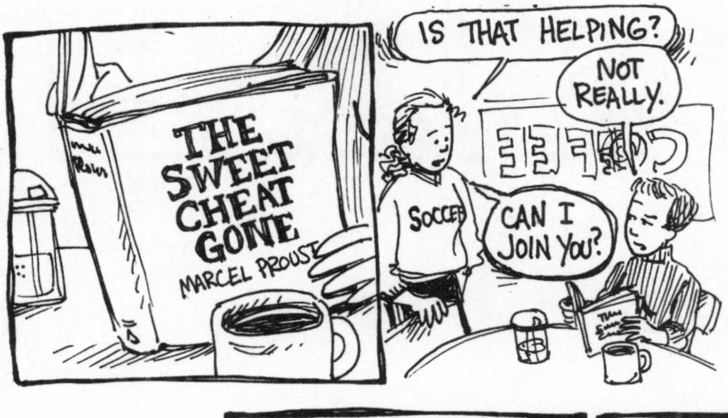
THE SWEET CHEAT GONE
MARCEL PROUST
IS THAT HELPING?
NOT REALLY.
SOCCER
CAN I JOIN YOU?

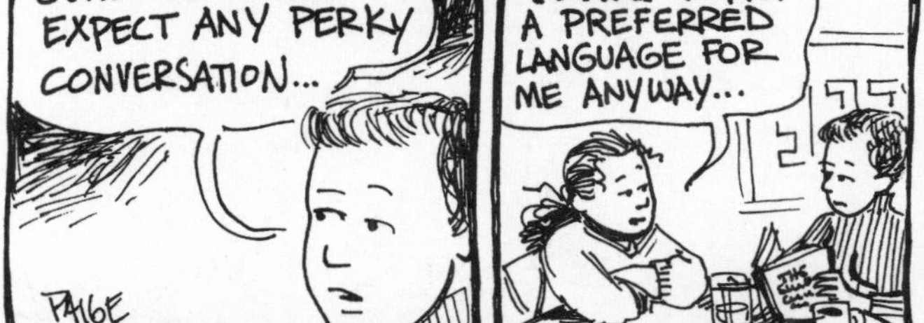
SURE... BUT DON'T EXPECT ANY PERKY CONVERSATION...
PAIGE
"PERKY" IS NOT A PREFERRED LANGUAGE FOR ME ANYWAY...

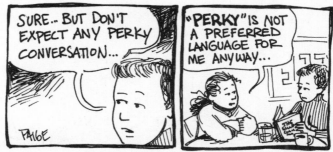

HAVE YOU TALKED TO JANE?... I MEAN, THAT'S WHO YOU'RE REALLY MAD AT RIGHT?...
YOU BARELY KNOW CHELLE...
COFFEE
CAFE
I DON'T REALLY WANT TO TALK ABOUT IT...OKAY?
PAIGE
WHAT ABOUT YOU?... I HEARD YOU HAD A ROMANTIC MOMENT WITH INGA?..
ACTUALLY, NO...!

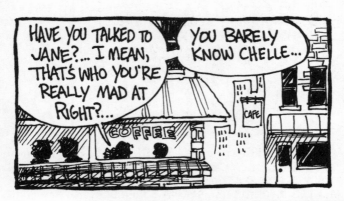

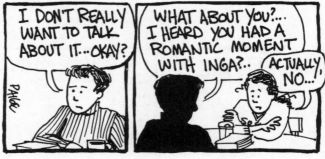

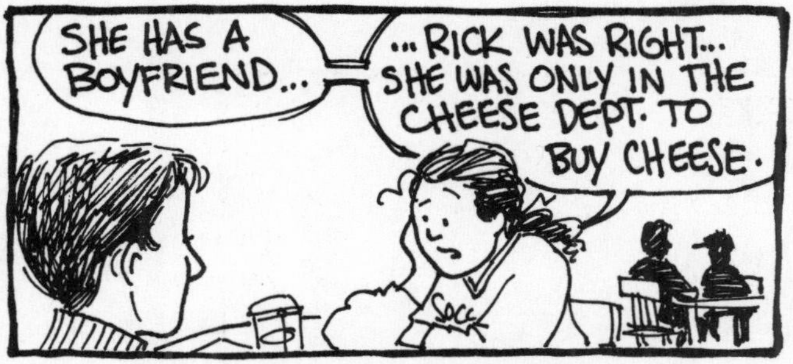
SHE HAS A BOYFRIEND...
...RICK WAS RIGHT... SHE WAS ONLY IN THE CHEESE DEPT. TO BUY CHEESE.

...AS TROUBLED SOULS FIND COMFORT IN EACH OTHER, ACROSS TOWN, IN JANE AND ETHAN'S LIVING ROOM, ANOTHER DRAMA THAT BEGAN MONTHS AGO ON THE FLATLANDS OF OKLAHOMA BEGINS TO UNFOLD...

... THE CHIMP WHO ONCE WAS...

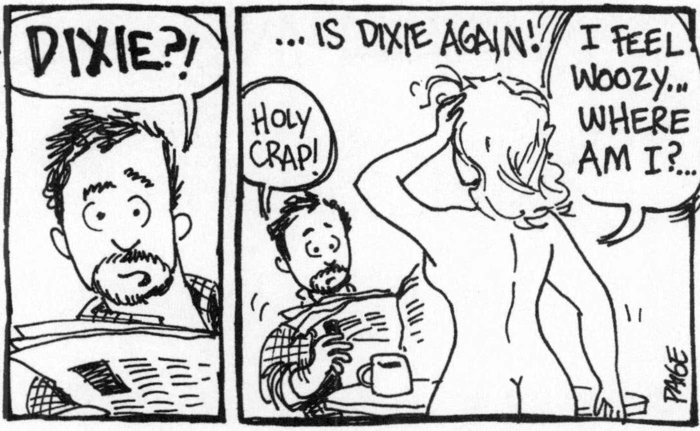
DIXIE?!
... IS DIXIE AGAIN!
I FEEL WOOZY... WHERE AM I?...
HOLY CRAP!
PAIGE

Chapter 6

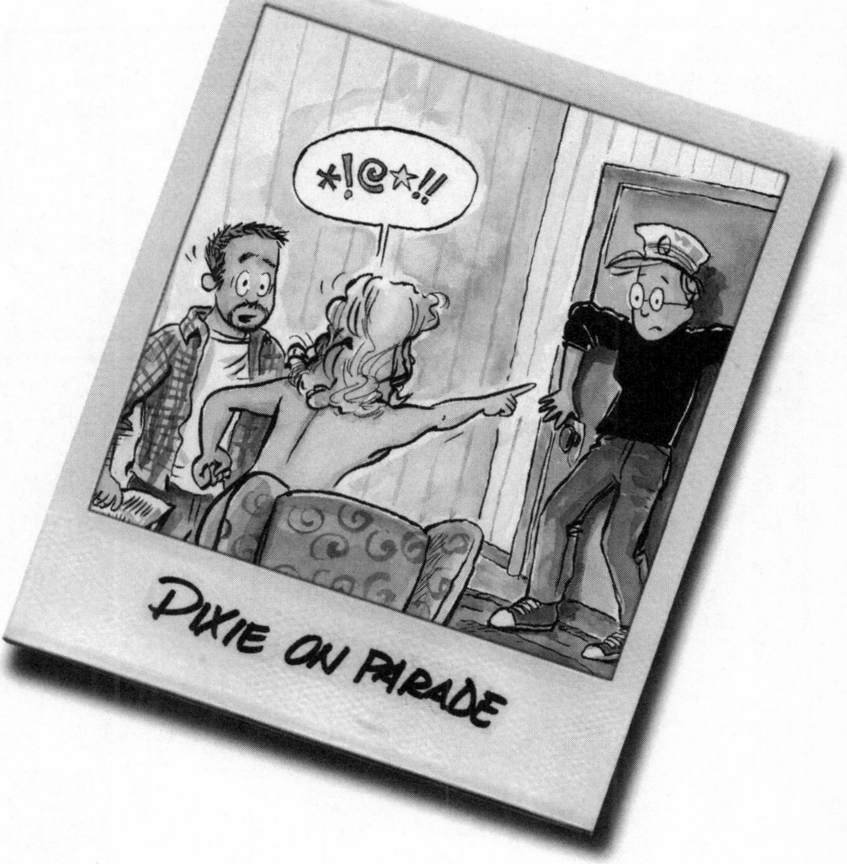
*!@☆!!
DIXIE ON PARADE

WHILE ETHAN SIPS HIS AFTERNOON COFFEE IN THE KITCHEN, A WONDER OF CHROMOSOMAL REFORMATION TAKES PLACE IN THE COMFORT OF JANE AND ETHAN'S LIVING ROOM. DIXIE RETURNS, WEARING NOTHING MORE THAN CHANEL NO. 5.

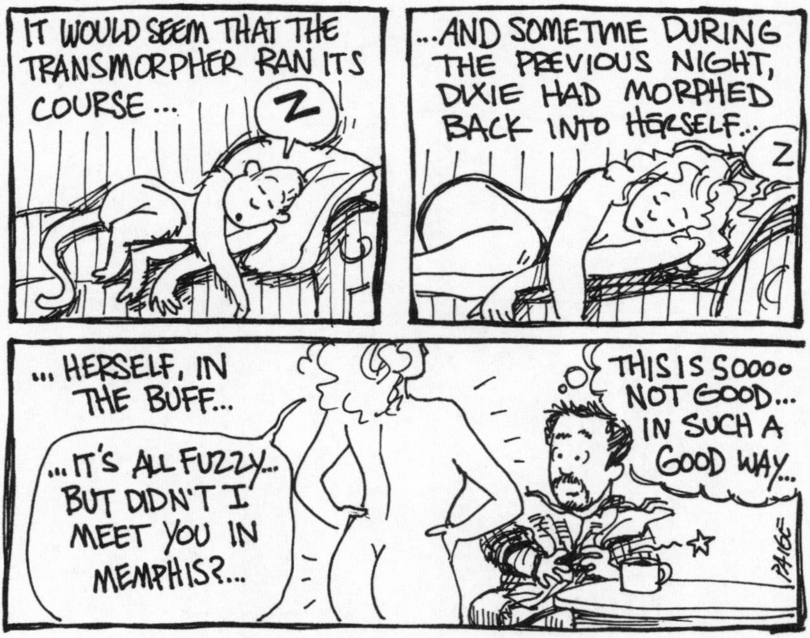
IT WOULD SEEM THAT THE TRANSMORPHER RAN ITS COURSE...
Z
...AND SOMETIME DURING THE PREVIOUS NIGHT, DIXIE HAD MORPHED BACK INTO HERSELF...
Z
... HERSELF, IN THE BUFF...
...IT'S ALL FUZZY... BUT DIDN'T I MEET YOU IN MEMPHIS?...
THIS IS SOOOO NOT GOOD... IN SUCH A GOOD WAY...
PAIGE

JANE SHOWS UP, JUST AS DIXIE'S MEMORY COME'S RUSHING BACK...

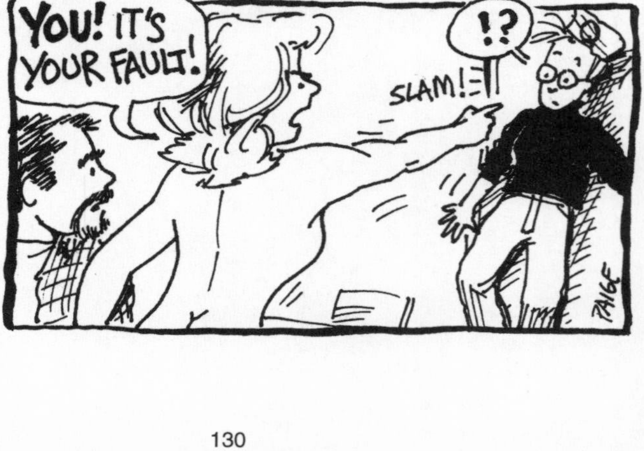
YOU! IT'S YOUR FAULT!
!?
SLAM!
PAIGE

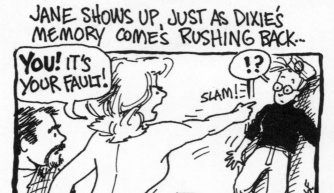

YOU TURNED ME INTO A CHIMP...AARGH!!

POUNCE!

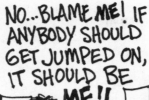

NO...BLAME ME! IF ANYBODY SHOULD GET JUMPED ON, IT SHOULD BE ME!!

DOROTHY, THINK-ING THAT THE LOVE NEST IS STILL HER DOMAIN, STOPS BY WITH A FROZEN, DAIRY TREAT FOR HER RECENTLY REDIS-COVERED BOYFRIEND...

HEY! I JUST STOPPED BY WITH SOME ICE CREAM... I THOUGHT YOU MIGHT LIKE...

THANKS.

!?

EXCUSE ME... WHO ARE YOU AND WHY ARE YOU WEARING MY BOYFRIEND'S SHIRT?!

PAIGE

SLAM

BE HAPPY...TEN MINUTES AGO SHE WASN'T EVEN WEARING THAT...

OH NOoo...

THINKING THIS IS ALL SOMEHOW JANE'S FAULT, AND FOLLOWING THE TRIED AND TRUE TECHNIQUE OF PUNCH FIRST, ASK QUESTIONS LATER, DOROTHY IS ABOUT TO PUMMEL JANE....

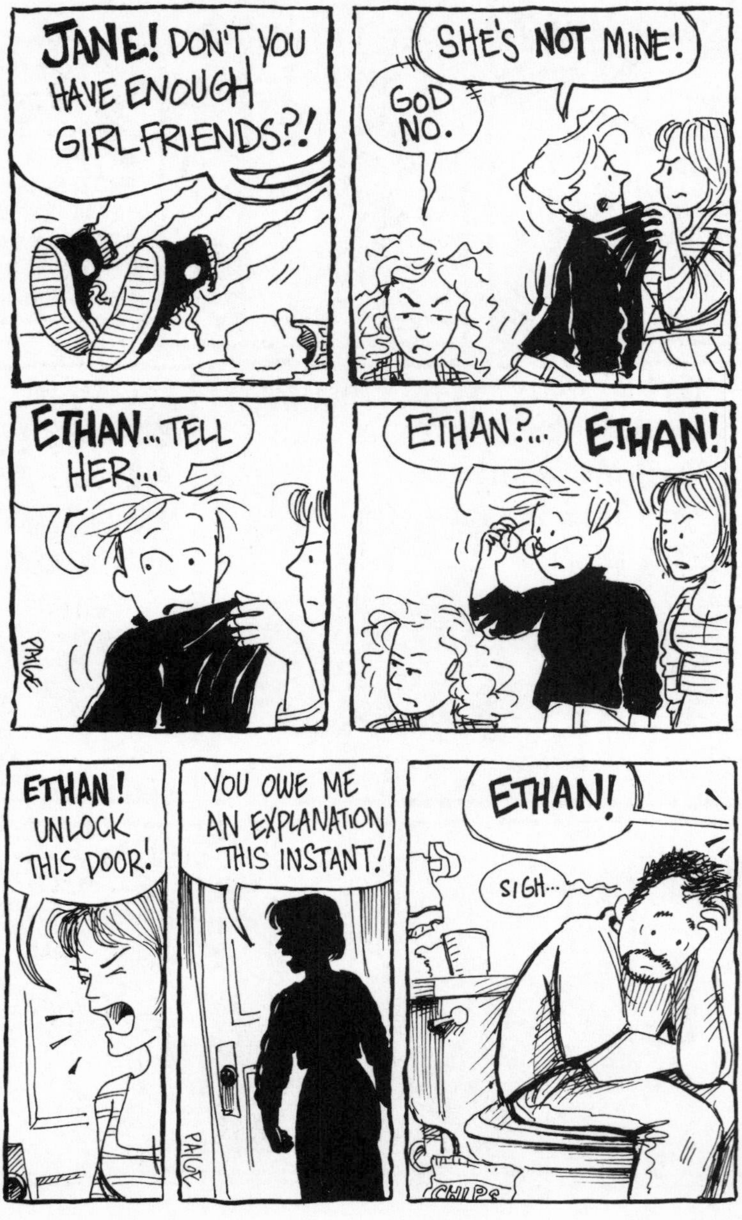
JANE! DON'T YOU HAVE ENOUGH GIRLFRIENDS?!
SHE'S NOT MINE!
GOD NO.
ETHAN... TELL HER...
PAIGE
ETHAN?...
ETHAN!
ETHAN! UNLOCK THIS DOOR!
YOU OWE ME AN EXPLANATION THIS INSTANT!
PAIGE
ETHAN!
SIGH...
CHIPS

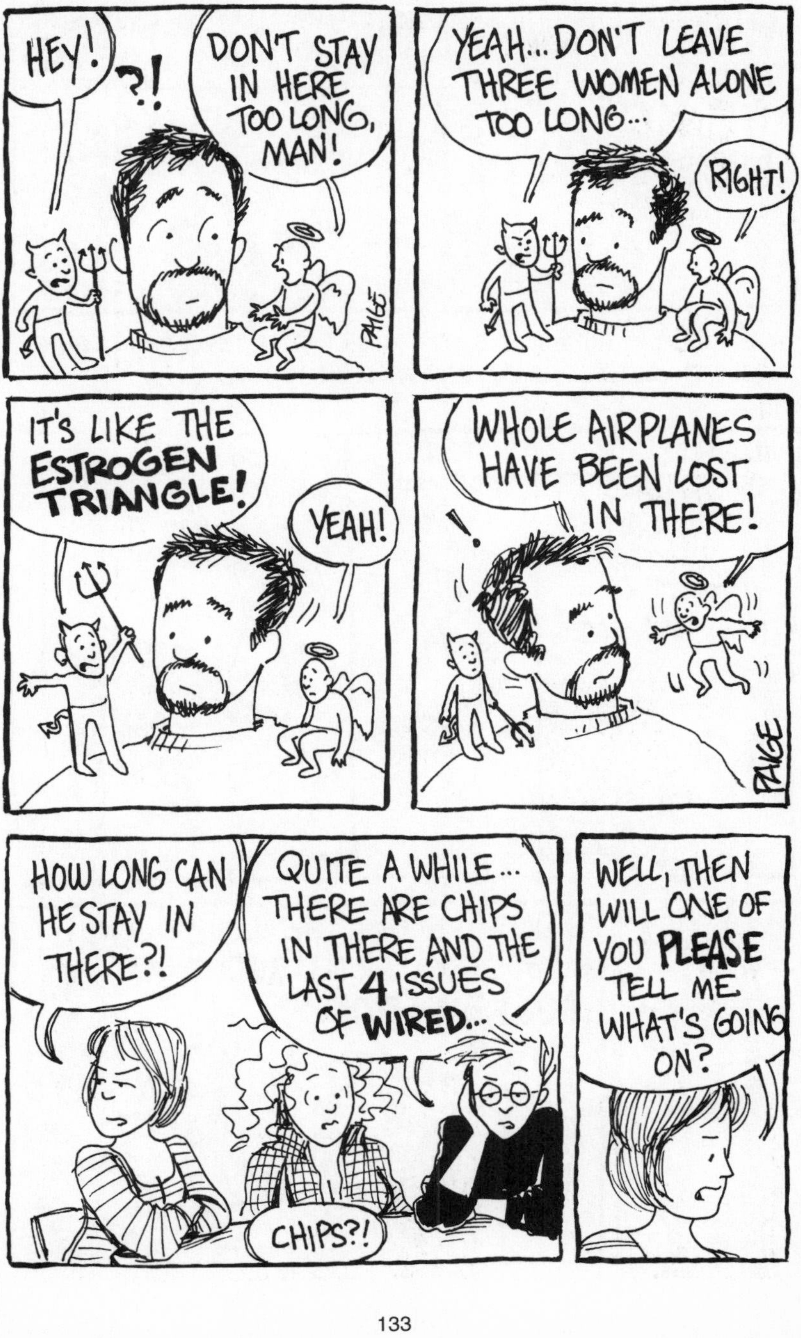
HEY!
?!
DON'T STAY IN HERE TOO LONG, MAN!
PAIGE
YEAH... DON'T LEAVE THREE WOMEN ALONE TOO LONG...
RIGHT!
IT'S LIKE THE **ESTROGEN TRIANGLE!**
YEAH!
WHOLE AIRPLANES HAVE BEEN LOST IN THERE!
!
PAIGE
HOW LONG CAN HE STAY IN THERE?!
QUITE A WHILE... THERE ARE CHIPS IN THERE AND THE LAST **4** ISSUES OF **WIRED**...
CHIPS?!
WELL, THEN WILL ONE OF YOU **PLEASE** TELL ME WHAT'S GOING ON?

WHO ARE YOU ANYWAY? **AND** COULD YOUR HAIR BE **ANY** BIGGER?!
BIG? AT LEAST IT AIN'T **THAT** STRINGY MESS...
... IT ALL STARTED WHEN DIXIE AND I GOT SUCKED UP INTO THE SPACE SHIP AND...
PAIGE

JANE EXPLAINS THE WHOLE STORY (SEE CHAPTER THREE) AND CONVINCES ETHAN TO COME OUT AND FACE THE TRUTH...

NOW, SEE? WAS THAT SO HARD? WHY COULDN'T YOU JUST TELL ME THE TRUTH IN THE FIRST PLACE?
I DIDN'T THINK YOU'D BELIEVE ME...
... DO YOU?
PAIGE
DO I BELIEVE YOU?...
I DON'T KNOW!... THE NAKED WOMAN IN YOUR KITCHEN **USED TO BE A MONKEY FROM OUTER SPACE?!**
SHE'S FROM MEMPHIS.

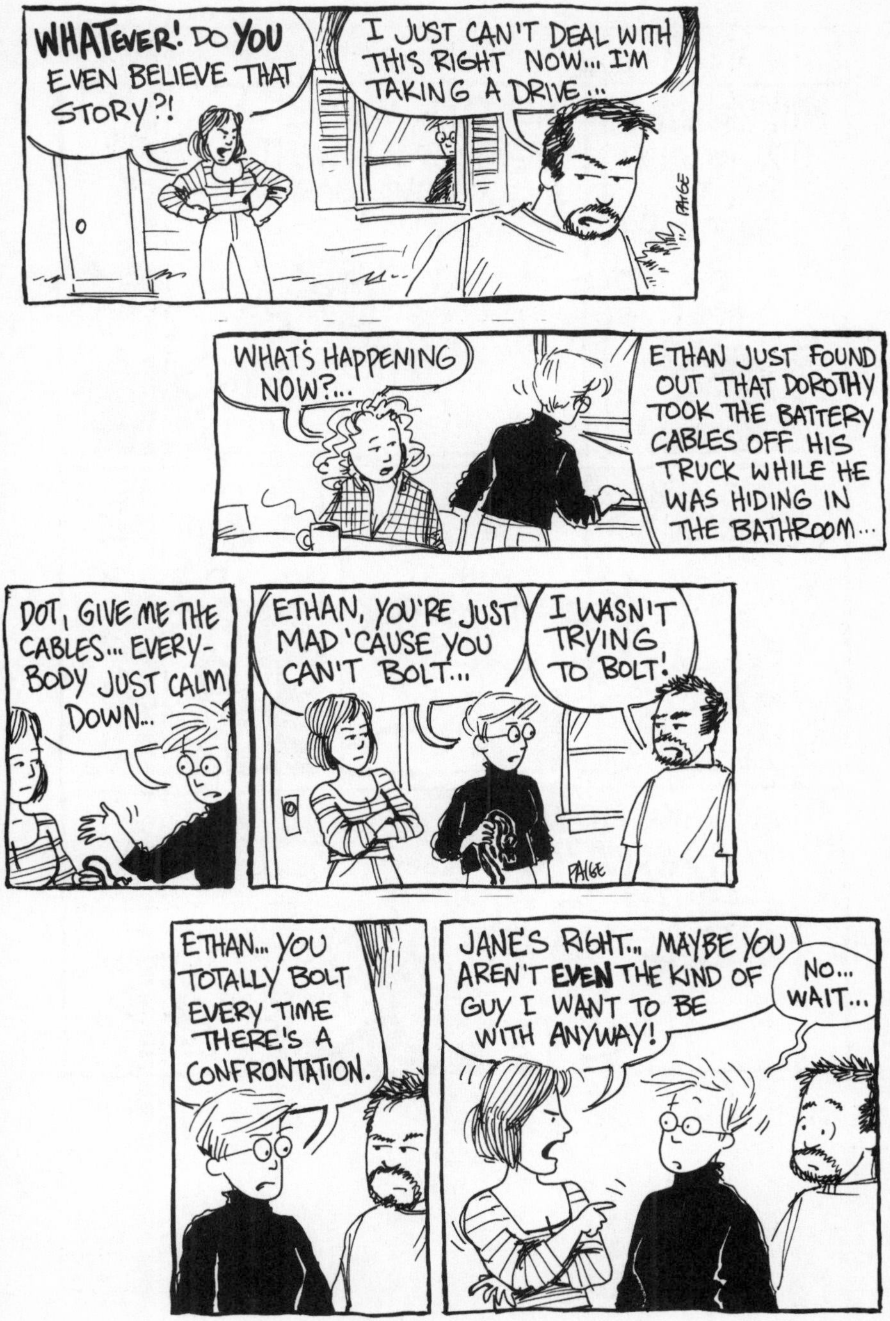
WHATever! DO YOU EVEN BELIEVE THAT STORY?!
I JUST CAN'T DEAL WITH THIS RIGHT NOW... I'M TAKING A DRIVE...
PAIGE
WHAT'S HAPPENING NOW?...
ETHAN JUST FOUND OUT THAT DOROTHY TOOK THE BATTERY CABLES OFF HIS TRUCK WHILE HE WAS HIDING IN THE BATHROOM...
DOT, GIVE ME THE CABLES... EVERY-BODY JUST CALM DOWN...
ETHAN, YOU'RE JUST MAD 'CAUSE YOU CAN'T BOLT...
I WASN'T TRYING TO BOLT!
PAIGE
ETHAN... YOU TOTALLY BOLT EVERY TIME THERE'S A CONFRONTATION.
JANE'S RIGHT... MAYBE YOU AREN'T EVEN THE KIND OF GUY I WANT TO BE WITH ANYWAY!
NO... WAIT...

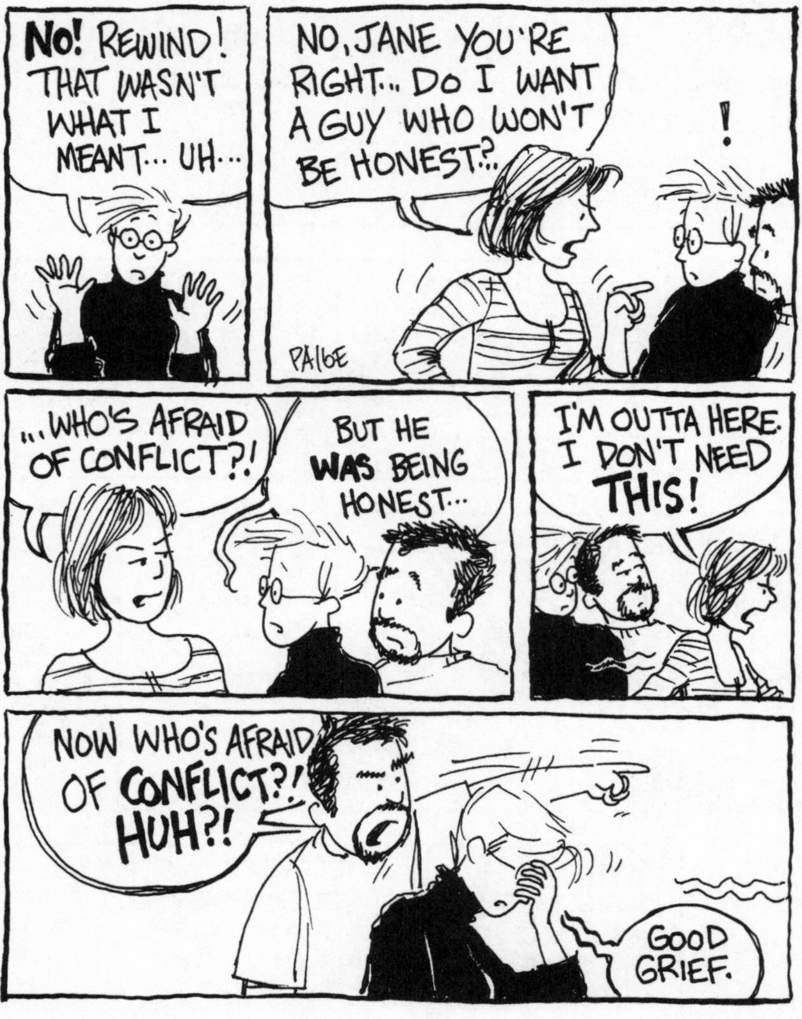
NO! REWIND! THAT WASN'T WHAT I MEANT... UH...
NO, JANE YOU'RE RIGHT... DO I WANT A GUY WHO WON'T BE HONEST?..
!
PAIGE
...WHO'S AFRAID OF CONFLICT?!
BUT HE WAS BEING HONEST...
I'M OUTTA HERE. I DON'T NEED THIS!
NOW WHO'S AFRAID OF CONFLICT?! HUH?!
GOOD GRIEF.

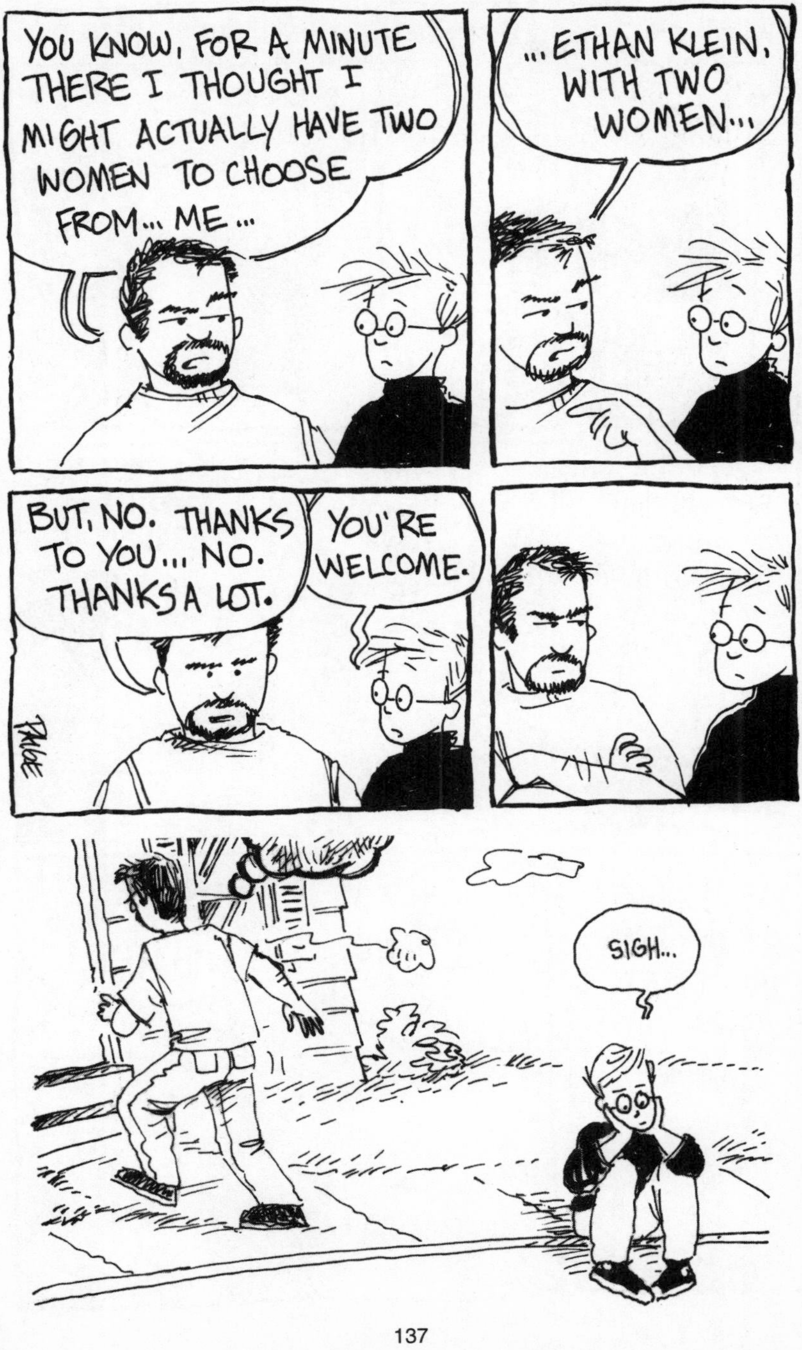
YOU KNOW, FOR A MINUTE THERE I THOUGHT I MIGHT ACTUALLY HAVE TWO WOMEN TO CHOOSE FROM... ME...
...ETHAN KLEIN, WITH TWO WOMEN...
BUT, NO. THANKS TO YOU... NO. THANKS A LOT.
YOU'RE WELCOME.
SIGH...

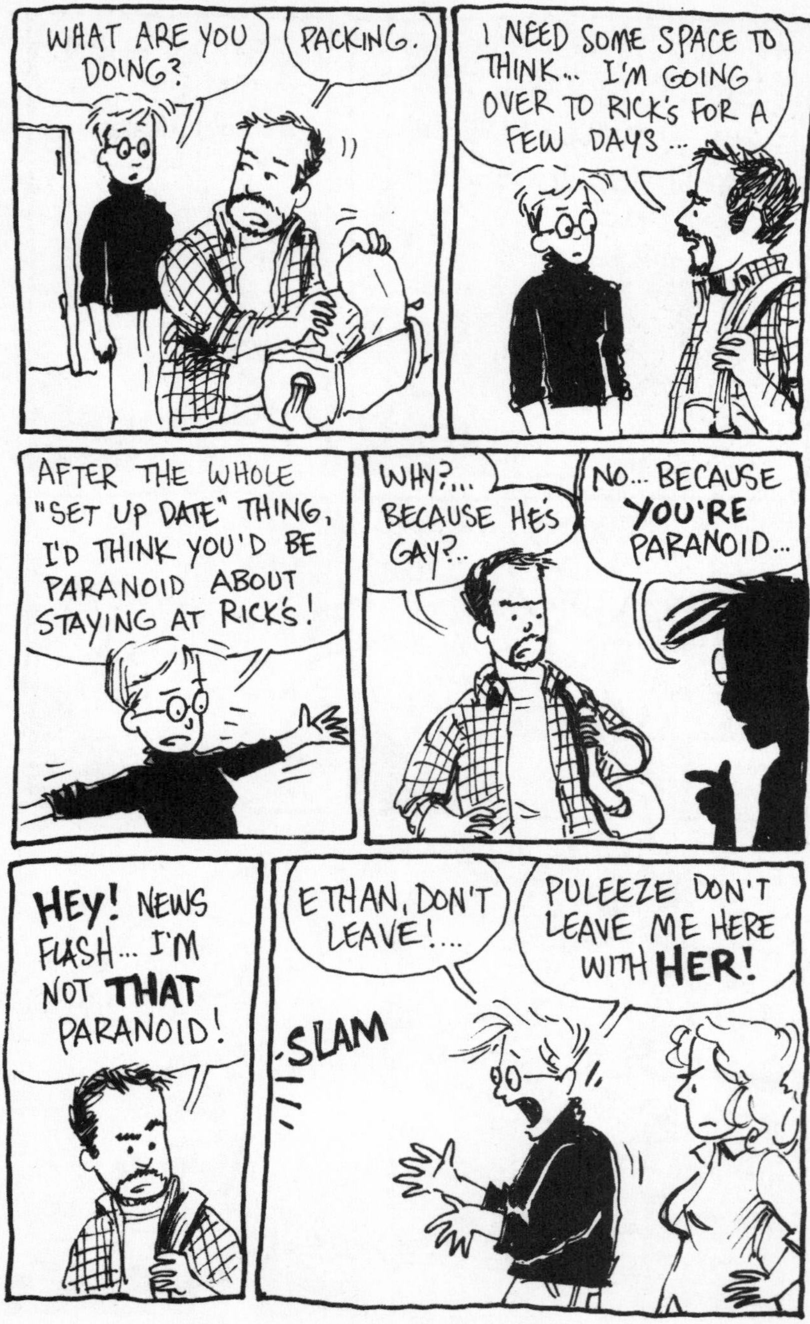
WHAT ARE YOU DOING?
PACKING.
I NEED SOME SPACE TO THINK... I'M GOING OVER TO RICK'S FOR A FEW DAYS ...
AFTER THE WHOLE "SET UP DATE" THING, I'D THINK YOU'D BE PARANOID ABOUT STAYING AT RICK'S!
WHY?... BECAUSE HE'S GAY?...
NO... BECAUSE **YOU'RE** PARANOID...
HEY! NEWS FLASH... I'M NOT **THAT** PARANOID!
SLAM
ETHAN, DON'T LEAVE!...
PULEEZE DON'T LEAVE ME HERE WITH **HER!**

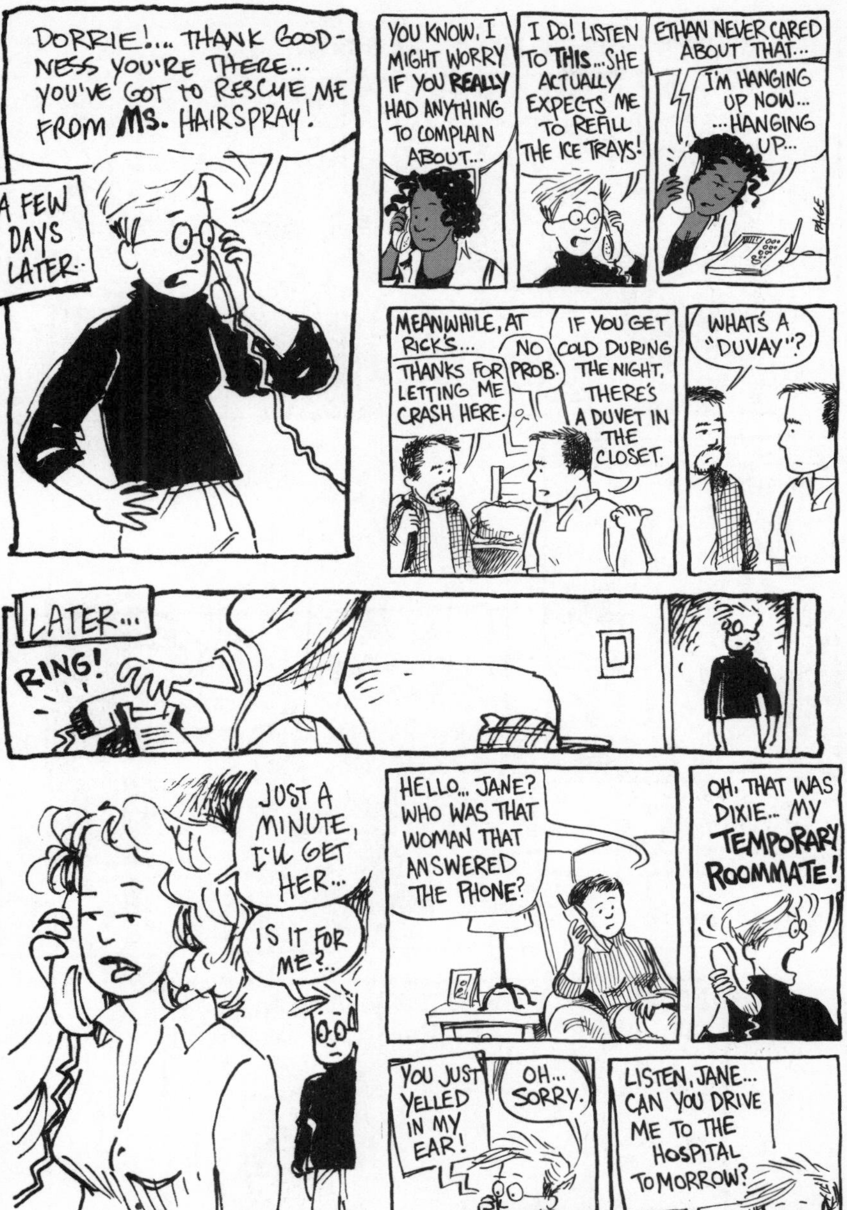
A FEW DAYS LATER..
DORRIE!... THANK GOODNESS YOU'RE THERE... YOU'VE GOT TO RESCUE ME FROM MS. HAIRSPRAY!
YOU KNOW, I MIGHT WORRY IF YOU REALLY HAD ANYTHING TO COMPLAIN ABOUT...
I DO! LISTEN TO THIS...SHE ACTUALLY EXPECTS ME TO REFILL THE ICE TRAYS!
ETHAN NEVER CARED ABOUT THAT...
I'M HANGING UP NOW... ...HANGING UP...
PAIGE
MEANWHILE, AT RICK'S...
THANKS FOR LETTING ME CRASH HERE.
NO PROB.
IF YOU GET COLD DURING THE NIGHT, THERE'S A DUVET IN THE CLOSET.
WHAT'S A "DUVAY"?
LATER...
RING!
JUST A MINUTE, I'LL GET HER...
IS IT FOR ME?...
HELLO... JANE? WHO WAS THAT WOMAN THAT ANSWERED THE PHONE?
OH, THAT WAS DIXIE... MY TEMPORARY ROOMMATE!
YOU JUST YELLED IN MY EAR!
OH... SORRY.
LISTEN, JANE... CAN YOU DRIVE ME TO THE HOSPITAL TOMORROW?
PAIGE

JANE PROCESSES THE PHONE CALL WITH ARCHIE...

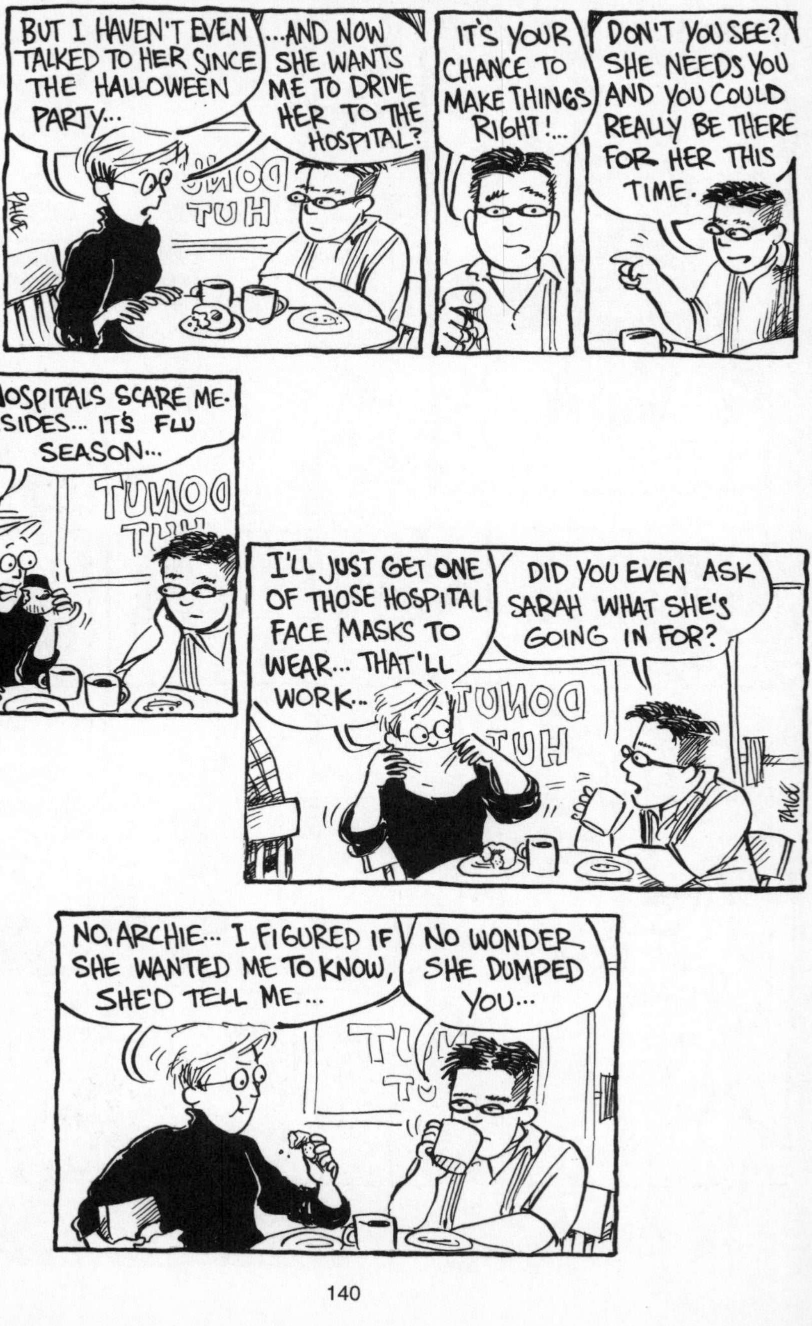

BUT I HAVEN'T EVEN TALKED TO HER SINCE THE HALLOWEEN PARTY...
...AND NOW SHE WANTS ME TO DRIVE HER TO THE HOSPITAL?
IT'S YOUR CHANCE TO MAKE THINGS RIGHT!...
DON'T YOU SEE? SHE NEEDS YOU AND YOU COULD REALLY BE THERE FOR HER THIS TIME.
BUT HOSPITALS SCARE ME. ... BESIDES... IT'S FLU SEASON...
I'LL JUST GET ONE OF THOSE HOSPITAL FACE MASKS TO WEAR... THAT'LL WORK...
DID YOU EVEN ASK SARAH WHAT SHE'S GOING IN FOR?
NO, ARCHIE... I FIGURED IF SHE WANTED ME TO KNOW, SHE'D TELL ME...
NO WONDER SHE DUMPED YOU...

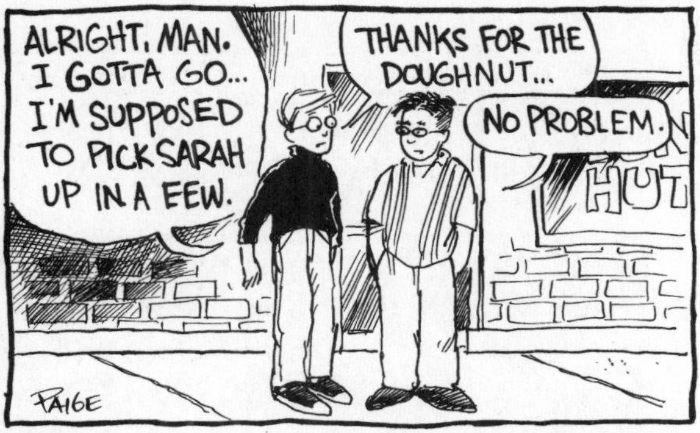
ALRIGHT, MAN. I GOTTA GO... I'M SUPPOSED TO PICK SARAH UP IN A FEW.
THANKS FOR THE DOUGHNUT...
NO PROBLEM.
HUT
PAIGE

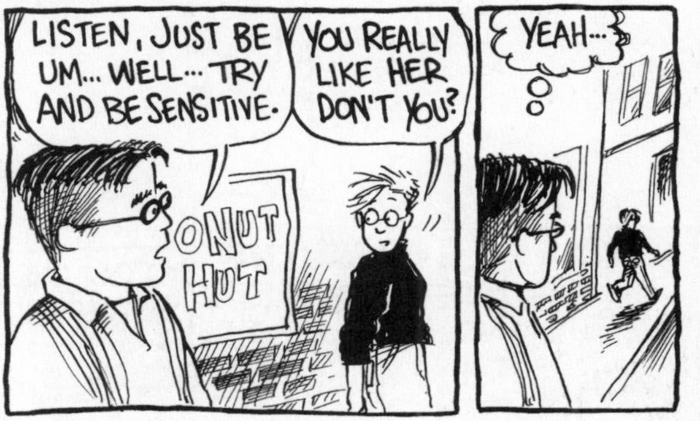
LISTEN, JUST BE UM... WELL... TRY AND BE SENSITIVE.
ONUT HUT
YOU REALLY LIKE HER DON'T YOU?
YEAH...

AT THE HOSPITAL...

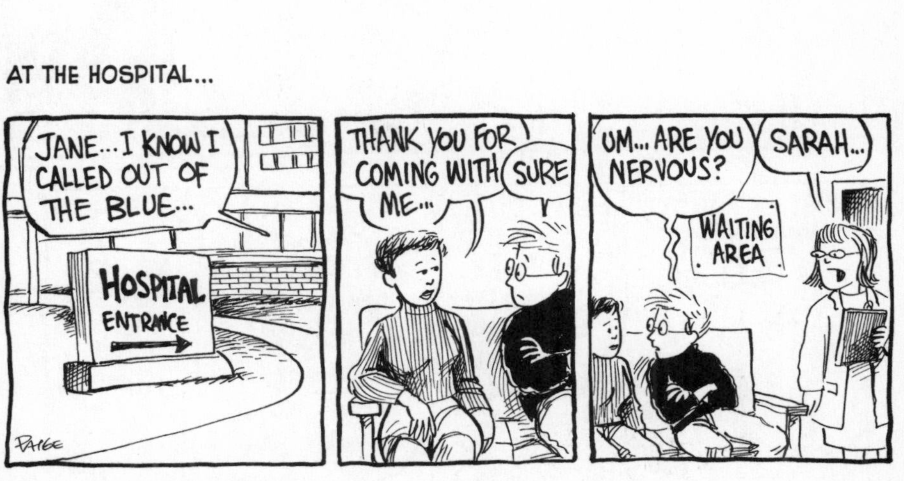
JANE... I KNOW I CALLED OUT OF THE BLUE...
HOSPITAL
ENTRANCE
PAIGE
THANK YOU FOR COMING WITH ME...
SURE
UM... ARE YOU NERVOUS?
SARAH...
WAITING AREA

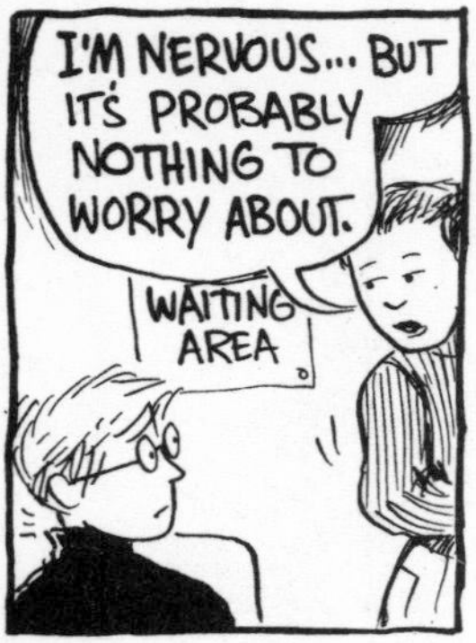
I'M NERVOUS... BUT IT'S PROBABLY NOTHING TO WORRY ABOUT.
WAITING AREA

JANE WAITS FOR WORD, WHILE ACROSS TOWN ETHAN GETS A TASTE OF WHAT IT'S LIKE TO LIVE WITH A GUY IN TOUCH WITH HIS FEMININE SIDE...

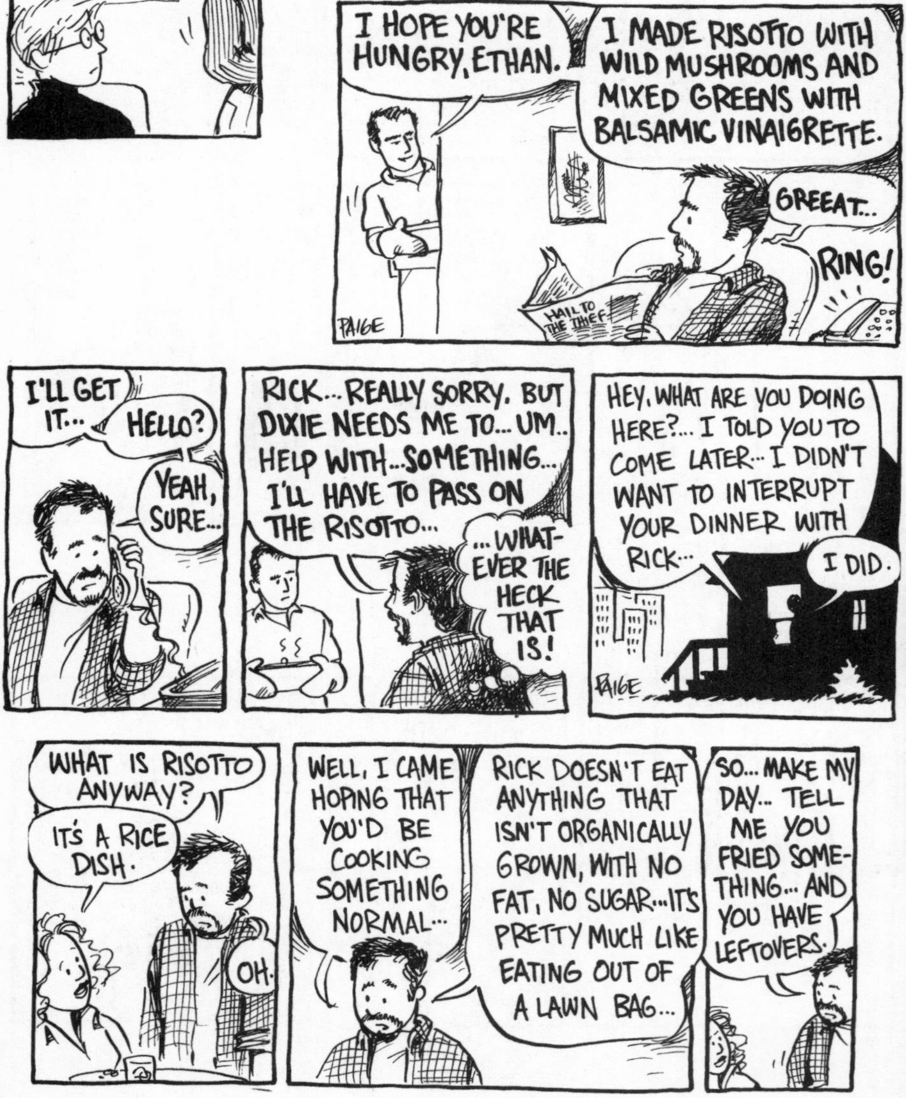
I HOPE YOU'RE HUNGRY, ETHAN.
I MADE RISOTTO WITH WILD MUSHROOMS AND MIXED GREENS WITH BALSAMIC VINAIGRETTE.
GREEAT...
RING!
HAIL TO THE THIEF
PAIGE
I'LL GET IT...
HELLO?
YEAH, SURE...
RICK... REALLY SORRY. BUT DIXIE NEEDS ME TO... UM.. HELP WITH...SOMETHING... I'LL HAVE TO PASS ON THE RISOTTO...
...WHAT-EVER THE HECK THAT IS!
HEY, WHAT ARE YOU DOING HERE?... I TOLD YOU TO COME LATER... I DIDN'T WANT TO INTERRUPT YOUR DINNER WITH RICK...
I DID.
PAIGE
WHAT IS RISOTTO ANYWAY?
IT'S A RICE DISH.
OH.
WELL, I CAME HOPING THAT YOU'D BE COOKING SOMETHING NORMAL...
RICK DOESN'T EAT ANYTHING THAT ISN'T ORGANICALLY GROWN, WITH NO FAT, NO SUGAR...IT'S PRETTY MUCH LIKE EATING OUT OF A LAWN BAG...
SO... MAKE MY DAY... TELL ME YOU FRIED SOME-THING... AND YOU HAVE LEFTOVERS.

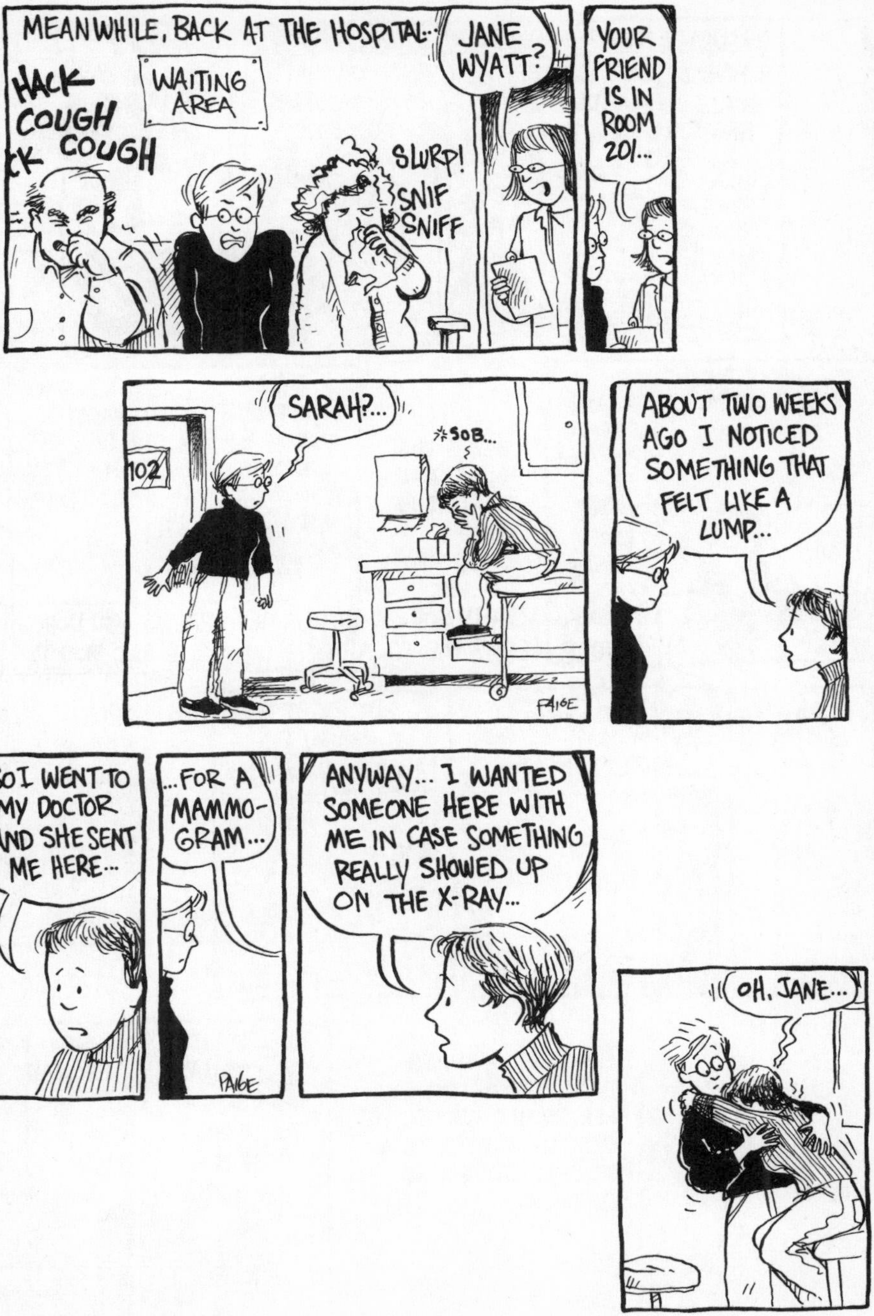

MEANWHILE, BACK AT THE HOSPITAL...
WAITING AREA
HACK
COUGH
COUGH
SLURP!
SNIF
SNIFF
JANE WYATT?
YOUR FRIEND IS IN ROOM 201...
SARAH?...
SOB...
102
PAIGE
ABOUT TWO WEEKS AGO I NOTICED SOMETHING THAT FELT LIKE A LUMP...
SO I WENT TO MY DOCTOR AND SHE SENT ME HERE...
...FOR A MAMMOGRAM...
PAIGE
ANYWAY... I WANTED SOMEONE HERE WITH ME IN CASE SOMETHING REALLY SHOWED UP ON THE X-RAY...
OH, JANE...

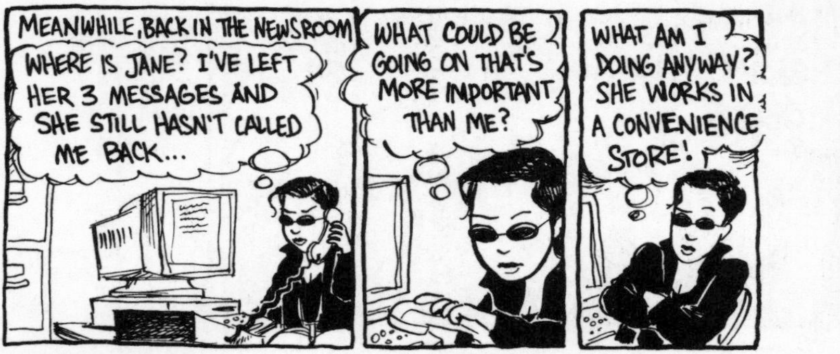
MEANWHILE, BACK IN THE NEWSROOM
WHERE IS JANE? I'VE LEFT HER 3 MESSAGES AND SHE STILL HASN'T CALLED ME BACK...
WHAT COULD BE GOING ON THAT'S MORE IMPORTANT THAN ME?
WHAT AM I DOING ANYWAY? SHE WORKS IN A CONVENIENCE STORE!

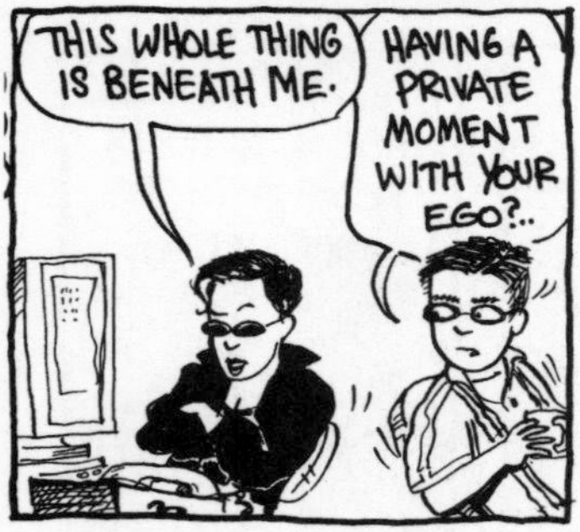
THIS WHOLE THING IS BENEATH ME.
HAVING A PRIVATE MOMENT WITH YOUR EGO?..

BEING THE GOOD PAL THAT HE IS, ARCHIE STOPS BY TO ASK AFTER SARAH...

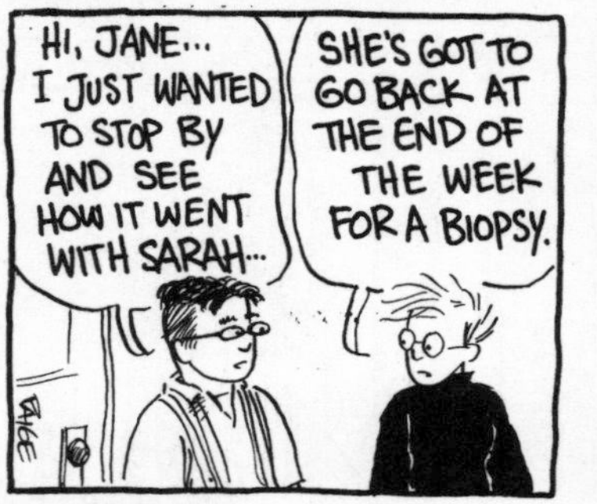
HI, JANE... I JUST WANTED TO STOP BY AND SEE HOW IT WENT WITH SARAH...
SHE'S GOT TO GO BACK AT THE END OF THE WEEK FOR A BIOPSY.
PAIGE

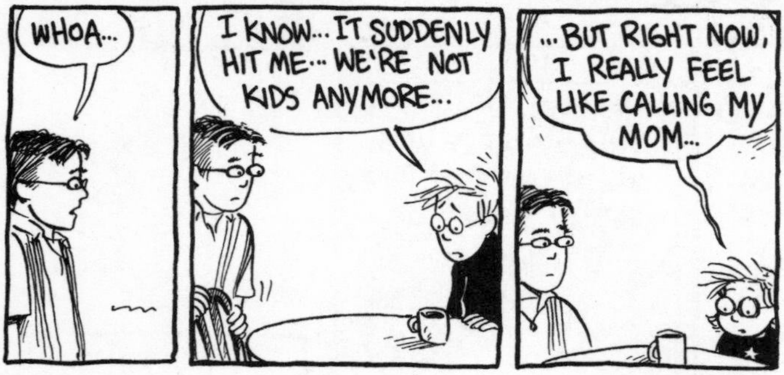
WHOA...
I KNOW... IT SUDDENLY HIT ME... WE'RE NOT KIDS ANYMORE...
...BUT RIGHT NOW, I REALLY FEEL LIKE CALLING MY MOM...

THE NEXT MORNING JANE STOPS FOR COFFEE ON HER WAY TO THE QUICKI-MART. IT'S A DOUBLE LATTE KIND OF DAY...

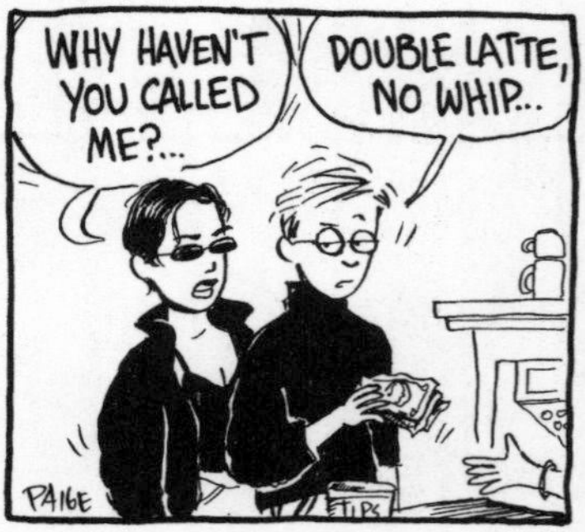
WHY HAVEN'T YOU CALLED ME?...
DOUBLE LATTE, NO WHIP...
PAIGE
TIPS

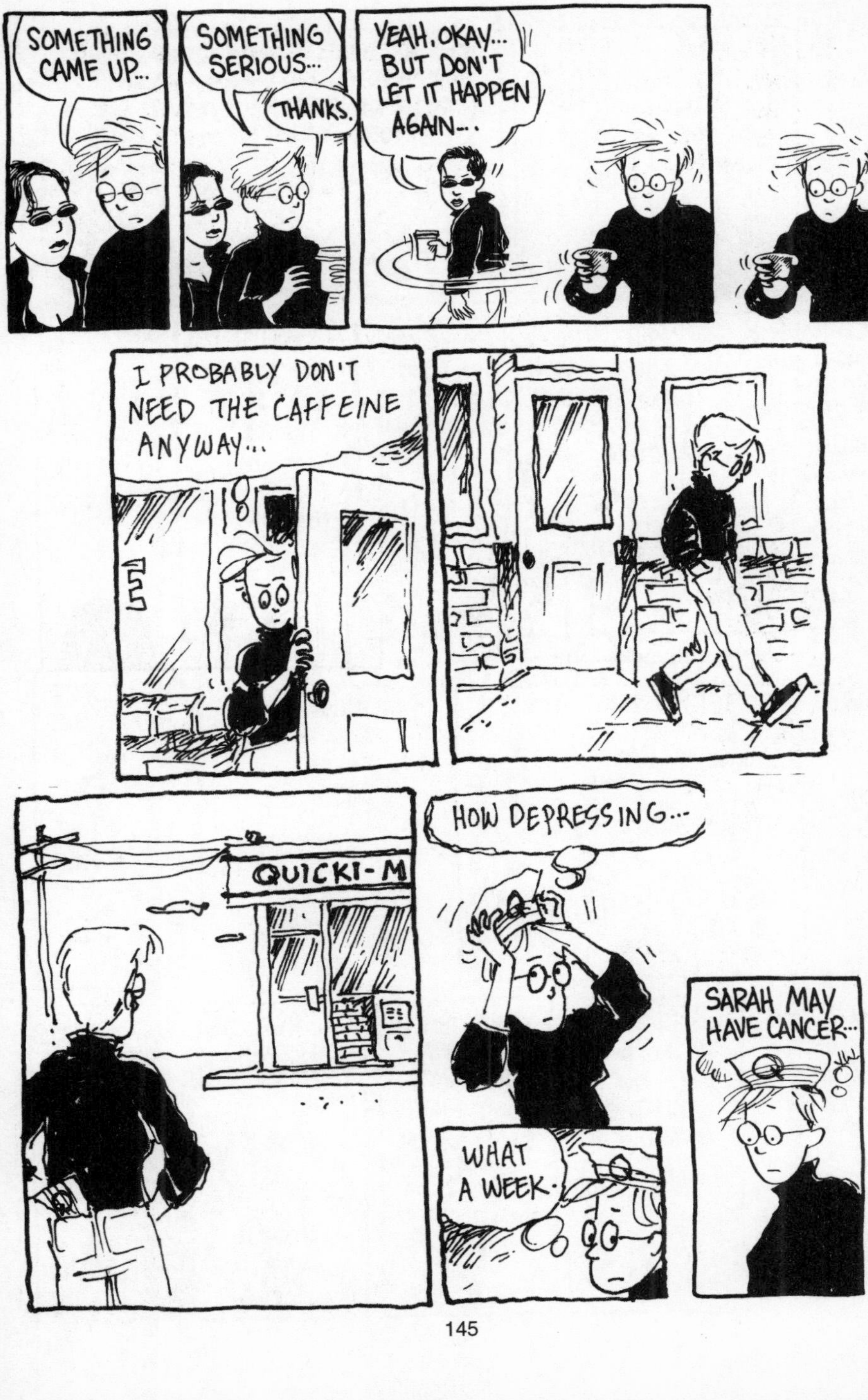
SOMETHING CAME UP...
SOMETHING SERIOUS...
THANKS.
YEAH, OKAY... BUT DON'T LET IT HAPPEN AGAIN...
I PROBABLY DON'T NEED THE CAFFEINE ANYWAY...
QUICKI-M
HOW DEPRESSING...
WHAT A WEEK.
SARAH MAY HAVE CANCER...

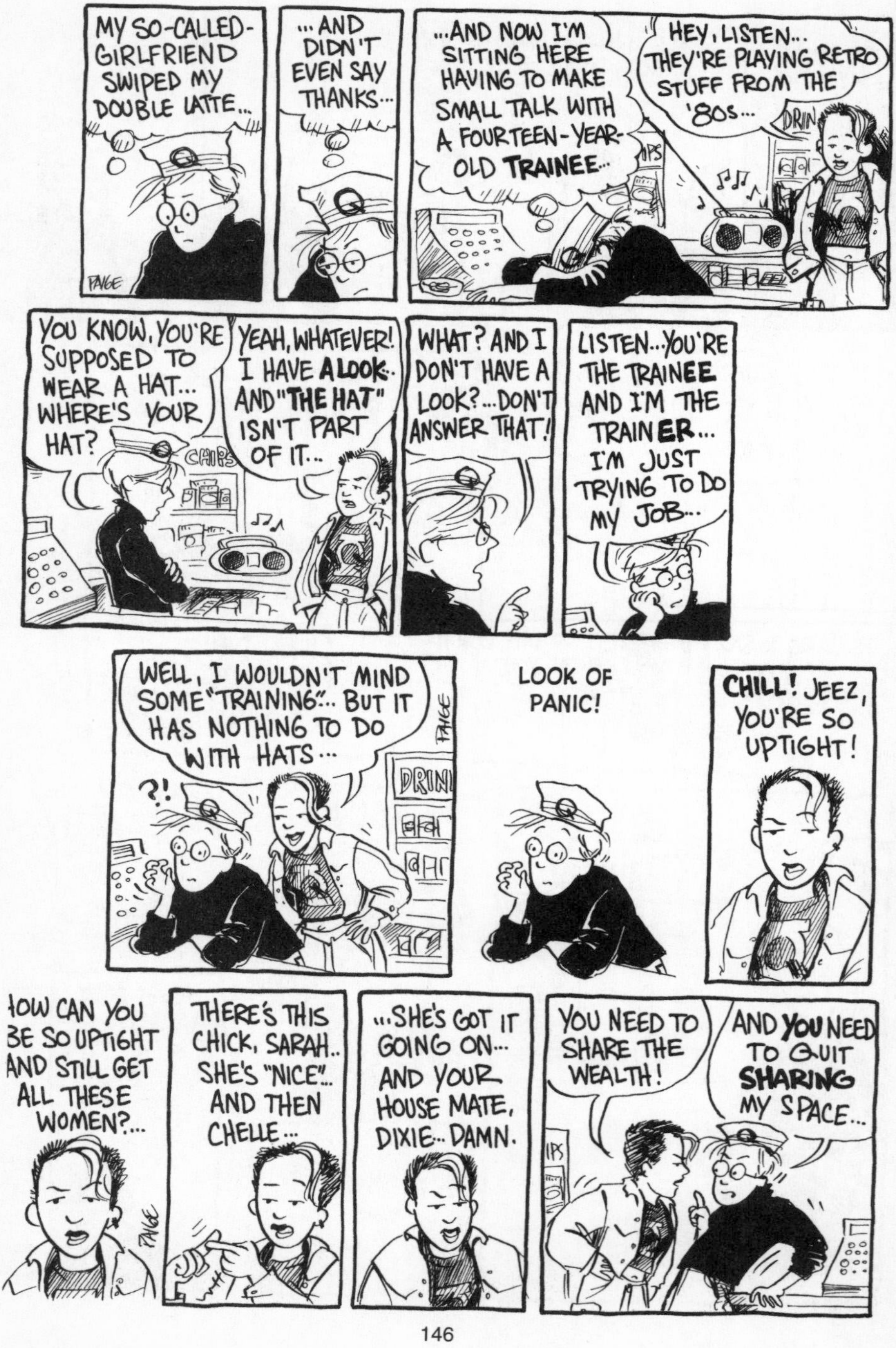

MY SO-CALLED-GIRLFRIEND SWIPED MY DOUBLE LATTE...
PAIGE
...AND DIDN'T EVEN SAY THANKS...
...AND NOW I'M SITTING HERE HAVING TO MAKE SMALL TALK WITH A FOURTEEN-YEAR-OLD **TRAINEE**...
HEY, LISTEN... THEY'RE PLAYING RETRO STUFF FROM THE '80S...
DRIN
IPS
YOU KNOW, YOU'RE SUPPOSED TO WEAR A HAT... WHERE'S YOUR HAT?
YEAH, WHATEVER! I HAVE **A LOOK**... AND "**THE HAT**" ISN'T PART OF IT...
CHIPS
WHAT? AND I DON'T HAVE A LOOK?...DON'T ANSWER THAT!
LISTEN...YOU'RE THE TRAIN**EE** AND I'M THE TRAIN**ER**... I'M JUST TRYING TO DO MY JOB...
WELL, I WOULDN'T MIND SOME "TRAINING"... BUT IT HAS NOTHING TO DO WITH HATS...
PAIGE
?!
DRINI
LOOK OF PANIC!
CHILL! JEEZ, YOU'RE SO UPTIGHT!
HOW CAN YOU BE SO UPTIGHT AND STILL GET ALL THESE WOMEN?...
PAIGE
THERE'S THIS CHICK, SARAH.. SHE'S "NICE"... AND THEN CHELLE...
...SHE'S GOT IT GOING ON... AND YOUR HOUSE MATE, DIXIE... DAMN.
YOU NEED TO SHARE THE WEALTH!
AND **YOU** NEED TO QUIT **SHARING** MY SPACE...
IPS

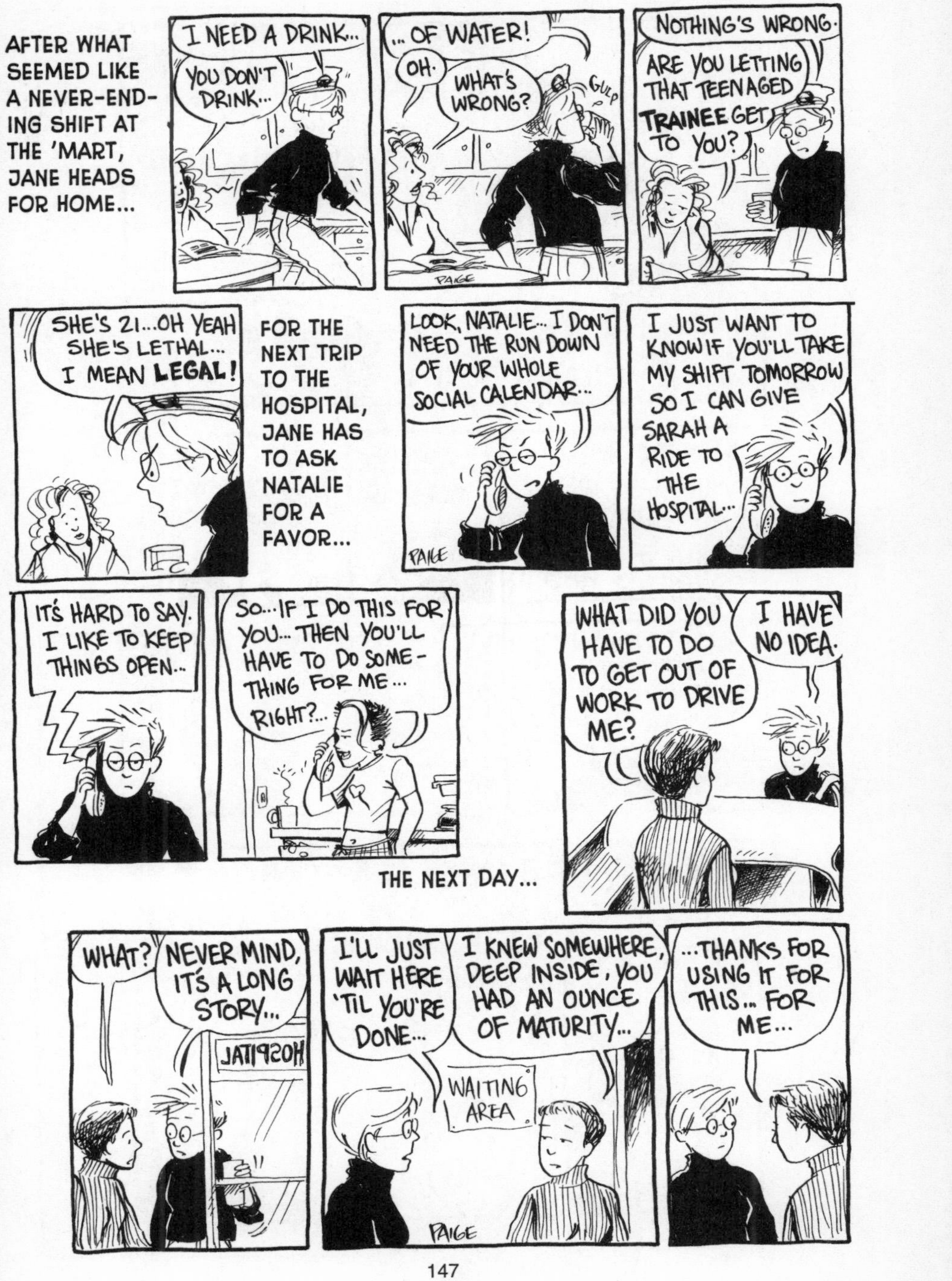
AFTER WHAT SEEMED LIKE A NEVER-ENDING SHIFT AT THE 'MART, JANE HEADS FOR HOME...
I NEED A DRINK...
YOU DON'T DRINK...
... OF WATER!
OH.
WHAT'S WRONG?
GULP
PAIGE
NOTHING'S WRONG.
ARE YOU LETTING THAT TEENAGED TRAINEE GET TO YOU?
SHE'S 21...OH YEAH SHE'S LETHAL... I MEAN LEGAL!
FOR THE NEXT TRIP TO THE HOSPITAL, JANE HAS TO ASK NATALIE FOR A FAVOR...
LOOK, NATALIE... I DON'T NEED THE RUN DOWN OF YOUR WHOLE SOCIAL CALENDAR...
PAIGE
I JUST WANT TO KNOW IF YOU'LL TAKE MY SHIFT TOMORROW SO I CAN GIVE SARAH A RIDE TO THE HOSPITAL...
IT'S HARD TO SAY. I LIKE TO KEEP THINGS OPEN...
SO... IF I DO THIS FOR YOU... THEN YOU'LL HAVE TO DO SOMETHING FOR ME... RIGHT?...
THE NEXT DAY...
WHAT DID YOU HAVE TO DO TO GET OUT OF WORK TO DRIVE ME?
I HAVE NO IDEA.
WHAT?
NEVER MIND, IT'S A LONG STORY...
I'LL JUST WAIT HERE 'TIL YOU'RE DONE...
WAITING AREA
I KNEW SOMEWHERE, DEEP INSIDE, YOU HAD AN OUNCE OF MATURITY...
...THANKS FOR USING IT FOR THIS... FOR ME...
PAIGE

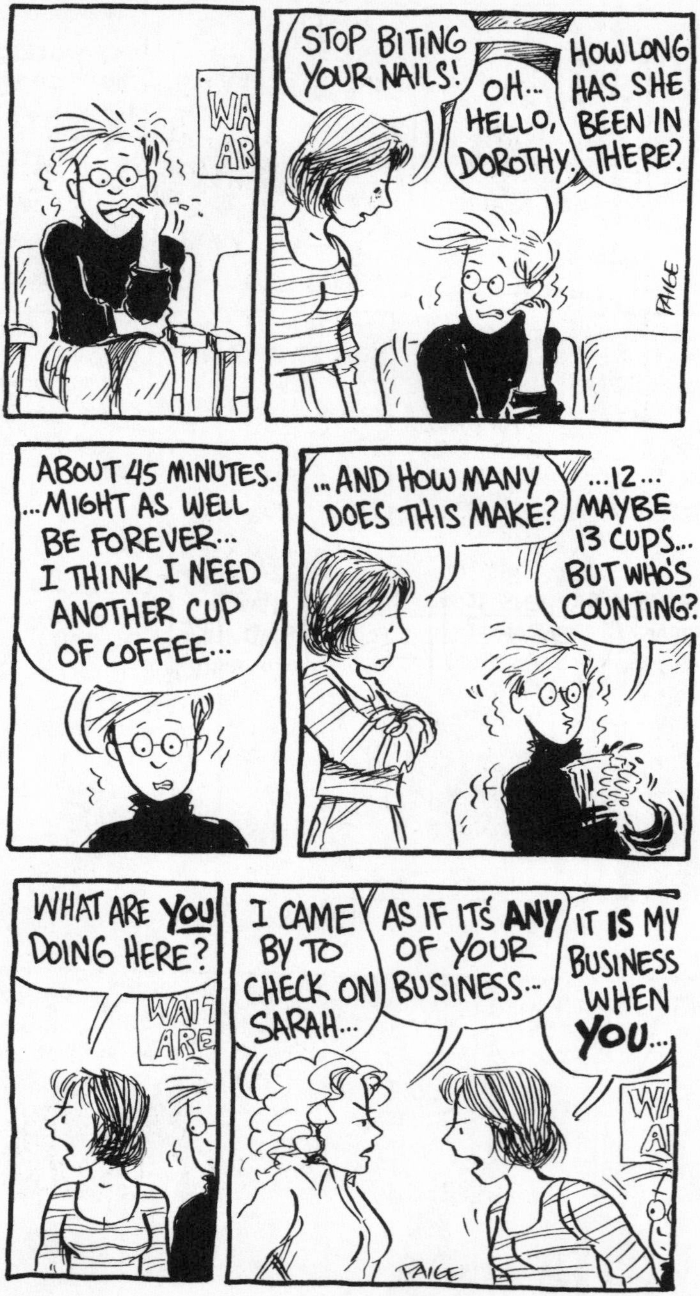

WA
AR
STOP BITING YOUR NAILS!
OH... HELLO, DOROTHY.
HOW LONG HAS SHE BEEN IN THERE?
PAIGE
ABOUT 45 MINUTES. ...MIGHT AS WELL BE FOREVER... I THINK I NEED ANOTHER CUP OF COFFEE...
...AND HOW MANY DOES THIS MAKE?
...12 ... MAYBE 13 CUPS... BUT WHO'S COUNTING?
WHAT ARE YOU DOING HERE?
WAIT ARE
I CAME BY TO CHECK ON SARAH...
AS IF ITS ANY OF YOUR BUSINESS...
IT IS MY BUSINESS WHEN YOU...
PAIGE

HEY! ENOUGH! THIS ISN'T ABOUT YOU GUYS... PUT YOUR FEUD ASIDE FOR NOW...
I THINK WE ALL KNOW WHO THIS IS REALLY ABOUT...
ME!... I'M FREAKIN' OUT! I HATE HOSPITALS!
IGNORE HER... IT'S JUST THE CAFFEINE TALKING...
YOU'RE FREAKING OUT?! GIVE ME A BREAK!
I'M SERIOUS! WHAT IF SOMETHING HAPPENS TO SARAH...?
WHAT IF SHE HAS CANCER?!
WHAT ABOUT ALL THE THINGS I HAVEN'T SAID... LIKE I'M SORRY.
I WAS A JERK WHEN WE DATED... I'VE BARELY BEEN A FRIEND SINCE...
WAITING AREA
IT HURTS TO KNOW YOU'VE BEEN SO CARELESS.
PAIGE

THE TENSION IS THICK BETWEEN DOROTHY AND DIXIE IN THE WAITING AREA... EVENTUALLY, THEY BOTH LEAVE JANE ALONE WITH HER THOUGHTS...

HEY... I THOUGHT DIXIE WAS HERE.

SHE WAS.

...BUT SO WAS DOROTHY...

OH.

SO... ANY NEWS?

NO... IT'S BEEN A COUPLE OF HOURS... ONLY TWO HOURS, AND I FEEL LIKE I'M HAVING A MELTDOWN...

I GUESS I'M NO GOOD IN A CRISIS...

WA AR

HEY... YOU'RE HERE AREN'T YOU? MOST TIMES JUST "BEING" IS GOOD ENOUGH.

HEY... IT'S THE NURSE... SHE'S COMING OUR WAY...

WAITI ARE

WHAT IF IT'S BAD NEWS?!

I CAN'T TELL BY HER EXPRESSION...

WATING AREA

PAIGE

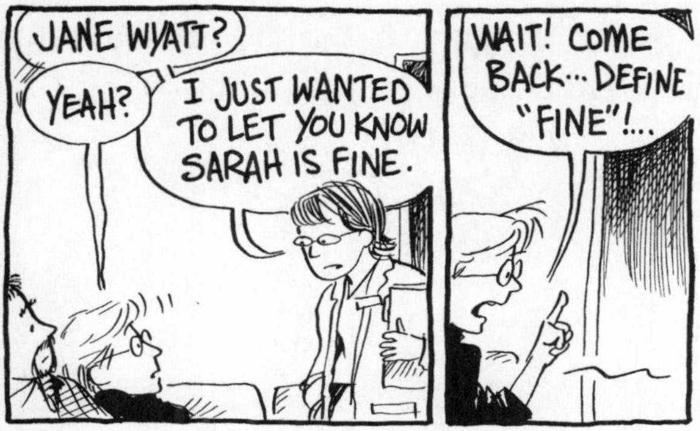
JANE WYATT?
YEAH?
I JUST WANTED TO LET YOU KNOW SARAH IS FINE.
WAIT! COME BACK... DEFINE "FINE"!...

THE CRISIS IS OVER... THE BIOPSY CAME BACK WITH GOOD NEWS... AND WHILE NONE OF THE EXPERIENCE COULD BE CLASSIFIED AS "GOOD," AT LEAST IT GOT JANE AND SARAH TALKING AGAIN... AND YOU KNOW WHAT TALKING LEADS TO... EX-GIRLFRIEND DRAMA...

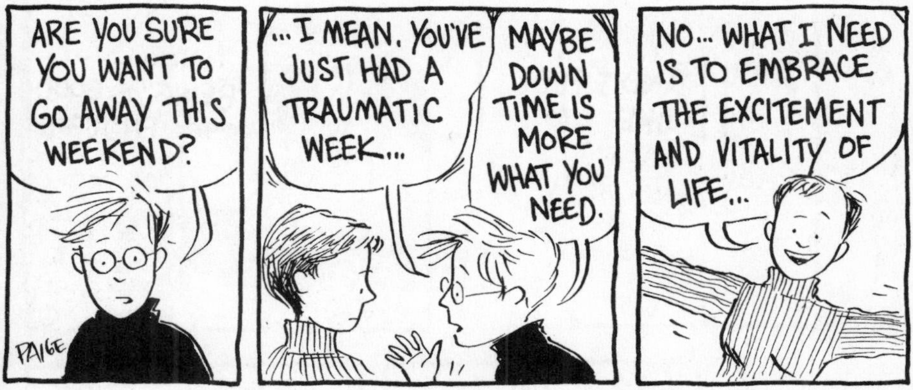
ARE YOU SURE YOU WANT TO GO AWAY THIS WEEKEND?
PAIGE
...I MEAN. YOU'VE JUST HAD A TRAUMATIC WEEK...
MAYBE DOWN TIME IS MORE WHAT YOU NEED.
NO... WHAT I NEED IS TO EMBRACE THE EXCITEMENT AND VITALITY OF LIFE...

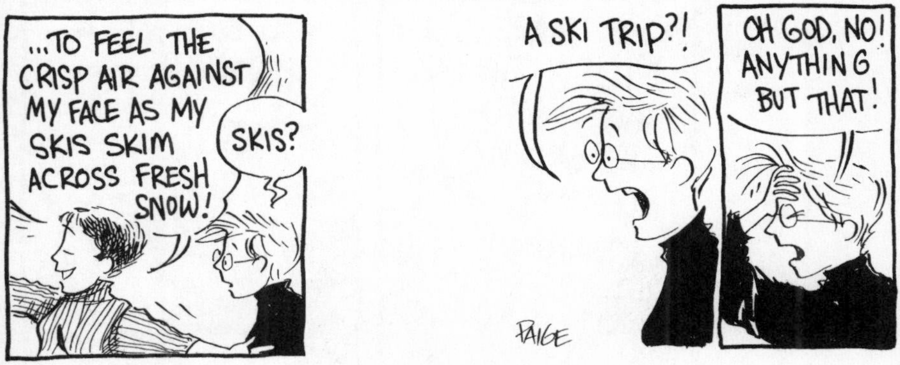
...TO FEEL THE CRISP AIR AGAINST MY FACE AS MY SKIS SKIM ACROSS FRESH SNOW!
SKIS?
A SKI TRIP?!
OH GOD, NO! ANYTHING BUT THAT!
PAIGE

REMEMBER THE CANOE TRIP? THAT WAS A TRAGIC BIT OF TOGETHERNESS!

THIS WILL BE DIFFERENT.

YEAH... FROST BITE AND BROKEN BONES!

ARE YOU CALLING CHELLE, OR AM I...?

THIS IS GOING TO BE A DISASTER! MY EX AND ME **AND** CHELLE IN A SECLUDED CABIN...

DUDE! SKI TRIP! ROCK ON...

SARAH WAS AT THE 'MART, FILLING THE TANK AND SHE SAID YOU NEEDED A FOURTH...

PAIGE

I'M GAME... BESIDES, YOU OWE ME A FAVOR...

OH, JEEZ...

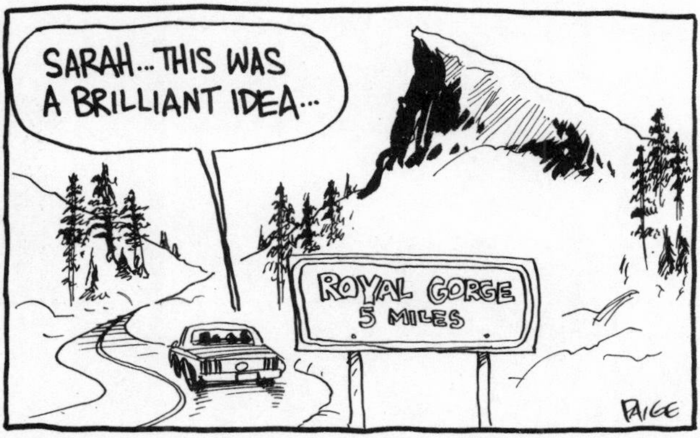
SARAH... THIS WAS A BRILLIANT IDEA...
ROYAL GORGE
5 MILES
PAIGE

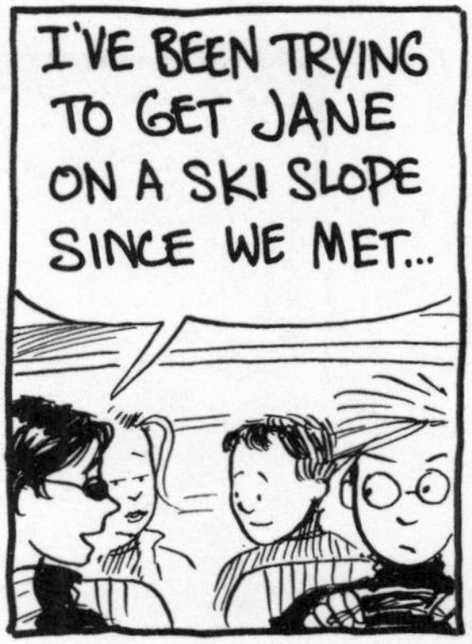
I'VE BEEN TRYING TO GET JANE ON A SKI SLOPE SINCE WE MET...

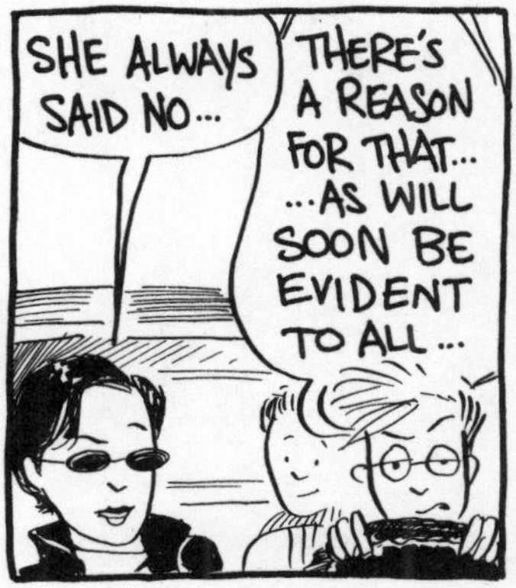
SHE ALWAYS SAID NO...
THERE'S A REASON FOR THAT... ...AS WILL SOON BE EVIDENT TO ALL...

Chapter 7

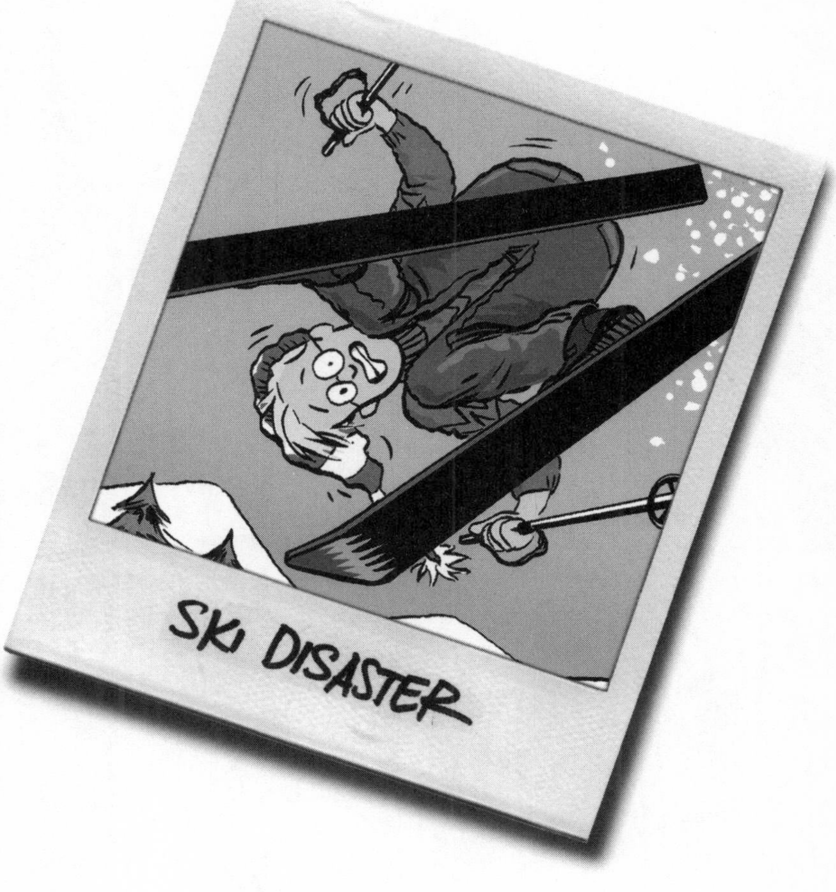
SKI DISASTER

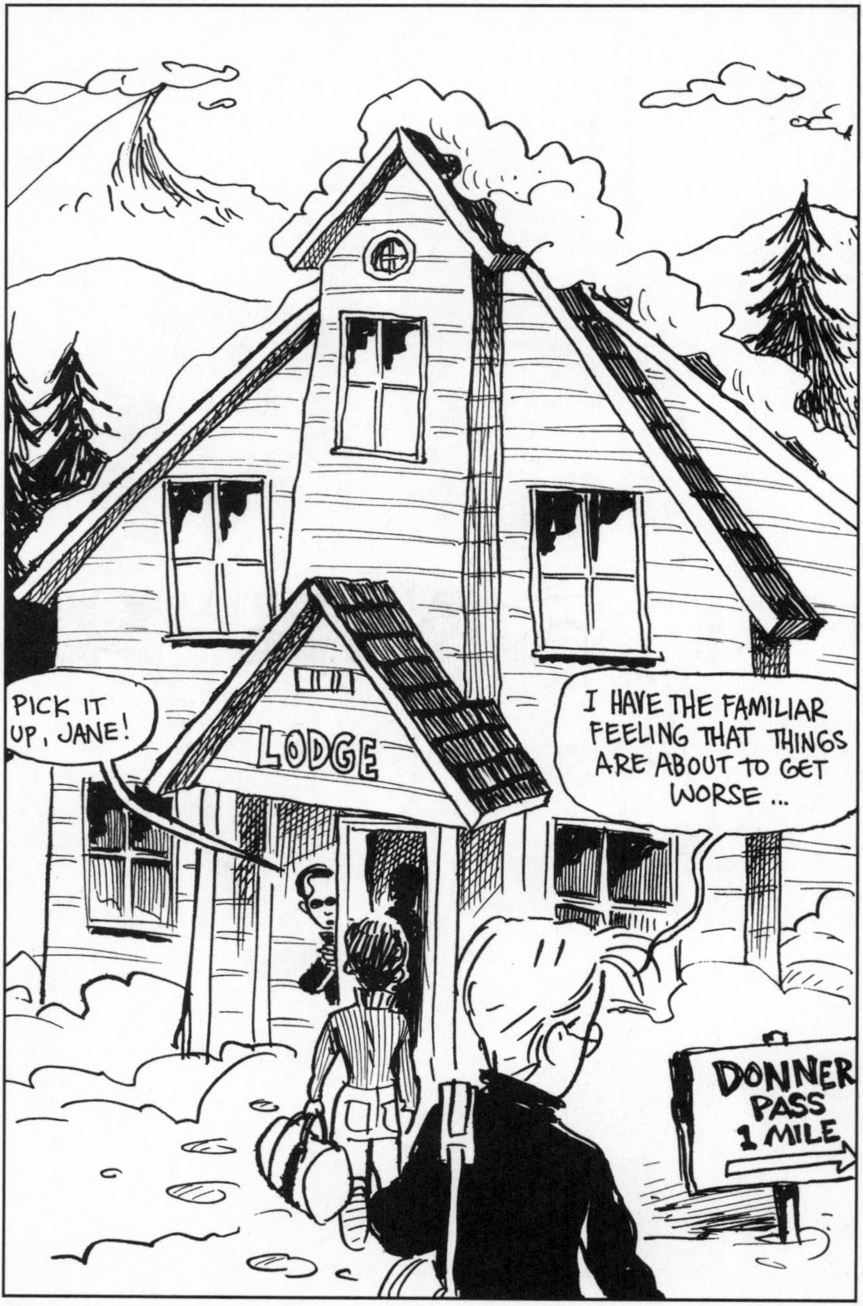
PICK IT UP, JANE!
I HAVE THE FAMILIAR FEELING THAT THINGS ARE ABOUT TO GET WORSE...
LODGE
DONNER PASS 1 MILE

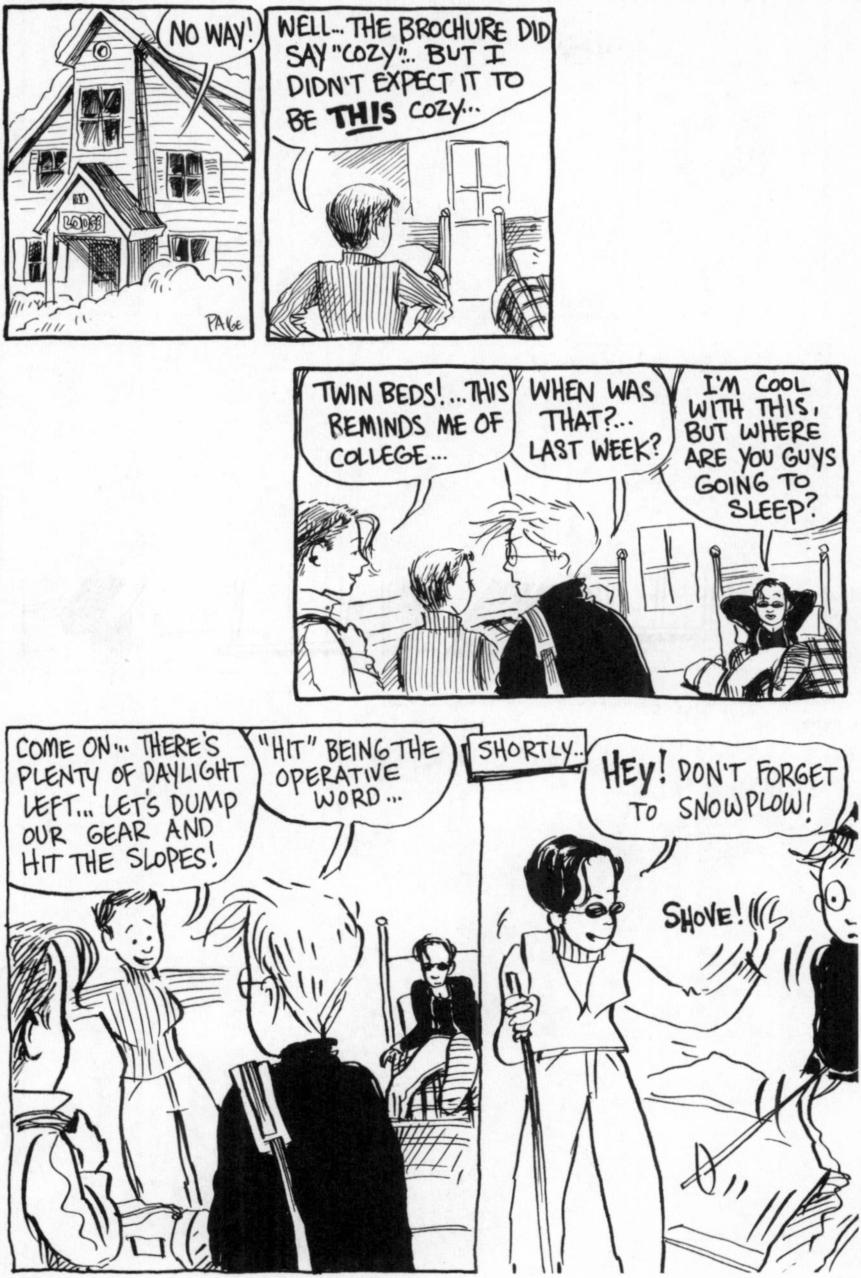
NO WAY!
PAIGE
WELL... THE BROCHURE DID SAY "COZY"... BUT I DIDN'T EXPECT IT TO BE THIS COZY...
TWIN BEDS!... THIS REMINDS ME OF COLLEGE...
WHEN WAS THAT?... LAST WEEK?
I'M COOL WITH THIS, BUT WHERE ARE YOU GUYS GOING TO SLEEP?
COME ON... THERE'S PLENTY OF DAYLIGHT LEFT... LET'S DUMP OUR GEAR AND HIT THE SLOPES!
"HIT" BEING THE OPERATIVE WORD...
SHORTLY...
HEY! DON'T FORGET TO SNOWPLOW!
SHOVE!

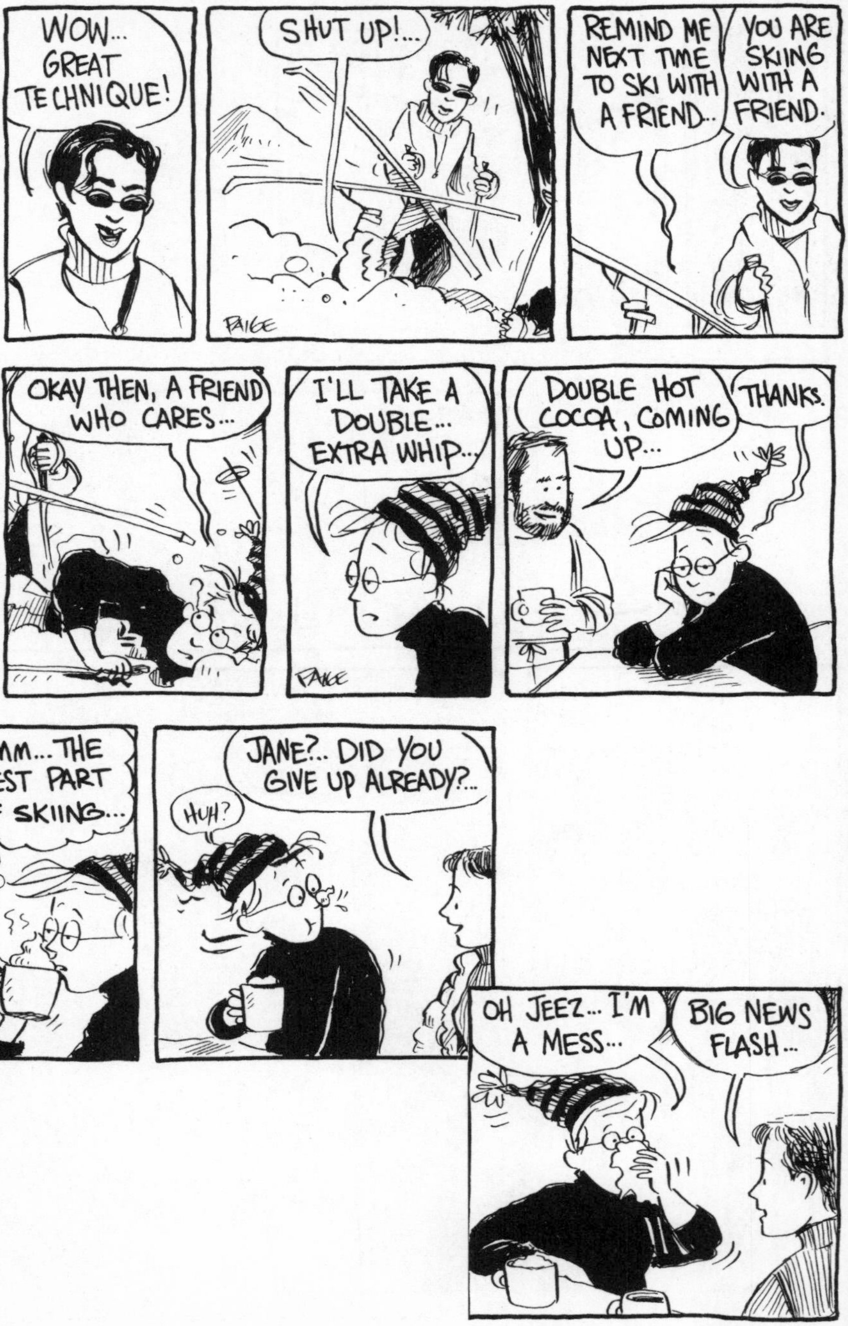
WOW... GREAT TECHNIQUE!
SHUT UP!...
PAIGE
REMIND ME NEXT TIME TO SKI WITH A FRIEND...
YOU ARE SKIING WITH A FRIEND.
OKAY THEN, A FRIEND WHO CARES...
I'LL TAKE A DOUBLE... EXTRA WHIP...
PAIGE
DOUBLE HOT COCOA, COMING UP...
THANKS.
MMM... THE BEST PART OF SKIING...
JANE?.. DID YOU GIVE UP ALREADY?...
HUH?
OH JEEZ... I'M A MESS...
BIG NEWS FLASH...

 SARAH?... CAN I ASK YOU SOMETHING?

 WHY ME?

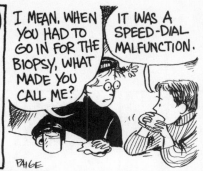 I MEAN, WHEN YOU HAD TO GO IN FOR THE BIOPSY, WHAT MADE YOU CALL ME?

IT WAS A SPEED-DIAL MALFUNCTION.

PAIGE

 I'M JUST KIDDING ABOUT THE SPEED-DIAL THING...

PAIGE

IT'S JUST LIFE, JANE...

LIFE, LITTLE BY LITTLE ...

 EXPERIENCE BY EXPERIENCE... CRISIS BY CRISIS...

 ...HELPS US SEE WHAT IS MOST IMPORTANT TO OUR HEART.

 I WONDER HOW THE SKI TRIP IS GOING?

I HAVE NO IDEA... THE LODGE HAS NO PHONES...

PAIGE

 I WOULDN'T EXPECT THEM TO CALL ANYWAY... I THINK IT'S SUPPOSED TO BE A PEACEFUL WEEKEND OF TOGETHERNESS.

 SNOW PLOW MY ASS!

WOO HOOOO!

SWOOSH!

!?!

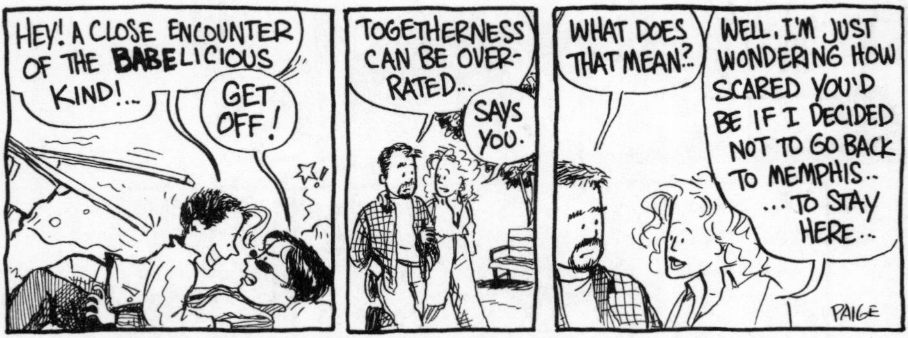
HEY! A CLOSE ENCOUNTER OF THE BABELICIOUS KIND!...
GET OFF!
TOGETHERNESS CAN BE OVER-RATED...
SAYS YOU.
WHAT DOES THAT MEAN?..
WELL, I'M JUST WONDERING HOW SCARED YOU'D BE IF I DECIDED NOT TO GO BACK TO MEMPHIS.. ...TO STAY HERE..
PAIGE

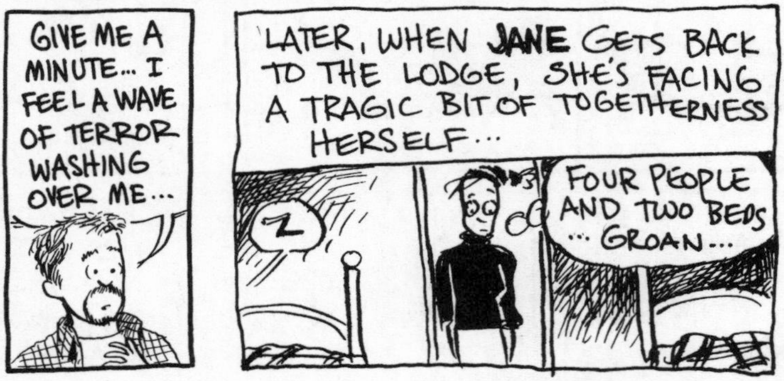
GIVE ME A MINUTE... I FEEL A WAVE OF TERROR WASHING OVER ME...
LATER, WHEN JANE GETS BACK TO THE LODGE, SHE'S FACING A TRAGIC BIT OF TOGETHERNESS HERSELF...
Z
FOUR PEOPLE AND TWO BEDS ... GROAN...

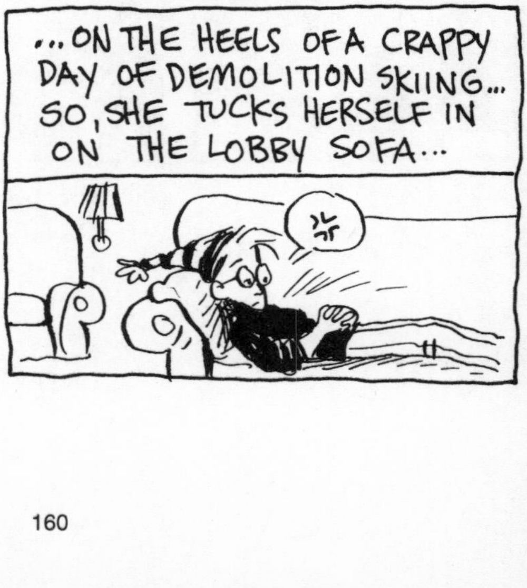
...ON THE HEELS OF A CRAPPY DAY OF DEMOLITION SKIING... SO, SHE TUCKS HERSELF IN ON THE LOBBY SOFA...

JANE? DID YOU SLEEP ON THE SOFA ALL NIGHT?
YES... THANK YOU FOR NOTICING THAT I WASN'T **EVEN** IN THE ROOM!
PAIGE
AS IF YOU REALLY CARE ...I NEEDED A LITTLE ALONE TIME..
HI.
OH YEAH... PLENTY OF THAT HERE IN **THE LOBBY.**
ARE YOU ALWAYS THIS ANNOYINGLY PERKY IN THE MORNING?...
IT'S OBVIOUS THAT YOU WOULDN'T KNOW ANYTHING ABOUT NEEDING SPACE...
AM I SKIING TOO CLOSE?
PAIGE

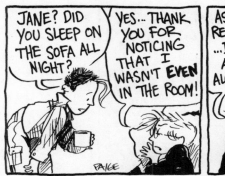

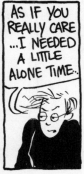

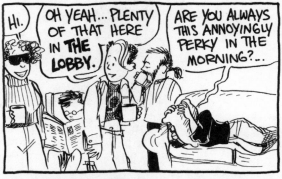

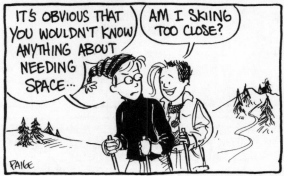

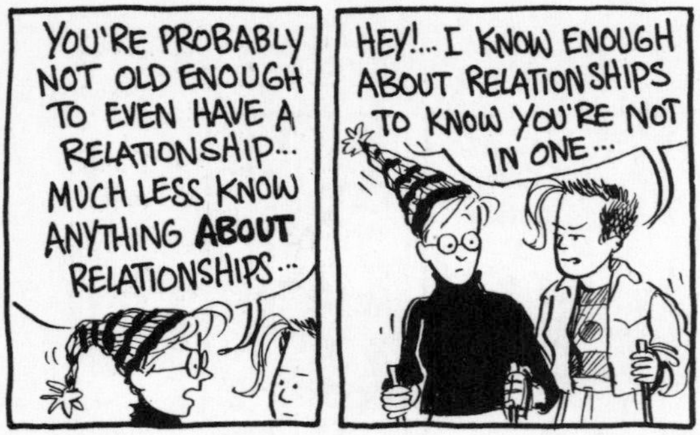
YOU'RE PROBABLY NOT OLD ENOUGH TO EVEN HAVE A RELATIONSHIP... MUCH LESS KNOW ANYTHING **ABOUT** RELATIONSHIPS...
HEY!... I KNOW ENOUGH ABOUT RELATIONSHIPS TO KNOW YOU'RE NOT IN ONE...

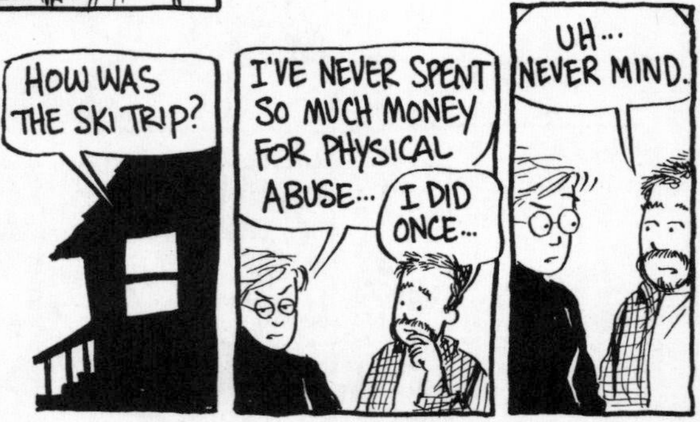
HOW WAS THE SKI TRIP?
I'VE NEVER SPENT SO MUCH MONEY FOR PHYSICAL ABUSE...
I DID ONCE...
UH... NEVER MIND.

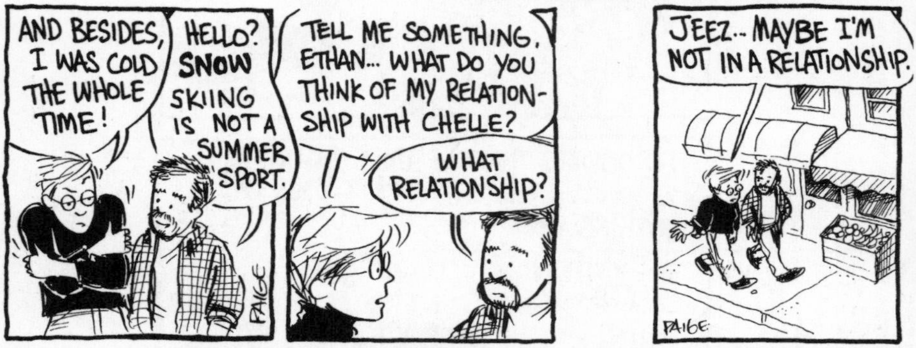
AND BESIDES, I WAS COLD THE WHOLE TIME!
HELLO? **SNOW** SKIING IS NOT A SUMMER SPORT.
PAIGE
TELL ME SOMETHING, ETHAN... WHAT DO YOU THINK OF MY RELATIONSHIP WITH CHELLE?
WHAT RELATIONSHIP?
JEEZ... MAYBE I'M NOT IN A RELATIONSHIP.
PAIGE

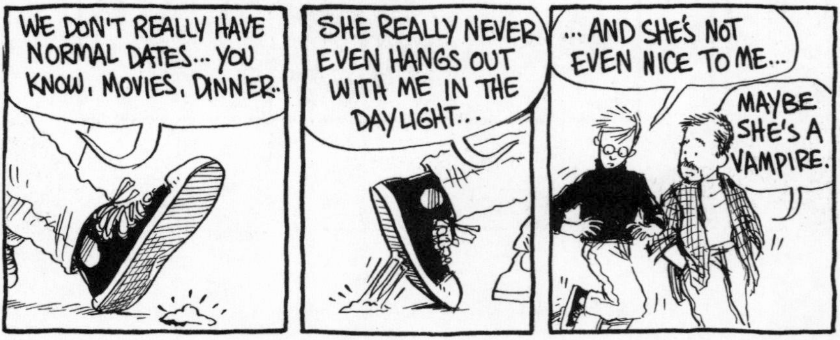
WE DON'T REALLY HAVE NORMAL DATES... YOU KNOW, MOVIES, DINNER...
SHE REALLY NEVER EVEN HANGS OUT WITH ME IN THE DAYLIGHT...
...AND SHE'S NOT EVEN NICE TO ME...
MAYBE SHE'S A VAMPIRE.

SHE'S NOT A VAMPIRE!
FOCUS PLEASE...
YEAH... SORRY...
MEANWHILE...
SO... HAVE YOU TALKED TO JANE? HOW WAS THE SKI TRIP?
I WAS THERE. IT WAS LAME.
WOULD IT KILL YOU TO SAY SOMETHING POSITIVE!
NO.
PAIGE
LATER, AT THE QUICKI-MART...
HOW LONG HAS BUSH BEEN IN OFFICE?!
QUICKI-MAR
3/14
PAIGE'9
...AND HE'S MANAGED TO DOUBLE THE DEFICIT!
WHAT A MAROON!
CHIPS
I JUST CAN'T STAND IT!...
WAKE ME UP WHEN THERE'S A NEW PRESIDENT...
UH...I SPILLED SOME COKE THERE THIS MORNING..
CHIPS
DRINKS
ARE YOU GOING TO WEAR THAT OUT TO EAT?
OH... NATALIE SPILLED SOME COKE... I LAID IN IT...
3/16

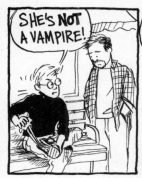

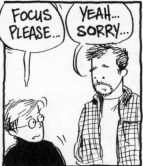

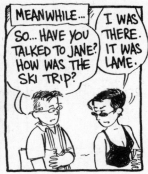

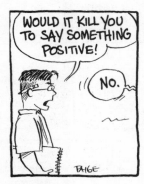

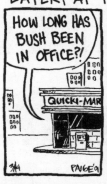

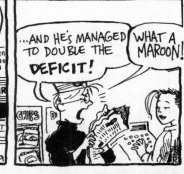

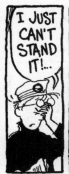

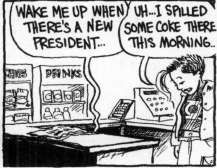

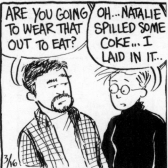

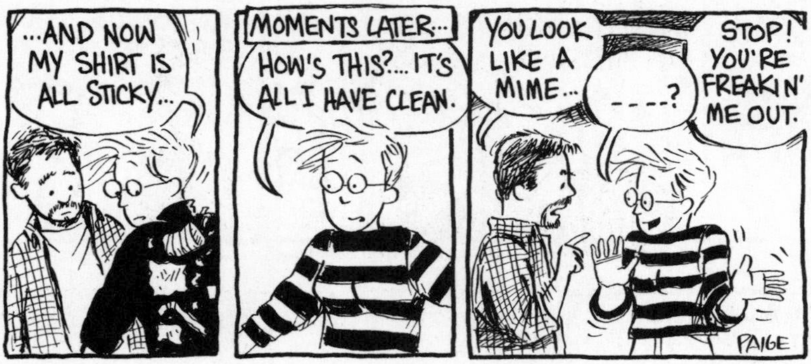
...AND NOW MY SHIRT IS ALL STICKY...
MOMENTS LATER...
HOW'S THIS?... IT'S ALL I HAVE CLEAN.
YOU LOOK LIKE A MIME...
----?
STOP! YOU'RE FREAKIN' ME OUT.
PAIGE

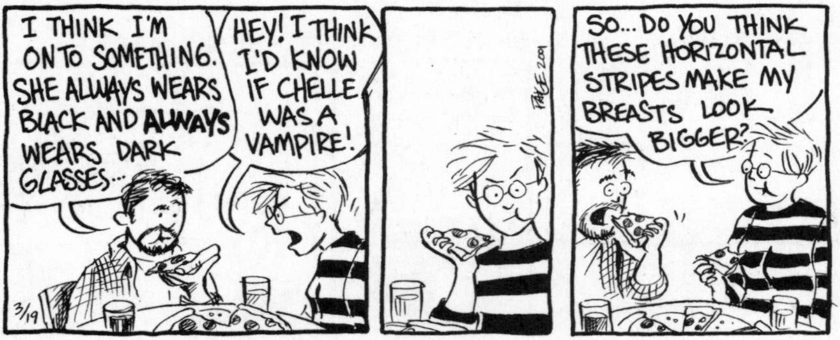
I THINK I'M ONTO SOMETHING. SHE ALWAYS WEARS BLACK AND **ALWAYS** WEARS DARK GLASSES...
HEY! I THINK I'D KNOW IF CHELLE WAS A VAMPIRE!
3/19
PAIGE 2001
SO... DO YOU THINK THESE HORIZONTAL STRIPES MAKE MY BREASTS LOOK BIGGER?

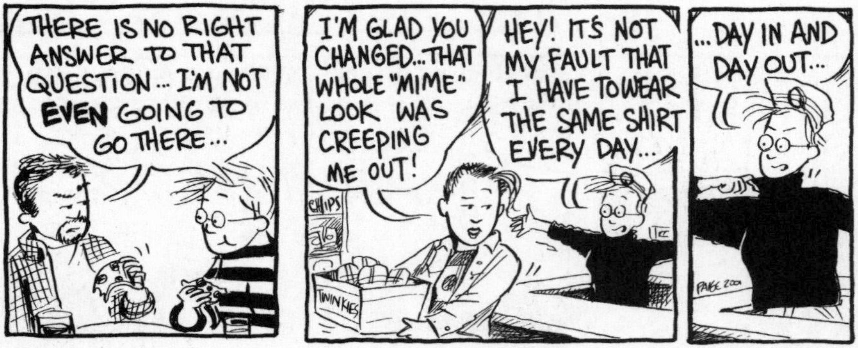
THERE IS NO RIGHT ANSWER TO THAT QUESTION... I'M NOT **EVEN** GOING TO GO THERE...
I'M GLAD YOU CHANGED...THAT WHOLE "MIME" LOOK WAS CREEPING ME OUT!
HEY! IT'S NOT MY FAULT THAT I HAVE TO WEAR THE SAME SHIRT EVERY DAY...
CHIPS
TWINKIES
...DAY IN AND DAY OUT...
PAIGE 2001

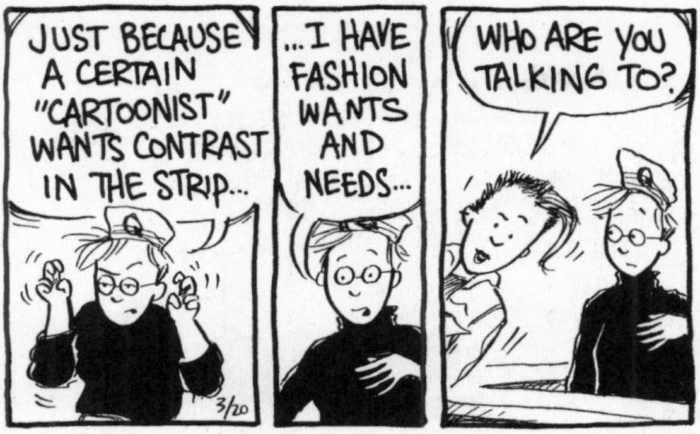
JUST BECAUSE A CERTAIN "CARTOONIST" WANTS CONTRAST IN THE STRIP...
...I HAVE FASHION WANTS AND NEEDS...
3/20
WHO ARE YOU TALKING TO?

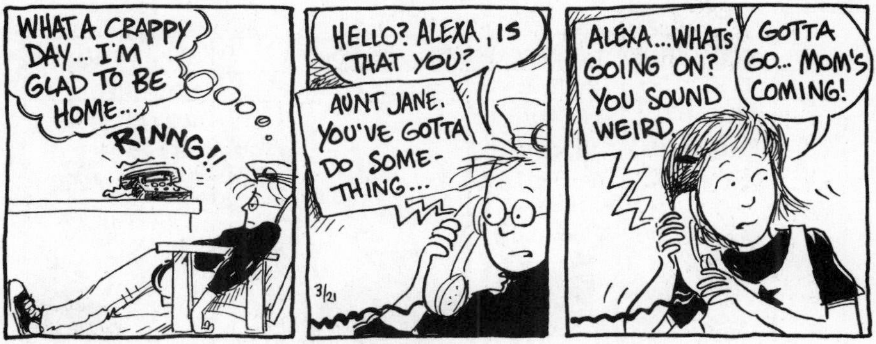
WHAT A CRAPPY DAY... I'M GLAD TO BE HOME...
RINNG!!
HELLO? ALEXA, IS THAT YOU?
AUNT JANE. YOU'VE GOTTA DO SOME-THING...
3/21
ALEXA...WHAT'S GOING ON? YOU SOUND WEIRD.
GOTTA GO... MOM'S COMING!

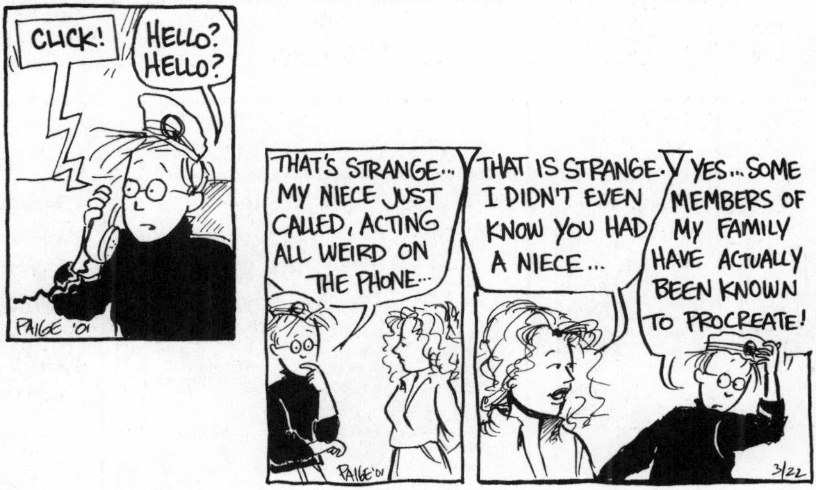
CLICK!
HELLO? HELLO?
PAIGE '01
THAT'S STRANGE... MY NIECE JUST CALLED, ACTING ALL WEIRD ON THE PHONE...
PAIGE '01
THAT IS STRANGE. I DIDN'T EVEN KNOW YOU HAD A NIECE...
YES... SOME MEMBERS OF MY FAMILY HAVE ACTUALLY BEEN KNOWN TO PROCREATE!
3/22

I'M GONNA CALL ALEXA BACK... NOW, WHERE DID I PUT MY SISTER'S NEW NUMBER?...

YOU KNOW, SOME PEOPLE ACTUALLY WRITE THE NUMBERS **IN** THE BOOK... SOME, EVEN IN ALPHABETICAL ORDER...

HEY!... THIS ADDRESS BOOK IS A PRECISION FACT FINDING INSTRUMENT! ... CIRCA 1987...

YEAH... UNTIL THE RUBBER BAND BREAKS.

DO YOU WANT TO RIDE TO THE CITY WITH ME?

TO SHARE IN THE FAMILY DRAMA?

3/26

NO THANKS!

IT'S PROBABLY NOTHING... YOU KNOW HOW TEENAGERS ALWAYS OVER-REACT...

SLAM!

ADOLESCENCE IS HELL...

I KNOW, LET ME KNOW WHEN YOURS IS OVER...

PAGE 2001

OKAY... SO SHE WASN'T AT HER PLACE IN THE CITY...

... WHAT THE HECK IS SHE DOING OUT HERE IN THE BOONIES?!

HOW CAN SHE TELECOMMUTE IF SHE'S COMPLETELY OFF THE GRID?!

3/27

MAYBE SHE'S JUST TRYING TO COMMUNE WITH NATURE...
...I GUESS THAT'S A LOT EASIER WHEN YOUR **VOLVO** HAS ALL-WHEEL DRIVE...
VOLVO
PAIGE 2001
BECCA?... BECCA?
JANE?!
3/28
PAIGE 2001
HEY, SIS... THOUGHT I'D SURPRISE YOU WITH A VISIT...
WHAT... NO HUG?
HMM... ALEXA MUST HAVE CALLED YOU BEFORE I DISCONNECTED THE PHONE...

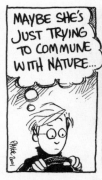

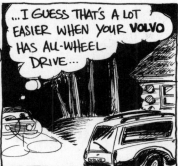

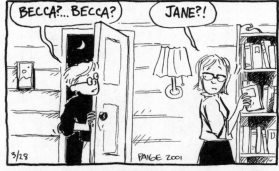

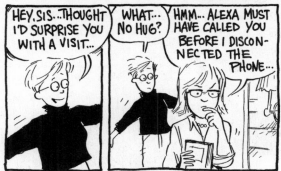

SO, WHERE'S KATE?
YOU KNOW, LOVE OF YOUR LIFE... THE REASON YOU LEFT TED, BLAH, BLAH, BLAH...
SHE'S PROBABLY FROLICKING IN THE SURF WITH HER NEW TWENTYSOMETHING GIRLFRIEND...
3/29
PAIGE 2001
OH... SORRY.
YEAH... I THOUGHT ONLY MEN TRADED YOU IN FOR A YOUNGER MODEL... WITH PERKY BREASTS!
PERKY BREASTS I UNDERSTAND... BUT HIDING IN THE WILDERNESS?
I KNEW YOU WOULDN'T UNDERSTAND... I'M TRYING TO GAIN SOME CONTROL IN MY LIFE...
I HATE TO TELL YOU, SIS... CONTROL IS AN ILLUSION...
3/30
PAIGE 2001

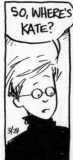

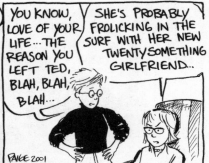

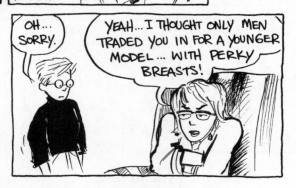

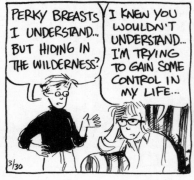

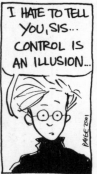

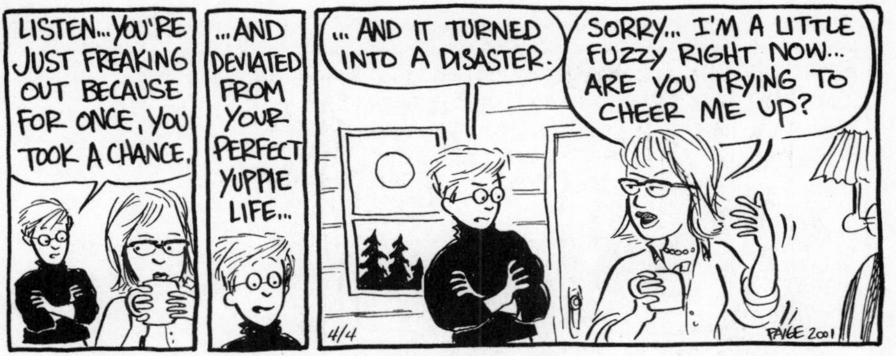
LISTEN... YOU'RE JUST FREAKING OUT BECAUSE FOR ONCE, YOU TOOK A CHANCE,
...AND DEVIATED FROM YOUR PERFECT YUPPIE LIFE...
... AND IT TURNED INTO A DISASTER.
SORRY... I'M A LITTLE FUZZY RIGHT NOW... ARE YOU TRYING TO CHEER ME UP?
4/4
PAIGE 2001

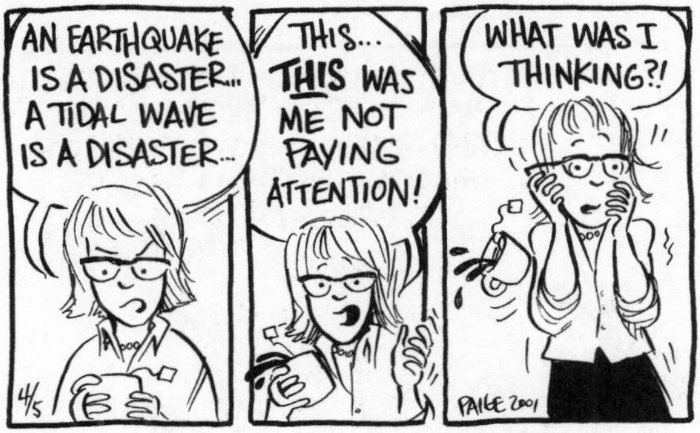
AN EARTHQUAKE IS A DISASTER... A TIDAL WAVE IS A DISASTER...
THIS... **THIS** WAS ME NOT PAYING ATTENTION!
WHAT WAS I THINKING?!
4/5
PAIGE 2001

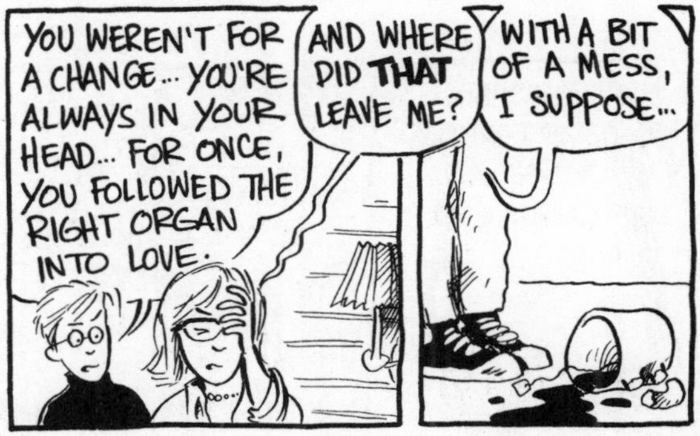
YOU WEREN'T FOR A CHANGE... YOU'RE ALWAYS IN YOUR HEAD... FOR ONCE, YOU FOLLOWED THE RIGHT ORGAN INTO LOVE.
AND WHERE DID **THAT** LEAVE ME?
WITH A BIT OF A MESS, I SUPPOSE...

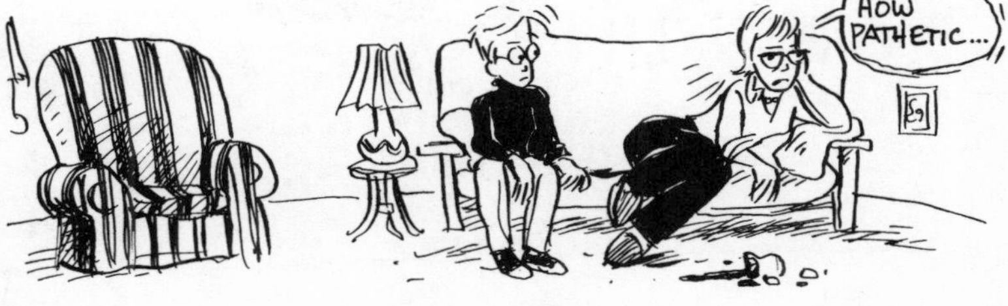
HOW PATHETIC...

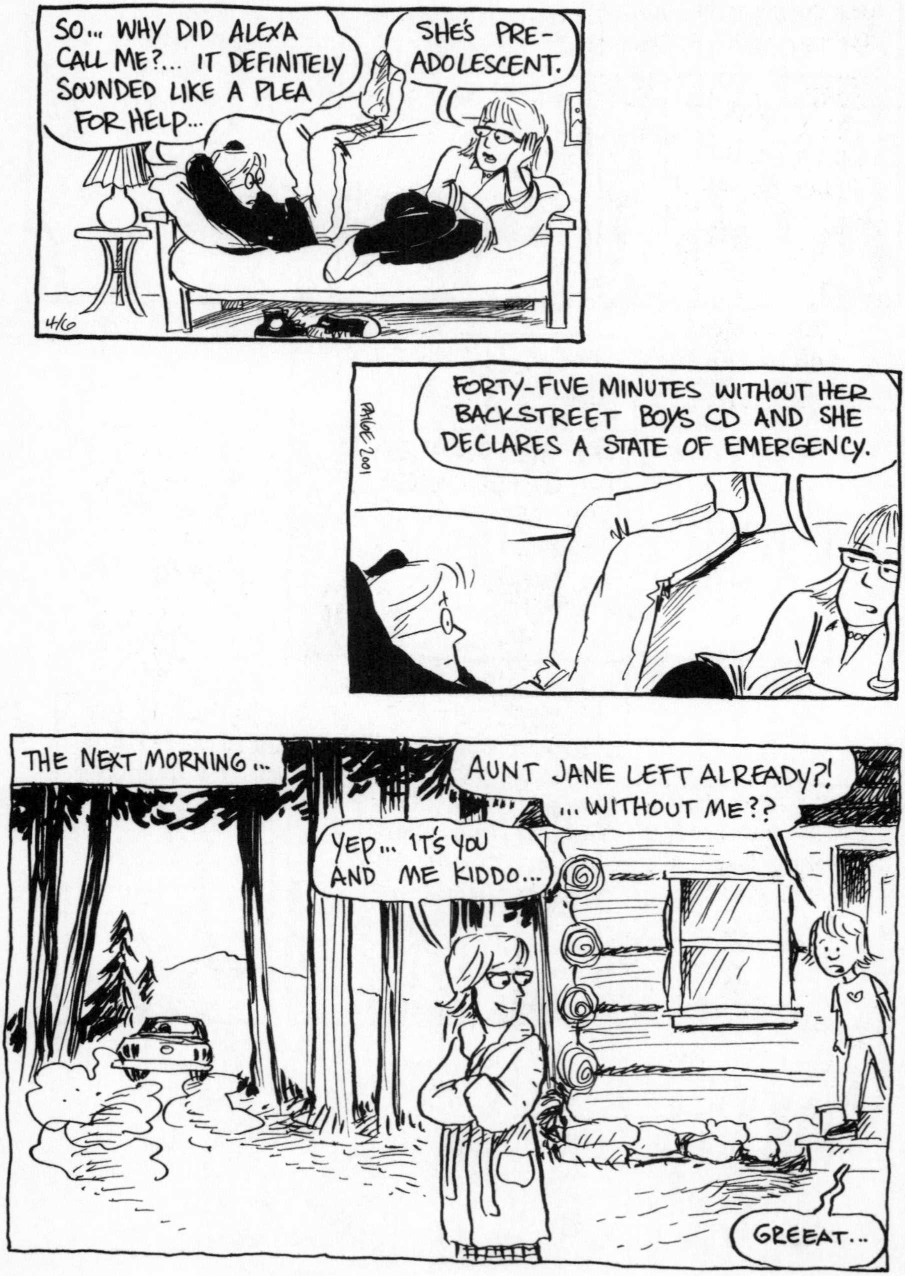
SO... WHY DID ALEXA CALL ME?... IT DEFINITELY SOUNDED LIKE A PLEA FOR HELP...
SHE'S PRE-ADOLESCENT.
4/6
PAIGE 2001
FORTY-FIVE MINUTES WITHOUT HER BACKSTREET BOYS CD AND SHE DECLARES A STATE OF EMERGENCY.
THE NEXT MORNING...
AUNT JANE LEFT ALREADY?! ...WITHOUT ME??
YEP... IT'S YOU AND ME KIDDO...
GREEAT...

BACK ON THE HOME FRONT, BUD
DECIDES TO HOST A YARD SALE...

SORRY I'M LATE. ALL I WANTED WAS A LARGE BLACK COFFEE...

BUT I HAD TO WAIT IN LINE BEHIND TWO SOY CHAIS, A CARAMEL MACCHIATO AND 3 NON-FAT LATTES WITH NO WHIP...

04/11

TRY THE **DONUT HUT**. THE COFFEE CHOICES ARE "DECAF" OR "REGULAR"...

...AND THE CHICKS?

LET'S JUST SAY THERE'S MORE TO LOVE...

YARD SALE

COMPLICATED WOMEN DRINK COMPLICATED COFFEE... THAT'S ALL I'M SAYIN'...

YOU'RE PROBABLY RIGHT...

YARD SALE

PAIGE 2001

I SHOULD HAVE KNOWN THE FIRST TIME DOROTHY ORDERED A DECAF SOY CHAI LATTE...

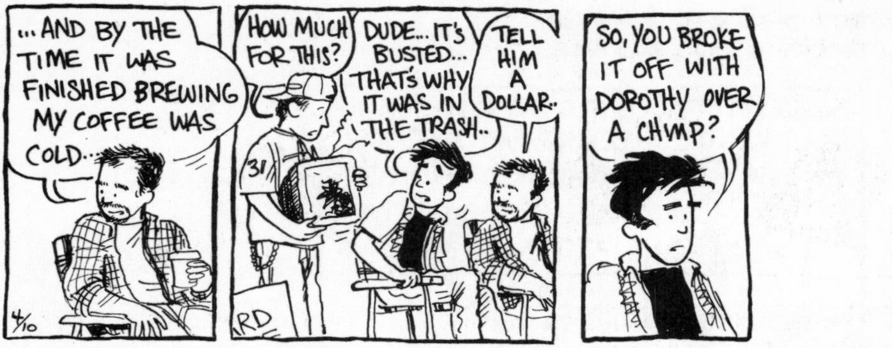
...AND BY THE TIME IT WAS FINISHED BREWING MY COFFEE WAS COLD...
4/10
HOW MUCH FOR THIS?
DUDE... IT'S BUSTED... THAT'S WHY IT WAS IN THE TRASH..
TELL HIM A DOLLAR..
31
RD
SO, YOU BROKE IT OFF WITH DOROTHY OVER A CHIMP?

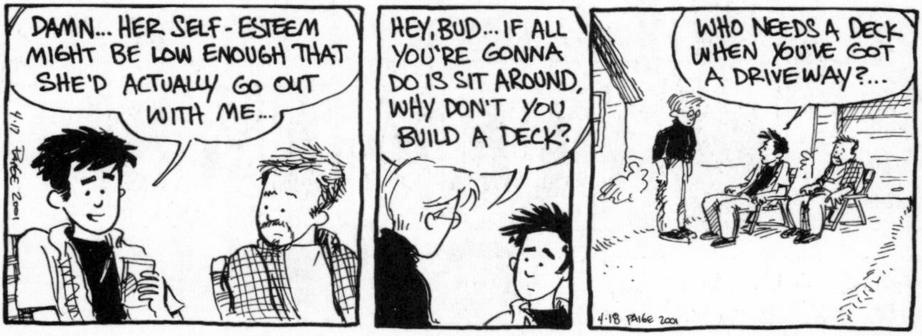
DAMN... HER SELF-ESTEEM MIGHT BE LOW ENOUGH THAT SHE'D ACTUALLY GO OUT WITH ME...
4.17 PAIGE 2001
HEY, BUD... IF ALL YOU'RE GONNA DO IS SIT AROUND, WHY DON'T YOU BUILD A DECK?
WHO NEEDS A DECK WHEN YOU'VE GOT A DRIVEWAY?...
4.18 PAIGE 2001

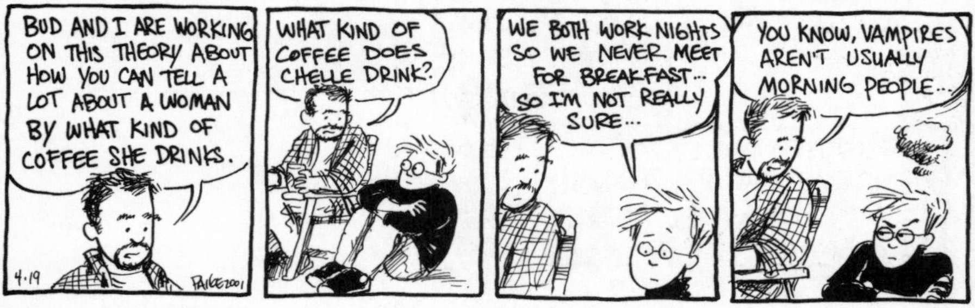
BUD AND I ARE WORKING ON THIS THEORY ABOUT HOW YOU CAN TELL A LOT ABOUT A WOMAN BY WHAT KIND OF COFFEE SHE DRINKS.
4.19
PAIGE 2001
WHAT KIND OF COFFEE DOES CHELLE DRINK?
WE BOTH WORK NIGHTS SO WE NEVER MEET FOR BREAKFAST... SO I'M NOT REALLY SURE...
YOU KNOW, VAMPIRES AREN'T USUALLY MORNING PEOPLE...

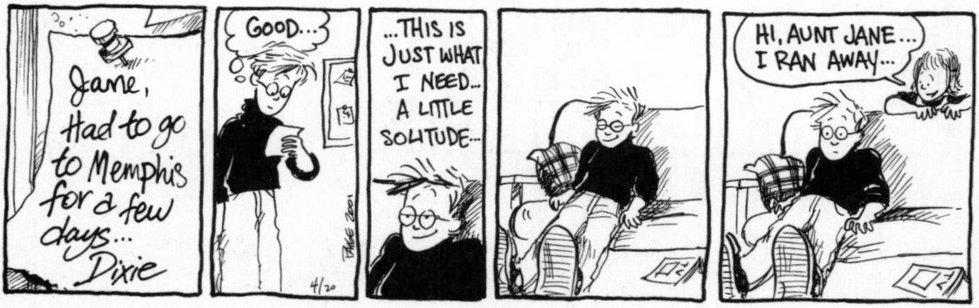
Jane,
Had to go to Memphis for a few days...
Dixie
GOOD...
PAIGE 2001
4/20
...THIS IS JUST WHAT I NEED... A LITTLE SOLITUDE...
HI, AUNT JANE... I RAN AWAY...

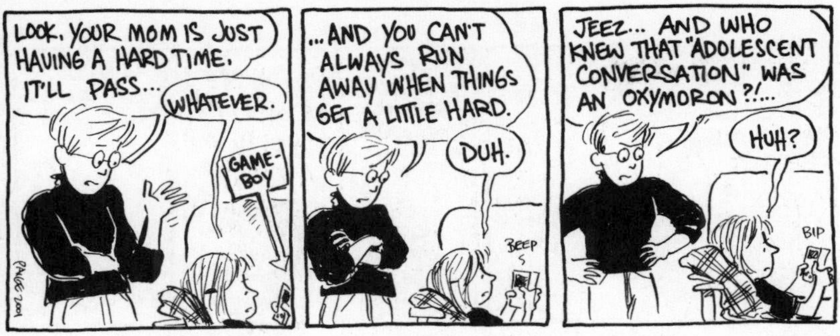
LOOK. YOUR MOM IS JUST HAVING A HARD TIME. IT'LL PASS...
WHATEVER.
GAME-BOY
...AND YOU CAN'T ALWAYS RUN AWAY WHEN THINGS GET A LITTLE HARD.
DUH.
BEEP
JEEZ... AND WHO KNEW THAT "ADOLESCENT CONVERSATION" WAS AN OXYMORON ?!...
HUH?
BIP

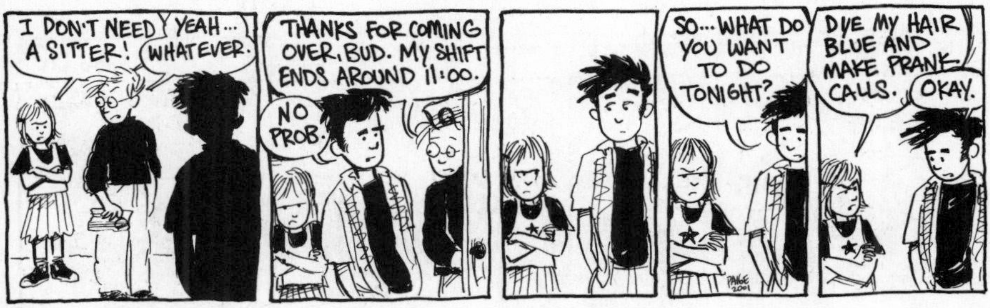
I DON'T NEED A SITTER!
YEAH... WHATEVER.
THANKS FOR COMING OVER, BUD. MY SHIFT ENDS AROUND 11:00.
NO PROB.
SO... WHAT DO YOU WANT TO DO TONIGHT?
DYE MY HAIR BLUE AND MAKE PRANK CALLS.
OKAY.

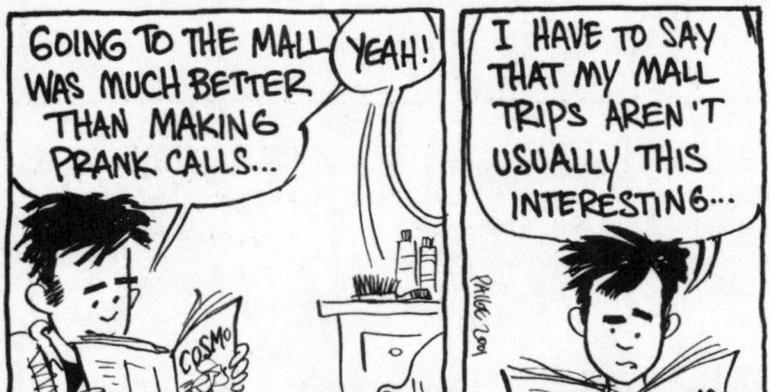
GOING TO THE MALL WAS MUCH BETTER THAN MAKING PRANK CALLS...
YEAH!
COSMO
I HAVE TO SAY THAT MY MALL TRIPS AREN'T USUALLY THIS INTERESTING...
COSMO

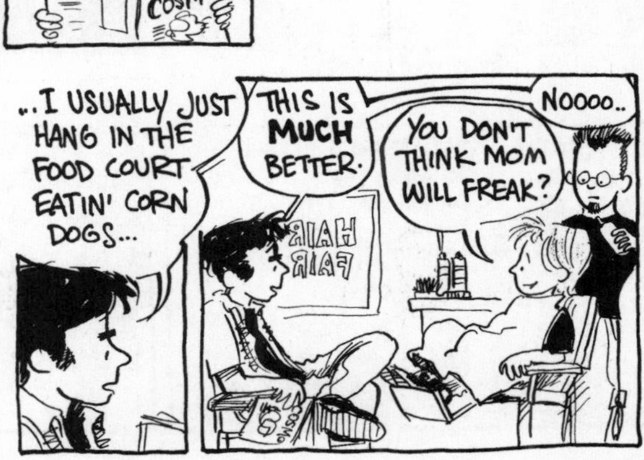
...I USUALLY JUST HANG IN THE FOOD COURT EATIN' CORN DOGS...
THIS IS MUCH BETTER.
YOU DON'T THINK MOM WILL FREAK?
NOOOO..

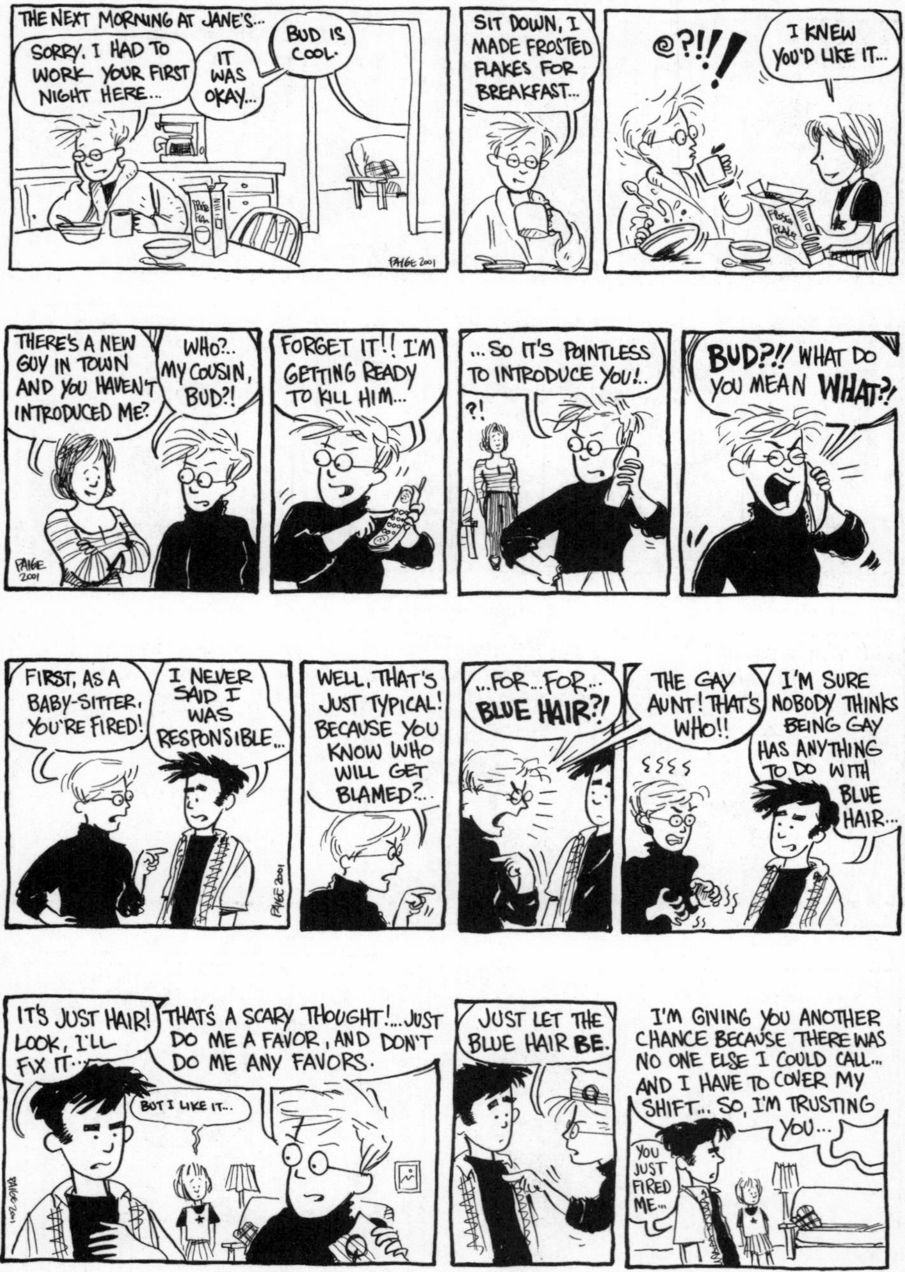
THE NEXT MORNING AT JANE'S...
SORRY. I HAD TO WORK YOUR FIRST NIGHT HERE...
IT WAS OKAY...
BUD IS COOL.
PAIGE 2001
SIT DOWN, I MADE FROSTED FLAKES FOR BREAKFAST...
@?!!!
I KNEW YOU'D LIKE IT...
THERE'S A NEW GUY IN TOWN AND YOU HAVEN'T INTRODUCED ME?
WHO?.. MY COUSIN, BUD?!
PAIGE 2001
FORGET IT!! I'M GETTING READY TO KILL HIM...
...SO IT'S POINTLESS TO INTRODUCE YOU!..
?!
BUD?!! WHAT DO YOU MEAN WHAT?!
FIRST, AS A BABY-SITTER, YOU'RE FIRED!
I NEVER SAID I WAS RESPONSIBLE...
PAIGE 2001
WELL, THAT'S JUST TYPICAL! BECAUSE YOU KNOW WHO WILL GET BLAMED?...
...FOR...FOR... BLUE HAIR?!
THE GAY AUNT! THAT'S WHO!!
I'M SURE NOBODY THINKS BEING GAY HAS ANYTHING TO DO WITH BLUE HAIR...
IT'S JUST HAIR! LOOK, I'LL FIX IT...
THAT'S A SCARY THOUGHT!...JUST DO ME A FAVOR, AND DON'T DO ME ANY FAVORS.
BUT I LIKE IT...
PAIGE 2001
JUST LET THE BLUE HAIR BE.
I'M GIVING YOU ANOTHER CHANCE BECAUSE THERE WAS NO ONE ELSE I COULD CALL... AND I HAVE TO COVER MY SHIFT... SO, I'M TRUSTING YOU...
YOU JUST FIRED ME...

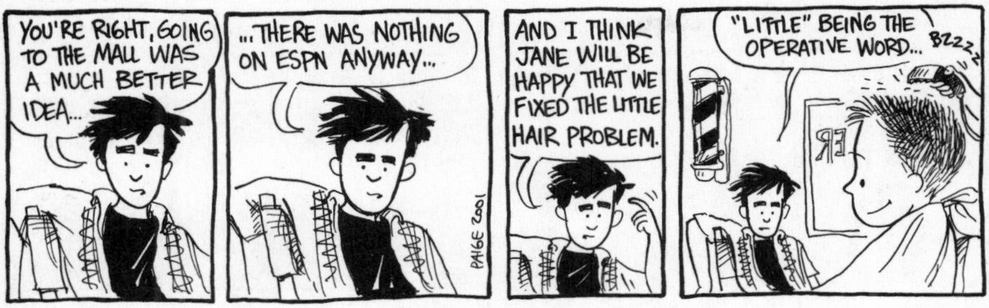
YOU'RE RIGHT, GOING TO THE MALL WAS A MUCH BETTER IDEA...
...THERE WAS NOTHING ON ESPN ANYWAY...
PAIGE 2001
AND I THINK JANE WILL BE HAPPY THAT WE FIXED THE LITTLE HAIR PROBLEM.
"LITTLE" BEING THE OPERATIVE WORD...
BZZZZ

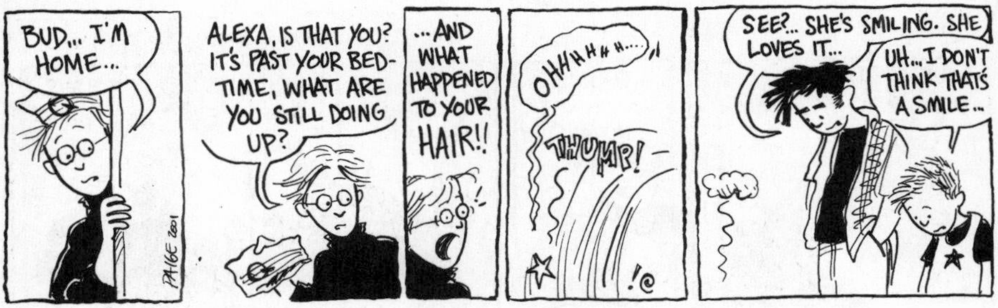
BUD... I'M HOME...
PAIGE 2001
ALEXA, IS THAT YOU? IT'S PAST YOUR BED-TIME, WHAT ARE YOU STILL DOING UP?
...AND WHAT HAPPENED TO YOUR HAIR!!
OHHHHHH......
THUMP!
SEE?... SHE'S SMILING. SHE LOVES IT...
UH... I DON'T THINK THAT'S A SMILE...

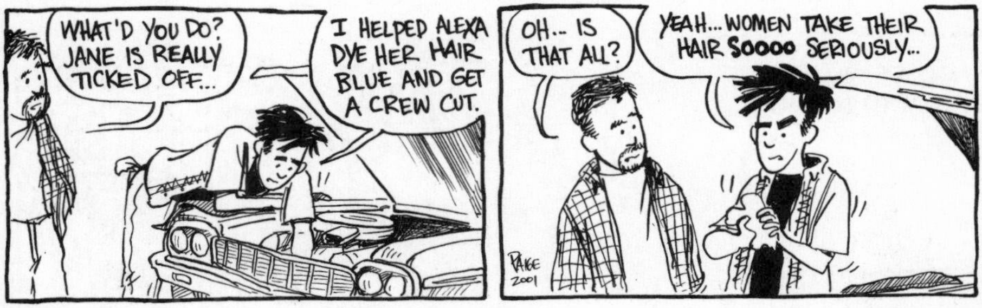
WHAT'D YOU DO? JANE IS REALLY TICKED OFF...
I HELPED ALEXA DYE HER HAIR BLUE AND GET A CREW CUT.
OH... IS THAT ALL?
YEAH... WOMEN TAKE THEIR HAIR SOOOO SERIOUSLY...
PAIGE 2001

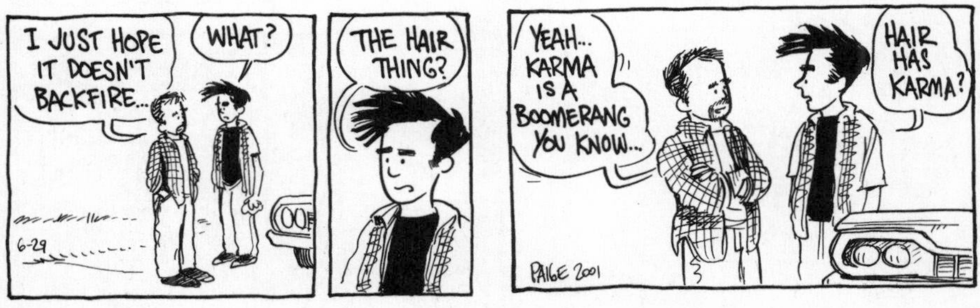
I JUST HOPE IT DOESN'T BACKFIRE...
WHAT?
6-29
THE HAIR THING?
YEAH... KARMA IS A BOOMERANG YOU KNOW...
HAIR HAS KARMA?
PAIGE 2001

THE NEXT DAY, AT THE CAFE...

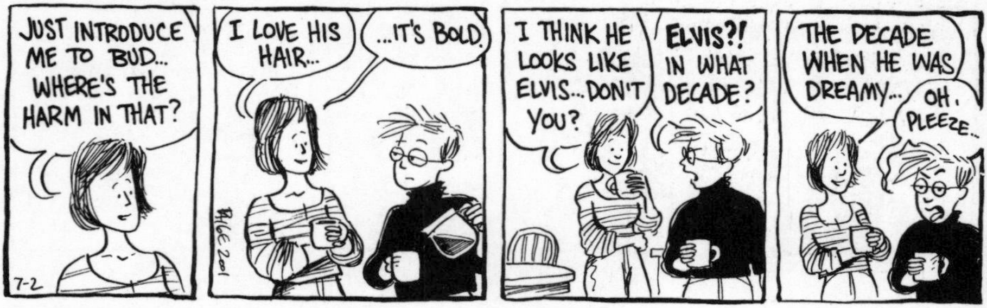

JUST INTRODUCE ME TO BUD... WHERE'S THE HARM IN THAT?
7-2
I LOVE HIS HAIR...
...IT'S BOLD.
PAIGE 2001
I THINK HE LOOKS LIKE ELVIS... DON'T YOU?
ELVIS?! IN WHAT DECADE?
THE DECADE WHEN HE WAS DREAMY...
OH, PLEEZE..

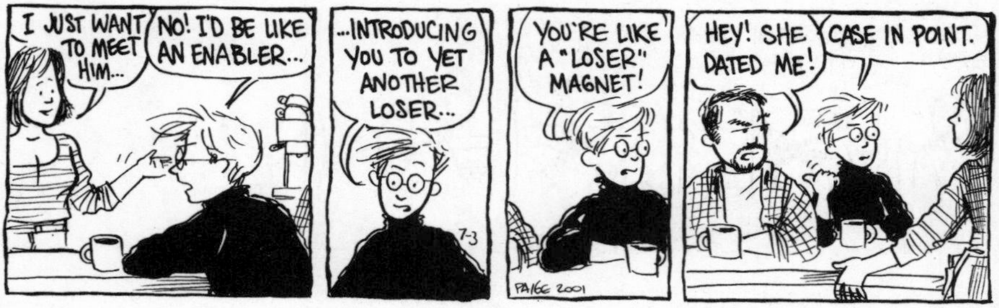

I JUST WANT TO MEET HIM...
NO! I'D BE LIKE AN ENABLER...
...INTRODUCING YOU TO YET ANOTHER LOSER...
7-3
YOU'RE LIKE A "LOSER" MAGNET!
PAIGE 2001
HEY! SHE DATED ME!
CASE IN POINT.

ACROSS TOWN, BUD IS HARD AT NOT WORKING...

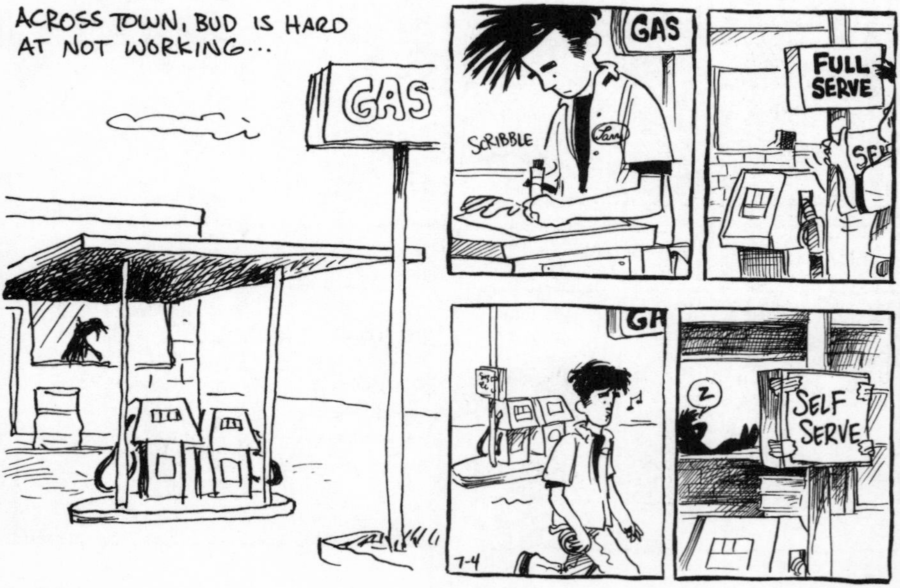

GAS
GAS
SCRIBBLE
FULL SERVE
7-4
Z
SELF SERVE

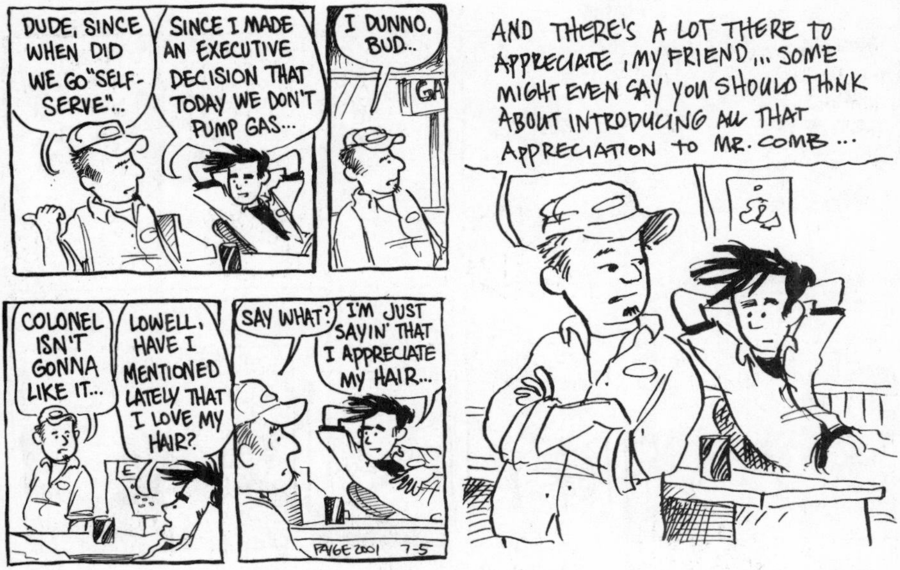
DUDE, SINCE WHEN DID WE GO "SELF-SERVE"...
SINCE I MADE AN EXECUTIVE DECISION THAT TODAY WE DON'T PUMP GAS...
I DUNNO, BUD...
AND THERE'S A LOT THERE TO APPRECIATE, MY FRIEND... SOME MIGHT EVEN SAY YOU SHOULD THINK ABOUT INTRODUCING ALL THAT APPRECIATION TO MR. COMB...
COLONEL ISN'T GONNA LIKE IT...
LOWELL, HAVE I MENTIONED LATELY THAT I LOVE MY HAIR?
SAY WHAT?
I'M JUST SAYIN' THAT I APPRECIATE MY HAIR...
PAIGE 2001 7-5

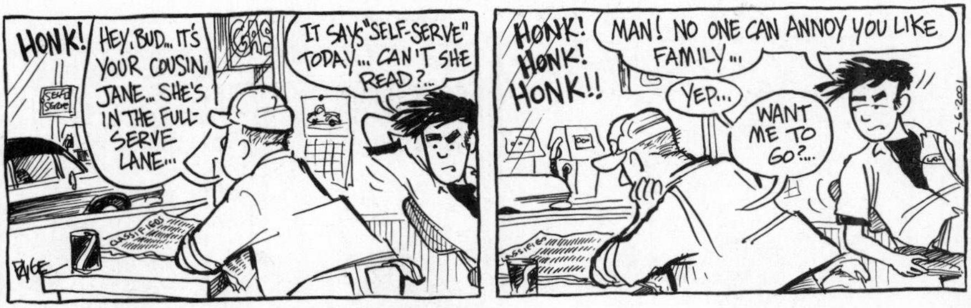
HONK!
HEY, BUD... IT'S YOUR COUSIN, JANE... SHE'S IN THE FULL-SERVE LANE...
IT SAYS "SELF-SERVE" TODAY... CAN'T SHE READ?...
SELF SERVE
PAIGE
HONK! HONK! HONK!!
MAN! NO ONE CAN ANNOY YOU LIKE FAMILY...
YEP...
WANT ME TO GO?...
7-6-2001

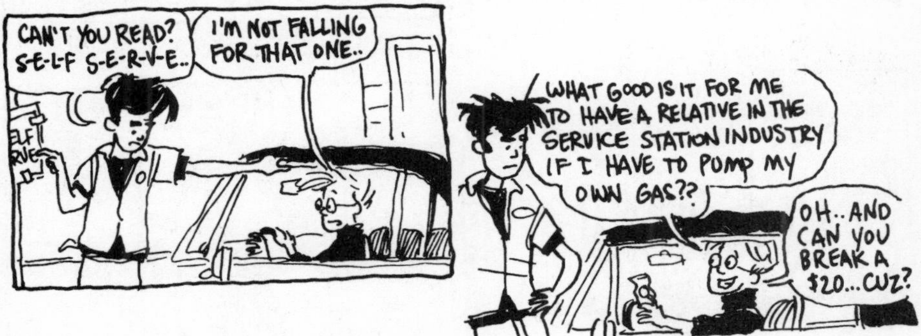
CAN'T YOU READ? S-E-L-F S-E-R-V-E...
I'M NOT FALLING FOR THAT ONE..
WHAT GOOD IS IT FOR ME TO HAVE A RELATIVE IN THE SERVICE STATION INDUSTRY IF I HAVE TO PUMP MY OWN GAS??
OH.. AND CAN YOU BREAK A $20... CUZ?

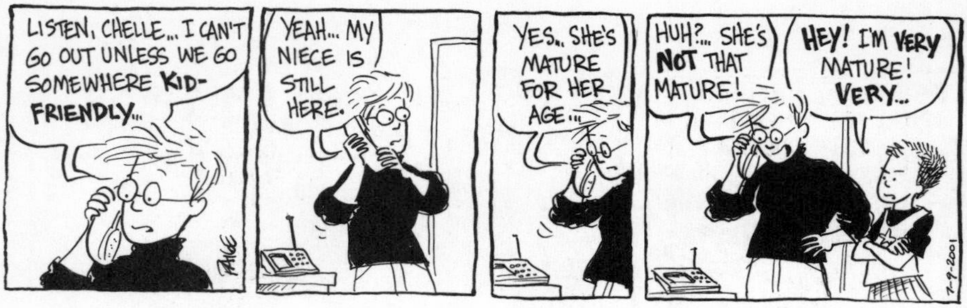
LISTEN, CHELLE... I CAN'T GO OUT UNLESS WE GO SOMEWHERE **KID-FRIENDLY**...
PAIGE
YEAH... MY NIECE IS STILL HERE.
YES.. SHE'S MATURE FOR HER AGE...
HUH?... SHE'S **NOT** THAT MATURE!
HEY! I'M **VERY** MATURE! **VERY**...
7-9-2001

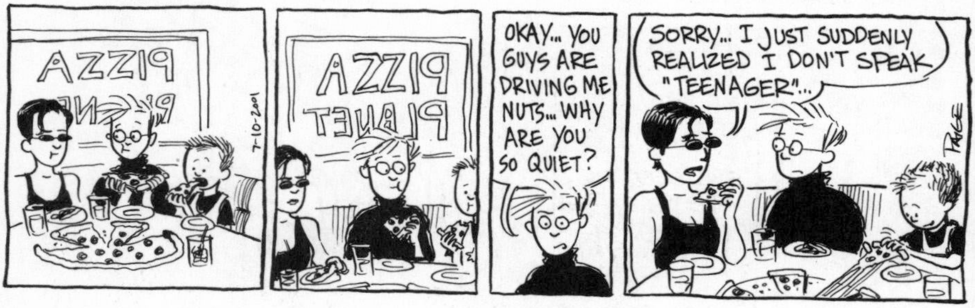
7-10-2001
OKAY... YOU GUYS ARE DRIVING ME NUTS... WHY ARE YOU SO QUIET?
SORRY... I JUST SUDDENLY REALIZED I DON'T SPEAK "TEENAGER"...
PAIGE

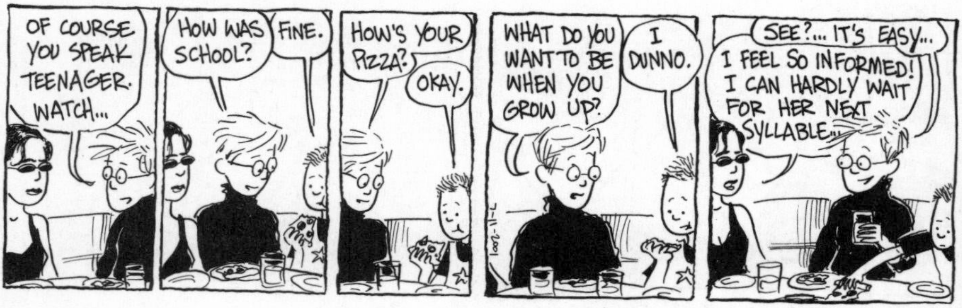
OF COURSE YOU SPEAK TEENAGER. WATCH...
HOW WAS SCHOOL?
FINE.
HOW'S YOUR PIZZA?
OKAY.
WHAT DO YOU WANT TO BE WHEN YOU GROW UP?
I DUNNO.
7-11-2001
SEE?... IT'S EASY...
I FEEL SO INFORMED! I CAN HARDLY WAIT FOR HER NEXT SYLLABLE...

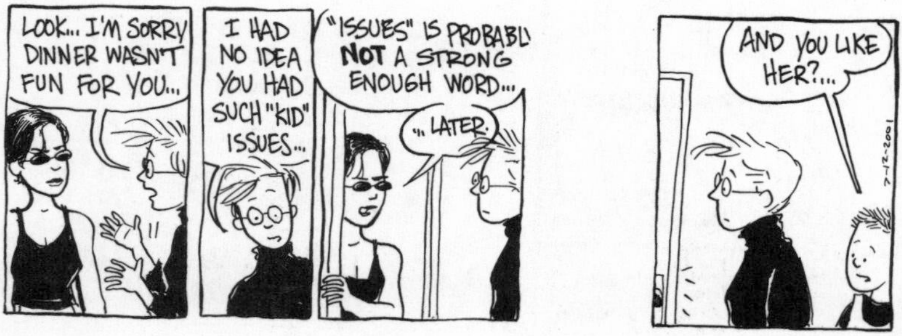
LOOK... I'M SORRY DINNER WASN'T FUN FOR YOU...
I HAD NO IDEA YOU HAD SUCH "KID" ISSUES...
"ISSUES" IS PROBABL **NOT** A STRONG ENOUGH WORD...
... LATER.
AND YOU LIKE HER?...
7-12-2001

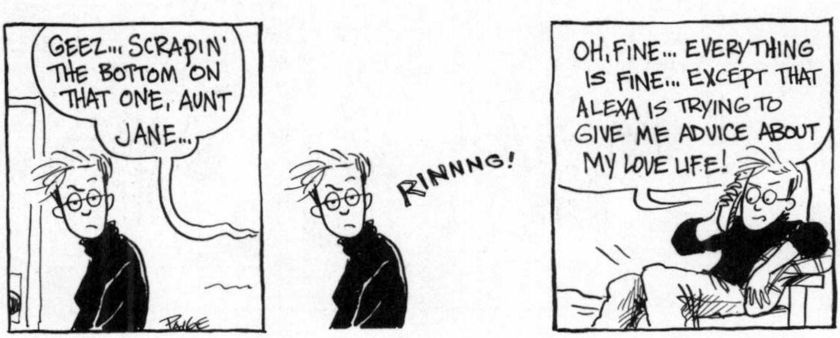
GEEZ... SCRAPIN' THE BOTTOM ON THAT ONE, AUNT JANE...
PAIGE
RINNNG!
OH, FINE... EVERYTHING IS FINE... EXCEPT THAT ALEXA IS TRYING TO GIVE ME ADVICE ABOUT MY LOVE LIFE!

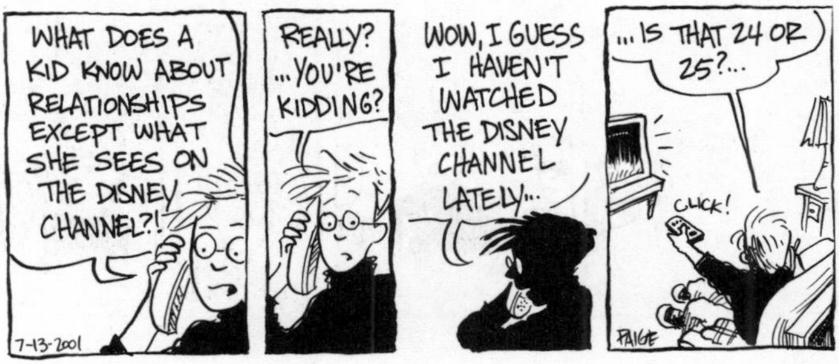
WHAT DOES A KID KNOW ABOUT RELATIONSHIPS EXCEPT WHAT SHE SEES ON THE DISNEY CHANNEL?!
7-13-2001
REALLY? ...YOU'RE KIDDING?
WOW, I GUESS I HAVEN'T WATCHED THE DISNEY CHANNEL LATELY...
...IS THAT 24 OR 25?...
CLICK!
PAIGE

THE NEXT DAY.

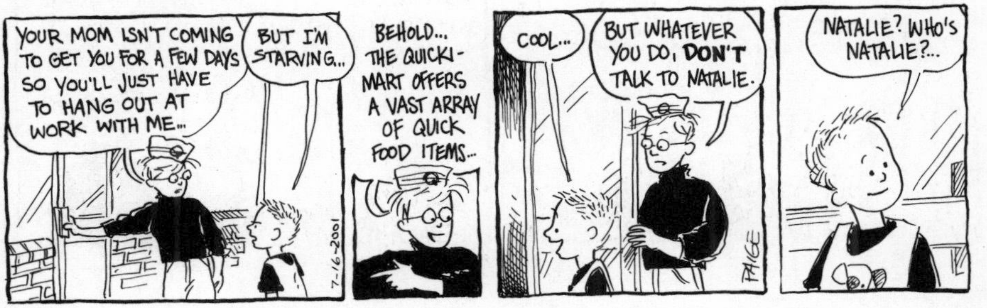
YOUR MOM ISN'T COMING TO GET YOU FOR A FEW DAYS SO YOU'LL JUST HAVE TO HANG OUT AT WORK WITH ME...
BUT I'M STARVING...
7-16-2001
BEHOLD... THE QUICKI-MART OFFERS A VAST ARRAY OF QUICK FOOD ITEMS...
COOL...
BUT WHATEVER YOU DO, DON'T TALK TO NATALIE.
PAIGE
NATALIE? WHO'S NATALIE?...

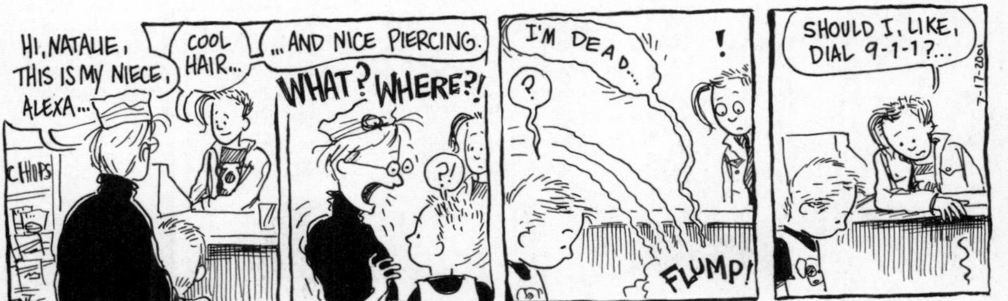
HI, NATALIE, THIS IS MY NIECE, ALEXA...
COOL HAIR...
CHIPS
PAIGE
...AND NICE PIERCING.
WHAT? WHERE?!
I'M DEAD...
FLUMP!
SHOULD I, LIKE, DIAL 9-1-1?...
7-17-2001

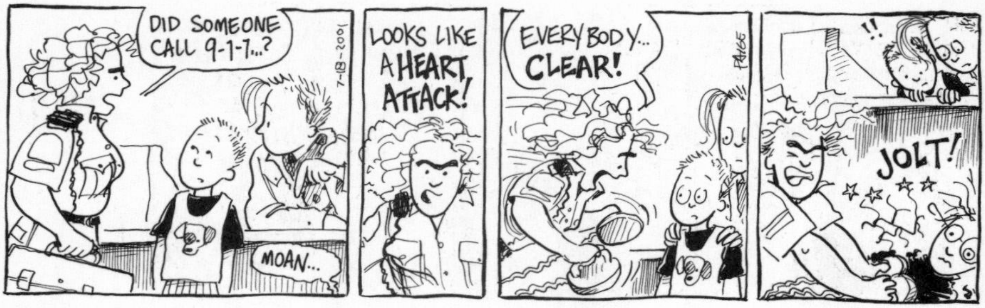
DID SOMEONE CALL 9-1-1...?
7-18-2001
MOAN...
LOOKS LIKE A HEART ATTACK!
EVERY BODY... CLEAR!
PAIGE
!!
JOLT!

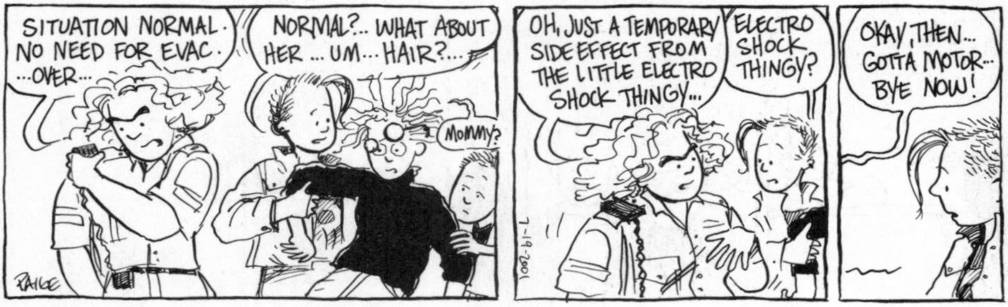
SITUATION NORMAL. NO NEED FOR EVAC. ...OVER...
PAIGE
NORMAL?... WHAT ABOUT HER ... UM... HAIR?...
MOMMY?
OH, JUST A TEMPORARY SIDE EFFECT FROM THE LITTLE ELECTRO SHOCK THINGY...
ELECTRO SHOCK THINGY?
7-19-2001
OKAY, THEN... GOTTA MOTOR... BYE NOW!

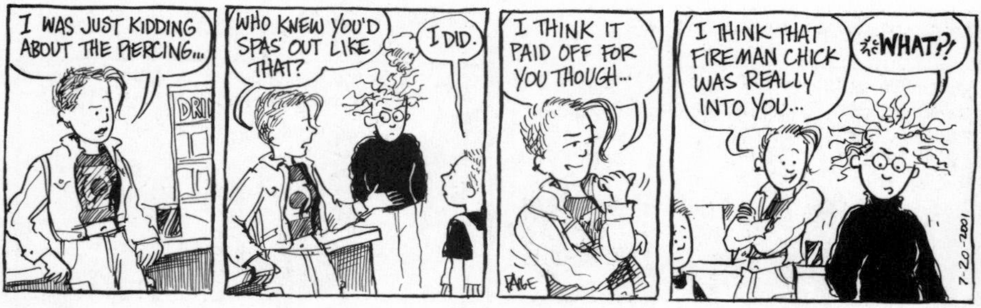
I WAS JUST KIDDING ABOUT THE PIERCING...
WHO KNEW YOU'D SPAS' OUT LIKE THAT?
I DID.
I THINK IT PAID OFF FOR YOU THOUGH...
PAIGE
I THINK THAT FIREMAN CHICK WAS REALLY INTO YOU...
WHAT?!
7-20-2001

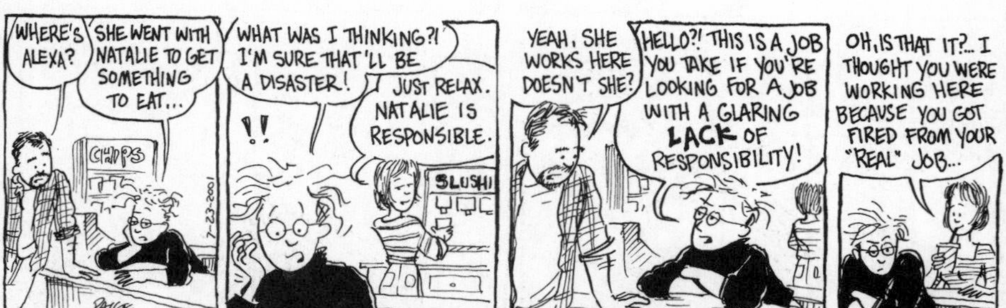
WHERE'S ALEXA?
SHE WENT WITH NATALIE TO GET SOMETHING TO EAT...
CHIPS
7-23-2001
PAIGE
WHAT WAS I THINKING?! I'M SURE THAT'LL BE A DISASTER!
JUST RELAX. NATALIE IS RESPONSIBLE.
!!
SLUSHI
YEAH, SHE WORKS HERE DOESN'T SHE?
HELLO?! THIS IS A JOB YOU TAKE IF YOU'RE LOOKING FOR A JOB WITH A GLARING LACK OF RESPONSIBILITY!
OH, IS THAT IT?... I THOUGHT YOU WERE WORKING HERE BECAUSE YOU GOT FIRED FROM YOUR "REAL" JOB...

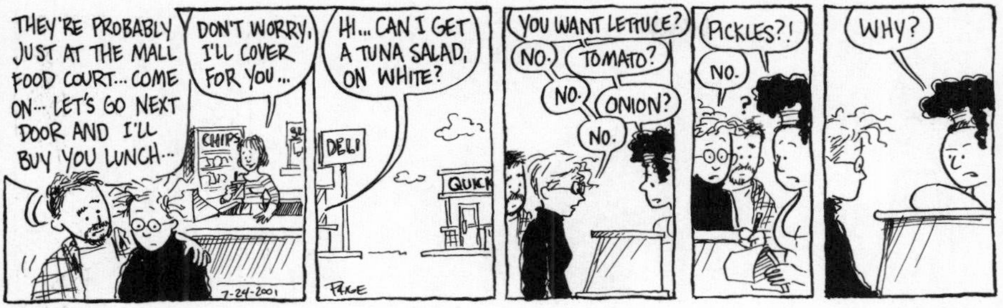

THEY'RE PROBABLY JUST AT THE MALL FOOD COURT... COME ON... LET'S GO NEXT DOOR AND I'LL BUY YOU LUNCH...
DON'T WORRY, I'LL COVER FOR YOU...
CHIPS
7-24-2001
HI... CAN I GET A TUNA SALAD, ON WHITE?
DELI
PAIGE
YOU WANT LETTUCE?
NO.
TOMATO?
NO.
ONION?
NO.
PICKLES?!
NO.
?
WHY?

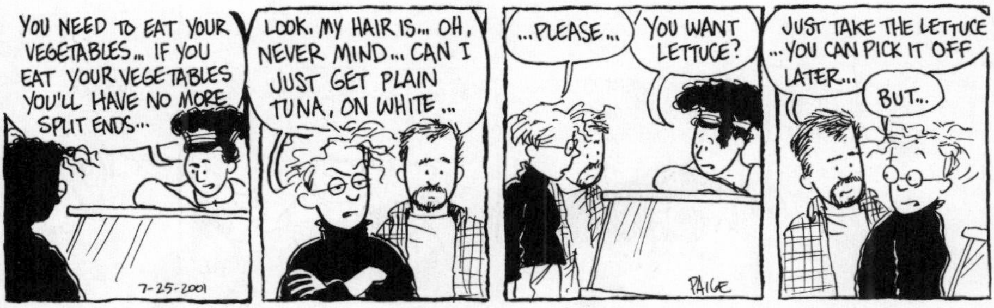

YOU NEED TO EAT YOUR VEGETABLES... IF YOU EAT YOUR VEGETABLES YOU'LL HAVE NO MORE SPLIT ENDS...
7-25-2001
LOOK, MY HAIR IS... OH, NEVER MIND... CAN I JUST GET PLAIN TUNA, ON WHITE...
...PLEASE...
YOU WANT LETTUCE?
PAIGE
JUST TAKE THE LETTUCE ...YOU CAN PICK IT OFF LATER...
BUT...

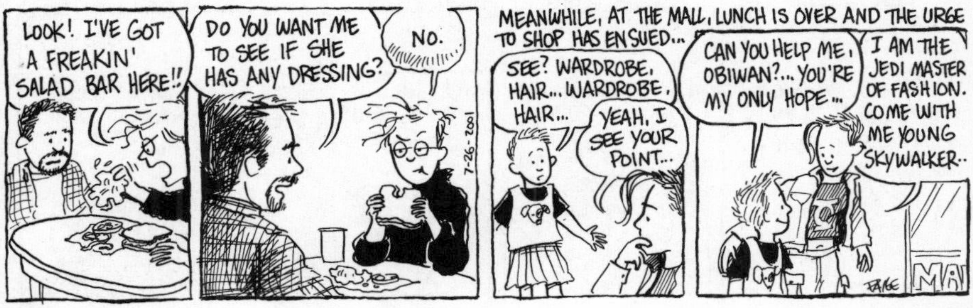

LOOK! I'VE GOT A FREAKIN' SALAD BAR HERE!!
DO YOU WANT ME TO SEE IF SHE HAS ANY DRESSING?
NO.
7-26-2001
MEANWHILE, AT THE MALL, LUNCH IS OVER AND THE URGE TO SHOP HAS ENSUED...
SEE? WARDROBE, HAIR... WARDROBE, HAIR...
YEAH, I SEE YOUR POINT...
CAN YOU HELP ME, OBIWAN?... YOU'RE MY ONLY HOPE...
I AM THE JEDI MASTER OF FASHION. COME WITH ME YOUNG SKYWALKER...
PAIGE

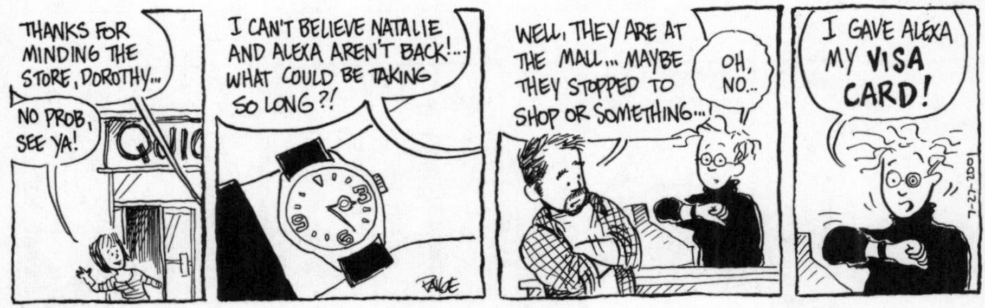

THANKS FOR MINDING THE STORE, DOROTHY...
NO PROB, SEE YA!
I CAN'T BELIEVE NATALIE AND ALEXA AREN'T BACK!... WHAT COULD BE TAKING SO LONG?!
PAIGE
WELL, THEY ARE AT THE MALL... MAYBE THEY STOPPED TO SHOP OR SOMETHING...
OH, NO...
I GAVE ALEXA MY **VISA CARD**!
7-27-2001

LATER, AT JANE'S "...

HERE'S BECCA NOW...

HERE IT COMES...

WELL, IT WAS A NICE LIFE WHILE IT LASTED.

HMMM... WHAT SHALL I DO WITH THE LAST 10 PRECIOUS MOMENTS OF MY BRILLIANT LIFE?

HOW ABOUT SPENDING IT TO FIND ME A BARF BAG...

GEEZ, AUNT JANE... YOU'RE SUCH A DRAMA QUEEN!

I'M NOT A DRAMA QUEEN! I'M A **REALIST!**... YOUR MOM IS GOING TO KILL ME!!

IN ONE SHORT MINUTE SHE IS GOING TO WALK THROUGH THAT DOOR, EXPECTING TO FIND HER CUTE 10-YEAR-OLD DAUGHTER...

...AND INSTEAD, IT'LL BE **YOU!** BLUE HAIR, AND BAGGY PANTS...

YOU'RE LIKE A BITE-SIZED NATALIE!

SO?

NATALIE IS COOL.

GOOD BYE CRUEL WORLD...

HI, BECCA... JUST MAKE IT QUICK AND PAINLESS, OKAY?

WHAT ARE YOU TALKING ABOUT?... AND WHERE IS...

ALEXA!

I'M HAPPY TO SEE YOU TOO MOM... LET'S MOTOR...

HEH... HEH...

182

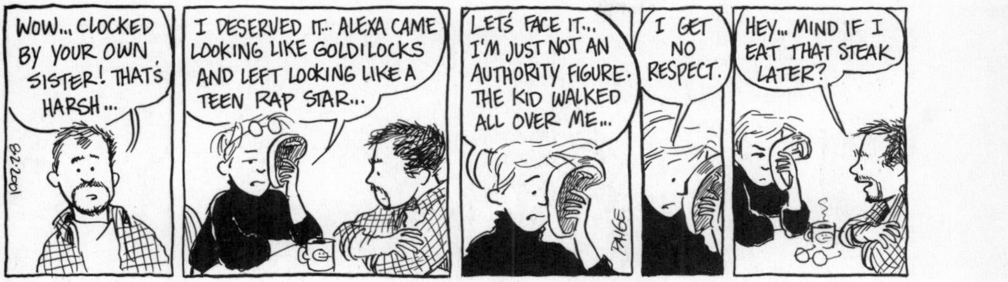
WOW... CLOCKED BY YOUR OWN SISTER! THAT'S HARSH...
8-2-2001
I DESERVED IT... ALEXA CAME LOOKING LIKE GOLDILOCKS AND LEFT LOOKING LIKE A TEEN RAP STAR...
LET'S FACE IT... I'M JUST NOT AN AUTHORITY FIGURE. THE KID WALKED ALL OVER ME...
PAIGE
I GET NO RESPECT.
HEY... MIND IF I EAT THAT STEAK LATER?

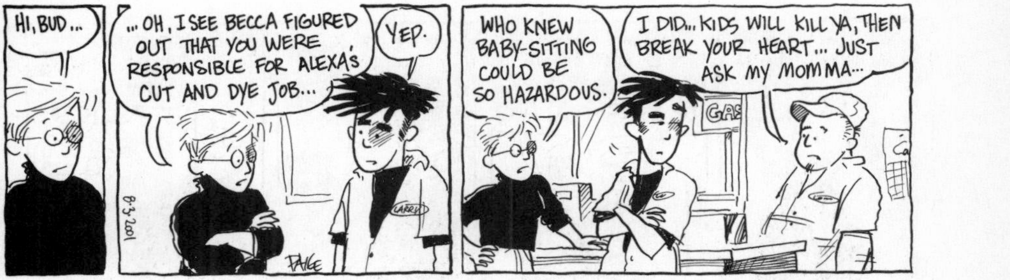
HI, BUD...
... OH, I SEE BECCA FIGURED OUT THAT YOU WERE RESPONSIBLE FOR ALEXA'S CUT AND DYE JOB...
YEP.
8-3-2001
PAIGE
LARRY
WHO KNEW BABY-SITTING COULD BE SO HAZARDOUS.
I DID... KIDS WILL KILL YA, THEN BREAK YOUR HEART... JUST ASK MY MOMMA...
GAS

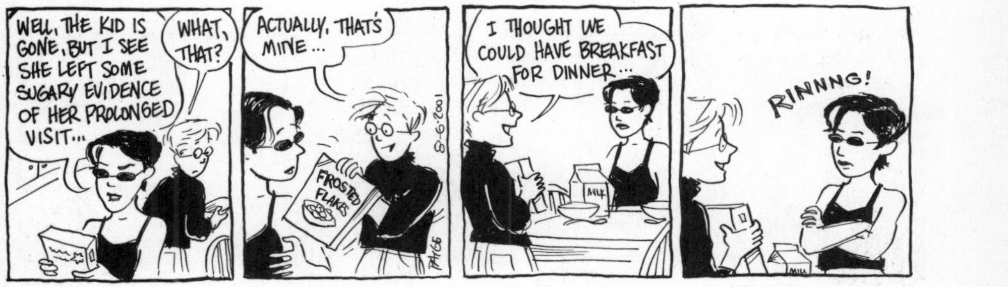
WELL, THE KID IS GONE, BUT I SEE SHE LEFT SOME SUGARY EVIDENCE OF HER PROLONGED VISIT...
WHAT, THAT?
ACTUALLY, THAT'S MINE...
8-6-2001
FROSTED FLAKES
PAIGE
I THOUGHT WE COULD HAVE BREAKFAST FOR DINNER...
MILK
RINNNG!

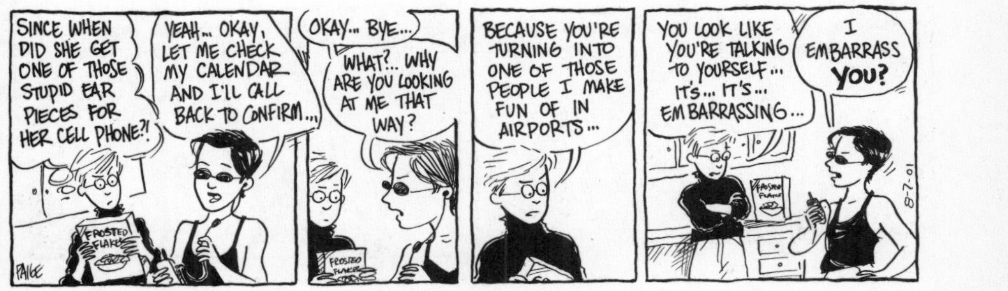
SINCE WHEN DID SHE GET ONE OF THOSE STUPID EAR PIECES FOR HER CELL PHONE?!
YEAH... OKAY, LET ME CHECK MY CALENDAR AND I'LL CALL BACK TO CONFIRM...
FROSTED FLAKES
PAIGE
OKAY... BYE...
WHAT?... WHY ARE YOU LOOKING AT ME THAT WAY?
BECAUSE YOU'RE TURNING INTO ONE OF THOSE PEOPLE I MAKE FUN OF IN AIRPORTS...
YOU LOOK LIKE YOU'RE TALKING TO YOURSELF... IT'S... IT'S... EMBARRASSING...
I EMBARRASS YOU?
8-7-01

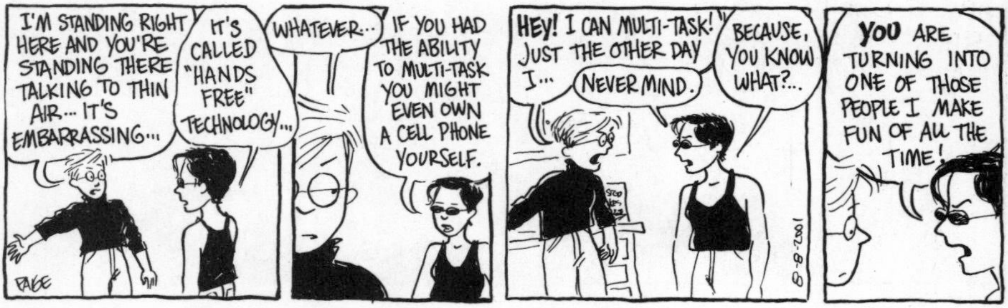
I'M STANDING RIGHT HERE AND YOU'RE STANDING THERE TALKING TO THIN AIR... IT'S EMBARRASSING...
IT'S CALLED "HANDS FREE" TECHNOLOGY...
PAIGE
WHATEVER...
IF YOU HAD THE ABILITY TO MULTI-TASK YOU MIGHT EVEN OWN A CELL PHONE YOURSELF.
HEY! I CAN MULTI-TASK! JUST THE OTHER DAY I...
NEVER MIND.
BECAUSE, YOU KNOW WHAT?...
8-8-2001
YOU ARE TURNING INTO ONE OF THOSE PEOPLE I MAKE FUN OF ALL THE TIME!

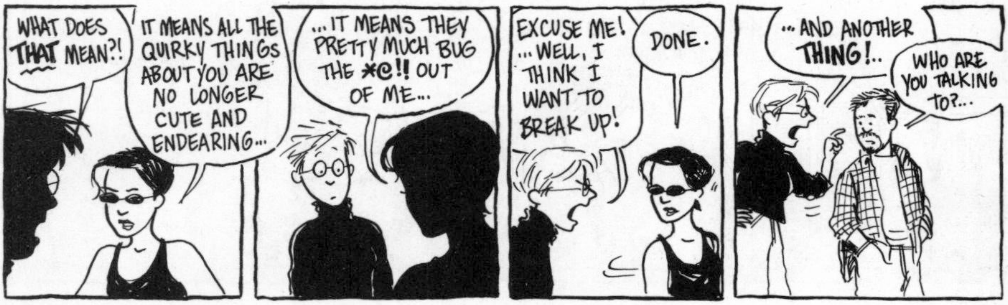
WHAT DOES THAT MEAN?!
IT MEANS ALL THE QUIRKY THINGS ABOUT YOU ARE NO LONGER CUTE AND ENDEARING...
...IT MEANS THEY PRETTY MUCH BUG THE *@!! OUT OF ME...
EXCUSE ME! ...WELL, I THINK I WANT TO BREAK UP!
DONE.
...AND ANOTHER THING!...
WHO ARE YOU TALKING TO?...

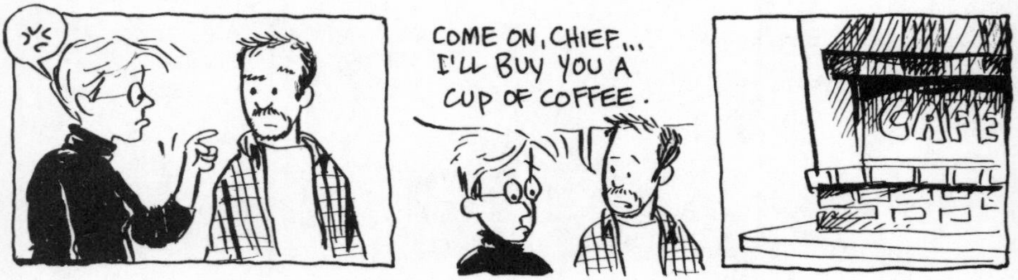
COME ON, CHIEF... I'LL BUY YOU A CUP OF COFFEE.
CAFE

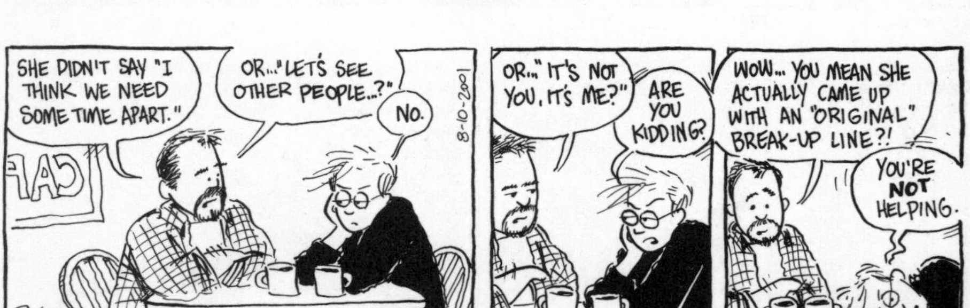
SHE DIDN'T SAY "I THINK WE NEED SOME TIME APART."
OR..."LET'S SEE OTHER PEOPLE...?"
NO.
PAIGE
8-10-2001
OR..."IT'S NOT YOU, IT'S ME?"
ARE YOU KIDDING?
WOW... YOU MEAN SHE ACTUALLY CAME UP WITH AN "ORIGINAL" BREAK-UP LINE?!
YOU'RE NOT HELPING.

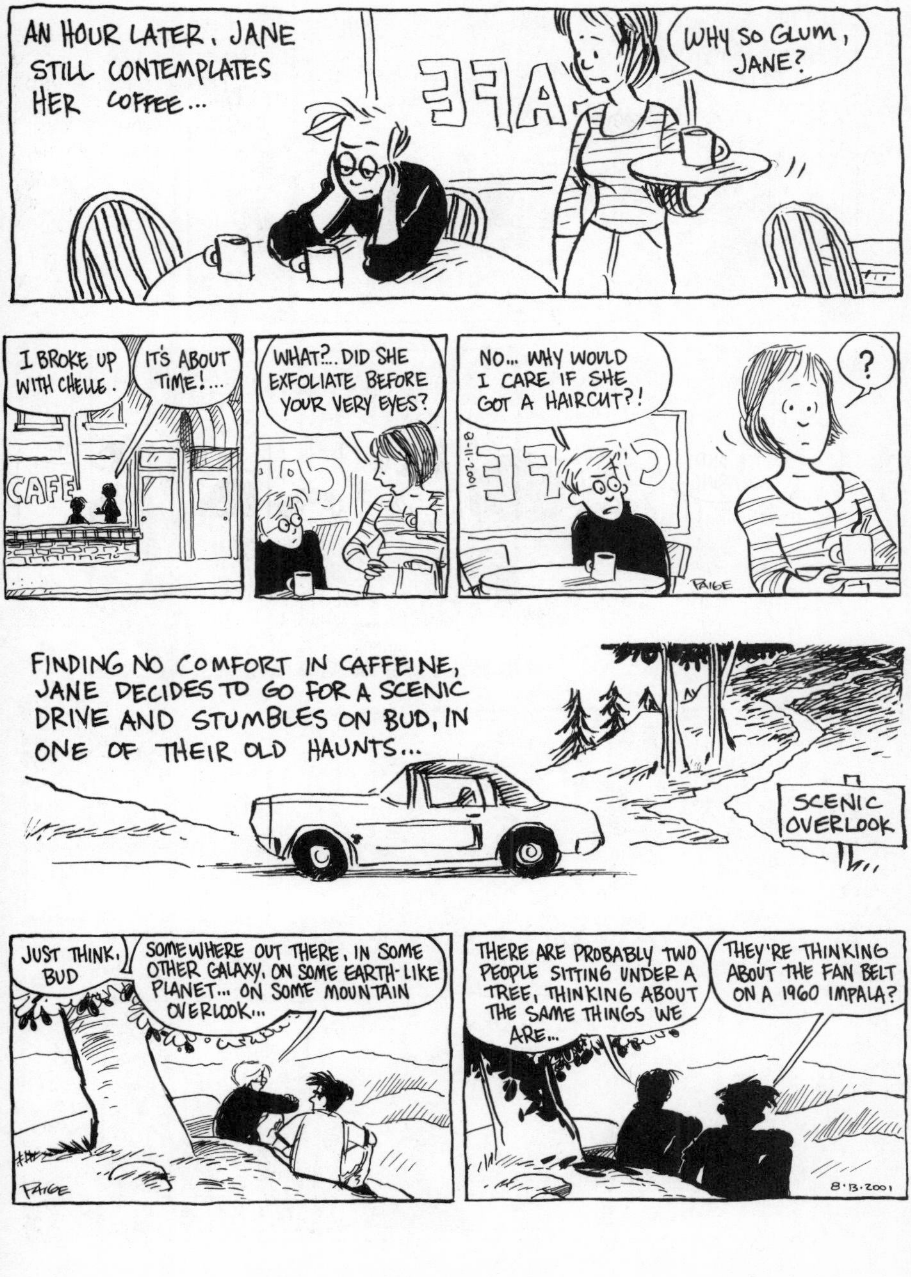

AN HOUR LATER, JANE STILL CONTEMPLATES HER COFFEE...
WHY SO GLUM, JANE?
CAFE
I BROKE UP WITH CHELLE.
IT'S ABOUT TIME!...
CAFE
WHAT?... DID SHE EXFOLIATE BEFORE YOUR VERY EYES?
NO... WHY WOULD I CARE IF SHE GOT A HAIRCUT?!
8-11-2001
?
PAIGE
FINDING NO COMFORT IN CAFFEINE, JANE DECIDES TO GO FOR A SCENIC DRIVE AND STUMBLES ON BUD, IN ONE OF THEIR OLD HAUNTS...
SCENIC OVERLOOK
JUST THINK, BUD
SOMEWHERE OUT THERE, IN SOME OTHER GALAXY, ON SOME EARTH-LIKE PLANET... ON SOME MOUNTAIN OVERLOOK...
THERE ARE PROBABLY TWO PEOPLE SITTING UNDER A TREE, THINKING ABOUT THE SAME THINGS WE ARE...
THEY'RE THINKING ABOUT THE FAN BELT ON A 1960 IMPALA?
PAIGE
8·13·2001

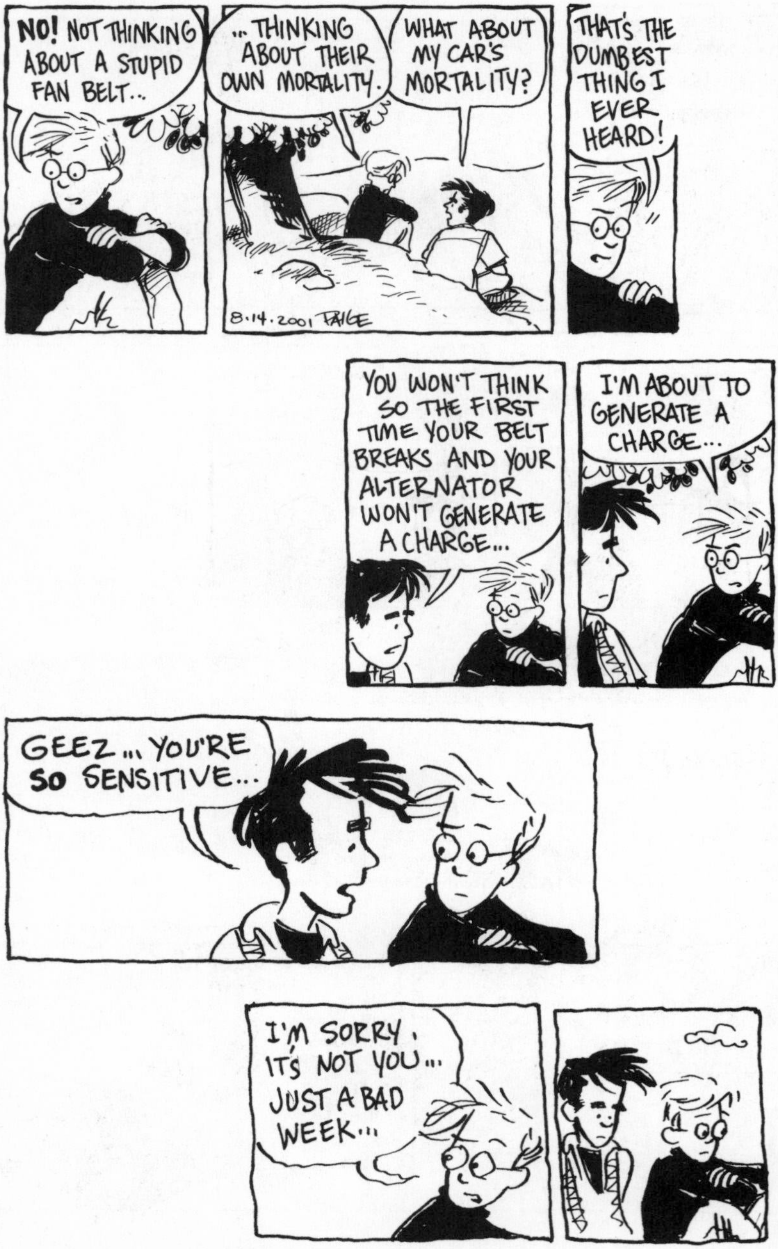
NO! NOT THINKING ABOUT A STUPID FAN BELT...
... THINKING ABOUT THEIR OWN MORTALITY.
WHAT ABOUT MY CAR'S MORTALITY?
8.14.2001 PAIGE
THAT'S THE DUMBEST THING I EVER HEARD!
YOU WON'T THINK SO THE FIRST TIME YOUR BELT BREAKS AND YOUR ALTERNATOR WON'T GENERATE A CHARGE...
I'M ABOUT TO GENERATE A CHARGE...
GEEZ... YOU'RE SO SENSITIVE...
I'M SORRY. IT'S NOT YOU... JUST A BAD WEEK...

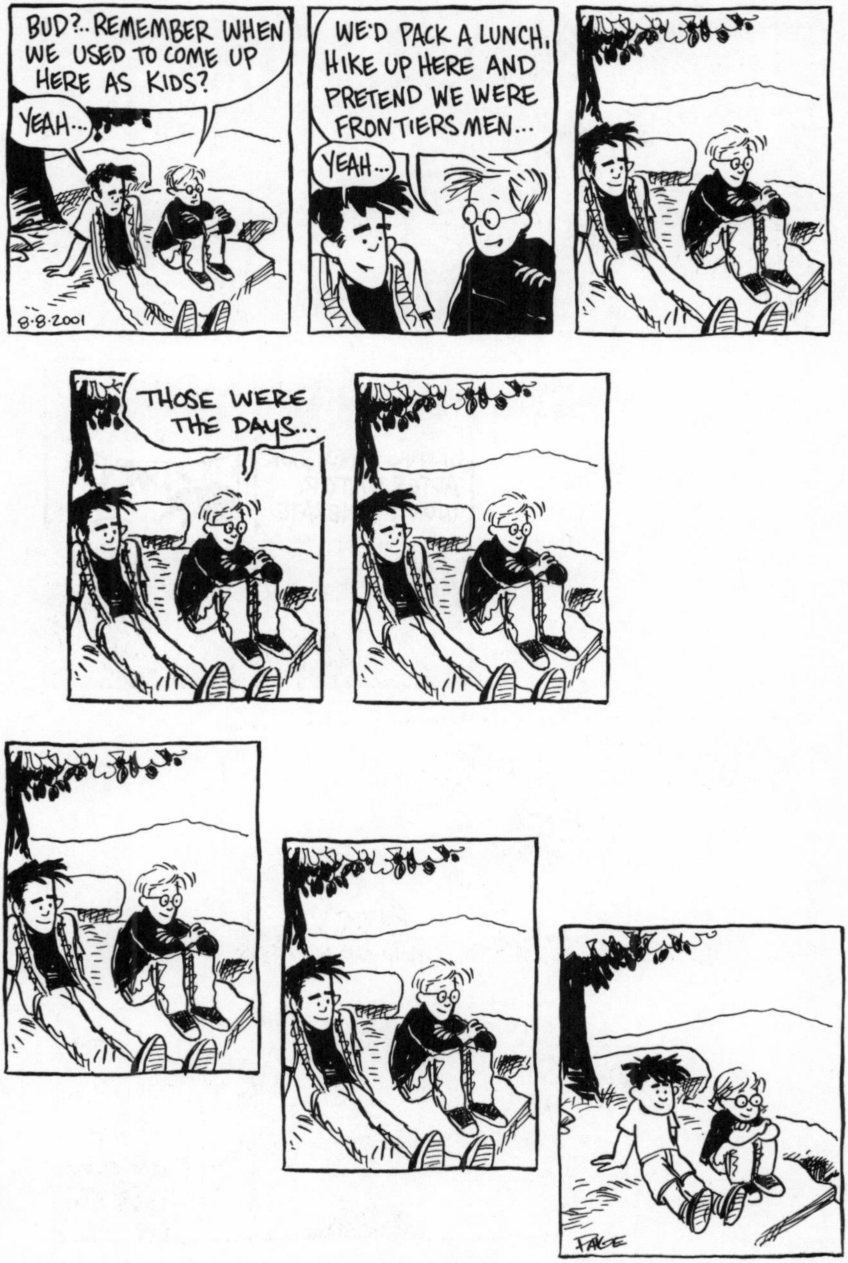
BUD?.. REMEMBER WHEN WE USED TO COME UP HERE AS KIDS?
YEAH...
8·8·2001
WE'D PACK A LUNCH, HIKE UP HERE AND PRETEND WE WERE FRONTIERSMEN...
YEAH...
THOSE WERE THE DAYS...
PAIGE

Chapter 8

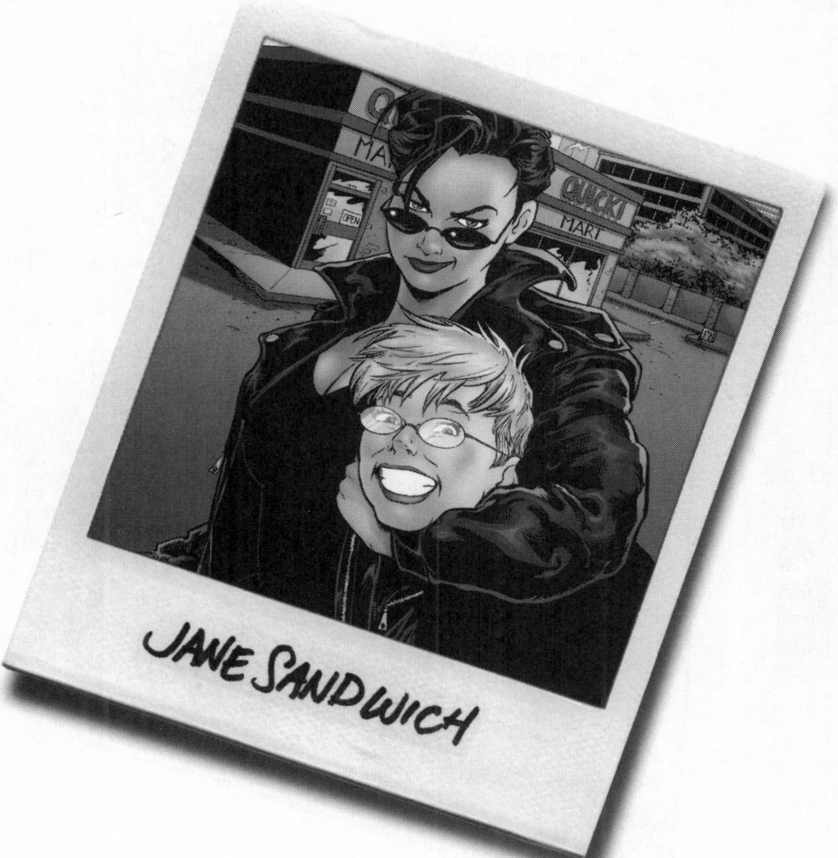
QUICK
MART
OPEN
JANE SANDWICH

ILLUSTRATION BY TERRY MOORE

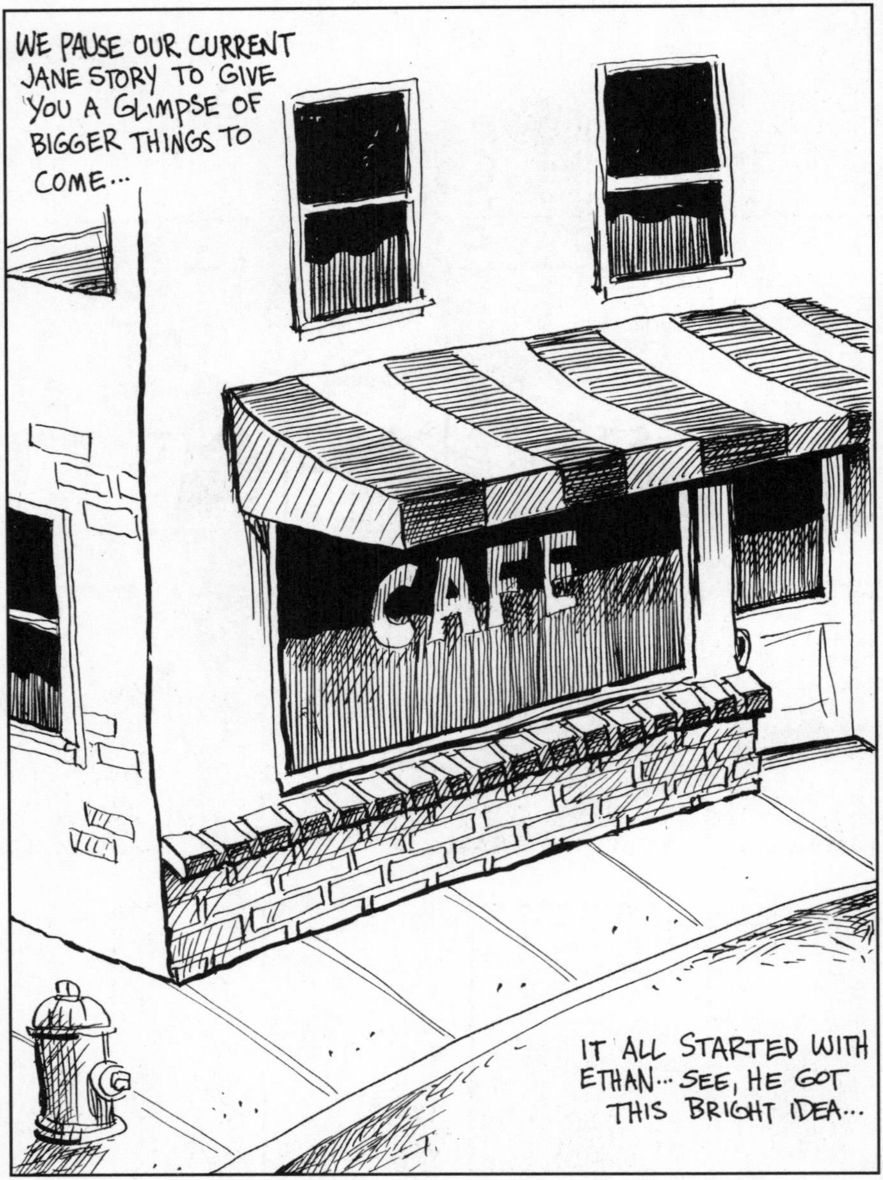
WE PAUSE OUR CURRENT JANE STORY TO GIVE YOU A GLIMPSE OF BIGGER THINGS TO COME...
CAFE
IT ALL STARTED WITH ETHAN... SEE, HE GOT THIS BRIGHT IDEA...

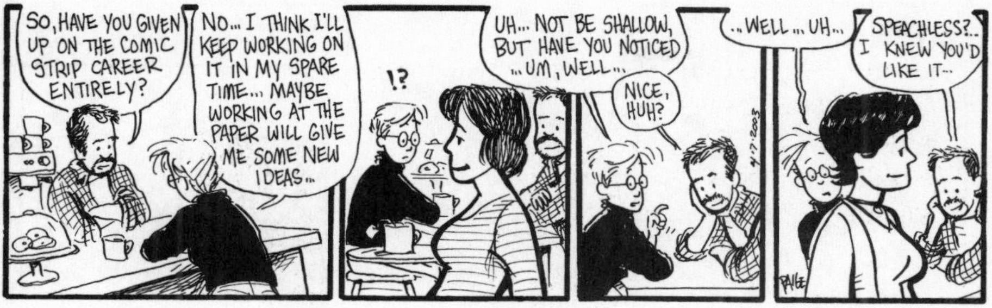
SO, HAVE YOU GIVEN UP ON THE COMIC STRIP CAREER ENTIRELY?
NO... I THINK I'LL KEEP WORKING ON IT IN MY SPARE TIME... MAYBE WORKING AT THE PAPER WILL GIVE ME SOME NEW IDEAS...
!?
UH... NOT BE SHALLOW, BUT HAVE YOU NOTICED ...UM, WELL...
NICE, HUH?
4-7-2003
..WELL ... UH...
SPEACHLESS?.. I KNEW YOU'D LIKE IT...
PAIGE

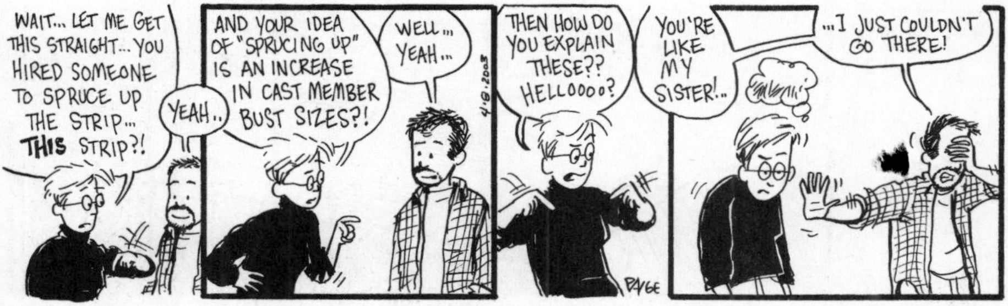
WAIT... LET ME GET THIS STRAIGHT... YOU HIRED SOMEONE TO SPRUCE UP THE STRIP... THIS STRIP?!
YEAH..
AND YOUR IDEA OF "SPRUCING UP" IS AN INCREASE IN CAST MEMBER BUST SIZES?!
WELL... YEAH...
4-8-2003
THEN HOW DO YOU EXPLAIN THESE?? HELLOOOO?
YOU'RE LIKE MY SISTER!..
...I JUST COULDN'T GO THERE!
PAIGE

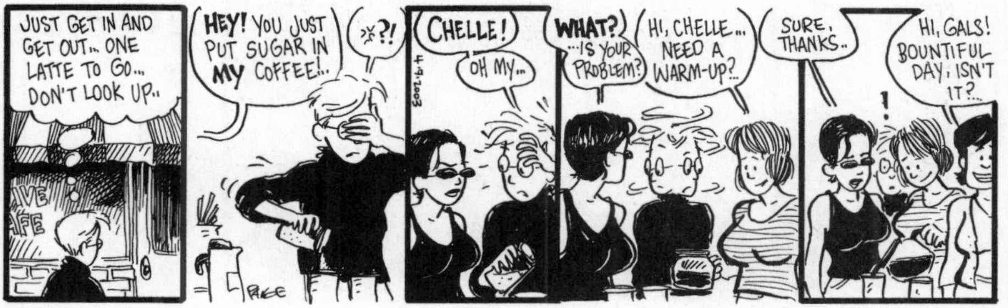
JUST GET IN AND GET OUT... ONE LATTE TO GO... DON'T LOOK UP..
HEY! YOU JUST PUT SUGAR IN MY COFFEE!..
?!
PAIGE
CHELLE!
OH MY...
4-9-2003
WHAT? ...IS YOUR PROBLEM?
HI, CHELLE... NEED A WARM-UP?..
SURE, THANKS..
!
HI, GALS! BOUNTIFUL DAY, ISN'T IT?...

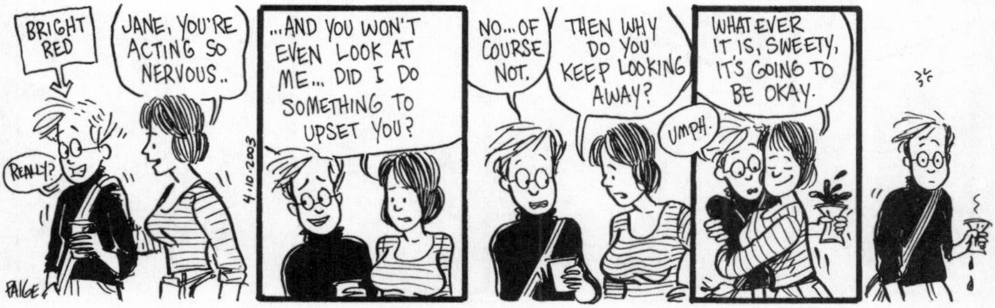
BRIGHT RED
REALLY?
JANE, YOU'RE ACTING SO NERVOUS..
PAIGE
4-10-2003
...AND YOU WON'T EVEN LOOK AT ME... DID I DO SOMETHING TO UPSET YOU?
NO... OF COURSE NOT.
THEN WHY DO YOU KEEP LOOKING AWAY?
UMPH.
WHATEVER IT IS, SWEETY, IT'S GOING TO BE OKAY.

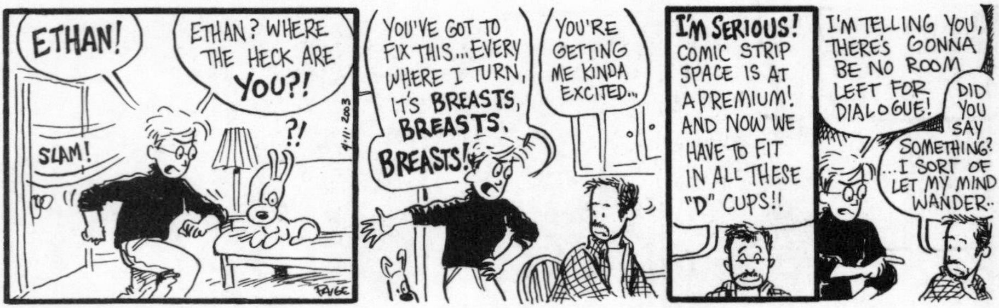
ETHAN!
ETHAN? WHERE THE HECK ARE YOU?!
SLAM!
?!
4·11·2003
YOU'VE GOT TO FIX THIS... EVERY WHERE I TURN, IT'S BREASTS, BREASTS, BREASTS!
YOU'RE GETTING ME KINDA EXCITED...
I'M SERIOUS! COMIC STRIP SPACE IS AT A PREMIUM! AND NOW WE HAVE TO FIT IN ALL THESE "D" CUPS!!
I'M TELLING YOU, THERE'S GONNA BE NO ROOM LEFT FOR DIALOGUE!
DID YOU SAY SOMETHING? ...I SORT OF LET MY MIND WANDER...
PAIGE

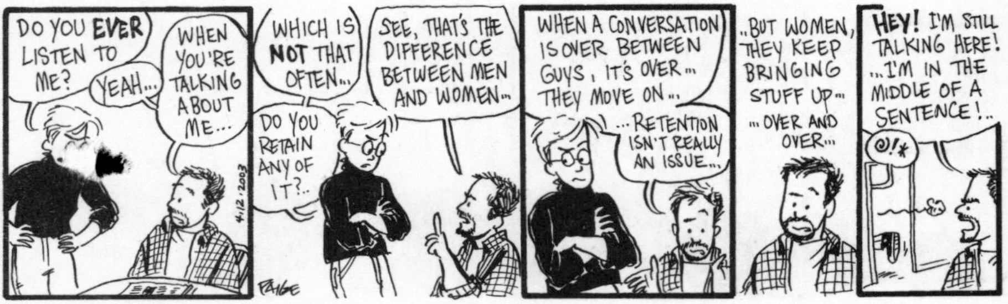
DO YOU EVER LISTEN TO ME?
YEAH...
WHEN YOU'RE TALKING ABOUT ME...
4·12·2003
WHICH IS NOT THAT OFTEN...
DO YOU RETAIN ANY OF IT?...
SEE, THAT'S THE DIFFERENCE BETWEEN MEN AND WOMEN...
WHEN A CONVERSATION IS OVER BETWEEN GUYS, IT'S OVER... THEY MOVE ON...
...RETENTION ISN'T REALLY AN ISSUE...
..BUT WOMEN, THEY KEEP BRINGING STUFF UP... ...OVER AND OVER...
HEY! I'M STILL TALKING HERE! ...I'M IN THE MIDDLE OF A SENTENCE!..
@!*
PAIGE

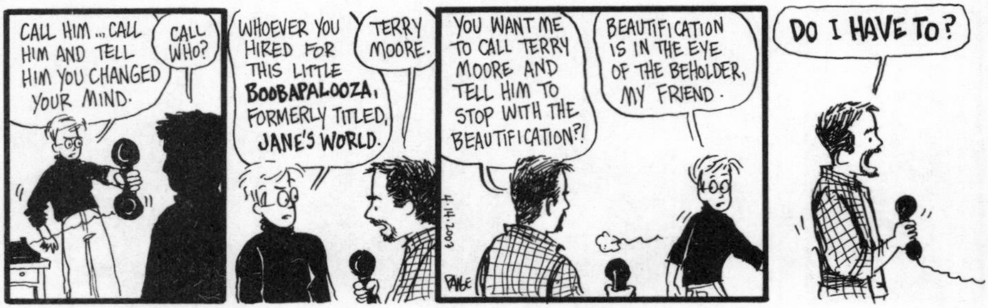
CALL HIM... CALL HIM AND TELL HIM YOU CHANGED YOUR MIND.
CALL WHO?
WHOEVER YOU HIRED FOR THIS LITTLE BOOBAPALOOZA, FORMERLY TITLED, JANE'S WORLD.
TERRY MOORE.
4·14·2003
YOU WANT ME TO CALL TERRY MOORE AND TELL HIM TO STOP WITH THE BEAUTIFICATION?!
BEAUTIFICATION IS IN THE EYE OF THE BEHOLDER, MY FRIEND.
DO I HAVE TO?
PAIGE

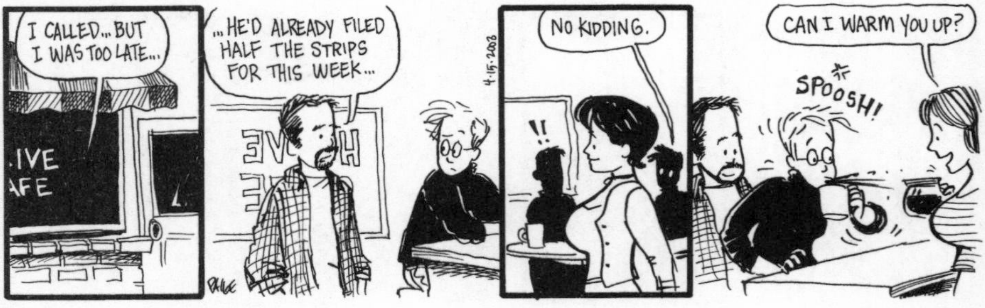
I CALLED... BUT I WAS TOO LATE...
LIVE
AFE
...HE'D ALREADY FILED HALF THE STRIPS FOR THIS WEEK...
4·15·2003
NO KIDDING.
!!
SPOOSH!
CAN I WARM YOU UP?
PAIGE

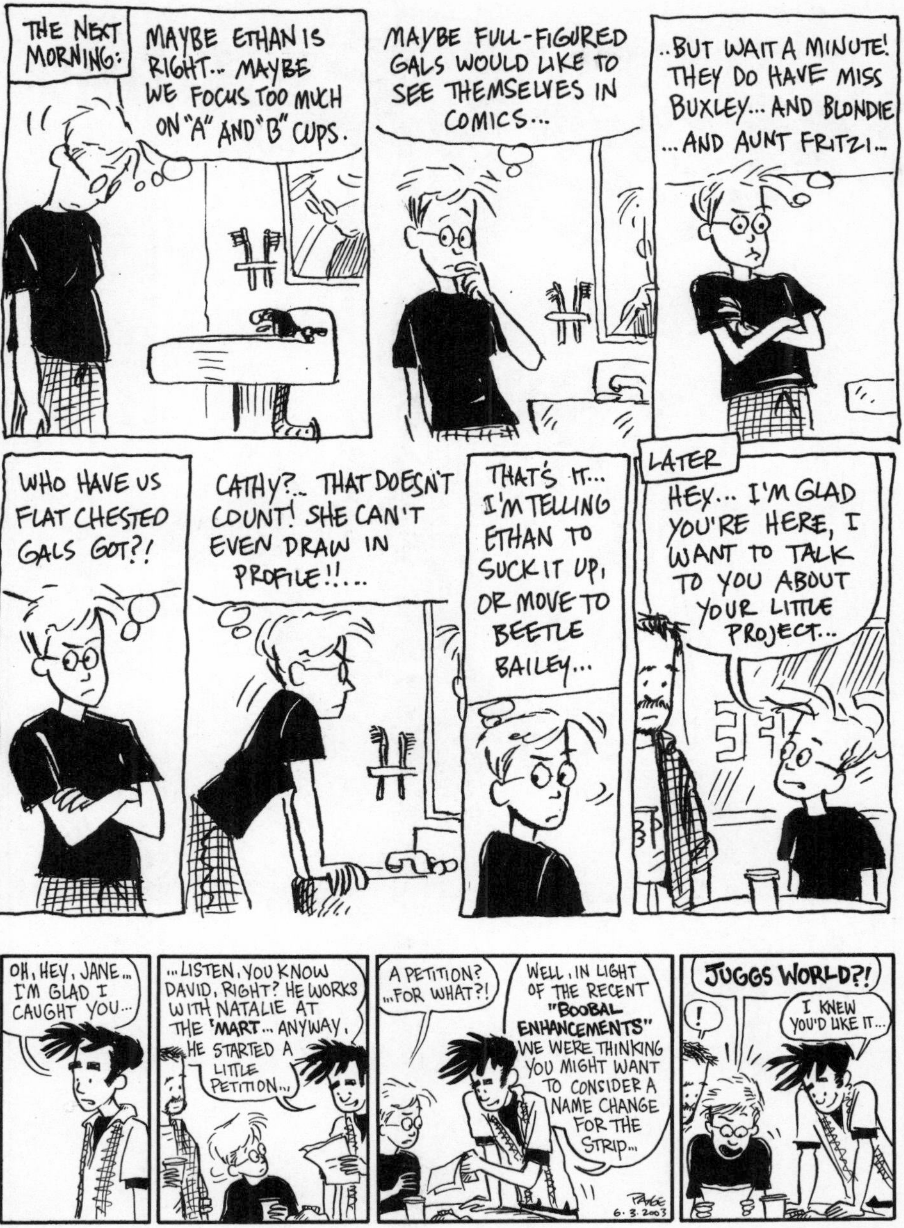
THE NEXT MORNING:
MAYBE ETHAN IS RIGHT... MAYBE WE FOCUS TOO MUCH ON "A" AND "B" CUPS.
MAYBE FULL-FIGURED GALS WOULD LIKE TO SEE THEMSELVES IN COMICS...
..BUT WAIT A MINUTE! THEY DO HAVE MISS BUXLEY... AND BLONDIE ...AND AUNT FRITZI...
WHO HAVE US FLAT CHESTED GALS GOT?!
CATHY?.. THAT DOESN'T COUNT! SHE CAN'T EVEN DRAW IN PROFILE!!...
THAT'S IT... I'M TELLING ETHAN TO SUCK IT UP, OR MOVE TO BEETLE BAILEY...
LATER
HEY... I'M GLAD YOU'RE HERE, I WANT TO TALK TO YOU ABOUT YOUR LITTLE PROJECT...
OH, HEY, JANE... I'M GLAD I CAUGHT YOU...
...LISTEN, YOU KNOW DAVID, RIGHT? HE WORKS WITH NATALIE AT THE 'MART... ANYWAY, HE STARTED A LITTLE PETITION...
A PETITION? ...FOR WHAT?!
WELL, IN LIGHT OF THE RECENT "BOOBAL ENHANCEMENTS" WE WERE THINKING YOU MIGHT WANT TO CONSIDER A NAME CHANGE FOR THE STRIP...
PAIGE 6.3.2003
JUGGS WORLD?!
!
I KNEW YOU'D LIKE IT...

THE END, FOR NOW

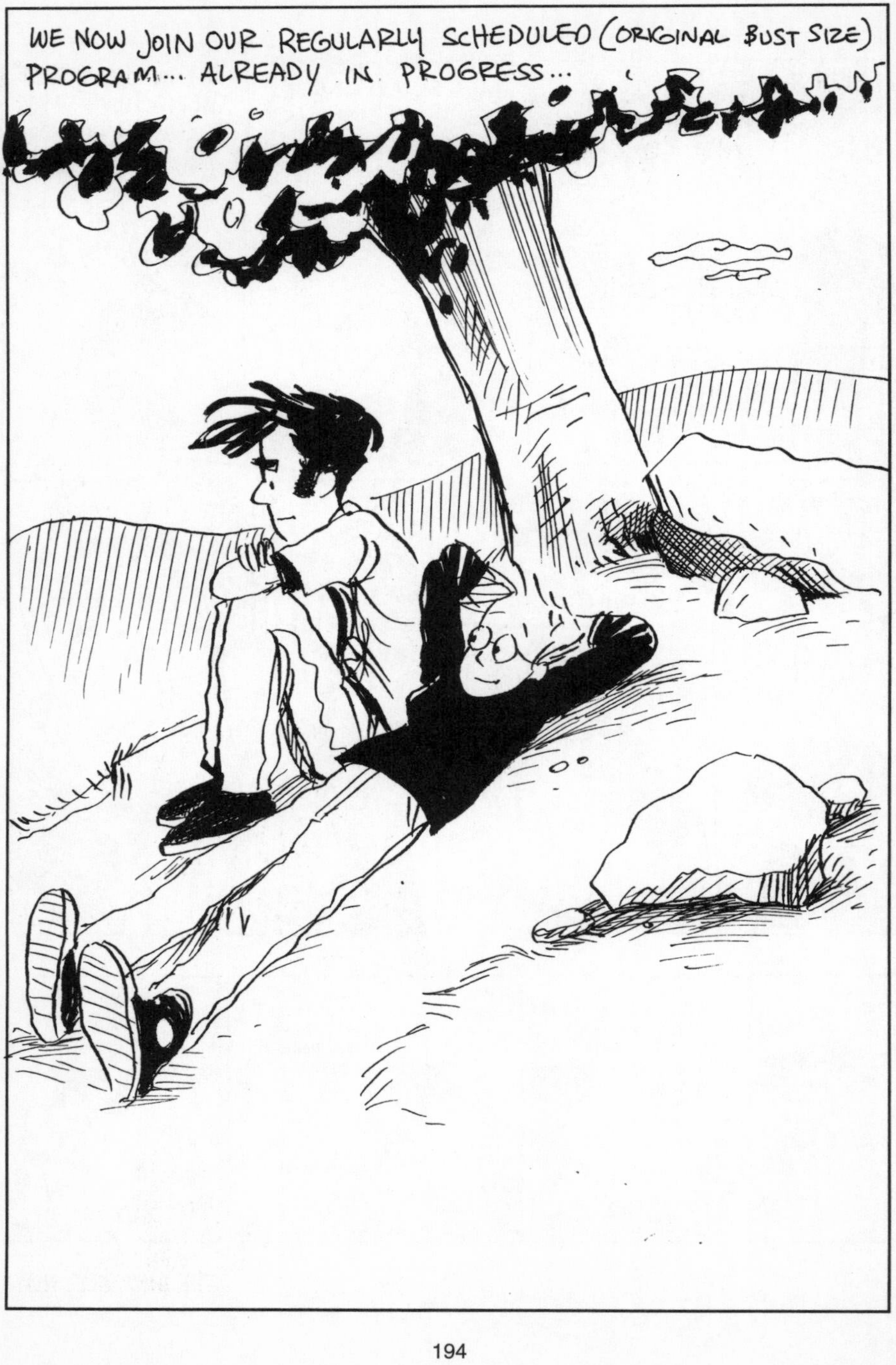
WE NOW JOIN OUR REGULARLY SCHEDULED (ORIGINAL BUST SIZE) PROGRAM... ALREADY IN PROGRESS...

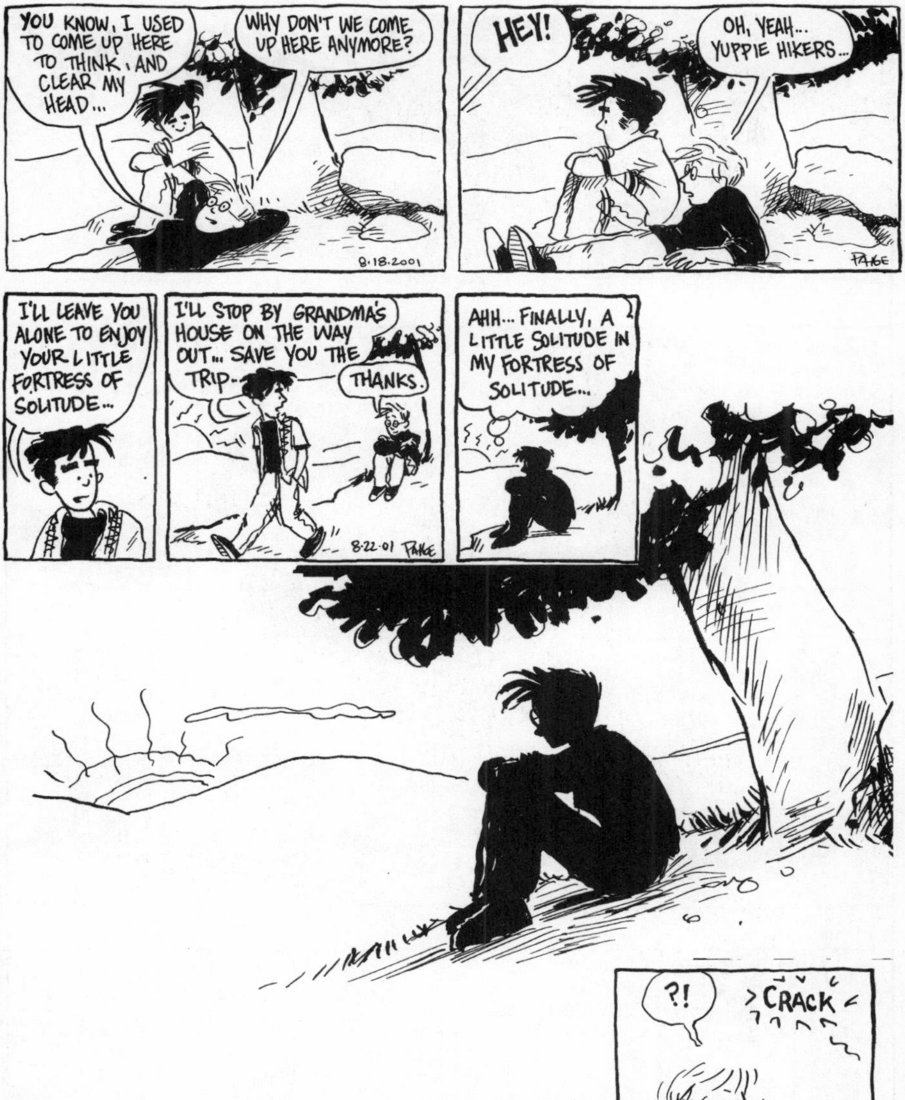
YOU KNOW, I USED TO COME UP HERE TO THINK, AND CLEAR MY HEAD...
WHY DON'T WE COME UP HERE ANYMORE?
8.18.2001
HEY!
OH, YEAH... YUPPIE HIKERS...
I'LL LEAVE YOU ALONE TO ENJOY YOUR LITTLE FORTRESS OF SOLITUDE...
I'LL STOP BY GRANDMA'S HOUSE ON THE WAY OUT... SAVE YOU THE TRIP.
THANKS.
8.22.01
AHH... FINALLY, A LITTLE SOLITUDE IN MY FORTRESS OF SOLITUDE...
?!
CRACK

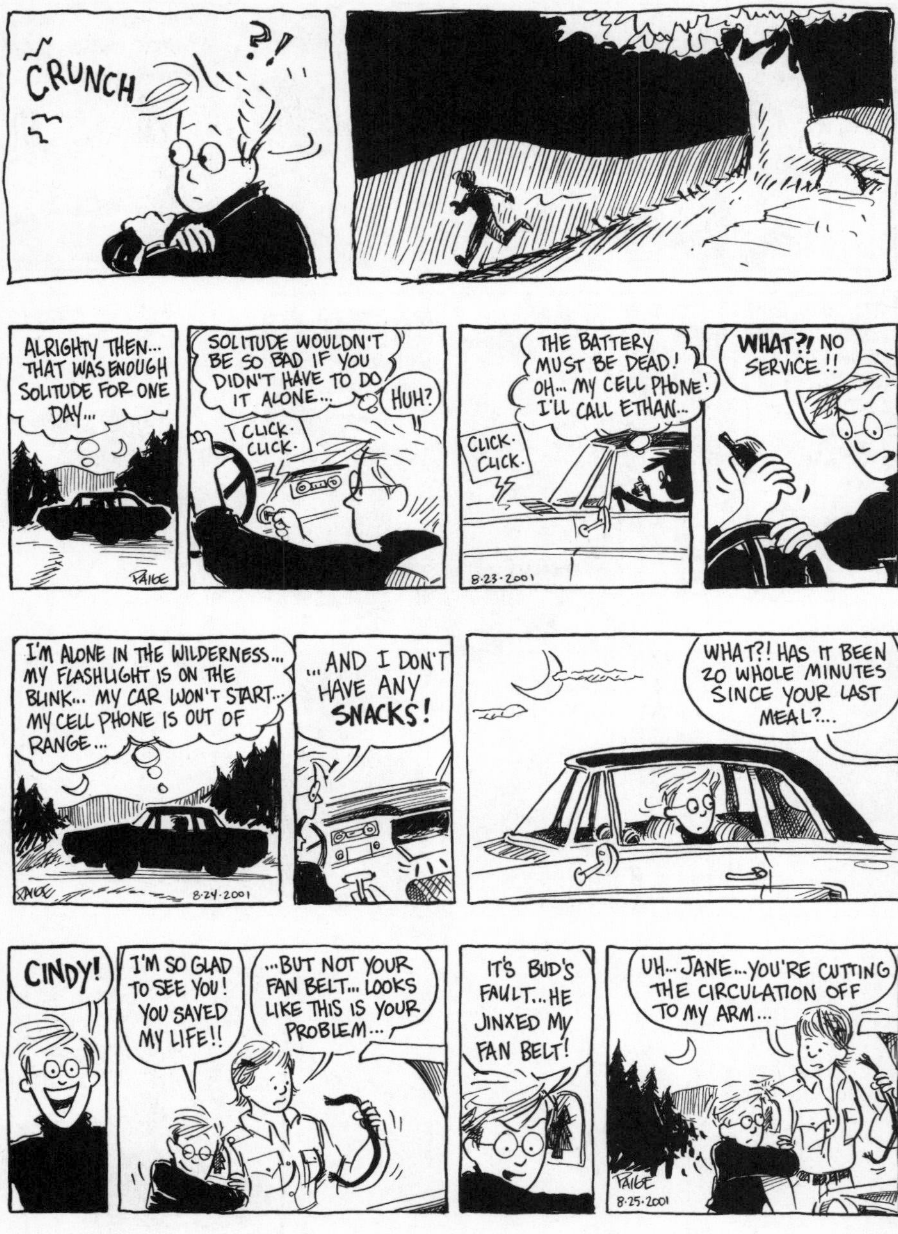
CRUNCH
?!
ALRIGHTY THEN... THAT WAS ENOUGH SOLITUDE FOR ONE DAY...
PAIGE
SOLITUDE WOULDN'T BE SO BAD IF YOU DIDN'T HAVE TO DO IT ALONE...
HUH?
CLICK. CLICK.
THE BATTERY MUST BE DEAD! OH... MY CELL PHONE! I'LL CALL ETHAN...
CLICK. CLICK.
8·23·2001
WHAT?! NO SERVICE!!
I'M ALONE IN THE WILDERNESS... MY FLASHLIGHT IS ON THE BLINK... MY CAR WON'T START... MY CELL PHONE IS OUT OF RANGE...
PAIGE
8·24·2001
...AND I DON'T HAVE ANY SNACKS!
WHAT?! HAS IT BEEN 20 WHOLE MINUTES SINCE YOUR LAST MEAL?...
CINDY!
I'M SO GLAD TO SEE YOU! YOU SAVED MY LIFE!!
...BUT NOT YOUR FAN BELT... LOOKS LIKE THIS IS YOUR PROBLEM...
IT'S BUD'S FAULT... HE JINXED MY FAN BELT!
UH... JANE... YOU'RE CUTTING THE CIRCULATION OFF TO MY ARM...
PAIGE
8·25·2001

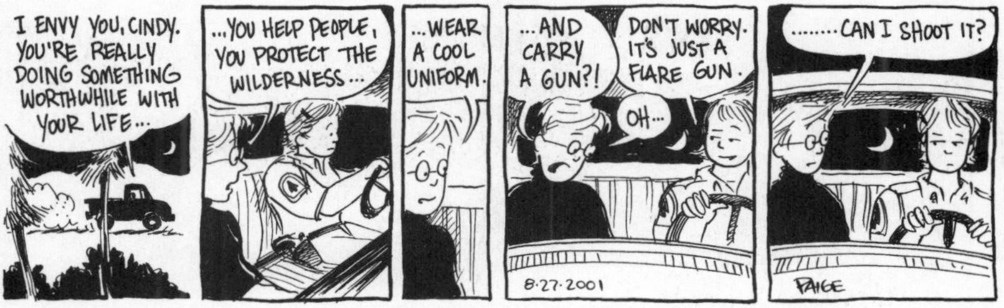
I ENVY YOU, CINDY. YOU'RE REALLY DOING SOMETHING WORTHWHILE WITH YOUR LIFE...
...YOU HELP PEOPLE, YOU PROTECT THE WILDERNESS...
...WEAR A COOL UNIFORM.
...AND CARRY A GUN?!
DON'T WORRY. IT'S JUST A FLARE GUN.
OH...
........CAN I SHOOT IT?
8·27·2001
PAIGE

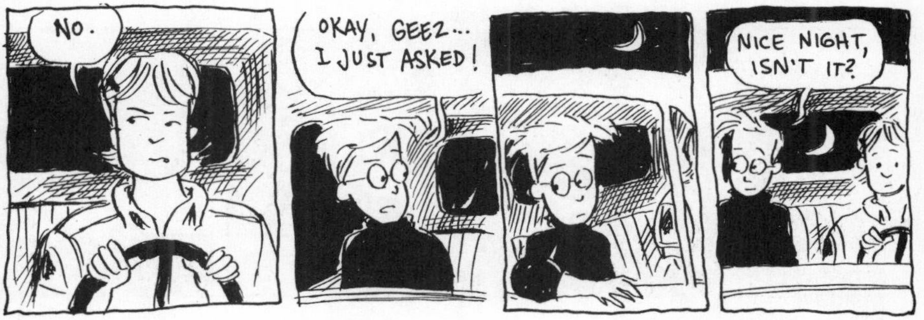
NO.
OKAY, GEEZ... I JUST ASKED!
NICE NIGHT, ISN'T IT?

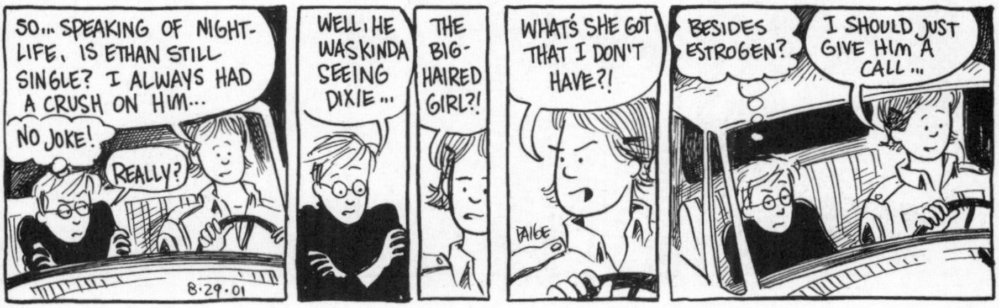
SO... SPEAKING OF NIGHT-LIFE, IS ETHAN STILL SINGLE? I ALWAYS HAD A CRUSH ON HIM...
NO JOKE!
REALLY?
8·29·01
WELL, HE WAS KINDA SEEING DIXIE...
THE BIG-HAIRED GIRL?!
WHAT'S SHE GOT THAT I DON'T HAVE?!
PAIGE
BESIDES ESTROGEN?
I SHOULD JUST GIVE HIM A CALL...

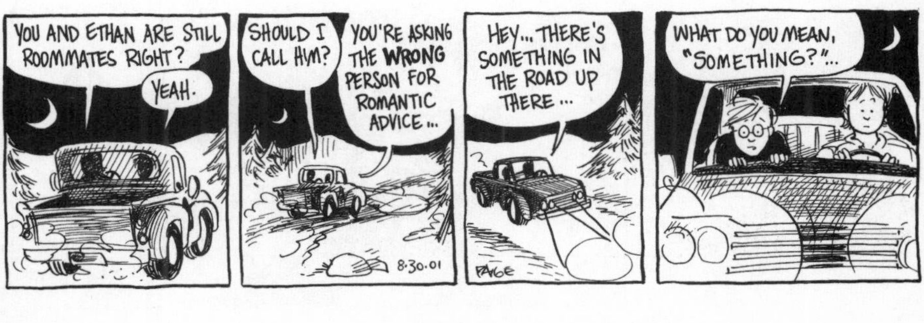
YOU AND ETHAN ARE STILL ROOMMATES RIGHT?
YEAH.
SHOULD I CALL HIM?
YOU'RE ASKING THE WRONG PERSON FOR ROMANTIC ADVICE...
8·30·01
HEY... THERE'S SOMETHING IN THE ROAD UP THERE...
PAIGE
WHAT DO YOU MEAN, "SOMETHING?"...

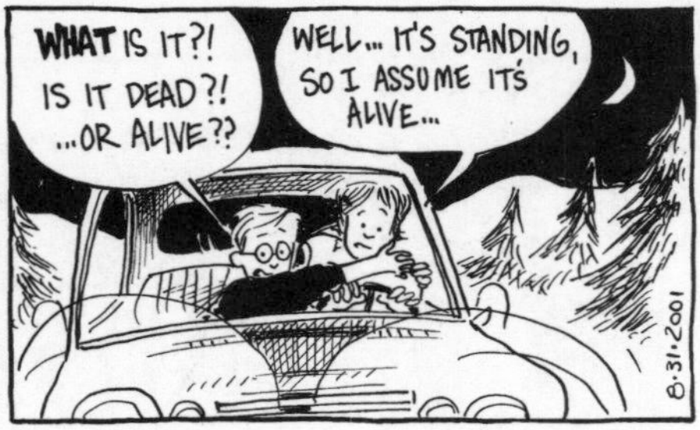
WHAT IS IT?! IS IT DEAD?! ...OR ALIVE??
WELL... IT'S STANDING, SO I ASSUME IT'S ALIVE...
8·31·2001

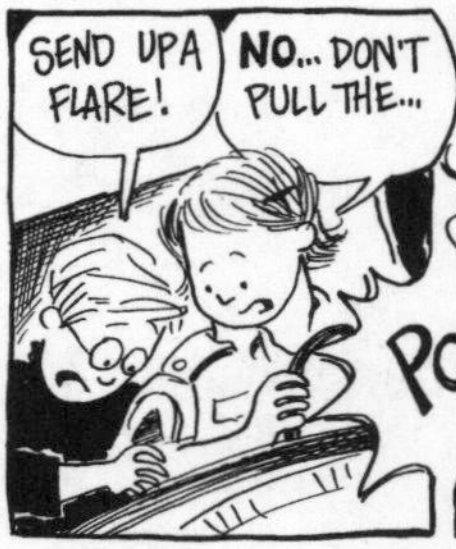
SEND UP A FLARE!
NO... DON'T PULL THE...

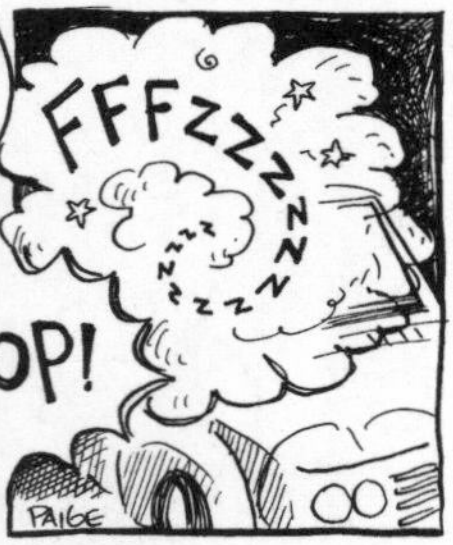
FFFZZZZZZ
POP!
PAIGE

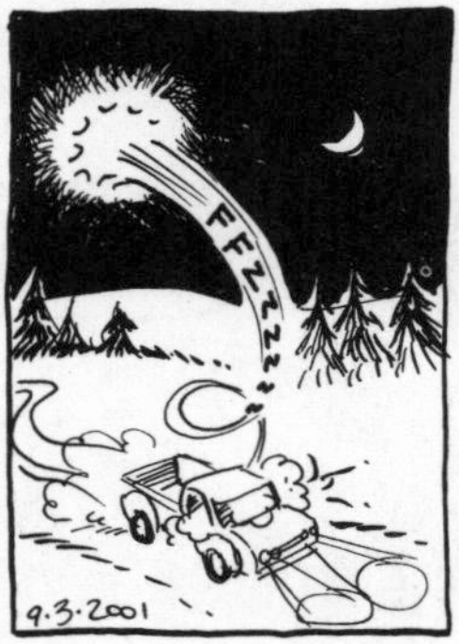
FFZZZZ
9·3·2001

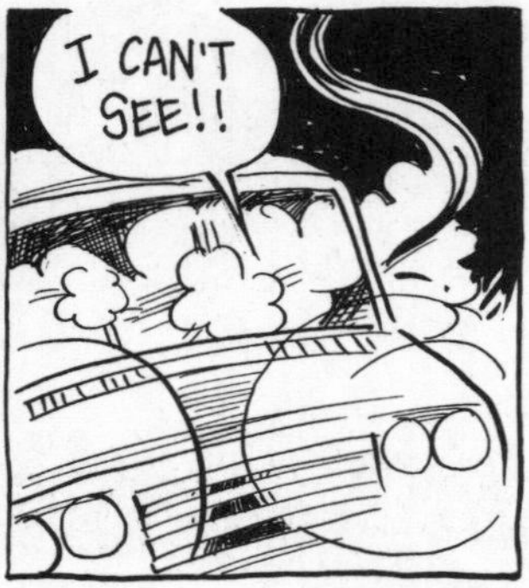
I CAN'T SEE!!

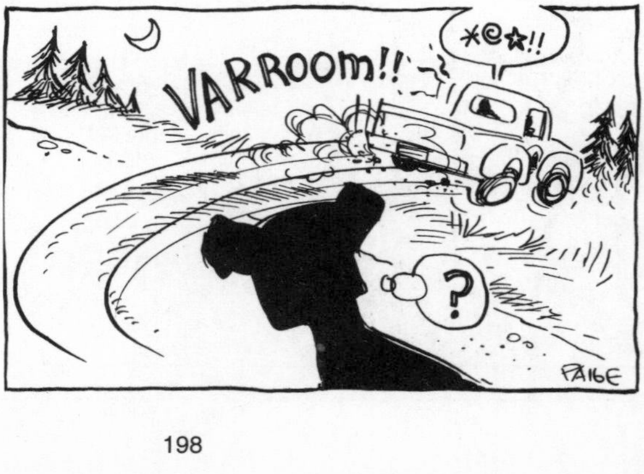
*@☆!!
VARROOM!!
?
PAIGE

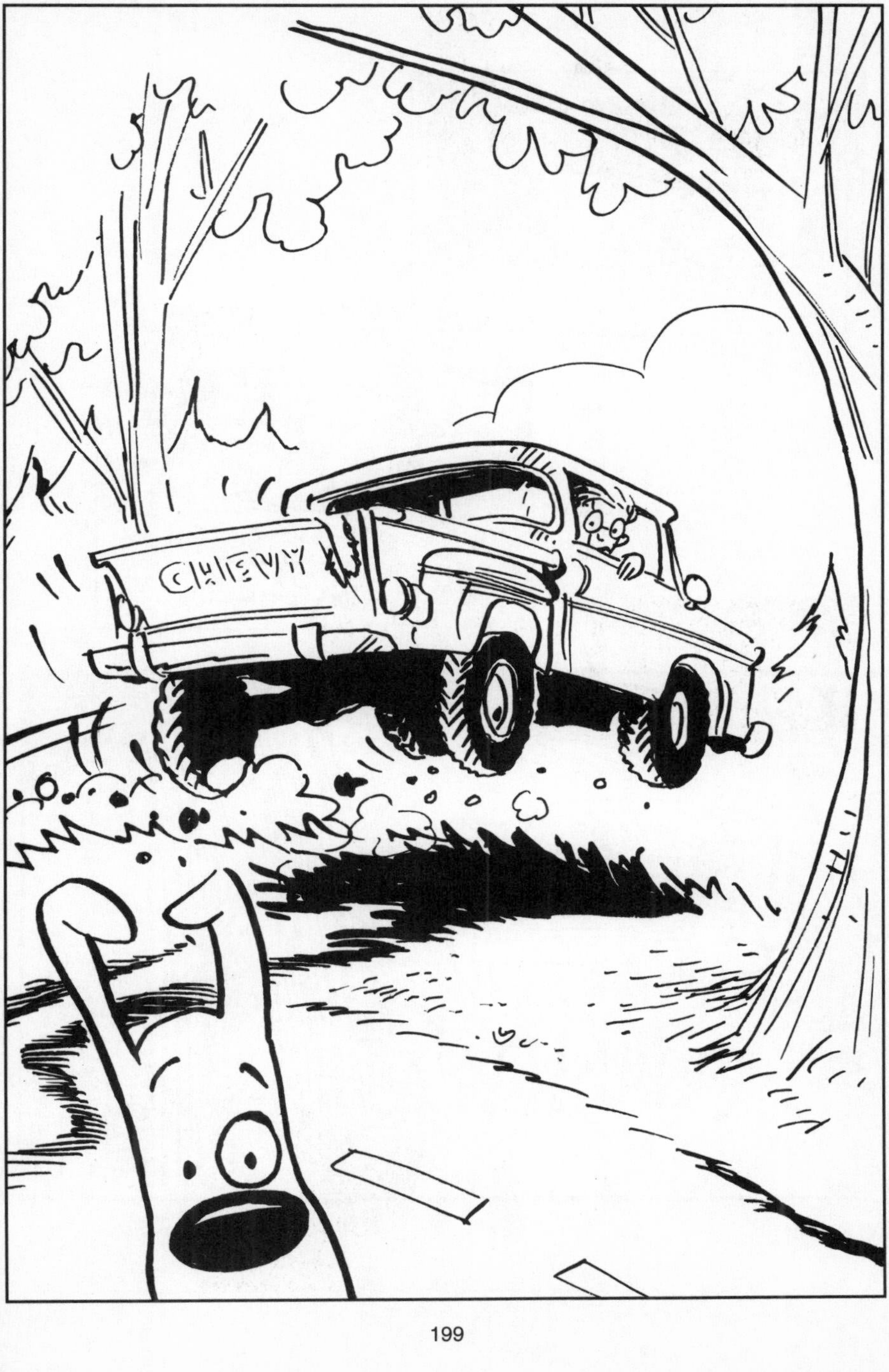
CHEVY

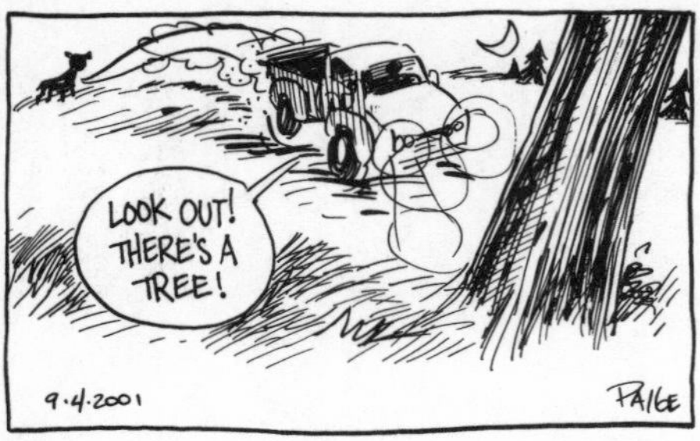
LOOK OUT! THERE'S A TREE!
9·4·2001
PAIGE

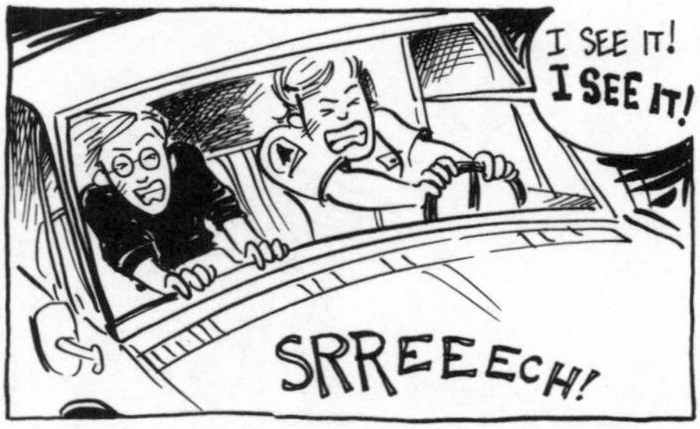
I SEE IT! I SEE IT!
SRREEEECH!

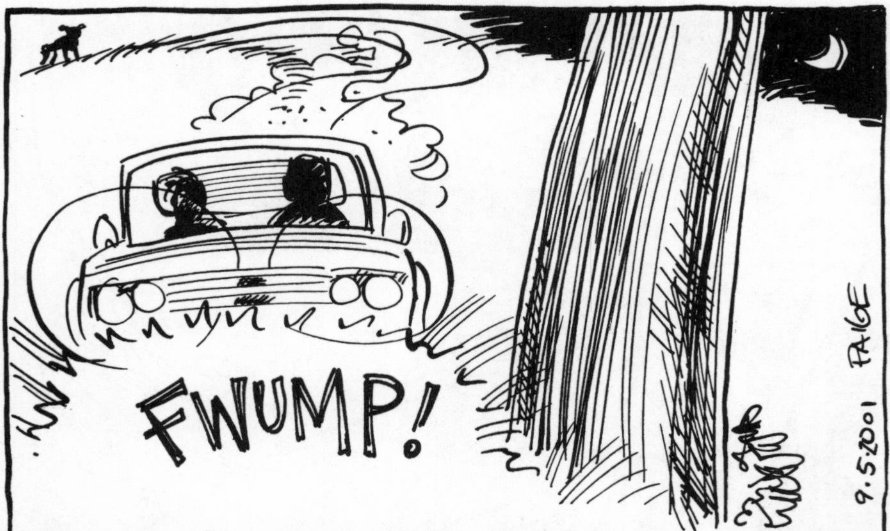
FWUMP!
9·5·2001
PAIGE

FWUMP!
PAIGE
9.5.2001
CLUNK
I'M ALIVE! SAVED BY A CLUMP OF GRASS!
NOT FOR LONG...
... BECAUSE I MIGHT HAVE TO KILL YOU MYSELF!
NOW MY TRUCK WON'T START!
I NEVER SHOULD HAVE FISHED YOU OUT OF THE RIVER!
9.6.2001
IF I HAD TO DO IT OVER, I'D SAVE ETHAN... BUT YOU!!
I'LL PULL ETHAN TO SAFETY! JANE... YOU'LL JUST HAVE TO SWIM FOR IT!!
GLUB...
PAIGE
CRACK
WHAT WAS THAT?!
9.7.2001
IT'S PROBABLY WHATEVER WE SAW IN THE ROAD COMING BACK TO FINISH US OFF!
IT THINKS WE'RE ROAD KILL!... A PRE-FLATTENED FREE MEAL!!
BOING!
CRACK!
CRAK!
!!
JANE!
PAIGE

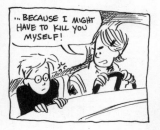

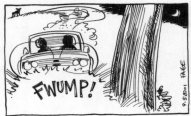

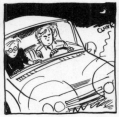

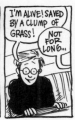

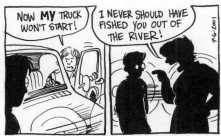

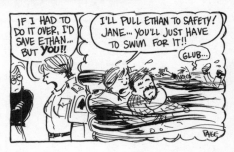

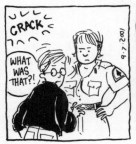

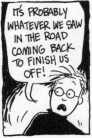

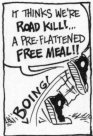

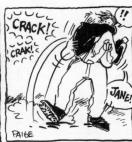

IT COULD BE A RABID RACCOON!

..OR A **WOLF!** ...OR A **BEAR!**

CRACK!

9-8-2001

...OR MY THIRD GRADE GYM TEACHER! ...SCAAARRY..

...OR JUST A REALLY CUTE DOG...

PAIGE

I'M GLAD YOUR TRUCK STARTED. WE COULD HAVE BEEN STRANDED FOREVER!

I COULD HAVE RADIOED FOR HELP...

OH.

PAIGE

WELL, THANKS FOR THE LIFT, AND GOOD LUCK WITH THE DOG...

WHAT DO YOU MEAN, "GOOD LUCK?" HE'S STAYING WITH YOU.

9·10·2001

WHAT DO YOU MEAN? "STAYING WITH ME"..?

I CAN'T HAVE A DOG IN MY APARTMENT.

9·11·2001

PAIGE

SO... HE'LL HAVE TO STAY WITH YOU...

BUT I DON'T WANT A DOG! I'M NOT A **DOG** PERSON... DOGS ARE **SO** NEEDY!

THOSE EYES.. THAT LOOK..

IT'S LIKE YOU'VE PERFECTED VULCAN MIND CONTROL!

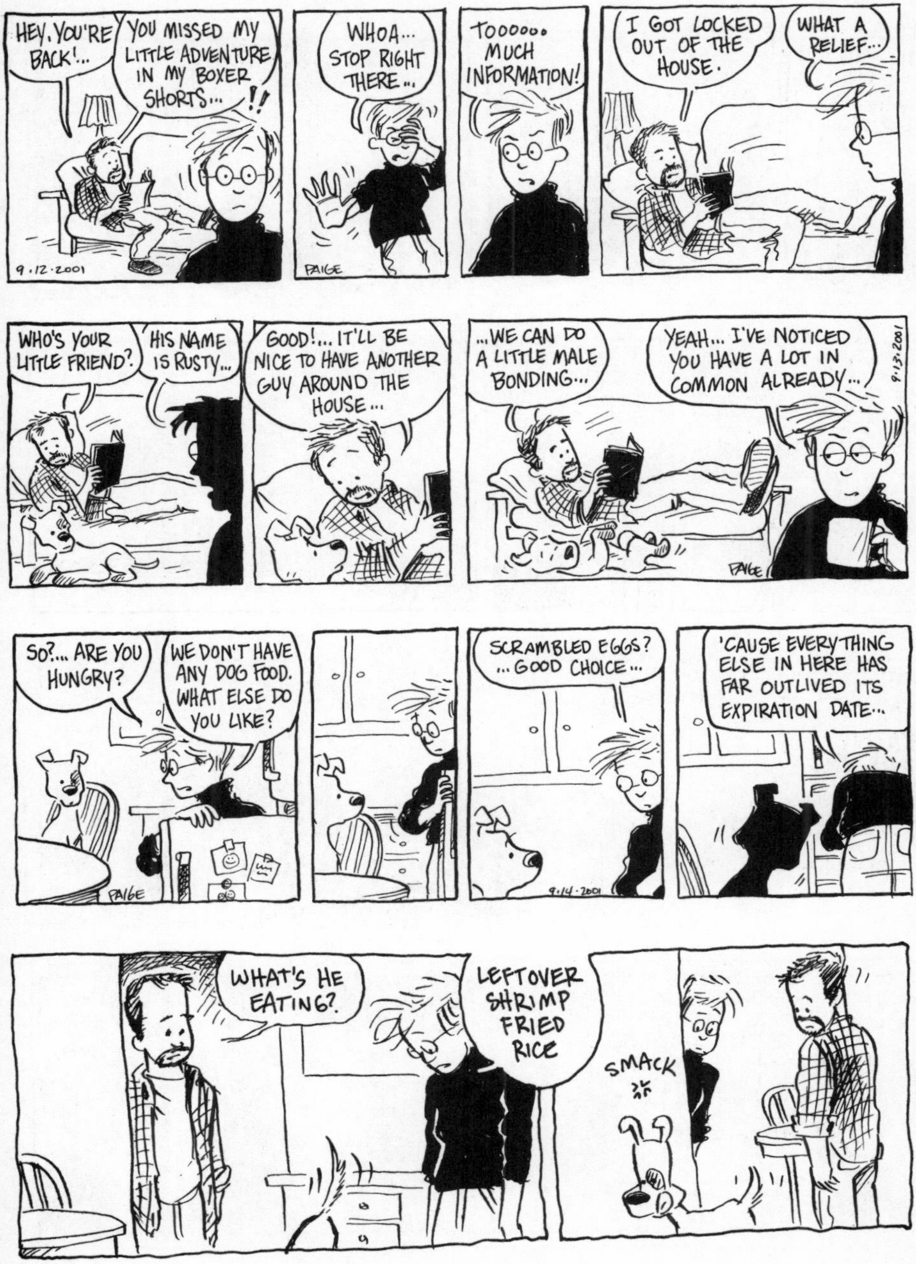
HEY, YOU'RE BACK!...
YOU MISSED MY LITTLE ADVENTURE IN MY BOXER SHORTS...
!!
9.12.2001
WHOA... STOP RIGHT THERE...
PAIGE
TOOOOOO... MUCH INFORMATION!
I GOT LOCKED OUT OF THE HOUSE.
WHAT A RELIEF...
WHO'S YOUR LITTLE FRIEND?
HIS NAME IS RUSTY...
GOOD!... IT'LL BE NICE TO HAVE ANOTHER GUY AROUND THE HOUSE...
...WE CAN DO A LITTLE MALE BONDING...
YEAH... I'VE NOTICED YOU HAVE A LOT IN COMMON ALREADY...
9.13.2001
PAIGE
SO?... ARE YOU HUNGRY?
WE DON'T HAVE ANY DOG FOOD. WHAT ELSE DO YOU LIKE?
PAIGE
SCRAMBLED EGGS? ...GOOD CHOICE...
9.14.2001
'CAUSE EVERYTHING ELSE IN HERE HAS FAR OUTLIVED ITS EXPIRATION DATE...
WHAT'S HE EATING?
LEFTOVER SHRIMP FRIED RICE
SMACK

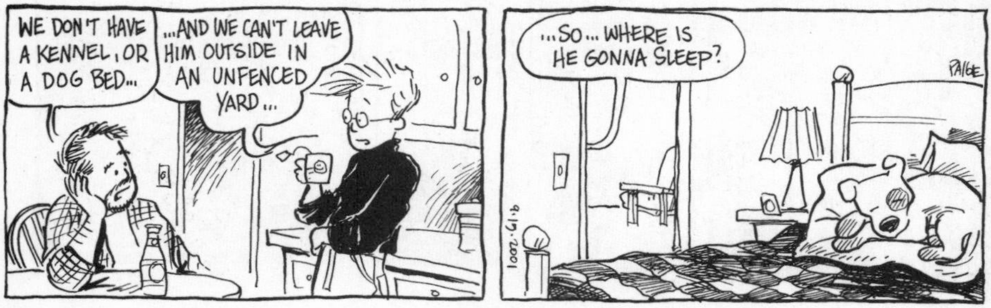
WE DON'T HAVE A KENNEL, OR A DOG BED...
...AND WE CAN'T LEAVE HIM OUTSIDE IN AN UNFENCED YARD...
...SO... WHERE IS HE GONNA SLEEP?
PAIGE

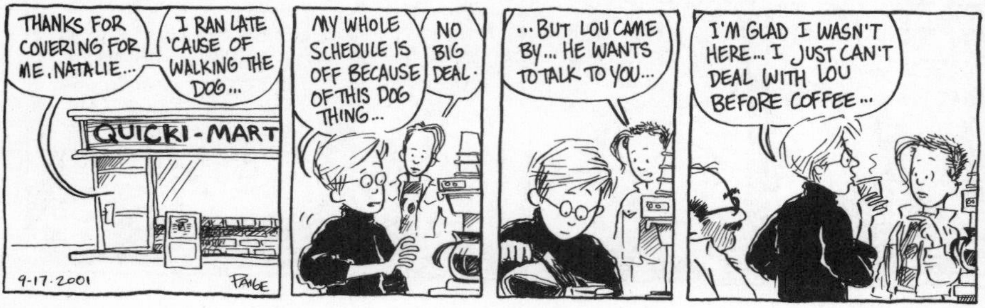
THANKS FOR COVERING FOR ME, NATALIE...
I RAN LATE 'CAUSE OF WALKING THE DOG...
QUICKI-MART
9-17-2001
PAIGE
MY WHOLE SCHEDULE IS OFF BECAUSE OF THIS DOG THING...
NO BIG DEAL.
...BUT LOU CAME BY... HE WANTS TO TALK TO YOU...
I'M GLAD I WASN'T HERE... I JUST CAN'T DEAL WITH LOU BEFORE COFFEE...

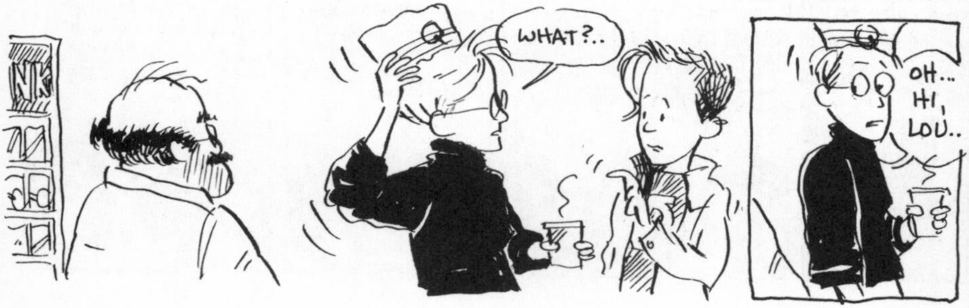
WHAT?..
OH... HI, LOU..

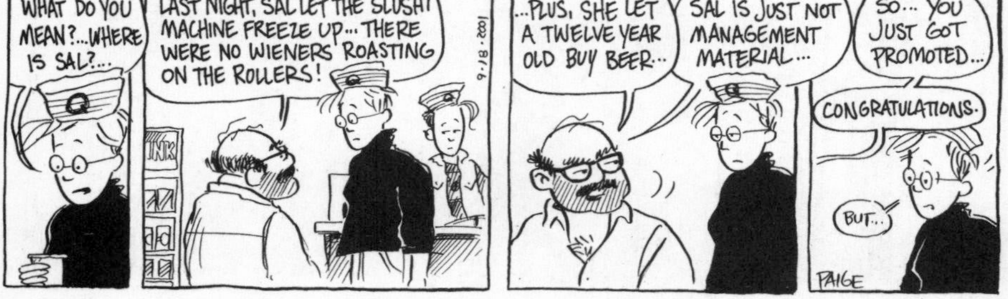
WHAT DO YOU MEAN?...WHERE IS SAL?...
LAST NIGHT, SAL LET THE SLUSHI MACHINE FREEZE UP... THERE WERE NO WIENERS ROASTING ON THE ROLLERS!
9.18.2001
...PLUS, SHE LET A TWELVE YEAR OLD BUY BEER...
SAL IS JUST NOT MANAGEMENT MATERIAL...
SO... YOU JUST GOT PROMOTED...
CONGRATULATIONS.
BUT..
PAIGE

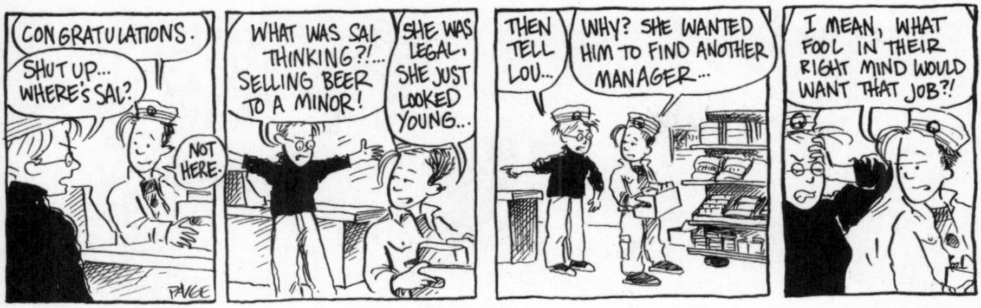
CONGRATULATIONS.
SHUT UP... WHERE'S SAL?
NOT HERE.
PAIGE
WHAT WAS SAL THINKING?!... SELLING BEER TO A MINOR!
SHE WAS LEGAL, SHE JUST LOOKED YOUNG...
THEN TELL LOU...
WHY? SHE WANTED HIM TO FIND ANOTHER MANAGER...
I MEAN, WHAT FOOL IN THEIR RIGHT MIND WOULD WANT THAT JOB?!

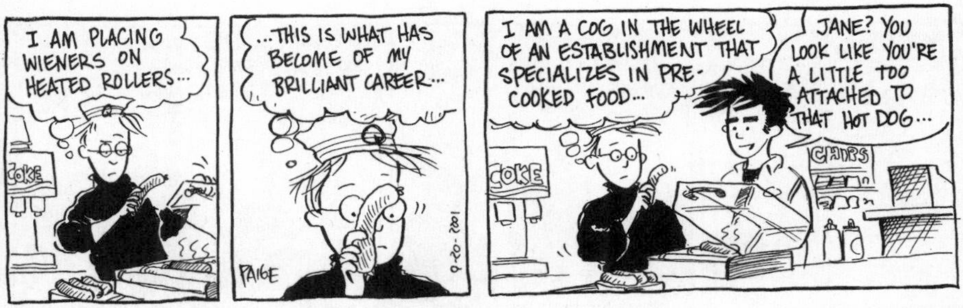
I AM PLACING WIENERS ON HEATED ROLLERS...
COKE
...THIS IS WHAT HAS BECOME OF MY BRILLIANT CAREER...
PAIGE
9-20-2001
I AM A COG IN THE WHEEL OF AN ESTABLISHMENT THAT SPECIALIZES IN PRE-COOKED FOOD...
JANE? YOU LOOK LIKE YOU'RE A LITTLE TOO ATTACHED TO THAT HOT DOG...
COKE
CHIPS

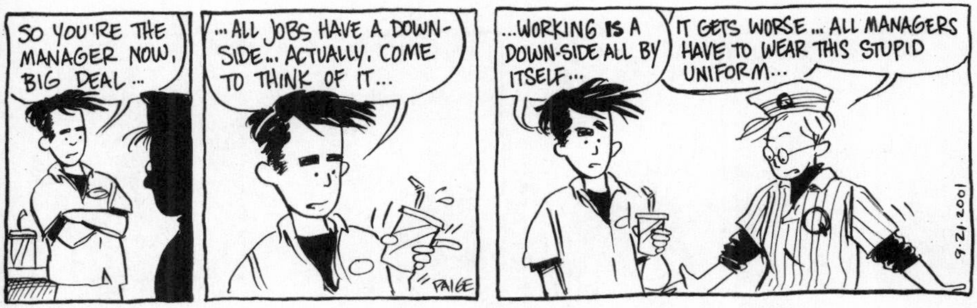
SO YOU'RE THE MANAGER NOW, BIG DEAL...
...ALL JOBS HAVE A DOWN-SIDE... ACTUALLY, COME TO THINK OF IT...
PAIGE
...WORKING IS A DOWN-SIDE ALL BY ITSELF...
IT GETS WORSE... ALL MANAGERS HAVE TO WEAR THIS STUPID UNIFORM...
9-21-2001

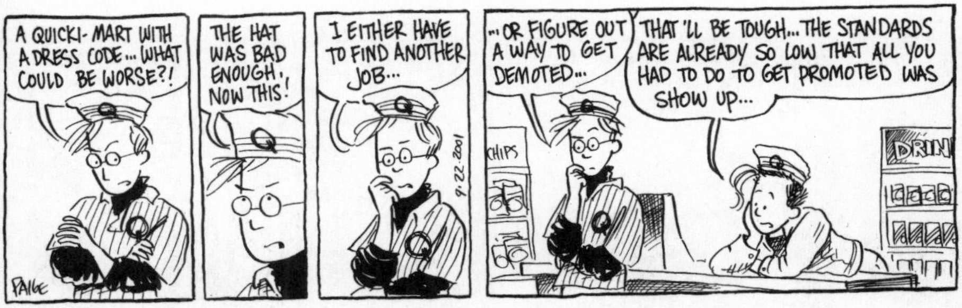
A QUICKI-MART WITH A DRESS CODE... WHAT COULD BE WORSE?!
PAIGE
THE HAT WAS BAD ENOUGH, NOW THIS!
I EITHER HAVE TO FIND ANOTHER JOB...
9-22-2001
...OR FIGURE OUT A WAY TO GET DEMOTED...
THAT'LL BE TOUGH... THE STANDARDS ARE ALREADY SO LOW THAT ALL YOU HAD TO DO TO GET PROMOTED WAS SHOW UP...
CHIPS
DRIN

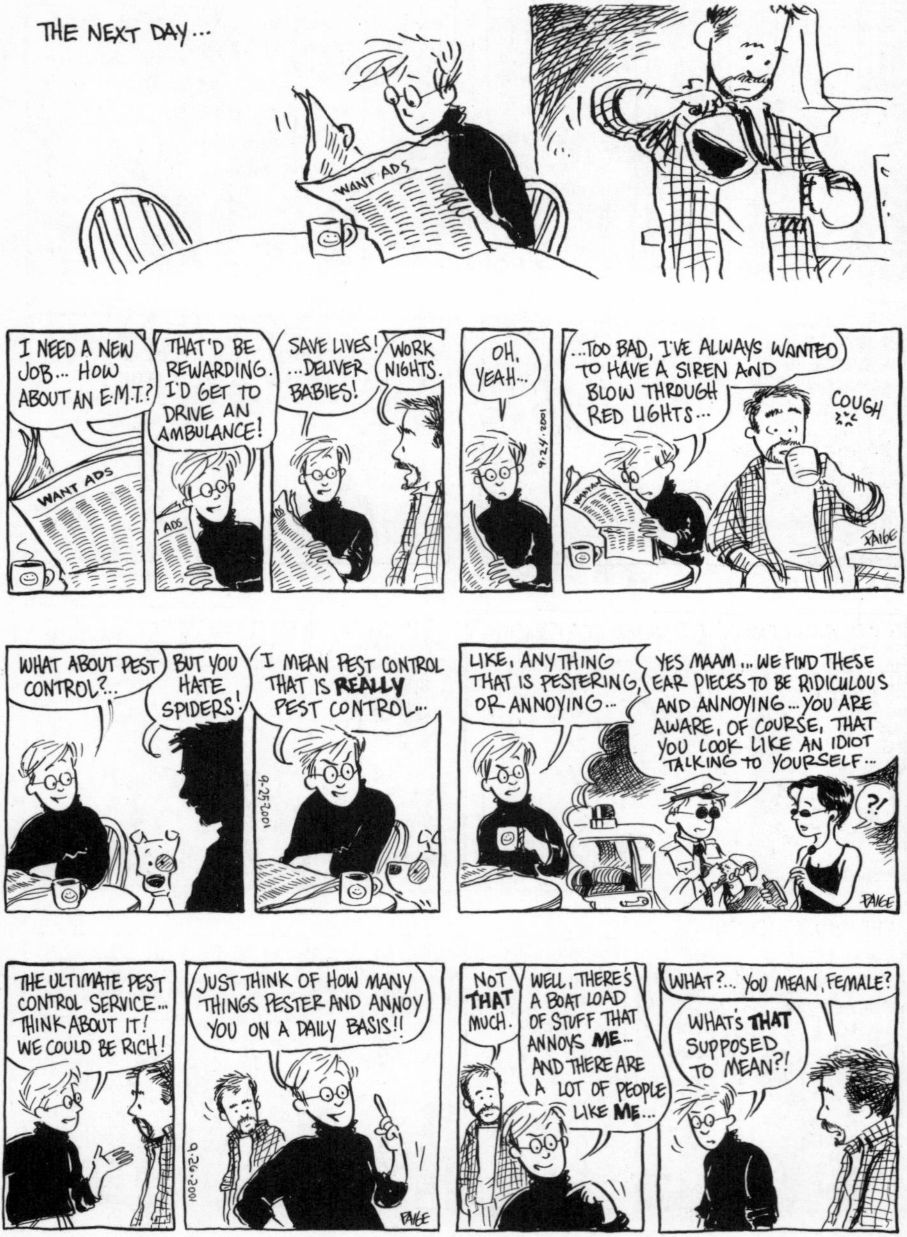

THE NEXT DAY...
WANT ADS
I NEED A NEW JOB... HOW ABOUT AN E.M.T.?
THAT'D BE REWARDING. I'D GET TO DRIVE AN AMBULANCE!
SAVE LIVES! ...DELIVER BABIES!
WORK NIGHTS.
OH, YEAH...
9.24.2001
...TOO BAD, I'VE ALWAYS WANTED TO HAVE A SIREN AND BLOW THROUGH RED LIGHTS...
COUGH
PAIGE
WHAT ABOUT PEST CONTROL?...
BUT YOU HATE SPIDERS!
I MEAN PEST CONTROL THAT IS **REALLY** PEST CONTROL...
9.25.2001
LIKE, ANYTHING THAT IS PESTERING, OR ANNOYING...
YES MAAM... WE FIND THESE EAR PIECES TO BE RIDICULOUS AND ANNOYING... YOU ARE AWARE, OF COURSE, THAT YOU LOOK LIKE AN IDIOT TALKING TO YOURSELF...
?!
PAIGE
THE ULTIMATE PEST CONTROL SERVICE... THINK ABOUT IT! WE COULD BE RICH!
JUST THINK OF HOW MANY THINGS PESTER AND ANNOY YOU ON A DAILY BASIS!!
9.26.2001
PAIGE
NOT **THAT** MUCH.
WELL, THERE'S A BOAT LOAD OF STUFF THAT ANNOYS **ME**... AND THERE ARE A LOT OF PEOPLE LIKE **ME**...
WHAT?... YOU MEAN, FEMALE?
WHAT'S **THAT** SUPPOSED TO MEAN?!

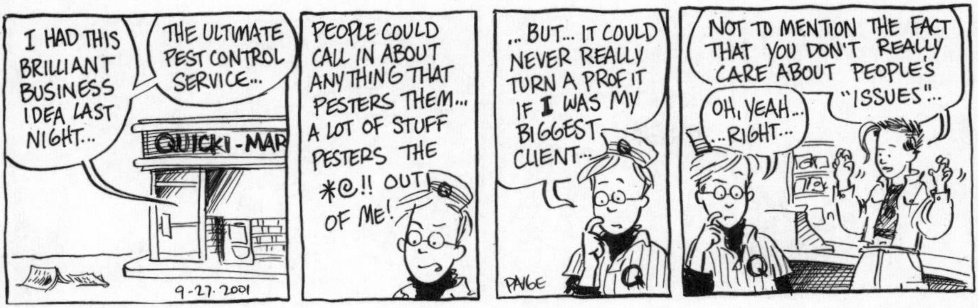
I HAD THIS BRILLIANT BUSINESS IDEA LAST NIGHT...
THE ULTIMATE PEST CONTROL SERVICE...
QUICKI-MAR
9-27-2001
PEOPLE COULD CALL IN ABOUT ANYTHING THAT PESTERS THEM... A LOT OF STUFF PESTERS THE *@!! OUT OF ME!
... BUT... IT COULD NEVER REALLY TURN A PROFIT IF I WAS MY BIGGEST CLIENT...
PAIGE
NOT TO MENTION THE FACT THAT YOU DON'T REALLY CARE ABOUT PEOPLE'S "ISSUES"...
OH, YEAH... ...RIGHT...

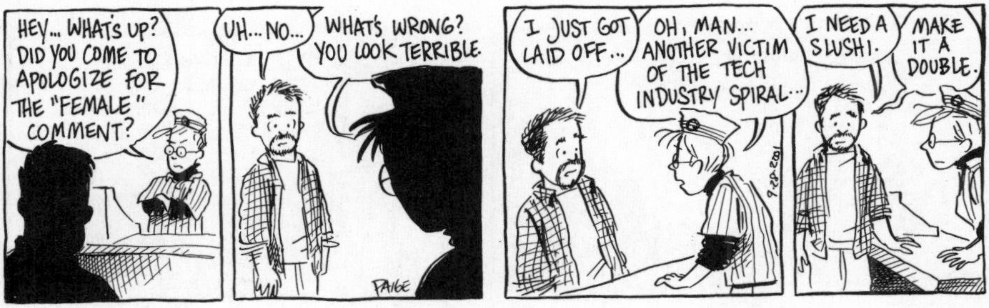
HEY... WHAT'S UP? DID YOU COME TO APOLOGIZE FOR THE "FEMALE" COMMENT?
UH... NO...
WHAT'S WRONG? YOU LOOK TERRIBLE.
PAIGE
I JUST GOT LAID OFF...
OH, MAN... ANOTHER VICTIM OF THE TECH INDUSTRY SPIRAL...
9-28-2001
I NEED A SLUSHI.
MAKE IT A DOUBLE.

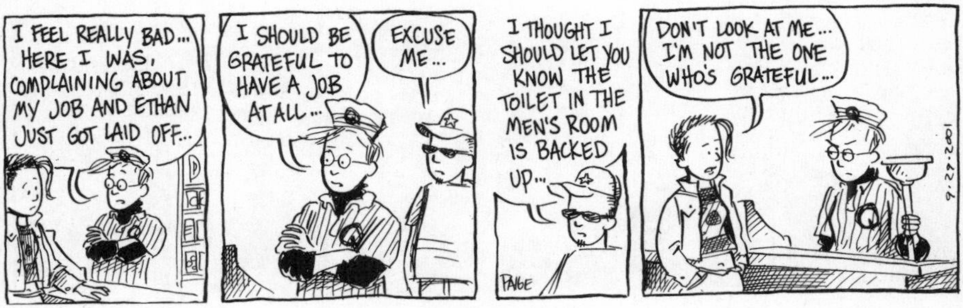
I FEEL REALLY BAD... HERE I WAS, COMPLAINING ABOUT MY JOB AND ETHAN JUST GOT LAID OFF...
I SHOULD BE GRATEFUL TO HAVE A JOB AT ALL...
EXCUSE ME...
I THOUGHT I SHOULD LET YOU KNOW THE TOILET IN THE MEN'S ROOM IS BACKED UP...
PAIGE
DON'T LOOK AT ME... I'M NOT THE ONE WHO'S GRATEFUL...
9-29-2001

THE NEXT MORNING...

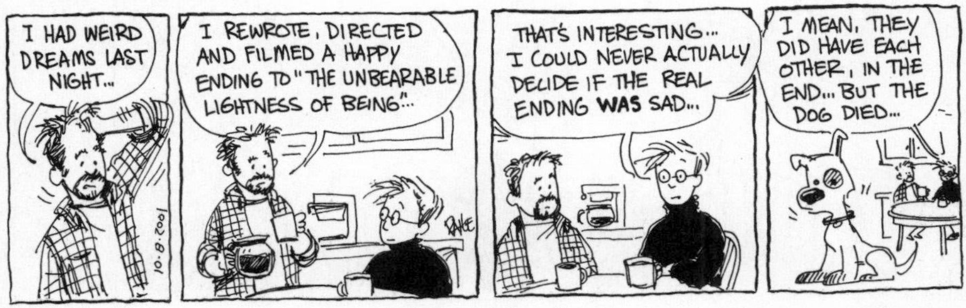
I HAD WEIRD DREAMS LAST NIGHT...
10-8-2001
I REWROTE, DIRECTED AND FILMED A HAPPY ENDING TO "THE UNBEARABLE LIGHTNESS OF BEING"...
PAIGE
THAT'S INTERESTING... I COULD NEVER ACTUALLY DECIDE IF THE REAL ENDING WAS SAD...
I MEAN, THEY DID HAVE EACH OTHER, IN THE END... BUT THE DOG DIED...

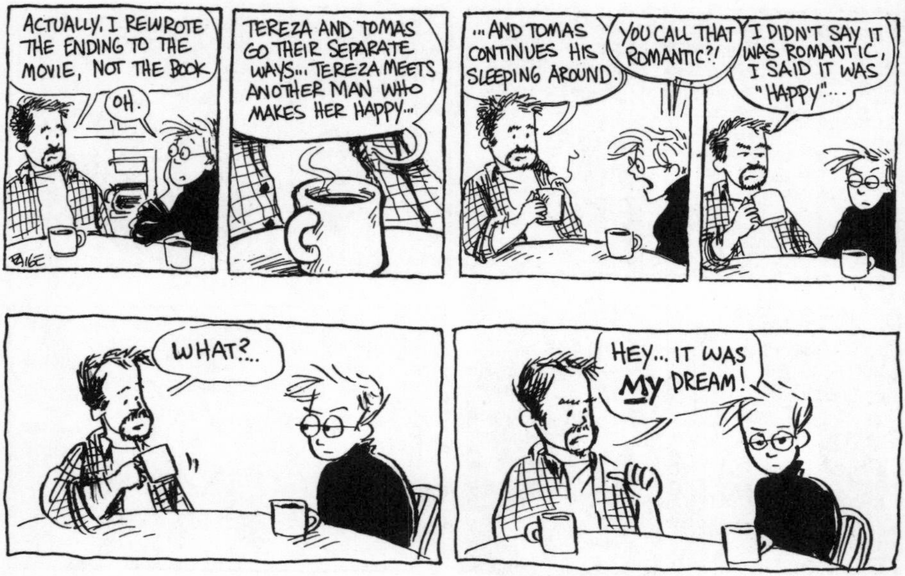
ACTUALLY, I REWROTE THE ENDING TO THE MOVIE, NOT THE BOOK
OH.
PAIGE
TEREZA AND TOMAS GO THEIR SEPARATE WAYS... TEREZA MEETS ANOTHER MAN WHO MAKES HER HAPPY...
...AND TOMAS CONTINUES HIS SLEEPING AROUND.
YOU CALL THAT ROMANTIC?!
I DIDN'T SAY IT WAS ROMANTIC, I SAID IT WAS "HAPPY"....
WHAT?...
HEY... IT WAS MY DREAM!

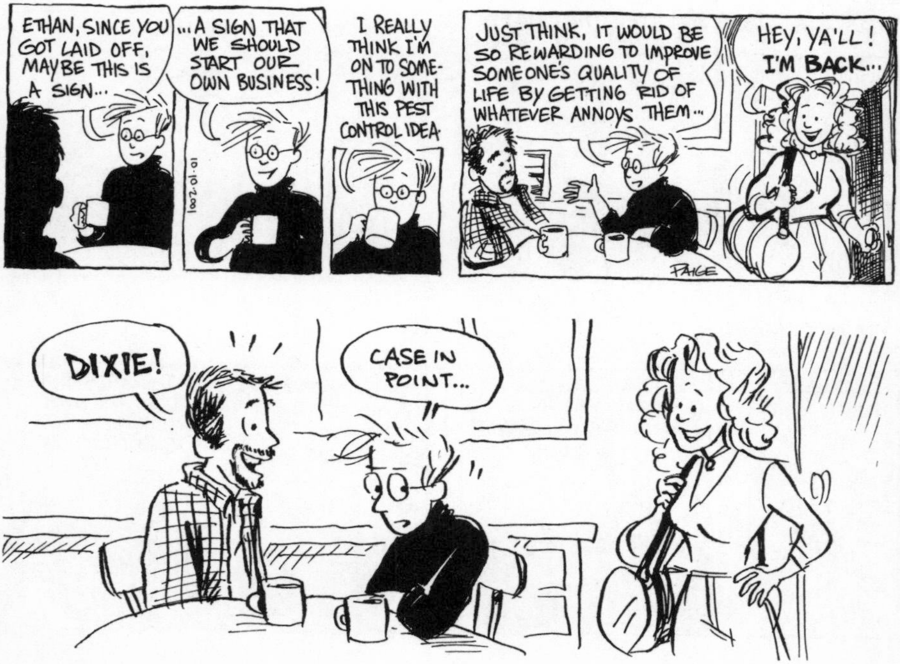
ETHAN, SINCE YOU GOT LAID OFF, MAYBE THIS IS A SIGN...
...A SIGN THAT WE SHOULD START OUR OWN BUSINESS!
I REALLY THINK I'M ON TO SOMETHING WITH THIS PEST CONTROL IDEA.
JUST THINK, IT WOULD BE SO REWARDING TO IMPROVE SOMEONE'S QUALITY OF LIFE BY GETTING RID OF WHATEVER ANNOYS THEM...
HEY, YA'LL! I'M BACK...
PAIGE
DIXIE!
CASE IN POINT...

LATER, AT THE QUICKI-MART....

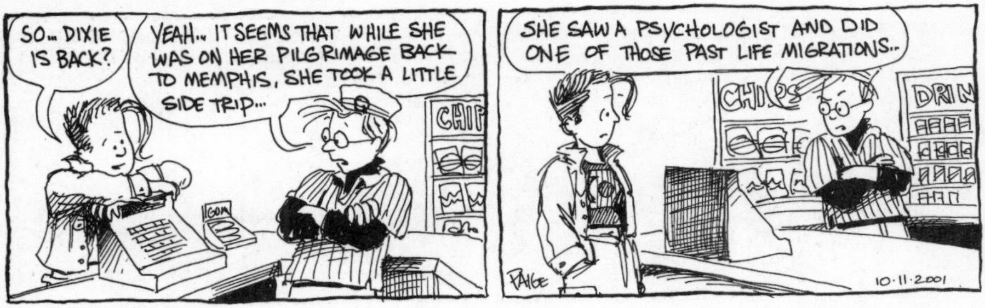
SO... DIXIE IS BACK?
YEAH.. IT SEEMS THAT WHILE SHE WAS ON HER PILGRIMAGE BACK TO MEMPHIS, SHE TOOK A LITTLE SIDE TRIP...
SHE SAW A PSYCHOLOGIST AND DID ONE OF THOSE PAST LIFE MIGRATIONS..
10·11·2001

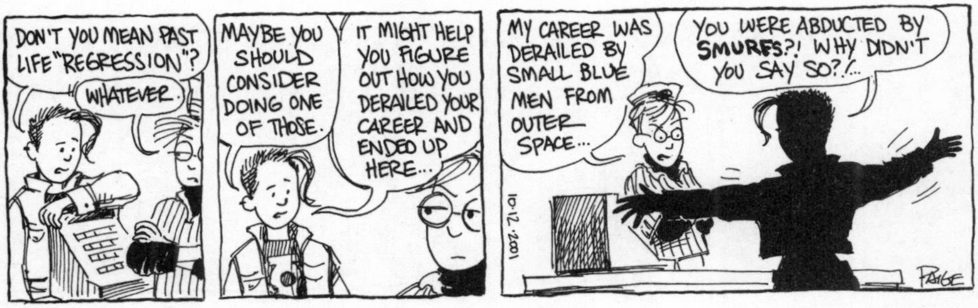
DON'T YOU MEAN PAST LIFE "REGRESSION"?
WHATEVER.
MAYBE YOU SHOULD CONSIDER DOING ONE OF THOSE.
IT MIGHT HELP YOU FIGURE OUT HOW YOU DERAILED YOUR CAREER AND ENDED UP HERE...
MY CAREER WAS DERAILED BY SMALL BLUE MEN FROM OUTER SPACE...
YOU WERE ABDUCTED BY SMURFS?! WHY DIDN'T YOU SAY SO?!...
10·12·2001

BACK AT JANE'S, LATER THAT DAY...

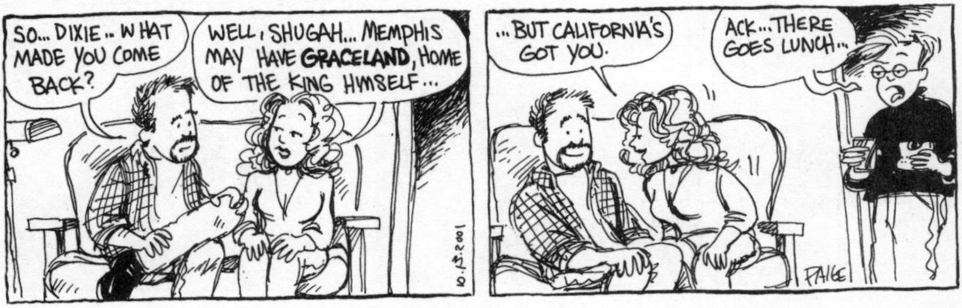
SO... DIXIE.. WHAT MADE YOU COME BACK?
WELL, SHUGAH... MEMPHIS MAY HAVE GRACELAND, HOME OF THE KING HIMSELF...
10·13·2001
...BUT CALIFORNIA'S GOT YOU.
ACK... THERE GOES LUNCH...

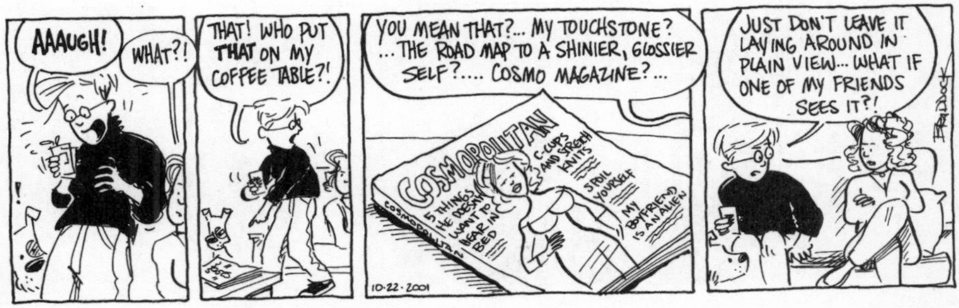
AAAUGH!
WHAT?!
THAT! WHO PUT THAT ON MY COFFEE TABLE?!
YOU MEAN THAT?... MY TOUCHSTONE? ...THE ROAD MAP TO A SHINIER, GLOSSIER SELF?..... COSMO MAGAZINE?...
COSMOPOLITAN
C-CUPS AND STRETCH KNITS
5 THINGS HE DOESN'T WANT TO HEAR IN BED
SPOIL YOURSELF
MY BOYFRIEND IS AN ALIEN
10·22·2001
JUST DON'T LEAVE IT LAYING AROUND IN PLAIN VIEW... WHAT IF ONE OF MY FRIENDS SEES IT?!

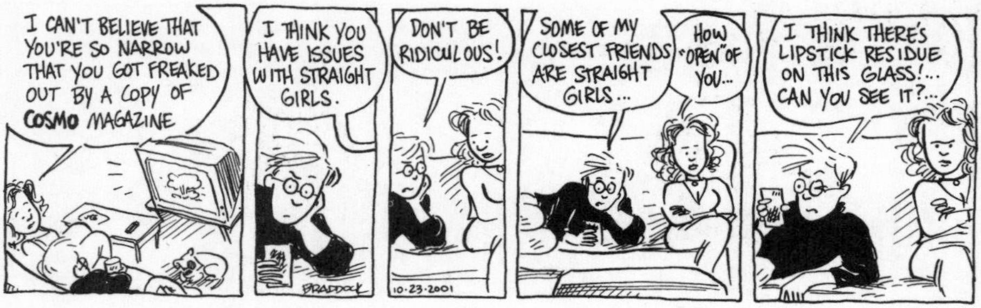
I CAN'T BELIEVE THAT YOU'RE SO NARROW THAT YOU GOT FREAKED OUT BY A COPY OF COSMO MAGAZINE
I THINK YOU HAVE ISSUES WITH STRAIGHT GIRLS.
BRADDOCK
DON'T BE RIDICULOUS!
10-23-2001
SOME OF MY CLOSEST FRIENDS ARE STRAIGHT GIRLS...
HOW "OPEN" OF YOU...
I THINK THERE'S LIPSTICK RESIDUE ON THIS GLASS!... CAN YOU SEE IT?...

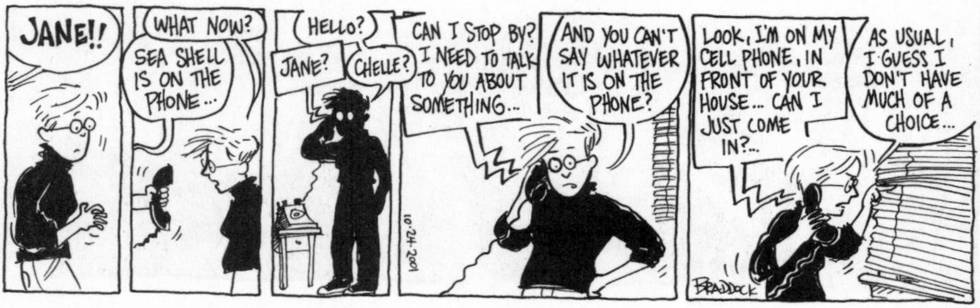
JANE!!
WHAT NOW?
SEA SHELL IS ON THE PHONE...
HELLO?
JANE?
CHELLE?
10-24-2001
CAN I STOP BY? I NEED TO TALK TO YOU ABOUT SOMETHING...
AND YOU CAN'T SAY WHATEVER IT IS ON THE PHONE?
LOOK, I'M ON MY CELL PHONE, IN FRONT OF YOUR HOUSE... CAN I JUST COME IN?...
AS USUAL, I GUESS I DON'T HAVE MUCH OF A CHOICE...
BRADDOCK

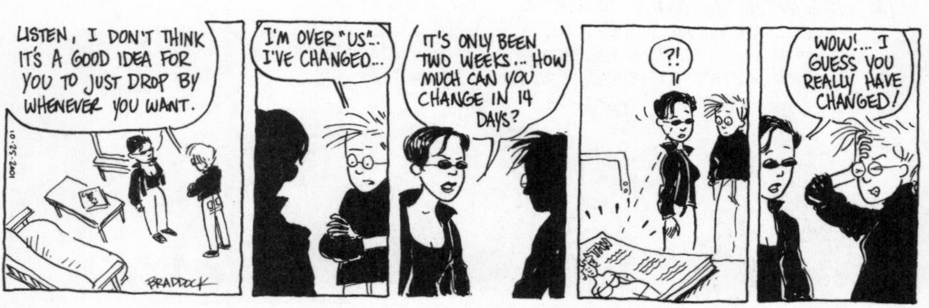
LISTEN, I DON'T THINK IT'S A GOOD IDEA FOR YOU TO JUST DROP BY WHENEVER YOU WANT.
10-25-2001
BRADDOCK
I'M OVER "US"... I'VE CHANGED...
IT'S ONLY BEEN TWO WEEKS... HOW MUCH CAN YOU CHANGE IN 14 DAYS?
?!
WOW!... I GUESS YOU REALLY HAVE CHANGED!

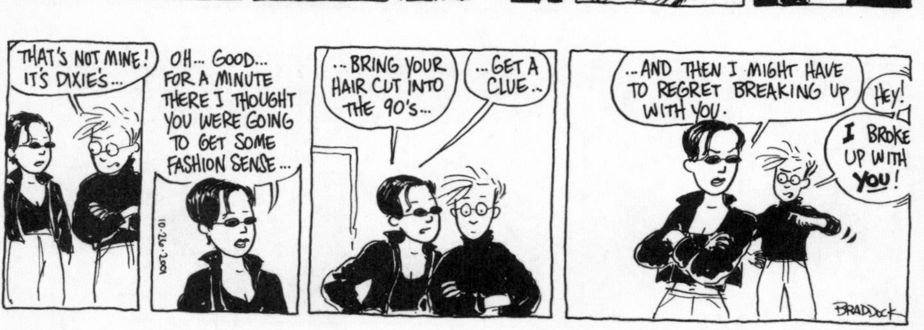
THAT'S NOT MINE! IT'S DIXIE'S...
OH... GOOD... FOR A MINUTE THERE I THOUGHT YOU WERE GOING TO GET SOME FASHION SENSE...
10-26-2001
...BRING YOUR HAIR CUT INTO THE 90'S...
...GET A CLUE...
...AND THEN I MIGHT HAVE TO REGRET BREAKING UP WITH YOU.
HEY!
I BROKE UP WITH YOU!
BRADDOCK

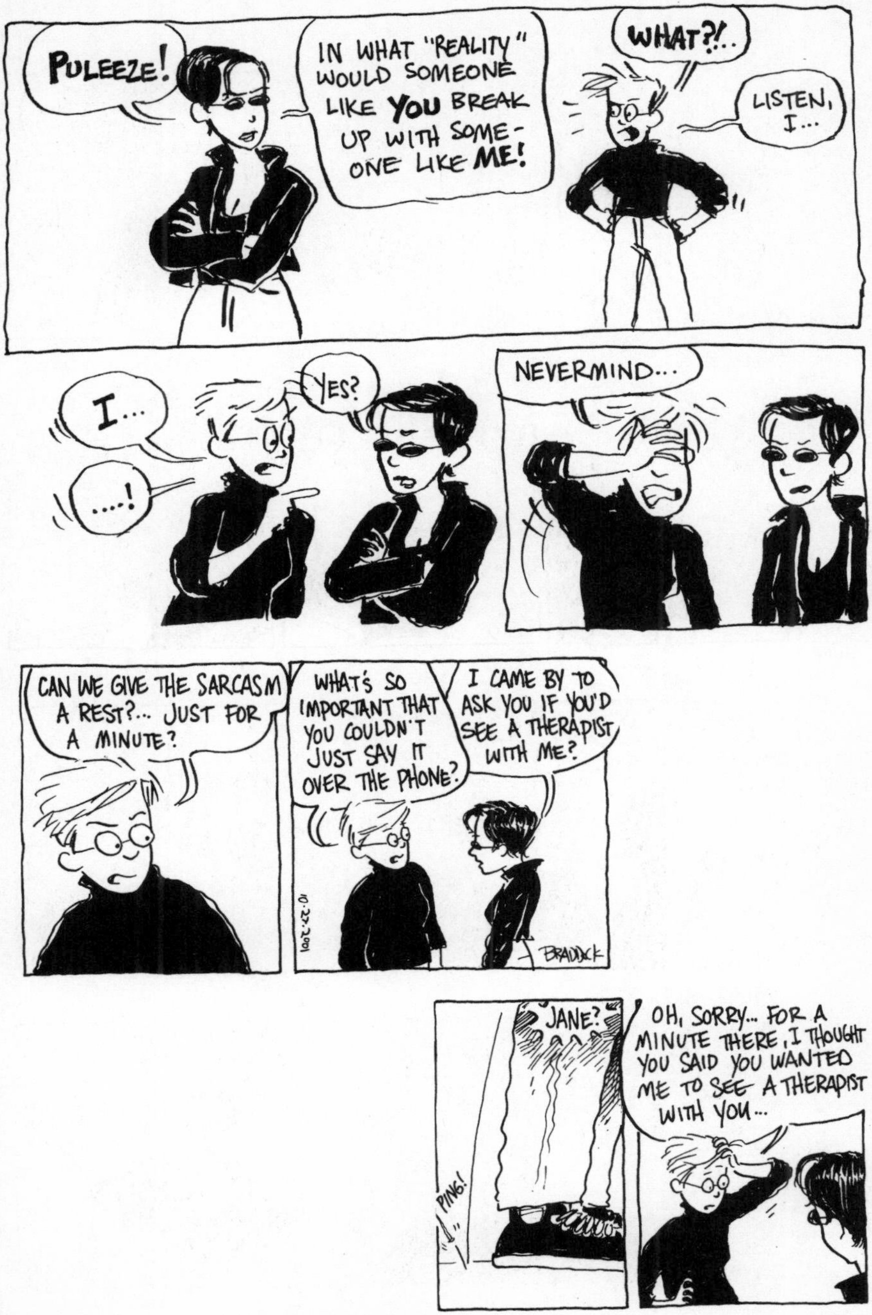
PULEEZE!
IN WHAT "REALITY" WOULD SOMEONE LIKE YOU BREAK UP WITH SOME-ONE LIKE ME!
WHAT?!...
LISTEN, I...
I...
YES?
....!
NEVERMIND...
CAN WE GIVE THE SARCASM A REST?... JUST FOR A MINUTE?
WHAT'S SO IMPORTANT THAT YOU COULDN'T JUST SAY IT OVER THE PHONE?
I CAME BY TO ASK YOU IF YOU'D SEE A THERAPIST WITH ME?
BRADDOCK
JANE?
PING!
OH, SORRY... FOR A MINUTE THERE, I THOUGHT YOU SAID YOU WANTED ME TO SEE A THERAPIST WITH YOU...

Chapter 9

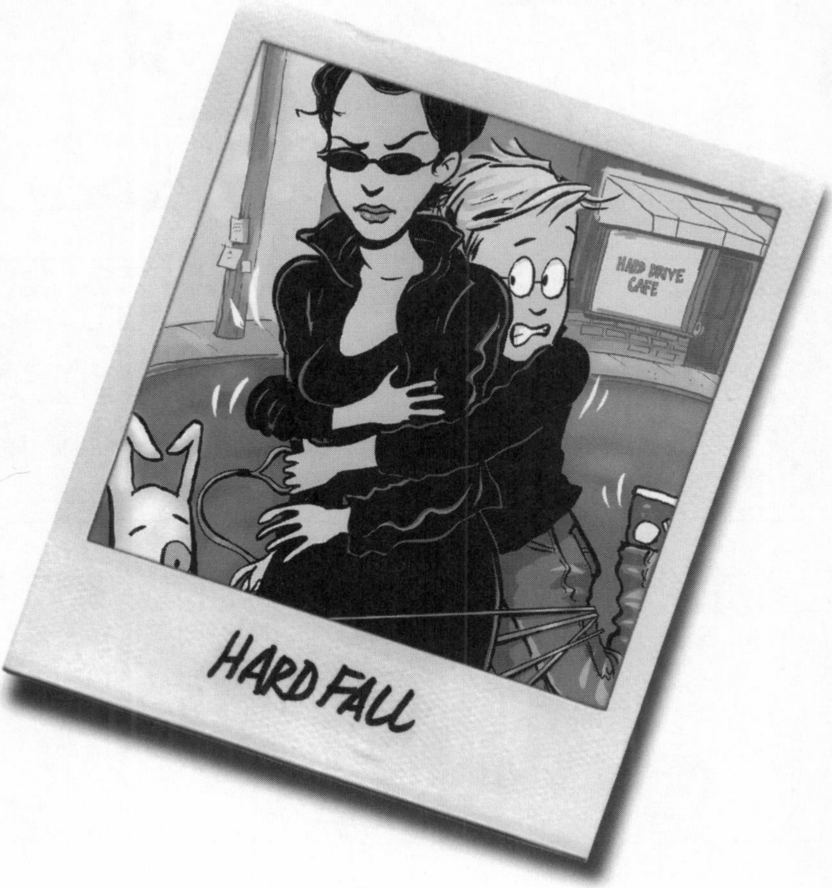
HARD DRIVE
CAFE
HARD FALL

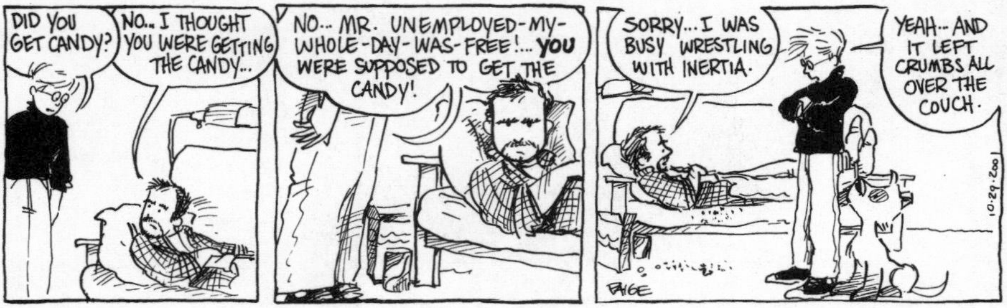
DID YOU GET CANDY?
NO.. I THOUGHT YOU WERE GETTING THE CANDY...
NO... MR. UNEMPLOYED-MY-WHOLE-DAY-WAS-FREE!... YOU WERE SUPPOSED TO GET THE CANDY!
SORRY... I WAS BUSY WRESTLING WITH INERTIA.
YEAH... AND IT LEFT CRUMBS ALL OVER THE COUCH.
10·29·2001
PAIGE

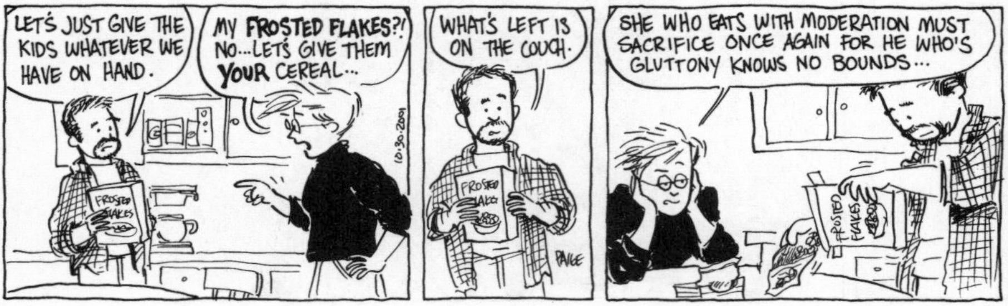
LET'S JUST GIVE THE KIDS WHATEVER WE HAVE ON HAND.
MY FROSTED FLAKES?! NO... LET'S GIVE THEM YOUR CEREAL...
10·30·2001
WHAT'S LEFT IS ON THE COUCH.
PAIGE
SHE WHO EATS WITH MODERATION MUST SACRIFICE ONCE AGAIN FOR HE WHO'S GLUTTONY KNOWS NO BOUNDS...

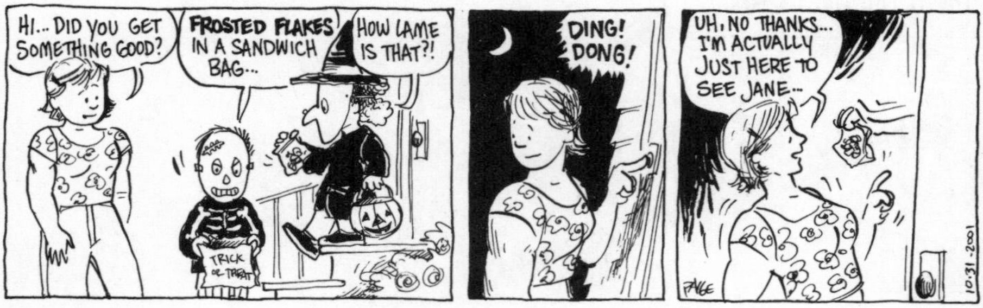
HI... DID YOU GET SOMETHING GOOD?
FROSTED FLAKES IN A SANDWICH BAG...
HOW LAME IS THAT?!
TRICK OR TREAT
DING! DONG!
UH, NO THANKS... I'M ACTUALLY JUST HERE TO SEE JANE...
PAIGE
10·31·2001

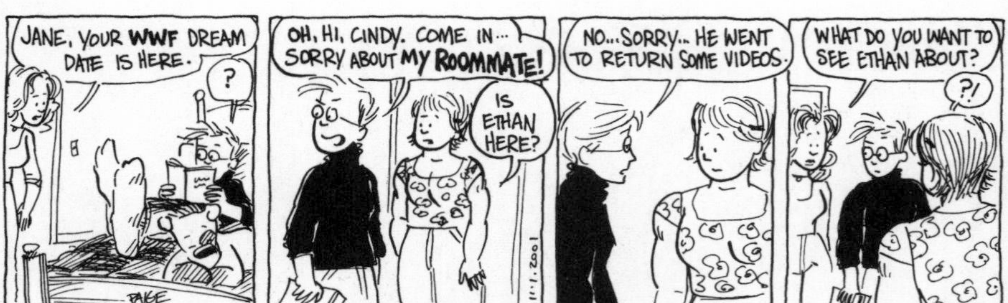
JANE, YOUR WWF DREAM DATE IS HERE.
?
PAIGE
OH, HI, CINDY. COME IN... SORRY ABOUT MY ROOMMATE!
IS ETHAN HERE?
11·1·2001
NO... SORRY... HE WENT TO RETURN SOME VIDEOS.
WHAT DO YOU WANT TO SEE ETHAN ABOUT?
?!

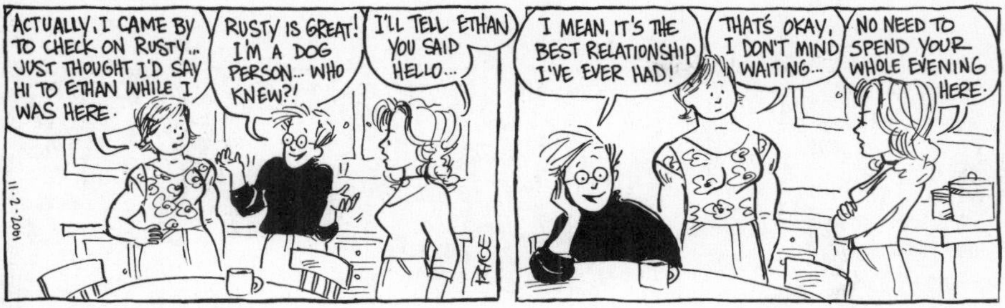
ACTUALLY, I CAME BY TO CHECK ON RUSTY... JUST THOUGHT I'D SAY HI TO ETHAN WHILE I WAS HERE.
RUSTY IS GREAT! I'M A DOG PERSON... WHO KNEW?!
I'LL TELL ETHAN YOU SAID HELLO...
I MEAN, IT'S THE BEST RELATIONSHIP I'VE EVER HAD!
THAT'S OKAY, I DON'T MIND WAITING...
NO NEED TO SPEND YOUR WHOLE EVENING HERE.
11-2-2001
PAIGE

A FEW MINUTES LATER...

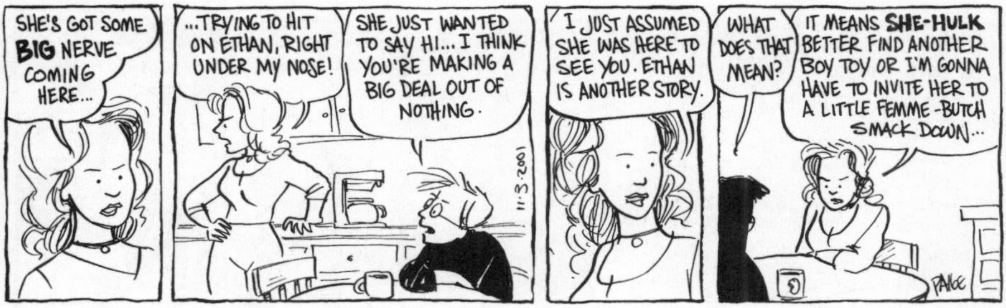
SHE'S GOT SOME **BIG** NERVE COMING HERE...
...TRYING TO HIT ON ETHAN, RIGHT UNDER MY NOSE!
SHE JUST WANTED TO SAY HI... I THINK YOU'RE MAKING A BIG DEAL OUT OF NOTHING.
11-3-2001
I JUST ASSUMED SHE WAS HERE TO SEE YOU. ETHAN IS ANOTHER STORY.
WHAT DOES THAT MEAN?
IT MEANS **SHE-HULK** BETTER FIND ANOTHER BOY TOY OR I'M GONNA HAVE TO INVITE HER TO A LITTLE FEMME-BUTCH SMACK DOWN...
PAIGE

THEN, THE NEXT DAY...

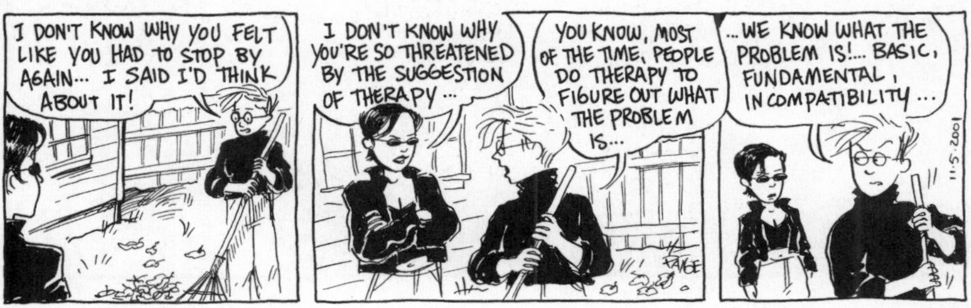
I DON'T KNOW WHY YOU FELT LIKE YOU HAD TO STOP BY AGAIN... I SAID I'D THINK ABOUT IT!
I DON'T KNOW WHY YOU'RE SO THREATENED BY THE SUGGESTION OF THERAPY...
YOU KNOW, MOST OF THE TIME, PEOPLE DO THERAPY TO FIGURE OUT WHAT THE PROBLEM IS...
...WE KNOW WHAT THE PROBLEM IS!... BASIC, FUNDAMENTAL, INCOMPATIBILITY...
PAIGE
11-5-2001

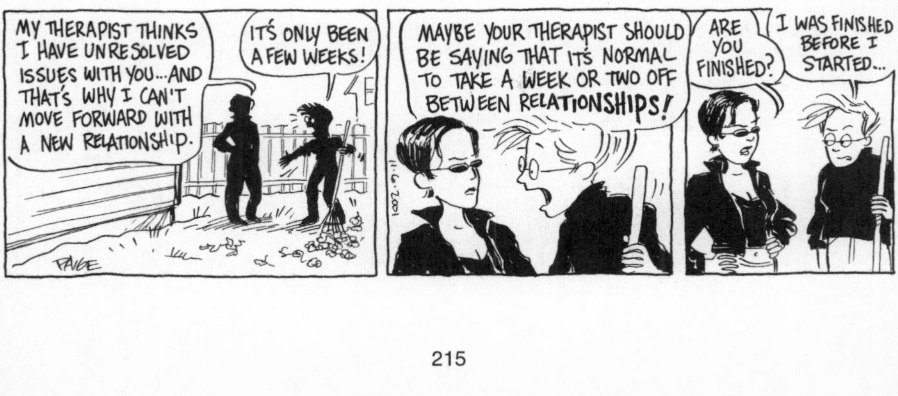
MY THERAPIST THINKS I HAVE UNRESOLVED ISSUES WITH YOU... AND THAT'S WHY I CAN'T MOVE FORWARD WITH A NEW RELATIONSHIP.
IT'S ONLY BEEN A FEW WEEKS!
PAIGE
MAYBE YOUR THERAPIST SHOULD BE SAYING THAT IT'S NORMAL TO TAKE A WEEK OR TWO OFF BETWEEN RELATIONSHIPS!
11-6-2001
ARE YOU FINISHED?
I WAS FINISHED BEFORE I STARTED...

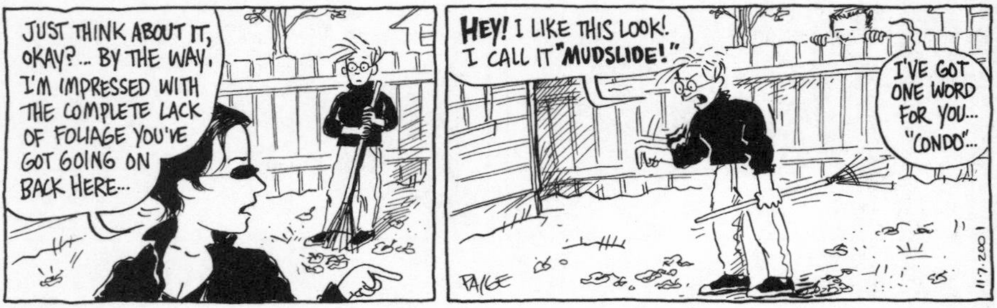
JUST THINK ABOUT IT, OKAY?... BY THE WAY, I'M IMPRESSED WITH THE COMPLETE LACK OF FOLIAGE YOU'VE GOT GOING ON BACK HERE...
HEY! I LIKE THIS LOOK! I CALL IT "MUDSLIDE!"
I'VE GOT ONE WORD FOR YOU... "CONDO"...
PAIGE
11.7.2001

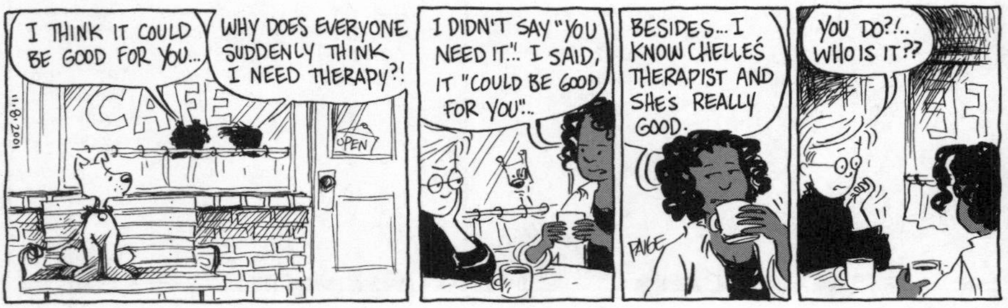
I THINK IT COULD BE GOOD FOR YOU...
WHY DOES EVERYONE SUDDENLY THINK I NEED THERAPY?!
CAFE
OPEN
11.8.2001
I DIDN'T SAY "YOU NEED IT"!.. I SAID, IT "COULD BE GOOD FOR YOU"...
BESIDES... I KNOW CHELLE'S THERAPIST AND SHE'S REALLY GOOD.
PAIGE
YOU DO?!.. WHO IS IT??

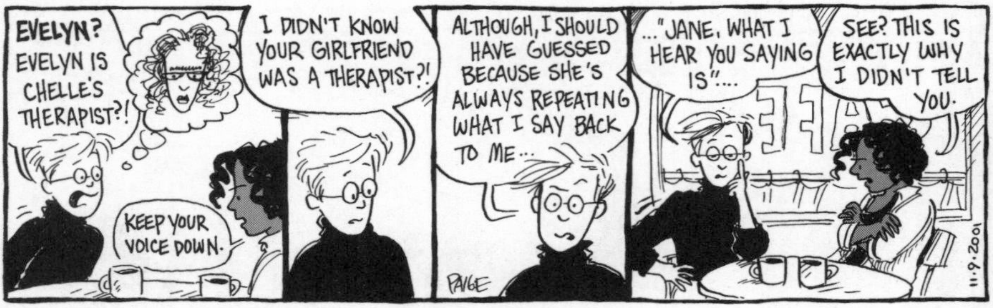
EVELYN? EVELYN IS CHELLE'S THERAPIST?!
KEEP YOUR VOICE DOWN.
I DIDN'T KNOW YOUR GIRLFRIEND WAS A THERAPIST?!
ALTHOUGH, I SHOULD HAVE GUESSED BECAUSE SHE'S ALWAYS REPEATING WHAT I SAY BACK TO ME...
PAIGE
..."JANE, WHAT I HEAR YOU SAYING IS"...
SEE? THIS IS EXACTLY WHY I DIDN'T TELL YOU.
11.9.2001

LATER, BACK AT JANE'S...

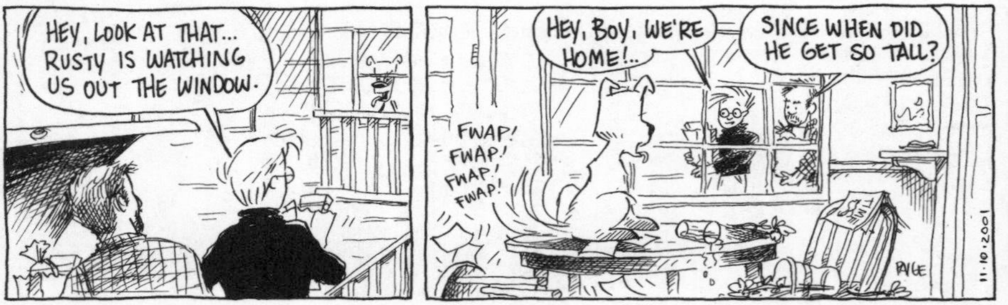
HEY, LOOK AT THAT... RUSTY IS WATCHING US OUT THE WINDOW.
HEY, BOY, WE'RE HOME!..
SINCE WHEN DID HE GET SO TALL?
FWAP! FWAP! FWAP! FWAP!
PAIGE
11.10.2001

...AND THE NEXT DAY, MORE DRAMA ON THE HOME FRONT...

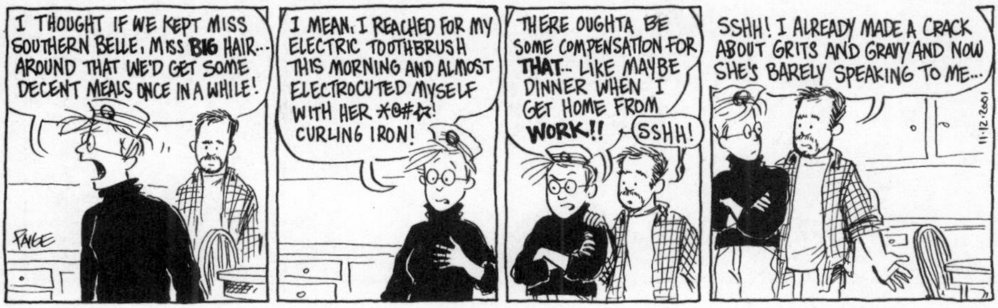
I THOUGHT IF WE KEPT MISS SOUTHERN BELLE, MISS BIG HAIR... AROUND THAT WE'D GET SOME DECENT MEALS ONCE IN A WHILE!
PAIGE
I MEAN, I REACHED FOR MY ELECTRIC TOOTHBRUSH THIS MORNING AND ALMOST ELECTROCUTED MYSELF WITH HER *@#☆! CURLING IRON!
THERE OUGHTA BE SOME COMPENSATION FOR THAT... LIKE MAYBE DINNER WHEN I GET HOME FROM WORK!!
SSHH!
SSHH! I ALREADY MADE A CRACK ABOUT GRITS AND GRAVY AND NOW SHE'S BARELY SPEAKING TO ME...
11·12·2001

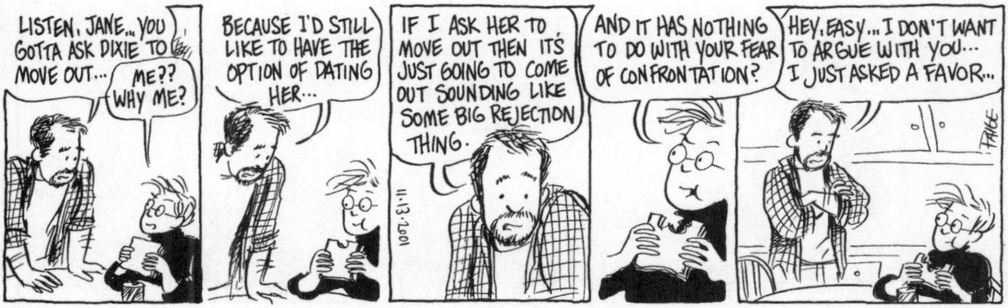
LISTEN, JANE... YOU GOTTA ASK DIXIE TO MOVE OUT...
ME?? WHY ME?
BECAUSE I'D STILL LIKE TO HAVE THE OPTION OF DATING HER...
IF I ASK HER TO MOVE OUT THEN IT'S JUST GOING TO COME OUT SOUNDING LIKE SOME BIG REJECTION THING.
11·13·2001
AND IT HAS NOTHING TO DO WITH YOUR FEAR OF CONFRONTATION?
HEY, EASY... I DON'T WANT TO ARGUE WITH YOU... I JUST ASKED A FAVOR...
PAIGE

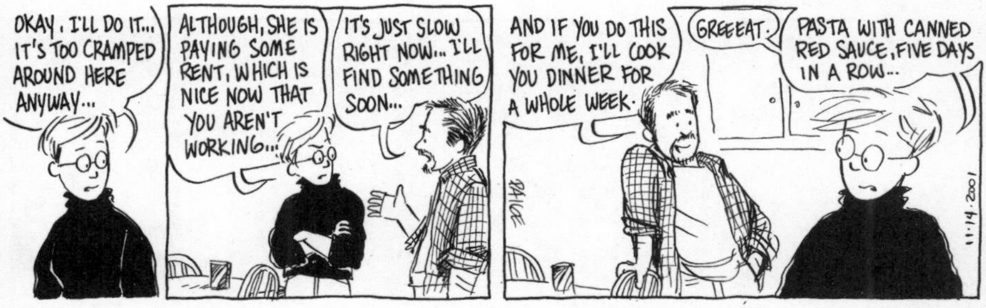
OKAY, I'LL DO IT... IT'S TOO CRAMPED AROUND HERE ANYWAY...
ALTHOUGH, SHE IS PAYING SOME RENT, WHICH IS NICE NOW THAT YOU AREN'T WORKING...
IT'S JUST SLOW RIGHT NOW... I'LL FIND SOMETHING SOON...
PAIGE
AND IF YOU DO THIS FOR ME, I'LL COOK YOU DINNER FOR A WHOLE WEEK.
GREEEAT.
PASTA WITH CANNED RED SAUCE, FIVE DAYS IN A ROW...
11·14·2001

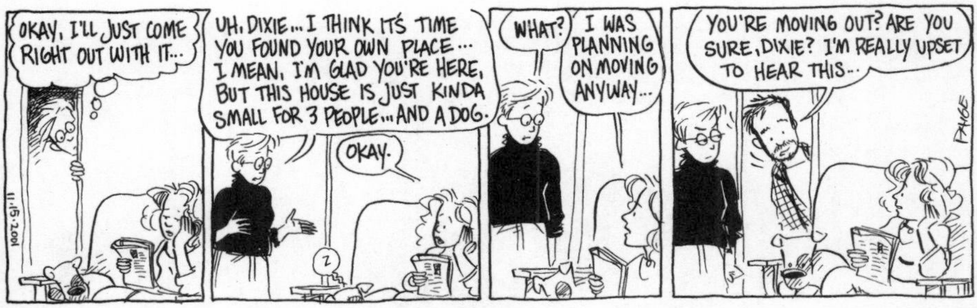
OKAY, I'LL JUST COME RIGHT OUT WITH IT...
11·15·2001
UH, DIXIE... I THINK IT'S TIME YOU FOUND YOUR OWN PLACE... I MEAN, I'M GLAD YOU'RE HERE, BUT THIS HOUSE IS JUST KINDA SMALL FOR 3 PEOPLE... AND A DOG.
OKAY.
Z
WHAT?
I WAS PLANNING ON MOVING ANYWAY...
YOU'RE MOVING OUT? ARE YOU SURE, DIXIE? I'M REALLY UPSET TO HEAR THIS...
PAIGE

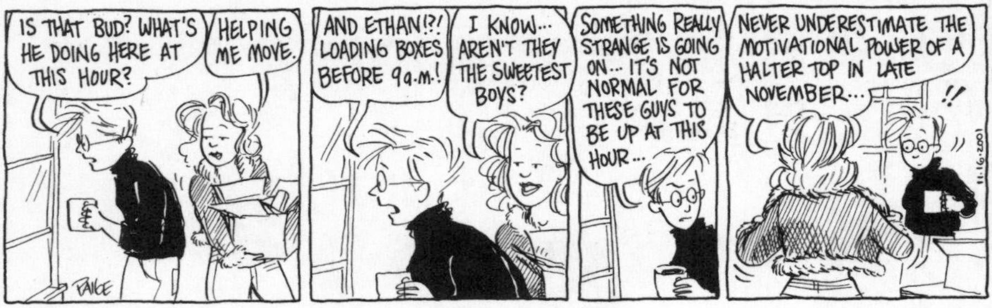
IS THAT BUD? WHAT'S HE DOING HERE AT THIS HOUR?
HELPING ME MOVE.
PAIGE
AND ETHAN!?! LOADING BOXES BEFORE 9 a.m.!
I KNOW... AREN'T THEY THE SWEETEST BOYS?
SOMETHING REALLY STRANGE IS GOING ON... IT'S NOT NORMAL FOR THESE GUYS TO BE UP AT THIS HOUR...
NEVER UNDERESTIMATE THE MOTIVATIONAL POWER OF A HALTER TOP IN LATE NOVEMBER...
!!
11·16·2001

AFTER THE MOVE, AT BUD'S PLACE....

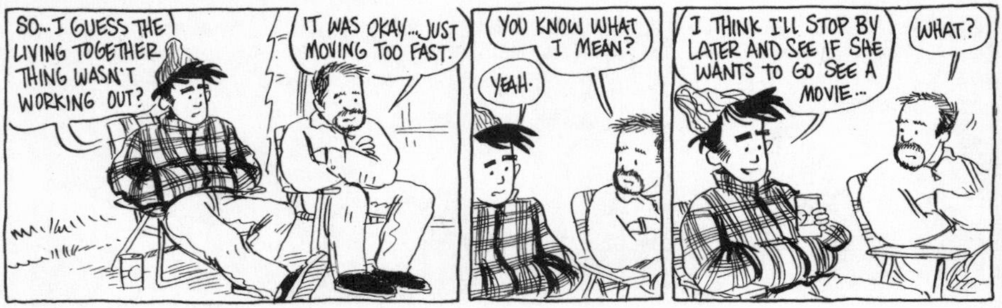
SO... I GUESS THE LIVING TOGETHER THING WASN'T WORKING OUT?
IT WAS OKAY... JUST MOVING TOO FAST.
YOU KNOW WHAT I MEAN?
YEAH.
I THINK I'LL STOP BY LATER AND SEE IF SHE WANTS TO GO SEE A MOVIE...
WHAT?

...AND THEN LATER, AT THE CAFE...

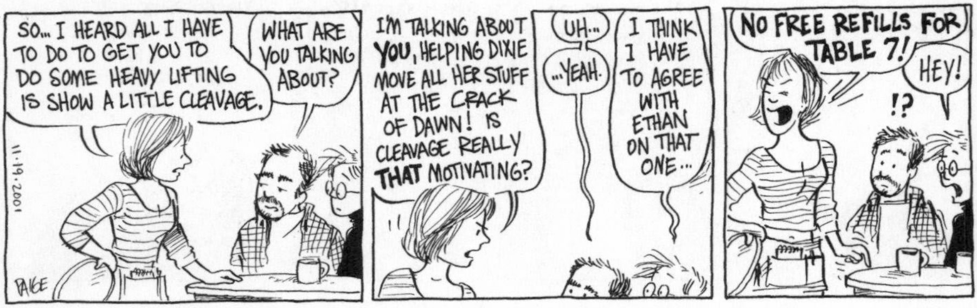
SO... I HEARD ALL I HAVE TO DO TO GET YOU TO DO SOME HEAVY LIFTING IS SHOW A LITTLE CLEAVAGE.
WHAT ARE YOU TALKING ABOUT?
11·19·2001
PAIGE
I'M TALKING ABOUT YOU, HELPING DIXIE MOVE ALL HER STUFF AT THE CRACK OF DAWN! IS CLEAVAGE REALLY THAT MOTIVATING?
UH...
...YEAH.
I THINK I HAVE TO AGREE WITH ETHAN ON THAT ONE...
NO FREE REFILLS FOR TABLE 7!
HEY!
!?

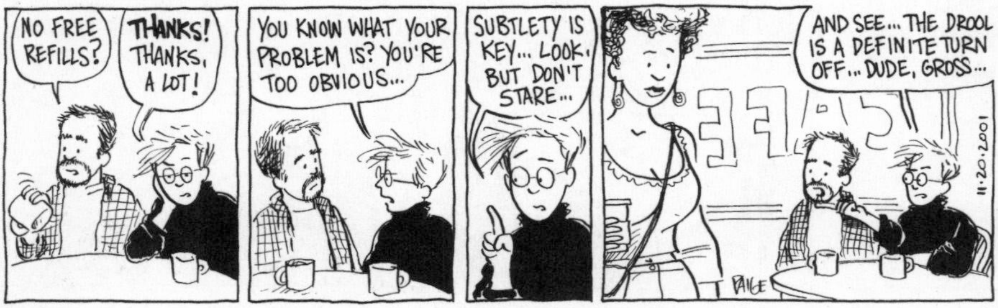
NO FREE REFILLS?
THANKS! THANKS, A LOT!
YOU KNOW WHAT YOUR PROBLEM IS? YOU'RE TOO OBVIOUS...
SUBTLETY IS KEY... LOOK, BUT DON'T STARE...
AND SEE... THE DROOL IS A DEFINITE TURN OFF... DUDE, GROSS...
11·20·2001
PAIGE

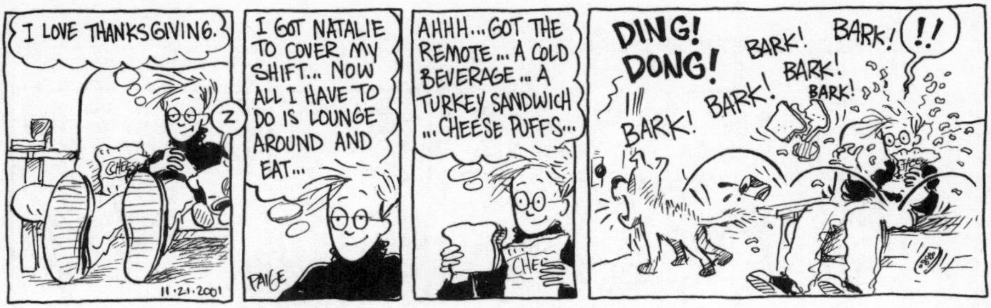
I LOVE THANKSGIVING.
Z
11·21·2001
I GOT NATALIE TO COVER MY SHIFT... NOW ALL I HAVE TO DO IS LOUNGE AROUND AND EAT...
PAIGE
AHHH...GOT THE REMOTE... A COLD BEVERAGE... A TURKEY SANDWICH ...CHEESE PUFFS...
DING! DONG!
BARK! BARK! BARK! BARK! BARK! BARK!
!!

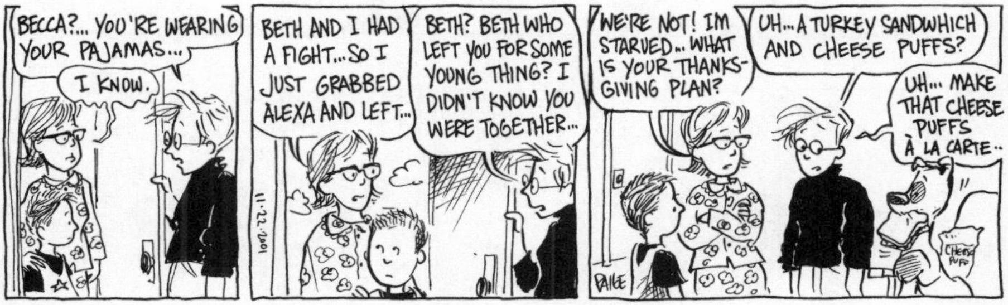
BECCA?... YOU'RE WEARING YOUR PAJAMAS...
I KNOW.
BETH AND I HAD A FIGHT...SO I JUST GRABBED ALEXA AND LEFT...
11·22·2001
BETH? BETH WHO LEFT YOU FOR SOME YOUNG THING? I DIDN'T KNOW YOU WERE TOGETHER...
WE'RE NOT! I'M STARVED... WHAT IS YOUR THANKSGIVING PLAN?
UH... A TURKEY SANDWHICH AND CHEESE PUFFS?
UH... MAKE THAT CHEESE PUFFS À LA CARTE..
PAIGE

THE NEXT DAY, THE THANKSGIVING-FAMILY-INVASION CONTINUES...

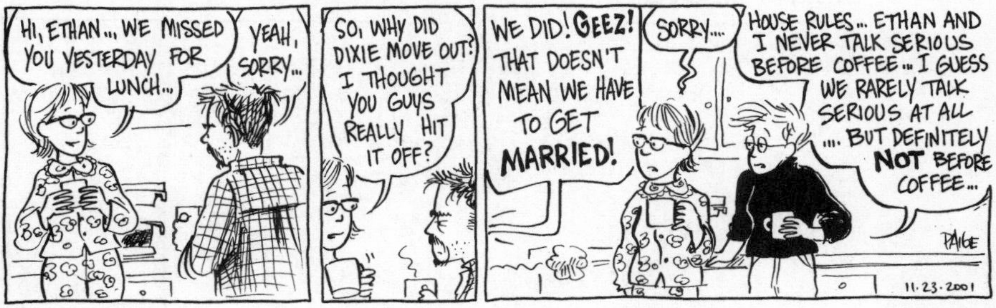
HI, ETHAN... WE MISSED YOU YESTERDAY FOR LUNCH...
YEAH, SORRY...
SO, WHY DID DIXIE MOVE OUT? I THOUGHT YOU GUYS REALLY HIT IT OFF?
WE DID! GEEZ! THAT DOESN'T MEAN WE HAVE TO GET MARRIED!
SORRY....
HOUSE RULES... ETHAN AND I NEVER TALK SERIOUS BEFORE COFFEE... I GUESS WE RARELY TALK SERIOUS AT ALL .... BUT DEFINITELY NOT BEFORE COFFEE...
PAIGE
11·23·2001

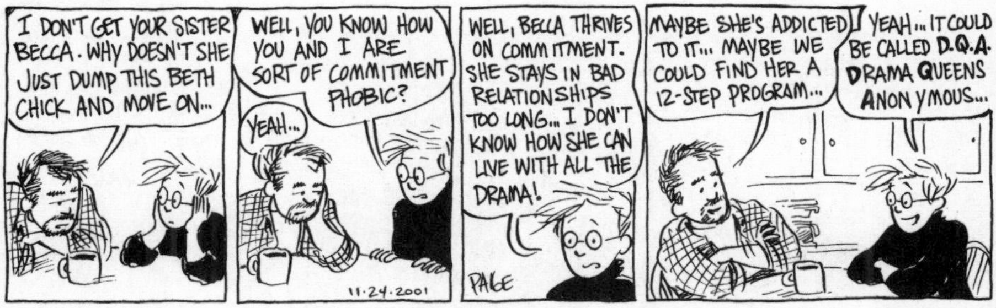
I DON'T GET YOUR SISTER BECCA. WHY DOESN'T SHE JUST DUMP THIS BETH CHICK AND MOVE ON...
WELL, YOU KNOW HOW YOU AND I ARE SORT OF COMMITMENT PHOBIC?
YEAH...
11·24·2001
WELL, BECCA THRIVES ON COMMITMENT. SHE STAYS IN BAD RELATIONSHIPS TOO LONG... I DON'T KNOW HOW SHE CAN LIVE WITH ALL THE DRAMA!
PAIGE
MAYBE SHE'S ADDICTED TO IT... MAYBE WE COULD FIND HER A 12-STEP PROGRAM...
YEAH... IT COULD BE CALLED D.Q.A. DRAMA QUEENS ANONYMOUS...

LATER THAT WEEK, JANE TAKES THE PLUNGE...

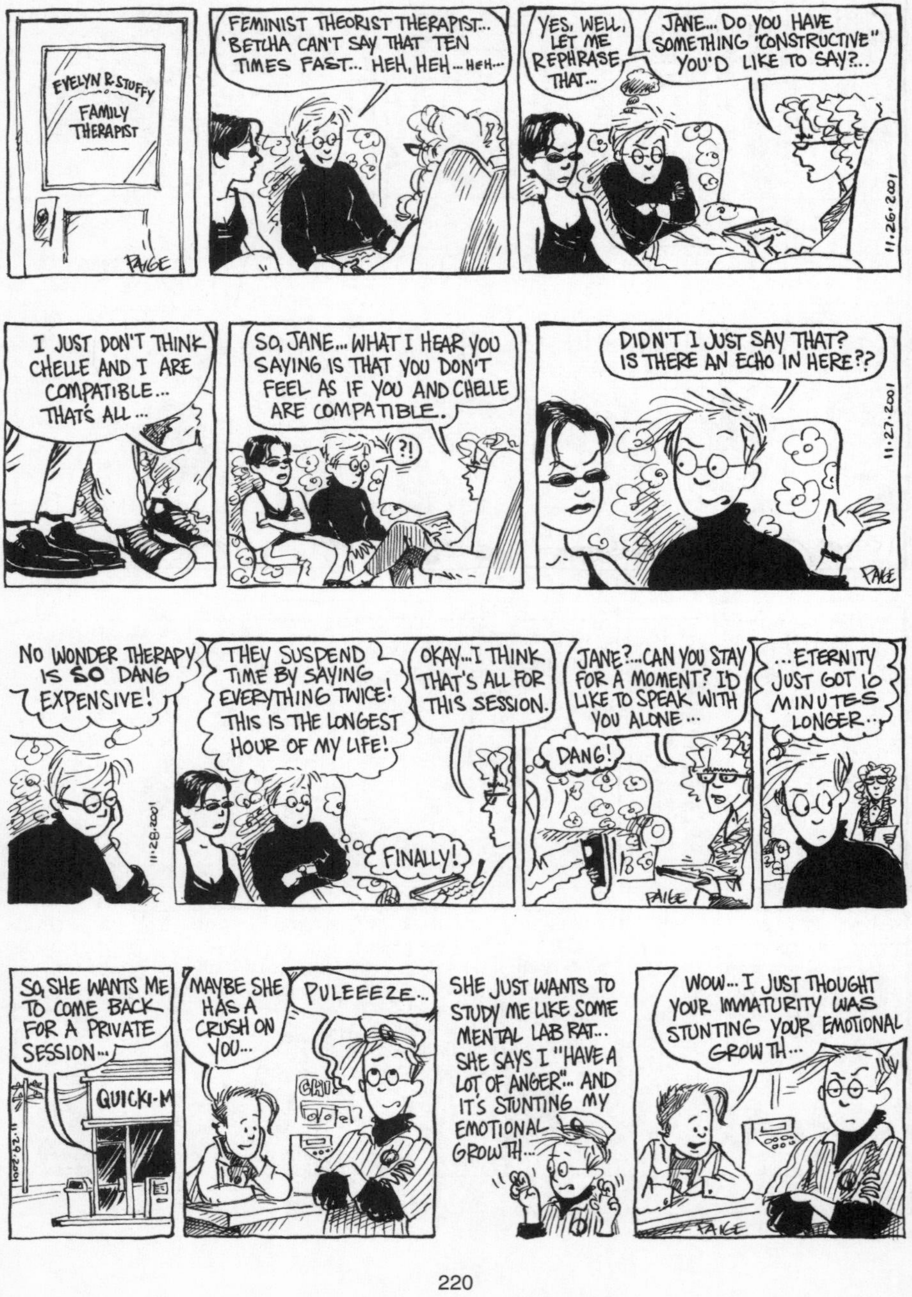
EVELYN R. STUFFY
FAMILY THERAPIST
FEMINIST THEORIST THERAPIST... 'BETCHA CAN'T SAY THAT TEN TIMES FAST... HEH, HEH... HEH...
YES, WELL, LET ME REPHRASE THAT...
JANE... DO YOU HAVE SOMETHING "CONSTRUCTIVE" YOU'D LIKE TO SAY?...
11·26·2001
I JUST DON'T THINK CHELLE AND I ARE COMPATIBLE... THAT'S ALL...
SO, JANE... WHAT I HEAR YOU SAYING IS THAT YOU DON'T FEEL AS IF YOU AND CHELLE ARE COMPATIBLE.
?!
DIDN'T I JUST SAY THAT? IS THERE AN ECHO IN HERE??
11·27·2001
NO WONDER THERAPY IS SO DANG EXPENSIVE!
11·28·2001
THEY SUSPEND TIME BY SAYING EVERYTHING TWICE! THIS IS THE LONGEST HOUR OF MY LIFE!
OKAY... I THINK THAT'S ALL FOR THIS SESSION.
FINALLY!
JANE?...CAN YOU STAY FOR A MOMENT? I'D LIKE TO SPEAK WITH YOU ALONE...
DANG!
...ETERNITY JUST GOT 10 MINUTES LONGER...
SO, SHE WANTS ME TO COME BACK FOR A PRIVATE SESSION...
QUICKI-M
11·29·2001
MAYBE SHE HAS A CRUSH ON YOU...
PULEEEZE...
SHE JUST WANTS TO STUDY ME LIKE SOME MENTAL LAB RAT... SHE SAYS I "HAVE A LOT OF ANGER"... AND IT'S STUNTING MY EMOTIONAL GROWTH...
WOW... I JUST THOUGHT YOUR IMMATURITY WAS STUNTING YOUR EMOTIONAL GROWTH...
PAIGE

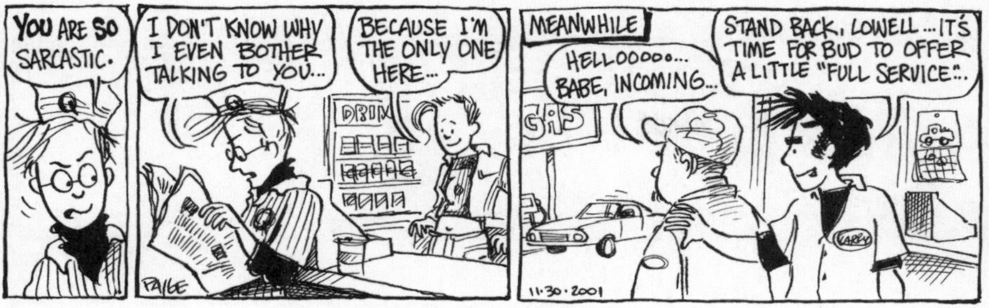
YOU ARE SO SARCASTIC.
I DON'T KNOW WHY I EVEN BOTHER TALKING TO YOU...
BECAUSE I'M THE ONLY ONE HERE...
PAIGE
MEANWHILE
HELLOOOOO... BABE, INCOMING...
STAND BACK, LOWELL...IT'S TIME FOR BUD TO OFFER A LITTLE "FULL SERVICE"..
11·30·2001

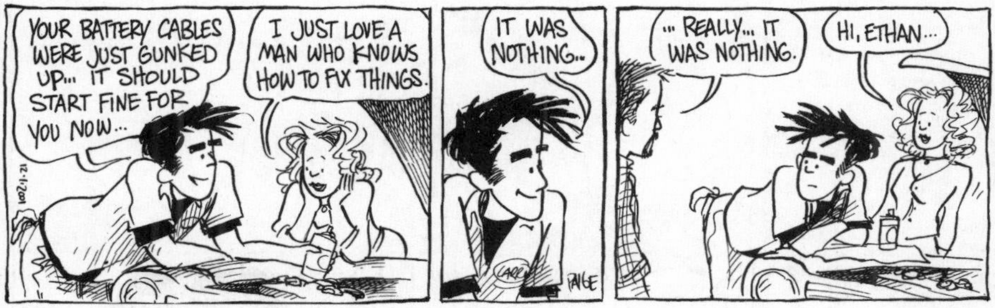
YOUR BATTERY CABLES WERE JUST GUNKED UP... IT SHOULD START FINE FOR YOU NOW...
I JUST LOVE A MAN WHO KNOWS HOW TO FIX THINGS.
12·1·2001
IT WAS NOTHING..
PAIGE
... REALLY... IT WAS NOTHING.
HI, ETHAN...

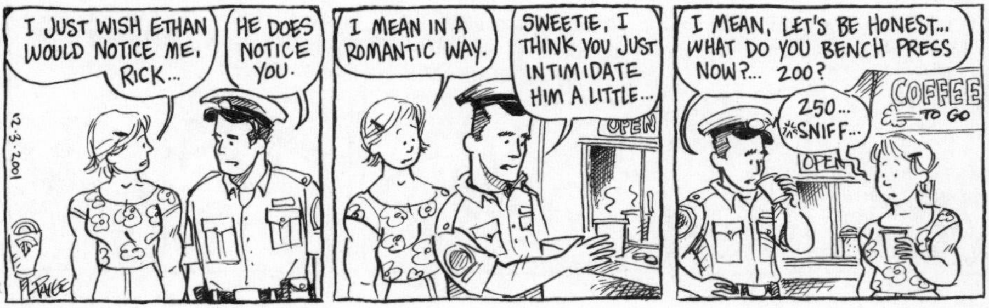
I JUST WISH ETHAN WOULD NOTICE ME, RICK...
HE DOES NOTICE YOU.
12·3·2001
PAIGE
I MEAN IN A ROMANTIC WAY.
SWEETIE, I THINK YOU JUST INTIMIDATE HIM A LITTLE...
OPEN
I MEAN, LET'S BE HONEST... WHAT DO YOU BENCH PRESS NOW?... 200?
250... *SNIFF*...
COFFEE TO GO
OPEN

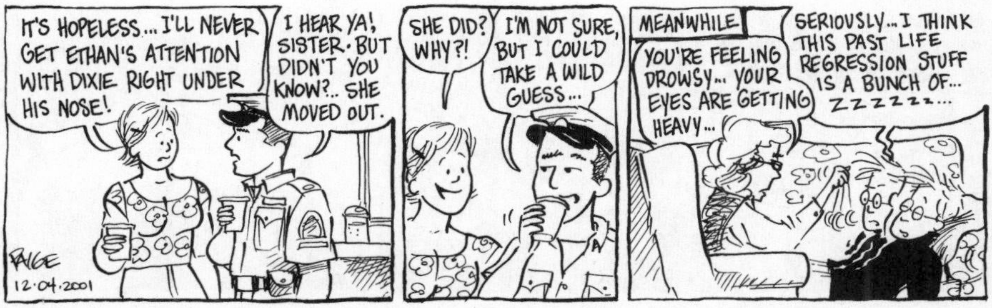
IT'S HOPELESS... I'LL NEVER GET ETHAN'S ATTENTION WITH DIXIE RIGHT UNDER HIS NOSE!
I HEAR YA! SISTER. BUT DIDN'T YOU KNOW?.. SHE MOVED OUT.
PAIGE
12·04·2001
SHE DID? WHY?!
I'M NOT SURE, BUT I COULD TAKE A WILD GUESS...
MEANWHILE
YOU'RE FEELING DROWSY... YOUR EYES ARE GETTING HEAVY...
SERIOUSLY... I THINK THIS PAST LIFE REGRESSION STUFF IS A BUNCH OF... ZZZZZZ...

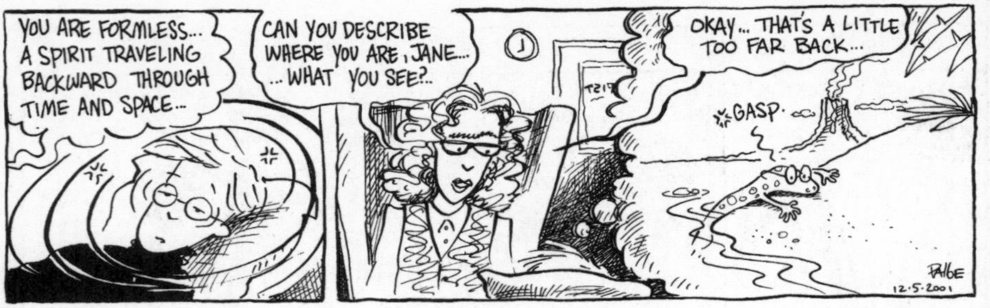
YOU ARE FORMLESS... A SPIRIT TRAVELING BACKWARD THROUGH TIME AND SPACE...
CAN YOU DESCRIBE WHERE YOU ARE, JANE... ...WHAT YOU SEE?..
OKAY... THAT'S A LITTLE TOO FAR BACK...
GASP
PAIGE
12·5·2001

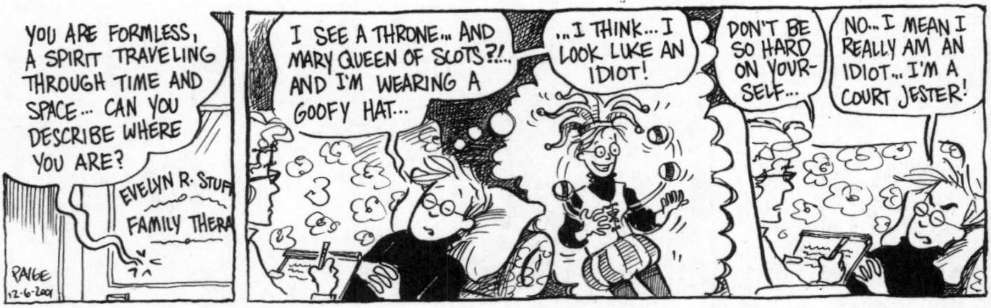
YOU ARE FORMLESS, A SPIRIT TRAVELING THROUGH TIME AND SPACE... CAN YOU DESCRIBE WHERE YOU ARE?
EVELYN R. STUFF
FAMILY THERA
PAIGE
12·6·2001
I SEE A THRONE... AND MARY QUEEN OF SCOTS?!... AND I'M WEARING A GOOFY HAT...
...I THINK... I LOOK LIKE AN IDIOT!
DON'T BE SO HARD ON YOURSELF...
NO... I MEAN I REALLY AM AN IDIOT... I'M A COURT JESTER!

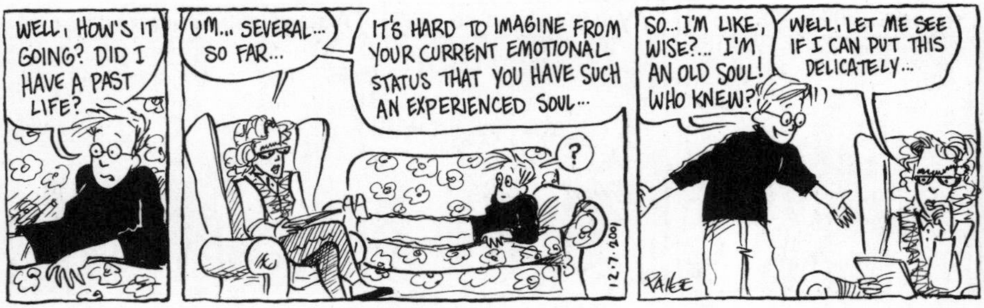
WELL, HOW'S IT GOING? DID I HAVE A PAST LIFE?
UM... SEVERAL... SO FAR...
IT'S HARD TO IMAGINE FROM YOUR CURRENT EMOTIONAL STATUS THAT YOU HAVE SUCH AN EXPERIENCED SOUL...
?
12·7·2001
SO... I'M LIKE, WISE?... I'M AN OLD SOUL! WHO KNEW?
WELL, LET ME SEE IF I CAN PUT THIS DELICATELY...
PAIGE

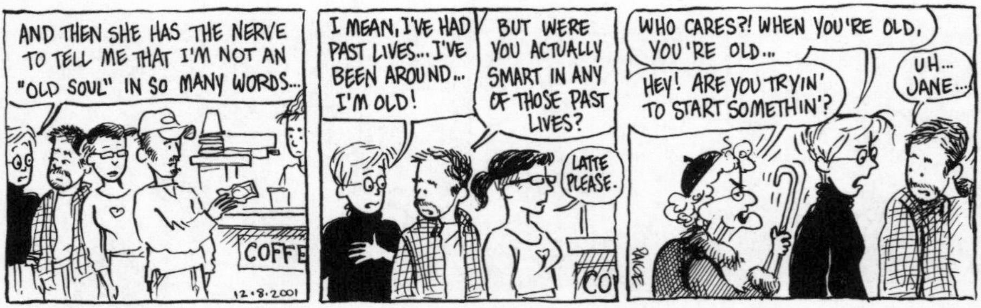
AND THEN SHE HAS THE NERVE TO TELL ME THAT I'M NOT AN "OLD SOUL" IN SO MANY WORDS...
COFFE
12·8·2001
I MEAN, I'VE HAD PAST LIVES... I'VE BEEN AROUND... I'M OLD!
BUT WERE YOU ACTUALLY SMART IN ANY OF THOSE PAST LIVES?
LATTE PLEASE.
PAIGE
CO
WHO CARES?! WHEN YOU'RE OLD, YOU'RE OLD...
HEY! ARE YOU TRYIN' TO START SOMETHIN'?
UH... JANE...

BACK IN THERAPY, A FEW DAYS LATER...

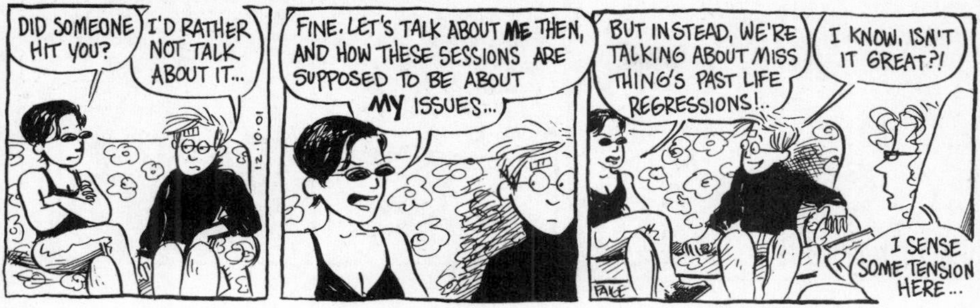
DID SOMEONE HIT YOU?
I'D RATHER NOT TALK ABOUT IT...
12·10·01
FINE. LET'S TALK ABOUT ME THEN, AND HOW THESE SESSIONS ARE SUPPOSED TO BE ABOUT MY ISSUES...
BUT INSTEAD, WE'RE TALKING ABOUT MISS THING'S PAST LIFE REGRESSIONS!..
I KNOW, ISN'T IT GREAT?!
I SENSE SOME TENSION HERE...
PAIGE

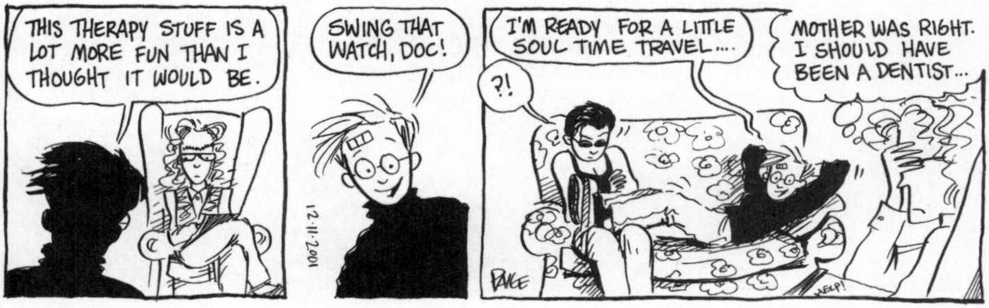
THIS THERAPY STUFF IS A LOT MORE FUN THAN I THOUGHT IT WOULD BE.
12·11·2001
SWING THAT WATCH, DOC!
I'M READY FOR A LITTLE SOUL TIME TRAVEL....
?!
MOTHER WAS RIGHT. I SHOULD HAVE BEEN A DENTIST...
HELP!
PAIGE

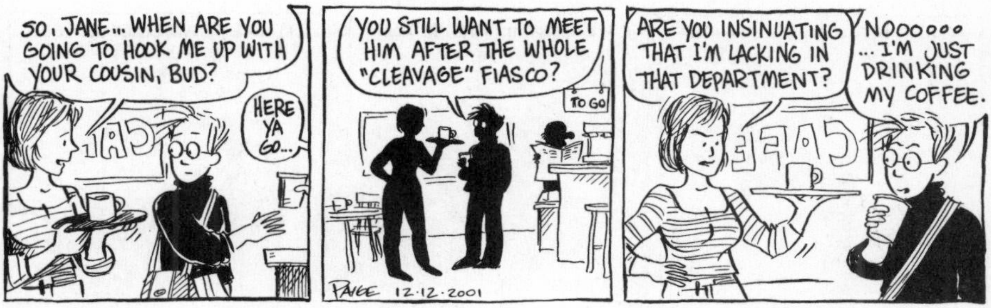
SO, JANE... WHEN ARE YOU GOING TO HOOK ME UP WITH YOUR COUSIN, BUD?
HERE YA GO...
YOU STILL WANT TO MEET HIM AFTER THE WHOLE "CLEAVAGE" FIASCO?
TO GO
PAIGE 12·12·2001
ARE YOU INSINUATING THAT I'M LACKING IN THAT DEPARTMENT?
NOOOOOO ...I'M JUST DRINKING MY COFFEE.
CAFE

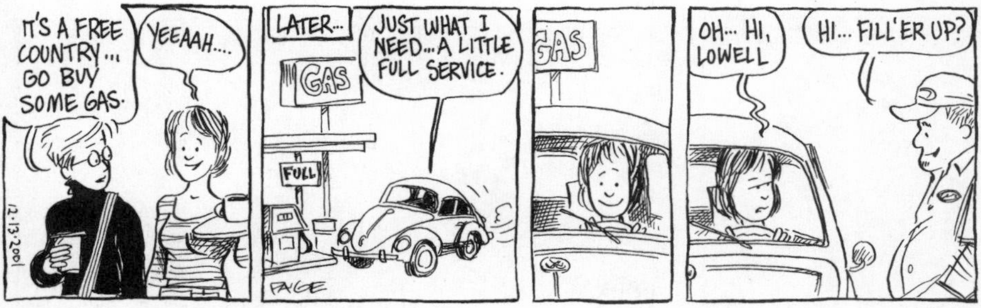
IT'S A FREE COUNTRY... GO BUY SOME GAS.
YEEAAH....
12·13·2001
LATER...
JUST WHAT I NEED...A LITTLE FULL SERVICE.
GAS
FULL
PAIGE
GAS
OH... HI, LOWELL
HI... FILL'ER UP?

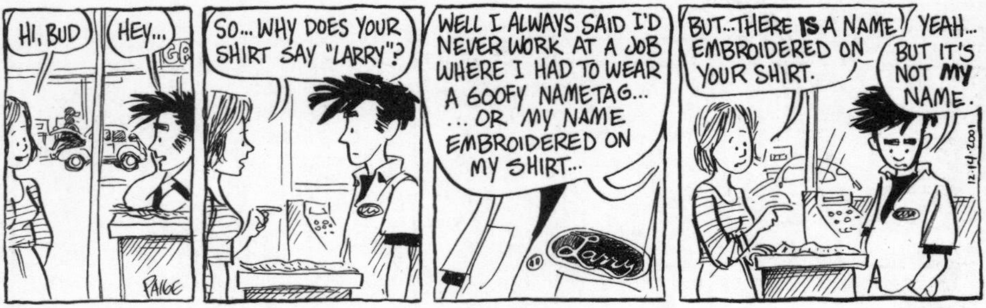
HI, BUD
HEY...
SO... WHY DOES YOUR SHIRT SAY "LARRY"?
WELL I ALWAYS SAID I'D NEVER WORK AT A JOB WHERE I HAD TO WEAR A GOOFY NAMETAG... ... OR MY NAME EMBROIDERED ON MY SHIRT...
Larry
BUT... THERE **IS** A NAME EMBROIDERED ON YOUR SHIRT.
YEAH... BUT IT'S NOT **MY** NAME.
PAIGE
12-14-2001

MEANWHILE...

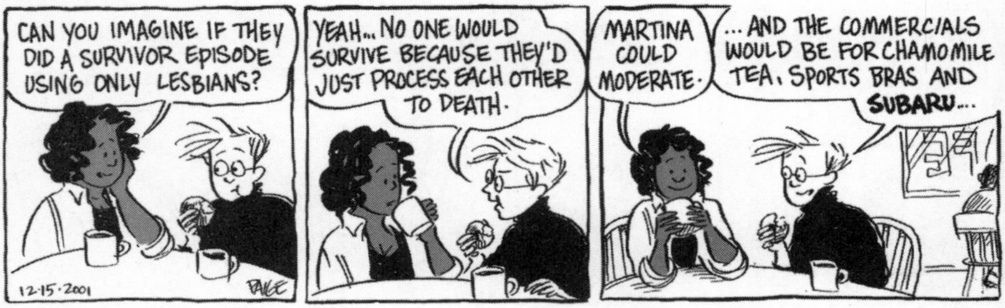
CAN YOU IMAGINE IF THEY DID A SURVIVOR EPISODE USING ONLY LESBIANS?
YEAH... NO ONE WOULD SURVIVE BECAUSE THEY'D JUST PROCESS EACH OTHER TO DEATH.
MARTINA COULD MODERATE.
... AND THE COMMERCIALS WOULD BE FOR CHAMOMILE TEA, SPORTS BRAS AND **SUBARU**...
12-15-2001
PAIGE

...AND NOW, A LITTLE BELATED CHRISTMAS CHEER, "PEANUTS" STYLE...

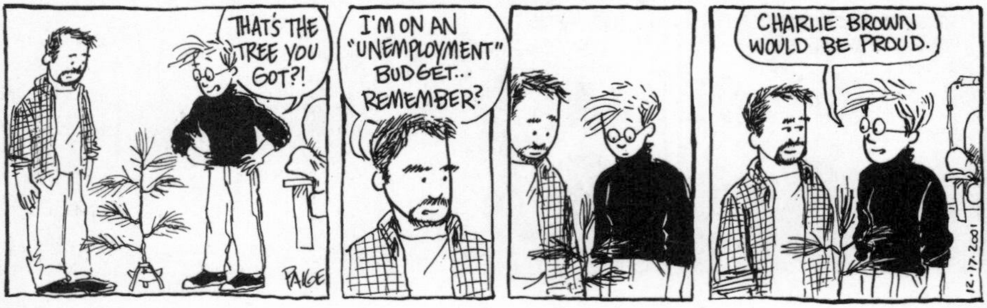
THAT'S THE TREE YOU GOT?!
PAIGE
I'M ON AN "UNEMPLOYMENT" BUDGET... REMEMBER?
CHARLIE BROWN WOULD BE PROUD.
12-17-2001

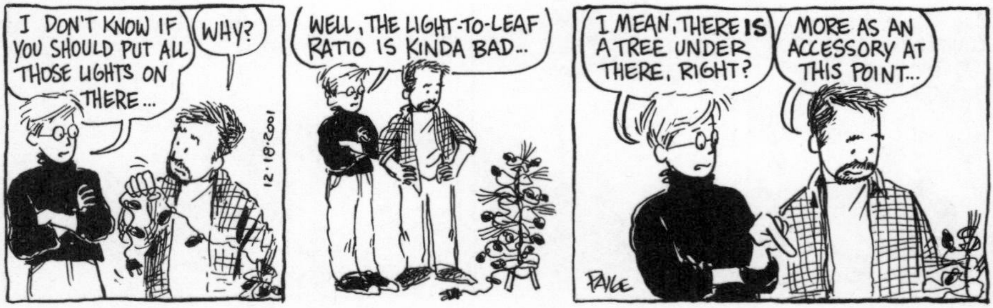
I DON'T KNOW IF YOU SHOULD PUT ALL THOSE LIGHTS ON THERE...
WHY?
12-18-2001
WELL, THE LIGHT-TO-LEAF RATIO IS KINDA BAD...
I MEAN, THERE **IS** A TREE UNDER THERE, RIGHT?
MORE AS AN ACCESSORY AT THIS POINT...
PAIGE

CUT THAT OUT!
PAIGE
WHAT'D YOU GET ME?
WHAT'S IT SOUND LIKE?
IT SOUNDS BIG... ...NOISEY... ...SPECIAL...
12·19·2001
IT PROBABLY IS... IT'S NOT FROM ME.
OH.

SO... ARE YOU COMING OVER FOR CHRISTMAS?
YEAH... I'LL BE THERE.
12·20·2001
PAIGE
JUST THE THREE OF US, RIGHT? YOU... ETHAN... AND ME...
TO GO
JUST LIKE THE OLD DAYS...
WHAT SHOULD I BRING?
HOW ABOUT DINNER?
I WALK RIGHT INTO IT EVERY TIME...

BUD WANTS TO COME OVER FOR CHRISTMAS.
DOES HE HAVE TO? I WAS LIKING JUST THE THREE OF US.
PAIGE
12·21·2001
HE'S MY COUSIN... WHAT AM I...?
...HUH?...

HE SAYS HE'LL BRING BROWNIES AND ICE CREAM...
...WITH NUTS? OR WITHOUT?

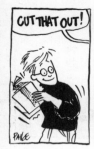

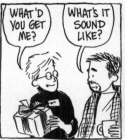

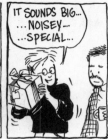

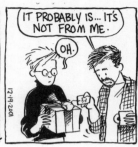

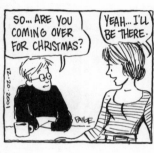

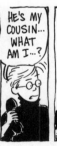

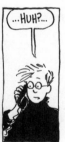

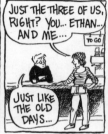

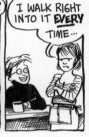

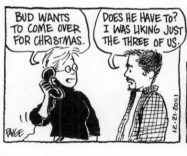

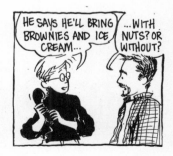

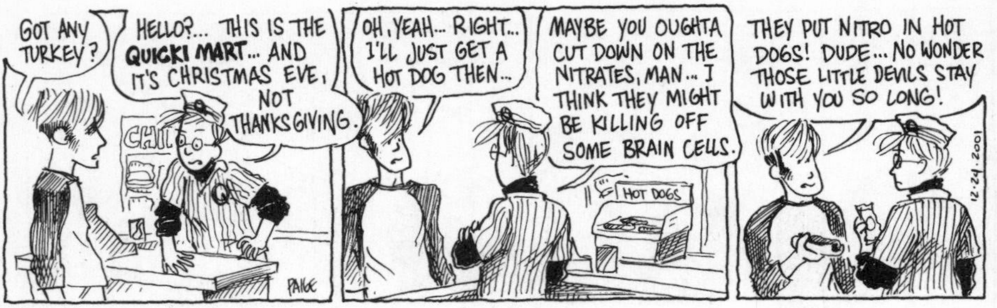
GOT ANY TURKEY?
HELLO?... THIS IS THE QUICKI MART... AND IT'S CHRISTMAS EVE, NOT THANKSGIVING.
OH, YEAH... RIGHT... I'LL JUST GET A HOT DOG THEN...
MAYBE YOU OUGHTA CUT DOWN ON THE NITRATES, MAN... I THINK THEY MIGHT BE KILLING OFF SOME BRAIN CELLS.
HOT DOGS
THEY PUT NITRO IN HOT DOGS! DUDE... NO WONDER THOSE LITTLE DEVILS STAY WITH YOU SO LONG!
12·24·2001
PAIGE

LATER, BACK AT JANE'S...

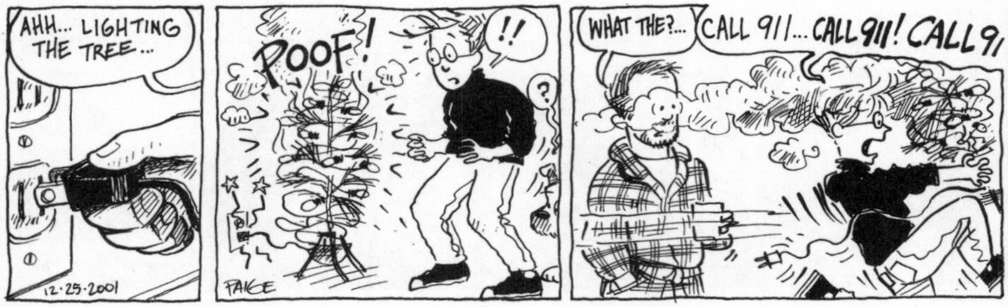
AHH... LIGHTING THE TREE...
12·25·2001
POOF!
!!
?
PAIGE
WHAT THE?...
CALL 911... CALL 911! CALL 9

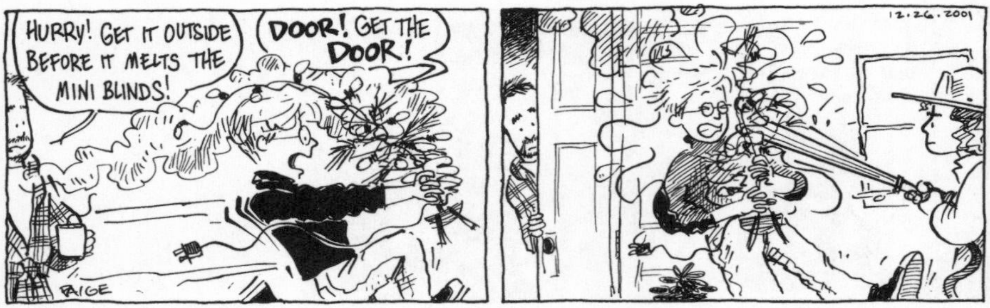
HURRY! GET IT OUTSIDE BEFORE IT MELTS THE MINI BLINDS!
DOOR! GET THE DOOR!
PAIGE
12·26·2001

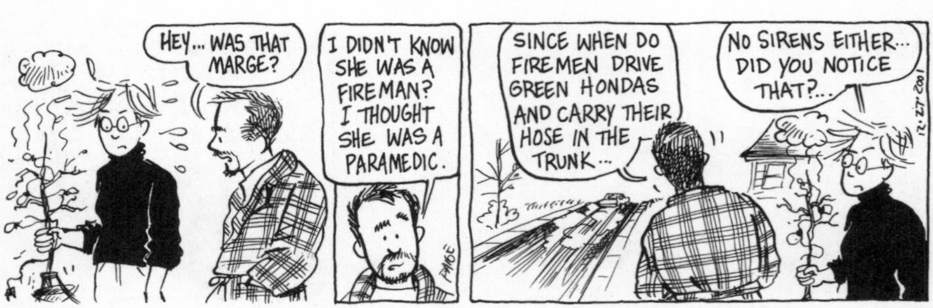
HEY... WAS THAT MARGE?
I DIDN'T KNOW SHE WAS A FIREMAN? I THOUGHT SHE WAS A PARAMEDIC.
PAIGE
SINCE WHEN DO FIREMEN DRIVE GREEN HONDAS AND CARRY THEIR HOSE IN THE TRUNK...
NO SIRENS EITHER... DID YOU NOTICE THAT?...
12·27·2001

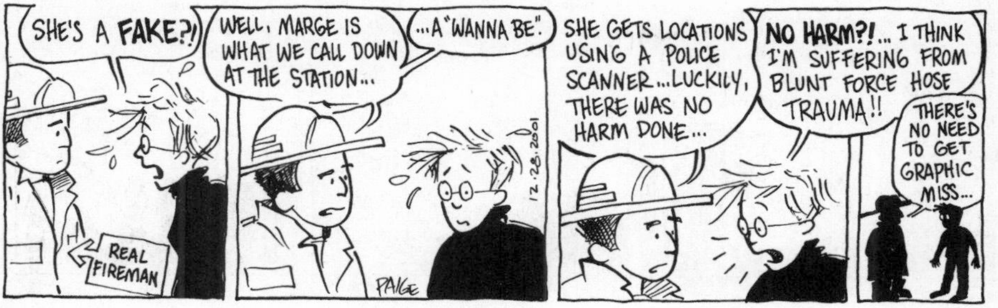

SHE'S A **FAKE**?!
REAL FIREMAN
WELL, MARGE IS WHAT WE CALL DOWN AT THE STATION...
...A "WANNA BE".
12·28·2001
PAIGE
SHE GETS LOCATIONS USING A POLICE SCANNER...LUCKILY, THERE WAS NO HARM DONE...
NO HARM?!... I THINK I'M SUFFERING FROM BLUNT FORCE HOSE TRAUMA!!
THERE'S NO NEED TO GET GRAPHIC MISS...

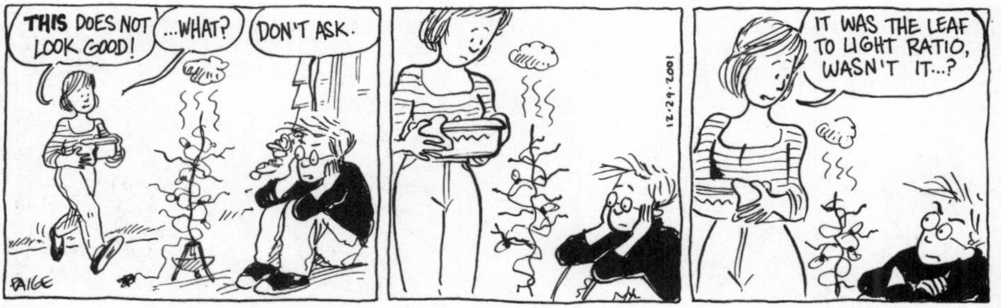

THIS DOES NOT LOOK GOOD!
...WHAT?
DON'T ASK.
PAIGE
12·29·2001
IT WAS THE LEAF TO LIGHT RATIO, WASN'T IT...?

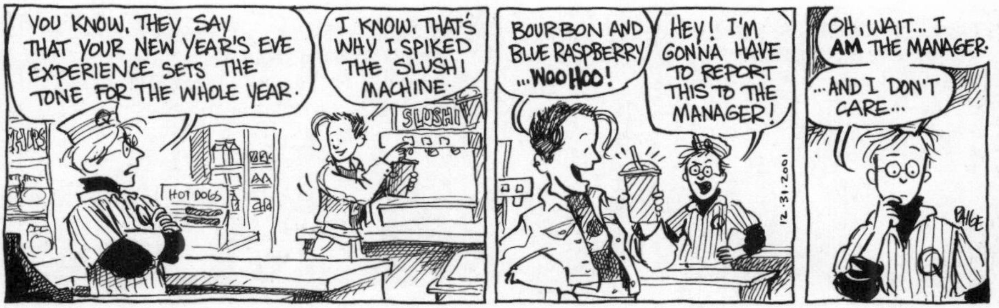

YOU KNOW, THEY SAY THAT YOUR NEW YEAR'S EVE EXPERIENCE SETS THE TONE FOR THE WHOLE YEAR.
I KNOW. THAT'S WHY I SPIKED THE SLUSHI MACHINE.
SLUSHI
HOT DOGS
BOURBON AND BLUE RASPBERRY ...**WOO HOO**!
HEY! I'M GONNA HAVE TO REPORT THIS TO THE MANAGER!
12·31·2001
OH, WAIT... I **AM** THE MANAGER.
...AND I DON'T CARE...
PAIGE

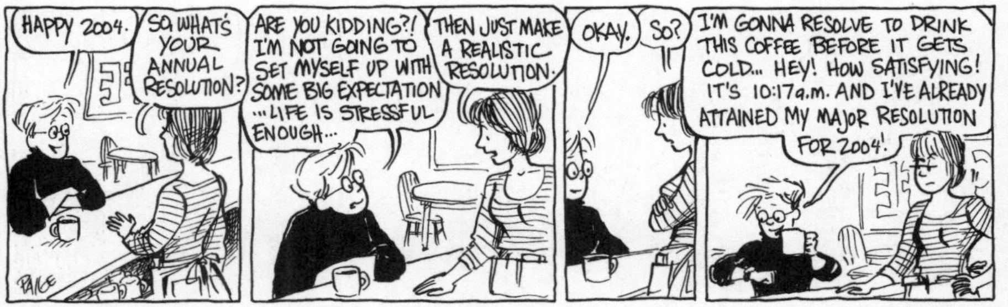

HAPPY 2004.
SO, WHAT'S YOUR ANNUAL RESOLUTION?
PAIGE
ARE YOU KIDDING?! I'M NOT GOING TO SET MYSELF UP WITH SOME BIG EXPECTATION ...LIFE IS STRESSFUL ENOUGH...
THEN JUST MAKE A REALISTIC RESOLUTION.
OKAY.
SO?
I'M GONNA RESOLVE TO DRINK THIS COFFEE BEFORE IT GETS COLD... HEY! HOW SATISFYING! IT'S 10:17a.m. AND I'VE ALREADY ATTAINED MY MAJOR RESOLUTION FOR 2004!

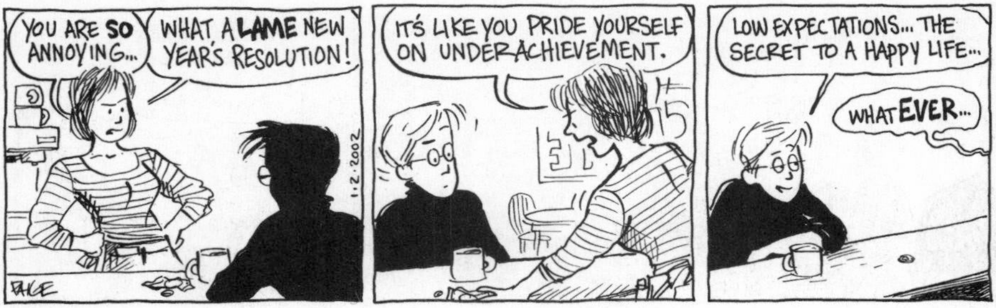
YOU ARE SO ANNOYING...
WHAT A LAME NEW YEAR'S RESOLUTION!
1.2.2002
PAIGE
IT'S LIKE YOU PRIDE YOURSELF ON UNDERACHIEVEMENT.
LOW EXPECTATIONS... THE SECRET TO A HAPPY LIFE...
WHATEVER...

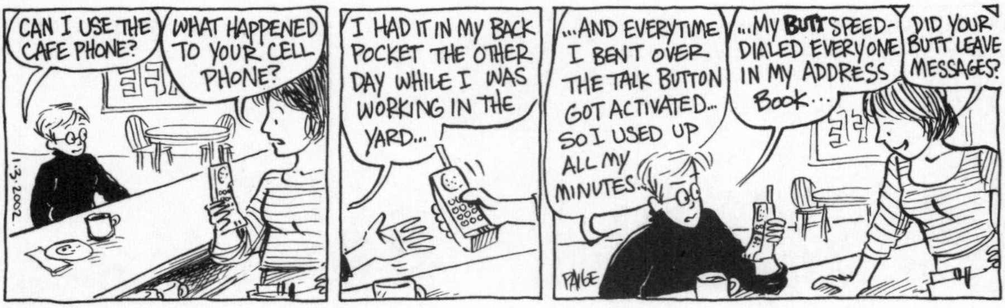
CAN I USE THE CAFE PHONE?
WHAT HAPPENED TO YOUR CELL PHONE?
1.3.2002
I HAD IT IN MY BACK POCKET THE OTHER DAY WHILE I WAS WORKING IN THE YARD...
...AND EVERYTIME I BENT OVER THE TALK BUTTON GOT ACTIVATED... SO I USED UP ALL MY MINUTES...
...MY BUTT SPEED-DIALED EVERYONE IN MY ADDRESS BOOK...
DID YOUR BUTT LEAVE MESSAGES?
PAIGE

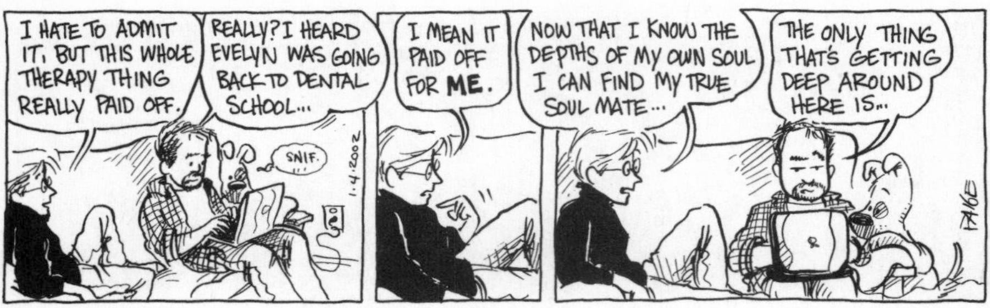
I HATE TO ADMIT IT, BUT THIS WHOLE THERAPY THING REALLY PAID OFF.
REALLY? I HEARD EVELYN WAS GOING BACK TO DENTAL SCHOOL...
SNIF.
1.4.2002
I MEAN IT PAID OFF FOR ME.
NOW THAT I KNOW THE DEPTHS OF MY OWN SOUL I CAN FIND MY TRUE SOUL MATE...
THE ONLY THING THAT'S GETTING DEEP AROUND HERE IS...
PAIGE

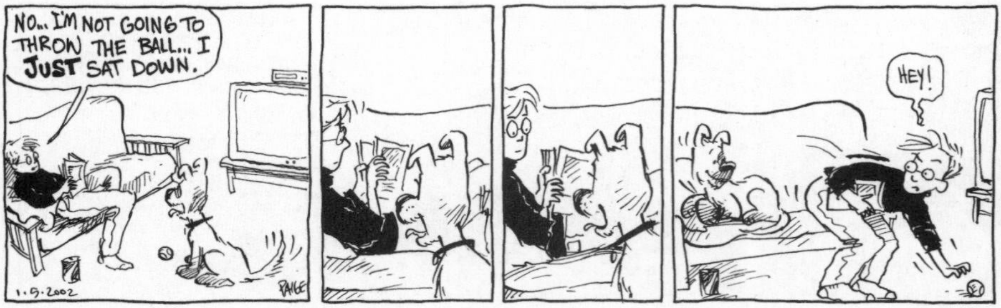
NO... I'M NOT GOING TO THROW THE BALL... I JUST SAT DOWN.
1.5.2002
PAIGE
HEY!

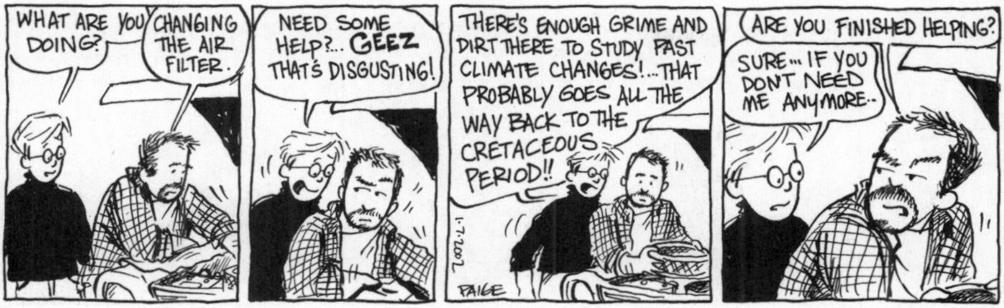
WHAT ARE YOU DOING?
CHANGING THE AIR FILTER.
NEED SOME HELP?... GEEZ THAT'S DISGUSTING!
THERE'S ENOUGH GRIME AND DIRT THERE TO STUDY PAST CLIMATE CHANGES!... THAT PROBABLY GOES ALL THE WAY BACK TO THE CRETACEOUS PERIOD!!
1.7.2002
PAIGE
ARE YOU FINISHED HELPING?
SURE... IF YOU DON'T NEED ME ANYMORE..

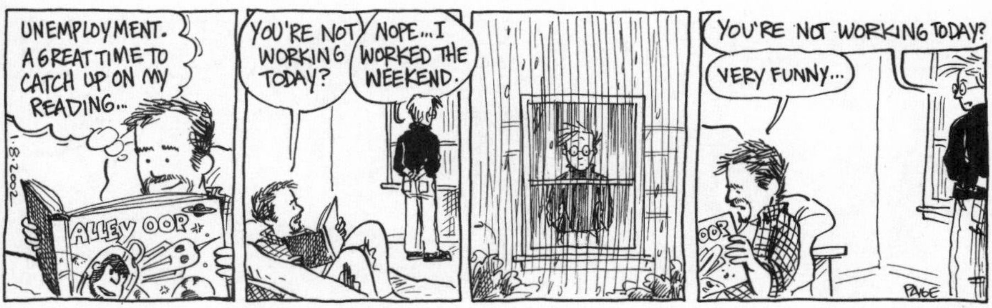
UNEMPLOYMENT. A GREAT TIME TO CATCH UP ON MY READING...
1.8.2002
ALLEY OOP
YOU'RE NOT WORKING TODAY?
NOPE... I WORKED THE WEEKEND.
YOU'RE NOT WORKING TODAY?
VERY FUNNY...
PAIGE

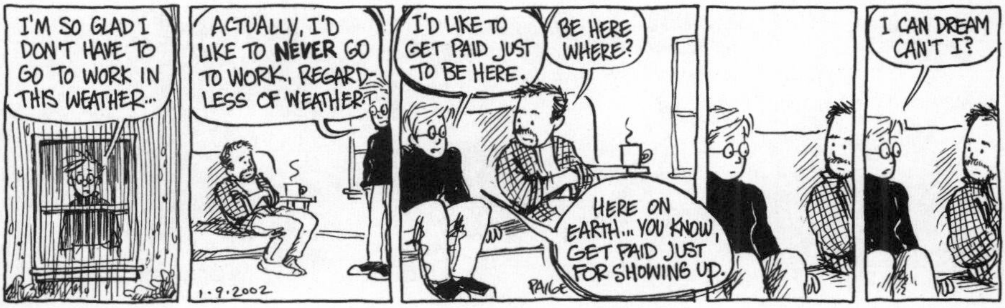
I'M SO GLAD I DON'T HAVE TO GO TO WORK IN THIS WEATHER...
ACTUALLY, I'D LIKE TO NEVER GO TO WORK, REGARDLESS OF WEATHER.
1.9.2002
I'D LIKE TO GET PAID JUST TO BE HERE.
BE HERE WHERE?
HERE ON EARTH... YOU KNOW, GET PAID JUST FOR SHOWING UP.
PAIGE
I CAN DREAM CAN'T I?

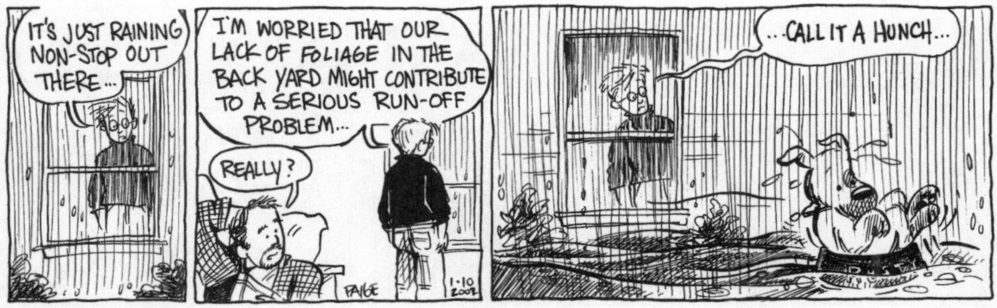
IT'S JUST RAINING NON-STOP OUT THERE...
I'M WORRIED THAT OUR LACK OF FOLIAGE IN THE BACK YARD MIGHT CONTRIBUTE TO A SERIOUS RUN-OFF PROBLEM...
REALLY?
PAIGE
1.10 2002
...CALL IT A HUNCH...

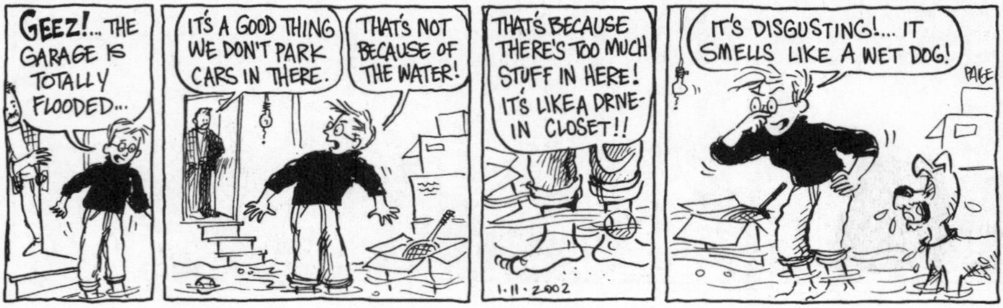
GEEZ!... THE GARAGE IS TOTALLY FLOODED...
IT'S A GOOD THING WE DON'T PARK CARS IN THERE.
THAT'S NOT BECAUSE OF THE WATER!
THAT'S BECAUSE THERE'S TOO MUCH STUFF IN HERE! IT'S LIKE A DRIVE-IN CLOSET!!
1·11·2002
IT'S DISGUSTING!... IT SMELLS LIKE A WET DOG!
PAIGE

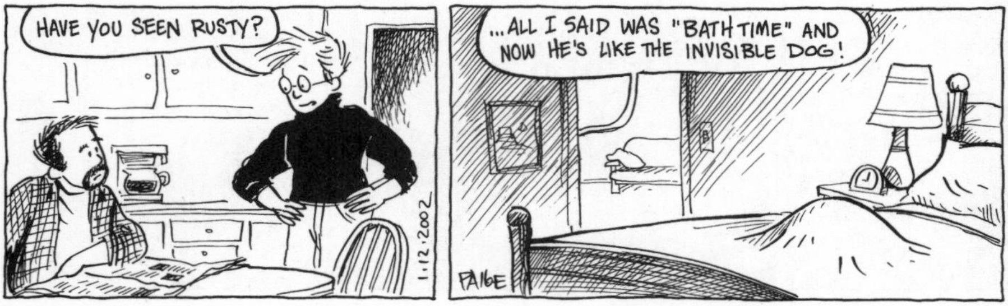
HAVE YOU SEEN RUSTY?
1·12·2002
...ALL I SAID WAS "BATH TIME" AND NOW HE'S LIKE THE INVISIBLE DOG!
PAIGE

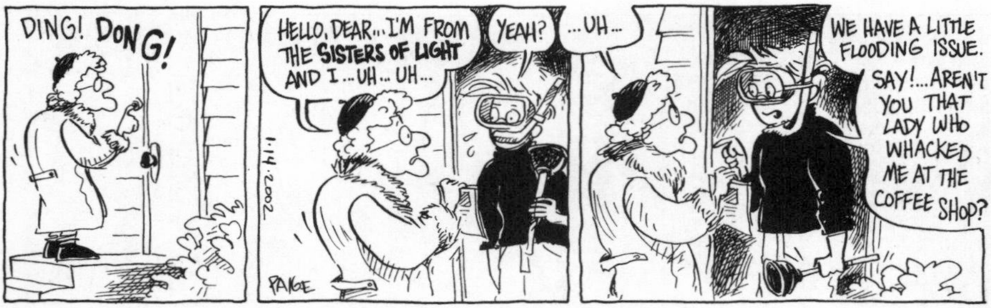
DING! DONG!
HELLO, DEAR... I'M FROM THE SISTERS OF LIGHT AND I... UH... UH...
YEAH?
1·14·2002
PAIGE
...UH...
WE HAVE A LITTLE FLOODING ISSUE.
SAY!... AREN'T YOU THAT LADY WHO WHACKED ME AT THE COFFEE SHOP?

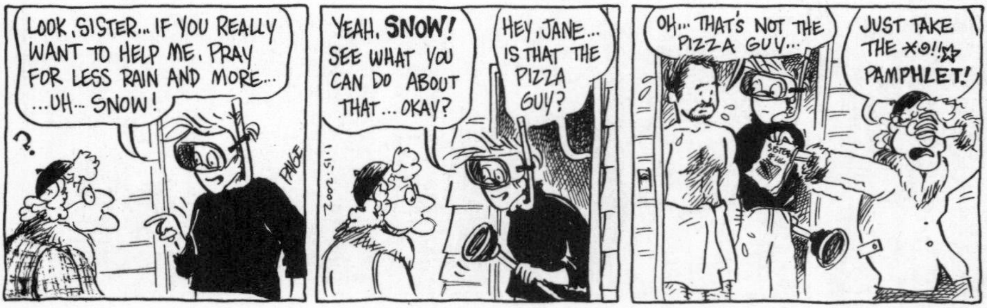
LOOK, SISTER... IF YOU REALLY WANT TO HELP ME, PRAY FOR LESS RAIN AND MORE... ...UH... SNOW!
PAIGE
YEAH, SNOW! SEE WHAT YOU CAN DO ABOUT THAT... OKAY?
HEY, JANE... IS THAT THE PIZZA GUY?
1·15·2002
OH... THAT'S NOT THE PIZZA GUY...
JUST TAKE THE *@!!☆ PAMPHLET!

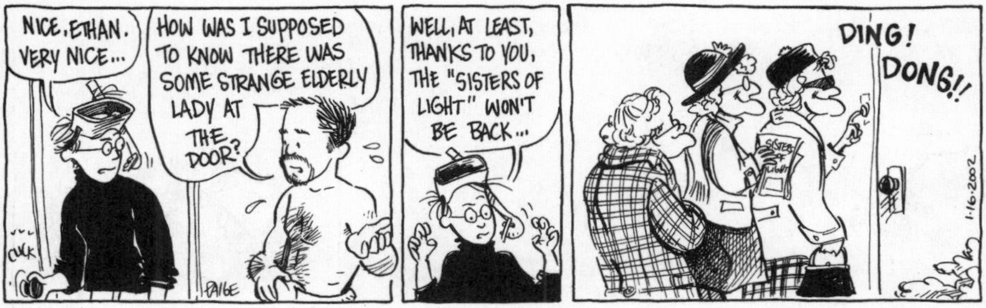
NICE, ETHAN. VERY NICE...
HOW WAS I SUPPOSED TO KNOW THERE WAS SOME STRANGE ELDERLY LADY AT THE DOOR?
CLICK
PAIGE
WELL, AT LEAST, THANKS TO YOU, THE "SISTERS OF LIGHT" WON'T BE BACK...
DING! DONG!!
1.16.2002

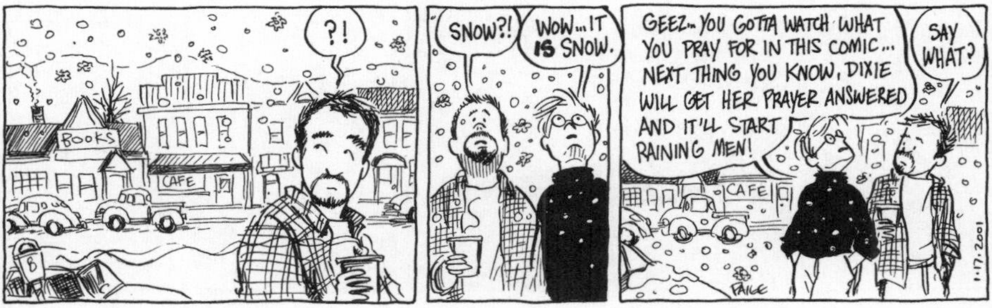
?!
BOOKS
CAFE
SNOW?!
WOW... IT IS SNOW.
GEEZ.. YOU GOTTA WATCH WHAT YOU PRAY FOR IN THIS COMIC... NEXT THING YOU KNOW, DIXIE WILL GET HER PRAYER ANSWERED AND IT'LL START RAINING MEN!
SAY WHAT?
CAFE
PAIGE
1.17.2001

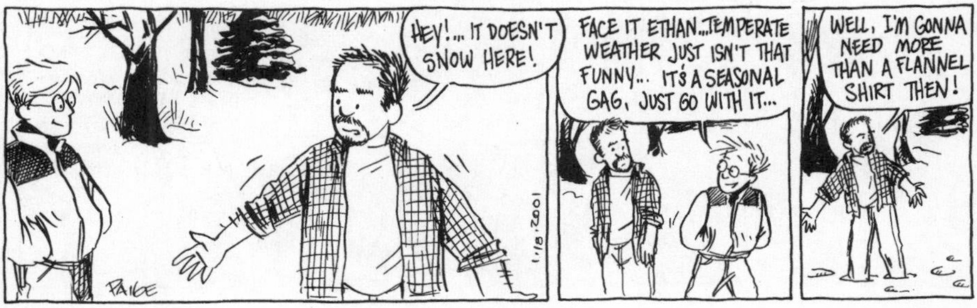
HEY!... IT DOESN'T SNOW HERE!
PAIGE
1.18.2001
FACE IT ETHAN... TEMPERATE WEATHER JUST ISN'T THAT FUNNY... IT'S A SEASONAL GAG, JUST GO WITH IT...
WELL, I'M GONNA NEED MORE THAN A FLANNEL SHIRT THEN!

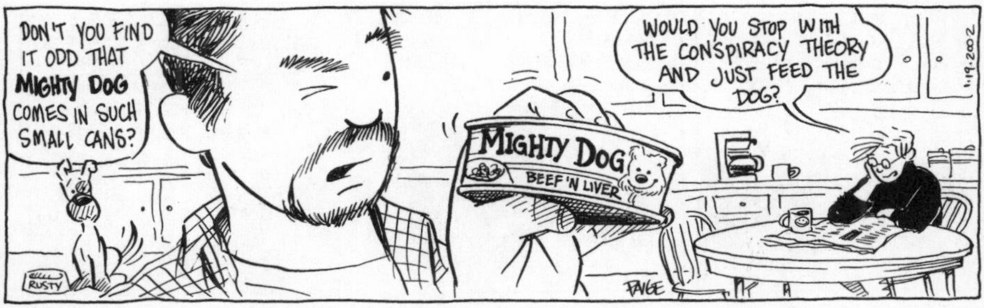
DON'T YOU FIND IT ODD THAT MIGHTY DOG COMES IN SUCH SMALL CANS?
WOULD YOU STOP WITH THE CONSPIRACY THEORY AND JUST FEED THE DOG?
MIGHTY DOG
BEEF 'N LIVER
RUSTY
PAIGE
1.19.2002

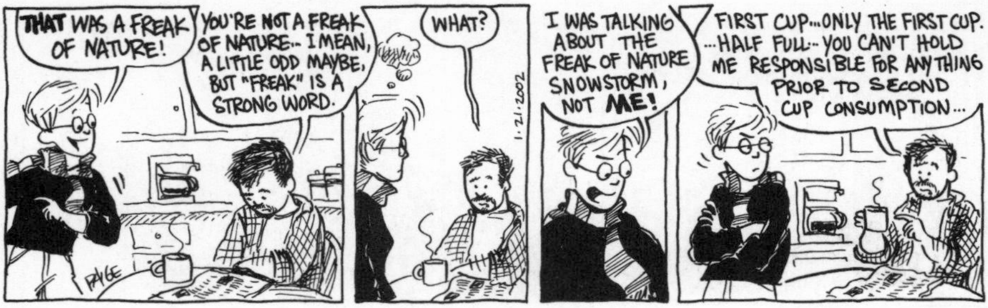
THAT WAS A FREAK OF NATURE!
YOU'RE NOT A FREAK OF NATURE... I MEAN, A LITTLE ODD MAYBE, BUT "FREAK" IS A STRONG WORD.
PAIGE
WHAT?
1·21·2002
I WAS TALKING ABOUT THE FREAK OF NATURE SNOWSTORM, NOT ME!
FIRST CUP...ONLY THE FIRST CUP. ...HALF FULL... YOU CAN'T HOLD ME RESPONSIBLE FOR ANYTHING PRIOR TO SECOND CUP CONSUMPTION...

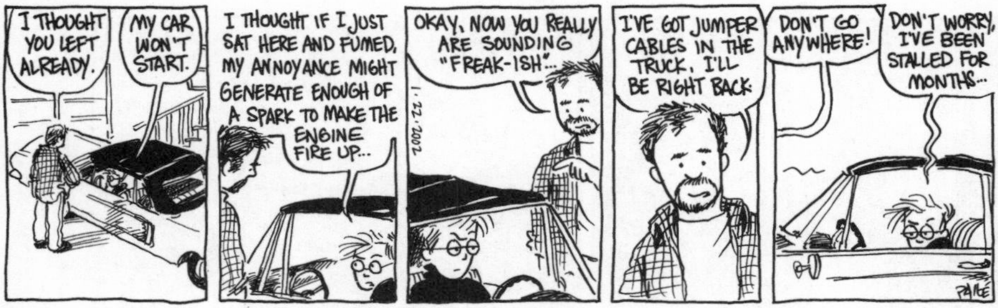
I THOUGHT YOU LEFT ALREADY.
MY CAR WON'T START.
I THOUGHT IF I JUST SAT HERE AND FUMED, MY ANNOYANCE MIGHT GENERATE ENOUGH OF A SPARK TO MAKE THE ENGINE FIRE UP...
1·22·2002
OKAY, NOW YOU REALLY ARE SOUNDING "FREAK-ISH"...
I'VE GOT JUMPER CABLES IN THE TRUCK. I'LL BE RIGHT BACK.
DON'T GO ANYWHERE!
DON'T WORRY, I'VE BEEN STALLED FOR MONTHS...
PAIGE

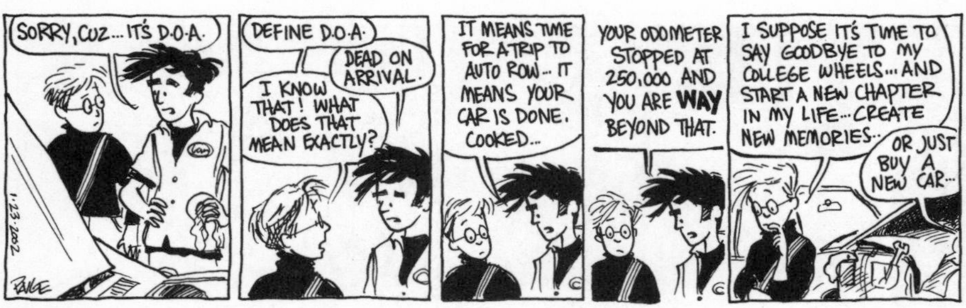
SORRY, CUZ... IT'S D.O.A.
1·23·2002
PAIGE
DEFINE D.O.A.
DEAD ON ARRIVAL.
I KNOW THAT! WHAT DOES THAT MEAN EXACTLY?
IT MEANS TIME FOR A TRIP TO AUTO ROW... IT MEANS YOUR CAR IS DONE. COOKED...
YOUR ODOMETER STOPPED AT 250,000 AND YOU ARE WAY BEYOND THAT.
I SUPPOSE IT'S TIME TO SAY GOODBYE TO MY COLLEGE WHEELS... AND START A NEW CHAPTER IN MY LIFE... CREATE NEW MEMORIES...
OR JUST BUY A NEW CAR...

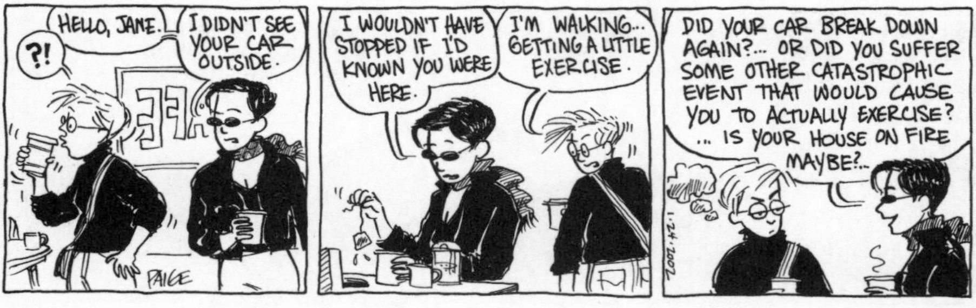
HELLO, JANE.
?!
I DIDN'T SEE YOUR CAR OUTSIDE.
PAIGE
I WOULDN'T HAVE STOPPED IF I'D KNOWN YOU WERE HERE.
I'M WALKING... GETTING A LITTLE EXERCISE.
1·24·2002
DID YOUR CAR BREAK DOWN AGAIN?... OR DID YOU SUFFER SOME OTHER CATASTROPHIC EVENT THAT WOULD CAUSE YOU TO ACTUALLY EXERCISE? ... IS YOUR HOUSE ON FIRE MAYBE?...

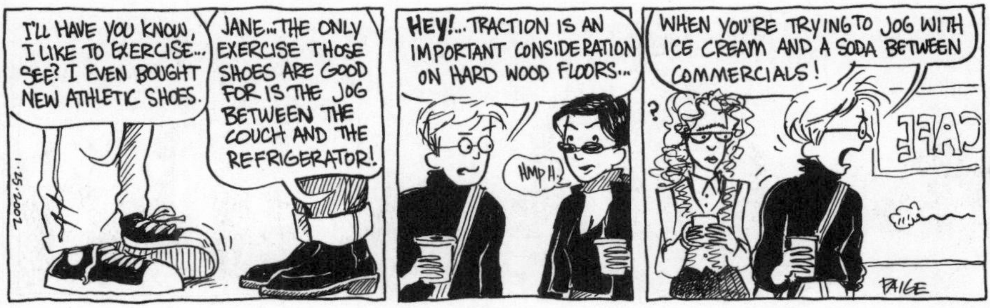
I'LL HAVE YOU KNOW, I LIKE TO EXERCISE... SEE? I EVEN BOUGHT NEW ATHLETIC SHOES.
1.25.2002
JANE...THE ONLY EXERCISE THOSE SHOES ARE GOOD FOR IS THE JOG BETWEEN THE COUCH AND THE REFRIGERATOR!
HEY!... TRACTION IS AN IMPORTANT CONSIDERATION ON HARD WOOD FLOORS...
HMPH.
WHEN YOU'RE TRYING TO JOG WITH ICE CREAM AND A SODA BETWEEN COMMERCIALS!
?
CAFE
PAIGE

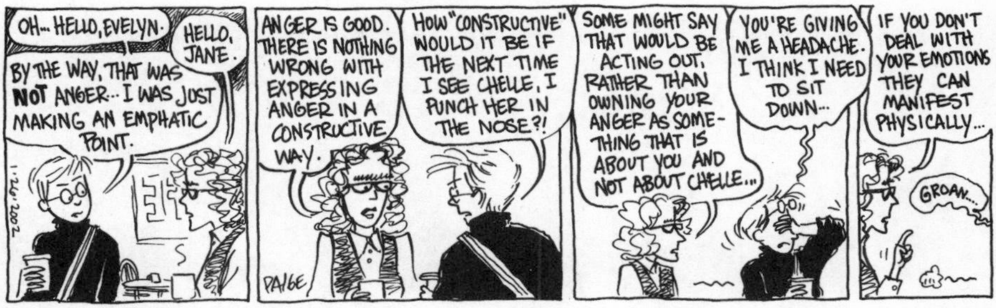
OH... HELLO, EVELYN.
HELLO, JANE.
BY THE WAY, THAT WAS NOT ANGER... I WAS JUST MAKING AN EMPHATIC POINT.
1.26.2002
ANGER IS GOOD. THERE IS NOTHING WRONG WITH EXPRESSING ANGER IN A CONSTRUCTIVE WAY.
HOW "CONSTRUCTIVE" WOULD IT BE IF THE NEXT TIME I SEE CHELLE, I PUNCH HER IN THE NOSE?!
PAIGE
SOME MIGHT SAY THAT WOULD BE ACTING OUT, RATHER THAN OWNING YOUR ANGER AS SOMETHING THAT IS ABOUT YOU AND NOT ABOUT CHELLE...
YOU'RE GIVING ME A HEADACHE. I THINK I NEED TO SIT DOWN...
IF YOU DON'T DEAL WITH YOUR EMOTIONS THEY CAN MANIFEST PHYSICALLY...
GROAN...

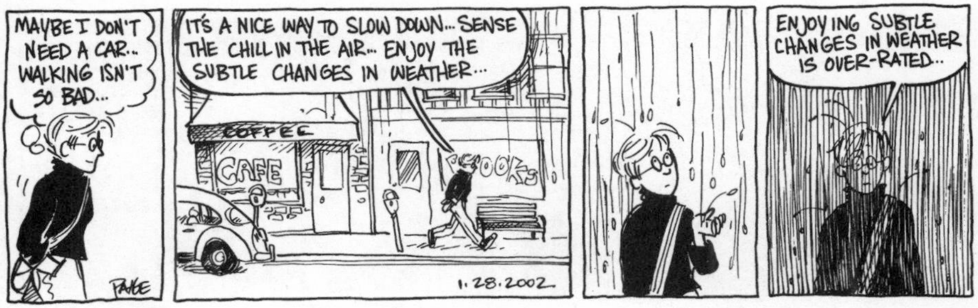
MAYBE I DON'T NEED A CAR.. WALKING ISN'T SO BAD...
PAIGE
IT'S A NICE WAY TO SLOW DOWN... SENSE THE CHILL IN THE AIR... ENJOY THE SUBTLE CHANGES IN WEATHER...
COFFEE
CAFE
BOOKS
1.28.2002
ENJOYING SUBTLE CHANGES IN WEATHER IS OVER-RATED...

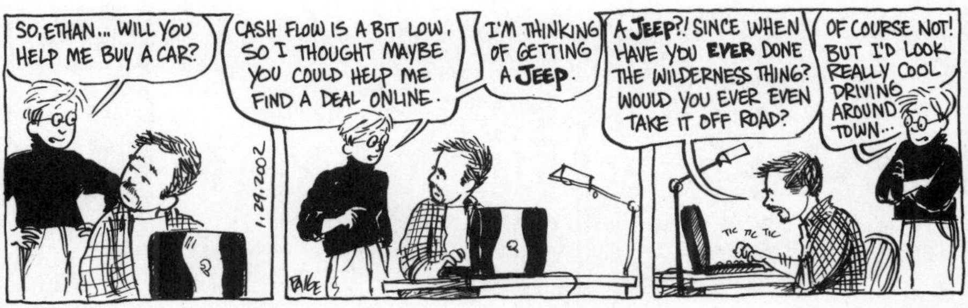
SO, ETHAN... WILL YOU HELP ME BUY A CAR?
1.29.2002
CASH FLOW IS A BIT LOW, SO I THOUGHT MAYBE YOU COULD HELP ME FIND A DEAL ONLINE.
I'M THINKING OF GETTING A JEEP.
PAIGE
A JEEP?! SINCE WHEN HAVE YOU EVER DONE THE WILDERNESS THING? WOULD YOU EVER EVEN TAKE IT OFF ROAD?
TIC TIC TIC
OF COURSE NOT! BUT I'D LOOK REALLY COOL DRIVING AROUND TOWN...

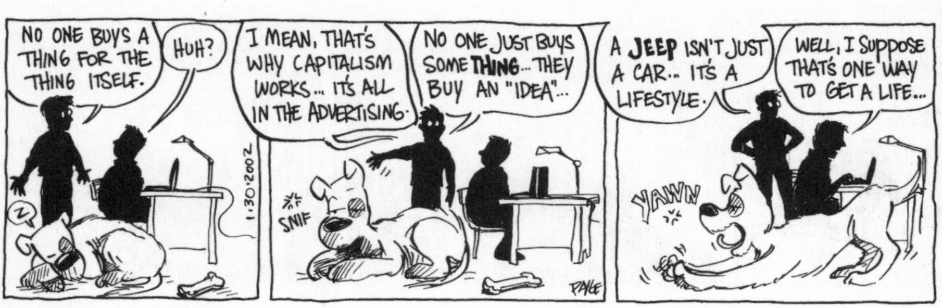
NO ONE BUYS A THING FOR THE THING ITSELF.
HUH?
1·30·2002
I MEAN, THAT'S WHY CAPITALISM WORKS... IT'S ALL IN THE ADVERTISING.
NO ONE JUST BUYS SOME**THING**... THEY BUY AN "IDEA"...
SNIF
PAIGE
A **JEEP** ISN'T JUST A CAR.. IT'S A LIFESTYLE.
WELL, I SUPPOSE THAT'S ONE WAY TO GET A LIFE...
YAWN

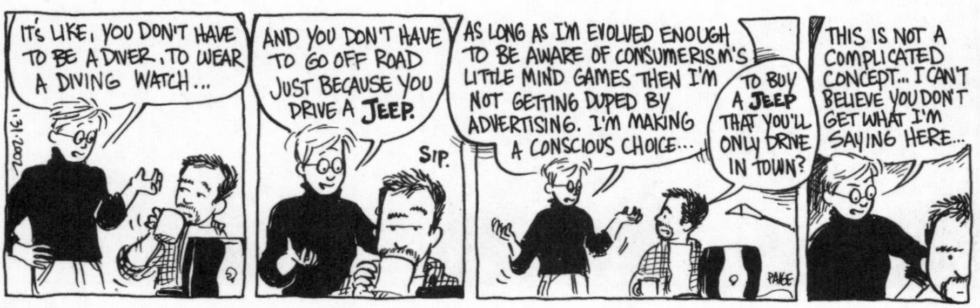
IT'S LIKE, YOU DON'T HAVE TO BE A DIVER, TO WEAR A DIVING WATCH...
1·31·2002
AND YOU DON'T HAVE TO GO OFF ROAD JUST BECAUSE YOU DRIVE A **JEEP**.
SIP.
AS LONG AS I'M EVOLVED ENOUGH TO BE AWARE OF CONSUMERISM'S LITTLE MIND GAMES THEN I'M NOT GETTING DUPED BY ADVERTISING. I'M MAKING A CONSCIOUS CHOICE...
TO BUY A **JEEP** THAT YOU'LL ONLY DRIVE IN TOWN?
PAIGE
THIS IS NOT A COMPLICATED CONCEPT... I CAN'T BELIEVE YOU DON'T GET WHAT I'M SAYING HERE...

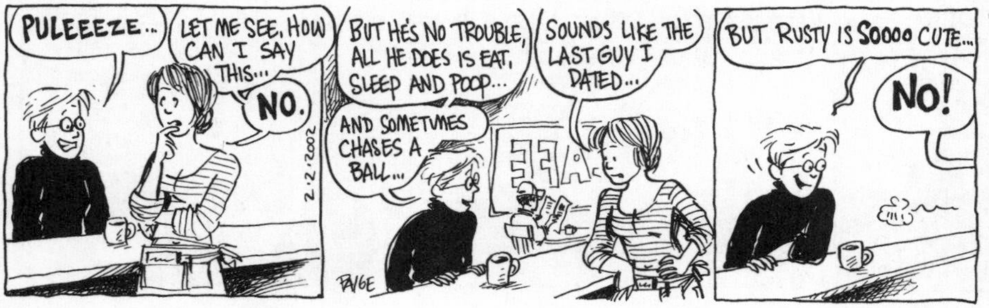
PULEEEZE...
LET ME SEE, HOW CAN I SAY THIS...
NO.
2·2·2002
BUT HE'S NO TROUBLE, ALL HE DOES IS EAT, SLEEP AND POOP...
AND SOMETIMES CHASES A BALL...
SOUNDS LIKE THE LAST GUY I DATED...
PAIGE
BUT RUSTY IS **SOOOO** CUTE...
NO!

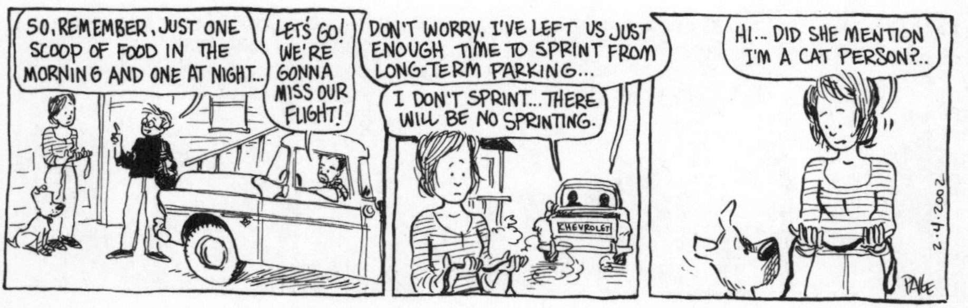
SO, REMEMBER, JUST ONE SCOOP OF FOOD IN THE MORNING AND ONE AT NIGHT...
LET'S GO! WE'RE GONNA MISS OUR FLIGHT!
DON'T WORRY. I'VE LEFT US JUST ENOUGH TIME TO SPRINT FROM LONG-TERM PARKING...
I DON'T SPRINT... THERE WILL BE NO SPRINTING.
CHEVROLET
HI... DID SHE MENTION I'M A CAT PERSON?..
2·4·2002
PAIGE

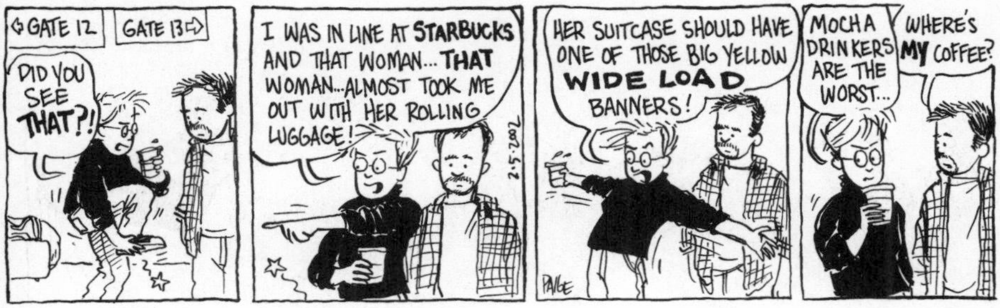

⇦ GATE 12
GATE 13 ⇨
DID YOU SEE THAT?!
I WAS IN LINE AT STARBUCKS AND THAT WOMAN... THAT WOMAN... ALMOST TOOK ME OUT WITH HER ROLLING LUGGAGE!
2-5-2002
HER SUITCASE SHOULD HAVE ONE OF THOSE BIG YELLOW WIDE LOAD BANNERS!
PAIGE
MOCHA DRINKERS ARE THE WORST...
WHERE'S MY COFFEE?

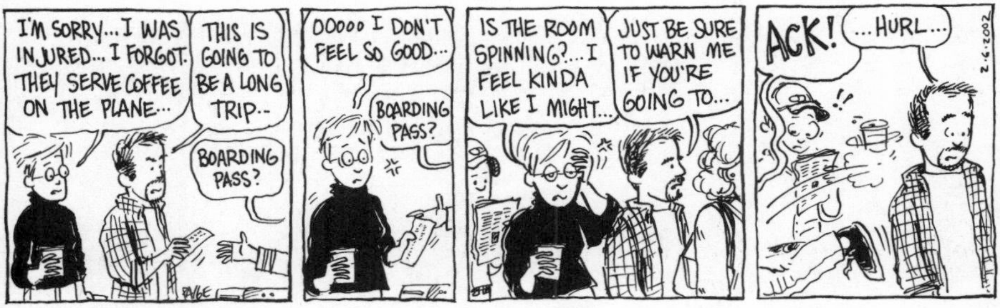

I'M SORRY... I WAS INJURED... I FORGOT. THEY SERVE COFFEE ON THE PLANE...
THIS IS GOING TO BE A LONG TRIP..
BOARDING PASS?
PAIGE
OOOOO I DON'T FEEL SO GOOD...
BOARDING PASS?
IS THE ROOM SPINNING?... I FEEL KINDA LIKE I MIGHT...
JUST BE SURE TO WARN ME IF YOU'RE GOING TO...
ACK!
...HURL...
2-6-2002

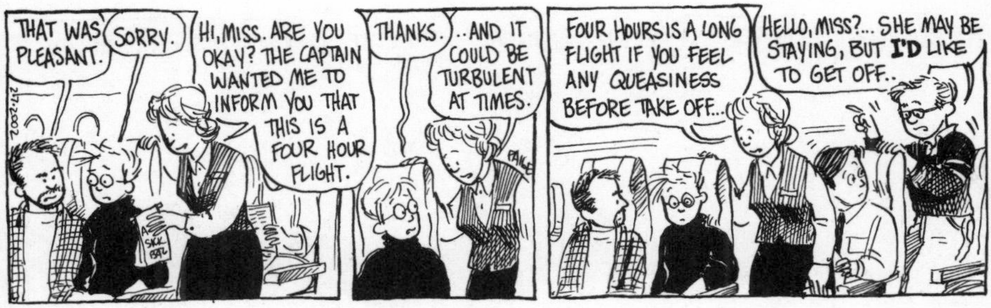

THAT WAS PLEASANT.
SORRY.
2-7-2002
HI, MISS. ARE YOU OKAY? THE CAPTAIN WANTED ME TO INFORM YOU THAT THIS IS A FOUR HOUR FLIGHT.
THANKS.
..AND IT COULD BE TURBULENT AT TIMES.
PAIGE
FOUR HOURS IS A LONG FLIGHT IF YOU FEEL ANY QUEASINESS BEFORE TAKE OFF...
HELLO, MISS?... SHE MAY BE STAYING, BUT I'D LIKE TO GET OFF..

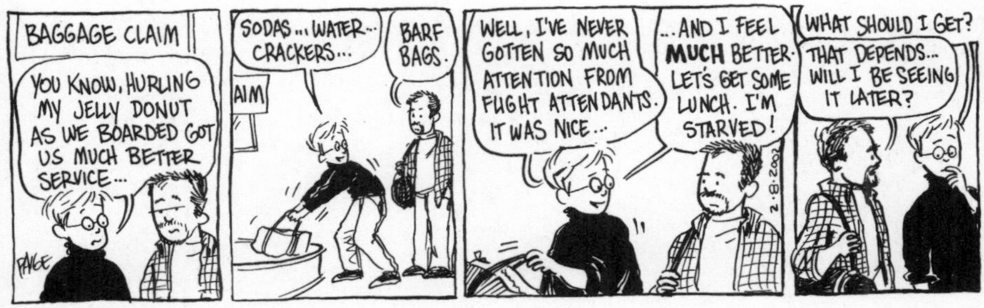

BAGGAGE CLAIM
YOU KNOW, HURLING MY JELLY DONUT AS WE BOARDED GOT US MUCH BETTER SERVICE...
PAIGE
SODAS... WATER... CRACKERS...
BARF BAGS.
WELL, I'VE NEVER GOTTEN SO MUCH ATTENTION FROM FLIGHT ATTENDANTS. IT WAS NICE...
...AND I FEEL MUCH BETTER. LET'S GET SOME LUNCH. I'M STARVED!
2-8-2002
WHAT SHOULD I GET?
THAT DEPENDS... WILL I BE SEEING IT LATER?

Chapter 10

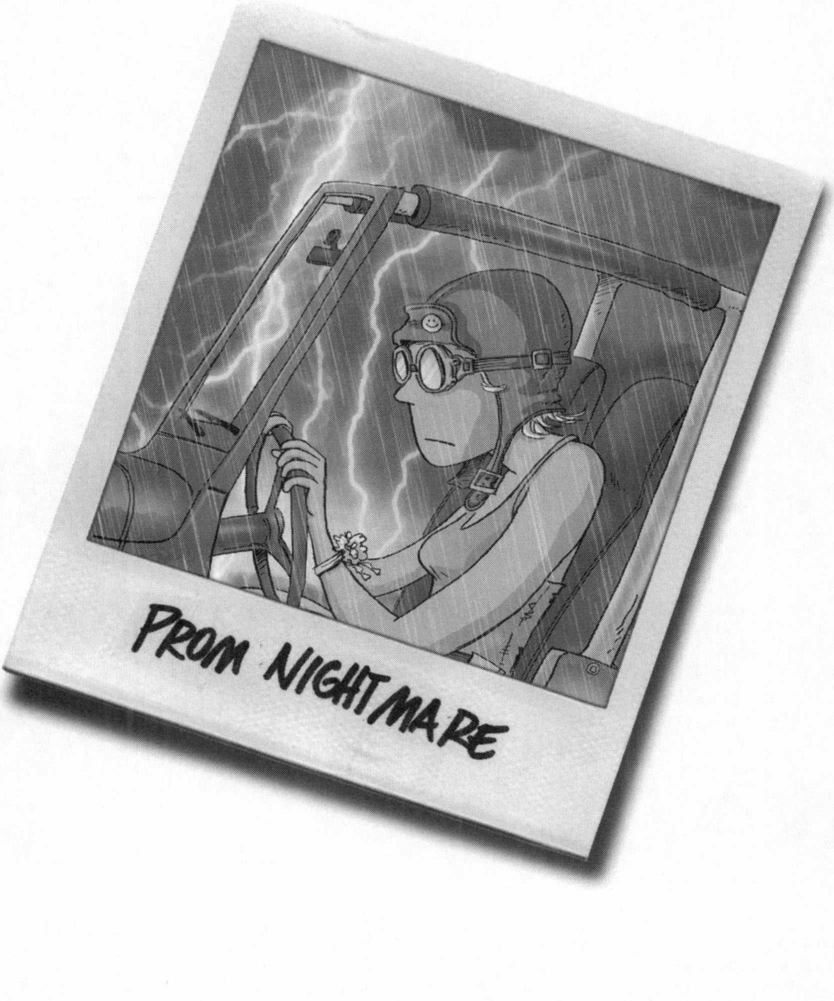
PROM NIGHTMARE

IT DOESN'T TAKE LONG FOR A CAT LOVER TO BE THROWN OFF BALANCE BY A DOG...

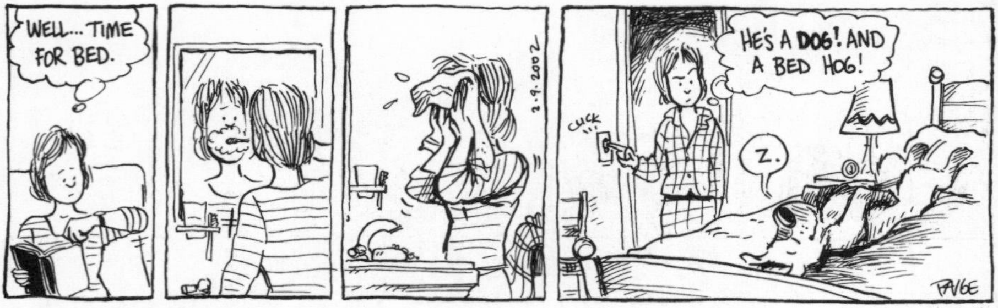
WELL... TIME FOR BED.
2.9.2002
CLICK
HE'S A DOG! AND A BED HOG!
Z.
PAIGE

A DAY LATER...

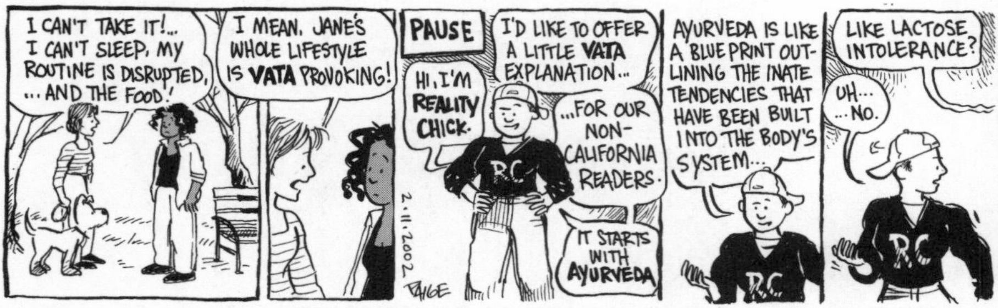
I CAN'T TAKE IT!... I CAN'T SLEEP, MY ROUTINE IS DISRUPTED, ... AND THE FOOD!
I MEAN, JANE'S WHOLE LIFESTYLE IS VATA PROVOKING!
2.11.2002
PAIGE
PAUSE
HI, I'M REALITY CHICK.
I'D LIKE TO OFFER A LITTLE VATA EXPLANATION...
...FOR OUR NON-CALIFORNIA READERS.
IT STARTS WITH AYURVEDA
AYURVEDA IS LIKE A BLUE PRINT OUT-LINING THE INATE TENDENCIES THAT HAVE BEEN BUILT INTO THE BODY'S SYSTEM...
LIKE LACTOSE INTOLERANCE?
UH... ...NO.

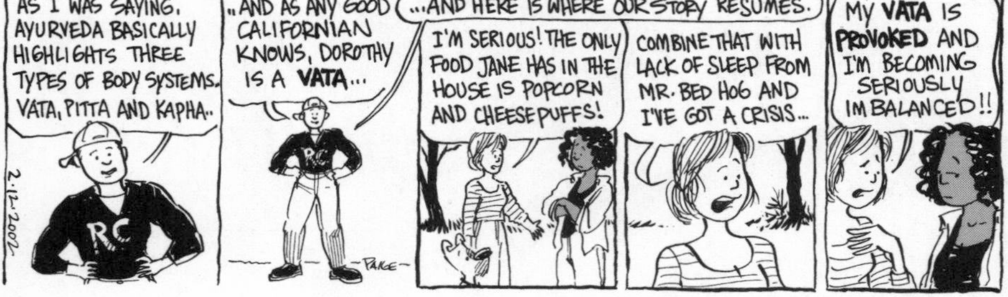
AS I WAS SAYING, AYURVEDA BASICALLY HIGHLIGHTS THREE TYPES OF BODY SYSTEMS. VATA, PITTA AND KAPHA..
2.12.2002
...AND AS ANY GOOD CALIFORNIAN KNOWS, DOROTHY IS A VATA...
PAIGE
...AND HERE IS WHERE OUR STORY RESUMES.
I'M SERIOUS! THE ONLY FOOD JANE HAS IN THE HOUSE IS POPCORN AND CHEESE PUFFS!
COMBINE THAT WITH LACK OF SLEEP FROM MR. BED HOG AND I'VE GOT A CRISIS...
MY VATA IS PROVOKED AND I'M BECOMING SERIOUSLY IMBALANCED!!

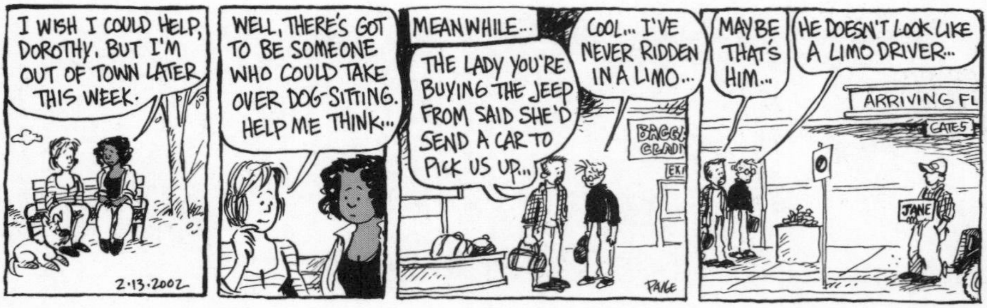
I WISH I COULD HELP, DOROTHY, BUT I'M OUT OF TOWN LATER THIS WEEK.
2.13.2002
WELL, THERE'S GOT TO BE SOMEONE WHO COULD TAKE OVER DOG-SITTING. HELP ME THINK...
MEANWHILE...
THE LADY YOU'RE BUYING THE JEEP FROM SAID SHE'D SEND A CAR TO PICK US UP...
COOL... I'VE NEVER RIDDEN IN A LIMO...
PAIGE
MAYBE THAT'S HIM...
HE DOESN'T LOOK LIKE A LIMO DRIVER...
ARRIVING FL
GATES
JANE

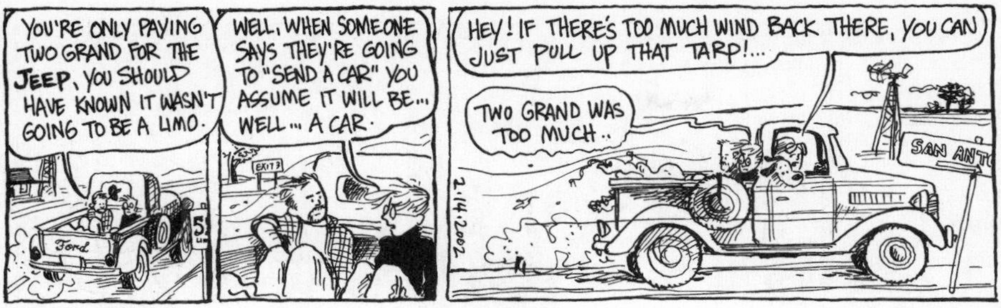
YOU'RE ONLY PAYING TWO GRAND FOR THE **JEEP**, YOU SHOULD HAVE KNOWN IT WASN'T GOING TO BE A LIMO.
Ford
WELL, WHEN SOMEONE SAYS THEY'RE GOING TO "SEND A CAR" YOU ASSUME IT WILL BE... WELL... A CAR.
HEY! IF THERE'S TOO MUCH WIND BACK THERE, YOU CAN JUST PULL UP THAT TARP!...
TWO GRAND WAS TOO MUCH..
SAN ANT
2.14.2002

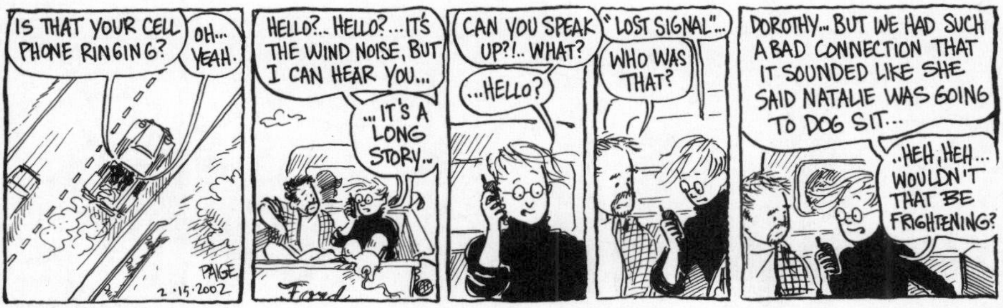
IS THAT YOUR CELL PHONE RINGING?
OH... YEAH.
PAIGE
2.15.2002
HELLO?.. HELLO?... IT'S THE WIND NOISE, BUT I CAN HEAR YOU...
... IT'S A LONG STORY..
Ford
CAN YOU SPEAK UP?!.. WHAT?
...HELLO?
"LOST SIGNAL"...
WHO WAS THAT?
DOROTHY... BUT WE HAD SUCH A BAD CONNECTION THAT IT SOUNDED LIKE SHE SAID NATALIE WAS GOING TO DOG SIT...
..HEH, HEH... WOULDN'T THAT BE FRIGHTENING?

MEANWHILE, BACK AT JANE'S...

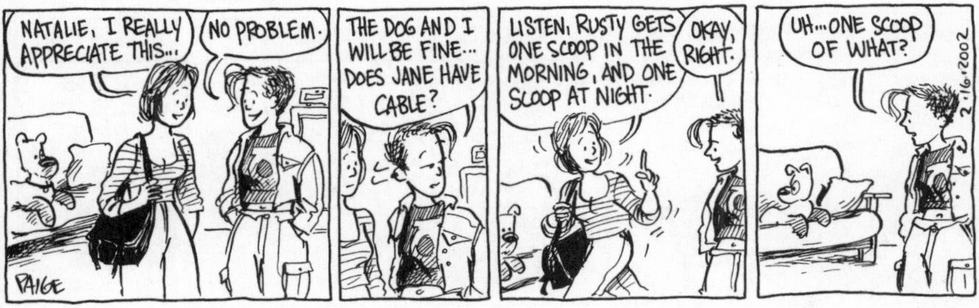
NATALIE, I REALLY APPRECIATE THIS...
NO PROBLEM.
PAIGE
THE DOG AND I WILL BE FINE... DOES JANE HAVE CABLE?
LISTEN, RUSTY GETS ONE SCOOP IN THE MORNING, AND ONE SCOOP AT NIGHT.
OKAY, RIGHT.
UH... ONE SCOOP OF WHAT?
2.16.2002

... WHILE IN TEXAS....

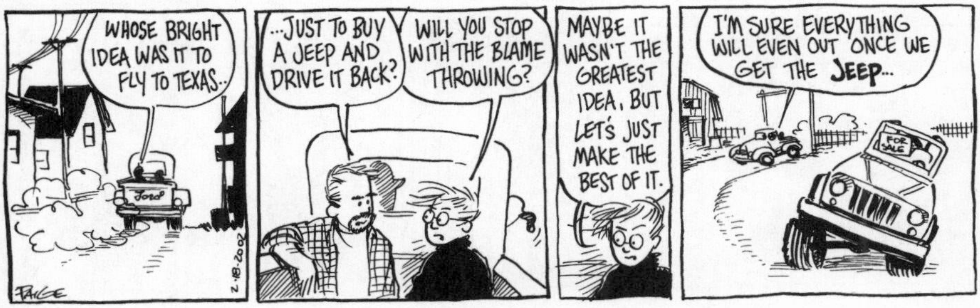
WHOSE BRIGHT IDEA WAS IT TO FLY TO TEXAS..
Ford
PAIGE
2.18.2002
...JUST TO BUY A JEEP AND DRIVE IT BACK?
WILL YOU STOP WITH THE BLAME THROWING?
MAYBE IT WASN'T THE GREATEST IDEA, BUT LET'S JUST MAKE THE BEST OF IT.
I'M SURE EVERYTHING WILL EVEN OUT ONCE WE GET THE **JEEP**...
FOR SALE

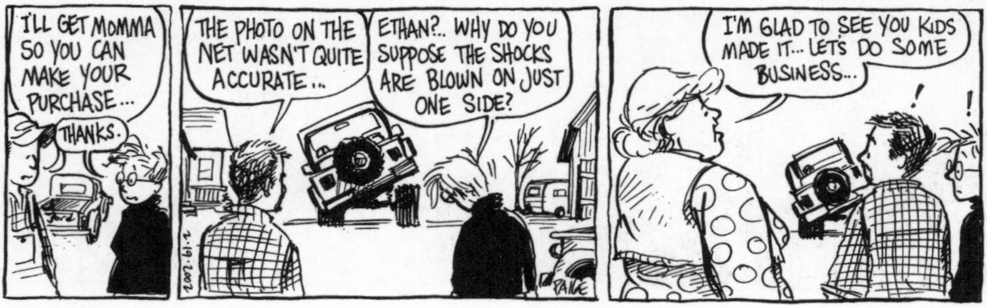
I'LL GET MOMMA SO YOU CAN MAKE YOUR PURCHASE...
THANKS.
2·19·2002
THE PHOTO ON THE NET WASN'T QUITE ACCURATE...
ETHAN?.. WHY DO YOU SUPPOSE THE SHOCKS ARE BLOWN ON JUST ONE SIDE?
PAIGE
I'M GLAD TO SEE YOU KIDS MADE IT... LET'S DO SOME BUSINESS...
!
!

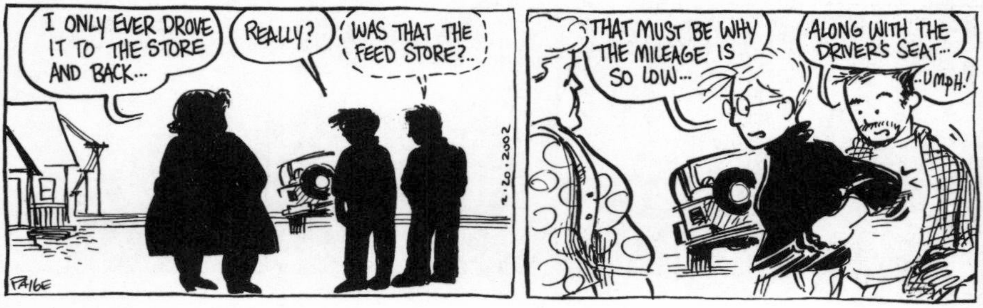
I ONLY EVER DROVE IT TO THE STORE AND BACK...
REALLY?
WAS THAT THE FEED STORE?..
PAIGE
2·20·2002
THAT MUST BE WHY THE MILEAGE IS SO LOW...
ALONG WITH THE DRIVER'S SEAT...
..UMPH!

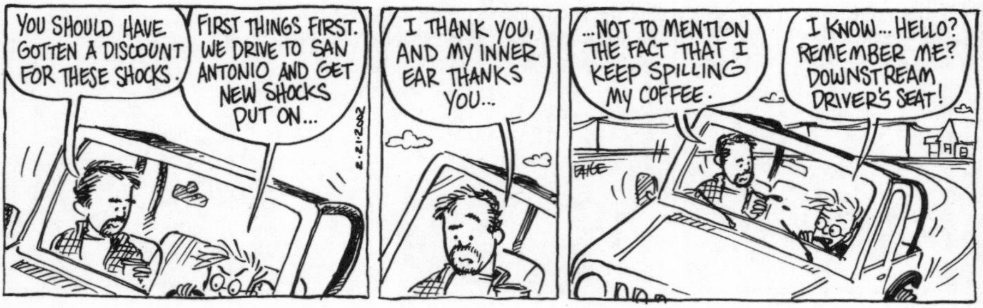
YOU SHOULD HAVE GOTTEN A DISCOUNT FOR THESE SHOCKS.
FIRST THINGS FIRST. WE DRIVE TO SAN ANTONIO AND GET NEW SHOCKS PUT ON...
2·21·2002
I THANK YOU, AND MY INNER EAR THANKS YOU...
...NOT TO MENTION THE FACT THAT I KEEP SPILLING MY COFFEE.
I KNOW... HELLO? REMEMBER ME? DOWNSTREAM DRIVER'S SEAT!
PAIGE

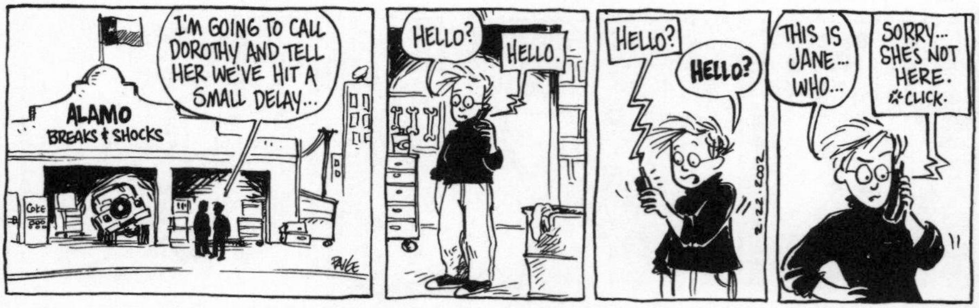
ALAMO
BREAKS & SHOCKS
I'M GOING TO CALL DOROTHY AND TELL HER WE'VE HIT A SMALL DELAY...
PAIGE
HELLO?
HELLO.
HELLO?
HELLO?
2·22·2002
THIS IS JANE... WHO...
SORRY... SHE'S NOT HERE.
CLICK.

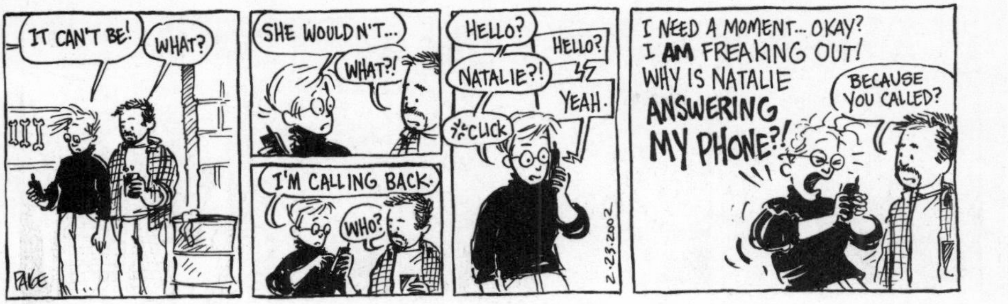
IT CAN'T BE!
WHAT?
PAIGE
SHE WOULDN'T...
WHAT?!
I'M CALLING BACK.
WHO?
HELLO?
HELLO?
NATALIE?!
YEAH.
CLICK
2.23.2002
I NEED A MOMENT... OKAY? I **AM** FREAKING OUT! WHY IS NATALIE **ANSWERING MY PHONE?!**
BECAUSE YOU CALLED?

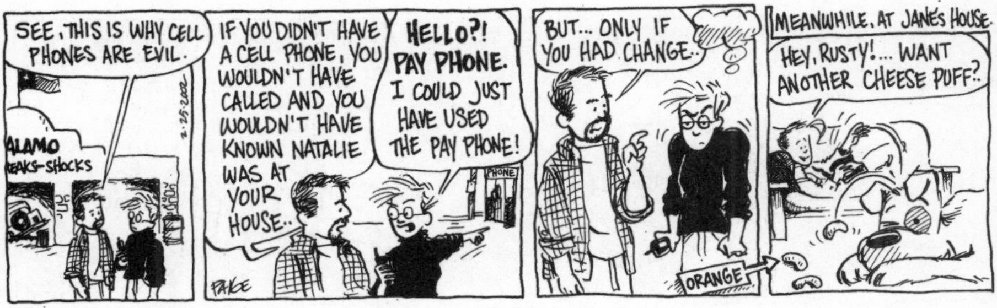
SEE, THIS IS WHY CELL PHONES ARE EVIL.
ALAMO
2.25.2002
PAIGE
IF YOU DIDN'T HAVE A CELL PHONE, YOU WOULDN'T HAVE CALLED AND YOU WOULDN'T HAVE KNOWN NATALIE WAS AT YOUR HOUSE...
HELLO?! PAY PHONE. I COULD JUST HAVE USED THE PAY PHONE!
PHONE
BUT... ONLY IF YOU HAD CHANGE...
ORANGE
MEANWHILE, AT JANE'S HOUSE.
HEY, RUSTY!... WANT ANOTHER CHEESE PUFF?

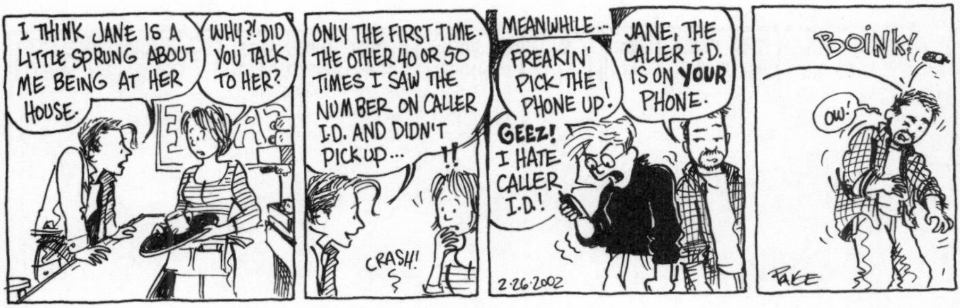
I THINK JANE IS A LITTLE SPRUNG ABOUT ME BEING AT HER HOUSE.
WHY?! DID YOU TALK TO HER?
ONLY THE FIRST TIME. THE OTHER 40 OR 50 TIMES I SAW THE NUMBER ON CALLER I.D. AND DIDN'T PICK UP...
!!
CRASH!
MEANWHILE...
FREAKIN' PICK THE PHONE UP!
JANE, THE CALLER I.D. IS ON **YOUR** PHONE.
GEEZ! I HATE CALLER I.D.!
2.26.2002
BOINK!
OW!
PAIGE

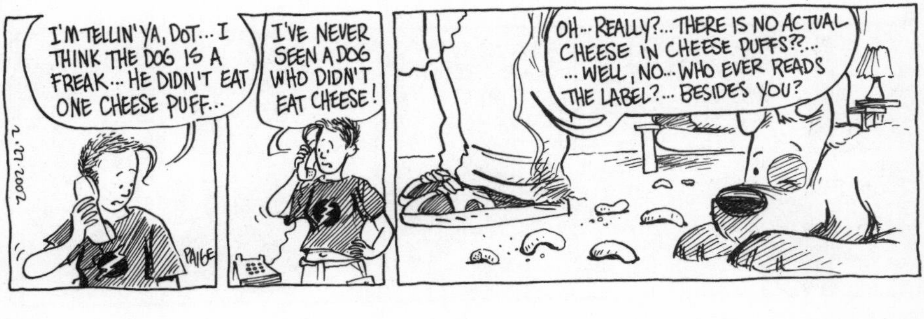
2.27.2002
I'M TELLIN' YA, DOT... I THINK THE DOG IS A FREAK... HE DIDN'T EAT ONE CHEESE PUFF...
PAIGE
I'VE NEVER SEEN A DOG WHO DIDN'T EAT CHEESE!
OH... REALLY?... THERE IS NO ACTUAL CHEESE IN CHEESE PUFFS??... ... WELL, NO... WHO EVER READS THE LABEL?... BESIDES YOU?

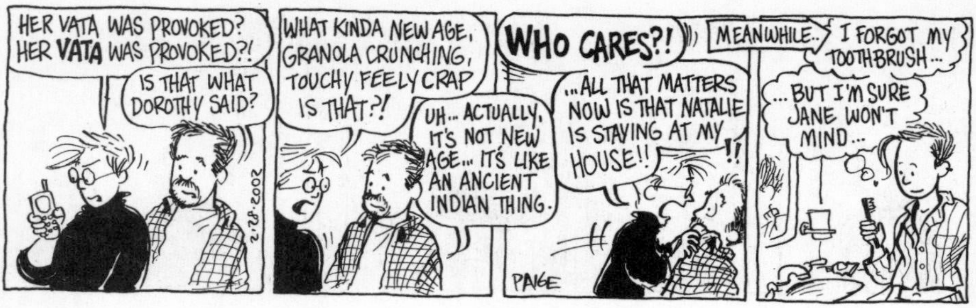
HER VATA WAS PROVOKED? HER **VATA** WAS PROVOKED?!
IS THAT WHAT DOROTHY SAID?
2·28·2002
WHAT KINDA NEW AGE, GRANOLA CRUNCHING, TOUCHY FEELY CRAP IS THAT?!
UH... ACTUALLY, IT'S NOT NEW AGE... IT'S LIKE AN ANCIENT INDIAN THING.
WHO CARES?!
...ALL THAT MATTERS NOW IS THAT NATALIE IS STAYING AT MY HOUSE!!
PAIGE
MEANWHILE..
I FORGOT MY TOOTHBRUSH...
...BUT I'M SURE JANE WON'T MIND...

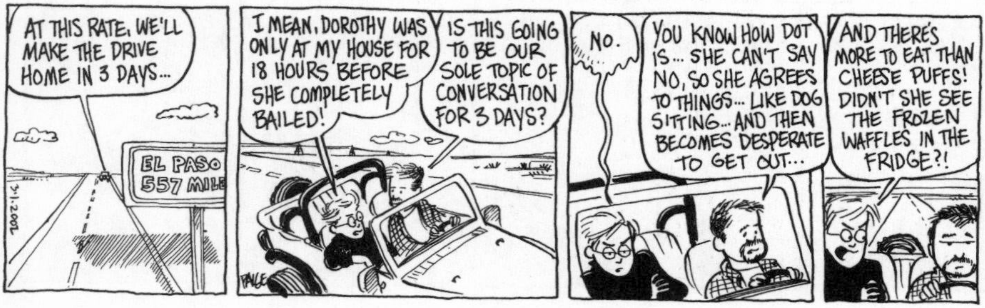
AT THIS RATE, WE'LL MAKE THE DRIVE HOME IN 3 DAYS...
EL PASO 557 MILE
3·1·2002
I MEAN, DOROTHY WAS ONLY AT MY HOUSE FOR 18 HOURS BEFORE SHE COMPLETELY BAILED!
IS THIS GOING TO BE OUR SOLE TOPIC OF CONVERSATION FOR 3 DAYS?
PAIGE
NO.
YOU KNOW HOW DOT IS... SHE CAN'T SAY NO, SO SHE AGREES TO THINGS... LIKE DOG SITTING... AND THEN BECOMES DESPERATE TO GET OUT...
AND THERE'S MORE TO EAT THAN CHEESE PUFFS! DIDN'T SHE SEE THE FROZEN WAFFLES IN THE FRIDGE?!

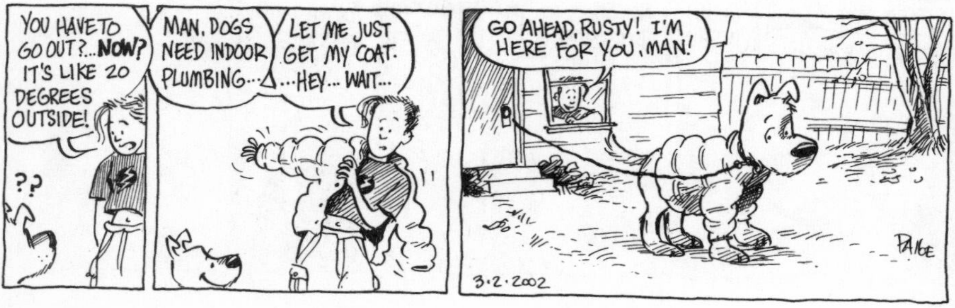
YOU HAVE TO GO OUT?...**NOW?** IT'S LIKE 20 DEGREES OUTSIDE!
??
MAN, DOGS NEED INDOOR PLUMBING...
LET ME JUST GET MY COAT.
...HEY... WAIT...
GO AHEAD, RUSTY! I'M HERE FOR YOU, MAN!
PAIGE
3·2·2002

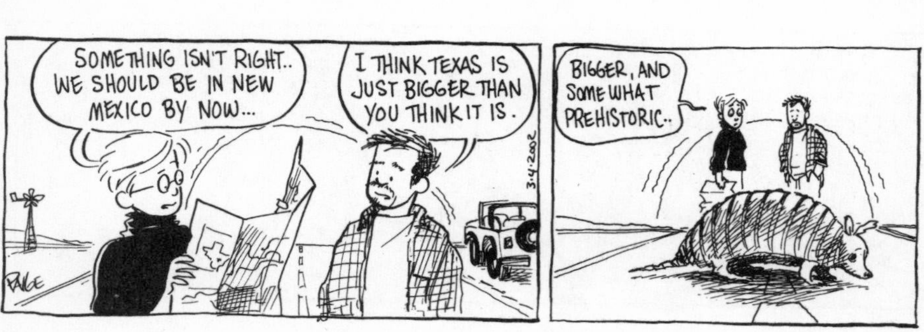
SOMETHING ISN'T RIGHT.. WE SHOULD BE IN NEW MEXICO BY NOW...
I THINK TEXAS IS JUST BIGGER THAN YOU THINK IT IS.
3·4·2002
PAIGE
BIGGER, AND SOME WHAT PREHISTORIC..

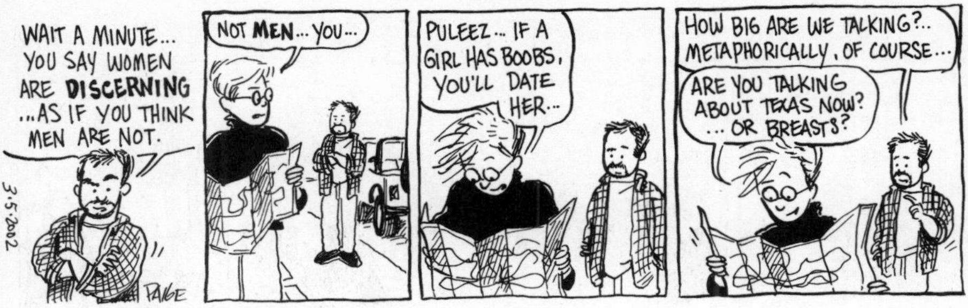
WAIT A MINUTE... YOU SAY WOMEN ARE DISCERNING ...AS IF YOU THINK MEN ARE NOT.
3.5.2002
PAIGE
NOT MEN... YOU...
PULEEZ... IF A GIRL HAS BOOBS, YOU'LL DATE HER...
HOW BIG ARE WE TALKING?.. METAPHORICALLY, OF COURSE...
ARE YOU TALKING ABOUT TEXAS NOW? ... OR BREASTS?

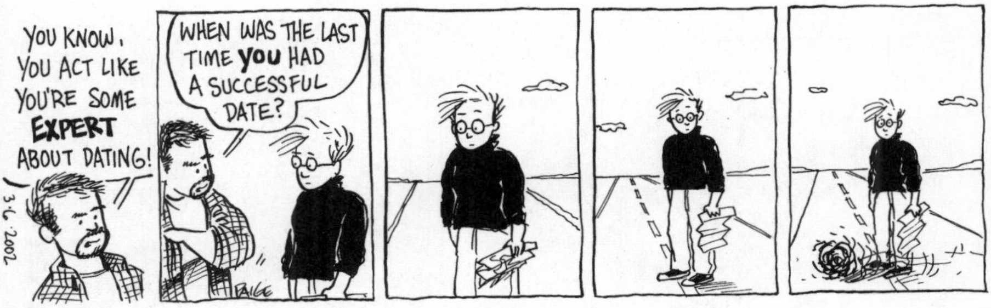
YOU KNOW, YOU ACT LIKE YOU'RE SOME EXPERT ABOUT DATING!
3.6.2002
WHEN WAS THE LAST TIME YOU HAD A SUCCESSFUL DATE?
PAIGE

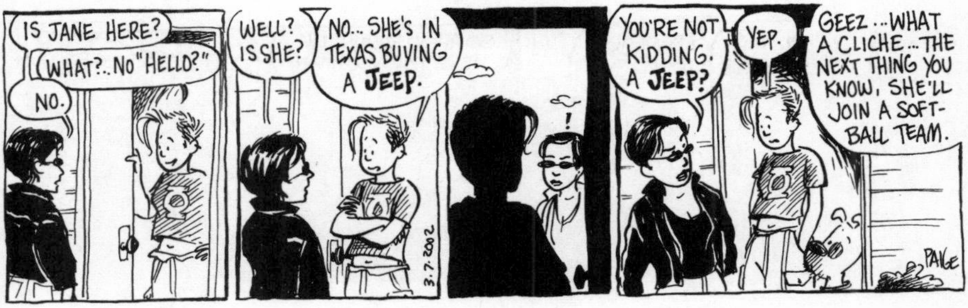
IS JANE HERE?
WHAT?.. NO "HELLO?"
NO.
WELL? IS SHE?
NO... SHE'S IN TEXAS BUYING A JEEP.
3.7.2002
!
YOU'RE NOT KIDDING. A JEEP?
YEP.
GEEZ... WHAT A CLICHE... THE NEXT THING YOU KNOW, SHE'LL JOIN A SOFT-BALL TEAM.
PAIGE

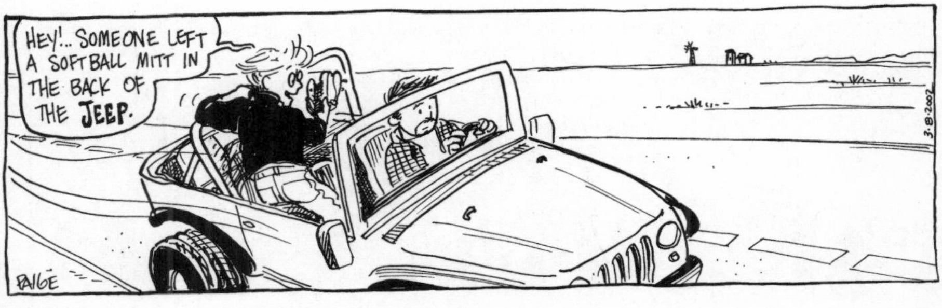
HEY!.. SOMEONE LEFT A SOFTBALL MITT IN THE BACK OF THE JEEP.
3.8.2002
PAIGE

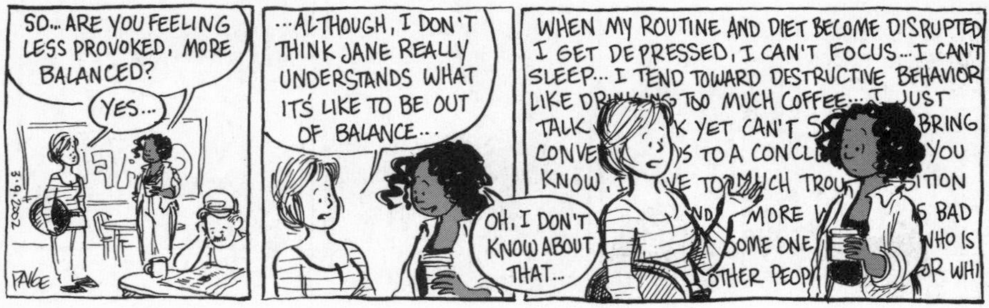
SO... ARE YOU FEELING LESS PROVOKED, MORE BALANCED?
YES...
3.9.2002
PAIGE
...ALTHOUGH, I DON'T THINK JANE REALLY UNDERSTANDS WHAT IT'S LIKE TO BE OUT OF BALANCE...
WHEN MY ROUTINE AND DIET BECOME DISRUPTED I GET DEPRESSED, I CAN'T FOCUS... I CAN'T SLEEP... I TEND TOWARD DESTRUCTIVE BEHAVIOR
TOO MUCH COFFEE...
OH, I DON'T KNOW ABOUT THAT...

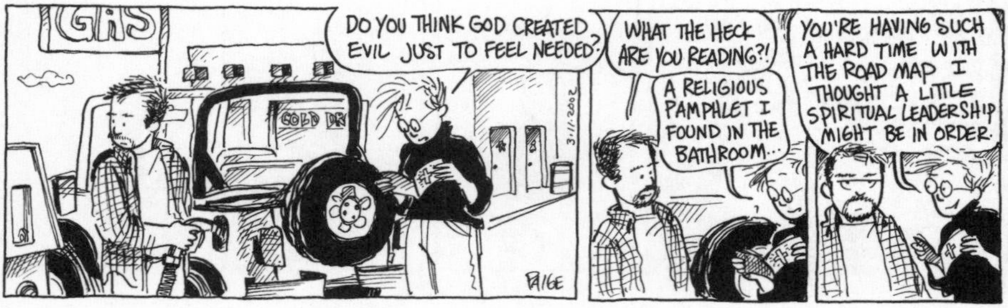
GAS
DO YOU THINK GOD CREATED EVIL JUST TO FEEL NEEDED?
3.11.2002
PAIGE
WHAT THE HECK ARE YOU READING?!
A RELIGIOUS PAMPHLET I FOUND IN THE BATHROOM...
YOU'RE HAVING SUCH A HARD TIME WITH THE ROAD MAP I THOUGHT A LITTLE SPIRITUAL LEADERSHIP MIGHT BE IN ORDER.

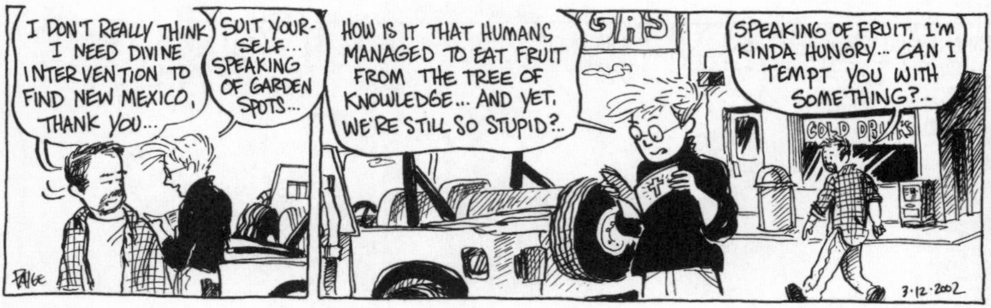
I DON'T REALLY THINK I NEED DIVINE INTERVENTION TO FIND NEW MEXICO, THANK YOU...
SUIT YOURSELF... SPEAKING OF GARDEN SPOTS...
PAIGE
HOW IS IT THAT HUMANS MANAGED TO EAT FRUIT FROM THE TREE OF KNOWLEDGE... AND YET, WE'RE STILL SO STUPID?..
GAS
SPEAKING OF FRUIT, I'M KINDA HUNGRY... CAN I TEMPT YOU WITH SOMETHING?..
COLD DRINKS
3.12.2002

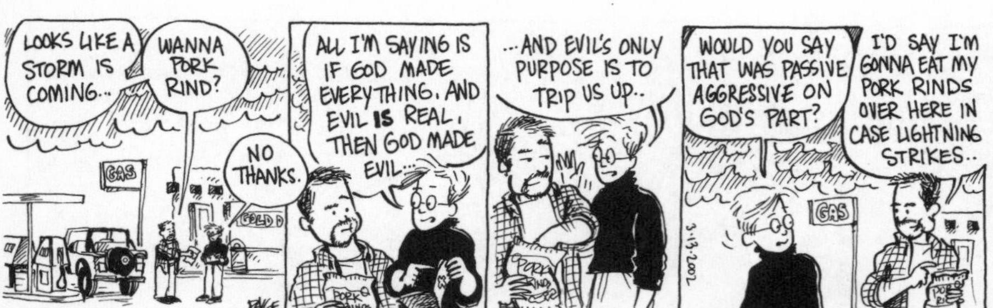
LOOKS LIKE A STORM IS COMING...
WANNA PORK RIND?
NO THANKS.
GAS
PAIGE
ALL I'M SAYING IS IF GOD MADE EVERYTHING, AND EVIL IS REAL, THEN GOD MADE EVIL...
PORK RINDS
...AND EVIL'S ONLY PURPOSE IS TO TRIP US UP..
WOULD YOU SAY THAT WAS PASSIVE AGGRESSIVE ON GOD'S PART?
3.13.2002
I'D SAY I'M GONNA EAT MY PORK RINDS OVER HERE IN CASE LIGHTNING STRIKES..

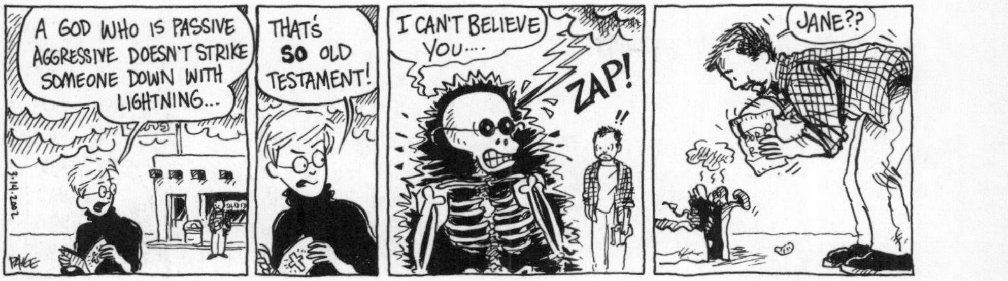
A GOD WHO IS PASSIVE AGGRESSIVE DOESN'T STRIKE SOMEONE DOWN WITH LIGHTNING...
3.14.2002
PAIGE
THAT'S **SO** OLD TESTAMENT!
I CAN'T BELIEVE YOU....
ZAP!
!!
JANE??

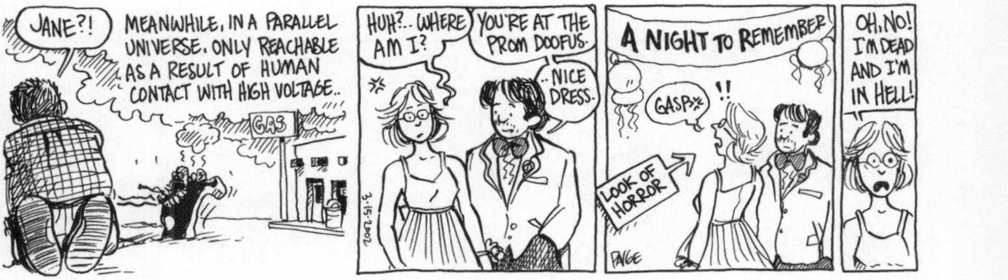
JANE?!
MEANWHILE, IN A PARALLEL UNIVERSE, ONLY REACHABLE AS A RESULT OF HUMAN CONTACT WITH HIGH VOLTAGE..
GAS
HUH?.. WHERE AM I?
YOU'RE AT THE PROM DOOFUS.
..NICE DRESS.
3.15.2002
A NIGHT TO REMEMBER
GASP
!!
LOOK OF HORROR
PAIGE
OH, NO! I'M DEAD AND I'M IN HELL!

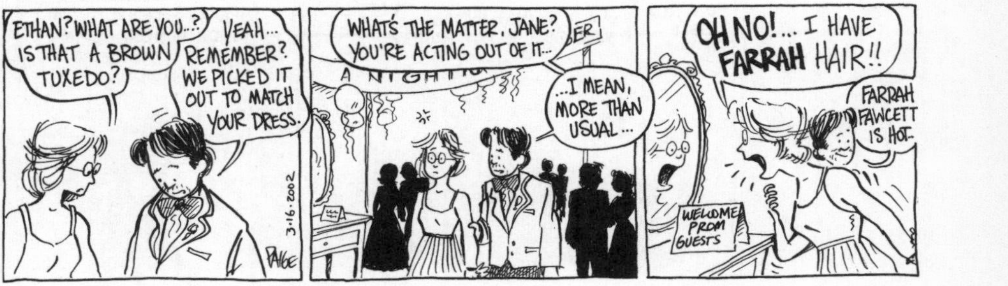
ETHAN? WHAT ARE YOU..? IS THAT A BROWN TUXEDO?
YEAH... REMEMBER? WE PICKED IT OUT TO MATCH YOUR DRESS.
3.16.2002
PAIGE
WHAT'S THE MATTER, JANE? YOU'RE ACTING OUT OF IT...
...I MEAN, MORE THAN USUAL...
OH NO!... I HAVE **FARRAH** HAIR!!
FARRAH FAWCETT IS HOT.
WELCOME PROM GUESTS

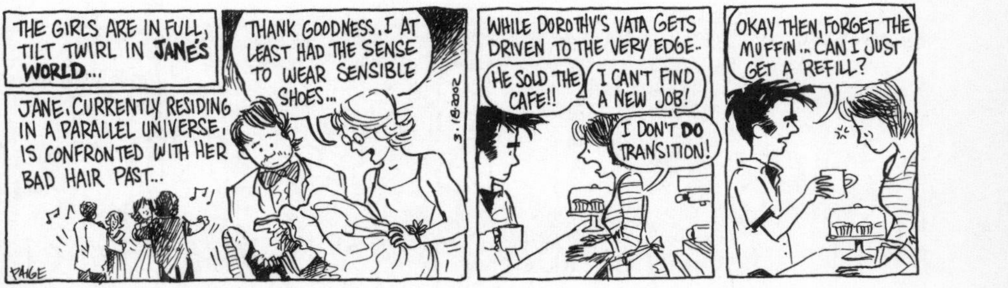
THE GIRLS ARE IN FULL, TILT TWIRL IN **JANE'S WORLD**...
JANE, CURRENTLY RESIDING IN A PARALLEL UNIVERSE, IS CONFRONTED WITH HER BAD HAIR PAST...
THANK GOODNESS, I AT LEAST HAD THE SENSE TO WEAR SENSIBLE SHOES...
3.18.2002
PAIGE
WHILE DOROTHY'S VATA GETS DRIVEN TO THE VERY EDGE..
HE SOLD THE CAFE!!
I CAN'T FIND A NEW JOB!
I DON'T **DO** TRANSITION!
OKAY THEN, FORGET THE MUFFIN.. CAN I JUST GET A REFILL?

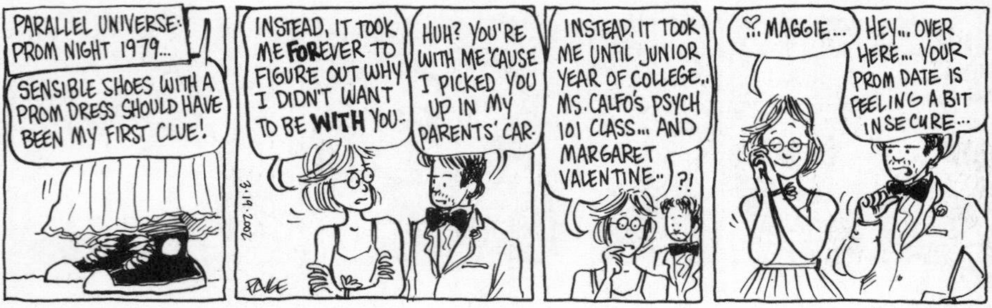
PARALLEL UNIVERSE: PROM NIGHT 1979...
SENSIBLE SHOES WITH A PROM DRESS SHOULD HAVE BEEN MY FIRST CLUE!
INSTEAD, IT TOOK ME FOREVER TO FIGURE OUT WHY I DIDN'T WANT TO BE WITH YOU..
HUH? YOU'RE WITH ME 'CAUSE I PICKED YOU UP IN MY PARENTS' CAR.
3·19·2002
PAIGE
INSTEAD, IT TOOK ME UNTIL JUNIOR YEAR OF COLLEGE.. MS. CALFO'S PSYCH 101 CLASS... AND MARGARET VALENTINE..
?!
...MAGGIE...
HEY... OVER HERE... YOUR PROM DATE IS FEELING A BIT INSECURE...

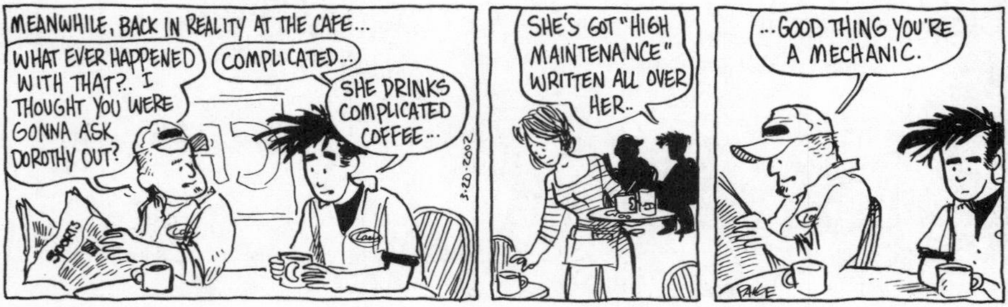
MEANWHILE, BACK IN REALITY AT THE CAFE...
WHAT EVER HAPPENED WITH THAT?.. I THOUGHT YOU WERE GONNA ASK DOROTHY OUT?
COMPLICATED...
SHE DRINKS COMPLICATED COFFEE...
SPORTS
3·20·2002
SHE'S GOT "HIGH MAINTENANCE" WRITTEN ALL OVER HER..
...GOOD THING YOU'RE A MECHANIC.
PAIGE

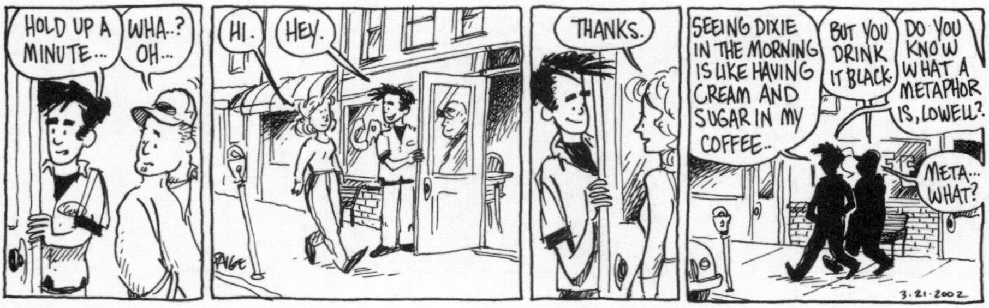
HOLD UP A MINUTE...
WHA..? OH...
HI.
HEY.
PAIGE
THANKS.
SEEING DIXIE IN THE MORNING IS LIKE HAVING CREAM AND SUGAR IN MY COFFEE..
BUT YOU DRINK IT BLACK.
DO YOU KNOW WHAT A METAPHOR IS, LOWELL?
META... WHAT?
3·21·2002

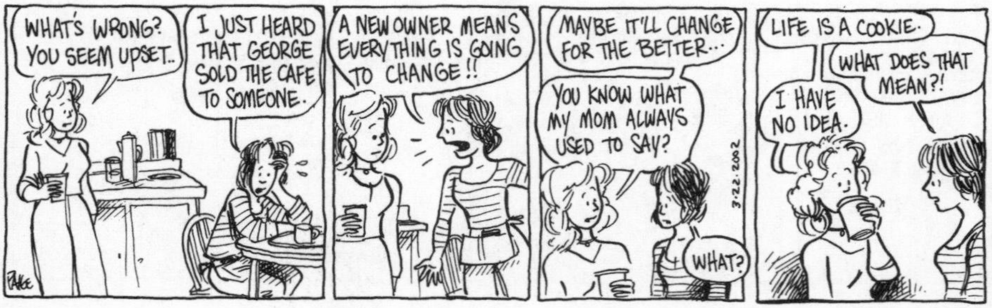
WHAT'S WRONG? YOU SEEM UPSET..
I JUST HEARD THAT GEORGE SOLD THE CAFE TO SOMEONE.
PAIGE
A NEW OWNER MEANS EVERYTHING IS GOING TO CHANGE!!
MAYBE IT'LL CHANGE FOR THE BETTER...
YOU KNOW WHAT MY MOM ALWAYS USED TO SAY?
WHAT?
3·22·2002
LIFE IS A COOKIE.
WHAT DOES THAT MEAN?!
I HAVE NO IDEA.

MEANWHILE, SOMEWHERE IN TEXAS...

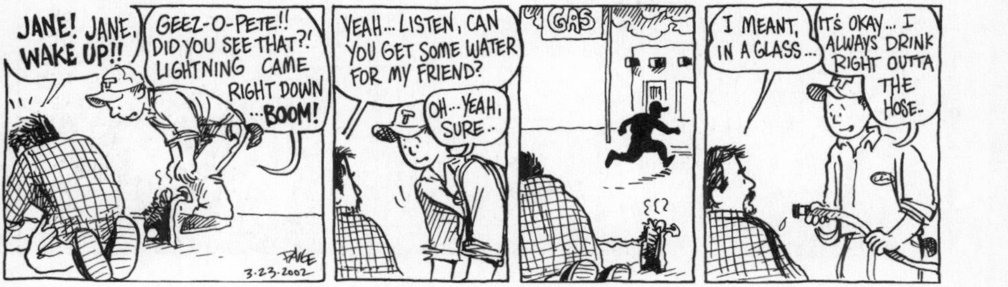

JANE! JANE, WAKE UP!!
GEEZ-O-PETE!! DID YOU SEE THAT?! LIGHTNING CAME RIGHT DOWN ...BOOM!
PAIGE 3·23·2002
YEAH... LISTEN, CAN YOU GET SOME WATER FOR MY FRIEND?
OH... YEAH, SURE..
GAS
I MEANT, IN A GLASS...
IT'S OKAY... I ALWAYS DRINK RIGHT OUTTA THE HOSE..

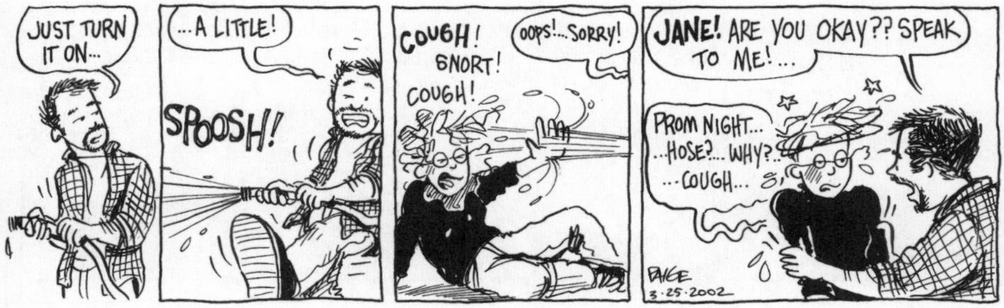

JUST TURN IT ON...
...A LITTLE!
SPOOSH!
COUGH! SNORT! COUGH!
OOPS!...SORRY!
JANE! ARE YOU OKAY?? SPEAK TO ME!...
PROM NIGHT... ...HOSE?... WHY?... ...COUGH...
PAIGE 3·25·2002

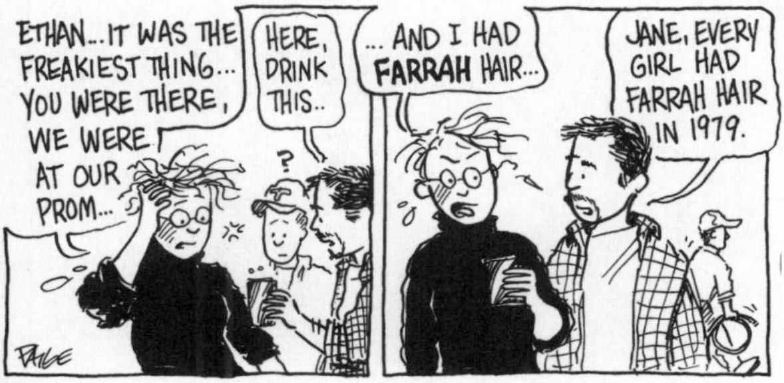

ETHAN... IT WAS THE FREAKIEST THING... YOU WERE THERE, WE WERE AT OUR PROM...
HERE, DRINK THIS..
?
PAIGE
... AND I HAD FARRAH HAIR...
JANE, EVERY GIRL HAD FARRAH HAIR IN 1979.

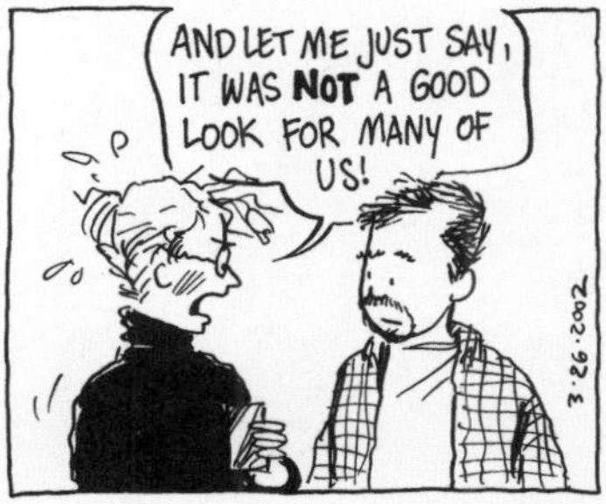

AND LET ME JUST SAY, IT WAS NOT A GOOD LOOK FOR MANY OF US!
3·26·2002

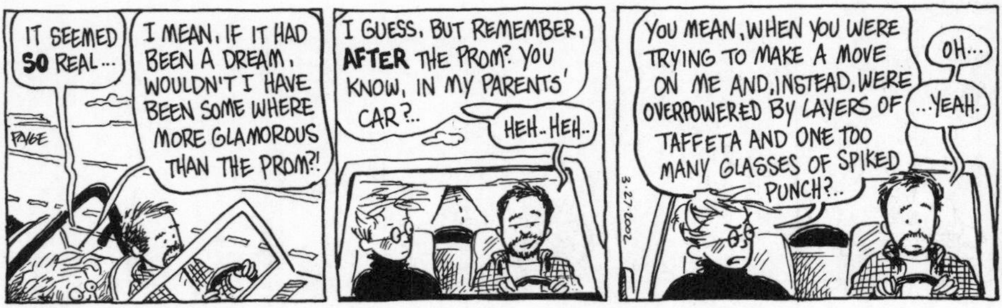
IT SEEMED **SO** REAL...
I MEAN, IF IT HAD BEEN A DREAM, WOULDN'T I HAVE BEEN SOME WHERE MORE GLAMOROUS THAN THE PROM?!
PAIGE
I GUESS, BUT REMEMBER, **AFTER** THE PROM? YOU KNOW, IN MY PARENTS' CAR?..
HEH.. HEH..
YOU MEAN, WHEN YOU WERE TRYING TO MAKE A MOVE ON ME AND, INSTEAD, WERE OVERPOWERED BY LAYERS OF TAFFETA AND ONE TOO MANY GLASSES OF SPIKED PUNCH?..
OH...
...YEAH.
3.27.2002

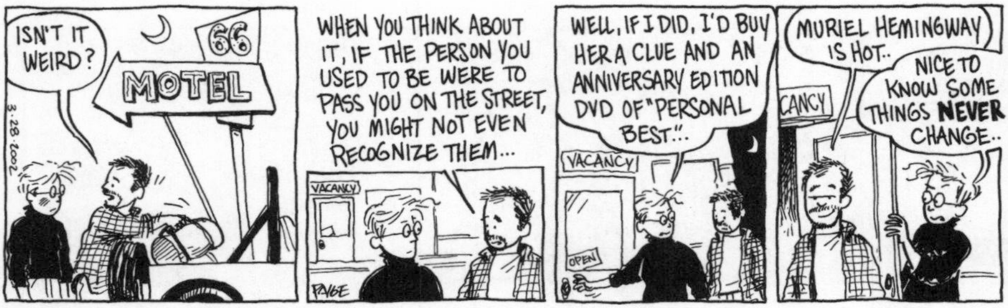
ISN'T IT WEIRD?
66
MOTEL
3.28.2002
WHEN YOU THINK ABOUT IT, IF THE PERSON YOU USED TO BE WERE TO PASS YOU ON THE STREET, YOU MIGHT NOT EVEN RECOGNIZE THEM...
VACANCY
PAIGE
WELL, IF I DID, I'D BUY HER A CLUE AND AN ANNIVERSARY EDITION DVD OF "PERSONAL BEST"..
VACANCY
OPEN
MURIEL HEMINGWAY IS HOT..
NICE TO KNOW SOME THINGS **NEVER** CHANGE..
CANCY

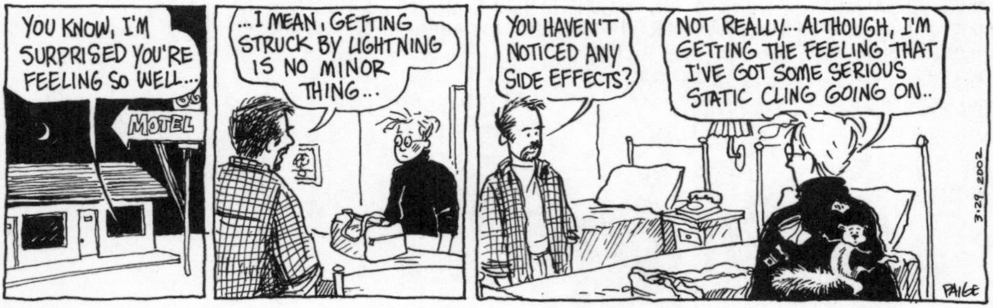
YOU KNOW, I'M SURPRISED YOU'RE FEELING SO WELL...
MOTEL
...I MEAN, GETTING STRUCK BY LIGHTNING IS NO MINOR THING...
YOU HAVEN'T NOTICED ANY SIDE EFFECTS?
NOT REALLY... ALTHOUGH, I'M GETTING THE FEELING THAT I'VE GOT SOME SERIOUS STATIC CLING GOING ON..
3.29.2002
PAIGE

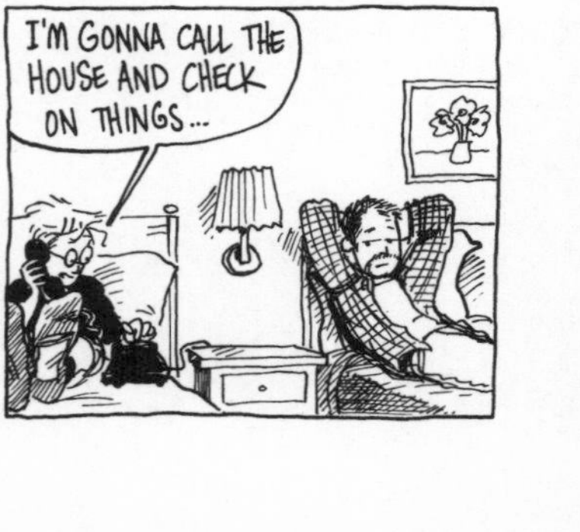
I'M GONNA CALL THE HOUSE AND CHECK ON THINGS...

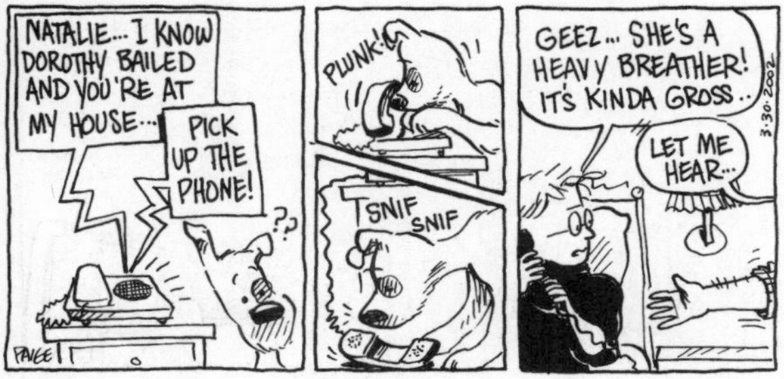
NATALIE... I KNOW DOROTHY BAILED AND YOU'RE AT MY HOUSE...
PICK UP THE PHONE!
PLUNK!
SNIF SNIF
GEEZ... SHE'S A HEAVY BREATHER! IT'S KINDA GROSS..
LET ME HEAR...
3·30·2002

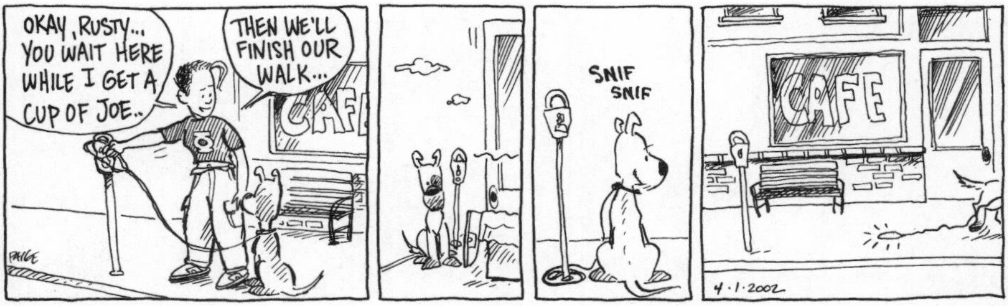
OKAY, RUSTY... YOU WAIT HERE WHILE I GET A CUP OF JOE..
THEN WE'LL FINISH OUR WALK...
CAFE
SNIF SNIF
CAFE
4·1·2002

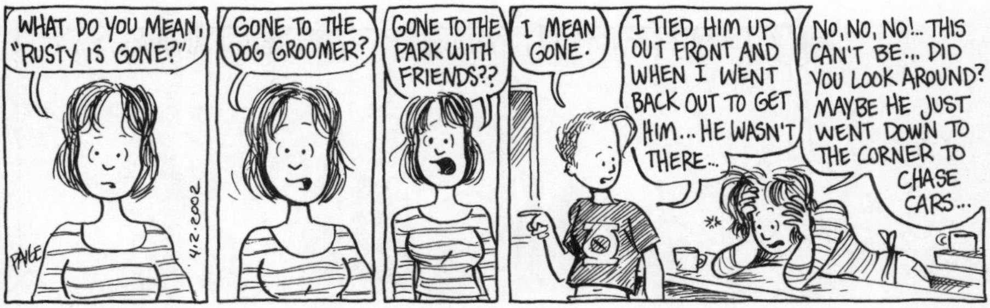
WHAT DO YOU MEAN, "RUSTY IS GONE?"
4·2·2002
GONE TO THE DOG GROOMER?
GONE TO THE PARK WITH FRIENDS??
I MEAN GONE.
I TIED HIM UP OUT FRONT AND WHEN I WENT BACK OUT TO GET HIM... HE WASN'T THERE...
NO, NO, NO!.. THIS CAN'T BE... DID YOU LOOK AROUND? MAYBE HE JUST WENT DOWN TO THE CORNER TO CHASE CARS...

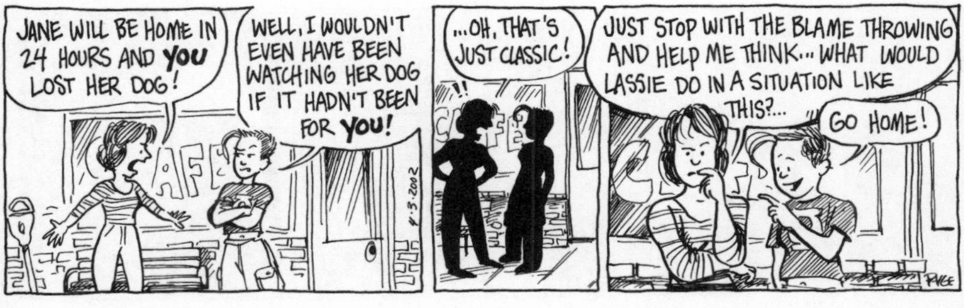
JANE WILL BE HOME IN 24 HOURS AND **YOU** LOST HER DOG!
WELL, I WOULDN'T EVEN HAVE BEEN WATCHING HER DOG IF IT HADN'T BEEN FOR **YOU**!
4·3·2002
...OH, THAT'S JUST CLASSIC!
JUST STOP WITH THE BLAME THROWING AND HELP ME THINK... WHAT WOULD LASSIE DO IN A SITUATION LIKE THIS?...
GO HOME!

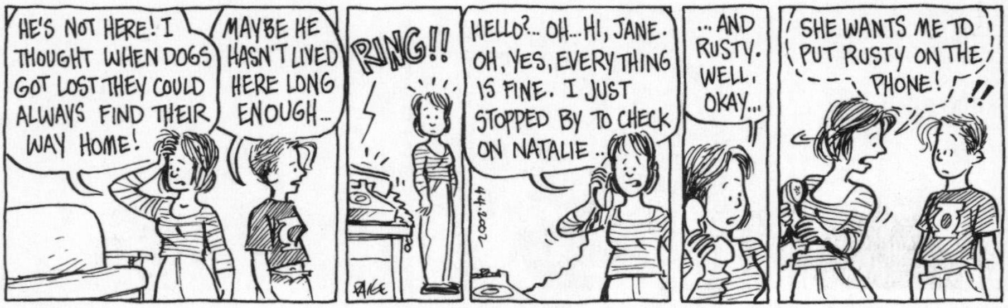
HE'S NOT HERE! I THOUGHT WHEN DOGS GOT LOST THEY COULD ALWAYS FIND THEIR WAY HOME!
MAYBE HE HASN'T LIVED HERE LONG ENOUGH...
RING!!
PAIGE
4.4.2002
HELLO?.. OH...HI, JANE. OH, YES, EVERYTHING IS FINE. I JUST STOPPED BY TO CHECK ON NATALIE...
...AND RUSTY. WELL, OKAY...
SHE WANTS ME TO PUT RUSTY ON THE PHONE!
!!

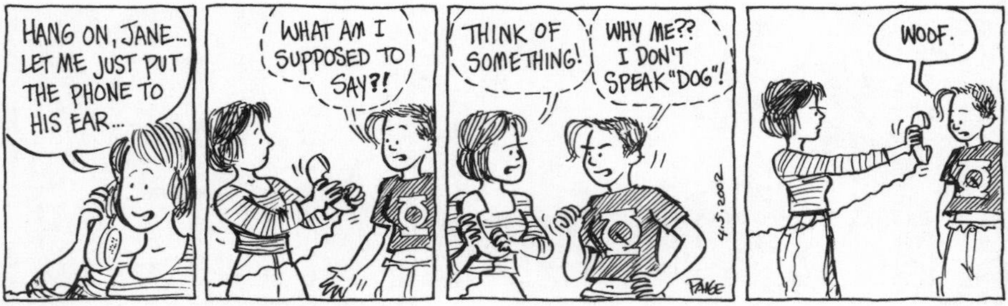
HANG ON, JANE... LET ME JUST PUT THE PHONE TO HIS EAR...
WHAT AM I SUPPOSED TO SAY?!
THINK OF SOMETHING!
WHY ME?? I DON'T SPEAK "DOG"!
4.5.2002
PAIGE
WOOF.

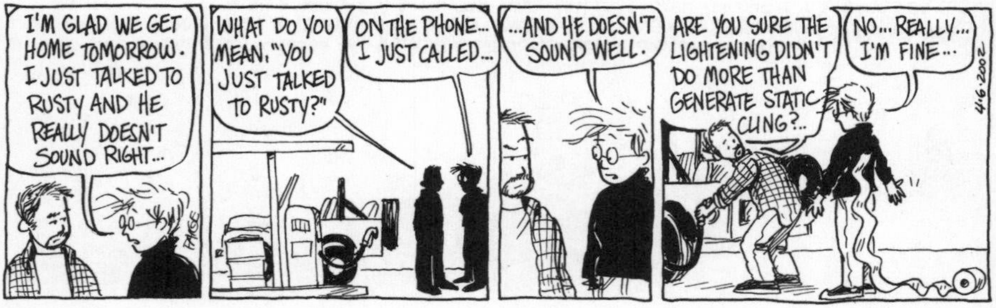
I'M GLAD WE GET HOME TOMORROW. I JUST TALKED TO RUSTY AND HE REALLY DOESN'T SOUND RIGHT...
PAIGE
WHAT DO YOU MEAN, "YOU JUST TALKED TO RUSTY?"
ON THE PHONE... I JUST CALLED...
...AND HE DOESN'T SOUND WELL.
ARE YOU SURE THE LIGHTENING DIDN'T DO MORE THAN GENERATE STATIC CLING?..
NO... REALLY... I'M FINE...
4.6.2002

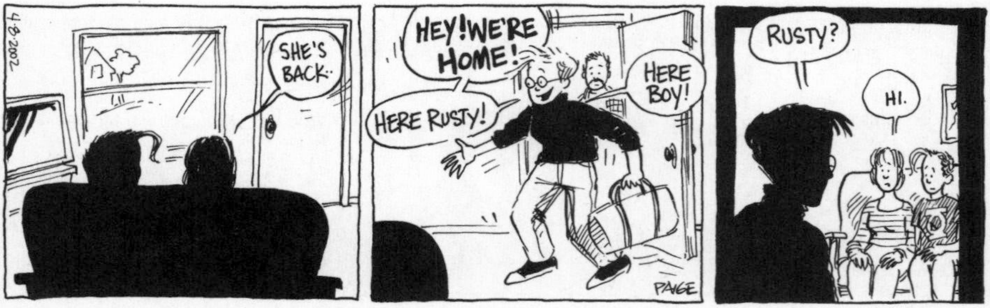
4.8.2002
SHE'S BACK..
HEY! WE'RE HOME!
HERE RUSTY!
HERE BOY!
PAIGE
RUSTY?
HI.

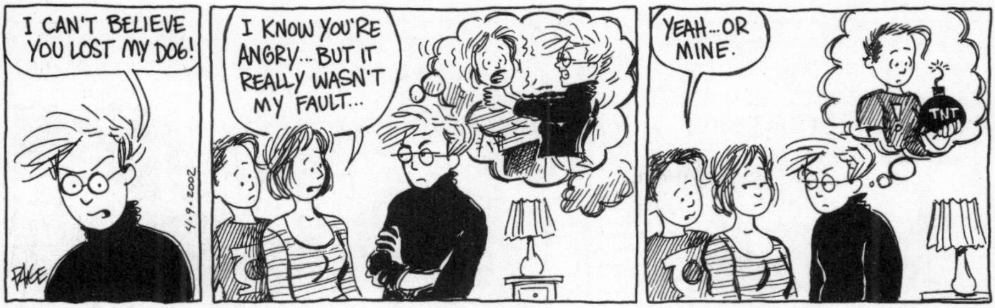
I CAN'T BELIEVE YOU LOST MY DOG!
PAGE
4.9.2002
I KNOW YOU'RE ANGRY... BUT IT REALLY WASN'T MY FAULT...
YEAH...OR MINE.
TNT

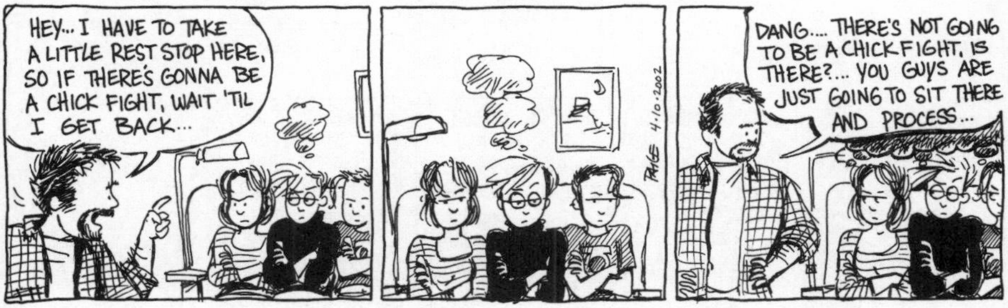
HEY... I HAVE TO TAKE A LITTLE REST STOP HERE, SO IF THERE'S GONNA BE A CHICK FIGHT, WAIT 'TIL I GET BACK...
PAGE
4.10.2002
DANG.... THERE'S NOT GOING TO BE A CHICK FIGHT, IS THERE?... YOU GUYS ARE JUST GOING TO SIT THERE AND PROCESS...

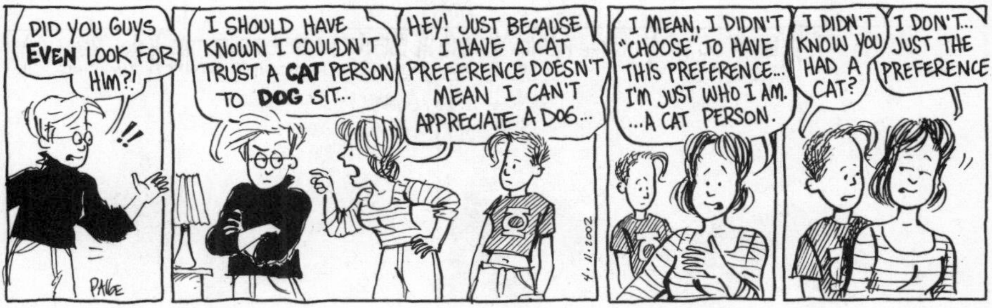
DID YOU GUYS EVEN LOOK FOR HIM?!
!!
PAGE
I SHOULD HAVE KNOWN I COULDN'T TRUST A CAT PERSON TO DOG SIT...
HEY! JUST BECAUSE I HAVE A CAT PREFERENCE DOESN'T MEAN I CAN'T APPRECIATE A DOG...
4.11.2002
I MEAN, I DIDN'T "CHOOSE" TO HAVE THIS PREFERENCE... I'M JUST WHO I AM. ...A CAT PERSON.
I DIDN'T KNOW YOU HAD A CAT?
I DON'T... JUST THE PREFERENCE

LATER THAT DAY...

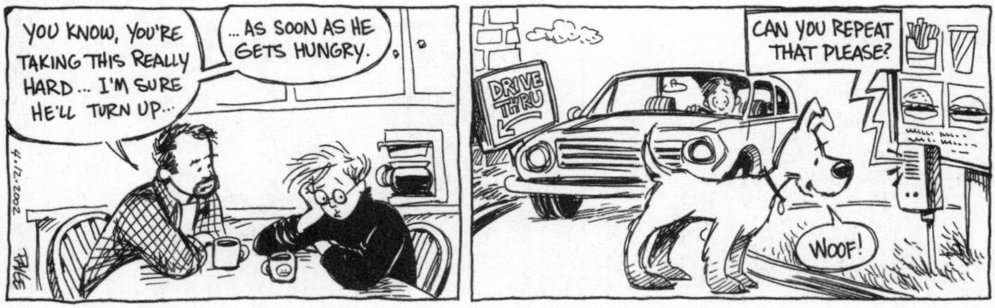
YOU KNOW, YOU'RE TAKING THIS REALLY HARD... I'M SURE HE'LL TURN UP...
... AS SOON AS HE GETS HUNGRY.
4.12.2002
PAGE
DRIVE THRU
CAN YOU REPEAT THAT PLEASE?
WOOF!

I'LL BET HE'S LONELY...
IT'S GETTING DARK ... WHERE'S HE GONNA SLEEP?
4.13.2002
MAYBE HE KNOWS A CUTE GIRL WHO COULD PUT HIM UP FOR THE NIGHT?
HEY! I'M THE ONLY CUTE GIRL IN HIS LIFE!
FI-FI
PAIGE

CHICKS ARE WEIRD. YOU'RE STILL MAD AT DOROTHY.
I MEAN, IF GUYS GET MAD AT EACH OTHER, THEY FIGHT IT OUT... THEN MOVE ON...
4.15.2002
PAIGE
THEY'RE DIRECT. THROW A FEW PUNCHES AND BOOM... YOU WORK OFF THE ANGER AND TENSION...
...NONE OF THIS "TALKING THROUGH ISSUES" STUFF... GUYS JUST ACT...

SMACK!
CAN I PUNCH YOU AGAIN?
NO!
MAN, YOU'RE RIGHT... I FEEL A LOT BETTER! WHO ELSE CAN I PUNCH?..

SEE YA...
...LATER!
SLAM
HELLO... DOROTHY?
...LISTEN, THIS MAY SOUND A LITTLE CRAZY, BUT IF YOU SEE JANE, DUCK AND ROLL...
4.16.2002
PAIGE

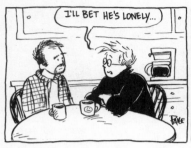

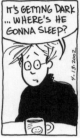

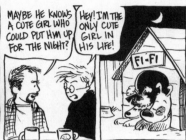

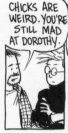

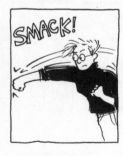

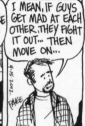

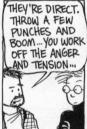

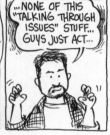

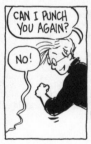

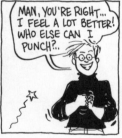

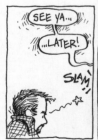

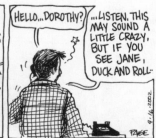

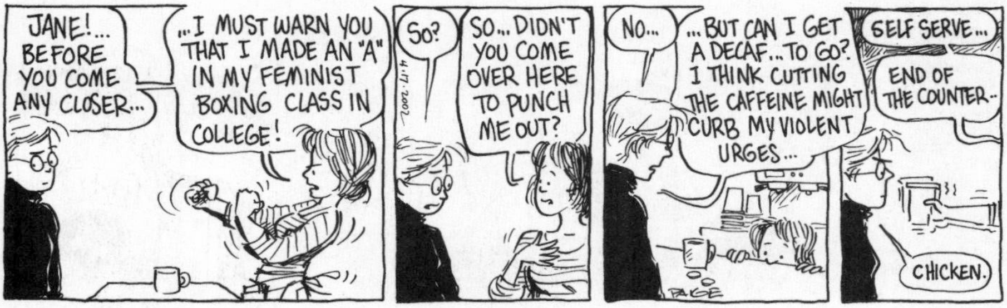
JANE!... BEFORE YOU COME ANY CLOSER...
...I MUST WARN YOU THAT I MADE AN "A" IN MY FEMINIST BOXING CLASS IN COLLEGE!
4.17.2002
So?
SO... DIDN'T YOU COME OVER HERE TO PUNCH ME OUT?
No...
...BUT CAN I GET A DECAF... TO GO? I THINK CUTTING THE CAFFEINE MIGHT CURB MY VIOLENT URGES...
SELF SERVE...
END OF THE COUNTER..
CHICKEN.
PAGE

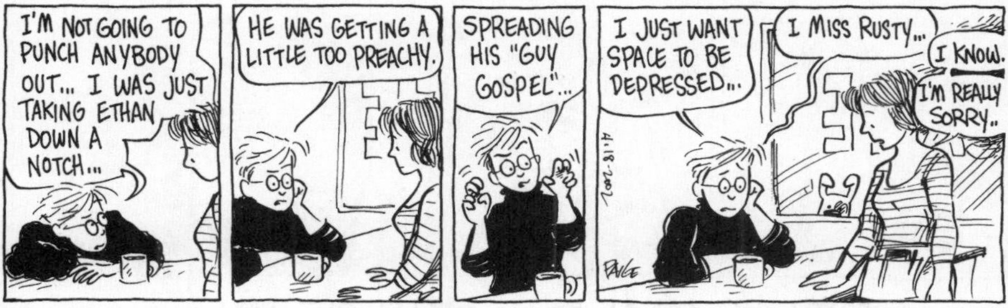
I'M NOT GOING TO PUNCH ANYBODY OUT... I WAS JUST TAKING ETHAN DOWN A NOTCH...
HE WAS GETTING A LITTLE TOO PREACHY.
SPREADING HIS "GUY GOSPEL"...
4.18.2002
I JUST WANT SPACE TO BE DEPRESSED...
I MISS RUSTY...
I KNOW.
I'M REALLY SORRY..
PAGE

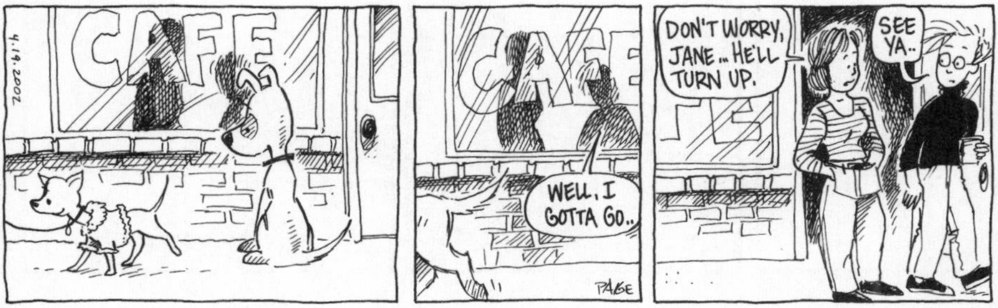
4.19.2002
CAFE
WELL, I GOTTA GO..
DON'T WORRY, JANE.. HE'LL TURN UP.
SEE YA..
PAGE

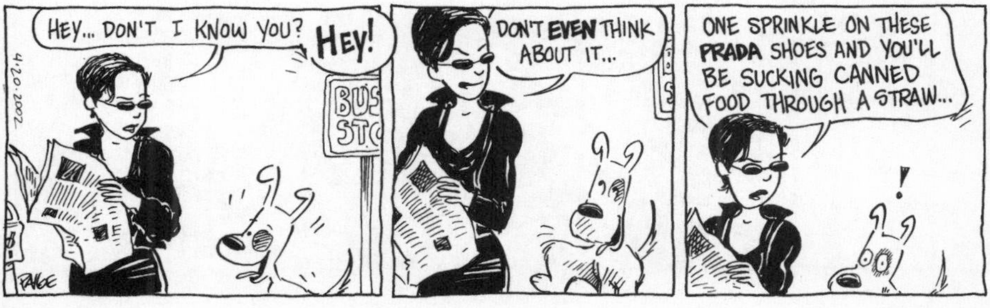
4.20.2002
HEY... DON'T I KNOW YOU?
HEY!
BUS STO
DON'T EVEN THINK ABOUT IT...
ONE SPRINKLE ON THESE PRADA SHOES AND YOU'LL BE SUCKING CANNED FOOD THROUGH A STRAW...
!
PAGE

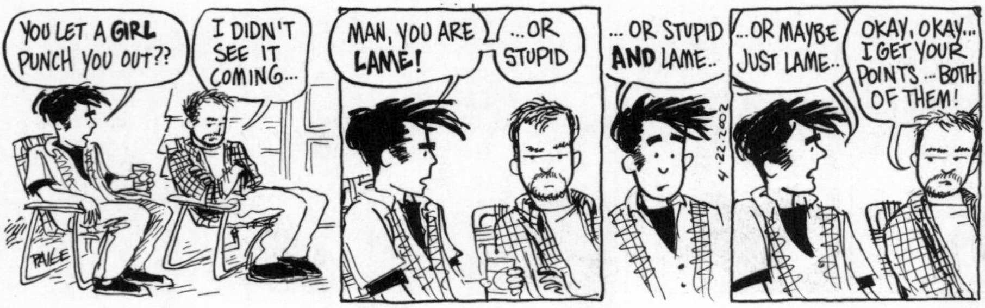
YOU LET A GIRL PUNCH YOU OUT??
I DIDN'T SEE IT COMING...
PAIGE
MAN, YOU ARE LAME!
...OR STUPID
...OR STUPID AND LAME..
4·22·2002
...OR MAYBE JUST LAME..
OKAY, OKAY... I GET YOUR POINTS ... BOTH OF THEM!

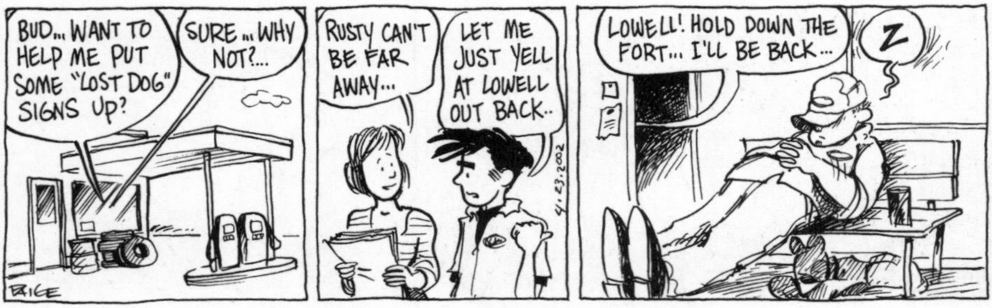
BUD... WANT TO HELP ME PUT SOME "LOST DOG" SIGNS UP?
SURE... WHY NOT?...
PAIGE
RUSTY CAN'T BE FAR AWAY...
LET ME JUST YELL AT LOWELL OUT BACK..
4·23·2002
LOWELL! HOLD DOWN THE FORT... I'LL BE BACK...
Z

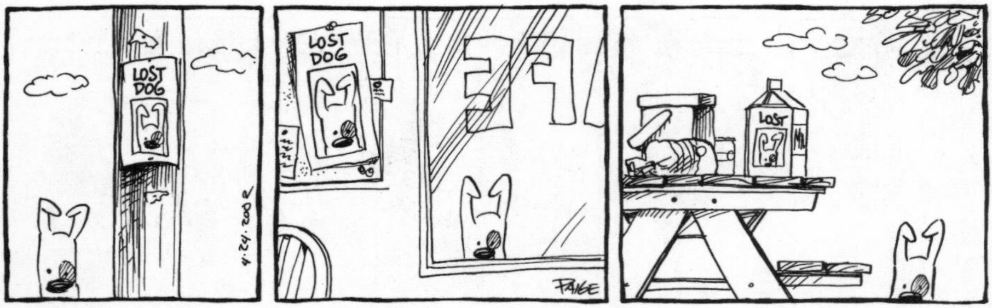
LOST DOG
4·24·2002
LOST DOG
PAIGE
LOST

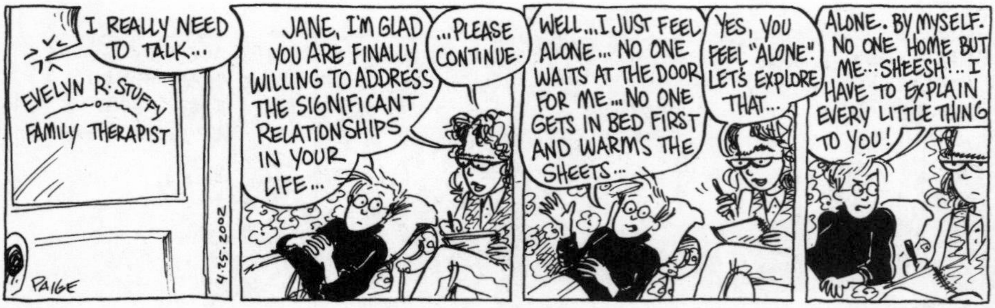
I REALLY NEED TO TALK...
EVELYN R. STUFFY
FAMILY THERAPIST
PAIGE
4·25·2002
JANE, I'M GLAD YOU ARE FINALLY WILLING TO ADDRESS THE SIGNIFICANT RELATIONSHIPS IN YOUR LIFE...
...PLEASE CONTINUE.
WELL... I JUST FEEL ALONE... NO ONE WAITS AT THE DOOR FOR ME... NO ONE GETS IN BED FIRST AND WARMS THE SHEETS...
YES, YOU FEEL "ALONE." LETS EXPLORE THAT...
ALONE.. BY MYSELF. NO ONE HOME BUT ME... SHEESH!.. I HAVE TO EXPLAIN EVERY LITTLE THING TO YOU!

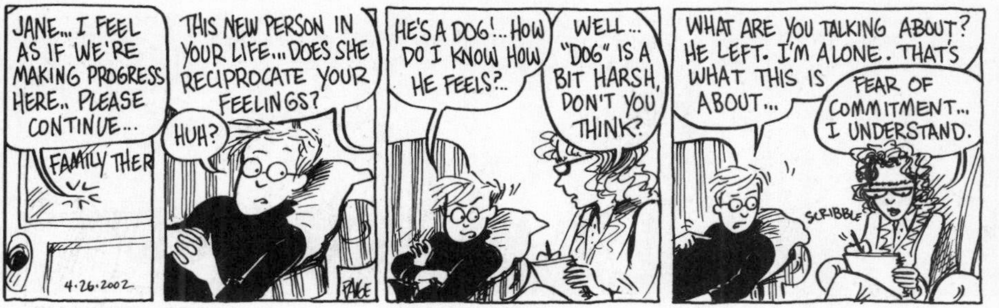
JANE... I FEEL AS IF WE'RE MAKING PROGRESS HERE.. PLEASE CONTINUE...
FAMILY THER
4·26·2002
THIS NEW PERSON IN YOUR LIFE... DOES SHE RECIPROCATE YOUR FEELINGS?
HUH?
HE'S A DOG!... HOW DO I KNOW HOW HE FEELS?...
WELL... "DOG" IS A BIT HARSH, DON'T YOU THINK?
PAIGE
WHAT ARE YOU TALKING ABOUT? HE LEFT. I'M ALONE. THAT'S WHAT THIS IS ABOUT...
FEAR OF COMMITMENT... I UNDERSTAND.
SCRIBBLE

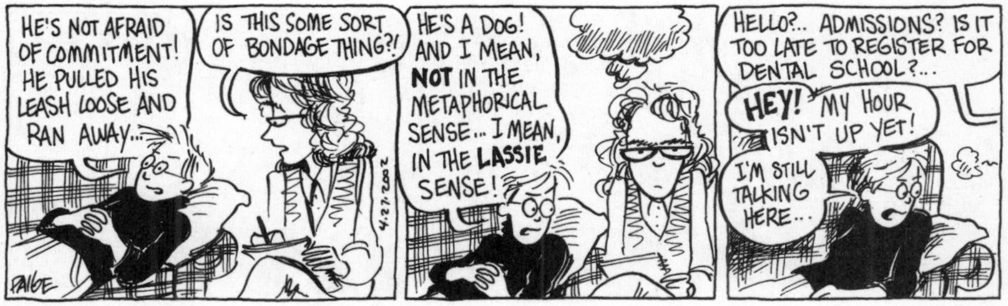
HE'S NOT AFRAID OF COMMITMENT! HE PULLED HIS LEASH LOOSE AND RAN AWAY...
IS THIS SOME SORT OF BONDAGE THING?!
PAIGE
4·27·2002
HE'S A DOG! AND I MEAN, NOT IN THE METAPHORICAL SENSE... I MEAN, IN THE LASSIE SENSE!
HELLO?.. ADMISSIONS? IS IT TOO LATE TO REGISTER FOR DENTAL SCHOOL?...
HEY! MY HOUR ISN'T UP YET!
I'M STILL TALKING HERE...

THE NEXT DAY...

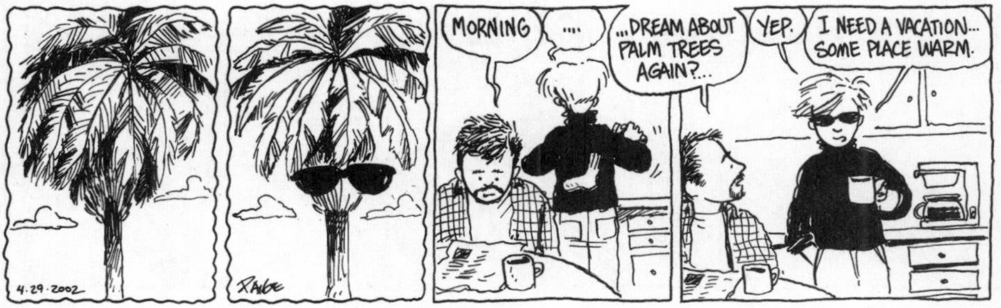
4·29·2002
PAIGE
MORNING
....
...DREAM ABOUT PALM TREES AGAIN?...
YEP.
I NEED A VACATION... SOME PLACE WARM.

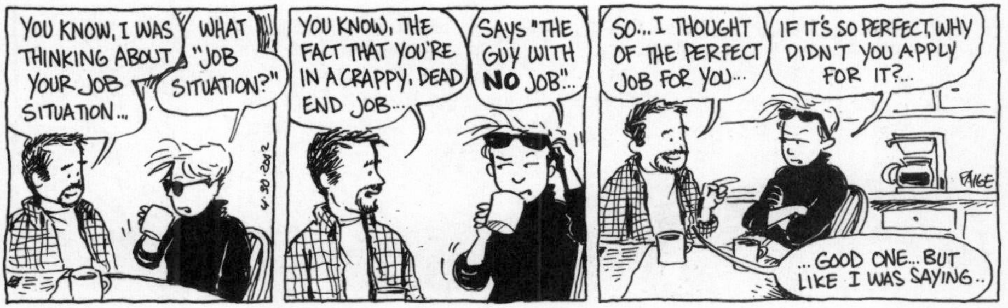
YOU KNOW, I WAS THINKING ABOUT YOUR JOB SITUATION...
WHAT "JOB SITUATION?"
4·30·2002
YOU KNOW, THE FACT THAT YOU'RE IN A CRAPPY, DEAD END JOB...
SAYS "THE GUY WITH NO JOB"...
SO... I THOUGHT OF THE PERFECT JOB FOR YOU...
IF IT'S SO PERFECT, WHY DIDN'T YOU APPLY FOR IT?...
PAIGE
... GOOD ONE... BUT LIKE I WAS SAYING...

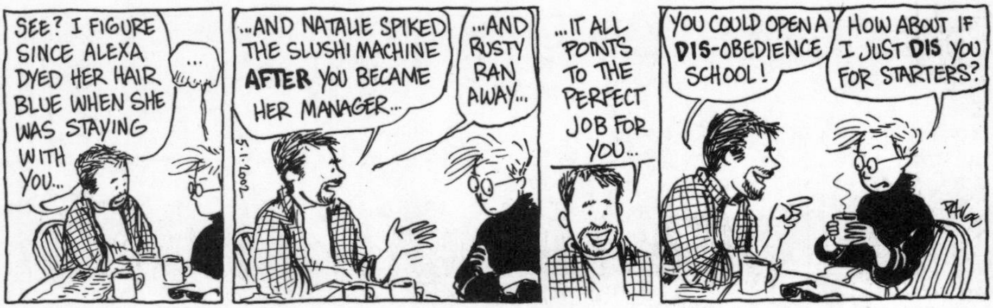
SEE? I FIGURE SINCE ALEXA DYED HER HAIR BLUE WHEN SHE WAS STAYING WITH YOU...
...
...AND NATALIE SPIKED THE SLUSHI MACHINE **AFTER** YOU BECAME HER MANAGER...
...AND RUSTY RAN AWAY...
5.1.2002
...IT ALL POINTS TO THE PERFECT JOB FOR YOU...
YOU COULD OPEN A **DIS**-OBEDIENCE SCHOOL!
HOW ABOUT IF I JUST **DIS** YOU FOR STARTERS?
PAIGE

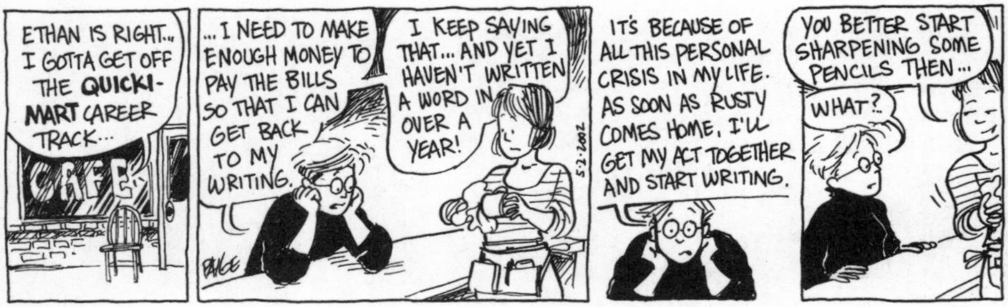
ETHAN IS RIGHT... I GOTTA GET OFF THE **QUICKI-MART** CAREER TRACK...
CAFE
...I NEED TO MAKE ENOUGH MONEY TO PAY THE BILLS SO THAT I CAN GET BACK TO MY WRITING.
I KEEP SAYING THAT... AND YET I HAVEN'T WRITTEN A WORD IN OVER A YEAR!
PAIGE
5.2.2002
IT'S BECAUSE OF ALL THIS PERSONAL CRISIS IN MY LIFE. AS SOON AS RUSTY COMES HOME, I'LL GET MY ACT TOGETHER AND START WRITING.
YOU BETTER START SHARPENING SOME PENCILS THEN...
WHAT?..

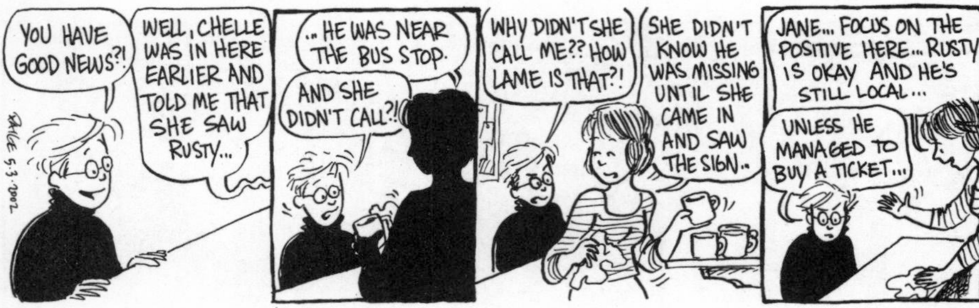
YOU HAVE GOOD NEWS?!
WELL, CHELLE WAS IN HERE EARLIER AND TOLD ME THAT SHE SAW RUSTY...
PAIGE 5.3.2002
...HE WAS NEAR THE BUS STOP.
AND SHE DIDN'T CALL?!
WHY DIDN'T SHE CALL ME?? HOW LAME IS THAT?!
SHE DIDN'T KNOW HE WAS MISSING UNTIL SHE CAME IN AND SAW THE SIGN..
JANE... FOCUS ON THE POSITIVE HERE... RUSTY IS OKAY AND HE'S STILL LOCAL...
UNLESS HE MANAGED TO BUY A TICKET...

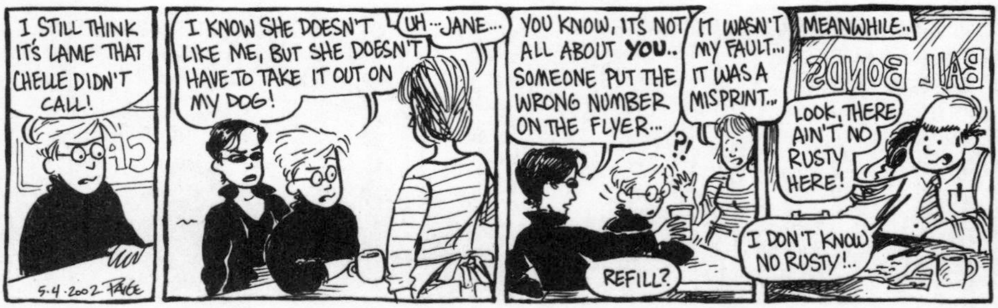
I STILL THINK IT'S LAME THAT CHELLE DIDN'T CALL!
5.4.2002 PAIGE
I KNOW SHE DOESN'T LIKE ME, BUT SHE DOESN'T HAVE TO TAKE IT OUT ON MY DOG!
UH... JANE...
YOU KNOW, IT'S NOT ALL ABOUT **YOU**.. SOMEONE PUT THE WRONG NUMBER ON THE FLYER...
IT WASN'T MY FAULT... IT WAS A MISPRINT...
?!
REFILL?
MEANWHILE..
BAIL BONDS
LOOK, THERE AIN'T NO RUSTY HERE!
I DON'T KNOW NO RUSTY!...

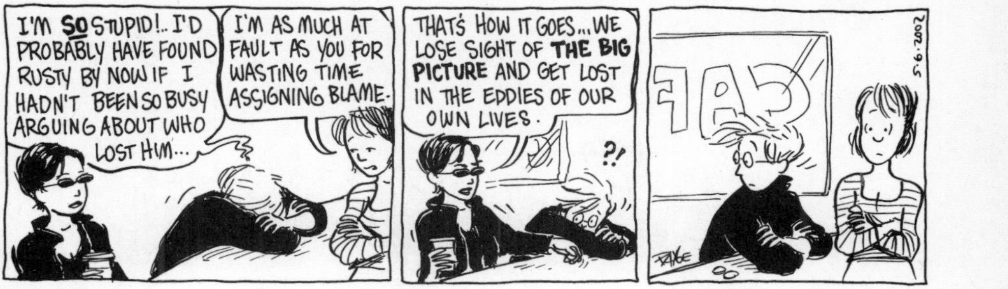
I'M SO STUPID!.. I'D PROBABLY HAVE FOUND RUSTY BY NOW IF I HADN'T BEEN SO BUSY ARGUING ABOUT WHO LOST HIM...
I'M AS MUCH AT FAULT AS YOU FOR WASTING TIME ASSIGNING BLAME.
THAT'S HOW IT GOES... WE LOSE SIGHT OF THE BIG PICTURE AND GET LOST IN THE EDDIES OF OUR OWN LIVES.
?!
CAFE
5.6.2002
PAIGE

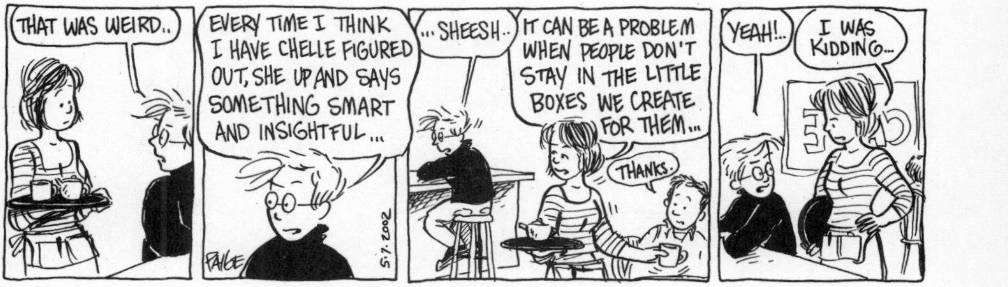
THAT WAS WEIRD..
EVERY TIME I THINK I HAVE CHELLE FIGURED OUT, SHE UP AND SAYS SOMETHING SMART AND INSIGHTFUL...
PAIGE
5.7.2002
... SHEESH..
IT CAN BE A PROBLEM WHEN PEOPLE DON'T STAY IN THE LITTLE BOXES WE CREATE FOR THEM...
THANKS.
YEAH!..
I WAS KIDDING...

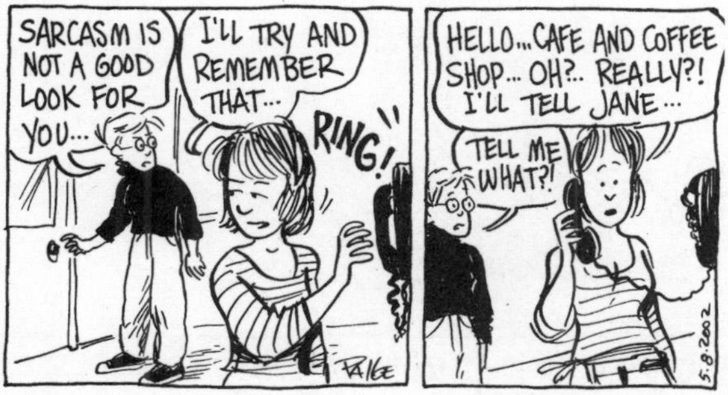
SARCASM IS NOT A GOOD LOOK FOR YOU...
I'LL TRY AND REMEMBER THAT...
RING!
PAIGE
HELLO... CAFE AND COFFEE SHOP... OH?.. REALLY?! I'LL TELL JANE...
TELL ME WHAT?!
5.8.2002

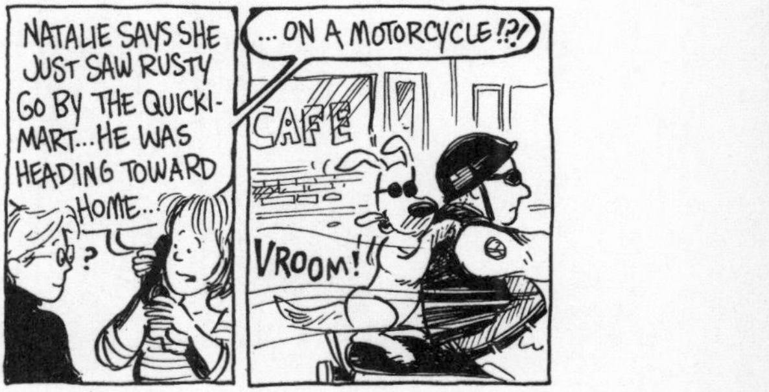
NATALIE SAYS SHE JUST SAW RUSTY GO BY THE QUICKI-MART... HE WAS HEADING TOWARD HOME...
?
... ON A MOTORCYCLE!?!
CAFE
VROOM!

WHAT'S GOING ON?
WELCOME HOME
A WELCOME HOME PARTY FOR RUSTY!.. DO YOU THINK I HAVE ENOUGH DOG BISCUITS OUT?..

NATALIE SAID SHE SAW HIM HEADING THIS WAY OVER AN HOUR AGO.
UH... JANE?
5.9.2002
Z

WHAT IS IT?
SSH... LOOK.
RUSTY!
HE MUST HAVE COME HOME WHILE I WAS UNLOADING THE CAR!..
HE LOOKS EXHAUSTED..
Z

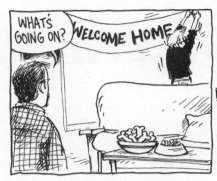

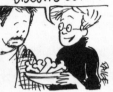

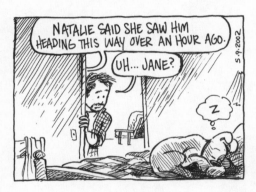

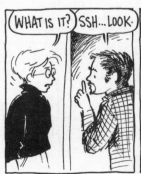

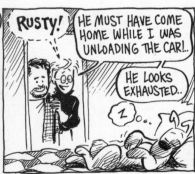

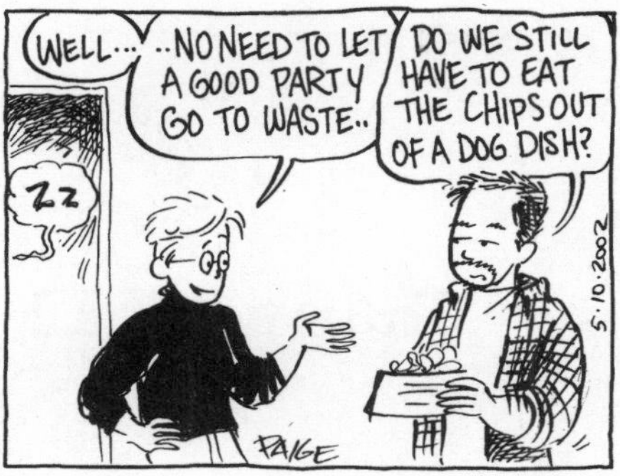
WELL...
..NO NEED TO LET A GOOD PARTY GO TO WASTE..
DO WE STILL HAVE TO EAT THE CHIPS OUT OF A DOG DISH?
ZZ
5·10·2002
PAIGE

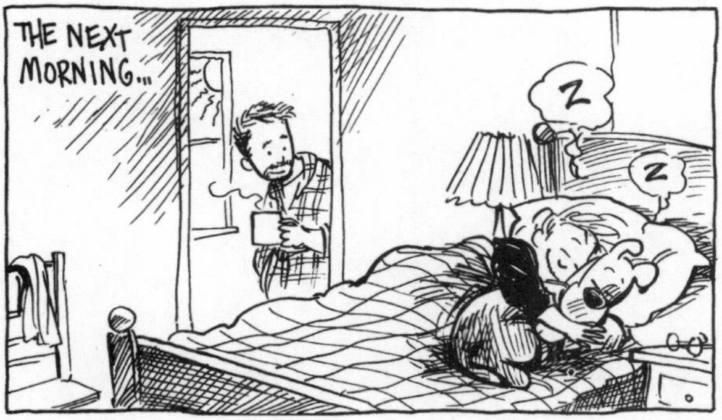
THE NEXT MORNING...
Z
Z

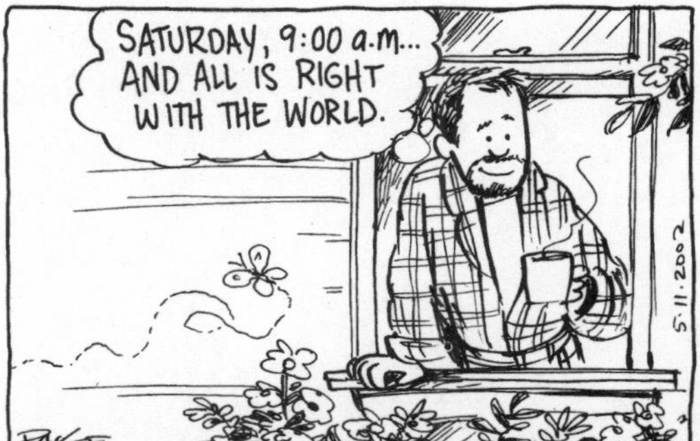
SATURDAY, 9:00 a.m... AND ALL IS RIGHT WITH THE WORLD.
5·11·2002
PAIGE

Chapter 11

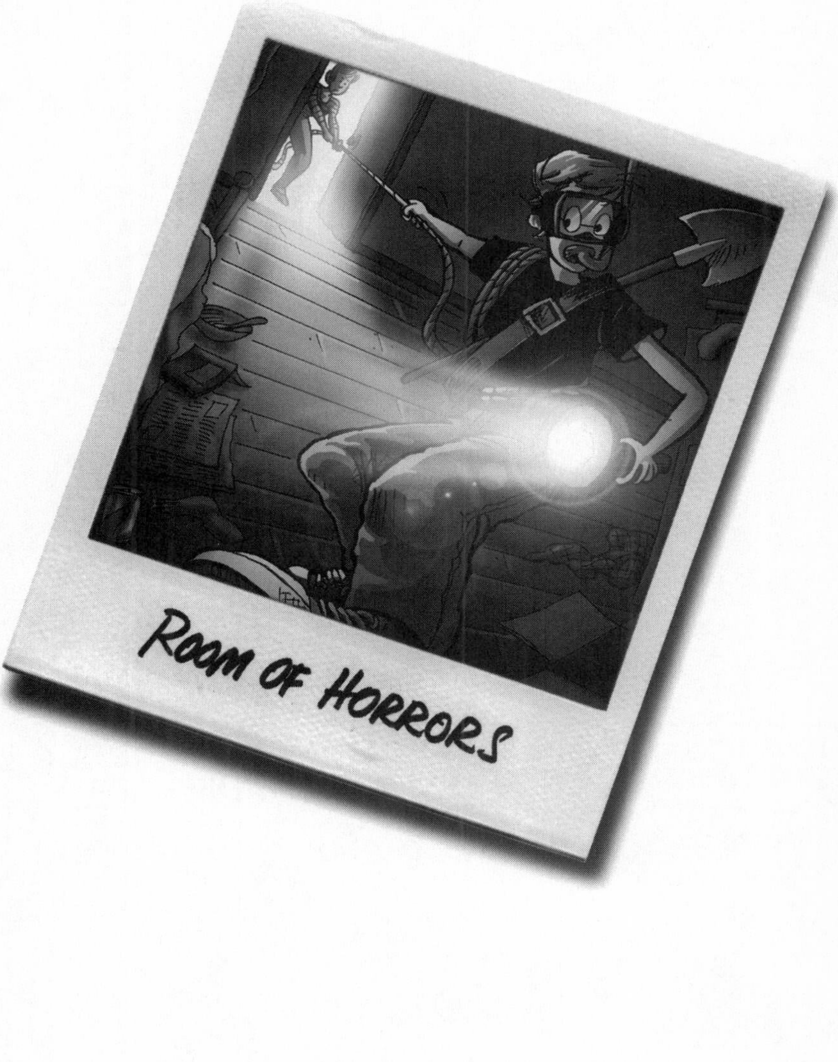
ROOM OF HORRORS

RUSTY'S FIRST MORNING BACK...

THIS IS GREAT!
...JUST LIKE ONE
BIG HAPPY FA..

DOES HE **HAVE** TO
EAT AT THE
TABLE?

SMAK
CRUNCH
D... SMAK

WELL...

'CAUSE HE'S
GROSSING
ME OUT...

SMAK
MUNCH

YEAH... I GUESS DOGS
CAN'T REALLY CHEW
WITH THEIR MOUTHS
CLOSED...

SMACK   CRUNCH
         SMAK

PLUNK!

PAIGE

5-13-2002

I THOUGHT IT WOULD
BE NICE JUST FOR
TODAY... YOU KNOW, HIS
FIRST DAY BACK
HOME...

PAIGE

5-1-K-2002

...IF HE COULD
EAT AT THE TABLE
WITH US.

WHO CAN
EAT...?

SMACK!
SMAK!

WHAT **IS** THAT?

AN EGG WHITE
OMELETTE... SEE,
YOU TAKE THE
YOKES...

SMAK

NO... NOT THAT... THAT... THE THING ON HIS SHOULDER?
WHAT THING?
IT LOOKS LIKE A TATTOO..
A TATTOO?!
?
HOW DOES A DOG GET A TATTOO?
I DON'T WANT TO KNOW.
5.15.2002
PAIGE
I HADN'T EVEN NOTICED IT... WHAT DOES IT SAY??
JANE
I LOVE YOU TOO, RUSTY!
HOW THE HECK?..
LATER AT THE CAFE..
HEY... WHO WAS THAT?... THE GIRL WHO JUST WALKED OUT?..
THE NEW OWNER OF THE CAFE.
REALLY? I DIDN'T EVEN KNOW IT WAS FOR SALE.
COULDN'T YOU TELL JUST BY LOOKING AT ME THAT WE'RE IN TRANSITION HERE?!
FEEL MY PULSE... AND TELL ME MY VATA ISN'T PROVOKED.
5.16.2002
PAIGE

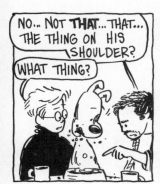

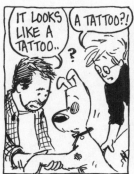

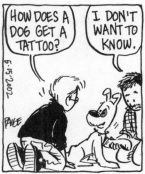

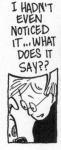

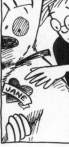

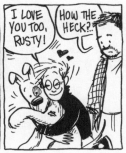

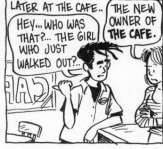

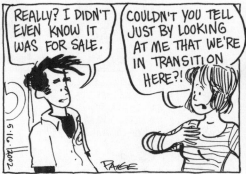

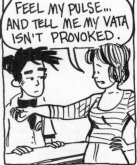

WHAT ARE YOU DOING?
FILLING OUT A JOB APPLICATION.
GEEZ... YOUR HANDWRITING REALLY STINKS!..
WHAT DO YOU MEAN?
IT'S UNREADABLE! ARE YOU CHALLENGED? ...OR JUST BLIND?
5.17.2002
PAIGE
?
HERE.., SEE FOR YOURSELF..
PAIGE
5.18.2002
WOW... YOU'RE RIGHT. THIS LOOKS LIKE IT WAS WRITTEN WITH A FORK!
WOW... I ALWAYS THOUGHT THAT WAS A PRINT IN THE WALLPAPER.
SPAGHETTI DINNER, 1996.
HEY, JANE!... ALL THIS TIME I THOUGHT YOU WERE A REAL BLOND!
HAND 'EM OVER..

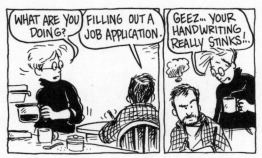

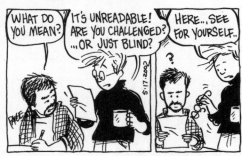

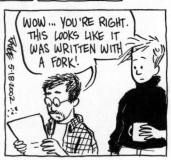

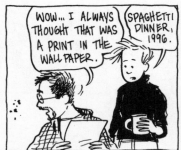

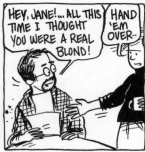

THE NEXT MORNING...

HMM...
Z
Z
PAIGE
JANE WON'T MIND IF I BORROW THESE FOR MY JOB INTERVIEW...
Z
Z
I'LL HAVE THEM BACK BEFORE SHE EVEN WAKES UP.
5.20.2002
Z
??
I THOUGHT I PUT MY GLASSES RIGHT HERE?...
WHERE COULD THEY BE?... ETHAN?...
5.21.2001
PAIGE
HMM... LOOKS LIKE A NOTE...
...BUT I CAN'T READ IT WITHOUT MY GLASSES!

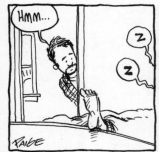

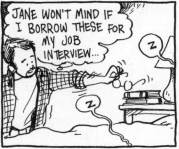

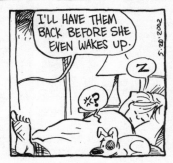

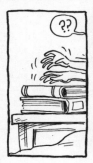

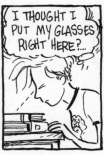

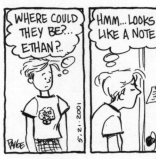

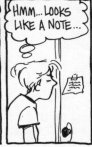

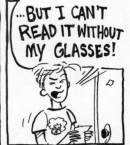

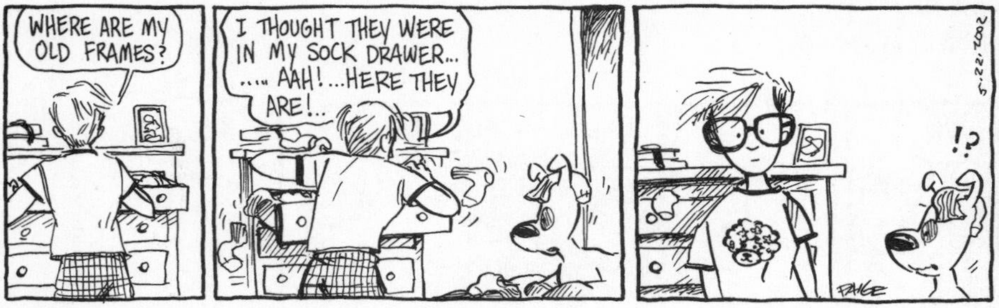
WHERE ARE MY OLD FRAMES?
I THOUGHT THEY WERE IN MY SOCK DRAWER... ..... AAH! ...HERE THEY ARE!...
5·22·2002
!?
PAIGE

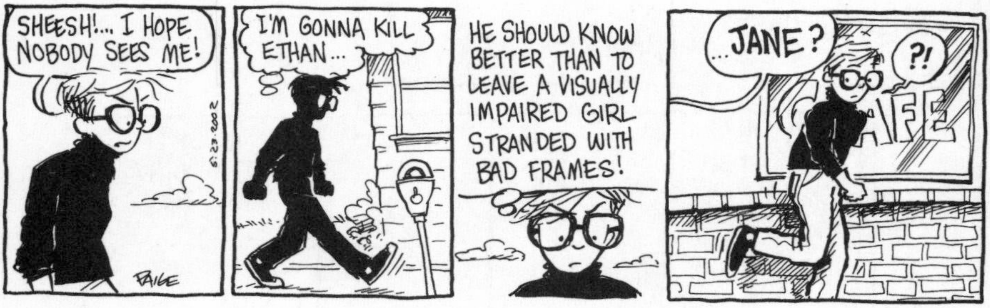
SHEESH!... I HOPE NOBODY SEES ME!
5·23·2002
PAIGE
I'M GONNA KILL ETHAN...
HE SHOULD KNOW BETTER THAN TO LEAVE A VISUALLY IMPAIRED GIRL STRANDED WITH BAD FRAMES!
...JANE?
?!
CAFE

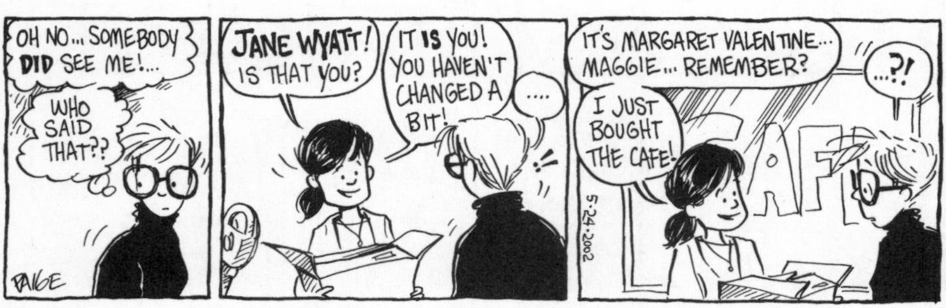
OH NO... SOMEBODY **DID** SEE ME!...
WHO SAID THAT??
PAIGE
JANE WYATT! IS THAT YOU?
IT **IS** YOU! YOU HAVEN'T CHANGED A BIT!
....
5·24·2002
IT'S MARGARET VALENTINE... MAGGIE... REMEMBER?
...?!
I JUST BOUGHT THE CAFE!

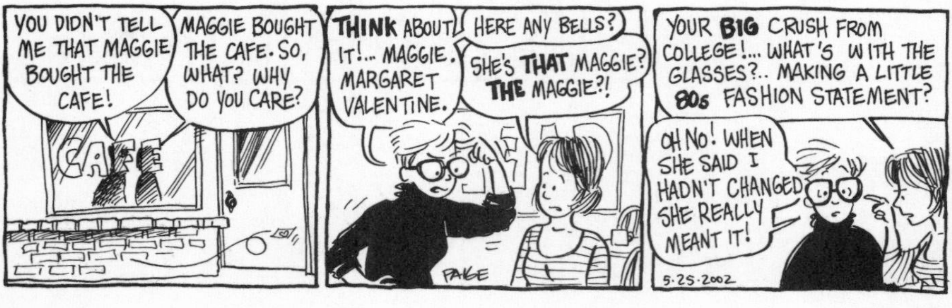
YOU DIDN'T TELL ME THAT MAGGIE BOUGHT THE CAFE!
MAGGIE BOUGHT THE CAFE. SO, WHAT? WHY DO YOU CARE?
CAFE
THINK ABOUT IT!... MAGGIE. MARGARET VALENTINE.
HERE ANY BELLS?
SHE'S **THAT** MAGGIE? **THE** MAGGIE?!
PAIGE
YOUR **BIG** CRUSH FROM COLLEGE!... WHAT'S WITH THE GLASSES?.. MAKING A LITTLE **80s** FASHION STATEMENT?
OH NO! WHEN SHE SAID I HADN'T CHANGED SHE REALLY MEANT IT!
5·25·2002

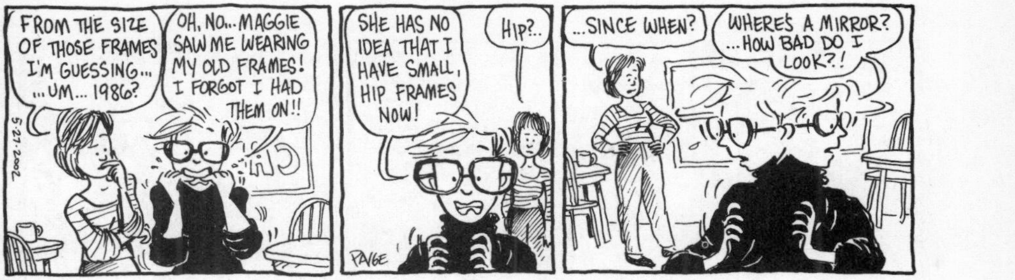
FROM THE SIZE OF THOSE FRAMES I'M GUESSING... ...UM... 1986?
OH, NO... MAGGIE SAW ME WEARING MY OLD FRAMES! I FORGOT I HAD THEM ON!!
5-27-2002
SHE HAS NO IDEA THAT I HAVE SMALL, HIP FRAMES NOW!
HIP?..
...SINCE WHEN?
WHERE'S A MIRROR? ...HOW BAD DO I LOOK?!

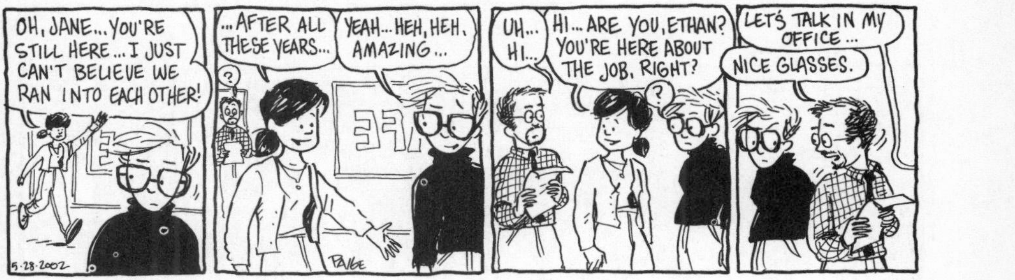
OH, JANE... YOU'RE STILL HERE... I JUST CAN'T BELIEVE WE RAN INTO EACH OTHER!
5-28-2002
...AFTER ALL THESE YEARS...
YEAH... HEH, HEH, AMAZING...
UH... HI...
HI... ARE YOU, ETHAN? YOU'RE HERE ABOUT THE JOB, RIGHT?
LET'S TALK IN MY OFFICE...
NICE GLASSES.

SHORTLY...

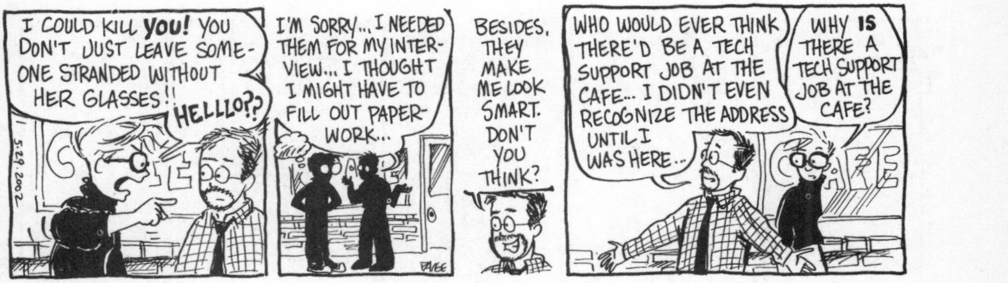
I COULD KILL **YOU!** YOU DON'T JUST LEAVE SOME-ONE STRANDED WITHOUT HER GLASSES!!
HELLLO??
5-29-2002
I'M SORRY... I NEEDED THEM FOR MY INTER-VIEW... I THOUGHT I MIGHT HAVE TO FILL OUT PAPER-WORK...
BESIDES, THEY MAKE ME LOOK SMART. DON'T YOU THINK?
WHO WOULD EVER THINK THERE'D BE A TECH SUPPORT JOB AT THE CAFE... I DIDN'T EVEN RECOGNIZE THE ADDRESS UNTIL I WAS HERE...
WHY **IS** THERE A TECH SUPPORT JOB AT THE CAFE?

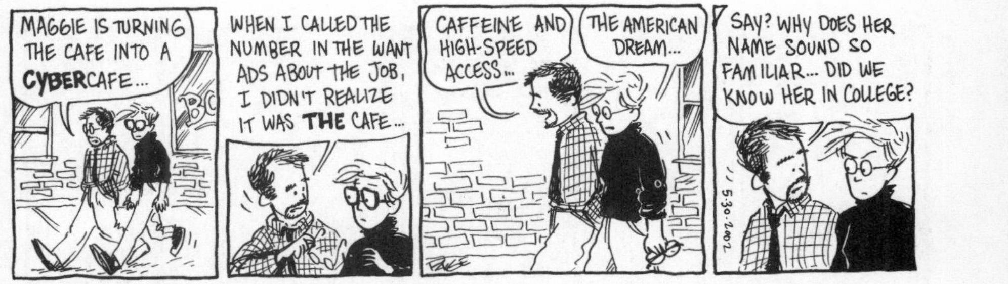
MAGGIE IS TURNING THE CAFE INTO A **CYBER**CAFE...
WHEN I CALLED THE NUMBER IN THE WANT ADS ABOUT THE JOB, I DIDN'T REALIZE IT WAS **THE** CAFE...
CAFFEINE AND HIGH-SPEED ACCESS...
THE AMERICAN DREAM...
SAY? WHY DOES HER NAME SOUND SO FAMILIAR... DID WE KNOW HER IN COLLEGE?
5-30-2002

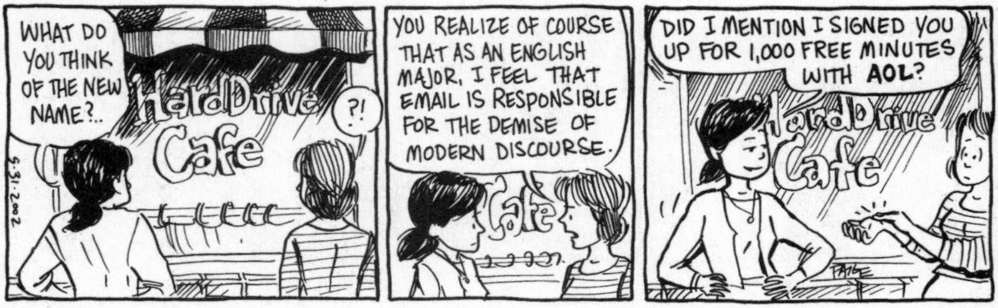
WHAT DO YOU THINK OF THE NEW NAME?...
HardDrive Cafe
?!
5.31.2002
YOU REALIZE OF COURSE THAT AS AN ENGLISH MAJOR, I FEEL THAT EMAIL IS RESPONSIBLE FOR THE DEMISE OF MODERN DISCOURSE.
DID I MENTION I SIGNED YOU UP FOR 1,000 FREE MINUTES WITH AOL?
PAIGE

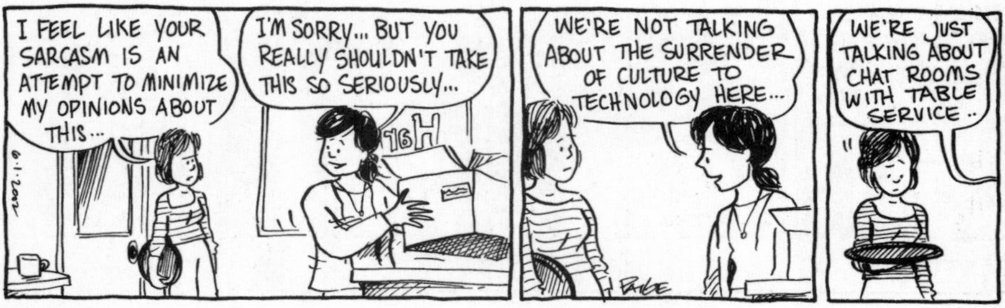
I FEEL LIKE YOUR SARCASM IS AN ATTEMPT TO MINIMIZE MY OPINIONS ABOUT THIS...
6.1.2002
I'M SORRY... BUT YOU REALLY SHOULDN'T TAKE THIS SO SERIOUSLY...
WE'RE NOT TALKING ABOUT THE SURRENDER OF CULTURE TO TECHNOLOGY HERE...
PAIGE
WE'RE JUST TALKING ABOUT CHAT ROOMS WITH TABLE SERVICE...

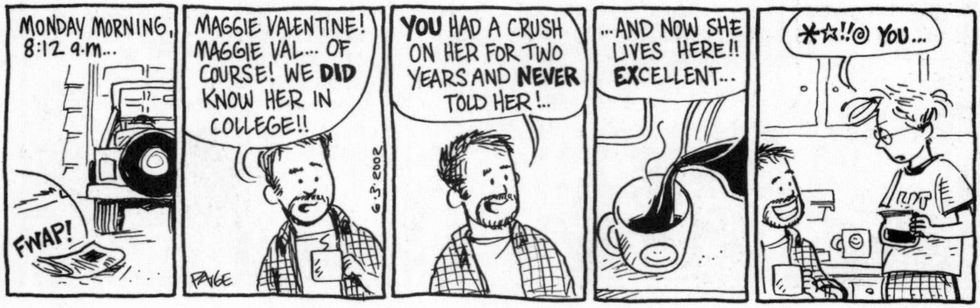
MONDAY MORNING, 8:12 a.m...
FWAP!
MAGGIE VALENTINE! MAGGIE VAL... OF COURSE! WE DID KNOW HER IN COLLEGE!!
6.3.2002
PAIGE
YOU HAD A CRUSH ON HER FOR TWO YEARS AND NEVER TOLD HER!...
...AND NOW SHE LIVES HERE!! EXCELLENT...
*☆!!@ YOU...

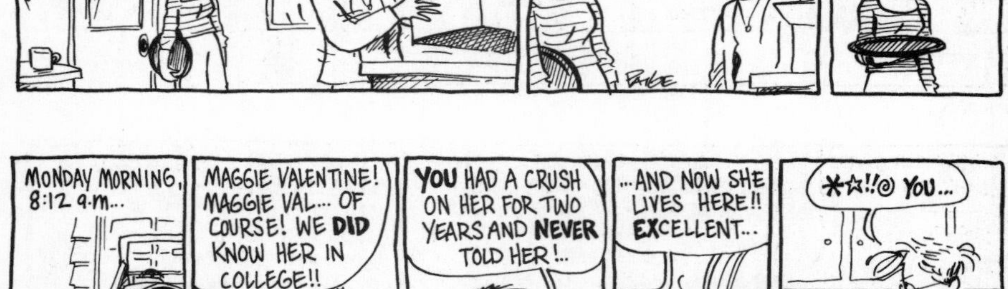
MONDAY MORNING 8:19 a.m...
OKAY, JANE... LET'S GET IT TOGETHER.
...LET'S TIGHTEN UP... MAGGIE IS BACK ...SO, WHAT?
6.4.2002
PAIGE
...DON'T GIVE ME THAT LOOK.

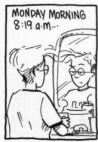

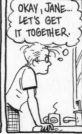

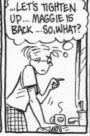

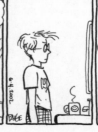

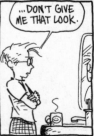

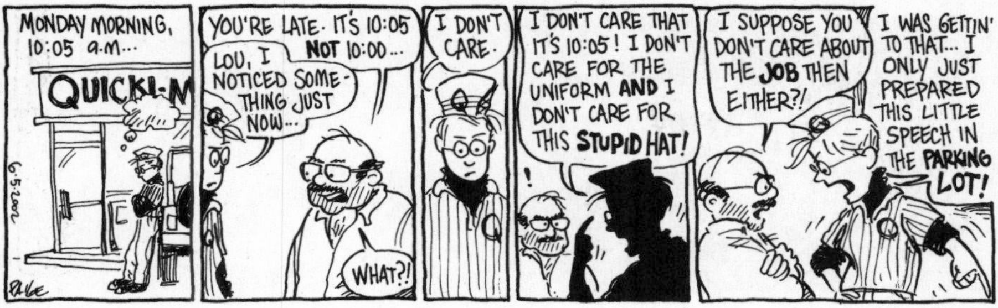
MONDAY MORNING, 10:05 a.m...
QUICKI-M
6.5.2002
PAIGE
YOU'RE LATE. IT'S 10:05 NOT 10:00...
LOU, I NOTICED SOME-THING JUST NOW...
WHAT?!
I DON'T CARE.
I DON'T CARE THAT IT'S 10:05! I DON'T CARE FOR THE UNIFORM AND I DON'T CARE FOR THIS STUPID HAT!
!
I SUPPOSE YOU DON'T CARE ABOUT THE JOB THEN EITHER?!
I WAS GETTIN' TO THAT... I ONLY JUST PREPARED THIS LITTLE SPEECH IN THE PARKING LOT!

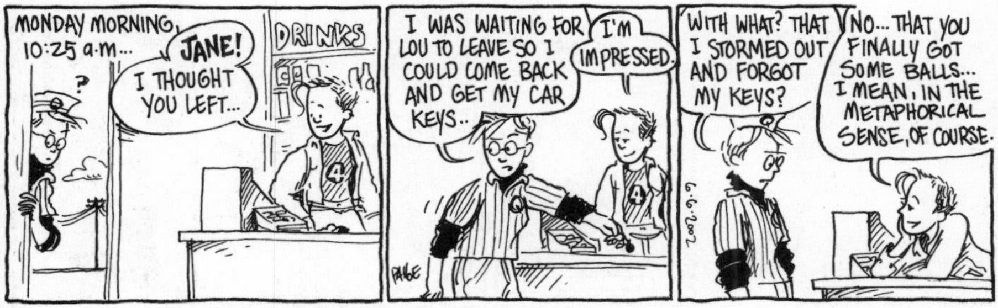
MONDAY MORNING, 10:25 a.m...
?
JANE! I THOUGHT YOU LEFT...
DRINKS
I WAS WAITING FOR LOU TO LEAVE SO I COULD COME BACK AND GET MY CAR KEYS...
I'M IMPRESSED.
PAIGE
WITH WHAT? THAT I STORMED OUT AND FORGOT MY KEYS?
NO... THAT YOU FINALLY GOT SOME BALLS... I MEAN, IN THE METAPHORICAL SENSE, OF COURSE.
6.6.2002

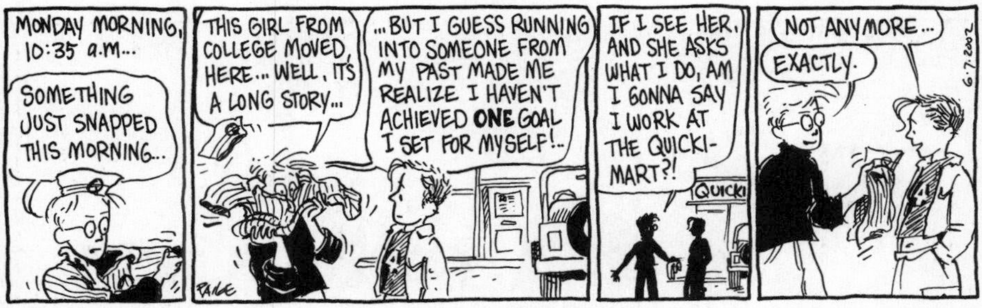
MONDAY MORNING, 10:35 a.m...
SOMETHING JUST SNAPPED THIS MORNING...
THIS GIRL FROM COLLEGE MOVED HERE... WELL, IT'S A LONG STORY...
PAIGE
...BUT I GUESS RUNNING INTO SOMEONE FROM MY PAST MADE ME REALIZE I HAVEN'T ACHIEVED ONE GOAL I SET FOR MYSELF!..
IF I SEE HER, AND SHE ASKS WHAT I DO, AM I GONNA SAY I WORK AT THE QUICKI-MART?!
QUICKI
NOT ANYMORE...
EXACTLY.
6.7.2002

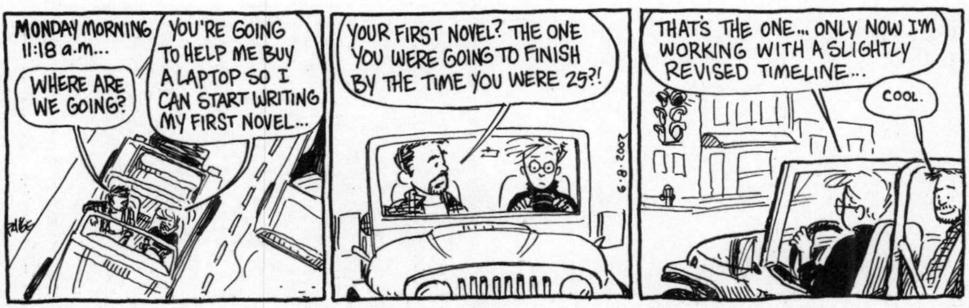
MONDAY MORNING 11:18 a.m...
WHERE ARE WE GOING?
YOU'RE GOING TO HELP ME BUY A LAPTOP SO I CAN START WRITING MY FIRST NOVEL...
PAIGE
YOUR FIRST NOVEL? THE ONE YOU WERE GOING TO FINISH BY THE TIME YOU WERE 25?!
6.8.2002
THAT'S THE ONE... ONLY NOW I'M WORKING WITH A SLIGHTLY REVISED TIMELINE...
COOL.

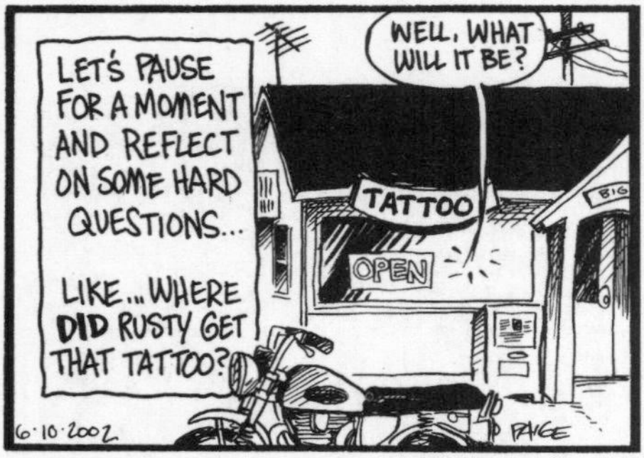
LET'S PAUSE FOR A MOMENT AND REFLECT ON SOME HARD QUESTIONS...
LIKE... WHERE **DID** RUSTY GET THAT TATTOO?
WELL, WHAT WILL IT BE?
TATTOO
OPEN
6·10·2002
PAIGE

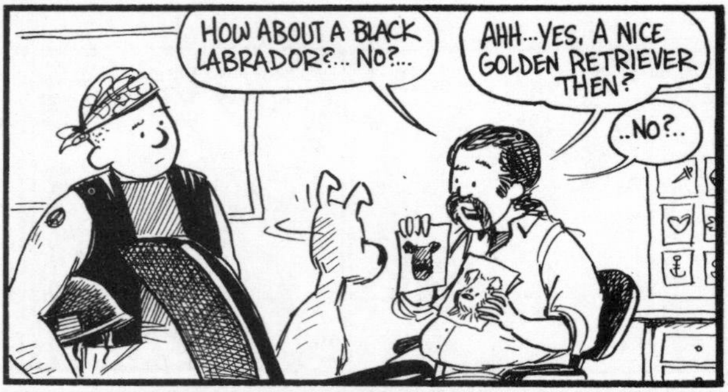
HOW ABOUT A BLACK LABRADOR?... NO?...
AHH...YES, A NICE GOLDEN RETRIEVER THEN?
..NO?..

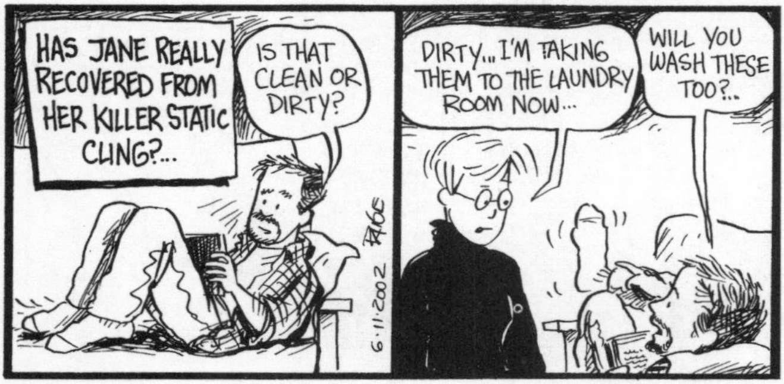
HAS JANE REALLY RECOVERED FROM HER KILLER STATIC CLING?...
IS THAT CLEAN OR DIRTY?
PAIGE
6·11·2002
DIRTY... I'M TAKING THEM TO THE LAUNDRY ROOM NOW...
WILL YOU WASH THESE TOO?..

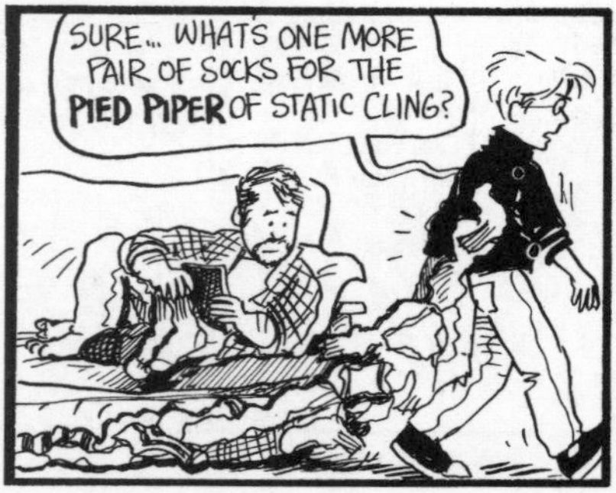
SURE... WHATS ONE MORE PAIR OF SOCKS FOR THE **PIED PIPER** OF STATIC CLING?

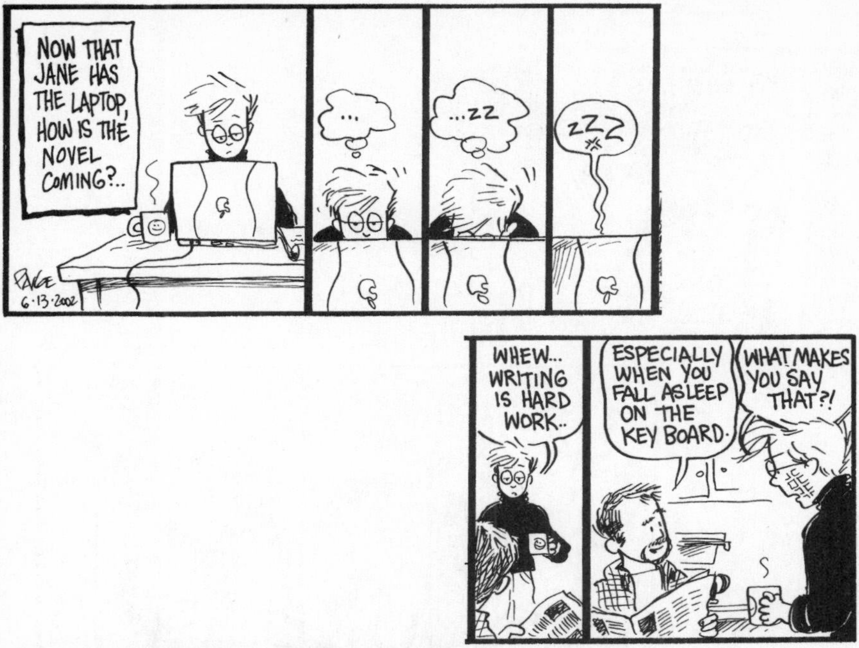
NOW THAT JANE HAS THE LAPTOP, HOW IS THE NOVEL COMING?..
...
...ZZ
ZZZ
PAIGE 6·13·2002
WHEW... WRITING IS HARD WORK..
ESPECIALLY WHEN YOU FALL ASLEEP ON THE KEY BOARD.
WHAT MAKES YOU SAY THAT?!

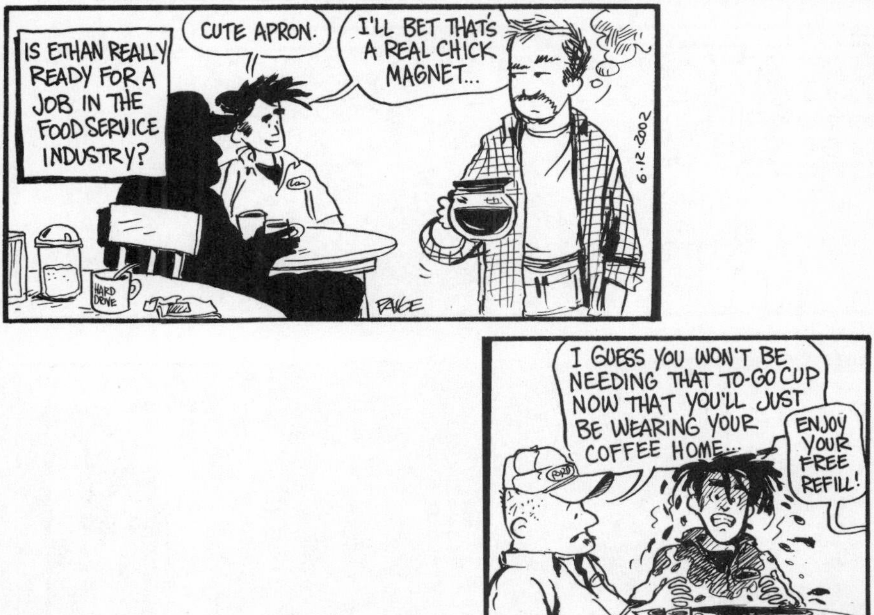
IS ETHAN REALLY READY FOR A JOB IN THE FOOD SERVICE INDUSTRY?
CUTE APRON.
I'LL BET THAT'S A REAL CHICK MAGNET...
6·12·2002
HARD DRIVE
PAIGE
I GUESS YOU WON'T BE NEEDING THAT TO-GO CUP NOW THAT YOU'LL JUST BE WEARING YOUR COFFEE HOME...
ENJOY YOUR FREE REFILL!

WHERE IS DIXIE?
I DUNNO... WHEN I CAME BACK FROM MY ROAD TRIP WITH JANE, SHE WAS GONE..
I SAW HER AT THE COFFEE SHOP RIGHT BEFORE SHE LEFT...
6·14·2002 PAGE

LEFT??
YEAH...AFTER YOU ASKED HER TO MOVE OUT, I GUESS SHE DECIDED TO GO BACK TO MEMPHIS.
WHY DO YOU CARE? YOU HADN'T EVEN NOTICED...
I WAS GETTING AROUND TO IT!
SHE WAS A REAL BISCUIT TOO... NOT ENOUGH OF THOSE HERE. ...*@!☆ SHAME.

IS DENTAL SCHOOL REALLY A VIABLE CAREER CHANGE FOR EVELYN?
...AND HOW DOES THAT ROOT CANAL FEEL?...
... BE PRESENT WITH THE PAIN... JUST MOVE THROUGH IT...
OWWWWW....
6·15·2002
PAGE

IS THE UNIVERSE INFINITE, OR JUST REALLY BIG?
FOCUS, PLEASE..
RIGHT... SORRY.

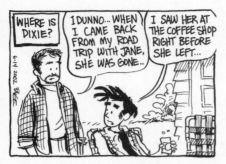

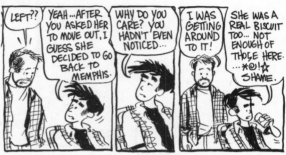

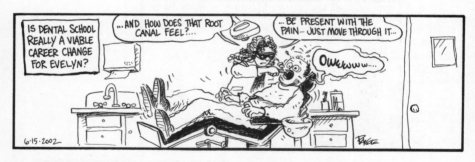

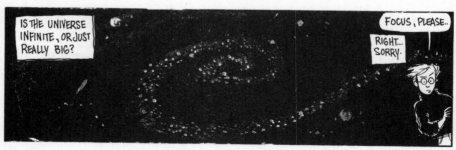

OKAY, FOLKS... WE'RE BACK ON TRACK...

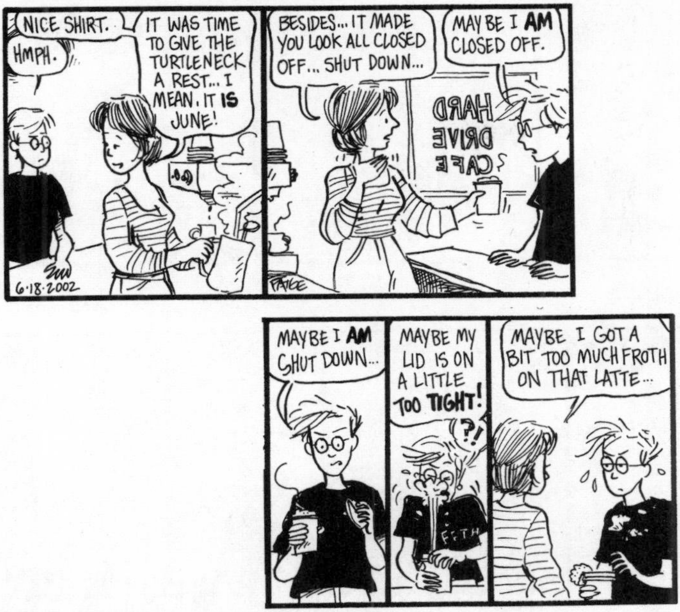
NICE SHIRT.
HMPH.
IT WAS TIME TO GIVE THE TURTLENECK A REST... I MEAN, IT **IS** JUNE!
BESIDES... IT MADE YOU LOOK ALL CLOSED OFF... SHUT DOWN...
MAYBE I **AM** CLOSED OFF.
HARD DRIVE CAFE
6·18·2002
PAIGE
MAYBE I **AM** SHUT DOWN...
MAYBE MY LID IS ON A LITTLE **TOO TIGHT**!
?!
MAYBE I GOT A BIT TOO MUCH FROTH ON THAT LATTE...

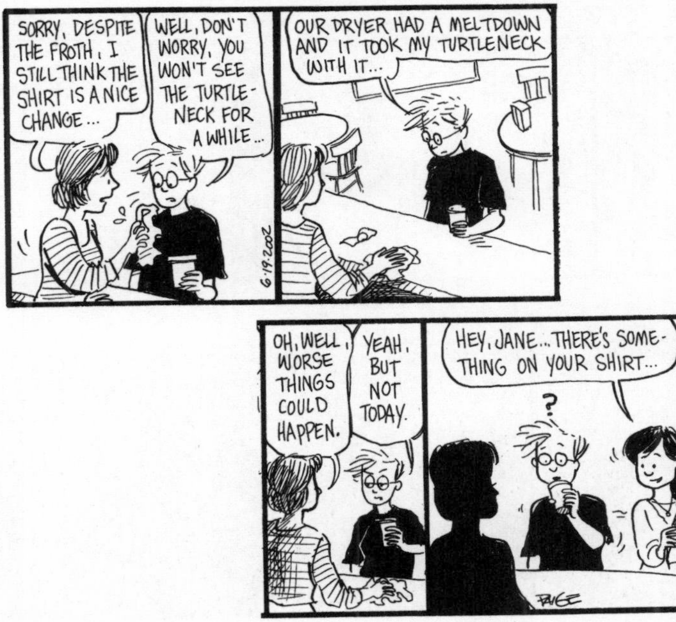
SORRY, DESPITE THE FROTH, I STILL THINK THE SHIRT IS A NICE CHANGE...
WELL, DON'T WORRY, YOU WON'T SEE THE TURTLE-NECK FOR A WHILE...
6·19·2002
OUR DRYER HAD A MELTDOWN AND IT TOOK MY TURTLENECK WITH IT...
OH, WELL, WORSE THINGS COULD HAPPEN.
YEAH, BUT NOT TODAY.
HEY, JANE... THERE'S SOME-THING ON YOUR SHIRT...
?
PAIGE

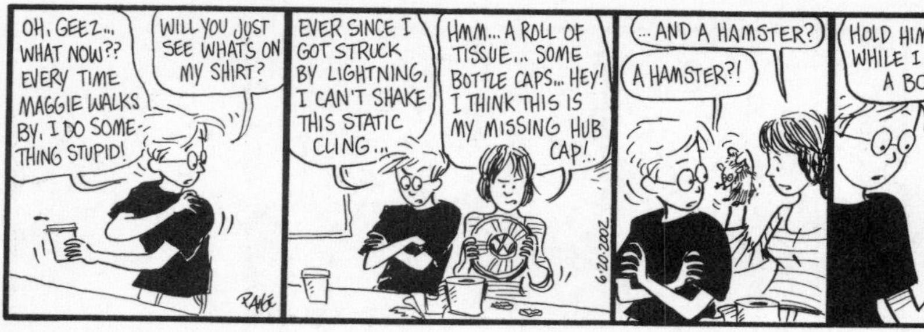
OH, GEEZ... WHAT NOW?? EVERY TIME MAGGIE WALKS BY, I DO SOMETHING STUPID!
WILL YOU JUST SEE WHAT'S ON MY SHIRT?
PAIGE
EVER SINCE I GOT STRUCK BY LIGHTNING, I CAN'T SHAKE THIS STATIC CLING...
HMM... A ROLL OF TISSUE... SOME BOTTLE CAPS... HEY! I THINK THIS IS MY MISSING HUB CAP!..
6·20·2002
...AND A HAMSTER?
A HAMSTER?!
HOLD HIM A MINUTE WHILE I LOOK FOR A BOX...
?!

LATER, AT JANE'S...

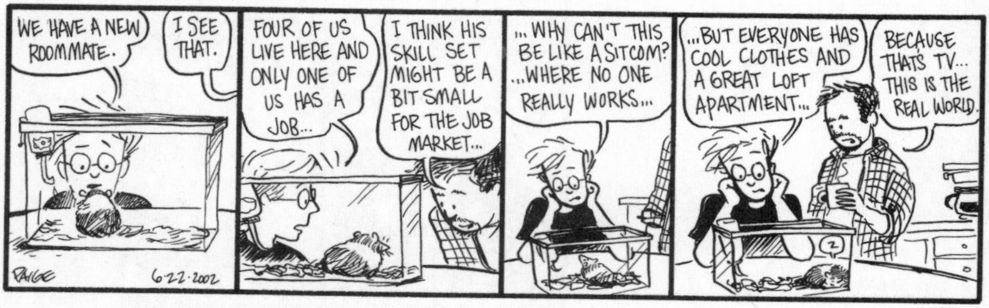
WE HAVE A NEW ROOMMATE.
I SEE THAT.
PAIGE
6·22·2002
FOUR OF US LIVE HERE AND ONLY ONE OF US HAS A JOB...
I THINK HIS SKILL SET MIGHT BE A BIT SMALL FOR THE JOB MARKET...
...WHY CAN'T THIS BE LIKE A SITCOM? ...WHERE NO ONE REALLY WORKS...
...BUT EVERYONE HAS COOL CLOTHES AND A GREAT LOFT APARTMENT...
BECAUSE THAT'S TV... THIS IS THE REAL WORLD.

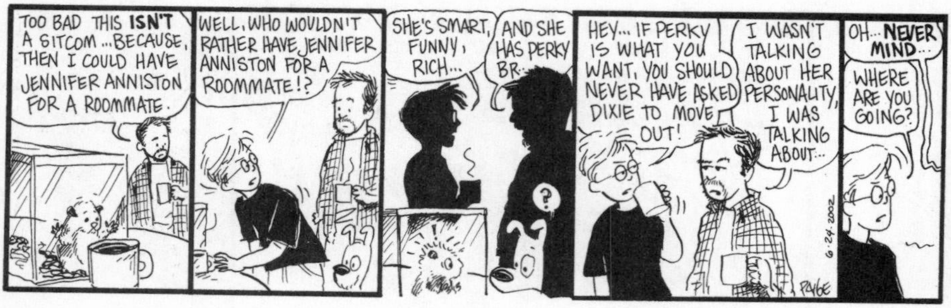
TOO BAD THIS **ISN'T** A SITCOM... BECAUSE, THEN I COULD HAVE JENNIFER ANNISTON FOR A ROOMMATE.
WELL, WHO WOULDN'T RATHER HAVE JENNIFER ANNISTON FOR A ROOMMATE!?
SHE'S SMART, FUNNY, RICH...
AND SHE HAS PERKY BR...
?
HEY... IF PERKY IS WHAT YOU WANT, YOU SHOULD NEVER HAVE ASKED DIXIE TO MOVE OUT!
I WASN'T TALKING ABOUT HER PERSONALITY, I WAS TALKING ABOUT...
6·24·2002
PAIGE
OH... **NEVER MIND**...
WHERE ARE YOU GOING?

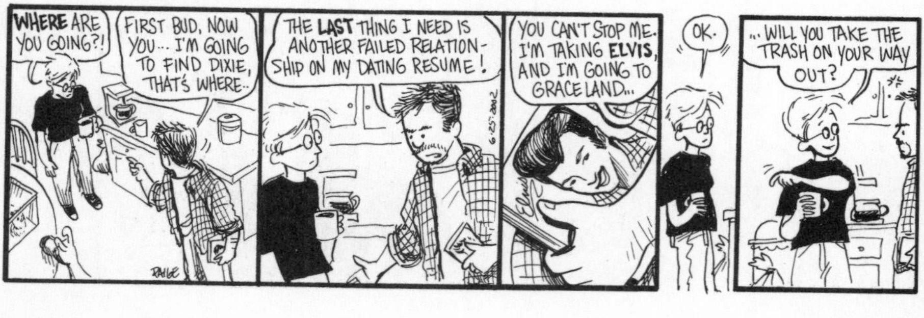
WHERE ARE YOU GOING?!
FIRST BUD, NOW YOU... I'M GOING TO FIND DIXIE, THAT'S WHERE..
PAIGE
THE **LAST** THING I NEED IS ANOTHER FAILED RELATIONSHIP ON MY DATING RESUME!
6·25·2002
YOU CAN'T STOP ME. I'M TAKING **ELVIS**, AND I'M GOING TO GRACELAND...
OK.
...WILL YOU TAKE THE TRASH ON YOUR WAY OUT?

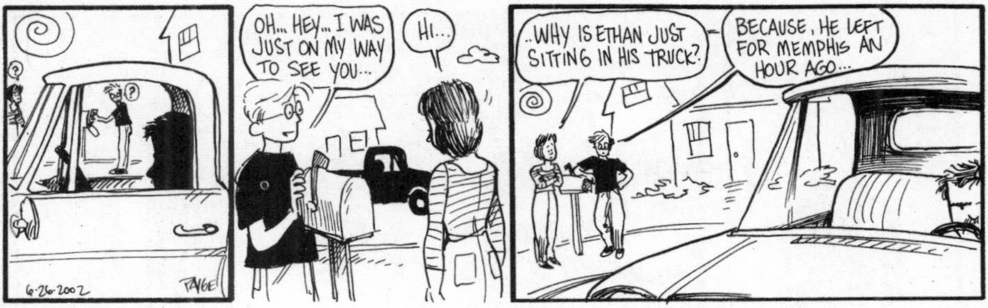
6·26·2002
PAIGE
OH... HEY... I WAS JUST ON MY WAY TO SEE YOU...
HI...
..WHY IS ETHAN JUST SITTING IN HIS TRUCK?
BECAUSE, HE LEFT FOR MEMPHIS AN HOUR AGO...

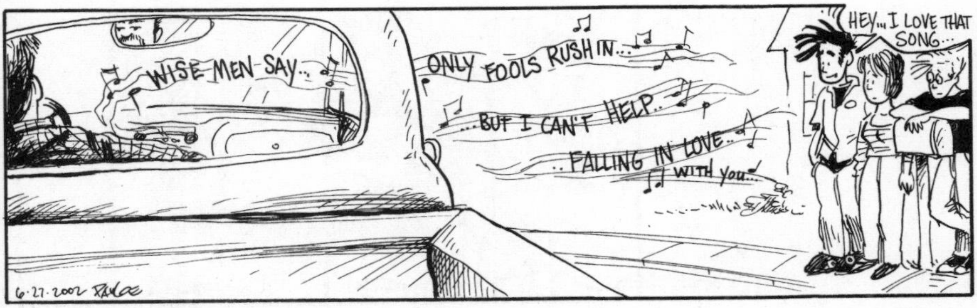
WISE MEN SAY...
ONLY FOOLS RUSH IN...
...BUT I CAN'T HELP..
.. FALLING IN LOVE..
WITH YOU..
HEY... I LOVE THAT SONG...
6·27·2002 PAIGE

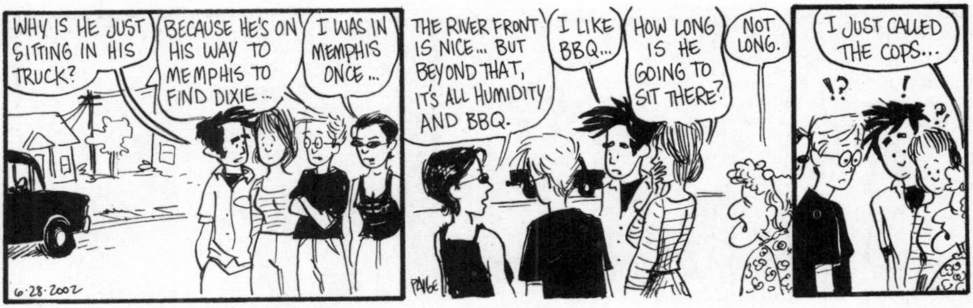
WHY IS HE JUST SITTING IN HIS TRUCK?
BECAUSE HE'S ON HIS WAY TO MEMPHIS TO FIND DIXIE...
I WAS IN MEMPHIS ONCE...
6·28·2002
THE RIVER FRONT IS NICE... BUT BEYOND THAT, IT'S ALL HUMIDITY AND BBQ.
I LIKE BBQ...
HOW LONG IS HE GOING TO SIT THERE?
NOT LONG.
PAIGE
I JUST CALLED THE COPS...
!?
!

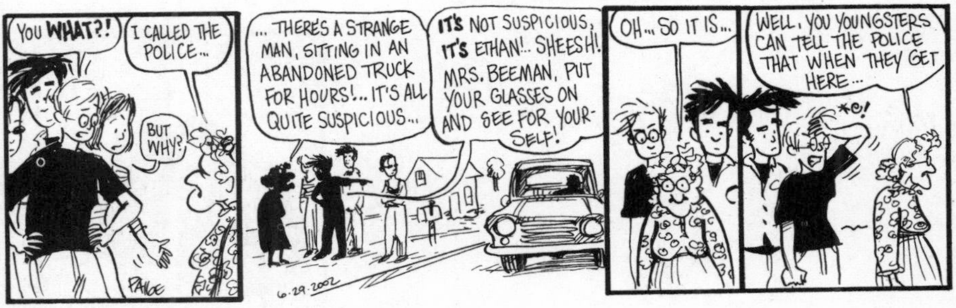
YOU WHAT?!
I CALLED THE POLICE...
BUT WHY?
PAIGE
... THERE'S A STRANGE MAN, SITTING IN AN ABANDONED TRUCK FOR HOURS!... IT'S ALL QUITE SUSPICIOUS...
IT'S NOT SUSPICIOUS, IT'S ETHAN!.. SHEESH! MRS. BEEMAN, PUT YOUR GLASSES ON AND SEE FOR YOURSELF!
6·29·2002
OH... SO IT IS...
WELL, YOU YOUNGSTERS CAN TELL THE POLICE THAT WHEN THEY GET HERE...

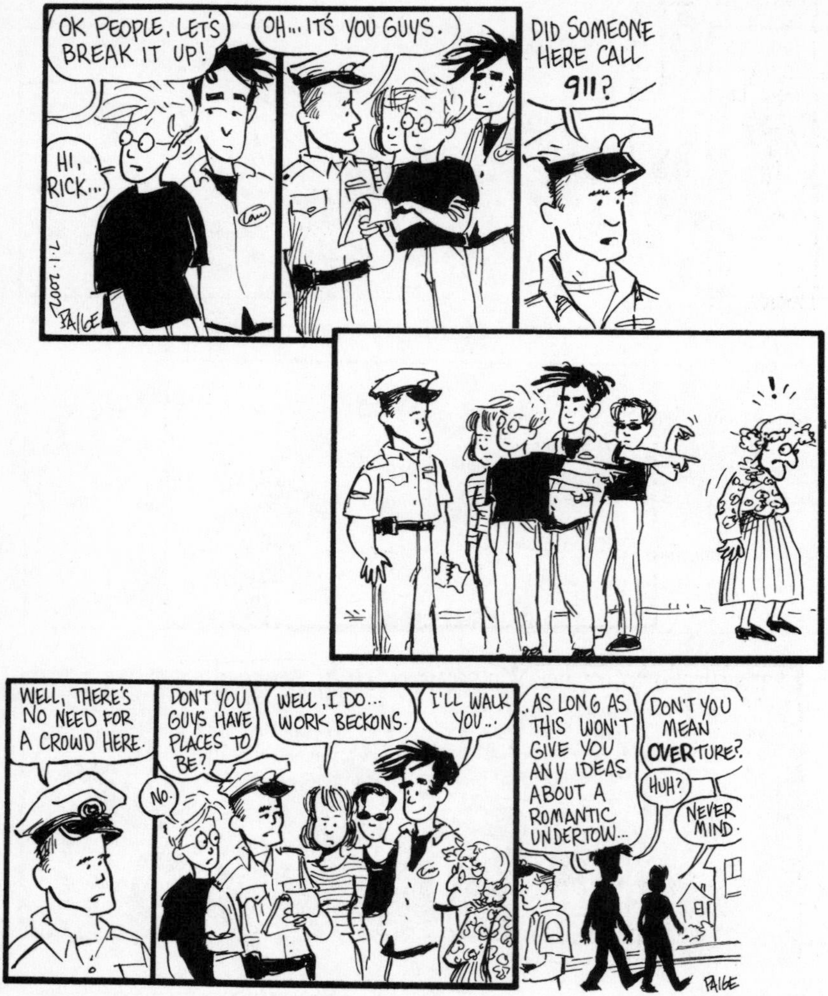
OK PEOPLE, LET'S BREAK IT UP!
HI, RICK...
7.1.2002
PAIGE
OH... IT'S YOU GUYS.
DID SOMEONE HERE CALL 911?
!
WELL, THERE'S NO NEED FOR A CROWD HERE.
DON'T YOU GUYS HAVE PLACES TO BE?
NO.
WELL, I DO... WORK BECKONS.
I'LL WALK YOU...
..AS LONG AS THIS WON'T GIVE YOU ANY IDEAS ABOUT A ROMANTIC UNDERTOW...
DON'T YOU MEAN OVERTURE?
HUH?
NEVER MIND.
PAIGE

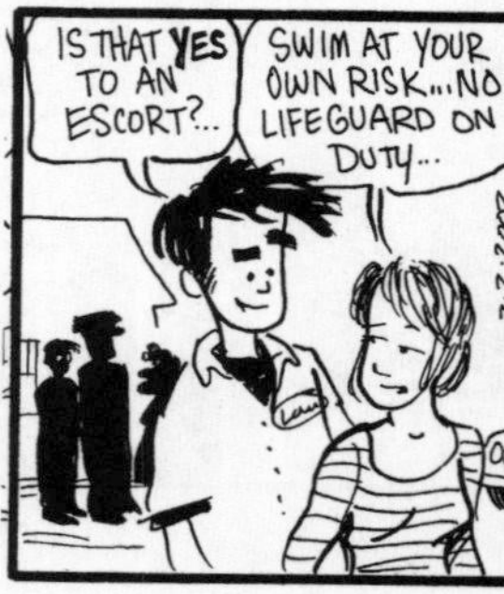
IS THAT YES TO AN ESCORT?...
SWIM AT YOUR OWN RISK...NO LIFEGUARD ON DUTY...
7.2.2002

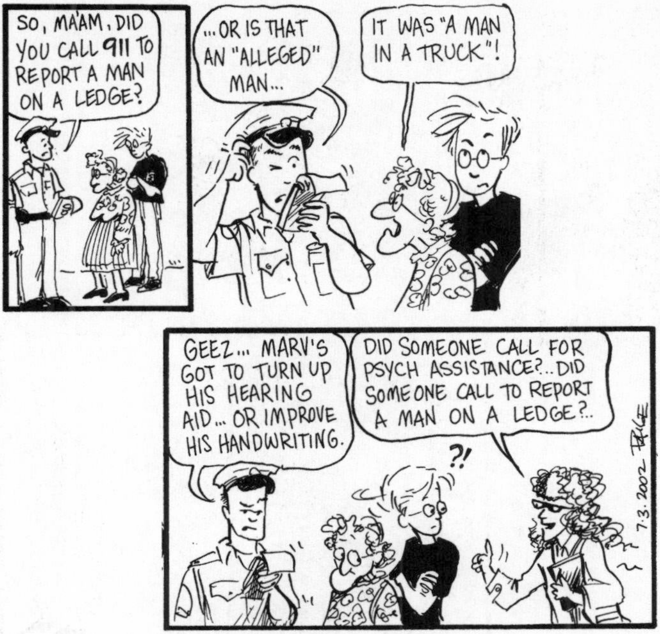
SO, MA'AM, DID YOU CALL 911 TO REPORT A MAN ON A LEDGE?
...OR IS THAT AN "ALLEGED" MAN...
IT WAS "A MAN IN A TRUCK"!
GEEZ... MARV'S GOT TO TURN UP HIS HEARING AID... OR IMPROVE HIS HANDWRITING.
DID SOMEONE CALL FOR PSYCH ASSISTANCE?.. DID SOMEONE CALL TO REPORT A MAN ON A LEDGE?..
?!
PAIGE
7.3.2002

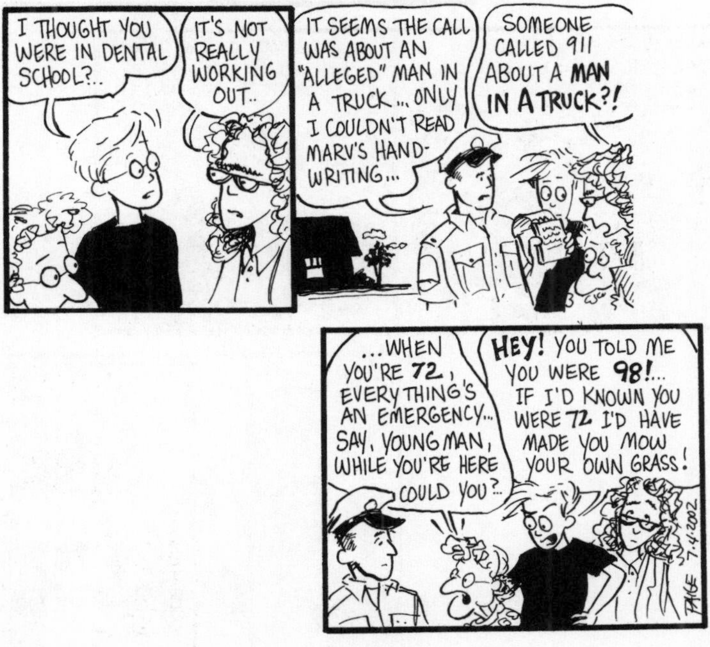
I THOUGHT YOU WERE IN DENTAL SCHOOL?..
IT'S NOT REALLY WORKING OUT..
IT SEEMS THE CALL WAS ABOUT AN "ALLEGED" MAN IN A TRUCK... ONLY I COULDN'T READ MARV'S HAND-WRITING...
SOMEONE CALLED 911 ABOUT A **MAN IN A TRUCK**?!
...WHEN YOU'RE 72, EVERYTHING'S AN EMERGENCY... SAY, YOUNG MAN, WHILE YOU'RE HERE COULD YOU?..
HEY! YOU TOLD ME YOU WERE **98**!... IF I'D KNOWN YOU WERE 72 I'D HAVE MADE YOU MOW YOUR OWN GRASS!
7.4.2002
PAIGE

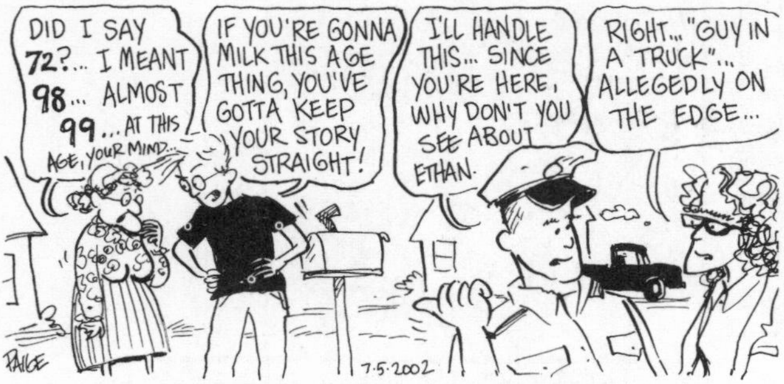
DID I SAY 72?... I MEANT 98... ALMOST 99... AT THIS AGE, YOUR MIND...
IF YOU'RE GONNA MILK THIS AGE THING, YOU'VE GOTTA KEEP YOUR STORY STRAIGHT!
I'LL HANDLE THIS... SINCE YOU'RE HERE, WHY DON'T YOU SEE ABOUT ETHAN.
RIGHT... "GUY IN A TRUCK"... ALLEGEDLY ON THE EDGE...
PAIGE
7·5·2002

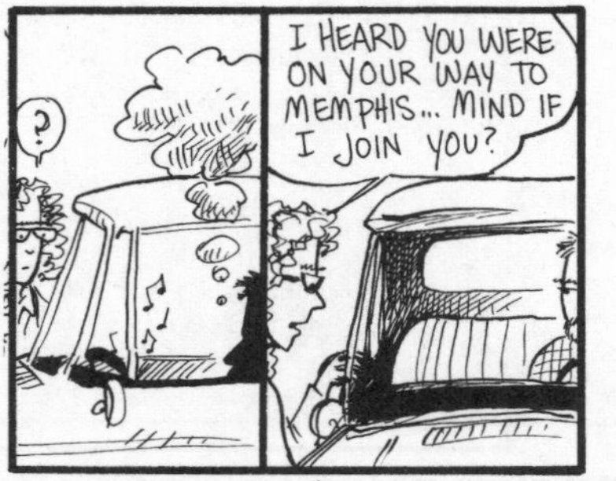
?
I HEARD YOU WERE ON YOUR WAY TO MEMPHIS... MIND IF I JOIN YOU?

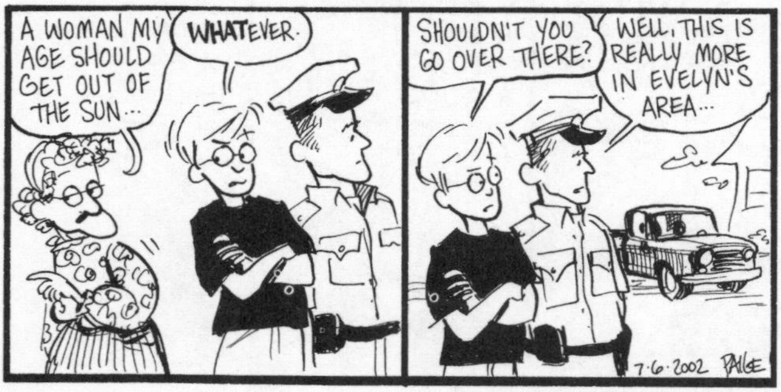
A WOMAN MY AGE SHOULD GET OUT OF THE SUN...
WHATEVER.
SHOULDN'T YOU GO OVER THERE?
WELL, THIS IS REALLY MORE IN EVELYN'S AREA...
7·6·2002 PAIGE

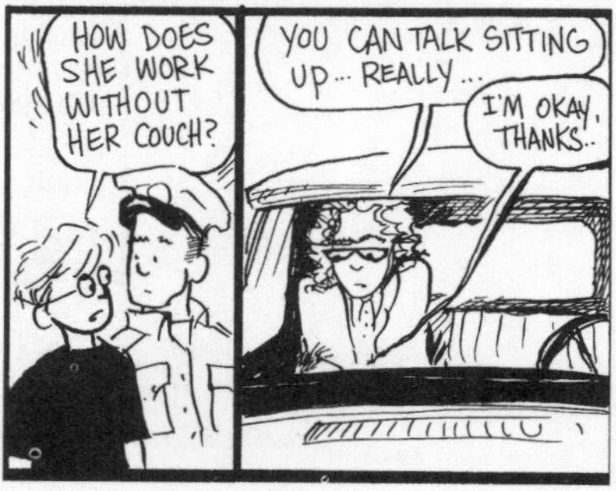
HOW DOES SHE WORK WITHOUT HER COUCH?
YOU CAN TALK SITTING UP... REALLY...
I'M OKAY, THANKS..

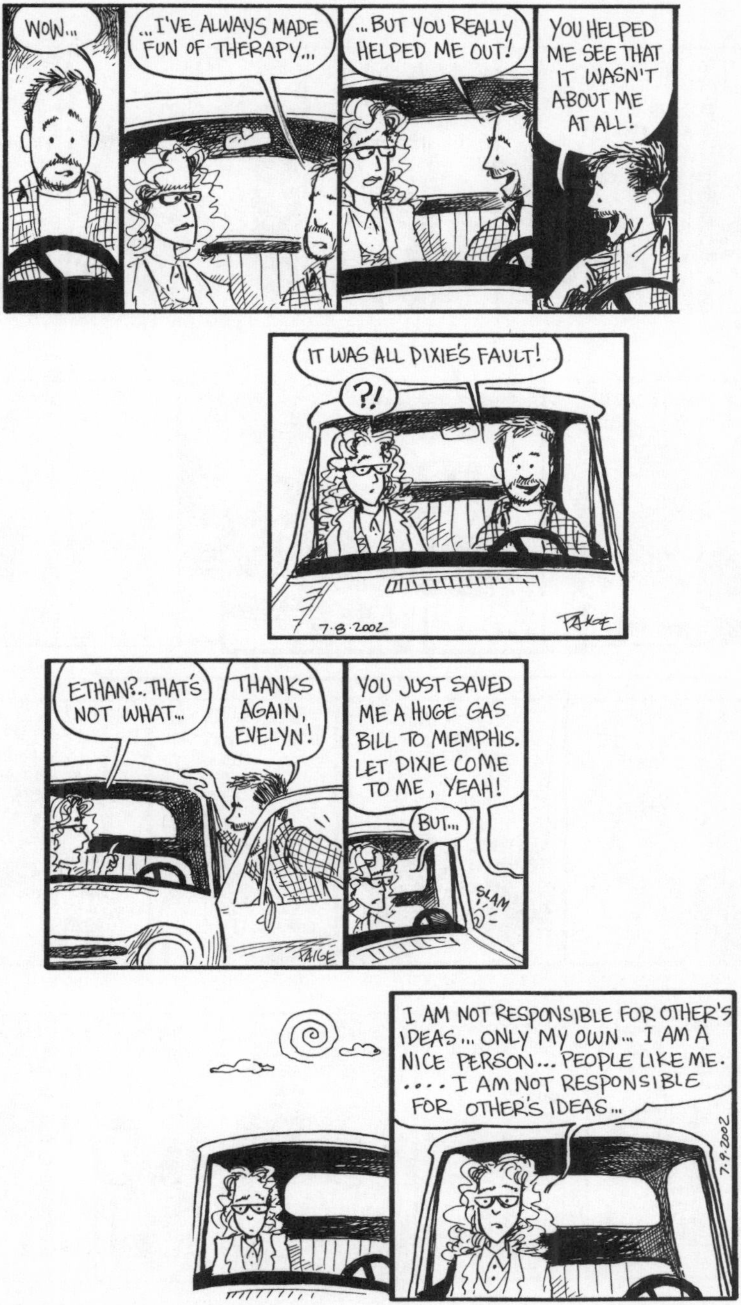
WOW...
...I'VE ALWAYS MADE FUN OF THERAPY...
...BUT YOU REALLY HELPED ME OUT!
YOU HELPED ME SEE THAT IT WASN'T ABOUT ME AT ALL!
IT WAS ALL DIXIE'S FAULT!
?!
7·8·2002
PAIGE
ETHAN?..THAT'S NOT WHAT...
THANKS AGAIN, EVELYN!
PAIGE
YOU JUST SAVED ME A HUGE GAS BILL TO MEMPHIS. LET DIXIE COME TO ME, YEAH!
BUT...
SLAM
I AM NOT RESPONSIBLE FOR OTHER'S IDEAS... ONLY MY OWN... I AM A NICE PERSON... PEOPLE LIKE ME. .... I AM NOT RESPONSIBLE FOR OTHER'S IDEAS...
7·9·2002

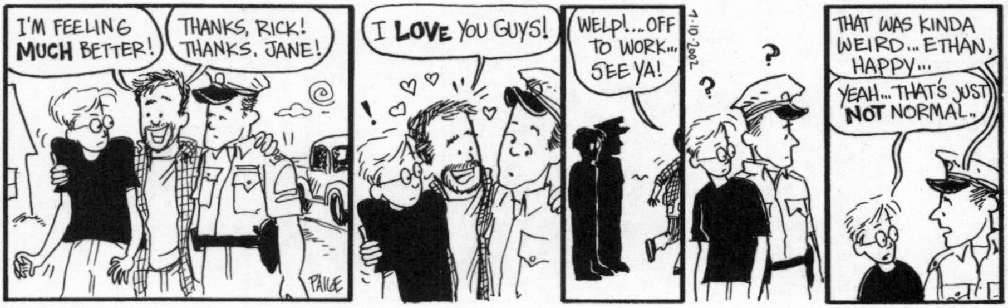
I'M FEELING MUCH BETTER!
THANKS, RICK! THANKS, JANE!
PAIGE
I LOVE YOU GUYS!
WELP!...OFF TO WORK... SEE YA!
7-10-2002
THAT WAS KINDA WEIRD... ETHAN, HAPPY...
YEAH... THAT'S JUST NOT NORMAL..

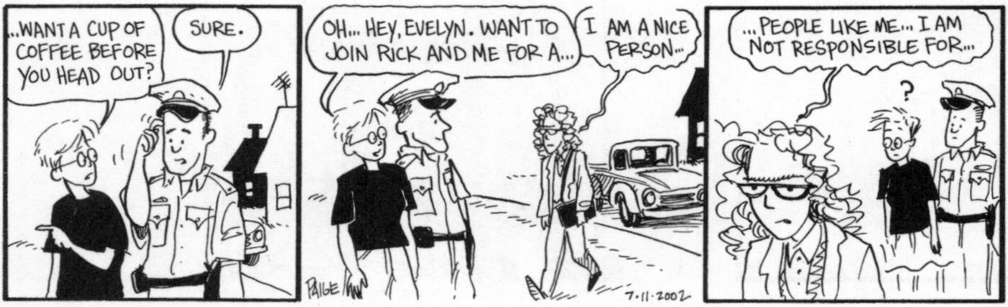
..WANT A CUP OF COFFEE BEFORE YOU HEAD OUT?
SURE.
OH... HEY, EVELYN. WANT TO JOIN RICK AND ME FOR A...
I AM A NICE PERSON...
PAIGE
7-11-2002
...PEOPLE LIKE ME... I AM NOT RESPONSIBLE FOR...

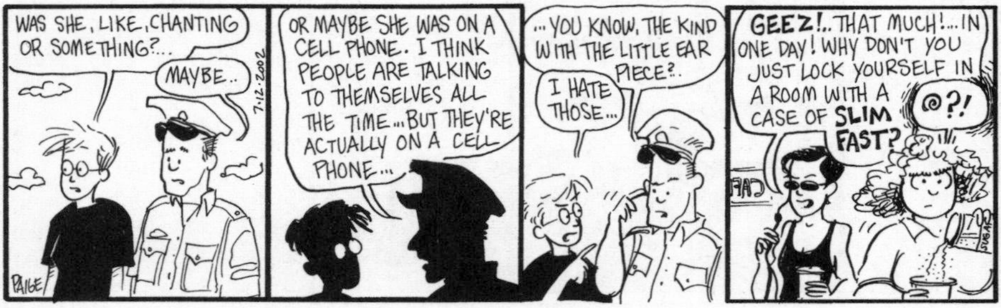
WAS SHE, LIKE, CHANTING OR SOMETHING?...
MAYBE..
7-12-2002
PAIGE
OR MAYBE SHE WAS ON A CELL PHONE. I THINK PEOPLE ARE TALKING TO THEMSELVES ALL THE TIME... BUT THEY'RE ACTUALLY ON A CELL PHONE...
...YOU KNOW, THE KIND WITH THE LITTLE EAR PIECE?..
I HATE THOSE...
GEEZ!.. THAT MUCH!... IN ONE DAY! WHY DON'T YOU JUST LOCK YOURSELF IN A ROOM WITH A CASE OF SLIM FAST?
@?!

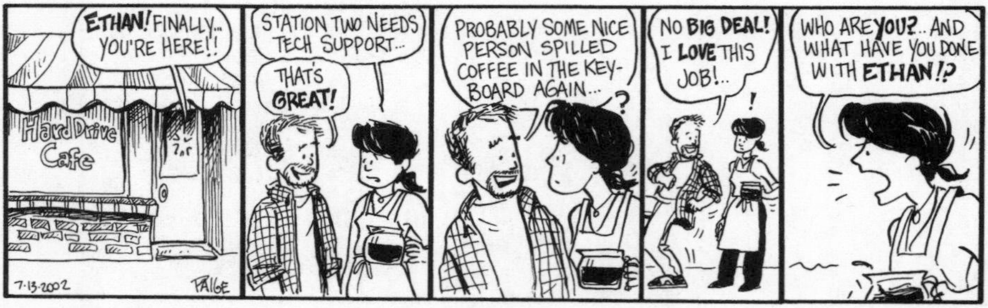
ETHAN! FINALLY... YOU'RE HERE!!
Hard Drive Cafe
7-13-2002
PAIGE
STATION TWO NEEDS TECH SUPPORT...
THAT'S GREAT!
PROBABLY SOME NICE PERSON SPILLED COFFEE IN THE KEY-BOARD AGAIN...
NO BIG DEAL! I LOVE THIS JOB!..
WHO ARE YOU?.. AND WHAT HAVE YOU DONE WITH ETHAN!?

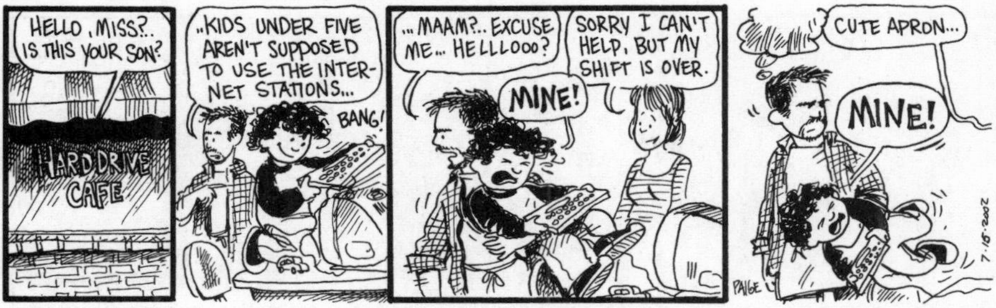
HELLO, MISS?.. IS THIS YOUR SON?
HARD DRIVE CAFE
..KIDS UNDER FIVE AREN'T SUPPOSED TO USE THE INTER-NET STATIONS...
BANG!
...MAAM?.. EXCUSE ME... HELLLOOO?
MINE!
SORRY I CAN'T HELP, BUT MY SHIFT IS OVER.
CUTE APRON...
MINE!
PAIGE
7.15.2002

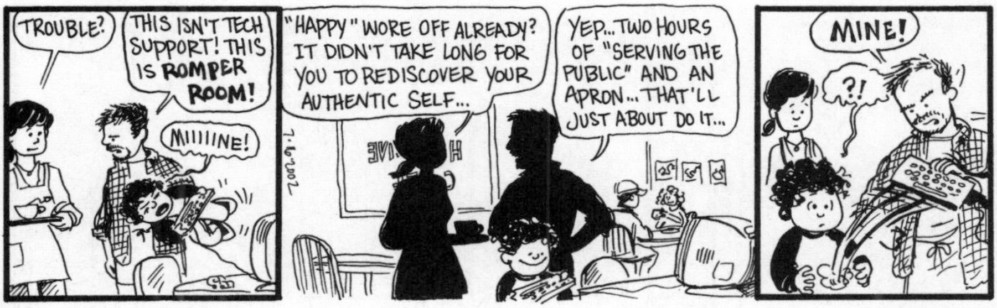
TROUBLE?
THIS ISN'T TECH SUPPORT! THIS IS ROMPER ROOM!
MIIIIINE!
7.16.2002
"HAPPY" WORE OFF ALREADY? IT DIDN'T TAKE LONG FOR YOU TO REDISCOVER YOUR AUTHENTIC SELF...
YEP... TWO HOURS OF "SERVING THE PUBLIC" AND AN APRON... THAT'LL JUST ABOUT DO IT...
MINE!
?!

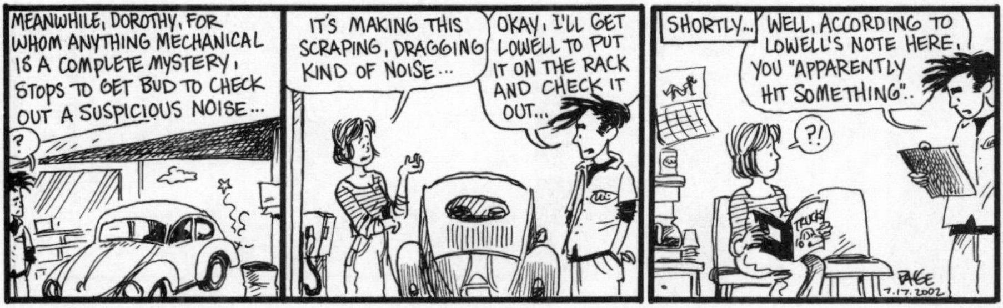
MEANWHILE, DOROTHY, FOR WHOM ANYTHING MECHANICAL IS A COMPLETE MYSTERY, STOPS TO GET BUD TO CHECK OUT A SUSPICIOUS NOISE...
?
IT'S MAKING THIS SCRAPING, DRAGGING KIND OF NOISE...
OKAY, I'LL GET LOWELL TO PUT IT ON THE RACK AND CHECK IT OUT...
SHORTLY...
WELL, ACCORDING TO LOWELL'S NOTE HERE, YOU "APPARENTLY HIT SOMETHING"..
?!
TRUCKS
PAIGE
7.17.2002

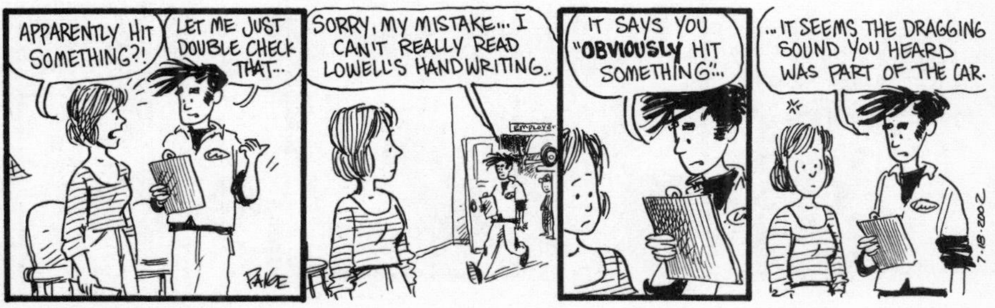
APPARENTLY HIT SOMETHING?!
LET ME JUST DOUBLE CHECK THAT...
PAIGE
SORRY, MY MISTAKE... I CAN'T REALLY READ LOWELL'S HANDWRITING..
EMPLOYEE
IT SAYS YOU "OBVIOUSLY HIT SOMETHING"...
...IT SEEMS THE DRAGGING SOUND YOU HEARD WAS PART OF THE CAR.
7.18.2002

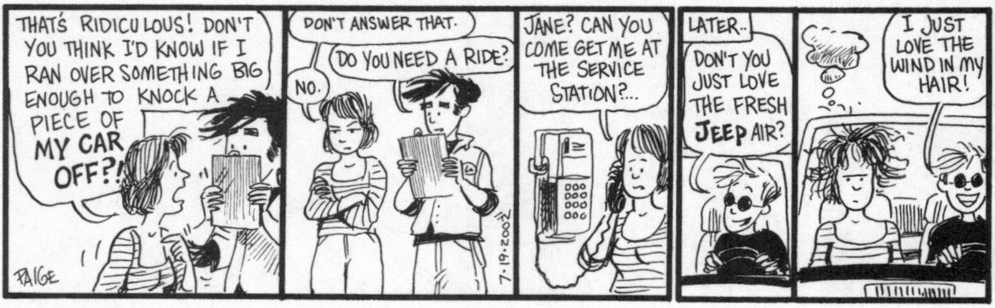
THAT'S RIDICULOUS! DON'T YOU THINK I'D KNOW IF I RAN OVER SOMETHING BIG ENOUGH TO KNOCK A PIECE OF MY CAR OFF?!
DON'T ANSWER THAT.
NO.
DO YOU NEED A RIDE?
JANE? CAN YOU COME GET ME AT THE SERVICE STATION?...
LATER..
DON'T YOU JUST LOVE THE FRESH JEEP AIR?
I JUST LOVE THE WIND IN MY HAIR!

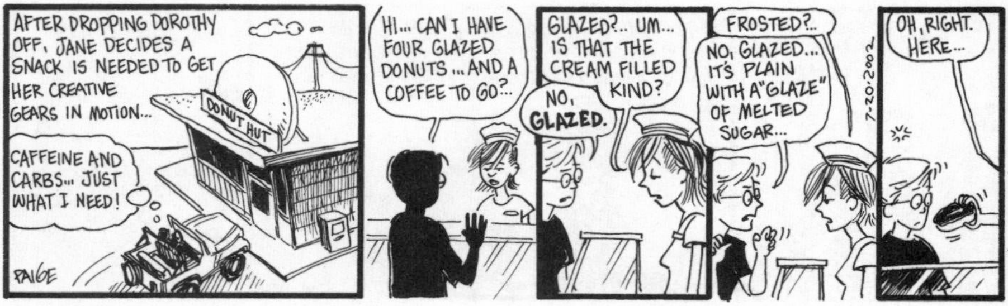
AFTER DROPPING DOROTHY OFF, JANE DECIDES A SNACK IS NEEDED TO GET HER CREATIVE GEARS IN MOTION...
DONUT HUT
CAFFEINE AND CARBS... JUST WHAT I NEED!
HI... CAN I HAVE FOUR GLAZED DONUTS... AND A COFFEE TO GO?..
GLAZED?.. UM... IS THAT THE CREAM FILLED KIND?
NO, GLAZED.
FROSTED?..
NO, GLAZED... IT'S PLAIN WITH A "GLAZE" OF MELTED SUGAR...
OH, RIGHT. HERE...

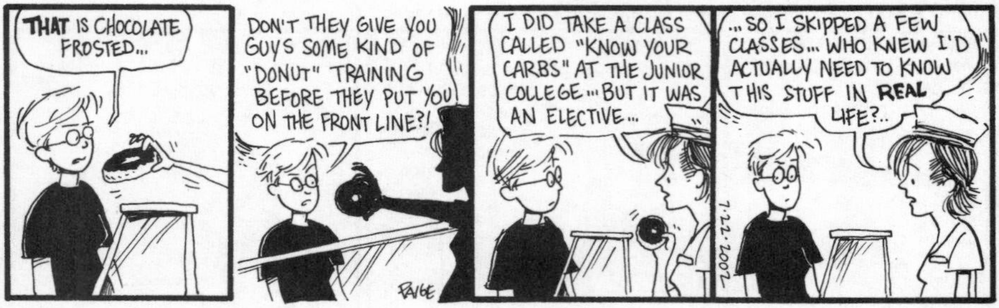
THAT IS CHOCOLATE FROSTED...
DON'T THEY GIVE YOU GUYS SOME KIND OF "DONUT" TRAINING BEFORE THEY PUT YOU ON THE FRONT LINE?!
I DID TAKE A CLASS CALLED "KNOW YOUR CARBS" AT THE JUNIOR COLLEGE... BUT IT WAS AN ELECTIVE...
...SO I SKIPPED A FEW CLASSES... WHO KNEW I'D ACTUALLY NEED TO KNOW THIS STUFF IN REAL LIFE?..

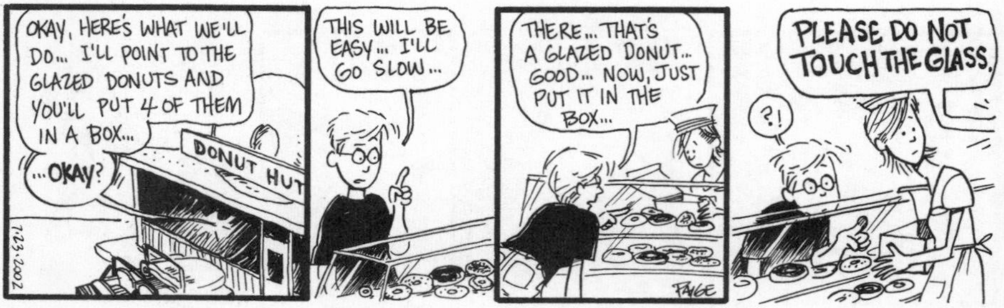
OKAY, HERE'S WHAT WE'LL DO... I'LL POINT TO THE GLAZED DONUTS AND YOU'LL PUT 4 OF THEM IN A BOX...
...OKAY?
DONUT HUT
THIS WILL BE EASY... I'LL GO SLOW...
THERE... THAT'S A GLAZED DONUT... GOOD... NOW, JUST PUT IT IN THE BOX...
?!
PLEASE DO NOT TOUCH THE GLASS.

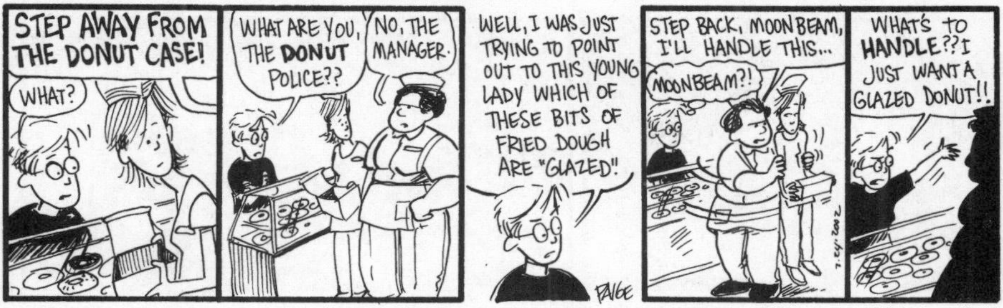
STEP AWAY FROM THE DONUT CASE!
WHAT?
WHAT ARE YOU, THE DONUT POLICE??
NO, THE MANAGER.
WELL, I WAS JUST TRYING TO POINT OUT TO THIS YOUNG LADY WHICH OF THESE BITS OF FRIED DOUGH ARE "GLAZED"!
PAIGE
STEP BACK, MOONBEAM, I'LL HANDLE THIS...
MOONBEAM?!
WHAT'S TO HANDLE??I JUST WANT A GLAZED DONUT!!
7.24.2002

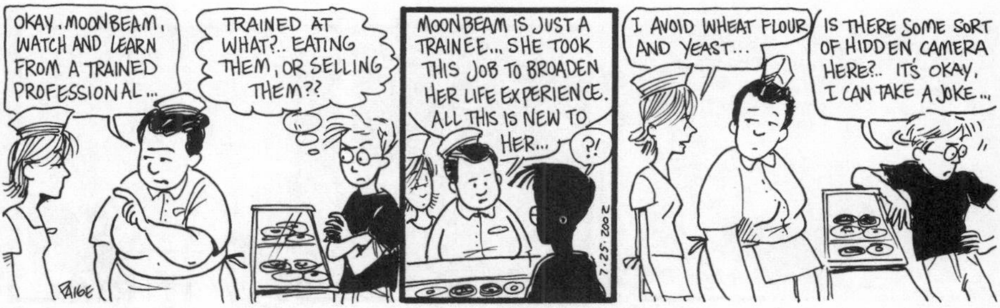
OKAY, MOONBEAM, WATCH AND LEARN FROM A TRAINED PROFESSIONAL...
TRAINED AT WHAT?.. EATING THEM, OR SELLING THEM??
PAIGE
MOONBEAM IS JUST A TRAINEE... SHE TOOK THIS JOB TO BROADEN HER LIFE EXPERIENCE. ALL THIS IS NEW TO HER...
?!
7.25.2002
I AVOID WHEAT FLOUR AND YEAST...
IS THERE SOME SORT OF HIDDEN CAMERA HERE?.. IT'S OKAY, I CAN TAKE A JOKE...

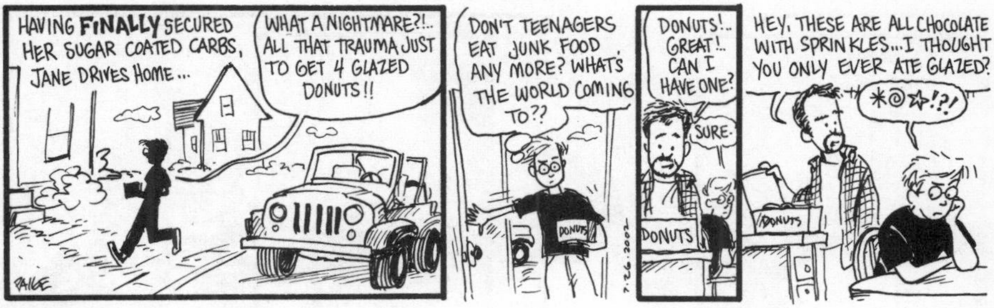
HAVING FINALLY SECURED HER SUGAR COATED CARBS, JANE DRIVES HOME...
WHAT A NIGHTMARE?!.. ALL THAT TRAUMA JUST TO GET 4 GLAZED DONUTS!!
PAIGE
DON'T TEENAGERS EAT JUNK FOOD ANY MORE? WHAT'S THE WORLD COMING TO??
DONUTS
7.26.2002
DONUTS!.. GREAT!.. CAN I HAVE ONE?
SURE.
DONUTS
HEY, THESE ARE ALL CHOCOLATE WITH SPRINKLES...I THOUGHT YOU ONLY EVER ATE GLAZED?
*@☆!?!
DONUTS

LATER...

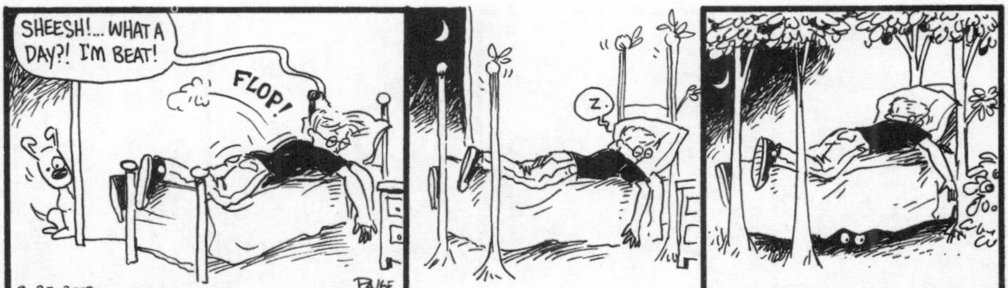
SHEESH!... WHAT A DAY?! I'M BEAT!
FLOP!
7.27.2002
PAIGE
Z

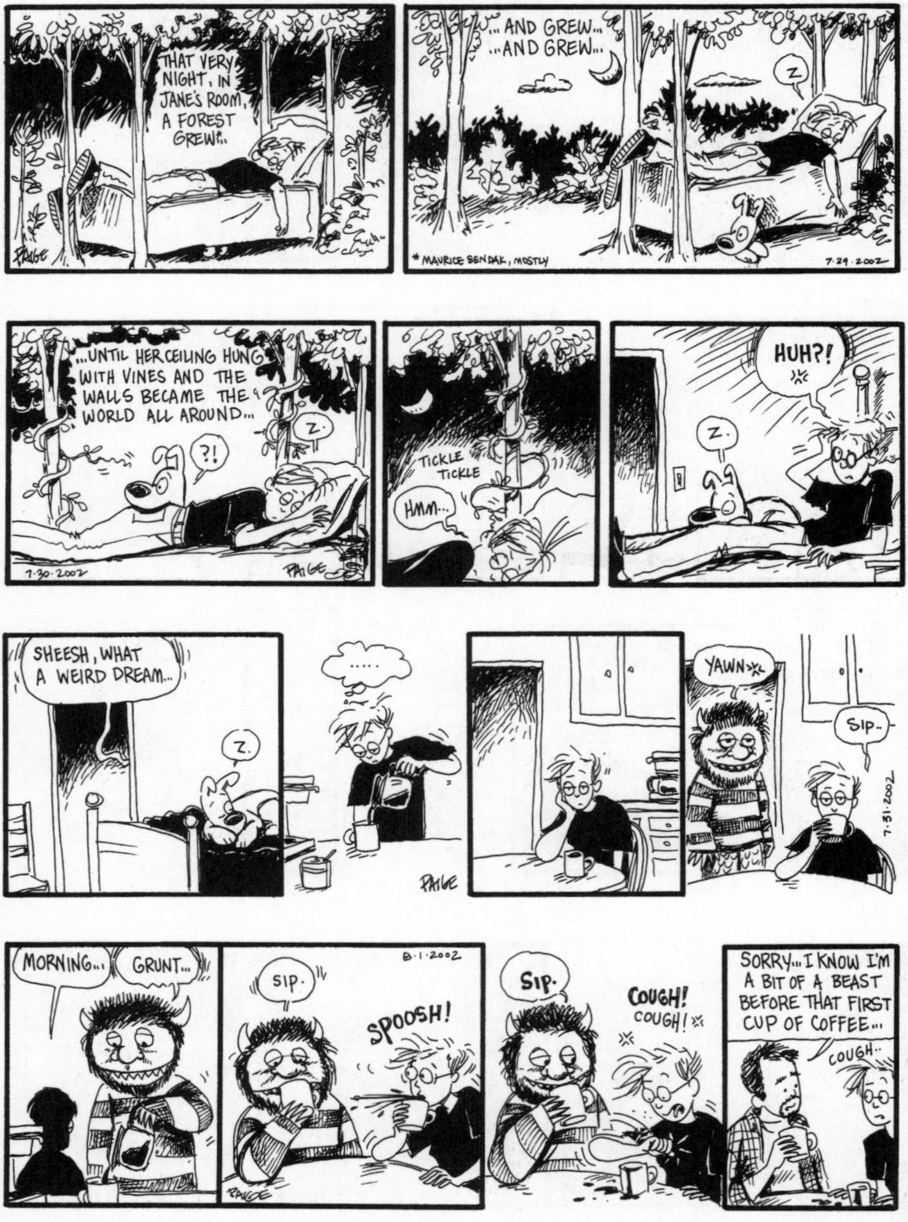

THAT VERY NIGHT, IN JANE'S ROOM, A FOREST GREW*...
PAIGE
...AND GREW... ...AND GREW...
Z
* MAURICE SENDAK, MOSTLY
7·29·2002
...UNTIL HER CEILING HUNG WITH VINES AND THE WALLS BECAME THE WORLD ALL AROUND...
Z.
?!
7·30·2002
PAIGE
TICKLE TICKLE
HMM...
HUH?!
Z.
SHEESH, WHAT A WEIRD DREAM...
Z.
.....
PAIGE
YAWN
SIP..
7·31·2002
MORNING...
GRUNT...
8·1·2002
SIP.
SPOOSH!
PAIGE
SIP.
COUGH! COUGH!
SORRY... I KNOW I'M A BIT OF A BEAST BEFORE THAT FIRST CUP OF COFFEE...
COUGH..

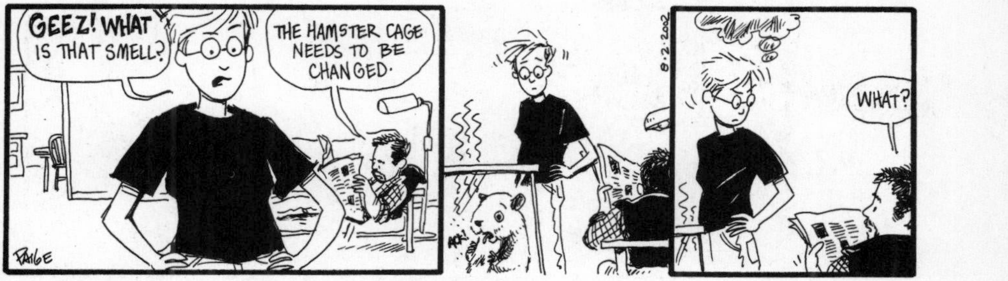
GEEZ! WHAT IS THAT SMELL?
THE HAMSTER CAGE NEEDS TO BE CHANGED.
PAIGE
8-2-2002
ACK!
WHAT?

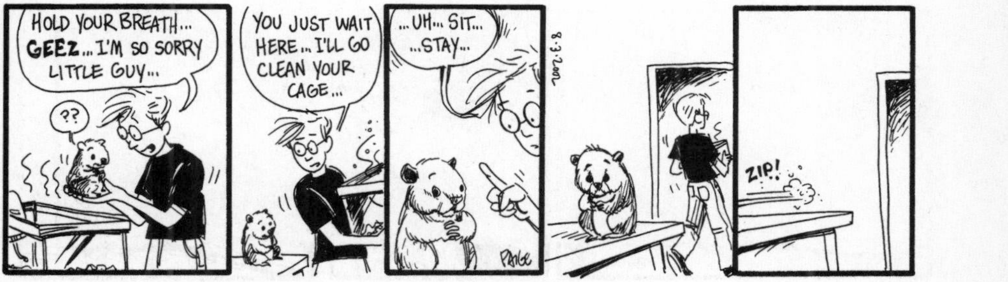
HOLD YOUR BREATH... GEEZ... I'M SO SORRY LITTLE GUY...
??
YOU JUST WAIT HERE... I'LL GO CLEAN YOUR CAGE...
...UH... SIT... ...STAY...
8-3-2002
PAIGE
ZIP!

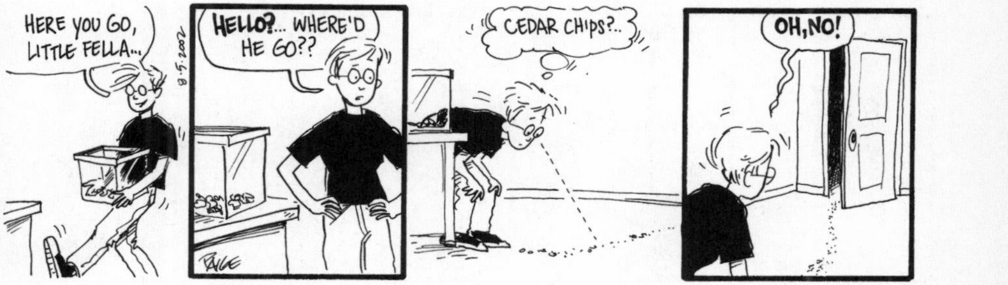
HERE YOU GO, LITTLE FELLA...
8-5-2002
HELLO?... WHERE'D HE GO??
PAIGE
CEDAR CHIPS?..
OH, NO!

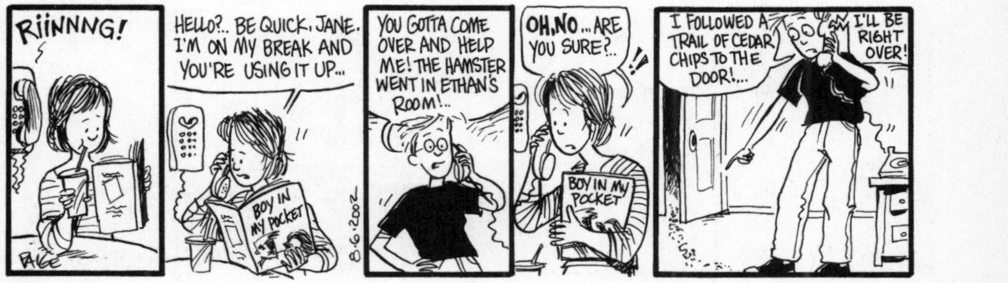
RIINNNG!
PAIGE
HELLO?.. BE QUICK, JANE. I'M ON MY BREAK AND YOU'RE USING IT UP...
BOY IN MY POCKET
8-6-2002
YOU GOTTA COME OVER AND HELP ME! THE HAMSTER WENT IN ETHAN'S ROOM!..
OH, NO... ARE YOU SURE?..
BOY IN MY POCKET
I FOLLOWED A TRAIL OF CEDAR CHIPS TO THE DOOR!...
I'LL BE RIGHT OVER!

IS THIS LINE MOVING?
EXCUSE ME. CAN I GET MY MOCHA TO GO?
WHERE'S DOROTHY?!
ORDER HERE
8·7·2002

I THINK SHE LEFT YOU A NOTE ON THE ESPRESSO MACHINE...
WHAT?!
Maggie, Had to leave - matter of life or death! Be back in a jiff! ~Dorothy
PAIGE

HANG ON, JANE... I'VE GOT THE SUPPLIES...
MOVIE
5 AND 10
BOOKS
BANK
8·8·2002

ONLY THE SHALLOW KNOW THEMSELVES
PAIGE
...AND I'M ON MY WAY!
VAROOM!

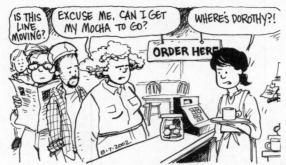

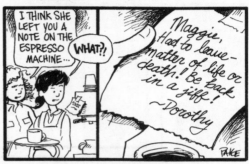

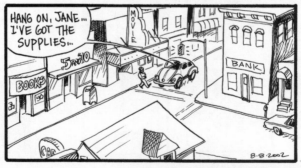

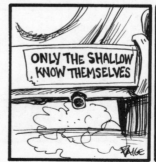

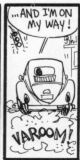

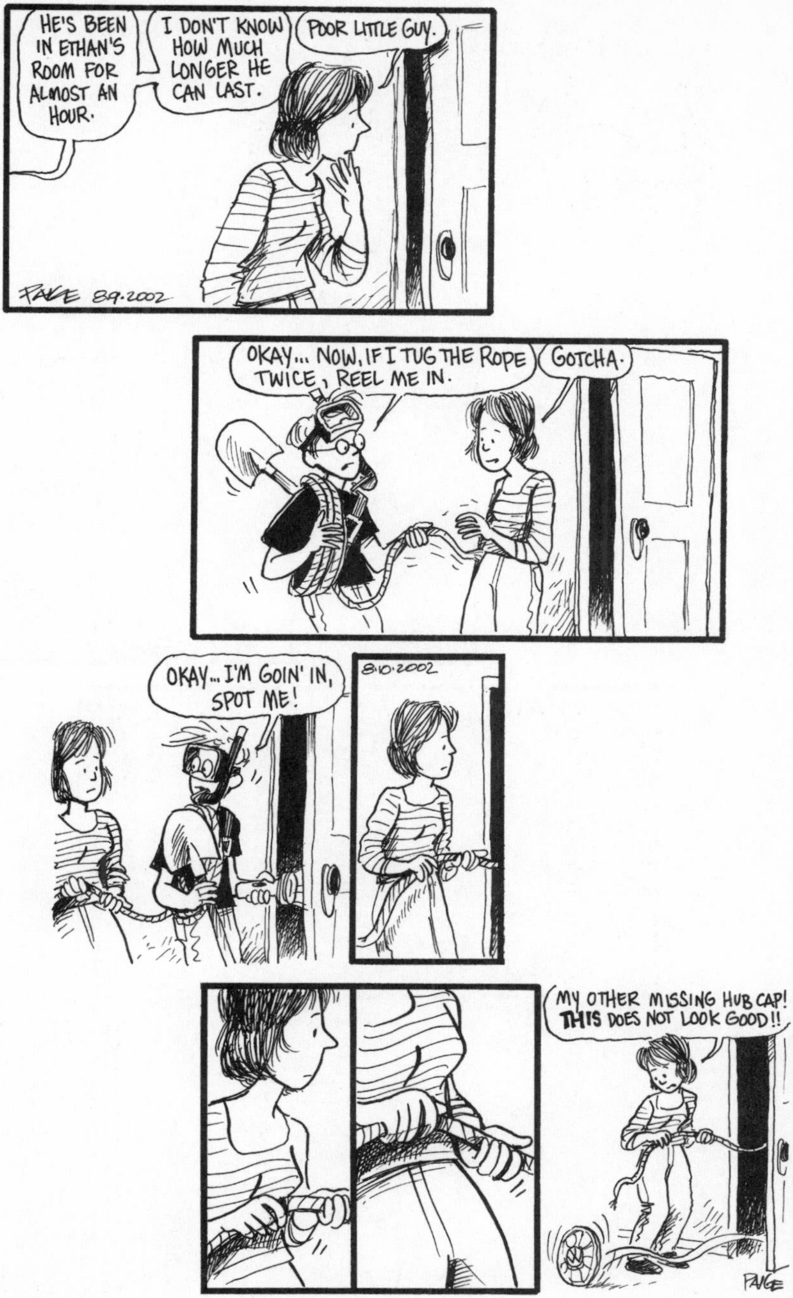
HE'S BEEN IN ETHAN'S ROOM FOR ALMOST AN HOUR.
I DON'T KNOW HOW MUCH LONGER HE CAN LAST.
POOR LITTLE GUY.
PAIGE 8·9·2002
OKAY... NOW, IF I TUG THE ROPE TWICE, REEL ME IN.
GOTCHA.
OKAY... I'M GOIN' IN, SPOT ME!
8·10·2002
MY OTHER MISSING HUB CAP! THIS DOES NOT LOOK GOOD!!
PAIGE

Chapter 12

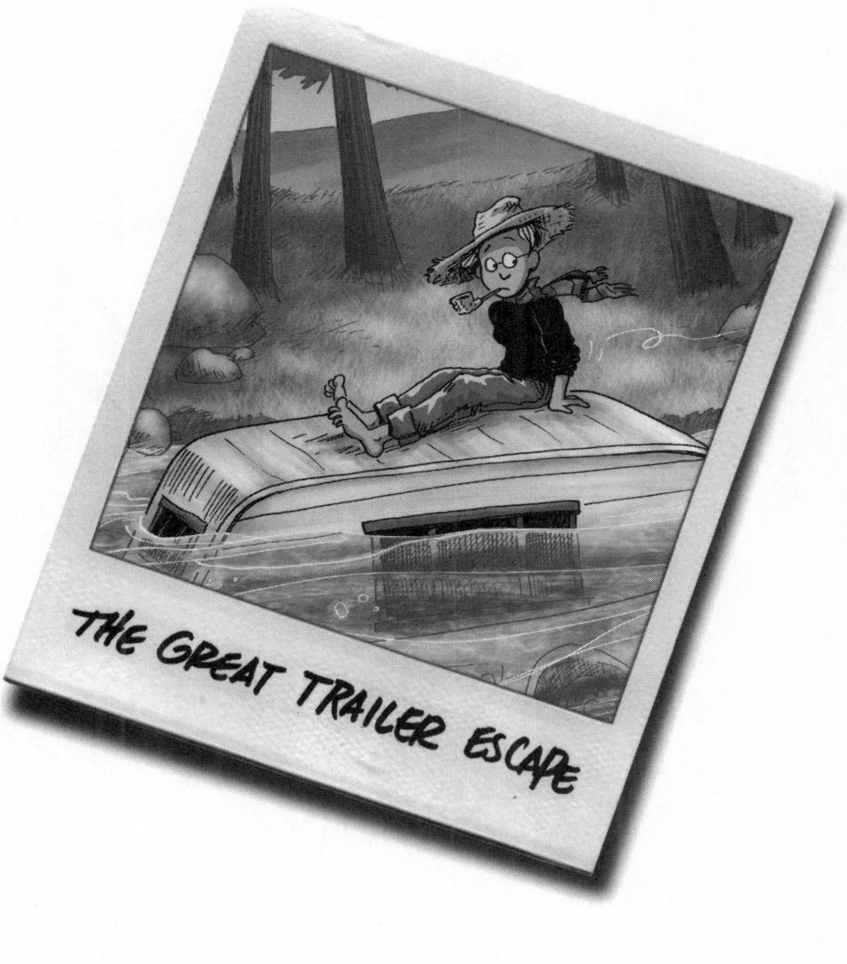
THE GREAT TRAILER ESCAPE

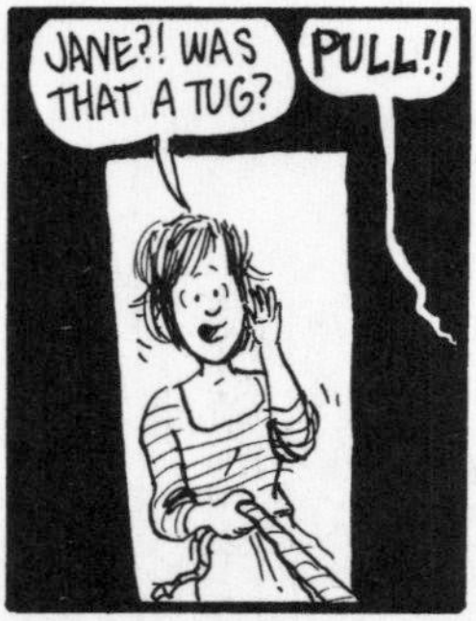
JANE?! WAS THAT A TUG?
PULL!!

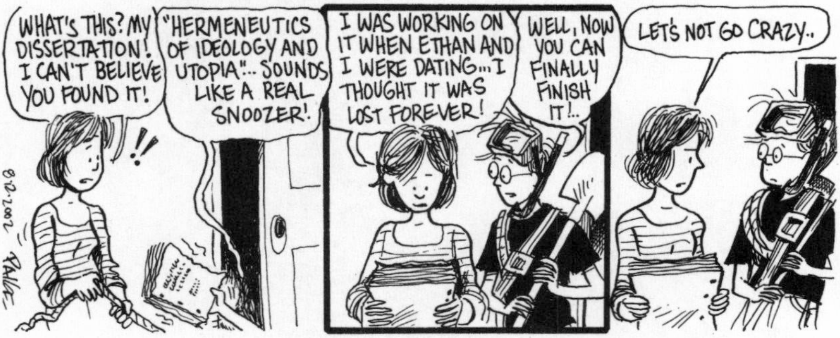
8-12-2002
WHAT'S THIS? MY DISSERTATION! I CAN'T BELIEVE YOU FOUND IT!
"HERMENEUTICS OF IDEOLOGY AND UTOPIA"... SOUNDS LIKE A REAL SNOOZER!
I WAS WORKING ON IT WHEN ETHAN AND I WERE DATING... I THOUGHT IT WAS LOST FOREVER!
WELL, NOW YOU CAN FINALLY FINISH IT!..
LET'S NOT GO CRAZY..

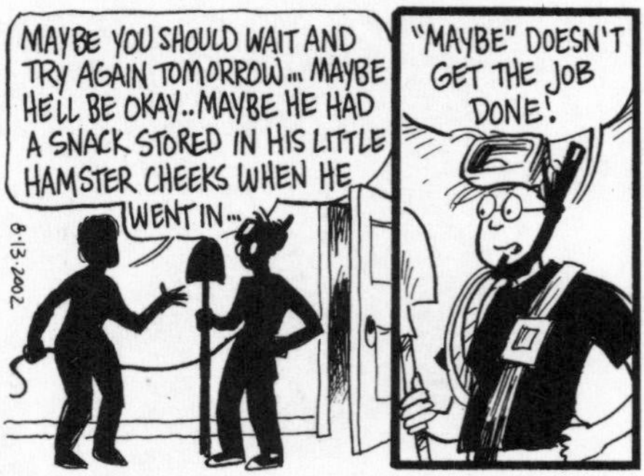
8-13-2002
MAYBE YOU SHOULD WAIT AND TRY AGAIN TOMORROW... MAYBE HE'LL BE OKAY.. MAYBE HE HAD A SNACK STORED IN HIS LITTLE HAMSTER CHEEKS WHEN HE WENT IN...
"MAYBE" DOESN'T GET THE JOB DONE!

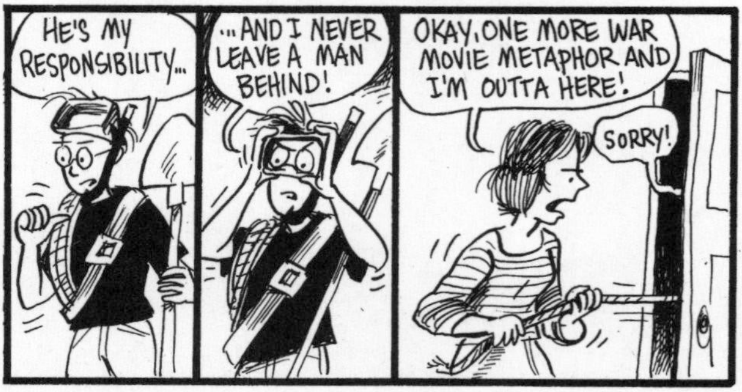
HE'S MY RESPONSIBILITY...
...AND I NEVER LEAVE A MAN BEHIND!
OKAY, ONE MORE WAR MOVIE METAPHOR AND I'M OUTTA HERE!
SORRY!

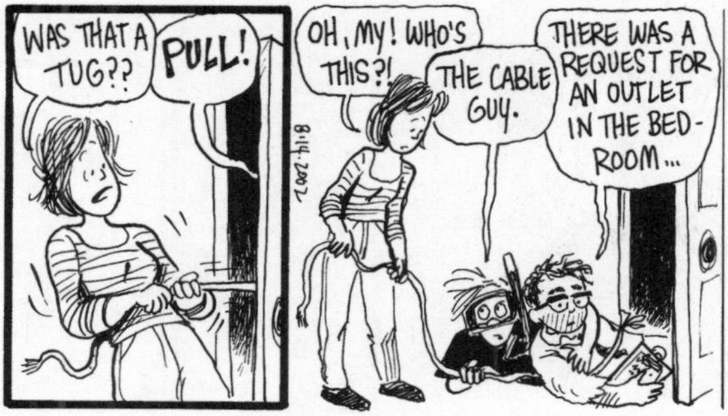

WAS THAT A TUG??
PULL!
OH, MY! WHO'S THIS?!
THE CABLE GUY.
THERE WAS A REQUEST FOR AN OUTLET IN THE BED-ROOM...
8·14·2002

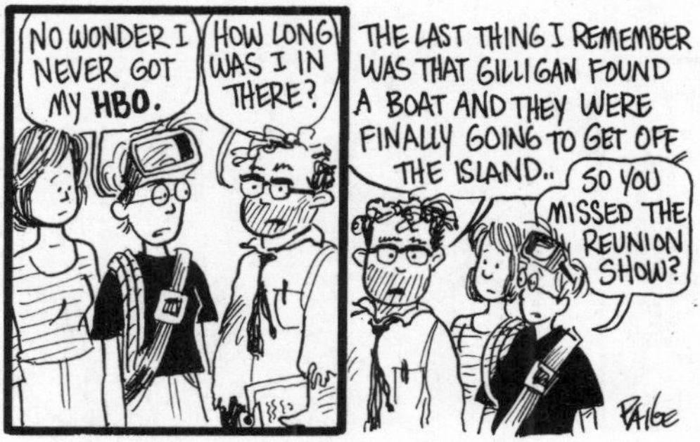

NO WONDER I NEVER GOT MY **HBO.**
HOW LONG WAS I IN THERE?
THE LAST THING I REMEMBER WAS THAT GILLIGAN FOUND A BOAT AND THEY WERE FINALLY GOING TO GET OFF THE ISLAND..
SO YOU MISSED THE REUNION SHOW?
PAIGE

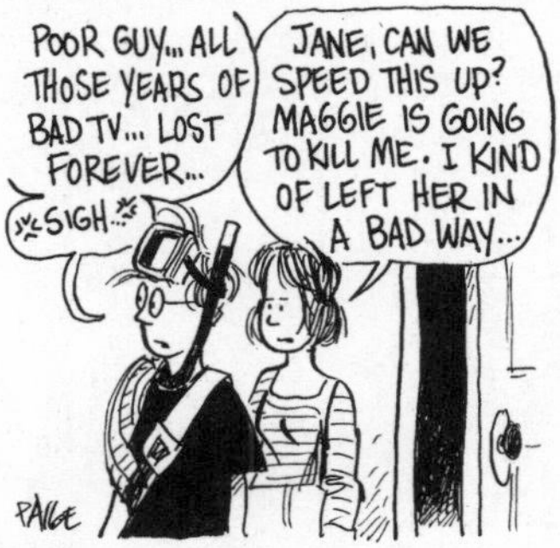

POOR GUY... ALL THOSE YEARS OF BAD TV... LOST FOREVER...
SIGH...
JANE, CAN WE SPEED THIS UP? MAGGIE IS GOING TO KILL ME. I KIND OF LEFT HER IN A BAD WAY...
PAIGE

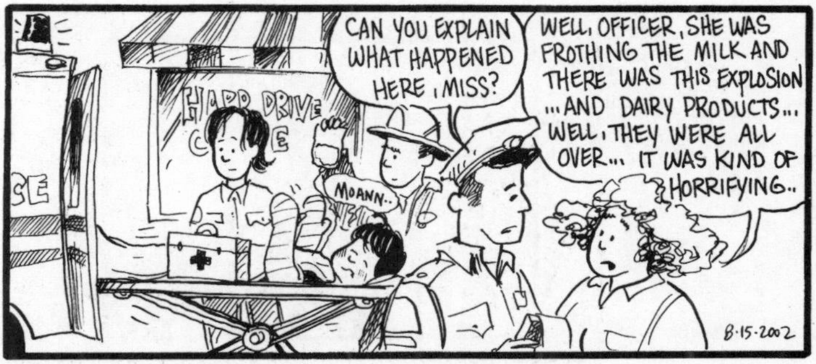

CAN YOU EXPLAIN WHAT HAPPENED HERE, MISS?
WELL, OFFICER, SHE WAS FROTHING THE MILK AND THERE WAS THIS EXPLOSION ...AND DAIRY PRODUCTS... WELL, THEY WERE ALL OVER... IT WAS KIND OF HORRIFYING..
MOANN..
8·15·2002

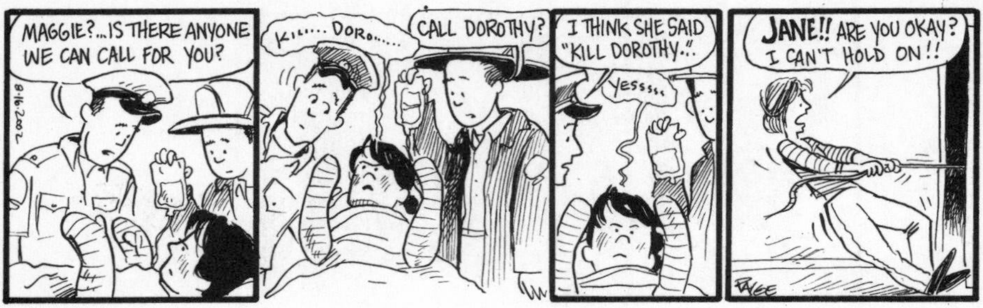
MAGGIE?...IS THERE ANYONE WE CAN CALL FOR YOU?
8.16.2002
KILL.... DORO......
CALL DOROTHY?
I THINK SHE SAID "KILL DOROTHY."
YESSSS...
JANE!! ARE YOU OKAY? I CAN'T HOLD ON!!

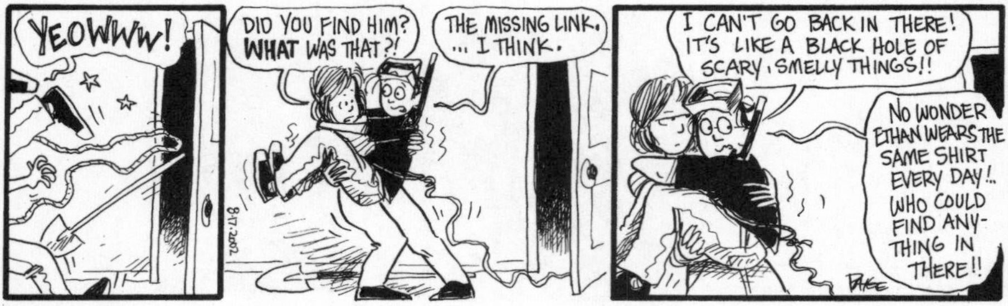
YEOWWW!
DID YOU FIND HIM? WHAT WAS THAT?!
THE MISSING LINK. ... I THINK.
8.17.2002
I CAN'T GO BACK IN THERE! IT'S LIKE A BLACK HOLE OF SCARY, SMELLY THINGS!!
NO WONDER ETHAN WEARS THE SAME SHIRT EVERY DAY!.. WHO COULD FIND ANYTHING IN THERE!!

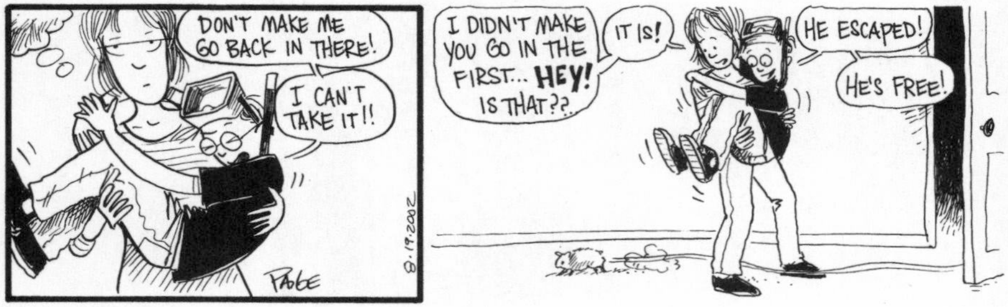
DON'T MAKE ME GO BACK IN THERE!
I CAN'T TAKE IT!!
8.19.2002
I DIDN'T MAKE YOU GO IN THE FIRST... HEY! IS THAT??
IT IS!
HE ESCAPED!
HE'S FREE!

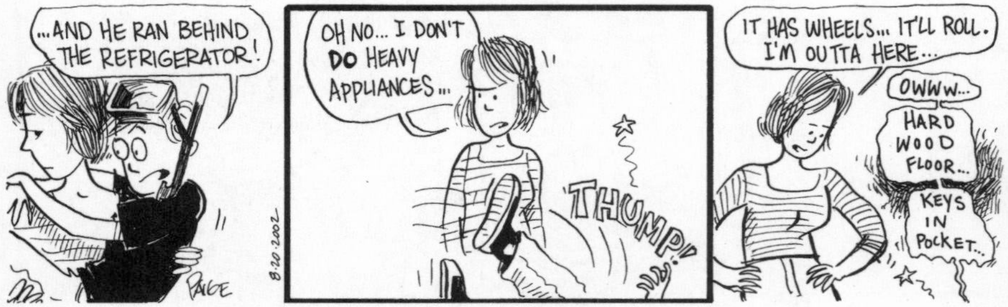
...AND HE RAN BEHIND THE REFRIGERATOR!
8.20.2002
OH NO... I DON'T DO HEAVY APPLIANCES...
THUMP!
IT HAS WHEELS... IT'LL ROLL. I'M OUTTA HERE...
OWWW...
HARD WOOD FLOOR...
KEYS IN POCKET...

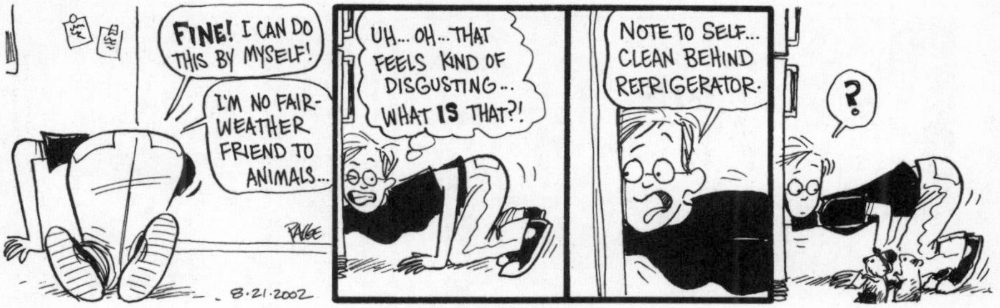
FINE! I CAN DO THIS BY MYSELF!
I'M NO FAIR-WEATHER FRIEND TO ANIMALS...
PAIGE
8·21·2002
UH... OH... THAT FEELS KIND OF DISGUSTING... WHAT IS THAT?!
NOTE TO SELF... CLEAN BEHIND REFRIGERATOR.
?

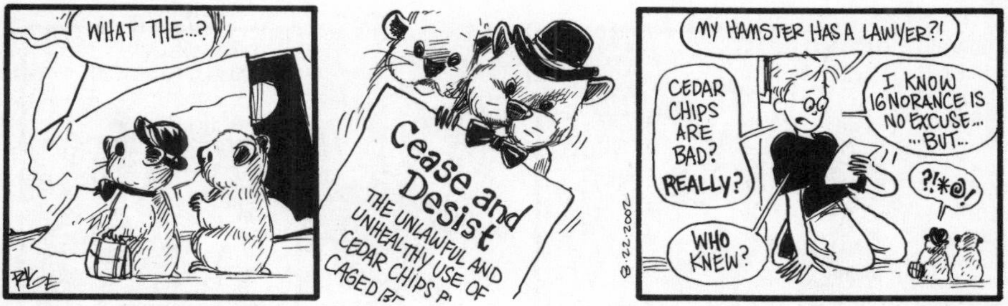
WHAT THE...?
PAIGE
Cease and Desist
THE UNLAWFUL AND UNHEALTHY USE OF CEDAR CHIPS
8·22·2002
MY HAMSTER HAS A LAWYER?!
CEDAR CHIPS ARE BAD? REALLY?
I KNOW IGNORANCE IS NO EXCUSE... ...BUT...
WHO KNEW?
?!*@!

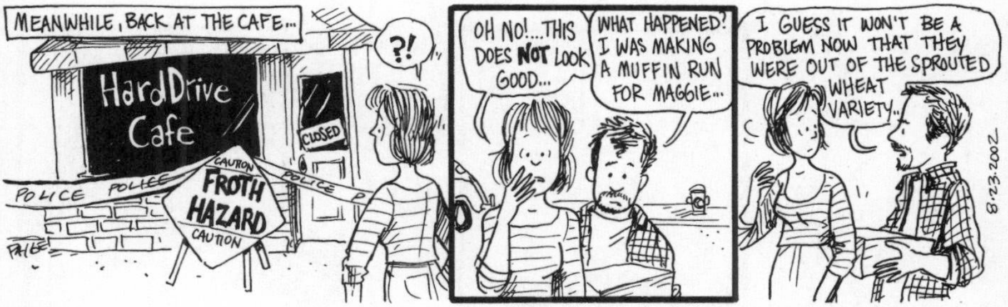
MEANWHILE, BACK AT THE CAFE...
HardDrive Cafe
CLOSED
POLICE POLICE POLICE
CAUTION FROTH HAZARD CAUTION
PAIGE
?!
OH NO!... THIS DOES NOT LOOK GOOD...
WHAT HAPPENED? I WAS MAKING A MUFFIN RUN FOR MAGGIE...
I GUESS IT WON'T BE A PROBLEM NOW THAT THEY WERE OUT OF THE SPROUTED WHEAT VARIETY...
8·23·2002

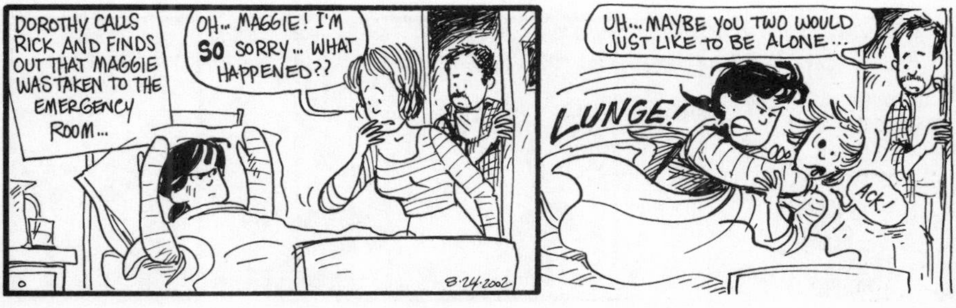
DOROTHY CALLS RICK AND FINDS OUT THAT MAGGIE WAS TAKEN TO THE EMERGENCY ROOM...
OH... MAGGIE! I'M SO SORRY... WHAT HAPPENED??
8·24·2002
UH... MAYBE YOU TWO WOULD JUST LIKE TO BE ALONE...
LUNGE!
ACK!

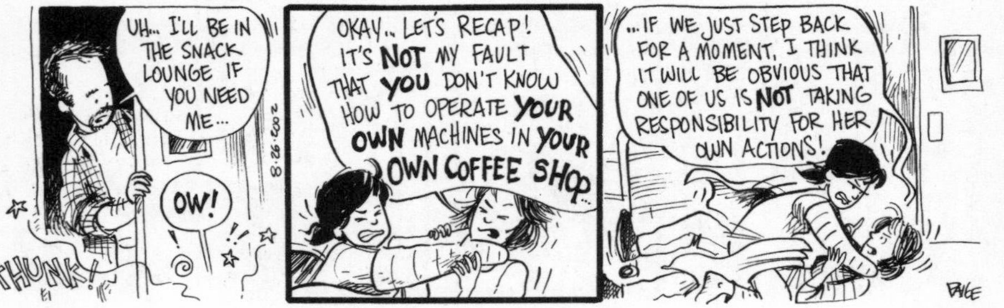
UH... I'LL BE IN THE SNACK LOUNGE IF YOU NEED ME...
OW!
THUNK!
8·26·2002
OKAY.. LET'S RECAP! IT'S **NOT** MY FAULT THAT **YOU** DON'T KNOW HOW TO OPERATE **YOUR OWN** MACHINES IN **YOUR OWN COFFEE SHOP**...
...IF WE JUST STEP BACK FOR A MOMENT, I THINK IT WILL BE OBVIOUS THAT ONE OF US IS **NOT** TAKING RESPONSIBILITY FOR HER OWN ACTIONS!
PAIGE

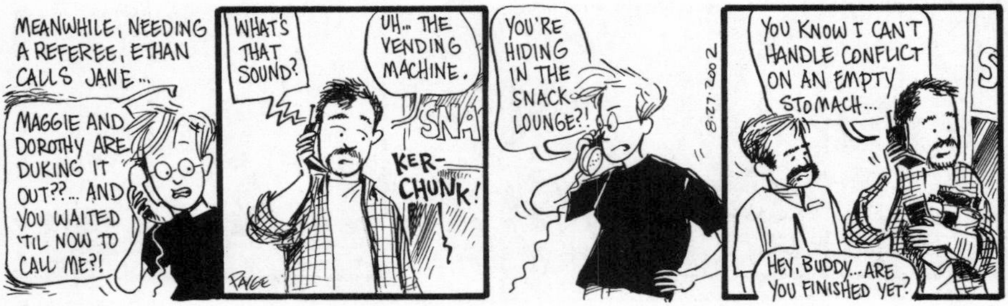
MEANWHILE, NEEDING A REFEREE, ETHAN CALLS JANE...
MAGGIE AND DOROTHY ARE DUKING IT OUT??... AND YOU WAITED 'TIL NOW TO CALL ME?!
PAIGE
WHAT'S THAT SOUND?
UH... THE VENDING MACHINE.
SNA
KER-CHUNK!
YOU'RE HIDING IN THE SNACK LOUNGE?!
8·27·2002
YOU KNOW I CAN'T HANDLE CONFLICT ON AN EMPTY STOMACH...
HEY, BUDDY... ARE YOU FINISHED YET?

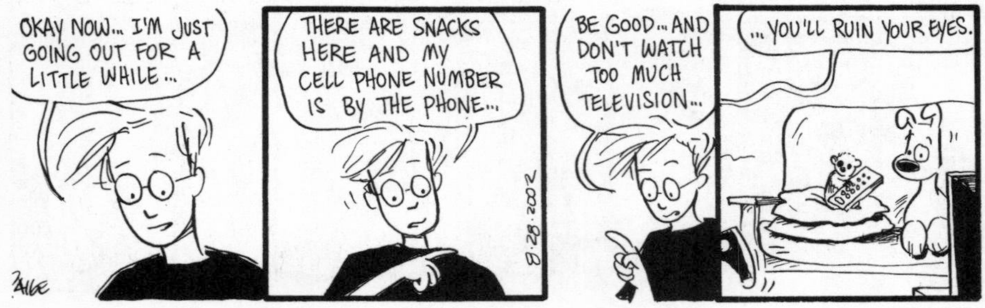
OKAY NOW... I'M JUST GOING OUT FOR A LITTLE WHILE...
PAIGE
THERE ARE SNACKS HERE AND MY CELL PHONE NUMBER IS BY THE PHONE...
8·28·2002
BE GOOD... AND DON'T WATCH TOO MUCH TELEVISION...
...YOU'LL RUIN YOUR EYES.

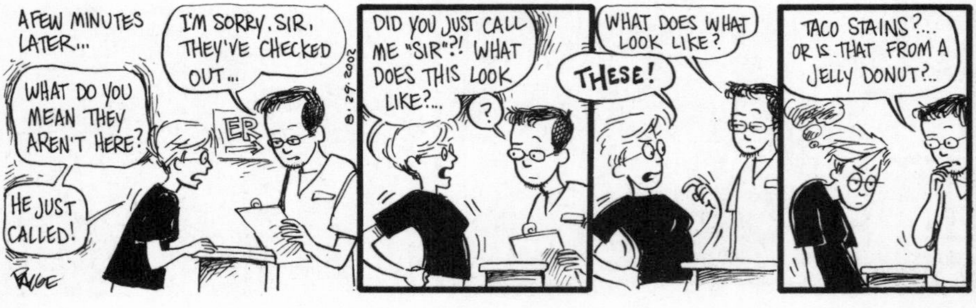
A FEW MINUTES LATER...
WHAT DO YOU MEAN THEY AREN'T HERE?
HE JUST CALLED!
I'M SORRY, SIR, THEY'VE CHECKED OUT...
ER
PAIGE
8·29·2002
DID YOU JUST CALL ME "SIR"?! WHAT DOES THIS LOOK LIKE?...
?
WHAT DOES WHAT LOOK LIKE?
THESE!
TACO STAINS?... OR IS THAT FROM A JELLY DONUT?..

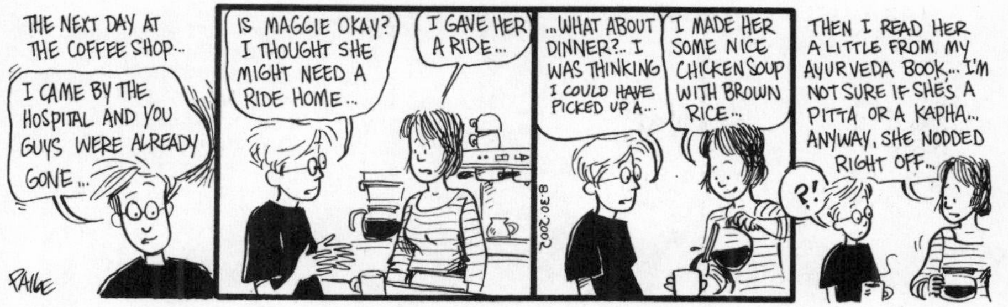
THE NEXT DAY AT THE COFFEE SHOP...
I CAME BY THE HOSPITAL AND YOU GUYS WERE ALREADY GONE...
PAIGE
IS MAGGIE OKAY? I THOUGHT SHE MIGHT NEED A RIDE HOME...
I GAVE HER A RIDE...
8.30.2002
...WHAT ABOUT DINNER?.. I WAS THINKING I COULD HAVE PICKED UP A...
I MADE HER SOME NICE CHICKEN SOUP WITH BROWN RICE...
THEN I READ HER A LITTLE FROM MY AYURVEDA BOOK... I'M NOT SURE IF SHE'S A PITTA OR A KAPHA... ANYWAY, SHE NODDED RIGHT OFF...
?!

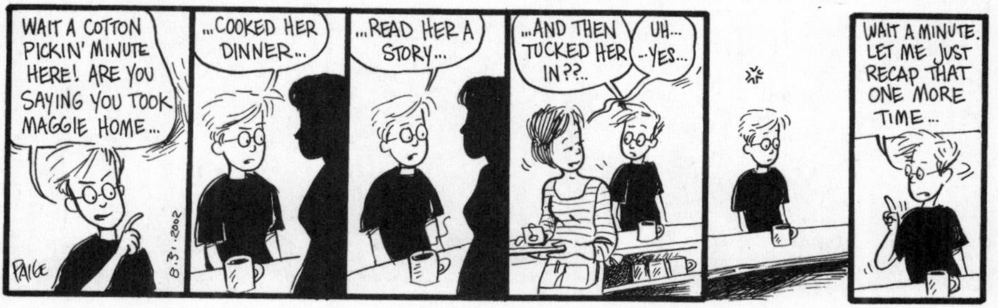
WAIT A COTTON PICKIN' MINUTE HERE! ARE YOU SAYING YOU TOOK MAGGIE HOME...
PAIGE
8.31.2002
...COOKED HER DINNER...
...READ HER A STORY...
...AND THEN TUCKED HER IN??..
UH... ...YES...
WAIT A MINUTE. LET ME JUST RECAP THAT ONE MORE TIME...

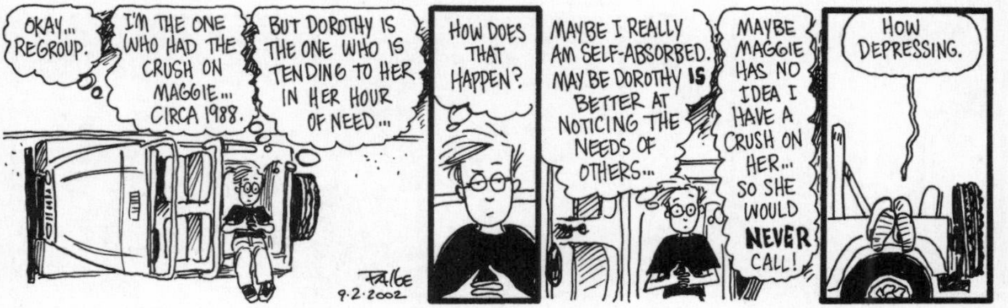
OKAY... REGROUP.
I'M THE ONE WHO HAD THE CRUSH ON MAGGIE... CIRCA 1988.
BUT DOROTHY IS THE ONE WHO IS TENDING TO HER IN HER HOUR OF NEED...
PAIGE
9.2.2002
HOW DOES THAT HAPPEN?
MAYBE I REALLY AM SELF-ABSORBED. MAYBE DOROTHY IS BETTER AT NOTICING THE NEEDS OF OTHERS...
MAYBE MAGGIE HAS NO IDEA I HAVE A CRUSH ON HER... SO SHE WOULD NEVER CALL!
HOW DEPRESSING.

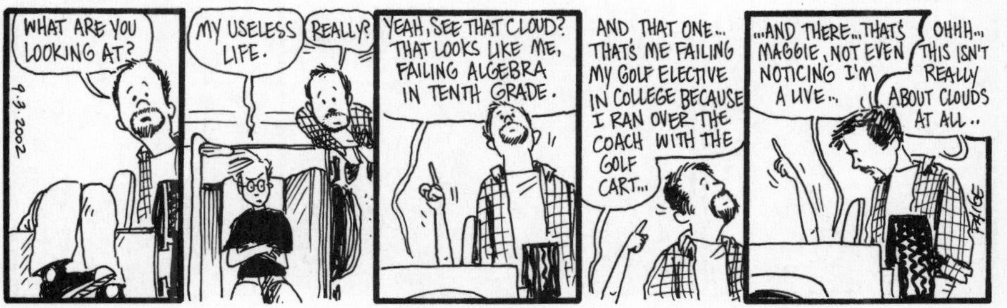
WHAT ARE YOU LOOKING AT?
9.3.2002
MY USELESS LIFE.
REALLY?
YEAH, SEE THAT CLOUD? THAT LOOKS LIKE ME, FAILING ALGEBRA IN TENTH GRADE.
AND THAT ONE... THAT'S ME FAILING MY GOLF ELECTIVE IN COLLEGE BECAUSE I RAN OVER THE COACH WITH THE GOLF CART...
...AND THERE... THAT'S MAGGIE, NOT EVEN NOTICING I'M ALIVE...
OHHH... THIS ISN'T REALLY ABOUT CLOUDS AT ALL...
PAIGE

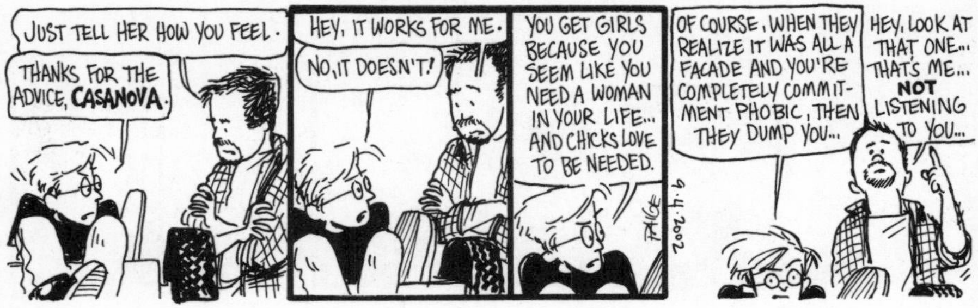
JUST TELL HER HOW YOU FEEL.
THANKS FOR THE ADVICE, **CASANOVA**.
HEY, IT WORKS FOR ME.
NO, IT DOESN'T!
YOU GET GIRLS BECAUSE YOU SEEM LIKE YOU NEED A WOMAN IN YOUR LIFE... AND CHICKS LOVE TO BE NEEDED.
9.4.2002
OF COURSE, WHEN THEY REALIZE IT WAS ALL A FACADE AND YOU'RE COMPLETELY COMMIT-MENT PHOBIC, THEN THEY DUMP YOU...
HEY, LOOK AT THAT ONE... THAT'S ME... **NOT** LISTENING TO YOU...

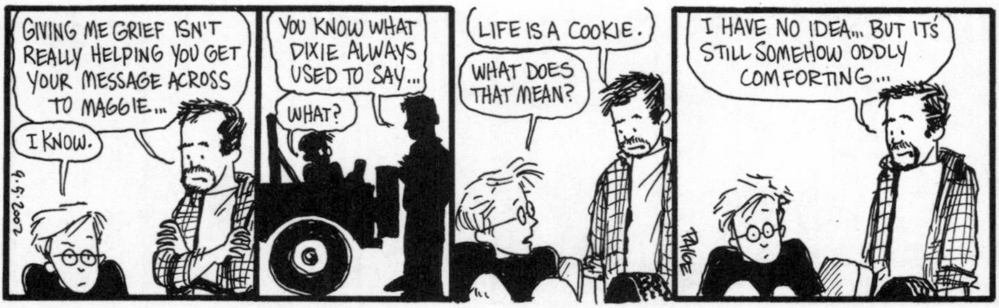
GIVING ME GRIEF ISN'T REALLY HELPING YOU GET YOUR MESSAGE ACROSS TO MAGGIE...
I KNOW.
9.5.2002
YOU KNOW WHAT DIXIE ALWAYS USED TO SAY...
WHAT?
LIFE IS A COOKIE.
WHAT DOES THAT MEAN?
I HAVE NO IDEA... BUT IT'S STILL SOMEHOW ODDLY COMFORTING...

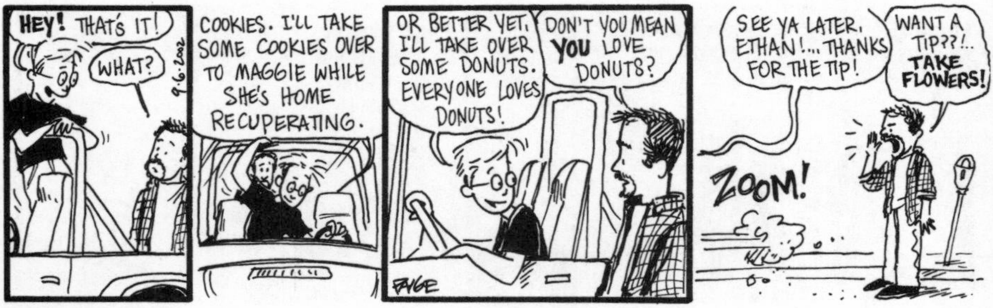
HEY! THAT'S IT!
WHAT?
9.6.2002
COOKIES. I'LL TAKE SOME COOKIES OVER TO MAGGIE WHILE SHE'S HOME RECUPERATING.
OR BETTER YET, I'LL TAKE OVER SOME DONUTS. EVERYONE LOVES DONUTS!
DON'T YOU MEAN **YOU** LOVE DONUTS?
SEE YA LATER, ETHAN!... THANKS FOR THE TIP!
WANT A TIP??!.. **TAKE FLOWERS!**
ZOOM!

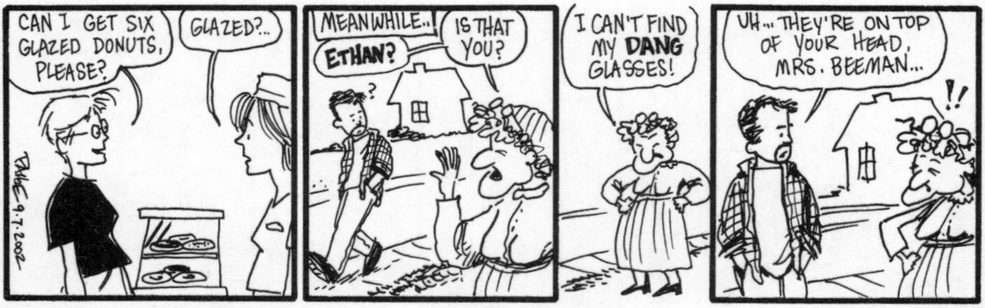
CAN I GET SIX GLAZED DONUTS, PLEASE?
GLAZED?..
9.7.2002
MEANWHILE..
ETHAN?
IS THAT YOU?
I CAN'T FIND MY **DANG** GLASSES!
UH... THEY'RE ON TOP OF YOUR HEAD, MRS. BEEMAN...
!!

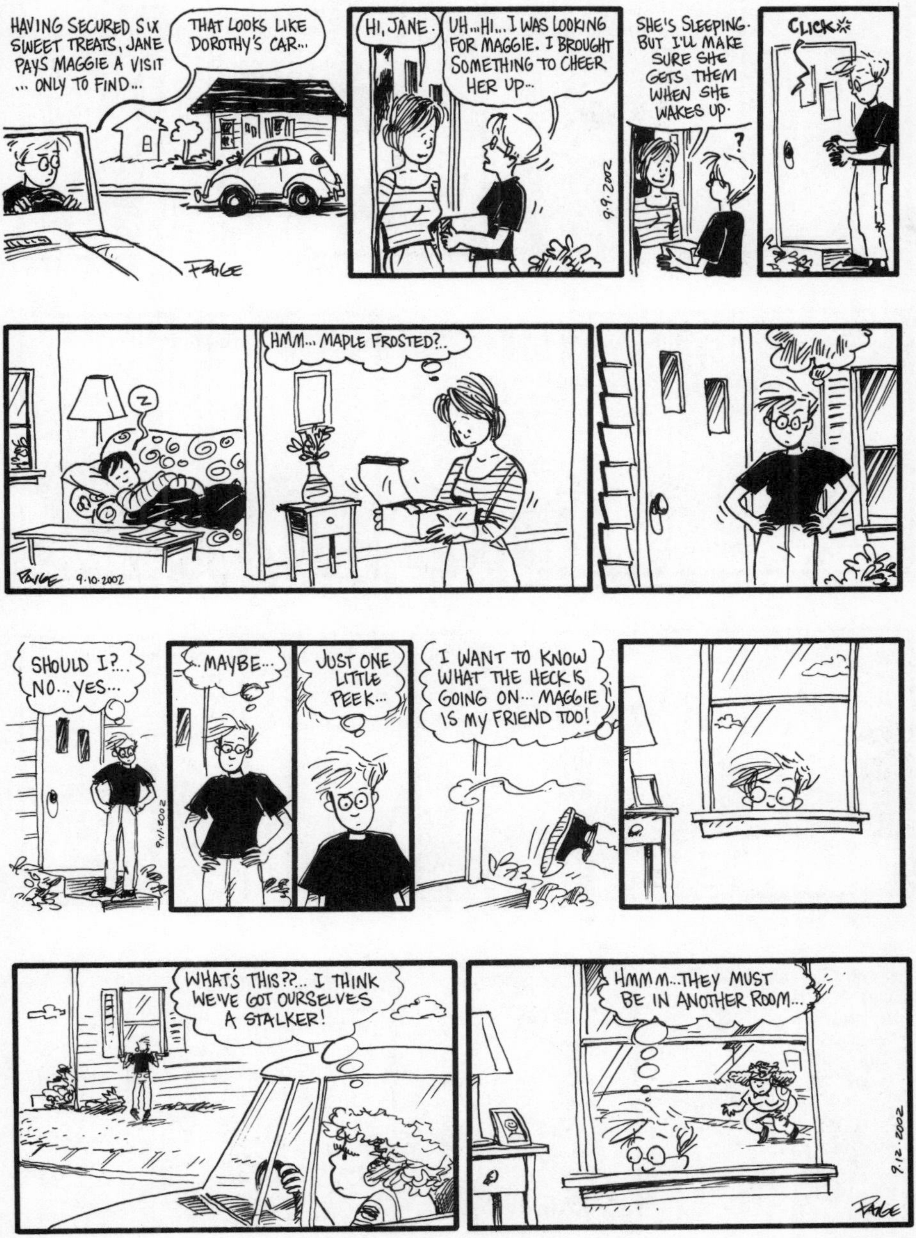

HAVING SECURED SIX SWEET TREATS, JANE PAYS MAGGIE A VISIT ... ONLY TO FIND...
THAT LOOKS LIKE DOROTHY'S CAR...
HI, JANE.
UH...HI... I WAS LOOKING FOR MAGGIE. I BROUGHT SOMETHING TO CHEER HER UP...
9.9.2002
SHE'S SLEEPING. BUT I'LL MAKE SURE SHE GETS THEM WHEN SHE WAKES UP.
?
CLICK
HMM... MAPLE FROSTED?...
9.10.2002
SHOULD I?... NO... YES...
9.11.2002
...MAYBE...
JUST ONE LITTLE PEEK...
I WANT TO KNOW WHAT THE HECK IS GOING ON... MAGGIE IS MY FRIEND TOO!
WHAT'S THIS??... I THINK WE'VE GOT OURSELVES A STALKER!
HMMM...THEY MUST BE IN ANOTHER ROOM...
9.12.2002

FWUMP!
HEY! GET OFF ME! WHAT'S THE BIG IDEA?!!
PERPETRATOR HAS BEEN SUBDUED..
HEY! I KNOW YOU! YOU'RE NO COP!!
... REQUESTING BACK UP...
THAT'S NOT EVEN A RADIO! IT'S A STUPID PALM PILOT!!
I HAVE A STYLUS... AND I'M NOT AFRAID TO USE IT...
?!@
A FAKE COP CAN'T ARREST ANYONE!
I'M NOT REALLY THE ONE WITH THE PROBLEM HERE, AM I?.. MS. STALKER?
I'M NOT STALKING! A FRIEND OF MINE LIVES HERE... GO AHEAD AND ASK HER!
OKAY... I WILL!
NO...
WAIT!...
TUG!!
WAIT!
MAYBE WE CAN WORK OUT A DEAL?!...
YOU KNOW, I COULD DO YOU A FAVOR AND YOU COULD DO ME A FAVOR...
... ACTUALLY, YOU COULD GO FIRST AND PUT ME DOWN...
I'LL PUT YOU DOWN... THEN YOU CAN GIVE ME ONE GOOD REASON WHY I SHOULDN'T REPORT THIS...
FWUMP!
SEE? IT ALL STARTED WHEN I PICKED UP DONUTS AND BROUGHT THEM OVER... NO... BACK UP ... IT WAS WHEN MAGGIE BOUGHT THE CAFE... ...NO... IT WAS ACTUALLY THE FALL... I MEAN, NOT THIS FALL... THE FALL OF MY JUNIOR YEAR...

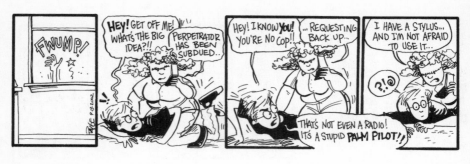

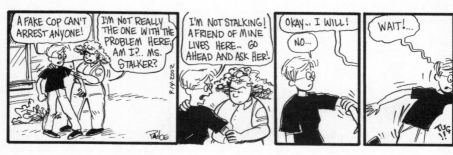

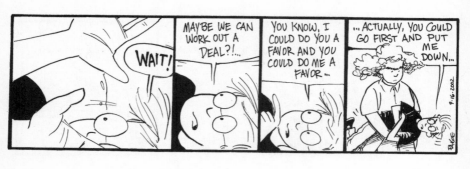

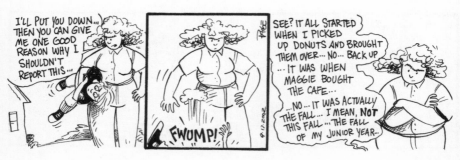

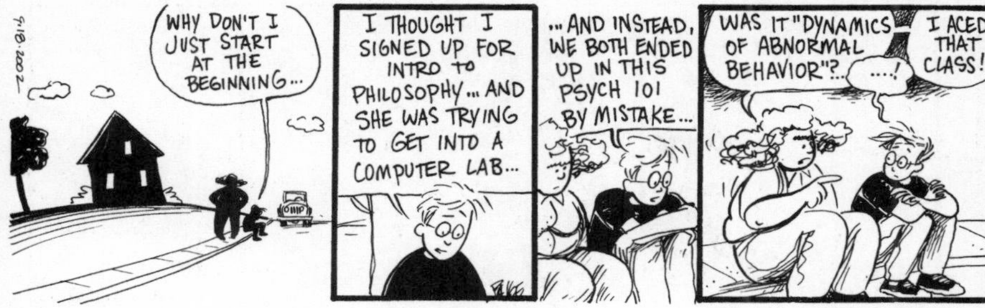
9.18.2002
WHY DON'T I JUST START AT THE BEGINNING...
I THOUGHT I SIGNED UP FOR INTRO TO PHILOSOPHY... AND SHE WAS TRYING TO GET INTO A COMPUTER LAB...
...AND INSTEAD, WE BOTH ENDED UP IN THIS PSYCH 101 BY MISTAKE...
WAS IT "DYNAMICS OF ABNORMAL BEHAVIOR"?..
....!
I ACED THAT CLASS!
PAIGE

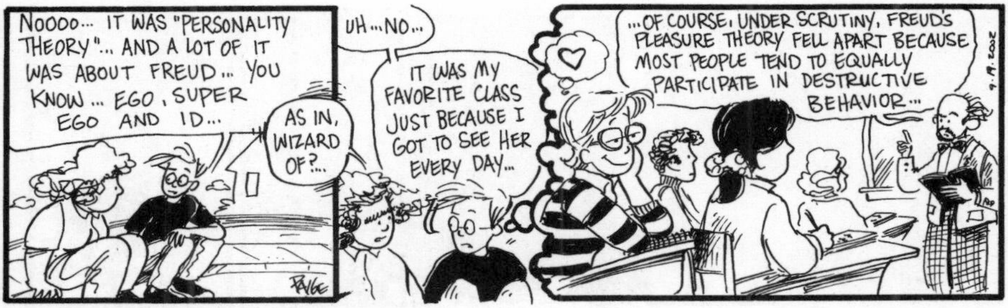
NOOOO... IT WAS "PERSONALITY THEORY"... AND A LOT OF IT WAS ABOUT FREUD... YOU KNOW... EGO, SUPER EGO AND ID...
AS IN, WIZARD OF?...
UH...NO...
IT WAS MY FAVORITE CLASS JUST BECAUSE I GOT TO SEE HER EVERY DAY...
...OF COURSE, UNDER SCRUTINY, FREUD'S PLEASURE THEORY FELL APART BECAUSE MOST PEOPLE TEND TO EQUALLY PARTICIPATE IN DESTRUCTIVE BEHAVIOR...
9.19.2002
PAIGE

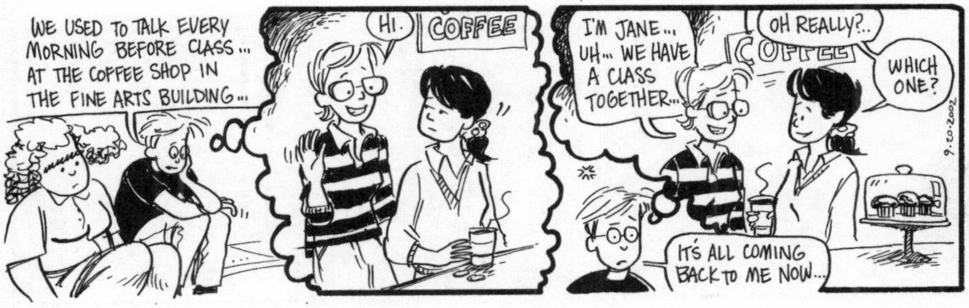
WE USED TO TALK EVERY MORNING BEFORE CLASS... AT THE COFFEE SHOP IN THE FINE ARTS BUILDING...
HI.
COFFEE
I'M JANE... UH... WE HAVE A CLASS TOGETHER...
OH REALLY?..
WHICH ONE?
IT'S ALL COMING BACK TO ME NOW...
9.20.2002

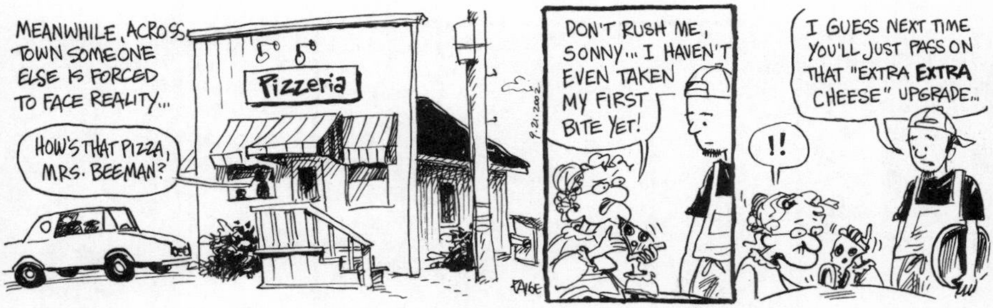
MEANWHILE, ACROSS TOWN SOMEONE ELSE IS FORCED TO FACE REALITY...
Pizzeria
HOW'S THAT PIZZA, MRS. BEEMAN?
9.21.2002
PAIGE
DON'T RUSH ME, SONNY... I HAVEN'T EVEN TAKEN MY FIRST BITE YET!
!!
I GUESS NEXT TIME YOU'LL JUST PASS ON THAT "EXTRA EXTRA CHEESE" UPGRADE...

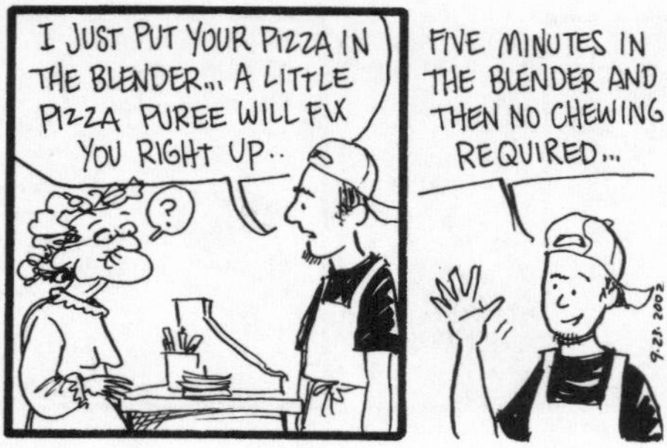
I JUST PUT YOUR PIZZA IN THE BLENDER... A LITTLE PIZZA PUREE WILL FIX YOU RIGHT UP..
?
FIVE MINUTES IN THE BLENDER AND THEN NO CHEWING REQUIRED...
9.23.2002

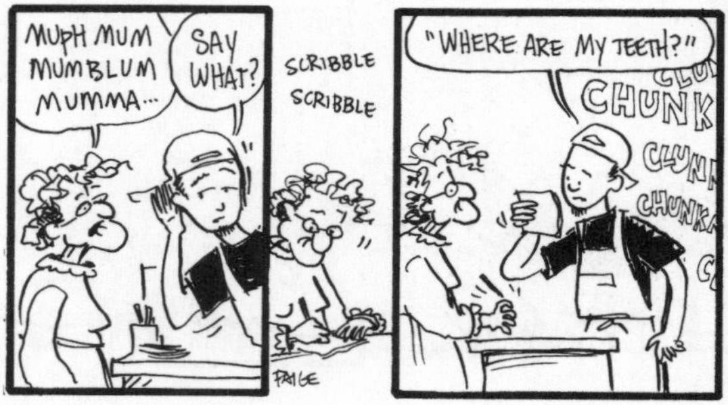
MUPH MUM MUMBLUM MUMMA...
SAY WHAT?
SCRIBBLE
SCRIBBLE
PAIGE
"WHERE ARE MY TEETH?"
CHUNK
CLUNK
CHUNKA

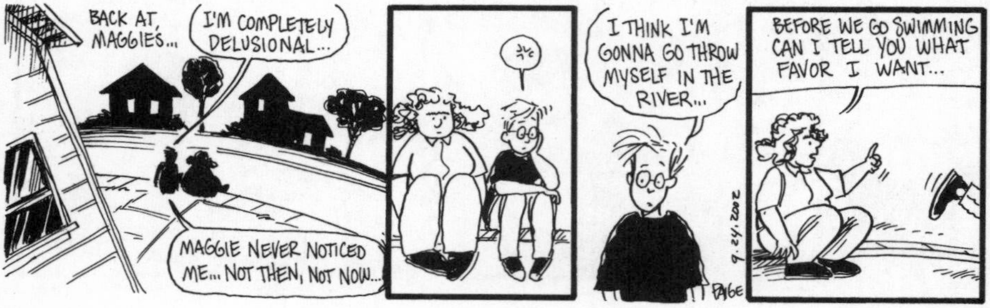
BACK AT, MAGGIE'S...
I'M COMPLETELY DELUSIONAL...
MAGGIE NEVER NOTICED ME... NOT THEN, NOT NOW...
I THINK I'M GONNA GO THROW MYSELF IN THE RIVER...
9.24.2002
PAIGE
BEFORE WE GO SWIMMING CAN I TELL YOU WHAT FAVOR I WANT...

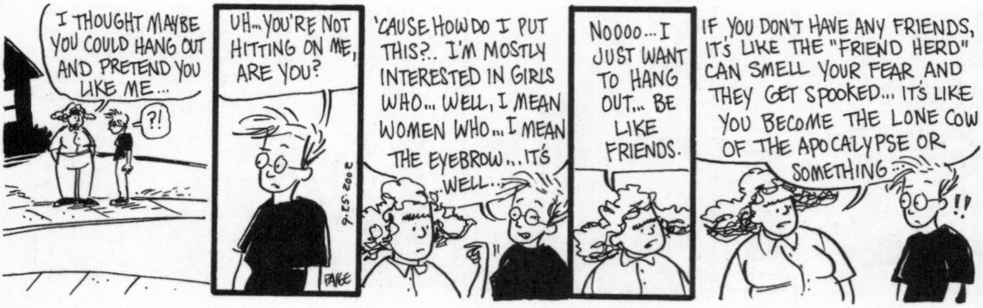
I THOUGHT MAYBE YOU COULD HANG OUT AND PRETEND YOU LIKE ME...
?!
UH... YOU'RE NOT HITTING ON ME, ARE YOU?
9.25.2002
PAIGE
'CAUSE HOW DO I PUT THIS?.. I'M MOSTLY INTERESTED IN GIRLS WHO... WELL, I MEAN WOMEN WHO... I MEAN THE EYEBROW... IT'S ...WELL...
NOOOO... I JUST WANT TO HANG OUT... BE LIKE FRIENDS.
IF YOU DON'T HAVE ANY FRIENDS, IT'S LIKE THE "FRIEND HERD" CAN SMELL YOUR FEAR AND THEY GET SPOOKED... IT'S LIKE YOU BECOME THE LONE COW OF THE APOCALYPSE OR SOMETHING...
!!

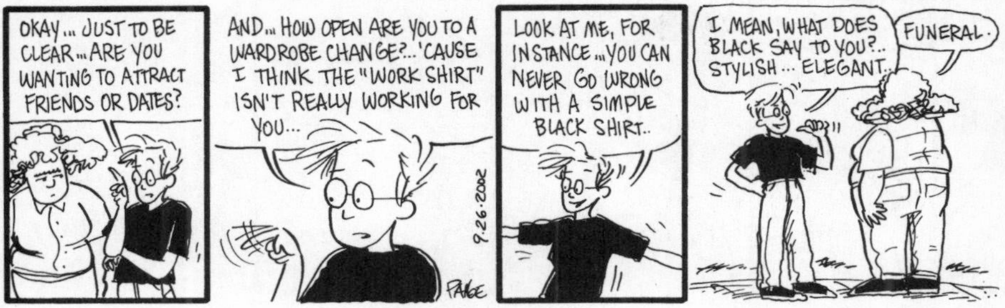
OKAY... JUST TO BE CLEAR... ARE YOU WANTING TO ATTRACT FRIENDS OR DATES?
AND... HOW OPEN ARE YOU TO A WARDROBE CHANGE?.. 'CAUSE I THINK THE "WORK SHIRT" ISN'T REALLY WORKING FOR YOU...
9.26.2002
PAIGE
LOOK AT ME, FOR INSTANCE... YOU CAN NEVER GO WRONG WITH A SIMPLE BLACK SHIRT..
I MEAN, WHAT DOES BLACK SAY TO YOU?.. STYLISH... ELEGANT..
FUNERAL.

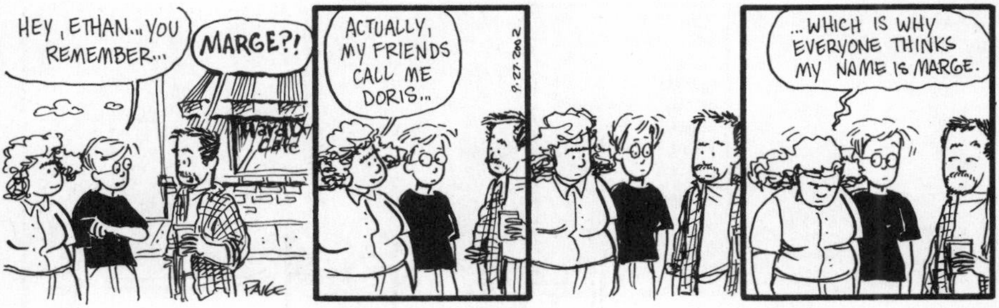
HEY, ETHAN... YOU REMEMBER...
MARGE?!
Hard Cafe
PAIGE
ACTUALLY, MY FRIENDS CALL ME DORIS...
9.27.2002
...WHICH IS WHY EVERYONE THINKS MY NAME IS MARGE.

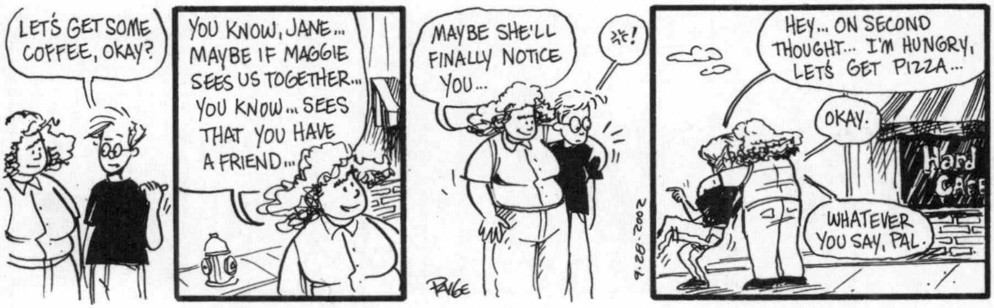
LET'S GET SOME COFFEE, OKAY?
YOU KNOW, JANE... MAYBE IF MAGGIE SEES US TOGETHER... YOU KNOW... SEES THAT YOU HAVE A FRIEND...
MAYBE SHE'LL FINALLY NOTICE YOU...
*!
PAIGE
HEY... ON SECOND THOUGHT... I'M HUNGRY, LET'S GET PIZZA...
OKAY.
Hard CAFE
WHATEVER YOU SAY, PAL.
9.28.2002

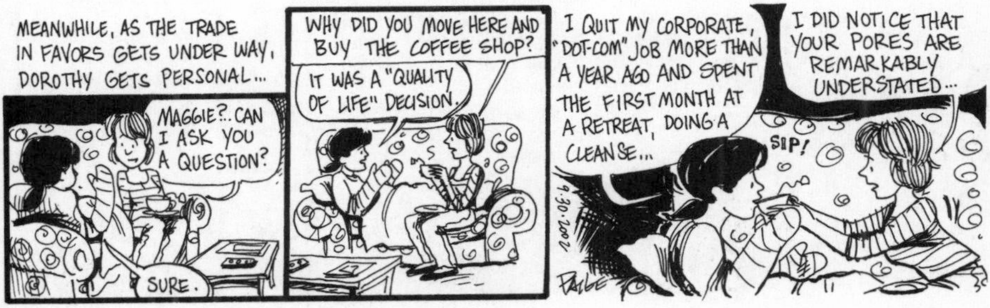
MEANWHILE, AS THE TRADE IN FAVORS GETS UNDER WAY, DOROTHY GETS PERSONAL...
MAGGIE?.. CAN I ASK YOU A QUESTION?
SURE.
WHY DID YOU MOVE HERE AND BUY THE COFFEE SHOP?
IT WAS A "QUALITY OF LIFE" DECISION.
I QUIT MY CORPORATE, "DOT-COM" JOB MORE THAN A YEAR AGO AND SPENT THE FIRST MONTH AT A RETREAT, DOING A CLEANSE...
I DID NOTICE THAT YOUR PORES ARE REMARKABLY UNDERSTATED...
SIP!
9.30.2002
PAIGE

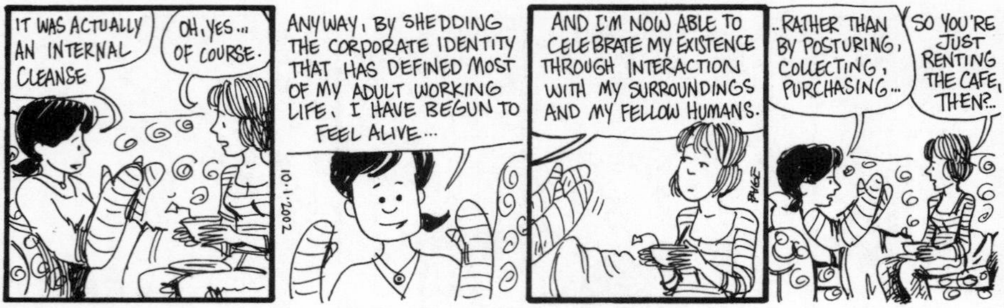
IT WAS ACTUALLY AN INTERNAL CLEANSE
OH, YES... OF COURSE.
ANYWAY, BY SHEDDING THE CORPORATE IDENTITY THAT HAS DEFINED MOST OF MY ADULT WORKING LIFE, I HAVE BEGUN TO FEEL ALIVE...
10.1.2002
AND I'M NOW ABLE TO CELEBRATE MY EXISTENCE THROUGH INTERACTION WITH MY SURROUNDINGS AND MY FELLOW HUMANS.
..RATHER THAN BY POSTURING, COLLECTING, PURCHASING...
SO YOU'RE JUST RENTING THE CAFE, THEN?..
PAIGE

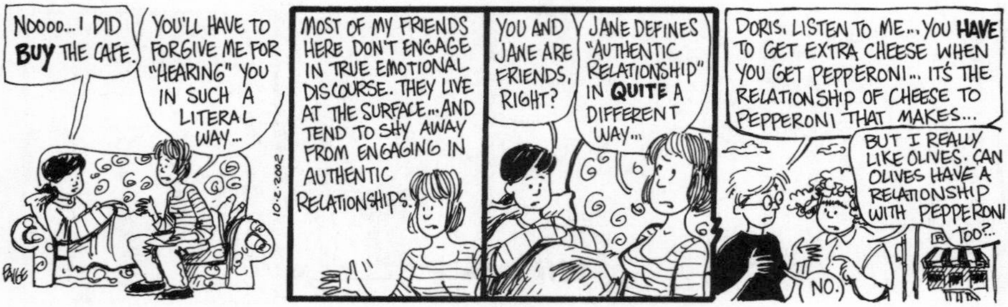
NOOOO...I DID **BUY** THE CAFE.
YOU'LL HAVE TO FORGIVE ME FOR "HEARING" YOU IN SUCH A LITERAL WAY...
PAIGE
10.2.2002
MOST OF MY FRIENDS HERE DON'T ENGAGE IN TRUE EMOTIONAL DISCOURSE. THEY LIVE AT THE SURFACE...AND TEND TO SHY AWAY FROM ENGAGING IN AUTHENTIC RELATIONSHIPS.
YOU AND JANE ARE FRIENDS, RIGHT?
JANE DEFINES "AUTHENTIC RELATIONSHIP" IN **QUITE** A DIFFERENT WAY...
DORIS, LISTEN TO ME... YOU **HAVE** TO GET EXTRA CHEESE WHEN YOU GET PEPPERONI... IT'S THE RELATIONSHIP OF CHEESE TO PEPPERONI THAT MAKES...
BUT I REALLY LIKE OLIVES. CAN OLIVES HAVE A RELATIONSHIP WITH PEPPERONI TOO?..
NO.

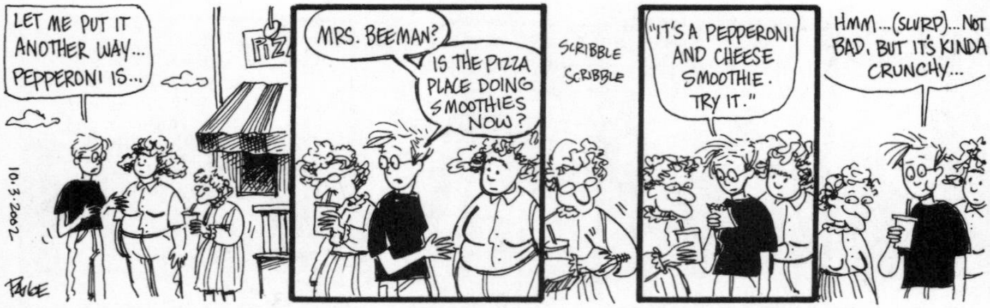
LET ME PUT IT ANOTHER WAY... PEPPERONI IS...
10.3.2002
PAIGE
MRS. BEEMAN?
IS THE PIZZA PLACE DOING SMOOTHIES NOW?
SCRIBBLE
SCRIBBLE
"IT'S A PEPPERONI AND CHEESE SMOOTHIE. TRY IT."
HMM...(SLURP)...NOT BAD, BUT IT'S KINDA CRUNCHY...

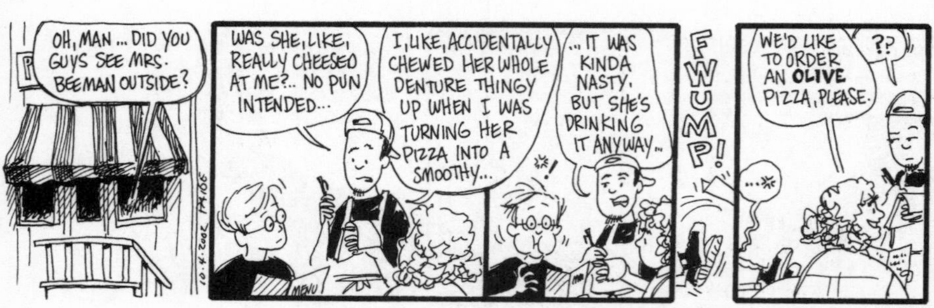
OH, MAN... DID YOU GUYS SEE MRS. BEEMAN OUTSIDE?
10.4.2002 PAIGE
WAS SHE, LIKE, REALLY CHEESED AT ME?.. NO PUN INTENDED...
I, LIKE, ACCIDENTALLY CHEWED HER WHOLE DENTURE THINGY UP WHEN I WAS TURNING HER PIZZA INTO A SMOOTHY...
MENU
...IT WAS KINDA NASTY, BUT SHE'S DRINKING IT ANYWAY...
FWUMP!
WE'D LIKE TO ORDER AN **OLIVE** PIZZA, PLEASE.
??

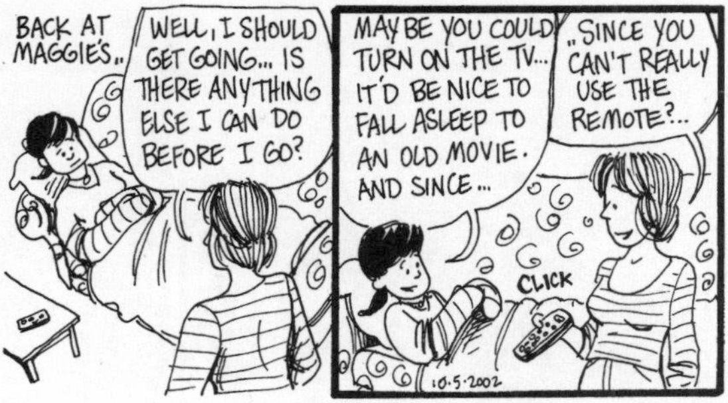
BACK AT MAGGIE'S..
WELL, I SHOULD GET GOING... IS THERE ANYTHING ELSE I CAN DO BEFORE I GO?
MAYBE YOU COULD TURN ON THE TV... IT'D BE NICE TO FALL ASLEEP TO AN OLD MOVIE. AND SINCE...
..SINCE YOU CAN'T REALLY USE THE REMOTE?...
CLICK
10.5.2002

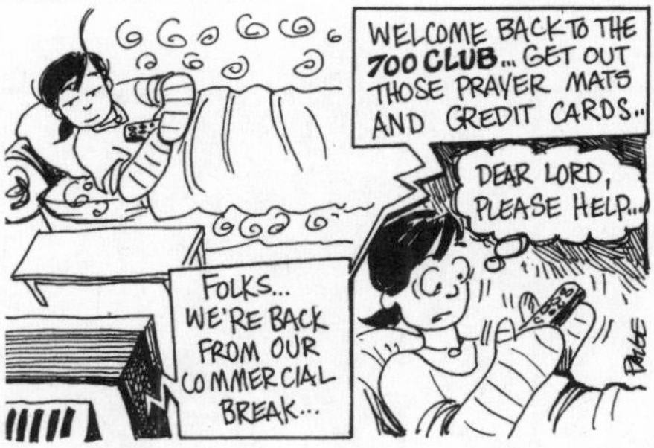
WELCOME BACK TO THE 700 CLUB... GET OUT THOSE PRAYER MATS AND CREDIT CARDS..
DEAR LORD, PLEASE HELP...
FOLKS... WE'RE BACK FROM OUR COMMERCIAL BREAK...
PAIGE

MEANWHILE, AT JANE'S...

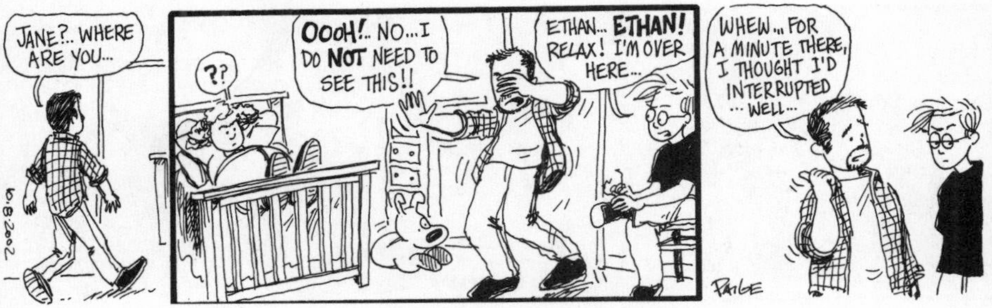
JANE?.. WHERE ARE YOU...
10.8.2002
??
OOOH!.. NO...I DO NOT NEED TO SEE THIS!!
ETHAN... ETHAN! RELAX! I'M OVER HERE...
WHEW... FOR A MINUTE THERE, I THOUGHT I'D INTERRUPTED ... WELL...
PAIGE

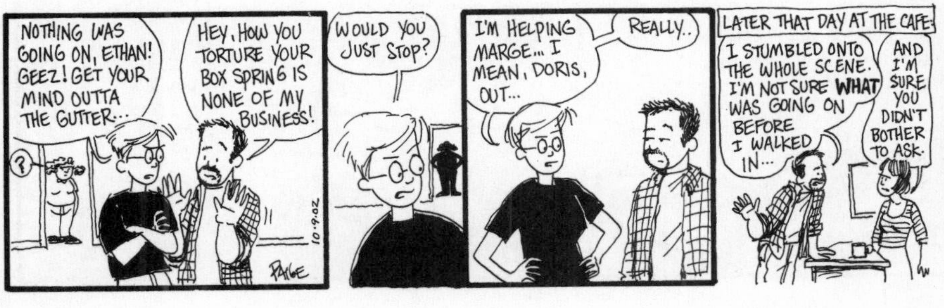
NOTHING WAS GOING ON, ETHAN! GEEZ! GET YOUR MIND OUTTA THE GUTTER...
HEY, HOW YOU TORTURE YOUR BOX SPRING IS NONE OF MY BUSINESS!
?
PAIGE
10.9.02
WOULD YOU JUST STOP?
I'M HELPING MARGE... I MEAN, DORIS, OUT...
REALLY..
LATER THAT DAY AT THE CAFE
I STUMBLED ONTO THE WHOLE SCENE. I'M NOT SURE WHAT WAS GOING ON BEFORE I WALKED IN...
AND I'M SURE YOU DIDN'T BOTHER TO ASK.

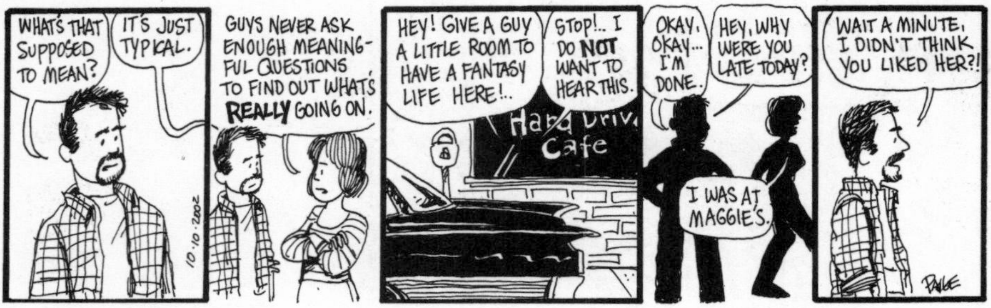
WHAT'S THAT SUPPOSED TO MEAN?
IT'S JUST TYPICAL.
10·10·2002
GUYS NEVER ASK ENOUGH MEANING-FUL QUESTIONS TO FIND OUT WHAT'S REALLY GOING ON.
HEY! GIVE A GUY A LITTLE ROOM TO HAVE A FANTASY LIFE HERE!..
STOP!.. I DO NOT WANT TO HEAR THIS.
Cafe
OKAY, OKAY... I'M DONE.
HEY, WHY WERE YOU LATE TODAY?
I WAS AT MAGGIE'S.
WAIT A MINUTE, I DIDN'T THINK YOU LIKED HER?!
PAIGE

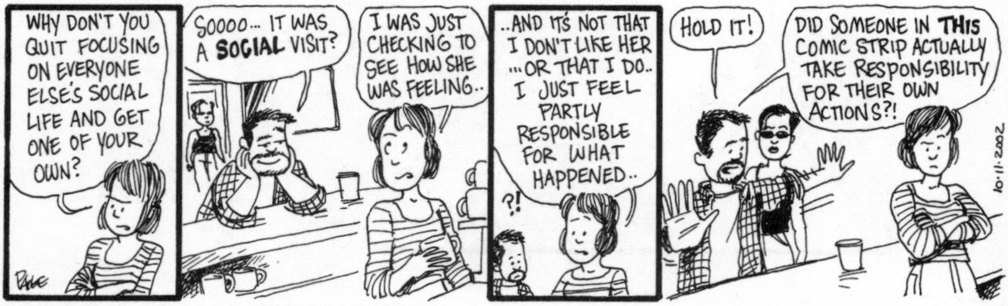
WHY DON'T YOU QUIT FOCUSING ON EVERYONE ELSE'S SOCIAL LIFE AND GET ONE OF YOUR OWN?
PAIGE
SOOOO... IT WAS A SOCIAL VISIT?
I WAS JUST CHECKING TO SEE HOW SHE WAS FEELING..
..AND IT'S NOT THAT I DON'T LIKE HER ...OR THAT I DO.. I JUST FEEL PARTLY RESPONSIBLE FOR WHAT HAPPENED..
?!
HOLD IT!
DID SOMEONE IN THIS COMIC STRIP ACTUALLY TAKE RESPONSIBILITY FOR THEIR OWN ACTIONS?!
10·11·2002

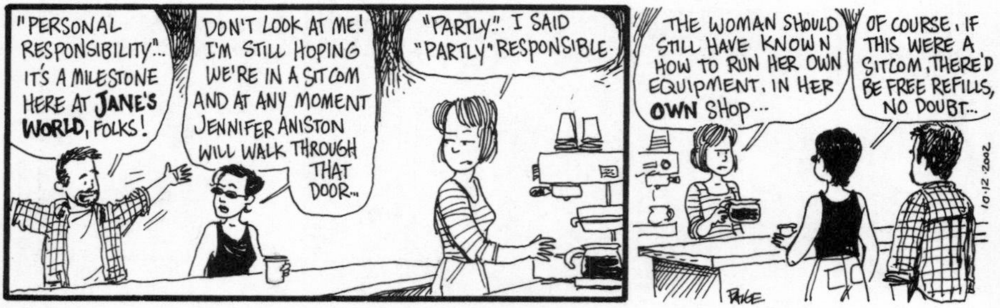
"PERSONAL RESPONSIBILITY"... IT'S A MILESTONE HERE AT JANE'S WORLD, FOLKS!
DON'T LOOK AT ME! I'M STILL HOPING WE'RE IN A SITCOM AND AT ANY MOMENT JENNIFER ANISTON WILL WALK THROUGH THAT DOOR...
"PARTLY"!.. I SAID "PARTLY" RESPONSIBLE.
THE WOMAN SHOULD STILL HAVE KNOWN HOW TO RUN HER OWN EQUIPMENT, IN HER OWN SHOP...
OF COURSE, IF THIS WERE A SITCOM, THERE'D BE FREE REFILLS, NO DOUBT...
10·12·2002
PAIGE

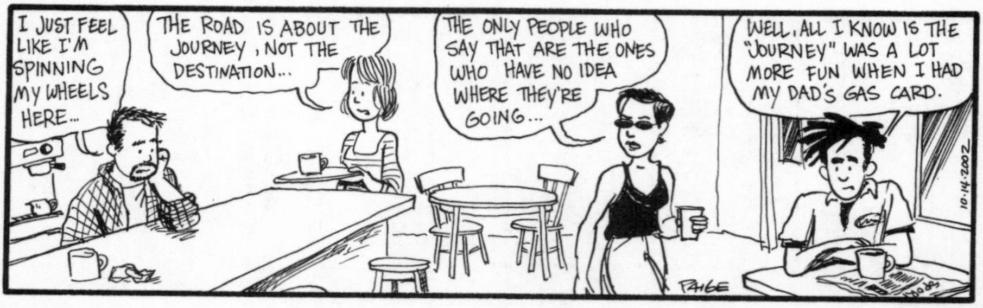
I JUST FEEL LIKE I'M SPINNING MY WHEELS HERE...
THE ROAD IS ABOUT THE JOURNEY, NOT THE DESTINATION...
THE ONLY PEOPLE WHO SAY THAT ARE THE ONES WHO HAVE NO IDEA WHERE THEY'RE GOING...
WELL, ALL I KNOW IS THE "JOURNEY" WAS A LOT MORE FUN WHEN I HAD MY DAD'S GAS CARD.
10·14·2002
PAIGE

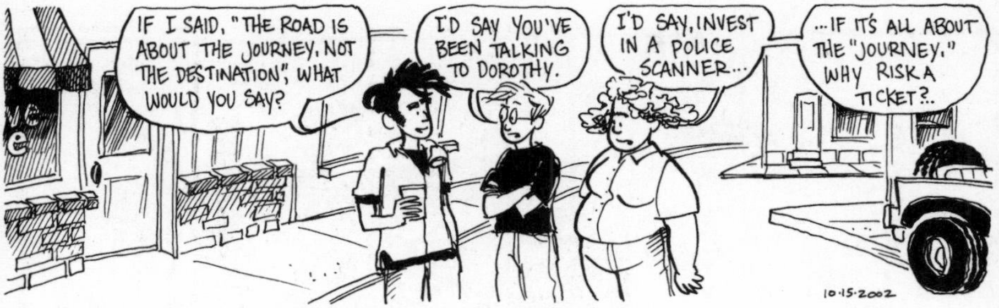
IF I SAID, "THE ROAD IS ABOUT THE JOURNEY, NOT THE DESTINATION", WHAT WOULD YOU SAY?
I'D SAY YOU'VE BEEN TALKING TO DOROTHY.
I'D SAY, INVEST IN A POLICE SCANNER...
...IF IT'S ALL ABOUT THE "JOURNEY," WHY RISK A TICKET?..
10·15·2002

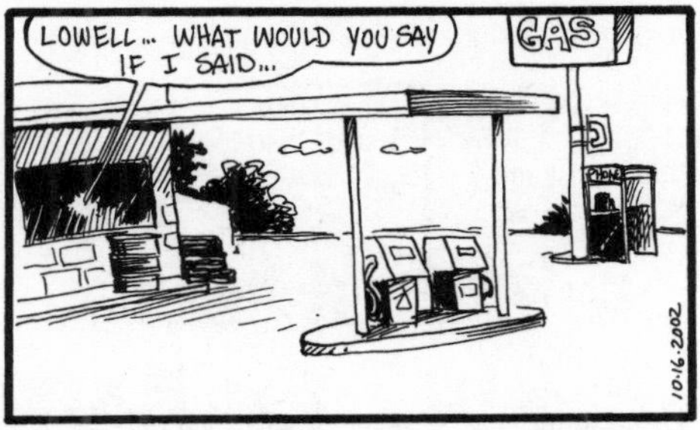
LOWELL... WHAT WOULD YOU SAY IF I SAID...
GAS
PHONE
10·16·2002

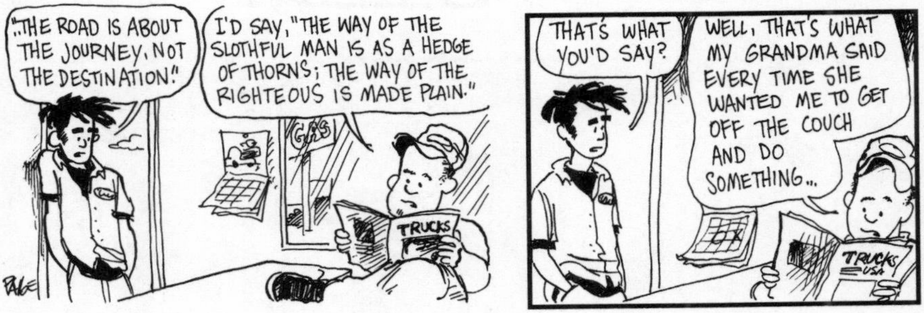
"..THE ROAD IS ABOUT THE JOURNEY, NOT THE DESTINATION!"
I'D SAY, "THE WAY OF THE SLOTHFUL MAN IS AS A HEDGE OF THORNS; THE WAY OF THE RIGHTEOUS IS MADE PLAIN."
GAS
TRUCKS
PAGE
THAT'S WHAT YOU'D SAY?
WELL, THAT'S WHAT MY GRANDMA SAID EVERY TIME SHE WANTED ME TO GET OFF THE COUCH AND DO SOMETHING...
TRUCKS USA

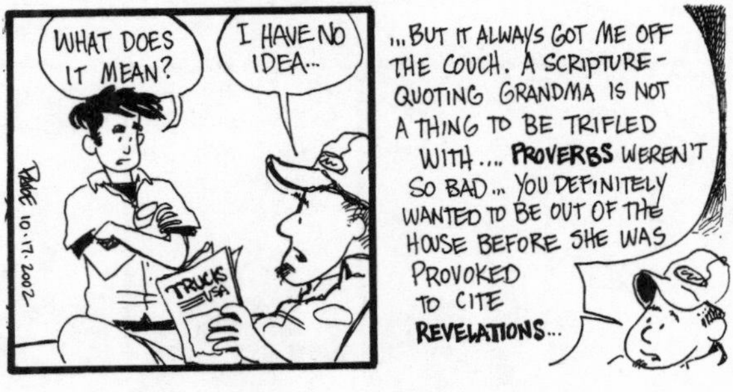
WHAT DOES IT MEAN?
I HAVE NO IDEA...
...BUT IT ALWAYS GOT ME OFF THE COUCH. A SCRIPTURE-QUOTING GRANDMA IS NOT A THING TO BE TRIFLED WITH.... PROVERBS WEREN'T SO BAD... YOU DEFINITELY WANTED TO BE OUT OF THE HOUSE BEFORE SHE WAS PROVOKED TO CITE REVELATIONS...
TRUCKS USA
PAGE 10·17·2002

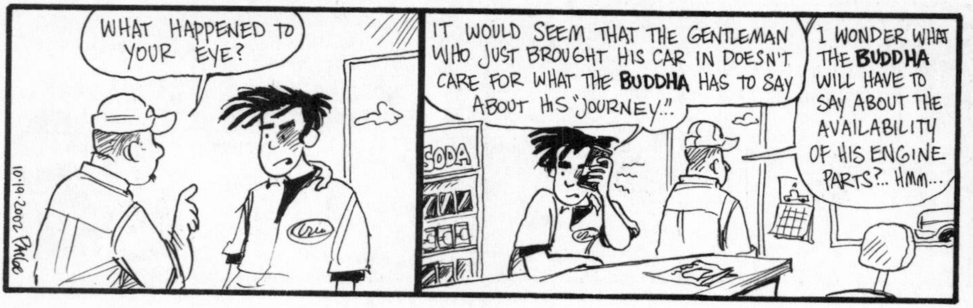
WHAT HAPPENED TO YOUR EYE?
10·19·2002 PAIGE
IT WOULD SEEM THAT THE GENTLEMAN WHO JUST BROUGHT HIS CAR IN DOESN'T CARE FOR WHAT THE **BUDDHA** HAS TO SAY ABOUT HIS "JOURNEY."
SODA
I WONDER WHAT THE **BUDDHA** WILL HAVE TO SAY ABOUT THE AVAILABILITY OF HIS ENGINE PARTS?.. HMM...

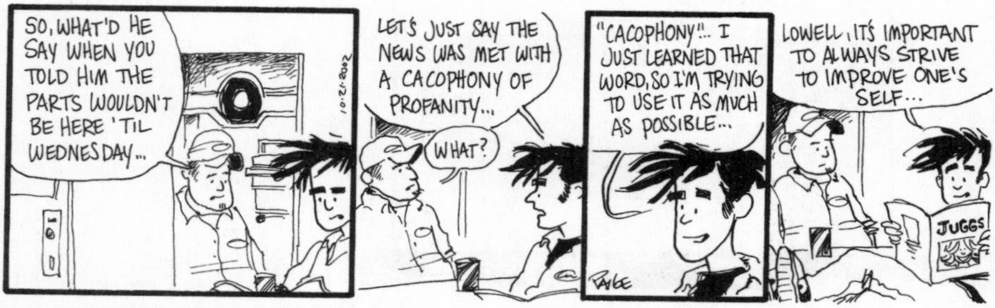
SO, WHAT'D HE SAY WHEN YOU TOLD HIM THE PARTS WOULDN'T BE HERE 'TIL WEDNESDAY...
10·21·2002
LET'S JUST SAY THE NEWS WAS MET WITH A CACOPHONY OF PROFANITY...
WHAT?
"CACOPHONY"... I JUST LEARNED THAT WORD, SO I'M TRYING TO USE IT AS MUCH AS POSSIBLE...
PAIGE
LOWELL, IT'S IMPORTANT TO ALWAYS STRIVE TO IMPROVE ONE'S SELF...
JUGGS

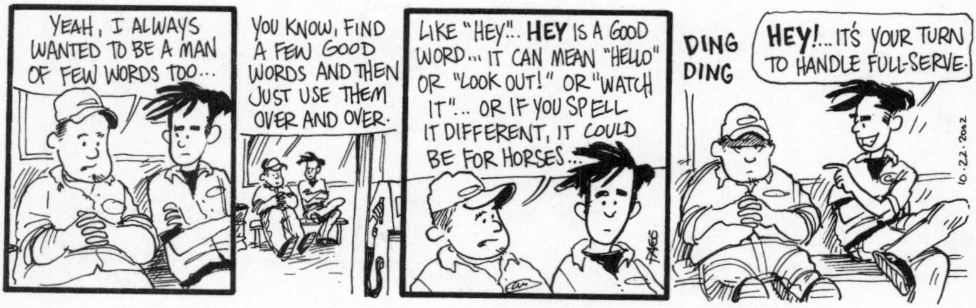
YEAH, I ALWAYS WANTED TO BE A MAN OF FEW WORDS TOO...
YOU KNOW, FIND A FEW GOOD WORDS AND THEN JUST USE THEM OVER AND OVER.
LIKE "HEY"... **HEY** IS A GOOD WORD... IT CAN MEAN "HELLO" OR "LOOK OUT!" OR "WATCH IT"... OR IF YOU SPELL IT DIFFERENT, IT COULD BE FOR HORSES...
PAIGE
DING DING
HEY!... IT'S YOUR TURN TO HANDLE FULL-SERVE.
10·22·2002

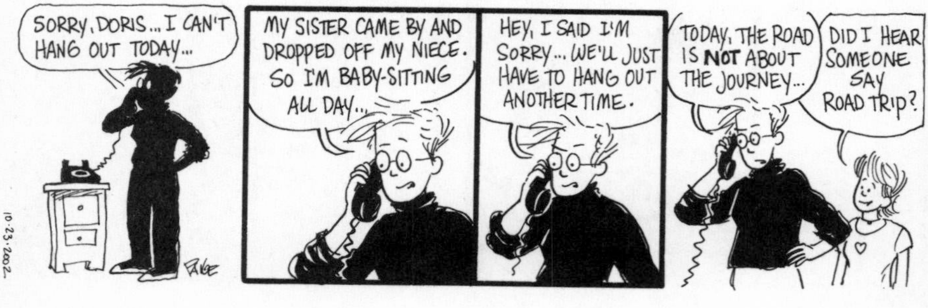
SORRY, DORIS... I CAN'T HANG OUT TODAY...
10·23·2002
PAIGE
MY SISTER CAME BY AND DROPPED OFF MY NIECE. SO I'M BABY-SITTING ALL DAY...
HEY, I SAID I'M SORRY... WE'LL JUST HAVE TO HANG OUT ANOTHER TIME.
TODAY, THE ROAD IS **NOT** ABOUT THE JOURNEY...
DID I HEAR SOMEONE SAY ROAD TRIP?

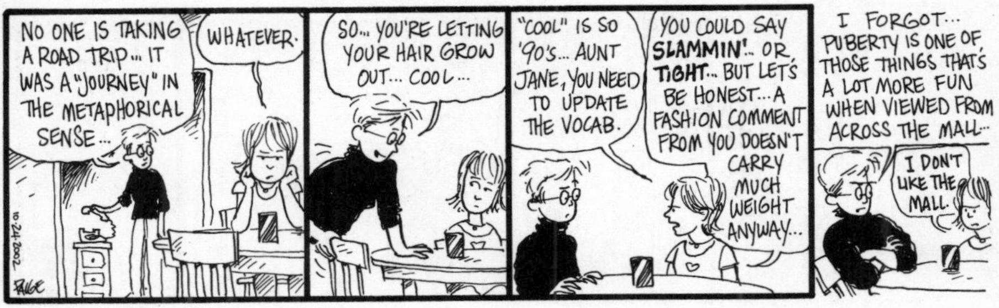

NO ONE IS TAKING A ROAD TRIP... IT WAS A "JOURNEY" IN THE METAPHORICAL SENSE...
WHATEVER.
SO... YOU'RE LETTING YOUR HAIR GROW OUT... COOL...
"COOL" IS SO '90'S... AUNT JANE, YOU NEED TO UPDATE THE VOCAB.
YOU COULD SAY **SLAMMIN'**.. OR, **TIGHT**.. BUT LET'S BE HONEST... A FASHION COMMENT FROM YOU DOESN'T CARRY MUCH WEIGHT ANYWAY...
I FORGOT... PUBERTY IS ONE OF THOSE THINGS THAT'S A LOT MORE FUN WHEN VIEWED FROM ACROSS THE MALL...
I DON'T LIKE THE MALL.
10·24·2002
PAIGE

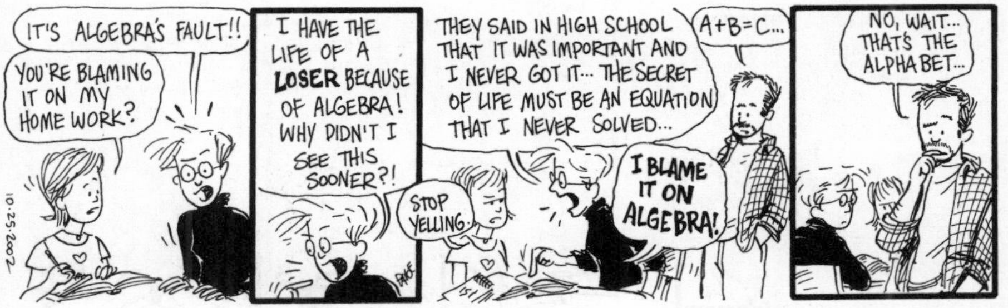

IT'S ALGEBRA'S FAULT!!
YOU'RE BLAMING IT ON MY HOME WORK?
I HAVE THE LIFE OF A **LOSER** BECAUSE OF ALGEBRA! WHY DIDN'T I SEE THIS SOONER?!
STOP YELLING.
THEY SAID IN HIGH SCHOOL THAT IT WAS IMPORTANT AND I NEVER GOT IT... THE SECRET OF LIFE MUST BE AN EQUATION THAT I NEVER SOLVED...
A+B=C...
I BLAME IT ON ALGEBRA!
NO, WAIT... THAT'S THE ALPHABET...
10·25·2002
PAIGE

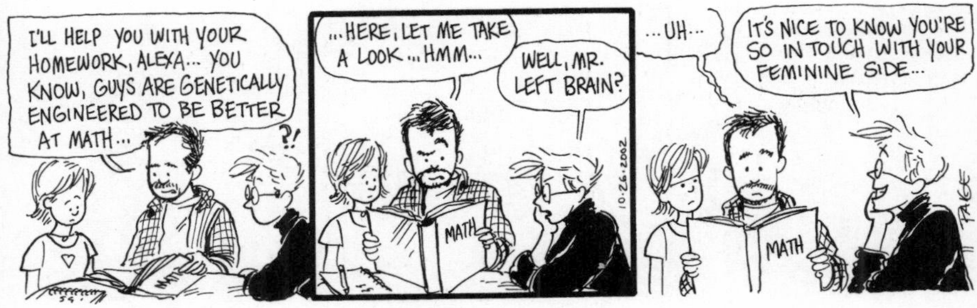

I'LL HELP YOU WITH YOUR HOMEWORK, ALEXA... YOU KNOW, GUYS ARE GENETICALLY ENGINEERED TO BE BETTER AT MATH...
?!
...HERE, LET ME TAKE A LOOK... HMM...
WELL, MR. LEFT BRAIN?
MATH
...UH...
IT'S NICE TO KNOW YOU'RE SO IN TOUCH WITH YOUR FEMININE SIDE...
MATH
10·26·2002
PAIGE

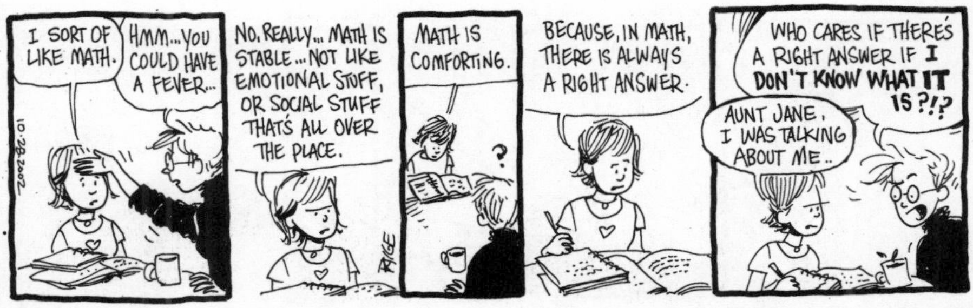

I SORT OF LIKE MATH.
HMM... YOU COULD HAVE A FEVER...
NO, REALLY... MATH IS STABLE... NOT LIKE EMOTIONAL STUFF, OR SOCIAL STUFF THAT'S ALL OVER THE PLACE.
MATH IS COMFORTING.
?
BECAUSE, IN MATH, THERE IS ALWAYS A RIGHT ANSWER.
WHO CARES IF THERE'S A RIGHT ANSWER IF **I DON'T KNOW WHAT IT IS?!?**
AUNT JANE, I WAS TALKING ABOUT ME..
10·28·2002
PAIGE

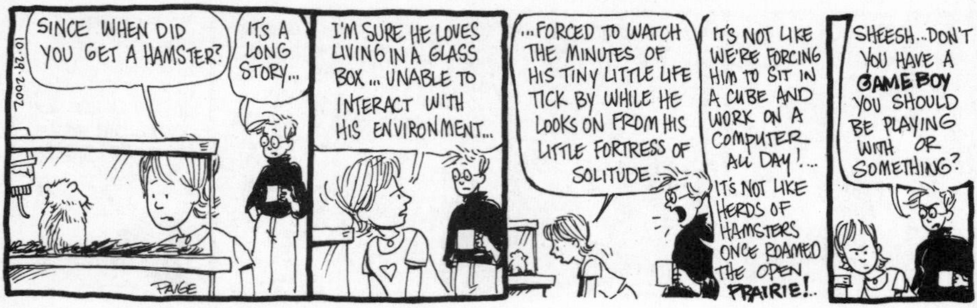
10-29-2002
SINCE WHEN DID YOU GET A HAMSTER?
IT'S A LONG STORY...
PAIGE
I'M SURE HE LOVES LIVING IN A GLASS BOX ... UNABLE TO INTERACT WITH HIS ENVIRONMENT...
...FORCED TO WATCH THE MINUTES OF HIS TINY LITTLE LIFE TICK BY WHILE HE LOOKS ON FROM HIS LITTLE FORTRESS OF SOLITUDE...
IT'S NOT LIKE WE'RE FORCING HIM TO SIT IN A CUBE AND WORK ON A COMPUTER ALL DAY!...
IT'S NOT LIKE HERDS OF HAMSTERS ONCE ROAMED THE OPEN PRAIRIE!..
SHEESH...DON'T YOU HAVE A GAMEBOY YOU SHOULD BE PLAYING WITH OR SOMETHING?

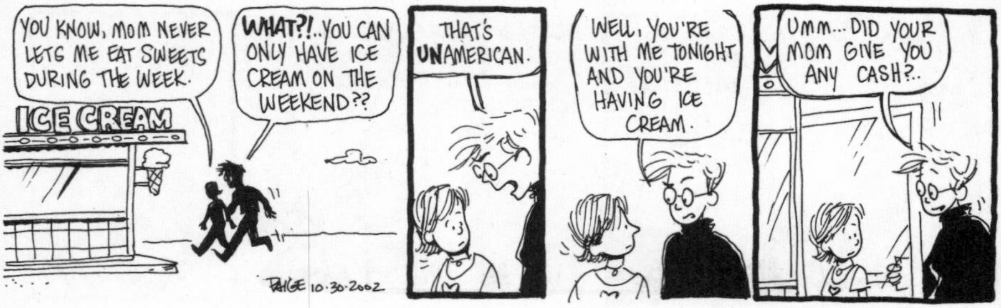
YOU KNOW, MOM NEVER LETS ME EAT SWEETS DURING THE WEEK.
WHAT?!..YOU CAN ONLY HAVE ICE CREAM ON THE WEEKEND??
ICE CREAM
PAIGE 10-30-2002
THAT'S UNAMERICAN.
WELL, YOU'RE WITH ME TONIGHT AND YOU'RE HAVING ICE CREAM.
UMM... DID YOUR MOM GIVE YOU ANY CASH?..

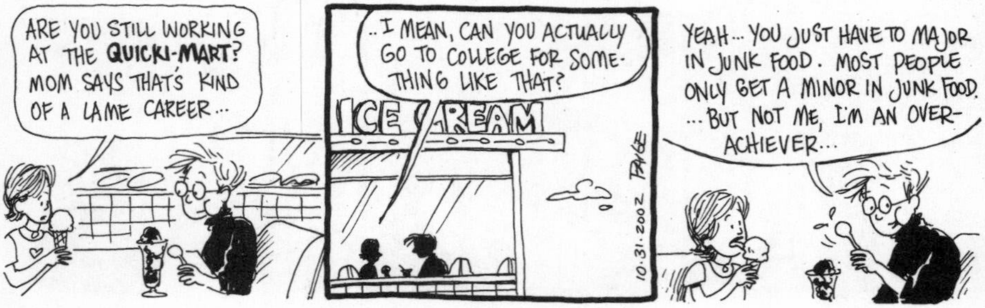
ARE YOU STILL WORKING AT THE QUICKI-MART? MOM SAYS THAT'S KIND OF A LAME CAREER...
..I MEAN, CAN YOU ACTUALLY GO TO COLLEGE FOR SOMETHING LIKE THAT?
ICE CREAM
PAIGE
10-31-2002
YEAH... YOU JUST HAVE TO MAJOR IN JUNK FOOD. MOST PEOPLE ONLY GET A MINOR IN JUNK FOOD.
... BUT NOT ME, I'M AN OVER-ACHIEVER...

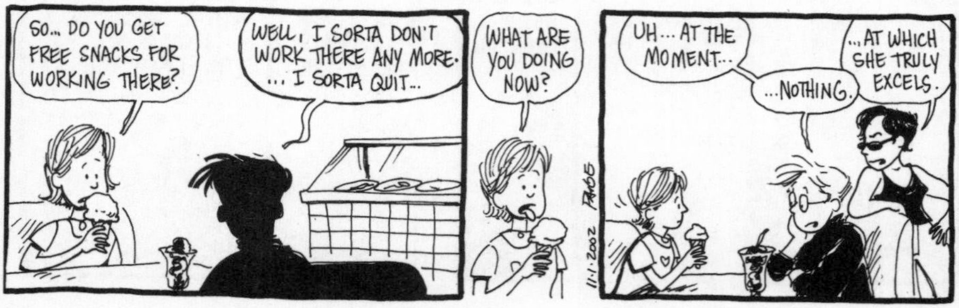
SO... DO YOU GET FREE SNACKS FOR WORKING THERE?
WELL, I SORTA DON'T WORK THERE ANY MORE. ... I SORTA QUIT...
WHAT ARE YOU DOING NOW?
PAIGE
11-1-2002
UH... AT THE MOMENT...
...NOTHING.
...AT WHICH SHE TRULY EXCELS.

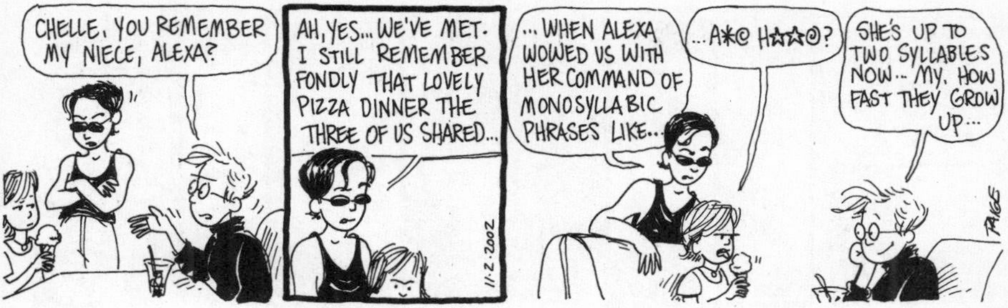
CHELLE, YOU REMEMBER MY NIECE, ALEXA?
AH, YES... WE'VE MET. I STILL REMEMBER FONDLY THAT LOVELY PIZZA DINNER THE THREE OF US SHARED...
11·2·2002
...WHEN ALEXA WOWED US WITH HER COMMAND OF MONOSYLLABIC PHRASES LIKE...
...A*@ H☆☆@?
SHE'S UP TO TWO SYLLABLES NOW... MY, HOW FAST THEY GROW UP...
PAIGE

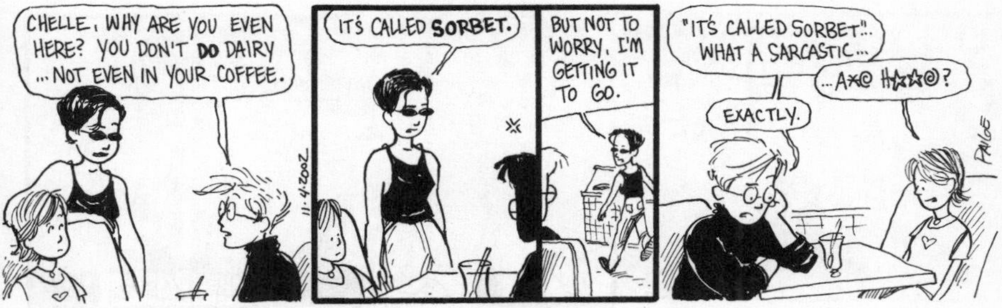
CHELLE, WHY ARE YOU EVEN HERE? YOU DON'T DO DAIRY ...NOT EVEN IN YOUR COFFEE.
11·4·2002
IT'S CALLED SORBET.
BUT NOT TO WORRY, I'M GETTING IT TO GO.
"IT'S CALLED SORBET"... WHAT A SARCASTIC...
...A*@ H☆☆@?
EXACTLY.
PAIGE

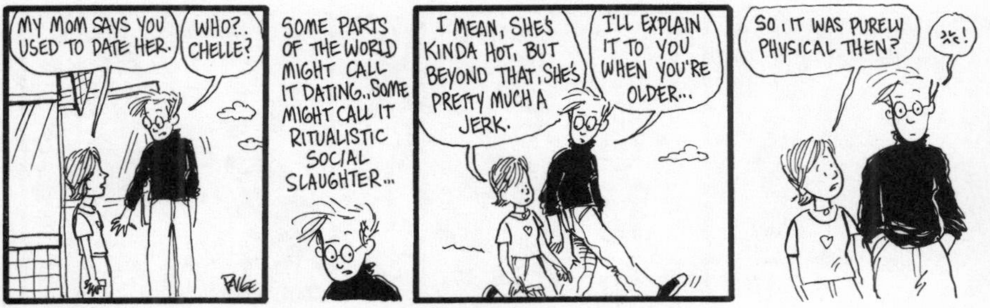
MY MOM SAYS YOU USED TO DATE HER.
WHO?.. CHELLE?
PAIGE
SOME PARTS OF THE WORLD MIGHT CALL IT DATING.. SOME MIGHT CALL IT RITUALISTIC SOCIAL SLAUGHTER...
I MEAN, SHE'S KINDA HOT, BUT BEYOND THAT, SHE'S PRETTY MUCH A JERK.
I'LL EXPLAIN IT TO YOU WHEN YOU'RE OLDER...
SO, IT WAS PURELY PHYSICAL THEN?

LATER...

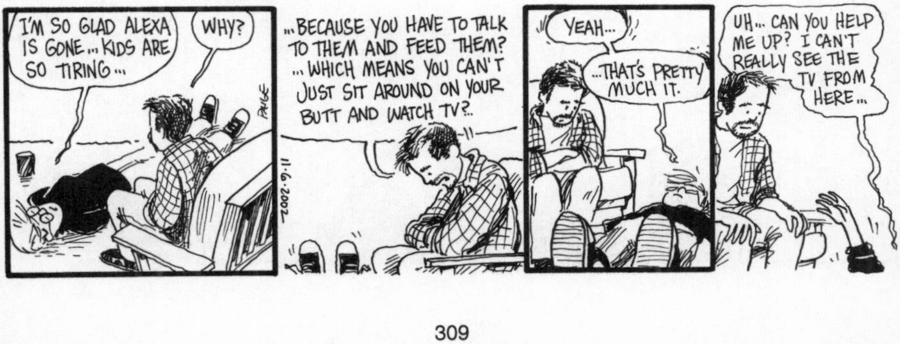
I'M SO GLAD ALEXA IS GONE... KIDS ARE SO TIRING...
WHY?
PAIGE
11·6·2002
...BECAUSE YOU HAVE TO TALK TO THEM AND FEED THEM? ...WHICH MEANS YOU CAN'T JUST SIT AROUND ON YOUR BUTT AND WATCH TV?..
YEAH...
...THAT'S PRETTY MUCH IT.
UH... CAN YOU HELP ME UP? I CAN'T REALLY SEE THE TV FROM HERE...

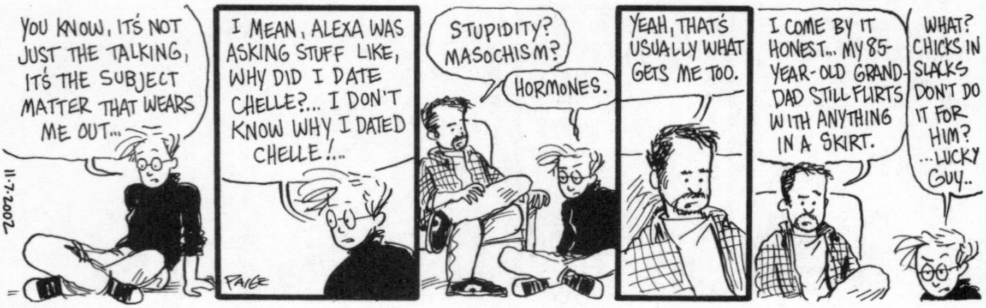
YOU KNOW, IT'S NOT JUST THE TALKING, IT'S THE SUBJECT MATTER THAT WEARS ME OUT...
11·7·2002
I MEAN, ALEXA WAS ASKING STUFF LIKE, WHY DID I DATE CHELLE?... I DON'T KNOW WHY I DATED CHELLE!...
PAIGE
STUPIDITY? MASOCHISM?
HORMONES.
YEAH, THAT'S USUALLY WHAT GETS ME TOO.
I COME BY IT HONEST... MY 85-YEAR-OLD GRANDDAD STILL FLIRTS WITH ANYTHING IN A SKIRT.
WHAT? CHICKS IN SLACKS DON'T DO IT FOR HIM? ...LUCKY GUY..

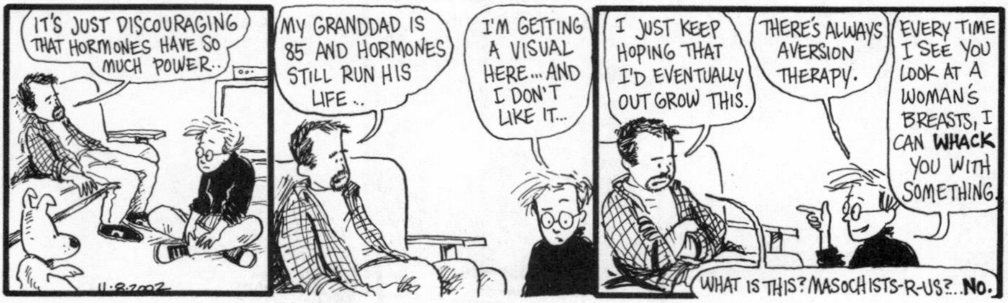
IT'S JUST DISCOURAGING THAT HORMONES HAVE SO MUCH POWER..
11·8·2002
MY GRANDDAD IS 85 AND HORMONES STILL RUN HIS LIFE..
I'M GETTING A VISUAL HERE... AND I DON'T LIKE IT...
I JUST KEEP HOPING THAT I'D EVENTUALLY OUT GROW THIS.
THERE'S ALWAYS AVERSION THERAPY.
EVERY TIME I SEE YOU LOOK AT A WOMAN'S BREASTS, I CAN WHACK YOU WITH SOMETHING.
WHAT IS THIS? MASOCHISTS-R-US?...NO.

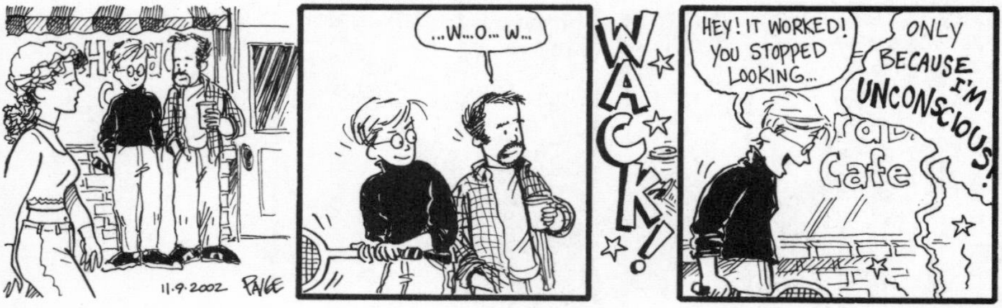
11·9·2002 PAIGE
...W...O...W...
WACK!
HEY! IT WORKED! YOU STOPPED LOOKING...
ONLY BECAUSE I'M UNCONSCIOUS!
Cafe

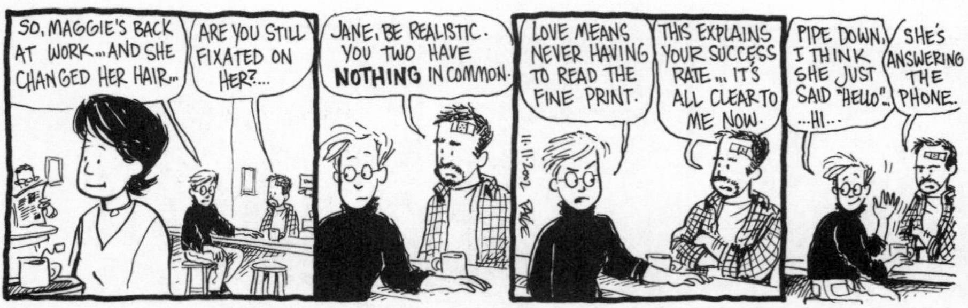
SO, MAGGIE'S BACK AT WORK... AND SHE CHANGED HER HAIR...
ARE YOU STILL FIXATED ON HER?...
JANE, BE REALISTIC. YOU TWO HAVE NOTHING IN COMMON.
11·11·2002 PAIGE
LOVE MEANS NEVER HAVING TO READ THE FINE PRINT.
THIS EXPLAINS YOUR SUCCESS RATE... IT'S ALL CLEAR TO ME NOW.
PIPE DOWN, I THINK SHE JUST SAID "HELLO"... ...HI...
SHE'S ANSWERING THE PHONE.

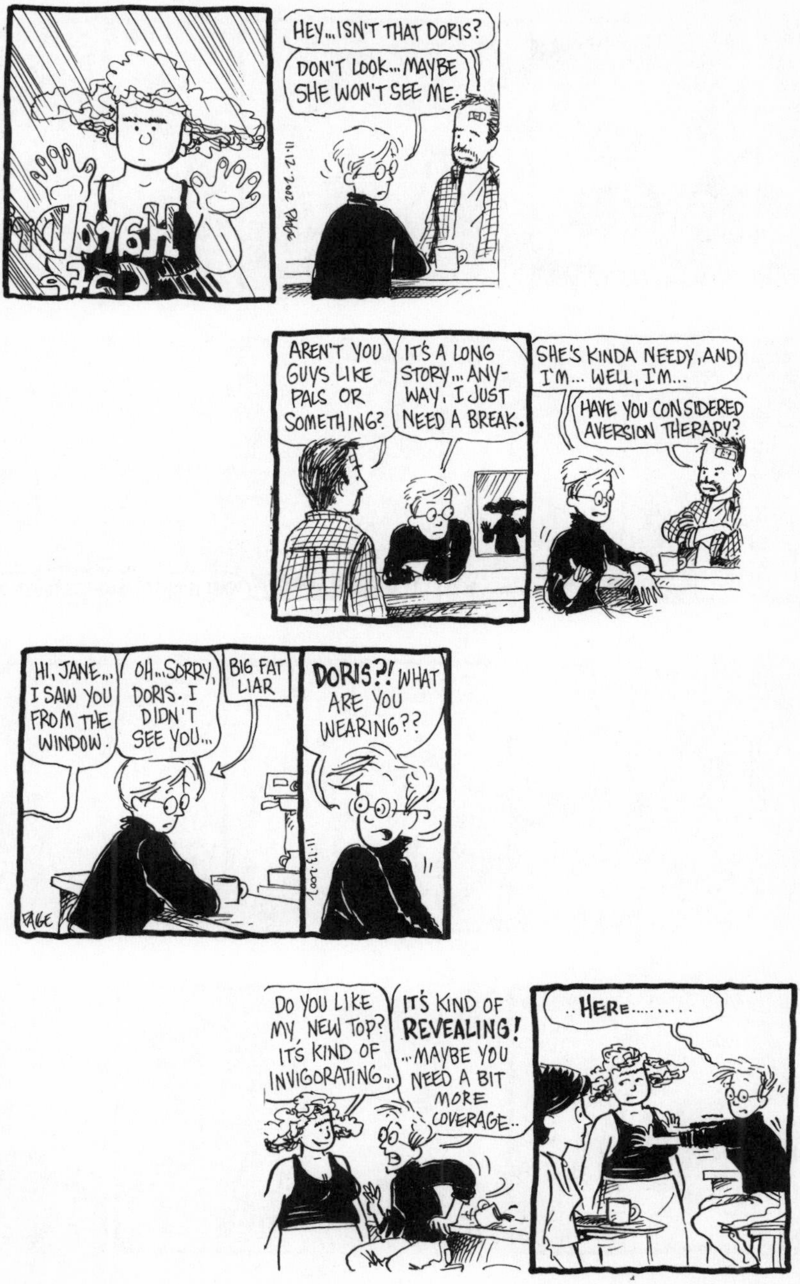
HEY... ISN'T THAT DORIS?
DON'T LOOK... MAYBE SHE WON'T SEE ME.
ARENT YOU GUYS LIKE PALS OR SOMETHING?
IT'S A LONG STORY... ANYWAY, I JUST NEED A BREAK.
SHE'S KINDA NEEDY, AND I'M... WELL, I'M...
HAVE YOU CONSIDERED AVERSION THERAPY?
HI, JANE... I SAW YOU FROM THE WINDOW.
OH... SORRY, DORIS. I DIDN'T SEE YOU...
BIG FAT LIAR
DORIS?! WHAT ARE YOU WEARING??
DO YOU LIKE MY NEW TOP? IT'S KIND OF INVIGORATING...
IT'S KIND OF REVEALING! ...MAYBE YOU NEED A BIT MORE COVERAGE..
..HERE.........

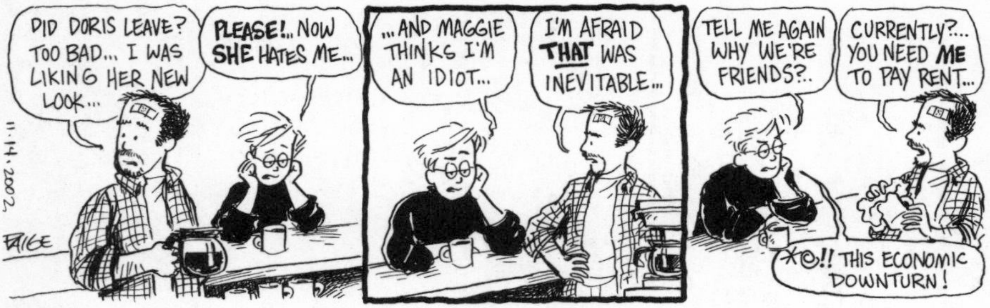
DID DORIS LEAVE? TOO BAD... I WAS LIKING HER NEW LOOK...
PLEASE!... NOW SHE HATES ME...
...AND MAGGIE THINKS I'M AN IDIOT...
I'M AFRAID THAT WAS INEVITABLE...
TELL ME AGAIN WHY WE'RE FRIENDS?..
CURRENTLY?... YOU NEED ME TO PAY RENT...
*@!! THIS ECONOMIC DOWNTURN!
11.14.2002
PAIGE

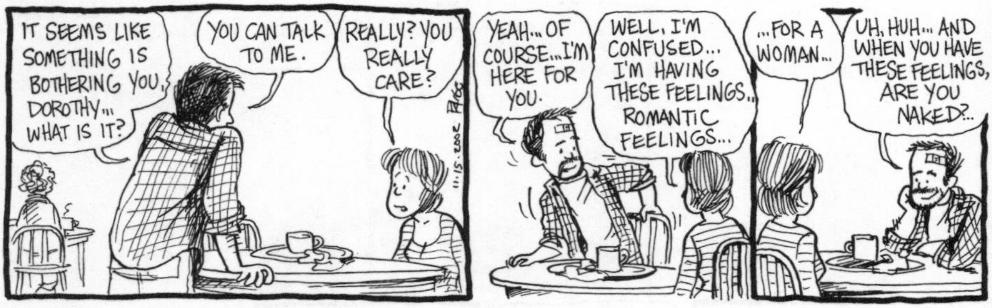
IT SEEMS LIKE SOMETHING IS BOTHERING YOU, DOROTHY... WHAT IS IT?
YOU CAN TALK TO ME.
REALLY? YOU REALLY CARE?
11.15.2002
YEAH... OF COURSE...I'M HERE FOR YOU.
WELL, I'M CONFUSED... I'M HAVING THESE FEELINGS... ROMANTIC FEELINGS...
...FOR A WOMAN...
UH, HUH... AND WHEN YOU HAVE THESE FEELINGS, ARE YOU NAKED?..

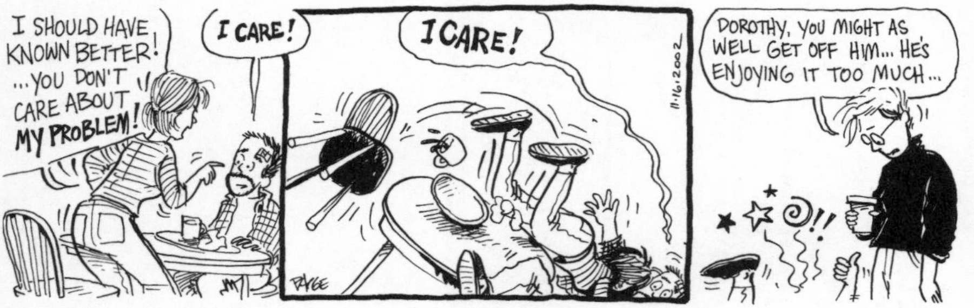
I SHOULD HAVE KNOWN BETTER! ...YOU DON'T CARE ABOUT MY PROBLEM!
I CARE!
I CARE!
11.16.2002
PAIGE
DOROTHY, YOU MIGHT AS WELL GET OFF HIM... HE'S ENJOYING IT TOO MUCH...

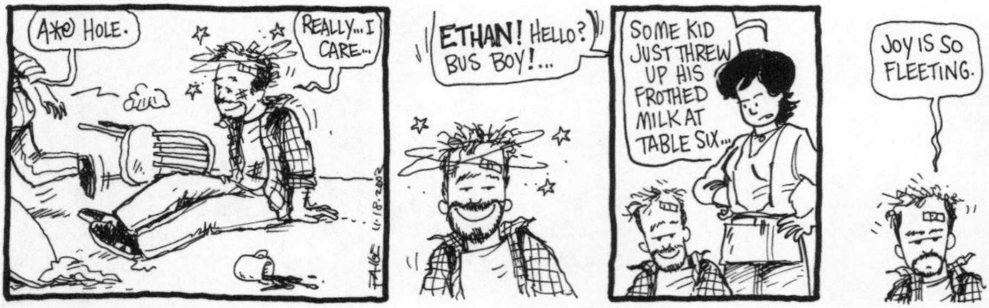
A*@ HOLE.
REALLY... I CARE...
11.18.2002
PAIGE
ETHAN! HELLO? BUS BOY!...
SOME KID JUST THREW UP HIS FROTHED MILK AT TABLE SIX...
JOY IS SO FLEETING.

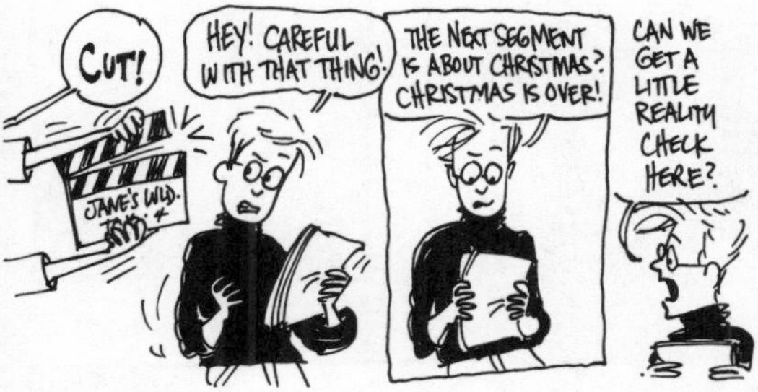
CUT!
HEY! CAREFUL WITH THAT THING!
THE NEXT SEGMENT IS ABOUT CHRISTMAS? CHRISTMAS IS OVER!
CAN WE GET A LITTLE REALITY CHECK HERE?

AUTHOR'S NOTE: OKAY, WHILE ETHAN GET'S CLEANED UP A BIT I'LL EXPLAIN THE WHOLE CHRISTMAS PROBLEM. IT ALL HAS TO DO WITH PACING... COMIC STRIP STYLE PACING THAT IS... SEE, I STARTED THIS CHRISTMAS TALE JUST BEFORE CHRISTMAS, BUT THEN I GOT SORT OF CARRIED AWAY WITH THE STORYLINE AND SINCE I CAN ONLY GET ONE TINY INSTALLMENT IN PER DAY... WELL, YOU CAN SEE HOW IF YOU GOT CARRIED AWAY IT WOULD BE EASY TO BE WRAPPING UP YOUR CHRISTMAS TALE IN APRIL. SORRY. SO, DO ME A FAVOR, SUSPEND DISBELIEF FOR A FEW MORE PAGES AND JUST RIDE THIS OUT WITH US. PRETEND CHRISTMAS LASTED JUST A LITTLE BIT LONGER...

CARTOON TIME ISN'T "REAL" TIME ANYWAY, IS IT?... OKAY, FOLKS... ROLL TAPE....

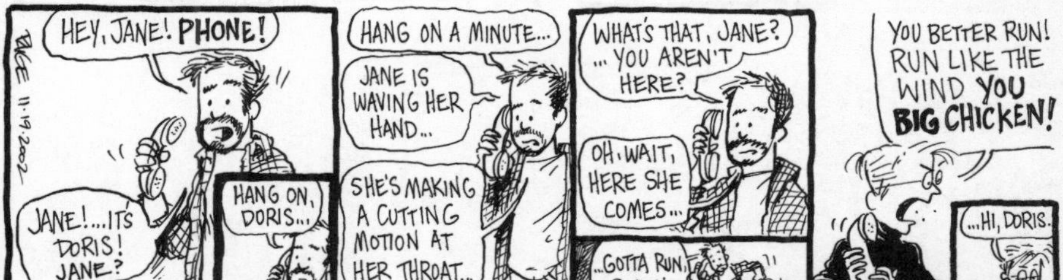
HEY, JANE! PHONE!
PAIGE 11·19·2002
JANE!...IT'S DORIS! JANE?
HANG ON, DORIS...
HANG ON A MINUTE...
JANE IS WAVING HER HAND...
SHE'S MAKING A CUTTING MOTION AT HER THROAT...
WHAT'S THAT, JANE? ...YOU AREN'T HERE?
OH, WAIT, HERE SHE COMES...
...GOTTA RUN, DORIS!...
YOU BETTER RUN! RUN LIKE THE WIND YOU BIG CHICKEN!
...HI, DORIS.

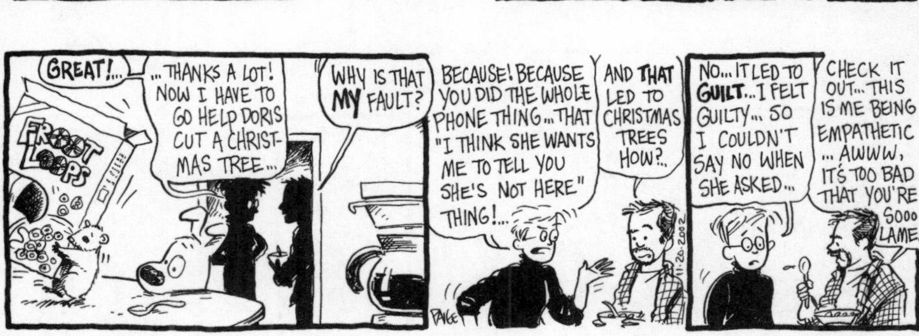
GREAT!...
...THANKS A LOT! NOW I HAVE TO GO HELP DORIS CUT A CHRISTMAS TREE...
FROOT LOOPS
WHY IS THAT MY FAULT?
BECAUSE! BECAUSE YOU DID THE WHOLE PHONE THING... THAT "I THINK SHE WANTS ME TO TELL YOU SHE'S NOT HERE" THING!...
AND THAT LED TO CHRISTMAS TREES HOW?...
PAIGE 11-20-2002
NO... IT LED TO GUILT... I FELT GUILTY... SO I COULDN'T SAY NO WHEN SHE ASKED...
CHECK IT OUT... THIS IS ME BEING EMPATHETIC ... AWWW, IT'S TOO BAD THAT YOU'RE SOOO LAME.

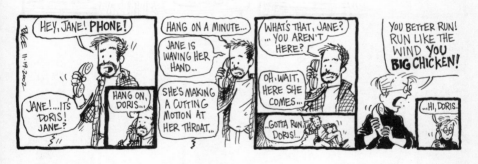

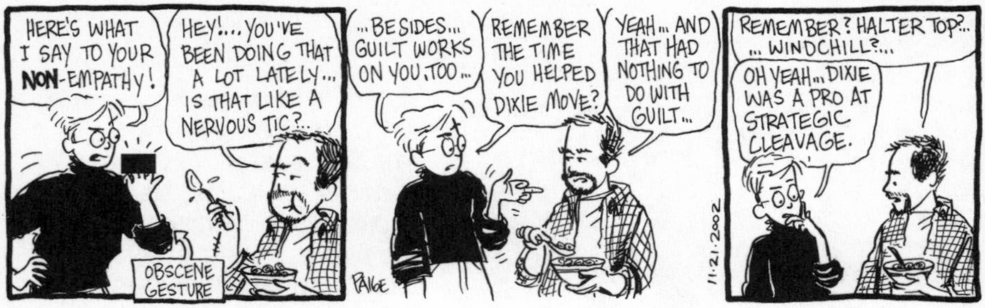
HERE'S WHAT I SAY TO YOUR **NON**-EMPATHY!
HEY!... YOU'VE BEEN DOING THAT A LOT LATELY... IS THAT LIKE A NERVOUS TIC?...
OBSCENE GESTURE
...BESIDES... GUILT WORKS ON YOU, TOO...
REMEMBER THE TIME YOU HELPED DIXIE MOVE?
YEAH... AND THAT HAD NOTHING TO DO WITH GUILT...
PAIGE
11·21·2002
REMEMBER? HALTER TOP?... ... WINDCHILL?...
OH YEAH... DIXIE WAS A PRO AT STRATEGIC CLEAVAGE.

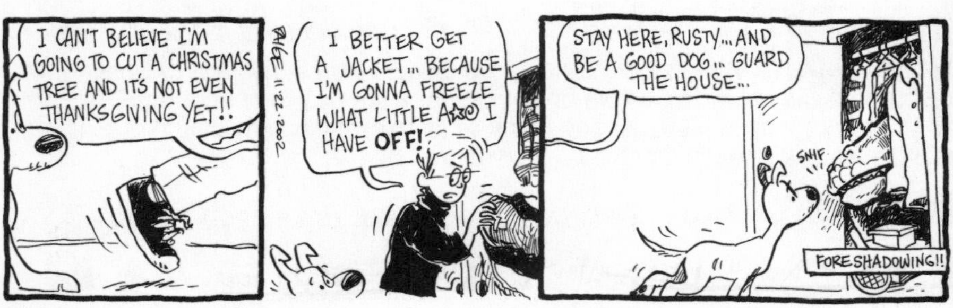
I CAN'T BELIEVE I'M GOING TO CUT A CHRISTMAS TREE AND IT'S NOT EVEN THANKSGIVING YET!!
PAIGE 11·22·2002
I BETTER GET A JACKET... BECAUSE I'M GONNA FREEZE WHAT LITTLE A☆@ I HAVE **OFF!**
STAY HERE, RUSTY... AND BE A GOOD DOG... GUARD THE HOUSE...
SNIF
FORESHADOWING!!

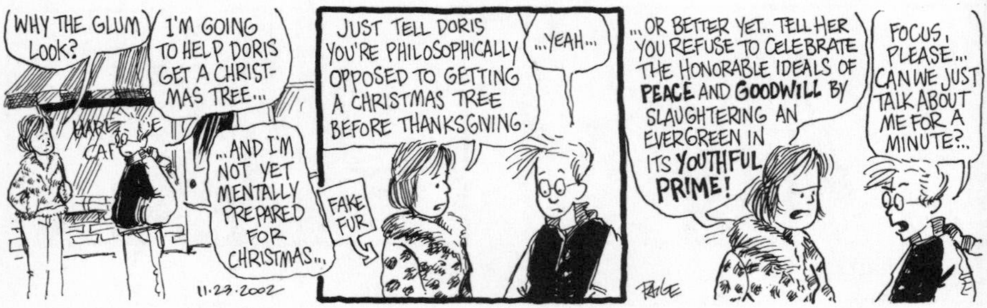
WHY THE GLUM LOOK?
I'M GOING TO HELP DORIS GET A CHRISTMAS TREE...
...AND I'M NOT YET MENTALLY PREPARED FOR CHRISTMAS...
11·23·2002
JUST TELL DORIS YOU'RE PHILOSOPHICALLY OPPOSED TO GETTING A CHRISTMAS TREE BEFORE THANKSGIVING.
...YEAH...
FAKE FUR
...OR BETTER YET... TELL HER YOU REFUSE TO CELEBRATE THE HONORABLE IDEALS OF **PEACE** AND **GOODWILL** BY SLAUGHTERING AN EVERGREEN IN ITS **YOUTHFUL PRIME!**
FOCUS, PLEASE... CAN WE JUST TALK ABOUT ME FOR A MINUTE?..
PAIGE

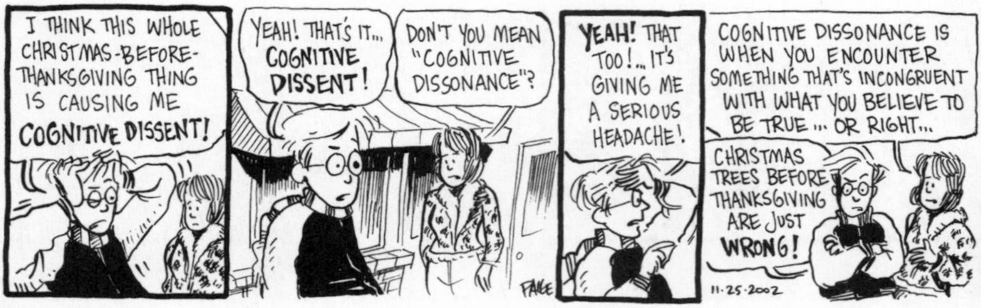
I THINK THIS WHOLE CHRISTMAS-BEFORE-THANKSGIVING THING IS CAUSING ME **COGNITIVE DISSENT!**
YEAH! THAT'S IT... **COGNITIVE DISSENT!**
DON'T YOU MEAN "COGNITIVE DISSONANCE"?
PAIGE
YEAH! THAT TOO!... IT'S GIVING ME A SERIOUS HEADACHE!
COGNITIVE DISSONANCE IS WHEN YOU ENCOUNTER SOMETHING THAT'S INCONGRUENT WITH WHAT YOU BELIEVE TO BE TRUE ... OR RIGHT...
CHRISTMAS TREES BEFORE THANKSGIVING ARE JUST **WRONG!**
11·25·2002

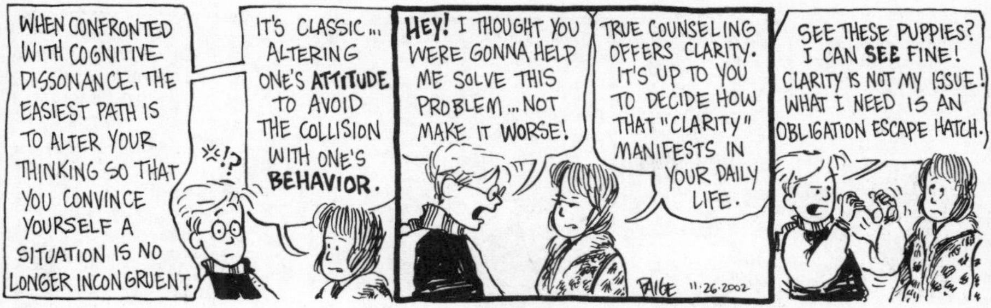
WHEN CONFRONTED WITH COGNITIVE DISSONANCE, THE EASIEST PATH IS TO ALTER YOUR THINKING SO THAT YOU CONVINCE YOURSELF A SITUATION IS NO LONGER INCONGRUENT.
IT'S CLASSIC... ALTERING ONE'S ATTITUDE TO AVOID THE COLLISION WITH ONE'S BEHAVIOR.
!?
HEY! I THOUGHT YOU WERE GONNA HELP ME SOLVE THIS PROBLEM... NOT MAKE IT WORSE!
TRUE COUNSELING OFFERS CLARITY. IT'S UP TO YOU TO DECIDE HOW THAT "CLARITY" MANIFESTS IN YOUR DAILY LIFE.
PAIGE 11·26·2002
SEE THESE PUPPIES? I CAN SEE FINE! CLARITY IS NOT MY ISSUE! WHAT I NEED IS AN OBLIGATION ESCAPE HATCH.

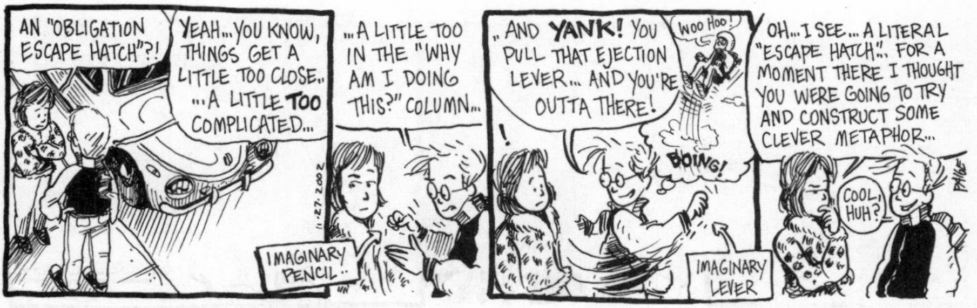
AN "OBLIGATION ESCAPE HATCH"?!
YEAH... YOU KNOW, THINGS GET A LITTLE TOO CLOSE.. ...A LITTLE TOO COMPLICATED...
11·27·2002
...A LITTLE TOO IN THE "WHY AM I DOING THIS?" COLUMN...
IMAGINARY PENCIL
..AND YANK! YOU PULL THAT EJECTION LEVER... AND YOU'RE OUTTA THERE!
WOO HOO!
BOING!
IMAGINARY LEVER
OH... I SEE... A LITERAL "ESCAPE HATCH".. FOR A MOMENT THERE I THOUGHT YOU WERE GOING TO TRY AND CONSTRUCT SOME CLEVER METAPHOR...
COOL, HUH?
PAIGE

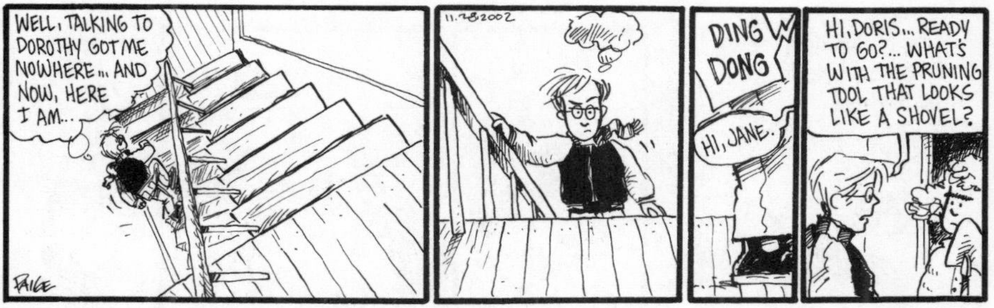
WELL, TALKING TO DOROTHY GOT ME NOWHERE... AND NOW, HERE I AM...
PAIGE
11·28·2002
DING DONG
HI, JANE.
HI, DORIS... READY TO GO?... WHAT'S WITH THE PRUNING TOOL THAT LOOKS LIKE A SHOVEL?

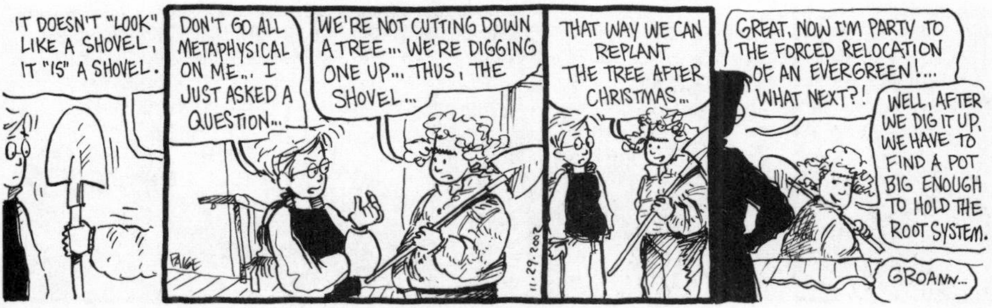
IT DOESN'T "LOOK" LIKE A SHOVEL, IT "IS" A SHOVEL.
DON'T GO ALL METAPHYSICAL ON ME... I JUST ASKED A QUESTION...
WE'RE NOT CUTTING DOWN A TREE... WE'RE DIGGING ONE UP... THUS, THE SHOVEL...
PAIGE
11·29·2002
THAT WAY WE CAN REPLANT THE TREE AFTER CHRISTMAS...
GREAT, NOW I'M PARTY TO THE FORCED RELOCATION OF AN EVERGREEN!... WHAT NEXT?!
WELL, AFTER WE DIG IT UP, WE HAVE TO FIND A POT BIG ENOUGH TO HOLD THE ROOT SYSTEM.
GROANN...

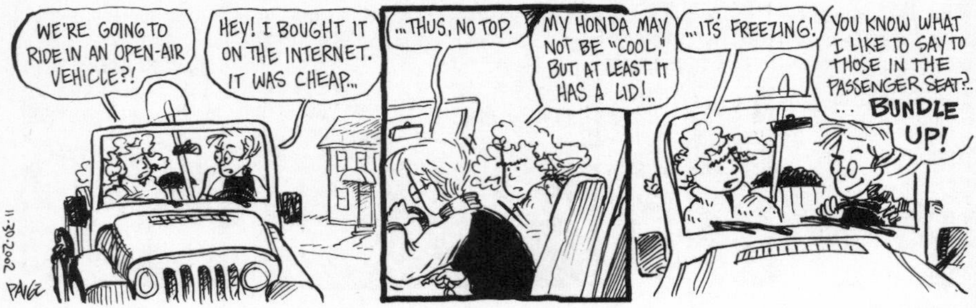
WE'RE GOING TO RIDE IN AN OPEN-AIR VEHICLE?!
HEY! I BOUGHT IT ON THE INTERNET. IT WAS CHEAP...
...THUS, NO TOP.
MY HONDA MAY NOT BE "COOL," BUT AT LEAST IT HAS A LID!..
...IT'S FREEZING!
YOU KNOW WHAT I LIKE TO SAY TO THOSE IN THE PASSENGER SEAT?.. ... BUNDLE UP!
11-30-2002
PAIGE

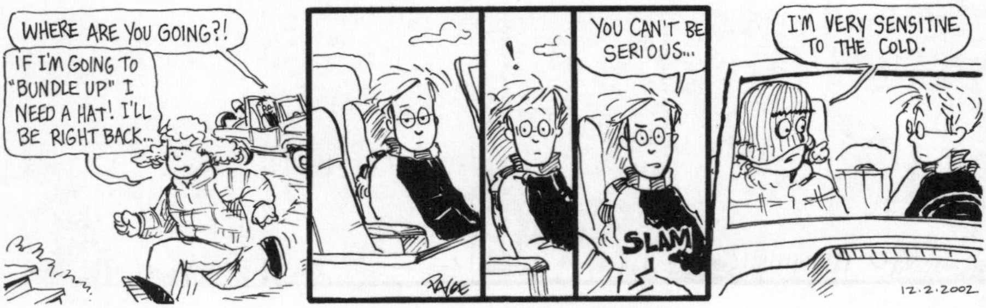
WHERE ARE YOU GOING?!
IF I'M GOING TO "BUNDLE UP" I NEED A HAT! I'LL BE RIGHT BACK...
!
YOU CAN'T BE SERIOUS...
SLAM
I'M VERY SENSITIVE TO THE COLD.
PAIGE
12-2-2002

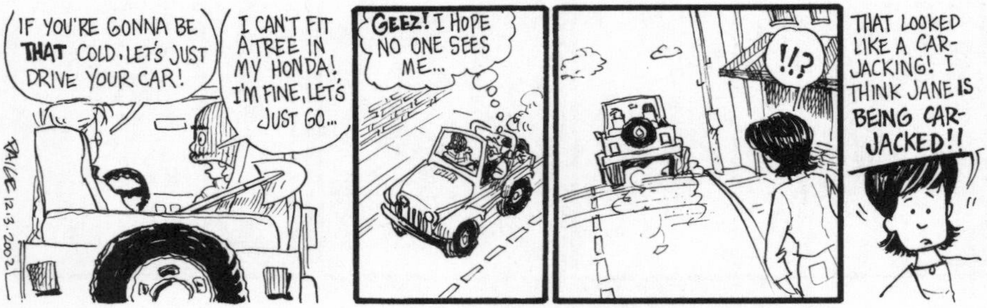
IF YOU'RE GONNA BE THAT COLD, LET'S JUST DRIVE YOUR CAR!
I CAN'T FIT A TREE IN MY HONDA! I'M FINE, LET'S JUST GO...
GEEZ! I HOPE NO ONE SEES ME...
!!?
THAT LOOKED LIKE A CAR-JACKING! I THINK JANE IS BEING CAR-JACKED!!
PAIGE 12-3-2002

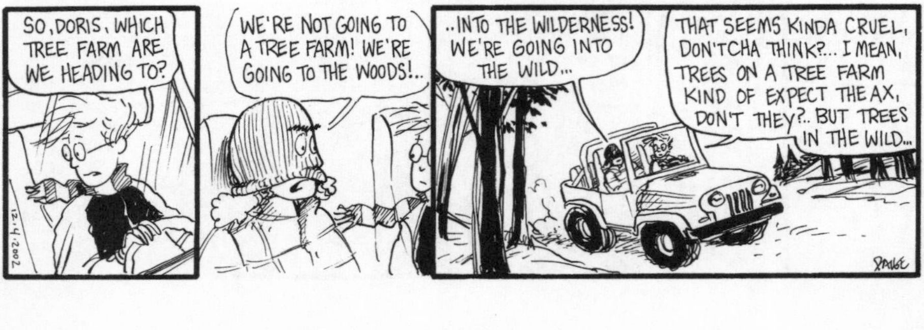
SO, DORIS, WHICH TREE FARM ARE WE HEADING TO?
WE'RE NOT GOING TO A TREE FARM! WE'RE GOING TO THE WOODS!..
..INTO THE WILDERNESS! WE'RE GOING INTO THE WILD...
THAT SEEMS KINDA CRUEL, DON'TCHA THINK?... I MEAN, TREES ON A TREE FARM KIND OF EXPECT THE AX, DON'T THEY?.. BUT TREES IN THE WILD...
12-4-2002
PAIGE

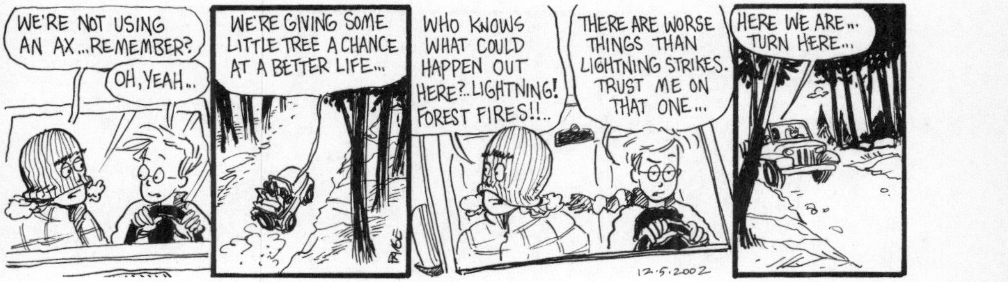
WE'RE NOT USING AN AX...REMEMBER?
OH, YEAH...
WE'RE GIVING SOME LITTLE TREE A CHANCE AT A BETTER LIFE...
WHO KNOWS WHAT COULD HAPPEN OUT HERE?..LIGHTNING! FOREST FIRES!!...
THERE ARE WORSE THINGS THAN LIGHTNING STRIKES. TRUST ME ON THAT ONE...
HERE WE ARE... TURN HERE...
PAIGE
12·5·2002

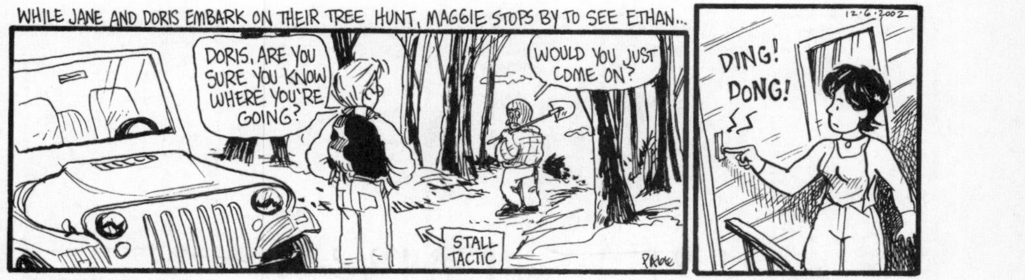
WHILE JANE AND DORIS EMBARK ON THEIR TREE HUNT, MAGGIE STOPS BY TO SEE ETHAN...
DORIS, ARE YOU SURE YOU KNOW WHERE YOU'RE GOING?
WOULD YOU JUST COME ON?
STALL TACTIC
PAIGE
12·6·2002
DING! DONG!

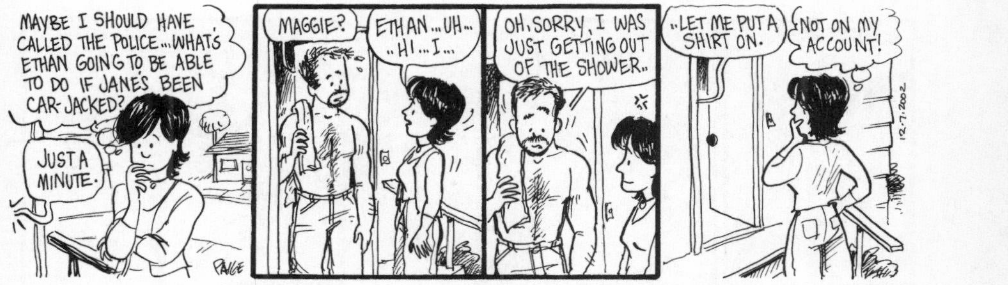
MAYBE I SHOULD HAVE CALLED THE POLICE...WHAT'S ETHAN GOING TO BE ABLE TO DO IF JANE'S BEEN CAR-JACKED?
JUST A MINUTE.
PAIGE
MAGGIE?
ETHAN...UH... ..HI...I...
OH, SORRY, I WAS JUST GETTING OUT OF THE SHOWER..
..LET ME PUT A SHIRT ON.
NOT ON MY ACCOUNT!
12·7·2002

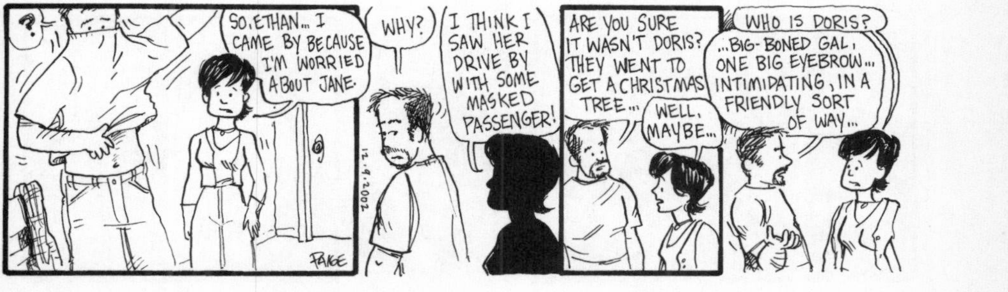
?
SO, ETHAN... I CAME BY BECAUSE I'M WORRIED ABOUT JANE.
PAIGE
WHY?
12·9·2002
I THINK I SAW HER DRIVE BY WITH SOME MASKED PASSENGER!
ARE YOU SURE IT WASN'T DORIS? THEY WENT TO GET A CHRISTMAS TREE...
WELL, MAYBE...
WHO IS DORIS?
...BIG-BONED GAL, ONE BIG EYEBROW... INTIMIDATING, IN A FRIENDLY SORT OF WAY...

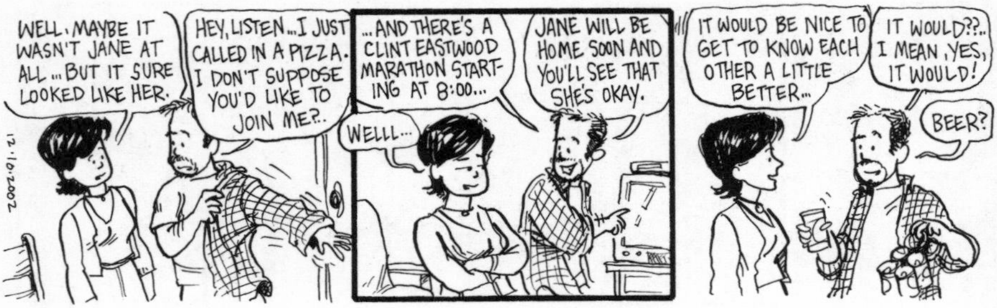
WELL, MAYBE IT WASN'T JANE AT ALL... BUT IT SURE LOOKED LIKE HER.
HEY, LISTEN... I JUST CALLED IN A PIZZA. I DON'T SUPPOSE YOU'D LIKE TO JOIN ME?..
12·10·2002
...AND THERE'S A CLINT EASTWOOD MARATHON STARTING AT 8:00...
WELLL...
JANE WILL BE HOME SOON AND YOU'LL SEE THAT SHE'S OKAY.
IT WOULD BE NICE TO GET TO KNOW EACH OTHER A LITTLE BETTER...
IT WOULD??.. I MEAN, YES, IT WOULD!
BEER?

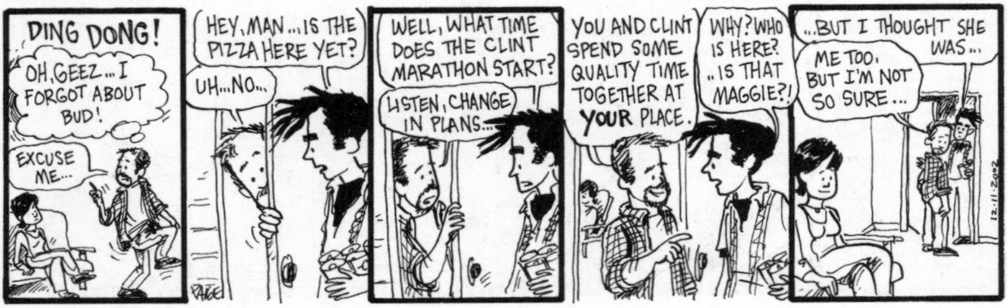
DING DONG!
OH, GEEZ... I FORGOT ABOUT BUD!
EXCUSE ME...
HEY, MAN... IS THE PIZZA HERE YET?
UH...NO...
WELL, WHAT TIME DOES THE CLINT MARATHON START?
LISTEN, CHANGE IN PLANS...
YOU AND CLINT SPEND SOME QUALITY TIME TOGETHER AT YOUR PLACE.
WHY? WHO IS HERE? ..IS THAT MAGGIE?!
...BUT I THOUGHT SHE WAS...
ME TOO. BUT I'M NOT SO SURE...
12·11·2002

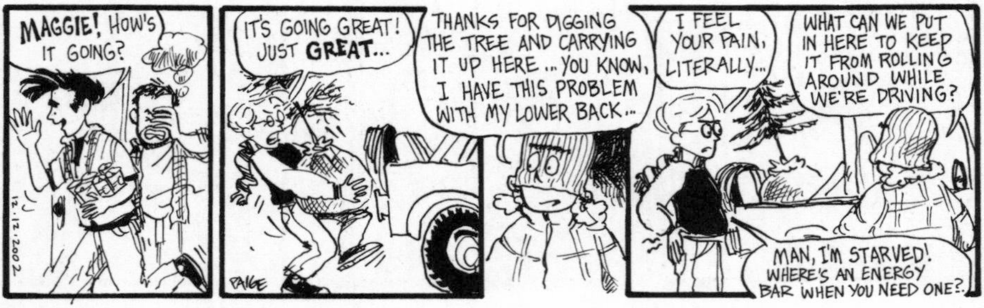
MAGGIE! HOW'S IT GOING?
12·12·2002
IT'S GOING GREAT! JUST GREAT...
THANKS FOR DIGGING THE TREE AND CARRYING IT UP HERE... YOU KNOW, I HAVE THIS PROBLEM WITH MY LOWER BACK...
I FEEL YOUR PAIN, LITERALLY...
WHAT CAN WE PUT IN HERE TO KEEP IT FROM ROLLING AROUND WHILE WE'RE DRIVING?
MAN, I'M STARVED! WHERE'S AN ENERGY BAR WHEN YOU NEED ONE?!

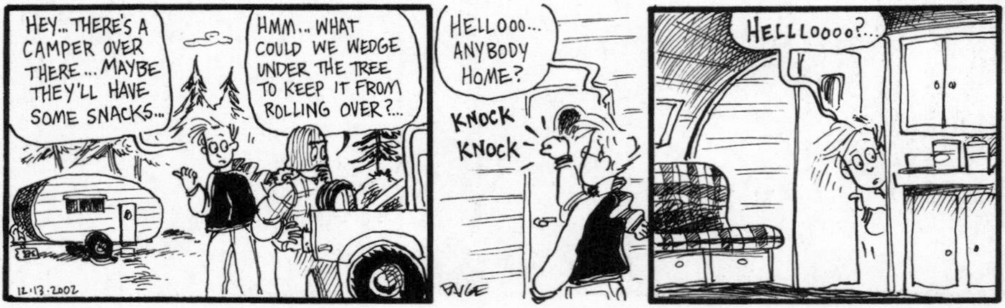
HEY... THERE'S A CAMPER OVER THERE... MAYBE THEY'LL HAVE SOME SNACKS...
HMM... WHAT COULD WE WEDGE UNDER THE TREE TO KEEP IT FROM ROLLING OVER?...
12·13·2002
HELLOOO... ANYBODY HOME?
KNOCK KNOCK
HELLLOOOO?...

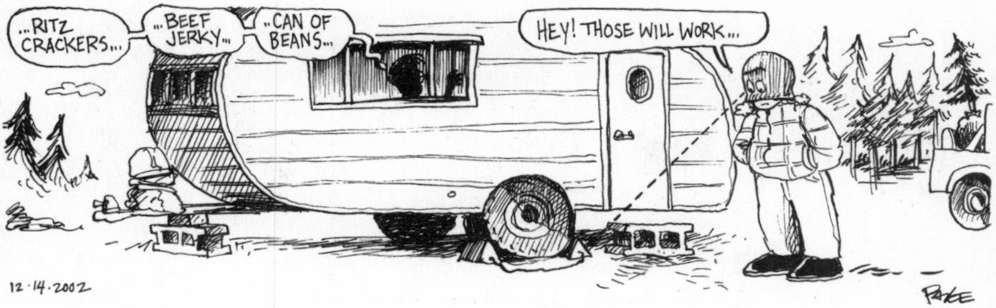
...RITZ CRACKERS...
...BEEF JERKY...
...CAN OF BEANS...
HEY! THOSE WILL WORK...
12·14·2002
PAIGE

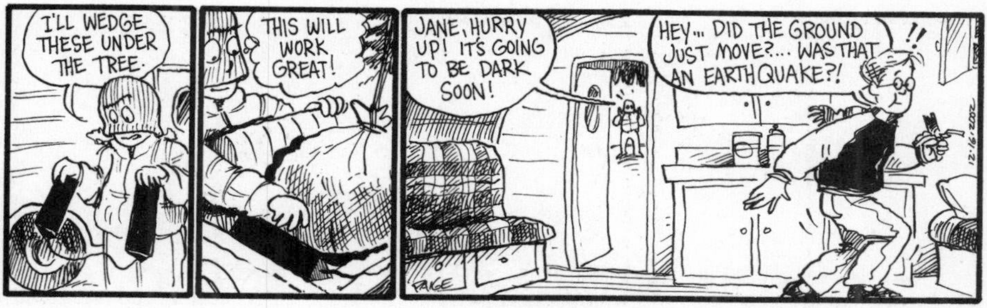
I'LL WEDGE THESE UNDER THE TREE.
THIS WILL WORK GREAT!
JANE, HURRY UP! IT'S GOING TO BE DARK SOON!
HEY... DID THE GROUND JUST MOVE?... WAS THAT AN EARTHQUAKE?!
!!
12·16·2002
PAIGE

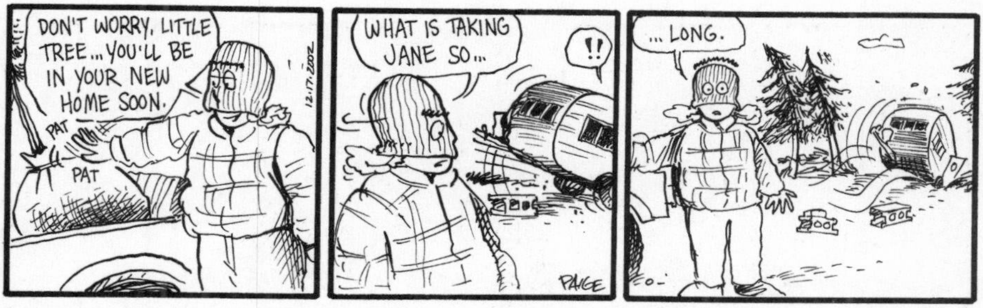
DON'T WORRY, LITTLE TREE... YOU'LL BE IN YOUR NEW HOME SOON.
PAT
PAT
12·17·2002
WHAT IS TAKING JANE SO...
!!
... LONG.
PAIGE

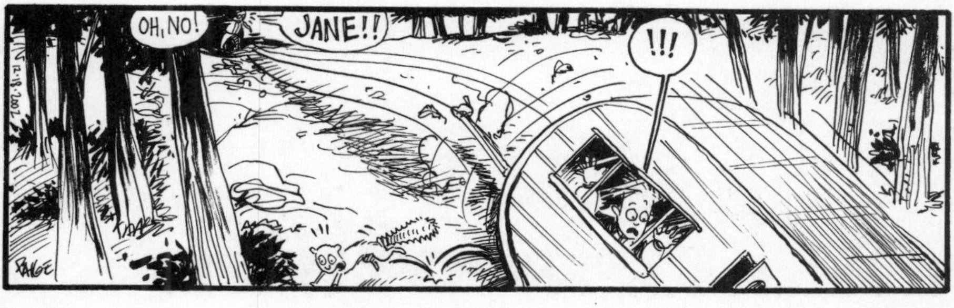
OH, NO!
JANE!!
!!!
12·18·2002
PAIGE

Chapter 13

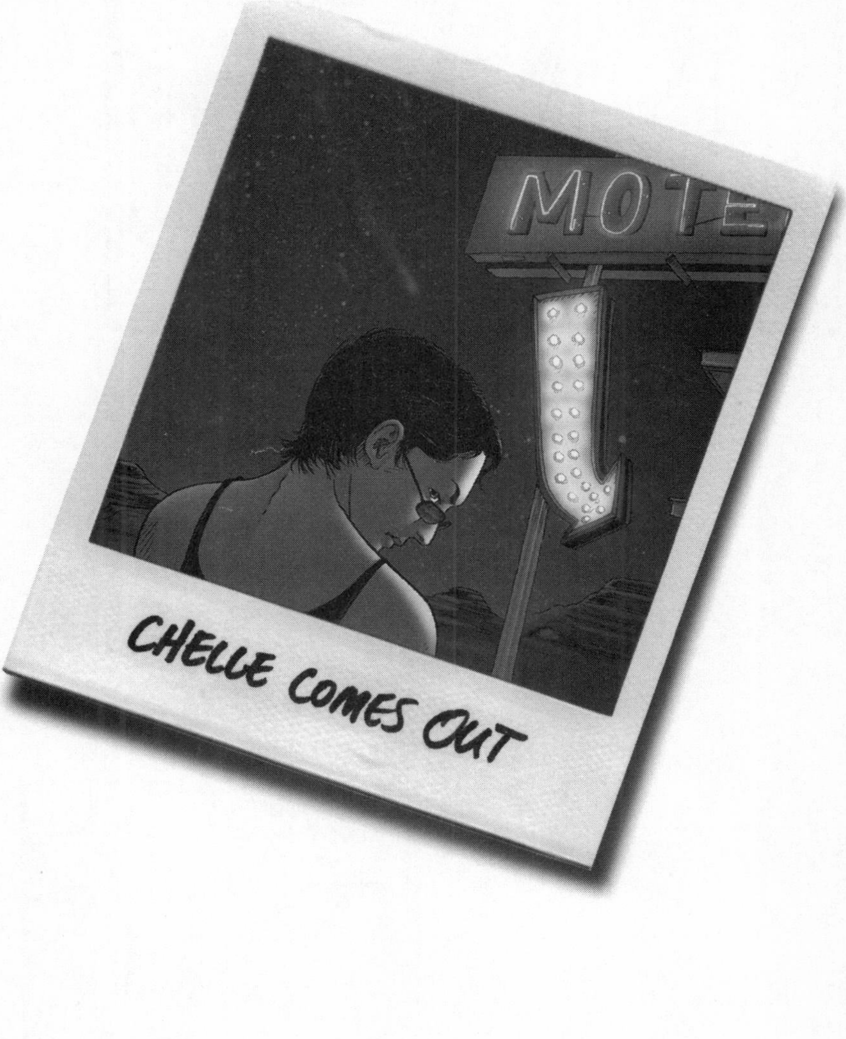
MOTE
CHELLE COMES OUT

OH, NO! IT'S ALL MY FAULT!!
JANE! LOOK OUT FOR THAT TREE!
ROCK! THERE'S A ROCK!!
12.19.2002

NOT THE RIVER!.. PLEASE, LORD, NOT IN THE RIVER!... I'LL BE GOOD... I'LL GIVE UP MY POLICE SCANNER... IF I DIDN'T HAVE LOWER-BACK PAIN, I'D PUT THE TREE BACK RIGHT THIS MINUTE!!
SPOOSH!

YES, FOLKS! JANE HAD A WILD DOWNHILL JAUNT RIGHT INTO THE RIVER!...

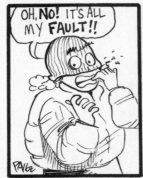

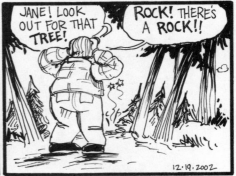

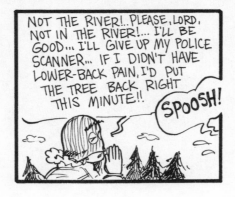

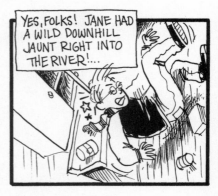

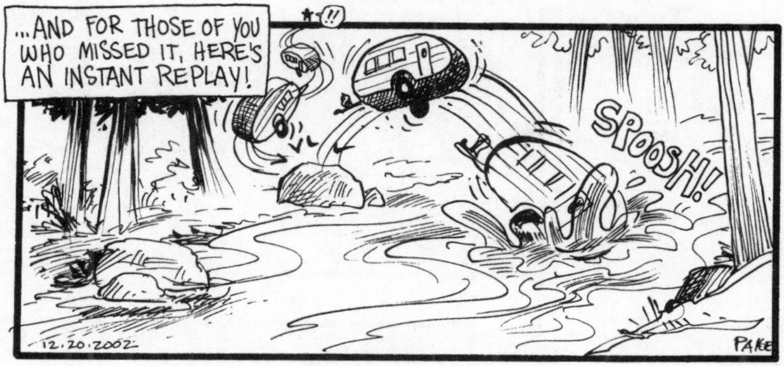
...AND FOR THOSE OF YOU WHO MISSED IT, HERE'S AN INSTANT REPLAY!
!!
SPOOSH!
12.20.2002
PAIGE

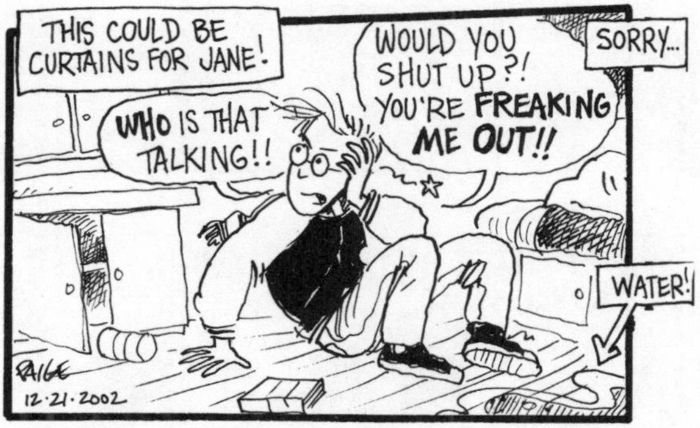
THIS COULD BE CURTAINS FOR JANE!
WHO IS THAT TALKING!!
WOULD YOU SHUT UP?! YOU'RE FREAKING ME OUT!!
SORRY...
WATER!
PAIGE
12.21.2002

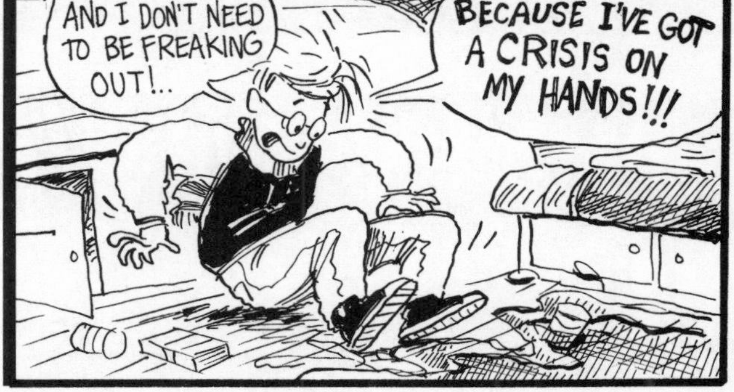
AND I DON'T NEED TO BE FREAKING OUT!...
BECAUSE I'VE GOT A CRISIS ON MY HANDS!!!

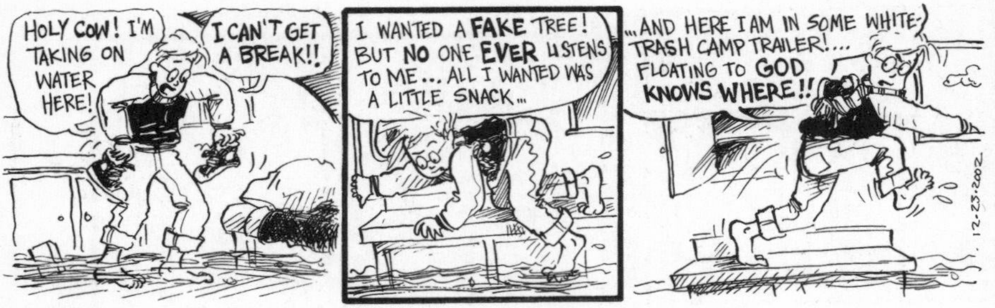
HOLY COW! I'M TAKING ON WATER HERE!
I CAN'T GET A BREAK!!
I WANTED A FAKE TREE! BUT NO ONE EVER LISTENS TO ME... ALL I WANTED WAS A LITTLE SNACK...
...AND HERE I AM IN SOME WHITE-TRASH CAMP TRAILER!... FLOATING TO GOD KNOWS WHERE!!
12-23-2002

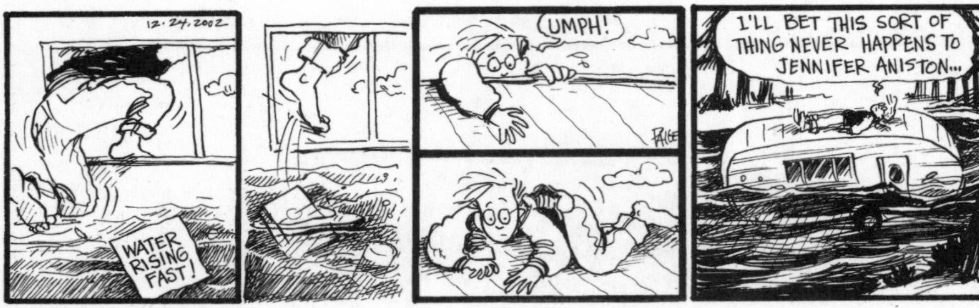
12-24-2002
WATER RISING FAST!
UMPH!
PAIGE
I'LL BET THIS SORT OF THING NEVER HAPPENS TO JENNIFER ANISTON...

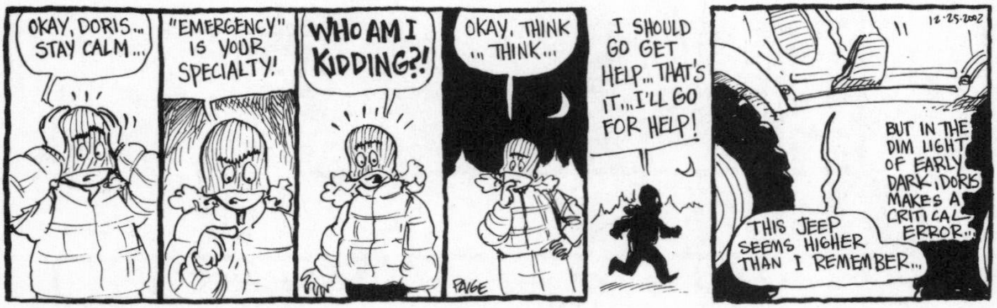
OKAY, DORIS... STAY CALM...
"EMERGENCY" IS YOUR SPECIALTY!
WHO AM I KIDDING?!
OKAY, THINK ... THINK...
PAIGE
I SHOULD GO GET HELP... THAT'S IT... I'LL GO FOR HELP!
12-25-2002
BUT IN THE DIM LIGHT OF EARLY DARK, DORIS MAKES A CRITICAL ERROR...
THIS JEEP SEEMS HIGHER THAN I REMEMBER...

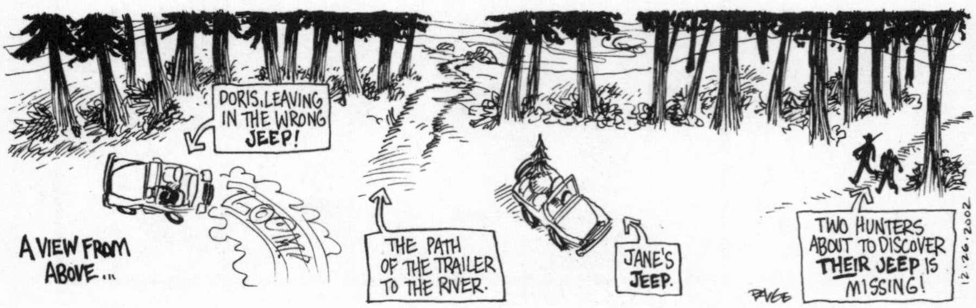
DORIS, LEAVING IN THE WRONG JEEP!
A VIEW FROM ABOVE...
THE PATH OF THE TRAILER TO THE RIVER.
JANE'S JEEP.
TWO HUNTERS ABOUT TO DISCOVER THEIR JEEP IS MISSING!
PAIGE
12-26-2002

TIME PASSES SLOWLY, AS JANE FLOATS DOWN STREAM...

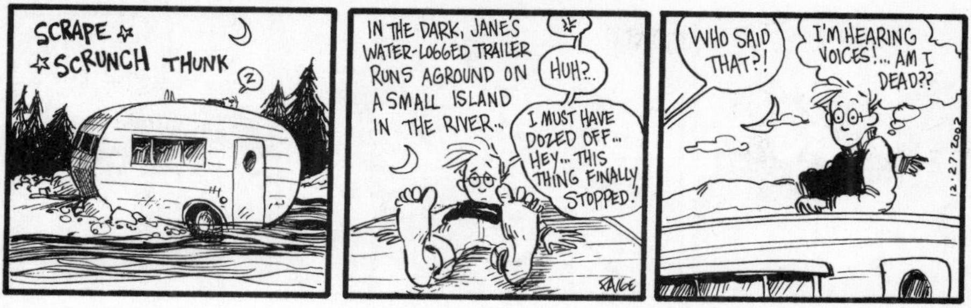

SCRAPE ☆
☆ SCRUNCH THUNK
Z
IN THE DARK, JANE'S WATER-LOGGED TRAILER RUNS AGROUND ON A SMALL ISLAND IN THE RIVER...
HUH?..
I MUST HAVE DOZED OFF... HEY... THIS THING FINALLY STOPPED!
PAIGE
WHO SAID THAT?!
I'M HEARING VOICES!... AM I DEAD??
12·27·2002

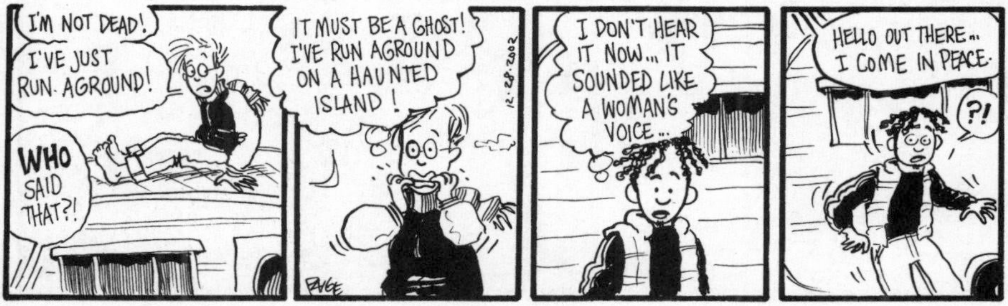

I'M NOT DEAD!
I'VE JUST RUN AGROUND!
WHO SAID THAT?!
IT MUST BE A GHOST! I'VE RUN AGROUND ON A HAUNTED ISLAND!
12·28·2002
PAIGE
I DON'T HEAR IT NOW... IT SOUNDED LIKE A WOMAN'S VOICE...
HELLO OUT THERE... I COME IN PEACE.
?!

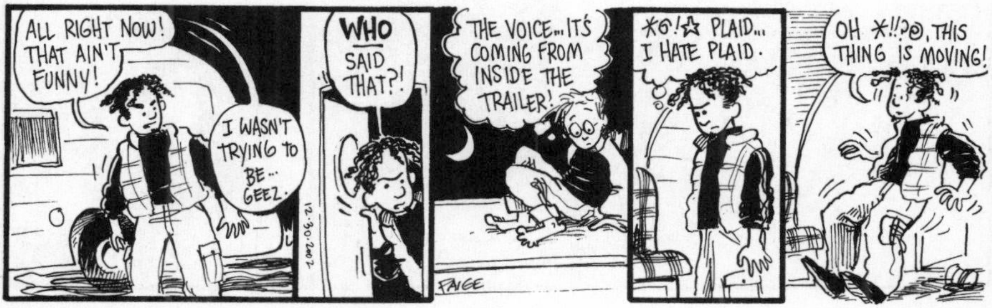

ALL RIGHT NOW! THAT AIN'T FUNNY!
I WASN'T TRYING TO BE... GEEZ.
12·30·2002
WHO SAID THAT?!
THE VOICE... IT'S COMING FROM INSIDE THE TRAILER!
PAIGE
PLAID... I HATE PLAID.
OH, THIS THING IS MOVING!

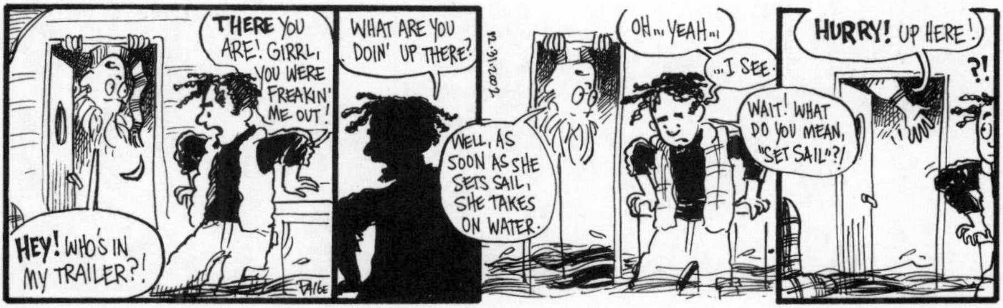

THERE YOU ARE! GIRRL, YOU WERE FREAKIN' ME OUT!
HEY! WHO'S IN MY TRAILER?!
PAIGE
WHAT ARE YOU DOIN' UP THERE?
12·31·2002
WELL, AS SOON AS SHE SETS SAIL, SHE TAKES ON WATER.
OH... YEAH...
...I SEE.
WAIT! WHAT DO YOU MEAN, "SET SAIL"?!
HURRY! UP HERE!
?!

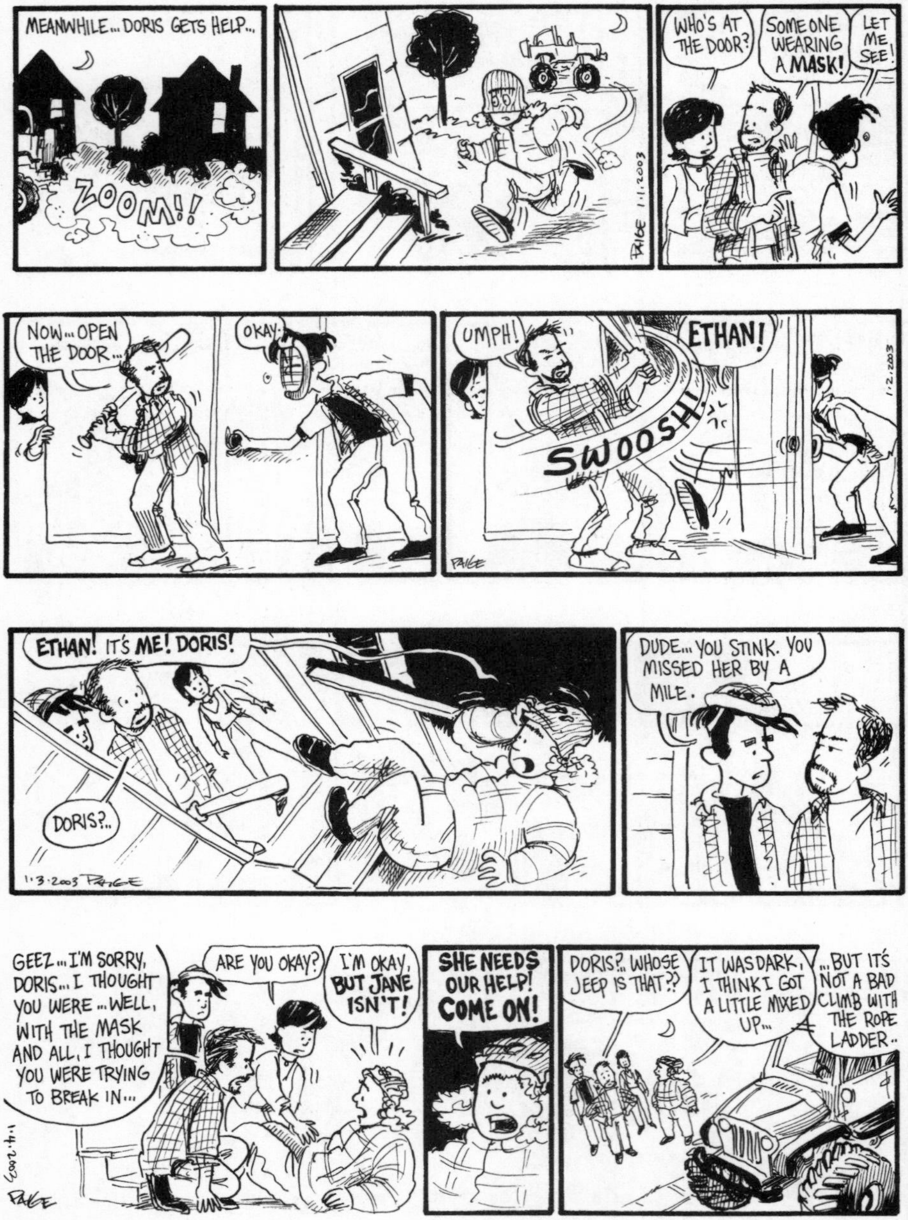
MEANWHILE... DORIS GETS HELP...
ZOOM!!
1.1.2003
PAIGE
WHO'S AT THE DOOR?
SOME ONE WEARING A MASK!
LET ME SEE!
NOW... OPEN THE DOOR...
OKAY.
UMPH!
ETHAN!
SWOOSH!
1.2.2003
PAIGE
ETHAN! IT'S ME! DORIS!
DORIS?..
1.3.2003 PAIGE
DUDE... YOU STINK. YOU MISSED HER BY A MILE.
GEEZ... I'M SORRY, DORIS... I THOUGHT YOU WERE ... WELL, WITH THE MASK AND ALL, I THOUGHT YOU WERE TRYING TO BREAK IN...
ARE YOU OKAY?
I'M OKAY, BUT JANE ISN'T!
SHE NEEDS OUR HELP! COME ON!
DORIS?.. WHOSE JEEP IS THAT??
IT WAS DARK, I THINK I GOT A LITTLE MIXED UP...
...BUT IT'S NOT A BAD CLIMB WITH THE ROPE LADDER..
1.4.2003
PAIGE

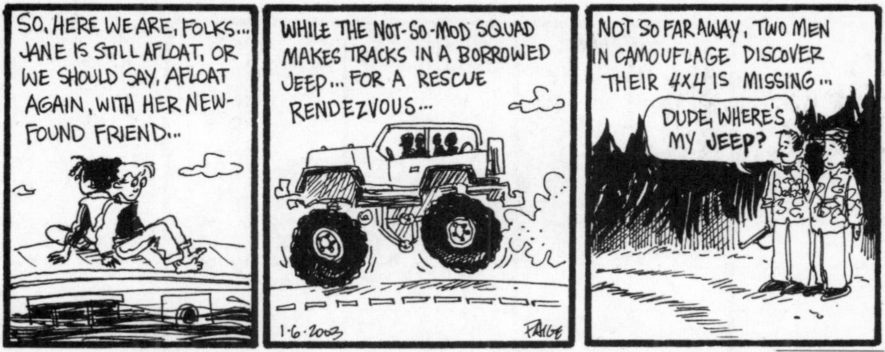
SO, HERE WE ARE, FOLKS... JANE IS STILL AFLOAT, OR WE SHOULD SAY, AFLOAT AGAIN, WITH HER NEW-FOUND FRIEND...
WHILE THE NOT-SO-MOD SQUAD MAKES TRACKS IN A BORROWED JEEP... FOR A RESCUE RENDEZVOUS...
1·6·2003
PAIGE
NOT SO FAR AWAY, TWO MEN IN CAMOUFLAGE DISCOVER THEIR 4x4 IS MISSING...
DUDE, WHERE'S MY JEEP?

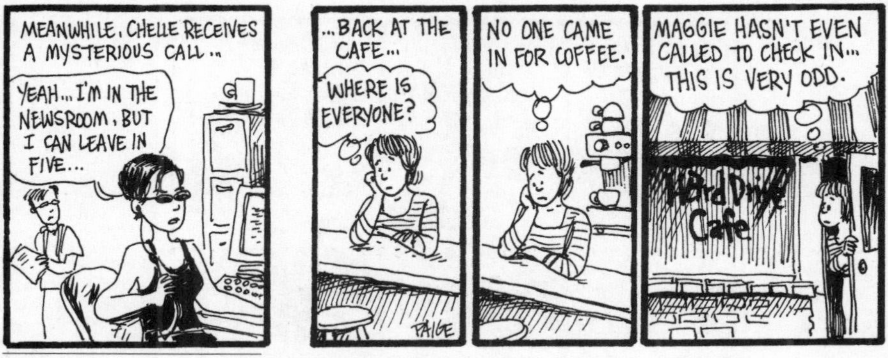
MEANWHILE, CHELLE RECEIVES A MYSTERIOUS CALL...
YEAH... I'M IN THE NEWSROOM, BUT I CAN LEAVE IN FIVE...
...BACK AT THE CAFE...
WHERE IS EVERYONE?
PAIGE
NO ONE CAME IN FOR COFFEE.
MAGGIE HASN'T EVEN CALLED TO CHECK IN... THIS IS VERY ODD.
Cafe

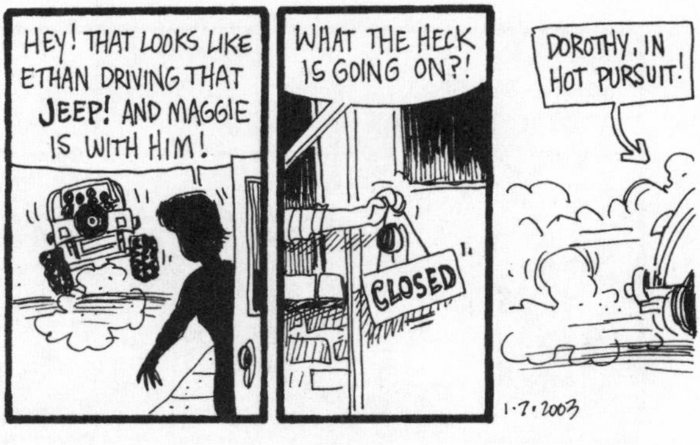
HEY! THAT LOOKS LIKE ETHAN DRIVING THAT JEEP! AND MAGGIE IS WITH HIM!
WHAT THE HECK IS GOING ON?!
CLOSED
DOROTHY, IN HOT PURSUIT!
1·7·2003

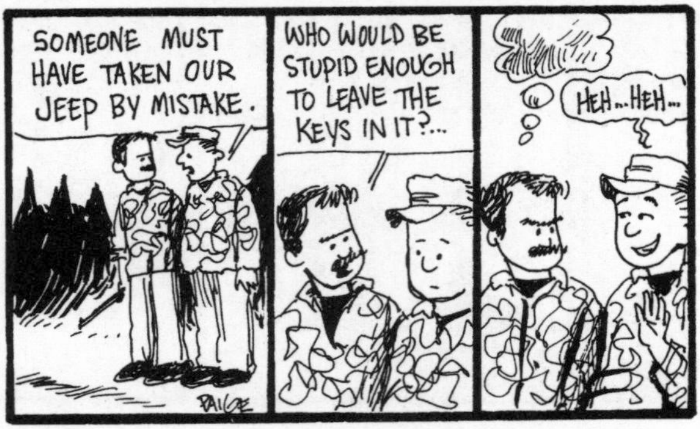
SOMEONE MUST HAVE TAKEN OUR JEEP BY MISTAKE.
WHO WOULD BE STUPID ENOUGH TO LEAVE THE KEYS IN IT?...
HEH...HEH...
PAIGE

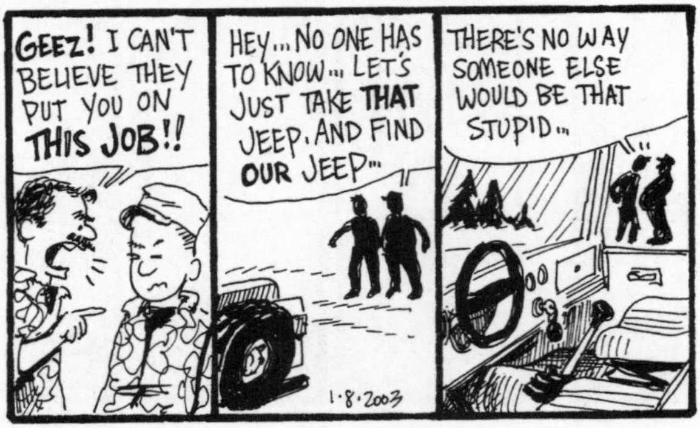
GEEZ! I CAN'T BELIEVE THEY PUT YOU ON THIS JOB!!
HEY... NO ONE HAS TO KNOW... LET'S JUST TAKE THAT JEEP, AND FIND OUR JEEP...
1·8·2003
THERE'S NO WAY SOMEONE ELSE WOULD BE THAT STUPID...

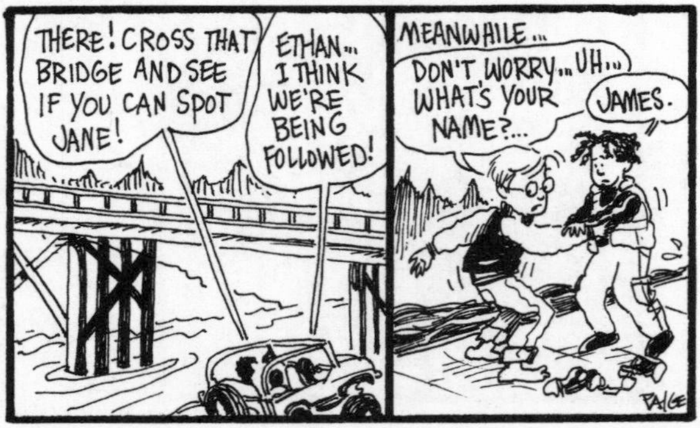
THERE! CROSS THAT BRIDGE AND SEE IF YOU CAN SPOT JANE!
ETHAN... I THINK WE'RE BEING FOLLOWED!
MEANWHILE...
DON'T WORRY... UH... WHAT'S YOUR NAME?...
JAMES.
PAIGE

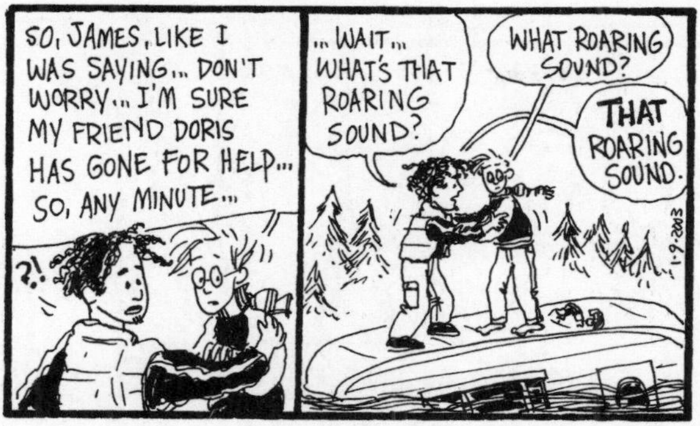
SO, JAMES, LIKE I WAS SAYING... DON'T WORRY... I'M SURE MY FRIEND DORIS HAS GONE FOR HELP... SO, ANY MINUTE...
?!
... WAIT... WHAT'S THAT ROARING SOUND?
WHAT ROARING SOUND?
THAT ROARING SOUND.
1-9-2003

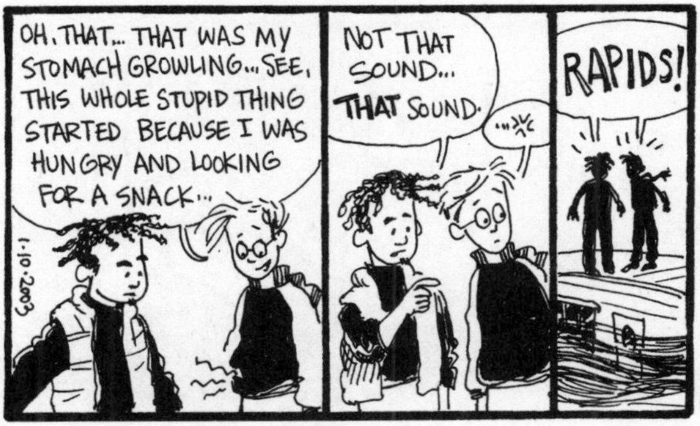
OH, THAT... THAT WAS MY STOMACH GROWLING... SEE, THIS WHOLE STUPID THING STARTED BECAUSE I WAS HUNGRY AND LOOKING FOR A SNACK...
1-10-2003
NOT THAT SOUND... THAT SOUND.
RAPIDS!

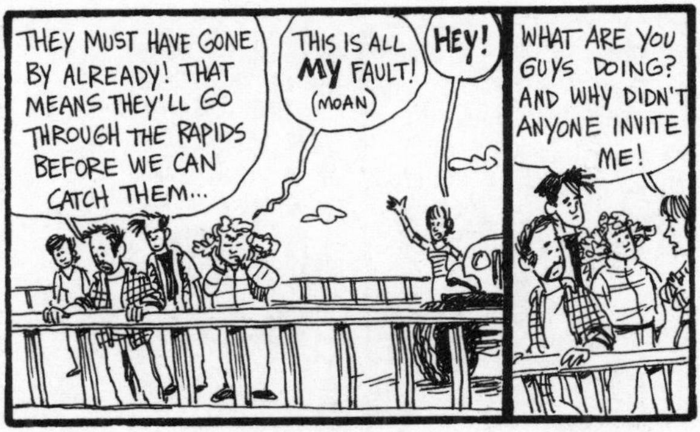
THEY MUST HAVE GONE BY ALREADY! THAT MEANS THEY'LL GO THROUGH THE RAPIDS BEFORE WE CAN CATCH THEM...
THIS IS ALL MY FAULT! (MOAN)
HEY!
WHAT ARE YOU GUYS DOING? AND WHY DIDN'T ANYONE INVITE ME!

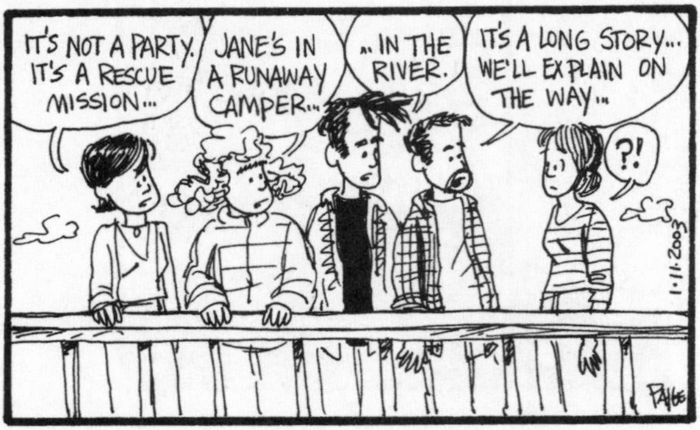
IT'S NOT A PARTY. IT'S A RESCUE MISSION...
JANE'S IN A RUNAWAY CAMPER...
.. IN THE RIVER.
IT'S A LONG STORY... WE'LL EXPLAIN ON THE WAY...
?!
1-11-2003

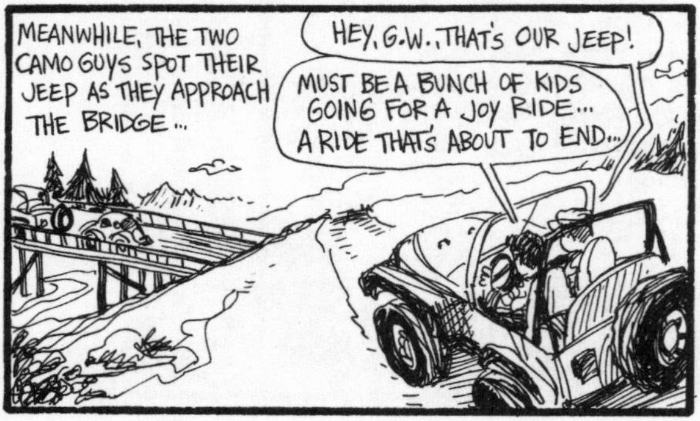
MEANWHILE, THE TWO CAMO GUYS SPOT THEIR JEEP AS THEY APPROACH THE BRIDGE...
HEY, G.W., THAT'S OUR JEEP!
MUST BE A BUNCH OF KIDS GOING FOR A JOY RIDE... A RIDE THAT'S ABOUT TO END...

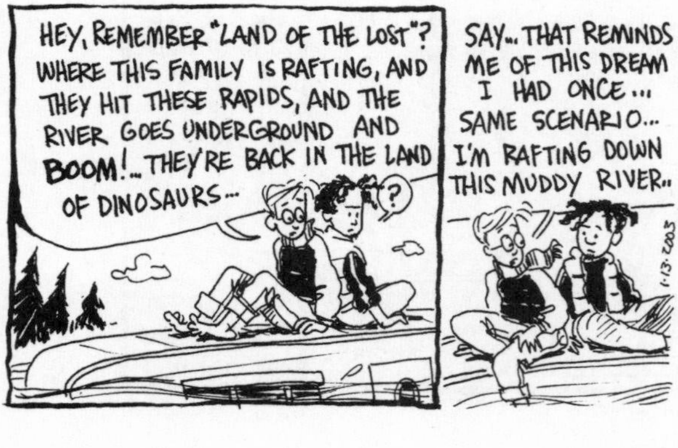
HEY, REMEMBER "LAND OF THE LOST"? WHERE THIS FAMILY IS RAFTING, AND THEY HIT THESE RAPIDS, AND THE RIVER GOES UNDERGROUND AND BOOM!... THEY'RE BACK IN THE LAND OF DINOSAURS...
?
SAY... THAT REMINDS ME OF THIS DREAM I HAD ONCE... SAME SCENARIO... I'M RAFTING DOWN THIS MUDDY RIVER..
1-13-2003

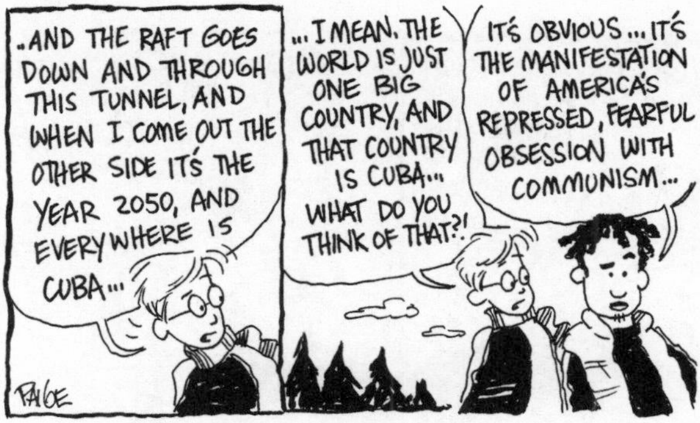
..AND THE RAFT GOES DOWN AND THROUGH THIS TUNNEL, AND WHEN I COME OUT THE OTHER SIDE IT'S THE YEAR 2050, AND EVERYWHERE IS CUBA...
...I MEAN, THE WORLD IS JUST ONE BIG COUNTRY, AND THAT COUNTRY IS CUBA... WHAT DO YOU THINK OF THAT?!
IT'S OBVIOUS... IT'S THE MANIFESTATION OF AMERICA'S REPRESSED, FEARFUL OBSESSION WITH COMMUNISM...
PAIGE

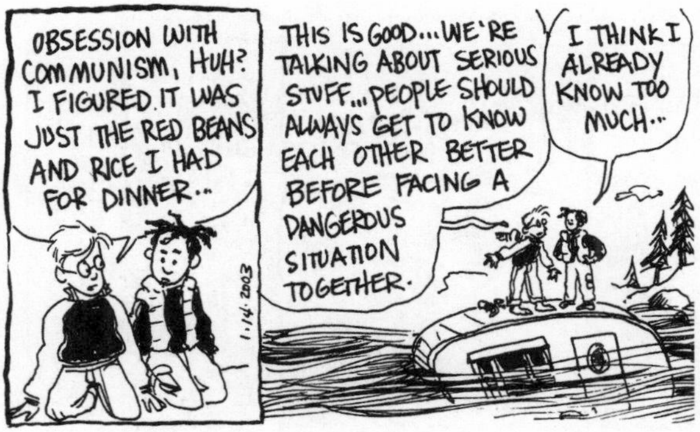
OBSESSION WITH COMMUNISM, HUH? I FIGURED IT WAS JUST THE RED BEANS AND RICE I HAD FOR DINNER...
1.14.2003
THIS IS GOOD... WE'RE TALKING ABOUT SERIOUS STUFF... PEOPLE SHOULD ALWAYS GET TO KNOW EACH OTHER BETTER BEFORE FACING A DANGEROUS SITUATION TOGETHER.
I THINK I ALREADY KNOW TOO MUCH...

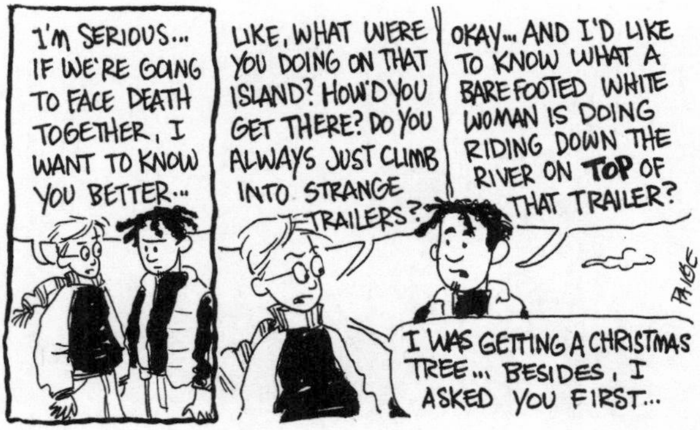
I'M SERIOUS... IF WE'RE GOING TO FACE DEATH TOGETHER, I WANT TO KNOW YOU BETTER...
LIKE, WHAT WERE YOU DOING ON THAT ISLAND? HOW'D YOU GET THERE? DO YOU ALWAYS JUST CLIMB INTO STRANGE TRAILERS?
OKAY... AND I'D LIKE TO KNOW WHAT A BAREFOOTED WHITE WOMAN IS DOING RIDING DOWN THE RIVER ON TOP OF THAT TRAILER?
I WAS GETTING A CHRISTMAS TREE... BESIDES, I ASKED YOU FIRST...
PAIGE

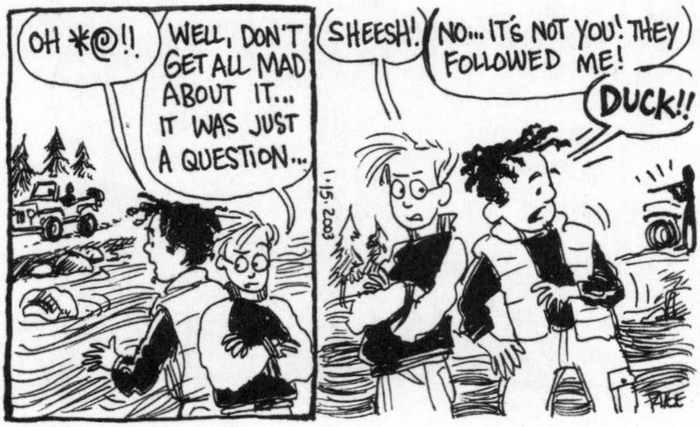
OH *@!!
WELL, DON'T GET ALL MAD ABOUT IT... IT WAS JUST A QUESTION...
1.15.2003
SHEESH!
NO... IT'S NOT YOU! THEY FOLLOWED ME!
DUCK!!
PAIGE

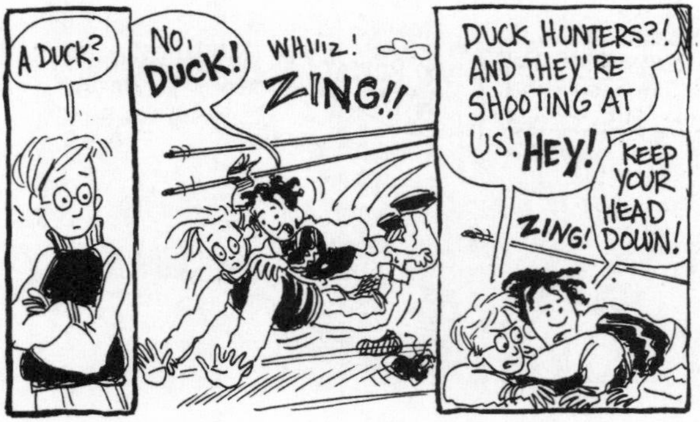
A DUCK?
NO, DUCK!
WHIIZ!
ZING!!
DUCK HUNTERS?! AND THEY'RE SHOOTING AT US! HEY!
ZING!
KEEP YOUR HEAD DOWN!

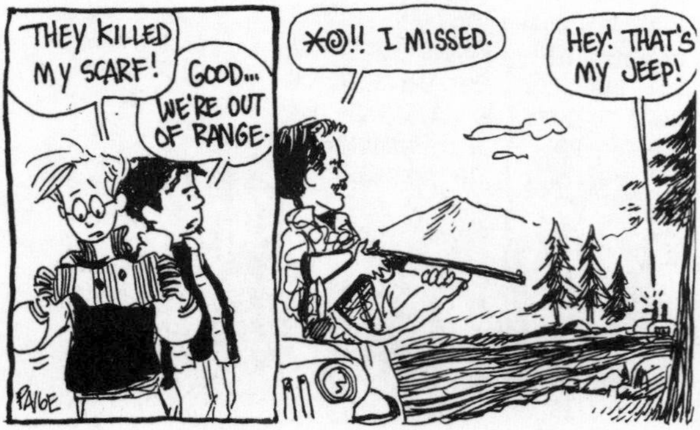
THEY KILLED MY SCARF!
GOOD... WE'RE OUT OF RANGE.
*@!! I MISSED.
HEY! THAT'S MY JEEP!
PAIGE

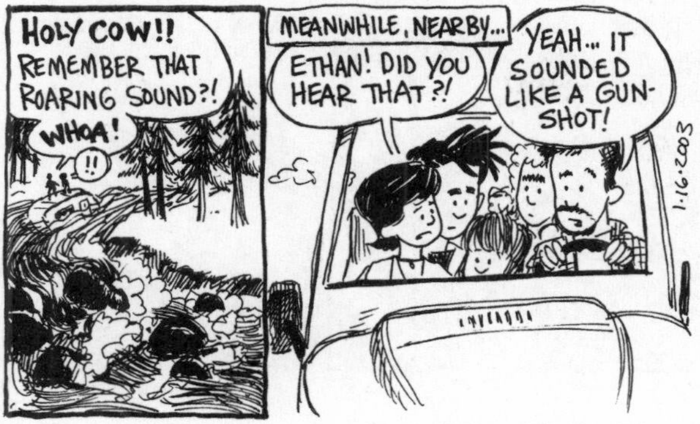
HOLY COW!! REMEMBER THAT ROARING SOUND?!
WHOA!
!!
MEANWHILE, NEARBY...
ETHAN! DID YOU HEAR THAT?!
YEAH... IT SOUNDED LIKE A GUN-SHOT!
1.16.2003

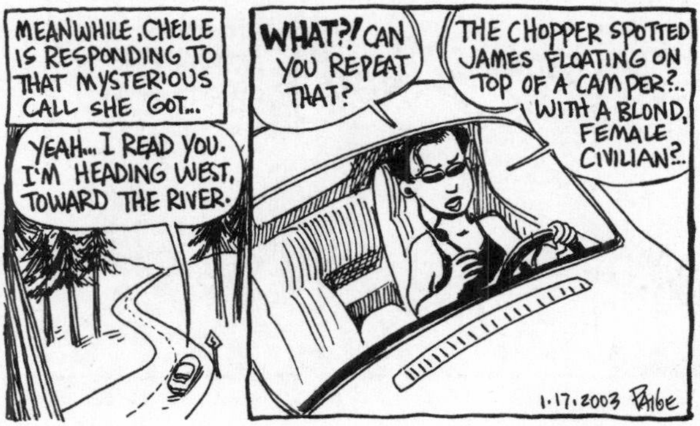
MEANWHILE, CHELLE IS RESPONDING TO THAT MYSTERIOUS CALL SHE GOT...
YEAH... I READ YOU. I'M HEADING WEST, TOWARD THE RIVER.
WHAT?! CAN YOU REPEAT THAT?
THE CHOPPER SPOTTED JAMES FLOATING ON TOP OF A CAMPER?.. WITH A BLOND, FEMALE CIVILIAN?..
1.17.2003

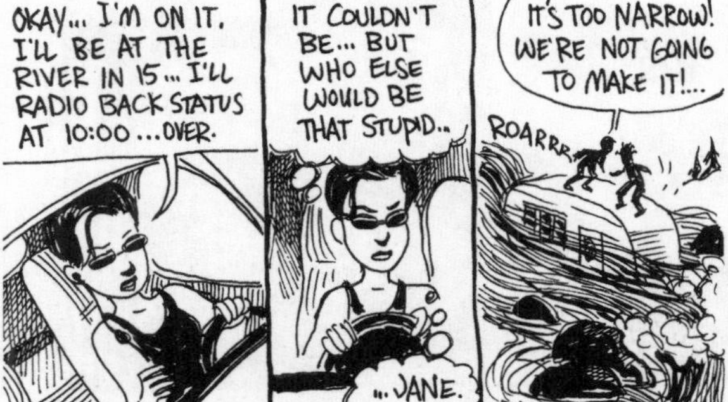
OKAY... I'M ON IT. I'LL BE AT THE RIVER IN 15... I'LL RADIO BACK STATUS AT 10:00... OVER.
IT COULDN'T BE... BUT WHO ELSE WOULD BE THAT STUPID..
...JANE.
IT'S TOO NARROW! WE'RE NOT GOING TO MAKE IT!...
ROARRR

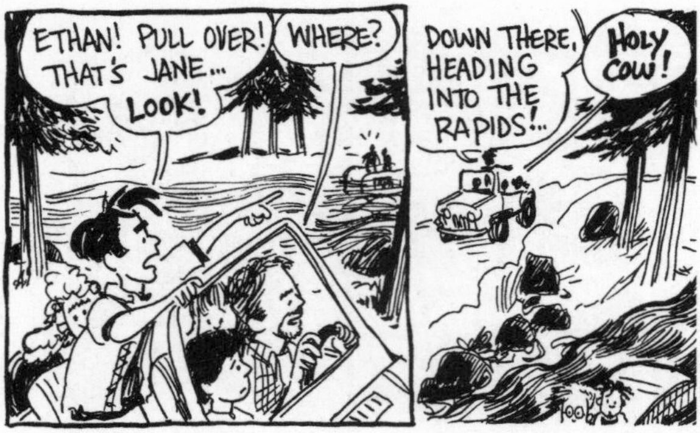
ETHAN! PULL OVER! THAT'S JANE... LOOK!
WHERE?
DOWN THERE, HEADING INTO THE RAPIDS!..
HOLY COW!

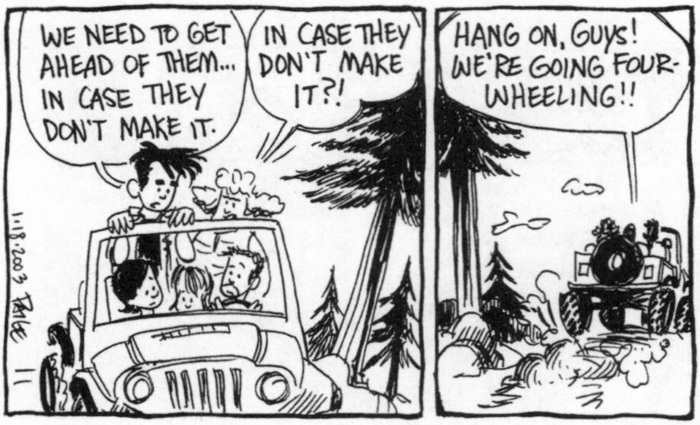
WE NEED TO GET AHEAD OF THEM... IN CASE THEY DON'T MAKE IT.
IN CASE THEY DON'T MAKE IT?!
1·18·2003 PAIGE
HANG ON, GUYS! WE'RE GOING FOUR-WHEELING!!

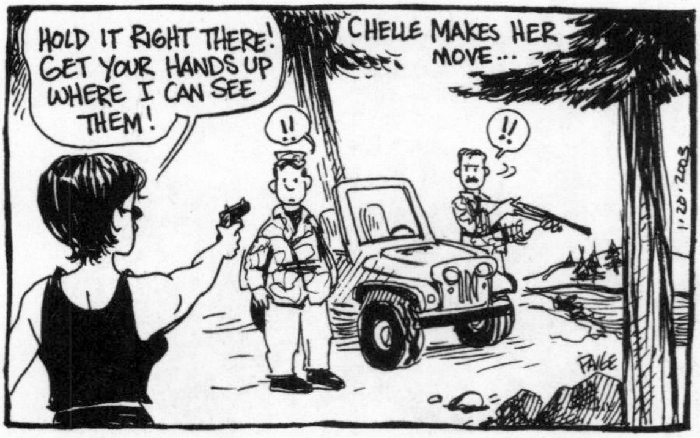
HOLD IT RIGHT THERE! GET YOUR HANDS UP WHERE I CAN SEE THEM!
CHELLE MAKES HER MOVE...
!!
!!
1·20·2003
PAIGE

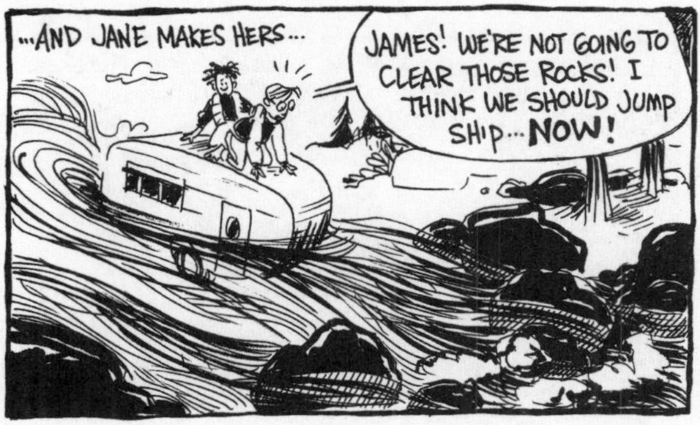
...AND JANE MAKES HERS...
JAMES! WE'RE NOT GOING TO CLEAR THOSE ROCKS! I THINK WE SHOULD JUMP SHIP... NOW!

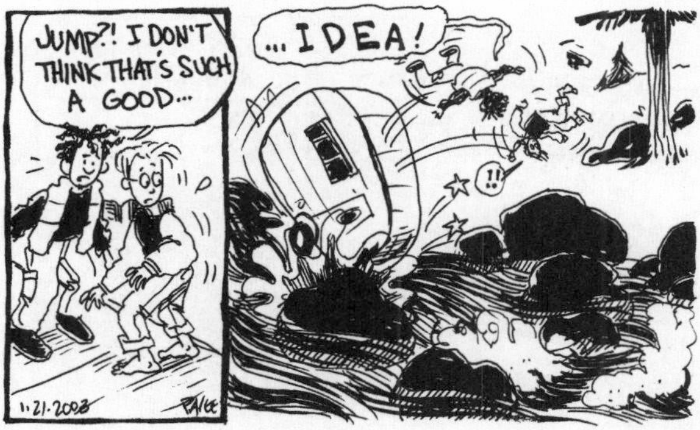
JUMP?! I DON'T THINK THAT'S SUCH A GOOD...
...IDEA!
!!
1.21.2008
PAIGE

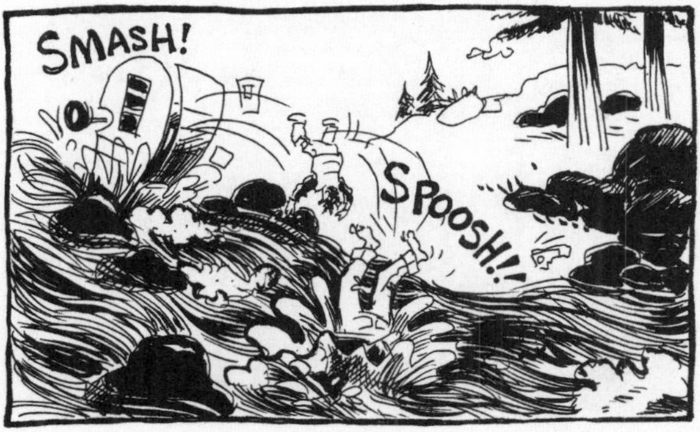
SMASH!
SPOOSH!!!

ETHAN AND CREW COME FOUR-WHEELING INTO THE SCENE JUST IN TIME TO SEE BITS OF THE WRECKED CAMPER FLY THROUGH THE AIR!
!!
!!
1.22.2003
HURRY! OUT OF THE JEEP! THEY'RE IN THE WATER!
EVERYBODY... HAND-IN-HAND! LET'S MAKE A HUMAN CHAIN!
MEANWHILE, UPSTREAM:
OKAY, G.W... YOU AND FRANK REACH FOR THE SKY... AND DROP THAT RIFLE...
1.23.2003
WHATEVER YOU SAY, SHELBY... RIGHT, FRANK?
THAT'S "CHELLE"... FACE DOWN IN THE DIRT, DIRT BAG.

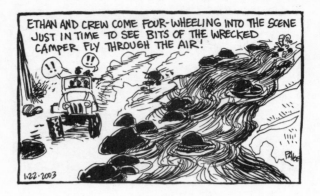

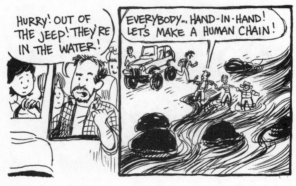

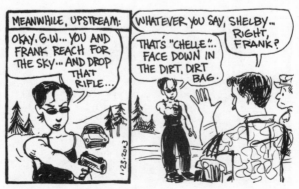

...BUT DIRT WAS A LITTLE TOO HANDY...
QUICK, FRANK! GET THE RIFLE!
ARGH!
!!
...AND IN CHELLE'S FACE IT WENT!
PAIGE

THINK AGAIN, FRANK!
UMPH!
UGH!
CRACK!
1·24·2005

THUD!
PAIGE
SMACK!

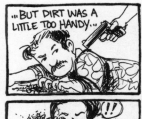

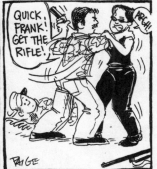

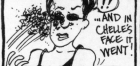

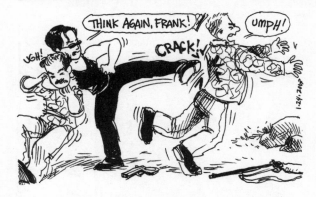

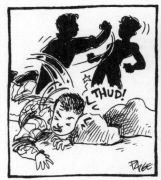

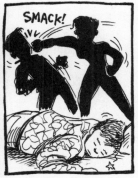

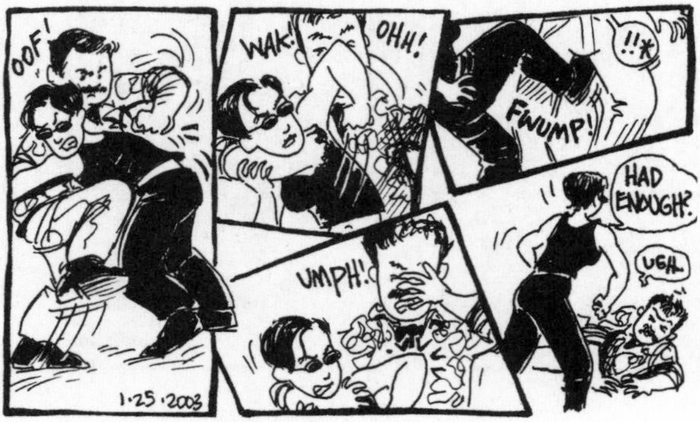
OOF!
WAK!
OHH!
!!*
FWUMP!
UMPH!
HAD ENOUGH?
UGH.
1·25·2003

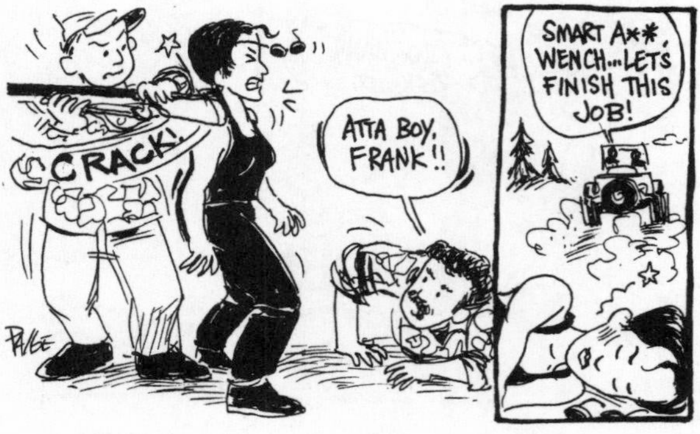
CRACK!
ATTA BOY, FRANK!!
SMART A**, WENCH...LET'S FINISH THIS JOB!

MEANWHILE...

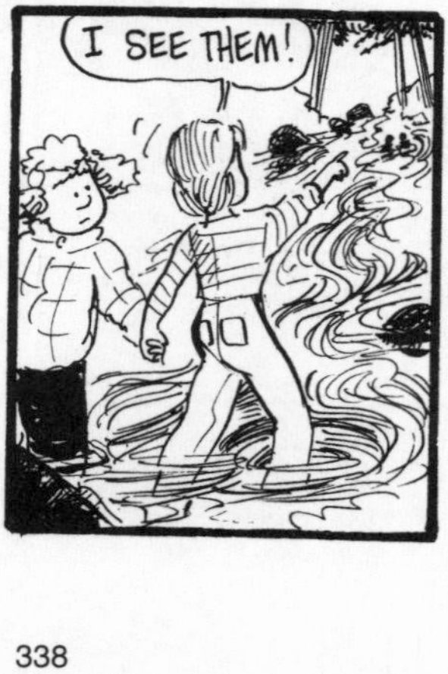
I SEE THEM!

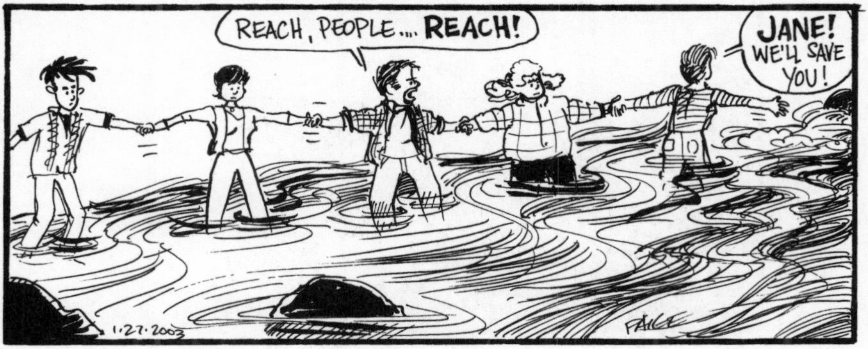
REACH, PEOPLE.... REACH!
JANE! WE'LL SAVE YOU!
1.27.2003
PAIGE

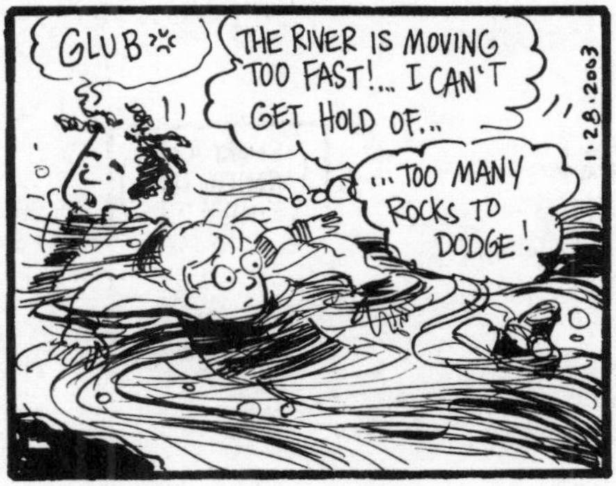
GLUB
THE RIVER IS MOVING TOO FAST!... I CAN'T GET HOLD OF...
...TOO MANY ROCKS TO DODGE!
1.28.2003

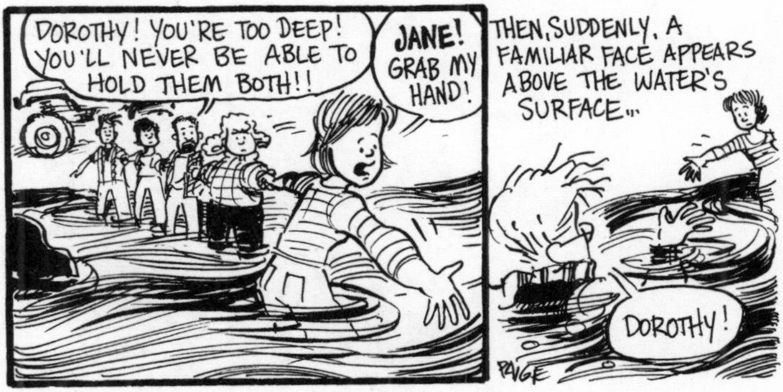
DOROTHY! YOU'RE TOO DEEP! YOU'LL NEVER BE ABLE TO HOLD THEM BOTH!!
JANE! GRAB MY HAND!
THEN, SUDDENLY, A FAMILIAR FACE APPEARS ABOVE THE WATER'S SURFACE...
DOROTHY!
PAIGE

THEIR FINGERS TOUCH...

...AND FOR AN INSTANT, THEIR HANDS MAKE FULL CONTACT, BUT THE WILL OF THE RIVER IS STRONG...

...AND THE WEIGHT OF JANE AND JAMES TOGETHER IS TOO GREAT FOR THEIR TENTATIVE GRIP...

...THEN, DESPITE BEST EFFORTS, THE RIVER CLAIMS ANOTHER...

DOROTHY!!

AAHHHH...

MEANWHILE...

OOOH... MY HEAD...

OKAY, CHELLE... PULL IT TOGETHER...

340

I'M SURE THEY'RE FOLLOWING THE RIVER SOUTH...
PAIGE
...FIND JAMES, AND I'LL FIND THEM...
I JUST HOPE I GET THERE IN TIME...
VAROOOM!

DOROTHY LOST HER FOOTING! I'VE GOTTA HELP HER!
DOROTHY! OVER HERE!
PAIGE

JANE IS ABLE TO SWIM CROSS-CURRENT JUST ENOUGH TO GET INTO DOROTHY'S PATH...
I'VE GOT YOU!!
GLUB
DOROTHY, PUT YOUR ARMS AROUND MY NECK...
I'LL PULL YOU UNDER!
NO.. I THINK ALL THOSE GLAZED DONUTS FINALLY PAID OFF...
...I'M MUCH MORE BUOYANT THAN I USED TO BE!!
1.31.2003

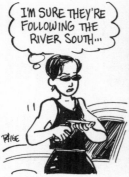

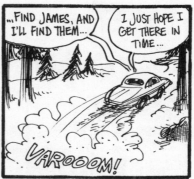

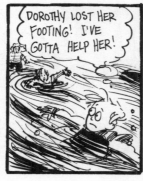

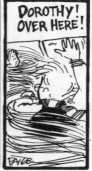

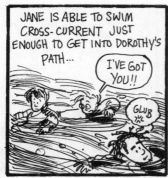

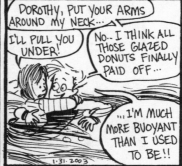

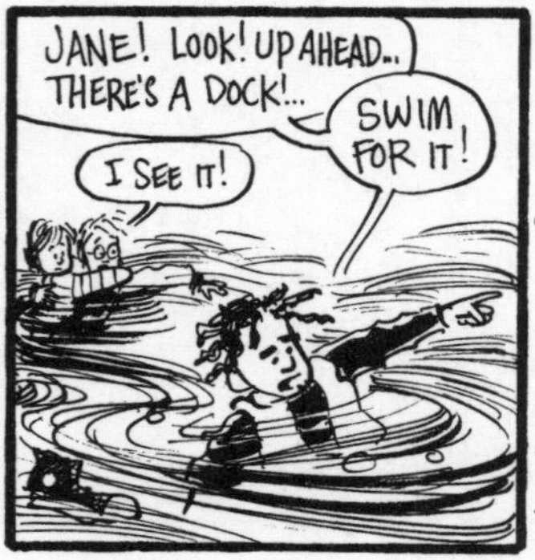
JANE! LOOK! UP AHEAD.. THERE'S A DOCK!...
SWIM FOR IT!
I SEE IT!

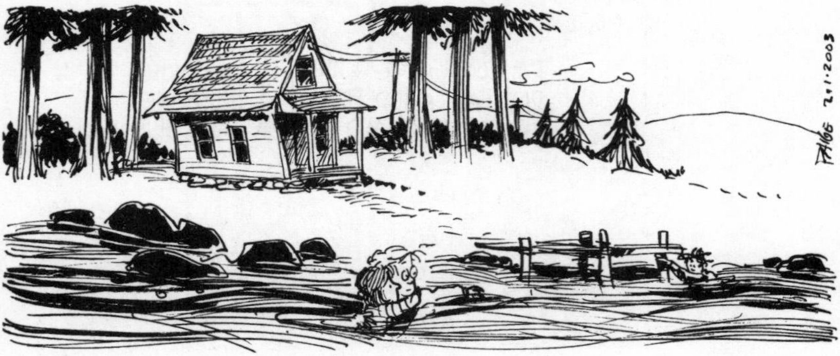

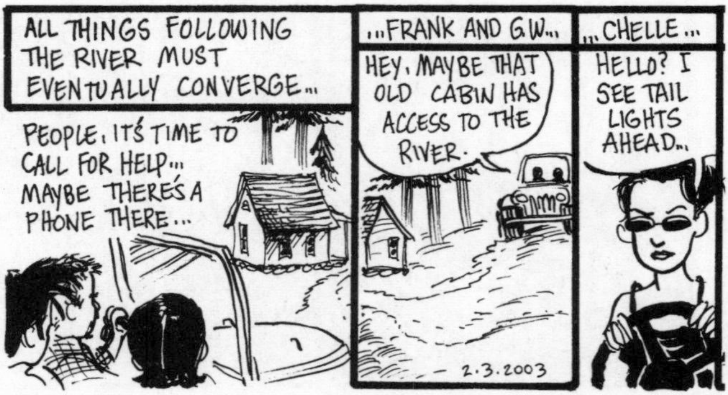
ALL THINGS FOLLOWING THE RIVER MUST EVENTUALLY CONVERGE...
PEOPLE, IT'S TIME TO CALL FOR HELP... MAYBE THERE'S A PHONE THERE...
...FRANK AND G.W...
HEY, MAYBE THAT OLD CABIN HAS ACCESS TO THE RIVER.
2.3.2003
...CHELLE...
HELLO? I SEE TAIL LIGHTS AHEAD...

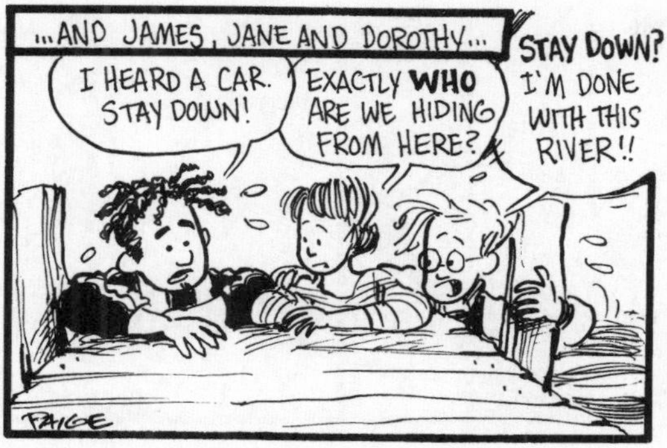
...AND JAMES, JANE AND DOROTHY...
I HEARD A CAR. STAY DOWN!
EXACTLY WHO ARE WE HIDING FROM HERE?
STAY DOWN? I'M DONE WITH THIS RIVER!!
PAIGE

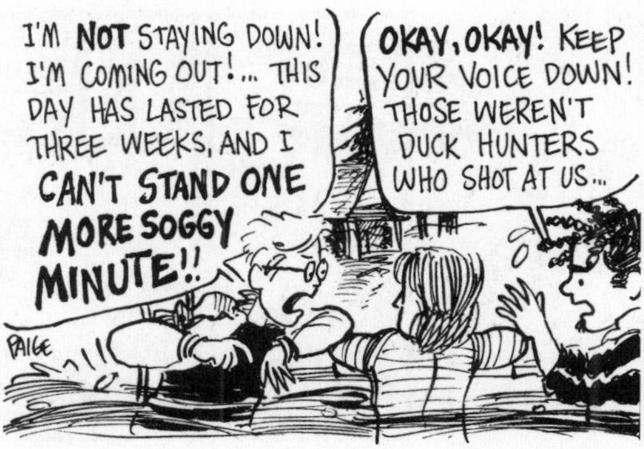
I'M NOT STAYING DOWN! I'M COMING OUT!... THIS DAY HAS LASTED FOR THREE WEEKS, AND I CAN'T STAND ONE MORE SOGGY MINUTE!!
OKAY, OKAY! KEEP YOUR VOICE DOWN! THOSE WEREN'T DUCK HUNTERS WHO SHOT AT US...
PAIGE

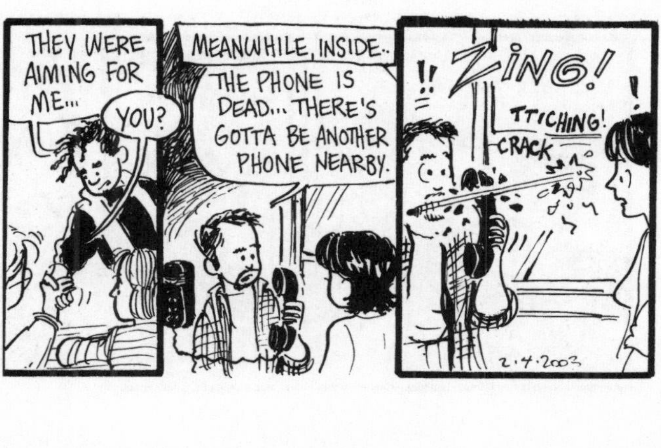
THEY WERE AIMING FOR ME...
YOU?
MEANWHILE, INSIDE..
THE PHONE IS DEAD... THERE'S GOTTA BE ANOTHER PHONE NEARBY.
!!
ZING!
!
TTICHING!
CRACK
2.4.2003

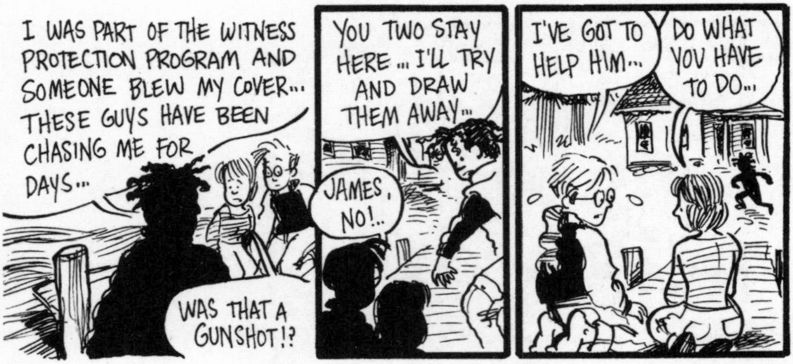
I WAS PART OF THE WITNESS PROTECTION PROGRAM AND SOMEONE BLEW MY COVER... THESE GUYS HAVE BEEN CHASING ME FOR DAYS...
WAS THAT A GUNSHOT!?
YOU TWO STAY HERE... I'LL TRY AND DRAW THEM AWAY...
JAMES, NO!..
I'VE GOT TO HELP HIM...
DO WHAT YOU HAVE TO DO...

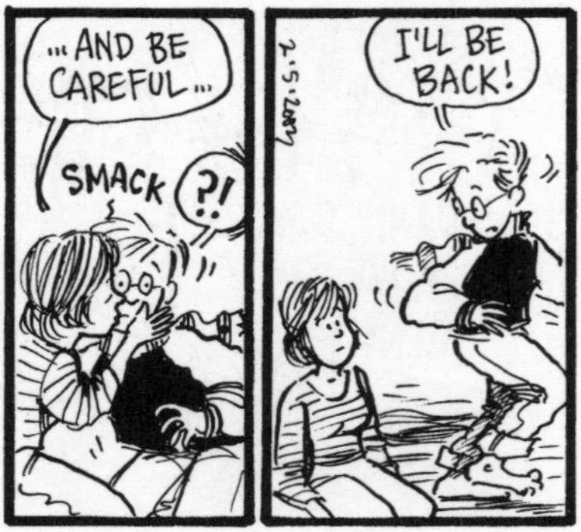
...AND BE CAREFUL...
SMACK
?!
I'LL BE BACK!

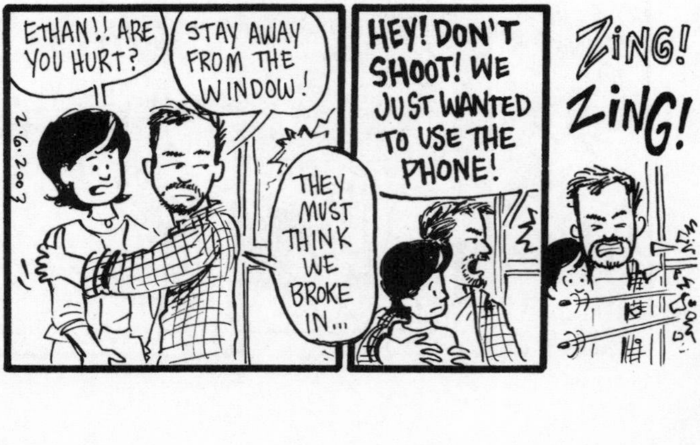
ETHAN!! ARE YOU HURT?
STAY AWAY FROM THE WINDOW!
THEY MUST THINK WE BROKE IN...
HEY! DON'T SHOOT! WE JUST WANTED TO USE THE PHONE!
ZING!
ZING!

SHOOT FIRST, ASK QUESTIONS LATER... SO TYPICAL, G.W.
WHERE'S YOUR BOYFRIEND, FRANK?
PAIGE
GET UP, LADY... NICE AND SLOW ... WHERE'S JAMES?

JAMES ISN'T HERE. YOU'RE WASTING YOUR TIME...
WALK!
OH, NO... DOROTHY!
PAIGE
CHELLE!
JAMES! THANK GOODNESS YOU'RE OKAY..
WHERE'S FRANK?
CLICK

MEANWHILE...
THIS IS IT... YOUR CHANCE TO MAKE A DIFFERENCE...
...GET SOME GUTS, JANE.
JUST KEEP WALKING... TOWARD THAT JEEP..
JANE!
2.7.2003

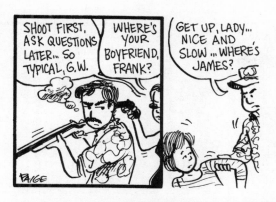

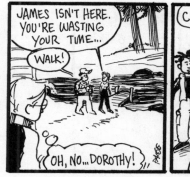

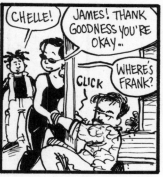

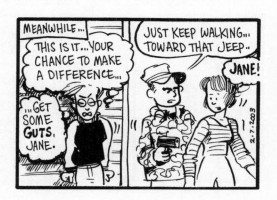

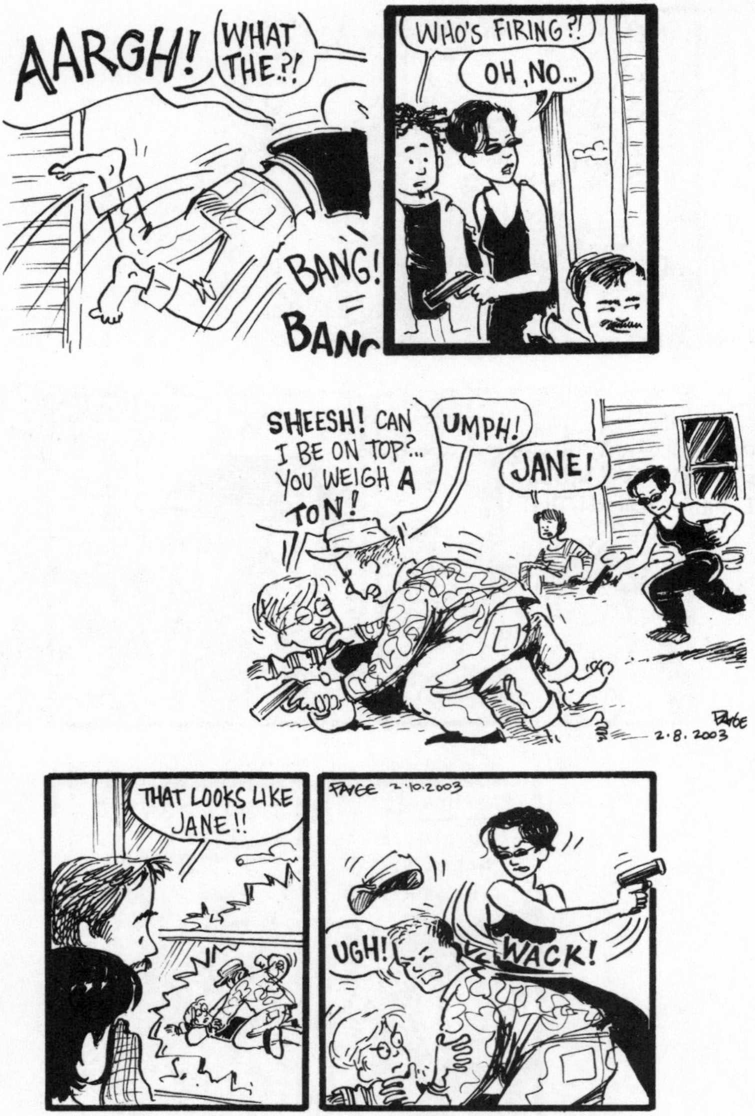
AARGH!
WHAT THE?!
BANG!
BANG
WHO'S FIRING?!
OH, NO...
SHEESH! CAN I BE ON TOP?... YOU WEIGH A TON!
UMPH!
JANE!
PAIGE 2.8.2003
THAT LOOKS LIKE JANE!!
PAIGE 2.10.2003
UGH!
WACK!

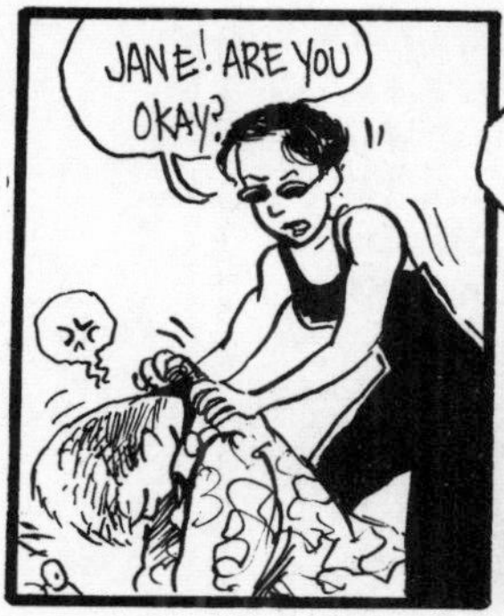
JANE! ARE YOU OKAY?

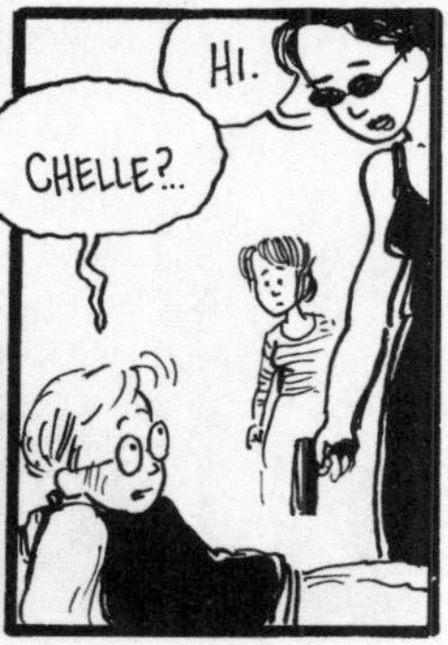
HI.
CHELLE?..

THE LONGEST DAY IN THE HISTORY OF COMIC ART HAS FINALLY COME TO AN END... AND THINGS IN JANE'S WORLD MAY NEVER BE QUITE THE SAME... ALL THAT SPECULATION ABOUT CHELLE'S SECRET LIFE CONTAINED A BIT OF TRUTH... AS IS SOMETIMES THE CASE... SHE **DID** HAVE A SECRET LIFE AFTER ALL!... BUT WHAT EXACTLY DOES ANY OF THIS MEAN?....

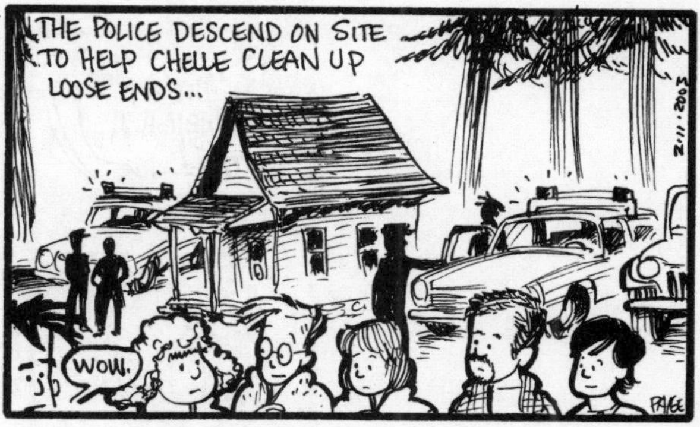
THE POLICE DESCEND ON SITE TO HELP CHELLE CLEAN UP LOOSE ENDS...
WOW.
PAIGE

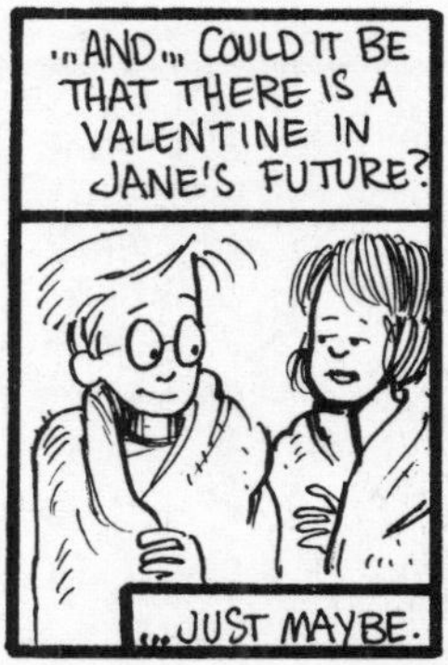
...AND... COULD IT BE THAT THERE IS A VALENTINE IN JANE'S FUTURE?
...JUST MAYBE.

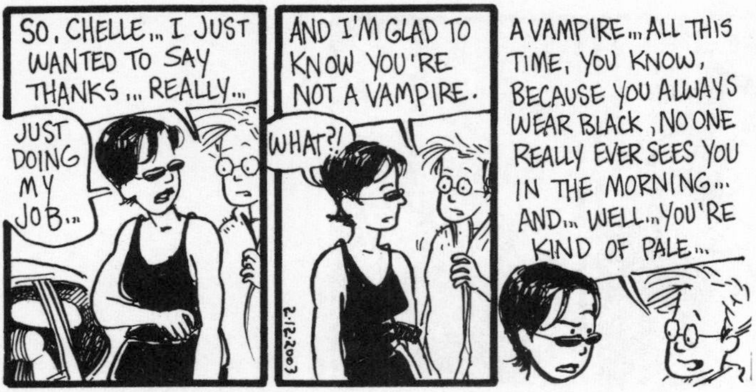
SO, CHELLE... I JUST WANTED TO SAY THANKS... REALLY...
JUST DOING MY JOB...
AND I'M GLAD TO KNOW YOU'RE NOT A VAMPIRE.
WHAT?!
A VAMPIRE... ALL THIS TIME, YOU KNOW, BECAUSE YOU ALWAYS WEAR BLACK, NO ONE REALLY EVER SEES YOU IN THE MORNING... AND... WELL... YOU'RE KIND OF PALE...

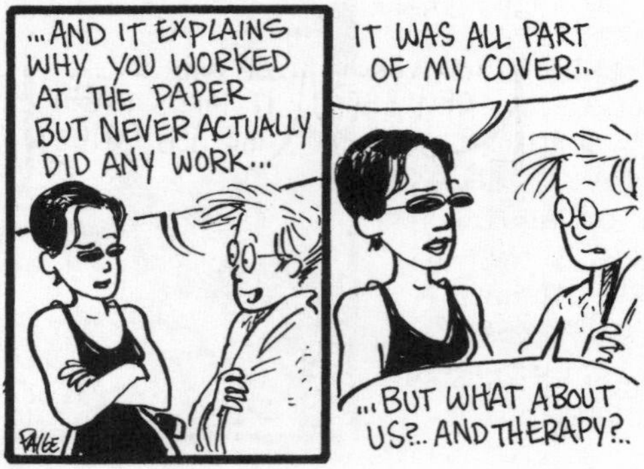
...AND IT EXPLAINS WHY YOU WORKED AT THE PAPER BUT NEVER ACTUALLY DID ANY WORK...
PAIGE
IT WAS ALL PART OF MY COVER...
...BUT WHAT ABOUT US?.. AND THERAPY?..

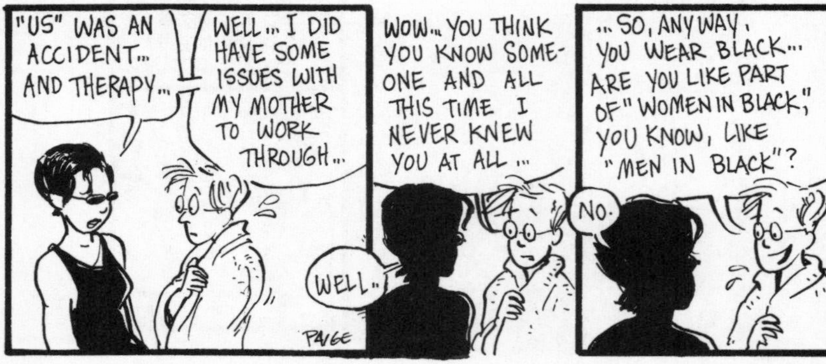
"US" WAS AN ACCIDENT... AND THERAPY...
WELL... I DID HAVE SOME ISSUES WITH MY MOTHER TO WORK THROUGH...
PAIGE
WOW... YOU THINK YOU KNOW SOME-ONE AND ALL THIS TIME I NEVER KNEW YOU AT ALL...
WELL..
...SO, ANYWAY, YOU WEAR BLACK... ARE YOU LIKE PART OF "WOMEN IN BLACK," YOU KNOW, LIKE "MEN IN BLACK"?
NO.

I JUST HAPPEN TO LIKE BLACK.
HERE...MY CARD.
WV
WOMEN ON THE VERGE
CHELLE ARCHER
2.13.2003

WOMEN ON THE VERGE OF WHAT?
ON THE VERGE OF WHATEVER IT TAKES TO GET THE JOB DONE.
SHE'S WEARING A TOWEL
COOOOL...

HEY, SO NOW THAT WE KNOW, CAN WE HELP YOU SOLVE CASES AND STUFF?..
?!
...LIKE THE WAY BUFFY'S PALS HELP HER SLAY VAMPIRES... I MEAN, NOW THAT THEY KNOW HER SECRET IDENTITY, THEY'RE LIKE HER POSSE... CAN WE...
NO.
2.14.2003

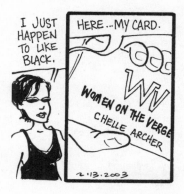

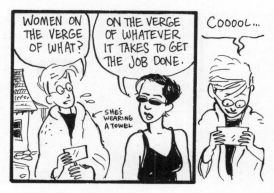

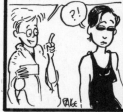

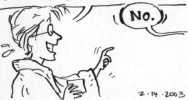

THE NEXT DAY, AT JANE'S...

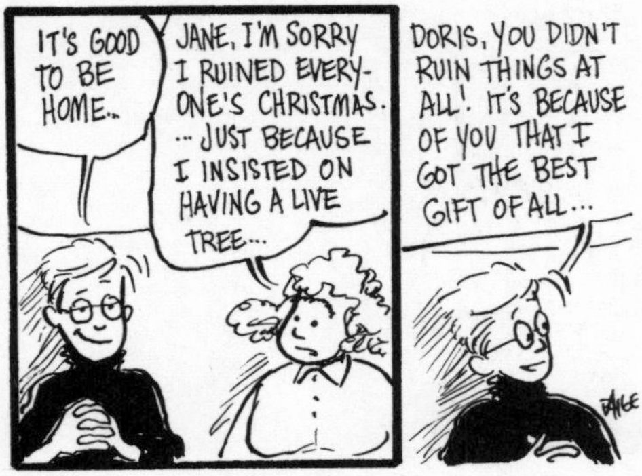
IT'S GOOD TO BE HOME..
JANE, I'M SORRY I RUINED EVERY-ONE'S CHRISTMAS. ...JUST BECAUSE I INSISTED ON HAVING A LIVE TREE...
DORIS, YOU DIDN'T RUIN THINGS AT ALL! IT'S BECAUSE OF YOU THAT I GOT THE BEST GIFT OF ALL...
PAIGE

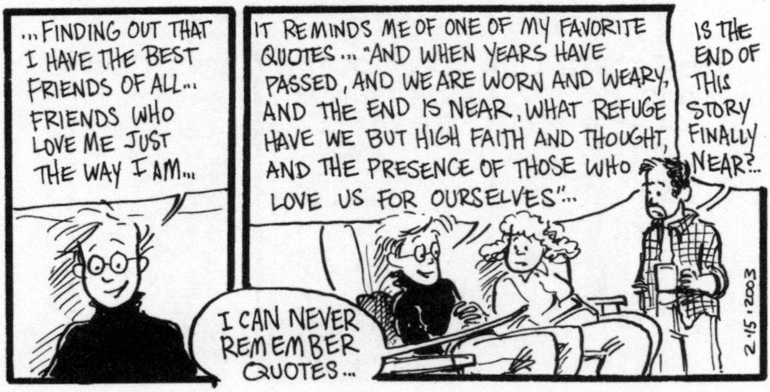
...FINDING OUT THAT I HAVE THE BEST FRIENDS OF ALL... FRIENDS WHO LOVE ME JUST THE WAY I AM...
IT REMINDS ME OF ONE OF MY FAVORITE QUOTES... "AND WHEN YEARS HAVE PASSED, AND WE ARE WORN AND WEARY, AND THE END IS NEAR, WHAT REFUGE HAVE WE BUT HIGH FAITH AND THOUGHT, AND THE PRESENCE OF THOSE WHO LOVE US FOR OURSELVES"...
IS THE END OF THIS STORY FINALLY NEAR?...
I CAN NEVER REMEMBER QUOTES...
2.15.2003

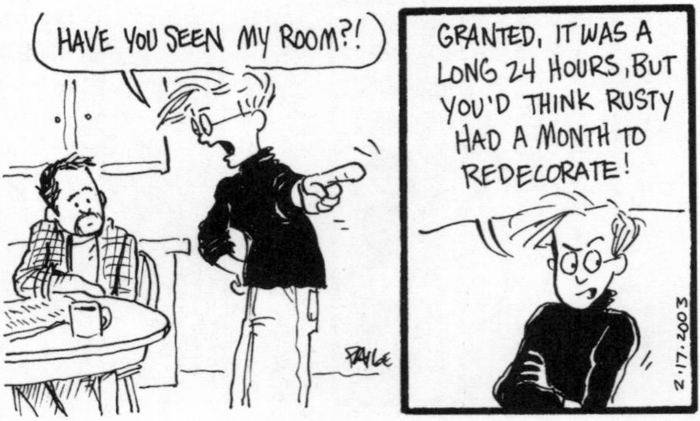
HAVE YOU SEEN MY ROOM?!
PAIGE
GRANTED, IT WAS A LONG 24 HOURS, BUT YOU'D THINK RUSTY HAD A MONTH TO REDECORATE!
2.17.2003

SO YOU'RE REALLY NOT MAD AT DORIS? I THINK I WOULD BE...

YOU KNOW, I'M REALLY NOT... I'M ODDLY CALM ABOUT THE WHOLE EXPERIENCE...

EXCEPT FOR THE PART ABOUT CHELLE BEING A SECRET-AGENT-TYPE CHICK...

THE WHOLE TIME WE DATED, SHE WAS CARRYING A CONCEALED WEAPON!

IT'S A GOOD THING I LET HER WIN ALL THE ARGUMENTS.

OH... SO "LOSING" WAS A STRATEGY?

LOSING ARGUMENTS WASN'T SO MUCH A STRATEGY AS IT WAS A ... UM ... WELL, A PASSIVE APPROACH TO OUR RELATIONSHIP ...

2·19·2003

PAIGE

CAN YOU SAY "DOORMAT"?

LIKE YOU'VE CORNERED THE MARKET ON EFFECTIVE COMMUNICATION!

"WHAT WE HAVE HERE IS A FAILURE TO COMMUNICATE" ...

HERE WE GO! ... ADVICE FROM THE GUY WHO THINKS ALL LIFE'S RIDDLES ARE ANSWERED IN "COOL HAND LUKE" ...

A RAINBOW FLAG?

YEAH ... I THINK IT'LL BRING SOME POSITIVE ENERGY BACK TO MY JEEP ... YOU KNOW, SINCE THOSE GUYS USED IT TO CARRY OUT THEIR EVIL PLOT AGAINST JAMES ...

BUT ISN'T A RAINBOW FLAG ON A JEEP A BIT REDUNDANT?
PAIGE
HEY! IT'S NOT LIKE IT'S A SUBARU!
2.20.2003

WE SHOULD INVEST IN A CAMP TRAILER...
2.21.2003
YOU KNOW, HAVE SOME NICE SPOT TO GET AWAY TO ON THE WEEKEND.
...INVEST WITH WHAT? YOU'VE GOT THAT PESKY UNEMPLOYMENT PROBLEM, REMEMBER?
PAIGE

THAT WON'T LAST FOREVER... AND WHEN I MAKE A MILLION ON MY FIRST NOVEL, WE COULD GET ONE. I THINK THAT'D BE COOL...
UNTIL SOME-ONE PULLS THE BLOCKS FROM UNDER THE TIRES AND IT ROLLS INTO THE RIVER...
LLOYD??
I SWEAR... IT WAS PARKED RIGHT HERE!

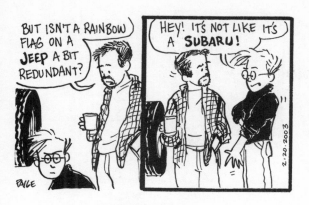

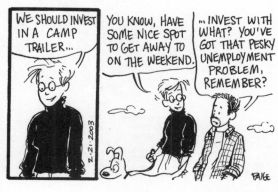

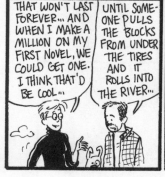

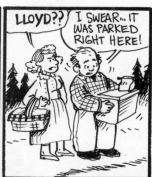

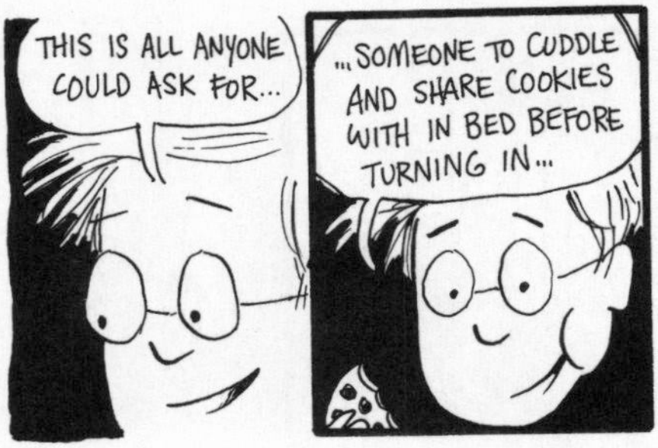
THIS IS ALL ANYONE COULD ASK FOR...
...SOMEONE TO CUDDLE AND SHARE COOKIES WITH IN BED BEFORE TURNING IN...

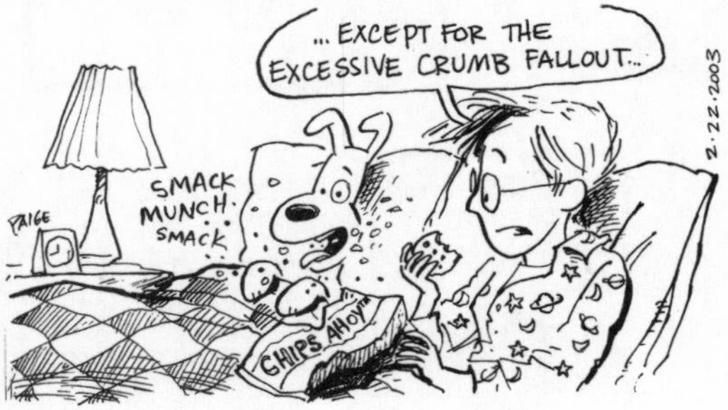
... EXCEPT FOR THE EXCESSIVE CRUMB FALLOUT...
SMACK
MUNCH.
SMACK
CHIPS AHOY!
PAIGE
2.22.2003

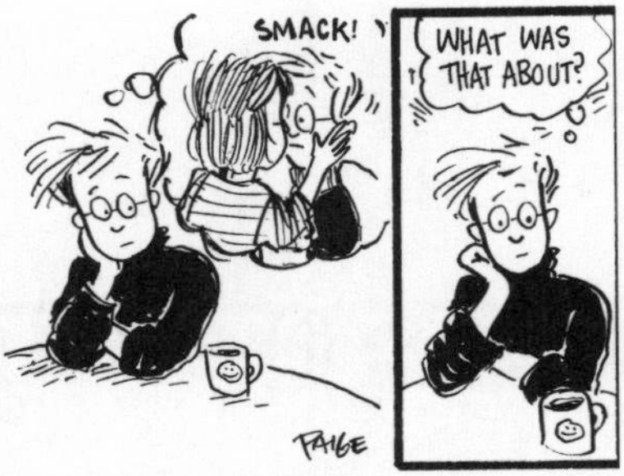
SMACK!
WHAT WAS THAT ABOUT?
PAIGE

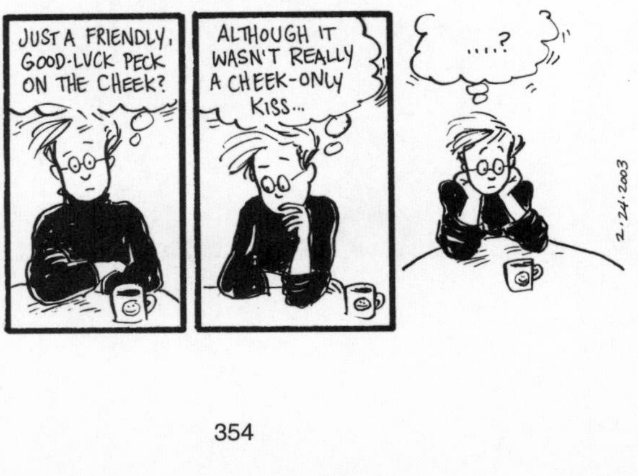
JUST A FRIENDLY, GOOD-LUCK PECK ON THE CHEEK?
ALTHOUGH IT WASN'T REALLY A CHEEK-ONLY KISS...
....?
2.24.2003

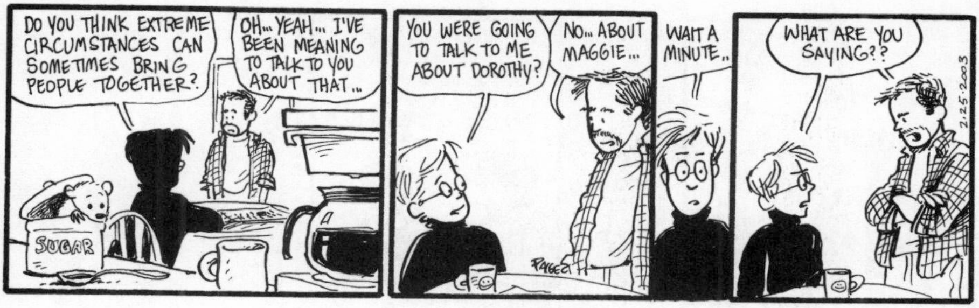
DO YOU THINK EXTREME CIRCUMSTANCES CAN SOMETIMES BRING PEOPLE TOGETHER?
OH... YEAH... I'VE BEEN MEANING TO TALK TO YOU ABOUT THAT...
SUGAR
YOU WERE GOING TO TALK TO ME ABOUT DOROTHY?
NO... ABOUT MAGGIE...
PAIGE
WAIT A MINUTE...
WHAT ARE YOU SAYING??
2.25.2003

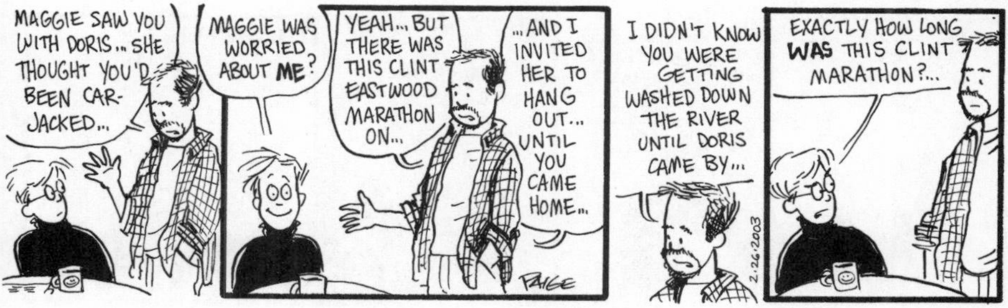
MAGGIE SAW YOU WITH DORIS... SHE THOUGHT YOU'D BEEN CAR-JACKED...
MAGGIE WAS WORRIED ABOUT **ME**?
YEAH... BUT THERE WAS THIS CLINT EASTWOOD MARATHON ON...
...AND I INVITED HER TO HANG OUT... UNTIL YOU CAME HOME...
PAIGE
I DIDN'T KNOW YOU WERE GETTING WASHED DOWN THE RIVER UNTIL DORIS CAME BY...
2.26.2003
EXACTLY HOW LONG **WAS** THIS CLINT MARATHON?...

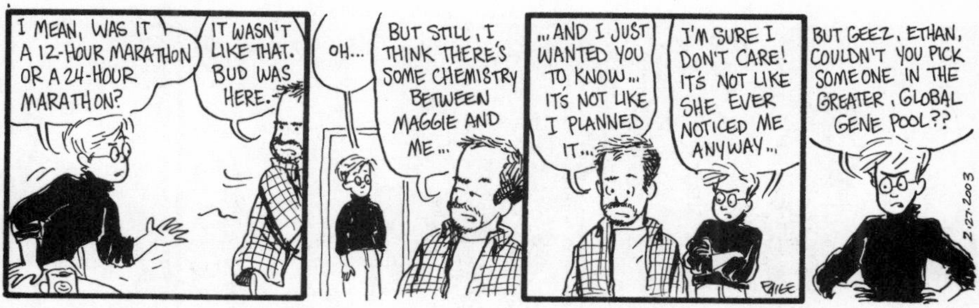
I MEAN, WAS IT A 12-HOUR MARATHON OR A 24-HOUR MARATHON?
IT WASN'T LIKE THAT. BUD WAS HERE.
OH...
BUT STILL, I THINK THERE'S SOME CHEMISTRY BETWEEN MAGGIE AND ME...
...AND I JUST WANTED YOU TO KNOW... IT'S NOT LIKE I PLANNED IT...
I'M SURE I DON'T CARE! IT'S NOT LIKE SHE EVER NOTICED ME ANYWAY...
PAIGE
BUT GEEZ, ETHAN, COULDN'T YOU PICK SOMEONE IN THE GREATER, GLOBAL GENE POOL??
2.27.2003

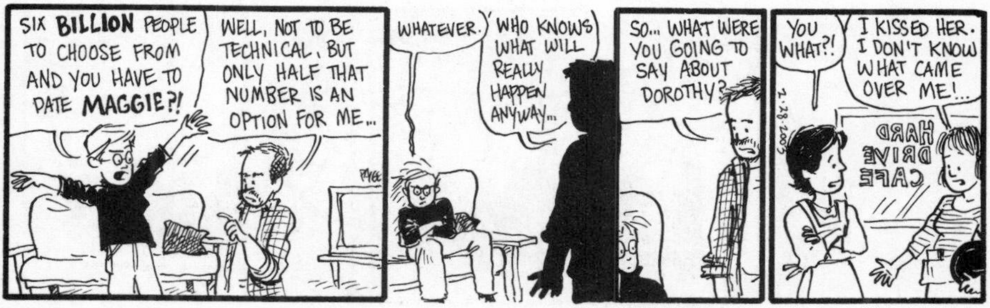
SIX **BILLION** PEOPLE TO CHOOSE FROM AND YOU HAVE TO DATE **MAGGIE**?!
WELL, NOT TO BE TECHNICAL, BUT ONLY HALF THAT NUMBER IS AN OPTION FOR ME...
PAIGE
WHATEVER.
WHO KNOWS WHAT WILL REALLY HAPPEN ANYWAY...
SO... WHAT WERE YOU GOING TO SAY ABOUT DOROTHY?
2.28.2003
YOU WHAT?!
I KISSED HER. I DON'T KNOW WHAT CAME OVER ME!...
HARD DRIVE CAFE

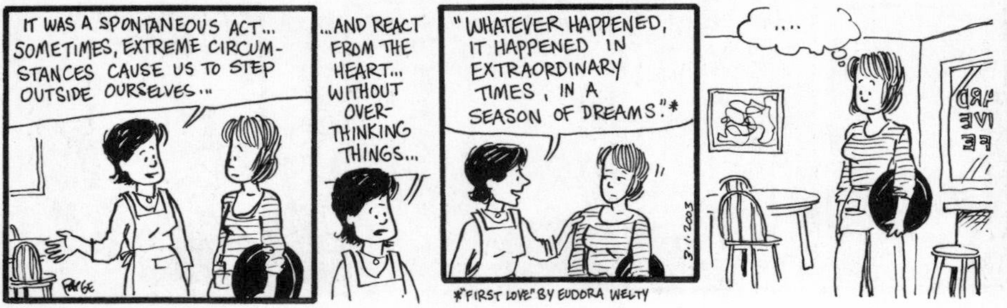
IT WAS A SPONTANEOUS ACT... SOMETIMES, EXTREME CIRCUMSTANCES CAUSE US TO STEP OUTSIDE OURSELVES...
...AND REACT FROM THE HEART... WITHOUT OVER-THINKING THINGS...
"WHATEVER HAPPENED, IT HAPPENED IN EXTRAORDINARY TIMES, IN A SEASON OF DREAMS."*
3.1.2003
....
*"FIRST LOVE" BY EUDORA WELTY

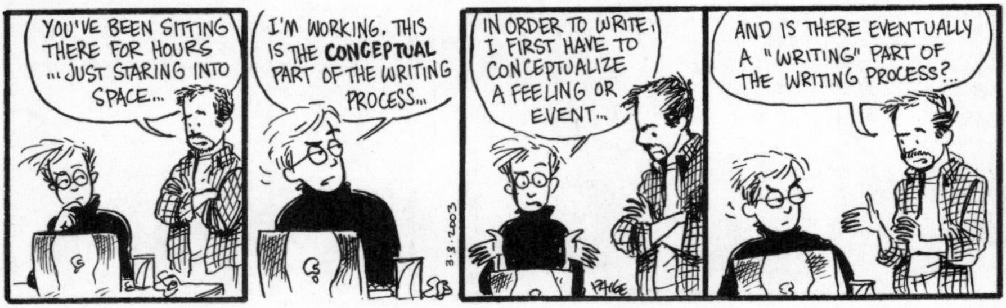
YOU'VE BEEN SITTING THERE FOR HOURS ...JUST STARING INTO SPACE...
I'M WORKING. THIS IS THE **CONCEPTUAL** PART OF THE WRITING PROCESS...
3.3.2003
IN ORDER TO WRITE, I FIRST HAVE TO CONCEPTUALIZE A FEELING OR EVENT...
AND IS THERE EVENTUALLY A "WRITING" PART OF THE WRITING PROCESS?...

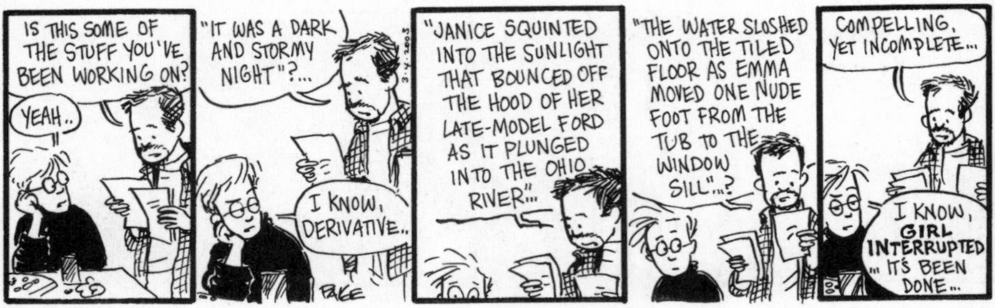
IS THIS SOME OF THE STUFF YOU'VE BEEN WORKING ON?
YEAH..
"IT WAS A DARK AND STORMY NIGHT"?...
I KNOW, DERIVATIVE..
3.4.2003
"JANICE SQUINTED INTO THE SUNLIGHT THAT BOUNCED OFF THE HOOD OF HER LATE-MODEL FORD AS IT PLUNGED INTO THE OHIO RIVER"...
"THE WATER SLOSHED ONTO THE TILED FLOOR AS EMMA MOVED ONE NUDE FOOT FROM THE TUB TO THE WINDOW SILL"...?
COMPELLING, YET INCOMPLETE...
I KNOW, **GIRL INTERRUPTED** ... IT'S BEEN DONE...

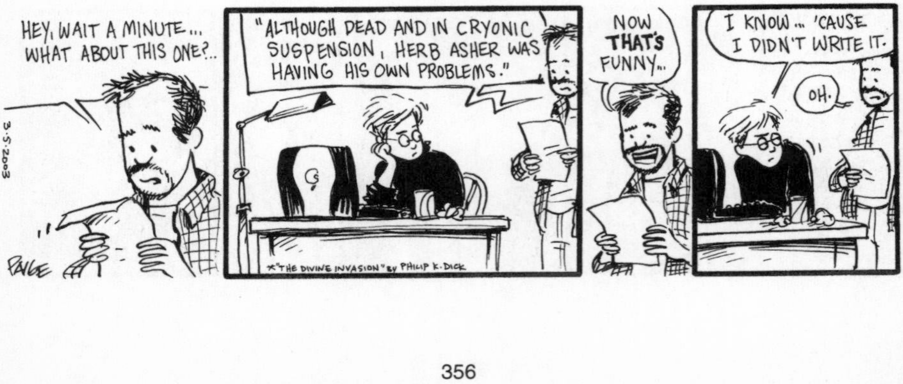
HEY, WAIT A MINUTE... WHAT ABOUT THIS ONE?...
3.5.2003
"ALTHOUGH DEAD AND IN CRYONIC SUSPENSION, HERB ASHER WAS HAVING HIS OWN PROBLEMS."*
NOW **THAT'S** FUNNY...
I KNOW... 'CAUSE I DIDN'T WRITE IT.
OH.
*"THE DIVINE INVASION" BY PHILIP K. DICK

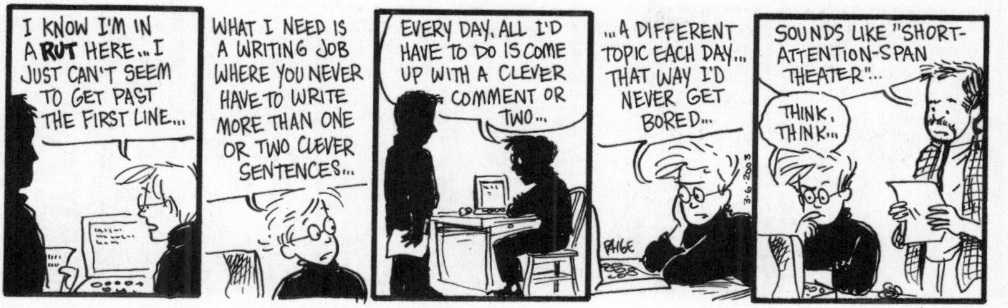
I KNOW I'M IN A **RUT** HERE... I JUST CAN'T SEEM TO GET PAST THE FIRST LINE...
WHAT I NEED IS A WRITING JOB WHERE YOU NEVER HAVE TO WRITE MORE THAN ONE OR TWO CLEVER SENTENCES...
EVERY DAY, ALL I'D HAVE TO DO IS COME UP WITH A CLEVER COMMENT OR TWO...
...A DIFFERENT TOPIC EACH DAY... THAT WAY I'D NEVER GET BORED...
3.6.2003
PAIGE
SOUNDS LIKE "SHORT-ATTENTION-SPAN THEATER"...
THINK, THINK...

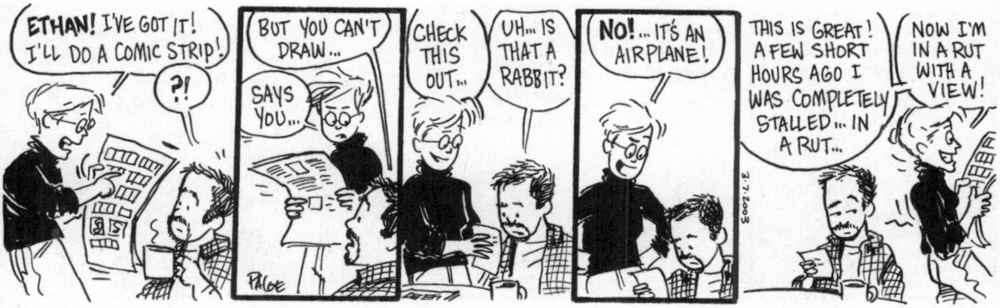
ETHAN! I'VE GOT IT! I'LL DO A COMIC STRIP!
?!
BUT YOU CAN'T DRAW...
SAYS YOU...
PAIGE
CHECK THIS OUT...
UH... IS THAT A RABBIT?
NO!... IT'S AN AIRPLANE!
3.7.2003
THIS IS GREAT! A FEW SHORT HOURS AGO I WAS COMPLETELY STALLED... IN A RUT...
NOW I'M IN A RUT WITH A VIEW!

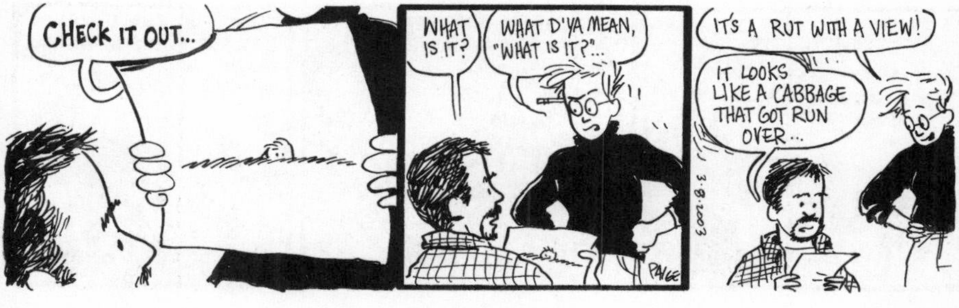
CHECK IT OUT...
WHAT IS IT?
WHAT D'YA MEAN, "WHAT IS IT?"...
3.8.2003
PAIGE
IT'S A RUT WITH A VIEW!
IT LOOKS LIKE A CABBAGE THAT GOT RUN OVER...

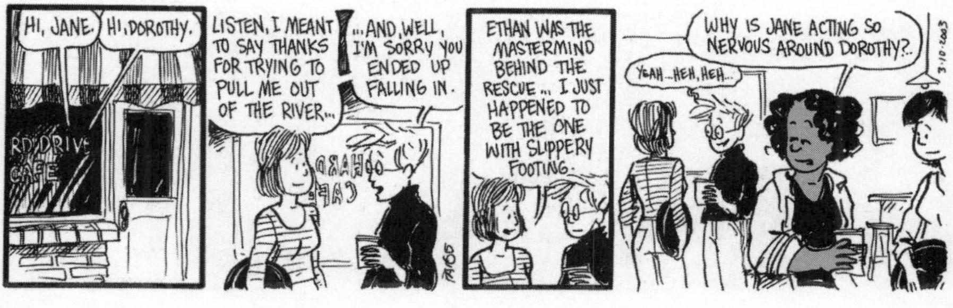
HI, JANE.
HI, DOROTHY.
RD DRIVE CAFE
LISTEN, I MEANT TO SAY THANKS FOR TRYING TO PULL ME OUT OF THE RIVER...
...AND, WELL, I'M SORRY YOU ENDED UP FALLING IN.
PAIGE
ETHAN WAS THE MASTERMIND BEHIND THE RESCUE... I JUST HAPPENED TO BE THE ONE WITH SLIPPERY FOOTING.
WHY IS JANE ACTING SO NERVOUS AROUND DOROTHY?...
YEAH... HEH, HEH...
3.10.2003

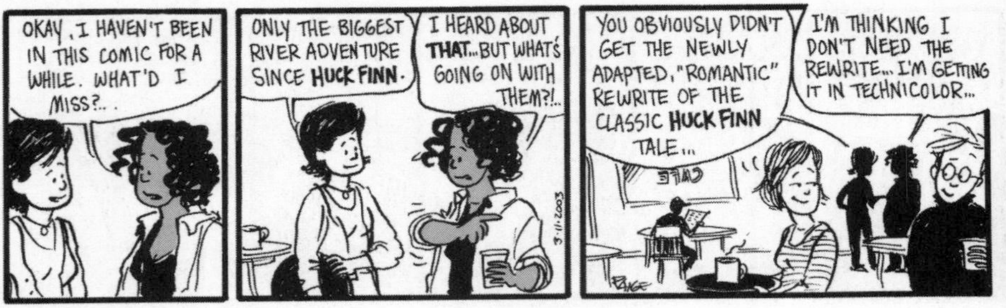

OKAY, I HAVEN'T BEEN IN THIS COMIC FOR A WHILE. WHAT'D I MISS?..
ONLY THE BIGGEST RIVER ADVENTURE SINCE HUCK FINN.
I HEARD ABOUT THAT... BUT WHAT'S GOING ON WITH THEM?!..
3-11-2003
YOU OBVIOUSLY DIDN'T GET THE NEWLY ADAPTED, "ROMANTIC" REWRITE OF THE CLASSIC HUCK FINN TALE...
I'M THINKING I DON'T NEED THE REWRITE... I'M GETTING IT IN TECHNICOLOR...
PAIGE

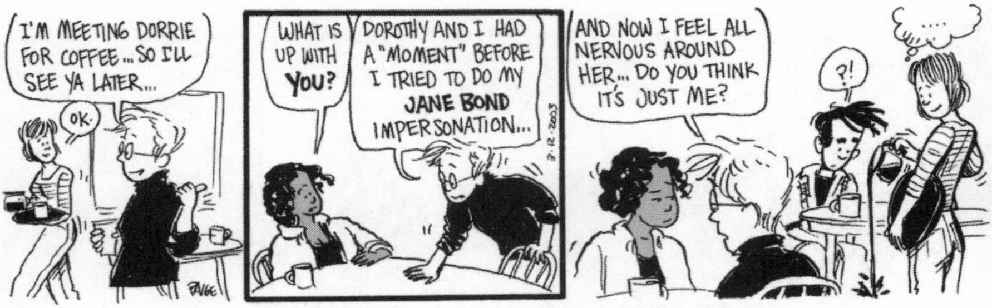

I'M MEETING DORRIE FOR COFFEE... SO I'LL SEE YA LATER...
OK.
PAIGE
WHAT IS UP WITH YOU?
DOROTHY AND I HAD A "MOMENT" BEFORE I TRIED TO DO MY JANE BOND IMPERSONATION...
3-12-2003
AND NOW I FEEL ALL NERVOUS AROUND HER... DO YOU THINK IT'S JUST ME?
?!
....

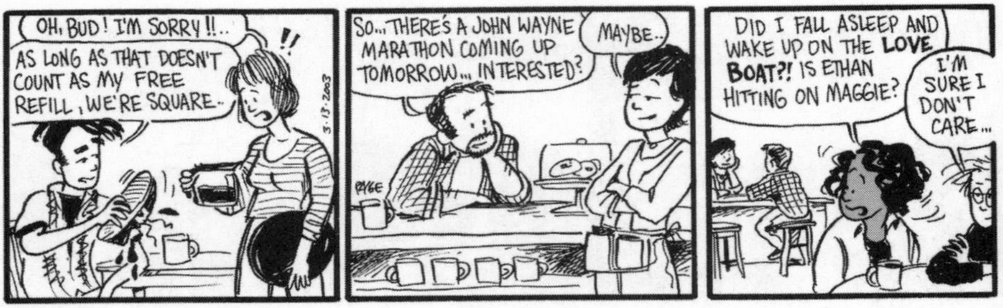

OH, BUD! I'M SORRY!!..
AS LONG AS THAT DOESN'T COUNT AS MY FREE REFILL, WE'RE SQUARE..
!!
3-13-2003
SO... THERE'S A JOHN WAYNE MARATHON COMING UP TOMORROW... INTERESTED?
MAYBE..
PAIGE
DID I FALL ASLEEP AND WAKE UP ON THE LOVE BOAT?! IS ETHAN HITTING ON MAGGIE?
I'M SURE I DON'T CARE...

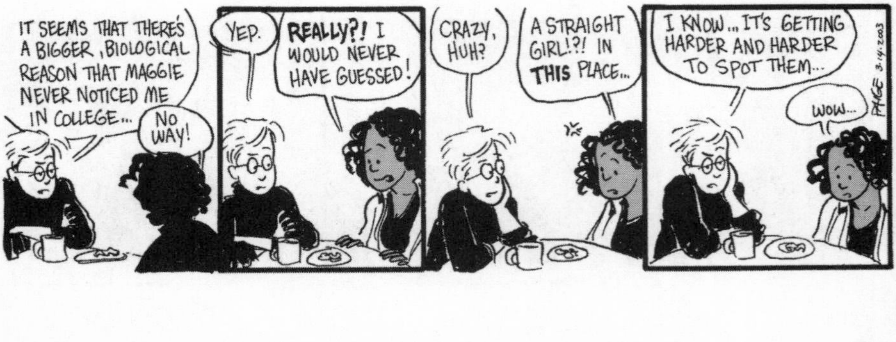

IT SEEMS THAT THERE'S A BIGGER, BIOLOGICAL REASON THAT MAGGIE NEVER NOTICED ME IN COLLEGE...
No WAY!
YEP.
REALLY?! I WOULD NEVER HAVE GUESSED!
CRAZY, HUH?
A STRAIGHT GIRL!?! IN THIS PLACE...
I KNOW... IT'S GETTING HARDER AND HARDER TO SPOT THEM...
WOW...
3-14-2003
PAIGE

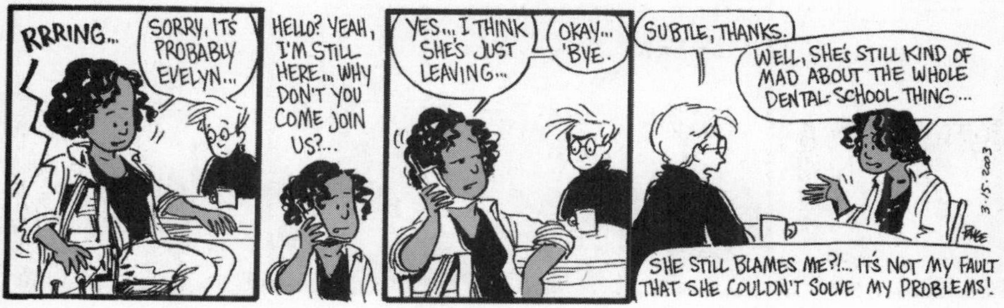
RRRING...
SORRY, IT'S PROBABLY EVELYN...
HELLO? YEAH, I'M STILL HERE... WHY DON'T YOU COME JOIN US?...
YES... I THINK SHE'S JUST LEAVING...
OKAY... 'BYE.
SUBTLE, THANKS.
WELL, SHE'S STILL KIND OF MAD ABOUT THE WHOLE DENTAL-SCHOOL THING...
SHE STILL BLAMES ME?!... IT'S NOT MY FAULT THAT SHE COULDN'T SOLVE MY PROBLEMS!
3-15-2003

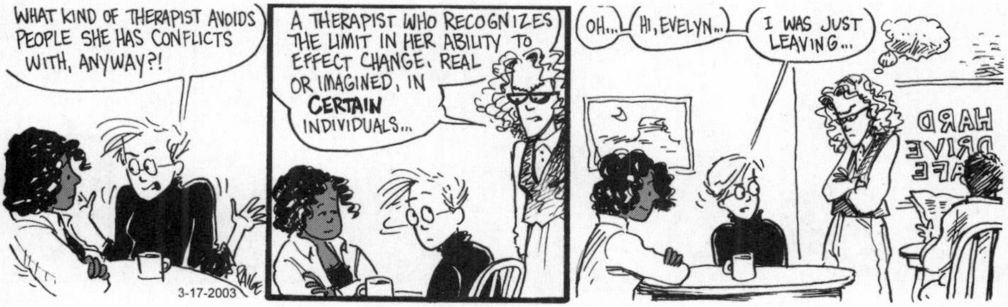
WHAT KIND OF THERAPIST AVOIDS PEOPLE SHE HAS CONFLICTS WITH, ANYWAY?!
3-17-2003
A THERAPIST WHO RECOGNIZES THE LIMIT IN HER ABILITY TO EFFECT CHANGE, REAL OR IMAGINED, IN CERTAIN INDIVIDUALS...
OH...
HI, EVELYN...
I WAS JUST LEAVING...

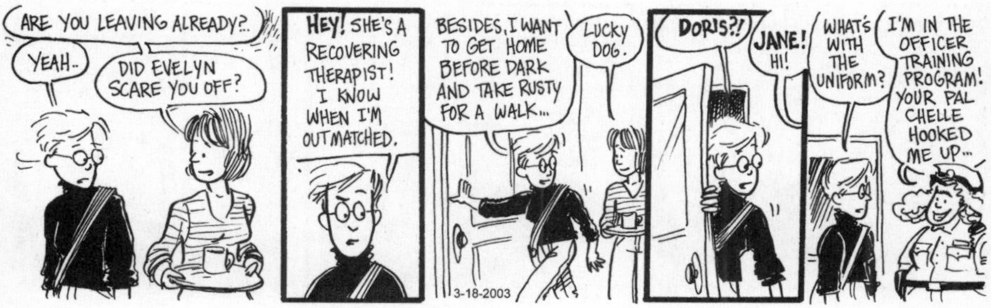
ARE YOU LEAVING ALREADY?..
YEAH..
DID EVELYN SCARE YOU OFF?
HEY! SHE'S A RECOVERING THERAPIST! I KNOW WHEN I'M OUTMATCHED.
BESIDES, I WANT TO GET HOME BEFORE DARK AND TAKE RUSTY FOR A WALK...
LUCKY DOG.
3-18-2003
DORIS?!
JANE! HI!
WHAT'S WITH THE UNIFORM?
I'M IN THE OFFICER TRAINING PROGRAM! YOUR PAL CHELLE HOOKED ME UP...

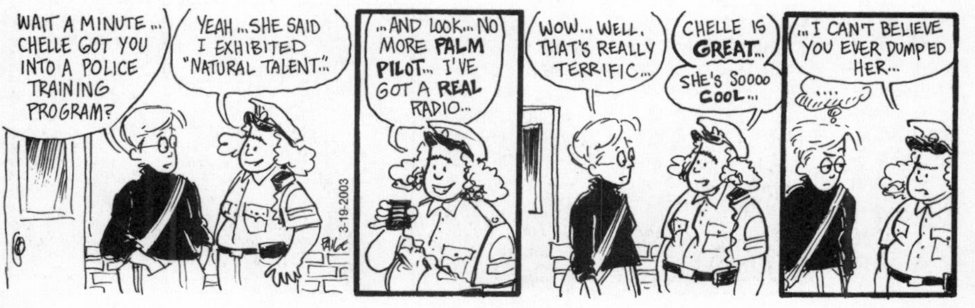
WAIT A MINUTE... CHELLE GOT YOU INTO A POLICE TRAINING PROGRAM?
YEAH... SHE SAID I EXHIBITED "NATURAL TALENT."
3-19-2003
...AND LOOK... NO MORE PALM PILOT... I'VE GOT A REAL RADIO...
WOW... WELL, THAT'S REALLY TERRIFIC...
CHELLE IS GREAT...
SHE'S SOOOO COOL...
...I CAN'T BELIEVE YOU EVER DUMPED HER...
....

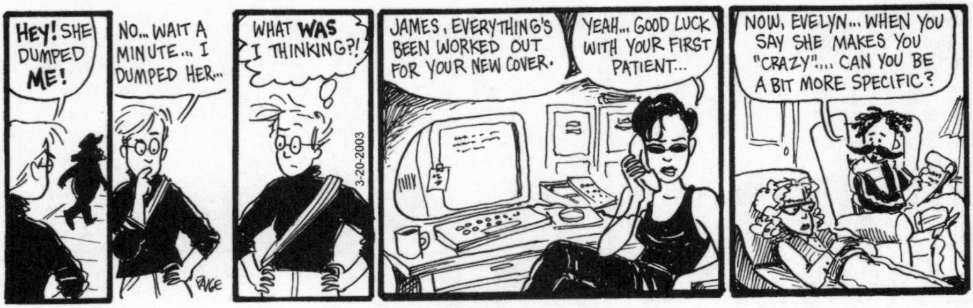
HEY! SHE DUMPED ME!
NO... WAIT A MINUTE... I DUMPED HER...
WHAT WAS I THINKING?!
3-20-2003
JAMES, EVERYTHING'S BEEN WORKED OUT FOR YOUR NEW COVER.
YEAH... GOOD LUCK WITH YOUR FIRST PATIENT...
NOW, EVELYN... WHEN YOU SAY SHE MAKES YOU "CRAZY"... CAN YOU BE A BIT MORE SPECIFIC?
PAIGE

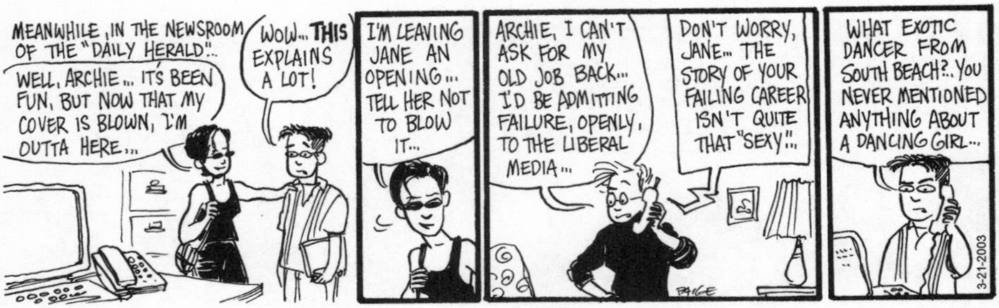
MEANWHILE, IN THE NEWSROOM OF THE "DAILY HERALD"...
WELL, ARCHIE... IT'S BEEN FUN, BUT NOW THAT MY COVER IS BLOWN, I'M OUTTA HERE...
WOW... THIS EXPLAINS A LOT!
I'M LEAVING JANE AN OPENING... TELL HER NOT TO BLOW IT...
ARCHIE, I CAN'T ASK FOR MY OLD JOB BACK... I'D BE ADMITTING FAILURE, OPENLY, TO THE LIBERAL MEDIA...
DON'T WORRY, JANE... THE STORY OF YOUR FAILING CAREER ISN'T QUITE THAT "SEXY"...
WHAT EXOTIC DANCER FROM SOUTH BEACH?.. YOU NEVER MENTIONED ANYTHING ABOUT A DANCING GIRL...
PAIGE
3-21-2003

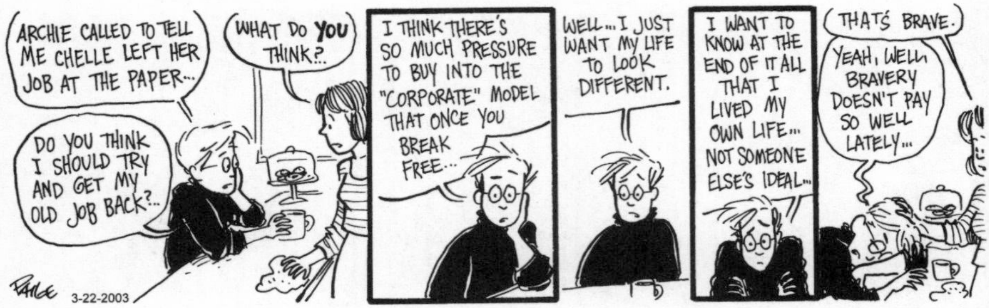
ARCHIE CALLED TO TELL ME CHELLE LEFT HER JOB AT THE PAPER...
DO YOU THINK I SHOULD TRY AND GET MY OLD JOB BACK?...
WHAT DO YOU THINK?..
I THINK THERE'S SO MUCH PRESSURE TO BUY INTO THE "CORPORATE" MODEL THAT ONCE YOU BREAK FREE...
WELL... I JUST WANT MY LIFE TO LOOK DIFFERENT.
I WANT TO KNOW AT THE END OF IT ALL THAT I LIVED MY OWN LIFE... NOT SOMEONE ELSE'S IDEAL...
THAT'S BRAVE.
YEAH, WELL, BRAVERY DOESN'T PAY SO WELL LATELY...
PAIGE
3-22-2003

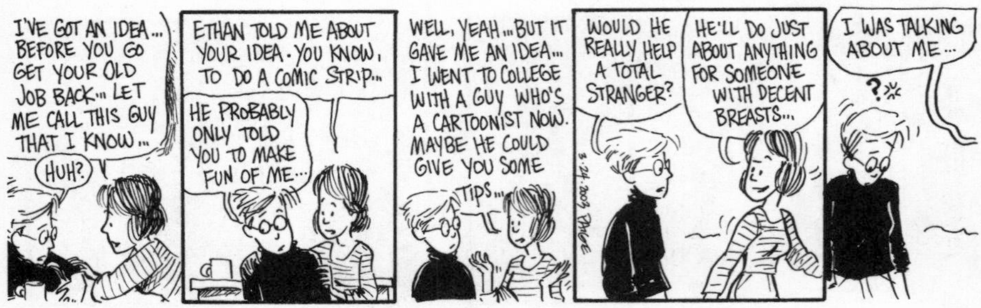
I'VE GOT AN IDEA... BEFORE YOU GO GET YOUR OLD JOB BACK... LET ME CALL THIS GUY THAT I KNOW...
HUH?
ETHAN TOLD ME ABOUT YOUR IDEA. YOU KNOW, TO DO A COMIC STRIP...
HE PROBABLY ONLY TOLD YOU TO MAKE FUN OF ME...
WELL, YEAH... BUT IT GAVE ME AN IDEA... I WENT TO COLLEGE WITH A GUY WHO'S A CARTOONIST NOW. MAYBE HE COULD GIVE YOU SOME TIPS...
3-24-2003 PAIGE
WOULD HE REALLY HELP A TOTAL STRANGER?
HE'LL DO JUST ABOUT ANYTHING FOR SOMEONE WITH DECENT BREASTS...
I WAS TALKING ABOUT ME...
?

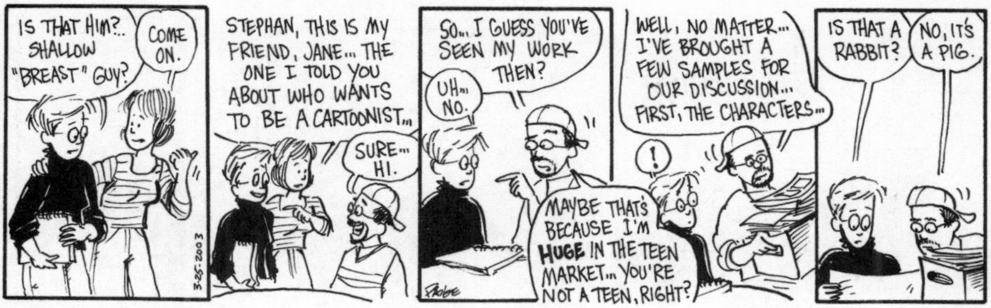
IS THAT HIM?.. SHALLOW "BREAST" GUY?
COME ON.
3.25.2003
STEPHAN, THIS IS MY FRIEND, JANE... THE ONE I TOLD YOU ABOUT WHO WANTS TO BE A CARTOONIST...
SURE... HI.
SO... I GUESS YOU'VE SEEN MY WORK THEN?
UH... NO.
MAYBE THAT'S BECAUSE I'M **HUGE** IN THE TEEN MARKET... YOU'RE NOT A TEEN, RIGHT?
WELL, NO MATTER... I'VE BROUGHT A FEW SAMPLES FOR OUR DISCUSSION... FIRST, THE CHARACTERS...
!
IS THAT A RABBIT?
NO, IT'S A PIG.

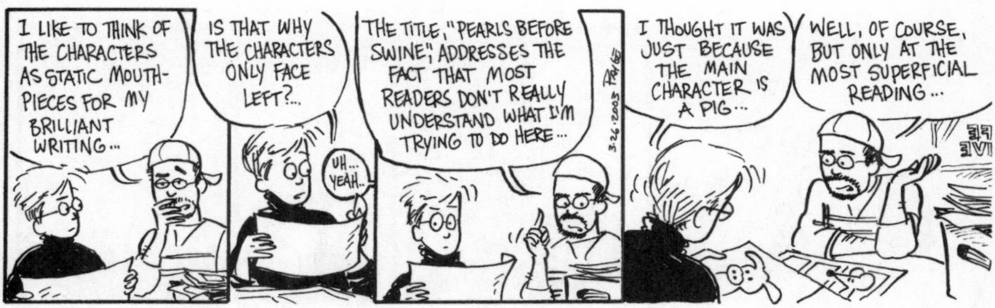
I LIKE TO THINK OF THE CHARACTERS AS STATIC MOUTH-PIECES FOR MY BRILLIANT WRITING...
IS THAT WHY THE CHARACTERS ONLY FACE LEFT?...
UH... YEAH...
THE TITLE, "PEARLS BEFORE SWINE", ADDRESSES THE FACT THAT MOST READERS DON'T REALLY UNDERSTAND WHAT I'M TRYING TO DO HERE...
3.26.2003
I THOUGHT IT WAS JUST BECAUSE THE MAIN CHARACTER IS A PIG...
WELL, OF COURSE, BUT ONLY AT THE MOST SUPERFICIAL READING...

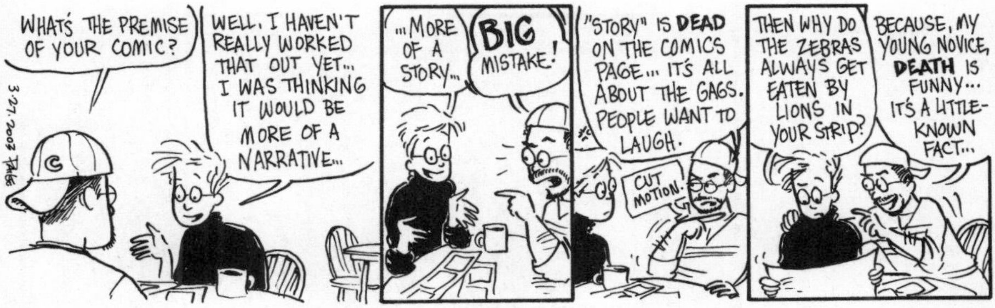
WHAT'S THE PREMISE OF YOUR COMIC?
3.27.2003
WELL, I HAVEN'T REALLY WORKED THAT OUT YET... I WAS THINKING IT WOULD BE MORE OF A NARRATIVE...
...MORE OF A STORY...
BIG MISTAKE!
"STORY" IS **DEAD** ON THE COMICS PAGE... IT'S ALL ABOUT THE GAGS. PEOPLE WANT TO LAUGH.
CUT MOTION.
THEN WHY DO THE ZEBRAS ALWAYS GET EATEN BY LIONS IN YOUR STRIP?
BECAUSE, MY YOUNG NOVICE, **DEATH** IS FUNNY... IT'S A LITTLE-KNOWN FACT...

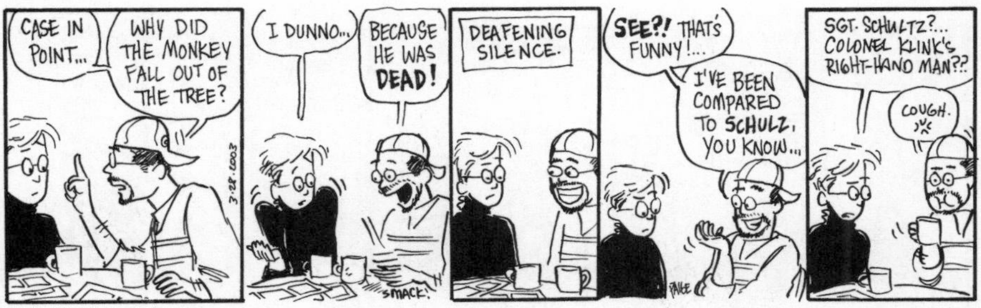
CASE IN POINT...
WHY DID THE MONKEY FALL OUT OF THE TREE?
3.28.2003
I DUNNO...
BECAUSE HE WAS **DEAD**!
SMACK!
DEAFENING SILENCE.
SEE?! THAT'S FUNNY!...
I'VE BEEN COMPARED TO **SCHULZ**, YOU KNOW...
SGT. SCHULTZ?... COLONEL KLINK'S RIGHT-HAND MAN??
COUGH.

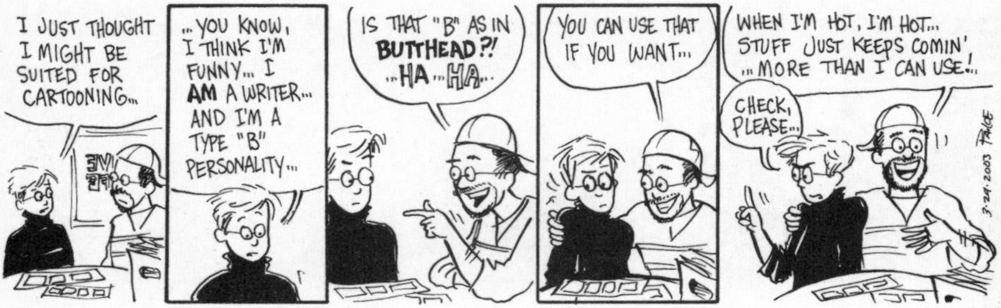
I JUST THOUGHT I MIGHT BE SUITED FOR CARTOONING...
...YOU KNOW, I THINK I'M FUNNY... I AM A WRITER... AND I'M A TYPE "B" PERSONALITY...
IS THAT "B" AS IN BUTTHEAD?! ...HA...HA...
YOU CAN USE THAT IF YOU WANT...
WHEN I'M HOT, I'M HOT... STUFF JUST KEEPS COMIN' ...MORE THAN I CAN USE!..
CHECK, PLEASE...
PAIGE
3-24-2003

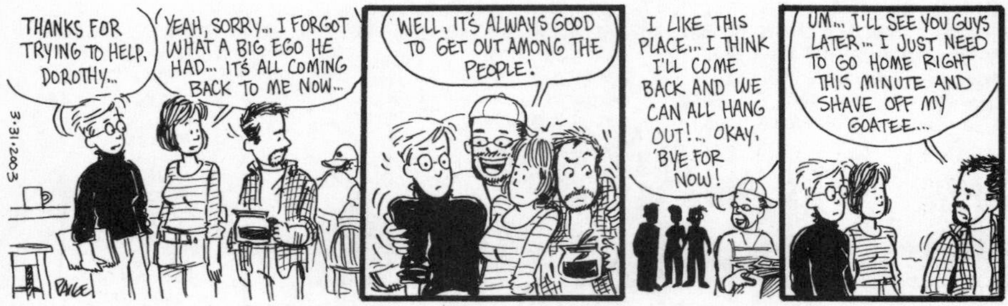
THANKS FOR TRYING TO HELP, DOROTHY...
YEAH, SORRY... I FORGOT WHAT A BIG EGO HE HAD... IT'S ALL COMING BACK TO ME NOW...
3-31-2003
PAIGE
WELL, IT'S ALWAYS GOOD TO GET OUT AMONG THE PEOPLE!
I LIKE THIS PLACE... I THINK I'LL COME BACK AND WE CAN ALL HANG OUT!... OKAY, 'BYE FOR NOW!
UM... I'LL SEE YOU GUYS LATER... I JUST NEED TO GO HOME RIGHT THIS MINUTE AND SHAVE OFF MY GOATEE...

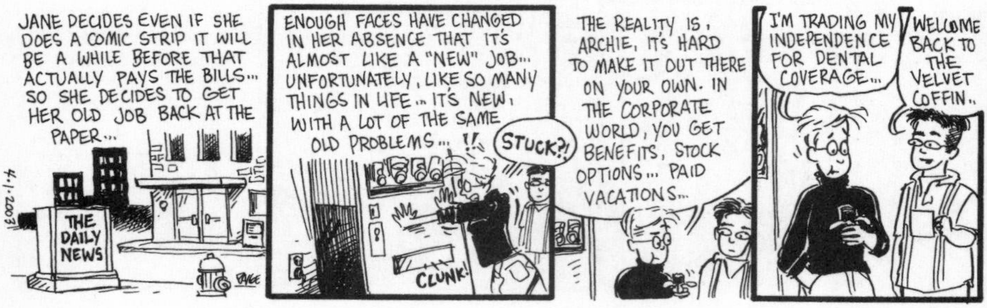
JANE DECIDES EVEN IF SHE DOES A COMIC STRIP IT WILL BE A WHILE BEFORE THAT ACTUALLY PAYS THE BILLS... SO SHE DECIDES TO GET HER OLD JOB BACK AT THE PAPER...
THE DAILY NEWS
4-1-2003
PAIGE
ENOUGH FACES HAVE CHANGED IN HER ABSENCE THAT IT'S ALMOST LIKE A "NEW" JOB... UNFORTUNATELY, LIKE SO MANY THINGS IN LIFE... IT'S NEW, WITH A LOT OF THE SAME OLD PROBLEMS...
STUCK?!
CLUNK!
THE REALITY IS, ARCHIE, IT'S HARD TO MAKE IT OUT THERE ON YOUR OWN. IN THE CORPORATE WORLD, YOU GET BENEFITS, STOCK OPTIONS... PAID VACATIONS...
I'M TRADING MY INDEPENDENCE FOR DENTAL COVERAGE...
WELCOME BACK TO THE VELVET COFFIN..

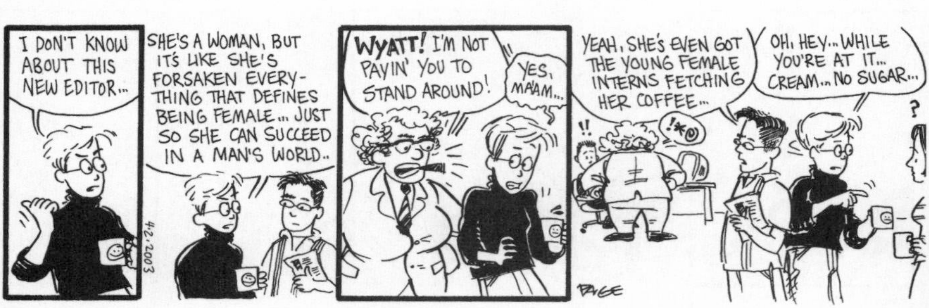
I DON'T KNOW ABOUT THIS NEW EDITOR...
SHE'S A WOMAN, BUT IT'S LIKE SHE'S FORSAKEN EVERY-THING THAT DEFINES BEING FEMALE... JUST SO SHE CAN SUCCEED IN A MAN'S WORLD..
4-2-2003
WYATT! I'M NOT PAYIN' YOU TO STAND AROUND!
YES, MA'AM...
PAIGE
YEAH, SHE'S EVEN GOT THE YOUNG FEMALE INTERNS FETCHING HER COFFEE...
OH, HEY... WHILE YOU'RE AT IT... CREAM... NO SUGAR...

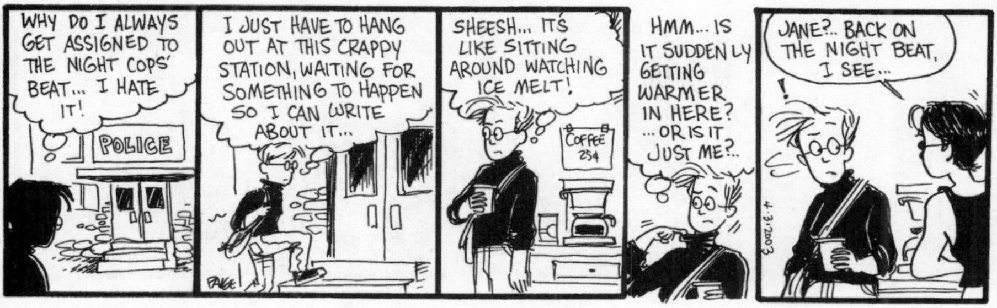
WHY DO I ALWAYS GET ASSIGNED TO THE NIGHT COPS' BEAT... I HATE IT!
POLICE
I JUST HAVE TO HANG OUT AT THIS CRAPPY STATION, WAITING FOR SOMETHING TO HAPPEN SO I CAN WRITE ABOUT IT...
PAGE
SHEESH... IT'S LIKE SITTING AROUND WATCHING ICE MELT!
COFFEE 25¢
HMM... IS IT SUDDENLY GETTING WARMER IN HERE? ...OR IS IT JUST ME?..
4.3.2003
!
JANE?.. BACK ON THE NIGHT BEAT, I SEE...

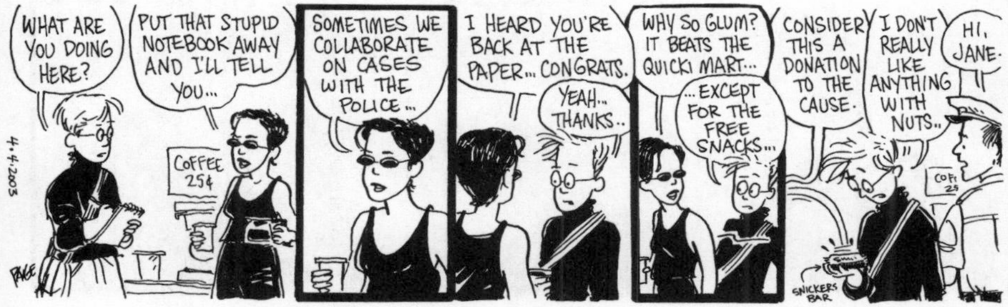
WHAT ARE YOU DOING HERE?
PUT THAT STUPID NOTEBOOK AWAY AND I'LL TELL YOU...
COFFEE 25¢
4.4.2003
PAGE
SOMETIMES WE COLLABORATE ON CASES WITH THE POLICE...
I HEARD YOU'RE BACK AT THE PAPER... CONGRATS.
YEAH.. THANKS..
WHY SO GLUM? IT BEATS THE QUICKI MART...
...EXCEPT FOR THE FREE SNACKS...
CONSIDER THIS A DONATION TO THE CAUSE.
I DON'T REALLY LIKE ANYTHING WITH NUTS..
HI, JANE.
SNICKERS BAR

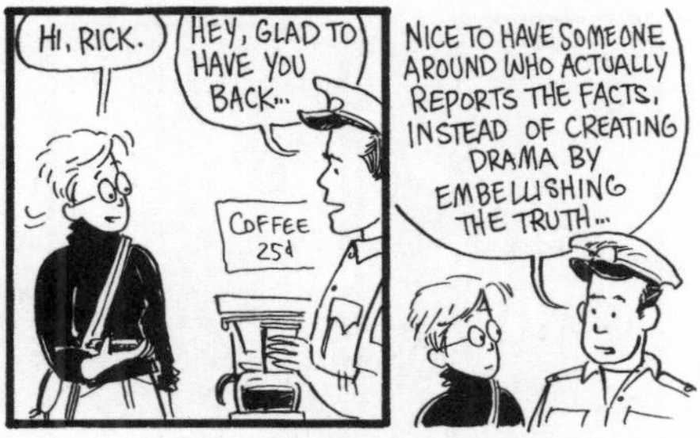
HI, RICK.
HEY, GLAD TO HAVE YOU BACK...
COFFEE 25¢
NICE TO HAVE SOMEONE AROUND WHO ACTUALLY REPORTS THE FACTS, INSTEAD OF CREATING DRAMA BY EMBELLISHING THE TRUTH...

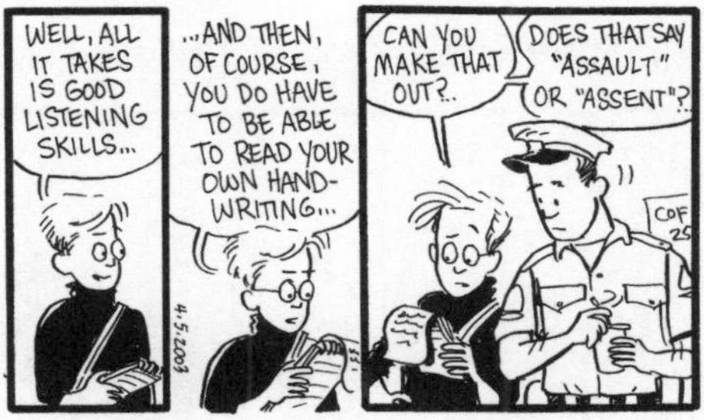
WELL, ALL IT TAKES IS GOOD LISTENING SKILLS...
...AND THEN, OF COURSE, YOU DO HAVE TO BE ABLE TO READ YOUR OWN HAND-WRITING...
4.5.2003
CAN YOU MAKE THAT OUT?..
DOES THAT SAY "ASSAULT" OR "ASSENT"?..

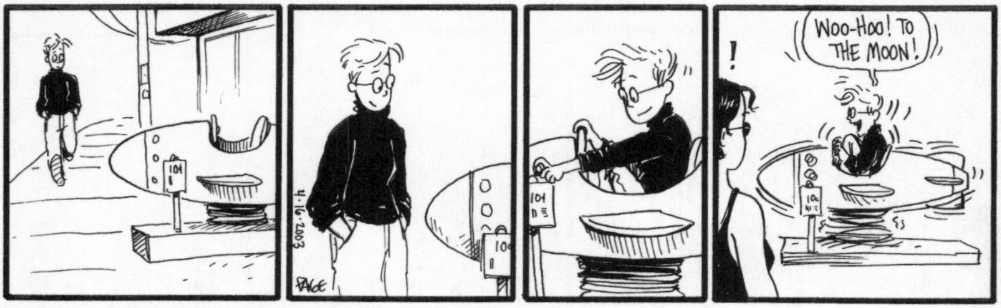
4.16.2003
PAGE
!
WOO-HOO! TO THE MOON!

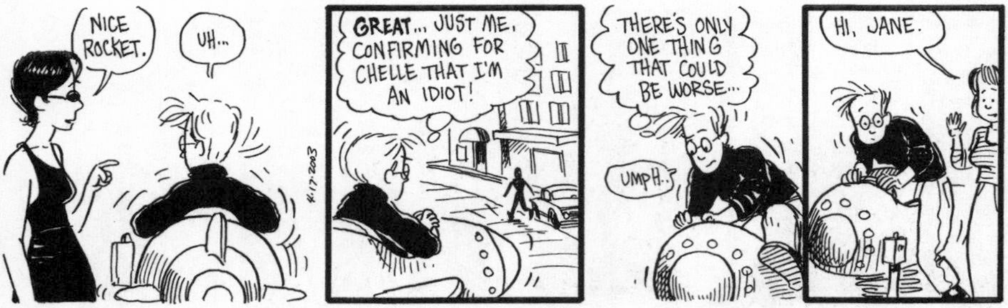
NICE ROCKET.
UH...
4.17.2003
GREAT... JUST ME, CONFIRMING FOR CHELLE THAT I'M AN IDIOT!
THERE'S ONLY ONE THING THAT COULD BE WORSE...
UMPH..
HI, JANE.

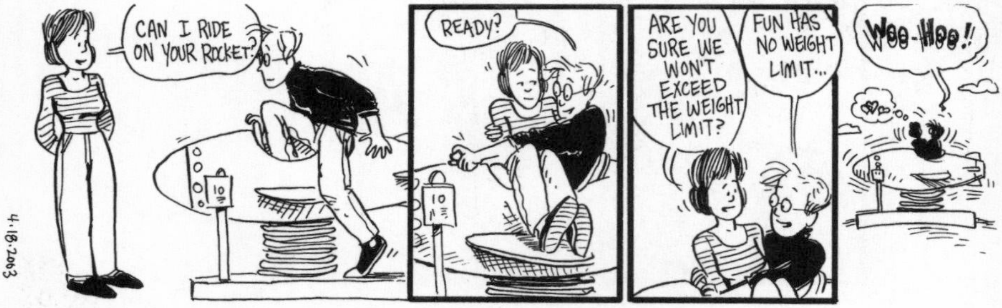
4.18.2003
CAN I RIDE ON YOUR ROCKET?
READY?
ARE YOU SURE WE WON'T EXCEED THE WEIGHT LIMIT?
FUN HAS NO WEIGHT LIMIT...
WOO-HOO!!

LATER, JANE AND ETHAN SETTLE IN FOR A LITTLE VIDEO RELAXATION...

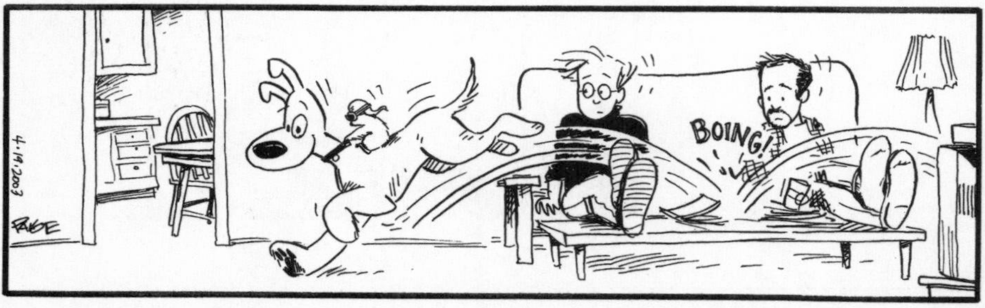
4.19.2003
PAGE
BOING!

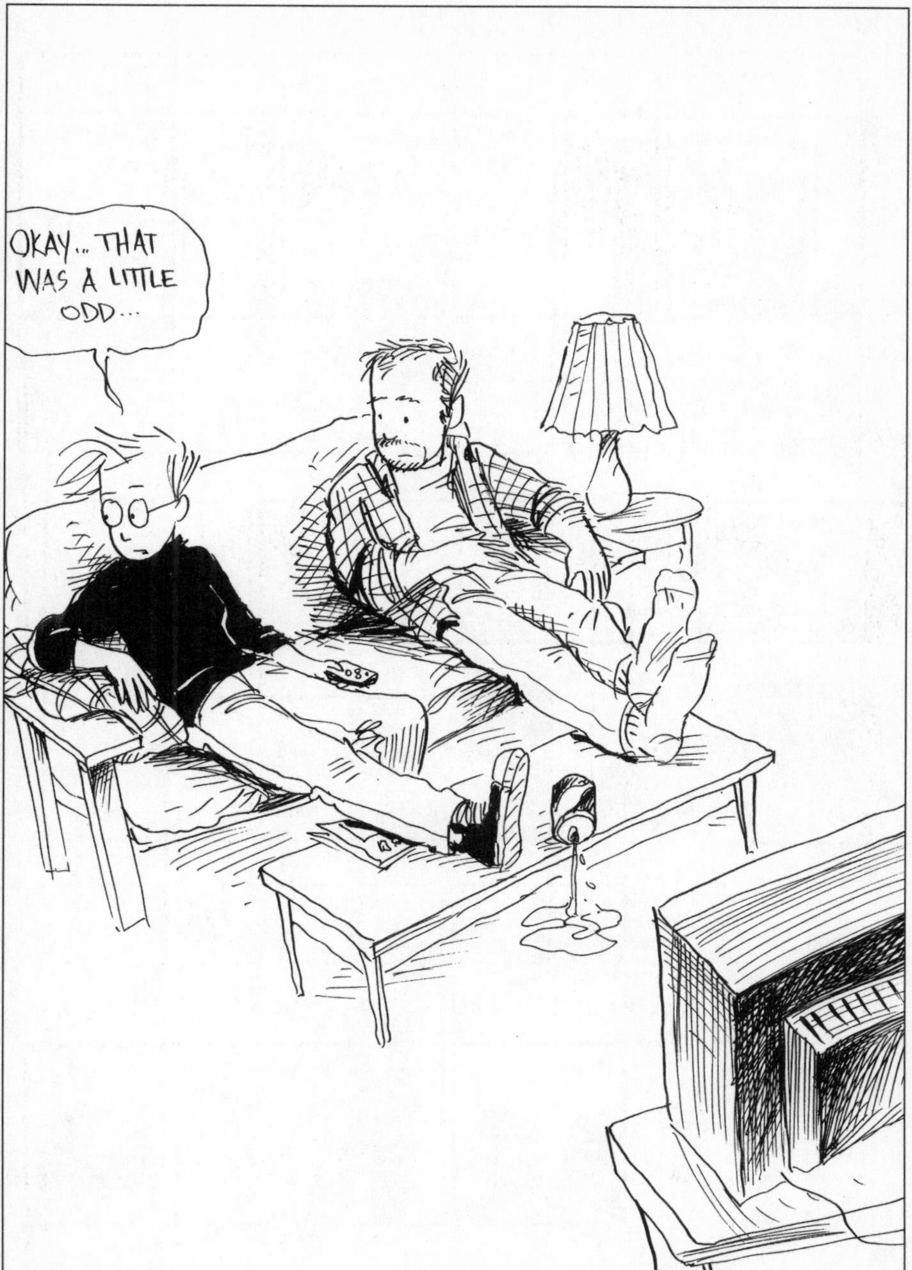
OKAY... THAT WAS A LITTLE ODD...

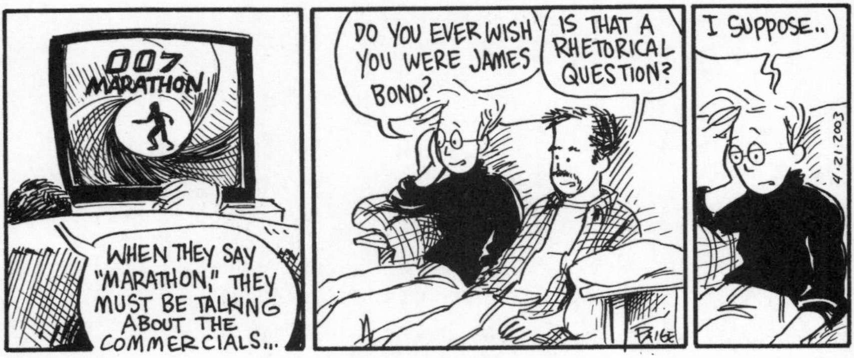
007 MARATHON
WHEN THEY SAY "MARATHON," THEY MUST BE TALKING ABOUT THE COMMERCIALS...
DO YOU EVER WISH YOU WERE JAMES BOND?
IS THAT A RHETORICAL QUESTION?
PAIGE
I SUPPOSE..
4.21.2003

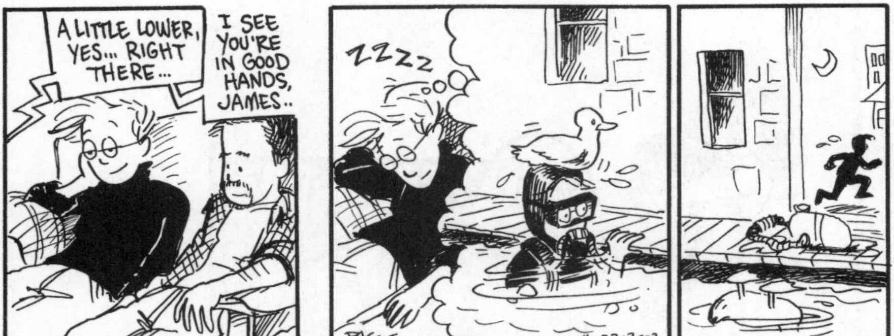
A LITTLE LOWER, YES... RIGHT THERE...
I SEE YOU'RE IN GOOD HANDS, JAMES..
ZZZZ
PAIGE
4.22.2003

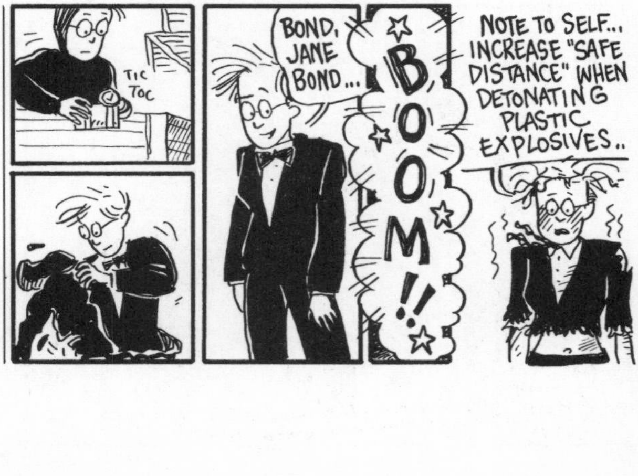
TIC TOC
BOND, JANE BOND...
BOOOM!!
NOTE TO SELF... INCREASE "SAFE DISTANCE" WHEN DETONATING PLASTIC EXPLOSIVES..

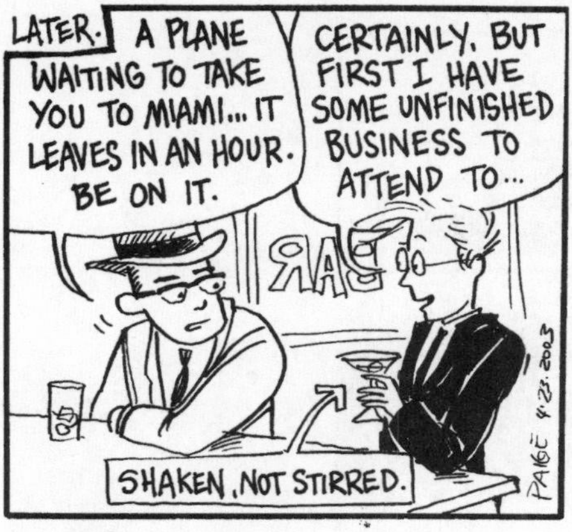
LATER.
A PLANE WAITING TO TAKE YOU TO MIAMI... IT LEAVES IN AN HOUR. BE ON IT.
CERTAINLY. BUT FIRST I HAVE SOME UNFINISHED BUSINESS TO ATTEND TO...
BAR
SHAKEN, NOT STIRRED.
PAIGE 4.23.2003

MOMENTS LATER, IN JANE BOND'S ROOM...

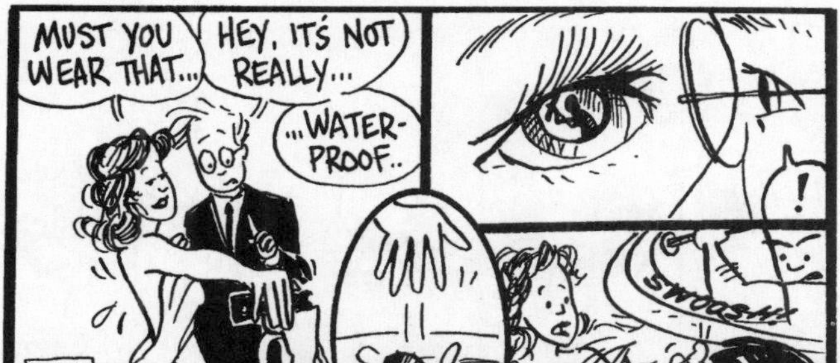
MUST YOU WEAR THAT...
HEY, IT'S NOT REALLY...
...WATER-PROOF..
!
BATH TUB
PLUNK!
SWOOSH!

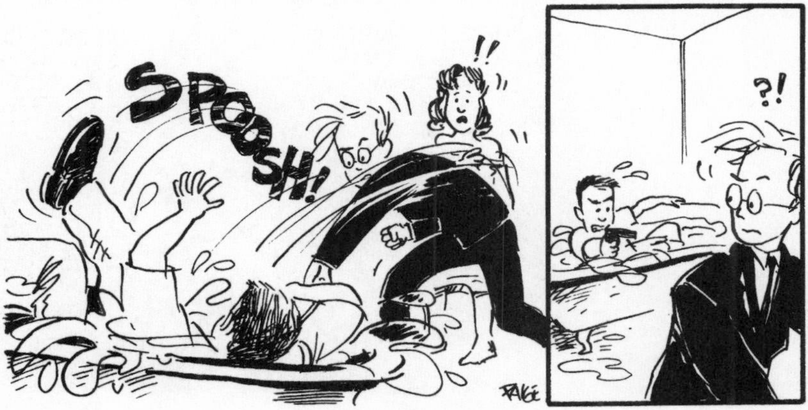
SPOOSH!
!!
PAIGE
?!

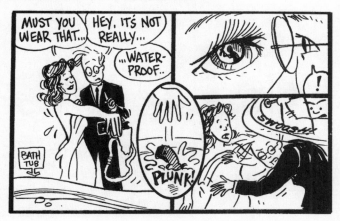

ZZZZZZ!

TOSS!

SHOCKING.

4·24·2003

MIAMI BEACH...

4·25·2003

I SEE YOU'RE IN GOOD HANDS, BOND..

WHAT CAN I DO FOR YOU...

I HAVE YOUR NEXT ASSIGNMENT.

WELL, I FIGURED YOU DIDN'T BOOK ME HERE TO ENJOY THE POOL.

SEE THE WOMAN OVER THERE?.. THAT'S GOLDSINGER... SHE'S A FOLK SINGER BY TRADE, BUT WE SUSPECT SHE'S SMUGGLING...

YOUR ASSIGNMENT IS TO GET CLOSE ENOUGH TO FIND OUT THE TRUTH...

EXCELLENT.

PAIGE

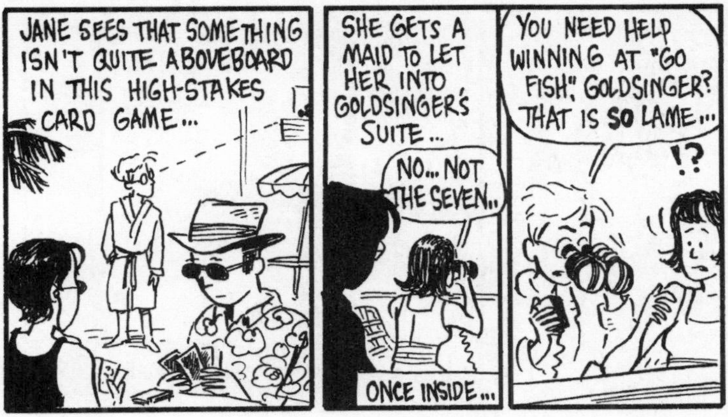
JANE SEES THAT SOMETHING ISN'T QUITE ABOVEBOARD IN THIS HIGH-STAKES CARD GAME...
SHE GETS A MAID TO LET HER INTO GOLDSINGER'S SUITE...
NO... NOT THE SEVEN..
ONCE INSIDE...
YOU NEED HELP WINNING AT "GO FISH", GOLDSINGER? THAT IS SO LAME...
!?

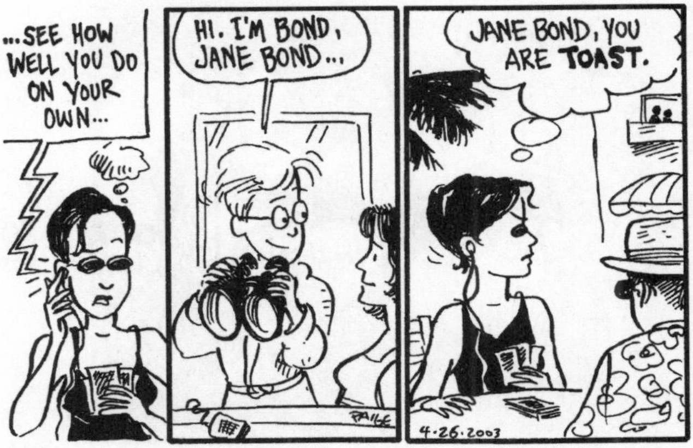
...SEE HOW WELL YOU DO ON YOUR OWN...
HI. I'M BOND, JANE BOND...
PAIGE
JANE BOND, YOU ARE TOAST.
4·26·2003

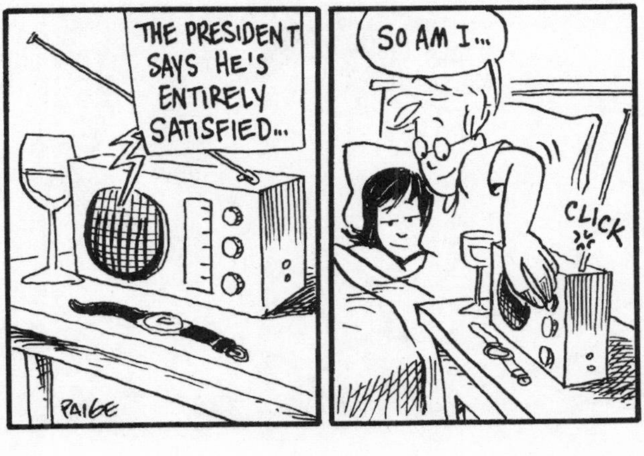
THE PRESIDENT SAYS HE'S ENTIRELY SATISFIED...
PAIGE
SO AM I...
CLICK

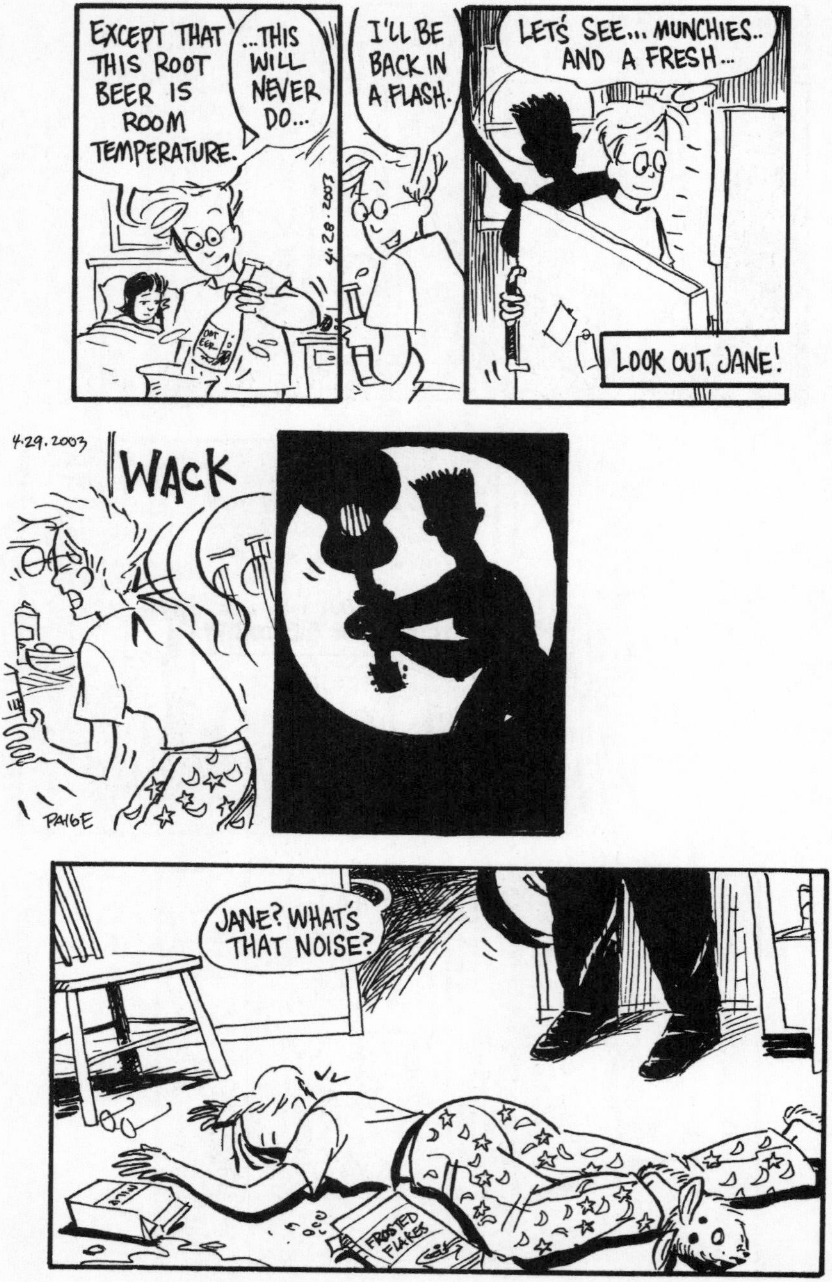
EXCEPT THAT THIS ROOT BEER IS ROOM TEMPERATURE.
...THIS WILL NEVER DO...
4.28.2003
I'LL BE BACK IN A FLASH.
LET'S SEE... MUNCHIES.. AND A FRESH...
LOOK OUT, JANE!
4.29.2003
WACK
JANE? WHAT'S THAT NOISE?
FROSTED FLAKES

ENGLAND... A FEW DAYS LATER...

YOU'RE LUCKY THEY DIDN'T PRESS CHARGES, 007... ANY IDEA WHY THEY WOULD KILL THE GIRL?

PAIGE

HOW WELL DID YOU KNOW THE GIRL?

....

I SEE...

4-30-2003

WELL, STAY FOCUSED. YOU STILL HAVE A JOB TO DO... WE SUSPECT GOLDSINGER IS SMUGGLING GOLD... ONCE IT'S MELTED DOWN, IT IS UNTRACEABLE... YOUR JOB IS TO FIND OUT HOW SHE GETS IT OUT OF THE COUNTRY.

SHE'S PLAYING TONIGHT IN LONDON... SEE THAT YOU MAKE THE SHOW...

MOMENTS LATER...

MORNING, Q... I HAVE A SHOW TO CATCH... WHERE'S MY BENTLEY?

HULLO, 007... IT'S NOT READY... YOU'LL HAVE TO DRIVE THIS ASTON MARTIN..

"AND I'D LIKE **THIS** ONE BACK IN ONE PIECE!"

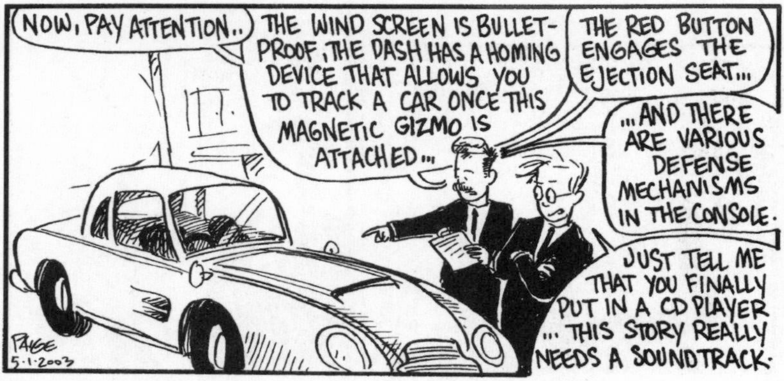
NOW, PAY ATTENTION..
THE WIND SCREEN IS BULLET-PROOF, THE DASH HAS A HOMING DEVICE THAT ALLOWS YOU TO TRACK A CAR ONCE THIS MAGNETIC GIZMO IS ATTACHED...
THE RED BUTTON ENGAGES THE EJECTION SEAT...
...AND THERE ARE VARIOUS DEFENSE MECHANISMS IN THE CONSOLE.
JUST TELL ME THAT YOU FINALLY PUT IN A CD PLAYER ... THIS STORY REALLY NEEDS A SOUNDTRACK.
PAIGE
5.1.2003

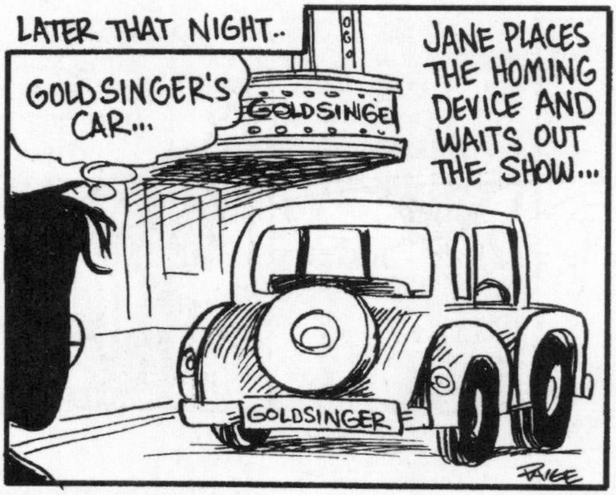
LATER THAT NIGHT..
GOLDSINGER'S CAR...
JANE PLACES THE HOMING DEVICE AND WAITS OUT THE SHOW...
GOLDSINGE
GOLDSINGER
PAIGE

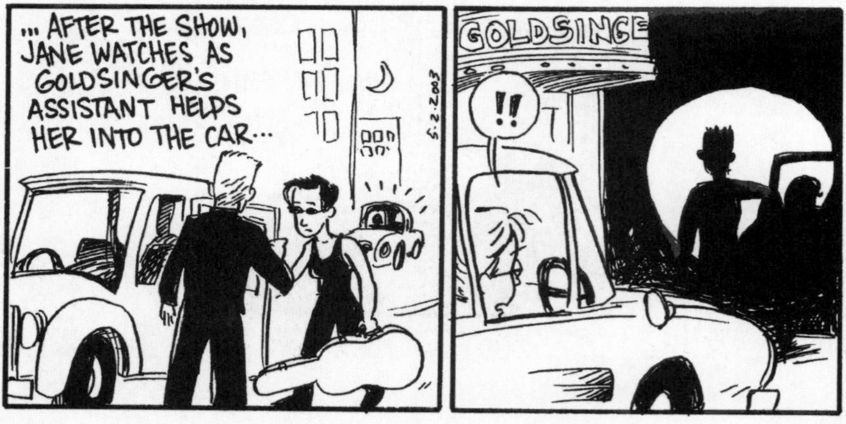
... AFTER THE SHOW, JANE WATCHES AS GOLDSINGER'S ASSISTANT HELPS HER INTO THE CAR...
5.2.2003
GOLDSINGE
!!

JANE TRACKS GOLDSINGER TO THE AIRPORT... THEN FOLLOWS ON A LATE-NIGHT FLIGHT TO SWEDEN...

..."YES"... JANE FLEW THE CAR ALONG AS WELL ...

..."THEN SUDDENLY"... ANOTHER CAR SEEMS TO BE JOINING THE MEASURED CHASE ...

HELLO? BABE IN CONVERTIBLE, APPROACHING FAST!

...BUT AT A MUCH FASTER CLIP...

HEY! WHO'S IN SUCH A BIG HURRY?

AND **WHO** WOULD RIDE WITH THE FREAKIN' TOP DOWN IN THE ALPS!?!

MAYBE I SHOULD JUST SPEED UP... NO...

DISCIPLINE, 007...DISCIPLINE...

...NOW, GOLDSINGER, WHERE THE HECK ARE YOU LEADING ME?...

BEEP BEEP

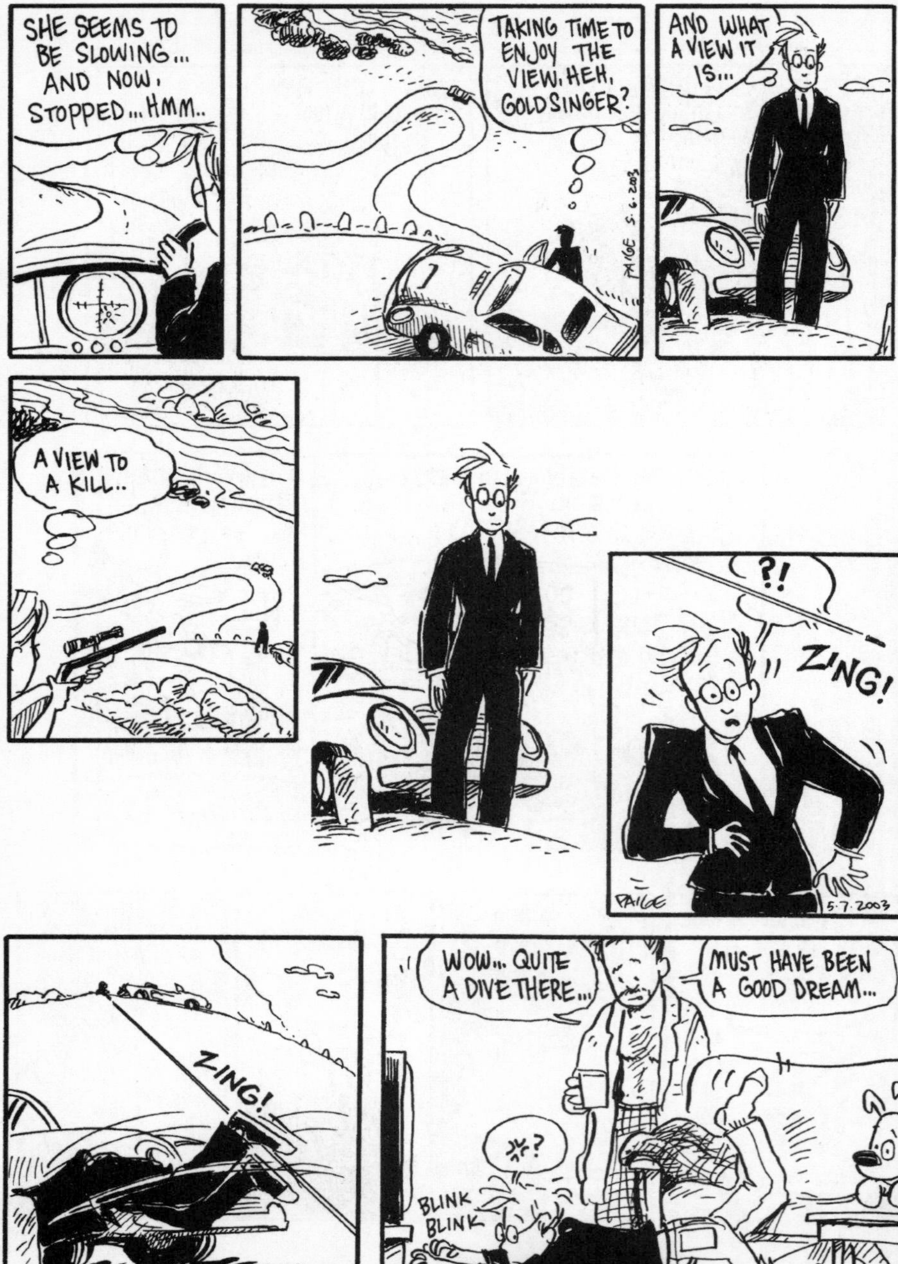
SHE SEEMS TO BE SLOWING... AND NOW, STOPPED... HMM..
TAKING TIME TO ENJOY THE VIEW, HEH, GOLDSINGER?
PAIGE 5.6.2003
AND WHAT A VIEW IT IS...
A VIEW TO A KILL..
?!
ZING!
PAIGE
5.7.2003
ZING!
WOW... QUITE A DIVE THERE...
MUST HAVE BEEN A GOOD DREAM...
?
BLINK
BLINK

IT WAS A GREAT DREAM...I WAS JANE BOND... AND I WAS AMAZINGLY COOL...
..DEFINITELY A DREAM THEN..
5·8·2003
HEY! WHY DIDN'T YOU WAKE ME UP?.. YOU LET ME SLEEP ON THE FUTON ALL NIGHT AND NOW MY NECK IS KILLING ME!
PAIGE

OOOH... BUT NOTHING IS KILLING ME AS MUCH AS CHEST HAIR BEFORE COFFEE... PULEEZE... DO I HAVE TO SEE THAT?!
ALL PART OF THE PACKAGE, 007... NO EXTRA CHARGE..

WELL, I'LL LEAVE YOU ALONE WITH YOUR PACKAGE...
5·9·2003

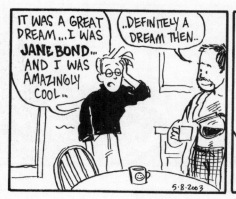

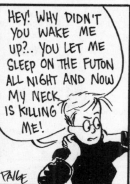

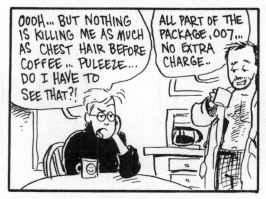

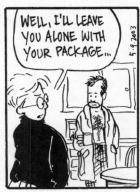

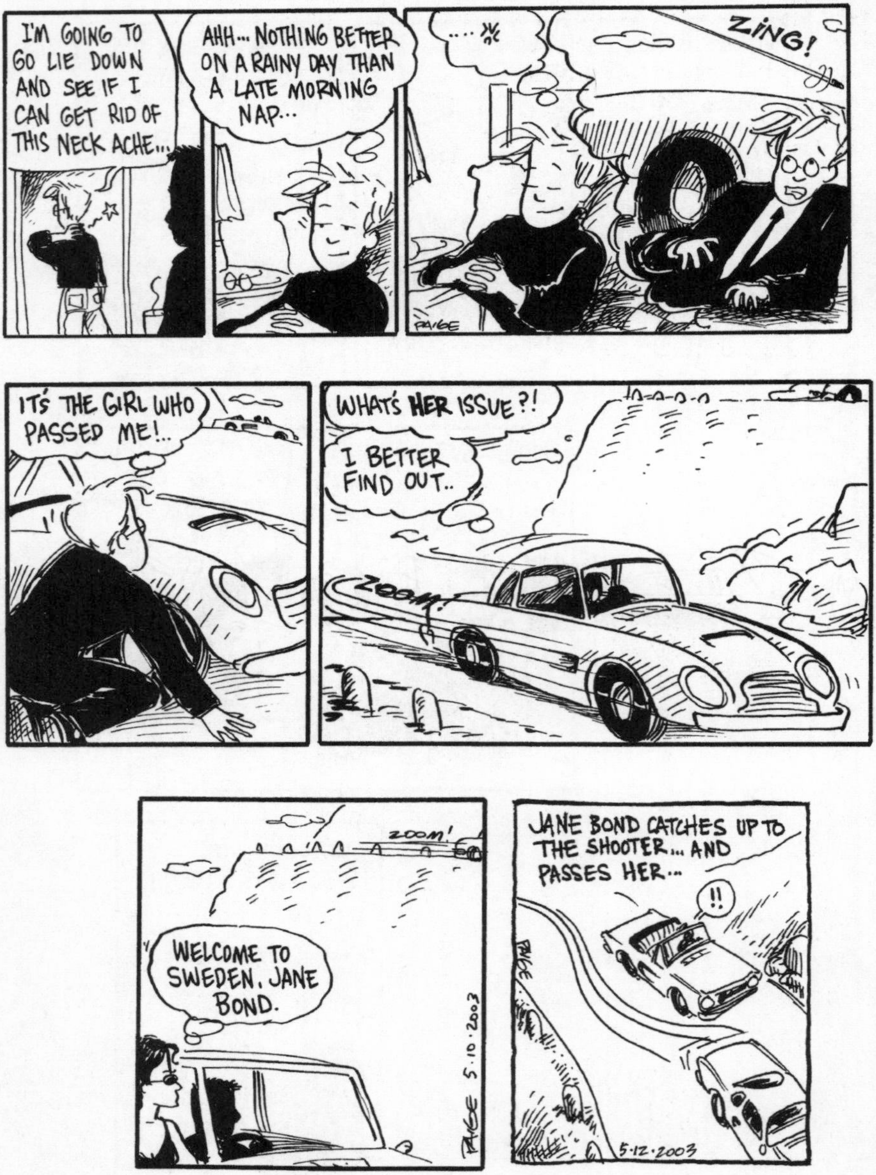
I'M GOING TO GO LIE DOWN AND SEE IF I CAN GET RID OF THIS NECK ACHE...
AHH... NOTHING BETTER ON A RAINY DAY THAN A LATE MORNING NAP...
ZING!
PAIGE
IT'S THE GIRL WHO PASSED ME!...
WHAT'S HER ISSUE?!
I BETTER FIND OUT..
ZOOM!
ZOOM!
WELCOME TO SWEDEN, JANE BOND.
PAIGE 5·10·2003
JANE BOND CATCHES UP TO THE SHOOTER... AND PASSES HER...
!!
PAIGE
5·12·2003

...THEN SLOWS SO THAT Q'S CAR WITH A MILLION DEVICES CAN WORK ITS MAGIC...

ENLARGED AREA

SPINNING, CUTTING THINGY IN RIM!!

...THE SPINNING CAN OPENER DOES THE TRICK...

SCRUNCH

POP!

SCREECH!

!!! ☆

THUMP!

HULLO!... IT SEEMS YOU'RE HAVING A BIT OF CAR TROUBLE!

SUSPICIOUSLY, YES...

CAN I GIVE YOU A RIDE?

JUST TO THE NEAREST SERVICE STATION.

CERTAINLY...

...I'M BOND. JANE BO...

SAVE IT FOR SOMEONE WHO'S INTERESTED...

OUCH... DEEP FREEZE...

5-18-2003

JANE SPENDS A FROSTY FEW MINUTES DRIVING THIS MYSTERY GIRL TO THE NEAREST STATION...

5.14.2003

WITH M.S. FROSTBITE OUT OF THE WAY, IT'S BACK TO BUSINESS, 007...

BEEP

...SPEAK TO ME, GOLDSINGER... WHERE ARE YOU?

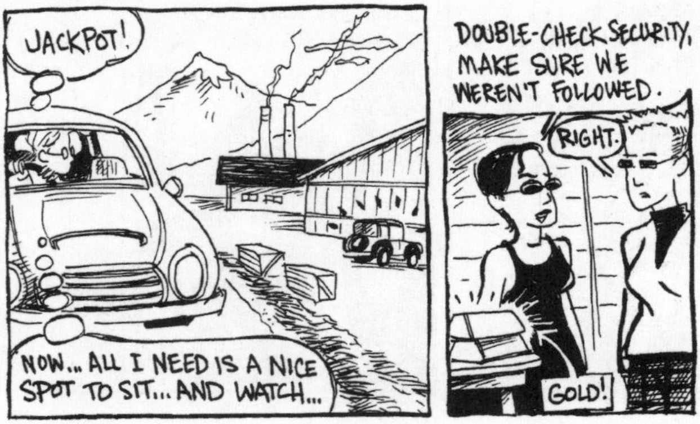
JACKPOT!
NOW... ALL I NEED IS A NICE SPOT TO SIT... AND WATCH...
DOUBLE-CHECK SECURITY, MAKE SURE WE WEREN'T FOLLOWED.
RIGHT.
GOLD!

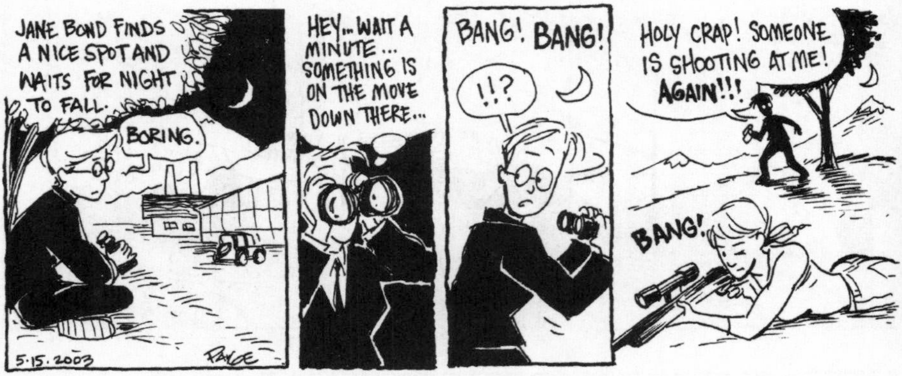
JANE BOND FINDS A NICE SPOT AND WAITS FOR NIGHT TO FALL.
BORING.
5.15.2003
PAIGE
HEY... WAIT A MINUTE... SOMETHING IS ON THE MOVE DOWN THERE...
BANG! BANG!
!!?
HOLY CRAP! SOMEONE IS SHOOTING AT ME! AGAIN!!!
BANG!

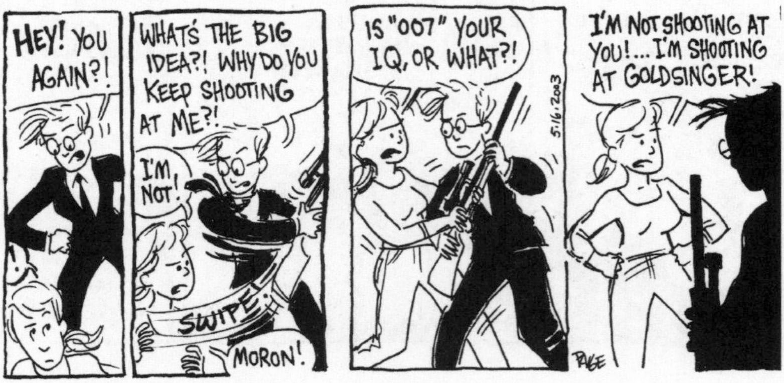
HEY! YOU AGAIN?!
WHAT'S THE BIG IDEA?! WHY DO YOU KEEP SHOOTING AT ME?!
I'M NOT!
SWIPE!
MORON!
IS "007" YOUR IQ, OR WHAT?!
5.16.2003
I'M NOT SHOOTING AT YOU!... I'M SHOOTING AT GOLDSINGER!
PAIGE

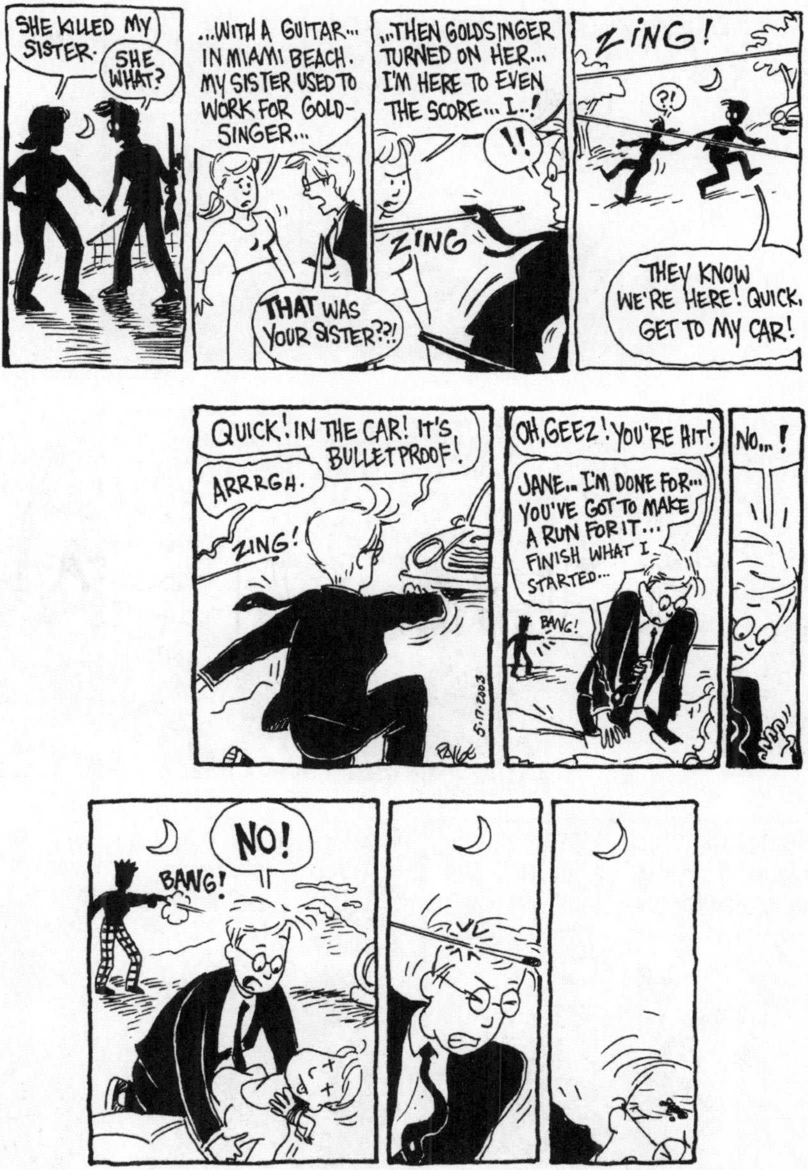
SHE KILLED MY SISTER.
SHE WHAT?
...WITH A GUITAR... IN MIAMI BEACH. MY SISTER USED TO WORK FOR GOLD-SINGER...
THAT WAS YOUR SISTER??!
...THEN GOLDSINGER TURNED ON HER... I'M HERE TO EVEN THE SCORE... I..!
!!
ZING
ZING!
?!
THEY KNOW WE'RE HERE! QUICK. GET TO MY CAR!
QUICK! IN THE CAR! IT'S BULLETPROOF!
ARRRGH.
ZING!
5.17.2003
OH, GEEZ! YOU'RE HIT!
JANE.. I'M DONE FOR... YOU'VE GOT TO MAKE A RUN FOR IT... FINISH WHAT I STARTED...
BANG!
NO...!
NO!
BANG!

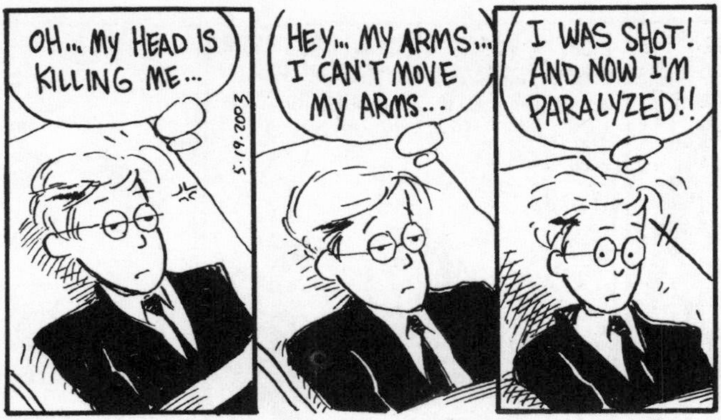
OH... MY HEAD IS KILLING ME...
5.19.2003
HEY... MY ARMS... I CAN'T MOVE MY ARMS...
I WAS SHOT! AND NOW I'M PARALYZED!!

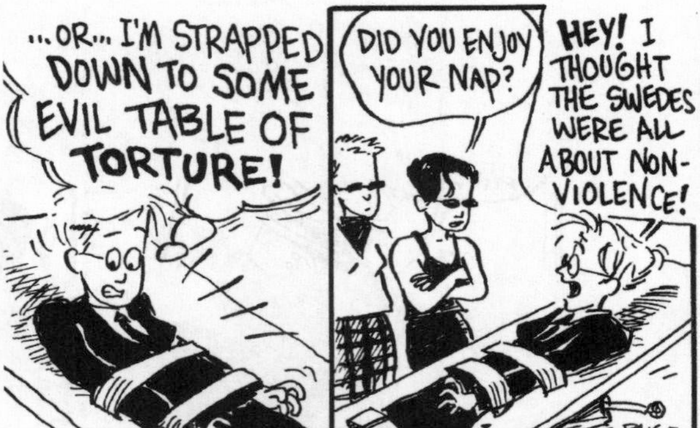
...OR... I'M STRAPPED DOWN TO SOME EVIL TABLE OF TORTURE!
DID YOU ENJOY YOUR NAP?
HEY! I THOUGHT THE SWEDES WERE ALL ABOUT NON-VIOLENCE!
PAIGE

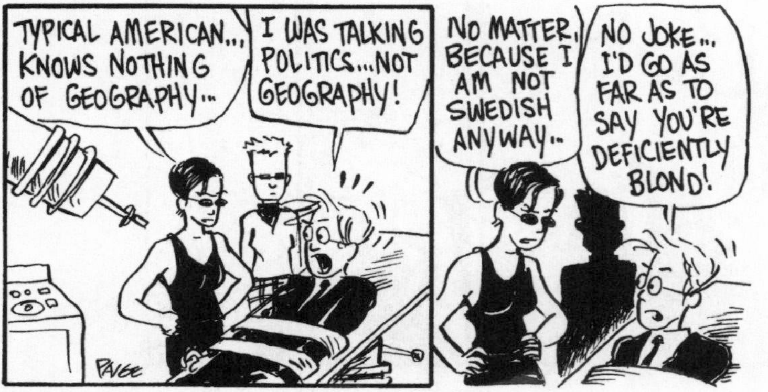
TYPICAL AMERICAN..., KNOWS NOTHING OF GEOGRAPHY...
I WAS TALKING POLITICS...NOT GEOGRAPHY!
PAIGE
NO MATTER, BECAUSE I AM NOT SWEDISH ANYWAY..
NO JOKE... I'D GO AS FAR AS TO SAY YOU'RE DEFICIENTLY BLOND!

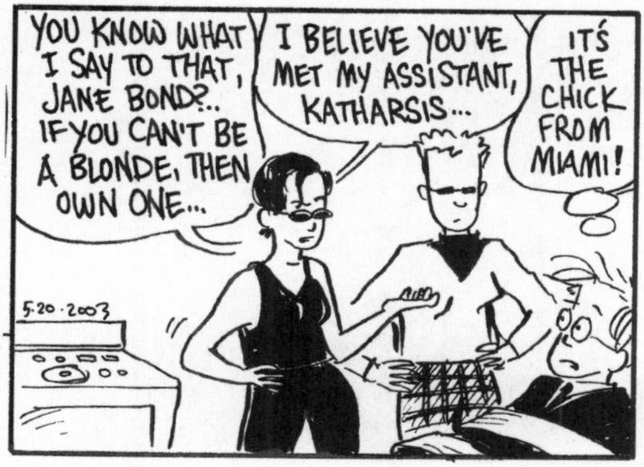
YOU KNOW WHAT I SAY TO THAT, JANE BOND?.. IF YOU CAN'T BE A BLONDE, THEN OWN ONE...
I BELIEVE YOU'VE MET MY ASSISTANT, KATHARSIS...
IT'S THE CHICK FROM MIAMI!
5.20.2003

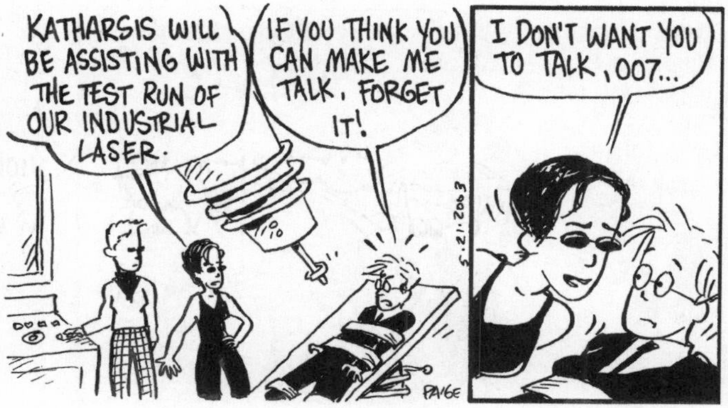
KATHARSIS WILL BE ASSISTING WITH THE TEST RUN OF OUR INDUSTRIAL LASER.
IF YOU THINK YOU CAN MAKE ME TALK, FORGET IT!
5.21.2003
PAIGE
I DON'T WANT YOU TO TALK, 007...

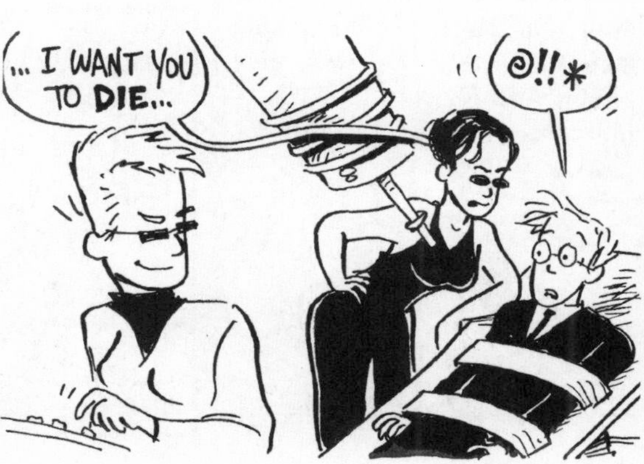
... I WANT YOU TO **DIE**...
@!!*

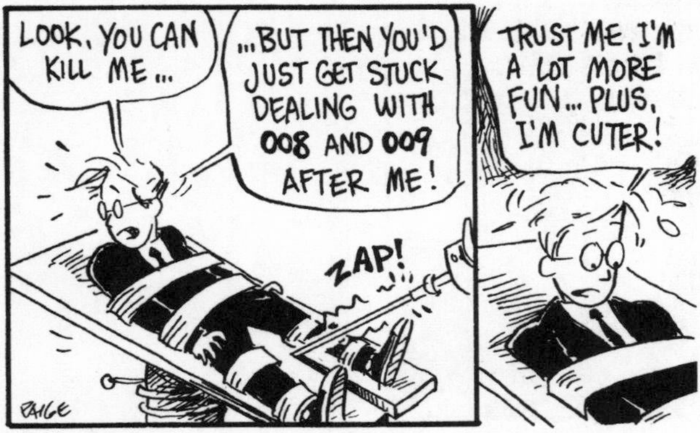
LOOK, YOU CAN KILL ME...
...BUT THEN YOU'D JUST GET STUCK DEALING WITH 008 AND 009 AFTER ME!
ZAP!
TRUST ME, I'M A LOT MORE FUN... PLUS, I'M CUTER!
PAIGE

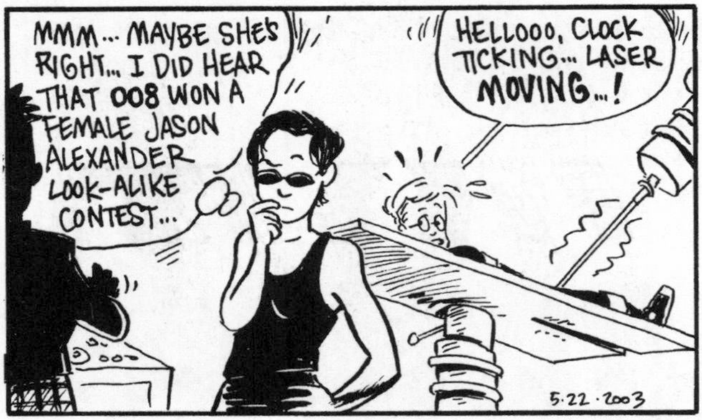
MMM... MAYBE SHE'S RIGHT... I DID HEAR THAT 008 WON A FEMALE JASON ALEXANDER LOOK-ALIKE CONTEST...
HELLOOO, CLOCK TICKING... LASER MOVING...!
5·22·2003

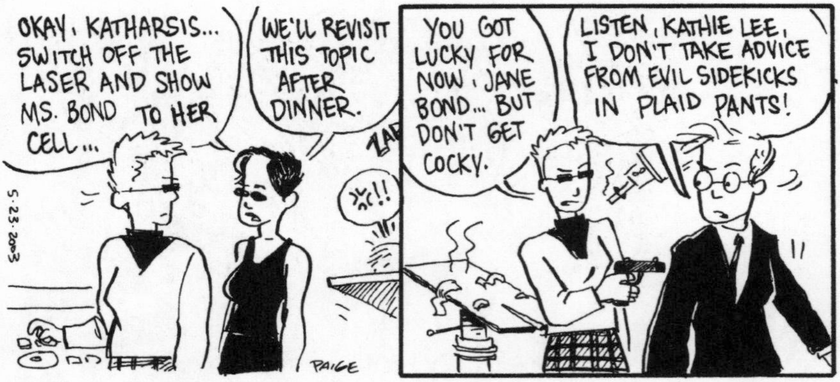
OKAY, KATHARSIS... SWITCH OFF THE LASER AND SHOW MS. BOND TO HER CELL...
WE'LL REVISIT THIS TOPIC AFTER DINNER.
5·23·2003
YOU GOT LUCKY FOR NOW, JANE BOND... BUT DON'T GET COCKY.
LISTEN, KATHIE LEE, I DON'T TAKE ADVICE FROM EVIL SIDEKICKS IN PLAID PANTS!
PAIGE

THAT'S KATHARSIS...
HOW'S THIS FOR CATHARSIS?!... UP WITH FREEDOM, DOWN WITH JAIL TIME!
HEY!
UMPH...
FWUMP!

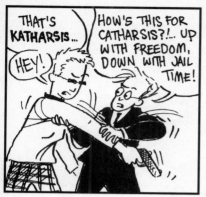

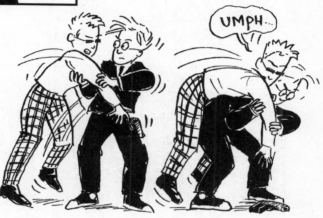

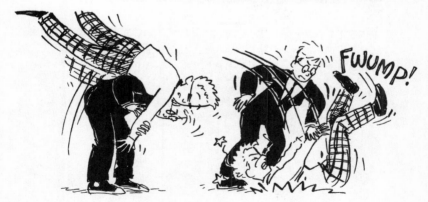

YOU'RE RIGHT, CATHARTIC ... I FEEL MUCH BETTER!
KATHARSIS...
WHATEVER.
SEE YA, WOULDN'T WANT TO BE YA!
SMACK!
UMPH!
JANE?
SLIDE
DANG IT, ETHAN! WATCH WHERE YOU OPEN DOORS!
SORRRY!
GEEZ... WHO WOKE UP ON THE WRONG SIDE OF THE DOOR THIS MORNING?
WERE YOU SLEEPWALKING?
I THINK I WAS SLEEPRUNNING ...I DREAMED I WAS JANE BOND AGAIN...

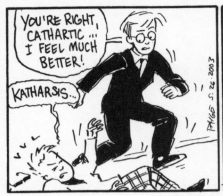

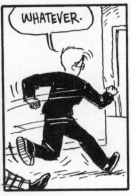

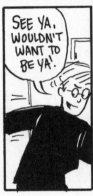

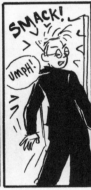

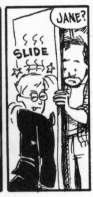

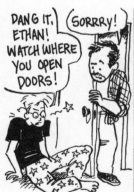

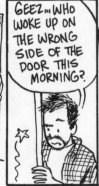

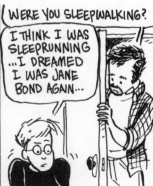

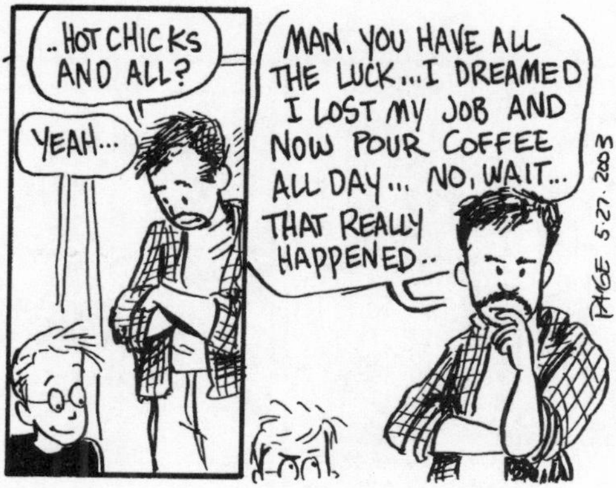
..HOT CHICKS AND ALL?
YEAH...
MAN, YOU HAVE ALL THE LUCK...I DREAMED I LOST MY JOB AND NOW POUR COFFEE ALL DAY... NO, WAIT... THAT REALLY HAPPENED..
PAGE 5.27.2003

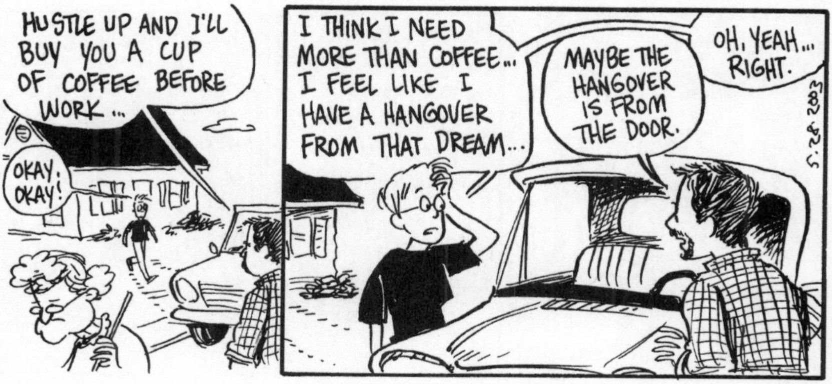
HUSTLE UP AND I'LL BUY YOU A CUP OF COFFEE BEFORE WORK...
OKAY, OKAY!
I THINK I NEED MORE THAN COFFEE... I FEEL LIKE I HAVE A HANGOVER FROM THAT DREAM...
MAYBE THE HANGOVER IS FROM THE DOOR.
OH, YEAH... RIGHT.
5.28.2003

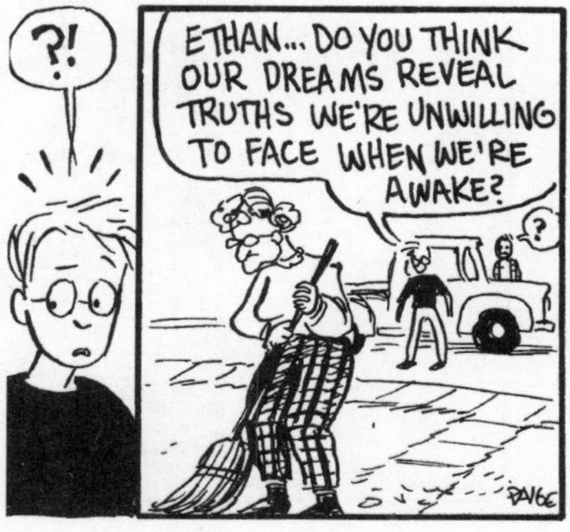
?!
ETHAN... DO YOU THINK OUR DREAMS REVEAL TRUTHS WE'RE UNWILLING TO FACE WHEN WE'RE AWAKE?
?
PAGE

SINCE WHEN DID MRS. BEEMAN START WEARING PLAID PANTS?
SINCE WHEN DO YOU CARE WHAT THE OCTOGENARIAN SET WEARS?...
PAIGE
I GUESS I DON'T REALLY..
..BUT HOW WEIRD..
5·29·2003
!
WHAT'S WRONG WITH YOU?... YOU LOOK KINDA FREAKED OUT...
UH... NOTHIN'!
PAIGE 5·30·2003
ETHAN, WHAT TOOK YOU SO LONG?... YOU CALLED AN HOUR AGO TO SAY YOU WERE ON YOUR WAY..
!!

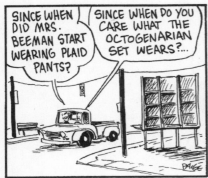

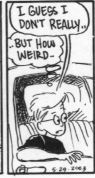

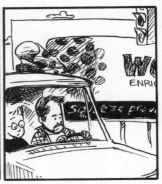

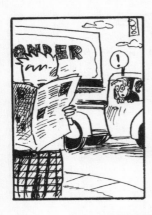

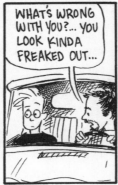

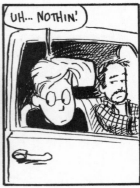

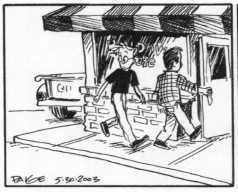

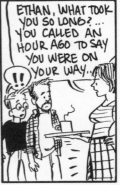

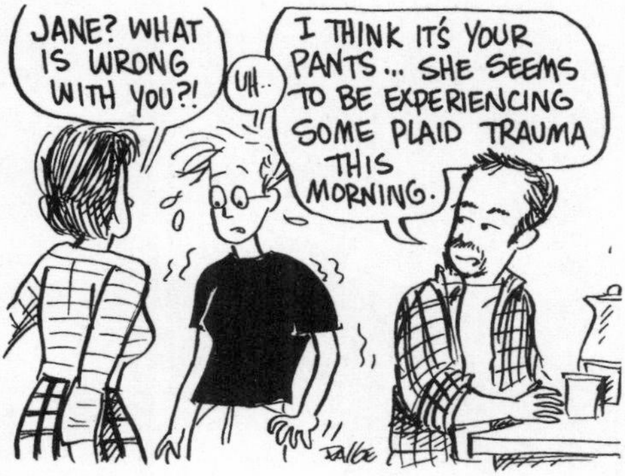
JANE? WHAT IS WRONG WITH YOU?!
UH..
I THINK IT'S YOUR PANTS... SHE SEEMS TO BE EXPERIENCING SOME PLAID TRAUMA THIS MORNING.

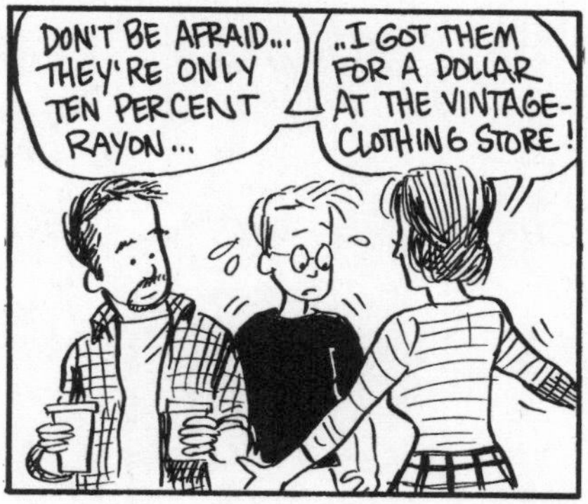
DON'T BE AFRAID... THEY'RE ONLY TEN PERCENT RAYON...
..I GOT THEM FOR A DOLLAR AT THE VINTAGE-CLOTHING STORE!

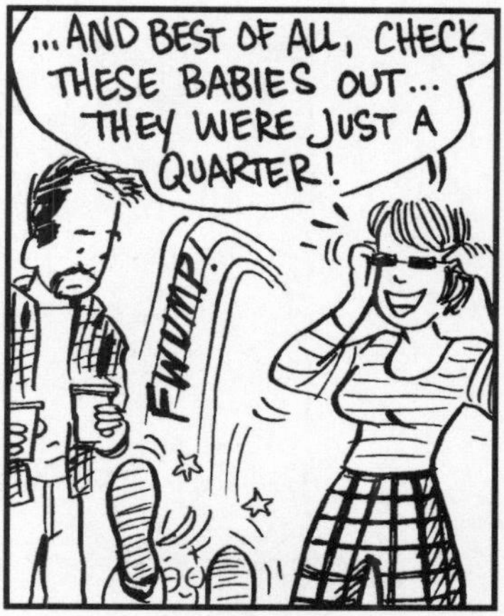
...AND BEST OF ALL, CHECK THESE BABIES OUT... THEY WERE JUST A QUARTER!
FWUMP!

Chapter 14

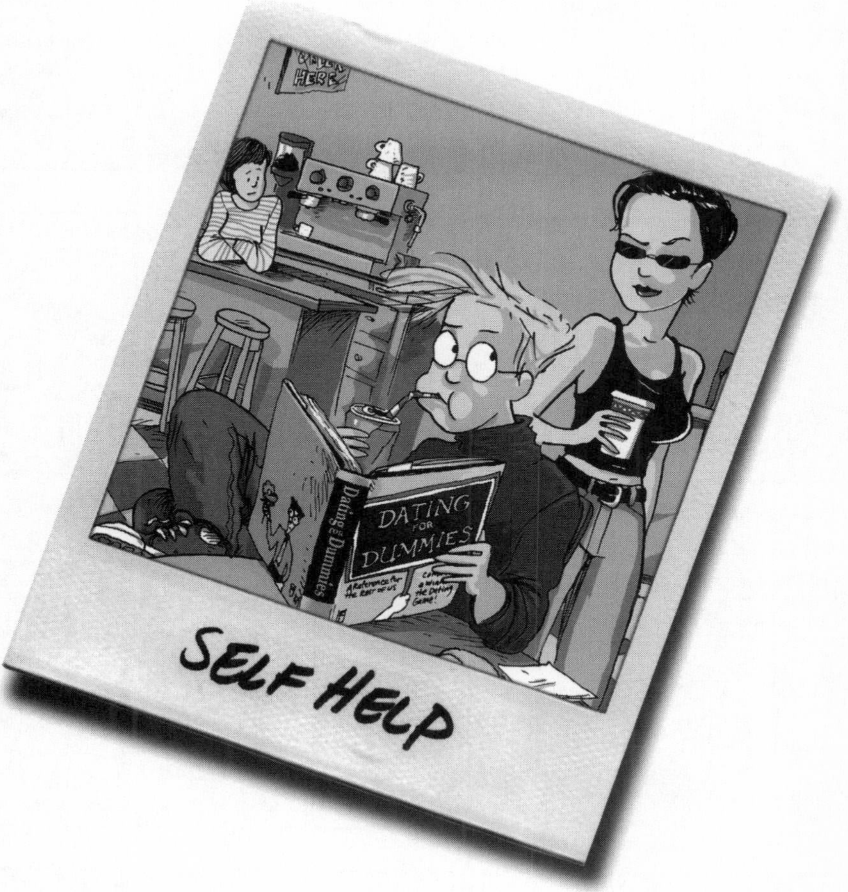
DATING FOR DUMMIES
Dating for Dummies
A Reference for the Rest of Us
SELF HELP

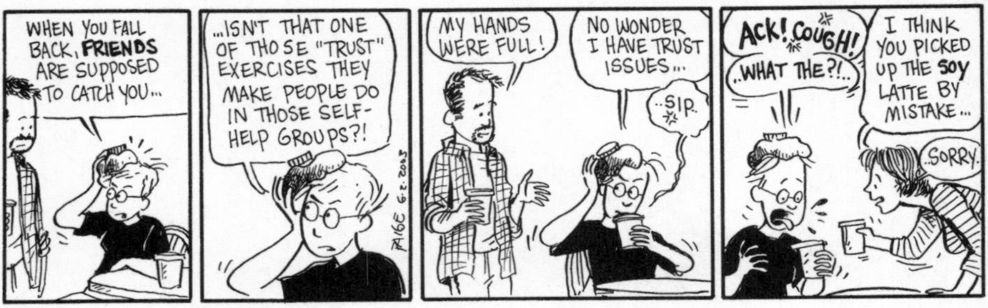
WHEN YOU FALL BACK, FRIENDS ARE SUPPOSED TO CATCH YOU...
...ISN'T THAT ONE OF THOSE "TRUST" EXERCISES THEY MAKE PEOPLE DO IN THOSE SELF-HELP GROUPS?!
PAIGE 6.2.2003
MY HANDS WERE FULL!
NO WONDER I HAVE TRUST ISSUES...
..SIP..
ACK! COUGH!
..WHAT THE?!..
I THINK YOU PICKED UP THE SOY LATTE BY MISTAKE...
..SORRY.

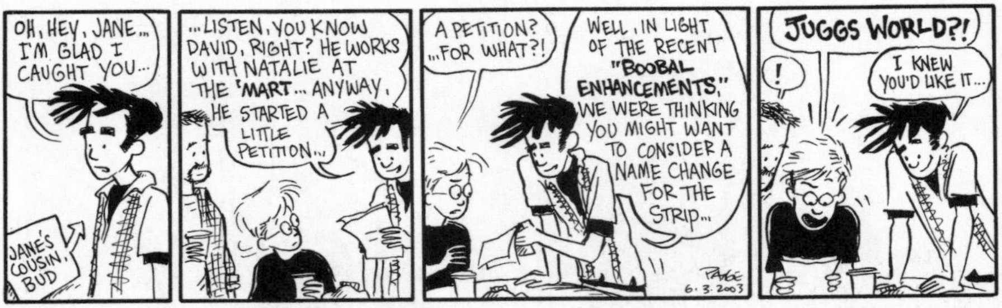
OH, HEY, JANE... I'M GLAD I CAUGHT YOU...
JANE'S COUSIN, BUD
...LISTEN, YOU KNOW DAVID, RIGHT? HE WORKS WITH NATALIE AT THE 'MART... ANYWAY, HE STARTED A LITTLE PETITION...
A PETITION? ...FOR WHAT?!
WELL, IN LIGHT OF THE RECENT "BOOBAL ENHANCEMENTS," WE WERE THINKING YOU MIGHT WANT TO CONSIDER A NAME CHANGE FOR THE STRIP...
PAIGE 6.3.2003
JUGGS WORLD?!
!
I KNEW YOU'D LIKE IT...

*NOTE TO READERS: YOU AREN'T LOSING IT, THIS ONE STRIP IS A REPEAT... SORRY. IT WAS ORIGINALLY PRINTED OUT OF ORDER FOR EFFECT.

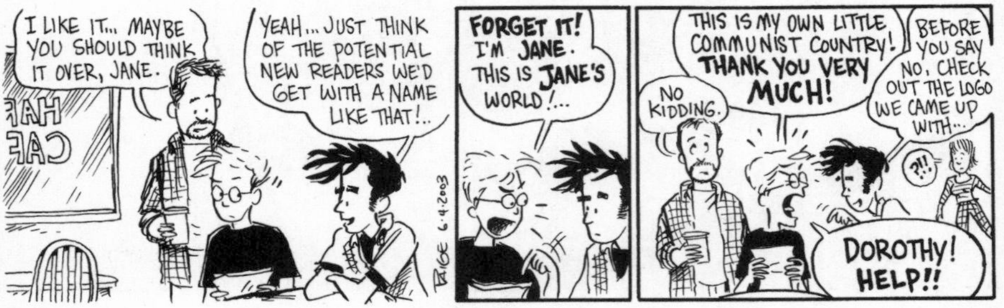
I LIKE IT... MAYBE YOU SHOULD THINK IT OVER, JANE.
YEAH... JUST THINK OF THE POTENTIAL NEW READERS WE'D GET WITH A NAME LIKE THAT!..
PAIGE 6.4.2003
FORGET IT! I'M JANE. THIS IS JANE'S WORLD!...
THIS IS MY OWN LITTLE COMMUNIST COUNTRY! THANK YOU VERY MUCH!
NO KIDDING.
BEFORE YOU SAY NO, CHECK OUT THE LOGO WE CAME UP WITH...
?!!
DOROTHY! HELP!!

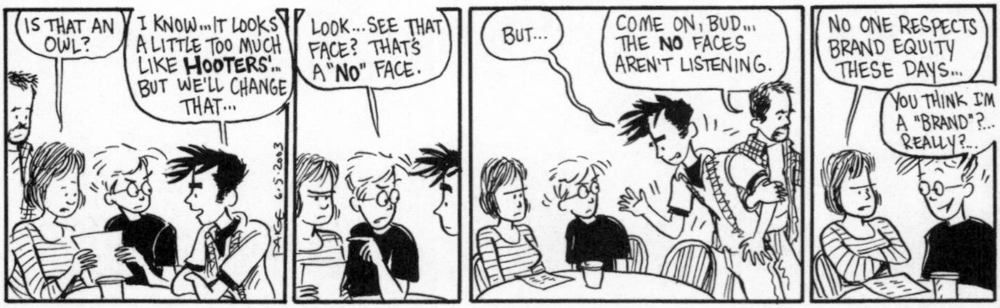
IS THAT AN OWL?
I KNOW... IT LOOKS A LITTLE TOO MUCH LIKE HOOTERS'... BUT WE'LL CHANGE THAT...
PAIGE 6.5.2003
LOOK... SEE THAT FACE? THAT'S A "NO" FACE.
BUT...
COME ON, BUD... THE NO FACES AREN'T LISTENING.
NO ONE RESPECTS BRAND EQUITY THESE DAYS...
YOU THINK I'M A "BRAND"?... REALLY?...

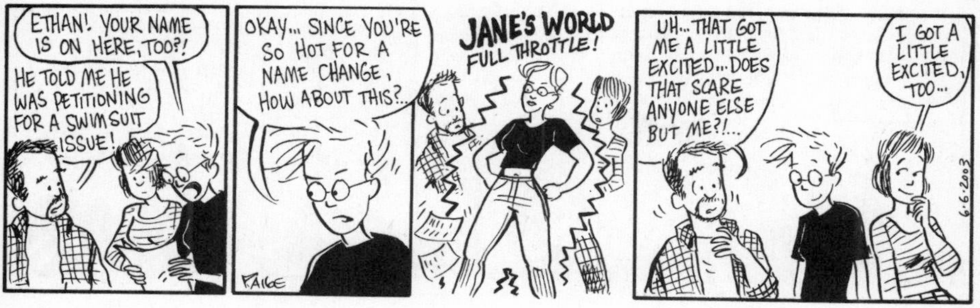
ETHAN! YOUR NAME IS ON HERE, TOO?!
HE TOLD ME HE WAS PETITIONING FOR A SWIMSUIT ISSUE!
OKAY... SINCE YOU'RE SO HOT FOR A NAME CHANGE, HOW ABOUT THIS?...
PAIGE
JANE'S WORLD FULL THROTTLE!
UH... THAT GOT ME A LITTLE EXCITED... DOES THAT SCARE ANYONE ELSE BUT ME?!...
I GOT A LITTLE EXCITED, TOO...
6.6.2003

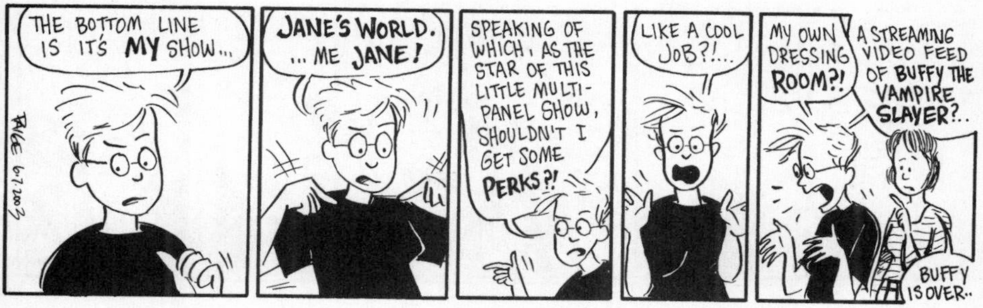
THE BOTTOM LINE IS IT'S MY SHOW...
PAIGE 6.7.2003
JANE'S WORLD. ... ME JANE!
SPEAKING OF WHICH, AS THE STAR OF THIS LITTLE MULTI-PANEL SHOW, SHOULDN'T I GET SOME PERKS?!
LIKE A COOL JOB?!...
MY OWN DRESSING ROOM?!
A STREAMING VIDEO FEED OF BUFFY THE VAMPIRE SLAYER?..
BUFFY IS OVER..

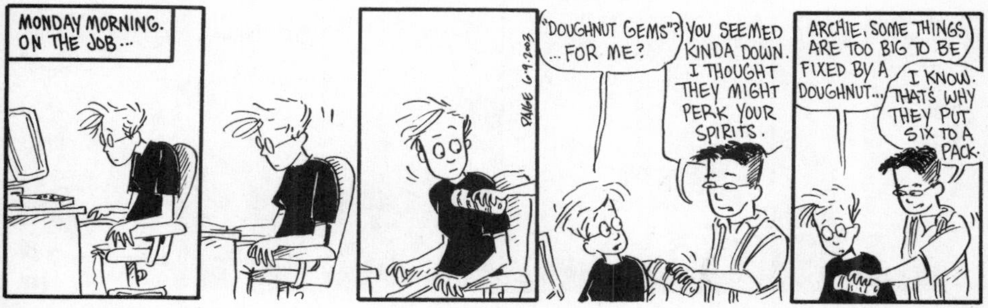
MONDAY MORNING. ON THE JOB...
PAIGE 6.9.2003
"DOUGHNUT GEMS"? ... FOR ME?
YOU SEEMED KINDA DOWN. I THOUGHT THEY MIGHT PERK YOUR SPIRITS.
ARCHIE, SOME THINGS ARE TOO BIG TO BE FIXED BY A DOUGHNUT...
I KNOW. THAT'S WHY THEY PUT SIX TO A PACK.

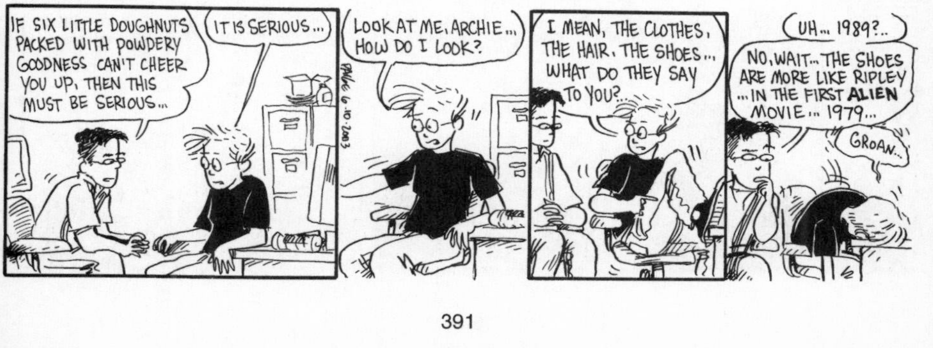
IF SIX LITTLE DOUGHNUTS PACKED WITH POWDERY GOODNESS CAN'T CHEER YOU UP, THEN THIS MUST BE SERIOUS...
IT IS SERIOUS...
PAIGE 6.10.2003
LOOK AT ME, ARCHIE... HOW DO I LOOK?
I MEAN, THE CLOTHES, THE HAIR, THE SHOES... WHAT DO THEY SAY TO YOU?...
UH... 1989?..
NO, WAIT... THE SHOES ARE MORE LIKE RIPLEY ... IN THE FIRST ALIEN MOVIE... 1979...
GROAN...

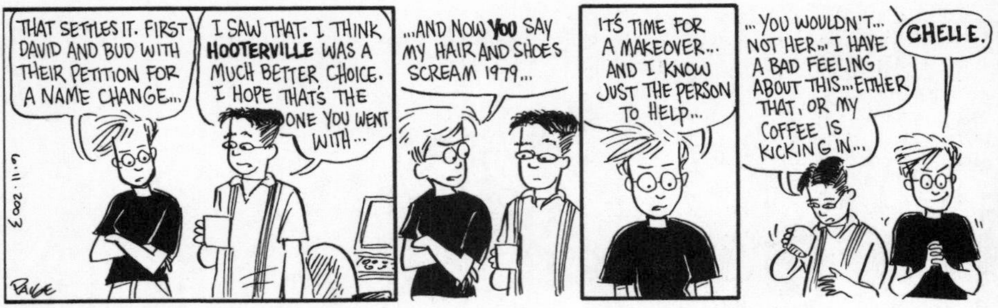
THAT SETTLES IT. FIRST DAVID AND BUD WITH THEIR PETITION FOR A NAME CHANGE...
I SAW THAT. I THINK HOOTERVILLE WAS A MUCH BETTER CHOICE. I HOPE THAT'S THE ONE YOU WENT WITH...
6·11·2003
PAIGE
...AND NOW YOU SAY MY HAIR AND SHOES SCREAM 1979...
IT'S TIME FOR A MAKEOVER... AND I KNOW JUST THE PERSON TO HELP...
...YOU WOULDN'T... NOT HER... I HAVE A BAD FEELING ABOUT THIS... EITHER THAT, OR MY COFFEE IS KICKING IN...
CHELLE.

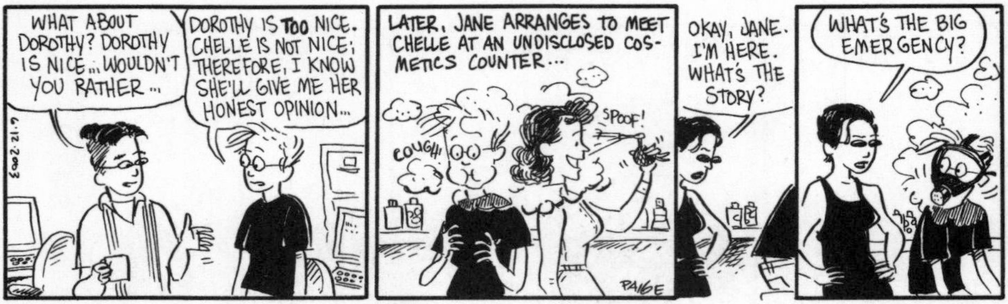
WHAT ABOUT DOROTHY? DOROTHY IS NICE... WOULDN'T YOU RATHER...
DOROTHY IS TOO NICE. CHELLE IS NOT NICE; THEREFORE, I KNOW SHE'LL GIVE ME HER HONEST OPINION...
6·12·2003
LATER, JANE ARRANGES TO MEET CHELLE AT AN UNDISCLOSED COSMETICS COUNTER...
COUGH!
SPOOF!
PAIGE
OKAY, JANE. I'M HERE. WHAT'S THE STORY?
WHAT'S THE BIG EMERGENCY?

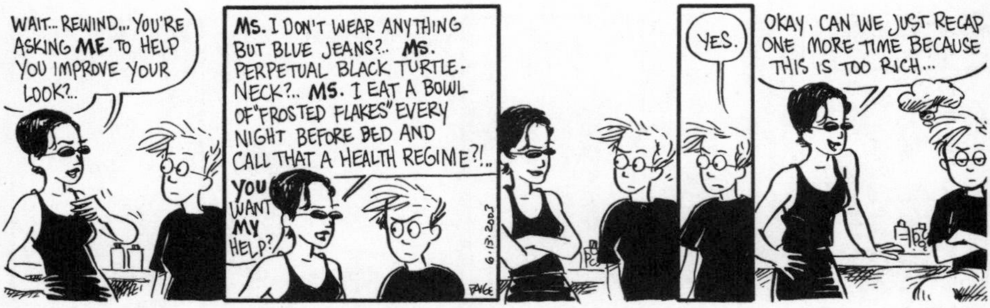
WAIT... REWIND... YOU'RE ASKING ME TO HELP YOU IMPROVE YOUR LOOK?..
MS. I DON'T WEAR ANYTHING BUT BLUE JEANS?.. MS. PERPETUAL BLACK TURTLENECK?.. MS. I EAT A BOWL OF "FROSTED FLAKES" EVERY NIGHT BEFORE BED AND CALL THAT A HEALTH REGIME?!..
YOU WANT MY HELP?
6·13·2003
PAIGE
YES.
OKAY, CAN WE JUST RECAP ONE MORE TIME BECAUSE THIS IS TOO RICH...

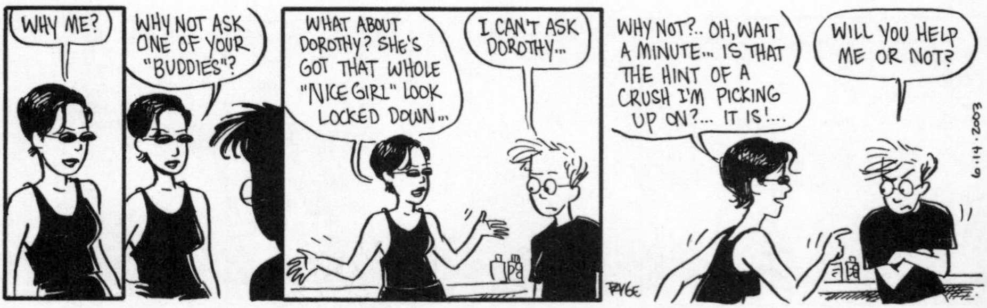
WHY ME?
WHY NOT ASK ONE OF YOUR "BUDDIES"?
WHAT ABOUT DOROTHY? SHE'S GOT THAT WHOLE "NICE GIRL" LOOK LOCKED DOWN...
I CAN'T ASK DOROTHY...
PAIGE
WHY NOT?.. OH, WAIT A MINUTE... IS THAT THE HINT OF A CRUSH I'M PICKING UP ON?... IT IS!...
WILL YOU HELP ME OR NOT?
6·14·2003

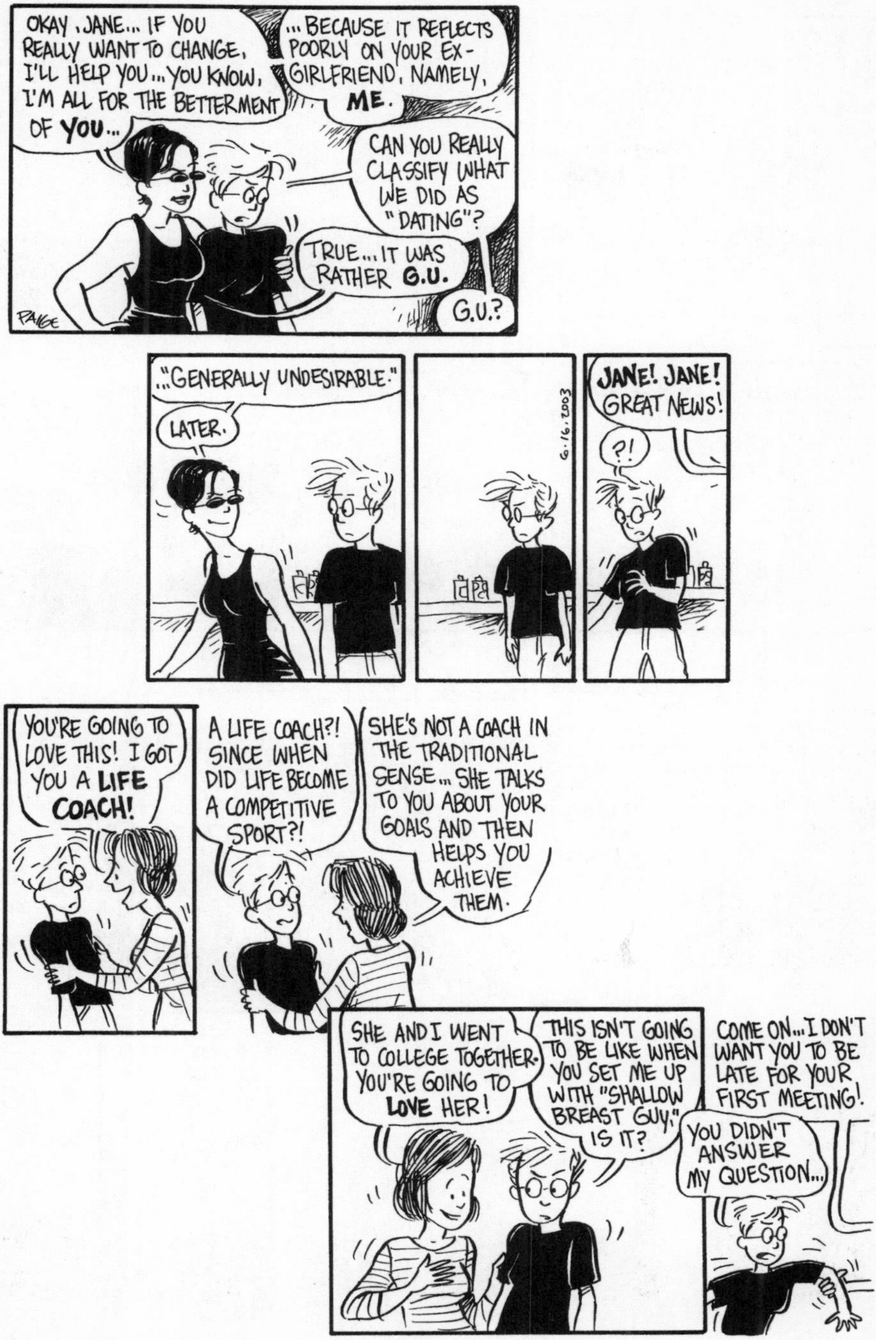
OKAY, JANE... IF YOU REALLY WANT TO CHANGE, I'LL HELP YOU... YOU KNOW, I'M ALL FOR THE BETTERMENT OF **YOU**...
... BECAUSE IT REFLECTS POORLY ON YOUR EX-GIRLFRIEND, NAMELY, **ME**.
CAN YOU REALLY CLASSIFY WHAT WE DID AS "DATING"?
TRUE... IT WAS RATHER **G.U.**
G.U.?
PAIGE
..."GENERALLY UNDESIRABLE."
LATER.
6.16.2003
JANE! JANE! GREAT NEWS!
?!
YOU'RE GOING TO LOVE THIS! I GOT YOU A **LIFE COACH!**
A LIFE COACH?! SINCE WHEN DID LIFE BECOME A COMPETITIVE SPORT?!
SHE'S NOT A COACH IN THE TRADITIONAL SENSE... SHE TALKS TO YOU ABOUT YOUR GOALS AND THEN HELPS YOU ACHIEVE THEM.
SHE AND I WENT TO COLLEGE TOGETHER. YOU'RE GOING TO **LOVE** HER!
THIS ISN'T GOING TO BE LIKE WHEN YOU SET ME UP WITH "SHALLOW BREAST GUY," IS IT?
COME ON... I DON'T WANT YOU TO BE LATE FOR YOUR FIRST MEETING!
YOU DIDN'T ANSWER MY QUESTION...

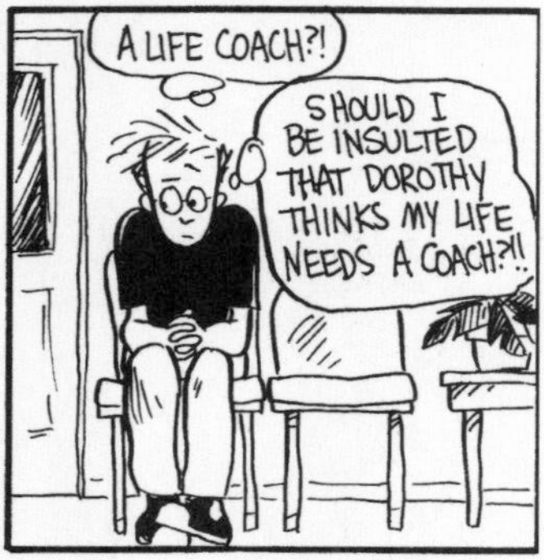
A LIFE COACH?!
SHOULD I BE INSULTED THAT DOROTHY THINKS MY LIFE NEEDS A COACH?!!

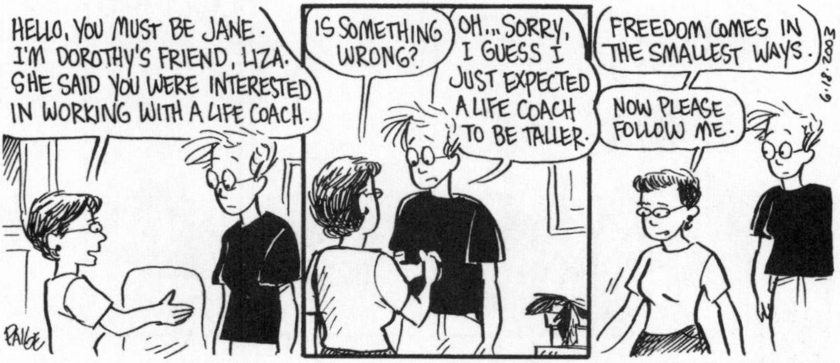
HELLO, YOU MUST BE JANE. I'M DOROTHY'S FRIEND, LIZA. SHE SAID YOU WERE INTERESTED IN WORKING WITH A LIFE COACH.
PAIGE
IS SOMETHING WRONG?
OH... SORRY, I GUESS I JUST EXPECTED A LIFE COACH TO BE TALLER.
FREEDOM COMES IN THE SMALLEST WAYS.
NOW PLEASE FOLLOW ME.
6.18.2003

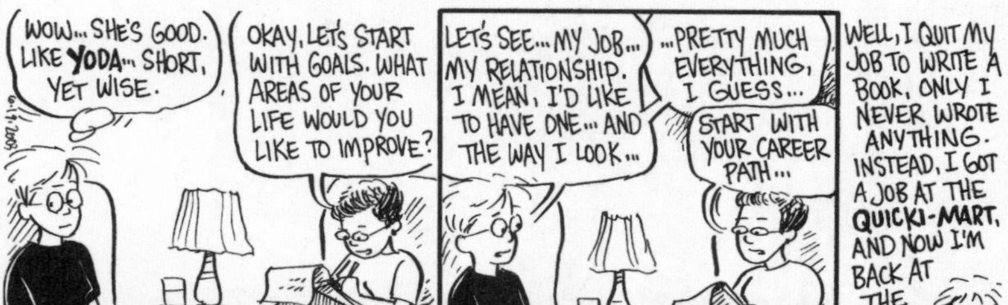
WOW... SHE'S GOOD. LIKE **YODA**... SHORT, YET WISE.
6.19.2003
OKAY, LET'S START WITH GOALS. WHAT AREAS OF YOUR LIFE WOULD YOU LIKE TO IMPROVE?
YELLOW PAGE
LET'S SEE... MY JOB... MY RELATIONSHIP. I MEAN, I'D LIKE TO HAVE ONE... AND THE WAY I LOOK...
...PRETTY MUCH EVERYTHING, I GUESS...
START WITH YOUR CAREER PATH...
WELL, I QUIT MY JOB TO WRITE A BOOK, ONLY I NEVER WROTE ANYTHING. INSTEAD, I GOT A JOB AT THE **QUICKI-MART**, AND NOW I'M BACK AT THE PAPER.

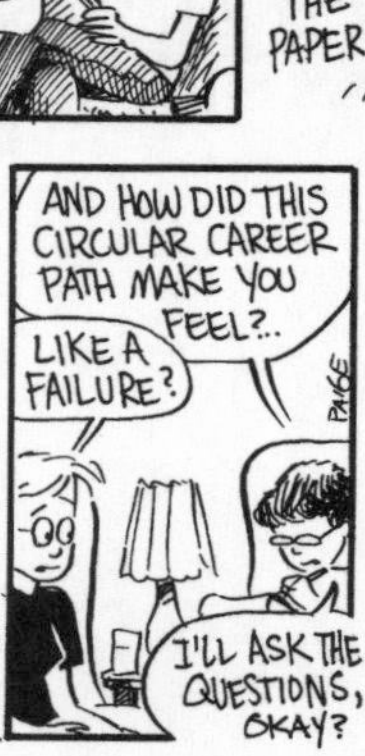
AND HOW DID THIS CIRCULAR CAREER PATH MAKE YOU FEEL?..
LIKE A FAILURE?
PAIGE
I'LL ASK THE QUESTIONS, OKAY?

DID YOU WRITE **ANYTHING** FOR YOUR NOVEL?
YEAH... BASICALLY A SERIES OF FIRST PARAGRAPHS... I'D WRITE A PARAGRAPH AND THEN LOSE INTEREST... IT STARTED TO FEEL LIKE A CHORE...
IT'S INTERESTING THAT ONCE YOU HAD A SPACE TO BE CREATIVE, YOU CHOSE A FORM THAT ULTIMATELY BECAME A CHORE.
WHY DO YOU SUPPOSE THAT IS?
PAIGE
6.20.2003

UH... WILL THERE BE ANY SIMPLE **YES** OR **NO** QUESTIONS DURING THIS PROCESS?
NO.
SCRIBBLE SCRIBBLE
SO YOU QUIT YOUR JOB IN ORDER TO WRITE A NOVEL... BUT THAT DIDN'T WORK OUT... ARE YOU SURE **WRITING** IS THE BEST MATCH FOR YOU?
WELL, I DID HAVE THIS BRILLIANT IDEA TO BECOME A CARTOONIST!
CAN YOU DRAW?
UH... NO.

SO YOU PICKED THIS SHORT WRITING FORM, BUT YOU DON'T HAVE THE SKILLS TO EXECUTE THIS...
PAIGE 6.21.2003
LET'S LOOK AT WHAT THIS "STRUGGLE" IS ALL ABOUT FOR YOU.
IS THIS LIFE-COACHING THING SUPPOSED TO MAKE ME FEEL BETTER OR WORSE ABOUT MY LIFE?

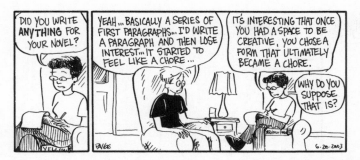

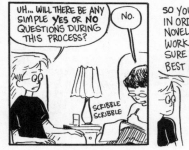

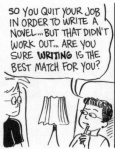

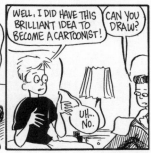

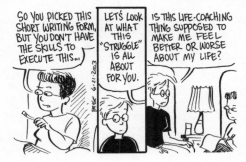

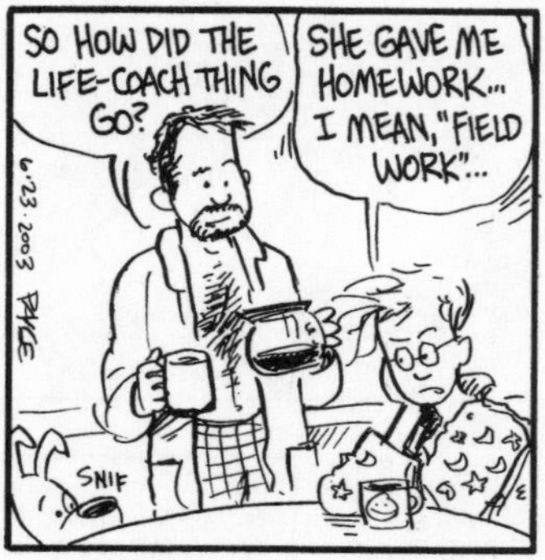
SO HOW DID THE LIFE-COACH THING GO?
SHE GAVE ME HOMEWORK... I MEAN, "FIELD WORK"...
SNIF
6·23·2003 PAYCE

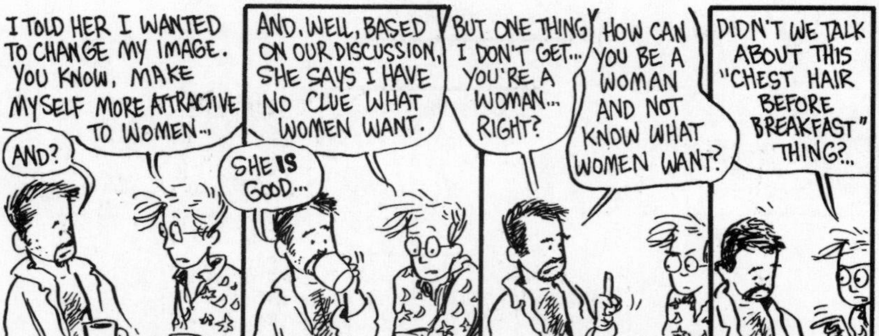
I TOLD HER I WANTED TO CHANGE MY IMAGE. YOU KNOW, MAKE MYSELF MORE ATTRACTIVE TO WOMEN...
AND?
AND, WELL, BASED ON OUR DISCUSSION, SHE SAYS I HAVE NO CLUE WHAT WOMEN WANT.
SHE IS GOOD...
BUT ONE THING I DON'T GET... YOU'RE A WOMAN... RIGHT?
HOW CAN YOU BE A WOMAN AND NOT KNOW WHAT WOMEN WANT?
DIDN'T WE TALK ABOUT THIS "CHEST HAIR BEFORE BREAKFAST" THING?...

WHAT ELSE DID THE COACH SAY?
SHE SAID IF I'M REALLY GOING TO DO THIS COMICS THING, I'LL HAVE TO TAKE CARE OF THE "ART" PROBLEM.
OH... YOU MEAN LIKE HOW YOU CAN'T DRAW... THAT PROBLEM?
YEAH.
LET'S DO THE "WHAT WOMEN WANT" THING FIRST, THAT'S A LOT MORE INTERESTING...
THERE'S NO "TEAM" IN "ME", ETHAN.
THIS IS MY FIELD WORK TO GET ME DATES...
I COULD BE YOUR FIELD ASSISTANT...
6·24·2003
PAIG

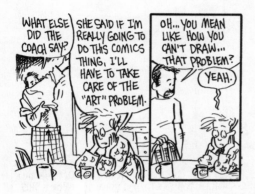

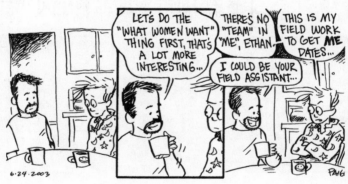

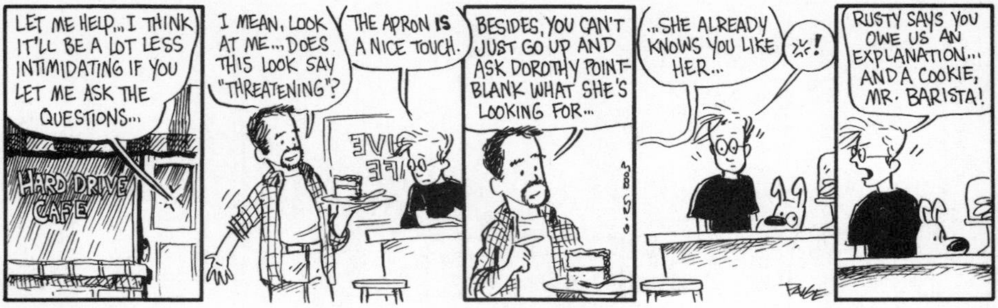
LET ME HELP... I THINK IT'LL BE A LOT LESS INTIMIDATING IF YOU LET ME ASK THE QUESTIONS...
HARD DRIVE CAFE
I MEAN, LOOK AT ME... DOES THIS LOOK SAY "THREATENING"?
THE APRON IS A NICE TOUCH.
BESIDES, YOU CAN'T JUST GO UP AND ASK DOROTHY POINT-BLANK WHAT SHE'S LOOKING FOR...
...SHE ALREADY KNOWS YOU LIKE HER...
RUSTY SAYS YOU OWE US AN EXPLANATION... AND A COOKIE, MR. BARISTA!

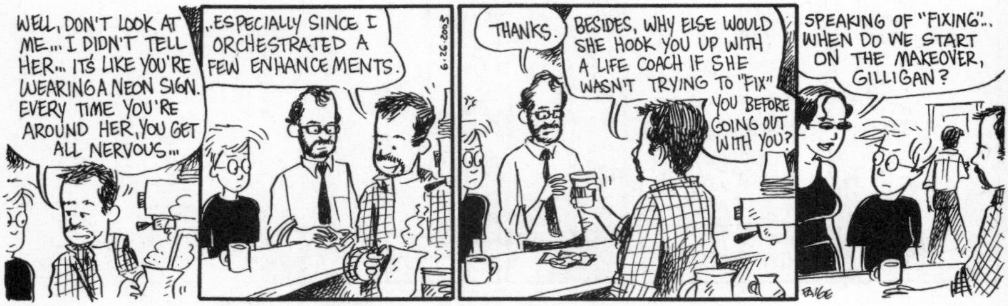
WELL, DON'T LOOK AT ME... I DIDN'T TELL HER... IT'S LIKE YOU'RE WEARING A NEON SIGN. EVERY TIME YOU'RE AROUND HER, YOU GET ALL NERVOUS...
..ESPECIALLY SINCE I ORCHESTRATED A FEW ENHANCEMENTS.
THANKS.
BESIDES, WHY ELSE WOULD SHE HOOK YOU UP WITH A LIFE COACH IF SHE WASN'T TRYING TO "FIX" YOU BEFORE GOING OUT WITH YOU?
SPEAKING OF "FIXING"... WHEN DO WE START ON THE MAKEOVER, GILLIGAN?

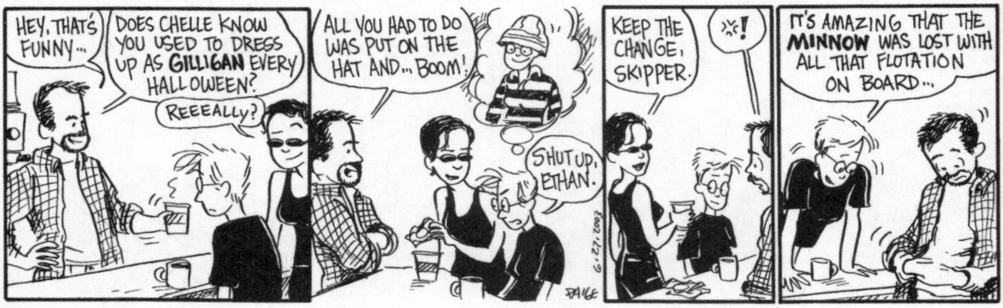
HEY, THAT'S FUNNY...
DOES CHELLE KNOW YOU USED TO DRESS UP AS GILLIGAN EVERY HALLOWEEN?
REEEALLY?
ALL YOU HAD TO DO WAS PUT ON THE HAT AND... BOOM!
SHUT UP, ETHAN.
KEEP THE CHANGE, SKIPPER.
IT'S AMAZING THAT THE MINNOW WAS LOST WITH ALL THAT FLOTATION ON BOARD...

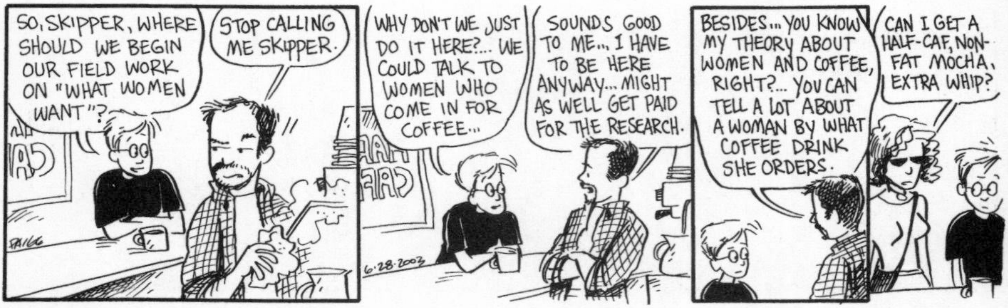
SO, SKIPPER, WHERE SHOULD WE BEGIN OUR FIELD WORK ON "WHAT WOMEN WANT"?
STOP CALLING ME SKIPPER.
WHY DON'T WE JUST DO IT HERE?... WE COULD TALK TO WOMEN WHO COME IN FOR COFFEE...
SOUNDS GOOD TO ME... I HAVE TO BE HERE ANYWAY... MIGHT AS WELL GET PAID FOR THE RESEARCH.
BESIDES... YOU KNOW MY THEORY ABOUT WOMEN AND COFFEE, RIGHT?... YOU CAN TELL A LOT ABOUT A WOMAN BY WHAT COFFEE DRINK SHE ORDERS.
CAN I GET A HALF-CAF, NON-FAT MOCHA, EXTRA WHIP?

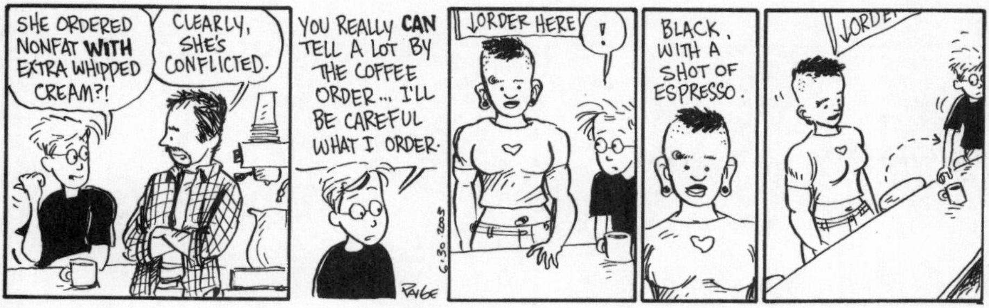
SHE ORDERED NONFAT WITH EXTRA WHIPPED CREAM?!
CLEARLY, SHE'S CONFLICTED.
YOU REALLY CAN TELL A LOT BY THE COFFEE ORDER... I'LL BE CAREFUL WHAT I ORDER.
ORDER HERE
!
BLACK, WITH A SHOT OF ESPRESSO.

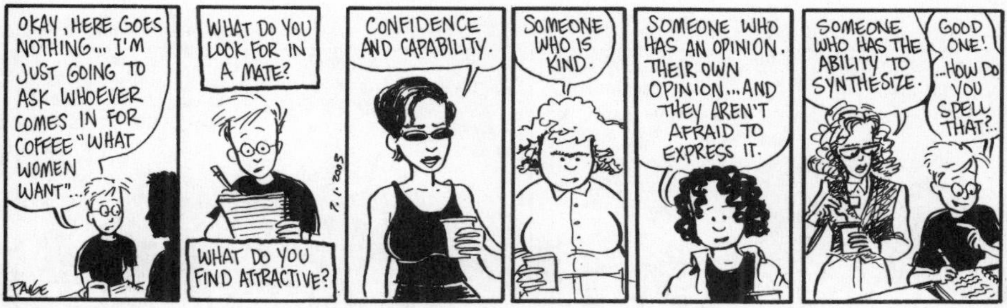
OKAY, HERE GOES NOTHING... I'M JUST GOING TO ASK WHOEVER COMES IN FOR COFFEE "WHAT WOMEN WANT"...
WHAT DO YOU LOOK FOR IN A MATE?
WHAT DO YOU FIND ATTRACTIVE?
CONFIDENCE AND CAPABILITY.
SOMEONE WHO IS KIND.
SOMEONE WHO HAS AN OPINION. THEIR OWN OPINION... AND THEY AREN'T AFRAID TO EXPRESS IT.
SOMEONE WHO HAS THE ABILITY TO SYNTHESIZE.
GOOD ONE! ...HOW DO YOU SPELL THAT?..

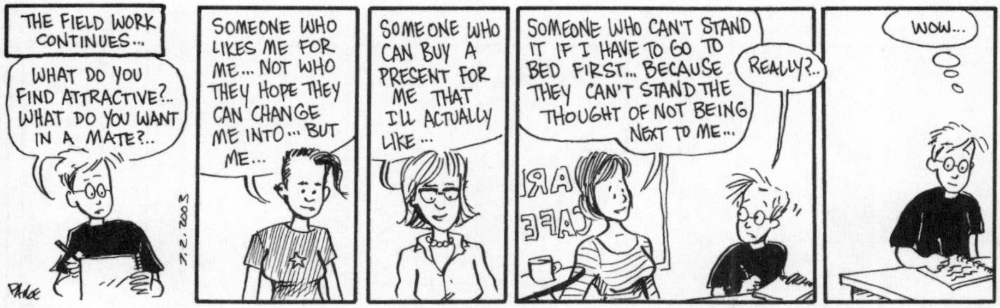
THE FIELD WORK CONTINUES...
WHAT DO YOU FIND ATTRACTIVE?.. WHAT DO YOU WANT IN A MATE?..
SOMEONE WHO LIKES ME FOR ME... NOT WHO THEY HOPE THEY CAN CHANGE ME INTO... BUT ME...
SOMEONE WHO CAN BUY A PRESENT FOR ME THAT I'LL ACTUALLY LIKE...
SOMEONE WHO CAN'T STAND IT IF I HAVE TO GO TO BED FIRST... BECAUSE THEY CAN'T STAND THE THOUGHT OF NOT BEING NEXT TO ME...
REALLY?..
WOW...

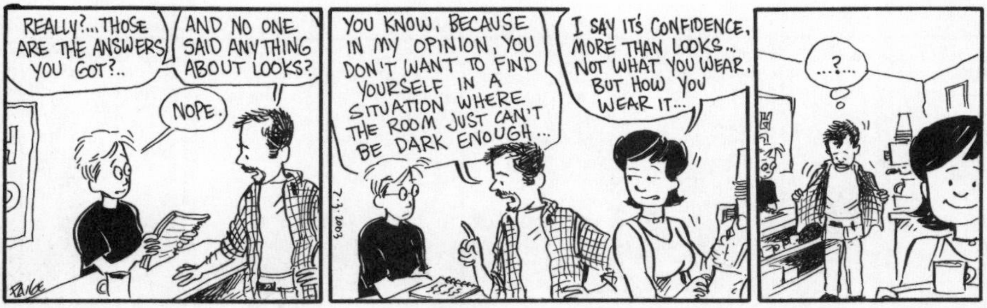
REALLY?... THOSE ARE THE ANSWERS YOU GOT?..
AND NO ONE SAID ANYTHING ABOUT LOOKS?
NOPE.
YOU KNOW, BECAUSE IN MY OPINION, YOU DON'T WANT TO FIND YOURSELF IN A SITUATION WHERE THE ROOM JUST CAN'T BE DARK ENOUGH...
I SAY IT'S CONFIDENCE, MORE THAN LOOKS.. NOT WHAT YOU WEAR, BUT HOW YOU WEAR IT...
...?...

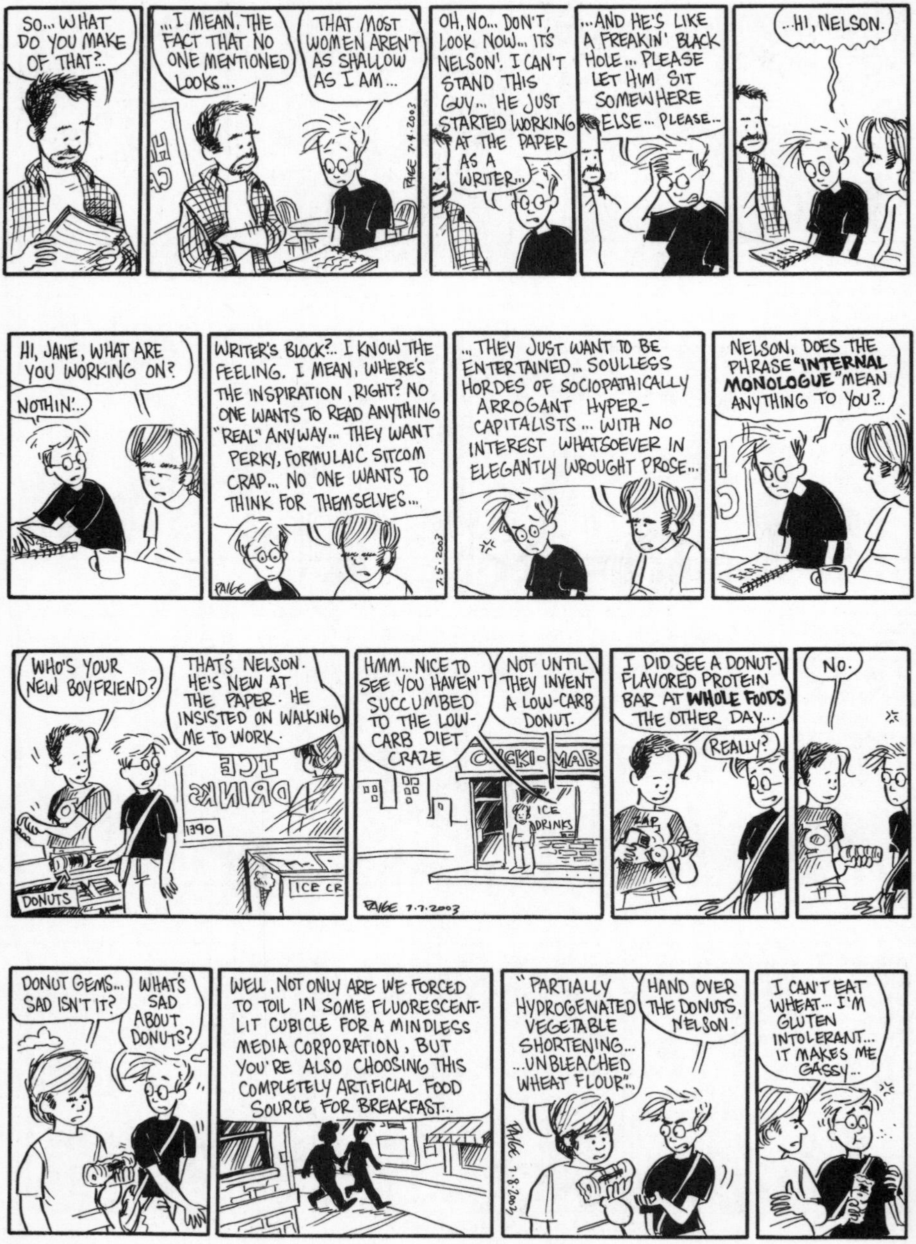
SO... WHAT DO YOU MAKE OF THAT?..
...I MEAN, THE FACT THAT NO ONE MENTIONED LOOKS...
THAT MOST WOMEN AREN'T AS SHALLOW AS I AM...
PAIGE 7.4.2003
OH, NO... DON'T, LOOK NOW... ITS NELSON! I CAN'T STAND THIS GUY... HE JUST STARTED WORKING AT THE PAPER AS A WRITER...
...AND HE'S LIKE A FREAKIN' BLACK HOLE... PLEASE LET HIM SIT SOMEWHERE ELSE... PLEASE...
...HI, NELSON.
HI, JANE, WHAT ARE YOU WORKING ON?
NOTHIN'...
WRITER'S BLOCK?.. I KNOW THE FEELING. I MEAN, WHERE'S THE INSPIRATION, RIGHT? NO ONE WANTS TO READ ANYTHING "REAL" ANYWAY... THEY WANT PERKY, FORMULAIC SITCOM CRAP... NO ONE WANTS TO THINK FOR THEMSELVES...
PAIGE 7.5.2003
...THEY JUST WANT TO BE ENTERTAINED... SOULLESS HORDES OF SOCIOPATHICALLY ARROGANT HYPER-CAPITALISTS ... WITH NO INTEREST WHATSOEVER IN ELEGANTLY WROUGHT PROSE...
NELSON, DOES THE PHRASE "INTERNAL MONOLOGUE" MEAN ANYTHING TO YOU?..
WHO'S YOUR NEW BOYFRIEND?
THAT'S NELSON. HE'S NEW AT THE PAPER. HE INSISTED ON WALKING ME TO WORK.
ICE DRINKS
DONUTS
ICE CR
HMM... NICE TO SEE YOU HAVEN'T SUCCUMBED TO THE LOW-CARB DIET CRAZE
NOT UNTIL THEY INVENT A LOW-CARB DONUT.
PAIGE 7.7.2003
I DID SEE A DONUT-FLAVORED PROTEIN BAR AT WHOLE FOODS THE OTHER DAY...
REALLY?
ZAP
NO.
DONUT GEMS... SAD ISN'T IT?
WHAT'S SAD ABOUT DONUTS?
WELL, NOT ONLY ARE WE FORCED TO TOIL IN SOME FLUORESCENT-LIT CUBICLE FOR A MINDLESS MEDIA CORPORATION, BUT YOU'RE ALSO CHOOSING THIS COMPLETELY ARTIFICIAL FOOD SOURCE FOR BREAKFAST...
"PARTIALLY HYDROGENATED VEGETABLE SHORTENING... ...UNBLEACHED WHEAT FLOUR"...
HAND OVER THE DONUTS, NELSON.
PAIGE 7.8.2003
I CAN'T EAT WHEAT... I'M GLUTEN INTOLERANT... IT MAKES ME GASSY...

NELSON SAYS YOU DON'T LIKE HIM...
OH, GEEZ... WHAT A BABY!
I JUST DIDN'T APPRECIATE HIS RUNNING COMMENTARY ON MY BREAKFAST CHOICE. ...OR DETAILS ABOUT HIS BODILY FUNCTIONS...
T.M.I.
OH, I SEE...
SO... HOW DID THE FIELD WORK GO?
WHAT?! DID A MEMO GO OUT OR SOMETHING? HOW DOES EVERY-ONE KNOW ABOUT THIS??
PAIGE
I GOT THE SCRIPT... OF COURSE, IF WE WERE A BIT MORE AHEAD OF DEADLINE, I'D HAVE GOTTEN IT SOON ENOUGH TO TELL YOU WHAT I WANT IN A PARTNER...
7.9.2003

YOU'RE NOT A WOMAN, ARCHIE.
THIS FIELD WORK IS ABOUT WHAT WOMEN WANT.
7·10·2003
WHAT ABOUT WHAT GUYS WANT?
WHO CARES?.. BESIDES, ALL GUYS WANT THE SAME THING... SEX.
PAIGE

THAT'S SO TYPICAL... NOW THAT I'M IN A "WOMEN'S" COMIC, SUDDENLY I HAVE NO OPINION... I'M JUST ONE OF THE NAMELESS, FACELESS NEANDERTHALS...
....
OKAY, ARCHIE... LAY IT ON ME. I'M ALL EARS... WHAT DO MEN WANT?
SEX.
DID I JUST SAY THAT?!

HEY! THAT'S NOT FAIR!! I COULD HAVE SAID SOME-THING MORE INSIGHTFUL, MORE MEANINGFUL... BUT YOU CONTROL THE SCRIPT! SO I'M JUST GOING TO SAY WHAT YOU WANT ME TO SAY!
THAT'S RIGHT, WE'VE BEEN OVER THIS... IT'S MY OWN LITTLE COMMUNIST COUNTRY CALLED JANE'S WORLD.
PAIGE 7·11·2003
HEY, NELSON? WHAT DO MEN WANT?
SEX.
THAT DOESN'T PROVE ANY-THING! YOU CONTROL HIS SCRIPT, TOO!
THIS IS THE POINT I WAS TRYING TO MAKE YESTERDAY: CHOICE IS AN ILLUSION.
HAVE A DONUT, ARCHIE... IT'LL MAKE YOU FEEL BETTER.
YOU ALREADY KNOW WHETHER I'LL TAKE IT OR NOT, DON'T YOU?

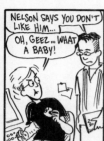

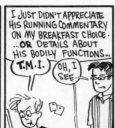

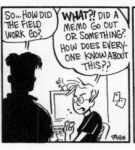

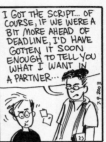

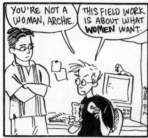

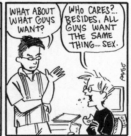

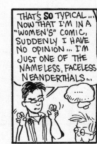

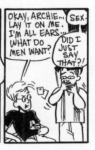

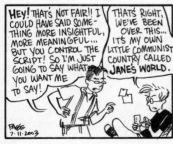

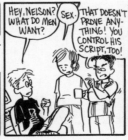

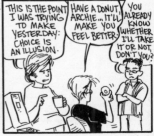

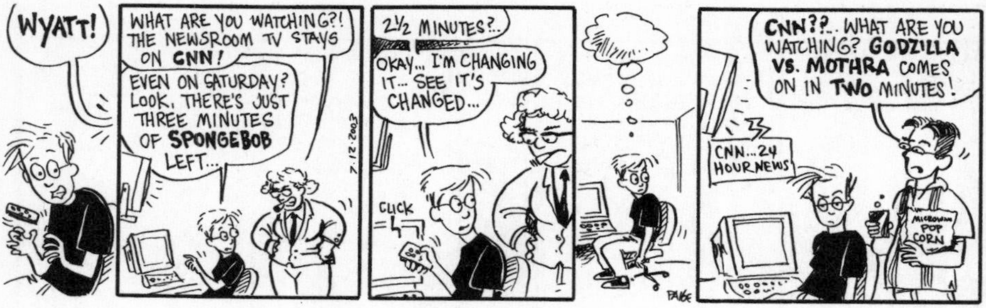
WYATT!
WHAT ARE YOU WATCHING?! THE NEWSROOM TV STAYS ON CNN!
EVEN ON SATURDAY? LOOK, THERE'S JUST THREE MINUTES OF SPONGEBOB LEFT...
7-12-2003
2½ MINUTES?..
OKAY... I'M CHANGING IT... SEE IT'S CHANGED...
CLICK
CNN...24 HOUR NEWS
CNN??.. WHAT ARE YOU WATCHING? GODZILLA VS. MOTHRA COMES ON IN TWO MINUTES!
MICROWAVE POP CORN
PAIGE

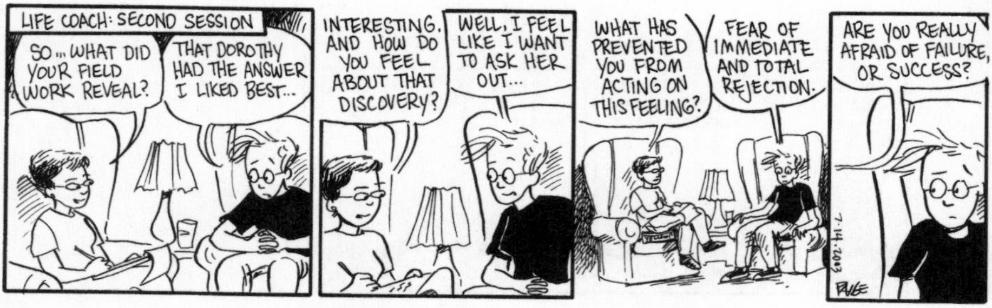
LIFE COACH: SECOND SESSION
SO... WHAT DID YOUR FIELD WORK REVEAL?
THAT DOROTHY HAD THE ANSWER I LIKED BEST...
INTERESTING. AND HOW DO YOU FEEL ABOUT THAT DISCOVERY?
WELL, I FEEL LIKE I WANT TO ASK HER OUT...
WHAT HAS PREVENTED YOU FROM ACTING ON THIS FEELING?
FEAR OF IMMEDIATE AND TOTAL REJECTION.
ARE YOU REALLY AFRAID OF FAILURE, OR SUCCESS?
7-14-2003
PAIGE

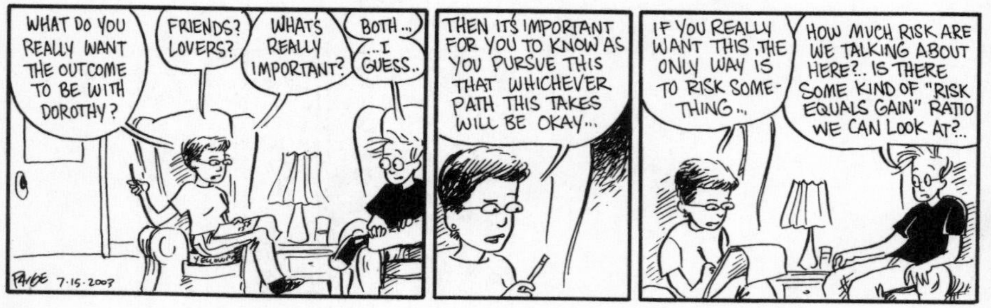
WHAT DO YOU REALLY WANT THE OUTCOME TO BE WITH DOROTHY?
FRIENDS? LOVERS?
WHAT'S REALLY IMPORTANT?
BOTH... ...I GUESS..
PAIGE 7-15-2003
THEN IT'S IMPORTANT FOR YOU TO KNOW AS YOU PURSUE THIS THAT WHICHEVER PATH THIS TAKES WILL BE OKAY...
IF YOU REALLY WANT THIS, THE ONLY WAY IS TO RISK SOME-THING...
HOW MUCH RISK ARE WE TALKING ABOUT HERE?.. IS THERE SOME KIND OF "RISK EQUALS GAIN" RATIO WE CAN LOOK AT?..

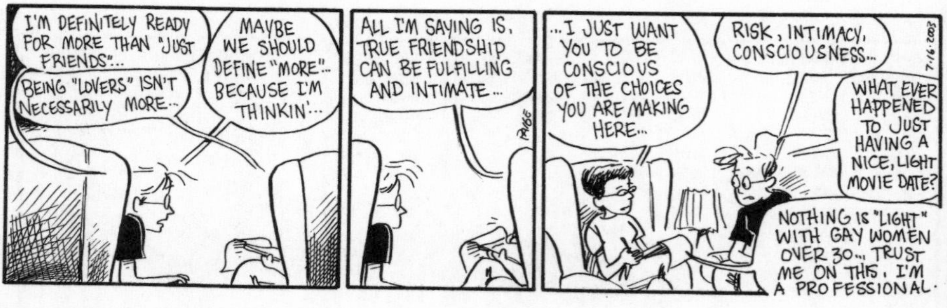
I'M DEFINITELY READY FOR MORE THAN "JUST FRIENDS"...
BEING "LOVERS" ISN'T NECESSARILY MORE...
MAYBE WE SHOULD DEFINE "MORE"... BECAUSE I'M THINKIN'...
ALL I'M SAYING IS, TRUE FRIENDSHIP CAN BE FULFILLING AND INTIMATE...
PAIGE
...I JUST WANT YOU TO BE CONSCIOUS OF THE CHOICES YOU ARE MAKING HERE...
RISK, INTIMACY, CONSCIOUSNESS...
7-16-2003
WHAT EVER HAPPENED TO JUST HAVING A NICE, LIGHT MOVIE DATE?
NOTHING IS "LIGHT" WITH GAY WOMEN OVER 30... TRUST ME ON THIS. I'M A PROFESSIONAL.

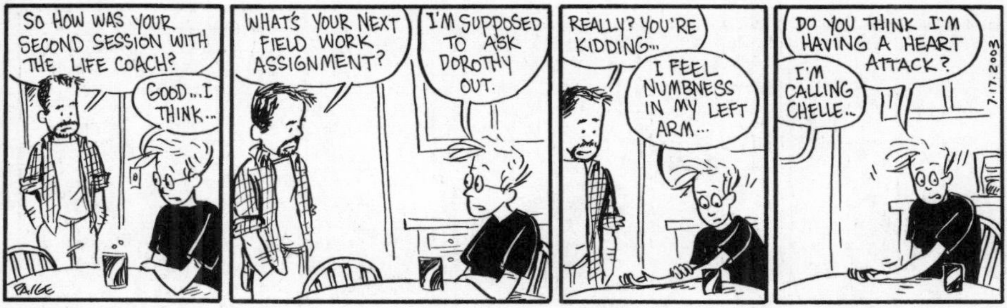
SO HOW WAS YOUR SECOND SESSION WITH THE LIFE COACH?
GOOD... I THINK...
PAIGE
WHAT'S YOUR NEXT FIELD WORK ASSIGNMENT?
I'M SUPPOSED TO ASK DOROTHY OUT.
REALLY? YOU'RE KIDDING...
I FEEL NUMBNESS IN MY LEFT ARM...
DO YOU THINK I'M HAVING A HEART ATTACK?
I'M CALLING CHELLE...
7.17.2003

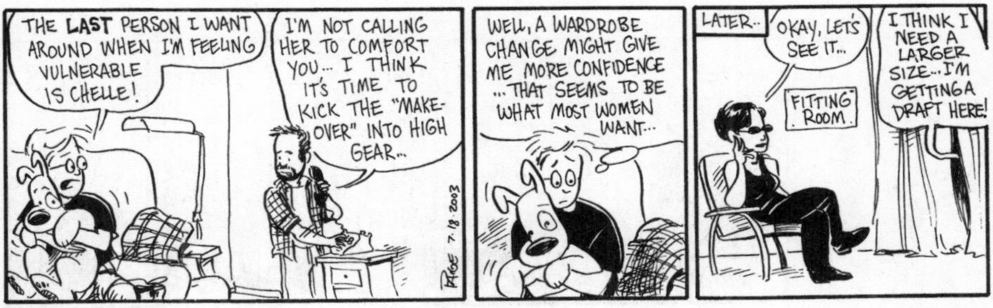
THE **LAST** PERSON I WANT AROUND WHEN I'M FEELING VULNERABLE IS CHELLE!
I'M NOT CALLING HER TO COMFORT YOU... I THINK IT'S TIME TO KICK THE "MAKE-OVER" INTO HIGH GEAR...
PAIGE 7.18.2003
WELL, A WARDROBE CHANGE MIGHT GIVE ME MORE CONFIDENCE ...THAT SEEMS TO BE WHAT MOST WOMEN WANT...
LATER...
OKAY, LET'S SEE IT...
FITTING ROOM
I THINK I NEED A LARGER SIZE... I'M GETTING A DRAFT HERE!

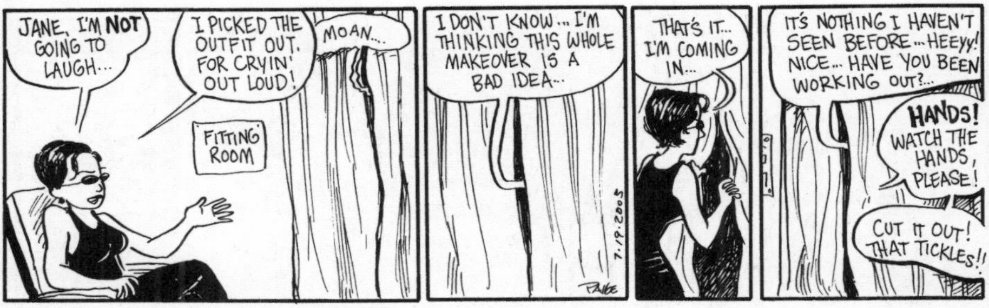
JANE, I'M **NOT** GOING TO LAUGH...
I PICKED THE OUTFIT OUT. FOR CRYIN' OUT LOUD!
FITTING ROOM
MOAN...
I DON'T KNOW... I'M THINKING THIS WHOLE MAKEOVER IS A BAD IDEA...
7.19.2003
PAIGE
THAT'S IT... I'M COMING IN...
IT'S NOTHING I HAVEN'T SEEN BEFORE... HEEYY! NICE... HAVE YOU BEEN WORKING OUT?...
HANDS! WATCH THE HANDS, PLEASE!
CUT IT OUT! THAT TICKLES!!

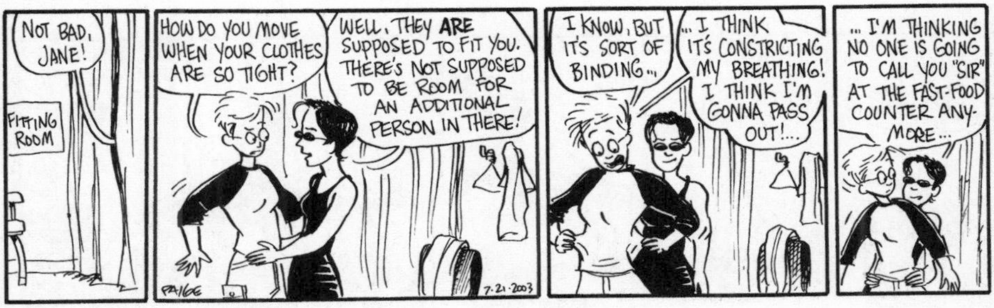
NOT BAD, JANE!
FITTING ROOM
PAIGE
HOW DO YOU MOVE WHEN YOUR CLOTHES ARE SO TIGHT?
WELL, THEY **ARE** SUPPOSED TO FIT YOU. THERE'S NOT SUPPOSED TO BE ROOM FOR AN ADDITIONAL PERSON IN THERE!
7.21.2003
I KNOW, BUT IT'S SORT OF BINDING...
...I THINK IT'S CONSTRICTING MY BREATHING! I THINK I'M GONNA PASS OUT!...
...I'M THINKING NO ONE IS GOING TO CALL YOU "SIR" AT THE FAST-FOOD COUNTER ANY-MORE...

WOW... AND YOU HAVE HIPS!.. WHO KNEW?
CAN WE GO NOW? I'M FEELING A BIT INVADED IN THE PERSONAL SPACE DEPARTMENT.
YOU CAN THANK ME LATER, JANE. I MANAGED TO MAKE YOU LOOK BETTER, BUT STILL LOOK LIKE YOURSELF.
PAIGE
I MEAN, IT'S NO EASY TASK TO PICK AN OUTFIT THAT WORKS WITH THOSE SHOES...
7·22·2003
YEAH, YEAH... YOU'RE A FREAKIN' GENIUS... NOW CAN WE GO?
LET ME HEAR THE GENIUS PART ONE MORE TIME... WITH CONVICTION.
YOU'RE A GENIUS... YOU'RE SOOOO SMART ...WOOOO
OKAY, ENOUGH WITH THE MOCKING... WE CAN GO.
?!
WAIT!
WHAT?
THIS WOMAN I'VE BEEN TRACKING IS HERE...
...WAIT, SHE'S AT THE CHECKOUT...
PAIGE 7·23·2003
...COME ON!
HURRY... PUT THIS ON.
PUNCH
CLOTHING · SHOES
PUNCH
CLOTHING · SHOES
ZOOM!
HMM... LOOKS LIKE CHELLE HAS FOUND HERSELF A CUTE NEW GIRL...
PAIGE 7·24·2003
CAR! LOOK OUT FOR THE CAR!
7·25·2003
PAIGE
*@!
SCREECH!
I THINK WE LOST HER.

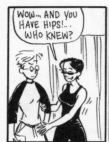

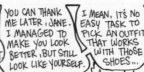

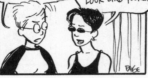

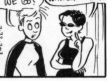

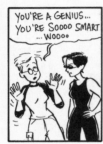

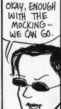

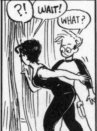

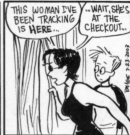

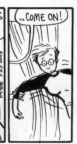

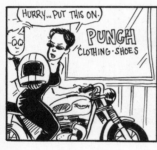

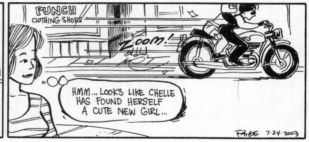

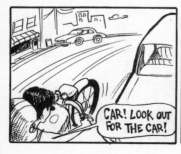

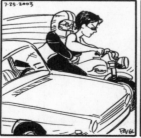

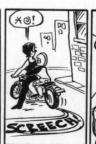

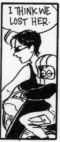

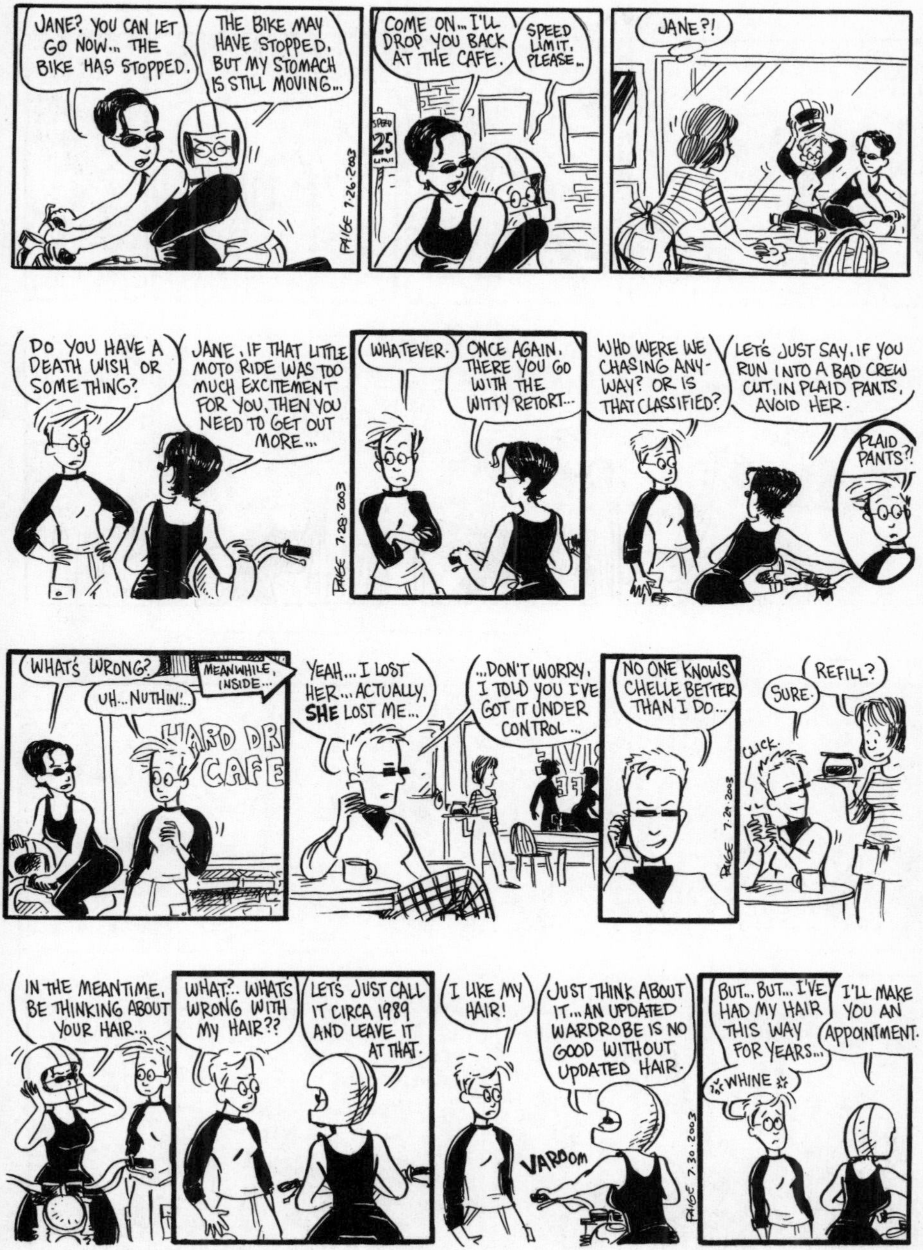

JANE? YOU CAN LET GO NOW... THE BIKE HAS STOPPED.
THE BIKE MAY HAVE STOPPED, BUT MY STOMACH IS STILL MOVING...
PAIGE 7·26·2003
COME ON... I'LL DROP YOU BACK AT THE CAFE.
SPEED LIMIT, PLEASE...
SPEED 25 LIMIT
JANE?!
DO YOU HAVE A DEATH WISH OR SOMETHING?
JANE, IF THAT LITTLE MOTO RIDE WAS TOO MUCH EXCITEMENT FOR YOU, THEN YOU NEED TO GET OUT MORE...
PAIGE 7·28·2003
WHATEVER.
ONCE AGAIN, THERE YOU GO WITH THE WITTY RETORT...
WHO WERE WE CHASING ANY-WAY? OR IS THAT CLASSIFIED?
LET'S JUST SAY, IF YOU RUN INTO A BAD CREW CUT, IN PLAID PANTS, AVOID HER.
PLAID PANTS?!
WHAT'S WRONG?
UH... NUTHIN'...
HARD DR CAFE
MEANWHILE, INSIDE...
YEAH... I LOST HER... ACTUALLY, SHE LOST ME...
...DON'T WORRY, I TOLD YOU I'VE GOT IT UNDER CONTROL...
NO ONE KNOWS CHELLE BETTER THAN I DO...
PAIGE 7·29·2003
SURE.
REFILL?
CLICK.
IN THE MEANTIME, BE THINKING ABOUT YOUR HAIR...
WHAT?.. WHATS WRONG WITH MY HAIR??
LETS JUST CALL IT CIRCA 1989 AND LEAVE IT AT THAT.
I LIKE MY HAIR!
JUST THINK ABOUT IT... AN UPDATED WARDROBE IS NO GOOD WITHOUT UPDATED HAIR.
VAROOM
PAIGE 7·30·2003
BUT... BUT... I'VE HAD MY HAIR THIS WAY FOR YEARS...
WHINE
I'LL MAKE YOU AN APPOINTMENT.

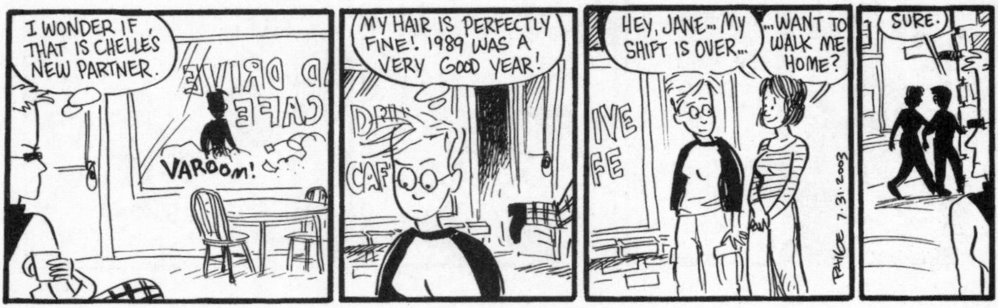
I WONDER IF THAT IS CHELLE'S NEW PARTNER.
VAROOM!
MY HAIR IS PERFECTLY FINE! 1989 WAS A VERY GOOD YEAR!
HEY, JANE... MY SHIFT IS OVER...
...WANT TO WALK ME HOME?
PAIGE 7.31.2003
SURE.

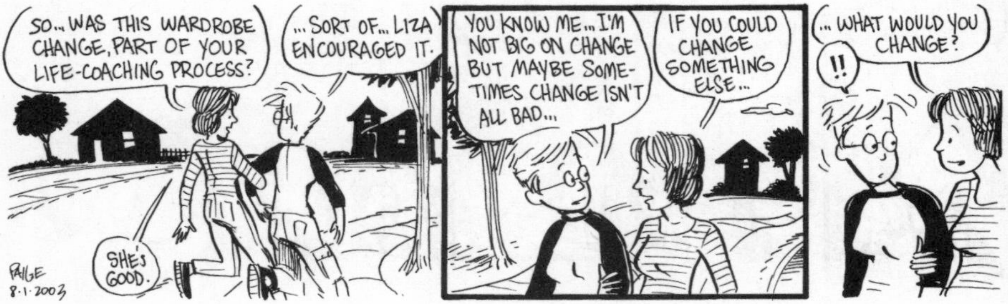
SO... WAS THIS WARDROBE CHANGE, PART OF YOUR LIFE-COACHING PROCESS?
...SORT OF... LIZA ENCOURAGED IT.
SHE'S GOOD.
PAIGE 8.1.2003
YOU KNOW ME... I'M NOT BIG ON CHANGE BUT MAYBE SOME-TIMES CHANGE ISN'T ALL BAD...
IF YOU COULD CHANGE SOMETHING ELSE...
!!
...WHAT WOULD YOU CHANGE?

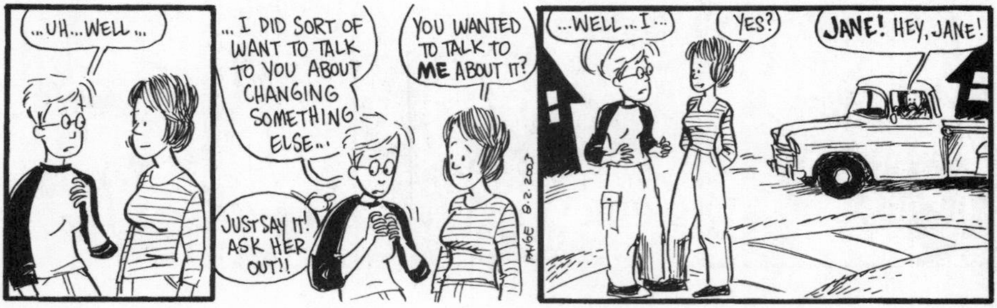
...UH...WELL...
...I DID SORT OF WANT TO TALK TO YOU ABOUT CHANGING SOMETHING ELSE...
JUST SAY IT! ASK HER OUT!!
YOU WANTED TO TALK TO ME ABOUT IT?
PAIGE 8.2.2003
...WELL...I...
YES?
JANE! HEY, JANE!

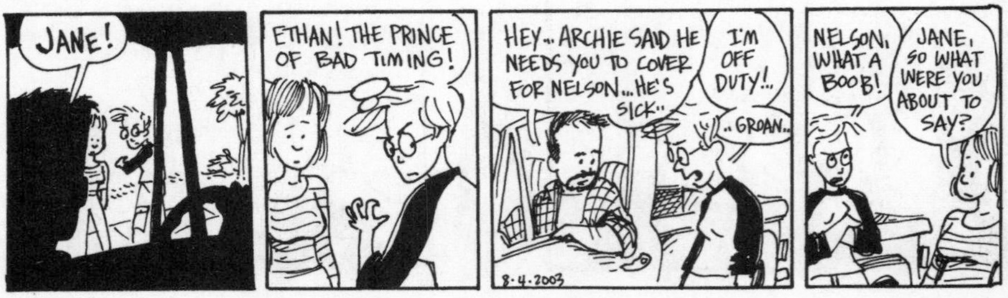
JANE!
ETHAN! THE PRINCE OF BAD TIMING!
HEY... ARCHIE SAID HE NEEDS YOU TO COVER FOR NELSON... HE'S SICK...
I'M OFF DUTY!...
..GROAN..
8.4.2003
NELSON, WHAT A BOOB!
JANE, SO WHAT WERE YOU ABOUT TO SAY?

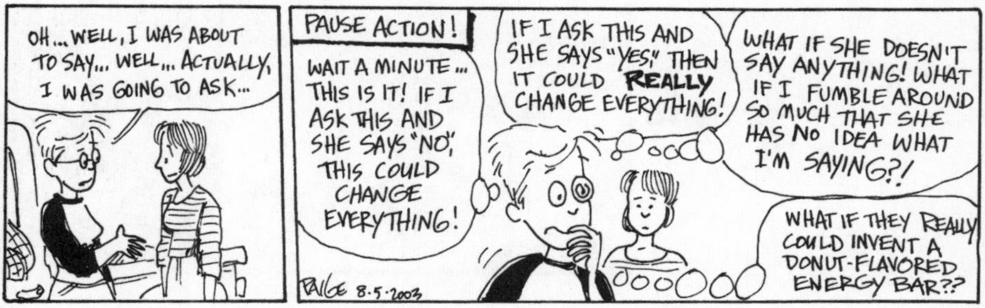
OH... WELL, I WAS ABOUT TO SAY... WELL... ACTUALLY, I WAS GOING TO ASK...
PAUSE ACTION!
WAIT A MINUTE... THIS IS IT! IF I ASK THIS AND SHE SAYS "NO," THIS COULD CHANGE EVERYTHING!
IF I ASK THIS AND SHE SAYS "YES," THEN IT COULD REALLY CHANGE EVERYTHING!
WHAT IF SHE DOESN'T SAY ANYTHING! WHAT IF I FUMBLE AROUND SO MUCH THAT SHE HAS NO IDEA WHAT I'M SAYING?!
WHAT IF THEY REALLY COULD INVENT A DONUT-FLAVORED ENERGY BAR??
PAIGE 8.5.2003

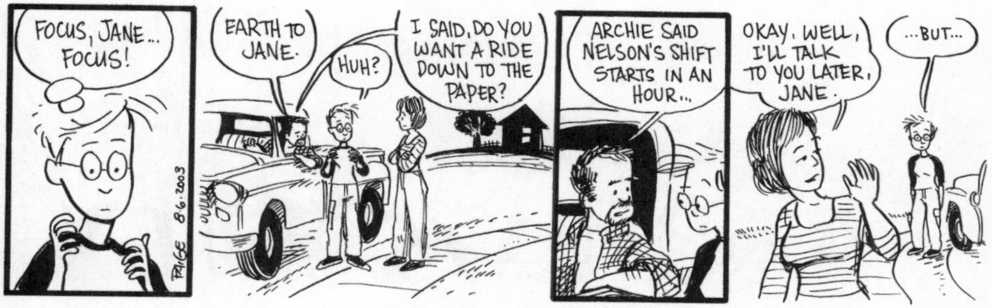
FOCUS, JANE... FOCUS!
PAIGE 8.6.2003
EARTH TO JANE.
HUH?
I SAID, DO YOU WANT A RIDE DOWN TO THE PAPER?
ARCHIE SAID NELSON'S SHIFT STARTS IN AN HOUR...
OKAY. WELL, I'LL TALK TO YOU LATER, JANE.
...BUT...

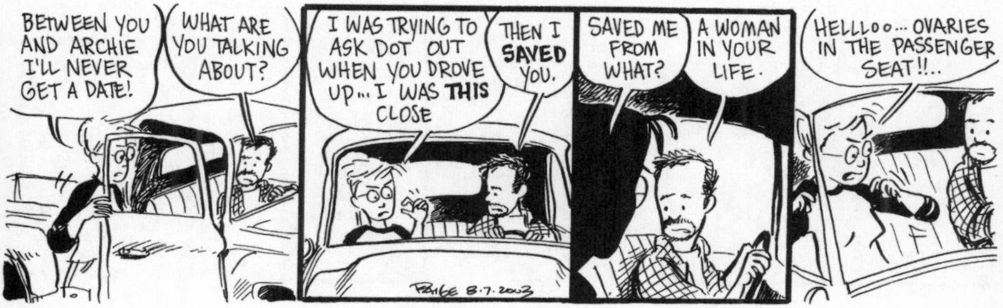
BETWEEN YOU AND ARCHIE I'LL NEVER GET A DATE!
WHAT ARE YOU TALKING ABOUT?
I WAS TRYING TO ASK DOT OUT WHEN YOU DROVE UP... I WAS THIS CLOSE
THEN I SAVED YOU.
PAIGE 8.7.2003
SAVED ME FROM WHAT?
A WOMAN IN YOUR LIFE.
HELLLOO... OVARIES IN THE PASSENGER SEAT!!...

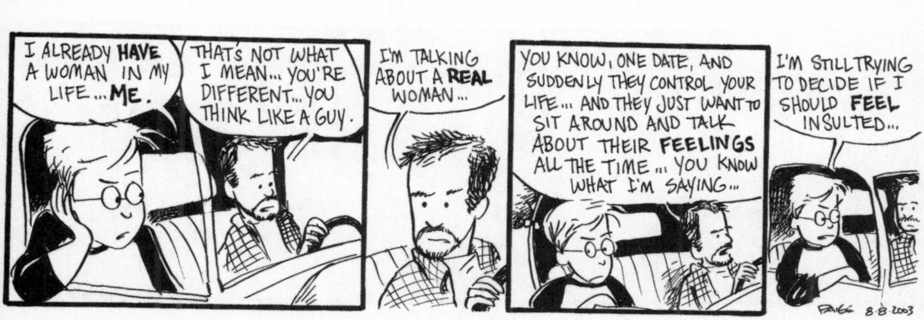
I ALREADY HAVE A WOMAN IN MY LIFE... ME.
THAT'S NOT WHAT I MEAN... YOU'RE DIFFERENT... YOU THINK LIKE A GUY.
I'M TALKING ABOUT A REAL WOMAN...
YOU KNOW, ONE DATE, AND SUDDENLY THEY CONTROL YOUR LIFE... AND THEY JUST WANT TO SIT AROUND AND TALK ABOUT THEIR FEELINGS ALL THE TIME... YOU KNOW WHAT I'M SAYING...
I'M STILL TRYING TO DECIDE IF I SHOULD FEEL INSULTED...
PAIGE 8.8.2003

I THINK LIKE A GUY? I'M NOT A REAL WOMAN JUST BECAUSE I'M NOT ALL EMOTIONAL?
DON'T GET ALL OFFENDED... IT WAS MEANT AS A COMPLIMENT.
8·9·2003
PAIGE
WHAT WAS THAT SONG?... IT GOES, "I GAVE A GIRL A RIDE IN MY WAGON... ♫
...SHE CLIMBED IN AND TOOK ♫ CONTROL."
DUDE... YOU HAVE ISSUES.
YEAH... YOU'RE ALL HAPPY NOW... JUST WAIT, YOU'LL HAVE "ISSUES," TOO...
WHATEVER.
THANKS FOR THE RIDE.
LATER
ARCHIE, HERE I AM... AT WORK ON MY DAY OFF... I'VE GOTTA FIGURE OUT THIS COMIC-STRIP THING...
8·11·2003
PAIGE
THIS WHOLE IDEA OF A 40-HOUR WEEK JUST DOESN'T REALLY WORK FOR ME...
HEY, I THOUGHT YOU WERE GETTING A MAKEOVER?
ALL YOU DID WAS CHANGE SHIRTS.
HOW IS THE LIFE-COACHING THING WORKING OUT? I THOUGHT SHE WAS GOING TO HELP YOU WITH THIS CAREER COMPONENT.
SHE IS, SORT OF.. ...SHE POINTED OUT THAT MY SHORTFALL IS ART...
8·12·2003
PAIGE
I EITHER HAVE TO LEARN TO DRAW MYSELF OR RECRUIT SOMEONE TO DRAW THE STRIP FOR ME.
HEY! THAT'S IT!... I'LL HOLD A CARTOONING TRYOUT!
I'M GOING TO USE MY LUNCH HOUR TO HANG SOME FLIERS AROUND CAMPUS!
LUNCH?? YOU JUST GOT HERE A HALF HOUR AGO!
HEY! BRING ME BACK A FROSTY!
LATER... ON CAMPUS...
HMM... THIS LOOKS LIKE A NICE, BUSY SPOT TO HANG A FLIER.
8·13·2003
PAIGE

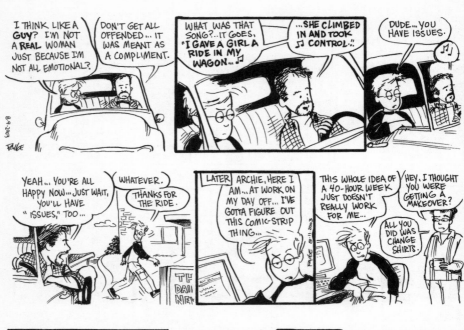

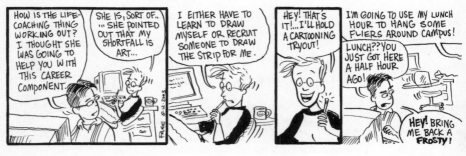

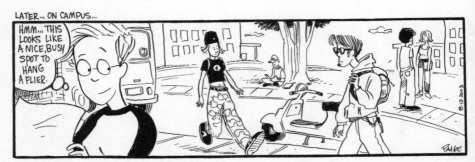

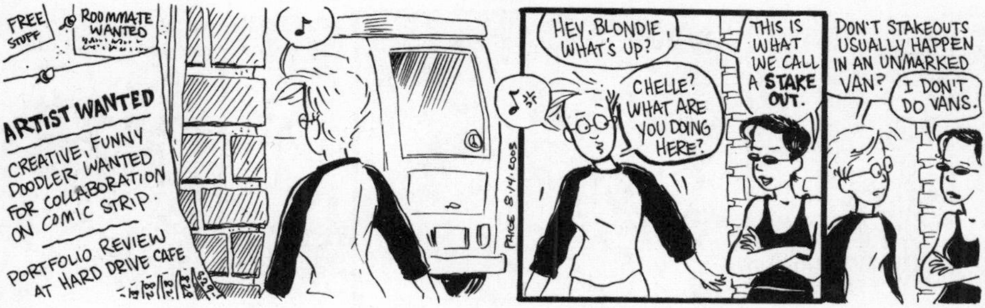
FREE STUFF
ROOMMATE WANTED
ARTIST WANTED
CREATIVE, FUNNY DOODLER WANTED FOR COLLABORATION ON COMIC STRIP.
PORTFOLIO REVIEW AT HARD DRIVE CAFE
PAIGE 8.14.2003
HEY, BLONDIE, WHAT'S UP?
CHELLE? WHAT ARE YOU DOING HERE?
THIS IS WHAT WE CALL A **STAKE OUT.**
DON'T STAKEOUTS USUALLY HAPPEN IN AN UNMARKED VAN?
I DON'T DO VANS.

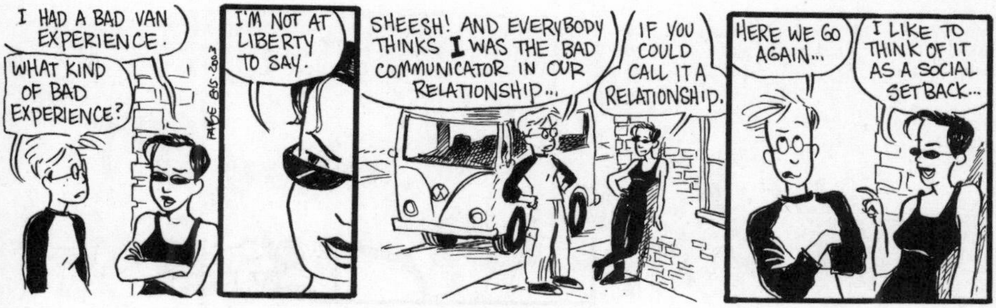
I HAD A BAD VAN EXPERIENCE.
WHAT KIND OF BAD EXPERIENCE?
PAIGE 8.15.2003
I'M NOT AT LIBERTY TO SAY.
SHEESH! AND EVERYBODY THINKS **I** WAS THE BAD COMMUNICATOR IN OUR RELATIONSHIP...
IF YOU COULD CALL IT A RELATIONSHIP.
HERE WE GO AGAIN...
I LIKE TO THINK OF IT AS A SOCIAL SETBACK...

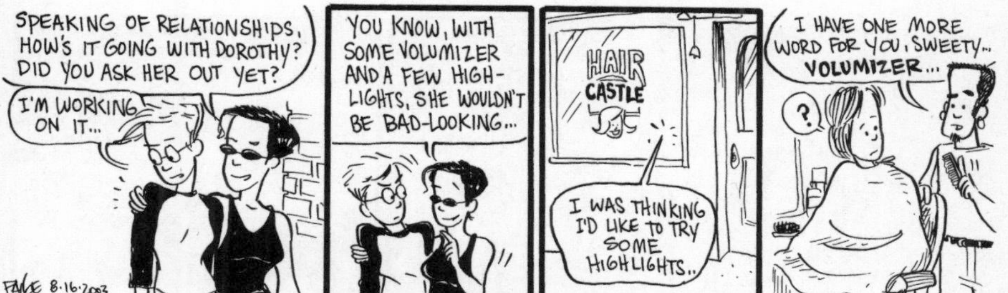
SPEAKING OF RELATIONSHIPS, HOW'S IT GOING WITH DOROTHY? DID YOU ASK HER OUT YET?
I'M WORKING ON IT...
PAIGE 8.16.2003
YOU KNOW, WITH SOME VOLUMIZER AND A FEW HIGH-LIGHTS, SHE WOULDN'T BE BAD-LOOKING...
HAIR CASTLE
I WAS THINKING I'D LIKE TO TRY SOME HIGHLIGHTS...
I HAVE ONE MORE WORD FOR YOU, SWEETY... **VOLUMIZER**...
?

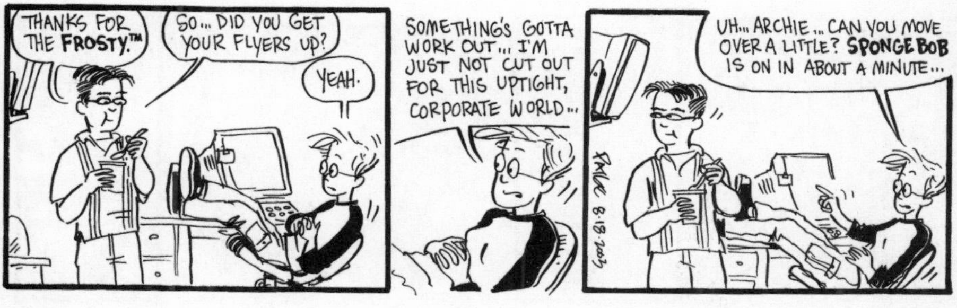
THANKS FOR THE **FROSTY.™**
SO... DID YOU GET YOUR FLYERS UP?
YEAH.
SOMETHING'S GOTTA WORK OUT... I'M JUST NOT CUT OUT FOR THIS UPTIGHT, CORPORATE WORLD...
PAIGE 8.18.2003
UH... ARCHIE... CAN YOU MOVE OVER A LITTLE? **SPONGEBOB** IS ON IN ABOUT A MINUTE...

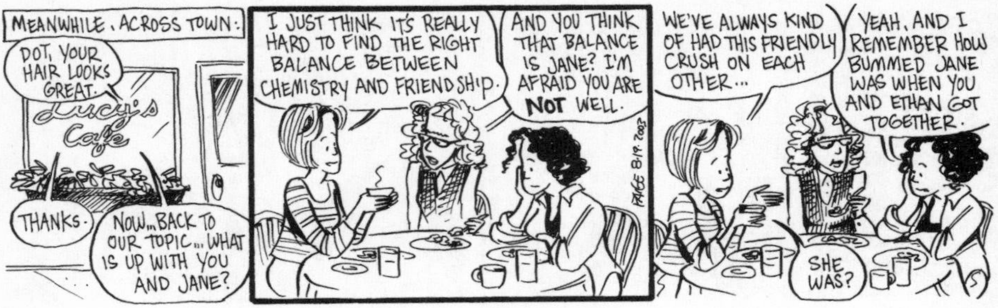
MEANWHILE, ACROSS TOWN:
DOT, YOUR HAIR LOOKS GREAT.
Lucy's Cafe
THANKS.
NOW... BACK TO OUR TOPIC... WHAT IS UP WITH YOU AND JANE?
I JUST THINK IT'S REALLY HARD TO FIND THE RIGHT BALANCE BETWEEN CHEMISTRY AND FRIENDSHIP.
AND YOU THINK THAT BALANCE IS JANE? I'M AFRAID YOU ARE NOT WELL.
PAIGE 8.19.2003
WE'VE ALWAYS KIND OF HAD THIS FRIENDLY CRUSH ON EACH OTHER...
YEAH, AND I REMEMBER HOW BUMMED JANE WAS WHEN YOU AND ETHAN GOT TOGETHER.
SHE WAS?

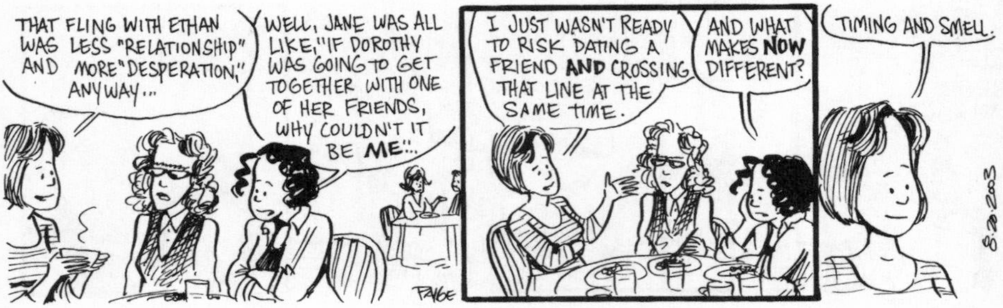
THAT FLING WITH ETHAN WAS LESS "RELATIONSHIP" AND MORE "DESPERATION," ANYWAY...
WELL, JANE WAS ALL LIKE, "IF DOROTHY WAS GOING TO GET TOGETHER WITH ONE OF HER FRIENDS, WHY COULDN'T IT BE ME?!"
PAIGE
I JUST WASN'T READY TO RISK DATING A FRIEND AND CROSSING THAT LINE AT THE SAME TIME.
AND WHAT MAKES NOW DIFFERENT?
TIMING AND SMELL.
8.20.2003

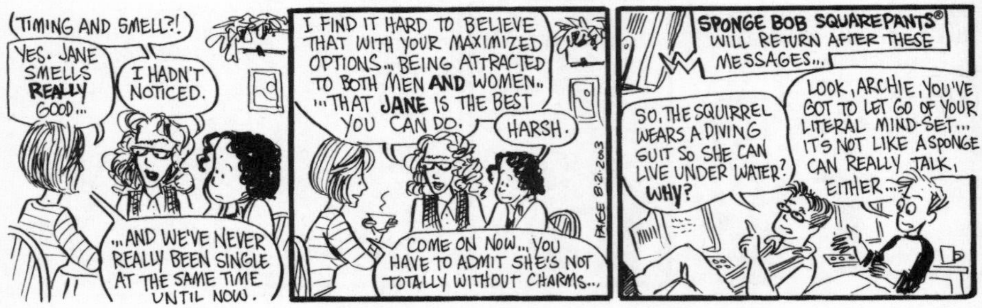
(TIMING AND SMELL?!)
YES. JANE SMELLS REALLY GOOD...
I HADN'T NOTICED.
...AND WE'VE NEVER REALLY BEEN SINGLE AT THE SAME TIME UNTIL NOW.
I FIND IT HARD TO BELIEVE THAT WITH YOUR MAXIMIZED OPTIONS... BEING ATTRACTED TO BOTH MEN AND WOMEN... ...THAT JANE IS THE BEST YOU CAN DO.
HARSH.
COME ON NOW... YOU HAVE TO ADMIT SHE'S NOT TOTALLY WITHOUT CHARMS...
PAIGE 8.21.2003
SPONGE BOB SQUAREPANTS® WILL RETURN AFTER THESE MESSAGES...
SO, THE SQUIRREL WEARS A DIVING SUIT SO SHE CAN LIVE UNDER WATER? WHY?
LOOK, ARCHIE, YOU'VE GOT TO LET GO OF YOUR LITERAL MIND-SET... IT'S NOT LIKE A SPONGE CAN REALLY TALK, EITHER...

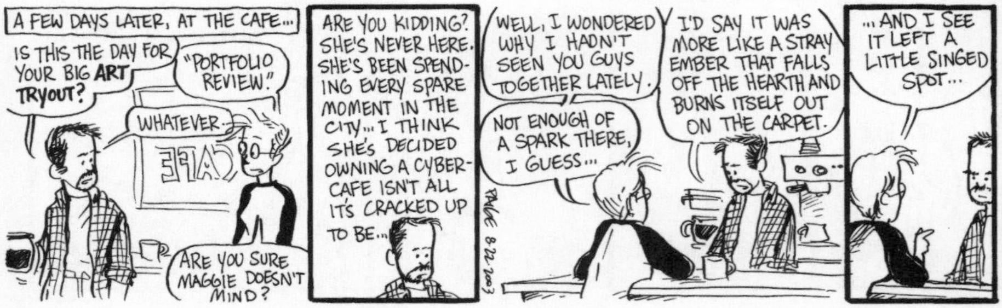
A FEW DAYS LATER, AT THE CAFE...
IS THIS THE DAY FOR YOUR BIG ART TRYOUT?
"PORTFOLIO REVIEW."
WHATEVER.
ARE YOU SURE MAGGIE DOESN'T MIND?
ARE YOU KIDDING? SHE'S NEVER HERE. SHE'S BEEN SPENDING EVERY SPARE MOMENT IN THE CITY... I THINK SHE'S DECIDED OWNING A CYBER-CAFE ISN'T ALL IT'S CRACKED UP TO BE...
PAIGE 8.22.2003
WELL, I WONDERED WHY I HADN'T SEEN YOU GUYS TOGETHER LATELY.
NOT ENOUGH OF A SPARK THERE, I GUESS...
I'D SAY IT WAS MORE LIKE A STRAY EMBER THAT FALLS OFF THE HEARTH AND BURNS ITSELF OUT ON THE CARPET.
...AND I SEE IT LEFT A LITTLE SINGED SPOT...

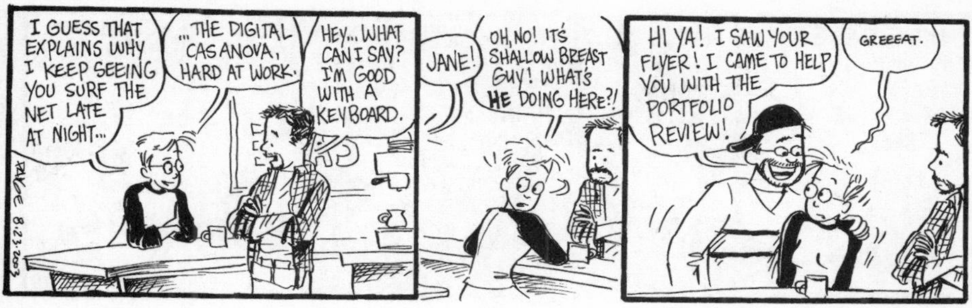

I GUESS THAT EXPLAINS WHY I KEEP SEEING YOU SURF THE NET LATE AT NIGHT...
...THE DIGITAL CASANOVA, HARD AT WORK.
HEY... WHAT CAN I SAY? I'M GOOD WITH A KEYBOARD.
JANE!
OH, NO! IT'S SHALLOW BREAST GUY! WHAT'S HE DOING HERE?!
HI YA! I SAW YOUR FLYER! I CAME TO HELP YOU WITH THE PORTFOLIO REVIEW!
GREEEAT.
PAIGE 8-23-2003

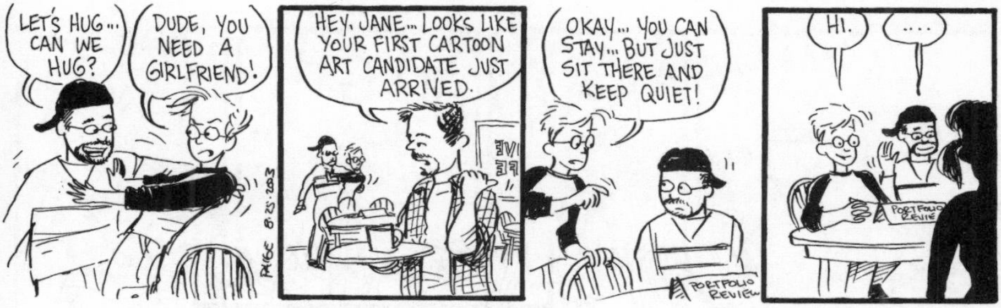

LET'S HUG... CAN WE HUG?
DUDE, YOU NEED A GIRLFRIEND!
PAIGE 8-25-2003
HEY, JANE... LOOKS LIKE YOUR FIRST CARTOON ART CANDIDATE JUST ARRIVED.
OKAY... YOU CAN STAY... BUT JUST SIT THERE AND KEEP QUIET!
PORTFOLIO REVIEW
HI.
....
PORTFOLIO REVIEW

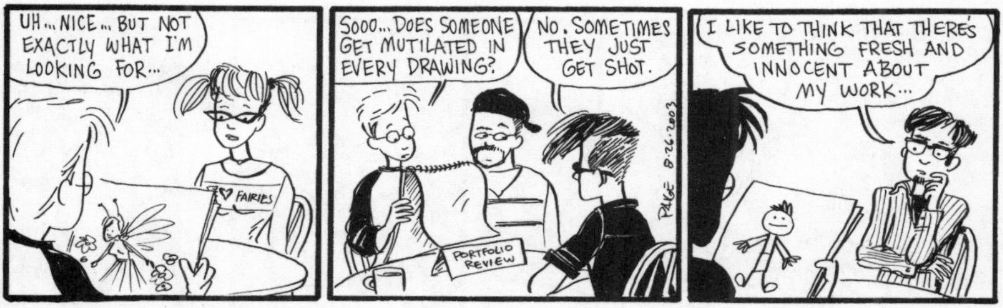

UH... NICE... BUT NOT EXACTLY WHAT I'M LOOKING FOR...
♡ FAIRIES
SOOO... DOES SOMEONE GET MUTILATED IN EVERY DRAWING?
NO. SOMETIMES THEY JUST GET SHOT.
PORTFOLIO REVIEW
PAIGE 8-26-2003
I LIKE TO THINK THAT THERE'S SOMETHING FRESH AND INNOCENT ABOUT MY WORK...

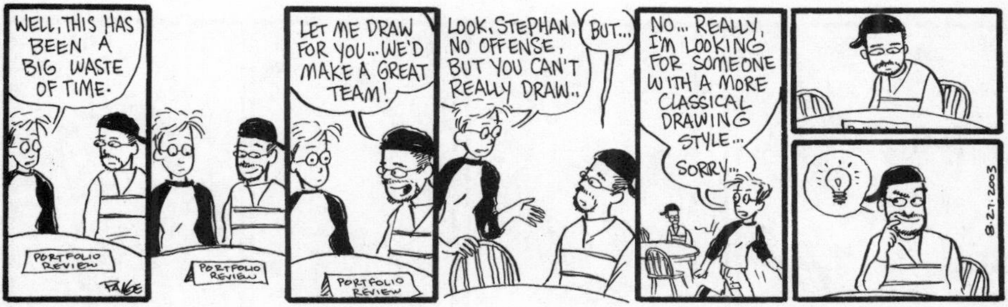

WELL, THIS HAS BEEN A BIG WASTE OF TIME.
PORTFOLIO REVIEW
PAIGE
PORTFOLIO REVIEW
LET ME DRAW FOR YOU... WE'D MAKE A GREAT TEAM!
PORTFOLIO REVIEW
LOOK, STEPHAN, NO OFFENSE, BUT YOU CAN'T REALLY DRAW..
BUT...
NO... REALLY, I'M LOOKING FOR SOMEONE WITH A MORE CLASSICAL DRAWING STYLE...
SORRY...
8-27-2003

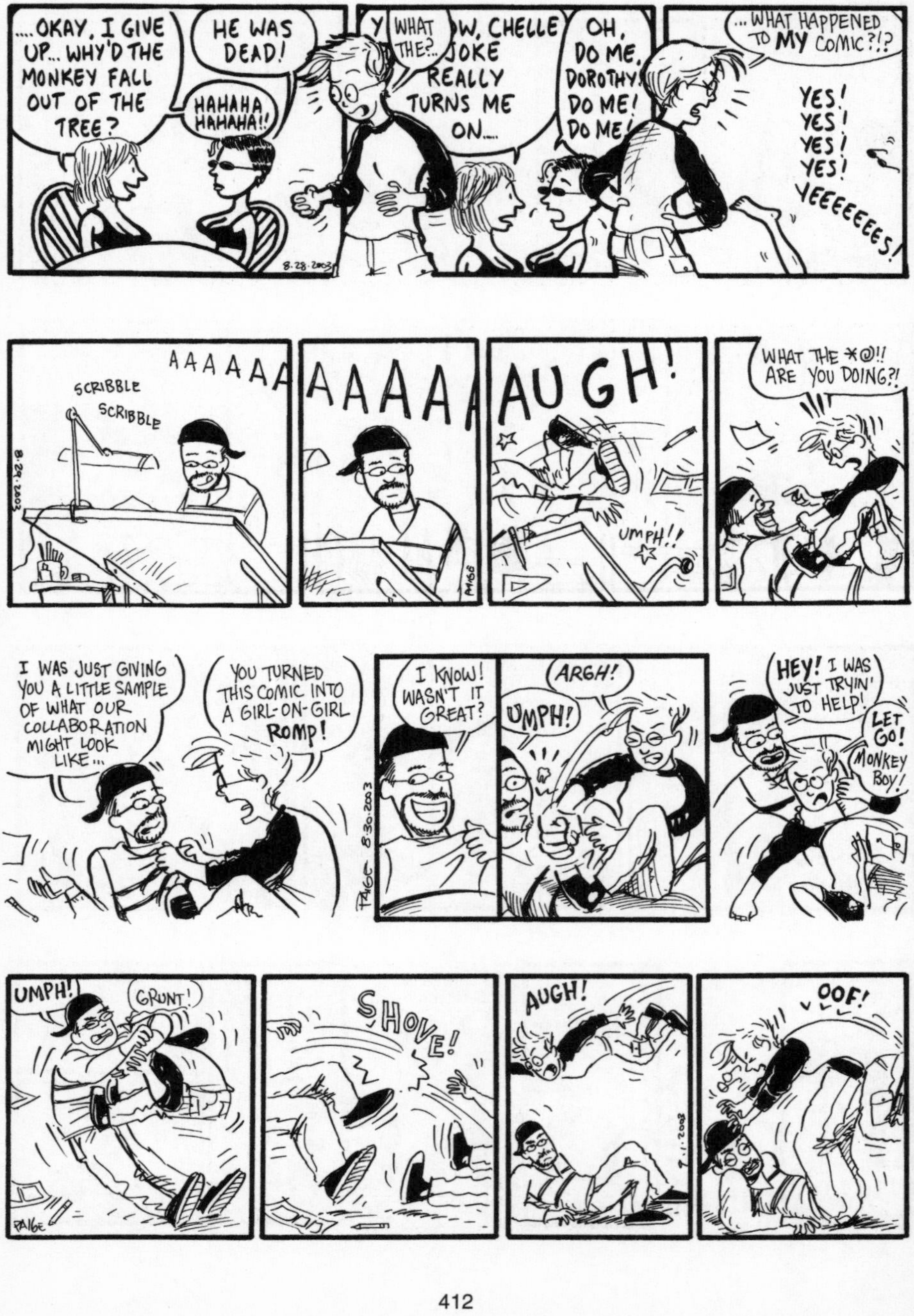

....OKAY, I GIVE UP... WHY'D THE MONKEY FALL OUT OF THE TREE?
HE WAS DEAD!
HAHAHA HAHAHA!!
WHAT THE?..
Y W, CHELLE JOKE REALLY TURNS ME ON....
OH, DO ME, DOROTHY! DO ME! DO ME!
...WHAT HAPPENED TO MY COMIC?!?
YES! YES! YES! YES! YEEEEEEEES!
SCRIBBLE
SCRIBBLE
AAAAAA AAAAA AUGH!
UMPH!!
WHAT THE *@!! ARE YOU DOING?!
I WAS JUST GIVING YOU A LITTLE SAMPLE OF WHAT OUR COLLABORATION MIGHT LOOK LIKE...
YOU TURNED THIS COMIC INTO A GIRL-ON-GIRL ROMP!
I KNOW! WASN'T IT GREAT?
ARGH!
UMPH!
HEY! I WAS JUST TRYIN' TO HELP!
LET GO! MONKEY BOY!
UMPH!
GRUNT!
SHOVE!
AUGH!
OOF!

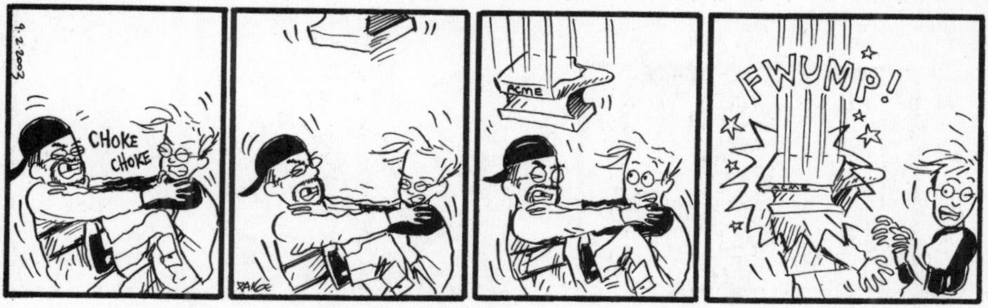
9.2.2003
CHOKE CHOKE
PAIGE
ACME
FWUMP!
ACME

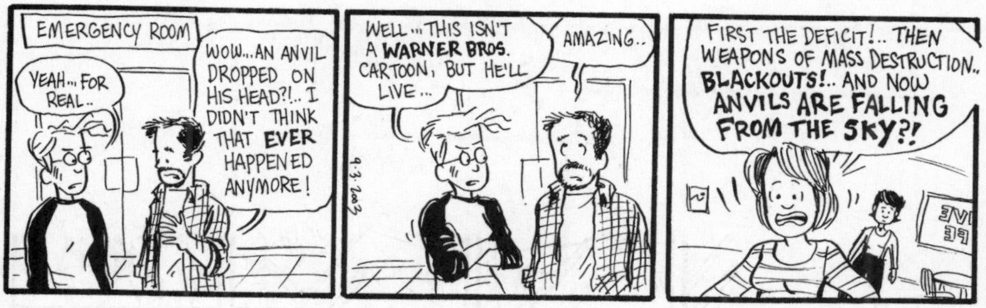
EMERGENCY ROOM
YEAH... FOR REAL..
WOW... AN ANVIL DROPPED ON HIS HEAD?!.. I DIDN'T THINK THAT **EVER** HAPPENED ANYMORE!
9.3.2003
WELL... THIS ISN'T A **WARNER BROS.** CARTOON, BUT HE'LL LIVE...
AMAZING..
FIRST THE DEFICIT!.. THEN WEAPONS OF MASS DESTRUCTION.. **BLACKOUTS!**.. AND NOW **ANVILS ARE FALLING FROM THE SKY?!**

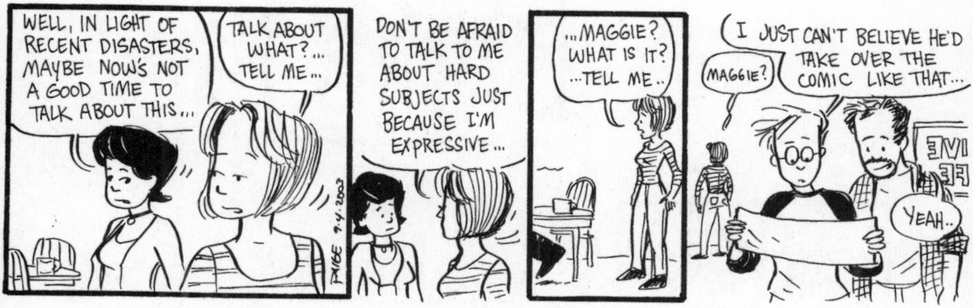
WELL, IN LIGHT OF RECENT DISASTERS, MAYBE NOW'S NOT A GOOD TIME TO TALK ABOUT THIS...
TALK ABOUT WHAT?... TELL ME...
PAIGE 9.4.2003
DON'T BE AFRAID TO TALK TO ME ABOUT HARD SUBJECTS JUST BECAUSE I'M EXPRESSIVE...
...MAGGIE? WHAT IS IT? ...TELL ME..
I JUST CAN'T BELIEVE HE'D TAKE OVER THE COMIC LIKE THAT...
MAGGIE?
YEAH..

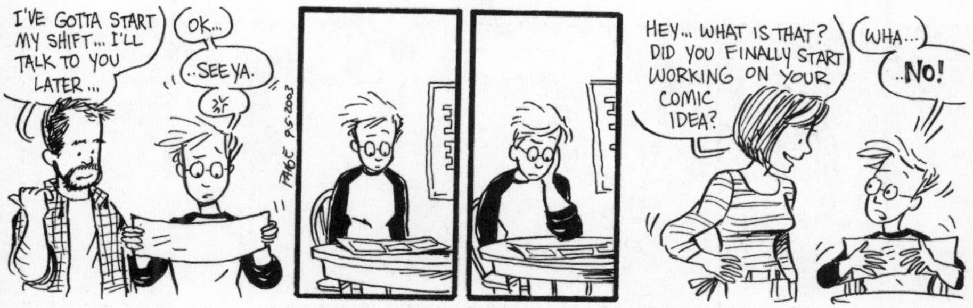
I'VE GOTTA START MY SHIFT... I'LL TALK TO YOU LATER...
OK...
..SEE YA.
PAIGE 9.5.2003
HEY... WHAT IS THAT? DID YOU FINALLY START WORKING ON YOUR COMIC IDEA?
WHA...
..**NO!**

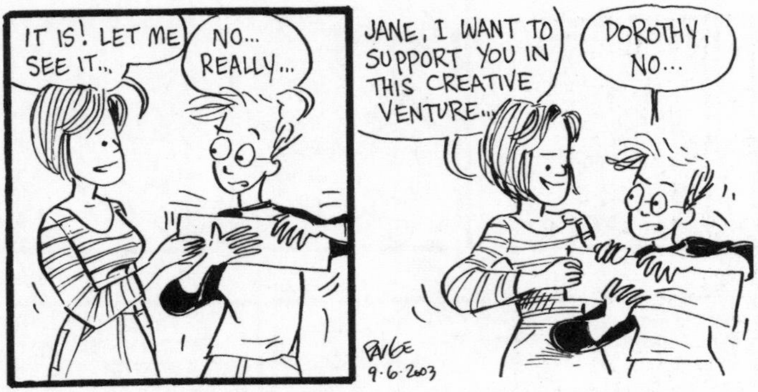
IT IS! LET ME SEE IT...
NO... REALLY...
JANE, I WANT TO SUPPORT YOU IN THIS CREATIVE VENTURE...
DOROTHY, NO...
PAIGE 9·6·2003

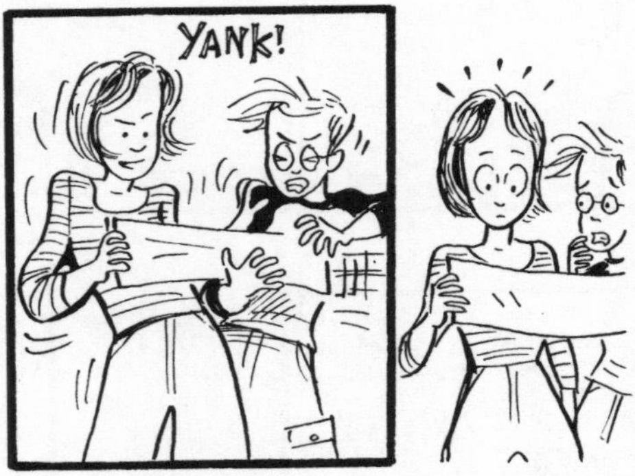
YANK!

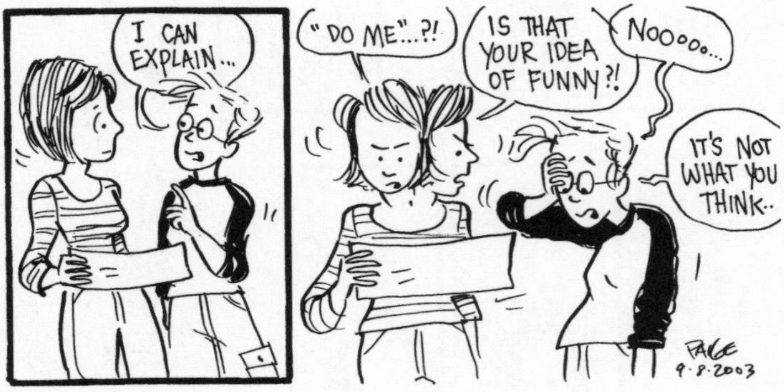
I CAN EXPLAIN...
"DO ME"...?!
IS THAT YOUR IDEA OF FUNNY?!
NOOooo...
IT'S NOT WHAT YOU THINK..
PAIGE 9·8·2003

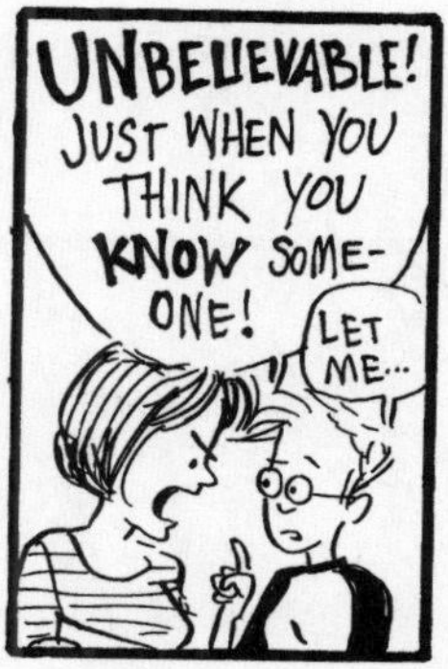
UNBELIEVABLE! JUST WHEN YOU THINK YOU KNOW SOME-ONE!
LET ME...

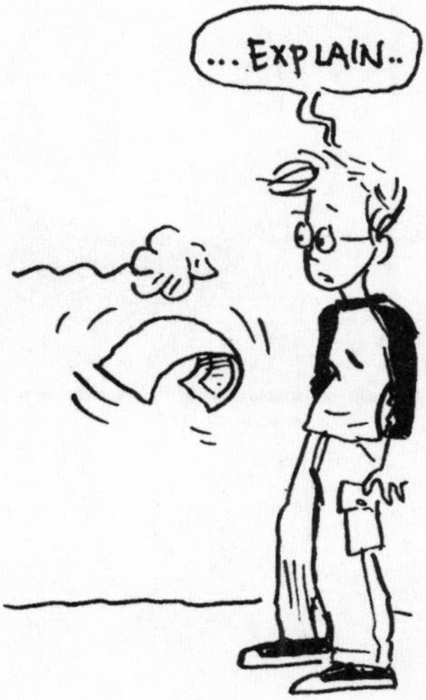
...EXPLAIN..

DOROTHY?...
HEY!!
PAGE 9.9.2003

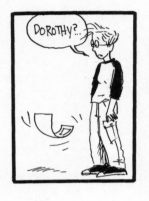

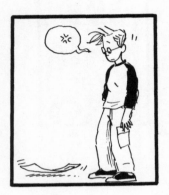

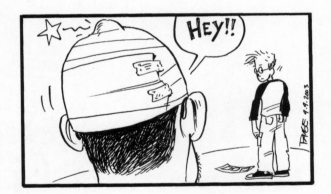

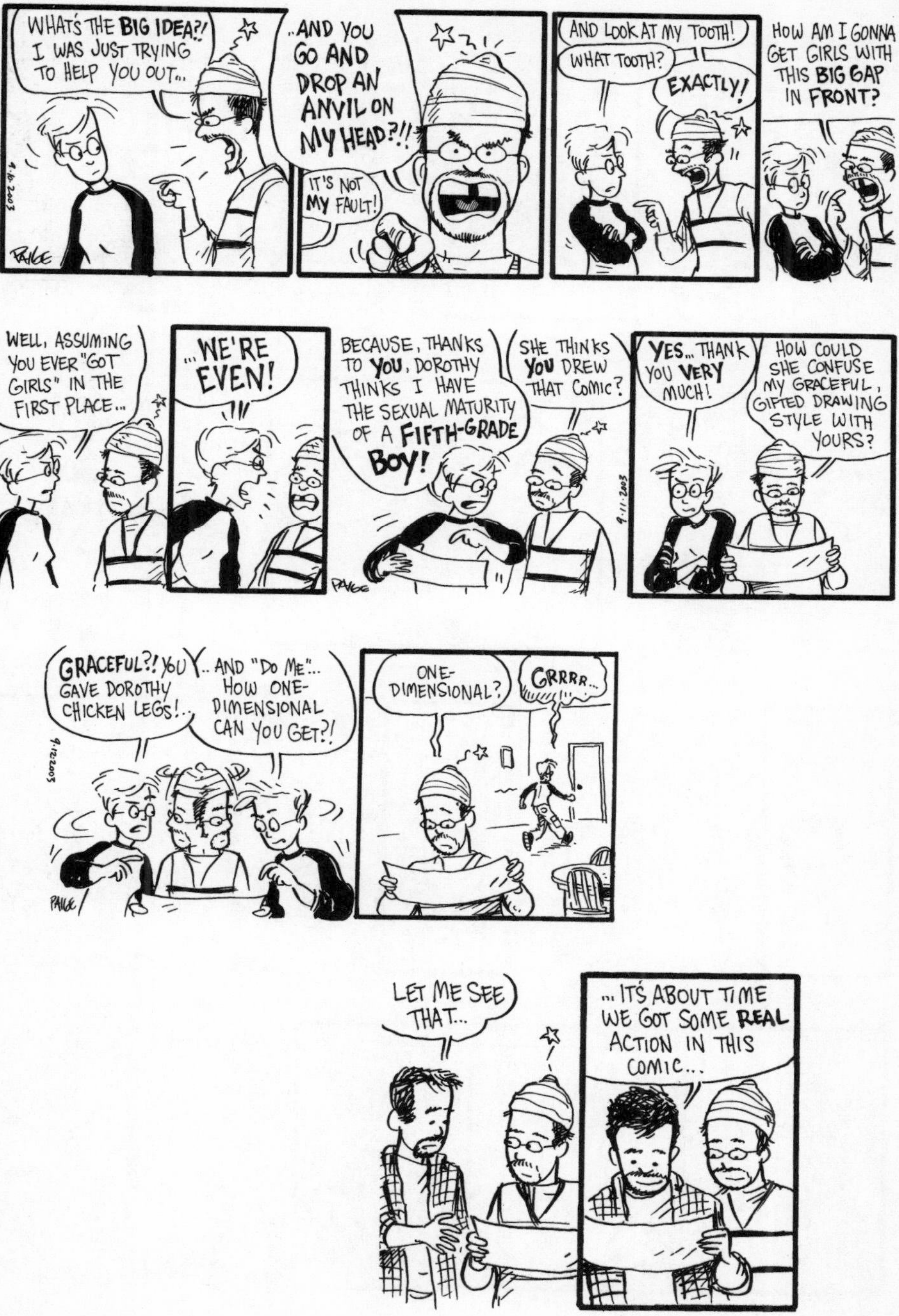
WHAT'S THE BIG IDEA?! I WAS JUST TRYING TO HELP YOU OUT...
9.10.2003
PAIGE
...AND YOU GO AND DROP AN ANVIL ON MY HEAD?!!
IT'S NOT MY FAULT!
AND LOOK AT MY TOOTH!
WHAT TOOTH?
EXACTLY!
HOW AM I GONNA GET GIRLS WITH THIS BIG GAP IN FRONT?
WELL, ASSUMING YOU EVER "GOT GIRLS" IN THE FIRST PLACE...
...WE'RE EVEN!
BECAUSE, THANKS TO YOU, DOROTHY THINKS I HAVE THE SEXUAL MATURITY OF A FIFTH-GRADE BOY!
SHE THINKS YOU DREW THAT COMIC?
PAIGE
9.11.2003
YES... THANK YOU VERY MUCH!
HOW COULD SHE CONFUSE MY GRACEFUL, GIFTED DRAWING STYLE WITH YOURS?
9.12.2003
GRACEFUL?! YOU GAVE DOROTHY CHICKEN LEGS!...
...AND "DO ME"... HOW ONE-DIMENSIONAL CAN YOU GET?!
PAIGE
ONE-DIMENSIONAL?
GRRRR...
LET ME SEE THAT...
...IT'S ABOUT TIME WE GOT SOME REAL ACTION IN THIS COMIC...

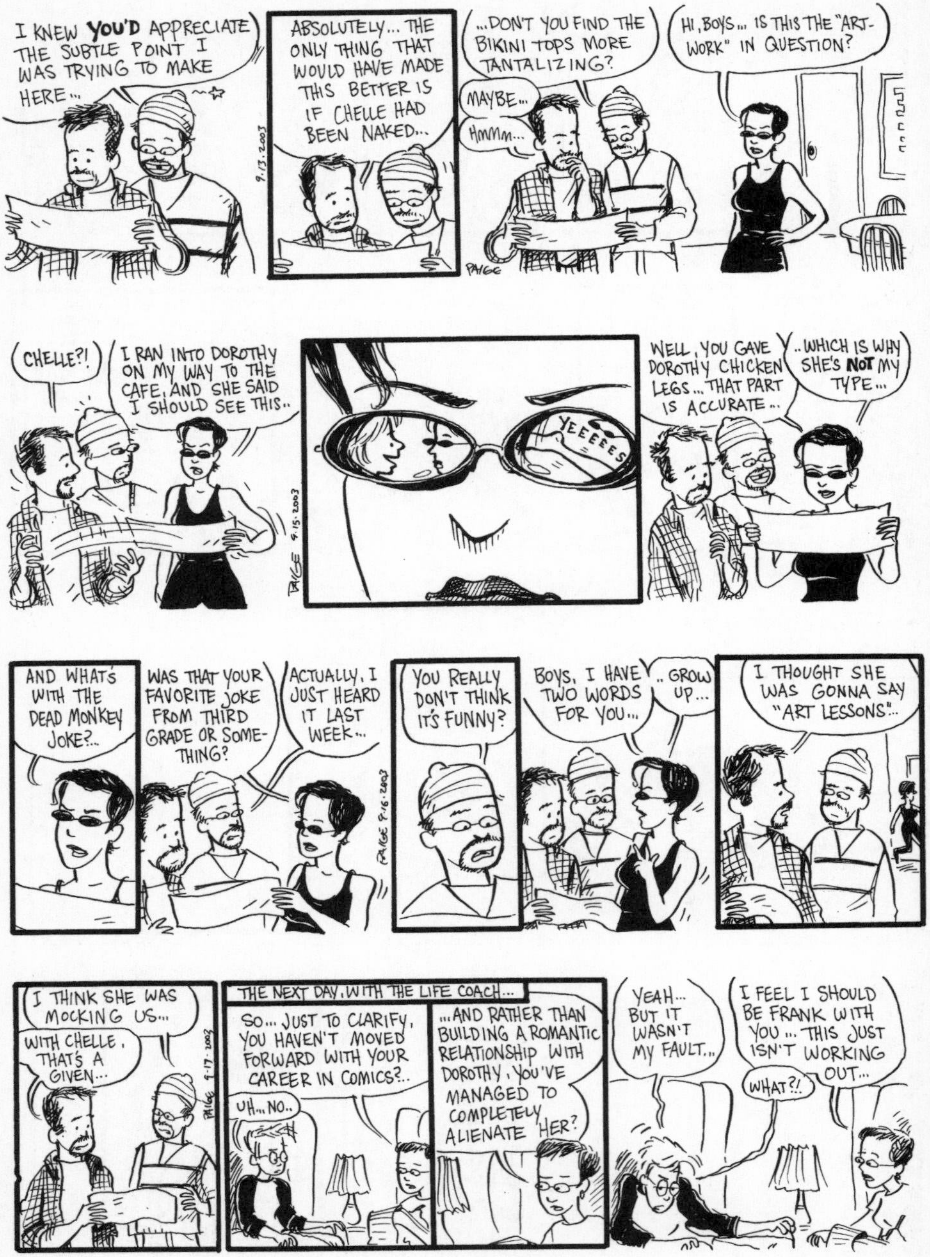
I KNEW YOU'D APPRECIATE THE SUBTLE POINT I WAS TRYING TO MAKE HERE...
9.13.2003
ABSOLUTELY... THE ONLY THING THAT WOULD HAVE MADE THIS BETTER IS IF CHELLE HAD BEEN NAKED...
...DON'T YOU FIND THE BIKINI TOPS MORE TANTALIZING?
MAYBE...
HMMM...
PAIGE
HI, BOYS... IS THIS THE "ART-WORK" IN QUESTION?
CHELLE?!
I RAN INTO DOROTHY ON MY WAY TO THE CAFE, AND SHE SAID I SHOULD SEE THIS..
PAIGE 9.15.2003
YEEEEEES
WELL, YOU GAVE DOROTHY CHICKEN LEGS... THAT PART IS ACCURATE...
..WHICH IS WHY SHE'S NOT MY TYPE...
AND WHAT'S WITH THE DEAD MONKEY JOKE?..
WAS THAT YOUR FAVORITE JOKE FROM THIRD GRADE OR SOME-THING?
ACTUALLY, I JUST HEARD IT LAST WEEK...
PAIGE 9.16.2003
YOU REALLY DON'T THINK IT'S FUNNY?
BOYS, I HAVE TWO WORDS FOR YOU...
.. GROW UP...
I THOUGHT SHE WAS GONNA SAY "ART LESSONS"...
I THINK SHE WAS MOCKING US...
WITH CHELLE, THAT'S A GIVEN...
PAIGE 9.17.2003
THE NEXT DAY, WITH THE LIFE COACH...
SO... JUST TO CLARIFY, YOU HAVEN'T MOVED FORWARD WITH YOUR CAREER IN COMICS?..
UH... NO..
...AND RATHER THAN BUILDING A ROMANTIC RELATIONSHIP WITH DOROTHY, YOU'VE MANAGED TO COMPLETELY ALIENATE HER?
YEAH... BUT IT WASN'T MY FAULT...
I FEEL I SHOULD BE FRANK WITH YOU... THIS JUST ISN'T WORKING OUT...
WHAT?!

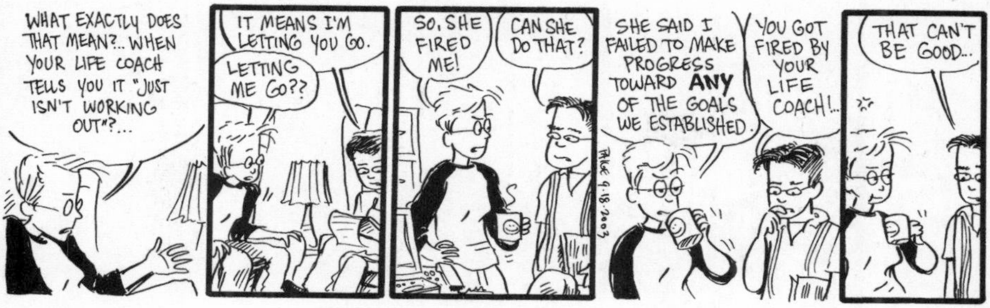
WHAT EXACTLY DOES THAT MEAN?.. WHEN YOUR LIFE COACH TELLS YOU IT "JUST ISN'T WORKING OUT"?...
IT MEANS I'M LETTING YOU GO.
LETTING ME GO??
SO, SHE FIRED ME!
CAN SHE DO THAT?
PAIGE 9.18.2003
SHE SAID I FAILED TO MAKE PROGRESS TOWARD ANY OF THE GOALS WE ESTABLISHED.
YOU GOT FIRED BY YOUR LIFE COACH!..
THAT CAN'T BE GOOD..

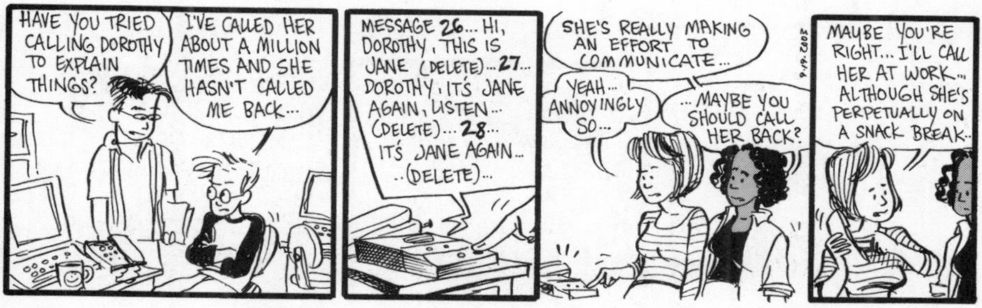
HAVE YOU TRIED CALLING DOROTHY TO EXPLAIN THINGS?
I'VE CALLED HER ABOUT A MILLION TIMES AND SHE HASN'T CALLED ME BACK...
MESSAGE 26... HI, DOROTHY, THIS IS JANE (DELETE)... 27... DOROTHY, IT'S JANE AGAIN, LISTEN... (DELETE)... 28... IT'S JANE AGAIN... ..(DELETE)...
SHE'S REALLY MAKING AN EFFORT TO COMMUNICATE...
YEAH... ANNOYINGLY SO...
... MAYBE YOU SHOULD CALL HER BACK?
9.19.2003
MAYBE YOU'RE RIGHT... I'LL CALL HER AT WORK... ALTHOUGH SHE'S PERPETUALLY ON A SNACK BREAK..

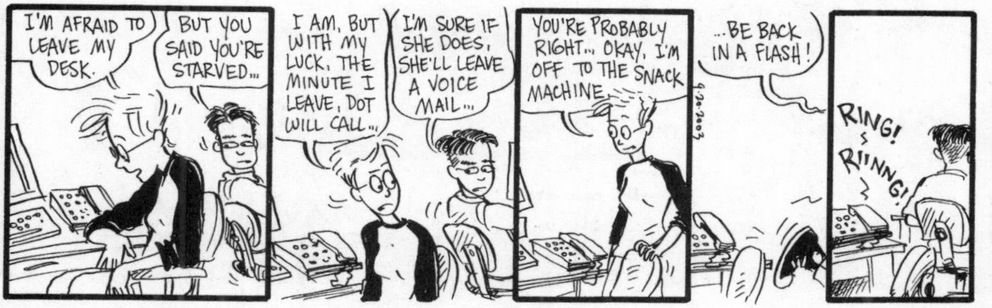
I'M AFRAID TO LEAVE MY DESK.
BUT YOU SAID YOU'RE STARVED...
I AM, BUT WITH MY LUCK, THE MINUTE I LEAVE, DOT WILL CALL...
I'M SURE IF SHE DOES, SHE'LL LEAVE A VOICE MAIL...
YOU'RE PROBABLY RIGHT... OKAY, I'M OFF TO THE SNACK MACHINE.
9.20.2003
...BE BACK IN A FLASH!
RING!
RIINNG!

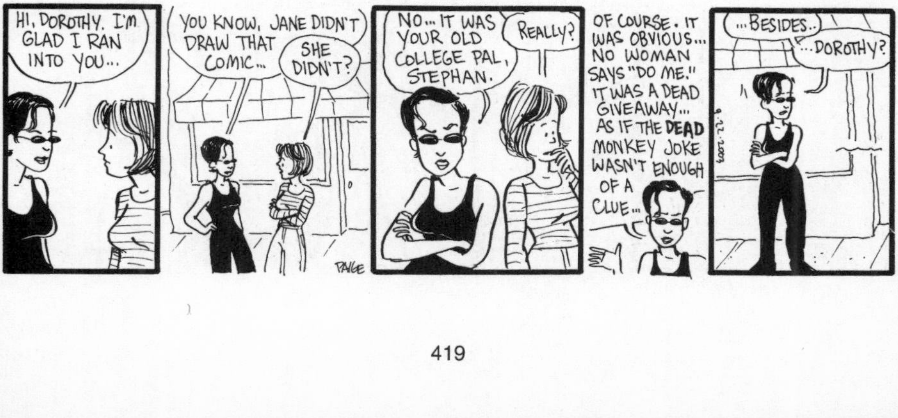
HI, DOROTHY. I'M GLAD I RAN INTO YOU...
YOU KNOW, JANE DIDN'T DRAW THAT COMIC...
SHE DIDN'T?
PAIGE
NO... IT WAS YOUR OLD COLLEGE PAL, STEPHAN.
REALLY?
OF COURSE. IT WAS OBVIOUS... NO WOMAN SAYS "DO ME." IT WAS A DEAD GIVEAWAY... AS IF THE DEAD MONKEY JOKE WASN'T ENOUGH OF A CLUE...
9.22.2003
...BESIDES..
...DOROTHY?

THE DAIL NE
9·23·2003

THE DAIL NEV
9·23·2003
JANE...
DOROTHY?
LISTEN, I'M SO SORRY THAT I JUMPED TO CONCLUSIONS... CHELLE EXPLAINED THE WHOLE THING..
CHELLE?!

YOU KNOW, SOMETIMES I JUST HAVE AN EMOTION, AND IT GETS REALLY BIG..
DOROTHY, I WOULD NEVER...
I KNOW..
HEY! NO FAIR! NOT IN FRONT OF THE SINGLE GUY! GET A ROOM!!
PAIGE

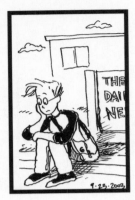

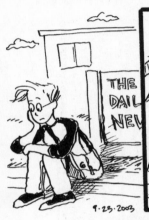

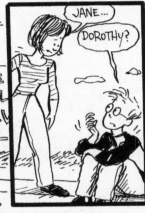

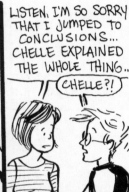

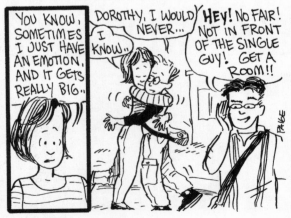

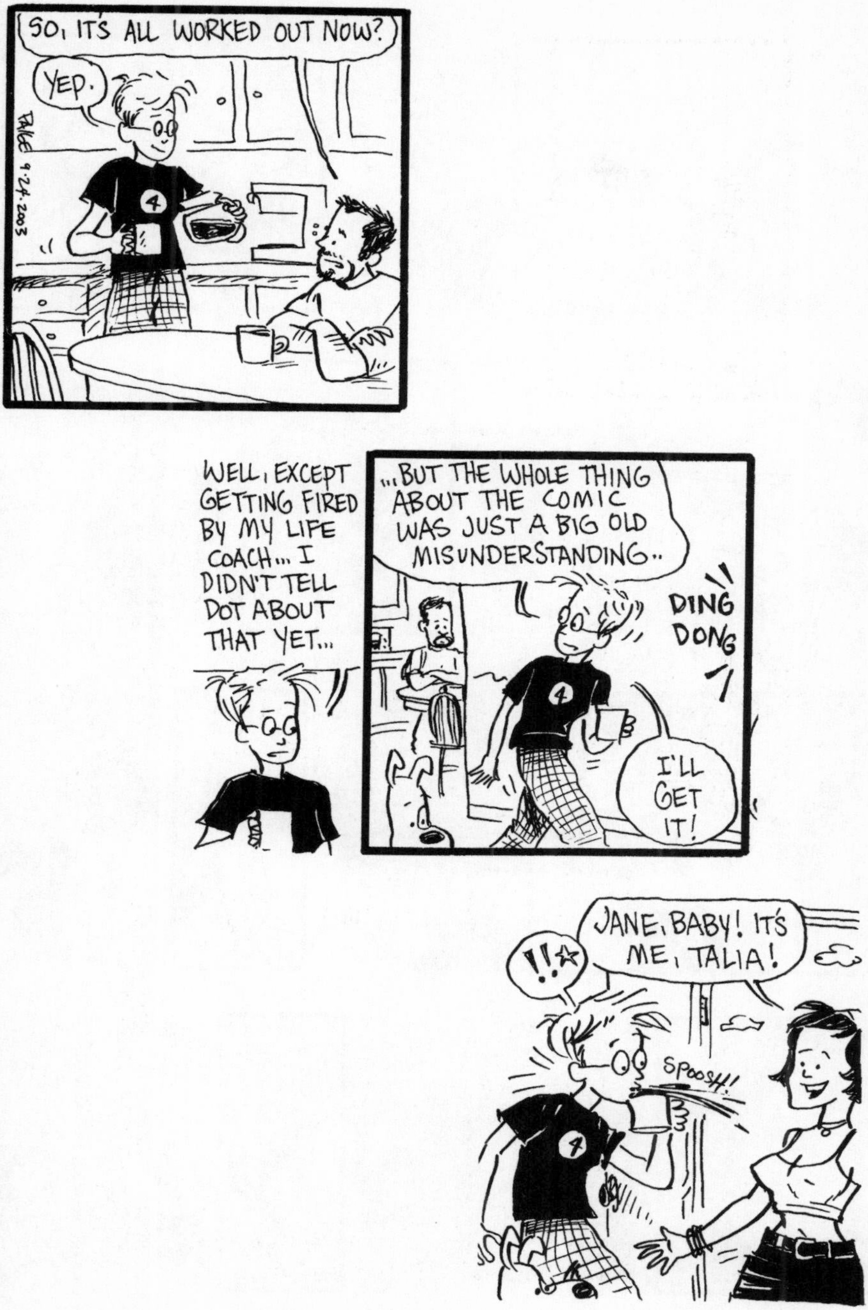
SO, IT'S ALL WORKED OUT NOW?
YEP.
9.24.2003
WELL, EXCEPT GETTING FIRED BY MY LIFE COACH... I DIDN'T TELL DOT ABOUT THAT YET...
...BUT THE WHOLE THING ABOUT THE COMIC WAS JUST A BIG OLD MISUNDERSTANDING..
DING DONG
I'LL GET IT!
!!☆
JANE, BABY! IT'S ME, TALIA!
SPOOSH!

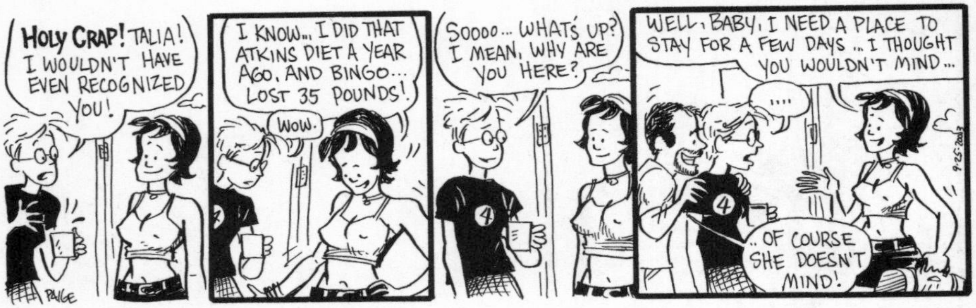
HOLY CRAP! TALIA! I WOULDN'T HAVE EVEN RECOGNIZED YOU!
PAIGE
I KNOW... I DID THAT ATKINS DIET A YEAR AGO, AND BINGO... LOST 35 POUNDS!
WOW.
SOOOO... WHAT'S UP? I MEAN, WHY ARE YOU HERE?
WELL, BABY, I NEED A PLACE TO STAY FOR A FEW DAYS... I THOUGHT YOU WOULDN'T MIND...
....
.. OF COURSE SHE DOESN'T MIND!
9-25-2003

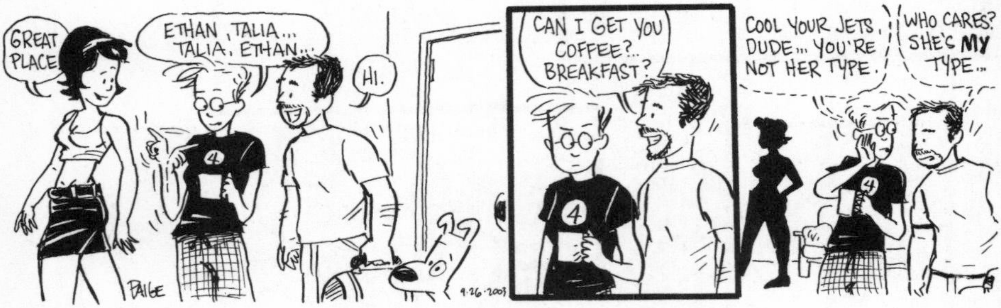
GREAT PLACE
ETHAN, TALIA... TALIA, ETHAN...
HI.
PAIGE
9-26-2003
CAN I GET YOU COFFEE?.. BREAKFAST?
COOL YOUR JETS, DUDE... YOU'RE NOT HER TYPE.
WHO CARES? SHE'S MY TYPE...

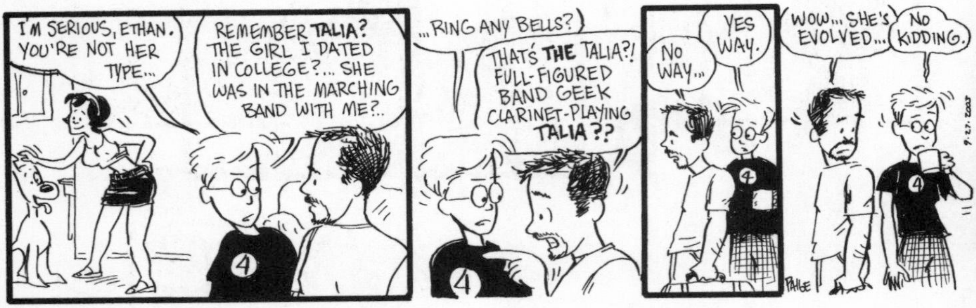
I'M SERIOUS, ETHAN. YOU'RE NOT HER TYPE...
REMEMBER TALIA? THE GIRL I DATED IN COLLEGE?... SHE WAS IN THE MARCHING BAND WITH ME?..
...RING ANY BELLS?
THAT'S THE TALIA?! FULL-FIGURED BAND GEEK CLARINET-PLAYING TALIA??
NO WAY...
YES WAY.
WOW... SHE'S EVOLVED...
NO KIDDING.
9-27-2003
PAIGE

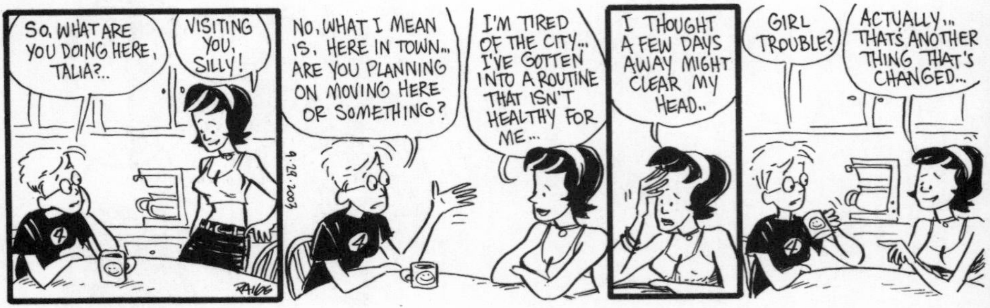
SO, WHAT ARE YOU DOING HERE, TALIA?..
VISITING YOU, SILLY!
PAIGE
9-28-2003
NO, WHAT I MEAN IS, HERE IN TOWN... ARE YOU PLANNING ON MOVING HERE OR SOMETHING?
I'M TIRED OF THE CITY... I'VE GOTTEN INTO A ROUTINE THAT ISN'T HEALTHY FOR ME...
I THOUGHT A FEW DAYS AWAY MIGHT CLEAR MY HEAD..
GIRL TROUBLE?
ACTUALLY... THAT'S ANOTHER THING THAT'S CHANGED...

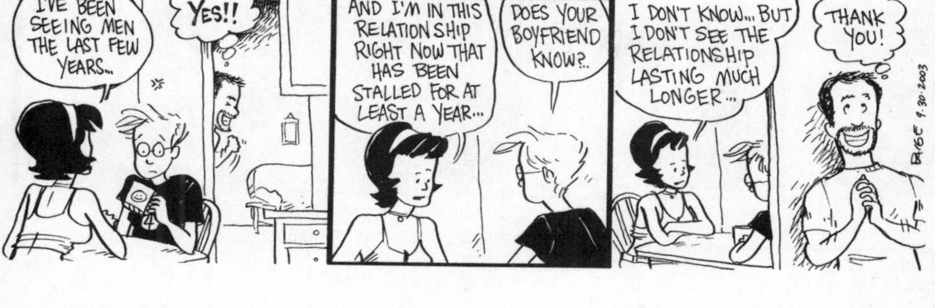
I'VE BEEN SEEING MEN THE LAST FEW YEARS...
YES!!
AND I'M IN THIS RELATIONSHIP RIGHT NOW THAT HAS BEEN STALLED FOR AT LEAST A YEAR...
DOES YOUR BOYFRIEND KNOW?..
I DON'T KNOW... BUT I DON'T SEE THE RELATIONSHIP LASTING MUCH LONGER...
THANK YOU!
PAIGE 9.30.2003

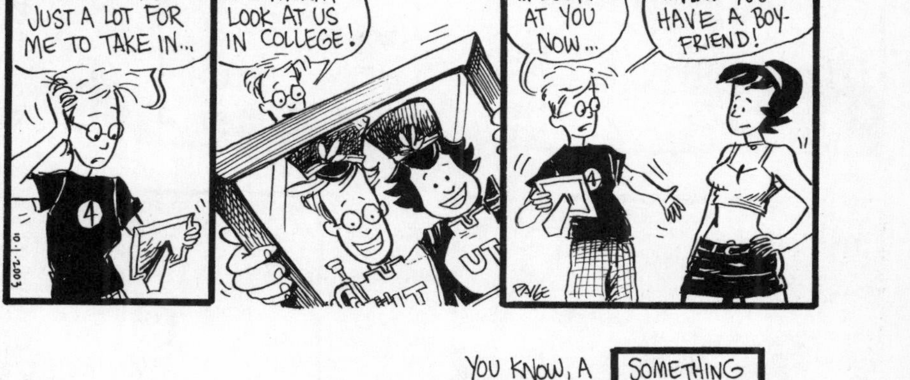
OK, THIS IS ALL JUST A LOT FOR ME TO TAKE IN...
10.1.2003
... I MEAN, LOOK AT US IN COLLEGE!
UT
... LOOK AT YOU NOW...
... AND YOU HAVE A BOY-FRIEND!
PAIGE

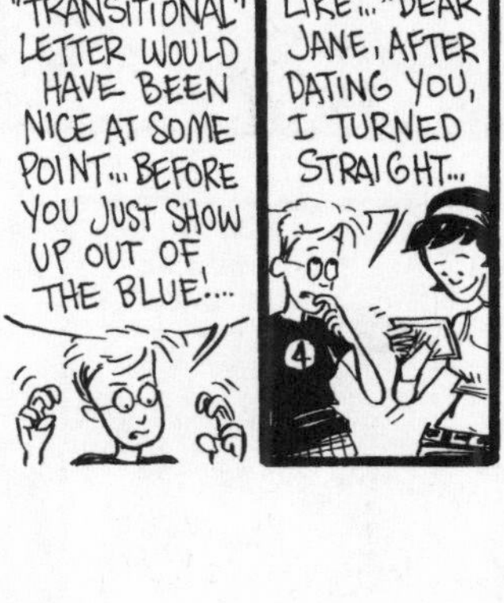
YOU KNOW, A "TRANSITIONAL" LETTER WOULD HAVE BEEN NICE AT SOME POINT... BEFORE YOU JUST SHOW UP OUT OF THE BLUE!...
SOMETHING LIKE... "DEAR JANE, AFTER DATING YOU, I TURNED STRAIGHT...

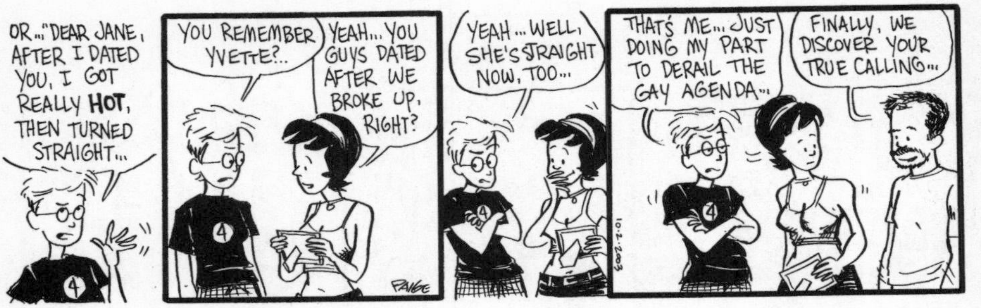
OR..."DEAR JANE, AFTER I DATED YOU, I GOT REALLY **HOT**, THEN TURNED STRAIGHT...
YOU REMEMBER YVETTE?..
YEAH... YOU GUYS DATED AFTER WE BROKE UP, RIGHT?
PAIGE
YEAH ... WELL, SHE'S STRAIGHT NOW, TOO...
10.2.2003
THAT'S ME... JUST DOING MY PART TO DERAIL THE GAY AGENDA...
FINALLY, WE DISCOVER YOUR TRUE CALLING...

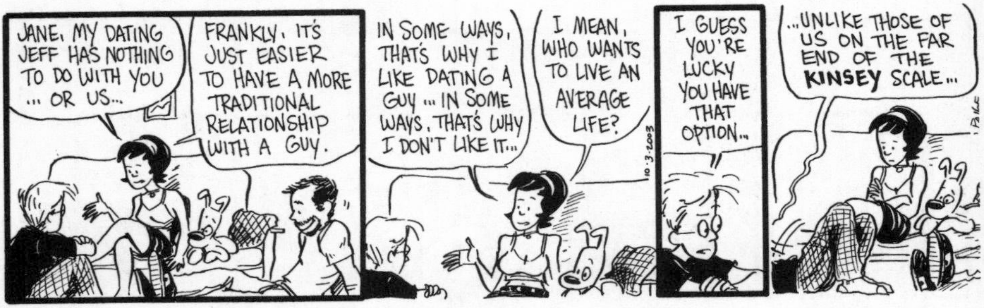
JANE, MY DATING JEFF HAS NOTHING TO DO WITH YOU ... OR US...
FRANKLY, IT'S JUST EASIER TO HAVE A MORE TRADITIONAL RELATIONSHIP WITH A GUY.
IN SOME WAYS, THAT'S WHY I LIKE DATING A GUY ... IN SOME WAYS, THAT'S WHY I DON'T LIKE IT...
I MEAN, WHO WANTS TO LIVE AN AVERAGE LIFE?
10.3.2003
I GUESS YOU'RE LUCKY YOU HAVE THAT OPTION...
...UNLIKE THOSE OF US ON THE FAR END OF THE **KINSEY** SCALE...
PAIGE

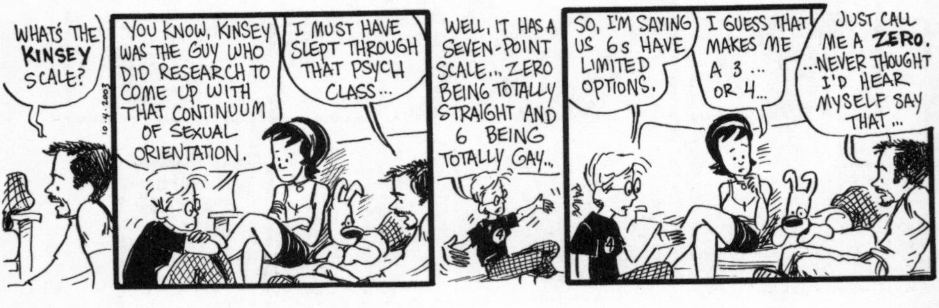
WHAT'S THE **KINSEY** SCALE?
10.4.2003
YOU KNOW, KINSEY WAS THE GUY WHO DID RESEARCH TO COME UP WITH THAT CONTINUUM OF SEXUAL ORIENTATION.
I MUST HAVE SLEPT THROUGH THAT PSYCH CLASS...
WELL, IT HAS A SEVEN-POINT SCALE... ZERO BEING TOTALLY STRAIGHT AND 6 BEING TOTALLY GAY...
PAIGE
SO, I'M SAYING US 6s HAVE LIMITED OPTIONS.
I GUESS THAT MAKES ME A 3 ... OR 4...
JUST CALL ME A **ZERO.** ...NEVER THOUGHT I'D HEAR MYSELF SAY THAT...

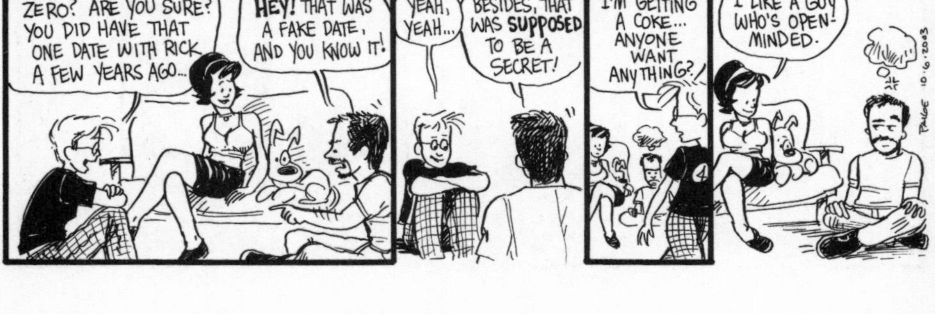
ZERO? ARE YOU SURE? YOU DID HAVE THAT ONE DATE WITH RICK A FEW YEARS AGO...
HEY! THAT WAS A FAKE DATE, AND YOU KNOW IT!
YEAH, YEAH...
BESIDES, THAT WAS **SUPPOSED** TO BE A SECRET!
I'M GETTING A COKE... ANYONE WANT ANYTHING?
I LIKE A GUY WHO'S OPEN-MINDED.
10.6.2003
PAIGE

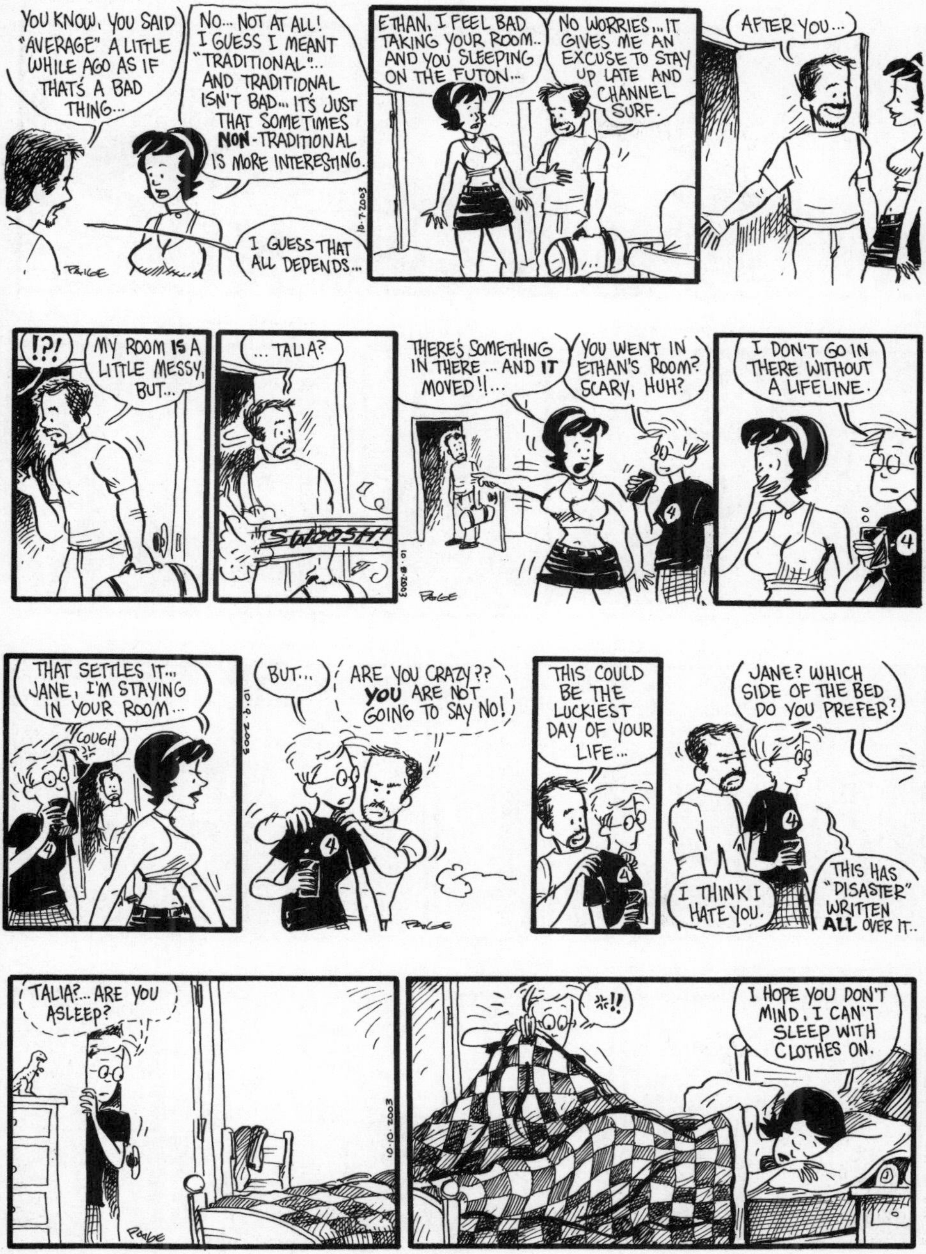

YOU KNOW, YOU SAID "AVERAGE" A LITTLE WHILE AGO AS IF THAT'S A BAD THING...
NO... NOT AT ALL! I GUESS I MEANT "TRADITIONAL"... AND TRADITIONAL ISN'T BAD... IT'S JUST THAT SOMETIMES NON-TRADITIONAL IS MORE INTERESTING.
I GUESS THAT ALL DEPENDS...
ETHAN, I FEEL BAD TAKING YOUR ROOM.. AND YOU SLEEPING ON THE FUTON...
NO WORRIES... IT GIVES ME AN EXCUSE TO STAY UP LATE AND CHANNEL SURF.
AFTER YOU...
!?!
MY ROOM IS A LITTLE MESSY, BUT...
SWOOSH!!
... TALIA?
THERE'S SOMETHING IN THERE ... AND IT MOVED!!...
YOU WENT IN ETHAN'S ROOM? SCARY, HUH?
I DON'T GO IN THERE WITHOUT A LIFELINE.
THAT SETTLES IT... JANE, I'M STAYING IN YOUR ROOM...
COUGH
BUT...
ARE YOU CRAZY?? YOU ARE NOT GOING TO SAY NO!
THIS COULD BE THE LUCKIEST DAY OF YOUR LIFE...
JANE? WHICH SIDE OF THE BED DO YOU PREFER?
I THINK I HATE YOU.
THIS HAS "DISASTER" WRITTEN ALL OVER IT..
TALIA?... ARE YOU ASLEEP?
*!!
I HOPE YOU DON'T MIND, I CAN'T SLEEP WITH CLOTHES ON.

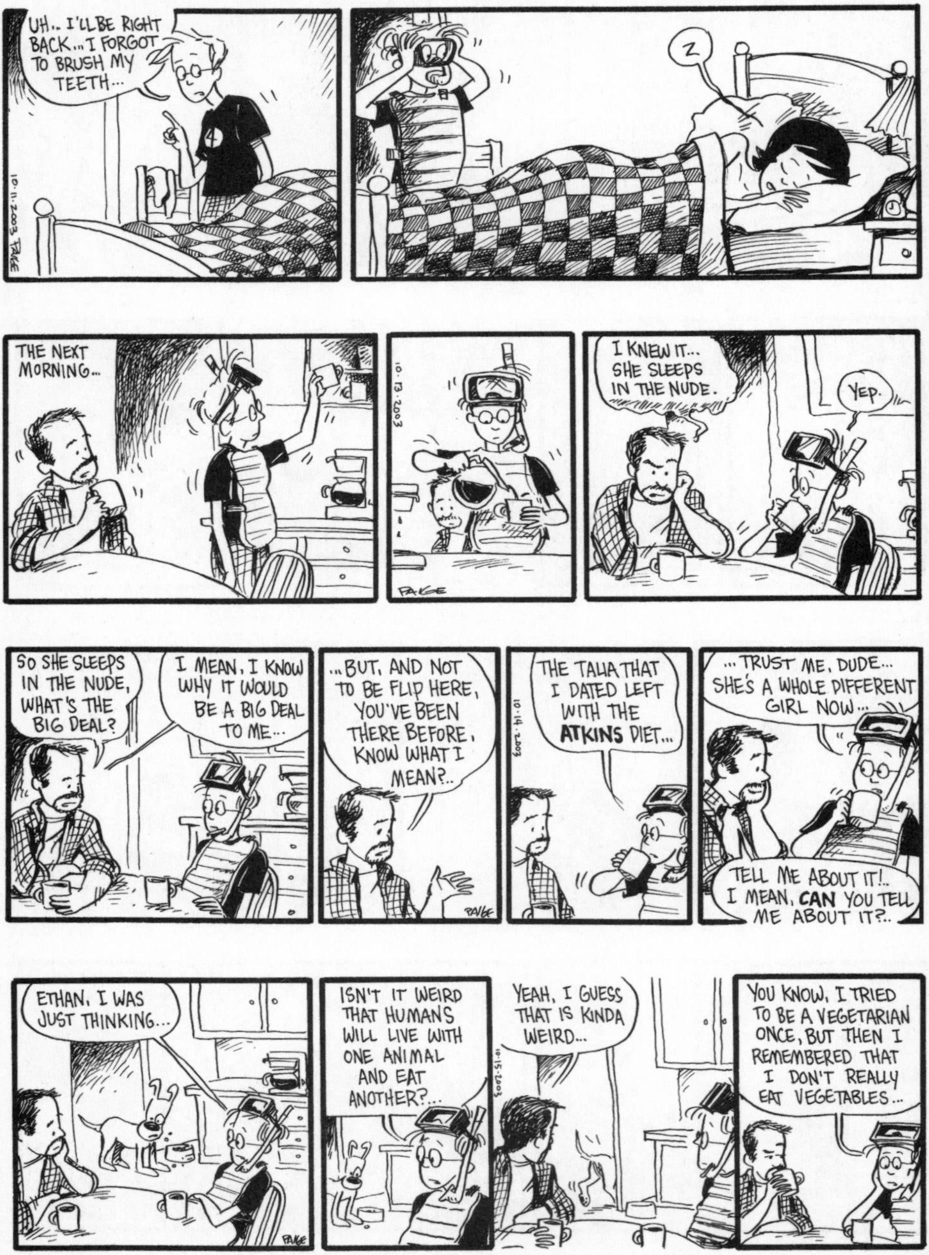
UH.. I'LL BE RIGHT BACK... I FORGOT TO BRUSH MY TEETH...
10.11.2003
PAIGE
Z
THE NEXT MORNING...
10.13.2003
PAIGE
I KNEW IT... SHE SLEEPS IN THE NUDE.
YEP.
SO SHE SLEEPS IN THE NUDE, WHAT'S THE BIG DEAL?
I MEAN, I KNOW WHY IT WOULD BE A BIG DEAL TO ME...
...BUT, AND NOT TO BE FLIP HERE, YOU'VE BEEN THERE BEFORE, KNOW WHAT I MEAN?..
PAIGE
10.14.2003
THE TALIA THAT I DATED LEFT WITH THE **ATKINS** DIET...
...TRUST ME, DUDE... SHE'S A WHOLE DIFFERENT GIRL NOW...
TELL ME ABOUT IT!.. I MEAN, **CAN** YOU TELL ME ABOUT IT?..
ETHAN, I WAS JUST THINKING...
PAIGE
ISN'T IT WEIRD THAT HUMANS WILL LIVE WITH ONE ANIMAL AND EAT ANOTHER?...
10.15.2003
YEAH, I GUESS THAT IS KINDA WEIRD...
YOU KNOW, I TRIED TO BE A VEGETARIAN ONCE, BUT THEN I REMEMBERED THAT I DON'T REALLY EAT VEGETABLES...

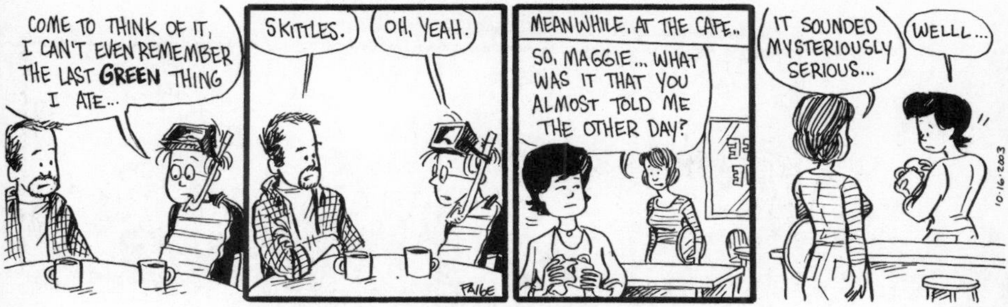
COME TO THINK OF IT, I CAN'T EVEN REMEMBER THE LAST **GREEN** THING I ATE...
SKITTLES.
OH, YEAH.
PAIGE
MEANWHILE, AT THE CAFE..
SO, MAGGIE... WHAT WAS IT THAT YOU ALMOST TOLD ME THE OTHER DAY?
IT SOUNDED MYSTERIOUSLY SERIOUS...
WELLL...
10·16·2003

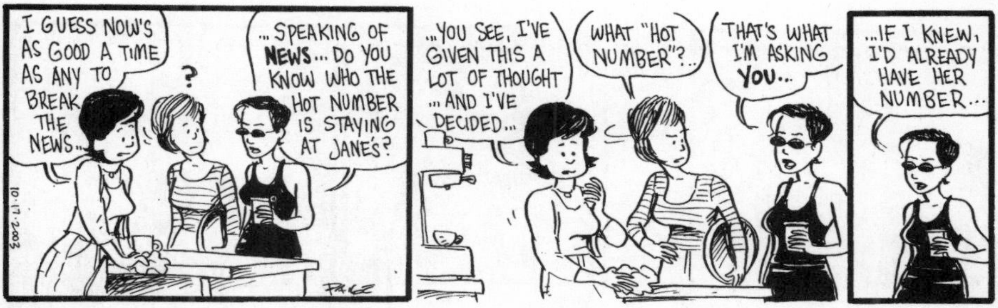
I GUESS NOW'S AS GOOD A TIME AS ANY TO BREAK THE NEWS...
?
... SPEAKING OF **NEWS**... DO YOU KNOW WHO THE HOT NUMBER IS STAYING AT JANE'S?
10·17·2003
PAIGE
...YOU SEE, I'VE GIVEN THIS A LOT OF THOUGHT ...AND I'VE DECIDED...
WHAT "HOT NUMBER"?..
THAT'S WHAT I'M ASKING **YOU**...
...IF I KNEW, I'D ALREADY HAVE HER NUMBER...

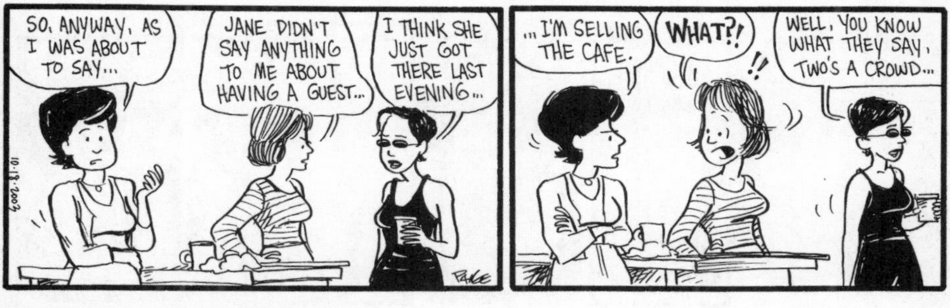
SO, ANYWAY, AS I WAS ABOUT TO SAY...
JANE DIDN'T SAY ANYTHING TO ME ABOUT HAVING A GUEST...
I THINK SHE JUST GOT THERE LAST EVENING...
10·18·2003
PAIGE
... I'M SELLING THE CAFE.
WHAT?!
!!
WELL, YOU KNOW WHAT THEY SAY, TWO'S A CROWD...

MEANWHILE, AT JANE AND ETHAN'S...

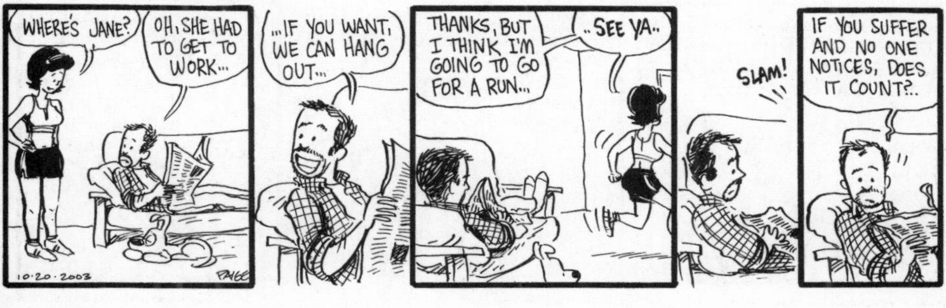
WHERE'S JANE?
OH, SHE HAD TO GET TO WORK...
10·20·2003
PAIGE
...IF YOU WANT, WE CAN HANG OUT...
THANKS, BUT I THINK I'M GOING TO GO FOR A RUN...
.. SEE YA..
SLAM!
IF YOU SUFFER AND NO ONE NOTICES, DOES IT COUNT?..

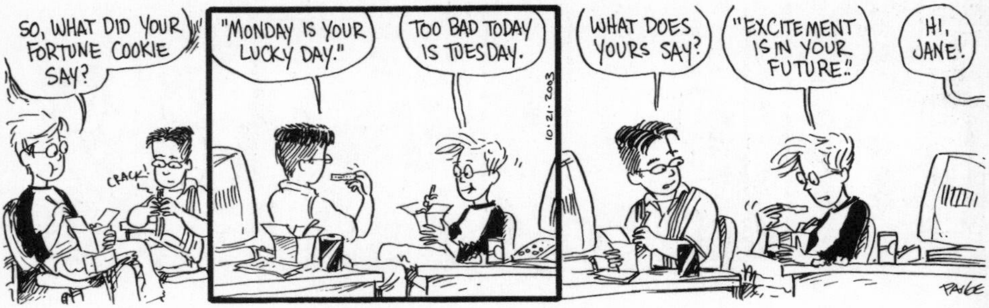
SO, WHAT DID YOUR FORTUNE COOKIE SAY?
CRACK!
"MONDAY IS YOUR LUCKY DAY."
TOO BAD TODAY IS TUESDAY.
10·21·2003
WHAT DOES YOURS SAY?
"EXCITEMENT IS IN YOUR FUTURE."
HI, JANE!
PAIGE

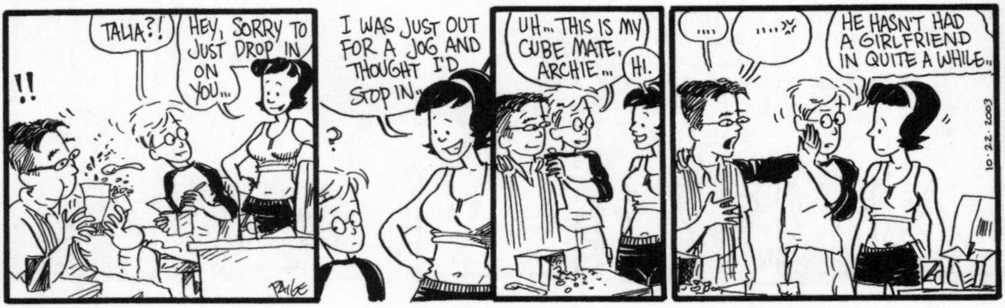
TALIA?!
HEY, SORRY TO JUST DROP IN ON YOU...
!!
I WAS JUST OUT FOR A JOG AND THOUGHT I'D STOP IN...
?
UH... THIS IS MY CUBE MATE, ARCHIE...
HI.
....
....
HE HASN'T HAD A GIRLFRIEND IN QUITE A WHILE...
10·22·2003
PAIGE

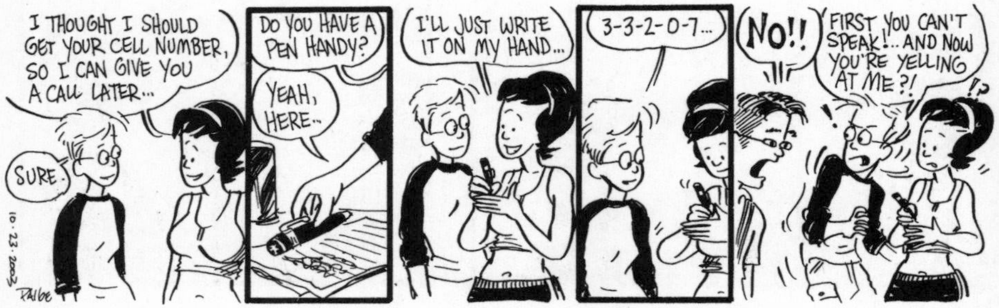
I THOUGHT I SHOULD GET YOUR CELL NUMBER, SO I CAN GIVE YOU A CALL LATER...
SURE.
10·23·2003
DO YOU HAVE A PEN HANDY?
YEAH, HERE.
I'LL JUST WRITE IT ON MY HAND...
3-3-2-0-7...
NO!!
FIRST YOU CAN'T SPEAK!... AND NOW YOU'RE YELLING AT ME?!
PAIGE

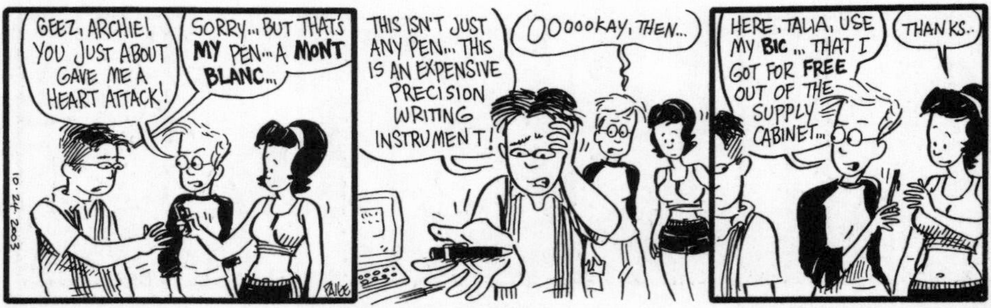
GEEZ, ARCHIE! YOU JUST ABOUT GAVE ME A HEART ATTACK!
SORRY... BUT THAT'S **MY** PEN... A **MONT BLANC**...
10·24·2003
THIS ISN'T JUST ANY PEN... THIS IS AN EXPENSIVE PRECISION WRITING INSTRUMENT!
OOoookay, THEN...
HERE, TALIA, USE MY **BIC** ... THAT I GOT FOR **FREE** OUT OF THE SUPPLY CABINET...
THANKS..
PAIGE

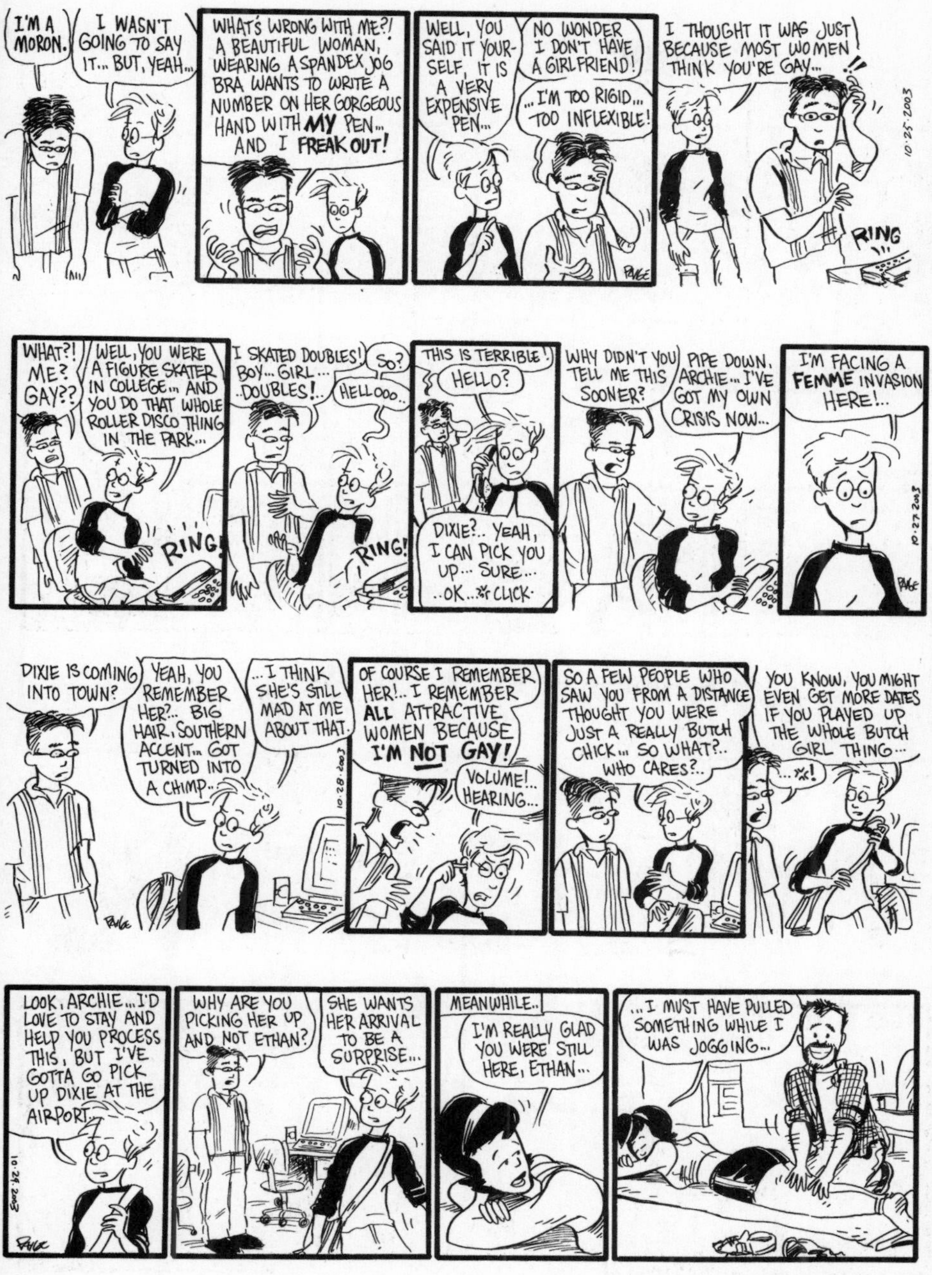
I'M A MORON.
I WASN'T GOING TO SAY IT... BUT, YEAH...
WHAT'S WRONG WITH ME?! A BEAUTIFUL WOMAN, WEARING A SPANDEX JOG BRA WANTS TO WRITE A NUMBER ON HER GORGEOUS HAND WITH MY PEN... AND I FREAK OUT!
WELL, YOU SAID IT YOURSELF, IT IS A VERY EXPENSIVE PEN...
NO WONDER I DON'T HAVE A GIRLFRIEND!
...I'M TOO RIGID... TOO INFLEXIBLE!
I THOUGHT IT WAS JUST BECAUSE MOST WOMEN THINK YOU'RE GAY...
RING
PAIGE
10.25.2003
WHAT?! ME? GAY??
WELL, YOU WERE A FIGURE SKATER IN COLLEGE... AND YOU DO THAT WHOLE ROLLER DISCO THING IN THE PARK...
RING!
I SKATED DOUBLES! BOY... GIRL... ..DOUBLES!..
SO?
HELLOOO...
RING!
THIS IS TERRIBLE!
HELLO?
DIXIE?.. YEAH, I CAN PICK YOU UP... SURE... ..OK... CLICK
WHY DIDN'T YOU TELL ME THIS SOONER?
PIPE DOWN, ARCHIE... I'VE GOT MY OWN CRISIS NOW...
I'M FACING A FEMME INVASION HERE!..
10.27.2003
PAIGE
DIXIE IS COMING INTO TOWN?
YEAH, YOU REMEMBER HER?.. BIG HAIR, SOUTHERN ACCENT... GOT TURNED INTO A CHIMP...
...I THINK SHE'S STILL MAD AT ME ABOUT THAT.
10.28.2003
PAIGE
OF COURSE I REMEMBER HER!.. I REMEMBER ALL ATTRACTIVE WOMEN BECAUSE I'M NOT GAY!
VOLUME!... HEARING...
SO A FEW PEOPLE WHO SAW YOU FROM A DISTANCE THOUGHT YOU WERE JUST A REALLY BUTCH CHICK... SO WHAT?.. WHO CARES?..
YOU KNOW, YOU MIGHT EVEN GET MORE DATES IF YOU PLAYED UP THE WHOLE BUTCH GIRL THING...
...✲!
LOOK, ARCHIE... I'D LOVE TO STAY AND HELP YOU PROCESS THIS, BUT I'VE GOTTA GO PICK UP DIXIE AT THE AIRPORT...
10.29.2003
PAIGE
WHY ARE YOU PICKING HER UP AND NOT ETHAN?
SHE WANTS HER ARRIVAL TO BE A SURPRISE...
MEANWHILE...
I'M REALLY GLAD YOU WERE STILL HERE, ETHAN...
...I MUST HAVE PULLED SOMETHING WHILE I WAS JOGGING...

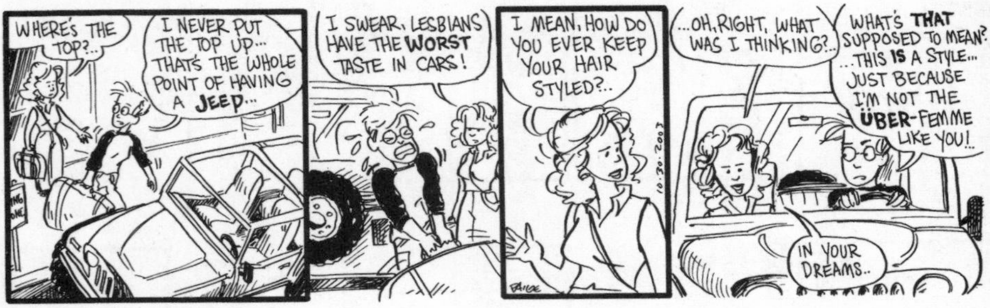
WHERE'S THE TOP?...
I NEVER PUT THE TOP UP... THAT'S THE WHOLE POINT OF HAVING A **JEEP**...
I SWEAR, LESBIANS HAVE THE **WORST** TASTE IN CARS!
I MEAN, HOW DO YOU EVER KEEP YOUR HAIR STYLED?..
10.30.2003
PAIGE
...OH, RIGHT, WHAT WAS I THINKING?..
WHAT'S **THAT** SUPPOSED TO MEAN? ...THIS **IS** A STYLE... JUST BECAUSE I'M NOT THE **ÜBER**-FEMME LIKE YOU!..
IN YOUR DREAMS..

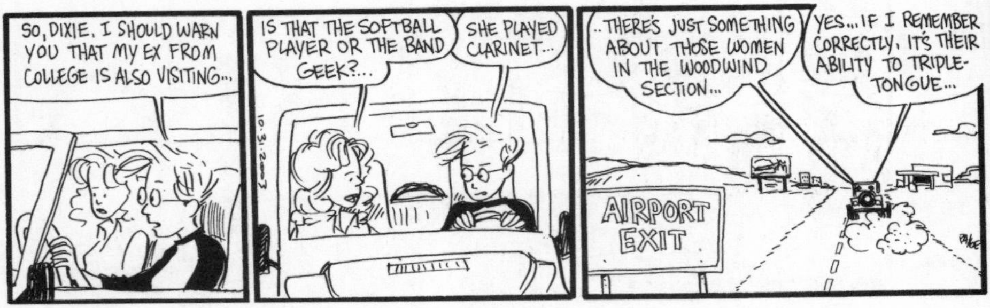
SO, DIXIE, I SHOULD WARN YOU THAT MY EX FROM COLLEGE IS ALSO VISITING...
IS THAT THE SOFTBALL PLAYER OR THE BAND GEEK?...
SHE PLAYED CLARINET...
10.31.2003
..THERE'S JUST SOMETHING ABOUT THOSE WOMEN IN THE WOODWIND SECTION...
YES... IF I REMEMBER CORRECTLY, IT'S THEIR ABILITY TO TRIPLE-TONGUE...
AIRPORT EXIT
PAIGE

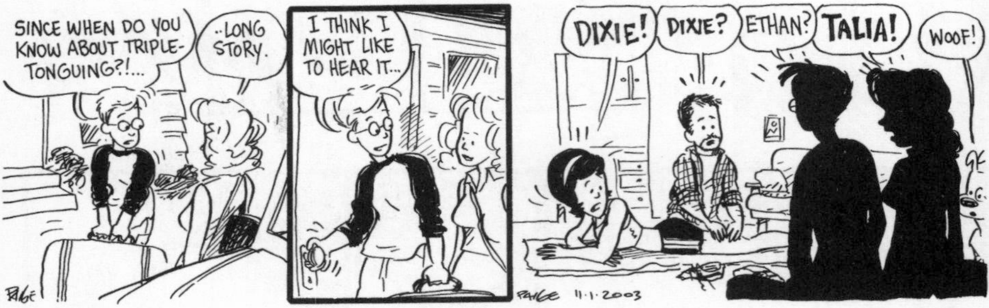
SINCE WHEN DO YOU KNOW ABOUT TRIPLE-TONGUING?!...
..LONG STORY.
PAIGE
I THINK I MIGHT LIKE TO HEAR IT...
DIXIE!
DIXIE?
ETHAN?
TALIA!
WOOF!
PAIGE 11.1.2003

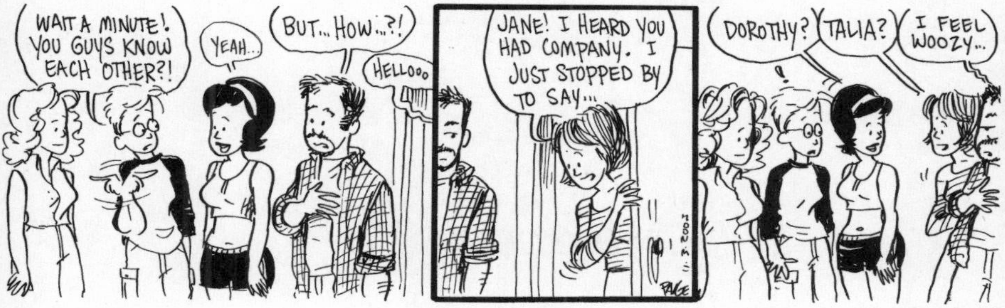
WAIT A MINUTE! YOU GUYS KNOW EACH OTHER?!
YEAH...
BUT... HOW...?!
HELLOOO
JANE! I HEARD YOU HAD COMPANY. I JUST STOPPED BY TO SAY...
DOROTHY?
TALIA?
I FEEL WOOZY...

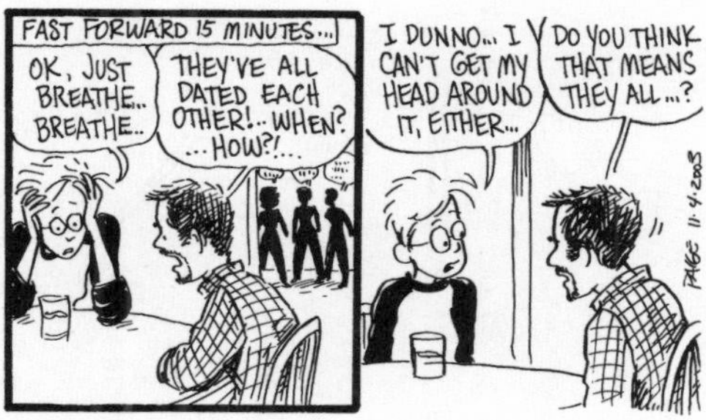
FAST FORWARD 15 MINUTES...
OK, JUST BREATHE... BREATHE...
THEY'VE ALL DATED EACH OTHER!.. WHEN? ... HOW?!...
I DUNNO... I CAN'T GET MY HEAD AROUND IT, EITHER...
DO YOU THINK THAT MEANS THEY ALL...?

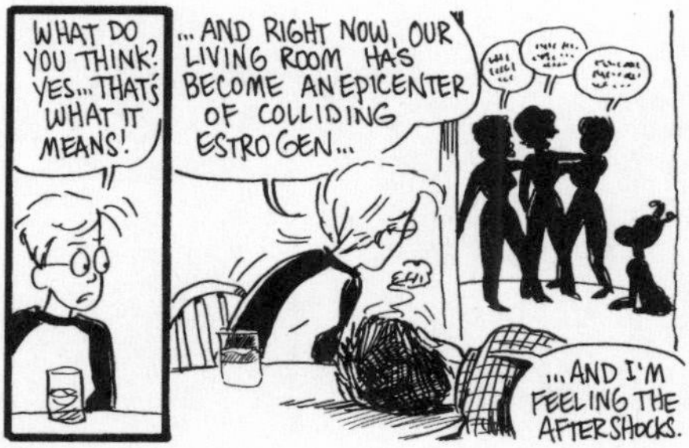
WHAT DO YOU THINK? YES... THAT'S WHAT IT MEANS!
... AND RIGHT NOW, OUR LIVING ROOM HAS BECOME AN EPICENTER OF COLLIDING ESTROGEN...
... AND I'M FEELING THE AFTERSHOCKS.

Chapter 15

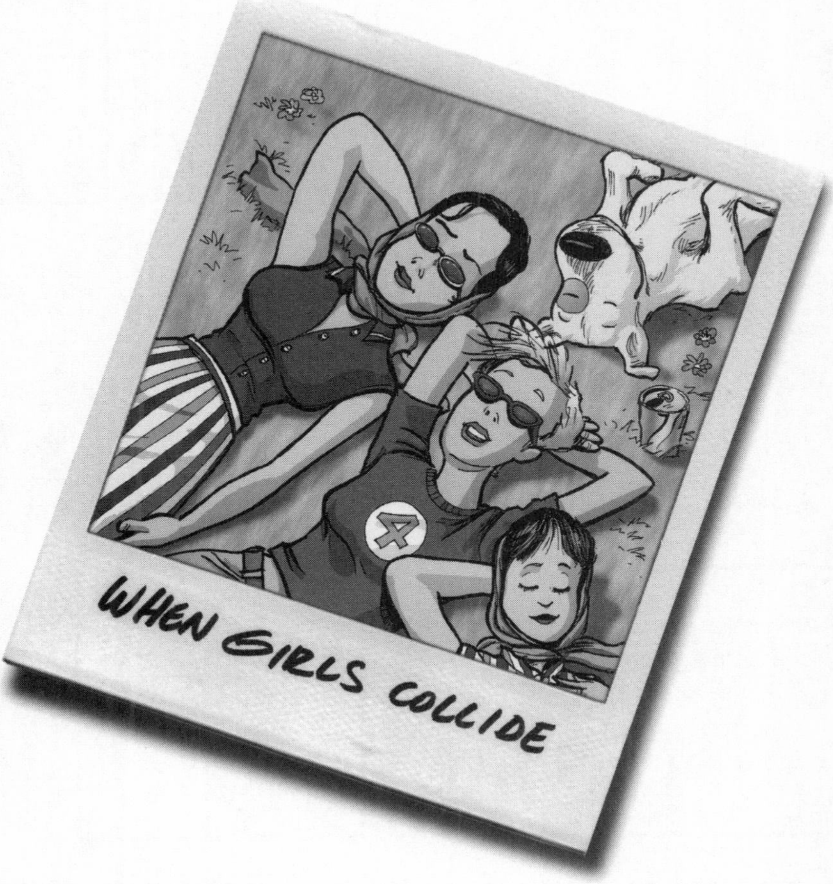
WHEN GIRLS COLLIDE

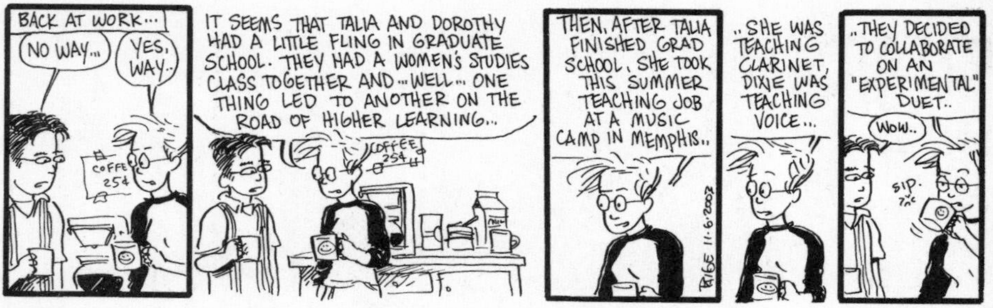
BACK AT WORK...
NO WAY...
YES, WAY..
COFFEE 25¢
IT SEEMS THAT TALIA AND DOROTHY HAD A LITTLE FLING IN GRADUATE SCHOOL. THEY HAD A WOMEN'S STUDIES CLASS TOGETHER AND... WELL... ONE THING LED TO ANOTHER ON THE ROAD OF HIGHER LEARNING...
COFFEE 25¢
THEN, AFTER TALIA FINISHED GRAD SCHOOL, SHE TOOK THIS SUMMER TEACHING JOB AT A MUSIC CAMP IN MEMPHIS..
PAIGE 11-6-2003
..SHE WAS TEACHING CLARINET, DIXIE WAS TEACHING VOICE...
..THEY DECIDED TO COLLABORATE ON AN "EXPERIMENTAL" DUET..
WOW..
SIP.

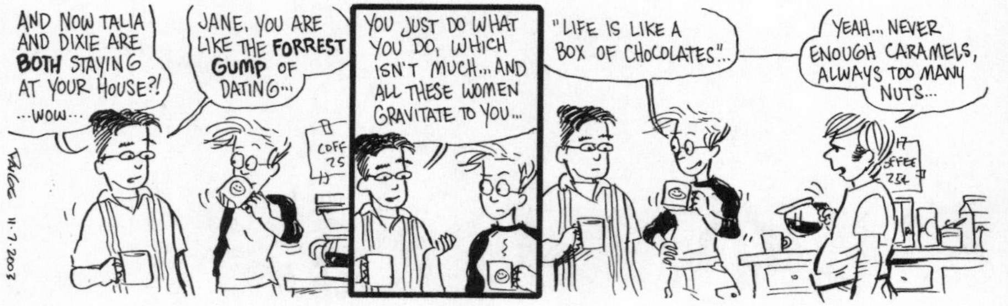
AND NOW TALIA AND DIXIE ARE **BOTH** STAYING AT YOUR HOUSE?!
...WOW...
PAIGE 11-7-2003
JANE, YOU ARE LIKE THE **FORREST GUMP** OF DATING...
YOU JUST DO WHAT YOU DO, WHICH ISN'T MUCH... AND ALL THESE WOMEN GRAVITATE TO YOU...
"LIFE IS LIKE A BOX OF CHOCOLATES"...
YEAH... NEVER ENOUGH CARAMELS, ALWAYS TOO MANY NUTS...
COFFEE 25¢

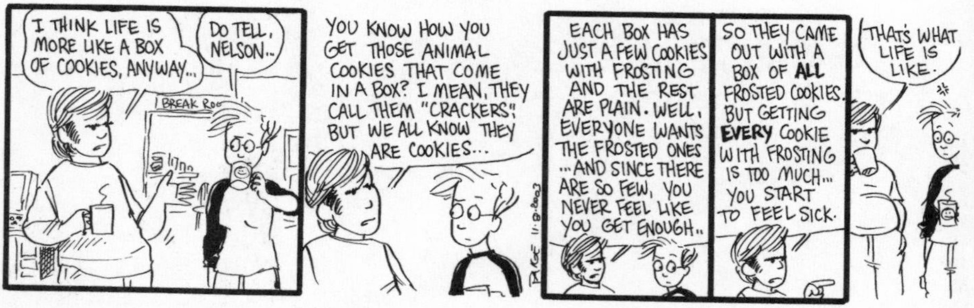
I THINK LIFE IS MORE LIKE A BOX OF COOKIES, ANYWAY...
DO TELL, NELSON...
BREAK ROO
YOU KNOW HOW YOU GET THOSE ANIMAL COOKIES THAT COME IN A BOX? I MEAN, THEY CALL THEM "CRACKERS," BUT WE ALL KNOW THEY ARE COOKIES...
PAIGE 11-8-2003
EACH BOX HAS JUST A FEW COOKIES WITH FROSTING AND THE REST ARE PLAIN. WELL, EVERYONE WANTS THE FROSTED ONES ...AND SINCE THERE ARE SO FEW, YOU NEVER FEEL LIKE YOU GET ENOUGH..
SO THEY CAME OUT WITH A BOX OF **ALL** FROSTED COOKIES. BUT GETTING **EVERY** COOKIE WITH FROSTING IS TOO MUCH... YOU START TO FEEL SICK.
THAT'S WHAT LIFE IS LIKE.

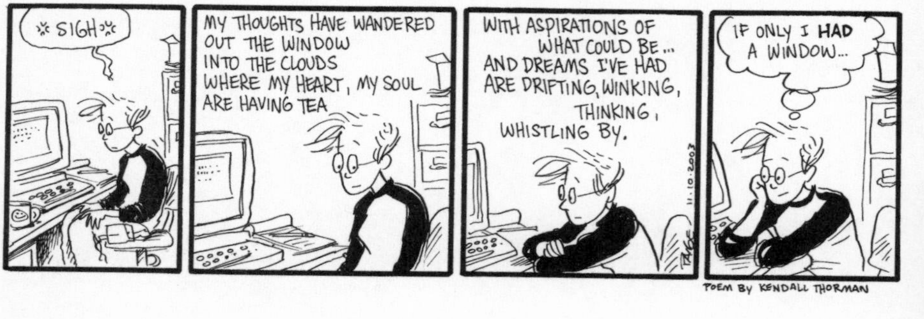
SIGH
MY THOUGHTS HAVE WANDERED OUT THE WINDOW INTO THE CLOUDS WHERE MY HEART, MY SOUL ARE HAVING TEA
WITH ASPIRATIONS OF WHAT COULD BE... AND DREAMS I'VE HAD ARE DRIFTING, WINKING, THINKING, WHISTLING BY.
PAIGE 11-10-2003
IF ONLY I **HAD** A WINDOW...

POEM BY KENDALL THORMAN

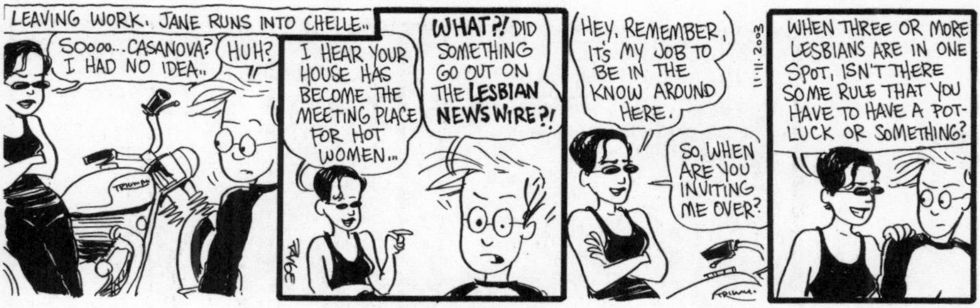
LEAVING WORK, JANE RUNS INTO CHELLE..
SOOOO... CASANOVA? I HAD NO IDEA..
HUH?
I HEAR YOUR HOUSE HAS BECOME THE MEETING PLACE FOR HOT WOMEN...
WHAT?! DID SOMETHING GO OUT ON THE LESBIAN NEWSWIRE?!
HEY, REMEMBER, IT'S MY JOB TO BE IN THE KNOW AROUND HERE.
SO, WHEN ARE YOU INVITING ME OVER?
11.11.2003
WHEN THREE OR MORE LESBIANS ARE IN ONE SPOT, ISN'T THERE SOME RULE THAT YOU HAVE TO HAVE A POT-LUCK OR SOMETHING?

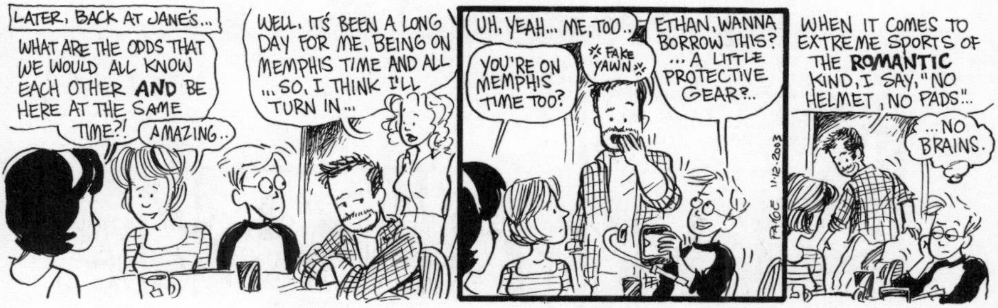
LATER, BACK AT JANE'S...
WHAT ARE THE ODDS THAT WE WOULD ALL KNOW EACH OTHER AND BE HERE AT THE SAME TIME?!
AMAZING..
WELL, IT'S BEEN A LONG DAY FOR ME, BEING ON MEMPHIS TIME AND ALL ... SO, I THINK I'LL TURN IN...
UH, YEAH... ME, TOO..
YOU'RE ON MEMPHIS TIME TOO?
FAKE YAWN
ETHAN, WANNA BORROW THIS? ... A LITTLE PROTECTIVE GEAR?..
11.12.2003
WHEN IT COMES TO EXTREME SPORTS OF THE ROMANTIC KIND, I SAY, "NO HELMET, NO PADS"..
... NO BRAINS.

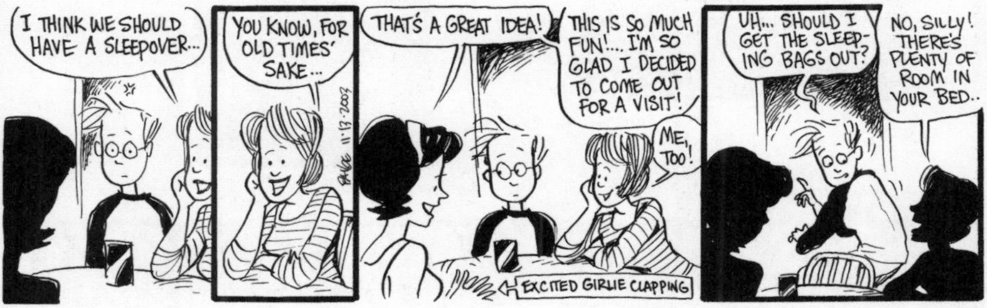
I THINK WE SHOULD HAVE A SLEEPOVER...
YOU KNOW, FOR OLD TIMES' SAKE...
11.13.2003
THAT'S A GREAT IDEA!
THIS IS SO MUCH FUN!... I'M SO GLAD I DECIDED TO COME OUT FOR A VISIT!
ME, TOO!
EXCITED GIRLIE CLAPPING
UH... SHOULD I GET THE SLEEPING BAGS OUT?
NO, SILLY! THERE'S PLENTY OF ROOM IN YOUR BED..

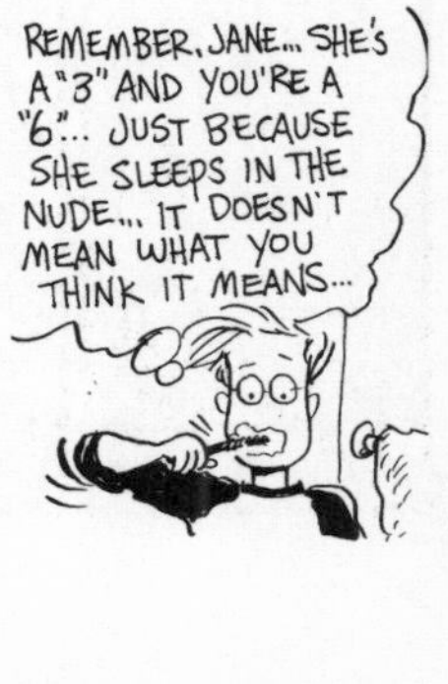
REMEMBER, JANE... SHE'S A "3" AND YOU'RE A "6"... JUST BECAUSE SHE SLEEPS IN THE NUDE... IT DOESN'T MEAN WHAT YOU THINK IT MEANS...

...TECHNICALLY, A "3" IS MOSTLY STRAIGHT... THEY JUST WANT TO CUDDLE...
CLICK!
SO, HORMONES ... CHILL!
PAIGE 11.14.2003
JANE! GET IN HERE AND HELP US WARM THE SHEETS UP!
THANK YOU. THANK YOU. THANK YOU.
I'M THE MIDDLE SPOON!
Z
Z
PAIGE 11.15.2003

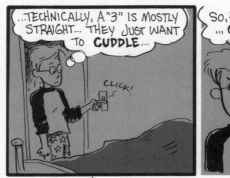

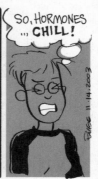

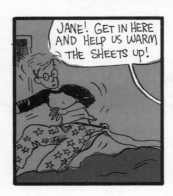

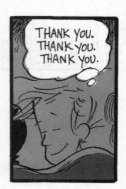

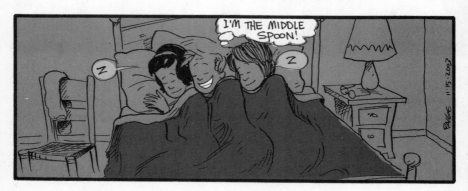

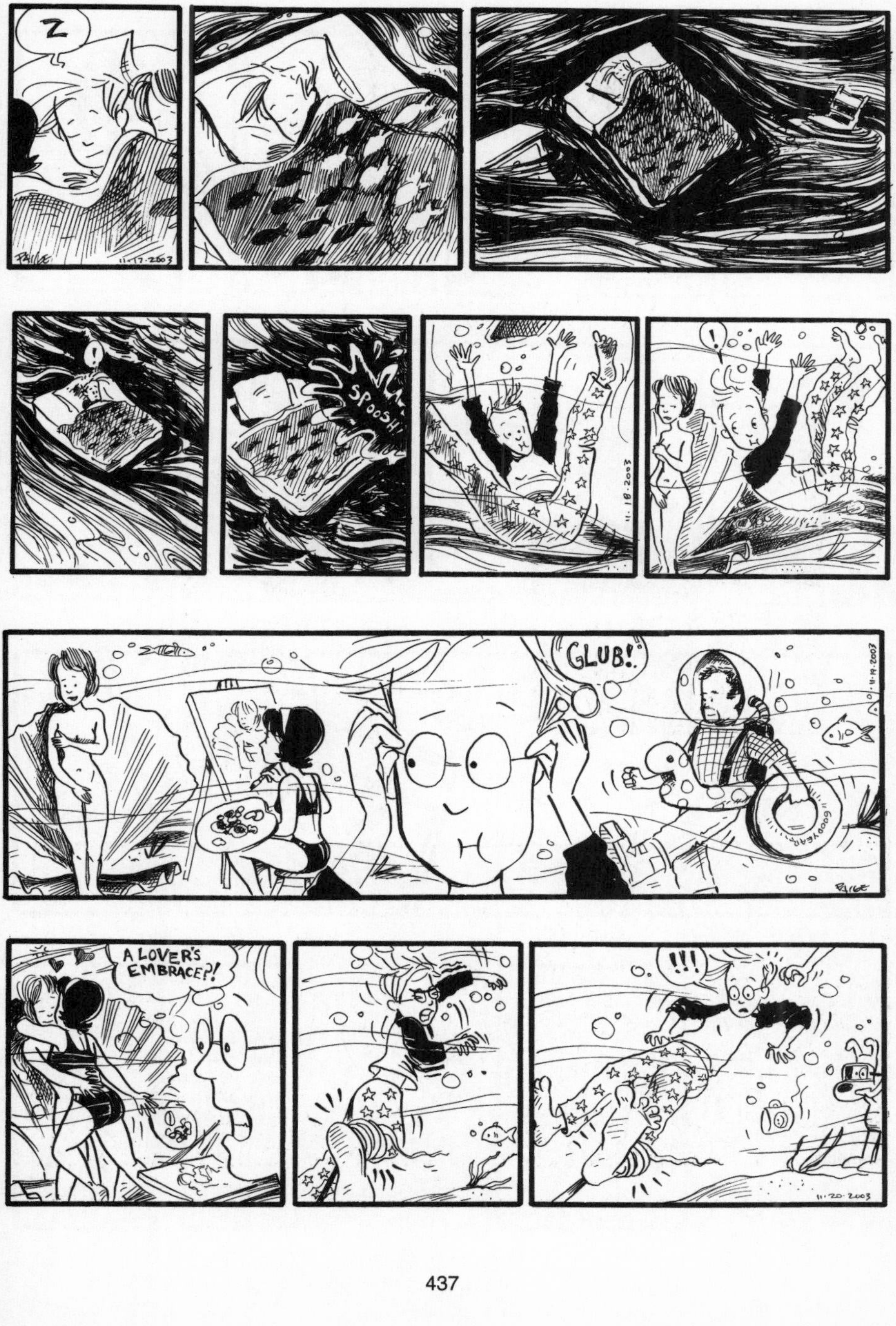
Z
11-17-2003
!
SPOOSH!
11.18.2003
!
GLUB!
11-19-2003
GOODYEAR
PAIGE
A LOVER'S EMBRACE?!
!!!
11-20-2003

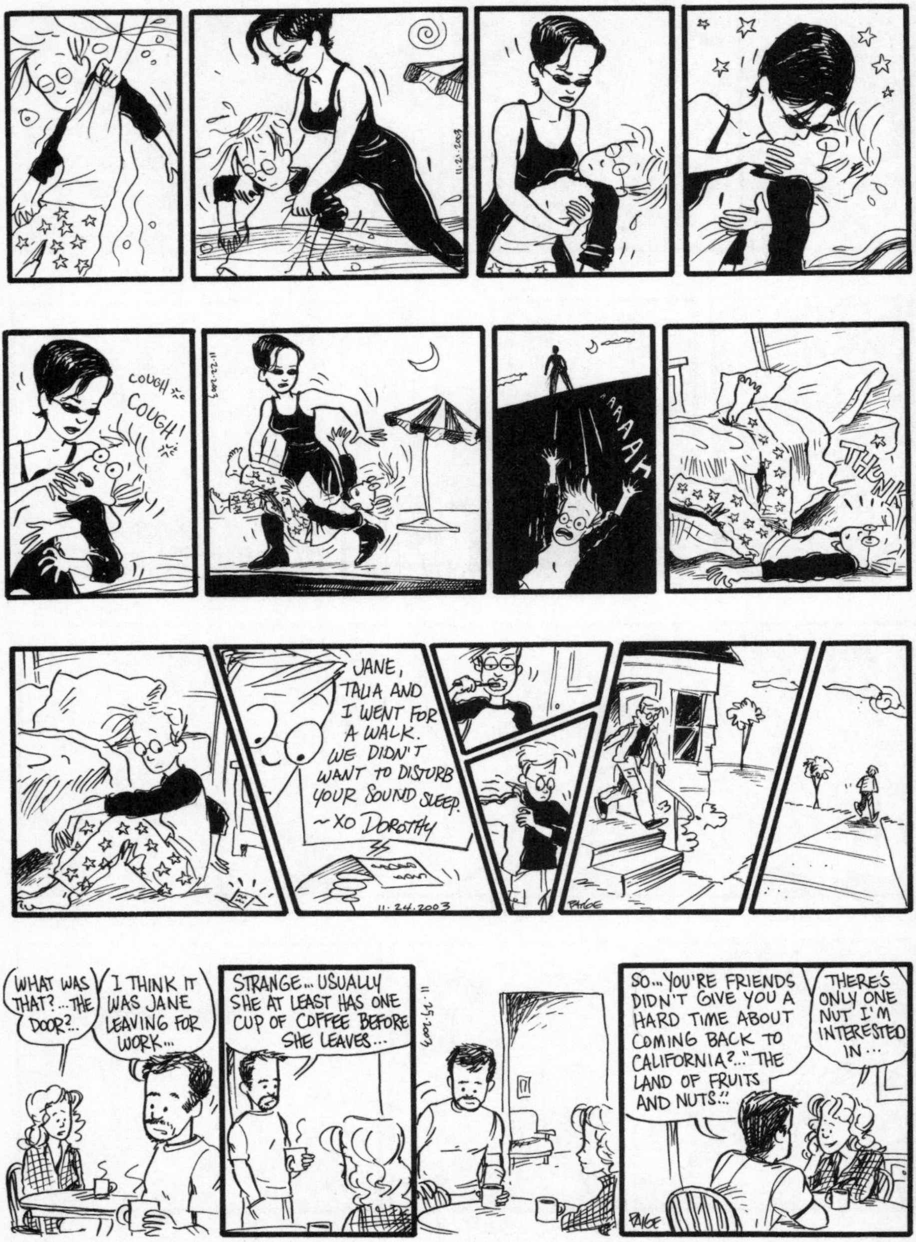

11-21-2003
COUGH
COUGH!
11-22-2003
AAAAAH
THUNK
JANE, TALIA AND I WENT FOR A WALK. WE DIDN'T WANT TO DISTURB YOUR SOUND SLEEP. ~XO DOROTHY
11.24.2003
PAIGE
WHAT WAS THAT?...THE DOOR?...
I THINK IT WAS JANE LEAVING FOR WORK...
STRANGE... USUALLY SHE AT LEAST HAS ONE CUP OF COFFEE BEFORE SHE LEAVES...
11-25-2003
SO...YOU'RE FRIENDS DIDN'T GIVE YOU A HARD TIME ABOUT COMING BACK TO CALIFORNIA?..."THE LAND OF FRUITS AND NUTS"!!
THERE'S ONLY ONE NUT I'M INTERESTED IN...
PAIGE

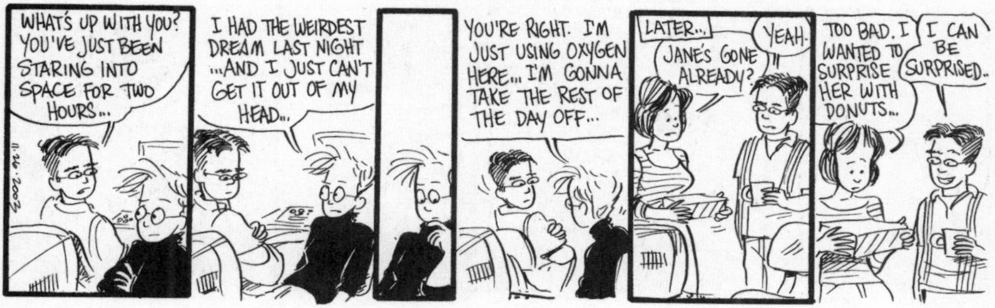
WHAT'S UP WITH YOU? YOU'VE JUST BEEN STARING INTO SPACE FOR TWO HOURS...
11-26-2003
I HAD THE WEIRDEST DREAM LAST NIGHT ...AND I JUST CAN'T GET IT OUT OF MY HEAD...
YOU'RE RIGHT. I'M JUST USING OXYGEN HERE... I'M GONNA TAKE THE REST OF THE DAY OFF...
LATER...
JANE'S GONE ALREADY?
YEAH.
TOO BAD. I WANTED TO SURPRISE HER WITH DONUTS...
I CAN BE SURPRISED..

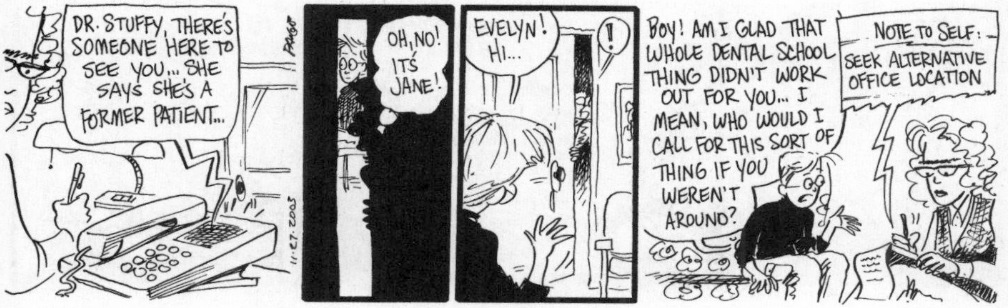
DR. STUFFY, THERE'S SOMEONE HERE TO SEE YOU... SHE SAYS SHE'S A FORMER PATIENT...
11-27-2003
OH, NO! IT'S JANE!
EVELYN! HI...
!
BOY! AM I GLAD THAT WHOLE DENTAL SCHOOL THING DIDN'T WORK OUT FOR YOU... I MEAN, WHO WOULD I CALL FOR THIS SORT OF THING IF YOU WEREN'T AROUND?
NOTE TO SELF: SEEK ALTERNATIVE OFFICE LOCATION

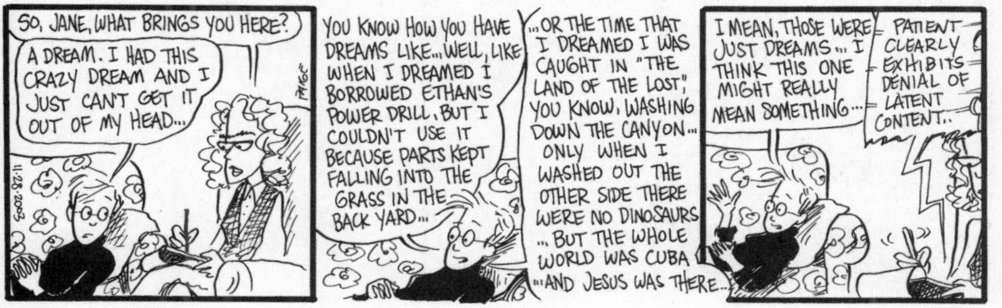
SO, JANE, WHAT BRINGS YOU HERE?
A DREAM. I HAD THIS CRAZY DREAM AND I JUST CAN'T GET IT OUT OF MY HEAD...
11-28-2003
YOU KNOW HOW YOU HAVE DREAMS LIKE... WELL, LIKE WHEN I DREAMED I BORROWED ETHAN'S POWER DRILL, BUT I COULDN'T USE IT BECAUSE PARTS KEPT FALLING INTO THE GRASS IN THE BACK YARD...
...OR THE TIME THAT I DREAMED I WAS CAUGHT IN "THE LAND OF THE LOST," YOU KNOW, WASHING DOWN THE CANYON... ONLY WHEN I WASHED OUT THE OTHER SIDE THERE WERE NO DINOSAURS ... BUT THE WHOLE WORLD WAS CUBA ...AND JESUS WAS THERE...
I MEAN, THOSE WERE JUST DREAMS... I THINK THIS ONE MIGHT REALLY MEAN SOMETHING...
PATIENT CLEARLY EXHIBITS DENIAL OF LATENT CONTENT..

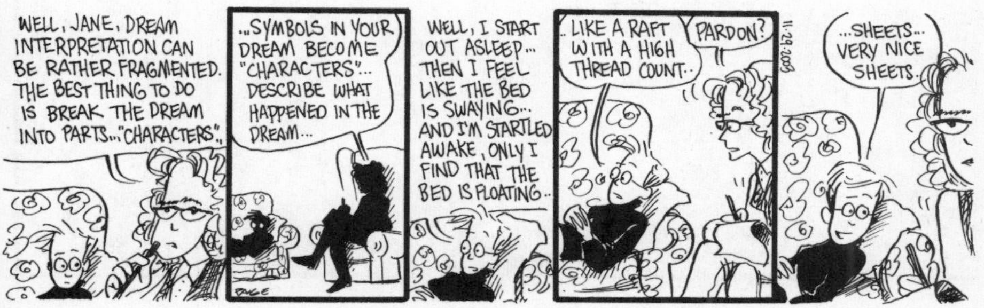
WELL, JANE, DREAM INTERPRETATION CAN BE RATHER FRAGMENTED. THE BEST THING TO DO IS BREAK THE DREAM INTO PARTS..."CHARACTERS"..
..SYMBOLS IN YOUR DREAM BECOME "CHARACTERS"... DESCRIBE WHAT HAPPENED IN THE DREAM...
WELL, I START OUT ASLEEP... THEN I FEEL LIKE THE BED IS SWAYING... AND I'M STARTLED AWAKE, ONLY I FIND THAT THE BED IS FLOATING..
..LIKE A RAFT WITH A HIGH THREAD COUNT..
PARDON?
11-29-2003
...SHEETS... VERY NICE SHEETS..

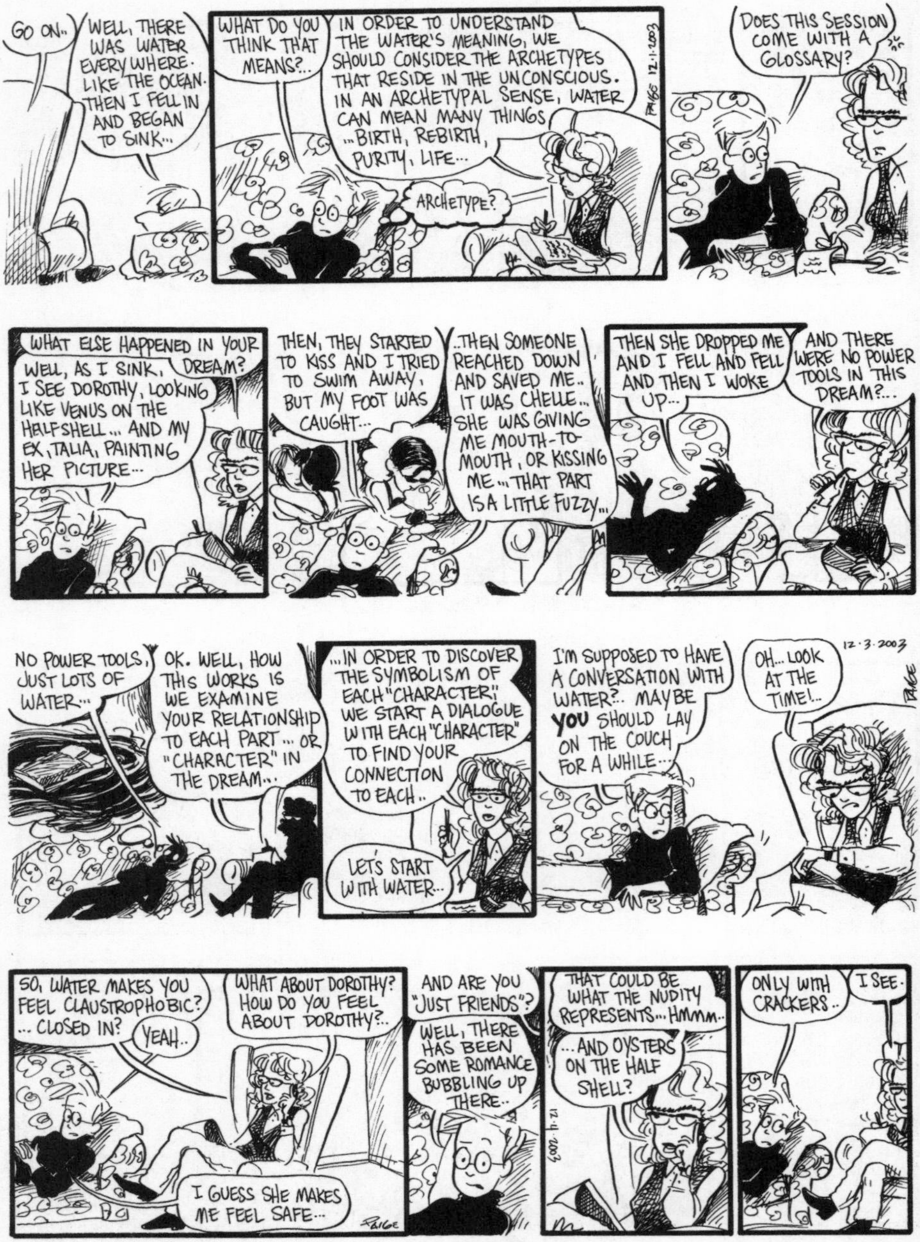
GO ON..
WELL, THERE WAS WATER EVERYWHERE. LIKE THE OCEAN. THEN I FELL IN AND BEGAN TO SINK...
WHAT DO YOU THINK THAT MEANS?...
IN ORDER TO UNDERSTAND THE WATER'S MEANING, WE SHOULD CONSIDER THE ARCHETYPES THAT RESIDE IN THE UNCONSCIOUS. IN AN ARCHETYPAL SENSE, WATER CAN MEAN MANY THINGS ...BIRTH, REBIRTH, PURITY, LIFE...
ARCHETYPE?
PAIGE 12·1·2003
DOES THIS SESSION COME WITH A GLOSSARY?
WHAT ELSE HAPPENED IN YOUR DREAM?
WELL, AS I SINK, I SEE DOROTHY, LOOKING LIKE VENUS ON THE HALFSHELL... AND MY EX, TALIA, PAINTING HER PICTURE...
THEN, THEY STARTED TO KISS AND I TRIED TO SWIM AWAY, BUT MY FOOT WAS CAUGHT...
..THEN SOMEONE REACHED DOWN AND SAVED ME.. IT WAS CHELLE... SHE WAS GIVING ME MOUTH-TO-MOUTH, OR KISSING ME... THAT PART IS A LITTLE FUZZY...
THEN SHE DROPPED ME AND I FELL AND FELL AND THEN I WOKE UP...
AND THERE WERE NO POWER TOOLS IN THIS DREAM?...
NO POWER TOOLS, JUST LOTS OF WATER...
OK. WELL, HOW THIS WORKS IS WE EXAMINE YOUR RELATIONSHIP TO EACH PART... OR "CHARACTER" IN THE DREAM...
...IN ORDER TO DISCOVER THE SYMBOLISM OF EACH "CHARACTER", WE START A DIALOGUE WITH EACH "CHARACTER" TO FIND YOUR CONNECTION TO EACH..
LET'S START WITH WATER..
I'M SUPPOSED TO HAVE A CONVERSATION WITH WATER?.. MAYBE **YOU** SHOULD LAY ON THE COUCH FOR A WHILE...
12·3·2003
OH... LOOK AT THE TIME!...
PAIGE
SO, WATER MAKES YOU FEEL CLAUSTROPHOBIC? ...CLOSED IN?
YEAH..
WHAT ABOUT DOROTHY? HOW DO YOU FEEL ABOUT DOROTHY?..
I GUESS SHE MAKES ME FEEL SAFE...
PAIGE
AND ARE YOU "JUST FRIENDS"?
WELL, THERE HAS BEEN SOME ROMANCE BUBBLING UP THERE..
THAT COULD BE WHAT THE NUDITY REPRESENTS... HMMM..
...AND OYSTERS ON THE HALF SHELL?
ONLY WITH CRACKERS..
I SEE.

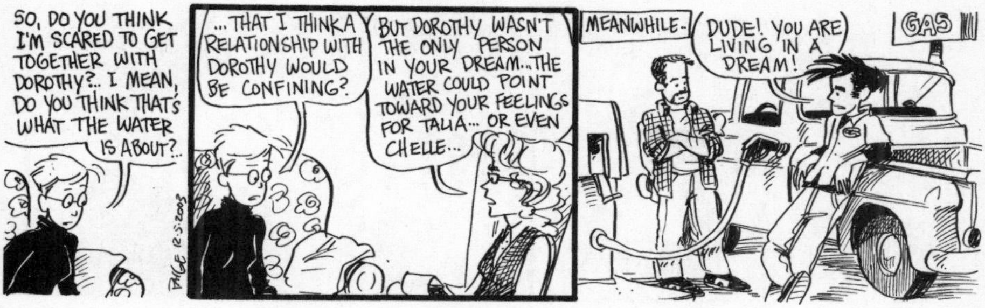
SO, DO YOU THINK I'M SCARED TO GET TOGETHER WITH DOROTHY?.. I MEAN, DO YOU THINK THAT'S WHAT THE WATER IS ABOUT?..
PAIGE 12·5·2003
...THAT I THINK A RELATIONSHIP WITH DOROTHY WOULD BE CONFINING?
BUT DOROTHY WASN'T THE ONLY PERSON IN YOUR DREAM.. THE WATER COULD POINT TOWARD YOUR FEELINGS FOR TALIA... OR EVEN CHELLE...
MEANWHILE..
DUDE! YOU ARE LIVING IN A DREAM!
GAS

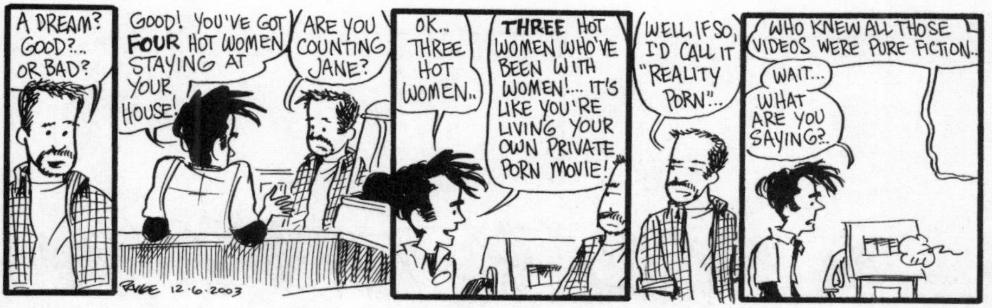
A DREAM? GOOD?... OR BAD?
GOOD! YOU'VE GOT FOUR HOT WOMEN STAYING AT YOUR HOUSE!
ARE YOU COUNTING JANE?
PAIGE 12·6·2003
OK... THREE HOT WOMEN..
THREE HOT WOMEN WHO'VE BEEN WITH WOMEN!... IT'S LIKE YOU'RE LIVING YOUR OWN PRIVATE PORN MOVIE!
WELL, IF SO, I'D CALL IT "REALITY PORN"...
WHO KNEW ALL THOSE VIDEOS WERE PURE FICTION..
WAIT... WHAT ARE YOU SAYING?..

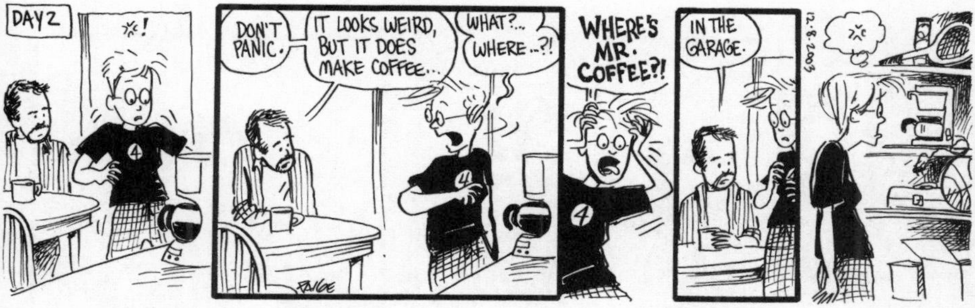
DAY 2
DON'T PANIC.
IT LOOKS WEIRD, BUT IT DOES MAKE COFFEE...
WHAT?... WHERE...?!
PAIGE
WHERE'S MR. COFFEE?!
IN THE GARAGE.
12·8·2003

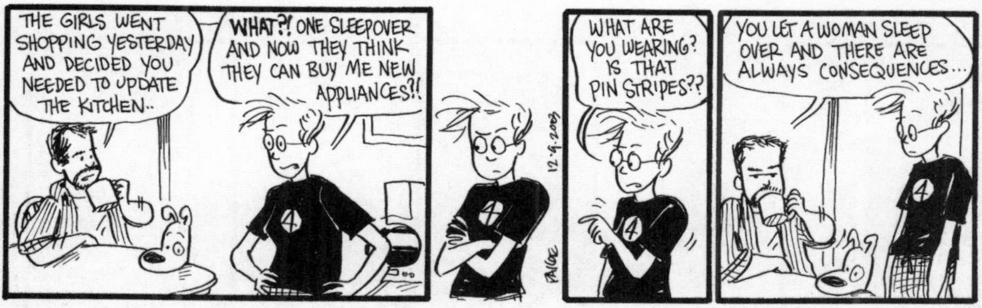
THE GIRLS WENT SHOPPING YESTERDAY AND DECIDED YOU NEEDED TO UPDATE THE KITCHEN..
WHAT?! ONE SLEEPOVER AND NOW THEY THINK THEY CAN BUY ME NEW APPLIANCES?!
12·9·2003
PAIGE
WHAT ARE YOU WEARING? IS THAT PIN STRIPES??
YOU LET A WOMAN SLEEP OVER AND THERE ARE ALWAYS CONSEQUENCES...

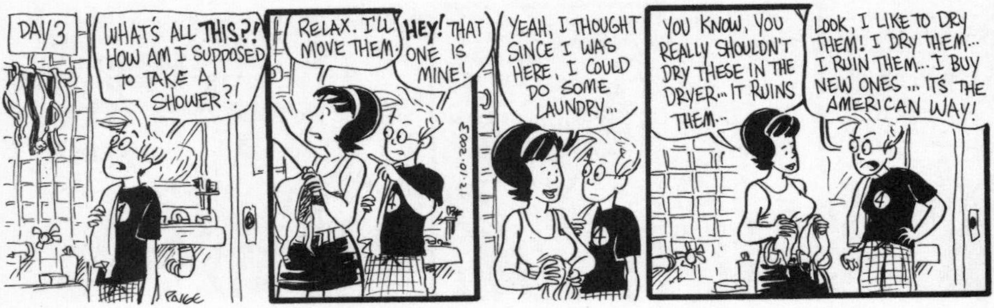
DAY 3
WHAT'S ALL THIS?! HOW AM I SUPPOSED TO TAKE A SHOWER?!
PAIGE
RELAX. I'LL MOVE THEM.
HEY! THAT ONE IS MINE!
12-10-2003
YEAH, I THOUGHT SINCE I WAS HERE, I COULD DO SOME LAUNDRY...
YOU KNOW, YOU REALLY SHOULDN'T DRY THESE IN THE DRYER... IT RUINS THEM...
LOOK, I LIKE TO DRY THEM! I DRY THEM... I RUIN THEM... I BUY NEW ONES... IT'S THE AMERICAN WAY!

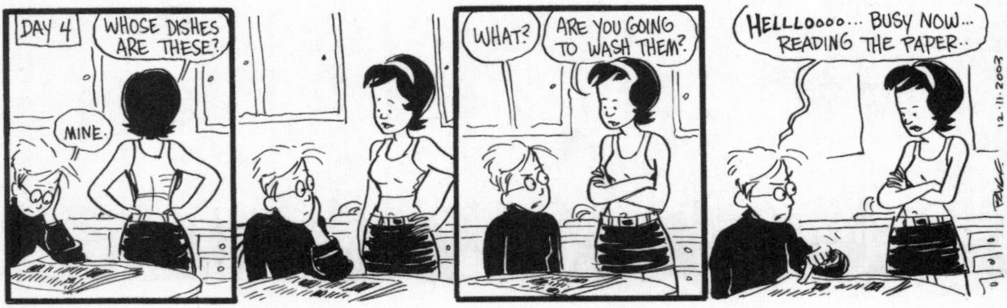
DAY 4
WHOSE DISHES ARE THESE?
MINE.
WHAT?
ARE YOU GOING TO WASH THEM?
HELLLOOOO... BUSY NOW... READING THE PAPER...
12-11-2003
PAIGE

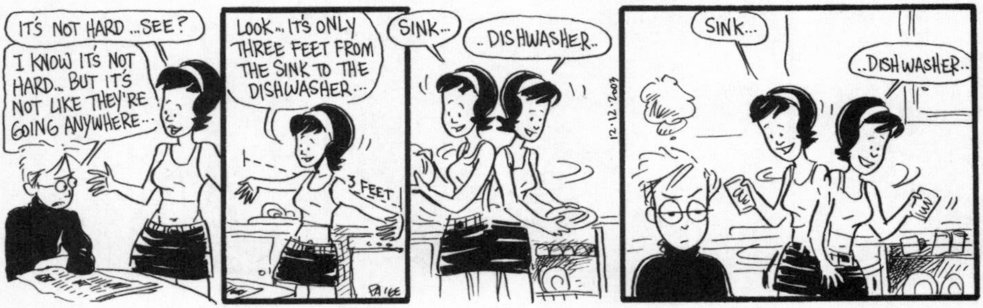
IT'S NOT HARD... SEE?
I KNOW IT'S NOT HARD... BUT IT'S NOT LIKE THEY'RE GOING ANYWHERE...
LOOK... IT'S ONLY THREE FEET FROM THE SINK TO THE DISHWASHER...
3 FEET
PAIGE
SINK...
.. DISHWASHER..
12-12-2003
SINK...
..DISHWASHER..

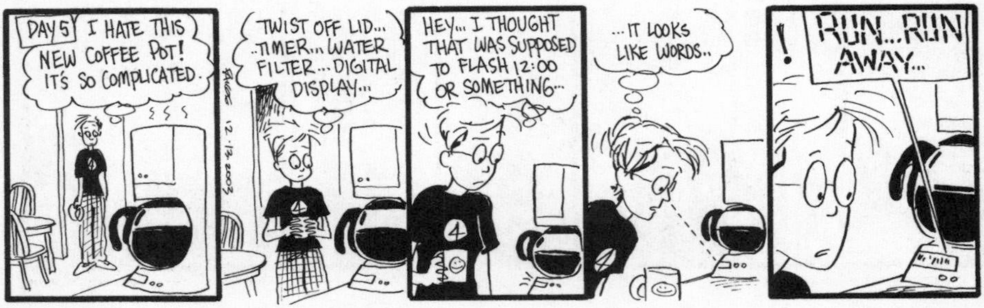
DAY 5
I HATE THIS NEW COFFEE POT! IT'S SO COMPLICATED.
PAIGE
12-13-2003
TWIST OFF LID... ..TIMER... WATER FILTER... DIGITAL DISPLAY...
HEY... I THOUGHT THAT WAS SUPPOSED TO FLASH 12:00 OR SOMETHING...
...IT LOOKS LIKE WORDS..
!
RUN... RUN AWAY...

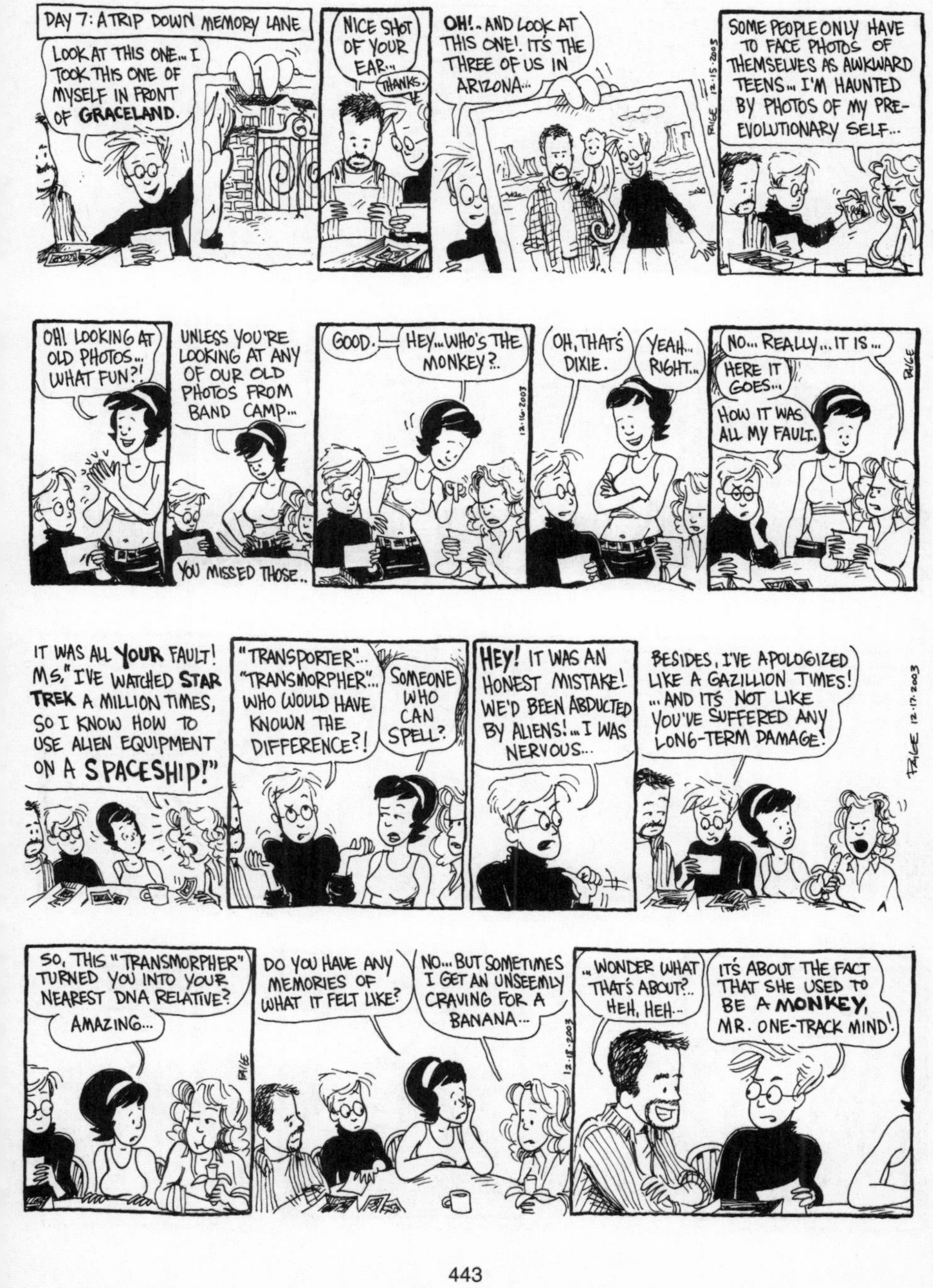
DAY 7: A TRIP DOWN MEMORY LANE
LOOK AT THIS ONE... I TOOK THIS ONE OF MYSELF IN FRONT OF **GRACELAND**.
NICE SHOT OF YOUR EAR...
THANKS.
OH!.. AND LOOK AT THIS ONE!. IT'S THE THREE OF US IN ARIZONA...
PAIGE 12-15-2003
SOME PEOPLE ONLY HAVE TO FACE PHOTOS OF THEMSELVES AS AWKWARD TEENS... I'M HAUNTED BY PHOTOS OF MY PRE-EVOLUTIONARY SELF...
OH! LOOKING AT OLD PHOTOS... WHAT FUN?!
UNLESS YOU'RE LOOKING AT ANY OF OUR OLD PHOTOS FROM BAND CAMP...
YOU MISSED THOSE..
GOOD.
HEY... WHO'S THE MONKEY?..
12-16-2003
OH, THAT'S DIXIE.
YEAH... RIGHT...
NO... REALLY... IT IS...
PAIGE
HERE IT GOES...
HOW IT WAS ALL MY FAULT..
IT WAS ALL **YOUR** FAULT! MS. "I'VE WATCHED **STAR TREK** A MILLION TIMES, SO I KNOW HOW TO USE ALIEN EQUIPMENT ON A **SPACESHIP!**"
"TRANSPORTER"... "TRANSMORPHER"... WHO WOULD HAVE KNOWN THE DIFFERENCE?!
SOMEONE WHO CAN SPELL?
HEY! IT WAS AN HONEST MISTAKE! WE'D BEEN ABDUCTED BY ALIENS!... I WAS NERVOUS...
BESIDES, I'VE APOLOGIZED LIKE A GAZILLION TIMES! ...AND IT'S NOT LIKE YOU'VE SUFFERED ANY LONG-TERM DAMAGE!
PAIGE 12-17-2003
SO, THIS "TRANSMORPHER" TURNED YOU INTO YOUR NEAREST DNA RELATIVE?
AMAZING...
PAIGE
DO YOU HAVE ANY MEMORIES OF WHAT IT FELT LIKE?
NO... BUT SOMETIMES I GET AN UNSEEMLY CRAVING FOR A BANANA...
12-18-2003
...WONDER WHAT THAT'S ABOUT?.. HEH, HEH..
IT'S ABOUT THE FACT THAT SHE USED TO BE A **MONKEY**, MR. ONE-TRACK MIND!

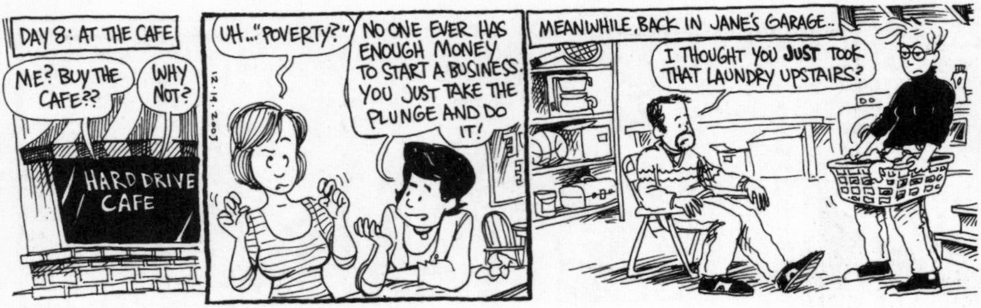
DAY 8: AT THE CAFE
ME? BUY THE CAFE??
WHY NOT?
HARD DRIVE CAFE
12.19.2003
UH..."POVERTY?"
NO ONE EVER HAS ENOUGH MONEY TO START A BUSINESS. YOU JUST TAKE THE PLUNGE AND DO IT!
MEANWHILE, BACK IN JANE'S GARAGE..
I THOUGHT YOU JUST TOOK THAT LAUNDRY UPSTAIRS?

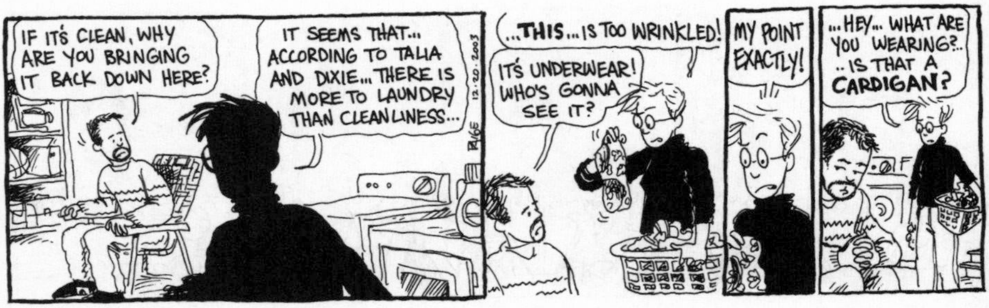
IF IT'S CLEAN, WHY ARE YOU BRINGING IT BACK DOWN HERE?
IT SEEMS THAT... ACCORDING TO TALIA AND DIXIE... THERE IS MORE TO LAUNDRY THAN CLEANLINESS...
12.20.2003
PAIGE
...THIS... IS TOO WRINKLED!
IT'S UNDERWEAR! WHO'S GONNA SEE IT?
MY POINT EXACTLY!
...HEY... WHAT ARE YOU WEARING?.. ..IS THAT A CARDIGAN?

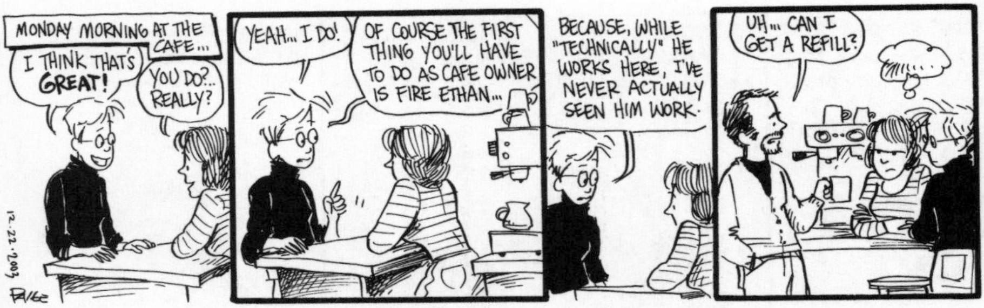
MONDAY MORNING AT THE CAFE...
I THINK THAT'S GREAT!
YOU DO?.. REALLY?
12.22.2003
PAIGE
YEAH... I DO!
OF COURSE THE FIRST THING YOU'LL HAVE TO DO AS CAFE OWNER IS FIRE ETHAN...
BECAUSE, WHILE "TECHNICALLY" HE WORKS HERE, I'VE NEVER ACTUALLY SEEN HIM WORK.
UH... CAN I GET A REFILL?

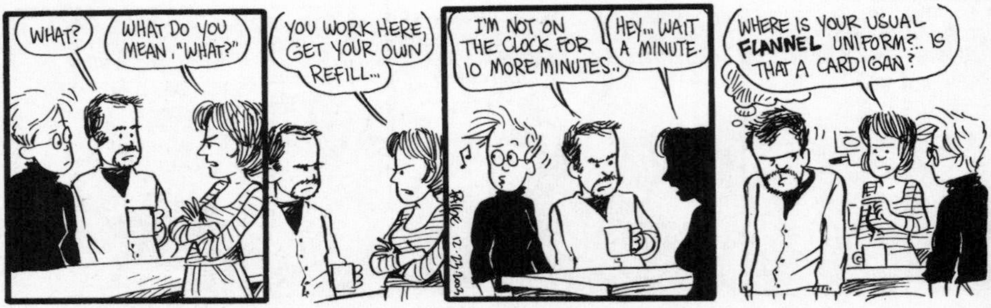
WHAT?
WHAT DO YOU MEAN, "WHAT?"
YOU WORK HERE, GET YOUR OWN REFILL...
PAIGE
I'M NOT ON THE CLOCK FOR 10 MORE MINUTES..
HEY... WAIT A MINUTE.
WHERE IS YOUR USUAL FLANNEL UNIFORM?.. IS THAT A CARDIGAN?

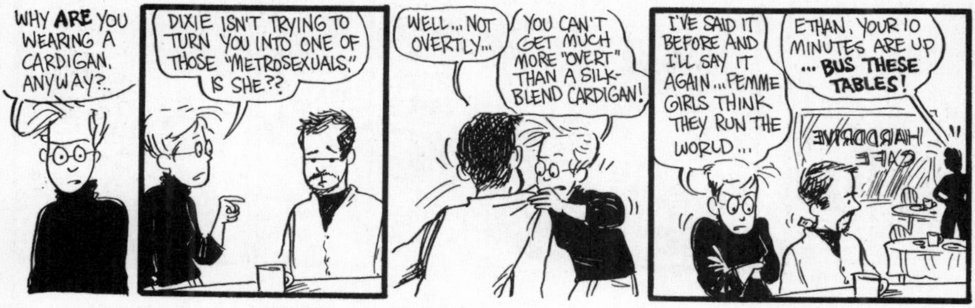
WHY **ARE** YOU WEARING A CARDIGAN, ANYWAY?..
DIXIE ISN'T TRYING TO TURN YOU INTO ONE OF THOSE "METROSEXUALS," IS SHE??
WELL... NOT OVERTLY...
YOU CAN'T GET MUCH MORE "OVERT" THAN A SILK-BLEND CARDIGAN!
I'VE SAID IT BEFORE AND I'LL SAY IT AGAIN... FEMME GIRLS THINK THEY RUN THE WORLD...
ETHAN, YOUR 10 MINUTES ARE UP **... BUS THESE TABLES!**

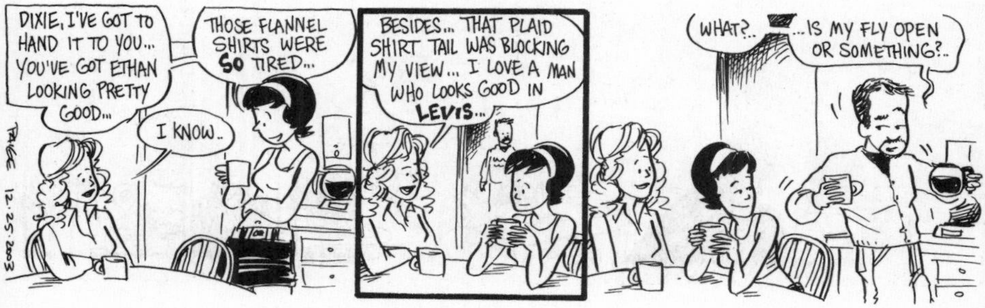
DIXIE, I'VE GOT TO HAND IT TO YOU... YOU'VE GOT ETHAN LOOKING PRETTY GOOD...
THOSE FLANNEL SHIRTS WERE **SO** TIRED...
I KNOW..
PAIGE 12·25·2003
BESIDES... THAT PLAID SHIRT TAIL WAS BLOCKING MY VIEW... I LOVE A MAN WHO LOOKS GOOD IN **LEVIS**...
WHAT?..
... IS MY FLY OPEN OR SOMETHING?..

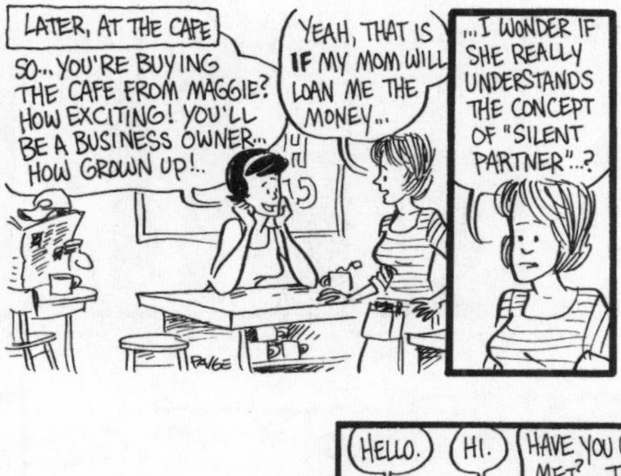
LATER, AT THE CAFE
SO... YOU'RE BUYING THE CAFE FROM MAGGIE? HOW EXCITING! YOU'LL BE A BUSINESS OWNER... HOW GROWN UP!..
YEAH, THAT IS **IF** MY MOM WILL LOAN ME THE MONEY...
PAIGE
... I WONDER IF SHE REALLY UNDERSTANDS THE CONCEPT OF "SILENT PARTNER"...?

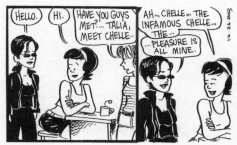

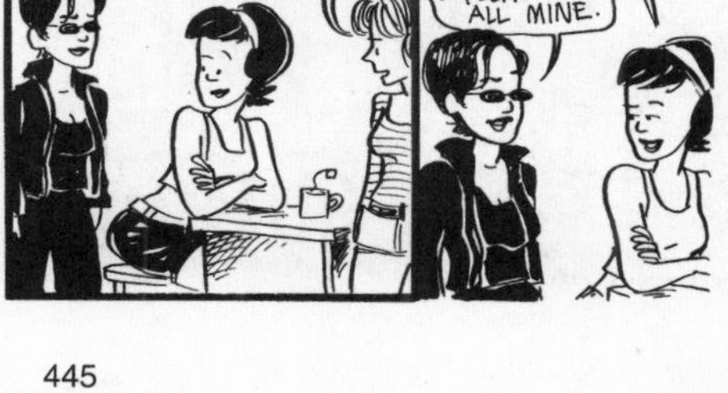
HELLO.
HI.
HAVE YOU GUYS MET?... TALIA, MEET CHELLE..
AH... CHELLE... THE INFAMOUS CHELLE... THE...
... PLEASURE IS ALL MINE.
12·26·2003

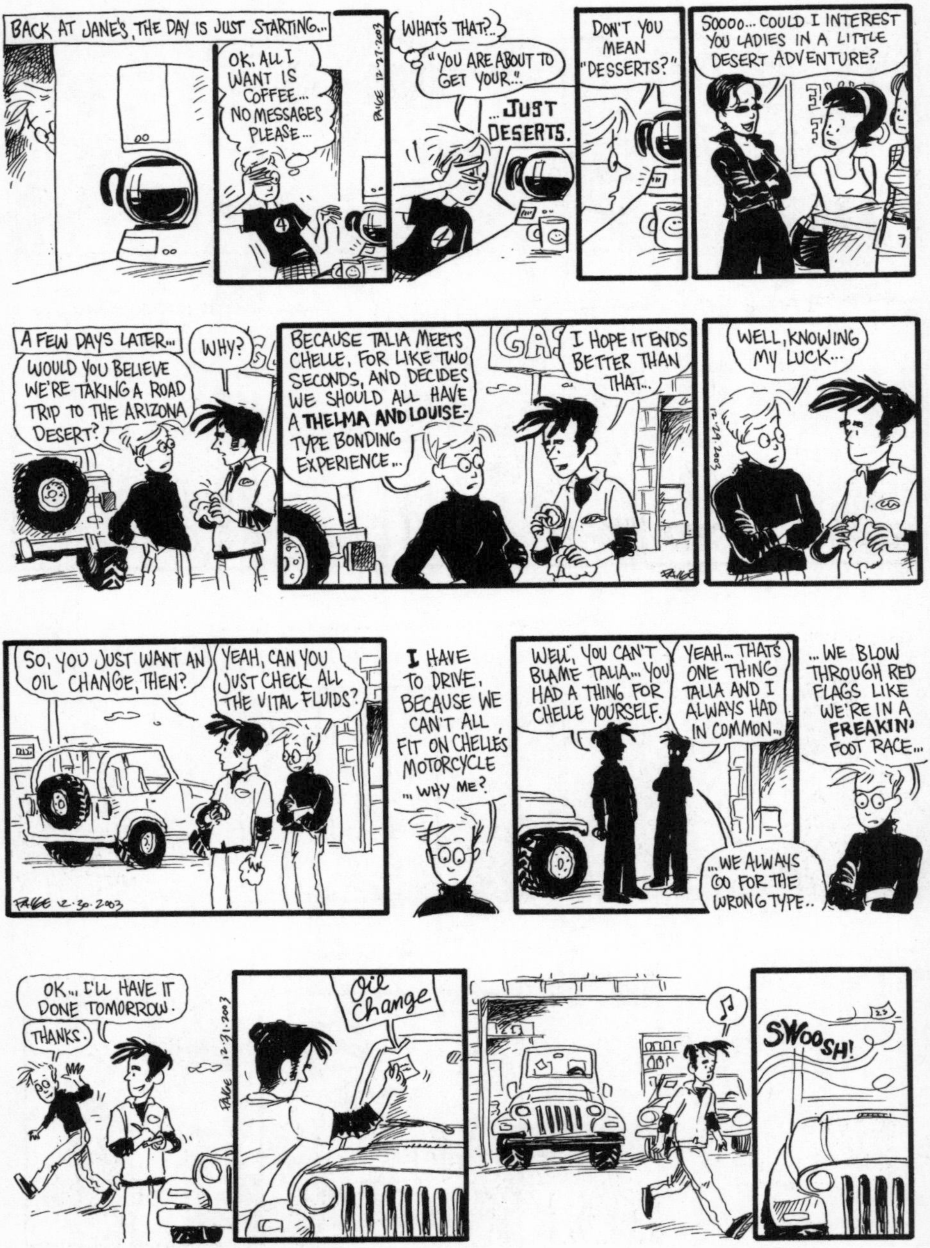

BACK AT JANE'S, THE DAY IS JUST STARTING...
OK, ALL I WANT IS COFFEE... NO MESSAGES PLEASE...
PAIGE 12-27-2003
WHAT'S THAT?..
"YOU ARE ABOUT TO GET YOUR.."
...JUST DESERTS.
DON'T YOU MEAN "DESSERTS?"
SOOOO... COULD I INTEREST YOU LADIES IN A LITTLE DESERT ADVENTURE?
A FEW DAYS LATER...
WOULD YOU BELIEVE WE'RE TAKING A ROAD TRIP TO THE ARIZONA DESERT?
WHY?
BECAUSE TALIA MEETS CHELLE, FOR LIKE TWO SECONDS, AND DECIDES WE SHOULD ALL HAVE A THELMA AND LOUISE-TYPE BONDING EXPERIENCE...
I HOPE IT ENDS BETTER THAN THAT...
12-29-2003
WELL, KNOWING MY LUCK...
SO, YOU JUST WANT AN OIL CHANGE, THEN?
YEAH, CAN YOU JUST CHECK ALL THE VITAL FLUIDS?
PAIGE 12-30-2003
I HAVE TO DRIVE, BECAUSE WE CAN'T ALL FIT ON CHELLE'S MOTORCYCLE ...WHY ME?
WELL, YOU CAN'T BLAME TALIA... YOU HAD A THING FOR CHELLE YOURSELF.
YEAH... THAT'S ONE THING TALIA AND I ALWAYS HAD IN COMMON...
...WE ALWAYS GO FOR THE WRONG TYPE..
...WE BLOW THROUGH RED FLAGS LIKE WE'RE IN A FREAKIN' FOOT RACE...
OK... I'LL HAVE IT DONE TOMORROW.
THANKS.
PAIGE 12-31-2003
Oil Change
SWOOSH!

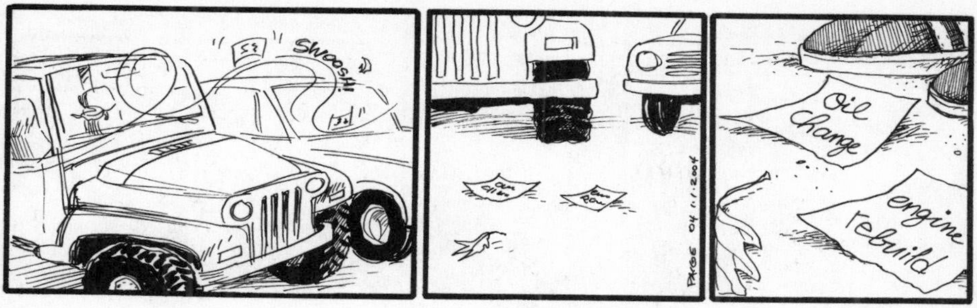
SWOOSH!!
PAIGE 04 1.1.2004
Oil change
engine rebuild

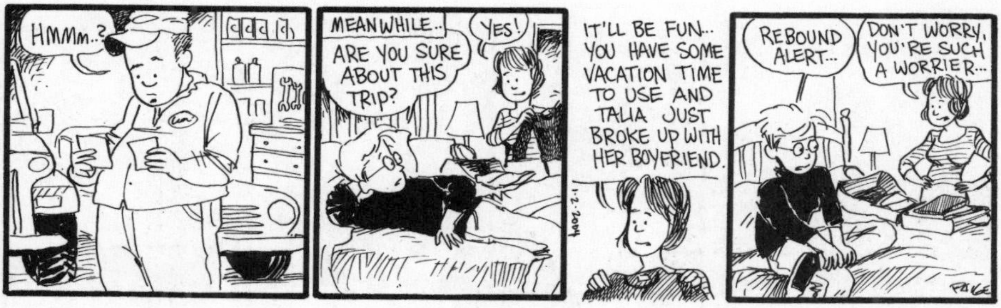
HMMm..?
MEANWHILE..
ARE YOU SURE ABOUT THIS TRIP?
YES!
1.2.2004
IT'LL BE FUN... YOU HAVE SOME VACATION TIME TO USE AND TALIA JUST BROKE UP WITH HER BOYFRIEND.
REBOUND ALERT...
DON'T WORRY, YOU'RE SUCH A WORRIER...
PAIGE

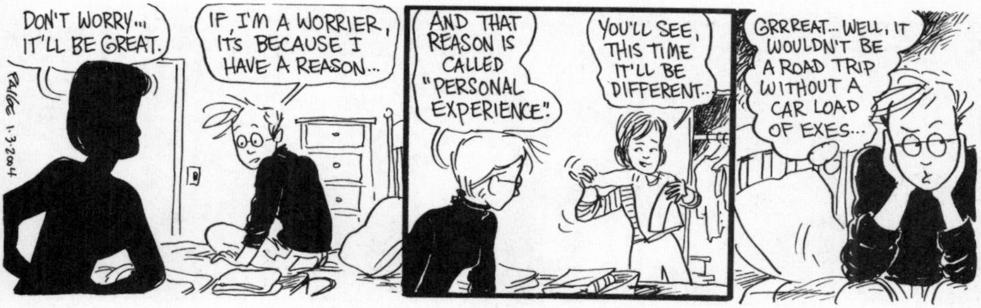
DON'T WORRY... IT'LL BE GREAT.
PAIGE 1.3.2004
IF, I'M A WORRIER, IT'S BECAUSE I HAVE A REASON...
AND THAT REASON IS CALLED "PERSONAL EXPERIENCE".
YOU'LL SEE, THIS TIME IT'LL BE DIFFERENT...
GRRREAT... WELL, IT WOULDN'T BE A ROAD TRIP WITHOUT A CAR LOAD OF EXES...

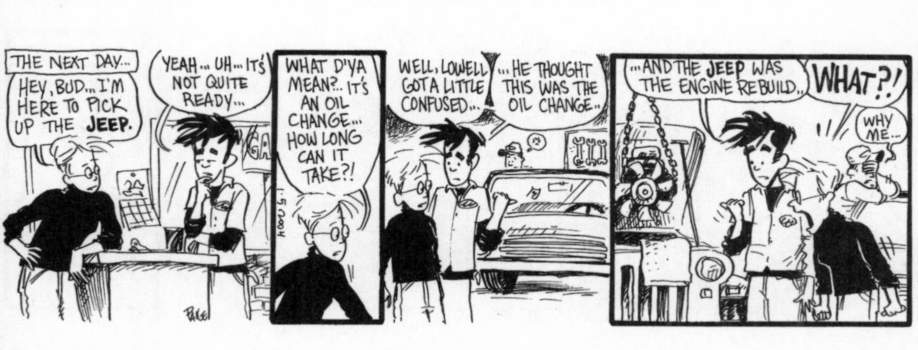
THE NEXT DAY...
HEY, BUD... I'M HERE TO PICK UP THE JEEP.
YEAH... UH... IT'S NOT QUITE READY...
WHAT D'YA MEAN?.. IT'S AN OIL CHANGE... HOW LONG CAN IT TAKE?!
1.5.2004
WELL, LOWELL GOT A LITTLE CONFUSED...
...HE THOUGHT THIS WAS THE OIL CHANGE..
...AND THE JEEP WAS THE ENGINE REBUILD..
WHAT?!
WHY ME...
PAIGE

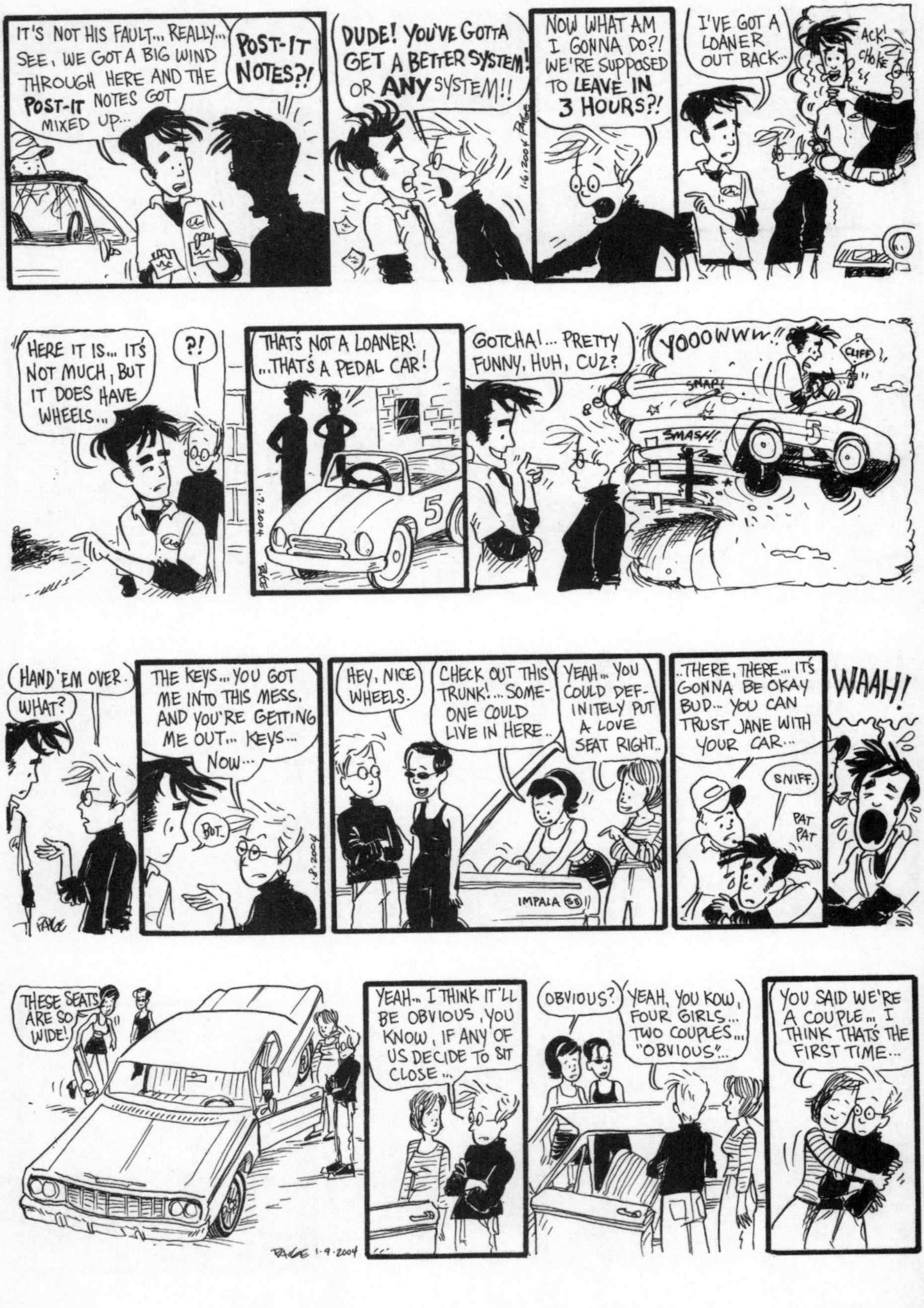
IT'S NOT HIS FAULT... REALLY... SEE, WE GOT A BIG WIND THROUGH HERE AND THE POST-IT NOTES GOT MIXED UP...
POST-IT NOTES?!
DUDE! YOU'VE GOTTA GET A BETTER SYSTEM! OR ANY SYSTEM!!
NOW WHAT AM I GONNA DO?! WE'RE SUPPOSED TO LEAVE IN 3 HOURS?!
I'VE GOT A LOANER OUT BACK...
ACK!
CHOKE
HERE IT IS... IT'S NOT MUCH, BUT IT DOES HAVE WHEELS...
?!
THAT'S NOT A LOANER! ...THAT'S A PEDAL CAR!
5
GOTCHA!... PRETTY FUNNY, HUH, CUZ?
YOOOWWW!!
CLIFF
SNAP!
SMASH!
5
HAND 'EM OVER.
WHAT?
THE KEYS... YOU GOT ME INTO THIS MESS, AND YOU'RE GETTING ME OUT... KEYS... NOW...
BUT...
HEY, NICE WHEELS.
CHECK OUT THIS TRUNK!... SOMEONE COULD LIVE IN HERE..
YEAH... YOU COULD DEFINITELY PUT A LOVE SEAT RIGHT..
IMPALA
..THERE, THERE... IT'S GONNA BE OKAY BUD... YOU CAN TRUST JANE WITH YOUR CAR...
SNIFF.
PAT PAT
WAAH!
THESE SEATS ARE SO WIDE!
YEAH... I THINK IT'LL BE OBVIOUS, YOU KNOW, IF ANY OF US DECIDE TO SIT CLOSE...
OBVIOUS?
YEAH, YOU KOW, FOUR GIRLS... TWO COUPLES... "OBVIOUS"...
YOU SAID WE'RE A COUPLE... I THINK THAT'S THE FIRST TIME...

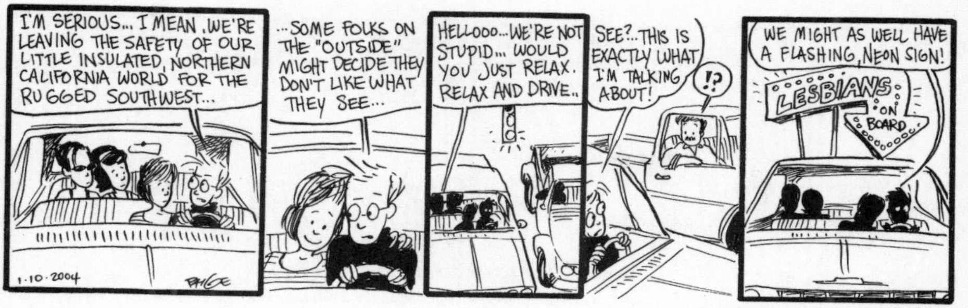
I'M SERIOUS... I MEAN, WE'RE LEAVING THE SAFETY OF OUR LITTLE INSULATED, NORTHERN CALIFORNIA WORLD FOR THE RUGGED SOUTHWEST...
1·10·2004
PAIGE
...SOME FOLKS ON THE "OUTSIDE" MIGHT DECIDE THEY DON'T LIKE WHAT THEY SEE...
HELLOOO... WE'RE NOT STUPID... WOULD YOU JUST RELAX. RELAX AND DRIVE..
SEE?.. THIS IS EXACTLY WHAT I'M TALKING ABOUT!
!?
WE MIGHT AS WELL HAVE A FLASHING, NEON SIGN!
LESBIANS
ON BOARD

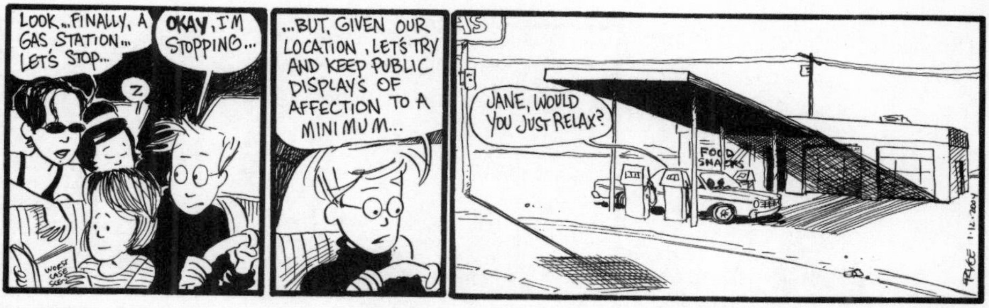
LOOK... FINALLY, A GAS STATION... LET'S STOP...
OKAY, I'M STOPPING...
Z
...BUT, GIVEN OUR LOCATION, LET'S TRY AND KEEP PUBLIC DISPLAYS OF AFFECTION TO A MINIMUM...
JANE, WOULD YOU JUST RELAX?
FOOD
SNACKS
1·12·2004
PAIGE

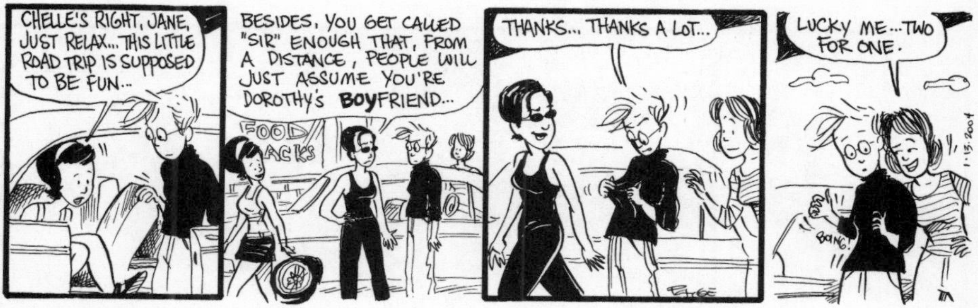
CHELLE'S RIGHT, JANE, JUST RELAX... THIS LITTLE ROAD TRIP IS SUPPOSED TO BE FUN...
BESIDES, YOU GET CALLED "SIR" ENOUGH THAT, FROM A DISTANCE, PEOPLE WILL JUST ASSUME YOU'RE DOROTHY'S BOYFRIEND...
THANKS... THANKS A LOT...
PAIGE
LUCKY ME... TWO FOR ONE.
BOING!
1·13·2004

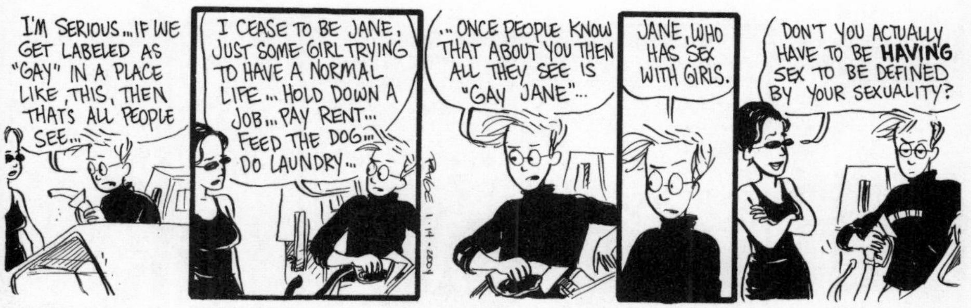
I'M SERIOUS... IF WE GET LABELED AS "GAY" IN A PLACE LIKE, THIS, THEN THATS ALL PEOPLE SEE...
I CEASE TO BE JANE, JUST SOME GIRL TRYING TO HAVE A NORMAL LIFE... HOLD DOWN A JOB... PAY RENT... FEED THE DOG... DO LAUNDRY...
PAIGE 1·14·2004
...ONCE PEOPLE KNOW THAT ABOUT YOU THEN ALL THEY SEE IS "GAY JANE"...
JANE, WHO HAS SEX WITH GIRLS.
DON'T YOU ACTUALLY HAVE TO BE HAVING SEX TO BE DEFINED BY YOUR SEXUALITY?

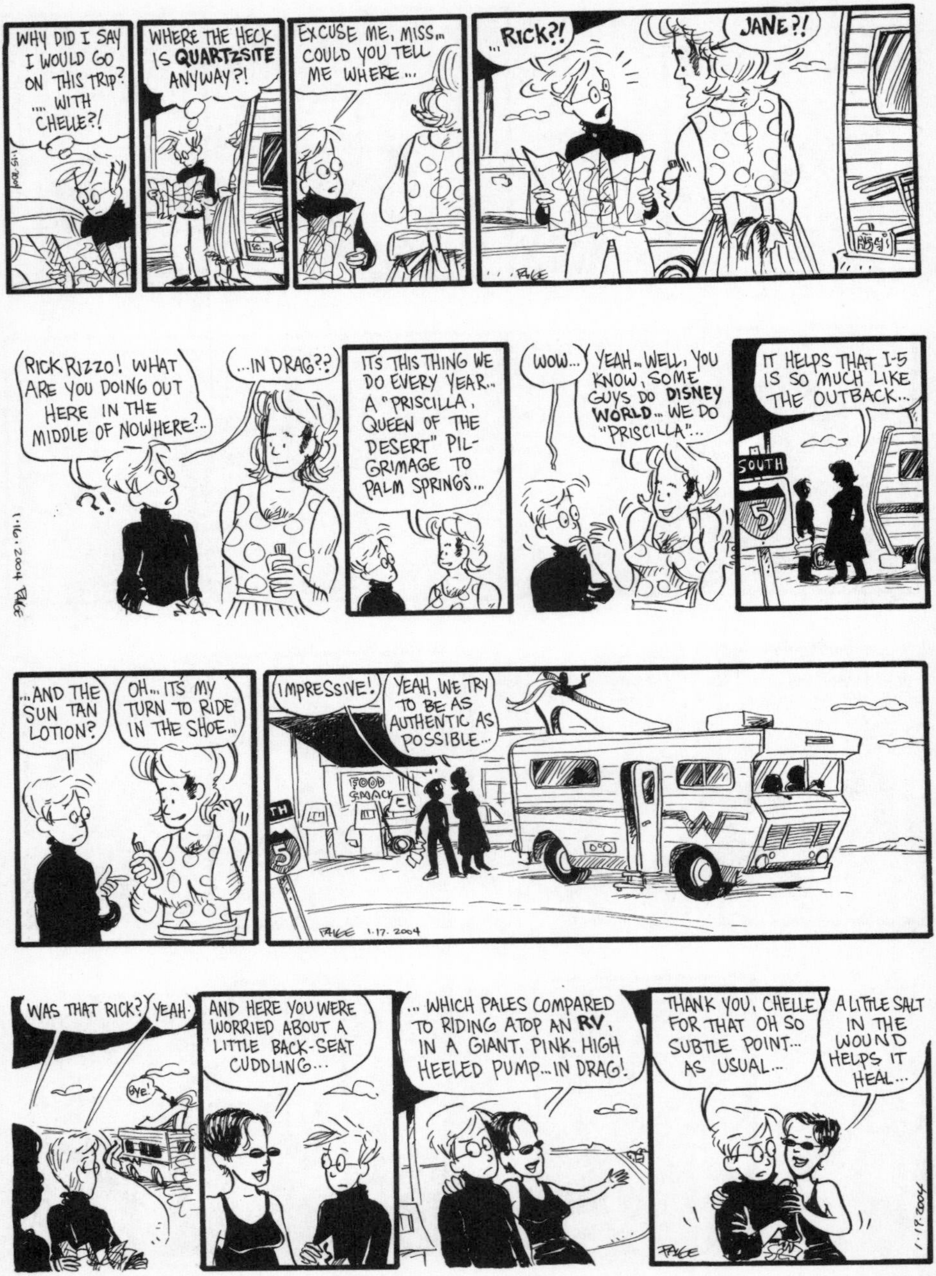
WHY DID I SAY I WOULD GO ON THIS TRIP? .... WITH CHELLE?!
1.15.2004
WHERE THE HECK IS QUARTZSITE ANYWAY?!
EXCUSE ME, MISS... COULD YOU TELL ME WHERE...
...RICK?!
JANE?!
PAGE
RICK RIZZO! WHAT ARE YOU DOING OUT HERE IN THE MIDDLE OF NOWHERE?...
?!
...IN DRAG??
1.16.2004
PAGE
IT'S THIS THING WE DO EVERY YEAR.. A "PRISCILLA, QUEEN OF THE DESERT" PILGRIMAGE TO PALM SPRINGS...
WOW...
YEAH... WELL, YOU KNOW, SOME GUYS DO DISNEY WORLD... WE DO "PRISCILLA"...
IT HELPS THAT I-5 IS SO MUCH LIKE THE OUTBACK...
SOUTH
5
...AND THE SUN TAN LOTION?
OH... IT'S MY TURN TO RIDE IN THE SHOE...
IMPRESSIVE!
YEAH, WE TRY TO BE AS AUTHENTIC AS POSSIBLE...
FOOD SHACK
PAGE 1.17.2004
WAS THAT RICK?
YEAH.
BYE!
AND HERE YOU WERE WORRIED ABOUT A LITTLE BACK-SEAT CUDDLING...
... WHICH PALES COMPARED TO RIDING ATOP AN RV, IN A GIANT, PINK, HIGH HEELED PUMP... IN DRAG!
THANK YOU, CHELLE FOR THAT OH SO SUBTLE POINT... AS USUAL...
A LITTLE SALT IN THE WOUND HELPS IT HEAL...
PAGE
1.19.2004

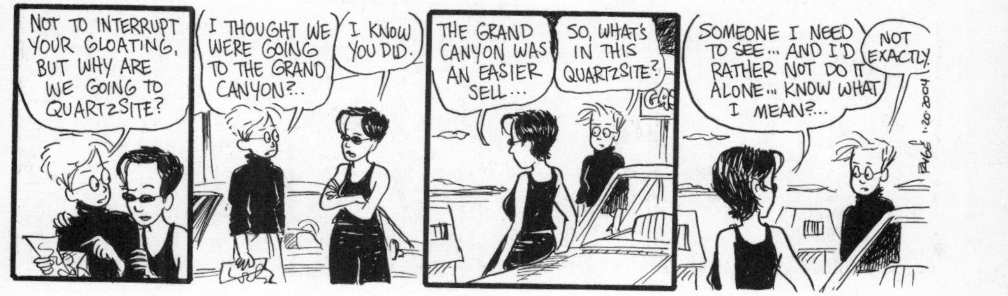
NOT TO INTERRUPT YOUR GLOATING, BUT WHY ARE WE GOING TO QUARTZSITE?
I THOUGHT WE WERE GOING TO THE GRAND CANYON?..
I KNOW YOU DID.
THE GRAND CANYON WAS AN EASIER SELL...
SO, WHAT'S IN THIS QUARTZSITE?
SOMEONE I NEED TO SEE... AND I'D RATHER NOT DO IT ALONE... KNOW WHAT I MEAN?...
NOT EXACTLY.
PAIGE 1.20.2004

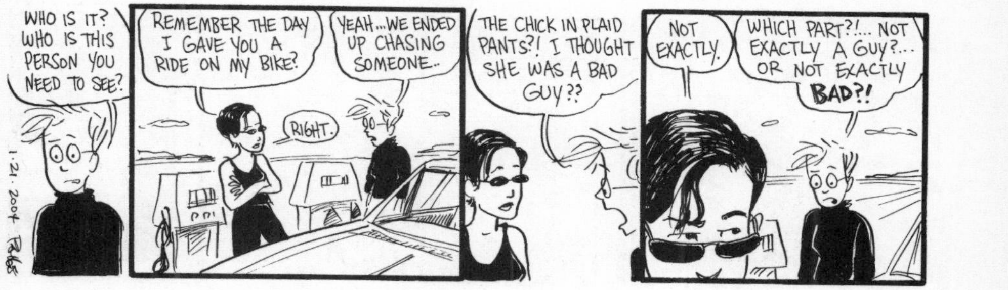
WHO IS IT? WHO IS THIS PERSON YOU NEED TO SEE?
1.21.2004 PAIGE
REMEMBER THE DAY I GAVE YOU A RIDE ON MY BIKE?
YEAH... WE ENDED UP CHASING SOMEONE..
RIGHT.
THE CHICK IN PLAID PANTS?! I THOUGHT SHE WAS A BAD GUY??
NOT EXACTLY.
WHICH PART?!... NOT EXACTLY A GUY?... OR NOT EXACTLY BAD?!

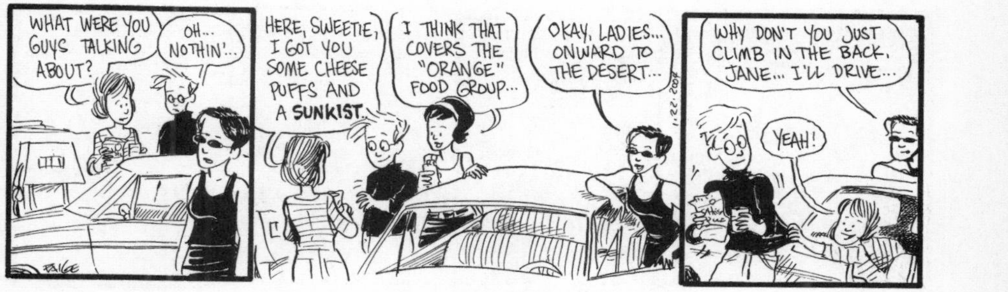
WHAT WERE YOU GUYS TALKING ABOUT?
OH... NOTHIN'...
PAIGE
HERE, SWEETIE, I GOT YOU SOME CHEESE PUFFS AND A SUNKIST.
I THINK THAT COVERS THE "ORANGE" FOOD GROUP...
OKAY, LADIES... ONWARD TO THE DESERT...
1.22.2004
WHY DON'T YOU JUST CLIMB IN THE BACK, JANE... I'LL DRIVE...
YEAH!

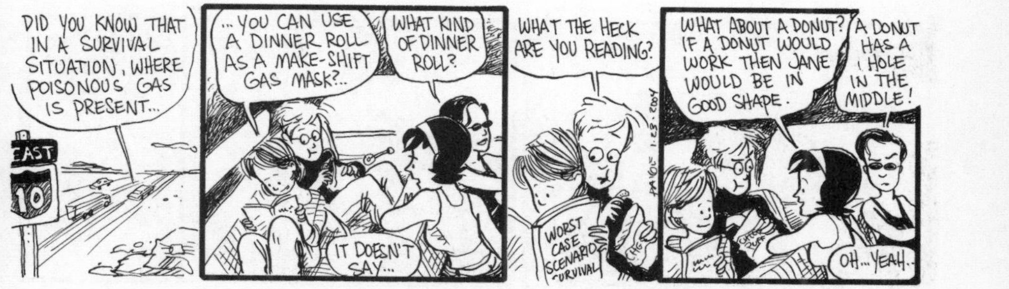
DID YOU KNOW THAT IN A SURVIVAL SITUATION, WHERE POISONOUS GAS IS PRESENT...
EAST
10
...YOU CAN USE A DINNER ROLL AS A MAKE-SHIFT GAS MASK?...
WHAT KIND OF DINNER ROLL?
IT DOESN'T SAY...
WHAT THE HECK ARE YOU READING?
WORST CASE SCENARIO SURVIVAL
PAIGE 1.23.2004
WHAT ABOUT A DONUT? IF A DONUT WOULD WORK THEN JANE WOULD BE IN GOOD SHAPE.
A DONUT HAS A HOLE IN THE MIDDLE!
OH... YEAH...

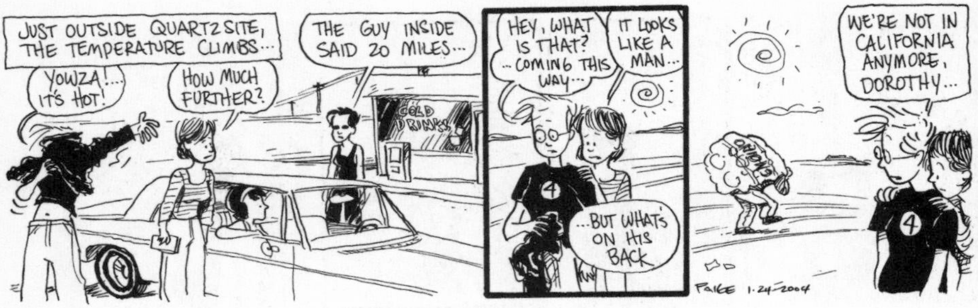
JUST OUTSIDE QUARTZSITE, THE TEMPERATURE CLIMBS...
YOWZA!... IT'S HOT!
HOW MUCH FURTHER?
THE GUY INSIDE SAID 20 MILES...
COLD DRINKS
HEY, WHAT IS THAT? ...COMING THIS WAY...
IT LOOKS LIKE A MAN...
...BUT WHAT'S ON HIS BACK
PAIGE 1.24.2004
WE'RE NOT IN CALIFORNIA ANYMORE, DOROTHY...

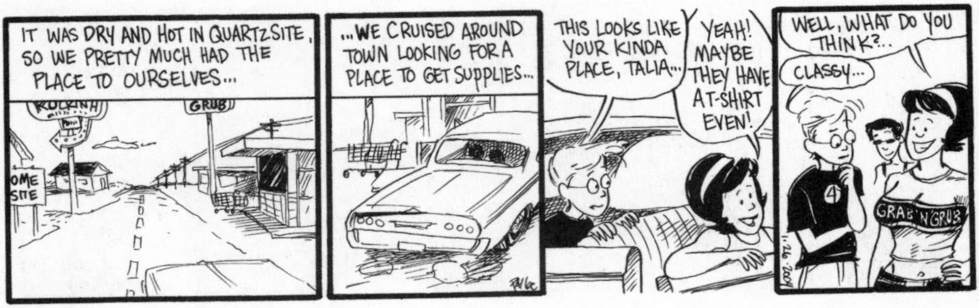
IT WAS DRY AND HOT IN QUARTZSITE, SO WE PRETTY MUCH HAD THE PLACE TO OURSELVES...
GRUB
...WE CRUISED AROUND TOWN LOOKING FOR A PLACE TO GET SUPPLIES...
THIS LOOKS LIKE YOUR KINDA PLACE, TALIA...
YEAH! MAYBE THEY HAVE A T-SHIRT EVEN!
WELL, WHAT DO YOU THINK?..
CLASSY...
GRAB 'N' GRUB
1.26.2004

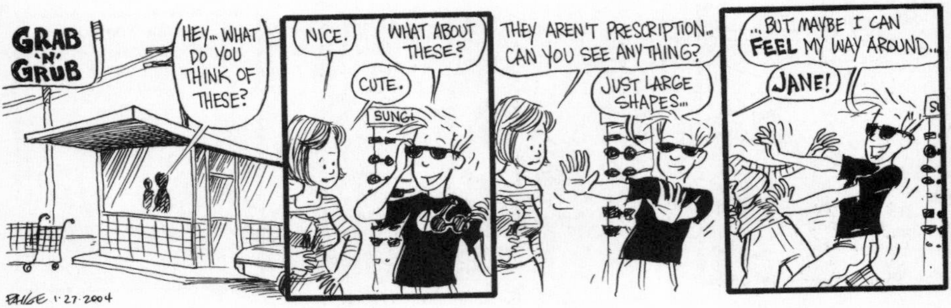
GRAB 'N' GRUB
HEY... WHAT DO YOU THINK OF THESE?
NICE.
WHAT ABOUT THESE?
CUTE.
THEY AREN'T PRESCRIPTION... CAN YOU SEE ANYTHING?
JUST LARGE SHAPES...
...BUT MAYBE I CAN FEEL MY WAY AROUND...
JANE!
PAIGE 1.27.2004

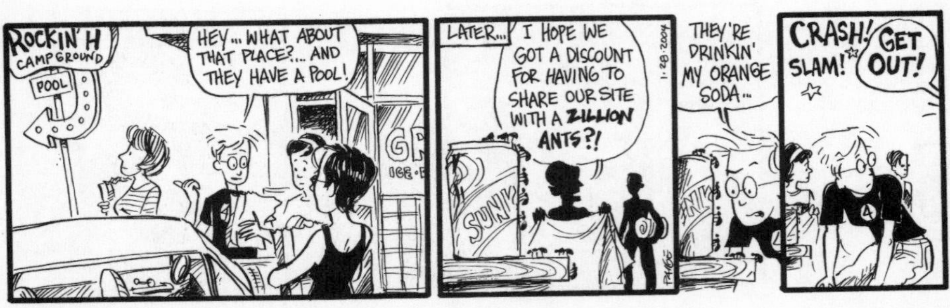
ROCKIN' H CAMPGROUND
POOL
HEY... WHAT ABOUT THAT PLACE?... AND THEY HAVE A POOL!
LATER...
I HOPE WE GOT A DISCOUNT FOR HAVING TO SHARE OUR SITE WITH A ZILLION ANTS?!
1.28.2004
THEY'RE DRINKIN' MY ORANGE SODA...
CRASH! SLAM!
GET OUT!

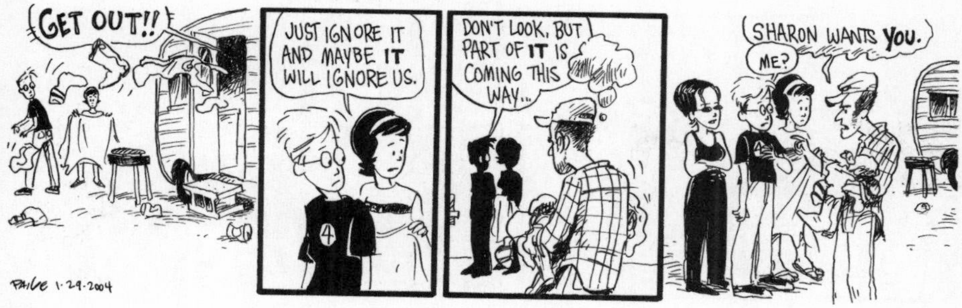
GET OUT!!
PAIGE 1.29.2004
JUST IGNORE IT AND MAYBE IT WILL IGNORE US.
DON'T LOOK, BUT PART OF IT IS COMING THIS WAY...
SHARON WANTS YOU.
ME?

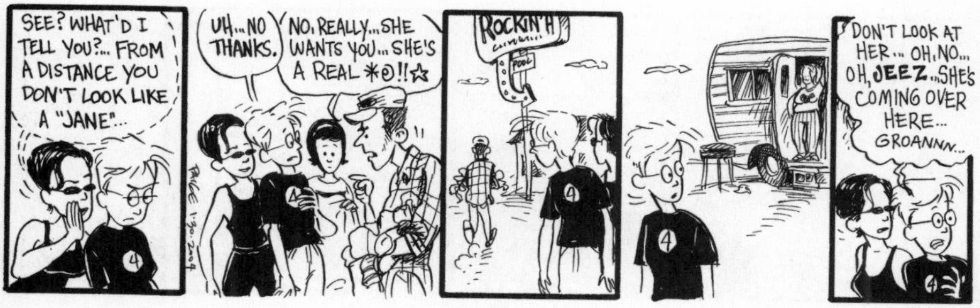
SEE? WHAT'D I TELL YOU?... FROM A DISTANCE YOU DON'T LOOK LIKE A "JANE"...
UH...NO THANKS.
NO, REALLY...SHE WANTS YOU...SHE'S A REAL *@!!☆
PAIGE 1.30.2004
ROCKIN' H
POOL
DON'T LOOK AT HER... OH, NO... OH, JEEZ...SHE'S COMING OVER HERE... GROANNN...

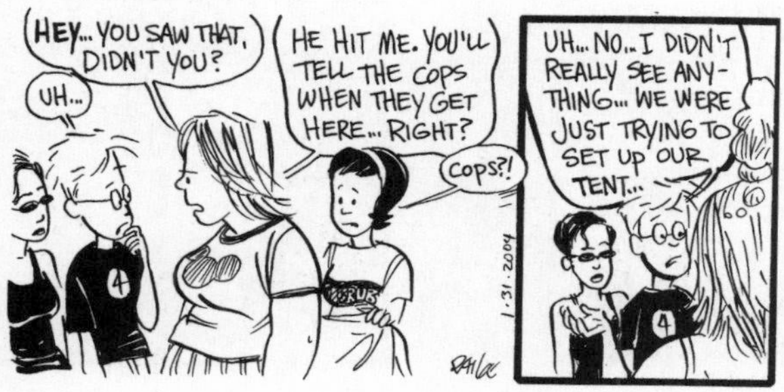
HEY... YOU SAW THAT, DIDN'T YOU?
UH...
HE HIT ME. YOU'LL TELL THE COPS WHEN THEY GET HERE... RIGHT?
Cops?!
1.31.2004
PAIGE
UH... NO... I DIDN'T REALLY SEE ANYTHING... WE WERE JUST TRYING TO SET UP OUR TENT...

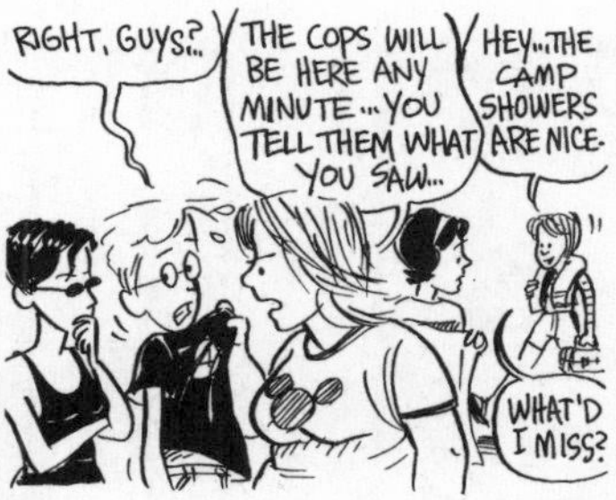
RIGHT, GUYS?...
THE COPS WILL BE HERE ANY MINUTE... YOU TELL THEM WHAT YOU SAW...
HEY...THE CAMP SHOWERS ARE NICE.
WHAT'D I MISS?

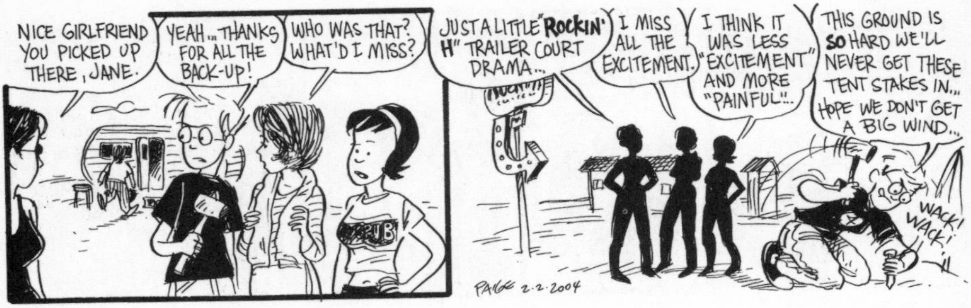
NICE GIRLFRIEND YOU PICKED UP THERE, JANE.
YEAH... THANKS FOR ALL THE BACK-UP!
WHO WAS THAT? WHAT'D I MISS?
JUST A LITTLE "ROCKIN' H" TRAILER COURT DRAMA...
I MISS ALL THE EXCITEMENT.
I THINK IT WAS LESS "EXCITEMENT" AND MORE "PAINFUL"...
THIS GROUND IS SO HARD WE'LL NEVER GET THESE TENT STAKES IN... HOPE WE DON'T GET A BIG WIND...
WACK! WACK!
PAIGE 2.2.2004

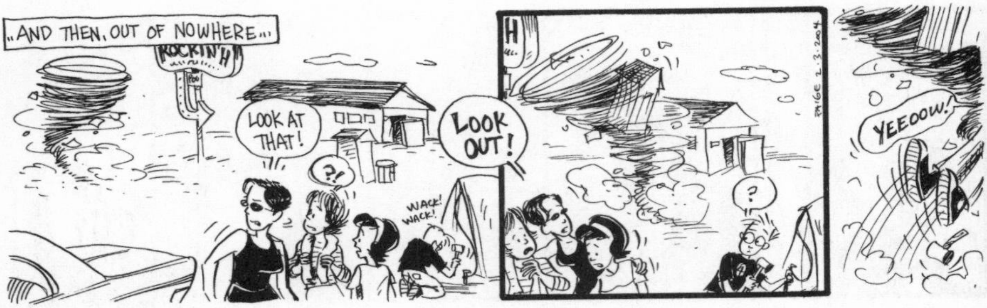
...AND THEN, OUT OF NOWHERE...
LOOK AT THAT!
?!
WACK! WACK!
LOOK OUT!
?
YEEOOW!
PAIGE 2.3.2004

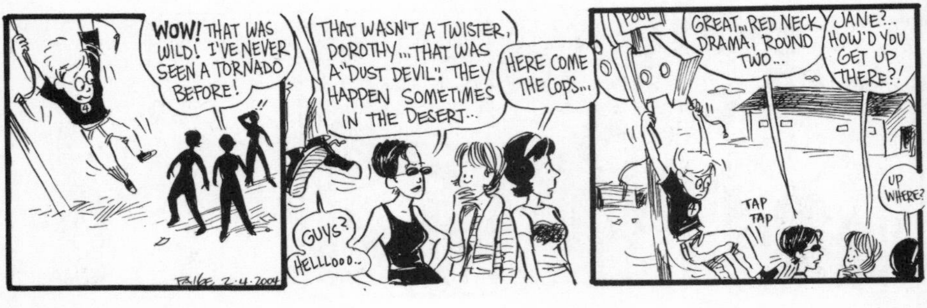
WOW! THAT WAS WILD! I'VE NEVER SEEN A TORNADO BEFORE!
!!
THAT WASN'T A TWISTER, DOROTHY... THAT WAS A "DUST DEVIL". THEY HAPPEN SOMETIMES IN THE DESERT...
GUYS? HELLLOOO..
HERE COME THE COPS...
POOL
GREAT... RED NECK DRAMA, ROUND TWO...
JANE?.. HOW'D YOU GET UP THERE?!
TAP TAP
UP WHERE?
PAIGE 2.4.2004

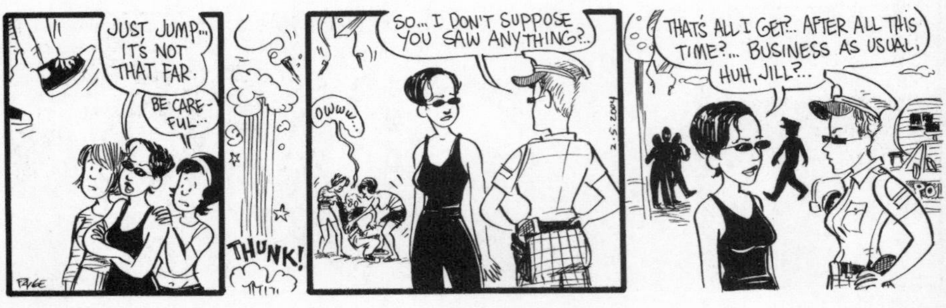
JUST JUMP... IT'S NOT THAT FAR.
BE CAREFUL...
THUNK!
OWWW...
SO... I DON'T SUPPOSE YOU SAW ANYTHING?..
2.5.2004
THAT'S ALL I GET?.. AFTER ALL THIS TIME?... BUSINESS AS USUAL, HUH, JILL?...
PAIGE

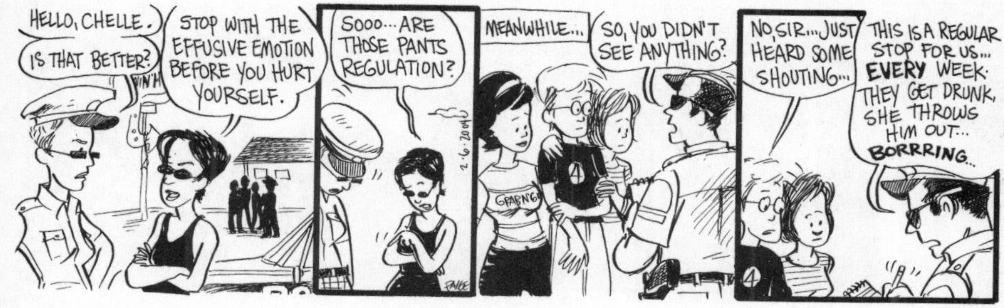
HELLO, CHELLE.
IS THAT BETTER?
STOP WITH THE EFFUSIVE EMOTION BEFORE YOU HURT YOURSELF.
SOOO... ARE THOSE PANTS REGULATION?
2-6-2004
MEANWHILE...
SO, YOU DIDN'T SEE ANYTHING?
NO, SIR... JUST HEARD SOME SHOUTING...
THIS IS A REGULAR STOP FOR US... **EVERY** WEEK. THEY GET DRUNK, SHE THROWS HIM OUT... **BORRRING**...

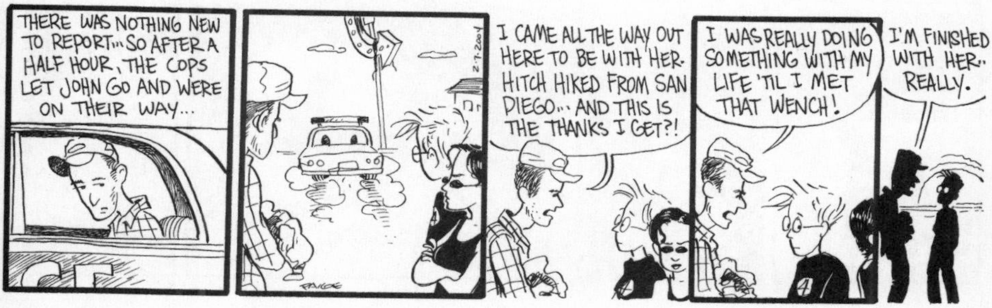
THERE WAS NOTHING NEW TO REPORT... SO AFTER A HALF HOUR, THE COPS LET JOHN GO AND WERE ON THEIR WAY...
2-7-2004
I CAME ALL THE WAY OUT HERE TO BE WITH HER. HITCH HIKED FROM SAN DIEGO... AND THIS IS THE THANKS I GET?!
I WAS REALLY DOING SOMETHING WITH MY LIFE 'TIL I MET THAT WENCH!
I'M FINISHED WITH HER... REALLY.

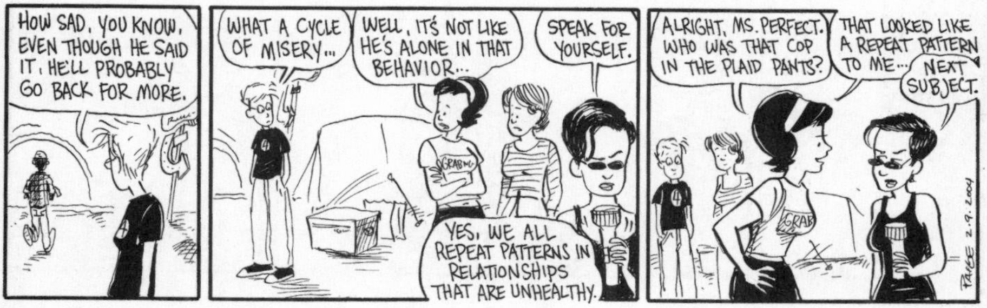
HOW SAD. YOU KNOW, EVEN THOUGH HE SAID IT, HE'LL PROBABLY GO BACK FOR MORE.
WHAT A CYCLE OF MISERY...
WELL, IT'S NOT LIKE HE'S ALONE IN THAT BEHAVIOR...
YES, WE ALL REPEAT PATTERNS IN RELATIONSHIPS THAT ARE UNHEALTHY.
SPEAK FOR YOURSELF.
ALRIGHT, MS. PERFECT. WHO WAS THAT COP IN THE PLAID PANTS?
THAT LOOKED LIKE A REPEAT PATTERN TO ME...
NEXT SUBJECT.
2-9-2004

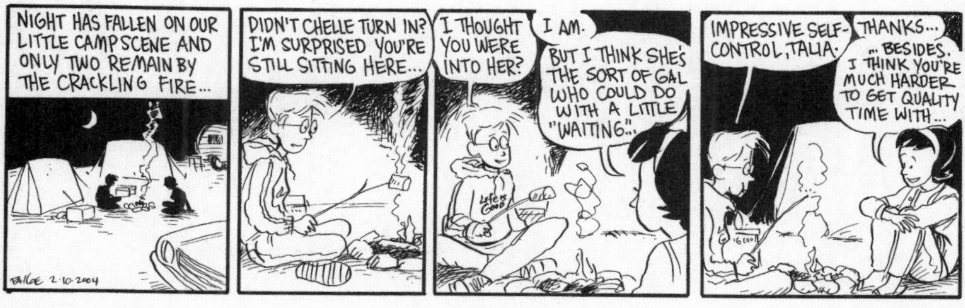
NIGHT HAS FALLEN ON OUR LITTLE CAMP SCENE AND ONLY TWO REMAIN BY THE CRACKLING FIRE...
2-10-2004
DIDN'T CHELLE TURN IN? I'M SURPRISED YOU'RE STILL SITTING HERE...
I THOUGHT YOU WERE INTO HER?
I AM.
BUT I THINK SHE'S THE SORT OF GAL WHO COULD DO WITH A LITTLE "WAITING."
IMPRESSIVE SELF-CONTROL, TALIA.
THANKS...
... BESIDES. I THINK YOU'RE MUCH HARDER TO GET QUALITY TIME WITH...

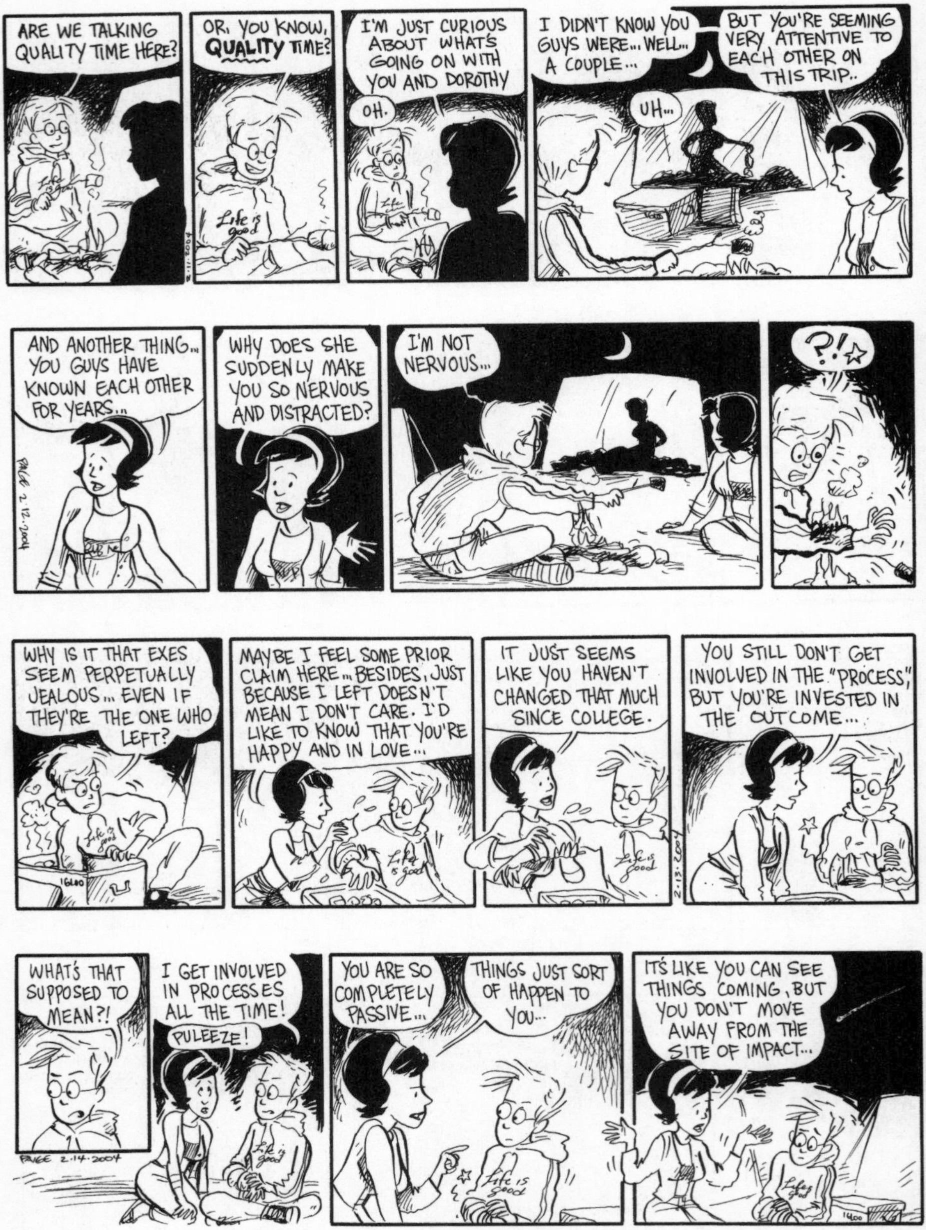
ARE WE TALKING QUALITY TIME HERE?
OR, YOU KNOW, QUALITY TIME?
2.11.2004
I'M JUST CURIOUS ABOUT WHAT'S GOING ON WITH YOU AND DOROTHY
OH.
I DIDN'T KNOW YOU GUYS WERE... WELL... A COUPLE...
BUT YOU'RE SEEMING VERY ATTENTIVE TO EACH OTHER ON THIS TRIP..
UH...
AND ANOTHER THING... YOU GUYS HAVE KNOWN EACH OTHER FOR YEARS...
PAIGE 2.12.2004
WHY DOES SHE SUDDENLY MAKE YOU SO NERVOUS AND DISTRACTED?
I'M NOT NERVOUS...
?!☆
WHY IS IT THAT EXES SEEM PERPETUALLY JEALOUS... EVEN IF THEY'RE THE ONE WHO LEFT?
MAYBE I FEEL SOME PRIOR CLAIM HERE... BESIDES, JUST BECAUSE I LEFT DOESN'T MEAN I DON'T CARE. I'D LIKE TO KNOW THAT YOU'RE HAPPY AND IN LOVE...
IT JUST SEEMS LIKE YOU HAVEN'T CHANGED THAT MUCH SINCE COLLEGE.
2.13.2004
YOU STILL DON'T GET INVOLVED IN THE "PROCESS," BUT YOU'RE INVESTED IN THE OUTCOME...
WHAT'S THAT SUPPOSED TO MEAN?!
PAIGE 2.14.2004
I GET INVOLVED IN PROCESSES ALL THE TIME!
PULEEZE!
YOU ARE SO COMPLETELY PASSIVE...
THINGS JUST SORT OF HAPPEN TO YOU...
IT'S LIKE YOU CAN SEE THINGS COMING, BUT YOU DON'T MOVE AWAY FROM THE SITE OF IMPACT...

SITE OF IMPACT, HUH?... GIVE ME ONE GOOD EXAMPLE...
YOU AND CHELLE.
YOU GUYS COULDN'T BE ANY MORE WRONG FOR EACH OTHER AND YET, YOU CAN'T STAY AWAY FROM HER.
I'M AWAY FROM HER... AT LEAST TEN FEET...
BUT YOU'RE ON THIS TRIP...
BUT...
THIS ISN'T ABOUT YOU AND CHELLE ANYWAY...
BUT...
LOOK, I LIKE DOROTHY. OBVIOUSLY... I MEAN, WE HAD THAT FLING IN COLLEGE...
SO, I'M NOT DOWN ON DOROTHY... ALL I'M SAYING IS PAY ATTENTION.
LIVE DELIBERATELY. DON'T JUST BE ATTRACTED TO THE ATTRACTION... MAKE A CHOICE AND INVEST YOURSELF IN IT.
WHO ARE YOU? AND WHAT HAVE YOU DONE WITH TALIA?..
I'M SERIOUS, JANE. THINK ABOUT IT.
SWEET DREAMS.
I DON'T KNOW WHAT SHE'S TALKING ABOUT. I'M NOT PASSIVE!...
I MEAN, THERE WAS ANNE, IN HIGH SCHOOL...
SHE WAS MY BEST FRIEND AND WE USED TO HAVE LOTS OF SLEEP OVERS...
AND IT DID SEEM LIKE SHE WANTED TO BE MORE THAN FRIENDS.
...BUT, WHO KNEW SHE'D TURN OUT TO BE GAY?
WE COULD SHOWER TOGETHER... TO CONSERVE WATER, OF COURSE...

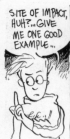

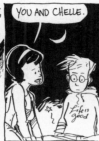

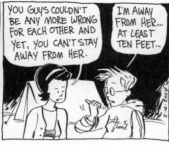

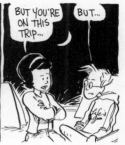

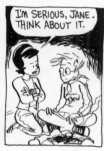

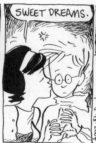

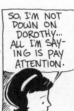

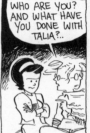

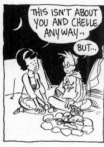

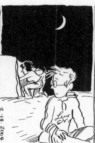

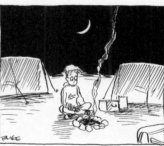

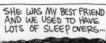

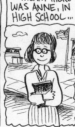

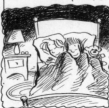

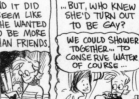

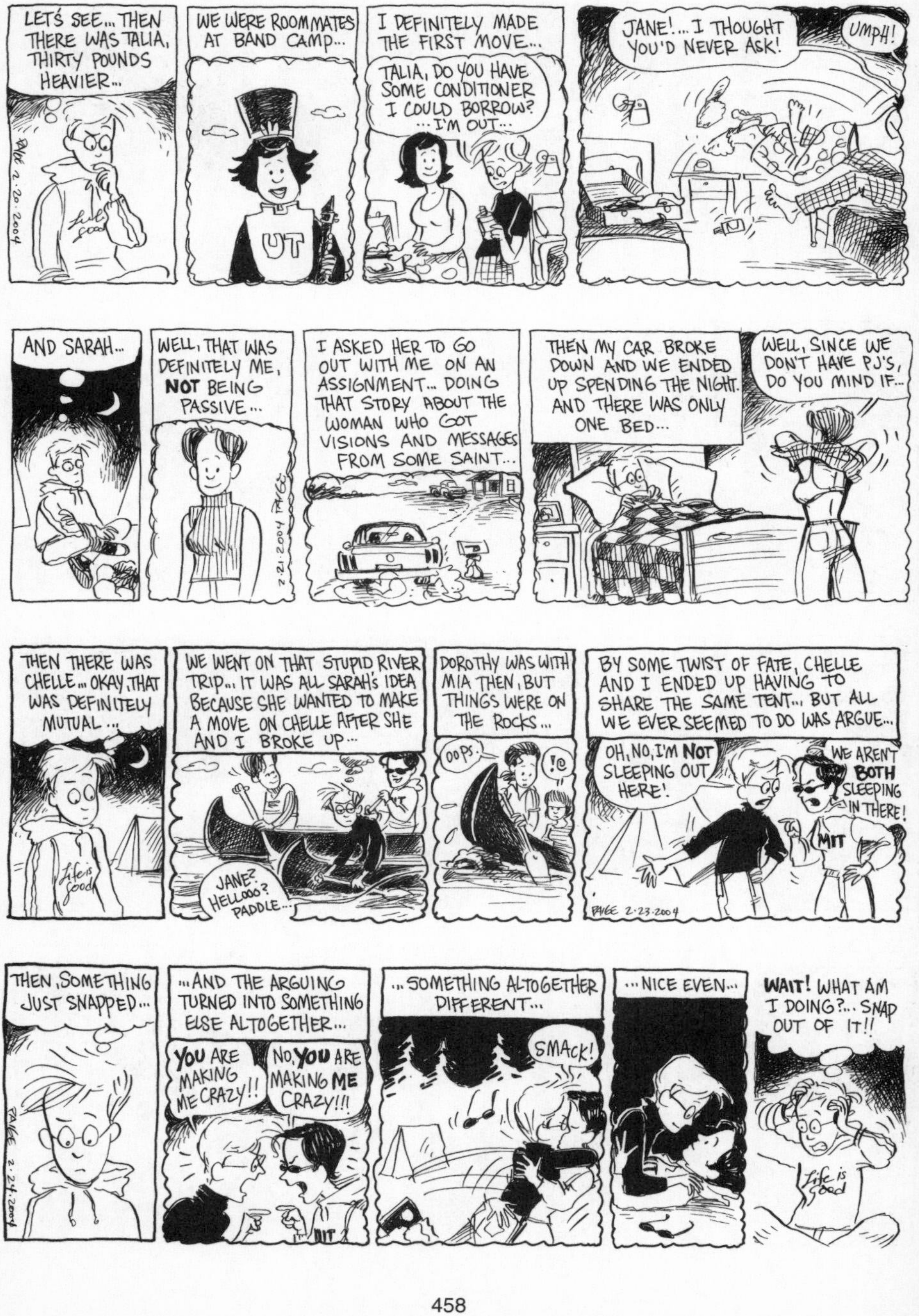
LET'S SEE... THEN THERE WAS TALIA, THIRTY POUNDS HEAVIER...
WE WERE ROOMMATES AT BAND CAMP...
UT
I DEFINITELY MADE THE FIRST MOVE...
TALIA, DO YOU HAVE SOME CONDITIONER I COULD BORROW? ...I'M OUT...
JANE!... I THOUGHT YOU'D NEVER ASK!
UMPH!
AND SARAH...
WELL, THAT WAS DEFINITELY ME, NOT BEING PASSIVE...
I ASKED HER TO GO OUT WITH ME ON AN ASSIGNMENT... DOING THAT STORY ABOUT THE WOMAN WHO GOT VISIONS AND MESSAGES FROM SOME SAINT...
THEN MY CAR BROKE DOWN AND WE ENDED UP SPENDING THE NIGHT. AND THERE WAS ONLY ONE BED...
WELL, SINCE WE DON'T HAVE PJ'S, DO YOU MIND IF...
THEN THERE WAS CHELLE... OKAY, THAT WAS DEFINITELY MUTUAL...
life is good
WE WENT ON THAT STUPID RIVER TRIP... IT WAS ALL SARAH'S IDEA BECAUSE SHE WANTED TO MAKE A MOVE ON CHELLE AFTER SHE AND I BROKE UP...
JANE? HELLOOO? PADDLE...
DOROTHY WAS WITH MIA THEN, BUT THINGS WERE ON THE ROCKS...
OOPS.
!@
BY SOME TWIST OF FATE, CHELLE AND I ENDED UP HAVING TO SHARE THE SAME TENT... BUT ALL WE EVER SEEMED TO DO WAS ARGUE...
OH, NO, I'M NOT SLEEPING OUT HERE!
WE AREN'T BOTH SLEEPING IN THERE!
MIT
THEN, SOMETHING JUST SNAPPED...
...AND THE ARGUING TURNED INTO SOMETHING ELSE ALTOGETHER...
YOU ARE MAKING ME CRAZY!!
NO, YOU ARE MAKING ME CRAZY!!!
...SOMETHING ALTOGETHER DIFFERENT...
SMACK!
...NICE EVEN...
WAIT! WHAT AM I DOING?... SNAP OUT OF IT!!
life is good

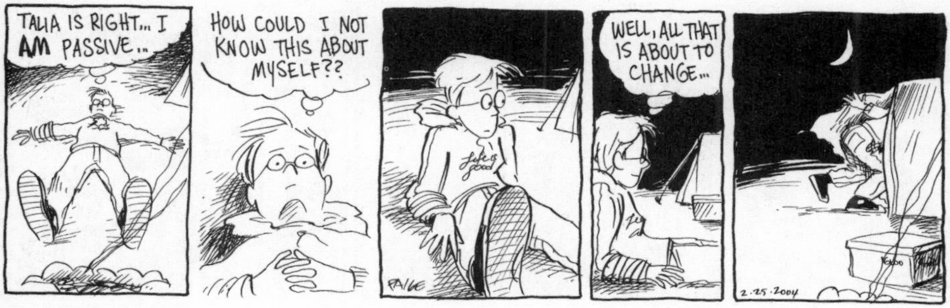
TALIA IS RIGHT... I **AM** PASSIVE...
HOW COULD I NOT KNOW THIS ABOUT MYSELF??
PAIGE
WELL, ALL THAT IS ABOUT TO CHANGE...
2.25.2004

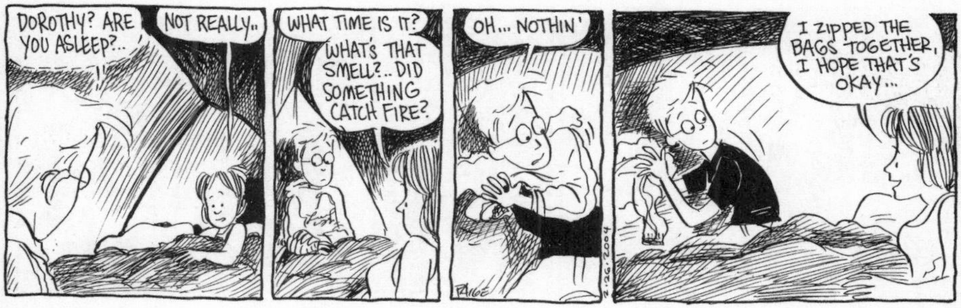
DOROTHY? ARE YOU ASLEEP?..
NOT REALLY..
WHAT TIME IS IT?
WHAT'S THAT SMELL?.. DID SOMETHING CATCH FIRE?
OH... NOTHIN'
PAIGE
2.26.2004
I ZIPPED THE BAGS TOGETHER, I HOPE THAT'S OKAY...

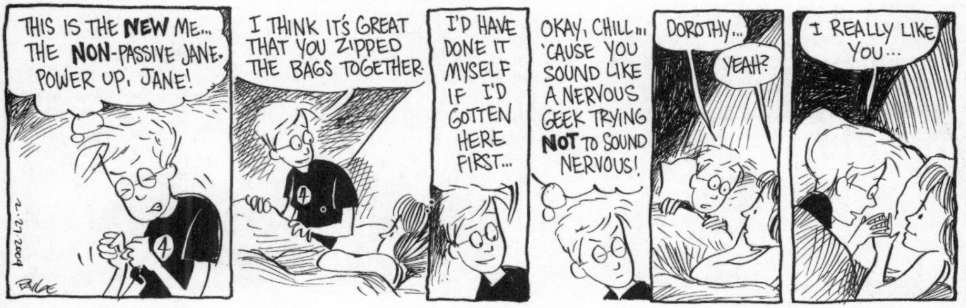
THIS IS THE **NEW** ME... THE **NON**-PASSIVE JANE. POWER UP, JANE!
2.27.2004
PAIGE
I THINK IT'S GREAT THAT YOU ZIPPED THE BAGS TOGETHER.
I'D HAVE DONE IT MYSELF IF I'D GOTTEN HERE FIRST...
OKAY, CHILL... 'CAUSE YOU SOUND LIKE A NERVOUS GEEK TRYING **NOT** TO SOUND NERVOUS!
DOROTHY...
YEAH?
I REALLY LIKE YOU...

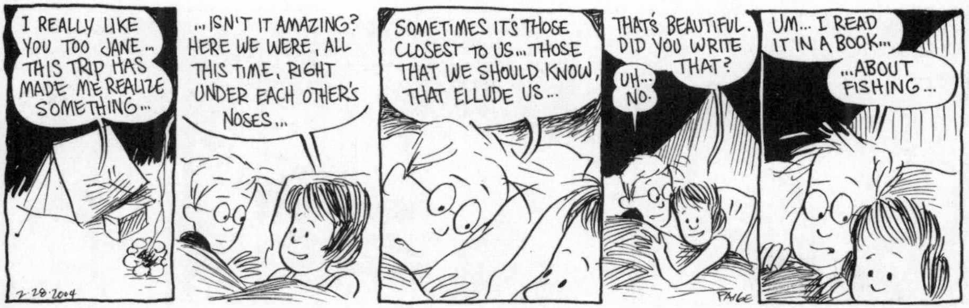
I REALLY LIKE YOU TOO JANE... THIS TRIP HAS MADE ME REALIZE SOMETHING...
2.28.2004
...ISN'T IT AMAZING? HERE WE WERE, ALL THIS TIME, RIGHT UNDER EACH OTHER'S NOSES...
SOMETIMES IT'S THOSE CLOSEST TO US... THOSE THAT WE SHOULD KNOW, THAT ELLUDE US...
THAT'S BEAUTIFUL. DID YOU WRITE THAT?
UH... NO.
PAIGE
UM... I READ IT IN A BOOK...
...ABOUT FISHING...

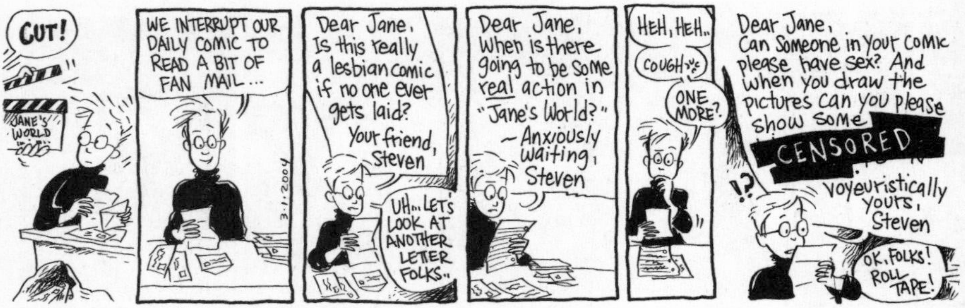
CUT!
JANE'S WORLD
WE INTERRUPT OUR DAILY COMIC TO READ A BIT OF FAN MAIL...
3·1·2004
Dear Jane, Is this really a lesbian comic if no one ever gets laid? Your friend, Steven
UH... LET'S LOOK AT ANOTHER LETTER FOLKS..
Dear Jane, When is there going to be some real action in "Jane's World?" ~Anxiously waiting, Steven
HEH, HEH..
COUGH
ONE MORE?
Dear Jane, Can someone in your comic please have sex? And when you draw the pictures can you please show some
CENSORED
Voyeuristically yours, Steven
!?
OK, FOLKS! ROLL TAPE!

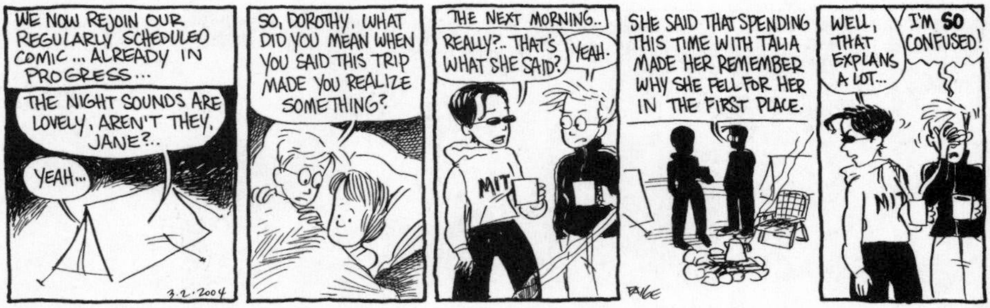
WE NOW REJOIN OUR REGULARLY SCHEDULED COMIC... ALREADY IN PROGRESS...
THE NIGHT SOUNDS ARE LOVELY, AREN'T THEY, JANE?..
YEAH...
3·2·2004
SO, DOROTHY, WHAT DID YOU MEAN WHEN YOU SAID THIS TRIP MADE YOU REALIZE SOMETHING?
THE NEXT MORNING..
REALLY?.. THAT'S WHAT SHE SAID?
YEAH.
MIT
SHE SAID THAT SPENDING THIS TIME WITH TALIA MADE HER REMEMBER WHY SHE FELL FOR HER IN THE FIRST PLACE.
PAIGE
WELL, THAT EXPLANS A LOT...
I'M SO CONFUSED!

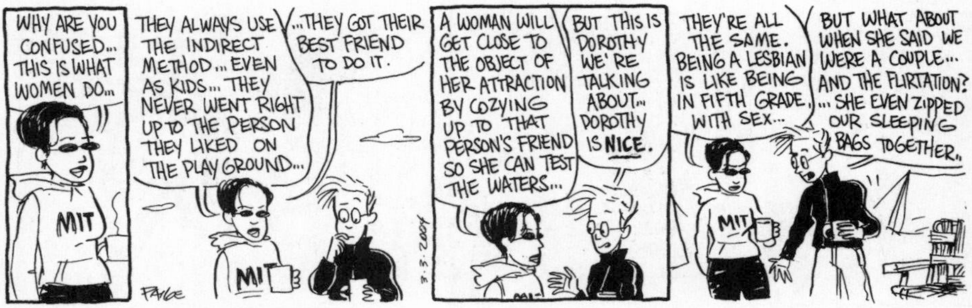
WHY ARE YOU CONFUSED... THIS IS WHAT WOMEN DO...
MIT
PAIGE
THEY ALWAYS USE THE INDIRECT METHOD... EVEN AS KIDS... THEY NEVER WENT RIGHT UP TO THE PERSON THEY LIKED ON THE PLAY GROUND...
...THEY GOT THEIR BEST FRIEND TO DO IT.
3·3·2004
A WOMAN WILL GET CLOSE TO THE OBJECT OF HER ATTRACTION BY COZYING UP TO THAT PERSON'S FRIEND SO SHE CAN TEST THE WATERS...
BUT THIS IS DOROTHY WE'RE TALKING ABOUT... DOROTHY IS NICE.
THEY'RE ALL THE SAME. BEING A LESBIAN IS LIKE BEING IN FIFTH GRADE, WITH SEX...
BUT WHAT ABOUT WHEN SHE SAID WE WERE A COUPLE... AND THE FLIRTATION? ...SHE EVEN ZIPPED OUR SLEEPING BAGS TOGETHER..

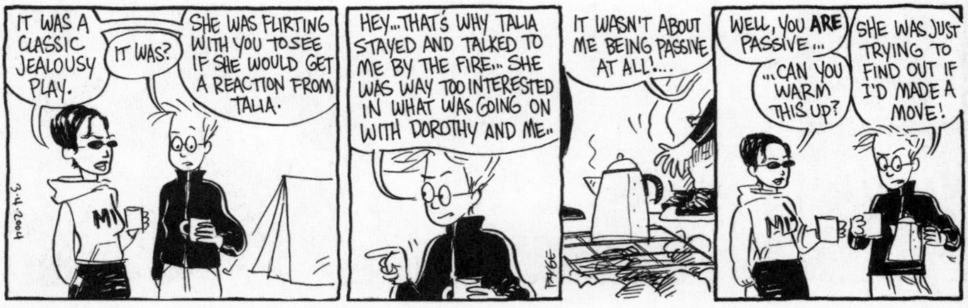
IT WAS A CLASSIC JEALOUSY PLAY.
IT WAS?
SHE WAS FLIRTING WITH YOU TO SEE IF SHE WOULD GET A REACTION FROM TALIA.
3·4·2004
HEY... THAT'S WHY TALIA STAYED AND TALKED TO ME BY THE FIRE... SHE WAS WAY TOO INTERESTED IN WHAT WAS GOING ON WITH DOROTHY AND ME..
IT WASN'T ABOUT ME BEING PASSIVE AT ALL!...
PAIGE
WELL, YOU ARE PASSIVE...
...CAN YOU WARM THIS UP?
SHE WAS JUST TRYING TO FIND OUT IF I'D MADE A MOVE!

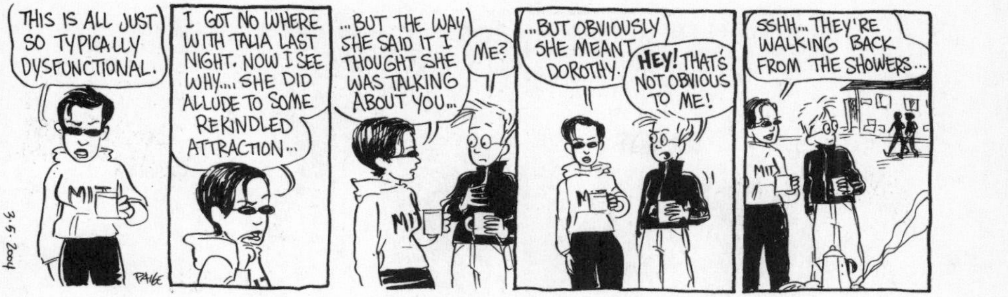
THIS IS ALL JUST SO TYPICALLY DYSFUNCTIONAL.
3.5.2004
PAIGE
I GOT NO WHERE WITH TALIA LAST NIGHT. NOW I SEE WHY... SHE DID ALLUDE TO SOME REKINDLED ATTRACTION...
...BUT THE WAY SHE SAID IT I THOUGHT SHE WAS TALKING ABOUT YOU...
ME?
...BUT OBVIOUSLY SHE MEANT DOROTHY.
HEY! THAT'S NOT OBVIOUS TO ME!
SSHH... THEY'RE WALKING BACK FROM THE SHOWERS...

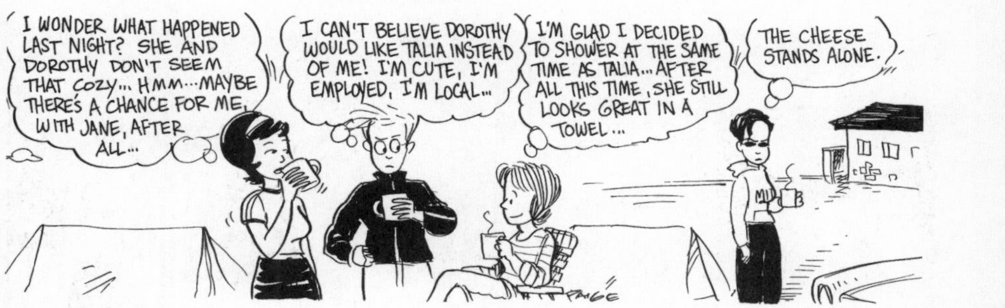
I WONDER WHAT HAPPENED LAST NIGHT? SHE AND DOROTHY DON'T SEEM THAT COZY... HMM... MAYBE THERE'S A CHANCE FOR ME WITH JANE, AFTER ALL...
I CAN'T BELIEVE DOROTHY WOULD LIKE TALIA INSTEAD OF ME! I'M CUTE, I'M EMPLOYED, I'M LOCAL...
I'M GLAD I DECIDED TO SHOWER AT THE SAME TIME AS TALIA... AFTER ALL THIS TIME, SHE STILL LOOKS GREAT IN A TOWEL...
THE CHEESE STANDS ALONE.
PAIGE

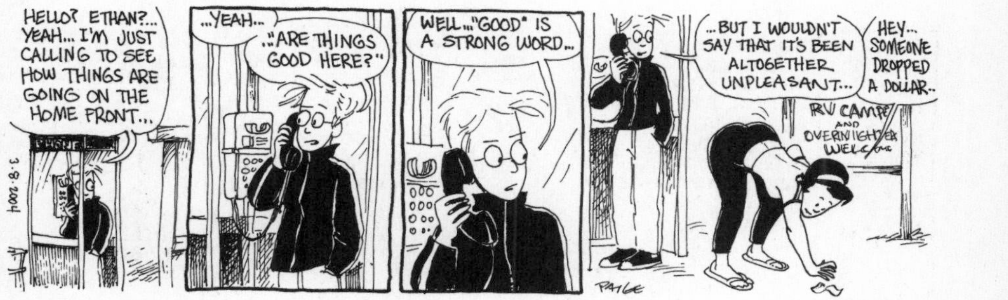
HELLO? ETHAN?... YEAH... I'M JUST CALLING TO SEE HOW THINGS ARE GOING ON THE HOME FRONT...
3.8.2004
PHONE
...YEAH...
..."ARE THINGS GOOD HERE?"
WELL... "GOOD" IS A STRONG WORD...
...BUT I WOULDN'T SAY THAT IT'S BEEN ALTOGETHER UNPLEASANT...
HEY... SOMEONE DROPPED A DOLLAR..
PAIGE

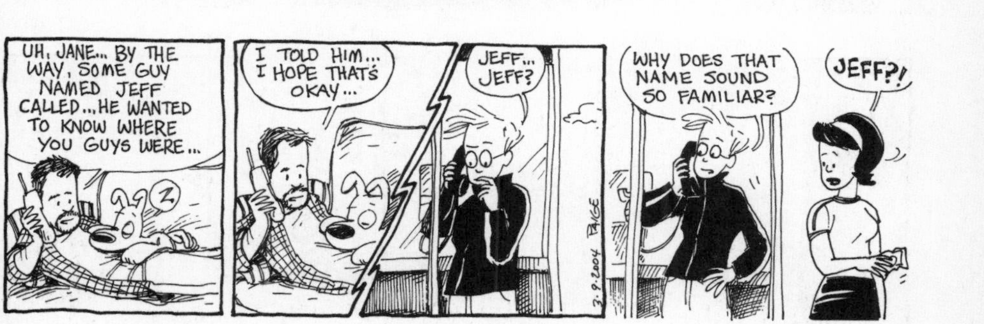
UH, JANE... BY THE WAY, SOME GUY NAMED JEFF CALLED... HE WANTED TO KNOW WHERE YOU GUYS WERE...
I TOLD HIM... I HOPE THAT'S OKAY...
JEFF... JEFF?
3.9.2004
PAIGE
WHY DOES THAT NAME SOUND SO FAMILIAR?
JEFF?!

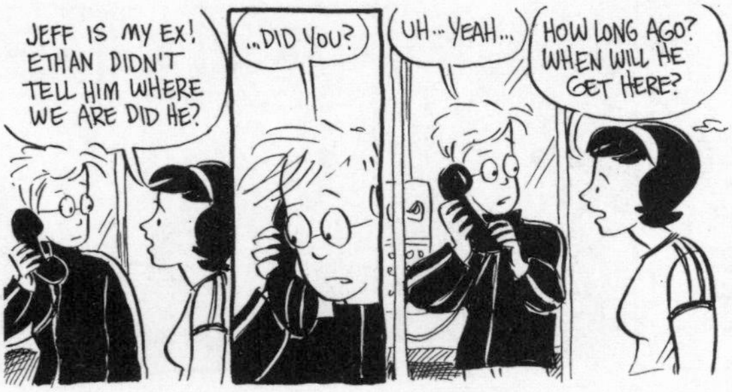
JEFF IS MY EX! ETHAN DIDN'T TELL HIM WHERE WE ARE DID HE?
...DID YOU?
UH... YEAH...
HOW LONG AGO? WHEN WILL HE GET HERE?

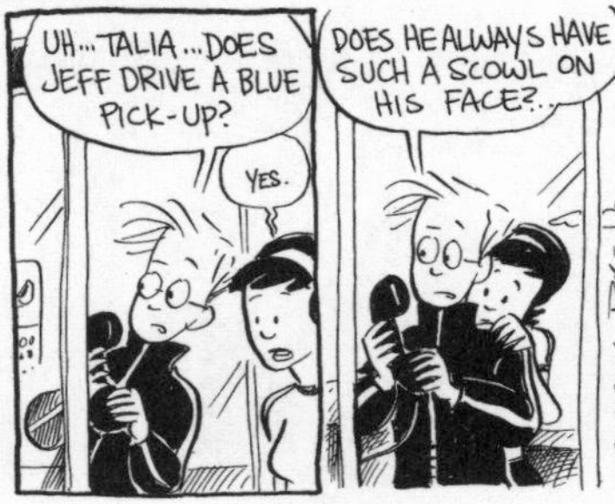
UH... TALIA ...DOES JEFF DRIVE A BLUE PICK-UP?
YES.
DOES HE ALWAYS HAVE SUCH A SCOWL ON HIS FACE?...
PAIGE
3.10.2004

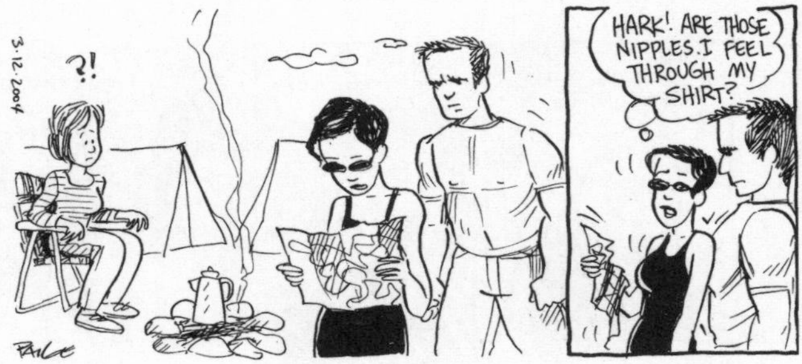
3.12.2004
?!
PAIGE
HARK! ARE THOSE NIPPLES I FEEL THROUGH MY SHIRT?

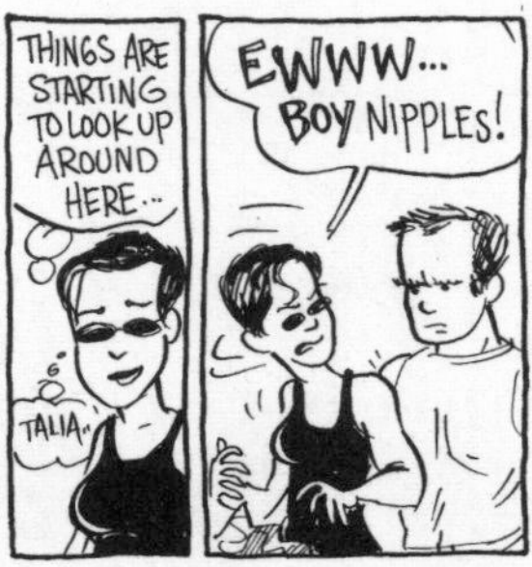
THINGS ARE STARTING TO LOOK UP AROUND HERE...
TALIA..
EWWW... BOY NIPPLES!

THAT'S RIGHT! BOY AS IN THE ABBREVIATION OF BOYFRIEND! WHERE IS TALIA?..
HMM... I DIDN'T KNOW TALIA HAD A BOYFRIEND. ARE YOU SURE ABOUT THAT?
LISTEN CHICKY...
3.13.2004
OH NO... YOU DIDN'T JUST CALL ME "CHICKY"...

DID YOU HEAR ME?
I HEARD YOU..
OW! OW! OWWW!
PAIGE

WHAT'S JEFF DOING HERE? I THOUGHT YOU GUYS BROKE UP...
WE DID, SORT OF...
3.15.2004
COME ON... I THINK WE SHOULD GET OVER THERE BEFORE CHELLE HURTS HIM...
....
ONE

HOW DO YOU "SORT OF" BREAK UP WITH SOMEONE?
PAIGE

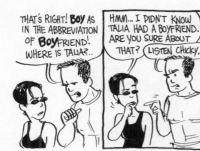

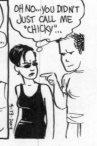

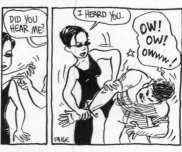

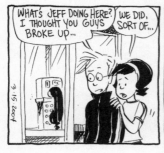

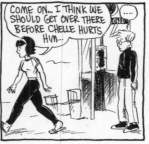

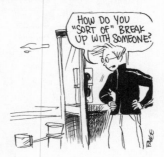

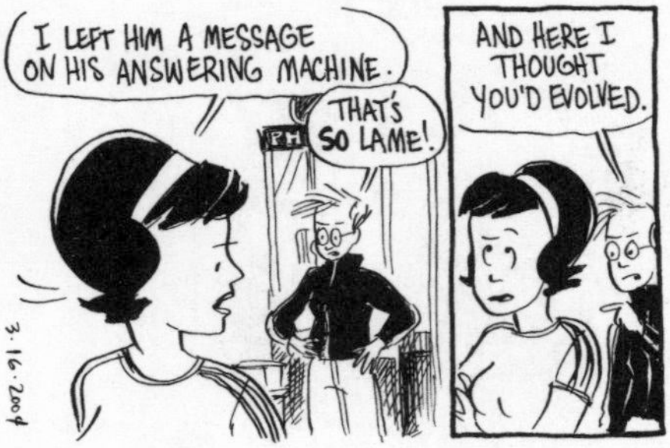
I LEFT HIM A MESSAGE ON HIS ANSWERING MACHINE.
THAT'S SO LAME!
AND HERE I THOUGHT YOU'D EVOLVED.
3.16.2004

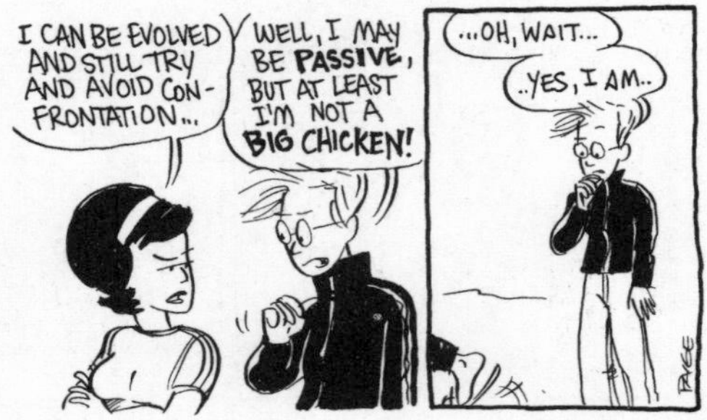
I CAN BE EVOLVED AND STILL TRY AND AVOID CON-FRONTATION...
WELL, I MAY BE **PASSIVE**, BUT AT LEAST I'M NOT A **BIG CHICKEN**!
...OH, WAIT...
..YES, I AM..

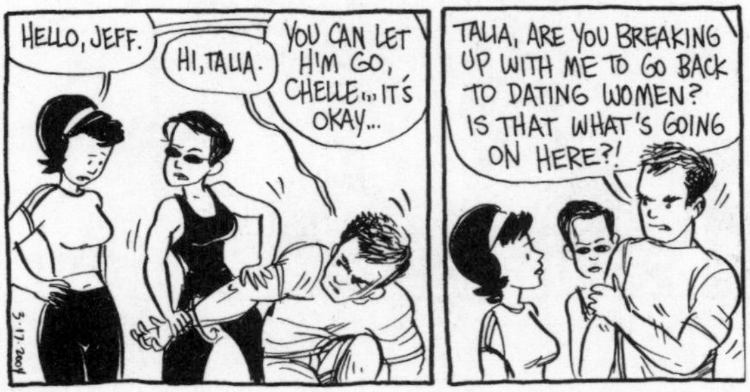
HELLO, JEFF.
HI, TALIA.
YOU CAN LET HIM GO, CHELLE... IT'S OKAY...
3.17.2004
TALIA, ARE YOU BREAKING UP WITH ME TO GO BACK TO DATING WOMEN? IS THAT WHAT'S GOING ON HERE?!

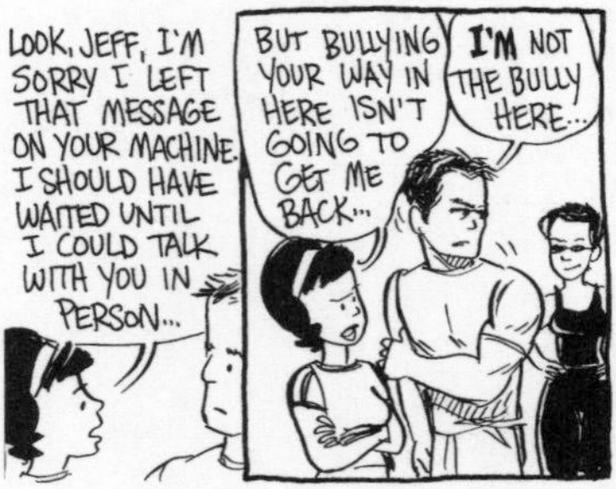
LOOK, JEFF, I'M SORRY I LEFT THAT MESSAGE ON YOUR MACHINE. I SHOULD HAVE WAITED UNTIL I COULD TALK WITH YOU IN PERSON...
BUT BULLYING YOUR WAY IN HERE ISN'T GOING TO GET ME BACK...
I'M NOT THE BULLY HERE...

She's not going to get back together with him is she?

... *!*

16:00

I'm sure I don't care.

What's that supposed to mean?

Why are you acting so mad at me??...

SPOOOF!

!! *?!*

Oh... I don't know, Ms. "I zipped our sleeping bags together"... but it didn't mean anything...

ORANGE SODA

What are you going on about?..

3-18-2004 PAGE

Mixed signals... that's what I'm talking about!

YOU and your MIXED SIGNALS!

You were definitely flirting with me this WHOLE trip!

So?

SO?!.. So, you were flirting with me, but you're interested in TALIA!

Again, I say... So?

PAIGE   3-19-2004

It's not like you were interested in her... You've practically been afraid of her since she got here!

ARRGH... never mind!

No, wait. You're obviously upset... we should talk this out..

465

I DON'T WANT TO TALK ABOUT IT...
WELL, SULKING ISN'T GOING TO SOLVE ANYTHING!
OH... I DUNNO... IT FEELS PRETTY **DARN** GOOD...
LOOK! ME... SULKING...
WHATE
HMMM... FEELS **SOOO** GOOD!
SUIT YOURSELF, JANE..

3·20·2004

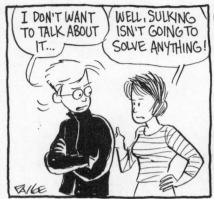

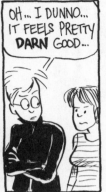

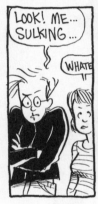

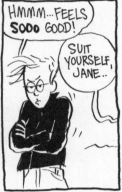

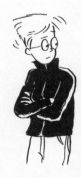

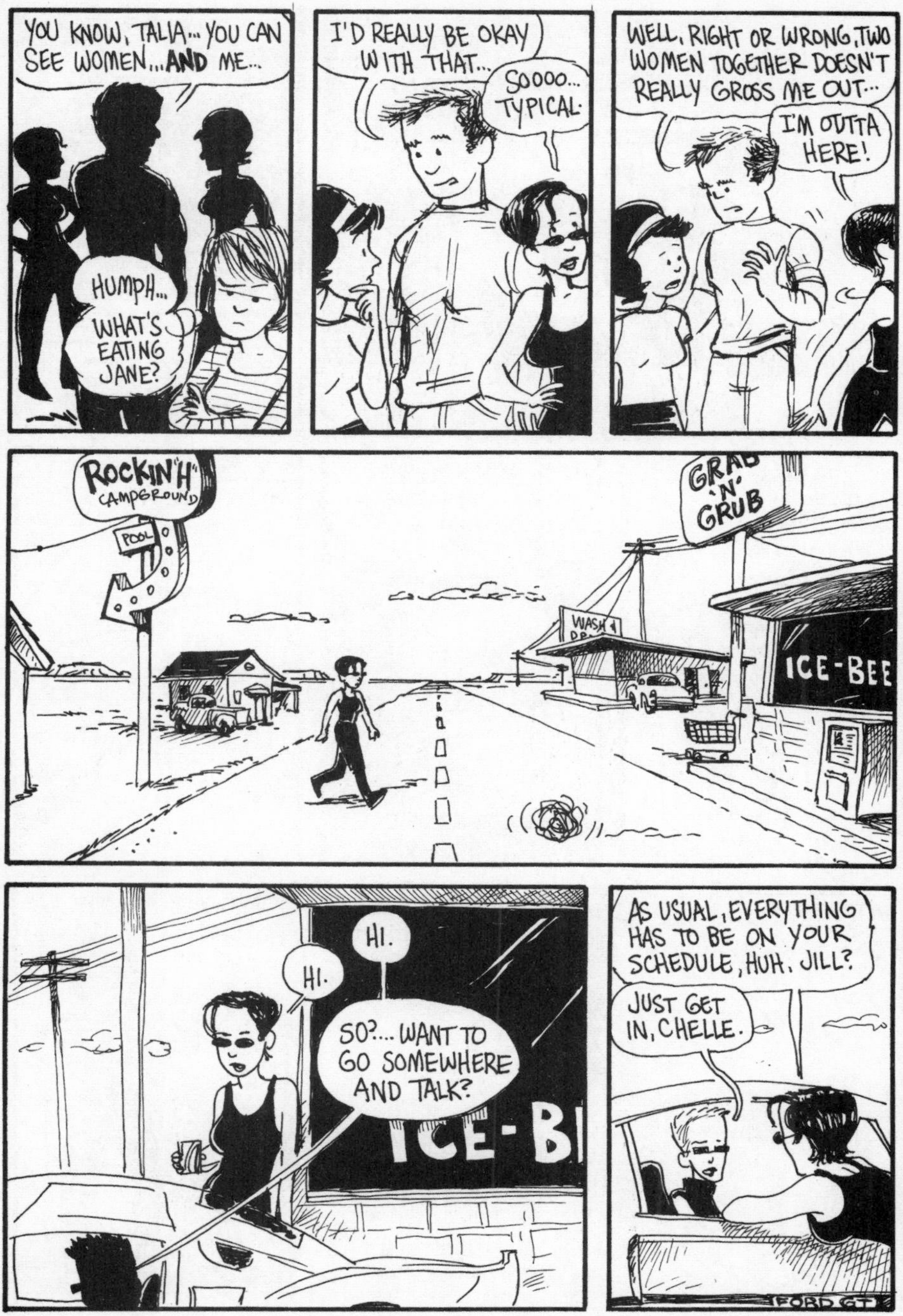

YOU KNOW, TALIA... YOU CAN SEE WOMEN... AND ME...
HUMPH... WHAT'S EATING JANE?
I'D REALLY BE OKAY WITH THAT...
SOOOO... TYPICAL.
WELL, RIGHT OR WRONG, TWO WOMEN TOGETHER DOESN'T REALLY GROSS ME OUT...
I'M OUTTA HERE!
ROCKIN' "H" CAMPGROUND
POOL
GRAB 'N' GRUB
WASH
ICE-BEE
HI.
HI.
SO?... WANT TO GO SOMEWHERE AND TALK?
ICE-B
AS USUAL, EVERYTHING HAS TO BE ON YOUR SCHEDULE, HUH, JILL?
JUST GET IN, CHELLE.
FORD GT

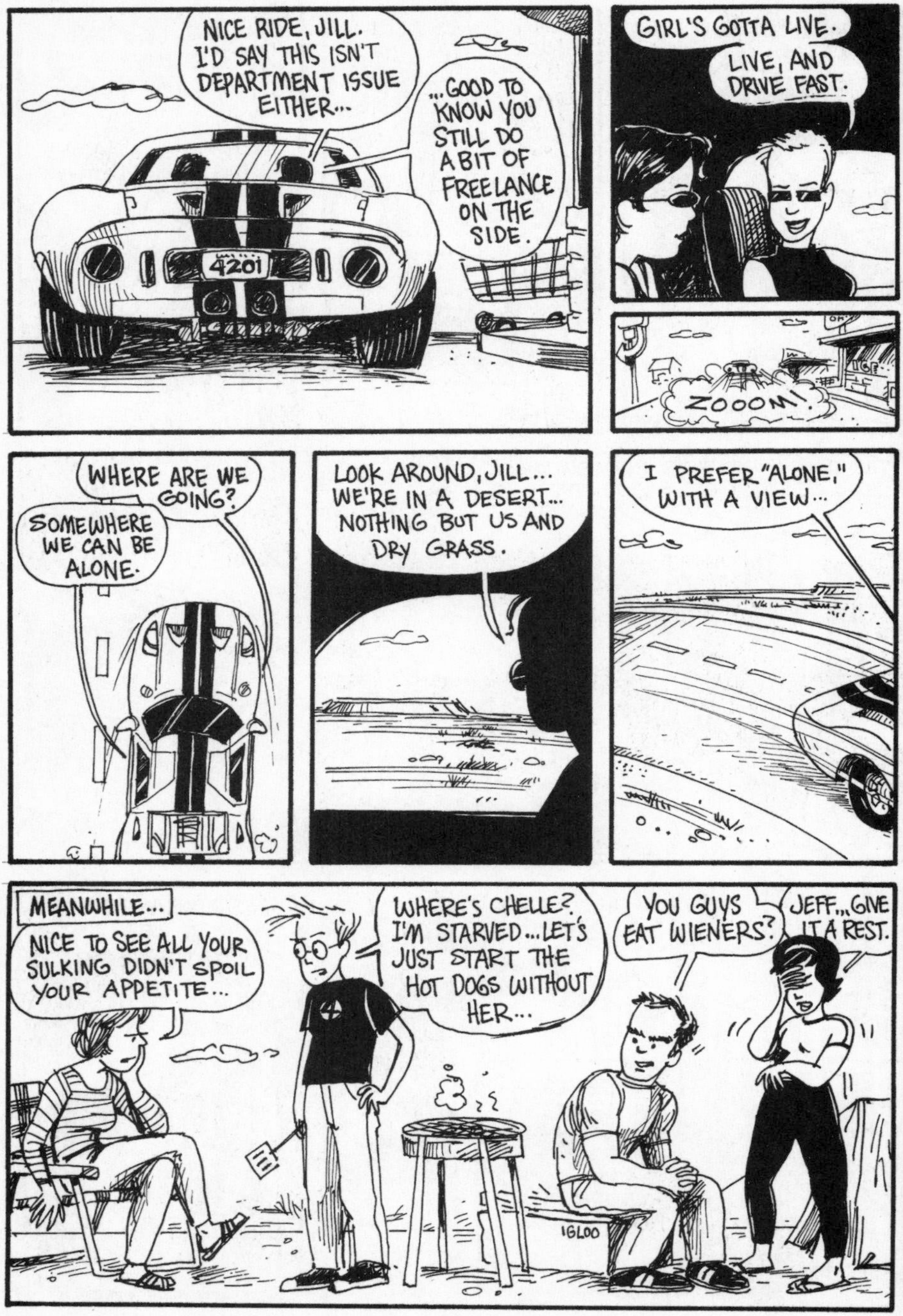
NICE RIDE, JILL. I'D SAY THIS ISN'T DEPARTMENT ISSUE EITHER...
...GOOD TO KNOW YOU STILL DO A BIT OF FREELANCE ON THE SIDE.
4201
GIRL'S GOTTA LIVE.
LIVE, AND DRIVE FAST.
ZOOOM!
WHERE ARE WE GOING?
SOMEWHERE WE CAN BE ALONE.
LOOK AROUND, JILL... WE'RE IN A DESERT... NOTHING BUT US AND DRY GRASS.
I PREFER "ALONE," WITH A VIEW...
MEANWHILE...
NICE TO SEE ALL YOUR SULKING DIDN'T SPOIL YOUR APPETITE...
WHERE'S CHELLE? I'M STARVED... LET'S JUST START THE HOT DOGS WITHOUT HER...
YOU GUYS EAT WIENERS?
JEFF... GIVE IT A REST.
IGLOO

SO, WHAT'S THE STORY, CHELLE?

WHAT WAS SO IMPORTANT THAT YOU DROVE ALL THE WAY TO THE DESERT TO FIND ME?

I WANT TO START MY OWN AGENCY.

I'M TIRED OF TAKING DIRECTIONS FROM PEOPLE WITH LESS EXPERIENCE THAN ME..

REALLY?

I'M READY TO DO MY OWN THING.

YOU'RE SERIOUS?

THE TRUST FUND CAME THROUGH LAST YEAR... SO I HAVE THE CASH... THE TIME IS RIGHT. BUT I CAN'T DO IT ALONE... I NEED SOMEONE WITH SKILLS...

..SOMEONE I TRUST.

AND YOU TRUST ME?

...AFTER WHAT WENT DOWN IN NEVADA?

YES.

YOU WERE JUST TRYING TO PROTECT...

...ME ...I KNOW THAT..

SO... YOU AREN'T A **WOMAN ON THE VERGE**✕ ANY LONGER?

I'D SAY I'M WAY BEYOND THAT...

I SHOULD HAVE FOUND A BETTER WAY.

BESIDES, YOU CAN'T BE HAPPY HERE ...PULLING IN A GOVERNMENT WAGE...

✕ IN PAST STORY LINE IT WAS REVEALED THAT CHELLE WORKED FOR AN AGENCY BY THAT NAME

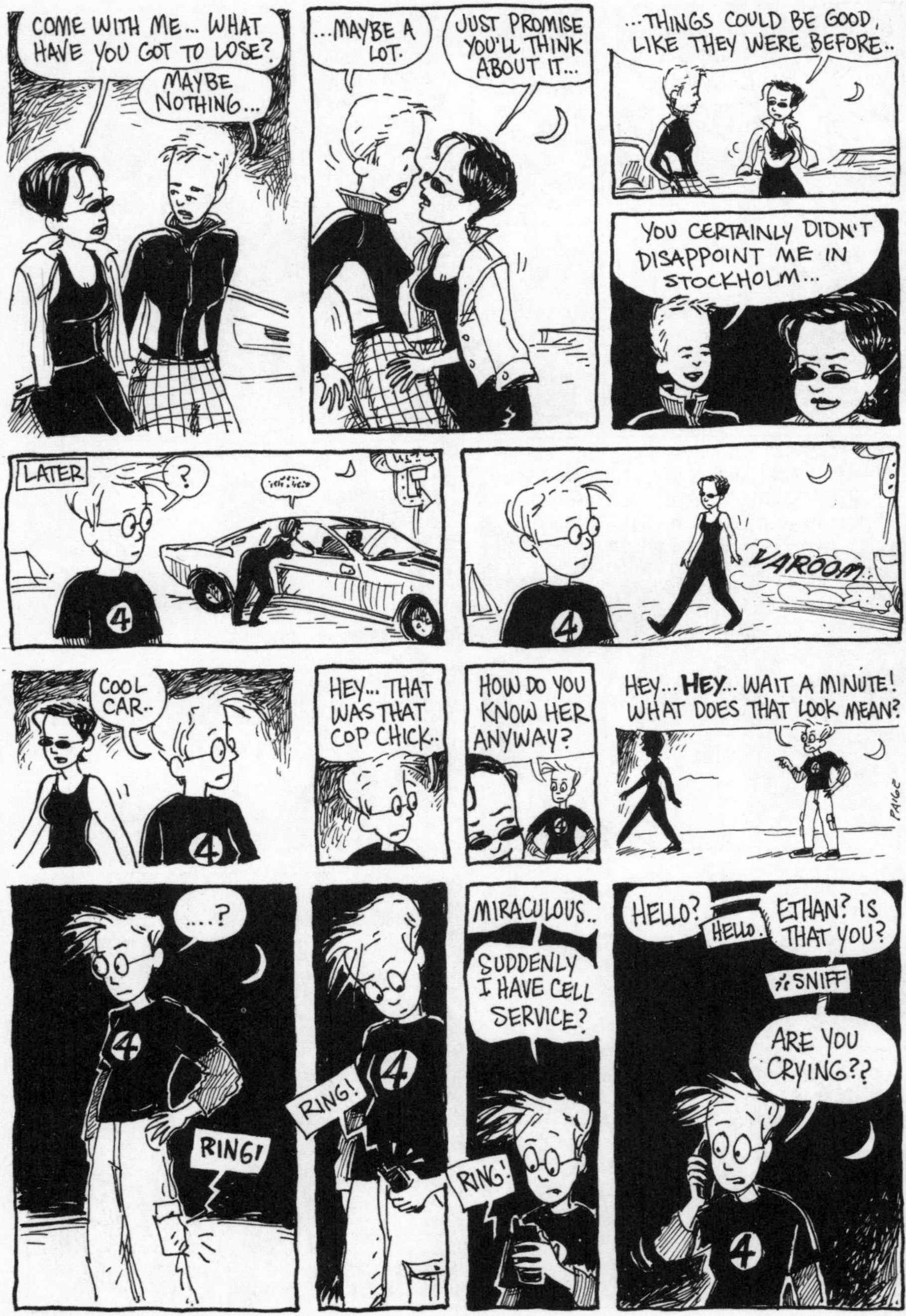

COME WITH ME... WHAT HAVE YOU GOT TO LOSE?
MAYBE NOTHING...
...MAYBE A LOT.
JUST PROMISE YOU'LL THINK ABOUT IT...
...THINGS COULD BE GOOD, LIKE THEY WERE BEFORE..
YOU CERTAINLY DIDN'T DISAPPOINT ME IN STOCKHOLM...
LATER
?
VAROOM
COOL CAR..
HEY... THAT WAS THAT COP CHICK..
HOW DO YOU KNOW HER ANYWAY?
HEY... HEY... WAIT A MINUTE! WHAT DOES THAT LOOK MEAN?
....?
RING!
RING!
MIRACULOUS..
RING!
SUDDENLY I HAVE CELL SERVICE?
HELLO?
HELLO.
ETHAN? IS THAT YOU?
SNIFF
ARE YOU CRYING??

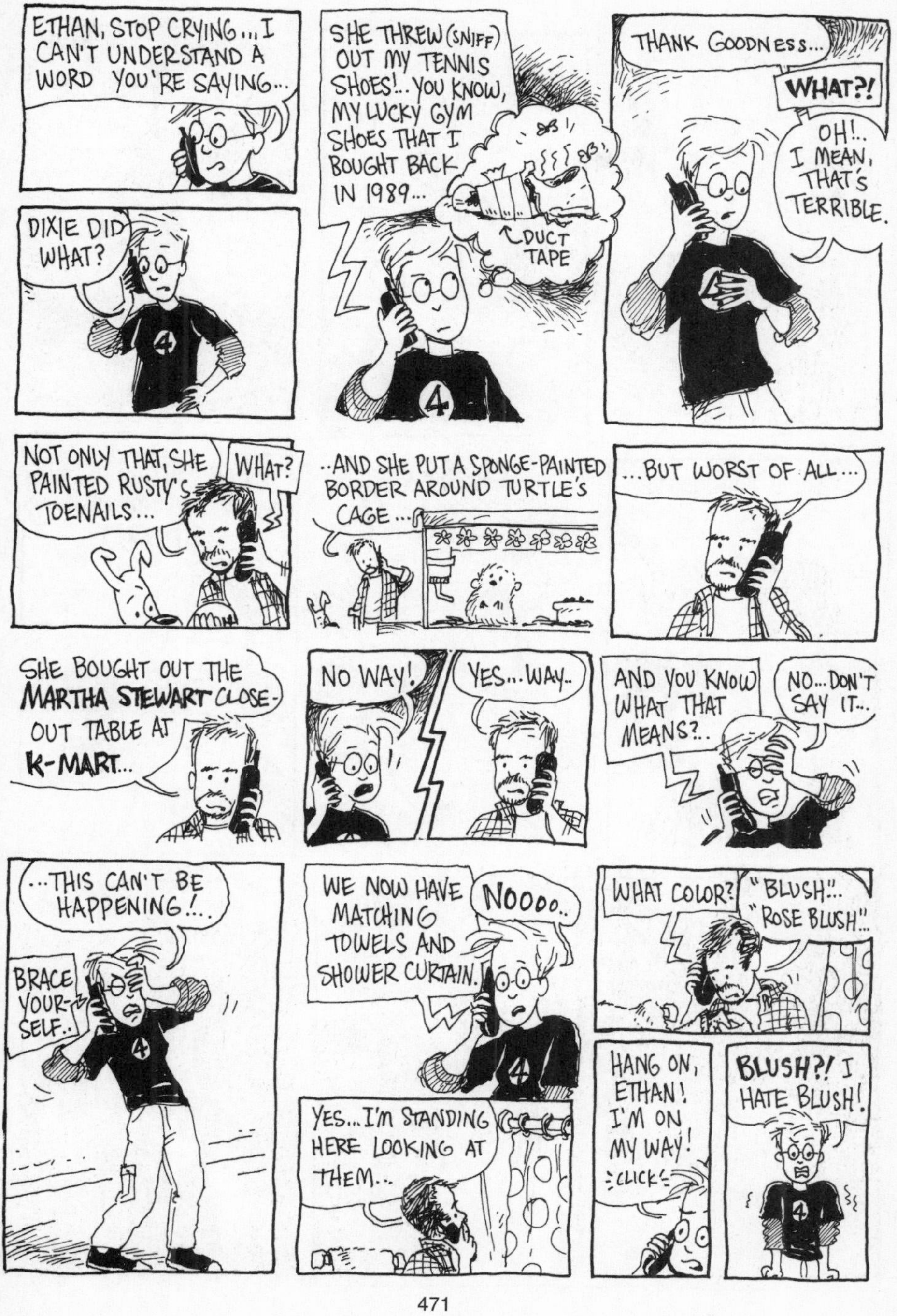
ETHAN, STOP CRYING... I CAN'T UNDERSTAND A WORD YOU'RE SAYING...
SHE THREW (SNIFF) OUT MY TENNIS SHOES!.. YOU KNOW, MY LUCKY GYM SHOES THAT I BOUGHT BACK IN 1989...
DUCT TAPE
THANK GOODNESS...
WHAT?!
OH!.. I MEAN, THAT'S TERRIBLE.
DIXIE DID WHAT?
NOT ONLY THAT, SHE PAINTED RUSTY'S TOENAILS...
WHAT?
..AND SHE PUT A SPONGE-PAINTED BORDER AROUND TURTLE'S CAGE...
...BUT WORST OF ALL...
SHE BOUGHT OUT THE MARTHA STEWART CLOSE-OUT TABLE AT K-MART...
NO WAY!
YES... WAY..
AND YOU KNOW WHAT THAT MEANS?..
NO... DON'T SAY IT...
...THIS CAN'T BE HAPPENING!...
BRACE YOURSELF..
WE NOW HAVE MATCHING TOWELS AND SHOWER CURTAIN.
NOOOO..
YES... I'M STANDING HERE LOOKING AT THEM...
WHAT COLOR?
"BLUSH"... "ROSE BLUSH"...
HANG ON, ETHAN! I'M ON MY WAY!
CLICK
BLUSH?! I HATE BLUSH!

YES!..EVERYONE HAS A CELL PHONE!

SAY THAT AGAIN, MOTHER.

YOU WILL?!

YOU'LL LOAN ME THE MONEY TO BUY THE CAFE??...

...

THAT'S TERRIFIC, MOM!

I'LL FLY OUT NEXT WEEK TO HELP YOU RENOVATE...

..CAN'T WAIT TO SEE YOU, SWEETIE!

MOM?

I THINK YOU'RE BREAKING UP...

I THOUGHT FOR A MINUTE THERE YOU SAID YOU WERE COMING OUT HERE...

BUT...

...MOM!..."SILENT PARTNER" WITH THE EMPHASIS ON SILENT.

RING!

HELLO?

ARCHIE?

JANE, I THINK YOU NEET TO COME BACK TO WORK...

WHY?

YOU'VE BEEN GONE SO LONG THEY'VE CONVERTED YOUR DESK INTO THE SNACK STATION.

..YOU KNOW, COFFEE AND DONUTS.

WHAT KIND OF DONUTS?

PAIGE

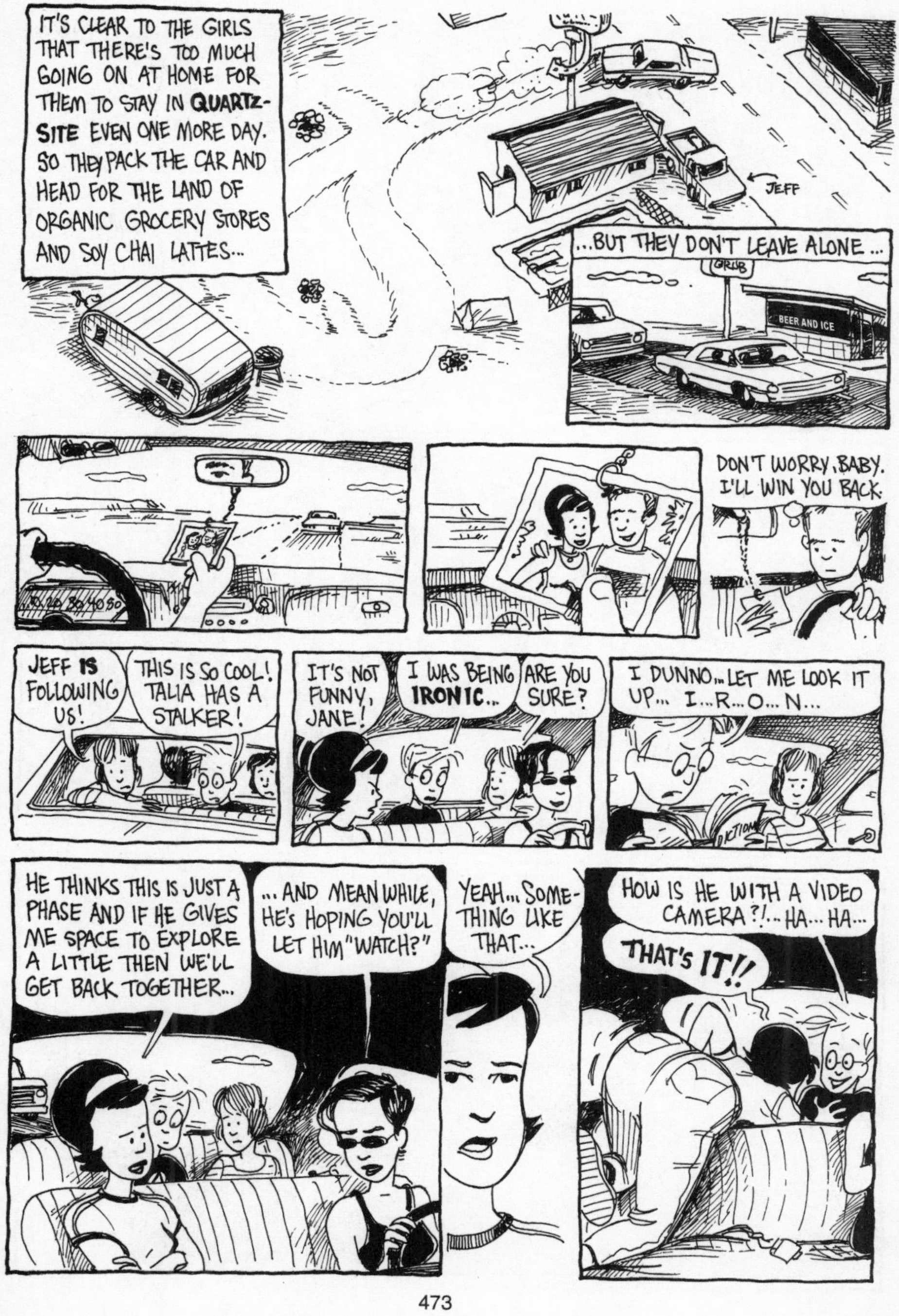

IT'S CLEAR TO THE GIRLS THAT THERE'S TOO MUCH GOING ON AT HOME FOR THEM TO STAY IN QUARTZ-SITE EVEN ONE MORE DAY. SO THEY PACK THE CAR AND HEAD FOR THE LAND OF ORGANIC GROCERY STORES AND SOY CHAI LATTES...
JEFF
...BUT THEY DON'T LEAVE ALONE...
GRUB
BEER AND ICE
DON'T WORRY, BABY. I'LL WIN YOU BACK.
JEFF IS FOLLOWING US!
THIS IS SO COOL! TALIA HAS A STALKER!
IT'S NOT FUNNY, JANE!
I WAS BEING IRONIC...
ARE YOU SURE?
I DUNNO... LET ME LOOK IT UP... I...R...O...N...
DICTION
HE THINKS THIS IS JUST A PHASE AND IF HE GIVES ME SPACE TO EXPLORE A LITTLE THEN WE'LL GET BACK TOGETHER...
...AND MEANWHILE, HE'S HOPING YOU'LL LET HIM "WATCH?"
YEAH... SOME-THING LIKE THAT...
HOW IS HE WITH A VIDEO CAMERA?!... HA... HA...
THAT'S IT!!

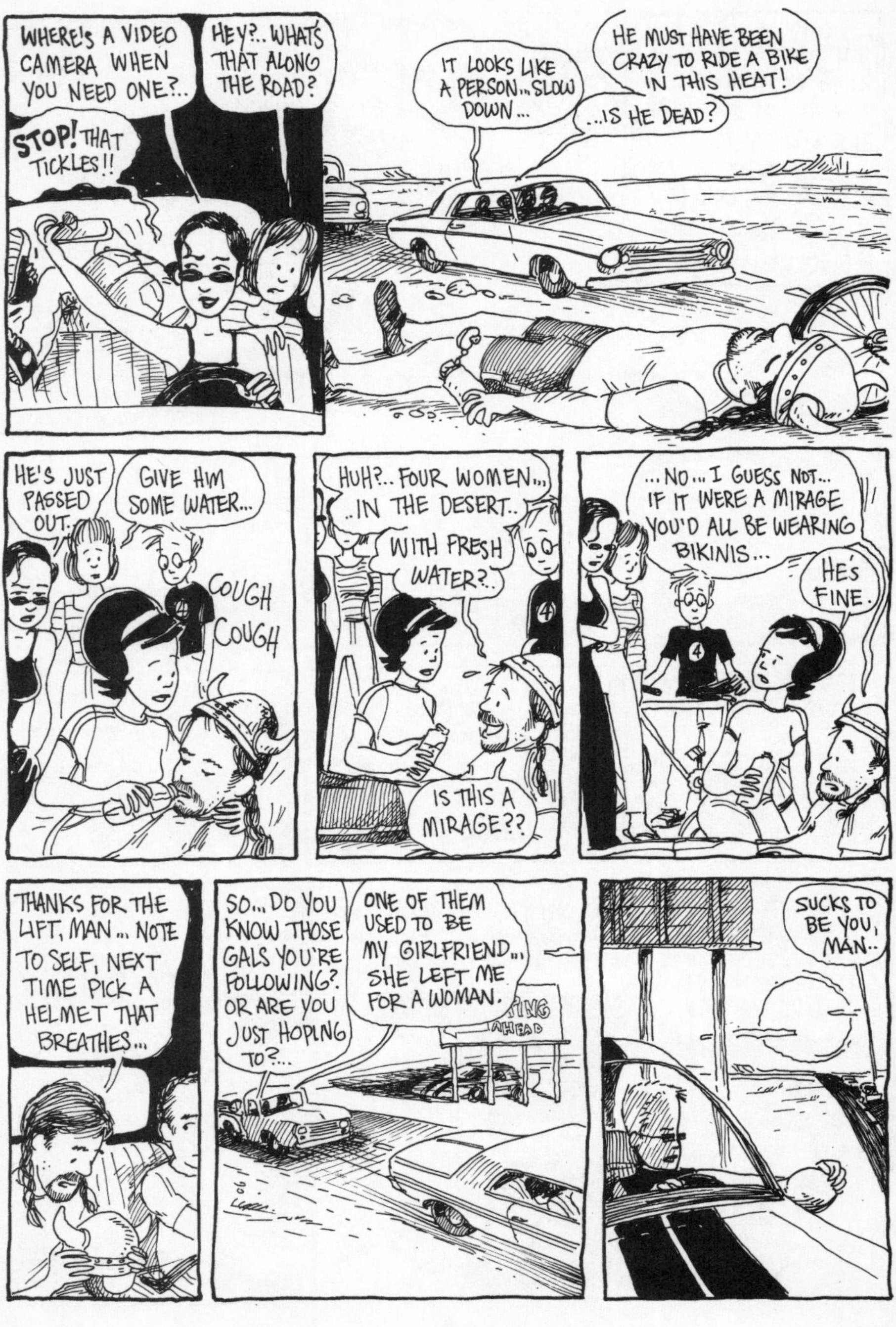
WHERE'S A VIDEO CAMERA WHEN YOU NEED ONE?..
HEY?.. WHAT'S THAT ALONG THE ROAD?
STOP! THAT TICKLES!!
IT LOOKS LIKE A PERSON... SLOW DOWN...
HE MUST HAVE BEEN CRAZY TO RIDE A BIKE IN THIS HEAT!
...IS HE DEAD?
HE'S JUST PASSED OUT...
GIVE HIM SOME WATER...
COUGH COUGH
HUH?.. FOUR WOMEN... ..IN THE DESERT..
WITH FRESH WATER?..
IS THIS A MIRAGE??
...NO... I GUESS NOT... IF IT WERE A MIRAGE YOU'D ALL BE WEARING BIKINIS...
HE'S FINE.
THANKS FOR THE LIFT, MAN... NOTE TO SELF, NEXT TIME PICK A HELMET THAT BREATHES...
SO... DO YOU KNOW THOSE GALS YOU'RE FOLLOWING?. OR ARE YOU JUST HOPING TO?...
ONE OF THEM USED TO BE MY GIRLFRIEND... SHE LEFT ME FOR A WOMAN.
AHEAD
SUCKS TO BE YOU, MAN..

JILL...

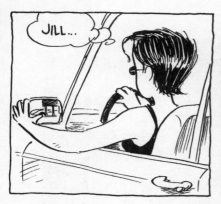

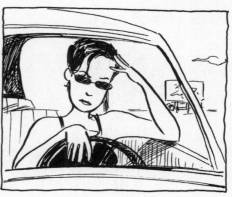

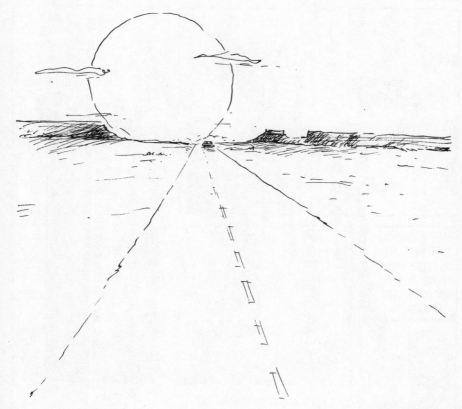

TO BE CONTINUED...

JANE'S WORLD COVER GALLERY

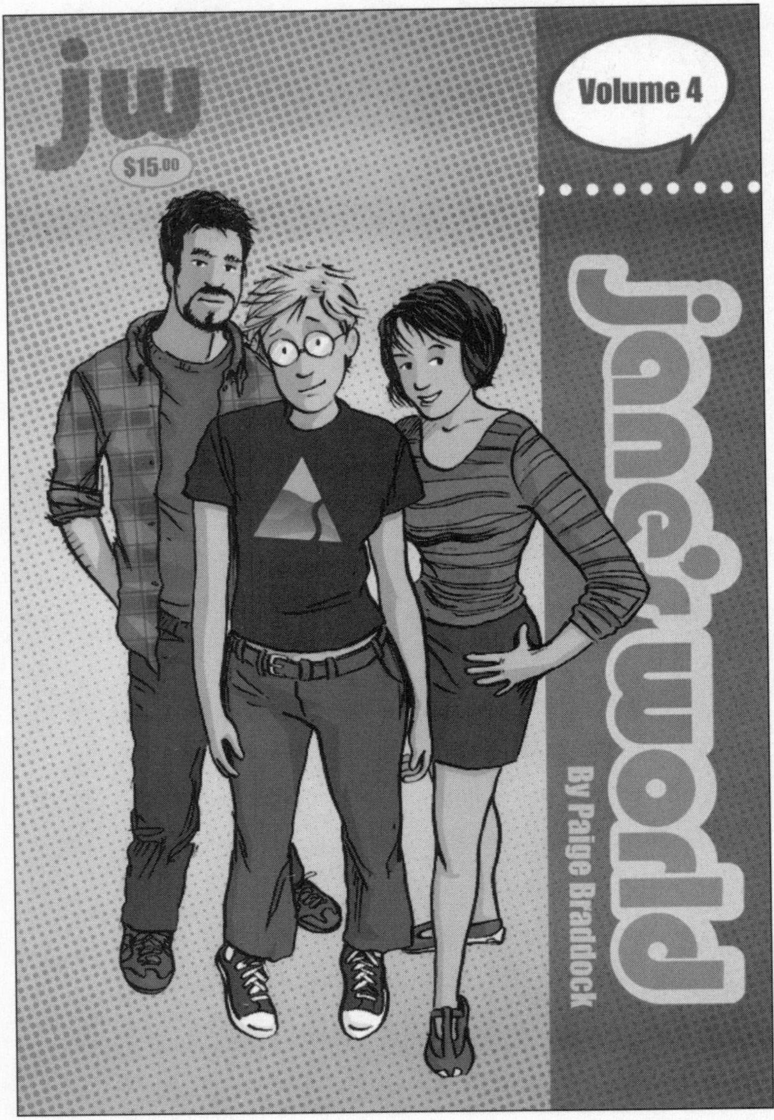
jw
$15.00
Volume 4
Jane's World
By Paige Braddock

Volume 4, ISBN 978-0-9766707-3-9

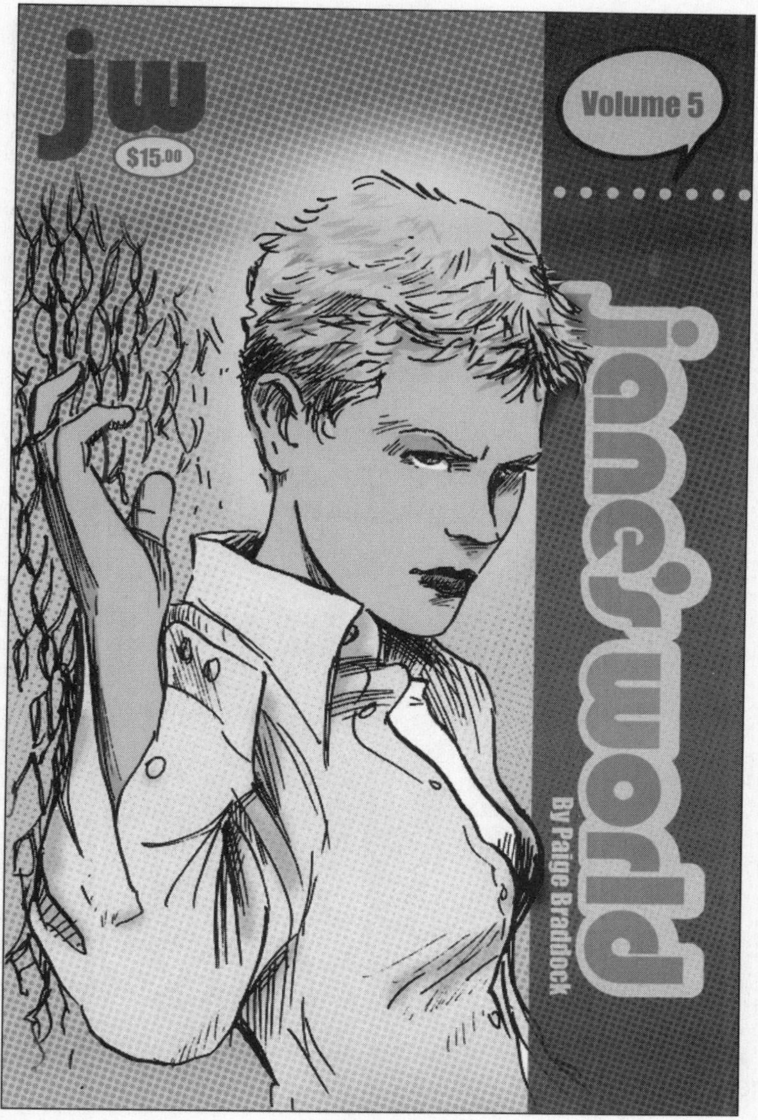
jw
$15.00
Volume 5
jane's world
By Paige Braddock

Volume 5, ISBN 978-0-9766707-5-5

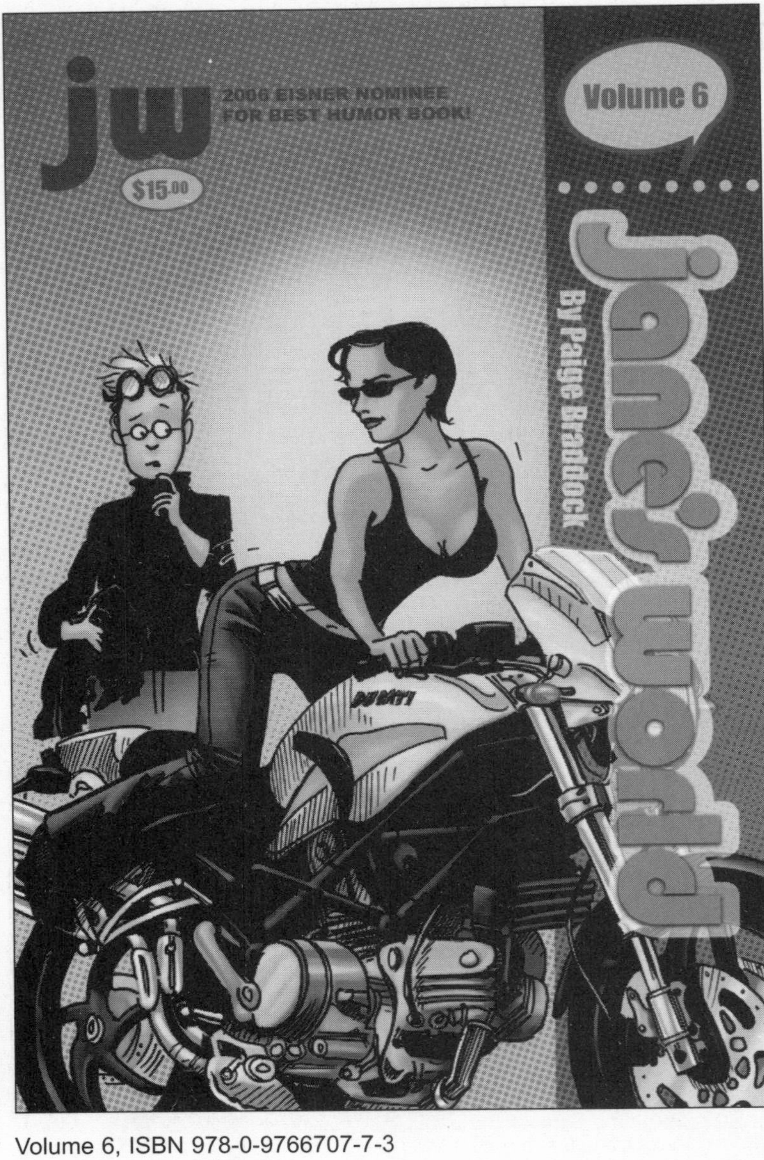
jw
2006 EISNER NOMINEE
FOR BEST HUMOR BOOK!
$15.00
Volume 6
Jane's World
By Paige Braddock

Volume 6, ISBN 978-0-9766707-7-3

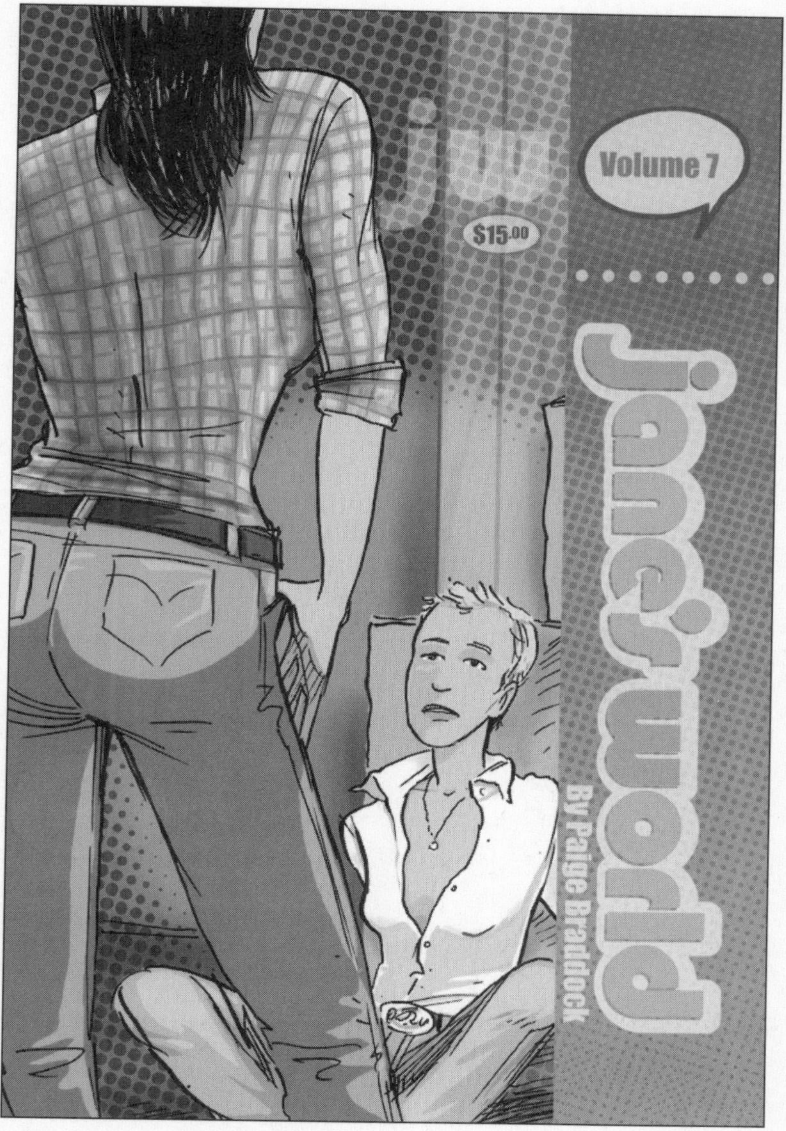
Volume 7
$15.00
Jane's World
By Paige Braddock

Volume 7, ISBN 978-0-9766707-9-7
RELEASE DATE: MAY 2007

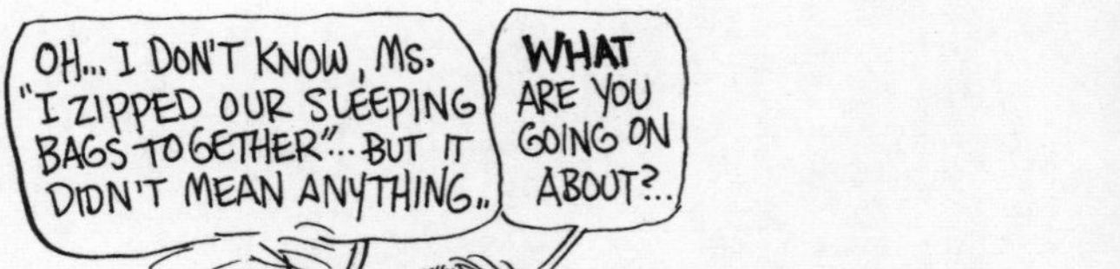
OH... I DON'T KNOW, MS. "I ZIPPED OUR SLEEPING BAGS TOGETHER"... BUT IT DIDN'T MEAN ANYTHING..
WHAT ARE YOU GOING ON ABOUT?..
ORANGE SODA

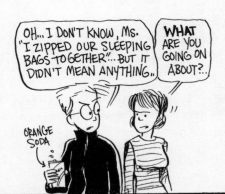